Twentieth-Century
Literary Criticism

Guide to Gale Literary Criticism Series

For criticism on	Consult these Gale series
Authors now living or who died after December 31, 1959	*CONTEMPORARY LITERARY CRITICISM (CLC)*
Authors who died between 1900 and 1959	*TWENTIETH-CENTURY LITERARY CRITICISM (TCLC)*
Authors who died between 1800 and 1899	*NINETEENTH-CENTURY LITERATURE CRITICISM (NCLC)*
Authors who died between 1400 and 1799	*LITERATURE CRITICISM FROM 1400 TO 1800 (LC)* *SHAKESPEAREAN CRITICISM (SC)*
Authors who died before 1400	*CLASSICAL AND MEDIEVAL LITERATURE CRITICISM (CMLC)*
Black writers of the past two hundred years	*BLACK LITERATURE CRITICISM (BLC)*
Authors of books for children and young adults	*CHILDREN'S LITERATURE REVIEW (CLR)*
Dramatists	*DRAMA CRITICISM (DC)*
Hispanic writers of the late nineteenth and twentieth centuries	*HISPANIC LITERATURE CRITICISM (HLC)*
Native North American writers and orators of the eighteenth, nineteenth, and twentieth centuries	*NATIVE NORTH AMERICAN LITERATURE (NNAL)*
Poets	*POETRY CRITICISM (PC)*
Short story writers	*SHORT STORY CRITICISM (SSC)*
Major authors from the Renaissance to the present	*WORLD LITERATURE CRITICISM, 1500 TO THE PRESENT (WLC)*

ISSN 0276-8178

Volume 68

Twentieth-Century Literary Criticism

**Excerpts from Criticism of the
Works of Novelists, Poets, Playwrights,
Short Story Writers, and Other Creative Writers
Who Lived between 1900 and 1960,
from the First Published Critical
Appraisals to Current Evaluations**

Scot Peacock
Editor

Thomas Ligotti
Associate Editor

GALE

DETROIT • NEW YORK • TORONTO • LONDON

STAFF

Scot Peacock, *Editor*

Thomas Ligotti, *Associate Editor*

Susan Trosky, *Permissions Manager*
Kim F. Smilay, *Permissions Specialist*
Sarah Chesney, *Permissions Associate*
Kelly H. Quin, *Permissions Assistant*

Victoria B. Cariappa, *Research Manager*
Laura C. Bissey, Julia C. Daniel, Michele P. LaMeau, Tamara C. Nott,
Tracie A. Richardson, Norma Sawaya, Cheryl L. Warnock,
Research Associates
Alfred A. Gardner, I, *Research Assistants*

Mary Beth Trimper, *Production Director*
Deborah L. Milliken, *Production Assistant*

Sherrell Hobbs, *Macintosh Artist*
Randy Bassett, *Image Database Supervisor*
Robert Duncan, *Imaging Specialist*
Pamela Hayes, *Photography Coordinator*

Library of Congress Catalog Card Number 76-46132
ISBN 0-7876-1168-9
ISSN 0276-8178

Printed in the United States of America
10 9 8 7 6 5 4 3 2 1

Contents

Preface vii

Acknowledgments xi

Preface

Since its inception more than fifteen years ago, *Twentieth-Century Literary Criticism* has been purchased and used by nearly 10,000 school, public, and college or university libraries. *TCLC* has covered more than 500 authors, representing 58 nationalities, and over 25,000 titles. No other reference source has surveyed the critical response to twentieth-century authors and literature as thoroughly as *TCLC*. In the words of one reviewer, "there is nothing comparable available." *TCLC* "is a gold mine of information—dates, pseudonyms, biographical information, and criticism from books and periodicals—which many libraries would have difficulty assembling on their own."

Scope of the Series

TCLC is designed to serve as an introduction to authors who died between 1900 and 1960 and to the most significant interpretations of these author's works. The great poets, novelists, short story writers, playwrights, and philosophers of this period are frequently studied in high school and college literature courses. In organizing and excerpting the vast amount of critical material written on these authors, *TCLC* helps students develop valuable insight into literary history, promotes a better understanding of the texts, and sparks ideas for papers and assignments. Each entry in *TCLC* presents a comprehensive survey of an author's career or an individual work of literature and provides the user with a multiplicity of interpretations and assessments. Such variety allows students to pursue their own interests; furthermore, it fosters an awareness that literature is dynamic and responsive to many different opinions.

Every fourth volume of *TCLC* is devoted to literary topics. These topic entries widen the focus of the series from individual authors to such broader subjects as literary movements, prominent themes in twentieth-century literature, literary reaction to political and historical events, significant eras in literary history, prominent literary anniversaries, and the literatures of cultures that are often overlooked by English-speaking readers.

TCLC is designed as a companion series to Gale's *Contemporary Literary Criticism,* which reprints commentary on authors now living or who have died since 1960. Because of the different periods under consideration, there is no duplication of material between *CLC* and *TCLC*. For additional information about *CLC* and Gale's other criticism titles, users should consult the Guide to Gale Literary Criticism Series preceding the title page in this volume.

Coverage

Each volume of *TCLC* is carefully compiled to present:

- criticism of authors, or literary topics, representing a variety of genres and nationalities

- both major and lesser-known writers and literary works of the period

- 6-12 authors or 3-6 topics per volume

- individual entries that survey critical response to each author's work or each topic in literary history, including early criticism to reflect initial reactions; later criticism to represent any rise or decline in reputation; and current retrospective analyses.

Organization of This Book

An author entry consists of the following elements: author heading, biographical and critical introduction, list of principal works, excerpts of criticism (each preceded by an annotation and a bibliographic citation), and a bibliography of further reading.

- The **Author Heading** consists of the name under which the author most commonly wrote, followed by birth and death dates. If an author wrote consistently under a pseudonym, the pseudonym will be listed in the author heading and the real name given in parentheses on the first line of the biographical and critical introduction. Also located at the beginning of the introduction to the author entry are any name variations under which an author wrote, including transliterated forms for authors whose languages use nonroman alphabets.

- The **Biographical and Critical Introduction** outlines the author's life and career, as well as the critical issues surrounding his or her work. References to past volumes of *TCLC* are provided at the beginning of the introduction. Additional sources of information in other biographical and critical reference series published by Gale, including *Short Story Criticism, Children's Literature Review, Contemporary Authors, Dictionary of Literary Biography,* and *Something about the Author,* are listed in a box at the end of the entry.

- Some *TCLC* entries include **Portraits** of the author. Entries also may contain reproductions of materials pertinent to an author's career, including manuscript pages, title pages, dust jackets, letters, and drawings, as well as photographs of important people, places, and events in an author's life.

- The **List of Principal Works** is chronological by date of first book publication and identifies the genre of each work. In the case of foreign authors with both foreign-language publications and English translations, the title and date of the first English-language edition are given in brackets. Unless otherwise indicated, dramas are dated by first performance, not first publication.

- Critical excerpts are prefaced by **Annotations** providing the reader with information about both the critic and the criticism that follows. Included are the critic's reputation, individual approach to literary criticism, and particular expertise in an author's works. Also noted are the relative importance of a work of criticism, the scope of the excerpt, and the growth of critical controversy or changes in critical trends regarding an author. In some cases, these annotations cross-reference excerpts by critics who discuss each other's commentary.

- A complete **Bibliographic Citation** designed to facilitate location of the original essay or book precedes each piece of criticism.

- **Criticism** is arranged chronologically in each author entry to provide a perspective on changes in critical evaluation over the years. All titles of works by the author featured in the entry are printed in boldface type to enable the user to easily locate discussion of particular works. Also for purposes of easier identification, the critic's name and the publication date of the essay are given at the beginning of each piece of criticism. Unsigned criticism is preceded by the title of the journal in which it appeared. Some of the excerpts in *TCLC* also contain translated material. Unless otherwise noted, translations in brackets are by the editors; translations in parentheses or continuous with the text are by the critic. Publication information (such as footnotes or page and line references to specific editions of works) have been deleted at the editor's discretion to provide smoother reading of the text.

- An annotated list of **Further Reading** appearing at the end of each author entry suggests secondary sources on the author. In some cases it includes essays for which the editors could not obtain reprint rights.

Cumulative Indexes

- Each volume of *TCLC* contains a cumulative **Author Index** listing all authors who have appeared in Gale's Literary Criticism Series, along with cross references to such biographical series as *Contemporary Authors* and *Dictionary of Literary Biography*. For readers' convenience, a complete list of Gale titles included appears on the first page of the author index. Useful for locating authors within the various series, this index is particularly valuable for those authors who are identified by a certain period but who, because of their death dates, are placed in another, or for those authors whose careers span two periods. For example, F. Scott Fitzgerald is found in *TCLC*, yet a writer often associated with him, Ernest Hemingway, is found in *CLC*.

- Each *TCLC* volume includes a cumulative **Nationality Index** which lists all authors who have appeared in *TCLC* volumes, arranged alphabetically under their respective nationalities, as well as Topics volume entries devoted to particular national literatures.

- Each new volume in Gale's Literary Criticism Series includes a cumulative **Topic Index**, which lists all literary topics treated in *NCLC, TCLC, LC 1400-1800,* and the *CLC* yearbook.

- Each new volume of *TCLC,* with the exception of the Topics volumes, includes a **Title Index** listing the titles of all literary works discussed in the volume. In response to numerous suggestions from librarians, Gale has also produced a **Special Paperbound Edition** of the *TCLC* title index. This annual cumulation lists all titles discussed in the series since its inception and is issued with the first volume of *TCLC* published each year. Additional copies of the index are available on request. Librarians and patrons will welcome this separate index; it saves shelf space, is easy to use, and is recyclable upon receipt of the following year's cumulation. Titles discussed in the Topics volume entries are not included *TCLC* cumulative index.

Citing *Twentieth-Century Literary Criticism*

When writing papers, students who quote directly from any volume in Gale's literary Criticism Series may use the following general forms to footnote reprinted criticism. The first example pertains to materials drawn from periodicals, the second to material reprinted from books.

[1]William H. Slavick, "Going to School to DuBose Heyward," *The Harlem Renaissance Re-examined,* (AMS Press, 1987); excerpted and reprinted in *Twentieth-Century Literary Criticism,* Vol. 59, ed. Jennifer Gariepy (Detroit: Gale Research, 1995), pp. 94-105.

[2]George Orwell, "Reflections on Gandhi," *Partisan Review,* 6 (Winter 1949), pp. 85-92; excerpted and reprinted in *Twentieth-Century Literary Criticism,* Vol. 59, ed. Jennifer Gariepy (Detroit: Gale Research, 1995), pp. 40-3.

Suggestions Are Welcome

In response to suggestions, several features have been added to *TCLC* since the series began, including annotations to excerpted criticism, a cumulative index to authors in all Gale literary criticism series, entries devoted to criticism on a single work by a major author, more extensive illustrations, and a title index listing all literary works discussed in the series since its inception.

Readers who wish to suggest authors or topics to appear in future volumes, or who have other suggestions, are cordially invited to write the editors.

Acknowledgments

The editors wish to thank the copyright holders of the excerpted criticism included in this volume and the permissions managers of many book and magazine publishing companies for assisting us in securing reproduction rights. We are also grateful to the staffs of the Detroit Public Library, the Library of Congress, the University of Detroit Mercy Library, Wayne State University Purdy/Kresge Library Complex, and the University of Michigan Libraries for making their resources available to us. Following is a list of the copyright holders who have granted us permission to reproduce material in this volume of *TCLC*. Every effort has been made to trace copyright, but if omissions have been made, please let us know.

COPYRIGHTED EXCERPTS IN *TCLC*, VOLUME 68, WERE REPRODUCED FROM THE FOLLOWING PERIODICALS:

American Quarterly, v. XII, Fall, 1960 for "Cultural History Written with Lightning: The Significance of 'The Birth of The Nation' " by Everett Carter. Copyright 1960, American Studies Association. Reproduced by permission of the publisher and the author.—*The American Scholar*, v. 59, Spring, 1990. Copyright (c) 1990 by the United Chapters of the Phi Beta Kappa Society. Reproduced by permission.—*American Studies*, v. 35, Spring, 1994 for "Ecstasy, Primitivism, Modernity: Isadora Duncan and Mary Wigman" by Melissa Ragona; v. 35, Spring, 1994 for "From Event to Monument: Modernism, Feminism and Isadora Duncan" by Elizabeth Francis. Copyright (c) Mid-America American Studies Association, 1994. Both reproduced by permission of the publisher and the authors.—*Ariel: A Review of International English Literature*, v. 13, October, 1982 for "Norman Douglas: The Willing Exile" by George Woodcock. Copyright (c) 1982 The Board of Governors, The University of Calgary. Reproduced by permission of the publisher and the author.—*Canadian Journal of History*, v. XXV, August, 1990. (c) Canadian Journal of History. Reproduced by permission.—*Commentary*, v. 34, March, 1963 for "Goebbels's Nature" by Werner J. Dannhauseer; v. 66, July, 1978 for "The End of the Road" by Dan Jacobson. Copyright (c) 1963, 1978 by the American Jewish Committee. All rights reserved. Both reproduced by permission of the publisher and the authors.—*The Commonweal*, v. XLVIII, June 25, 1948. Copyright 1948 Commonweal Publishing Co., Inc. Reproduced by permission of Commonweal Foundation.—*Critical Inquiry*, v. 15, Spring, 1989. Copyright (c) 1989 by The University of Chicago. Reproduced by permission of the author and publisher.—*The D. H. Lawrence Review*, v. 9, Summer, 1976. (c) James C. Cowan. Reproduced with the permission of The D. H. Lawrence Review.—Reprinted from *ETC.: A Review of General Semantics*, v. 36, no. 2, Summer, 1979, with permission of the International Society for General Semantics, Concord, CA.—*Film Comment*, v. 10, March-April, 1974. Copyright (c) 1974 by Film Comment Publishing Corporation. Reproduced by permission.—*Film Quarterly*, v. XXVIII, Fall, 1974; v. XLVI, Winter, 1992-93. (c) 1974, 1992-93 by The Regents of the University of California. Both reproduced by permission of the Regents.—*The Journal of Modern History*, v. 63, December, 1991. (c) 1991 by The University of Chicago. Reproduced by permission of The University of Chicago Press and the author.—*The Kentucky Review*, v. VI, Fall, 1986. Copyright (c) 1986 by the University of Kentucky Libraries. Reproduced by permission.—First published in *The Kenyon Review*, OS v. XIV, No. 4, Autumn, 1952 for "Norman Douglas" by R. W. Flint. Copyright 1952 by Kenyon College. All rights reserved. Reproduced by permission of the publisher and author.—*Los Angeles Times Book Review*, October 25, 1987. Copyright, 1987, Los Angeles Times. Reproduced by permission.—*The Markham Review*, v. 2, September, 1969. Reproduced by permission.—*Michigan Quarterly Review*, v. XVI, Winter, 1977 for "Time's Own River: The Three Major Novels of Elizabeth Madox Roberts" by Wade Tyree. Copyright (c) The University of Michigan, 1977. Reproduced by permission of the author.—*The Mississippi Quarterly*, v. XL, Spring, 1987. Copyright 1987 Mississippi State University. Reproduced by permission.—Copyright (c) by George Steiner. *The New Yorker*, v. LXXI, April 17, 1995. Reproduced by permission of Georges Borchardt, Inc. for the author. —*The New York Review of Books*, v. XXXV, July 21, 1988; v. XXXV, September 27, 1988. Copyright (c) 1988 Nyrev, Inc. Both reproduced with permission from The New York Review of Books.—*The New York Times Book Review*, April 10, 1988. Copyright (c) 1988 by The New York Times Company. Reproduced by permission.—*Orbis Litterarum*, v. 41, 1986. Reproduced by permission.—*The Register of the Kentucky Historical Society*, v. 64, April, 1966. Reproduced by permission.—*Sight and Sound*, v. 15, Autumn, 1946. Copyright 1946 by The British Film Institute. Reproduced by permission.—*South Atlantic Quarterly*, v. 49, April, 1950. Copyright 1950 by Duke University Press, Durham, NC. Reproduced with permission.—*The Southern Literary Journal*, v. XVIII, Fall, 1985. Copyright 1985 by the Department of English, University of North Carolina at Chapel Hill. Reproduced by permission.—From *The Spyglass: Views and Reviews, 1924-1930*, by Davidson, Donald. Edited by John Tyree Fain. Vanderbilt University Press, 1963. Copyright (c) 1963 by John Tyree Fain. Reproduced by permission.

COPYRIGHTED EXCERPTS IN *TCLC,* VOLUME 68, WERE REPRODUCED FROM THE FOLLOWING BOOKS:

Auchincloss, Louis. From *Pioneers & Caretakers: A Study of 9 American Women Novelists.* University of Minnesota Press, 1965. (c) copyright 1961, 1964, 1965 by the University of Minnesota. All rights reserved. Reproduced by permission.—Bangerter, Lowell A. From *Robert Musil.* The Continuum Publishing Company, 1988. Copyright (c) 1988 by Lowell A. Bangerter. All rights reserved. Reproduced by permission.—Campbell, Harry Modean and Ruel E. Foster. From *Elizabeth Madox Roberts: American Novelist.* University of Oklahoma Press, 1956. Copyright 1956 by the University of Oklahoma Press, Publishing Division of the University. Reproduced by permission.—Copyright (c) 1963 Connelly, Cyril. From *Previous Convictions.* Reproduced by permission of the Estate of Cyril Connolly c/o Rogers, Coleridge & White Ltd.—Crowther, Bosley. From *The Great Films: Fifty Golden Years of Motion Pictures.* G. P. Putnam's Sons, 1967. Copyright (c) 1967 by Bosley Crowther. Copyright (c) The New York Times Co. All rights reserved. Reproduced by permission of The Putnam Publishing Group and The New York Times Co.—Dorris, George E. From "Griffith in Retrospect," in *Man and Movies.* Edited by W. R. Robinson. Louisiana State University Press, 1967. Copyright (c) 1967 by Louisiana State University Press. Reproduced by permission.—Drew, William M. From *D. W. Griffith's Intolerance: Its Genesis and Its Vision.* McFarland & Company, Inc., 1986. (c) 1986 William M. Drew. All rights reserved. Reproduced by permission.—From *My Life,* by Isadora Duncan. Copyright, 1927 by Horace Liveright, Inc., renewed (c) 1955 by Liveright Publishing Corporation. Reproduced by permission of Liveright Publishing Corporation.—"Dickens, Griffith, and the Film Form" from *Film Form: Essays in Film Theory* by Sergei Eisenstein, copyright 1949 by Harcourt Brace & Company and renewed 1977 by Jay Leyda, reprinted by permission of the publisher.—Enright, D. J. From *A Mania for Sentences.* Chatto & Windus, 1983. (c) D. J. Enright 1983. All rights reserved. Reproduced by permission of Watson, Little Limited for the author.—From *The Face of the Third Reich: Portraits of the Nazi Leadership* by Joachim C. Fest, translated by Michael Bullock. Copyright (c) 1970 by Weidenfeld and Nicolson Limited. Reprinted by permission of Pantheon Books, a Division of Random House, Inc.—Fussell, Paul. From *Abroad: British Literary Traveling Between the Wars.* Oxford University Press, 1980. Copyright (c) 1980 by Paul Fussell. Reproduced by permission of Oxford University Press, Inc.—Goebbels, Joseph. From *The Goebbels Diaries: 1942-1943* by Goebbels. Copyright (c) 1948 by The Fireside Press, Inc. Used by permission of Doubleday, a division of Bantam Doubleday Dell Publishing Group, Inc. All rights reserved. Used by permission of Doubleday, the publisher.—Greene, Graham. From *Collected Essays.* The Viking Press, 1969. Copyright 1951, (c) 1966, 1968, 1969 by Graham Greene. All rights reserved. Reproduced by permission of Viking Penguin, a division of Penguin Books USA, Inc. Reproduced by permission of David Higham Associates Limited for Graham Greene.—Guggenheimer, Richard. From *Sight and Insight: A Prediction of New Perceptions in Art.* Harper & Brothers Publishers, 1945. Copyright, 1945, by HarperCollins Publishers, Inc. All rights reserved. Reproduced by permission of HarperCollins Publishers, Inc.—Heiber, Helmut. From an introduction to *The Early Goebbels Diaries: The Journal of Joseph Goebbels from 1925-1926.* Edited by Helmut Heiber, translated by Oliver Watson. Weidenfeld and Nicolson, 1962. English translation (c) 1962 by George Weidenfeld & Nicolson, Ltd. All rights reserved. Reproduced by permission.—Kael, Pauline. From "A Great Folly, and a Small One," in *Going Steady.* Atlantic-Little, Brown, 1970. Reprinted by permission of Curtis Brown, Ltd. Copyright (c) 1968 by Pauline Kael, renewed.

Norman Douglas

1869–1952

Full name George Norman Douglas. Austrian-born English travel-writer, novelist, essayist, short story writer, scientist, poet, and critic.

INTRODUCTION

A writer of varied talents, Douglas is best known for his travel books that capture the mood and atmosphere of Mediterranean Europe in the first fcw decades of the twentieth century and for his novel *South Wind* (1917), which enjoyed widespread popularity in America during the 1920s and 1930s. As a travel-writer, Douglas is remembered for his erudite and highly expressive prose style in such works as *Fountains in the Sand* (1912) and *Old Calabria* (1915). Douglas's novels—characterized by his sardonic wit and trenchant satire—are meditations on hedonism, amorality, and the inadequacies of modern religion, and, like his travel books, are distinguished by his often brilliant evocations of natural setting. In his life and writings Douglas, an aesthete and an aristocrat by birth, adopted a pose of haughty disdain intermingled with flashes of humane concern, and dramatized his adage that "leisure is the key to artistic creation and appreciation."

Biographical Information

Douglas was born in Thüringen, Austria on December 8, 1868. His mother Vanda (Von Poellnitz) Douglass was the daughter of an Austrian Baron and his father Sholto Douglass, who died when Douglas was five years old, owned a local cotton mill. After her husband's death, Douglas's mother sent her son to preparatory school in England, though he later returned to the European continent in 1883 to attend the Karlsruhe Gymnasium. He spent six years at Karlsruhe, learning languages and expanding his youthful interest in the natural sciences—he published several scientific papers in his younger years, the most significant being *On the Darwinian Hypothesis of Sexual Selection* (1895). After graduating in 1889, Douglas spent the next several years traveling in Mediterranean Europe and North Africa and studying to enter the British Diplomatic Service. He passed his examinations in 1893 and after a year at the Foreign Office was transferred to St. Petersburg. Two and one half years later Douglas left the Diplomatic Service and resumed his travels. In 1898 he married Elsa FitzGibbon, with whom he collaborated on his first literary work, *Unprofessional Tales* (1901), a collection of short stories published under the joint pseudonym, "Normyx." The two experienced a bitter divorce, however, in 1903, and Douglas soon after left for the island of Capri. By 1907 his fortunes had largely

evaporated and Douglas turned to writing to maintain his livelihood. He began to write articles and reviews for several periodicals, including the *Atlantic Monthly*, *Cornhill Magazine*, and *Putnam's*, and to put together his first travel book, *Siren Land* (1911). He moved back to London in 1910 to find a publisher for the work, and spent three months in Tunisia during that year, a trip he described in *Fountains in the Sand*. Between 1913 and 1916 he worked as an assistant editor for the *English Review*. In 1917 Douglas published his most successful novel, *South Wind*, and two years later took up residence in Florence, were he would stay for the next two decades. In the early 1930s, Douglas experienced some troubles with the fascist government in Italy, especially because of the overtly erotic poetry of *Some Limericks* (1928). He fled to Lisbon, Portugal and later to London rather than face charges, but eventually returned to Italy after the Second World War. He continued to write and travel during this period, spending a great deal of time on the isle of Capri, the subject of his last work, *Footnote on Capri*, published shortly after his death (rumored to be the result of a self-induced overdose of medication) on February 9, 1952.

1

Major Works

While he wrote short stories, poetry, criticism, and scientific monographs, Douglas's significant literary works are generally limited to his travel books and three novels. In the former, Douglas presented many vivid descriptive passages of beautiful Mediterranean regions, including Capri (*Siren Land*, 1911), Tunisia (*Fountains in the Sand: Rambles Among the Oases of Tunisia*, 1912), Italy (*Old Calabria*, 1915, and *Alone*, 1922), and Greece (*One Day*, 1929). In his novels he more fully demonstrated his cynical and hedonistic sensibility, as well as varying degrees of humor, ranging from sarcasm to outright brutality. Douglas's first and best known novel, *South Wind*, was set on the fictional island of Nepenthe (patterned after the author's sometime home of Capri). The novel explores the influence of the Mediterranean atmosphere as a powerful inducement to hedonism, amorality, and ultimately happiness. In *They Went* (1921), a short novel set in a mythic city in Brittany during the late Roman era, Douglas presents an allegory of goodness pitted against beauty. *In the Beginning* (1927), similar in tone to the previous work, is an anti-religious fable in which Man, victimized by the disease of "goodness," forsakes a life of pleasure and eventually destroys itself. Among his other writings, Douglas produced several book-length essays, such as a survey of childhood imagination entitled *London Street Games* (1916) and a virulent reproach of bourgeois values in *Good-bye to Western Culture* (1929). Other works include *Experiments* (1925), a collection of formerly published stories, articles, and reviews; *Birds and Beasts of the Greek Anthology* (1927), a commentary on these animals, both mythic and real; *Looking Back: An Autobiographical Excursion* (1933), reminiscences and anecdotes about Douglas's friends; *An Almanac* (1941), a series of epigrams from his books; and *Late Harvest* (1946), containing personal commentary on his previously published writings.

Critical Reception

As a novelist, Douglas's reputation rests on *South Wind*, which is thought to have influenced a generation of young writers in America with its stylized characters, witty dialogue, and glorification of hedonism. Still, charges of poor characterization and a weak plot have since been leveled against the novel. Overall, Douglas's standing has declined considerably since the 1930s, the period of his greatest popularity. Some of his later works, particularly *Good-bye to Western Culture*, have been called excessively bitter; and some critics have observed that Douglas produced very little that was new in his last decades, opting instead to republish portions of earlier writings. For his travel writing, however, Douglas has been consistently praised, with many critics numbering him among the outstanding authors in the genre for his powerful and evocative descriptions of natural beauty.

PRINCIPAL WORKS

On the Darwinian Hypothesis of Sexual Selection (scientific monograph) 1895
Unprofessional Tales [as Normyx, with Elsa FitzGibbon] (short stories) 1901
Siren Land (travelogue) 1911
Fountains in the Sand: Rambles Among the Oases of Tunisia (travelogue) 1912
Old Calabria (travelogue) 1915
London Street Games (essay) 1916
South Wind (novel) 1917
They Went (novel) 1920
Alone (travelogue) 1922
Together (travelogue) 1923
D. H. Lawrence and Maurice Magnus: A Plea for Better Manners (essay) 1925
Experiments (essays, reviews, and stories) 1925
In the Beginning (novel) 1927
Birds and Beasts of the Greek Anthology (essays) 1927
Some Limericks (poetry) 1928
Nerinda (short story) 1929
One Day (travelogue) 1929
How About Europe? Some Footnotes on East and West [republished as *Good-bye to Western Culture*, 1930] (essay) 1929
Capri: Materials for a Description of the Island (travelogue) 1930
Paneros. Some Words on Aphrodisiacs and the Like (essay) 1932
Summer Islands: Ischia and Ponza (travelogue) 1931
Looking Back: An Autobiographical Excursion (reminiscences) 1933
An Almanac (epigrams) 1941
Late Harvest (essays) 1946
Footnote on Capri (travelogue with photographs) 1952

CRITICISM

Elizabeth D. Wheatley (essay date 1932)

SOURCE: "Norman Douglas," in *The Sewanee Review*, Vol. XL, No. 1, January, 1932, pp. 55-67.

[*In the following essay, Wheatley surveys such major works by Douglas as* South Wind, Experiments, *and* Goodbye to Western Culture, *commenting favorably on his main themes and style and comparing his writings to those of other authors, both contemporary and classical.*]

Here in America and perhaps in general elsewhere, Norman Douglas has suffered from neglect. Except for the attention paid to *South Wind* and the rather craven acceptance of *Goodbye to Western Culture,* he has not been properly introduced to a public who could reasonably enjoy him by taking pains to do so. There have been few articles in American magazines: the best of them was "The Early Work of Norman Douglas", by Edward D. McDonald, in *The Bookman* for September, 1927. There have been reviews of his books, ephemeral tributes. And there is always, for the Douglas lover and student, the *Centaur Bibliography of the Writings of Norman Douglas,* (Centaur Book Shop, Philadelphia, 1927), also by Edward D. McDonald. While this is now incomplete, since it ends, as to the books, with *Experiments* published in 1925, it is an enviably careful record of all printed matter up to 1927. Nevertheless, Mr. Douglas has not been adequately received here. The neglect may in part be attributed to the difficulty of reading him, and to the fact that he is totally unlike any other living writer. He has incalculable depths of culture and knowledge under his feet, and the magnetism of his work rests largely on that hard stratum.

One appears to find, on approaching Mr. Douglas, that a great deal of erudition is necessary to enjoy him. If one wishes to absorb him, one is led, like Mr. Eames, annotating the work of Monsignor Perrelli in *South Wind,* into a multitude of divergent roads of learning, into: "minerals, medicine, strategy, heraldry, navigation, palaeography, statistics, politics, botany", and into letters, philosophy, psychology, history, biology, bibliography, and all the arts. It seems too difficult to reach æsthetic relaxation by such a hard road. But that difficulty is Mr. Douglas' tonic quality, the thing that makes him perennially interesting. One cannot wallow in him as in Cabell or Erskine, in Hemingway, or Faulkner. He requires to be met by the spirit alert, erect, and stubborn. He is the touch of earth that renews Antœus. His claim to immortality rests upon his difficulty as well as upon his crystalline hardness and fragrance. He who wishes to understand the firm splendor of the Douglas spirit can do so by a process of patient innoculation. He should begin with *Experiments*. He should read the first chapter on Doughty's *Arabia Deserta,* the chapter on Isabelle Eberhart, the essay on Poe, and above all things, the pamphlet on Lawrence and Magnus, most fortunately included. He should leave the rest of *Experiments* and go on to *Alone*. And with convenient intervals of rest from so much vigor, he should read *Together, South Wind,* and *Old Calabria*. Now he is ready for anything. He has imbued himself with a master, and he will always be coming back for more.

And what will the reader of Douglas find? He will find that Norman Douglas stands out in the field of contemporary letters like an historic pine, divorced from its forest fellows, lofty and alone on a mountain slope; an erect, wind-warped figure from which emanates an aromatic spice. And yet, there is too much that is turbid, restless, homeless, and voracious, about Mr. Douglas to let such a static comparison remain unchallenged. He is more like a torrential, flood-swollen river, a stream that

in its onward rush carries away hindering banks, devours fields, scours out caverns, and bears in its breast innumerable forms of strange life; a stream that splits the solid earth with its terrible silver beauty. But whether he be compared to a tree, or to living waters, the fact of his solitary uniqueness remains. In spite of his many and opposing phases of character, there is still a oneness, a "uniquity", a marked and over-powering personality which differentiates him from the diffused and nervous intellects of modern literature. It is said of him that he does not like analogies drawn between himself and other writers. And to compare him with the moderns is impossible. One must go back to the giants of other times; to Voltaire, Darwin, and Nietzsche. These men and their like, and Douglas are the center of a storm of which the moderns are the diminishing and weary waves. Norman Douglas himself has been, so it seems, a follower in one case only. He has absorbed Nietzschean principles, perhaps unconsciously, and has made of himself a super-man. His last works indicate that he has reached that point of cold sanity which borders perilously on insanity. In fact, one might, not unreasonably, think on reading *In the Beginning,* that the leaf had fallen which turns the scale. In times past Douglas had a thousand Protean shapes both terrible and sweet. He has become by the strictures of time, and, one fears, of neglect, a stiffening figure, sometimes negatively and peevishly ferocious. He is hardening into a grinning garden god, a battered Priapus. And still he stands alone, superior in golden, Hellenic vitality. It is as if Priapus stood in a glade of eternal sunshine.

I

The work of Norman Douglas divides itself roughly into three classes; scientific, critical, and creative. It covers intermittently a period of over forty years. The first printed thing was a small contribution to *The Zoologist, a Monthly Journal of Natural Science,* in 1886. The last was *Goodbye to Western Culture,* in 1930. The early treatises on natural science, (1886-95), can have little interest for letters, except as an indication of their author's inexhaustible, insatiate zest for curious knowledge, and as a clue to his continuous preference for nature over man. The archaeological studies of Capri, (1904-15), may long continue to interest the leisured and scholarly traveler; but a great deal of the material from them has been incorporated in *Siren Land,* and *Old Calabria*. The *Centaur Bibliography* gives the information that hints from *The Forestal Conditions of Capri* found their way into the second chapter of *Siren Land*: and that the monograph on "Tiberius", and the *Life of the Venerable Suor Serafino Di Dio,* became respectively the fourth and ninth chapters of *Siren Land*: and that material on the "Saracens in Italy" became chapter eighteen of *Old Calabria*. Some of the Capri work was also rewritten for various magazines. This reworking of material is very characteristic of Mr. Douglas. He seems loath to part with anything which his brain has tested and moulded. He is constantly scrutinizing, perfecting, and giving new birth to those of his writings for which he has most respect. One might be tempted to deduce from this that he exhibits a scientist's hunger for infallibility, rather than a creator's exuberance.

It would be an interesting and profitable labor to extract from all his critical writings that entity, Mr. Douglas the critic. One may venture the supposition from what little is known, that he could not be proven an originator or creator in the field of criticism. He would be a follower, but a follower of what has been most noble in the past. He would be found a commentator, rather than a critic; and his mind charged with Hellenism would be a touchstone to determine the intrinsically pure from the base. He would be discovered, perhaps, as the last exemplar of Renaissance Humanism, as it has been explained by Santayana in *The Genteel Tradition at Bay.*

Norman Douglas' critical work contributed chiefly to the *English Review* over a period of about four years, (1912-16), and to several other journals up until 1925, has been scantily collected. He seems to value it less than other kinds of his writing. When one reads the list of reviews tabulated by McDonald in the *Centaur Bibliography* one wishes profoundly that more of them had been put into book form. What, for instance, has he said about Francis Brett Young's critical study of *Robert Bridges;* what about Irving Babbitt's *Masters of French Criticism;* or about Van Wyck Brooks' *John Addington Symonds?* It seems a shame that the activity of his mind on these subjects and others of equal importance should be contained only in the comparatively ephemeral records of a journal. A few samples of reviewing work are included in *Experiments,* which is entirely a collection of early writings. By comparison with the really critical essays in the same book, these reviews seem sketchy and impatient. That is no great wonder, however, when one observes the trivial subjects which he has, for the most part, dealt with. It is like seeing a giant play with a child's jack-straws. Why were these inept things saved at the expense of what must have been better? Why have they been allowed to encumber a book otherwise radiant with charm? That is one of the peculiar Douglas mysteries of which there are many. These reviews are fragile little hooks upon which to hang reflections and prejudices that are more firmly expressed elsewhere.

It is not wrenching the natural order of things to put *Experiments* and *Goodbye to Western Culture* side by side. The ideas that are the backbone of *Experiments* have become lively with time, and have broken out in the later book into an angry flame that gives forth acrid and sulphurous odors; a flame in which prance ribald and ridiculous devils. Mr. Douglas reminds us here of another uneasy, sulphurous, and revolting soul of an earlier generation, Mark Twain. Both of these men are rebels against material stagnation, against bourgeois

primness, and the fawning habits of a people who are uncertain of their culture and nervous about their safety in this world and the next. Mr. Douglas has advanced in courage beyond Twain, and attacks both Christianity and its legal institutions with blundering ferocity. He is beside himself with rage, like a man devoured by ants. And he succeeds in leaving the general impression with the puzzled reader of *Goodbye to Western Culture,* that Christianity is an evil spirit flown out of India, a demon exorcised which has left behind it, in that pleasant Eastern land, a life and society entirely wholesome, excellent, and righteous. It is a very amusing book; and some of it is sadly true. But one must finally feel that the shoe pinches Mr. Douglas somewhere or he would not have troubled to write his tirade. He is not sufficiently in love with human beings to care very much what absurdities they commit. With the exception of his very righteous remarks on reform schools and education, he is furious only about those annoyances that interfere with his comfort, and quite complacent about others that do not. *Goodbye to Western Culture* has the ear-marks of a private spleen. It is something of a sport from the rest of Douglas' work.

However, were Norman Douglas, speaking in literary manner, always perfect, he would be as intolerable as Emerson. When he takes the pains to be genuinely critical, (and that is when he honors his subject), the result of his thought is a penetrative rightness which comes, not so much from fixed or original critical principles, as from what is naturally right and vigorous in Douglas himself. In Doughty's *Arabia Deserta,* for example, he appreciates those qualities which are most firmly imbedded in his own nature, and which break forth again and again in his own writing, like the craggy out-cropping of an upland pasture. He says of Doughty: "What drove him, besides an Homeric love of adventure, to endure those hardships was pure intellectual curiosity, the longing of a brain that feeds on disinterested thought." The Homeric quality, the intellectual longing—that is Douglas. Speaking of authors of travel literature, he says: "Those earlier ones were gentlemen scholars who saw things from their own individual angle. Their leisurely, aristocratic flavor, their wholesome discussions about this or that, their waywardness, and all their mercurial touch of a bygone generation, where is it now?" It is kept in Douglas. But in one respect what he says about Doughty will not do for himself. He remarks upon Doughty's reserve and his sublime detachment. Mr. Douglas is at times neither reserved not detached. He has moments of submitting to his own crustacean prejudices, of hysterically bowing to his own idols, that constitute a sort of temporary blind staggers, an intoxication of bitterness such as has occasionally infected our frantic Mr. Mencken.

II

And now the lesser, and still great Mr. Douglas can be left for the time, firm in the superior qualities of his scientific curiosity, his endless knowledge, his generosity for the things he trusts, his outrageous and sometimes medicating sanity. Leaving his irritations, his flair for the reversed platitude, we can pass on to the truly immortal Mr. Douglas, he who creates. Under the head of creative writing must come, not only his short stories and novels, but also and in particular, his reminiscences, his memoirs of wandering: *Siren Land, Fountains in the Sand, Old Calabria, Alone,* and *Together*. Creative memoirs! There is no better word for these things in their golden fullness. They are the kind of memoirs that Douglas is always asking other people to write, the revelations of a rich, various, an instinctively noble personality.

The first effect of these travel books and the others is that Douglas is a non-creative and purely exploratory writer. That impression persists for a long time, because he has a trick of repeating his work as if at loss for new material. Nearly all of his few short stories have had several printings, each with an improving revision. And the material of the Capri studies has entered not only into *Siren Land* and *Old Calabria,* but into the structure of *South Wind*. Mr. Douglas has apparently only one poem to his credit, and no plays, unless he himself undertook the dramatization of *South Wind*. He is not a plot maker; and his characters, however vigorous, are few. The best of them may be discovered to be emanations from his own variegated personality. But when one puts side by side Mr. Douglas' work as a whole, and the judgment of Mr. Edward D. McDonald, who has named him reasonably and truly a realist and stylist, the creative element comes to light by contrast. It is true that Mr. Douglas is a realist in his inexhaustible and thoughtful observations. It is also true that he is a stylist in the perfect impact of thought and word and in mellow sequences. But he is more; he has something beyond the nervous modern fad for minutiae. This something is mythopoesis, the ability, the need to invest natural phenomena with sprites and demons, to shroud the bones of life with fair flesh, and breathe an individual spirit into the body of his creation. He has, in short, the Coleridgean esemplastic imagination. Let us take his own word for it.

> To hear the "subtle harmony" and respond to the gentle promptings of the *genius loci,* the unseen presence, is what Doughty found to be a talisman. So might others find, but never will among the unseemly and restless conditions of modern life . . . The drying up of the fountains of mythopoesis, the elimination of mystery might well sadden and sterilize a poetic soul.
> —*Experiments,* "Arabia Deserta."

> I have only a diary of dates to go upon, out of which with the help of memory and imagination have been extracted these pages . . . Imagination— why not? Truth blends well with untruth, and phantasy has been so sternly banned of late from travelers' tales that I am growing tenderhearted toward the poor old dame; quite chivalrous in fact, especially on those rather frequent occasions

> when I find myself unable to dispense with her services.
> —*Alone*.

The elusive fascination and magnetism of Mr. Douglas' writing, the compulsion of it, lie in his refulgent poetic quality. He is a maker of dreams and dragons. These travel books are full of such infectious moments of beauty as only the creative genius can produce. Consider two extracts from *Together,* perhaps the most personal and revealing of the books of reminiscence, if not the finest.

> They dig peat here as in many of these upland bogs, and the rank vegetation with its pungent odours, sweet and savage, has not yet been mowed down—a maze of tall blue gentians, and mint and mare's tail, and flame-like pyramids of ruby color, and meadowsweet, and the two yellows, the lusty and the frail, all tenderly confused among the mauve mist of flowering reeds.

> Stars are out; the Tschallenga hill confronting us has become pitch black; those Rhaetian peaks are like steel, and their snow-patches have a dead look at this hour. Tawny exhalations as of lingering day, flit about the Swiss mountains on our west. Some grass has been mown up here, during the host afternoon; the air is full of its fragrance.

Simple things these two quotations, but how difficult to do without over-doing! They are *alive!* Only the creative hand can so master the color in prose and weave it into a vital entity. It is not every one who will think of snow gone dead at twilight, of tawny exhalations, of frail and lusty yellows. There is a jewel-H like quality about this writing, as if it were a diamond with an eternity of light playing in its depths.

Norman Douglas is creative also in his writing of men, whether they be garnered from the past, or men of his own knowing. He seems to have held few women in sufficient respect to make living personalities of them in his books: Ouida, Isabelle Eberhardt, his dour old grandmother, the housewife from whom he extracts the information that she roasts coffee "to the color of a capuchin's frock". That is his method of creating with people. He extracts something of their individuality, or their oddity, something dear to his heart, and embodies in it an ever fresh fragment of his writing. There is Ramage, for example, author of that ripe companion of Douglas' Italian wanderings, *The Nooks and Byways of Italy;* and there are the guides, the innkeepers, the stray acquaintances, those rural Italian family men, and all the innumerable people of the distant past upon whom he touches so frequently. They all live for us under his hand, and require a returning, a constant renewal of their friendship. This is creation; it is not realism, which hands you actualities as a stone for bread.

And now we come to creation as it is more usually understood, the synthesis of plot, the birth of characters.

Mr. Douglas' record is slender but glowing. It begins with the short stories which were first published pseudonymously in *Unprofessional Tales,* (1901). In the Centaur Bibliography, Mr. McDonald tells us that all of these tales but one had a collaborator, and that they were, "tentative and derivative work". They were obviously little flowers offered on the altar of Poe. In later years they were frequently worked over, and must have been invested with the peculiar Douglas originality. Those that are included in *Experiments* have become deft and elvish little intaglios, sometimes grotesque and terrible, sometimes weirdly beautiful, but always delicate.

There are two novels and one long mythological tale, *In the Beginning,* (1928). The writing of this last seems to have been rather a mistake on Mr. Douglas' part. The particular kind of ribaldry which is its essence has become a little stale since *Candide,* and *Penguin Island;* and it has been much overworked by Cabell. But even *In the Beginning* has its moments of beauty; for Mr. Douglas cannot touch anything without imparting to it a fiery phoenix charm.

How many mistakes a man may be forgiven for the sake of *They Went* and *South Wind*! Innumerable literary errors may be allowed to slip into the blackness of forgetting, while one remembers: Theophilus, and the green Princess; Keith, Count Caloveglia, Don Francesco, and the decent Eames who loved the "ballon captif". These two novels are glowing things, full of seductive poetry and summer enchantment. Mr. Douglas is said to have remarked of *South Wind* that it took a long period of happiness to write. He must have had that happiness for *They Went,* also. The two books are different in music and color. They are greatly differentiated by the fact that *They Went,* which should have been named "Theophilus" after its Miltonic fiend, is pure fantasy, the frothy incarnation of a legend. *South Wind* has the dash of reality that makes its illusion credible. The one is a fairy tale; the other might have happened. *They Went* is, however, the firmer book of the two, the more severely patterned; it has a backbone in the character of Theophilus which is lacking to the other. In spite of the fact that Douglas is constantly using a leif-motif of rainbow mist; it is hard, green, and malicious like an emerald. *South Wind* is hot and multicolored. Both of these books are invaded by the sea, the ever-beloved companion of Mr. Douglas, the great and joyous philosopher who is never troubled by categorical imperatives, whose moods, terrible, devouring, playful or serene, reflect his own.

There was quite a little commotion, at least in the author's mind, about the plot of *South Wind.* Some unfortunate reviewers said that it had none. It is presumable that they could give honest reasons for their opinion, but Mr. Douglas' ire was aroused. In a subsequent book, *Alone,* he proved that *South Wind* was all plot from beginning to end. The plot, he says, was to provide subtle means whereby a Bishop should be fuddled into overlooking a murder. The very fineness of the plot lay in its obscurity. It is indeed so obscure that one is tempted to believe Mr. Douglas thought about it after the book was written. The Bishop was to be secretly unravelled and unmoralized by the langorous airs, and by the savage beauty of the island of Nepenthe, until the murder, committed by a woman for whom he had great respect, seemed of no importance. In short, the poor Bishop was the butt of Douglas' Voltairean priesthatred. He made the mistake, however, of creating in the Bishop a flexible dummy instead of a man. It is child's play to knock down a dummy. Had Mr. Douglas faced a real Bishop with his golden absurdities, he would have met an *impasse.* For it is the business of Bishops to forgive and forget more terrible crimes than murder.

There are numbers of little plots in *South Wind,* elusive things, perfect for short stories, but almost lost in the glowing mass of the whole. The best of them is the story of Count Caloveglia, the Hellenic impostor, the creator of that glorious fraud, the Locri Faun. There is no one plot for the whole book; but it does not need one. Its fascinations are endless without. I have said that it is real, and so it is, in the sense that it might happen, but the very name of the island which is its scenic background, gives it the unsubstantiality of a summer dream; Nepenthe, surcease of sorrow. It is a holiday performance; a masque, a revel, into which are poured all of the author's most joyous pagan humours and no small share of his learning. The torrential Mr. Douglas has become playful and serene, content for sunny hours to spray his wit in deathless conversations.

One puzzles a little about the fiftieth and last chapter of *South Wind.* It seems at first sight an obvious afterthought, but one realizes, finally, that the book could end only so, with the disintegration of the whole Nepenthe crowd, except Caloveglia, in an orgie of drunkeness. It strikes a fair balance for the disintegration of the straw Bishop. One particularly rejoices in the last feebleness of Keith, the Bishop's anti-type. An admirable conversationalist is Mr. Keith; a poor pagan, with his Achilles heel of fear. One feels no little contempt for him, and his life carefully garnered for ever more and more peculiar pleasures of the senses. He is really likable only when he is naïve and boring. Caloveglia, on the other hand, is a man with a cult of perfection in moderation, and with genius. He is one of the few persons upon whom Mr. Douglas has not exercised his malicious desire for defamation and detraction. Perhaps because Caloveglia has from the beginning the unmoral gift for regal lying, his creator feels no need to unpedestal him as he does so many other estimable people. Eames is an example of it. To rip away the pitiful tatters of self-respect, to undermine the foundations of pomposity, and find worms in fair roses—that is Douglas' particular notion of irony. *South Wind* is not a book to be comprehended in a day. One must put oneself in a receptive and amiable mood for it, and then paradoxically be on guard against too much receptiveness. In all his work Douglas can never be submitted to, and particularly in this. Summer madness as it is, **South Wind** requires continuous agility on the part of the reader lest he, too, be fuddled by the sirocco. This playful ocean mood of Mr. Douglas is very treacherous.

Something is the matter with both **South Wind** and **They Went**. Something they lack. Urbanity, distinction, beauty, they have all this, and a highly charged life. They have also a disarming naiveté. They lack ultimate emotions. These books are the products of hedonism; they are the embodiment of the æsthetic moment for its own sake. Let is be said with truth that to embody such a moment is the artist's goal. Is it enough? The answer to that is, of course, that both **South Wind** and **They Went** are only a glorious kind of fooling, like *The Shaving of Shagpat*. But the fooling is so large and impressive that one is cajoled into taking it seriously, and into hunting for the germ of a truth such as is to be found in *Shagpat*. One must take care to remember that **They Went** and **South Wind** are the unwinding of all truth by a summer hurricane. It is useless to look to Douglas for any emotional satisfaction; he is too experimental. One wearies at last of the metallic and bitter beauty of **They Went,** and of the hot commotion of **South Wind**. One must go back to **Alone,** and **Old Calabria** for completer satisfaction.

III

Innumerable essays and books could be written about Mr. Douglas to dissect, analyse, and track to their source the infinite facets and contradictions of his literary personality. One of his chief values to modern literature is that Renaissance zest which supplies for the aspiring critic an inexhaustible field of creative work. One might write a complete book replete with quotations, on the Douglas humour, which is ever present, either boisterously or under the surface. It is as varied as the rest of his personality, sometimes heavy-treading and ponderous, sometimes illusive and glancing as marsh lights. One might write an amusing monograph on Mr. Douglas' preferences in inns, and wines, and his taste in food. Much could be written on his contradictions: on the hermaphroditic character of him by which he is at times, brusque and "robustious", even goatish, and at other times, more tender and winsome than a woman; on the fact that he calls all religious symbols absurd, and yet is constantly making of everything that he touches into beauty, a symbol of some ghostly quality; and on the still greater contradiction that he is at once modest, almost shy, and yet highly egotistical. In the last analysis, Mr. Douglas writes of little but himself. He never interprets anything human except in the flood of his own personality. Like all Nietzschean folk, who are terribly afraid of dissolving in the crowd, he will listen with infinite, sweet patience to the unseen sprites of wood, and water, and mountain, and to the shy talk of animals; but never will he quite surrender himself to the human mood. Like all complete egotists, he is insentient to the murmur of the human heart, unless it beats

in tune with his own. That is why his creation, which is the liquefaction of external things in his own chemistry, exists chiefly in memoirs, rather than in poems, or plays, or novels.

Mr. Douglas' ultimate value for modern literature lies in the fact that, although he is a rebel, he is not one of the disillusioned. Life is not bleak for him, never a thing to whine about. He escapes, it is true, but into such things as may profitably offer themselves with infinite variety, to any one; into mountain and woodland fastnesses, into the cleansing lore of antiquity. He freshens such sour humours as produce a Sinclair Lewis, or a Faulkner, with the wind of wider horizons. His philosophy seems to be a mingling of Epicureanism, Nietzscheanism, and fortitude; and fortitude is the greater part. He is assuredly one of the immortals. So much vitality, so much "terrific sunshine" cannot soon die away. In the introduction to Wyndham Lewis' *Francois Villon,* Hilaire Belloc speaks of a quality of "hardness" in Villon, which assures him deathless literary value. It is by this same kind of hardness that Douglas also will survive the erosions of time. And by that other quality named by Nietzsche in speaking of himself, fragrance. Douglas works not in butter, nor yet in oak, but in veined marble and crystal; and his work gives forth a myriad of living scents, as if it had the warmth of flesh. In years to come, some one taking down **Old Calabria** from a dusty shelf of antiquities, will find in it that timeless summer odor, that resilient unsubmissiveness.

H. T. Webster (essay date 1950)

SOURCE: "Norman Douglas: A Reconsideration," in *South Atlantic Quarterly,* Vol. 49, No. 2, April, 1950, pp. 226-36.

[*In the following essay, Webster examines Douglas's reputation and the reception of his works by critics and the general reading public. He concludes that the autobiographical nature of Douglas's work accounts for its abiding energy and vibrancy.*]

In the burgeoning of the 1920's, when every publisher's list seemed to make literary history, few writers enjoyed a greater *succès d'estime* than Norman Douglas. Everybody who thought of himself as belonging to the cognoscenti, the intelligentsia, the sophisticates, or even the intelligent minority, admired **South Wind**. For the American tourist-third bound for Europe this book must have been almost the familiar traveling companion that Joyce's *Ulysses* was on the return voyage. Less temperate Douglas devotees read all of his books and bought them too—often in expensive limited editions. As one satisfied purchaser of **Birds and Beasts of the Greek Anthology** remarked: "I believe he could write a book about the alphabet and make it interesting." These words adequately sum up the initial reaction to Douglas of many aging admirers. They suggest exceptional virtues, for even the best authors are usually guilty of *longueurs* that the most appreciative reader must meet with resignation. But Norman Douglas's early scientific writings became valued collectors' items, and his casual review articles were reprinted in anticipation of the scholar's gleanings.

The 1940's have seen a good many reputations, dazzling a couple of decades ago, fade into the light of common day. Yet Norman Douglas appears to have suffered an unreasonably drastic eclipse of fame. A generation has reached maturity that knows of *South Wind* only by hearsay. This was to be expected. But Mr. Douglas's most recent book, *Late Harvest* (London, 1946), did not even find a publisher in this country, which seems a little hard on a person who once counted Joseph Conrad and Lytton Strachey among his admirers. Worst of all, the literary historian, who has among his duties that of keeping alive the names of eminent authors that nobody reads, has demoted Douglas from a complimentary line or two in Légouis and Cazamian's revised *History of English Literature* (1935) to a dismal footnote in the new and authoritative *Literary History of England* edited by Professor Albert C. Baugh in 1948. In a short outline history composed by Professor Bernard Grebanier, Douglas's name is not mentioned. Thus, his writing is at present officially considered inconsequential beside that of Lytton Strachey, E. M. Forster, Virginia Woolf, and R. B. Cunninghame Graham, to mention the names of a few esteemed figures who seemed at best no more than his peers a few years ago. On the whole this is rather cavalier treatment of a man whose position in English literature was lately regarded as assured by a discriminating public and distinguished fellow craftsmen. It is a state of affairs which provokes comments and can hardly be expected to persist. Meanwhile, a near octogenarian, Douglas in *Late Harvest* makes a brief appearance before the curtain, and he is almost better than ever.

There can be little doubt that the present neglect of Douglas arises in part from the fact that the basic appeal of his work cannot be described in the critical terminology it has suggested. Most of the critics and historians who have tackled him have done so with a slightly puzzled air, and Douglas has remained a controversial figure, not so much because his literary merits are disputed, as because they have been given no satisfactory definition. Meanwhile, his more enthusiastic readers sense virtues which the critics have not clarified.

It was inevitable in an age which associates major literary activity with the novel that he would be known and judged chiefly by *South Wind*. What can the literary historian say of such a book? That it is a twentieth-century version of the fantastic discussion novel, resembling Peacock and foreshadowing Aldous Huxley and Evelyn Waugh? This hardly constitutes a recommendation. Peacock is today little more than a literary curiosity, and people who are reading Huxley and Waugh are not likely to turn back to a precursor. Besides, the scholar may well contest the historic importance of *South Wind* as a refurbishing of the discussion novel. Anatole France, Remy de Gourmont, and Maurice Barrès had produced a variety of modern examples of it which anticipated much of the form and ideational character of *South Wind*. Clearly, the literary historian, following his usual grooves of thought and comment, will fail to describe *South Wind* adequately even if he likes it. The more philosophic commentator, attempting to define the book's immediate appeal in the days of its first popularity, will hardly do better. In the perspective of thirty years, he might observe that it provided an escape of fantasy more robust than Mr. Cabell's Poictesme for a generation that found escape fantasies one way to deal with a reality which seemed crass when it was not dreary; that it gave actuality and body to the confused Hellenism which had been set even in Matthew Arnold's time as a corrective to the rigors of the Puritans; that it offered the Anglo-American reader an initiation into the Mediterranean viewpoint as Madame de Staël's *Corinne, ou L'Italie* and Stendhal's *Rôme, Naples et Florence* had done for the French a hundred years before. Still, no great recommendation for *South Wind*; still nothing to distinguish it from a hundred volumes that most of us feel no vocation to read.

Perhaps the luxuriance of wit and sophistication with which *South Wind* is embellished has encouraged an oversophisticated view of it, which blinds us to cruder and more fundamental virtues. At any rate, Mr. Douglas suggests a more naïve approach in *Late Harvest*. It seems to require little critical penetration to note that *South Wind* is an uproariously funny book, one of the few in the language that can reasonably be expected to shake people with laughter when it is read aloud. Yet in all the more intellectualized claims made for it, critics have characteristically overlooked this simple and basic one. Few writers have the genuine comic vocation. For comedy in the grand style, irrepressible high spirits must survive wide worldly experience, erudition, and a literary technic that must usually be acquired laboriously. In the perspective of thirty-odd years we may now suspect that Mr. Douglas belongs among the comic writers in the grand style. The ideas that he advanced in his novel were never as original as they appeared to be to early readers, but Mr. Freddy Parker, Miss Wilberforce, Signor Malipizzo, and a host of other genial burlesques are as peculiarly Douglas's figures as Uncle Toby and the Widow Wadman and Mr. Pickwick are figures of their creators. Moreover, Douglas's comic characters are classic types, likely to be recognizable in any foreseeable future. Time may change the terms in which a pompous, incompetent fraud like Mr. Freddy Parker and a rancorous man like Signor Malipizzo express themselves, but future readers will still see Freddy Parkers and Signor Malipizzos around them. Nor is the humor of *South Wind* that of character alone. No author has turned erudition to better purpose of comedy. Ben Jonson, Samuel Butler, and even Sterne puzzle us with obscurities of learning, but Douglas sticks to the highways most of us travel, and his travesty of the renaissance autocrat in the Good Duke Alfred, of more extravagant saints legends in Saint Dodekanus, and of the very geology of Nepenthe in the account of the mineral springs are not likely to need the illumination of footnotes in the future.

South Wind, then, seems to have a very good chance of taking its place in literature as a masterpiece of English comic writing rather than as the tendential presentation of a point of view, which has been the quality most noted in it to date. Perhaps we may even have future scholarly monographs on the Shandean delicacy of the Cave of Mercury episodes, the slapstick note of Mr. Keith's misfortune with the lime receptacle, the transatlantic touch in Cornelius van Koppen's adventure with the overgrown peas, the Caledonian absurdity of Mr. Keith and the committee to restrict Miss Wilberforce, the Mediterranean local color of the "nice old mans" and the "dam' fool foreigner." The scholar might want to compare the alcoholic festivities at the club with inebriate incidents in *Pickwick* or Shirley's *Lady of Pleasure* or Congreve's *Love for Love.* Such matters can be carried pretty far afield, but it is sufficient in the present article to observe that Douglas's humor is robust enough to bear such handling.

If *South Wind* introduced Douglas to a wide reading public, it also helped to distort the critical appreciation of his other books. An author, like an actor, is likely to pay for popular success by being "typed" in the minds of his readers. Douglas's critics and admirers approached his later works with the hope that these would resemble *South Wind.* Though new *South Wind*'s were forthcoming in due course, they were not from the pen of Norman Douglas. There can be no doubt that the failure to do another *South Wind* cost him immediate popularity. In *Looking Back* he included two chapters of a discarded novel, almost as though to demonstrate how easily he could have gratified his public's wishes, but for better or worse he did not himself fall a victim to the sirocco worship which prevailed at the time. Instead, he departed into new territory.

His two later novels, *They Went* and *In the Beginning,* were puzzling and not entirely successful excursions into the sort of anthropological fiction which Thomas Mann has recently written in a more solemn vein. If such imaginative recreations of the dawn of civilization become a recognized literary type, these books may retain some historic importance. *In the Beginning* certainly has enough artistic vitality to hold a few future readers, as does *Vathek,* a remotely comparable example. Yet both novels promise more than they perform, and Douglas would deserve to be demoted to the footnotes of literary history if he had nothing less eccentric to recommend him. Other books, nonfiction these, did little to clarify his position. *Together, Alone,* and *Experiments* were clearly not very much like earlier travel books such as *Siren Land* and *Old Calabria,* and in fact, taken out of the context of the rest of Douglas's work, they are hard to label at all. Yet when they were published, they continued to attract a

small but faithful and discriminating public to their author.

The precipitous decline of Douglas's reputation dates from the volume called **How About Europe?** in England and **Goodbye to Western Culture** in America. This book on its publication seemed like a long and tedious coda to *South Wind* and out of date as well. In 1930 even the newspapers were printing more discouraging reports of Western civilization than anything Mr. Douglas had to record. Possibly a few traveled Americans could not resist a smile at the splenetic summary of the discomforts of the tourist in England, but this is about the best that can be said for it. When **Looking Back,** Douglas's autobiography, was published in 1933, the murk of depression and war already enveloped us, and the author seemed to be speaking from a different planet. In the early 1930's Douglas was thus the victim not so much of a critical revaluation as of a lapse in that special sort of appeal writers occasionally have for the public when they are in the favored position of putting into the reader's mouth exactly what the reader himself wants to say. Books like **South Wind** and **Old Calabria** could hardly have been better designed to anticipate and ingratiatingly express the distaste for the sanctioned values of an Anglo-American way of life, which began to turn the stomachs of rebels on both sides of the Atlantic in the next decade.

Professor Samuel C. Chew speaks of "the boldness of Douglas's assault upon conventional moral standards" (*A Literary History of England,* 1948). Needless to say, most authors of that period who still interest us were holding these same moral standards up to critical scrutiny. The scrutiny had really begun as far back as Matthew Arnold, who first raised the problem. Douglas's attack on conventions was bold in the sense that it was uncompromising and showed none of that ambivalence of sympathy which characterized certain of his generation, but it delighted its early readers more by its skilful flanking tactics than by its impetuosity. While H. L. Mencken abused the evangelists, Douglas suavely cajoled his Bishop of Bampopo into approving a well-justified murder. There was a marked difference in social tone and literary skill. Douglas may very well have been the most effective of this iconoclastic generation. He marshaled an enormous amount of erudition, wit, worldly experience, and common sense against Philistia's whole way of life and even managed to persuade good manners to turn traitor in the enemy's camp. He had the advantage that he really meant his assault. One had the uneasy suspicion that many of his brothers-in-arms were seeing only the reverse of the medal, but it was clear that Douglas had no lingering emotional attachment to the things he ridiculed. Moreover, alone among the critics of the puritan-industrial way of life in the 1920's, he had an understandable set of positive values to offer his reader. It was an age of misty and somewhat ridiculous Utopias, in which D. H. Lawrence's almost occult instinctivism vied with Eliot's mannered attachment to church, king, and John Dryden, and Hemingway's cult of blood and courage was strikingly contrasted with Ronald Firbank's perfumed fairyland. Small wonder that for the more balanced sort of reader Douglas's tempered epicureanism with his savor of the past and present, his delight in a visible world of flora and fauna, his wholehearted acceptance of empiric science in all its implications, and all this in a brilliantly colored Mediterranean setting, seemed by far the best answer to the more dreary actualities of the Anglo-American scene.

The way of life Douglas exemplified and recommended had the disadvantage that to be lived successfully it required some of his own genius and something of a private income, but neither of these things seemed insuperable obstacles to malcontents in those days. As an ideal, it had been quite capable of being realized in many periods of human history. The cosmopolitan sage that Douglas typified came to be at an awkward disadvantage in the 1930's and still is today. Nevertheless, Norman Douglas remains as the yea-sayer of a dispirited generation, pointing out the many blessings of this life which we perversely make unavailable to ourselves. The first ten pages of **Late Harvest** alone should assure his literary immortality as a moving expression of the by no means solemn serenity of extreme old age. "How have I spent my days?" asks Mr. Douglas as a preface to retrospective notes on his books. Most people who know something of his books will answer—enviably.

While a literary artist is never a formal philosopher, Norman Douglas's work represents a clear enough pattern of ideas which still have their bearing on a troubled present, though the bearing is a little obscured by the complexity of our problems, and also by our author's frequent eccentricities of opinion. Douglas bristles with these, but as with Samuel Johnson they often generate a sort of affection. Perhaps it flatters the reader's self-esteem to find such gifted figures so harmlessly wrong. But with Douglas, as with Samuel Johnson, common sense is likely to triumph in any real pinch. If he gets ridiculously excited about the suggestive fashion with which the canaille of the French customs finger the lingerie of genuine British ladies, we find him again on firm ground when he writes of the inhumanity of French orphan asylums. Better still, in his famous controversy with D. H. Lawrence about Maurice Magnus and other matters we note that though Douglas appears to be the touchy eccentric, stirred in his shell by the luminous common sense of Lawrence, it is also Douglas who maintains the principle that authors have no right lightly to expose recognizable people to contempt on the basis of personal dislike. The principle is admitted in general practice and should be, though Douglas's own **Looking Back** would be almost better without it. In spite of a battle-scarred career, he treats nearly everyone except a few anonymous magistrates with a forbearance which increases one's admiration for the man and occasionally detracts from the interest of the book.

Lawrence himself is let off with the spirited and nettled account of a personal relationship, which Douglas does not confuse with Lawrence's undoubted genius. Such things as this give one confidence in the balance of a very individual and sometimes wayward personality.

Douglas's personality: The words bring us to a new and very important facet of his work. Few writers are personally as interesting as their creations. No one would expect Shakespeare to be as fascinating as Hamlet or Falstaff, or Dickens to be half as funny as Sam Weller. Perhaps this abnegation of the author in the character is the final expression of genius. But most of Douglas's readers have suspected that the author is personally more interesting than his creations. In **Late Harvest** he encourages us to look on the whole canon of his work as an autobiography. "Now, having reached nearly twice the age at which Platen died, I no longer complain of how I squandered my days; my one regret is that I have not many more of them to squander. If one has enjoyed life and contrived to extract matter of mirth even out of its not infrequent mishaps, one cannot be said to have squandered one's days. . . . And there is this advantage in the writing of books when they are in some measure autobiographical, describing events from early childhood onwards; instead of being confused memories they are authentic documents which allow a man to live his life over again. . . . For Platen's exclamation point I substitute a question mark. How have you spent your days?"

So Mr. Douglas puts the word *autobiographical* into our mouths. It is the obvious term which no one thought to apply to **Together** and **Alone** when they were published, and which also would have explained satisfactorily the basic literary impulse in **Siren Land** and **Old Calabria**. It brings his work into new perspective and even accounts for his wish to preserve such trivial things as the review articles which he reprints in **Experiments** and **Late Harvest**. These are inconsequential in themselves but an important record of a period in their author's life and of his war with Mrs. Grundy. There is indeed an almost organic relationship between all of Douglas's books which gives the whole canon an unusual degree of unity. The early Capri pamphlets are recapitulated in **Siren Land** and to some extent in **Old Calabria;** **Summer Islands** furnishes a good part of the topography of **South Wind. Together** fills in the background of the early zoological pamphlets. **Alone** anticipates the more candid autobiographic note of **Looking Back,** and the privately published book of limericks amplifies it with some bawdry which is dull unless one likes limericks, but still a characteristic expression of the man who compiled them. **London Street Games** gives an account of its author's period of poverty in London, which is not amplified in **Looking Back**. Even **Birds and Beasts of the Greek Anthology** is prefaced by Will Percy's biographical sketch, showing the subject in a pose which he neglects in the self-portrait. Except for the three novels, there is no book from Douglas's pen in which interest in the material is not shared in an exceptional degree with interest in the writer himself. This essentially is autobiographic writing, as Mr. Douglas himself suggests.

It was interest in following the threads of his complex and fascinating personality that led people to collect his early scientific pamphlets, to read him on the fauna of antiquity, on old aphrodisiacs, on the iniquities of modern Europe. His essential appeal was obscured even from his most affectionate readers as much by the unprecedented form his autobiography assumed as by the fact that a writer who had produced a novel of high merit was inescapably labeled a novelist in an age which thought of the novel as the literary norm. He is still classed as a novelist by our literary historians, which means that most of his work is thrown out of consideration. The unexpected and puzzling nature of his autobiographic writing may readily be illustrated by **Looking Back,** the most conventionally autobiographic book he has written, which, proceeding in no chronological order, is thus, among other things, the random associations called up by many years' accumulation of calling cards.

Norman Douglas may thus be seen as a sort of twentieth-century Samuel Johnson, who is also his own Boswell. If the essentially autobiographic nature of his work is accepted, and I think it must be by those who know it well, **Looking Back** lies at the center of it; the lines of interest radiate through Douglas's own books and into such works as D. H. Lawrence's *Aaron's Rod* and *A Portrait of M. M.,* Muriel Draper's *Music at Midnight,* G. Orioli's *Adventures of a Bookseller,* Compton Mackenzie's *Vestal Fire,* Louis Golding's *Sunward,* and other bits of Douglasiana, which booksellers used to recommend to enthusiasts.

A multi-volumed autobiography which has attracted such devoted readers is sure to have something out of the ordinary to recommend it. The mere facts of Douglas's life, as distinct from his literary genius, would guarantee an interesting record, though he tantalizes us with reticences about them as much as he nourishes our curiosity with revelations. However, the main outlines of an unusual career can be pieced together readily enough. It yields a sketch something like this: A Scotch county-family father and a German mother; a cosmopolitan education on the Continent, mainly in Karlsruhe; early scientific and musical interests; a period in London as a young gentleman of well-gloved and tailored leisure; a brief period in the diplomatic service in Russia; wide and observant travel, to Greece, to Turkey, to India; marriage and the purchase of a villa in Capri; an absorption with the present and past of the Mediterranean world; then a period of bankruptcy and privation (the marriage was evidently dissolved); from the elegant and accomplished amateur, G. Norman Douglass, had emerged Norman Douglas, professional man of letters,

assistant editor of the *English Review,* and a minor figure in London literary circles. World War I and a new personal cataclysm of some sort turned Douglas into the picturesque expatriate bohemian described in *Aaron's Rod* and more glowingly painted in *Alone.* A few years later, and the bohemian had become the sage and esteemed literary artist. A strange, improbable sort of life, veiled by inexplicable obscurities; illuminated by unexpected bits of picaresque candor, most striking of all in the satisfaction it gave the man who lived it. It offers enough "problems" to keep a dozen scholars happy. One hopes that before very many years someone informed of these matters will tell us how Norman Douglas happened to go broke—a significant fact in his literary career. And how about certain "emotional difficulties" which J. H. Retinger refers to in *Joseph Conrad and his Friends?* We have occasional hints of such things in Douglas's books, but they would seem to have been by no means the decisive force in his life that they were in Gide's or Proust's, which is fortunate from the point of view of his larger public. Then it would be interesting to trace his financial affairs as co-publisher with Signor Orioli. And how about his relations with various literary celebrities?

The facts in Douglas's life are interesting, quite as interesting as those of Stendhal's, who might serve as an understandable parallel, as a man whose work also has a strong autobiographic motive. But facts alone can never make great biographic writing. Perhaps the root of Douglas's charm lies in an irrepressible, youthful *élan,* which in **Late Harvest** hardly seems wearied by the weight of eight decades. This quality gives coherence to the many-sided and perplexing individuality which emerges in his own books and those of other men. Douglas, the not-too-earnest gentleman, giving Mrs. Conrad a courtly arm to lead her away from the unspeakable Frank Harris; Douglas, the pedant grumbling about footnotes; Douglas, the shady bohemian swindling a tailor; Douglas, the amateur scientist, impassioned about tree conservation; Douglas, the *bon vivant* approving or abusing the vintage; Douglas, the Hellenist, recapturing the past Mediterranean world in its brightly colored present; Douglas, the controversialist, denouncing a bad manner. And all this, with a vigor and copiousness of experience, bookish and otherwise, that belongs to the heroic scale. Where other men write their books, Douglas seems to live his. What is more, he makes his reader live them too, with a vividness and intimacy that eludes our "stripped style" and "immediate impact" experts, who are already beginning to seem a little dated.

What should the uninitiated reader do about this situation? He can start with the justly popular **South Wind.** If he likes it and wishes to know his author better, he might turn to **Old Calabria, London Street Games,** and **Looking Back**. When he has read these, he will know a man who has lived a favored life and one quite largely of his own contriving. This is a considerable feat, particularly in the first half of the twentieth century, when the more articulate people too often give the impression that they have wasted their time, not spent it. Douglas has no such regrets. "Externalize yourself," Count Caloveglia tells the youthful Dennis in *South Wind*. Douglas externalized himself. His life is a record of interest in the past and present, in such diverse human activities as street games and hagiology, in the visible surface of the earth and the animal and vegetable life it bears. He seems to have lived with a minimum of family ties. As for friends, "I like to taste my friends, not to eat them." His behavior has been independent of any group. In an age when we reject old social values and distrust new ones, Douglas has left the account of a bold individual experiment in living, which by no means answers all human aspirations, but which assuredly has much to teach a generation that is still seeking new bearings. Those readers who come to this conclusion will probably abandon escorted tours of the author for a personal exploration, which they can hardly fail to find rewarding.

R. W. Flint   (essay date 1952)

SOURCE: "Norman Douglas," in *The Kenyon Review,* Vol. XIV, No. 4, Autumn, 1952, pp. 660-68.

[*In the following essay, Flint surveys Douglas's career, praising his travel writings but concluding: "his literary reputation must remain a small one."*]

> So, while her arm rested lightly on mine, we wandered about those gardens, the saintly lady and myself; her mind dwelling, maybe, on memories of her one classic love-adventure and the part she came nigh to playing in the history of Europe, while mine was lost in a maze of vulgar love-adventures which came nigh to making me play a part in the police courts of Rome.
> —*from* **Alone**, *referring to Malida von Meyserberg the mystic.*

Norman Douglas died last spring on Capri, a handsome, white-haired, venerably boisterous old gentlemen of eighty-four who had survived many reverses of fortune, including official banishment from Italy by the Fascists from the mid-thirties until 1946. Like Lawrence and several other writers of the between-wars period, Douglas was taken more literally than dramatically or critically by his American readers. That is, one took (or rejected) his more declamatory ideas about modern civilization, as put into the mouths of the two principal spokesmen of *South Wind,* straight, so to speak, and read the fiction and memoirs as more or less successful illustrations of these ideas. But this, as is often the case with Lawrence and Faulkner on the superficial levels of criticism, is to miss his proper substance and flavor altogether. Douglas was no Lawrence or Faulkner, but neither was he merely a British version of Cabell, Hergesheimer or Van Vechten. *South Wind,* which everyone knows, contains at least as much of his worst writing as it does of his best. My epigraph comes from

his own favorite among the books of memoirs (and mine too, if one overlooks his extravagant praise of Ouida) and is a fair specimen of the Douglas manner—mildly ritualized, mildly literary, mildly incongruous—the gallant and scholarly old scamp. It is a minor version of the Augustan comic style, a cultivated anachronism, an encompassing, outlandish, amateur talent, one that frames an era rather than dominating it.

What with "peace," *Volkswagens* and superhighways, the Grand Tour of Europe is once again a lure for writers. Every valley has been exalted and the rough places planed. One has little protection against seeing more than eye can see and feeling more than heart can feel. So many of the useful old bogies are gone—each city cleaner than New York or Boston, every guide a Ph.D. in *turismo!* (How few *buildings* Dante was obliged to admire in his spiritual travels!) No one foresaw all this better than Douglas, and few exiles of his generation knew better how to play host among the newly-weeded ruins. For Douglas knew how to take his time; he was first of all a memoirist, historian, scientist, scholar, last of all a "creative" artist. V. S. Pritchett in his memorial essay (in *The New Statesman and Nation*), commenting on Douglas' "very original contribution to landscape in literature," on the superb scientific conscience which got its effect without the overt poetic organization of Joyce, Lawrence or Hemingway, finds that it comes "from the mastery of a defect of temperament, a defect of heart." Let us say at any rate a *difference* of temperament, and let hearts go for a moment.

"Indeed, any volume of European travels, however dull, is interesting provided that it be written before the age of railways and Ruskin," wrote Aldous Huxley. But Huxley, like Symonds and Symons before him, had played the cultural circuit in the time-worn spirit of Oxford Greats. Huxley's rage at the Church of Brou, for example, would be unthinkable without Arnold's poem or Ruskin's polemics. Each of these university wits has something solid to give us, but it is not what Douglas can or wants to provide. Like D. H. Lawrence, an admirable sidestepper and bypasser of the Ruskinian *agon,* he finds his subject not by taking a donkey-cart when a railway is available nor by ignoring Ruskin, but simply by having a life of his own. Doughty, T. E. Lawrence, Conrad, Gregorovius, Burkhardt, Darwin, Gibbon, Lucian, Pausanias, the Greek Anthologists were the kind of writers who fed his mind. *Inglese italianato e vero diavolo.* Such a devil was Norman Douglas, "an autocthonous gentleman of the north country."

In his generally sympathetic essay, Mr. Pritchett summarizes the best and the worst that can be said of Douglas without quite making the two sides seem the answers to the same question, namely, why read him at all? "It was a mere irony," he writes, "that *South Wind* became the Apocrypha of a younger generation of sophisticates and cads in the Twenties, for sophistication is not a word one would think of applying to this author." So much for the rather shallow popular obituaries. But Mr.

Pritchett is fresh from a series of papers on the French pagans of the *fin-de-siècle* and after and likes to take a jocular tone toward their English opposites, finding a *paganisme voulu,* jackdaws strutting in peacocks' feathers. The scheme which fits a Wilde or a Chesterton, those thoroughly domesticated exotics, serves less well, however, for Douglas, who escaped into a larger actual world precisely because he lived in a narrower world of phantasy and craft. We don't see Douglas spinning about, no hands, on a bicycle called Paradox, but we do see a corner of the spinning world. "Compared to Anatole France," continues Mr. Pritchett, "he's a dom-inie . . . a muscular non-Christian, a hardened sceptic, an immoralist by sheer tirelessness, even assertion, of the Scottish conscience, a powerful egotistical nagger in continuous moral argument, and filled with the sectary's fine palate for ethical conundrums." And so on. Which would all be ghastly enough, were it essentially rather than peripherally, incidentally, true. It would make Douglas as wearisome as Carlyle, without the Carlyle élan. But Douglas was more a Gibbon than a Carlyle, more a Boswell than a Wilde. His "solution" to the ills of the world, to which Mr. Pritchett gives so much more importance than it deserves, is like the tea the Chinese use to pack the real tea in, a borrowed ethos not brought up to literary date, a rhetoric to make the party go until fresh drinks are mixed. For Douglas was a courtly Mynheer Peeperkorn who went a little more deeply into the tears of things than Mann's circus-master. Nor did he *make* people drunk. Even his scorn was affectionate.

The best critics of Hawthorne, of Emily Dickinson, of Arnold, Ruskin and D. H. Lawrence have seen that "Puritanism" need not always be a source of limitation. Mr. Pritchett admits his ignorance of Douglas' early life and accuses him of over-reacting to Puritan influences. But these early years are amply recorded and seem to have been providentially free of any sort of extreme except health and energy. His true extremes were not so much metaphysical and religious as geographical—his hearty Scotch-Bavarian ancestry and his classical-scientific education at Heidelberg—and temperamental, his immense gusto. Before starting to write seriously, Douglas had read widely, composed briefly, put in three years as Third Secretary at Moscow, written articles for the zoological and geological magazines, sent a number of specimens home to the British Natural History Museum (Darwin had said that toads don't grow on volcanic islands, and Douglas had submitted a toad from a volcanic island), founded and helped manage a cut-rate London nightclub called "Gardenia" until the police closed it, served as British representative for a scheme to drain the Pontine Marshes until the Italian government sat on it, acted as assistant editor and copious reviewer for *The English Review* under Austin Harrison, where he became friendly with Conrad and the Georgians. His first book was a genial and thorough account of London street games, his first printed essay a study of Poe. Not the career one would expect from a man battling with the ghost of Calvin! He was forty-six when the 1914 war broke out. **South Wind,** which made him famous, appeared in 1917 when England was at its dreariest. But Douglas had something better than gusto and curiosity; he had a generously lyric sense of life ("tragic" might be too strong a word), a *molle et facetum in-genium*. He was the host of British and American exiles in Italy as Landor once had been. The list of his acquaintance with impoverished scholars, professors, librarians, poets, popular novelists and noble ne'er-do-wells is astonishing, and he beheld the spectacle of Lord Roseberry removing a flea from his person with the same relish as when he heard a Calabrian wine-seller's story for the twentieth time. His *pietas* brought him with flowers to the graves of such erstwhile friends as Rupert Brooke and D. H. Lawrence, though he had a famous public spat with Lawrence and had found Brooke's conversation "a collection of radiant platitudes."

Whatever may have been Douglas' "palate" for "ethical conundrums," his own efforts in that line were meager, the very opposite of "fine." "Let there be no virgins in the land!" is a typical *mot* of this class, convivial outbursts not worth the irritation one might feel at the cockier sayings of Voltaire. He was not really a "hardened" anything; his scepticism never crystallizes out. He took the scepticisms of other and *applied* them, to history, to the world around him. Dilettantism was his true specialty, an attitude of the heart and manners as well as of the mind, stiffened by a scholarly conscience, a professional dilettantism which made him shy of every other sort of professionalism. In time, indeed, he became (how could he help it in Southern Italy?) something of a connoisseur of fraud, but it is utterly untrue to say that he didn't care for its opposite or its cure. It was easy and specious humanism which annoyed him, not the real thing. "There's enough goodness in the world without putting it into our books," was his reply to a particularly fatuous critic. His ideal of the "gentleman" was substantially Chesterfield's, softened and narrowed perhaps by Victorian domestic chivalry and Edwardian clubmanism. Douglas' gentleman does not betray his living friends in his books, speaks no evil of his family, is scrupulous of the honor of those ladies, usually volunteers of lower station, whom he happens to seduce. This code was no "myth" for Douglas, as Mr. Pritchett infers: it was the way he lived, and he rose above it to an impersonal sense of nature and history. "What is the lyric temper?" he wrote in **Looking Back**. "I should describe it as a sympathetic feeling for the myriad processes of Nature and the application of this gift towards interpreting human phenomena with concision and poignancy." A post-romantic toughness about that, as well as the slight dullness of all Douglas' abstract thinking. He gives us what he admired in others ". . . a loving and accurate student both of plants and animals and their literature . . . an affectionate waiting upon nature," a sense of *affairs*. Of his 18th Century prototype Craufurd Tait Ramage, L.L.D., a Scot who travelled Italy as purposefully as Johnson travelled Scotland, Douglas keens, "Where are they gone, those candid inquirers, so full of gentlemanly curiosity, so informative and yet so shrewdly human?"

D. H. Lawrence was certainly no gentleman after the Douglas model and very much more of a Puritan, but he had a too-little-appreciated humor and gallantry which made his clash with Douglas over the head of the unfortunate Maurice Magnus an amusing and revealing episode. Magnus was a moderately talented essayist and eccentric from Baltimore who had a grueling time as a volunteer in the Foreign Legion and had repaid Douglas extravagantly for some small earlier help. When he ran afoul of Lawrence by twice touching him for a loan, he was distracted and planning suicide. (He used to carry a small capsule of poison about with him and crack macabre jokes about it to his friends.) Lawrence somehow became literary executor (another of Magnus' jokes?) of the posthumous *Memoirs of the Foreign Legion* and wrote an introduction which contained one of his typically brilliant portraits of a man about whom he knew almost nothing. Naturally it drew blood from Douglas, who knew both men well, and was well aware of his antagonist's powers. "I commend this short paragraph," he wrote of the Lawrence Introduction, "to those simpletons who say that friend Lawrence cannot write: it is a perfect etching—not a stroke too much or too little: there he is, M. M. in matutinal garb, once and forever." But Lawrence had committed a breach of candor as well as of manners. Ignoring what he could easily have discovered of his victim's extraordinary generosity and scrupulousness in money matters, he thought he had found just enough shiftiness in Magnus to set him up as yet another object-lesson in that endless assault on the parasitic classes, that exhilarating *proces moral* which spared nobody, least of all Lawrence himself. In the abstract, I think one can prefer the magnificent disdain of the mythical and posthumous Magnus to Douglas' sometimes petulant reproaches against the living Lawrence, whose difficulties he knew and whom he genuinely admired. But more than the mere issue of Magnus entered into the quarrel. Lawrence had mildly caricatured Douglas, and although Douglas took it in fairly good part he couldn't understand Lawrence's literary "professionalism" because he drastically underestimated the place of the modern novel. Poetic justice, therefore, earned him a frivolous fame for his two resorts to a despised form, in *South Wind* and *They Went,* satirical novels very seriously marred by heavy moralizing. To cap the irony, we find Douglas grumbling in print, not too seriously perhaps, about the critics who found *South Wind* "plotless," as if the question were more than academic. To Aldington, Lawrence once confessed that his own father and Douglas had been the two figures in his experience who seemed most to live out of a natural joy in life; and Aldington adds, of their first talks in Florence: "After the bloodless abstractions of Russell and Murray, a course of Douglas, whose sole object was to live and enjoy life, was most salutary." More than Aldington was equipped to see or to care, both these men were also political idealists in the old English tradition. Both of them, no matter how far they might lose control of themselves on occasion, liked their hedonism in a framework of decency and just dealing. But Douglas couldn't grasp the way in which the novel is an

exorcism of the evils it represents, though perhaps no "cure" in the popular sense. Lawrence knew that however "one sheds one's sickness in one's books," one does not cease to be sick. The cure, surely, is that a new life comes into being in which the sickness no longer undermines the glory and order of the world, a life granted only to those who care more for glory and order than for the baleful distinctions of being sick. ". . . it is no use appealing to his better nature," Douglas wrote of Lawrence, "since he has no nature at all; he is a *cloaca maxima* for the discharge of objectionable personalities." And so he is. This is "his antithetical self, perverse, destructive, hating, hateful, conceited as a gutter Lucifer," not the whole self, but as real and necessary a part of Lawrence as the gifted lyrist, the devoted impersonal literary craftsman, the valuable and difficult friend.

In avoiding the splendid but often rather glib rhetorical channels down which Ruskin and his school of literary travellers moved, Douglas made his work episodic, personal, reminiscent. Out of his half-dozen or so best books, one fat volume might be compounded worthy to stand with Stendhal on Lombardy and Rome, with Heine's *Reisebilder* or Lawrence's *Twilight in Italy*. He was less a poet, less an imaginative writer, less a man of the world, really, than these three. His comments on art in general, though often shrewd, never reach the first interest. "Only think: never to have vexed one's soul with Plato and Cimabue and Categorical Imperatives and the thousand other 'essentials' of Western Culture—what would one not give to feel really Russian for half an hour!" Russia in this case was the admirable Isabelle Eberhardt, one of those brooding, nobly ruined lady-profligates for whom Douglas had a great *tendre* and whom he hauntingly portrayed in Miss Wilberforce of *South Wind*. I doubt whether Douglas' attitude towards these women was *wholly* gallant; it seems to me the weakest point in his armor. He was a writer for whom a succession of not-quite-satisfying lady-loves had to serve. The "innocent" Lawrence was probably luckier.

One must realize what it cost Douglas in literal outlandishness to arrive at his (sometimes) cool gallantry ("I like to taste my friends, not to eat them") towards a collapsing world, how he struggled to save himself by various kinds of respectable *askesis* from the terrible over-intimacy, over-knowledge (as he saw it) which isolated his greater contemporaries. But in so doing he made one corner of the world thoroughly his own. He forever lays the island-nostalgia which has teased European thought since Sappho at least, and he becomes very angry at anyone who plays loose with Tiberius merely for taking his baths in a grotto. "How one stumbles upon delightful folks! Set me down in furthest Cathay and I will undertake to find soon afterwards some person with whom I am quite prepared to spend the remaining years of my life." A bit menacing, this gusto. What one remembers in Douglas are not "characters" in the sharp Dickensian sense, but mixtures of people and things, people and history, an endless humane ragging of the scholars. We remember the love-letters of Calabrian boys, the shower of ashes on "Nepenthe" (an amalgam of some dozen Mediterranean islands), the mountain festival of Pollino, the politics of Southern sainthood, the ingredients of the notorious *Zuppa di Pesce,* and finally, the life of caves, fountains, forests, dragons, cliffs and oases—all with an elegiac tinge. "And now, at the other end of life, one returns anew to Rosenegg on a sunny afternoon, purged of the mists of middle years, and delving into memories of that clear dawn and seeking to recapture its spirit, one marvels at the feverish joy which greeted discoveries such as these degenerate little garnets, not a single one of which had the right colour, nor made the slightest pretense at being the rhombic dodecahedron it should have been. How one changes!"

However richly and forthrightly he lived on the European stage of the early 20th Century, his literary reputation must remain a small one. He knew as much himself and used to tell a story about a certain very deaf Mrs. Whitbread who once accosted him on the street: ". . . for want of something better to say, I bawled into her ear: 'What wonderful weather we're having for November.' She said: 'Oh, you naughty man. . . .'"

Graham Greene (essay date 1952)

SOURCE: "Norman Douglas," in *Collected Essays,* The Bodley Head, 1969, pp. 362-65.

[*Greene was one of the most popular and respected authors of the twentieth century. A prolific novelist, dramatist, critic, and essayist, he is perhaps best known for the novels* Brighton Rock (*1938*), The Power and the Glory (*1940*), *and* The Third Man (*1950*). *In the following essay, originally published in 1952, he fondly recalls Douglas's life and discusses what* South Wind *meant to his generation of writers.*]

In those last years you would always find him between six and dinner-time in the Café Vittoria, unfashionably tucked away behind the Piazza. Through the shabby windows one stared across at Naples—one could go only a few steps further without tumbling off the island altogether. Crouched over an aperitif (too often in the last years almost unalcoholic), his fingers knotted with rheumatism, squawking his 'Giorgio, Giorgio' to summon the devoted waiter who could hear that voice immediately above all the noises of Capri, snow-white hair stained here and there a kind of butterfly-yellow with nicotine, Norman Douglas sat on the borders of the kingdom he had built house by house, character by character, legend by legend.

One remembers him a few months before he died, handling the typescript of this book, [*Venus in the Kitchen*], resorting the loose carbon pages: there wasn't enough room on the café table what with the drinks, the old blue beret, the snuff-box, the fair copy; the wind would keep on picking up a flimsy carbon leaf and shifting it out of place, but the old ruler was back at the old game of ruling. He wouldn't have given even the menial task of assembly to another. With a certain fuss of pleasure and a great tacit pride he was handling a new book of his own again. There hadn't been a new book for—how many years? Sometimes something seemed to be wrong with the typescript: a monologue of exaggerated grumbles marked the misprints—not one of those earlier misprints carefully preserved in proof, to be corrected later in manuscript gratis for a friend and at a price for collectors—'Cost him a tenner, my dear'—and that sudden laugh would break like an explosion in a quarry, over before the noise has reached you.

My generation was brought up on *South Wind,* although I suppose the book was already five years old before we opened it and read the first sentence, 'The bishop was feeling rather sea-sick', which seemed to liberate us from all the serious dreary immediate wartime past. Count Caloveglia, Don Francesco, Cornelius van Koppen, Miss Wilberforce, Mme Steynlin, Mr Eames, Saint Dodekanus, the Alpha and Omega Club: Nepenthe had not been Capri, but Capri over half a century has striven with occasional success to be Nepenthe. *South Wind* appeared in 1917, superbly aloof from the catastrophes of the time: it was the age of Galsworthy, Wells, Bennett, Conrad: of a sometimes inflated, of a sometimes rough-and-ready prose. Novelists were dealing with 'big' subjects—family panoramas, conflicts of loyalty. How reluctantly we came to the last sentence: 'For it was obvious to the meanest intelligence that Mr Keith was considerably drunk.' This wasn't the world of Lord Jim or the Forsytes or the dreary Old Wives.

South Wind was to have many inferior successors: a whole Capri school. Douglas was able to convey to others some of his tolerance for human foibles: characters like Mr Parker and Mr Keith were taken up like popular children and spoiled. It became rather easy to write a novel, as the reviewers would say, 'in the manner of *South Wind*'. None of Douglas's disciples had learnt to write as he had. Nearly a quarter of a century of clean, scholarly, exact writing, beginning so unrewardingly with a Foreign Office report on the Pumice Stone Industry of the Lipari Islands by the Third Secretary of Her Majesty's Embassy in St Petersburg, published by the Stationery Office at a halfpenny, went to the creation of Perelli's Antiquities and 'the unpublished chronicle of Father Capocchio, a Dominican friar of licorous and even licentious disposition, a hater of Nepenthe. . . .'

Douglas died in the middle eighties after a life consistently open, tolerant, unashamed. 'Ill spent' it has been called by the kind of judges whose condemnation is the highest form of praise. In a sense he had created Capri: there have been suicides, embezzlements, rapes, thefts, bizarre funerals and odd processions which we feel would not have happened exactly in that way if Douglas had not existed, and some of his tolerance perhaps touched even the authorities when they came to deal with those events.

It is fitting, I think, that his last book should be as unserious and shameless as this collection of aphrodisiac recipes, to close a life in which he had enjoyed varied forms of love, left a dozen or so living tokens here and there, and been more loved himself than most men. (One remembers the old gypsy family from northern Italy who travelled all the way to Capri to spend an afternoon with Douglas and proudly exhibit to him another grandchild.) With its air of scholarship, its blend of the practical—the almond soup—and the wildly impracticable—Rôti sans Pareil, the crispness of the comments (we only have to add his customary endearments to hear the ghost speak): 'Very stimulating, my dear', 'Much ado about nothing', 'Not very useful for people of cold temperament', with a certain dry mercilessness in the introduction, this book will be one of my favourite Douglases: it joins **Old Calabria, Fountains in the Sand, They Went, Looking Back, London Street Games,** the forbidden anthology of limericks.

He will be delighted in the shades at any success we may have with his recipes and bark with laughter at our ignominious failures, and how pleased he will be at any annotations and additions, so long as they are exact, scholarly, uninflated, and do not carpingly rise from a cold temperament. For even his enormous tolerance had certain limits. He loved life too well to have much patience with puritans or fanatics. He was a gentleman and he disliked a boor. One of the finest passages of invective written in our time is his pamphlet against D. H. Lawrence in defence of Maurice Magnus, and an echo of that old controversy can be found in these pages.

> 'Not many years ago I met in the South of France a Mr D. H. Lawrence, an English painter, whom I interested in this subject and who certainly looked as if his own health would have been improved by a course of such recipes as I had gathered together.

There are said to be certain Jewish rabbis who perform the operation of circumcision with their thumbnail so rapidly and painlessly that the child never cries. So without warning Douglas operates, and the victim has no time to realize in what purgatorio of lopped limbs he is about to awake, among the miserly, the bogus, the boring, and the ungenerous.

Cyril Connolly (essay date 1963)

SOURCE: "Norman Douglas," in *Previous Convictions,* Hamish Hamilton, 1963, pp. 224-26.

[Connolly was a very influential English critic, nonfiction writer, and literary journal editor. In the following positive review of Old Calabria, *he praises Douglas's talents as a travel writer.]*

This would seem to be the first edition of **Old Calabria** for twenty-five years. It belongs to the great tradition of English travel books: it is more solid than all the author's other work, and may well be that for which he is longest remembered.

It is introduced by Mr. John Davenport, who has some robust and original comments to make on the author. I knew him quite well myself, though I do not suppose I penetrated far beneath the surface. He was a happy man and though, I expect, very selfish, he managed to make others feel happy. This serene, ironic gaiety was not a pose nor did it proceed from an abdication of life: 'One can make just as big a fool of oneself at seventy as at thirty,' he once assured me at a time when infatuation for some young person caused him to spend painful evenings on the Big Wheels and switchbacks of a Paris circus.

Happiness is so rare among intellectuals that one wanted to know more about it. What philosophy had engendered it? What teachers, what lovers, what books? It was here that 'Uncle Norman's' reserve became impenetrable. The philosophers he admired most were those who had lived longest: Democritus, Xenophanes, Xenophilos of whom nothing is known but some hundred and fifty-odd summers.

I am inclined to think the source of his inner content was his Scots temperament and his good breeding which made him not expect too much from himself but assume the rôle of privileged onlooker without self-questioning. And he was very Scottish, with a pawky and dreadful humour, as when he re-entered a Capri café to ask 'Has anyone found a toothpick tasting of ham?' I remember seeing him set off with some younger men on an expedition to the Chartreuse de la Verne. They had not taken provisions because there was supposed to be a restaurant nearby, but Douglas lingered behind a moment, gave out his extraordinary dry crackle of a laugh and with a clownish leer revealed the end of an enormous salami under his jacket.

No author was less literary; he never rolled words or gargled quotations yet his silvery tones could infuse a fine nuance of melancholy. His scientific training was the source of his thoroughness as an observer and even of his originality. For, on the whole, he did not always write very well. Time and again in enjoying his sensibility one is brought up short by a cliché or some tritely poetic expression. For this reason he is more memorable in attack than eulogy, though here too a hint of journalism would creep in.

On the eucalyptus:

> I never lose an opportunity of saying exactly what I think about this particularly odious representative of the brood, this eyesore, this grey-haired scarecrow, this reptile of a growth with which a pack of misguided enthusiasts have

disfigured the entire Mediterranean basin. . . .
A single eucalyptus will ruin the fairest landscape.
No plant on earth rustles in such a horribly metallic
fashion when the wind blows through those ever-
lastingly withered branches; the noise chills one to
the marrow; it is like the sibilant chattering of ghosts;
its oil is called 'medicinal' only because it happens
to smell rather nasty. . . .

And so for another hundred lines, an uneven *tour de
force* which never comes to a head. Here is a more
poetic, but, even so, strangely tawdry piece on Croton:

> The temple has vanished, together with the sacred
> grove that once embowered it; the island of Cal-
> ypso, where Swinburne took his ease (if such it
> was), has sunk into the purple realms of Glaucus;
> the corals and sea-beasts that writhed among its
> crevices are engulfed under mounds of submarine
> sand. There was life, once, at this promontory.
> Argosies touched here, leaving priceless gifts;
> fountains flowed, and cornfields waved in the
> genial sunshine. Doubtless there will be life again;
> earth and sea are only waiting for the enchanter's
> wand.

No, it is not as a writer of prose but as a human observer, historian, master of dialects, wine-bibber, walker
and botanist that Douglas shines in *Old Calabria*. Even
as a controversialist he is beginning to date: 'The quaint
Alexandrian *tutti-frutti* known as Christianity.' Well, let
it pass.

His travel books have a quality we lack today; he knew
not only the languages but the dialects, he met people
the hard way by walking and by being alone, he frequented the vanishing world of priest, mayor, chemist
and village schoolmaster—then cabined and confined
by poverty and malaria, now self-consciously Hollywood.

Who now in those once remote parts could find such
wine (symbol of humanist tradition and sociability) so
cleverly:

> To this end, I generally apply to the priests; not
> because they are the greatest drunkards (far from
> it; they are mildly Epicurean or even abstemious)
> but by reason of their unrivalled knowledge of
> personalities. They know exactly who has been
> able to keep his liquor of such and such a year,
> and who has been obliged to adulterate it. . . .
> And failing the priests I go to an elderly individual
> of that tribe of red-nosed connoisseurs, the coach-
> men, ever thirsty and mercenary souls. . . .

Ralph D. Lindeman   (essay date 1965)

SOURCE: "The Novels," in *Norman Douglas,* Twayne
Publishers, 1965, pp. 121-58.

[*In the following excerpt, Lindeman examines Douglas's
novels, discussing their plots and main themes, and*
*relating some of the critical commentary they gener-
ated.*]

Douglas' three novels—*South Wind, They Went,* and *In
the Beginning*—are usually considered satirical. Satire
is difficult of definition. Its tone is one of disapproba-
tion; its tools are irony, wit, humor, and exaggeration.
And it is theoretically didactic, since its implied purpose
is the renovation of society. Douglas' novels are witty
and humorous, employing the kind of exaggerated characterization associated with satire and striking at human
foibles and self-delusion. Certainly Douglas would have
been scandalized by the suggestion that he intended to
reform society. And such a suggestion needs qualification. But it is clear that he held values which he believed to be better than those of most of his fellow men
and that the approach of his novels—indeed, of everything he wrote—was designed, consciously or otherwise,
to influence the intelligent reader to his way of thinking. Like all satirists, he saw clearly that men fall short
of the moral and social standards to which they profess
allegiance; and, like all satirists, he scorned the hypocrisy with which men pretend to lofty ideals while they
live lives based on selfishness and egotism.

Of course Douglas hated the selfishness and egotism
less than he hated the hypocrisy. . . . [He] believed that
the individual should be self-sustaining and that pleasure was a justifiable end. He advocated an approach to
life in which few values were absolute and in which
actions were deemed good or bad in relation to their
ends; whatever did not conduce to a leisurely, undisturbed existence and to a controlled exploitation of the
senses was humbug. What he deplored most was that
intelligent men should fail to recognize these facts and
hence sacrifice the natural pleasures to a set of absurd
and outmoded ethical values to which the great majority
of people paid only lip service. Disapproving attitudes,
expressed in a tone and manner that would probably be
called satiric, had appeared incidentally in the travel
books, but they first received full treatment in satiric
fiction in *South Wind*.

I **South Wind:** *a Bishop Mediterraneanized*

The material of *South Wind* (1917) was a remarkably
felicitous selection, and Douglas was never again to find
a subject so perfectly suited to his talent and temperament. Its themes were ideas that Douglas had long cherished—the relativity of morals, the futility of false ideals, the importance of climate as a factor in social and
cultural conditions. Its setting enabled him to exploit
his practiced ability to describe Mediterranean scenery.
And its plot was such that atmospheric factors, which
Douglas always handled adeptly, played a more important role than narrative or dramatic action, which did
not come so easily for him.

Joseph Conrad had written Douglas in 1908: ". . . think
seriously of writing a novel. . . . Place it in southern
Italy if that will help. . . . Don't make it a novel of

Italian peasant life—not yet! . . . Place European personalities in Italian frame. European here means an international crowd. Try and make it a novel of analysis on the basis of some strong situation" [*Joseph Conrad: Life and Letters,* edited by G. Jean-Aubry, 1927]. Some years later, when Douglas undertook **South Wind,** he followed Conrad's advice almost entirely. He wrote a novel of analysis with a setting that fit Conrad's suggestion, although perhaps the situation was not so strong as his friend might have desired. The scene was a fictitious island named Nepenthe, a Mediterranean island with an Italianate populace and near a mainland on which there was a volcano. It was peopled with a cosmopolitan crowd, mostly English. Its model was plainly Capri.

On Nepenthe, Douglas created his own kind of Utopia—a device familiar to the satiric tradition—where people lived, for the most part, a casual, leisurely existence, doing the things they wanted to do and attaching importance only to things that Douglas thought important. Many of the characters represented aspects of Douglas' own personality—one was a hedonist, one a Classicist, one a recluse-scholar, one a geologist. It was as if the author's own personality had been passed through a spectrum and separated into its various components.

Perhaps the most important character in **South Wind** is the atmosphere of Nepenthe, which seems to have a life of its own. By deft handling of the geological features of the island, exaggerated from those of Ponza which he had described in **Summer Islands,** and by clever allusions to the sirocco which blew incessantly, Douglas created a strange and infectious mood, at once attractive and sinister, salubrious and debilitating. But whatever the ambiguous properties of the climate and the south wind, the salient feature of Nepenthe's atmosphere was its power to induce clear-sightedness. As Mr. Keith explained:

> This coast-line alone—the sheer effrontery of its mineral charm—might affect some natures to such an extent as to dislocate their stability. Northern minds seem to become fluid here, impressionable, unstable, unbalanced—what you please. There is something in the brightness of this spot which decomposes their old particles and arranges them into fresh and unexpected patterns. That is what people mean when they say they "discover themselves" here. You discover a mechanism, you know, when you take it to pieces.

Into this atmosphere comes Mr. Heard, English Bishop of Bampopo in Africa, who is stopping over on Nepenthe to visit his cousin and to escort her back to England, since her second husband, Mr. Meadows, cannot leave his post in India. A reasonable and intelligent man, Mr. Heard cannot become overly perturbed about the waywardness and the ethical eccentricities of the African natives. But he still labors under some "serious delusions": he idealizes women, and he clings to the beliefs of his church.

Don Francesco, a genial but lascivious priest met on the boat, introduces the Bishop to the American Mrs. Steynlin, called the Duchess of San Martino, a leader of Nepenthean society who is about to become a Catholic through the influence of Don Francesco, and to her guest Denis Phipps, a pleasantly naïve and impressionable English student. Bishop Heard subsequently meets other unusual Nepentheans, such as Mr. Keith, a wealthy hedonist with a penchant for exotic cookery; Count Caloveglia, a Classicist and antiquarian who professes Hellenic values; Eames, an amiable and innocuous bibliographer of the island's literature; Edward Marten, an indigent Jewish minerologist; Freddy Parker, supposedly the Commissioner of Finance from Nicaragua but actually the devious proprietor, along with his "barn-like" step sister, of the local drinking club; the Commissioner's friend, the red-headed, Mephistophelian magistrate, Malipizzo; and the alcoholic Englishwoman, Miss Wilberforce, who undresses in public.

The first days of the Bishop's fortnight visit to Nepenthe are filled only with leisurely conversation in which the distinctive qualities and interests of the various inhabitants are revealed. He attends the colorful festival of the local saint, St. Dodekanus, and calls on his cousin, who is strangely displeased to see him. Then he discovers that "things are beginning to happen." There are ominous reports that one of the island's springs has dried up and that unusual births have occurred; Freddy Parker's stepsister dies of a mosquito bite and that suspicious personage learns that his patron in the Nicaraguan government has also died and that his empty but esteemed title of Commissioner of Finance may be revoked. Finally, the volcano begins to erupt, raining ashes on the island. Miraculously, further catastrophe is averted by a procession in honor of St. Dodekanus proposed by Commissioner Parker, who is not even a Catholic.

The mysterious dangers past, the life of Nepenthe becomes again a series of friendly gatherings and rambling conversations. Bishop Heard hears about Van Koppen, the American millionaire who yearly visits Nepenthe on his yacht, which is always the scene of disreputable parties. He learns of Denis Phipps' inability to find a purpose in life, and of the plan to build a clinic for Miss Wilberforce, a project disapproved by Mr. Keith, who believes everyone should be permitted to do as he pleases. He watches Count Caloveglia, dignified pronouncer of virtuous principles, sell a fake antique statue to the millionaire Van Koppen, who knows that it is a fake but admires the Count's ability to dupe the experts. And finally, while sitting among the cliffs with Denis, Mr. Heard sees his cousin, Mrs. Meadows, walk out of her house with a man he recognizes as one Mr. Muhlen he met on the ship and has since learned is actually a blackmailer named Retlow. And he sees his cousin push this man off the cliff. Remembering how unpleasant Retlow had been and remembering that Mrs. Meadows' first husband had been named Retlow, the Bishop concludes that his cousin has been the victim of an obnoxious blackmailer and that her act was justified.

Unfortunately, a native boy is accused of the murder when a gold piece that had belonged to Retlow is found in his possession. The evil Malipizzo hopes, by convicting the native, to discredit the Church, since the boy's cousin is the village priest. But a lawyer named Morena, famous as a member of the Black Hand, is called in by the priest to defend the boy and is successful through his sentimental eloquence. And under these conditions, despite the ostensible immorality of the events, the Bishop does not feel it necessary to divulge his knowledge of the matter.

Denis, having also been worked upon by the atmosphere of the place, is "beginning to know his own mind," and asserts himself to stop the windy harangues of Mr. Keith, thus performing "the first virile achievement" of his young life.

Heard's stay on Nepenthe produces the necessary change. The provocative conversation of the articulate Mr. Keith, who insidiously propounds his rationalistic hedonism, has its effect. And Bishop Heard watches various situations which mellow his point of view. But most important of all, the magical atmosphere of the place permeates him, and the south wind sweeps the cobwebs from his mind. The transformation is complete when he is able to face the act of murder, performed by one whom he considers an epitome of the English womanly ideal, and not only overlooks it as a trivial matter but justifies it as a moral necessity.

In *Late Harvest* Douglas described the purposes of *South Wind* as follows: "*South Wind* was the result of my craving to escape from the wearisome actualities of life. To picture yourself living in a society of such instability, of such 'jovial immoderation' and 'frolicsome perversity' that even a respectable bishop can be persuaded to approve of murder—this was my aim." The "wearisome actuality"—the stodgy, complacent social mores and the impractical ethical code upon which they were supposed to be based—is the true target of the satire. Thus Douglas sets up a society which flouts stability and respectability—a society which is his kind of utopia. Bishop Heard, "respectable but rather drab . . . whose tastes and needs are fashioned to reflect those of the average drab reader," is introduced into this society, and it is demonstrated that such a person cannot resist its influence. The Bishop—the observer and interpreter of the events—sees, as the reader is expected to, that a reasonable person should live a reasonable existence in a carefree pursuit of civilized pleasures with no pretense of subscribing to outmoded and false conceptions. The reader is being asked, implicitly, "Could you resist?"

H. M. Tomlinson, discussing *South Wind,* concludes that the only practical suggestion which the book makes is:

> that the more likeable of us should migrate to the sunny south, to be thawed out—loosened from the frost of the north, and Christianity and other inhibiting elements. The suggestion approaches the diabolical, for we know it cannot be only a matter of climate; he himself notes elsewhere the mortification of the flesh, which to him is the sin against the light, may be witnessed as frequently under the warmer skies of the south as where northern blasts chill us into a miserable apprehension of our sins.

And, of course, the theme should not be interpreted as the insistence that only a Mediterranean sun can make possible the kind of rebellion against Christian morality which *South Wind* sympathetically depicts. That the southern climate is no complete panacea is part of the irony, and it is a "diabolical" irony because it includes the unstated but always plausible possibility that nothing is really of much help. The atmosphere is artificial; Nepenthe is as unreal as Erewhon. But that it is more like Italy than like any place else is not surprising, since Douglas assuredly believed that the sunny south was the best hope of civilized men; other men—most men—had no hope.

While Douglas may have been under no illusions as to the possibility of universal amelioration, his Mediterraneanism was deep seated. It was to be expected, as Conrad saw, that this attitude would form part of Douglas' first serious effort at fiction. As we have already noted, Douglas believed that climate and region influenced the human outlook. In *Siren Land* he had written: "The landscape . . . and not only the hour and the man, plays a part when gods are to be created." And now in *South Wind*: "But certainly the sun which colours our complexion and orders our daily habits, influences at the same time our character and outlook. The almost hysterical changes of light and darkness, summer and winter, which have impressed themselves upon the literature of the North, are unknown here." He had likewise spoken in *Siren Land* of the cathartic properties of the southern Italian regions:

> Here, on these odorous Siren heights, far removed from duty's sacred call—for duty has become the Moloch of modern life—it may not be amiss to build a summer hut wherein to undergo a brief *katharsis,* of purgation and readjustment. For we do get sadly out of perspective with our environment in the fevered North, out of touch with elemental and permanent things. . . .
>
> . . . many of us would do well to *mediterraneanise* ourselves for a season, to quicken those ethic roots from which has sprung so much of what is best in our natures. To dream in Siren Land, pursuing the moods and memories as they shift in labyrinthine mazes, like shadows on a woodland path in June; to stroll among the hills and fill the mind with new images upon which to browse at leisure, casting off outworn weeds of thought with the painless ease of a serpent and unperplexing, incidentally, some of those "questions of the day" of which the daily papers nevertheless know nothing—this is an antidote

for many ills. There is repose in Siren Land; there is none of that delirious massing-together in which certain mortals, unable to stand alone, can lean up against one another and so gain, for a moment, a precarious condition of equipoise.

This is the atmosphere Douglas attempted to recreate in *South Wind*—the repose, the solitude, the naïve light, the nearness to elemental things. By following the process of the mediterraneanizing of Bishop Heard, we can learn something of how Douglas managed his problem.

To begin with, Bishop Heard is not a hopeless case; if he were, Douglas would not be interested in him. Having spent considerable time in Africa, the Bishop is somewhat mellowed. The natives there had something of the same "spirit of unconquerable playfulness in grave concerns" that he now notes in the Nepentheans. His favorites were the Bulanga: "And the Bulanga. . . . Really the Bulanga were the worst of the lot. Not fit to be talked about. And yet, somehow or other, one could not help liking them. . . ." Bishop Heard is a reasonable man; and he is ripe for Nepenthe. When he has been on the island only a few days he is already reflecting on the new, open-minded attitude of which he has become aware:

> Happiness—an honourable, justifiable happiness—how was it to be attained? Not otherwise, he used to think than through the two-fold agency of Christianity and civilization. That was his old College attitude. Imperceptibly his outlook had shifted since then. Something had been stirring within him; new points of view had floated into his ken. He was no longer so sure about things. The structure of his mind had lost that old stability; its elements seemed to be held in solution, ready to form new combinations. China had taught him that men can be happy and virtuous while lacking, and even scorning, the first of these twin blessings. Then had come Africa, where his notions had been further dislocated by those natives who derided both the one and the other—such fine healthy animals, all the same! A candid soul, he allowed his natural shrewdness and logic to play freely with memories of his earlier experiences among the London poor. Those experiences now became fraught with a new meaning. The solemn doctrines he had preached in those days: were they really a panacea for all the ills of the flesh? He thought upon the gaunt bodies, starved souls, and white faces—the dirt, the squalor of it! Was that Christianity, civilization?

Before long the Bishop feels himself on the verge of something:

> Whatever it was he seemed to be no longer his own master, as in former days. Fate had caused his feet to stray towards something new—something alarming. He was poised, as it were on the brink of a gulf. Or rather, it was as if that old mind of his, like a boat sailing hitherto briskly before the wind, had suddenly encountered a bank

of calm, of utter and ominous calm; it was a thing spellbound; a toy of circumstances beyond human control. The canvas hung in the stagnant air. From which quarter would the quickening breeze arrive? Whither would it bear him?

The influence of new and unusual friends, of a new sense of leisure, and of the omnipresent south wind makes of his mind a pliable and impressionable thing, giving his own good sense a chance to operate. Old conceptions are beginning to vanish, the rigid sense of duty to dissolve, and an insidious doubt to enter:

> He tried to get himself into perspective. "I must straighten myself out," he thought. Assuredly it was a restful place, this Nepenthe, abounding in kindly people; his affection for it grew with every day. Rest without; but where was that old rest within, that sense of plain tasks plainly to be performed, of tangible duty? Whither had it gone? Alien influences were at work upon him. Something new had insinuated itself into his blood, some demon of doubt and disquiet which threatened his old-established conceptions. Whence came it? The effect of changed environment—new friends, new food, new habits? The unaccustomed leisure which gave him, for the first time, a chance of thinking about non-professional matters? The South Wind acting on his still weakened health? All these together? Or had he reached an epoch in his development, the termination of one of those definite life-periods when all men worthy of the name pass through some cleansing process of spiritual desquamation, and slip their outworn weeds of thought and feeling.

Soon afterwards we find him entertaining a new realization of the importance of the individual and of the inevitability of individual weakness. He thinks to himself that perhaps the American millionaire Van Koppen, who reportedly keeps a number of young ladies on his yacht, cannot help being what he is; perhaps this very coarseness in Van Koppen has helped him to become a renowned philanthropist. And most startling of all, perhaps even ladies have such coarse impulses:

> Certain human attributes were mutually exclusive—avarice and generosity, for instance; others no doubt mysteriously but inextricably intertwined. A man was an in-dividual [sic]; he could not be divided or taken to pieces; he could not be expected to possess virtues incompatible with the rest of his mental equipment, however desirable such virtues might be. Who knows? Van Koppen's doubtful acts might be an unavoidable expression of his personality, an integral part of that nature under whose ferocious stimulus he had climbed to his present enviable position. And Mr. Heard was both shocked and amused to reflect that but for the co-operation of certain coarse organic impulses to which these Nepenthe legends testified, the millionaire might never have been able to acquire the proud title of "Saviour of his Country." [Van Koppen's fortune was the result of his monopoly of certain ingeniously contrived rubber goods.]

"That's queer," he mused. "It never struck me before. Shows how careful one must be. Dear me! Perhaps the ladies have inevitable organic impulses of a corresponding kind. Decidedly queer. H'm. Ha. Now I wonder. . . . And perhaps, if the truth were known, these young persons are having quite a good time of it—"

Various other incidents and impressions have their effect on Bishop Heard. There are the Russians, the simplehearted sect of "Little White Cows," and their demagogic leader who show him what incredible "chimaeras" the "hyperborean mists" of northern Europe can engender. And there is the murder trial, with its comic opera confusion, which shows him how undependable is the justice of organized society. Everything prepares him for the climactic situation in which he witnesses the murder and, far from being outraged, he is able to take the matter in stride and to attribute it to the "immutable instincts of mankind." "One dirty blackmailer more or less; what on earth did it matter to anybody? . . . A contemptible little episode! He decided to relegate it into the category of unimportant events."

His conclusive view is that Nepenthe has done him good:

> There was something bright and diabolical in the tone of the place, something kaleidoscopic,—a frolicsome perversity. Purifying, at the same time. It swept away the cobwebs. It gave you a measure, a standard, whereby to compute earthly affairs. Another landmark passed; another milestone on the road to enlightenment. That period of doubt was over. His values had righted themselves. He had carved out new and sound ones; a workable, up-to-date theory of life. He was in fine trim. His liver—he forgot that he ever had one. Nepenthe had done him good all round. And he knew exactly what he wanted. A return to the Church, for example, was out of the question. His sympathies had outgrown the ideals of that establishment; a wave of pantheistic benevolence had drowned its smug little teachings. The Church of England! What was it still good for? A stepping stone, possibly towards something more respectable and humane; a warning to all concerned of the folly of idolizing dead men and their delusions. The Church? Ghosts!

A criticism to which **South Wind** is probably open is the weakness of its story line. One reviewer [Arthur Eckersley, *English Review,* August, 1917] said, "There is no story, or none that matters." And Richard Aldington is quite severe on this matter:

> . . . there was a theme for an extravaganza or short story of novelette length if properly constructed, but the author doesn't know his trade. True, he has created here and there an ambience and "atmosphere" of genial and irresponsible paganism, for which I praise him. But about one third of his chapters are irrelevant to his theme

and therefore from an artistic point of view useless excrescences, however excellent they may be in themselves as essays. The author's real problem was admittedly a difficult one, and, in view of its preposterous nature, the Bishop's conversion from Christianity to low-class South Italian immoralism could only take place in an extravaganza. The Bishop ought to have been shown by a series of skilfully contrived and interwoven incidents and experiences, gradually condoning one by one breaches of Anglican morals until he arrives at murder. . . . [*Pinorman,* 1954]

Douglas, annoyed by the reviewers' charges concerning the weakness of the plot of **South Wind,** undertook to answer them in **Alone** with a rather lengthy discussion of the novel:

> I see no reason why a book should have a plot. In regard to this one, it would be nearer the truth to say it is nothing but plot from beginning to end. How to make a murder palatable to a bishop: that is the plot. How? You must unconventionalise him and instil into his mind the seeds of doubt and revolt. You must shatter his old notions of what is right. It is the only way to achieve this result, and I would defy the critic to point to a single incident or character or conversation in the book which does not further the object in view. The good bishop soon finds himself among new influences; his sensations, his intellect, are assailed from within and without. Figures such as those in Chapters 11, 19, and 35 [these are respectively the story of Bashakuloff and the Little White Cows, that of the Good Duke Alfred, and that of Commendatore Giustino Morena]; the endless dialogues in the boat; the even more tedious happenings in the local law-court; the very externals—relaxing wind and fantastic landscape and volcanic phenomena—the joval immoderation of everything and everybody; they foster a sense of violence and insecurity; they all tend to make the soil receptive to new ideas.
>
> If that was your plot, the reviewer might say, you have hidden it rather successfully. I have certainly done my best to hide it. For although the personalities of the villain and his legal spouse crop up periodically, with ominous insistence, from the first chapter onwards, they are always swallowed up again. The reason is given in the penultimate chapter, where the critic might have found a *résumé* of my intentions and the key to this plot—to wit, a murder under those particular circumstances is not only justifiable and commendable but—insignificant. Quite insignificant! Not worth troubling about. Hundreds of decent and honest folk are being destroyed every day; nobody cares tuppence; "one dirty blackmailer more or less—what does it matter to anybody?" There are so many more interesting things on earth. That is why the bishop—*i.e.* the reader—here discovers the crime to be a "contemptible little episode," and decides to "relegate it into the category of unimportant events." *He was glad that the whole affair had*

remained in the background, so to speak, of his local experiences. It seemed appropriate. . . . That is the heart, the core, of the plot. And that is why all those other happenings find themselves pushed into the foreground.

There is little that can be said to contradict this explanation—or to support it. Douglas' assertion that *everything* contributes in some way to the central problem is rather strong, but it could probably be defended. Final recourse must be to the response of the individual reader; and, while the effect of the book is not particularly one of economy, most readers probably find it, in the main, unified. Nevertheless, the structure of the novel is not so strong as that of many less important novels. Almost the entire first half is devoted to exposition, establishment of characters, and development of atmosphere. With the threatened eruption of the volcano, accompanied by various fantastic portents, a tension is created which subsequently snaps. Dramatic things then begin to happen: the Little White Cows riot; Mrs. Meadows murders her first husband; Freddy Parker dies; and finally the Count sells his fake statue. The resolution of the plot takes place within the mind of the Bishop, and the denouement appropriately involves everyone's getting quietly and whimsically tipsy.

II *The Gallery of Eccentrics*

Douglas was more interested in the souls of places than in the souls of individuals. He preferred to observe life generally rather than to study psychology and individual behavior. As a result, his characters do not have the kind of depth and verisimilitude that we have come to expect in the modern novel, where the naturalistic tradition is strong and where subtle psychology is demanded. One cannot chart their unconscious minds or follow the various hereditary factors and traumatic incidents which make them what they are. In this sense, they might be considered superficial and lacking in realism. V. S. Pritchett writes:

> Douglas is an observer of human nature who depends upon his first impression for his effect; he is not a novelist in the sense that he proceeds any deeper into his people. He certainly is not "in" them and has little sympathy. He is a brilliant satirical talker, the egotist who is the unrelaxing circus master displaying his own power as a trainer, not the real power of the animals. How, the human reader asks, have these grotesques been trained to the master's will? There is, unnoticed by him but patent to us, a pathos in their fixed gaze, as they watch the whip.

It may be that Douglas' characters are too contrived to be completely realistic, but it seems clear also that Pritchett has allowed his metaphor to get out of control. The picture of Mr. Keith or Miss Wilberforce gazing pathetically at the Cipolla-like figure of their creator and pleading for more individuality is amusing. It is just as important that characters function harmoniously and effectively in the total scheme of the novel as that they seem to live a life of their own. If all characters ran away from their authors, as Becky Sharp is supposed to have run away from Thackeray, novels would be chaotic affairs. Characters should be what their author wants them to be, or as nearly so as he can make them. Some are created with close attention to subsurface factors and hence give an impression of many dimensions. Others are intentionally and necessarily superficial.

Douglas' characters have the quality of caricature, each representing some particular tendency to an extreme degree. They thus approach the nature of symbols. E. M. Forster in *Aspects of the Novel* has written astutely about characters of this type, which he calls "flat" characters. He points out that they are built around "a single idea or quality" and can often be expressed in one sentence. He finds two principal advantages to "flat" characters. First, they are easily recognized by the reader: "It is a convenience for an author when he can strike with his full force at once, and flat characters are very useful to him, since they never need reintroducing, never run away, have not to be watched for development, and provide their own atmosphere—little luminous disks of a pre-arranged size, pushed hither and thither like counters across the void or between the stars; most satisfactory."

A second advantage is that such characters are easily remembered by the reader after he has finished the book: "They remain in his mind as unalterable for the reason that they were not changed by circumstances; they moved through circumstances, which gives them in retrospect a comfortable quality, and preserves them when the book that produced them may decay. . . . All of us, even the sophisticated, yearn for permanence, and to the unsophisticated permanence is the chief excuse for a work of art. We all want books to endure, to be refuges, and their inhabitants to be always the same, and flat characters tend to justify themselves on this account."

Forster cites Dickens as an example of a "big" writer who employed "flat" characters almost exclusively and produced a "wonderful feeling of human depth" through them. Although such characters as Mr. Micawber and Mr. Pickwick are, if looked at edgeways, "no thicker than a gramaphone record," Dickens presented them so ingeniously that the reader never gets "the sideway view." Moreover, Dickens' immense vitality caused his characters "to vibrate a little, so that they borrow his life and appear to live one of their own." Forster concludes that "Dickens' success with types suggests that there may be more in flatness than the severer critics admit."

The interpretation of humanity produced by Douglas' characters may be, in some senses, a shallower and less adequate one than that of Dickens, even though it has in some ways, greater complexity. Yet, in the main, Forster's observations about Dickens apply to Douglas. Douglas' characters are memorable, despite their flatness; and they do embody some of their creator's intellectual vitality. The kind of world that Douglas' fiction created—and all three novels bear this out—is a stylized world. It contains, somehow, one dimension less than the worlds of Henry James, D. H. Lawrence, or James Joyce—to cite diverse examples. Douglas' characters are at home in this world, as "rounder" characters would not be. They serve his purposes. He will not "pry" into them beyond a certain depth, as he would not "pry" into himself for his reader's benefit.

It is ironic that Forster chooses to quote, as an example of critical disapproval of the kind of flat characters that he is defending, "one of our foremost writers, Mr. Norman Douglas." The passage which he quotes is from *A Plea for Better Manners*. Douglas is taking to task writers like D. H. Lawrence who, he claims, place their friends in novels and falsify them with "the novelist's touch." He defines this as follows:

> It consists, I should say in a failure to realize the profundities and complexities of the ordinary human mind; it selects for literary purposes two or three facets of a man or woman, generally the most spectacular and therefore "useful" ingredients of their character, and disregards all the others. Whatever fails to fit in with these specially chosen traits is eliminated; must be eliminated, for otherwise the description would not hold water. Such and such are the data; everything incompatible with those data has to go by the board. It follows that the novelist's touch argues, often logically, from a wrong premise; it takes what it likes and leaves the rest. The facts may be correct so far as they go, but there are too few of them; what the author says may be true, and yet by no means the truth. That is the novelist's touch. It falsifies life.

This is in some ways shortsighted criticism; perhaps it reflects Douglas' chagrin at Lawrence's characterization of him in *Aaron's Rod* and certainly it reflects the conviction which he often expressed that the individual's privacy should always be respected. Douglas should certainly have realized that the artist can never disclose everything but must choose the details which serve his artistic ends. A large part of the *dramatis personae* of any novel must consist of characters who are considerably less than completely developed. The novelist's art should not photograph life but epitomize it.

In violation of the principles Douglas had announced in his attack on Lawrence's methods, he seems to have put living people into his own novels. There is hardly an important character in *South Wind* who did not have a living counterpart. And, although Douglas claimed that all of them were idealized and that no one was maligned or offensively depicted, some characters, such as Malipizzo and Freddy Parker, have been construed as rancorous attacks on their models.

Mr. Heard must be considered the protagonist of *South Wind,* for it is to him that the important things happen. He is a good deal "rounder" than most of Douglas'

people—as a protagonist must necessarily be—and does undergo a development. As a protagonist he has not been well received by all readers. Those critics who disapprove of Mr. Heard seem to do so on the absurd basis that if he had been another kind of bishop, instead of the kind he was, the story would have had a different outcome. Elizabeth Wheatley, [in "Norman Douglas," *Sewanee Review,* January, 1932] for instance, calls him a "flexible dummy instead of a man." "It is child's play to knock down a dummy. Had Mr. Douglas faced a real bishop with his golden absurdities, he would have met an *impasse.* For it is the business of bishops to forgive and forget more terrible crimes than murder." And Pelham Edgar in *The Art of the Novel,* [1933] complains that, by making Heard an easy target for the island's message, Douglas had stacked the cards. Edgar says that, though Heard is the only character in the book "capable of a critical reaction," he is "an unsatisfactory reagent." Needless to say, a better bishop would have been another story; but it would not have been written by Norman Douglas. These are actually criticisms of Douglas' values rather than of his characterization. Bishop Heard is the kind of bishop that Douglas' purpose required. A "real" bishop would be out of place in *South Wind,* or in any other satire for that matter.

Among the characters in *South Wind* is the confused student, Denis Phipps. He comes to Nepenthe unsure of his values—timorous, idealistic, and too English. The atmosphere takes its effect:

> All was not well with Denis. And the worst of it was, he had no clear notion of what was the matter. He was changing. The world was changing too. It had suddenly expanded. He felt that he, also, ought to expand. There was so much to learn, to see, to know—so much, that it seemed to paralyse his initiative. Could he absorb all this? Would he ever get things into order once more, and recapture his self-possession? Would he ever again be satisfied with himself? It was an invasion of his tranquillity, from within and without. He was restless.

Like the bishop, Denis too has been somewhat prepared: "The novel impressions of Florence had helped in the disintegration. Nepenthe—its sunshine, its relentless paganism—had done the rest. It shattered his earlier outlook and gave him nothing in exchange. Nothing and yet everything." Denis supplements the Bishop because, being younger, he can have a love affair and give Douglas an opportunity to comment on this aspect of things. Thus Denis falls in love with a sensuous and amoral servant girl, the essence of southern beauty; but he is crushed when the less idealistic and more aggressive Edgar Marten wins her promiscuous love. Then Denis receives advice from Mr. Keith:

> "He said I made a mistake in paying attention to what human beings said and did, and that I ought to forsake mankind for a while, and art and books, and so on. You know the way he talks! He said

it would give me a stronger individuality if I came into contact with nature and thought things out for myself instead of listening to other people. He advised me to sit among the rocks at midnight and in the hot afternoons, conversing with the genii of earth and air. It would correct my worldly perspective."

Having followed Keith's advice, Denis, like Bishop Heard, is regenerated at the end the story.

Of the several characters who seem to represent aspects of Douglas' own point of view, Mr. Keith is the most important. He is a rationalist, a pagan, an individualist, a hedonist—and he is strikingly articulate. He also has Douglas' reverence for nature, his hunger for knowledge, and his worship of facts:

> Keith was a pertinacious and omnivorous student; he sought knowledge not for a set purpose but because nothing was without interest for him. He took all learning to his province. He read for the pleasure of knowing what he did not know before; his mind was usually receptive because, he said, he respected the laws which governed his body. Facts were his prey. He threw himself into them with a kind of piratical ardour; took them by the throat, wallowed in them, worried them like a terrier, and finally assimilated them. They gave him food for what he liked best on earth: "disinterested thought." They "formed a rich loam." He had an encyclopaedic turn of mind; his head, as somebody once remarked, was a lumber-room of useless information. He could tell you how many public baths existed in Geneva in pre-Reformation days, what was the colour of Mehemet Ali's whiskers, why the manuscript of Virgil's friend Gallius had not been handed down to posterity, and in what year, and what month, the decimal system was introduced into Finland. Such aimless incursions into knowledge were a puzzle to his friends, but not to himself. They helped him to build up a harmonious scheme of life—to round himself off.

Mr. Keith further has Douglas' liking for solitude: he contended "that no garden on earth, however spacious, was large enough for more than one man." He even shows the note of pagan melancholy which we have seen Douglas display. A kind of chorus, Mr. Keith serves to develop the moral implications of the plot. And, though his long and frequent conversations about human conduct might easily have become tedious, Douglas has made him sufficiently eloquent to avoid this danger.

Count Caloveglia is also a spokesman for the author. He is a Classicist, a Hellenist, a lover of the Mediterranean, and something of a Machiavellian: "There was sunshine in his glance—a lustrous gem-like grace; one realized from his conversation, from his every word, that he had discarded superfluities of thought and browsed for a lifetime, in leisurely fashion, upon all that purifies and exalts the spirit. Nothing one felt, would avail to ruffle that deep pagan content." The crowning achievement of the Count's life is the sale of his faked antique to the

American millionaire, Van Koppen; the money will secure a dowry for his daughter. But, even when this success is assured, he does not forget the "golden mean": "The cheque would be in his pocket that night. Three hundred and fifty thousand francs—or nearly. That is what made him not exactly grave, but reserved. Excess of joy, like all other excess, is not meet to be displayed before men. All excess is unseemly. Nothing overmuch. Measure in everything."

Douglas had known people who sold fake antiques as Count Caloveglia did. Orioli describes a man named Martin, whom Douglas undoubtedly also knew, who made a business of such nefarious dealings. Douglas also knew a man who had some of the characteristics of Mr. Eames, the scholar of Nepenthe. This was John Ellington Brooks, to whom Douglas dedicated ***Birds and Beasts of the Greek Anthology.*** Brooks, who lived alone on Capri, never returned to the mainland. He was content to play with his cat, strum his piano, and enjoy his scholarly pursuits. Included in his pile of unpublished manuscripts were, according to Orioli, original poetry and prose as well as translations from Greek, Latin, and French. His only publication, apart from the translations Douglas used in ***Birds and Beasts*** was a sonnet which he once sold for a few pounds. Brooks may have contributed to several of the characters in ***South Wind,*** but he was clearly a model for Mr. Eames, who is described as "this man of single aim and purpose, this monk of literature. . . . Happy mortal! Free from all superfluities and encumbrances of the flesh! Enviable mortal! He reduced earthly existence to its simplest and most effective terms; he owed no man anything; he kept alive, on a miserable income, the sacred flame of enthusiasm. To aspire, that was the secret of his life."

Miss Wilberforce, the Englishwoman with an addiction to alcohol and a habit of disrobing in public, is an amusing, sympathetically presented character. In his introduction to the Modern Library edition of ***South Wind,*** Douglas said of her creation: "Miss Wilberforce has been put together out of some twelve dames of that particular alcoholic temperament whom it has been my privilege to know, and each of whom has contributed her mite; she is a synthetic lady-sot—a type I fervently pray God may never die out." Miss Wilberforce's sailor fiancé had died at sea. His death had been a "twist," and she had tried to drown herself several times.

> Then, gradually, she put on a new character altogether and relapsed into queer ancestral traits, stripping off, like so many worthless rags, the layers of laboriously acquired civilization.
>
> . . . . .
>
> . . . Staggering about the lanes of Nepenthe in the silent hours before dawn, she was liable to be driven, at the bidding of some dark primeval impulse, to divest herself of her rainment—a singularity which perturbed even the hardiest of social nightbirds who had the misfortune to

encounter her. Taxed with this freakish behaviour, she would refer to the example of St. Francis of Assisi who did the same, and brazenly ask whether he wasn't good enough for them?

Douglas had an affection for this sort of gentle, ruined profligate. Miss Wilberforce provides a humorous continuity and allows an opportunity for Mr. Keith to give an exposition of his laissez-faire social attitudes when he eloquently thwarts an attempt of local "do-gooders" to put the poor lady in a private asylum.

Another character, the Duchess, is patterned after an American lady named Mrs. Snow. In referring to this lady in *Looking Back,* Douglas reiterated his view that novelists should not take their characters from life without thoroughly remodeling them:

> Mrs. Snow. She finally returned to America. A vision of her helped me to portray the "Duchess" in a certain story; other ladies contributed their share of suggestion; imagination also played its part. I have never tried to draw a figure from life, as they say. My creed is that a human character, however engrossing, however convincing and true to itself, must be modelled anew before it can become material for fiction. It must be licked into shape, otherwise its reactions in a world of fictitious characters, would be out of focus. No authentic child of man will fit into a novel.
>
> History is the place for such people; history or oblivion.

Freddy Parker and his lady, Douglas confessed to have intended as Mr. and Mrs. Harold Trower. Trower was the author of *The Book of Capri* and hence a kind of rival of Douglas. Signor Malipizzo ("Ha, the animal! He has the Evil Eye. He is also scrofulous, rachitic") was a magistrate named Capolozzi, who, Douglas said, "very nearly had me in the lock-up once or twice." Orioli calls Capolozzi "a horrible creature . . . , lame and sickly and red-haired, and hated to such an extent by everybody . . . that he asked to be transferred to another post in the nick of time to save himself from a stab in the belly. . . ." Muhlen (or Retlow), the blackmailing husband of Mrs. Meadows, was suggested by Baron Fritz Von Meltheim, who was apparently both a blackmailer and a murderer. And Bazhakuloff was based on Rasputin and other Russian "imposters."

A great part of Douglas' characterization and plot development is dependent upon conversation. Many of the ideas in *South Wind* receive their development through the dialogue of such "spokesman" characters as Mr. Keith and Count Caloveglia. And the advancement of the plot—that is, the evolution of the Bishop's outlook—is in part effected through the provocative conversation of these characters who insinuate ideas into his mind. Mr. Keith is so astute in his reading of character and so articulate in his explanations that his discussions with the Bishop form a kind of choral commentary on the atmosphere, the incidents, and the other

characters. *South Wind* has been called a conversational novel in the tradition of Peacock.

Douglas' dialogue has been deemed stylized, the criticism being that all characters speak with the same voice and that that voice is Douglas' own. Aldington writes that Douglas ". . . had a stylized dialogue which was fatal to the living word, so that almost everyone who talks in his books is Douglas-ised into similarity, a monotony of flippantly doggish worldliness." It is true that the dialogue often lacks what might be called "realism," because the characters are all somewhat too eloquent. But realism was not Douglas' object, nor would it have been especially appropriate to his novels. He was not attempting to present a "slice of life" but to produce the well-made novel in which everything contributed to his intentions. In *Looking Back,* he criticized Lawrence's dialogue, which is ordinarily praised as lifelike: "Lawrence never divined that conversations and dialogue are precious contrivances, to be built up *con amore;* that they should suggest a clue to character and carry forward the movement instead of retarding it; that they should be sparkling oases, not deserts of tiresome small-talk."

Some further defense can be made against the charge that Douglas' characters are less than real and individualized in their speech. Many of the characters in *South Wind*—Mr. Keith, Caloveglia, Don Francesco—can be eloquent without being inconsistent to their characters in other respect. Others—the Bishop, Denis, the Duchess, and Mrs. Steynlin—would also be expected to speak as correctly and as well as they do. Edgar Marten, on the other hand, is depicted as somewhat coarse. His language reflects this; notice, for instance, his reaction to the Russian fanatic Bazhakuloff; "He's a beauty! Eyes like a boiled haddock. And that thing has the cheek to call itself a Messiah. Thank God I'm a Jew; it's no business of mine. But if I were a Christian, I'd bash his blooming head in. Damned if I wouldn't. The frowsy, fetid, fly-blown fraud. Or what's the matter with the Dog's Home?" It must be admitted, however, that Douglas himself had several "voices," and that even this was one of them. The expression of Douglas' characters, like their ideas, is usually recognizable as that of the author. The differentiating features are too superficial to hide Douglas' mannerisms, his liking for epigram, and even some of his favorite words. One must be content with the fact that their conversation is usually interesting and witty and that its stylized quality is not out of keeping with the atmosphere in which it is set.

South Wind appears to have been a sort of consummation of Douglas' particular possibilities. Although there are always readers who prefer *Old Calabria, Siren Land,* or even *They Went,* most grant *South Wind* to be Douglas' best book and the most consummate display of his powers. It allowed him to present some of his eccentric Capri friends in an idealized form and to project his own personality into several characters; it permitted him to talk casually and eloquently about many of his favorite topics—geology, history, and even saints' legends.

And amazingly enough, through his felicitous style and ironic wit, he was able to inform the whole with a unity of mood and purpose. Less than a decade after the publication of **South Wind,** an influential critic, writing in the *New York Times* [Herbert Gorman, *The New York Times Book Review,* February 8, 1975], summarized the basis of the critical esteem in which the book had already come to be held: "The high engrossment in atmosphere delineation, the almost flawless projection of character, the steady stream of faintly ironic humor, the philosophical undercurrent, the sense of completeness and, above all, the achievement of a colorful and melodious prose that is both pleasant and fastidious, combine together in a work that has won for itself a small but vociferous body of admirers who insist upon denominating it as one of the smaller classics."

But this critic added, prophetically, that "**South Wind** is his triumph and vindication as a writer, and somehow one suspects that it will remain so; that another such work would be impossible from him for the simple reason that he has put all of himself in it. He is not a great creative writer, but for once his powers fused at their best and the result is one that should accord him a place in the minds of those readers who love what are termed 'the delicacies of literature.'"

III **They Went**: *Beauty Over Betterment*

They Went (1920) Douglas' second full-length novel, was written during the lean years after World War I. Begun at St. Malo, it was "interrupted owing to lack of food," and finished at Mentone after the war "when I was feeling comfortable again" [*Late Harvest*]. In *Looking Back* Douglas described the circumstances of its writing and the thoughts which prompted it:

> At Mentone I was already drifting away from humanity pure and simple, with its odd little loves and hates and ambitions; into the regions beyond, and saying to myself as I actually wrote later: "How many avenues of delight are closed to the mere moralist or immoralist who knows nothing of things extra-human; who remains absorbed in mankind and its half-dozen motives of conduct, so unstable yet forever the same, which we all fathomed before we were twenty!" There is an infusion of the extra-human in **They Went,** which depicts the conflict between beauty and betterment, art and morality. Betterment wins, despite the extra-human intervention of Theophilus. It is apt to win. In the shape of priestcraft, it extinguished art and science in Egypt; in the shape of Plato and his followers, it extinguished them in Greece. That city, the thing of beauty, lies drowned under the waves, while betterment remains perched on its granite rock.

They Went is a short, whimsical tale, set sometime in the dim past. Its pseudo-legendary form and austere style produce an effect far different from that of **South Wind.** Description is kept to a minimum; conversation plays a much less prominent part than in the earlier novel; the mood is less bright and sparkling; and despite a strong humorous element, the tone is more serious and less tolerant.

The setting is a strange, mist-shrouded city on the rugged northern coast, presumably Brittany, in the fifth or sixth century. The heroic age of the city is past; it is in a period of decadence—of splendor, luxury, and immorality. The King, now an old and doddering man, has memories of great conquests over the Vikings; but now the weapons and armor are rusting, and the old smith Lelian is reduced to making trinkets for the beautiful but cruel Princess.

The King's last great victory has been over the sea, for he has caused a mighty sea wall to be constructed by an exiled Roman engineer. The sea has been pushed back, a flooded plain drained, and a city built on a spit of reclaimed land. Now, at the King's belt hangs the key to the sluice gates which hold back the angry ocean that thunders at the city's foundation, eager to take back what was once its own.

The Princess, whom all men adore at first sight, is a lover of beauty and has rebuilt the city, transforming the plain functional buildings of the Roman engineer by adding exotic towers and porticoes. The control of the city is hers, for her personality and intellect are far stronger than those of her senile father or her innocuous mother. It is the Princess who has made the city a center of world commerce and an object of wide interest by bringing skillful craftsmen and artisans from distant lands. She toys with the city as she does with the men who make the mistake of offering her their adulation, and her private tower is known to contain rare secrets and to have been the scene of strange orgies. It has a stairway opening on the great drain; when her lovers begin to bore her, or when her favorites have been gleaned of all their knowledge, *they go.*

The Princess was not actually the child of the king. Once Aithryn, the great ruler of the north whom people thought to be a sea god, had become jealous of the city beside the sea and had sailed there in his green ship. He did not enter the city, but found the Queen seated on the sea wall embroidering and took her on his ship for a brief visit. Thus the element of discord entered the city; now, nineteen years later, Aithryn's spies carefully watch the maturing of the strong-willed young Princess who seems so unlike the King.

The religious life of the city is dominated by Manthis, a harsh old druidess and worshiper of Belen who keeps a girls' school on an island in the bay and who propagates her doctrines of betterment, social utility, and the superiority of women. The last Christian missionary had been treated tolerantly; but, when he proved to be a bigot and hacked down the sacred druidical grove, the King and Manthis decided that he had to go. He went, but in his dying malediction he had mentioned "retribution from the sea." Manthis scrutinized the missionary's entrails to read the future and promptly moved her girls to the island.

The new missionary, a handsome young man named Kenwyn with a weakness in matters of sex, proves acceptable to Manthis and attractive to the Princess. But even more appealing to this self-willed young lady is a mysterious Greek named Theophilus, who, though ugly and diabolical, has a vast knowledge of architecture and the other arts that the Princess lives for. He is able to make workmen and materials appear as if by magic, and he is the only person whose fate Manthis has been unable to read.

With Theophilus, whose resources of knowledge are unlimited, the Princess is happy for the first time in her life. Together they make the city beautiful. From him she learns not only new methods and crafts, but also new qualities of kindness and mercy that temper her former callousness; for the pragmatic Theophilus knows well that nothing is accomplished by unnecessary cruelty. But now the Princess is to learn the meaning of sacrifice as well, for Theophilus finds it necessary to ask recompense for his help. He explains to her that people like them, lovers of beauty, have dangerous enemies—, the forces of betterment and the All-Highest. He explains that Aithryn, her real father, is now leagued with the All-Highest. Suffering a kind of senility as a result of an old head wound, Aithryn has fallen under the power of the Christians, who promise him a future life in return for extensive grants of land to the Church. And now the Christians insist that Aithryn destroy the evil city by the sea, whose Princess, rumor has it, has sold her soul to the evil one. The first measures which Theophilus requires the Princess to take are the disposal of the Christian missionary and the securing of the great key from her irresponsible father.

The Princess, half in love with Kenwyn, at first refuses Theophilus' request; but, when he threatens to leave, she complies. The lovesick young missionary is easily lured to her tower at night, as others before him have been; and, like them, "he *went*." The great drain tells no tales. Now the Princess, who has shed tears for the first time in her life, knows what it means to sacrifice for something one loves. But she has failed to secure the key to the sluice gates. The green ship comes again; Aithryn enters the palace during the nightly revelry; the Queen is so excited that she forgets to put the old King to bed when he reaches "high water mark"; and Aithryn leaves with the key.

The ocean surges over the city. Aithryn is waiting outside the tower for his daughter, but Theophilus easily destroys him. Theophilus is dejected to see his magnificent work destroyed, but he is accustomed to such disappointment. The All-Highest, who prefers a preacher to a portico, is always ready to destroy thousands of innocent people in order to accomplish his whims. But Theophilus will take the Princess to his own land, where they can rear a new city without the interference of the forces of betterment. The princess is happy and willing. "They went."

Manthis, safe with her girls on the island, realizes that her hopes of some kind of an alliance with Christianity were futile because they depended on men, and Kenwyn has proved that men are too weak for such high purposes. She is happy in the realization that the sinful city is gone and, with it all, the annoyances and frustrations. Now she will be able to develop her own ideas of betterment: "She felt like some sagacious gardener who holds in his hands a seed scarcely visible, and already contemplates, with the mind's eye, the tall and seemly growth which must inevitably spring therefrom."

The loss of the city's population—and hence of all the men—disturbs Manthis' pupils, who ask, "If all the men are drowned, and even the young ones, and even the tiny little boys, how shall we ever—" But Manthis is undisturbed. "Belen will provide," she announces gravely. And thus "the thing of beauty lies drowned under the wave, while betterment remains perched on its granite rock."

The book received some favorable reviews. The *Athenaeum* [8 October 1920] said, ". . . Mr. Douglas has developed and transformed the Peacockian novel, carrying it to a point far beyond that charming if uneven writer. . . ." And Rebecca West wrote in the *New Statesman* [2 October 1920] that Douglas' talent had found a more appropriate expression than in **South Wind** or in **Old Calabria**. A few other critics have since echoed this preference. Raymond Mortimer [in *Nation and Athenaeum* 22 September 1928] considers **They Went** Douglas' best novel, and Elizabeth Wheatly considers it "finer" than **South Wind** and "more severely patterned."

Some reviewers were confused about the interpretation of the story. The American *Bookman* [21 May 1921] said:

> Perhaps Mr. Douglas is taking a crack at family life. . . . perhaps it is love that annoys him. Maybe he means her [the Princess] to be woman incarnate.
>
> Let me warn you against this novel if you are the sort of person who must know the exact meaning of your story books.

And another review:

> Perhaps it is the tragedy of a womanhood that is simply the will to have and to enjoy, and which so becomes in the end its own victim. Or is the princess a symbol of paganism successfully resisting the lures and the threats of a religion of sacrifice? Or do you take her (with me) as the child with the dormant soul whose interest for the cold and cruel destruction of warm things has carried her so far that the moment of possible awakening has come too late? [H.W. Boynton, in *Weekly Review,* 30 April 1921]

Light is thrown upon the meaning of the novel, or at least upon the intention of its author, in the prefatory letter which Douglas prefixed to the third printing. He explained that while visiting Brittany he had discovered that the country was saturated with legends and had decided to "dissect a handful of these for a scientific purpose." His goal was to prove the theory that a myth is "the slow product of ages . . . a kind of palimpsest . . . overscored at various periods of its growth by the fresh experience of the race." Although Douglas makes no claim for the absolute originality of these views of the nature of myth, he seems to have considered them more startling than they were. He chose the *Roi d'Ys* story, the drowned city motif which had appeared in a number of plays and poems, as well as in the "melodiously saccharine opera by Lalo." Working with the Breton variant of the legend, he found "that primordial or autochtonous note—the domineering and lustful woman, as well as another aboriginal feature which I proposed, just for the sake of the theory, to attribute to the old dolichocephalous inhabitants of Brittany: the personification of wild nature forces—in this case a revengeful ocean." Next he discerned "the *brachycephalic* contribution" (in the metals, craftsmanship, and so on); then a Roman element; and last, the "Christian patina—the intervention of a saint." Thus, six thousand years of accretions, "Q.E.D. Pure guess work, you perceive."

In considering these legends, Douglas was disturbed—as might be expected—by the intrusion of saints and angels and by the admixture of Christian values: "It dulls their pristine vigour and originality and even, by appearing as *deus ex machina* at a critical moment, renders them almost *jejune*—nonsensical. . . ." He relates that he tried to strip off these "adventitious wrappings" and to reconstruct the legend in "pagan garb." But he soon lost sight of his original problem and began to wonder what version offered most artistic merit, what improvements might be made, which characters were superfluous, and what new ones might be added. And thus **They Went** came into being. Douglas called it therefore ". . . not a phantasy of my own, but an adaptation from a familiar legend which keeps alive, maybe, the memory of some actual historical occurrence, some inroad of the sea destructive to the works of man."

As to the meaning of his novel Douglas wrote:

> In this little allegory of beauty *versus* betterment into which the Roi d'Ys has developed (you see what happens when I take a legend in hand for "scientific purposes") I have tried to remain aloof and to hold the balance evenly. It is true that the All-Highest wins by a rather tortuous device. He does; and not for the first time in history. For this exalted personage would be unendurable had he not likewise his curse, his tragedy, his cloven hoof. He is omnipresent and yet not invariably wise; he blunders now and then (*see* Genesis) and is streaked, moreover, by a curious little vein of senile malice. Which of us, at one time or another, has not suffered from it? Kindly note, nevertheless, that the catastrophe would not have occurred and that the All-Highest would have been delightfully outwitted, but for the refusal of the princess to ask for the key. What made her refuse? "Sheer wrongness—wrongness and pride." Pride—hybris: that unforgivable sin which brings about the downfall of mortals.

Thus Douglas attempted, with indifferent success, to maintain a balance between the opposing teams. Both sides have weaknesses. The All-Highest has the incongruities characteristic of anthropomorphic deities. He has, from the human point of view, that disconcerting flaw that poor Job discovered: he is neither just nor consistent. The Princess has the flaw of humanity which the Greeks discovered: she is proud, immoderate, and shortsighted. It is obvious that Theophilus contains much of Douglas' own character and temperament. He is the lover of beauty, the Machiavellian, the gentleman of perfect taste. But he has the problem that all Satans in literature have faced: he is by definition unable to overcome his adversary.

Although the deepest conflicts of the plot are those between the antithetical cosmic forces, the little weaknesses of men play their parts in the turn of events. Without the personality of the King, the needs of the Queen, the hybris of the Princess, and the flawed mind of Aithryn, things would not have come about as they did. Thus Douglas apparently tried to keep a balance also between fate and human responsibility—the kind of balance which forms part of the achievement of Greek tragedy and epic. The people in **They Went** make their own fate to a degree, but their very nature makes it impossible for the best that is in them to win out. They get the god they deserve. Manthis is right in her perception of human weakness; but she has her own flaw, and the handling of the story makes her flaw perhaps the worst of all. She is allied with the forces of betterment which will always thwart man in his efforts to fulfill his potentialities for beauty and civilization, and these latter values are clearly the ones to which the author gives his nod of approval. Rebecca West has adroitly summed up what happens in the story and what the outcome implies:

> . . . this struggle between the artist and the moralist is illusory. It comes to no decisions; it merely embellishes the pattern of life by adding to the intricacy of events, and the course of history is settled by things quite other. The city was washed away not by any machination of the devil or the missionary, but because the barbarian king, jealous of this rival kingdom and barred from any constructive belligerent policy by the effects of a crack on the skull, sent spies overseas to tamper with the embankment. It is stupidity that always finishes the argument between the artist and the saint, the cracked skull of humanity that is the decisive factor in the affairs of men. [*New Statesman*, 2 October 1920]

Concerning the principal characters, Douglas had something to say also. Theophilus, unlike the Princess and her parents, had no precedent in other versions of the legend. He was introduced because "the semi-savage Princess Ahes could never have reared a town surpassing Paris in splendour "without the help of the great Master-Builder of medieval days. . . ." In regard to the devil Douglas had written in **Siren Land**: "And what lends the devil his charm? His quasi-human attributes; his bargainings, his ill-treatment at the hands of heaven. Beings wholly divine are inevitably endowed with qualities of good and evil identical with our own: they are mere caricatures of good or bad men." Douglas made his devil in **They Went** human and appealing. Though astute and masterful, Theophilus is also tactful and sympathetic; he does not push himself in where he is not wanted. Hc is sensitive to beauty, kind when it is not necessary to be otherwise, and much affected by the sight of suffering. And, despite a few outbursts, he is resigned and relatively humble before the state of things—as far from the proud rebel of the earlier books of *Paradise Lost* as from the suave Voltarian of Goethe's *Faust*. A true gentleman, Theophilus has the sense of proportion that Douglas admired. Douglas' own analysis of this character emphasizes the commendable human qualities of enlightenment and creativity, but it emphasizes also the tragic dimension: "Ever to aspire and ever to be thwarted; that is the curse, the tragedy, of Theophilus and other Light-bringers. Well may they 'despair of mankind!' I grant he is not the devil of the schoolmen. He is the devil as he ought to be."

Princess Ahes was not intended to be as sympathetic a character as Theophilus: she is coarser and less self-sufficient. But she demonstrates a facet of Douglas that is sometimes overlooked; she represents an effort to show that pure intellectuality, without some tincture of warmheartedness, is objectionable. Douglas described her:

> . . . a cold, earthly thinker, an egoist predestined from birth to fall under his [Theophilus'] influence, which moulds her character in singular fashion, softening it here, and hardening it there. She too has troubles, troubles that move her to tears. Yet they fail to enlist our compassion; we find it a strain to sympathize with the griefs, however acute, however sincere, of those whose head controls their heart. Many tragic figures were murderers; none has ever been a pure intellectual.

They Went has serious defects, not the least of which is the obtrusive repetition which will be discussed elsewhere. There are elements of preciousness and snideness of tone which are at times offensive to the most kindly disposed reader. But it has the saving qualities of Douglas' felicitous prose and his potent wit, as well as remarkable economy—thanks to its author's pithy style and his belief in the unities—and a bizarre and engaging mood. Its tone—a peculiar compound of sophistication, cynicism, and equanimity—is distinctively Douglas.

IV In the Beginning

In the Beginning (1927) was also based on legendary material: the tale of Ninus and Semiramis, the mythological founders of the Assyrian Empire. They are mentioned by Herodotus, and their story is discussed by Sir James Frazer in *The Golden Bough*. Douglas claimed in **Late Harvest** that he had consulted all the ancient writers and "not a few of their modern commentators. . . ." But the legend itself is so slight and vague that the plot of **In the Beginning** can be considered original with Douglas. It is, in fact, his most sustained and complex plot; and a detailed summary of this little-known novel is necessary to make discussion possible.

The story takes place long ago, when mankind lived naked and unashamed and the gods took their pleasures not only in their own celestial halls but among the sons of men. Young Linus, a goatherd, is in love with Ayra, the daughter of a fisherman. They know little, but both feel some mysterious need. Often Linus draws the girl to a shady forest glen and caresses her clumsily, saying to himself, "This time, yes!" But her answer is always, "Oh, Linus, another day."

Ayra's father disturbed by the boy's slowness, also wonders about his wits because Linus has often reported seeing a fish of prodigious size and splendid hue, and the old man knows of no such monster. Ayra excuses her lover as a "dreamy boy" and secretly wonders whether he has not seen some immortal.

Linus has also seen a giant figure stepping across the jagged white spires which are visible halfway up the eastern sky and which are, unknown to men, a great chain of mountains. This figure is indeed the Earth god, off to pay a visit to the distant Colocynthians, whom he likes to tease with earthquakes. The Colocynthians have an advanced culture: they cultivate their land, build tall buildings, and powder their hair. It is they who have given the Earth god the nickname "O-Boum"—the Clatterer—which he resents.

The gods live in leisurely pleasure. They are immortal and fearless—but not passionless—and thrive on the worship of mortals. There are multitudes of them, peopling earth and sky, and also many half-gods products of "tender dalliance" between gods and mortals. These half-gods live on earth. They are fair and, like their divine parents, lazy, frivolous, and mischievous. Poor human beings, subject to the divine caprices of their deities, toil, suffer, and die; but they are always trying, usually in vain, to propitiate the gods.

There is, at the moment, great merriment in the celestial halls because Menetha the Maiden, cleverest of the goddesses and favorite daughter of the Great Father of the gods, has fallen in love with the young moon, who, alone among immortals, is sterile. The Clatterer laughs especially heartily, because Menetha has often chided him about his diversions, but she claims that her love for the moon is of another kind. Some of the gods think that the clever Menetha has chosen well, for she will not have to bear the pangs of childbirth from which gods are not immune. The Great Mother is pleased; there are too many philanderings with mortals and too many half-gods about. The moon, for his part, says it is all a rumor and the fault of the gossiping wind. It is quickly agreed that the wind shall be bottled up and rolled about again—one of the favorite sports in the celestial halls. It is left to Menetha to "put the moon to rights."

The Great Father has long since lapsed into lethargy and is no longer as jovial and as inventive as he once was. He is enveloped in a starry mist from which his stainless hand occasionally emerges to grasp a cup of myut, the wondrous liquor of the gods.

Linus, who is an orphan, lives with his grandmother, a woman with a reputation for great wisdom. One day he returns to their hut to find the old woman dead and learns from the First One, eldest of the three rulers of the village, that her last instructions were for the boy to visit Neahuni, the satyr.

The satyrs were a race of semidivine creatures who once peopled the earth. They were master builders, agriculturists, and scientists; but the Great Father became jealous and fearful of them and cursed them with sterility. Although their race was long-lived, the satyrs finally died out; now only Nea-huni remains. Rather than leave the earth unpeopled, the Great Father, who loved to invent things, created the race of men, fashioning them from the dung of Hapso, the loathly fowl. They are subservient creatures, good for nothing but to be laughed at. But before the satyrs disappeared, they taught many of their arts to the Colocynthians.

Nea-huni dwells alone, having outlived his beloved companion Azdhubal, fighter of demons. For a time Nea-huni was respected as a seer and healer, but now a rumor has circulated among men that this peaceful vegetarian satyr is a cannibal, and no one dares to approach him.

Linus and the First One spend several days with the gentle satyr and learn from him that Linus is a half-god, son of the Clatterer himself, and that he will one day cultivate the desolate plains again as they were cultivated in the days of the satyrs. Nea-huni also tells them of a visit he has had from the Earth god, who asked his help in capturing the demon Aroudi, haunter of outskirts, hater of men, and maker of floods and droughts. Nea-huni gave the Clatterer a magic potion with which to drug Aroudi and in return received a promise that his old friend Azdhubal would be returned to life and that the plain would be cultivated again.

In Eskion, a dusky old village at the other end of the world, something is wrong. A terrible drought is destroying the land. Heat is radiating from the temple of Derco, the maiden fish-goddess, a moody, vindictive creature who has caused this sort of thing before. When the disquieted populace is about to burn the temple, they notice that the flame which denotes the presence of the goddess has disappeared from its place.

At this instant, far away, Linus is resting on a river bank after his visit to the sanctuary of the satyr. Once again he sees the great spangled fish, and this time there is a sudden flash of light and Derco stands before him, gloriously beautiful. She tells the youth that he alone can quench her flames. Linus, who is after all his father's son, proves an apt pupil; and Derco has never in her age-long experience known such transport. Linus awakes from a refreshing slumber no longer a dreamy boy. He sets out to find Ayra, muttering to himself, "This time, yes."

Derco returns to Eskion confident that her latest lover will soon die as do all mortals who lie with gods. Prosperity and happiness return to Eskion, and the merchant Babramolok, an old Derco-worshiper, donates money for a new temple. Then one day the flame disappears again. Derco is with child. New miseries are in store. Babramolok is exiled.

Now all the gods laugh at Derco, who has been driven from her temple because the Eskions prefer a virgin goddess and have replaced her with another protector. Neither Menetha, nor the Great Father, nor Nea-huni can help her. She pays a visit to Linus, is at first surprised to find him alive, and then is enraged to learn that he has taken a mortal in his arms after lying with a divine lover. Transforming herself into a monstrous worm, she sucks out his blood and then burns the hut of Ayra and her father. But before the soul of Linus can flit away, it is caught up by the Earth god, taken to his workshop under the earth, and there revived.

Later, in a lonely cave where Derco is awaiting the birth of her child, she receives a visit from the gossipy wind, who tells her that Linus is the son of the Clatterer, who has rescued him. In return for the information, Derco agrees to help the wind the next time the gods decide to bottle him up and roll him about.

After reviving Linus in the subterranean laboratory, the Clatterer stops a while to taunt Aroudi, where the powerful demon is chained. The desert maker, whom the gods can never kill, strains at his bonds and swears revenge. He threatens the god with what will happen if men are not held in check: "I foresee the day when you will grow out of your fondness for such groveling creatures, when every fair spot has been scarred by their hands and deformed to their mean purposes, the rivers made turbid and hills and forests leveled away and all the wild green places smothered under cities full of smoke and clanking metal; when the Sun himself, the steadiest of your inconstant breed, will refuse to peer down through their foul vapors. . . ."

The Clatterer, remembering his promise to Nea-huni, returns Adzhubal to life. He also gives Linus great wisdom and sends him to the two satyrs to learn how to cultivate the plains. In two years the young man is a great king; he has cleared jungles, drained marshes, irrigated deserts, invented many new devices, and gathered great armies about him.

Derco gives birth to a daughter whom she leaves on a mountain to be found and raised in the traditional fashion by a goatherd. The girl, Symira, is much like her mother; and, growing up among lascivious goats and doves, she becomes extraordinarily hot-blooded and impulsive. When she reaches young womanhood, her foster mother gives her to Oannes, a powerful and savage chieftain of a primitive army. Symira diligently learns the arts of war from Oannes, then strangles him and declares herself chief. With her vast army of warriors, one or another of whom is brought to her tent every night only to depart in disgrace in the morning, she descends upon the lands of Linus and conquers them. But after one night in Symira's tent, Linus proves to the savage queen that he is superior to other men; thereafter, the two rule the earth together.

Derco has been able to return to Eskion, for Babramolok, back from his exile, has sent to the city an unsatisfactory god, an old woman-chaser whom the Colocynthians brought down from heaven especially to foist upon their unsuspecting enemies. The Eskions soon have enough of him and are ready to bring back Derco, who has been changed by motherhood from a capricious virgin goddess to a kindly mother goddess, full of love and joy. All is well now. The new motto of the city is "Nobody should be a virgin." The goddess has given up her sport with mortals, and the wind is known to blow strangely often within her temple.

Linus and Symira build a magnificent kingdom, vying with each other for new and fruitful ideas. Symira builds the temple of the doves to house the flocks of those birds which have followed her since her birth. In it she installs sixty-nine dancing girls known as the Doves or the Pleasant Ones. In charge of Fatutta, a pleasure-loving old harlot, their duty is to teach the art of love to the young men of the kingdom. So successful is the institution that even those who need no lessons, even Linus himself, patronize the Doves. Symira gratifies her old instincts by frequently visiting the House of the Doves and playing the part of a Pleasant One herself. But since this is not completely satisfactory, at the suggestion of Fatutta there is established a personal bodyguard for the Queen, composed of ninety-nine chosen warriors.

Then one day Linus conceives the notion of building a temple to the Great Father. The languishing old deity is so pleased that he becomes gay again. He is seen sporting about the earth in goatish disguises and is even known to be inventing things once more, producing oddities such as a star with a ring around it, a comet without a tail, and bearded women.

Once while hunting, Linus is seized by Aroudi, who has been released by the Clatterer for the sake of a little excitement. The demon warns Linus to stay out of the wilderness, which is his. After this fright, Linus changes. He gives up hunting and begins to devote more and more time to the Pleasant Ones. Despite his godlike powers, he becomes weak from overindulgence and reduces himself to a senile spendthrift and a danger to the kingdom. Moreover, he begins to think himself a god. Taking advantage of this eccentricity, Symira, who sees that her consort will have to go, convinces him that he should have himself burned to death so that he can soar to the celestial halls and visit the other immortals.

Things go well for a time, with Symira ruling the kingdom alone; then she too begins to change, developing a dislike for men and becoming herself more mannish. The ninety-nine warriors are cast aside and Symira "begins to develop longings as ardent as they are outrageous." Fatutta tries to keep the changes secret, but this is impossible. Soon there are tales abroad "—unpleasant tales about dwarfs, and apes, and horses, and other abominations. . . ."

It is just at this time that the Great Father looks down, sees what is happening, and loses his temper. He straightway lets loose upon the earth a terrible dust or powder which taints the wits of mortals. It infects them with prepostrous ideas about good and evil, which have hitherto been none of their business, and with a passion for quarreling. People are sick for only a few days, but they are left sadly altered: "They called themselves good, and forthwith began to act in accordance with frantic notions engendered by the disease." They cease to cultivate the fields and spend all their time arguing about the welfare of their souls, "as though it were something quite apart from the welfare of their bodies. . . ."

A new race of men grows up from among those who have not contracted the disease. These call themselves "dreamers" and love to think about old times and about the future, searching for some more reasonable way of life. They look to Aroudi as their savior. And the haunter of outskirts, enemy of toilers and quarrelers but friend to solitaries like these, is not asleep. Obliterating the vestiges of human folly, he gladdens the dreamers by charming the world once more into desert.

Meanwhile the malady rages. Men lose their capacity for joy and learn what it means to fear. A band of prophets and lawgivers arises who capitalize on men's fear and promulgate thousands of laws concerning good and evil which no one could possibly abide by. "All delight fled from earth, and mortals, for the most part, grew to be the fools and cowards they have since remained."

Symira herself takes the infection and becomes "better" than anyone else. It is plain that any subjects who wish to retain their lives must contract the disease. The Pleasant Ones and the ninety-nine warriors are condemned to death, but Fatutta saves them and herself by reporting erroneously that they have all taken the illness.

Symira gives up worldly pursuits and retires to rule the House of Doves. She enforces strict rules requiring that the sixty-nine Pleasant Ones, now known as the Good Ones, wear only sack cloth and eat only the most meager of rations. In effect, she establishes the first convent.

In a few years the kingdom has gone to pieces; the few remaining sane people escape to Eskion, where pleasure can still be had. The Queen dies one night, a bitter and abstemious old woman. In a final feverish wakefulness, she cries out: "Such horrible dreams, Fatutta! About horses. . . ." She leaves a sack of rubies, which are to be used to build a monument to her memory. But Fatutta spends the money on a tremendous banquet for the sixty-nine Good Ones, for old time's sake. She even invites the ninety-nine guards, who do their duty nobly.

The novel ends with a conversation between Nea-huni and Adzhubal. Nea-huni has given men up as a complete loss and both express their views concerning men and gods: "To the crocodiles, with both of them!"

The reviewers of *In the Beginning* were not kind to the book. They were disturbed by what seemed to them pornographic passages. The English *Saturday Review* said, "dull, spiritless impropriety." [L. P. Harley, 22 September 1928]. The American *New Republic* [6 June 1928] said, "Professional salaciousness." Regretting that Douglas' "refreshing paganism" had given way to "shrill impatience," the reviewer found that "The sexual debaucheries of his characters are drawn into the narrative so gratuitously and so often that they end by attracting our attention for their own sake instead of contributing to a satirical picture." The most severe attack came from the *Saturday Review of Literature*:

> *In the Beginning* is a feeble specimen of that chirping pornography that passes for strength among the weak. . . . A sort of cancerous proud-flesh has been forced to attach itself to the dry bones of the legend. If Herodotus, or Ctesius . . . alludes to some amiable sexual aberration, Mr. Douglas enlarges, envelops and expatiates. He seems completely unaware of the beauty and dignity and wonder that once were the attributes of the principle of generation. And his tone as he narrates the procreant exploits of his gods and heros and heroines is a vulgar cross between the hysterical smirking of an ill-bred fifth former and the gross crackle of a worn-out boulevardier. . . . It will bore anyone it could conceivably hurt. [Leonard Bacon, "Norman Douglas' Latest," June, 1928]

It is difficult to defend Douglas against accusations that the disturbing passages in the book were there for their own sake. Indeed, he would no doubt have rejected such defense just as Aristophanes or Rabelais would have

done. Moreover, from the perspective of a different cultural climate, and in light of the kinds of literary themes and scenes that are now accepted as a matter of course, an elaborate defense of Douglas' practice would be pointless. Douglas himself had an explanation for the critics' disapproval of *In the Beginning*. He wrote of the book in *Looking Back*:

> It lacks the admixture of saccharine which is prescribed by the taste of today. Its anti-democratic and uncompromising outlook is disquieting: "Too awful to contemplate," writes one of them, "especially the last chapter." How seriously these humans take themselves and their affairs! I do not find it awful; I find it good fun, especially the last chapter. But I understand his state of mind. I know what he wants. He wants his comforter, his treacle, his dose of irrationalism. He would have liked me to insert a touch of that "hopefulness" with which the present generation likes to delude itself, in defiance of the teaching of all history.

Late Harvest contained a few comments concerning the composition of *In the Beginning*: "The book was a strain on my inventive faculties. Some twenty new words were coined, and a fresh heaven had to be created with eight major deities, as well as half-gods and demons and a brace of gentle satyrs, not to speak of hitherto unknown races of men. Lucian was of some help in regard to the divine members of this community, while the Great Father himself is modelled upon my conception of that old Javeh of the Jews." There is also the suggestion that part of the "moral" of *In the Beginning* is that "Nothing on earth is permanent save only change, unless, of course, we include the changeless race of Gods, the Great Father and his more or less disreputable brood of children—call him Jupiter if you like—those phantasms whom we create in our own image, and endow with our own facets of good or bad humour, of lust and wisdom and inconstancy."

The book presents no great problems of interpretation. Douglas hated the Jewish God, who was a spying, "upstairs" God created by the proletariat which "loves to humiliate itself." He preferred the Classical "downstairs" gods who "were invented by intellectuals who felt themselves capable of maintaining a kind of comradeship with their deities [south wind]." Hence the happier days of *In the Beginning* are of the period when unconcerned and pleasure-loving anthropomorphic gods roamed the world.

The important aspects of the theme are the exaltation of amoral individualism and free sensuous living, the condemnation of the practice of separating body and soul, and the satire of humanity's practice of making gods. There is also present the primitivistic strain which caused Douglas to seek the refreshment of lonely places. In his essay on Doughty's *Arabia Deserta*, Douglas had made significant remarks concerning the Great Red Desert:

We learn . . . that the so-called *Empty Quarter,* the Great Red Desert, has not yet been seen by western eyes. Long may it remain invisible, a solace for future generations! Deserts have their uses, and the *Empty Quarter,* let us hope, will sooner or later demonstrate its *raison d'être* by stirring that first intrepid beholder as he gazes down upon its trackless ocean of billowing dunes, into some rare utterance—a paragraph or two, a sonnet, or some poignant little epigram: an epigram that shall justify the existence of a million leagues of useless sand, and the non-existence of several myriad useful cultivators. [*Experiments*]

Thus we find Aroudi, the maker of deserts, presented as a cleansing savior to a world which has been corrupted by the fanatical practices of men.

In its largest effect **In the Beginning** is a satirical history of human folly as Douglas saw it. It is unreasonable and uncompromising as is most satire. Presenting all sides of the story is not the job of the satirist; if it were, Douglas could never have been one. There is, indeed, a note of bitterness. Perhaps the aging libertine, losing his ability to enjoy the sensuous life, found gratification in indulging his hedonism by presenting it written large in these prodigious and carefree gods and half-gods, and in aiming some spiteful shafts at the dullards who so stubbornly refused to exploit life as he no longer could.

Not all critics have deplored the book. Edward Garnett liked it and wrote to Douglas, "I am glad you have nailed our colours to the mast." He called the supper party of the harlots "pure gorgonzola," "which," said Douglas, "was exactly what I intended it to be [**Late Harvest**]." Rachel Taylor, reviewing the book for the *Spectator* [18 September 1928], praised the "limpid, iridescent prose," which Douglas himself considered among his best writing, and called it the nearest thing in the language to the manner of Anatole France. Edward McDonald, a staunch Douglas admirer, found Linus a character who touches the heart more than any character in **South Wind**. But his final judgment of the book echoed the consensus of critics: "Perhaps a travesty designed on so huge a scale must inevitably fall of its own weight. In any event, fall it certainly does, and in the midst of its scaffolding."

Keath Fraser (essay date 1976)

SOURCE: "Norman Douglas and D. H. Lawrence: A Sideshow in Modern Memoirs," in *The D. H. Lawrence Review,* Vol. 9, No. 2, Summer, 1976, pp. 283-95.

[*In the following essay, Fraser examines the dispute between Douglas and Lawrence over the memoirs of Maurice Magnus,* Memoirs of the Foreign Legion (1924), *which Douglas wrote about in* D. H. Lawrence and Maurice Magnus: A Plea for Better Manners.]

The cause of the breach between the two novelists whom E. M. Forster called [in *Aspects of the Novel,* 1962] "a

doughty pair of combatants, the hardness of whose hitting makes the rest of us feel like a lot of ladies up in a pavilion," is summed up in two words: Maurice Magnus. The dispute between Norman Douglas and D. H. Lawrence which arose in 1924, over Magnus' suicide in Malta in 1920, is a curious and unresolved sideshow in modern literary biography. The outline of the story is well known, for each of the combatants has had numerous defenders since the twenties—the staunchest two publishing their memoirs of Douglas simultaneously in 1954. Nancy Cunard, a Douglas supporter, pointed out that the pamphlet Douglas wrote against Lawrence, in answer to Lawrence's Introduction to "M. M.'s" *Memoirs of the Foreign Legion* (1924), "was a red-hot polemical coal for a long time in the twenties. It is no cinder now—nor ever will be to anyone interested in literary and human integrity as well as literary energy, and also in the utterly opposite characters of Douglas and D. H. Lawrence" [*Grand Man: Memories of Norman Douglas,* 1954]. Lawrence's chief supporter, Richard Aldington, has stated quite frankly that "warfare between two such free spirits and great writers as Norman Douglas and D. H. Lawrence was a misfortune for both literature and themselves" [*Pinorman: Personal Recollections of Norman Douglas, Pino Orioli, and Charles Prentice,* 1954]. To be sure, without the prominent personalities of Douglas and Lawrence engaged in public debate over the issue of biographical distortion, it is unlikely that such a dispute would have become the minor but rancorous spectacle it did. Yet given its unavoidable interest it seems important to come to a conclusion concerning the dispute which so far no one has convincingly resolved.

This odd story begins with the extraordinary eighty-three page Introduction Lawrence wrote for a manuscript left behind by Magnus. "Introduction" hardly describes what Lawrence's account is, for its relation to the memoirs of the Foreign Legion which follow is somewhat tenuous. Lawrence's Introduction is cast in the form of a narrative, complete with dialogue, and it recounts Lawrence's acquaintance with M—, over a period of twelve months. It is an evocative piece of writing that maintains the precision, even sinisterness, with which it begins: "On a dark, wet, wintry evening in November, 1919, I arrived in Florence, having just got back to Italy for the first time since 1914." Lawrence relates how he first meets M— through the man M— appears to be waiting on hand and foot, but a man who seems to despise him nonetheless, N— D—. M—, once an actor-manager and now a journalist, is described as rather flighty: "He looked a man of about forty, spruce and youngish in his deportment, very pink-faced, and very clean, very natty, very alert, like a sparrow painted to resemble a tom-tit." Later on, after sending M— five pounds, Lawrence tells of a visit he pays to the famous monastery (Monte Cassino) where M— is temporarily residing, in the mountains south of Rome. Subsequently, the fastidious American turns up in Sicily, on the run from the carabinieri who are after him for failing to pay a hotel bill. Lawrence, living in Taormina with Frieda, here discovers that M— expects him to pay for his expenses at a local first-class hotel. Lawrence reluctantly agrees. He also advances M— seven pounds to cover further room and board during the rest of his stay. A week later in Syracuse, coincidentally on the way to Malta himself, Lawrence finds that M— has not yet sailed for the island, and consequently is compelled to pay for his hotel once more. M—, who refuses to live in other than first-class style, continues to run up debts, eventually swallowing poison in Malta (following Lawrence's departure from the island), when police arrive to extradite him for defrauding a hotel in Rome.

Such a summary, I fear, is conspicuously inadequate. Lawrence's Introduction has generally been neglected as literature, in deference to its significance as biography, or, perhaps more importantly, autobiography. Although the essay is an unbroken flow of writing, there are six clearly defined sections: in Florence, where Douglas lives; at the monastery with its magnificent setting which Lawrence renders; in Sicily, both at Taormina and Syracuse; on the ship to Malta where Lawrence and Frieda, travelling second-class, discover Magnus, thanks to their money, parading himself on the first-class deck; in Malta itself—most of which is related in a letter to Lawrence from a Maltese friend of Magnus' about the suicide; and, finally, a section that summarizes Magnus' history and character, of which Lawrence is eloquently and passionately disapproving. The essay pleased Lawrence. It was, he told Catherine Carswell, "the best single piece of writing, as _writing,_ that he had ever done" [Carswell, _The Savage Pilgrimage: A Narrative of D. H. Lawrence_ 1932].

Douglas' reply, **D. H. Lawrence and Maurice Magnus: A Plea for Better Manners** (completed in Syracuse on December 24, 1924), was a damning rebuttal of Lawrence's portrait of Magnus, coming as it did from an eminent fellow author. "Now, at the risk of being longwinded, I will try to straighten this affair out definitely." Breezily dismissing the unflattering portrait of himself, by admitting to it, Douglas accounts for Magnus' servitude (as Lawrence describes it) by calling it a willing fulfillment of a financial obligation, the paying back of a pound and a half Douglas had given Magnus in Capri a decade before. (Evidently Magnus still cherished such an obligation in 1919, even though he had already re-met Douglas in 1917, and had at that time helped Douglas over a difficult period of poverty.) However, Douglas' main and legitimate concern in his pamphlet is with what he calls "the novelist's touch"—this is what Forster was interested in—the novelist's selection of biographical facts which falsify the truth of living or, in Magnus' case, dead acquaintances. This involves "a failure to realize the profundities and complexities of the ordinary human mind. . . . The facts may be correct so far as they go, but there are too few of them: what the author says may be true, and yet by no means the truth. That is the novelist's touch. It falsifies life." It should perhaps be noted that Douglas isn't entirely consistent in his discussion of the novelist's

touch. On the one hand, the hand he emphasizes, the novelist's touch is quite a conscious and deliberate thing. On the other hand, and this is how he describes Lawrence's Introduction, it is "a masterpiece of unconscious misrepresentation." Adamantly Douglas contends, with some justification, that Magnus "was a far more civilized and multifaceted person" than Lawrence depicts. Then he goes on to suggest that the indignation Lawrence reveals in his Introduction, towards Magnus and his suicide, was caused by Lawrence's annoyance at having lost a few pounds, which Magnus owed him. With his Introduction, however, Lawrence will admirably have recouped his losses.

> It seems to me [argues Douglas] that even such a writing man should have some manners, some reserve, though his mentality be of the nonhuman order and his ethos immeasurably inferior to that of the butcher or grocer; that if he cannot respect his neighbours, he ought at least to respect himself. But he has forgotten what self-respect means; everything is grist to his mill—including himself; he chronicles your postprandial effusions as rapturously and scrupulously as he chronicles his own nocturnal emissions and it is no use appealing to his better nature, since he has no nature at all; he is a _cloaca maxima_ for the discharge of objectionable personalities.

The pamphlet was reprinted more than once, and anthologized by Douglas in _Experiments_ (1925). Lawrence answered Douglas in 1926. His letter to _The New Statesman_ complains of being slandered, and contradicts a hope expressed by Douglas that he might, as Magnus' literary executor, receive something from the publication of the _Memoirs._ Lawrence quotes a letter received from Douglas in 1921, telling Lawrence (and this Douglas has italicized) _to pocket all the cash himself._ In this letter we learn that Douglas had given Lawrence permission to put him (Douglas) into the Introduction; we learn, too, that Douglas was thinking of doing his own memoir of Magnus. Lawrence claims that he might indeed have made a considerable sum of money out of Magnus, had he been willing to sell his Introduction as a separate piece of writing. This he refused to do, shopping around for two years—following his completion of the Introduction in 1922—until he found a publisher willing to publish Magnus' _Memoirs_ as part of the package. Then, after paying off Magnus' debt to his Maltese creditor (an obligation Lawrence nevertheless refuses to admit is his, in spite of what the Maltese who befriended Magnus appeared to believe as a result of Lawrence's association with Magnus in Malta), Lawrence declares he may have received as much as he would for selling a short story in America: far short of a thousand dollars. "As for Mr Douglas, he must gather himself haloes where he may" [letter to _The New Statesman,_ 20 February 1976].

On the face of it the case for Lawrence's credibility seems pretty sound. Yet a careful study of the entire dispute is a study in the relativity of biographical truth. E. M. Forster agreed that the novelist's touch, as Douglas defined it, was a bad thing for biography—though not necessarily for the novel ("a novel that is at all complex often requires flat people as well as round, and the outcome of their collisions parallels life more accurately than Mr Douglas implies"). Since Lawrence was a novelist, as a biographer it might well seem instinctive for him to have sought what may be called substantial, rather than literal, truth. If this is what he did with Magnus, it would appear that Douglas was right: "What the author says may be true, and yet by no means the truth." If so, what were Lawrence's motives in selecting the facts he did about Magnus? Was it merely a good story he wished to tell, one whose suicidal climax sat well with the protagonist's dodgy life-style? Was he, as Douglas alleges, angry at having lost money to Magnus, and consequently avenging himself? Or is it possible that Lawrence's portrait of Magnus is literally true? "The whole circumstances of my acquaintance with Maurice Magnus, and the facts of his death, are told in my introduction as truthfully as a man can tell a thing." We now know that Lawrence's memory was highly developed, and that the precise and vivid *Sea and Sardinia,* for example, written not long before his Introduction, was written after Lawrence's brief visit to Sardinia, and evidently without notes. Naturally there is no blame to be attached for Magnus' suicide, except of course to the spendthrift Magnus himself. (I shall, however, return to the suicide.) What remains to be decided is whether Lawrence is more nearly correct in what he reveals about Magnus and Douglas, or whether Douglas is closer to the "whole" truth in refuting Lawrence and supporting Magnus. Given that biographical truth— even as "round" as it may be offered—is still relative to the facts selected to describe a man, then I believe Douglas comes out of the dispute more soiled than Lawrence.

Aldington's account of the affair in *Pinorman* is interesting though incomplete. By sifting through Aldington's evidence, and speculating on evidence never noticed before, one is able with the benefit of hindsight to reach a tentative conclusion about the merits of the conflicting claims over Magnus and his accurate portrayal. Douglas is possibly right in his contention that Lawrence had misrepresented Magnus' character. Even Aldington admits this possibility in his very readable autobiography, *Life for Life's Sake* (1941). And later in his biography of Lawrence. *Portrait of a Genius, But . . .* (1950), Aldington discloses lapses in Lawrence's memory of the affair, with respect to how poor Lawrence actually was. Of course none of this, as Aldington recognized, alters the fact of Lawrence's innocence concerning Magnus' fate. Although Lawrence evidently enjoyed Magnus' company—something he never really accounts for in his Introduction—he found himself paying for this pleasure, either by lending him money, or by helping to find Magnus outlets for his writings. The weakness of Lawrence's portrait of Magnus lies in its obvious antagonism toward Magnus.

Alternatively, there are two charges that can be made to challenge Douglas' apparently disinterested memoir of

Magnus. To Douglas' annoyance Aldington made one of these charges in *Life for Life's Sake,* as he did later and at greater length in *Pinorman*. The real reason for Douglas' resentment against Lawrence, Aldington contended, was the unflattering portrait of Douglas as Argyle, in *Aaron's Rod* (1922). Aldington might also have emphasized the equally damaging portrait of Douglas in Lawrence's Introduction to the *Memoirs*. In spite of Douglas' words to the contrary, both portraits must have smarted; especially since Aldington for one has attested to the vividness of Lawrence's view of the author of **South Wind** (also a satirist and user of people for fictional purposes). Douglas did nothing to refute the accuracy of either portrait, preferring (probably wisely) to discount them playfully in his pamphlet on Magnus, and in **Looking Back** (1934), where his final assessment of Lawrence is rather an arrogant one. "He sometimes turned up at the *English Review* office," recalled Douglas, "with stories like the *Prussian Officer* written in that impeccable handwriting of his. They had to be cut down for magazine purposes; they were too redundant; and I was charged with the odious task of performing the operation." In the same book he concluded that "Scholars and men of the world will not find much inspiration in . . . [his] novels. Lawrence opened a little window for the bourgeoisie. That is his life-work." It should be noted that in **Looking Back** the emphasis of Douglas' thesis falls on Lawrence's "love of scoring off people to whom he is under an obligation." And Douglas uses *Aaron's Rod* to illustrate this aspect of Lawrence's character, a character unable to accept the burden of patronage without maintaining his independence by striking back. Just how this explains Lawrence's specific use of Douglas in *Aaron's Rod,* or his treatment of Magnus in the Introduction, is not clear. For certainly if the novelist's touch in the Introduction to Magnus' *Memoirs* is one of resentment, even Douglas would have had to admit that this resentment could hardly have arisen from Lawrence's being under any obligation to Magnus, financial or otherwise. It may be that, apart from the two days he spent as Magnus' guest at the monastery in Italy, Lawrence accepted from Magnus more hospitality in Malta than he cared to admit. Yet the evidence seems to suggest that Magnus did his best to sponge off Lawrence everywhere, and certainly the fact that he died owing Lawrence money does not argue for Lawrence's feeling resentment against Magnus, because of any obligation he felt himself under. Or does it? Perhaps there was an obligation to clear himself, in his own eyes, of having been made to look a fool by putting up with Magnus.

More plausible, however, is the likely notion by Lawrence that he had a duty to clear himself of an *apparent* obligation. The second charge against Douglas, more difficult to prove, is one Aldington only skirts the edges of. It must be suggested, I think, that the reason for Lawrence's very strong distaste expressed for Magnus in his Introduction was his own awareness that he might be accused unjustly of having caused Magnus' death, by having refused to give him "half my money," the lack of which precipitated his suicide. This Douglas declined to accuse Lawrence of, preferring instead to attribute Lawrence's anger to the loss of a few pounds. Is it possible that Douglas adopted this approach because his own hands in the incident were not as clean as his pamphlet would have us believe (nor indeed as Douglas' own letter which Lawrence quotes in *The New Statesman* suggests: "I'm out of it and, *for once in my life,* with a clean conscience")? Had Douglas accused Lawrence of precipitating Magnus' suicide, by refusing to lend Magnus money, he himself may well have had to answer the same charge. In fact, this very nearly had been Aldington's allegation against Douglas in *Life for Life's Sake:* of not helping Magnus, who was *his* friend and not Lawrence's. A few years later, in **Late Harvest** (1946), Douglas dragged in a red herring—as Aldington points out in *Pinorman*—in an unconvincing attempt to refute Aldington's implication by quoting from an article Aldington wrote about Douglas, for *Esquire* in 1941, in which he refers to Douglas' generosity to old friends.

Yet the important evidence, either never seen or forgotten about by Aldington, is offered in a letter Nancy Cunard innocently quotes in her panegyric *Grand Man*—in which Douglas, in 1942, attempts to confute Aldington's allegation for the first time.

> Speaking of money, and of Aldington's further suggestion that I refused to lend it to Magnus in his distress, I was careful to point out in my pamphlet that I knew nothing of "this particular embarrassment" which was to cost him his life and which the dispatch of money might have removed. Often low-spirited and hard up and full of bitter complaints, like many of his sanguinary temperament, Maurice invariably contrived by hard work to straighten his affairs out again and give his friends a good time. He had done this all his life, and would have done so once more but for the embarrassment—that bolt from the blue which led to his suicide within three minutes. "If only"—so I wrote—"he had told me the complete truth! But he was always shy about disclosing his troubles to me, etc."

Apart from the rather unappealing picture of Magnus, there is in this, one feels, a subtle admission by Douglas that he was indeed asked by Magnus for money before his suicide (as Lawrence admits he himself had been). Is there not also an attempt to conceal this by a general reference to Magnus' frequent and "bitter complaints" which, it would appear, Douglas preferred invariably to let him resolve for himself, before accepting once more from Magnus "a good time"? Douglas tells us that in this particular case, however, he might have done something, had Magnus told him "the complete truth." At this point one wonders whether the letters Douglas claims, in his pamphlet, he sent to Magnus on November 6, 8, 14 and 15 were not in answer to some pretty truthful and naked letters from Magnus, about his financial, if not mental, state. At any rate Magnus evidently came to expect no help from Douglas either. His suicide

occurred on November 4, and Douglas' last letters were returned unopened.

Although in his will Magnus left his manuscripts to Douglas, it was the Maltese friend from whom Magnus borrowed heavily—and into whose hands as creditor Magnus' possessions naturally fell—who refused to send these manuscripts to Douglas. Why? Apparently Borg (Mazzaiba in Lawrence's Introduction) did not trust Douglas, or at least did not feel that Douglas would be willing to reimburse him the fifty-five pounds lent to Magnus. Is it conceivable that Magnus' Maltese friend may have come across earlier letters from Douglas to Magnus, and if in these he saw no financial help was forthcoming at a time prior to the suicide, was hardly likely to feel that Douglas would be willing to help an unknown recover his losses afterwards? Alternatively, Magnus might well have told Borg of his inability to convince his friend in Florence to send money. At least with Lawrence, even if he would have nothing more to do with Magnus' debts, the Maltese had met him. And it was to Lawrence that Borg sent the manuscript of the *Foreign Legion,* holding it back from Douglas, the literary executor. It was his hope, in due course justified, that Lawrence would be able to sell it to a publisher and so reimburse him his losses.

Now it is less than necessary to point out once more that when it comes to the reason for Magnus' suicide neither Douglas nor Lawrence is to be implicated. Magnus had been so often, as Douglas implies, in debt, or escaping from something, that yet another threat of arrest—such as one he had experienced deserting from the Foreign Legion in France—does not really seem sufficient motivation for such a drastic action as suicide by so enterprising a man. Obviously fear and depression, compounded by the intangible nature of Magnus' homosexuality and parasitism, erupted in some unknowable fission inside the spirit of an intelligent yet self-deceiving man. My own purpose is not to lay blame on either novelist—although both Douglas and Lawrence, as I have shown, seem to have felt it necessary to clear themselves of responsibility for Magnus' misfortune—but simply to decide who of Douglas and Lawrence is biographically more accurate in his memoir of the man who accounted for a good deal of bitterness not only between both novelists but also among those who later wrote their own memoirs and biographies of Lawrence and Douglas.

The two novelists did not remain unreconciled enemies. They met again in Florence when *Lady Chatterley's Lover* was published by Pino Orioli, in 1928, and they at least buried their hatchets. But evidently Douglas, to judge from his acerbic comments in **Looking Back** and **Late Harvest,** never came to think very highly of Lawrence either as a person or a writer. This is rather a pity because biographers of Lawrence such as Aldington, who had long admired Douglas, or others such as Frieda who genuinely responded to Douglas' charm, have been unable to let themselves forget Douglas' attacks on Lawrence, and this has not helped to enhance the reputation of a remarkable, if now increasingly forgotten, author.

So it has been that the case to support either Lawrence or Douglas has often seemed to depend on unequivocal preference rather than the equivocal character of biographical truth. Certainly all the facts about Magnus can never be known, since the ultimate fact of a man's character is invariably subjective. Is one to support Lawrence, whose brilliant Introduction leaves the attractive "wistfulness" (and this word recurs half a dozen times) of Magnus unexplained, in preference for an emphatic account of Magnus' unattractiveness? Is it a legitimate ambivalence, Lawrence's peculiar regard for Magnus' courage in death, but not for his nervous posing in life? Or will one accept Douglas, whose gruff affection for Magnus leaves unexplained his own role with respect to Magnus' poverty, in preference for his disvaluation of Lawrence's creation? Was Douglas perhaps right, as Forster believed, about the novelist's tendency to falsify biography? To read any biographer on either novelist is to have the case resolved staunchly in favour of his subject. Yet biographical truth is relative to the facts one chooses to have at hand—biography as much as fiction requiring a selection and a shaping by the author. In spite of what Forster wrote, the novelist's touch is not really different from the biographer's, since the biographer is as responsible as the novelist for creating a "round" protagonist. Douglas' portrait of Magnus, for all its purported accuracy, is a flat one. That Lawrence's is round—if only in the sense of nuance—not even Douglas would deny. To be sure "truth" is not determined merely by roundness or flatness; as Forster would argue, Mr. Micawber (that other getter-into-debt) is a flat yet truthful portrait. Obviously there is truth in both memoirs of Magnus, even though truth in biography, like truth in fiction, will always be the servant of the author's disposition. In the case of Lawrence and Douglas, each was disposed—considerably more than the "objective" biographer—to put his account in such a way as to place himself, an acquaintance of the suicide, in a favourable light. In the case of Magnus, rather an unusual case, one is forced to decide which light throws fewer shadows of doubt. For all Lawrence's crossness, his enthusiasm for the task—if not for his subject—would seem to burn the more brightly.

Paul Fussell (essay date 1980)

SOURCE: "Norman Douglas's Temporary Attachments," in *Abroad: British Literary Traveling Between the Wars*, Oxford University Press, 1980, pp. 119-30.

[*Fussell is an outspoken American nonfiction writer, essayist, and critic whose best-known works—including* The Great War and Modern Memory (*1975*), Class: A Guide through the American Class System (*1983*), *and* BAD: or, the Dumbing of America (*1991*)—*are noted for their scrupulous scholarship, accomplished prose style, and often polemical tone. In the following excerpt, he examines Douglas's travel writings in light of his pederastic relationships with young boys.*]

The titles of the two travel books Douglas published in the 20's, *Alone* (1921) and *Together* (1923), will suggest the alliance in his mind between companionship and the impulse to record perceptions of abroad. According to Acton, "He told me that each of his books had ripened under the warm rays of some temporary attachment: unless he was in love he had little or no impulse to write. Each of his books, therefore, was mingled with the happiest associations of a life-time." Or to put it another way, each of his books becomes a way of talking about pederastic satisfactions—not all of them sexual—with boys like Eric and René in an atmosphere where such things are not discussed, or if discussed, discussed in such terms as those of George V's reputed assertion, "I won't knight buggers."

Douglas's is a pre-modern sensibility. He was born in 1868, and although he lived until 1952, nothing in his emotional outlook or literary posture prompted him to any interest in Joyce, Yeats, Eliot, or Pound. Darwin and Herbert Spencer were his thinkers, Conrad his writer. He was a Scottish late-Victorian, a sort of Field Marshal Sir Douglas Haig turned inside out. Such a formulation at least would recognize the importance of his Germano-Scottish origins while doing justice to the Puritan determination of his atheism and hedonism, the stubborn assiduity of his pederasty, and the strongmindedness of his performance as a British eccentric abroad. His Nietzschean brand of naughtiness is of the 90's: like Shaw's or Samuel Butler's, his subversiveness does not threaten the *status quo*, it teases it and requires it. His reputation for shadiness is like Frank Harris's (born 1856), as is his conviction that the Mediterranean is the natural locale for the seduction of very young persons. His Italy is the Italy of Pater, Symonds, and Baron Corvo. His improper limericks (with of course their perverse geography) suggest an Edward Lear who has cast off all restraint except verse-form, just as his pleasure in little boys resembles Dodgson's in little girls. If rough-trade homosexuality of the Genet stamp is one sign of the self-consciously modern or post-modern, pederasty—Douglas seems to have been fondest of children ten to twelve—is pre-modern. Maurice Richardson remembers lunching with Douglas in 1943: "By the end of the lunch Norman was enthusing about the smell of children's armpits and I got faintly embarrassed."

The pattern of his life was a series of flights abroad. So often was he obliged to decamp across frontiers, or, as he says, "put a slice of sea" between himself and outraged parents, that he became learned in the details of European extradition treaties. "Burn your boats," he advised. "This has ever been my system in times of stress." His first precipitate departure was in 1896, from St. Petersburg, where, having impregnated a lady, he abandoned his post as Third Secretary in the Embassy and took off for Naples. In those days he was fond of ladies, marrying one in 1898 and fathering two boys. But his tastes had changed probably by 1908, when he lived with a peasant boy in Italy while writing **Siren Land** (1911), and certainly by 1916, when he was arrested in the South Kensington tube station for paying a boy too much attention and fled to Italy to escape trial. In the 30's there were two more similar flights, one from Austria, one from Florence. He finally came to rest, much passion spent, in southern France, only to be forced by the Second World War to Portugal and then back to London, which he hated. (In London under the bombings of 1943, with little drink and terrible food, and in appalling cold, he and Nancy Cunard would sit on a sofa and solace themselves by pretending it was the seat of a wagon-lit speeding across Italy to France in the old days of sun and freedom.) Despite poverty and age, his halcyon period began in 1946. He was now an Honorary Citizen of Capri (the only other one was Benedetto Croce) and one of the local sights, and he lived there in a handsome villa provided by his friend Kenneth Macpherson. He was attended by the ten-year-old Neapolitan Ettore, tenderly beloved by Douglas although denominated "a little tart" by some. His happiness was only slightly tarnished by the badgerings of somewhat faded American fans of **South Wind**. Near the end he had a few regrets but no apologies: "If I had stuck in the Dipl. Service," he wrote, "I should certainly have become an Ambassador and be now living on a pension of £5,000 a year." Instead he was raggedy, although he managed to maintain, Acton recalls, "the elegance of a Scottish Jacobite in exile." His constitution was rugged—another Scotticism. After a lifetime of excesses—confronted by temptation, he always followed his own favorite suggestion, "Why not, my dear?"—he apparently couldn't die, even at the age of 84, and finally had to put himself down with an overdose of pills.

He had a remarkable mind and vast learning, the result in part, as he liked to notice, of his having escaped a university education. His school was the Karlsruhe Gymnasium, and he was there in the 80's, when a German education meant languages (Russian, French, Italian), music (piano), and science. It did not include absorption in the self. The objectivity and curiosity Douglas learned at Karlsruhe made him an ideal traveler, and he started early. At the age of 19, he wrote his grandmother before his first trip to Naples: "I have been studying my Baedeker very diligently, and already *seem* to know my way about Naples quite well." Grown up and preparing for a trip to Greece, he writes: "I read one book on Greece every day, and will soon know the country and the language so intimately that it will be sheer waste of time and money going there." He grew up a scholarly, meticulous young mineralogist, taxidermist, and scrutinizer of lizards, author of the treatise **On the Herpetology of the Grand Duchy of Baden** (1891) and later scholar of the geology, archeology, and history of Capri, the Sorrentine Peninsula, and Calabria. "Externalize yourself!" enjoins the Count in **South Wind**. Douglas's curiosity about "out there" is Aristotelian,

like his empiricism about sex, drink, food, and study. He was a scientist, a dissector. "Finding everything wonderful," as Mark Holloway says, "but nothing miraculous," he was that rare creature, "a happy man, who has got his values right for himself and knows it." In this he's like the other literary travelers of this period: all superbly know what they're doing, an achievement some will find refreshing.

If Douglas resembles any other twentieth-century writer it is Nabokov. The two share a similar erudition and devotion to natural history (Nabokov's lepidoptery is Douglas's herpetology), a similar secure individuality and contempt for the modern world, a similar commitment to the value of the aristocratic intellect, and a similar playfulness and waggery. Douglas's sense of security when he commends something resembles Robert Byron's, but he is a little like Lawrence too in his instinct to make literature out of his sense of being embattled and his tendency to visit verbal violence upon the English. As in this Lawrentian moment from **How About Europe?** (1939):

> Ribald persons used to say: Wake up, Britain! Easier said then done. The Anglo-Saxon is hard to wake up, being phlegmatic and self-righteous to such a degree that the only thing which will really wake him up is brute force. Sad, but true.

His literary and historical admirations offer a key to his own character and talent. One of his favorites was the nineteenth-century German historian of Rome, Ferdinand Gregorovius, some of whose chapters Douglas translated into Italian while a student at Karlsruhe. "I liked Gregorovius even then," he wrote 40 years later, "and in later years learned to appreciate more fully his humanism, his alloy of learning and descriptive power." Likewise he never forgot the model of Count Campo Alegre, whom he had known at the Spanish Embassy in St. Petersburg, "scholar and man of the world, [who] impressed his character on all he possessed and all he said. . . . He belonged to an almost forgotten race, the humanist; the man of boundless curiosity and boundless tolerance—of that tolerance which derives from satisfied curiosity, and can derive from nothing else." What he liked about the translations of Petrarch by another of his idols, Frederick Wharton Mann, is that they had nothing touristic about them: "His work was meticulous and refined, exclusive, anti-vulgarian."

It was in the spirit of these admirations that he traveled, not just in Russia and Italy, but to Africa (with Nancy Cunard), Greece, Turkey (he loved the beautiful, studious town of Bursa), India, Ceylon, Syria, and Kenya. He was accompanied everywhere by "Alfred" (sometimes "Alfredino")—the small hard pillow necessary to his sleep. But he spent more than half his life in Italy, and it is as an interpreter of the Italian mode of abroad to a grey, hangdog Anglo-Saxonry that he finds his career. He began before the war with **Siren Land,** a consideration of the ancient Siren myth in relation to the topographical and archeological features of the Bay of

Naples. Here he achieves what will be his lifelong method of grasping "a place": he moves eye and mind rapidly over the whole, like someone "reading" a painting, in order to possess all the elements at once and unite them, no matter how contradictory the details or how puzzling the result. In aid of this method, his prose attains a wonderful dynamics. It is full of exclamations, assertions, and queries as he moves back and forth from present datum to past association. And in **Siren Land** he develops his personal structure for the travel book: narrative and description interrupted by frequent interlarded essays—on the ethics derivable from ruins, the local winds and their folklore, the character of Tiberius, local spooks and saints, caves and their traditional narratives, leisure, local wines. The method is a form of geographical gossip. Underlying the whole busy performance is the theme that he will develop a hundred different ways, the nastiness of positing "the antagonism of flesh and spirit, the most pernicious piece of crooked thinking which has ever oozed out of our poor deluded brain." That's a way of talking about his delight in the company of the peasant boy he took up with at Nerano while writing **Siren Land,** whose conversation gave Douglas most of what he needed of local folklore for the book. (This boy later cooked for Douglas on Capri while he was writing **South Wind**.) His next travel book, **Fountains in the Sand** (1912), follows the same method in its treatment of Tunisia. Here his companion was a German schoolmaster, "tall, young, and attractive." Despite Douglas's technique of associative impressionism, the book is topographically precise, and he was pleased to be told by an army Colonel in 1943 that his book had been more useful to the planners of the North African campaign than any official materials.

His companion while touring southern Italy for **Old Calabria** (1915) was the twelve-year-old Eric (Ernest Frederick Eric Wolton), a Cockney he picked up (his words) at the Crystal Palace. The grown-up Eric continued as Douglas's friend and ended as a police official in East Africa, retiring finally as Chief Superintendent of the Tanganyikan police. Eric kept his own diary of the trip ("Salami is a kind of sausage it is very beastly"), and seems to have enjoyed everything but the food and the malaria. "His curly hair dropped out," Douglas notes, "till he was nearly bald."

Douglas once said, speaking of the Great War: "A continent which can make such an exhibition of itself is not to be taken seriously." **South Wind** (1917) was designed in part as an uncontaminated island's rebuke to northern Europe, a plea for youth and sun and tolerance addressed to nations at suicidal war apparently contemptuous of these things. The novel is sometimes taken as a satyr's mere naughty recommendation of pleasure as the end of life, but seeing it in the context of the war makes it appear a more thoughtful critique. And a more subtle one than sometimes imagined. For example, its implicit celebration of the institution of conversation, especially conversation about ideas liberally conceived, makes its own comment on the nationalistic rigidities

presiding up north, exposing the incivility of the noisy, wordless confrontation occurring in Belgium and France (as Count Caloveglia says, "Northern people, whether from climatic or other causes, are prone to extremes"). **South Wind** appears to be "a novel," but its earliest readers, like Arthur Eckersley writing in the *English Review,* sensed its proximity to the travel book: "One knew already that Mr. Norman Douglas was the ideal writer of travel volumes; the setting of **South Wind** enables him to give some vivid pictures of Italian scenes, so vividly realized that the book may be regarded as a kind of holiday substitute." There is a plot, a boyishly subversive one, but it's there less for its own sake than as a justification for the "travel" essays, which treat Nepenthe like an actual island visited by an actual curious traveler. Thus we are told about its topography, geology, and mineralogy, its customs, antiquities, and floraculture, sometimes almost in guidebook idiom. We encounter essays on aesthetics, fanaticism, comparative theology, folk-medicine, and cookery; as well as numerous character-sketches and even a mock saint's life. But **South Wind** is most like a travel book in its wonder about the magic of place, its curiosity about the intercourse between place and character. It is the anomalous sirocco, inseparable from Nepenthe, that tempts foreigners there to "strange actions," just as in *A Passage to India,* the work of another traveler and one of Douglas's admirers, it is the echo in a strange "place," the Marabar Caves, that changes everything.

In 1919, arriving in Menton by train, Douglas met a sweet-tempered boy of fourteen, René Mari, who helped him carry his suitcase. One thing led to another, and it was René (his parents approving) who accompanied Douglas on most of the walking tours in Italy recalled in **Alone,** published in 1921. Since he's toured with a companion, Douglas, in a footnote at the end, acknowledges that his title is "rather an inapt one." But, he concludes, "Let it stand!" It has the merit of some ironic concealment, as well as implying the author's aloneness as the last remaining honest man with aristocratic tastes and scorn for the modern world. The Introduction (first published as **"The Tribulations of a Patriot"**) helps explain what this odd, strongminded Briton is doing in Italy. It details with rich sarcasm and anger his frustrations trying to get some kind of war work at home in the autumn of 1914. Rejected everywhere, he naturally packs his bags and takes off, alone. From Menton he proceeds to Levanto, Siena, Pisa, the resort town Viareggio, dead in February but awakening in May, and thence to Rome, "the most engaging capital in Europe." Off again to Olevano, Valmontone, Sorrento, and back to Rome again. Then finally to Soriano and Alatri. Douglas's method is to invite the places visited to cover their associations of earlier trips and earlier visitants, with the results that the book blends, as Holloway observes, "fact, fiction, and semi-fiction in a completely satisfying whole." As usual, Douglas throws in what interests him and ties it to a place. We meet characters, mostly rascals or nice children. We get natural-history notes on snakes, lizards, and birds; exotic speculations

about human motives or institutions, examined historically; accounts of flirtations with young girls; renderings of walks and conversations with intelligent and
unschooled—and therefore sensitive—young boys; hedonistic notes on local wine and food; quasi-dirty jokes,
set forth so shrewdly they could pass for clean; anti-
Puritan diatribes, focussing on "over-legislation" everywhere; an attack on gross-feeders (most of them British), who betray coarseness of soul by not caring what
they eat; an excursus on the delusions of the mob and
the orthodoxies and public pieties threatening the first-
rate man; and observations on the corruption of rural
life by cities and machinery. There is an essay on
whether youth should drink wine at all or should leave
it to age, which needs it more and knows how to manage it better. There are half-whimsical anthropological
inquiries: why do the French develop noses that make
them resemble rats? whence their devotion to scent?
There are invectives against telephones, trams, noise,
"progress"; and plans for outré literary projects, like an
anti-fly anthology. All these excursions are realizations
of curiosity in action, showing the reader what it's like
to be interested in something for its own sake. They are
exercises in a "liberal" kind of noticing, which misses
no nuance and treasures associations because experience
is blank without them. He once knew a lady in California whose fondness for the large, lurid wild flowers
there prompted her to contemn the European varieties. If flowers were mere objects, Douglas says, she'd be
right. He tried to explain to her that European flowers
bear about them seven millenia of literary, mythological, and historical associations, which constitute their
meaning: "a nimbus of lore had gathered around the
humblest of them; they were hallowed; they had a
past, an ancestry. There was nothing, I insisted, at
the back of California flowers; no memories, no associations. . . . What poet had ever sung their praises? What
legend had twined about them? She was deaf to this argument. . . ."

In *Alone* Douglas exploits virtually all literary methods,
producing even mock-proverbs: "Consider well your
neighbor, what an imbecile he is. Then ask yourself
whether it be worth while paying any attention to what
he thinks of you." Douglas divided up and scattered
through the text of *Alone* essays already prepared, and
the reader encountering the sentence, "Whoever suffers
from insomnia will find himself puzzling at night over
questions which have no particular concern for him at
other times," might think himself embarked on an essay
by Hazlitt or Lamb or Stevenson. Douglas has just described the disappointing Arno at Pisa, and is making
one of his "transitions" to what he thought last night
about heredity. With *Alone* Douglas begins his practice
of making his own vigorous comic indexes:

> Acqua santa, mineral fountain, its appalling
>   effects
> Alpenglühen, an abomination
> Bacon, *misquoted*
> Beds in England, neolithic features of

Cement floors, a detestable invention
Ghosts, mankind surrounded by, 111; away with
   them, 137
Imagination, needful to travel literature
Shelley, . . . recommends caverns to his readers,
   but lives comfortably himself
Viareggio, an objectionable place
Whistling, denotes mental vacuity,

and finally, with deep irony,

> Zürich, its attractions.

He returned to the technique of the comic index in
Together, and the index to *Some Limericks* (1928) provided ample opportunity for associating the outrageous
with abroad:

> Australia, floral design by a native of
> Coblenz, a lucky kitchen-maid of
> Horn, Cape, hypochondria among its aborigenes,
>   86; imports French goods, *Ibid.*
> Madras, indelicate behavior of local cobra
> Stamboul, case of varicose veins at.

(It's like Nabokov, we notice, in his comic index to *Pale
Fire,* where fanciful geography joins mock-scholarship
and wry mock-*Sehnsucht:*

> Kalixhaven, a colorful seaport on the Western
>   coast, a few miles north of Blawick (*q.v.*), 171;
>   many pleasant memories.
> Kobaltana, a once fashionable mountain resort
>   near the ruins of some old barracks, now a
>   cold and desolate spot of difficult access and
>   no importance but still remembered in military
>   families and forest castles, not in the text.)

If *Alone* is about intellectual curiosity satisfied in proximity to a beloved person, *Together,* while affecting to
be about a walking tour in the Austrian Vorarlberg, is
a tour in time back to Douglas's childhood in that area.
His companion is again René (here, "Mr. R."), whose
young fondness for milk and eggs at inns is disclosed in
the third paragraph. "I am past his stage," writes Douglas, "though still young enough to revel in that delicious raspberry jelly." Thus the theme of the book, the
sweet conflict between youth and age, is set in motion.
Douglas dedicated *Together* to his two sons, and it is
full of memories and anecdotes about fathers and sons,
families and heredity, and always the affectionate abra-
sion between young and old. To Douglas, Mr. R. appears pig-headed; to Mr. R., Douglas's problem is, as he
puts it, "*troppo vino*. You comprehend?" The odd thing
is that Douglas used to be Mr. R. "How one changes!"
Now, in every one of his perceptions, Douglas is conscious of the perceptions of the boy beside him. Maybe
it was this feature that appealed so strongly to Lytton
Strachey and Forster, both fervent admirers of *Together*.
"The thrill that only you can give," Strachey wrote him,
"goes down my back."

Every literary traveler has an habitual practice. Douglas's is climbing up to an eminence whose height allows

him to see something special in the prospect before him or to learn something inaccessible to ground-dwellers. In both *Alone* and *Together,* he performs this action numerous times; in *South Wind* the Count avails himself of it as a figure for arguing the loss of a former extensiveness of thought. The disappearance of Latin and of European commonality, he says, has led to narrowness and provincialism, to everyone's retreat behind the frontiers of his own vernacular. Modern commerce "has demarcated our frontiers with a bitterness hitherto unknown. The world of thought has not expanded; it has contracted and grown provincial. Men have lost sight of distant horizons. Nobody writes for humanity . . . they write for their country, their sect; to amuse their friends or annoy their enemies." On the other hand, "Pliny or Linnaeus or Humboldt—they sat on mountain-tops; they surveyed the landscape at their feet, and if some little valley lay shrouded in mist, the main outlines of the land yet lay clearly distanced before them." Over and over Douglas ascends to mountain- or hill-tops, and thence, like the speaker in an eighteenth-century prospect poem, surveys the land below, inviting it to serve now as matter for metaphor, now as data for historical speculation, now as a trigger of associative recall. His travel essay *One Day* (1929) is the record of trying to pack into a final twelve hours an indelible image of Greece. His method is to climb up: "Why not scramble in earliest morning, before breakfast, up the stony steps of the Lykabettus . . . for the sake of the view, and to watch the town at one's feet beginning to throb with life once more?" Why not, indeed. At the top, his felicity is complete, for in addition to the view he is vouchsafed the company of two schoolboys, typical of the Greek variety: "If you . . . care for their society, they will take you for walks singly, or in couples, or by the dozen, and ask sensible questions and impart useful and even edifying information. . . ."

These were his friends and his lovers, the temporary attachments he traveled for. "He could endure the society of fewer and fewer people over the age of fourteen," Acton reports of him in the 30's, by which time his main work was finished. Brigit Patmore asked him why he wasn't writing anything now. "I can only write if I have *this*," he said, gripping her arm tightly. "I knew he didn't mean *my* arm or me," she says, "but the confiding closeness, that ardent heightening of mind and senses through love or passion." In *Aaron's Rod* Lawrence delivered a portrait of Douglas as "James Argyle." Some of it is caricature, but some is not. Argyle says to the Marchese:

> "A man is drawn—or driven. Driven, I've found it. Ah, my dear fellow, what is life but a search for a friend? A search for a friend—that sums it up."

> "Or a lover," said the Marchese, grinning.

> "Same thing. Same thing. . . ."

George Woodcock   (essay date 1982)

SOURCE: "Norman Douglas: the Willing Exile," in *Ariel*, Vol. 13, No. 4, October, 1982, pp. 87-101.

[*Woodcock was a highly respected and influential Canadian literary critic. In the following essay, he discusses the theme of exile in Douglas's works and in his life.*]

To talk of exile writers is to cover an extraordinary range of experience, for even when one has excluded those who have observed poignantly on their wanderings but have returned to their spiritual and physical homes to record those observations, like André Gide and Graham Greene and the classic nineteenth-century scientific wanderers, there remains the fundamental division between those one can call outcasts and those one can call expatriates.

The division seemed especially apparent to me when, in studying Norman Douglas' writings, I read what at first seemed to me a surprising passage in which he approved of Ouida's referring to Oscar Wilde as a *cabotin* (roughly, a ham actor), though he immediately qualified that slighting remark by condemning the judicial manoeuvres that had caused Wilde's downfall and the deterioration after release from prison that brought about his relatively early death. On the surface there seemed so much in common between Douglas and Wilde that such a clear expression of dissociation was at first surprising. Clearly it was not because of the fear of being linked with the homosexual fraternity that Wilde then symbolically represented, since Douglas was a known pederast and made no serious effort to conceal the fact, though he adroitly evaded its consequences. While Wilde foolishly stayed in England to face the music after the collapse of his case against the Marquis of Queensbury, Douglas—caught in very similar tangles—"bolted" no less than four times; on two of these occasions it was because of his involvement with boys.

Here, it seems to me, we have the essential clue. Wilde and Douglas were both practicing pederasts, and according to the law as it existed in their times—1890's in Wilde's case and the period between 1916 and 1936 in Douglas' case—were both culpable. Indeed, given the fact that they were both attracted to minors, they might even be hypothetically culpable under such laws as touch on homosexual behaviour in the 1980's. It is their differing reactions to similar predicaments that are germane to the present discussion. Wilde, after his libel action failed, had sufficient time to escape to France; his friends urged him to do so; the public prosecutor even allowed a reasonable interval to elapse before he issued the warrant for Wilde's arrest and set the detectives on the trail. In other words, the scene in the Cadogan Hotel that has become part of literary history and even poetry (celebrated by the incumbent laureate, Sir John Betjeman, in impeccable Georgian verses) was unnecessary except in terms of Wilde's personal myth—reinforced by the urgings of Speranza and of Willie Wilde—which told him he must stay on whatever the consequences. Wilde really stayed on because the very world that was rejecting him—the world of the Mayfair salons and the country houses ("the unspeakable in pursuit of the uneatable")—was the world he had wished to inhabit and to dominate. He could not willingly leave that world; he was expelled by public clamour at the time of his trial, and later, when he was released and went to live out his exile's existence in France, by ostracism. He knew a return to England was impossible, since despite the loyalty of a few individuals like the admirable Ada Leverson, he could never have re-established that position as the lion of the salons (Ouida's *cabotin*) which was so important to him; he was wounded even in France by the hostility of English visitors whom he would normally have regarded with contempt, while to gain what publication he achieved after his release from prison he had to rely on the seedy pornographer, Leonard Smithers, of whom he said: "He is rather dreadful; I suppose many of us are rather dreadful now and do not realize to what we have come."

The difference between Wilde and Douglas can be found in that last sentence. Wilde felt his own degradation. As *De Profundis* demonstrated, on one level he accepted his conviction; he saw it as a fitting punishment for his attempt to gain the protection of society when his whole life had been based on a systematic defiance of accepted standards. He saw himself at the end, with a mixture of acquiescence and self-pity, in the role of the outcast, and there is little doubt that it was himself rather than the cricket-capped guardsman he had in mind when he wrote that poignant stanza of *The Ballad of Reading Goal,* which his friends appropriately engraved on the monument Epstein made for him in Père Lachaise:

> Yet all is well: he has but passed
>   To Life's appointed bourne;
> And alien tears will fill for him
>   Pity's long broken urn,
> For his mourners will be outcast men,
>   And outcasts always mourn.

Wilde saw himself as an outcast, lived his few remaining years as an outcast, and was buried as an outcast by men and veiled women who came furtively to his funeral. That is one of the several personae in which he haunts us even to this day, and it represented in its most eloquently rendered form one of the two principal kinds of exile—the tragic kind.

Norman Douglas could in no way be considered an outcast or a tragic exile, and this reflects in the most obvious way his difference from Wilde, whom he otherwise resembled in many ways, even apart from the pederastic inclinations they shared. Douglas, who spent his life "bolting," as he put it, from one comic scrape to another, never showed any sign of acquiescing in society's condemnation. There was no music seductive enough for Douglas to feel impelled to face it, and nothing delighted him so much as the exercise of jumping

bail. He refused society and the state any claim on him; on the other hand he seems never to have pitied himself for the troubles into which the defiance of society sometimes led him.

Undoubtedly one of the reasons for Douglas' persistent non-acceptance of conventional social rules and of any laws that inconvenienced him was the special character of his exile. He did not see himself as an outcast, for there was no community to which he felt enough attachment or loyalty for his casting out from it to affect him emotionally. He was indeed perhaps the best example among English-speaking writers of the other kind of literary exile: the expatriate. His expatriation, I suggest, was manifest on two levels. He lived by far the greater part of his life away from both the land of his birth, which was the Austrian province of Vorarlberg, and the land of his legal citizenship and his ancestry, which was Scotland. On the other level, he had developed the true wanderer's inclination to agree with Milton that "the mind is its own place," and to find a home wherever the ambient culture for the time being most strongly appealed to him.

The origins of this role of the exile as multiple expatriate which Douglas continued to play to the end of a long life (he lived hard and survived to eighty-four) are to be found in a history that almost destined him to a wanderer's life. He was born in 1862 in a village of the Vorarlberg, that outlying province which, isolated to the west of the great mountain wall of the Arlberg, is itself a land almost exiled from its country of Austria. Douglas' mother was by ancestry half-Scottish and half-German; his father, James Sholto Douglas, was a Scottish cotton miller who had become virtually naturalized in this far corner of the already decaying Austro-Hungarian empire. It was not until after his father died in a mountaineering accident that Norman Douglas, at the age of six, first saw Scotland, and in later years he rarely visited it. For nine years of boyhood he endured an unsatisfying range of English educational approaches (a preparatory school in Staffordshire, private tuition in a Leicestershire vicarage, and low-grade public school training at Uppingham), but it was only in the less insular atmosphere of the Gymnasium at Karlsruhe in Germany that he was happy in his studies; in the six years there—he did not leave until he was twenty—he became an exceptional linguist (adding Latin, Greek, French, Italian and Russian to the English he had learnt in childhood), a good pianist and an accomplished field naturalist in the nineteenth-century tradition; shortly afterwards he was in active correspondence with Alfred Russell Wallace.

Douglas made his first visit to Italy and to an unspoilt Capri in 1888, long before he celebrated the island in literature or even contemplated writing as a career, and though for most of the next few years (from 1890 to 1894) he lived in Kensington, this was also the period when he visited Greece and the Lipari Islands and formed the attachments to the Mediterranean world and especially to Magna Graecia that were to dominate the rest of his life.

But there were interludes in which his restless nature led him to experience other countries and cultures. He joined the British Foreign Office and from 1894 to 1896 served in St. Petersburg, "evaporating" hurriedly when he got into the first of his notable scrapes, this time a heterosexual one with a lady of the Russian court whose identity is still a matter of speculation. After leaving Russia, he acquired a villa at Posilipo near Naples; restless as ever, he travelled to Tunis (the first of four trips) and to Ceylon, married in 1898 and divorced six years afterwards, and in 1904 moved to Capri. Even before he was married he had shown evidence of homosexual inclinations and now, after his divorce, they began to manifest themselves in pederasty as the Greeks understood it, the love of boys. It was during this period on Capri that the image of Naughty Uncle Norman began to emerge.

Parallel to it emerged the reality of the writer. Douglas was already in his fortieth year when, in 1908, he started to write *Siren Land,* the first of his books, which was published in 1911. Up to this time his writings had been the essays of an accomplished amateur scientist, such as *On the Herpetology of the Grand Duchy of Baden* (he harboured an enduring interest in reptiles) and *On the Darwinian Hypothesis of Sexual Selection,* which earned him the respect of professional biologists and showed an inclination towards scientific humanism that was to influence his writings when, in travel books and novels, he turned to the evocation of human characters and the depiction of landscapes.

The scientific essays, born of a passionate observation of the natural environment, were Douglas' apprentice work. *Siren Land* was the book of a man who had already reached the beginning of his prime as a writer; he knew what he wanted to say, and he was eminently aware of how it should be said. It set the tone for all his later work, since it was the testament of a willing expatriate, a celebration of the Graeco-Latin world that henceforward Douglas would regard as his spiritual homeland. It offered a pattern that was to be repeated in later books, of visually evocative descriptions of landscape, sketches of individuals and incidents that not only evoke persons encountered but also outline the shape of a culture, and historical interludes that often present us with revisionist views of episodes and personalities of the past, like the rehabilitation of the Emperor Tiberius into one of the most modest and clement figures of the ancient world that is one of the more controversial passages of *Siren Land.* And all the time, in the tone and style of the book as well as in the opinions expressed, one is aware of an insistent personality breaking through.

A decade afterwards, in *The London Mercury,* Douglas wrote a long essay on Doughty's *Arabia Deserta,* and

there he outlined his view of the essential qualities of a good travel writer:

> It seems to me that the reader of a good travel-book is entitled not only to an exterior voyage, to descriptions of scenery and so forth, but to an interior, a sentimental or temperamental voyage, which takes place side by side with that outer one; and that the ideal book of the kind offers us, indeed, a triple opportunity of exploration— abroad, into the author's brain, and into our own. The writer should therefore possess a brain worth exploring; some philosophy of life—not necessarily, though by preference, of his own forging—and the courage to proclaim it and put it to the test; he must be naif and profound, both child and sage. (*Experiments,* 1925)

At their best, and notably in the earlier works like *Siren Land, Fountains in the Sand* (1912) and especially *Old Calabria* (1915), Douglas' own travel books certainly meet these desiderata. The later travel narratives, *Alone* (1921) and *Together* (1923), while they retain the limpidity of style and the classical scholarship with its haunting implications for the modern world that make *Old Calabria* and *Siren Land* still so engaging seventy years after they were written, lack the tension between the subjective and the objective elements that sustained one's interest even in the most erudite passages of *Siren Land* and *Old Calabria.* Similarly, there was a lapsing of the intellectual tension, which even in Douglas' fiction is the most vital element, in the later novels—*They Went* (1920) and *In the Beginning* (1928), so that in this field *South Wind,* written in the same period as *Old Calabria* and published two years later (in 1917) has remained the book by which Douglas is known to the widest public—a book that has shown an amazing durability as a popular classic.

When one has sorted out Douglas' books, there is perhaps only one out of more than a score that can be dismissed as bad—an uninspired collection of opinionated notes about English and French hypocrisies called *How About Europe* (1930) which Douglas wrote as a kind of political pot boiler after the appearance of a sensational attack on Hindu ways of life, *Mother India,* by an American writer, Katherine Mayo. But even this book has its relevance to the attitudes which Douglas' expatriation fostered.

Douglas defended the Hindus, but his main aim was to attack European hypocrisies. Most of what he says in *How About Europe,* when he is not dredging through newspaper quotations for examples of the perfidy of Albion or Gaul, is related to the themes of his major books, and particularly to the kind of genial hedonism which in *Old Calabria* he attributed to the ancient Ionian philosopher Xenocrates, whose philosophy he summed up as the belief that "happiness consists not only in the possession of human virtues, but *in the accomplishment of natural acts.*" Douglas' definition of "natural acts" was broader than his reputation as a libertine might suggest, for he harboured an unexpected vein of practical and non-pharisaical humanitarianism that is defined in **How About Europe** when he comes to talk about moral busybodies:

> A commendable form of meddlesomeness is that of a Howard or a Shaftesbury. One cannot blame Christianity for originating the most discommendable form—that which preoccupies itself with other people's spiritual well-being. It started so far as we are concerned, with Pythagoras, though the Christians, once they began to exist, soon claimed it as a specialty of their own invention.

Pythagoras was Douglas' antique *bête noire;* he saw him as the hypocritical mystagogue who was responsible for the destruction of hedonistic Sybaris and displayed for him an unreserved and—in my view—entirely deserved contempt. But it will seem curious to most readers of Douglas to find Howard and Shaftesbury among the people he approved, unless they read his eccentric autobiography, **Looking Back** (1934), and learn of his actions during the great Messina earthquake of 1908. Douglas, then in Capri, learnt of the suffering of the survivors, and knew enough about Italy to realize that—then as in more recent natural disasters in that country—"the money filtered through committees, and many families might be starving before they received their share." So Douglas determined to go personally to the site of the disaster and to give money directly to the victims:

> With this end in view, and knowing nearly all the foreigners on the island at that time, I managed to cajole or blackmail most of them into giving something, however little.

> During this operation I had occasion to observe, not for the first time, that when it is a question of relieving distress the poorer folk are more generous, relatively speaking, than the wealthy ones.

Nevertheless, it was a rich American woman who topped off Douglas' collection by giving him twice as much as the other Capri foreigners combined, and he went off with a friend to seek out personally the people who needed help and to thrust the money into their hands in defiance of committees and bureaucrats.

The significance of the incident is not merely anecdotal. It is, I suggest, particularly germane to the theme of this essay, since it shows the extent to which Douglas was by this time identifying with the people of southern Italy, not only in the way they accepted the joys of life, but also in the way they endured its sorrows. This the Italians realized, to the extent that the people of Capri regarded him as one of their own and made him one of their few honorary citizens; there is an extraordinary description by Bryher, quoted by Mark Holloway in his *Norman Douglas* (1976), of his return to the island in 1921 after having been several years away:

> The news of his arrival spread from mouth to mouth. I have never seen a political leader enjoy so great a triumph. Men offered him wine, women with babies in their arms rushed up so that he might touch them, the children brought him flowers. I slipped away as he walked slowly through a crowd of several hundred people, shouting jokes in ribald Italian, kissing equally the small boys and girls and patting the babies as if they were kittens. The *signore* had deigned to return to his kingdom and I am sure that they believed that the crops would be abundant and the cisterns full of water as a result.

In the opening lines of **Old Calabria,** when he is talking of the Apulian town of Lucera at the start of his journey through the mountains and plains of Italy's foot, Douglas says that "the character is there, if one could but seize it, for every place has its genius." And it is clear—if one compares **Fountains in the Sand,** good as it is, with **Old Calabria** and **Siren Land** and even **South Wind**—that the local genii whose characters Douglas most easily seized upon were of places in southern Italy. **Fountains in the Sand** evokes the Tunisian scene with great visual conviction; it makes one feel in an almost physical way the discomforts of desert travel; it discourses intelligently on the peculiar flaws of French colonialism; it sharply characterizes the people encountered and projects the author's personality through his reactions to people and to experiences. Yet, while in this book Douglas shows himself very much *in* this bizarre marginal world through which he travels, one never has the sense that he is *of* it. There is never the sense of naturalization into a land, a culture, a tradition, of which one is so often aware in the Italian books. "It is good," Douglas said of East Africa in recollection, "to live in strange places, in places where, a day's march distant, there are districts marked as 'unexplored' on the map." But he could not live *for long* in such places; they remained "strange" to him, and Italy—one feels—never was.

Here we return in another way to the difference between the exile as outcast and the exile as expatriate. The exile as outcast never really finds a new home. He longs to return to the places he has been forced to leave, and if he cannot, his life is irremediably unhappy. The exile as expatriate, already an alien in his own country, finds a new home which he prefers to that he has abandoned, as Henry James and T. S. Eliot and Joseph Conrad did in England. In a similar way Douglas found his true and new home in those parts of Italy that bear indelibly the mark of the Greek beginnings of their civilization. There is something fated, something even of deliberation (however unconscious), in his departures from Russia in 1896, from England in 1917, from his native Vorarlberg in 1936, departures precipitated by scandals that prevented his return. "Burn your boats!" he remarked when he considered his past in **Looking Back,** "This has ever been my system in times of stress." He burnt his boats even in Florence when in 1937 he was forced to flee after he had departed temporarily from pederastic adventuring and had become involved with a small girl instead of a small boy. But, significantly, he burnt no boats in southern Italy. Capri was always safe for him to return to like a homecoming prince, and even though in 1934 he lamented that it had become "too cosmopolitan, too meretricious," he went back there to die.

Thinking of his childhood, Douglas once said, "Some few of us are born centrifugal. The head-system and team-life, congenial to many, went against my grain" (*Looking Back*). And centrifugal, in terms of Anglo-Saxon society and its mores, he remained. Yet so far as southern Italy is concerned one might almost call him centripetal, returning always to that still centre of his prime which I think was most eloquently and figuratively localized, not in *Old Calabria,* which offers one the panorama of a whole region and its traditions, nor in *South Wind,* which proceeds by fictional indirection, but in one of the earlier passages of that indispensable Douglas source book, *Looking Back,* where he describes the spot on Capri—a boulder-strewn tract leading to a pine-grove—that became for a long time his image of refuge, the heart of the island *patria chica* to which his attachment ran so much deeper than honorary citizenship:

> As to that secluded grove of pines—what an inspiring place to spend the evening of one's days! One of many attractions was its inaccessibility. And yet, I thought, once a path has been constructed across that wilderness of boulders and through a rocky spur of the hill, where a gate should be placed, you are within a few minutes' walk of the piazza, the centre of such life as there is. Go to that centre, if you wish to see fellow-creatures; lock your gate, and wall up that fissure in the rock higher up, and only a bird can reach you. An aerial situation; you are posed between earth and sky. Here, if anywhere, one might still find peace from the world; here one might gather together the wreck of one's belongings and dream away the hours, drinking the heady perfume of the pines and listening to that Theocritean melody of theirs, which is not truly a whisper, but an almost inaudible breathing: summer music. Here, if anywhere, one might—

Douglas bought the Petrara in 1907 and hoped to build a villa there in which he might live out his life. He failed to raise enough money for the building, and eventually circumstances forced him to sell the pine wood. But he never forgot the place, just as he never departed, in mind, far from the Italy of the Greeks. It is perhaps evidence of the intensity of the feeling he retained for them that he wrote his best Italian books—*Old Calabria* and *South Wind*—during the period between 1912 and 1916 when he was living not very happily in England and working for the *English Review;* the writing was a kind of surrogate presence.

Even more than *Siren Land,* which celebrated the relatively small island which was the heart of Douglas' Italy, *Old Calabria* stands as his real testament to the

land he made his home. Once, reviewing a book of travel sketches by Lowes Dickinson in the early 1920's, Douglas came very near to defining the virtues of his own narratives of journeys when he remarked: "That capacity of assimilating the ideas of strange folk, of remaining true to his own standard while unravelling an alien mentality with sympathetic discernment—that gift of insight is the Englishman's prerogative" (*Experiments*). Whether or not that is true in a general sense, or true even of Lowes Dickinson, it was certainly true of Douglas, for one is perpetually surprised in *Old Calabria,* following his progress from Apulia down to the toe-point of Reggio de Calabria, by the way he seems to enter the minds of the people he encounters even when he is forced into confrontations with them through their obstinacy or their failure to understand his needs; there is a triumph of empathy in the way he projects a collective portrait of a people, as well as many individual sketches, whose truth came from sympathetic external observation.

In *Old Calabria* Douglas' ever-active curiosity is transferred from the reptiles of his boyhood to the oddities of human behaviour in the ancient world and the middle ages, which remain presences in the country he traverses and whose physical shape he renders so vividly. But one is not provided merely with amusing tales from history or reflections on history, though both of these are there in abundance. The ultimate fascination of *Old Calabria* comes from two of its features: Douglas' travelling persona, curious, complaining, enduring, and constantly mediating between those he meets and those he addresses; and the philosophy of life, with the courage to maintain it, of which he had talked in praising *Arabia Deserta.* He does not attempt to reconstruct the pagan life of ancient Magna Graecia, though he touches on some of the historical questions evoked by visiting its almost obliterated sites. But he does draw, out of his experience of the landscape and his knowledge of what happened there, a neo-pagan personal stance which he relates to the setting and the ways of life men have evolved within it. There is a noble serenity to the fine last paragraphs of *Old Calabria* that belies the pose of amoral egotism which Douglas sometimes liked to affect, and shows how in this setting he had found not merely a physically appealing, but also a spiritually stimulating home:

> This corner of Magna Graecia is a severely parsimonious manifestation of nature. Rocks and waters! But these rocks and waters are actualities; the stuff whereof man is made. A landscape so luminous, so resolutely scornful of accessories, hints at brave and simple forms of expression; it brings us to the ground, where we belong; it medicines to the disease of introspection and stimulates a capacity which we are in danger of unlearning amid our morbid hyperborean gloom— the capacity for honest contempt: contempt of that scarecrow of a theory which would have us neglect what is earthly, tangible. What is life well lived but a blithe discarding of primordial husks, of

those comfortable intangibilities that lurk about us, waiting for our weak moments?

> The sage, that perfect savage, will be the last to withdraw himself from the influence of these radiant realities. He will strive to knit closer the bond, and to devise a more durable and affectionate relationship between himself and them. Let him open his eyes. For a reasonable adjustment lies at his feet. From these brown stones that seam the tranquil Ionian, from this gracious solitude, he can carve out, and bear away into the cheerful din of cities, the rudiments of something clean and veracious and wholly terrestrial—some tonic philosophy that shall foster sunny mischiefs and farewell regret.

As with most good writers, the division between fiction and travel narrative in Douglas' work is somewhat blurred. For formal reasons the good travel writer will arrange and adjust his material so that the patterns of a journey as they emerge from his book will not be exactly those that the chance of the road imposed on them in real life. Similarly, individuals encountered on the way will often be reshaped and enlarged. That Douglas followed this practice is shown by an odd little note in **Looking Back** in which he mentions an engineer named Robert Duterme encountered in Tunis, and remarks: ". . . he helped, I think, to form the character of 'Paul Dufrénois' in my **Fountains in the Sand**." Now **Fountains in the Sand** passes for a travel book, and undoubtedly its basis and its general structure were provided by the Tunisian journey which Douglas undertook, but within the frame he introduced persons fictional enough to be described as "characters" and clearly based on individuals in real life rather than being exact portraits.

Douglas' best novel, and the only one to survive in public esteem, is **South Wind**. Its successors, **They Went** (1920) and **In the Beginning** (1928) move away from the present world into the realm of historical fantasy, in the case of **They Went,** which is set in the Merovingian age, and reconstituted myth, in the case of **In the Beginning,** which is based on Middle Eastern religious tales. It is only in a far-fetched way, by nothing their distance from contemporary reality, that one can relate these books to Douglas' exile. **South Wind,** on the other hand, is clearly both the product and the expression of his expatriation.

In form **South Wind** belongs to a slender but respectable tradition within English fiction. In its concern with propagating ideas, and also in its considerable dependence on conversation as a means of revealing character and precipitating action it is clearly descended, perhaps in part via George Meredith for whom Douglas appears to have had some admiration, from Thomas Love Peacock. (Eventually, through **South Wind,** the Peacockian tradition would be transmitted to writers emerging in the early 1920's, like Aldous Huxley and Evelyn Waugh.) Like Peacock, Douglas gathered a number of

characters into a limited area for a short stretch of time, choosing an island favoured by expatriate strangers rather than a Peacockian country house. In such a restricted locale the eccentricities of the characters, and hence their reactions to each other, become more pronounced, and conversation provides the means by which their *idées fixes* are revealed in conflict. The author does not sit in judgement; he allows the drama of ideas and temperaments to play itself out, with some assistance from nature, in the form of the volcano which sends a night of falling ash over the island of Nepenthe. Those who are permanent residents, like the opinionated Keith, a kind of Norman Douglas with the unlikely attribute of great wealth, are not much changed by the events that take place in the novel. But those who come to Nepenthe and depart at the end of **South Wind,** are "changed utterly," the Anglican bishop Heard finding that his set prejudices have been replaced by a liberating moral relativism which allows him to condone the murder of an evil man, while the naif young man Denis sheds his romanticism for an unsentimental pagan realism. He has learnt the wisdom of Keith's exhortation:

> Of course I live sensibly. Shall I give you my recipe for happiness? I find everything wonderful and nothing miraculous. I reverence the body. I avoid first causes like the plague. You will find that a pretty good recipe, Denis.

How far Douglas made **South Wind** from his observation and experience of life on Capri it is difficult to say with any accuracy, and it is made no more easy by his own pronouncements. Clearly, an autobiographical fiction, it has deficiencies, since there are aspects of Naughty Uncle Norman's life on Capri that could not, in 1917, be safely described in print. But geographically Nepenthe resembles Capri, and the mixture of natives, foreign residents and tourists that Douglas presents is plausible enough. As for his characters, he seems to have built them up in the same way, though rather more elaborately, as those who figure in his travel books. One of the leading figures in **South Wind** is an American woman who has acquired by marriage the Italian title of Duchess. In **Looking Back,** commenting on a visiting card receiving long ago from a "Mrs. Snow," Douglas remarks:

> She finally returned to America. A vision of her helped me to portray the 'Duchess' in a certain story; other ladies contributed their share of suggestion; imagination also played its part. I have never tried to draw a figure from life, as they say. My creed is that a human character, however engrossing, however convincing and true to itself, must be modelled anew before it can become material for fiction. It must be licked into shape, otherwise its reactions, in a world of fictitious characters, would be out of focus. No authentic child of man will fit into a novel.
>
> History is the place for such people; history, or oblivion.

Even so, one can say that generically the characters of *South Wind* are taken from life. They form a living gallery of expatriate types, all of them exiles in a double sense. Their natures or their personal histories have made their former homes either unsatisfying or inhospitable. And their experience of exile has changed them into the willing denizens of strange lands. For the ultimate in-tent of *South Wind* is to show the transforming effects on Gothic temperaments of a warm and beautiful southern land steeped in Hellenic traditions. The people of *South Wind* are not outcasts; they are glad exiles, as Douglas was.

FURTHER READING

Bibliography

Woolf, Cecil. *A Bibliography of Norman Douglas*. London: Rupert Hart-Davis, 1954, 210 p.
    Comprehensive bibliography of Douglas's works, including his books, pamphlets, and journal articles.

Biography

Holloway, Mark. *Norman Douglas: A Biography*. London: Secker & Warburg, 1976, 519 p.
    Standard biography of Douglas.

Criticism

FitzGibbon, Constantine. *Norman Douglas: A Pictorial Record*. London: The Richard's Press, 1953, 71 p.
    Includes a critical consideration of Douglas's life and career.

Leary, Lewis. *Norman Douglas*. New York: Columbia University Press, 1968, 48 p.
    Introductory study of Douglas's life and works.

Low, D. M., "Introduction." In *Norman Douglas: A Selection from His Works,* pp. 9-24. Chatto & Windus, 1955.
    Traces Douglas's literary career and discusses the main characteristics of his writing.

Orel, Harold. "Norman Douglas's *South Wind* (1917)." In *Popular Fiction in England, 1914-1918*, pp. 65-77. London: Harvester Wheatsheaf, 1992.
    Presents a biographical interpretation of Douglas's most popular novel.

Wilson, Edmund. "The Nietzschean Line." In *The Shores of Light: A Literary Chronicle of the Twenties and Thirties*, pp. 485-91. New York: Farrar, Straus, and Giroux, 1979.
    Calls the social criticism of Douglas's *Good-bye to Western Culture* "essentially trivial."

Additional coverage of Douglas's life and career is available in the following sources published by Gale Research: *Contemporary Authors,* Vol. 119; *Dictionary of Literary Biography*, Vol. 34.

Isadora Duncan

1877(?)-1927

American dancer and autobiographer.

INTRODUCTION

Considered a proto-feminist for her unconventional lifestyle and for the promotion of herself as a "liberated" woman, Duncan is best known as one of the originators of modern dance. She was also a teacher of dance and wrote on its techniques and cultural significance. Her autobiography, *My Life* (1927), is a revealing self-portrait of Duncan's artistic and emotional life.

Biographical Information

Duncan was born in San Francisco and raised by her mother. Duncan's father abandoned the family when she was still an infant, forcing her mother to support the children from her earnings as a music teacher. Allowed to leave school at the age of ten to pursue an interest in dancing, Duncan began her career in Chicago and then moved to New York. Her provocative dances shocked American sensibilities of the day, however, and in 1899 she left the United States for Europe, where her improvisational, free-spirited dance performances met with widespread approval. In the first two decades of the century Duncan successfully toured most of western and eastern Europe. She opened short-lived but influential dancing schools in France and Germany and became both a popular public personality and a critically respected innovator of modern dance. Because she danced in Russia before the revolution and had a decisive impact on the ballet styles of Mikhail Fokine and Sergei Diaghilev, Duncan was invited in 1921 by the government of the Soviet Union to found and run a school for dancing in that country. While in Russia she married poet Sergei Esenin and became a Soviet citizen. Esenin, who was twenty years younger than Duncan, committed suicide in 1924. Three years later, after having completed most of her autobiography, Duncan was killed in an automobile accident when the scarf she was wearing became entangled in the wheels of her car.

Major Works

Commentators note that Duncan's most significant accomplishments were her own celebrity and her dancing; and of the latter—save for still photographs of her on stage—there is no surviving record. *My Life* and *The Art of the Dance* (1928), which collects some of her essays and other writings, present her thoughts on dancing and on the creative process. Given its perfunctory glosses on certain aspects of her life, and Duncan's tendency to mythologize herself, *My Life* has been de-

scribed as a somewhat inaccurate and self-serving memoir. The volume has also been criticized for its banal prose style; most critics agree with Linda Pannill that Duncan's "medium was movement, not words." Nonetheless, *My Life* is considered valuable for its glimpses of Duncan struggling with the demands of her art, her career, and her personal life. Despite the fact that her greatest successes were in Europe, Duncan believed that her dance was quintessentially American in nature. She felt that her movements were the direct expression of her soul. From this followed her teaching that women should learn to control their bodies and spirits through dance, gaining for themselves a measure of the autonomy enjoyed by men. Critics have likened her belief in self-reliance and inner inspiration to American transcendental romanticism. Pannill argues that Duncan was much like poet Walt Whitman in this regard—both "rejected the duality of the soul and body." Stuart Samuels concluded: "Isadora Duncan's death was mourned by many. She left no work that could be performed again, no school or teaching method, and few pupils, but with her new view of movement she had revolutionized dance."

PRINCIPAL WORKS

Der tanz der zukunft / The Dance of the Future (nonfiction) 1903
The Dance (nonfiction) 1909
My Life (autobiography) 1927
†*The Art of the Dance* (essays) 1928
‡*"Your Isadora": The Love Story of Isadora Duncan and Gordon Craig* (letters) 1974
§*Isadora Speaks* (essays, lectures) 1981; also published as *Selections: 1981,* 1981

*This work was published in Germany in both German and English.

†This work was edited by Sheldon Cheney.

‡This work was edited by Francis Steegmuller.

§This work was edited by Franklin Rosemont.

CRITICISM

Isadora Duncan (essay date 1927)

SOURCE: "Introduction," in *My Life,* Liveright Publishing Corp., 1927, pp. 1-8.

[*In the following introduction to* My Life, *Duncan explains her difficulties writing an autobiography.*]

I confess that when it was first proposed to me I had a terror of writing [*My Life*]. Not that my life has not been more interesting than any novel and more adventurous than any cinema and, if really well written, would not be an epoch-making recital, but there's the rub—the writing of it!

It has taken me years of struggle, hard work and research to learn to make one simple gesture, and I know enough about the Art of writing to realise that it would take me again just so many years of concentrated effort to write one simple, beautiful sentence. How often have I contended that although one man might toil to the Equator and have tremendous exploits with lions and tigers, and try to write about it, yet fail, whereas another, who never left his verandah, might write of the killing of tigers in their jungles in a way to make his readers feel that he was actually there, until they can suffer his agony and apprehension, smell lions and hear the fearful approach of the rattle-snake. Nothing seems to exist save in the imagination, and all the marvellous things that have happened to me may lose their savour because I do not possess the pen of a Cervantes or even of a Casanova.

Then another thing. How can we write the truth about ourselves? Do we even know it? There is the vision our friends have of us; the vision we have of ourselves, and the vision our lover has of us. Also the vision our enemies have of us—and all these visions are different. I have good reason to know this, because I have had served to me with my morning coffee newspaper criticisms that declared I was beautiful as a goddess, and that I was a genius, and hardly had I finished smiling contentedly over this, than I picked up the next paper and read that I was without any talent, badly shaped and a perfect harpy.

I soon gave up reading criticisms of my work. I could not stipulate that I should only be given the good ones, and the bad were too depressing and provocatively homicidal. There was a critic in Berlin who pursued me with insults. Among other things he said that I was profoundly unmusical. One day I wrote imploring him to come and see me and I would convince him of his errors. He came and as he sat there, across the tea-table, I harangued him for an hour and a half about my theories of visional movement created from music. I noticed that he seemed most prosaic and stolid, but what was my uproarious dismay when he produced from his pocket a deafaphone and informed me he was quite deaf and even with his instrument could hardly hear the orchestra; although he sat in the first row of the stalls! This was the man whose views on myself had kept me awake at night!

So, if at each point of view others see in us a different person how are we to find in ourselves yet another personality of whom to write in this book? Is it to be the Chaste Madonna, or the Messalina, or the Magdalen, or the Blue Stocking? Where can I find the woman of all these adventures? It seems to me there was not one, but hundreds—and my soul soaring aloft, not really affected by any of them.

It has been well said that the first essential in writing about anything is that the writer should have no experience of the matter. To write of what one has actually experienced in words, is to find that they become most evasive. Memories are less tangible than dreams. Indeed, many dreams I have had seem more vivid than my actual memories. Life is a dream, and it is well that it is so, or who could survive some of its experiences? Such, for instance, as the sinking of the *Lusitania.* An experience like that should leave forever an expression of horror upon the faces of the men and women who went through it, whereas we meet them everywhere smiling and happy. It is only in romances that people undergo a sudden metamorphosis. In real life, even after the most terrible experiences, the main character remains exactly the same. Witness the number of Russian princes who, after losing everything they possessed, can be seen any evening at Montmartre supping as gaily as ever with chorus girls, just as they did before the war.

Any woman or man who would write the truth of their lives would write a great work. But no one has dared to write the truth of their lives. Jean-Jacques Rousseau made this supreme sacrifice for Humanity—to unveil the truth of his soul, his most intimate actions and thoughts. The result is a great book. Walt Whitman gave his truth to America. At one time his book was forbidden to the mails as an "immoral book." This term seems absurd to us now. No woman has ever told the whole truth of her life. The autobiographies of most famous women are a series of accounts of the outward existence, of petty details and anecdotes which give no realisation of their real life. For the great moments of joy or agony they remain strangely silent.

My Art is just an effort to express the truth of my Being in gesture and movement. It has taken me long years to find even one absolutely true movement. Words have a different meaning. Before the public which has thronged my representations I have had no hesitation. I have given them the most secret impulses of my soul. From the first I have only danced my life. As a child I danced the spontaneous joy of growing things. As an adolescent, I danced with joy turning to apprehension of the first realisation of tragic undercurrents; apprehension of the pitiless brutality and crushing progress of life.

When I was sixteen I danced before an audience without music. At the end some one suddenly cried from the audience, "It is Death and the Maiden," and the dance was always afterwards called "Death and the Maiden." But that was not my intention, I was only endeavouring to express my first knowledge of the underlying tragedy in all seemingly joyous manifestation. The dance, according to my comprehension, should have been called "Life and the Maiden."

Later on I danced my struggle with this same life, which the audience had called death, and my wresting from it its ephemeral joys.

Nothing is further from the actual truth of a personality than the hero or heroine of the average cinema play or novel. Endowed generally with all the virtues, it would be impossible for them to commit a wrong action. Nobility, courage, fortitude, etc. . . . etc. . . ; for *him*. Purity, sweet temper, etc. . . . for *her*. All the meaner qualities and sins for the villain of the plot and for the "Bad Woman," whereas in reality we know that no one is either good or bad. We may not all break the Ten Commandments, but we are certainly all capable of it. Within us lurks the breaker of all laws, ready to spring out at the first real opportunity. Virtuous people are simply those who have either not been tempted sufficiently, because they live in a vegetative state, or because their purposes are so concentrated in one direction that they have not had the leisure to glance around them.

I once saw a wonderful film called "The Rail." The theme was that the lives of human beings are all as the engine running on a set track. And if the engine jumps the track or finds an insurmountable object in its way, there comes disaster. Happy those drivers who, seeing a steep descent before them, are not inspired with a diabolical impulse to take off all brakes and dash to destruction.

I have sometimes been asked whether I consider love higher than art, and I have replied that I cannot separate them, for the artist is the only lover, he alone has the pure vision of beauty, and love is the vision of the soul when it is permitted to gaze upon immortal beauty.

Perhaps one of the most wonderful personalities of our times is Gabriel d'Annunzio, and yet he is small and, except when his face lights up, can hardly be called beautiful. But when he talks to one he loves, he is transformed to the likeness of Phœbus Apollo himself, and he has won the love of some of the greatest and most beautiful women of the day. When D'Annunzio loves a woman, he lifts her spirit from this earth to the divine region where Beatrice moves and shines. In turn he transforms each woman to a part of the divine essence, he carries her aloft until she believes herself really with Beatrice, of whom Dante has sung in immortal strophes. There was an epoch in Paris when the cult of D'Annunzio rose to such a height that he was loved by all the most famous beauties. At that time he flung over each favourite in turn a shining veil. She rose above the heads of ordinary mortals and walked surrounded by a strange radiance. But when the caprice of the poet ended, this veil vanished, the radiance was eclipsed, and the woman turned again to common clay. She herself did not know what had happened to her, but she was conscious of a sudden descent to earth, and looking back to the transformation of herself when adored by D'Annunzio, she realised that in all her life she would never again find this genius of love. Lamenting her fate, she became more and more desolate, until people, looking at her, said, "How could D'Annunzio love this commonplace and red-eyed woman?" So great a lover was Gabriel d'Annunzio that he could transform the most commonplace mortal to the momentary appearance of a celestial being.

Only one woman in the life of the poet withstood this test. She was the re-incarnation of the divine Beatrice herself, and over her D'Annunzio needed to throw no veil. For I have always believed that Eleanore Duse was the actual Beatrice of Dante re-incarnated in our days, and so before her D'Annunzio could only fall upon his knees in adoration, which was the unique and beatific experience of his life. In all other women he found the material which he himself transmitted; only Eleanore soared above him, revealing to him the divine inspiration.

How little do people know of the power of subtle flattery! To hear oneself praised with that magic peculiar to D'Annunzio is, I imagine, something like the experience of Eve when she heard the voice of the serpent in Paradise. D'Annunzio can make any woman feel that she is the centre of the universe.

I remember a wonderful walk I had with him in the Forêt. We stopped in our walk and there was silence. Then D'Annunzio exclaimed, "Oh, Isadora, it is only possible to be alone with you in Nature. All other women destroy the landscape, you alone become part of it." (Could any woman resist such homage?) "You are part of the trees, the sky, you are the dominating goddess of Nature."

That was the genius of D'Annunzio. He made each woman feel she was a goddess in a different domain.

Lying here on my bed at the Negresco, I try to analyse this thing that they call memory. I feel the heat of the sun of the Midi. I hear the voices of children playing in a neighbouring park. I feel the warmth of my own body. I look down on my bare legs—stretching them out. The softness of my breasts, my arms that are never still but continually waving about in soft undulations, and I realise that for twelve years I have been weary, this breast has harboured a never-ending ache, these hands before me have been marked with sorrow, and when I am alone these eyes are seldom dry. The tears have flowed for twelve years, since that day, twelve years ago, when, lying on another couch, I was suddenly awakened by a great cry and, turning, saw L. like a man wounded: "The children have been killed."

I remember a strange illness came upon me, only in my throat I felt a burning as if I had swallowed some live coals. But I could not understand. I spoke to him very softly; I tried to calm him; I told him it could not be true. Then other people came, but I could not conceive what had happened. Then entered a man with a dark beard. I was told he was a Doctor. "It is not true," he said, "I will save them."

I believed him. I wanted to go with him but people held me back. I know since that this was because they did not wish me to know that there was indeed no hope. They feared the shock would make me insane, but I was, at that time, lifted to a state of exaltation. I saw every one about me weeping, but I did not weep. On the contrary I felt an immense desire to console every one. Looking back, it is difficult for me to understand my strange state of mind. Was it that I was really in a state of clairvoyance, and that I knew that death does not exist—that those two little cold images of was were not my children, but merely their cast-off garments? That the souls of my children lived on in radiance, but always lived? Only twice comes that cry of the mother which one hears as without one's self—at Birth and at Death—for when I felt in mine those little cold hands that would never again press mine in return I heard my cries—the same cries as I had heard at their births. Why the same—since one is the cry of supreme joy and the other of Sorrow? I do not know why but I know they are the same. Is it that in all the Universe there is but one Great Cry containing Sorrow, Joy, Ecstasy, Agony, the Mother Cry of Creation?

H. L. Mencken (essay date 1928)

SOURCE: "Two Enterprising Ladies," in *American Mercury,* Vol. XIII, No. 52, April, 1928, pp. 506-08.

[*In the following review, Mencken excoriates Duncan's autobiography, her dancing, and her lifestyle.*]

[*My Life*] I assume, was planned as the first of two volumes. It stops short with the fair (and, by that time, somewhat fat) author's invasion of Russia in 1921. That invasion turned out to be as ill-starred as Napoleon's, and she was presently back in France, where she was to die in 1927. What she has to say in her first volume about her curiously banal love affairs has made the book a roaring success, and it is now being read by all the flappers who devoured *The President's Daughter* six months ago. But what gives it solid interest is not this pathetic and almost mannish mulling over cold amours, but the author's laborious and vain effort to explain the principles of her so-called Art. This effort leaves it revealed as precisely what it was: a mass of puerilities, without any more rational basis than golf or spiritualism. Isadora simply loved to prance around in a shift; all the rest was afterthought. The daughter of a music-teacher, she began this prancing very early in life and to the tune of relatively respectable music: in the fact lay the seeds of her future success. It gave the world, and especially the world of artists, a pleasant shock to see the shift waving and billowing to the tunes of Chopin and Tschaikovsky; there was another shock later on when it began to flap to the tunes of Wagner and Brahms. It was an era of painfully correct ballet-dancing, and to worn-out, tin-pan music. Here, at least, was something new—and straightway it became converted into something portentous. But its meaning, at bottom, was exactly that of any other dancing, which is to say it had scarcely any meaning at all.

Isadora lived and died without anything properly describable as an education, but she was quick, woman-like, to take color from her surroundings, and so she picked up a great deal of profound prattle, and some of it she unloaded into her book. On analysis, it turns out to be very hollow. With one breath she connects her dancing with the figures on Greek urns, and with the next she protests that it was completely American, and had Walt Whitman for its pa. At other times she talks darkly of Beethoven, Wagner and Nietzsche—"the first dancing philosopher." But what had Nietzsche to do with her melodramatic performance of *The Marseillaise,* and what had Wagner to do with her writhing to *The Beautiful Blue Danube*—her two most solid successes?

The more she goes into this matter, in fact, the more absurd she becomes. Her tragedy was that she was not content to be a first-rate bare-legged dancer: she also yearned to be an intellectual. The same folly has engulfed many other ladies of the stage. It is responsible for the ghastly Ibsen revivals that drive dramatic critics to cocaine and heroin, and it is responsible too for the dreadful memoirs that their Heddas and Noras write. Let it be said for La Duncan that her own tome, though it is full of buncombe, is nevertheless very interesting. In it, for the first time, a lady of many loves discusses them realistically, if at the same time somewhat gurglingly. It presents one fact hitherto unnoticed by science: that even a professional charmer sometimes finds it immensely difficult to snare her man. Isadora conquered a great many, but her flops were almost as numerous as her conquests. It was her ambition to bear children to men of eminence, and to that end (according to her own account) she tackled such whales of science as Ernst Haeckel and such sound artists as George Grey Barnard. But they were beyond her seductions, and so, of her actual offspring, two out of three were fathered by dismal nonentities. A foolish woman, and a sad life. . . .

Richard Guggenheimer   (essay date 1945)

SOURCE: "The Grace of Continuity," in *Sight and Insight: A Prediction of New Perceptions in Art,* Harper & Brothers Publishers, 1945, pp. 32-41.

[*In the following essay, Guggenheimer discusses Duncan's dancing in the context of poetry and painting.*]

One may well be reproached for introducing metaphysics into the study or the appreciation of works of art. Resentment frequently and understandably arises when a "pure emotion" expressed by some "intuitive" artist is subjected to tampering analysis at the hands of inquiring "intellectuals." This revulsion against dissection of the mysterious flower is similar to the pain one might feel if an inquisitive anatomist were to halt the expressive miracle of an Isadora Duncan in the act of dancing in order to investigate the skeletal processes of her motions. Such investigation would surely yield no explanation of her peculiarly exalted grace. Yet an understanding of her mentality might reveal at least some attributes of the spirit animating her gestures. For the compulsion, the power to move us, possessed by a great dancer does not lie in the nature of her beautiful body or in the mere grace of its movement. These qualities may constitute a welcome part of the equipment and functioning of a Duncan but, without the animating genius behind these gracious accessories, they are capable of producing only the mediocre achievement of a pleasing but uninspired spectacle.

In this connection, it is interesting to recall from both the Platonic and the Xenophonic dialogues the fact that Socrates himself, despite the handicap of what seems to have been by his own admission an almost revoltingly ugly body, endeavored to express himself occasionally through the medium of the dance. He insisted that he need feel in no way hampered by the apparent disadvantages of an ill-formed body. He was persuaded that any body, motivated by lofty sentiment, could be the medium for beautiful expression. Indeed, is it not an obvious fact that out of the plainest, most ill-favored visage may shine a heavenly light when, from the inner spirit, comes an inspiring and benevolent message? Vapid and inconsequential remains the prettiness of a merely pretty face; stirring to the depths of the soul will be the coun-

tenance animated by the virtues of gentle understanding and illimitable love. Thus, with Socrates, it was his logical conviction that if he ardently yearned to convey a noble sentiment by grace of an "ungraceful" body, the intensity of his will so to do would surmount the handicap of his bodily awkwardness and achieve a spiritual grace.

This was at the heart of Isadora Duncan's so-called genius, a variety of saintliness that lies at the bottom of so much of humanity's highest endeavor. As mysticism falls away from religion in these modern eras of science and skepticism, the saint of other ages will be found in some of the artists of today. Here is the field of renunciation of worldly vanities, the embracing of the three interchangeable virtues. For, where the unregenerate worldlings will have, time and again, rejected goodness out of vanity, and ignored truth out of willfulness, they are still touched by beauty and inspired, if only ephemerally, to a renewed love of virtue. A pointed illustration of the intimate connection between the concepts of beauty and virtue is contained in the *Causeries Florentins* of Klaczko: "The short epoch which traverses the times of Leonardo to the death of Raphael was one of the most radiant of human history. The matter of Beauty preoccupied almost exclusively, animated and bore along the greatest and most elevated spirits; it had become the unique end, the vast business and ultimate reason in all things. And it is from this period, if I am not mistaken, that art, ingenuity, skill acquired amongst us so generally the name of Virtue." Once again we see that beauty may manifestly be a visible radiation of the form of Truth, of God, of whatever humanity may choose to call the ineffable Virtue.

Isadora liked to consider the human soul in the vernacular of her own time, as a radio receiver and transmitter. Her message of universal love, she believed, was best conveyed far and wide by her "tuning in" on the ethereal omniscience, and radiating out of herself to her fellow beings the love impulse that she sensed to be the humanized version of this godly vibration. She felt this comprehension to be unutterable in words, but believed that it could be shown, or at least implied, by gestures of a human body receptive to the impulse of this ineffable power and capable of becoming a medium for its transmission. Nor did she feel this capability to be anything more special than a consecration of the human will. As with so many saintly characters, her fanatical devotion to this specific concept endowed her with ever-growing persuasiveness, so that gradually her vision gained vast empire over herself and over those who were privileged to receive her communication. The result was that finally she had but to make a simple gesture, without even the necessity to move her feet, and there came forth from her almost stationary dancing a hypnotic force laden with gifts of purifying magic. This was a religious experience of the most elevated nature; to behold this type of transport is to be lifted out of all the selfish encumbrances of world preoccupation, of inertia, of fear, of all the manifold obstructions to which the spirit ordinarily is subjected by the substance; and, transcending these, to answer love with love, bereft of any other passion, rendered too pure in essence to give or to receive any radiation other than this most ultimate grace.

It will not be digressive to study for a moment the mental processes which nurtured the talent and fructified the genius of such an artist as Isadora Duncan. According to her own description, she was animated by the dominant conviction that love is the essential force by which human nature can and must fulfill its highest destiny. She regarded all obstacles to the sustained possession of this dynamic sentiment as symptomatic of the world neurosis from which we all suffer to greater and lesser degree. She wished, above all else, to purge her fellow beings and to purge herself of the multitudes of obstructive vanities and fears which so encumber and so vitiate the conduct of worthy lives. She understood intuitively as a psychiatrist understands analytically the obsessive fears and lusts which envelop us in such unhappy, dark confusion. She felt that, in succumbing to these incapacitating degenerations of our spiritual stamina, we bind ourselves hopelessly in the fetters of our own malignant folly. And so it was clear to her that if she could demonstrate the futility of selfishness she would deliver humanity from frustration into a regenerative flowering. It is neither necessary nor fitting to investigate here the logic by which Isadora persuaded herself and her communicants of the divine indispensability of this truth, since it is an ethic that has been beatifically revealed and expounded to the world of lethargic mortals time and again by its loftiest and most inspired thinkers. This was the vast blessing that Jesus strove with all his anguished heart to give to us.

Isadora was sensitive to the analogy between the morally and the aesthetically noxious. The offensive behavior of the impure human being constitutes a blemish on the pattern of what is good, and the corruption of the pattern of goodness is as ugly a catastrophe as can befall a God-aspiring world. In other words, an unloving spirit is an unlovely spirit, and the world of unlovely spirits is an ugly thing. It is probable that when Isadora was a young girl starting upon her difficult career as a dancer, few if any of these thoughts were in her mind. At that time she was more virginally unaware of her deep intuitions and not analytical of them. She loved the idea of the dance and she wanted to dance as beautifully as she could. She studied the figures on ancient Grecian vases, feeling that she derived much inspiration from the elevated achievement of the classical age. The dynamic quality of her temperament ensured her against any tendency to mere imitations or sterile resurrections of past splendors. She was simply beginning her own young life with a healthy susceptibility to the almost hypnotic communication that comes to all sensitive earthlings from the creativity of their forebears. This, contrary to much illusory cavil on the part of individuals who dread an empire of the past over the present, has always been the way of growth in the evolution of human genius. Our Cézanne and our Van Gogh were as mightily enamored

of what they sought and found in the Musée du Louvre as many an uncreative amateur, and the structure of their own original works was only enhanced by these stirring messages from their fathers and their brothers. As the infant matures by the accumulation of its own experience, so does the human race; and every one of its creative members emerges in the advancing flow, by the cumulative force of the historic current plus his own striving. So it was with Isadora. By every means available to her, out of the past and from her contemporaries, she sought to make of herself as good a dancer as by the grace of God, of man, and of her own efforts she possibly could. She knew that she yearned to dance beautifully and she did not at that time greatly question why.

And she did dance beautifully, to such an extent that her name was celebrated and loved. The art of the dance was revived by her into an experience that stirred great numbers to a quickened enthusiasm. The current of her artistry charged her audiences with responsive emotion as though electrified, and the whole metabolism of their souls arose to a new vigor. And as she went on accomplishing this fine performing in the early flower of her youth, she did little philosophizing about her art and little proselytizing. Her message at this time was in the form of a great, spontaneous outpouring of pure movement. In her hour on the stage she sought, by the exquisitely responsive medium of her body, to execute a noble architecture in time and space. The unimpeded grace with which her motion suggested a transcendent rhythm released her audiences from their self-imposed bondage of egoistic restraints and anxieties. By an empathic surge they felt themselves drawn and lifted into an effortless communion and identification with the dancer.

We are all more or less acquainted with the illusion of ease that a great artist produces by the perfection of his own performance. A beautiful singer makes us feel that we ourselves have but to open wide our eager mouths to sing as well. In the hearing of operatic cadences one sometimes has to exert a self-restraint, so great is the impulsion to fling oneself into the gloriously fluent stream of sound. One reads a sonnet of Dante, of Milton, of Shakespeare, and one feels ready to add a sonnet of one's own. In a less restricted field, what mediocre amateur of tennis has not felt, when watching a Tilden in the easy stride and swing of his masterly performing, that he might readily step upon the court and enter into an exalted version of his usual game? The compelling grace of the master tends to lift us out of our frustrating sense of mediocrity. Nor is this merely tempting us into a momentarily happy illusion from which we are to be rudely awakened each time into the sordid reality of our little selves again. If this is all the artist could do for us—raise us up a moment to the airy altitudes of his attainment and drop us down again to the depressive level of our everyday torpidity—we could not profit greatly. Fortunately, the contrary is the case. Every time an average mortal is privileged to come within the aura or direct influence of a more articulate, superior mortal he is affected by the experience. We are all to a great extent the products of our environment. If we wish to be connoisseurs of good wine we have to do much wine tasting in order to emerge from complete ignorance of wines to extensive familiarity with them. If we wish to know enough about the art of music or of painting or of any human expression to be enabled to receive from music, paintings or other communications what they have to give to us, we must hear much music, see many pictures, make many efforts to increase our capacity of comprehension. And similarly, the more often and the more intensively we are exposed to the influential grace of a fine artist the more apt we become to assimilate and to reincarnate much of that grace. Hence those who saw Isadora dance only once had already an inkling of some further dimension to the human soul, and those who saw her many times expanded that much further into the wider spaces of her reaching.

It is not surprising that Isadora found in Walt Whitman a kindred spirit. Here was a pioneer American poet who sang at the top of his lusty voice about his beloved America dancing with all the fervor of its youthful strength. He too felt that the young and pure of heart must dance their dreams, in the full joy of universal love. All men were his brothers, children under the same sky and out of the same mother earth; and if he could fling aside the encumbering robes of selfishness in which we all-too-often wrap ourselves, freeing himself for the exuberant way of life, why not all his brothers and his sisters? He identified himself with all of them, he loved them all, and wanted all of them to love as he loved. To move with love is to dance, is to sing, is to be gay. And so Walt Whitman called out to all America and to all the world to join the dance of the good life. He lifted up the lame and the halt by the strength of his fellowship and by the force of his will. There was an exhilarating and a healing energy in his joyful wisdom that swept through the stiff joints and interstices of many a diseased spirit, restoring it to health and happiness. This was the "gai savoir" of which Nietzsche at times so wistfully and at times so feverishly sang.

One of the earliest as well as most enduring impulses of man seems to be this gesturing with his body as a means of expressing emotion, exorcising demons, supplicating gods. It is one of our earliest and most elemental languages. And at the summit of its perfection it affords a tangible display of human grace in fullest actuality. It is so potent an instinct that its semblance often appears in other forms of art. For instance, this same majestic dance rhythm so literally rendered by an Isadora is to be found almost ecstatically revealed in the marvels of El Greco. In his paintings, Christ and his apostles are in an endless swirl of what, in the behavior of ordinary people, would seem to be an excessive movement. It is true that "ordinary people" do not move like that. When they walk they do not seem to dance, nor when they are eager do they soar like flames. But El Greco's Christians dance and soar because they and El Greco are not "ordinary people." They are imbued with that vehe-

mence of character which, in men of lesser wisdom and integrity, is called fanaticism. The ardor with which they seek to purify themselves and their fellow beings, to transcend the paralyzing effects of mortal iniquity, causes them to think and to act in a mood of urgency. They live in the conviction that every transgression is a morbid profanity of the life that is given man to live, and their own accelerated activity is the result of their striving to purge humanity of its inherent poisons. The tremendous exercise of will required by a sound mind to guide an impaired mind toward health, the torment that so inevitably accompanies this herculean task of overcoming resistance and inertia, rouses the stronger will to a higher and higher pitch of endeavor.

This, at bottom, is the motivating power of the saint, dominated by the unique resolve to free himself and his brothers of every impediment which from the impure flesh confounds the spirit. And in the ultimate sense of the words, it is the ascension from death to life. Is there much wonder, then, that men like these, bent upon celestial business all their lives, should acquire some of the heavenly idiom? Is it not to be expected that these men who come to understand the grace of humble love and wisdom will move with grace along the ways of their benevolence? Thus, in the human idiom, to move with grace is to dance, particularly when it is a movement of aspirational intensity and joyful reward. A child will leap and dance for joy, and so, by his own testimony, did Socrates. Why, then, will he not dance in the fervid exertion of his spiritual flight? El Greco says he will, and he shows us Jesus in a passion against the sinners who violate the temple. In a transport of righteous indignation Christ lashes out at the impurity of mankind, scourging and purging himself as well as his brother men of the corruptions that impede a better human destiny. For he loves them as he loves his Father, and the greater his love the more violent the ecstasy of his castigation. His exalted emotion is pictured by El Greco in a tumultuous creativity of ethereal motion, essentially a dance of good surmounting evil, of life casting out death. Here is form beyond aesthetic, Nature in her divinely plastic mood!

As the spirit and mentality of Isadora emerged from the chaste virtues of adolescence into the more matured experience of adult years, her art expanded. Virtuosity became less and less sufficient to the conscience of the artist. As she encountered the passions and prejudices of a troubled world, she was no longer content with the enthusiastic but rather sterile reactions of her audiences. She wanted her dancing to produce more than acclamation. She was ashamed of the vanity in her that caused her to enjoy the triumph of wild applause. Her conscience did not want applause. The doctor does not seek applause from his patient, nor the teacher from his pupil, nor God from his children. Humble silence were a better sign. Beauty and truth prosper best in the tranquillity of listening spirits. She became distrustful of the prima donna role that life was forcing upon her. And it was by the combination of this pure intuition and the sorrowful tribulations to which her sensitive spirit was subjected by the accidents and incidents of her life that Isadora at last mounted to the apogee of her genius. With a brief description of this final phase of her being I shall be describing at the same time the process by which so much of the world's best genius has flowered.

Isadora's final hope was to induce all humanity to dance as she danced, and so to be in a universal communion of feeling and gesture. She believed that it was most practical to start with little children, and she envisaged a dance of mutual love spreading over the world, bearing with it the blessings of serenity and self-evolving felicity. When asked how she hoped to be able to teach any ordinary child to dance as beautifully as she danced, and by just what process this might be done, her explanation was simpler than the achievement. Because she did not always see how little of her own integrity and generosity could be permanently inculcated into the frail vessels that were her brother and sister children. However, though we cannot all be Isadoras, we can all receive and give forth in the measure of our individual capacities the grace of her ampler benevolence. Her explanation of how to dance involved no systematic physical training, no program of laborious technique. This she felt would develop of itself by the constant exercise of the body in pursuit of and in response to its motivating idea. The first thing she taught each child was to consider that the motivating force of a human being, the soul, or whatever one might call it, is situated at the center of one's breast, and then she had each child hold her hands one upon the other over this central place. She then explained that there were children all over the world who, though they spoke different languages and lived materially separated lives, nevertheless stood in the same way with their hands gently folded over their breasts. These were all brothers and sisters, everywhere and at all times. And the first gesture she asked them to make was to reach forth their arms to these brothers and sisters with only one idea in their minds, that this stretching forth of arms was a greeting, a silent, far-reaching message of love. Animated by this thought, and this thought alone, the gesture was always a beautiful one. It is amazing to see with what grace the most untutored person will perform such a gesture when actuated by this impelling mood, automatically released from the awkward restraints of self-consciousness and the other impediments of habitual egoism. Whereas if one were to set about making the same gracious movement by skill alone, uninspired by the urgency of the communication, the result might be what we call pretty but it would not be beautiful. It would be only the copy of an original, without any of the sublime emotional impact.

On this alone a volume might be written, and we have but to look at a Parisian Madeleine or a New York St. Patrick's Cathedral in contrast to a Grecian temple and a cathedral at Chartres to understand the full implication. Even a certain vulgar mawkishness of a well-intentioned but shallow Murillo when compared to such spirits as Cimabue, Duccio, Giotto, Fra Angelico—to mention only an outstanding few of the galaxy of love-inspired ones—illustrates the world of difference between talent and genius, skill and spontaneity. The flower of grace has to be watered with tears of love. And that is why Isadora held out her hands to give herself to her children and to receive them in her arms. This was her mature smile.

Franklin Rosemont (essay date 1981)

SOURCE: "Introduction: Isadora Duncan," in *Isadora Speaks* by Isadora Duncan, edited by Franklin Rosemont, City Lights Books, 1981, pp. ix-xvii.

[*In the following essay, Rosemont praises Duncan's revolutionary approach to her art and her life.*]

Dancer, adventurer, revolutionist, ardent defender of the poetic spirit, Isadora Duncan (1877-1927) has been one of the most enduring influences on twentieth century culture. Ironically, the very magnitude of her achievements as an artist, as well as the sheer excitement and tragedy of her life, have tended to dim our awareness of the originality, depth and boldness of her thought. But Isadora always was a thinker as well as a doer, gifted with a lively poetic imagination, critical lucidity, a radical defiance of "things as they are," and the ability to express her ideas with verve and humor.

[*Isadora Speaks*] brings together, for the first time, dozens of her essays, speeches, interviews, letters-to-the-editor and statements to the press that until now have remained inaccessible in old newspapers, obscure periodicals and out-of-print books. This material adds to our understanding of Isadora as dancer and theorist of dance; as critic of modern society, culture, education; and as champion of the struggles for women's rights, social revolution and the realization of poetry in everyday life.

. . . . .

Born in San Francisco, Isadora spent her childhood in the Bay Area in the years that a wide-ranging aggregate of poets, artists and inspired "characters" were turning the former gold-rush settlement into one of the most vital creative centers in the world. In the raucous, freewheeling ethos that brought forth *The Call of the Wild* and *The Devil's Dictionary,* Isadora provoked the "awakening," as she put it, of "an art that has slept for two thousand years." Virtually alone, she restored *dance* to a high place among the arts.

Breaking with all conventions, Isadora traced the art of dance back to its roots as a *sacred* art—universally symbolic of the act of creation. With characteristic lack of equivocation, she proclaimed herself "an enemy of ballet"—an enemy, indeed, of all the insipid dance of her time. She scorned the restrictive garb and other artifices of the stage-dancer, and developed free and natural movements. In her diaphanous tunic and bare feet, she restored to the human body its vital actuality as an expressive instrument. Her celebrated "simplicity" was oceanic in its depth. Returning to ancient modes of apprehension relating bodily movements to cosmogony and magic, Isadora invented what later came to be known as *modern dance.*

Her success in this domain, of course, needs no emphasis. Within a few years she became the inspiration of millions of people, including the leading poets and artists of her time. She danced in dozens of countries before audiences rarely if ever exceeded. Indeed, she is the only dancer who can truly be called, in Hegel's sense, a *world-historical figure.*

Interestingly, Hegel in his *Aesthetics* classified dance among the "imperfect arts," along with gardening. But the most encyclopedic man of an encyclopedic age nonetheless conceded at least the *possibility* of dance as a major vehicle of human expression:

> If some spiritual expression is to glint through this mere dexterity, which nowadays has wandered into an extreme of senselessness and intellectual poverty, what is required is not only a complete conquest of all the technical difficulties but measured movement in harmony with our emotions, and a freedom and grace that are extremely rare.

Does this not read like a veritable prophecy of our young Californian? Significantly, this striking passage occurs in Hegel's discussion of *poetry,* the "universal art" which embraces the totality of the human spirit and unifies all forms of artistic expression. Among the arts, poetry was the first to comprehend the modern spirit; dance was the last. Throughout the modern period dance has been, as Doris Humphrey observed, "ten to fifty years behind the other arts." The reasons for this retardation are not difficult to discern. The poetic instrument is the *word,* the most portable of all substances, and the least affected by repression. In dance, however, the instrument is precisely the *body,* on which repression is most heavily concentrated.

It is no accident, in any case, that Isadora was inspired not by dancers—much less by "dance masters"—but, on the contrary, by *poets!* Blake, Whitman, Rousseau, Nietzsche, Keats, Shelley, Byron, Poe, the Pre-Raphaelites, the great French Romantics and Symbolists: These were key sources of the new dance. Isadora situated herself in that grand poetic tradition which—from Shakespeare and the great Elizabethans all the way to the surrealists—is distinguished above all by its insistence on the primacy of the *unfettered imagination.*

She was influenced, too, by painters, sculptors and musicians. A close student of everything alive in ancient and "classical" art, she became an inspiration to innovative currents as varied as the New York "Ashcan School," the Yiddish "Die Yunge," Italian Futurism,

Russian Imaginism and Parisian Dadaism. She who revolutionized the art of dance began by assimilating the revolutions in other forms of expression. The first to apply poetic imperatives to dance, she in turn became a major influence on poetry and the other arts.

. . . . .

Isadora had the highest hopes for dance—as an art, as a new educational force, and even as a means of social transformation. But she did not regard herself, and did not wish to be regarded by others, as "merely a dancer." Her approach never was narrowly esthetic; her aspirations went far beyond the stage. *Revolt* was the hallmark of all that she did. "I am not a dancer," she insisted. "What I am interested in doing is finding and expressing a new form of life."

Exceptionally rebellious even as a child, Isadora grew more radical each passing year. Her unconventional dance inevitably brought her into conflict with the forces of puritanism and other manifestations of cultural/political sclerosis. Like most authentic poets, she repeatedly found herself in trouble with the police, and slandered in the bourgeois press. The insults hurled at her by Bible-thumping evangelists, tinhorn politicians, the American Legion and the Ku Klux Klan—not to mention aristocratic patrons of ballet—doubtless helped her develop a critique of capitalist/christian hypocrisy, and led her to identify herself with currents seeking radical social change. Her motto, she affirmed, was *"sans limites,"* and she set out to combat the limits imposed by bourgeois law'n'order. With the same freedom and grace that characterized her dance, she took up the whole gamut of radical and revolutionary causes.

Isadora's social views covered a wide field, indeed—her "program" included at one time or another everything from dress reform to vegetarianism to birth control. But her radicalism was by no means flighty or frivolous, as some critics have pretended. On the contrary, she demonstrated over a long period a serious, consistent and practical dedication to the struggles she upheld as particularly her own: the women's movement; opposition to organized religion; a new educational system; and the abolition of wage-slavery.

Throughout her life she was a vigorous exemplar of woman's emancipation, and her writings are important documents of that struggle. To our knowledge, she never called herself a feminist, or belonged to any feminist group, but it is not surprising that she came into contact with Antoinette Konikow, Sylvia Pankhurst, Alexandra Kollontai and Klara Zetkin, whose program for women's liberation included socialist revolution. Isadora always maintained that her dance was, more than anything else, "symbolic of the freedom of woman." She looked ahead bravely to the coming "new woman . . . more glorious than any woman that has yet been . . . the highest intelligence in the freest body!"

Brought up in a free-thinking family, Isadora remained a sharp critic of organized religion. This did not prevent her from invoking now and then the central figures in various ancient religious myths. Moreover, like Shelley, Rimbaud, Breton and other poets noted for their vehement atheism, she was deeply interested in "occult" theories, heretical doctrines and psychical research. Like the poets, she trespassed on religious ground whenever it pleased her to do so, and for purely poetic purposes. Always she could have declared, with Luis Buñuel, "I'm still an atheist, thank God!"

Isadora's views on education were developed in considerable detail; undoubtedly they comprise her most original work as a social theorist. Taking as her point of departure her own school experiences as a child, which she recalled were "as humiliating as a penitentiary," reflecting "a brutal incomprehension of childhood," she elaborated a profound critique of modern educational institutions which even today, alas! has lost none of its timeliness. Her own School was designed to be completely different from, and opposed to, all other schools. She did not regard it as a "school of dance," in the usual sense, but rather as a kind of organizing center for what she called a "general reform of the world." In her educational ideas, Isadora rejoins the great utopians, especially Charles Fourier, genial theorist of *passional attraction*.

Political radicals of all kinds—anarchists, socialists, single-taxers—long constituted a majority of her friends, but Isadora's own radicalism did not assume a clear political orientation until relatively late in her life. She was profoundly affected by what she saw of the aftermath of "Bloody Sunday" during the Russian Revolution of 1905, and it was the overthrow of Czarism twelve years later that led her to begin thinking of herself as a communist. "On the night of the Russian Revolution," she wrote in **My Life,** "I danced with a terrible fierce joy." During the last years of her life, her allegiance to the cause of the Third International was unwavering.

To make Isadora appear more "respectable," some commentators have scoffed at, or even entirely ignored, her avowed support for the workers' movement. Fortunately, however, it is impossible to misread her own crystal-clear pronouncements on the subject. In the great contest between Capital and Labor, Isadora left not the smallest doubt as to which side she was on. "In my red tunic," she wrote, "I have always danced the Revolution."

It is true that she was little inclined to the narrower varieties of ideological disputation, and it seems unlikely that she made much of an effort to master the finer points of Marxist theory. Her adherence to the revolutionary cause may have been largely romantic and even utopian—but in the best sense of those terms. Disdaining the old forms of address, "Miss" and "Mademoiselle," she insisted on being called Comrade. Her

zeal for Bolshevik Russia, for Lenin, for the International, was beyond question. Later, as the workers' councils succumbed to blows from the vast privileged bureaucracy consolidated by Stalin (who, incidentally, admired the decadent ballet), she grew more critical. But her solidarity with the basic aims and achievements of the Revolution never diminished; indeed, it grew continually stronger.

The fact that she never joined any revolutionary organization does not mean that her support for revolution was merely verbal. On the contrary, Isadora was always very much an activist. In the early 1900s, long before Dadaism systematized such provocations, she harangued the youth of Berlin to tear down the ugly militaristic statues that disfigured that city's parks. She who could write so lyrically of the workers' May Day was a ready participant in street demonstrations. She agitated for Russian famine-relief, for the independence of Ireland, for the release of class war prisoners. Near the end of her life her Paris apartment served as meetingplace for the committee to defend Sacco and Vanzetti, and she herself took an active part in the tumultuous protests against the judicial murder of these two anarchist workers.

Isadora's greatest services to the revolution, of course, lay elsewhere—in her dance, her teaching, her *example*. These were her own unique contributions to the overthrow of the old society and the building of the new. That she herself tended to view them in this light is made plain in many of her utterances. But how few critics have been willing to admit that this great dancer intended her life's work to be, not a source of amusement for the rich, but a lever of human emancipation!

Not one of Isadora's biographers has mentioned the efforts of Juliette Poyntz, of the International Ladies' Garment Workers Union in New York, in 1915, to establish a school for working-class children under Isadora's direction. The project regrettably did not materialize; her School was always plagued with misfortune. Even later when, with the aid of the Soviet government, she opened a School in Moscow, it fell far short of her hopes. She dreamed of a big School, with a thousand children in spacious surroundings. But like Fourier's Phalanstery, Isadora's School remained more dream than reality. It persists nonetheless, like the dream of Fourier, on a near-mythic plane, as a grand appeal for a life made marvelous. For Isadora's vision did not stop at a School; the School, for her, was only a beginning. To Walt Whitman's "I hear America singing," she added "I see America dancing." Internationalist that she was, she could truly have said that she saw the *whole world* dancing.

In her dance, in her teaching, in her life, Isadora communicated a wildly generous, all-embracing revolutionary spirit, a passionate enthusiasm for a new and exalted life of creativity and freedom. Some idea of the *universality* implicit in her revolutionary élan—her ability to transcend the temporal, sectarian, strategic and tactical differences that divide those whose common aim is to transform the world—may be gauged from the enthusiasm that she and her work evoked in partisans whose views were otherwise strongly opposed. We know that Lenin, for instance, "liked Isadora Duncan very much," and that he was "deeply interested" in her work. "The more attention we pay to what she is doing," he said, "the better the results will be." She was also a good friend of the anarchist Alexander Berkman. An outspoken critic of Bolshevism, Berkman was a warm admirer of Isadora's, and called her "a great and noble character." But perhaps it was the socialist Floyd Dell, writing in the *The Masses* in 1916, who best expressed the ardor Isadora inspired for a whole generation of radicals.

> A strange and dark century, the nineteenth! . . . It does not console me to remember that through that darkness there flamed such meteors as Nietzsche and Whitman, Darwin and Marx, prophetic of the splendors of millennium. When I think that if I had lived and died in the darkness of that century I should never have seen with these eyes the beauty and terror of the human body, I am glad of the daylight of my own time. It is not enough to throw God from his pedestal, and dream of superman and the co-operative commonwealth: One must have *seen* Isadora Duncan to die happy.
>
> · · · · ·

Isadora did not think of herself as a writer; in *My Life* she bemoaned the fact that she lacked "the pen of a Cervantes or even of a Casanova." In truth, she wrote and spoke with clarity, and a sparkle all her own. *My Life* is probably the most widely read autobiography in the English language, after Benjamin Franklin's. Surely no *dancer* has had so much to say, and has said it so well, on such a wide range of subjects.

Too many biographies of Isadora have reduced her to caricature, or legend, or a mere fragment of her true self. Here she is *in her own words:* anti-puritanical, eros-affirming, libertarian, radical in everything, an authentic *free spirit,* one of the boldest condemners of miserabilism in all its forms—an inspiration for all who dream of a better world, all who strive to make that dream a reality.

Lillian Loewenthal   (essay date 1993)

SOURCE: "La Presse," in *The Search for Isadora: The Legend & Legacy of Isadora Duncan,* Dance Horizons Books, 1993, pp. 129-53.

[*In the following essay, Loewenthal recounts Duncan's reception by the press in Paris.*]

The importance of France in the formulation of Isadora Duncan's artistic image was emphasized to me by artist Abraham Walkowitz during a conversation at his Brooklyn home. He spoke of France's esteem and respect for creative people; how "without France, Isadora would not be Isadora . . . the French created her and the French got the best out of her." No other country had the opportunity to accumulate the quantity and variety of documentation concerning Isadora, who established the longest residency of her quasi-nomadic existence in Paris.

Writer George Delaquys reminisced how Isadora seemed to have dropped in on Paris in 1900, from out of nowhere, so to speak. She was not French; she was a foreigner. He pondered if she was even necessary. Parisian culture lacked for nothing; there were operas, café-concerts, and ballerinas galore. The suddenness of Isadora's appearance caught Parisians off guard, and after a brief display of her dancing before private gatherings, she took off as mysteriously as she had come.

Isadora's first public appearance in Paris took place at the Théâtre Sarah Bernhardt during May and June 1903. "She was not successful," Delaquys noted. Objecting to "payoffs," Isadora earned herself a press who were "indifferent or hostile . . . the critics who lived on their reputation for making discoveries of persons of genius discovered nothing that year . . . not Isadora Duncan." Nevertheless, curiosity about this mysterious young woman and her mysterious dance had begun. Rumors circulated "like the flying winds," but the dancer eluded reporters who pursued her. "The truth is," said Delaquys, "Miss Duncan doesn't give a damn."

Isadora pulled off some adroit capers to safeguard her privacy. Wherever she was sought she proved to be elsewhere, but the shadows of stalking journalists were to hover permanently over her extraordinary life's events. With the increase of her concert activities, her fame flowered. She came under the scrutiny and judgment of the many writers and critics who penned the staggering quantity of printed material available to early twentieth-century Parisians.

On the subject of Isadora Duncan, these writers swung a wide critical pendulum, from full-blown emotionalism and adoration to fierce cynicism and rejection; few were middle of the road. One might parody, extol, or lampoon her efforts, but one rarely, if ever, was dispassionate. Journalists, on occasion, were known to make use of their newspaper column to take a serious "poke" at an irksome colleague for either his overenthusiasm or underappreciation of the dancer. Isadora herself became a "journalist" at crucial times. Responding to unflattering remarks, she was always ready to offer her "corrections" in a letter to the press.

It took Isadora one year to convert the 1903 setback at the Théâtre Sarah Bernhardt into a 1904 conquest at the Trocadéro Palace. No less than the titan of music, Beethoven, now graced her expanded repertory. For her *Soirée Beethoven* she included two piano sonatas (the

Pathétique, Opus 13 in C minor and the *Moonlight* (*Quasi una Fantasia*) Opus 27 no. 2 in C-sharp minor), some minuets (arranged by Hans von Bülow), and two movements from the Seventh Symphony (Opus 92 in A major)—her first attempt at symphonic choreography. She was assisted by the famous Colonne Orchestra and its venerable conductor, Edouard Colonne.

A cavernous theater, the Trocadéro was filled to overflowing. The musicians in the audience were especially wary of choreographed Beethoven. Afterward, composer Gustave Charpentier commented that "she has understood that the most elusive, complex, and evanescent movements of the human spirit can be mirrored through the contours and lines of the dancer's body. With her, dance encompasses everything . . . the drama, the symphony. . . . With all the refinement of her own person, her leaps, her languors, the tremblings of the nakedness beneath the veils, she has created a new vocabulary, an ensemble of metaphors capable of speaking in the most immediate and musical of languages."

Musicologist and critic Louis Laloy indicated that he was usually reluctant to apply a term like "genius" to the dance, in view of the deteriorated state of the ballet of his time, but found Isadora's dance altogether a different matter. He had come to her concert fully expecting to find the manner of her dance "poor and puerile compared to the sumptuous music she wished to interpret. It was nothing like that."

Like other arts that reveal the most beautiful secrets of life, Laloy referred to Isadora's new dance as "mute music and moving sculpture." He was impressed that the presence of a full orchestra was not able to eclipse the dancer; she sustained full interest in her dance. Furthermore, in the more subtle, underlying themes of the "Adagio" of the sonata *Pathétique* and the "Adagio Sostenuto" of the *Moonlight,* her gestures transmitted the more profound human emotions that existed in the music.

For Laloy, the interest and beauty of Isadora's performance lay in the personal nature of her expressiveness through movements that were "nowhere to be found in any prior or existing textbook on dance. . . . Here a spirit is sensed and materialized before us." Laloy assured his readers that Isadora Duncan was a priestess "worthy of her God . . . she has piety, purity, and nobility of thought."

The swift-moving dances in close rapport with the music roused the critic's enthusiasm: "Melody and movement are here as twin flowers of the supporting rhythm. One does not know which of these flowers has the most grace and perfume." The minuets, he said, revealed a virginal face; Isadora's turnings were delicate, somewhat demure, and reminiscent of the maidens of the Parthenon. Finally, Laloy commented on the Beethoven symphony, after first subduing those who protested Isadora's use of the composer's music. The symphony, Laloy conceded, was in itself a complete work that re-quired no supplemental clarification from another medium, such as dance, but the dance of Isadora Duncan was also to be regarded as "a work of art."

Beginning with the second movement (the first was an orchestral prelude), Laloy remarked on "the mystic weeping, which invokes in her alone a whole procession of moods, alternately sad and weary, or bathed in elysian light." In the rondo, "one imagines seeing nymphs reaching for one another's hand." Finally, there was the "seraphic bacchanale" of the last movement, in which Isadora's brisk movements and the accentuated bounce of her body on the final note of the main phrase infused the music with "fine images of nymphs dancing at the festivals of Dionysus."

Other European performances, motherhood, and her first tour of her native United States in 1908 consumed the almost five years until Isadora once again appeared in concert in the French capital from late January into February 1909, at the Théâtre-Lyrique Municipal de la Gaîté. Two distinctive premières took place on that occasion: Gluck's *Iphigénie* (which had first been presented in Germany in late 1904) and the Paris debut of the children from her first school of dance in Grunewald (the children had already been widely seen in Germany and throughout Europe).

Gluck's two operas—*Iphigénie en Aulide* (1774) and *Iphigénie en Tauride* (1779)—were revered by the dancer and were long a choreographic preoccupation of hers. From them, she fashioned a single concert-length production. Into the second section ("Tauride") she interpolated an orchestral arrangement by Felix Mottl from yet another Gluck opera, *Armide,* which furnished the accelerating mood of celebration in the closing portion with dances of an added joyous character. With *Iphigénie,* another block of Isadora's broadening exploration into music for her dance was set in place. It was possibly her *chef-d'oeuvre,* the apex of her lyric-dramatic style, and remained an actively integral part of her repertory.

At the Gaîté-Lyrique Isadora was assisted in her series of performances by the Concerts Lamoureux Orchestra, conducted by Camille Chevillard, under the artistic management of Lugné-Poë. A second engagement at this theater, with a seating capacity of approximately 2,200, took place in May and June 1909, when she was accompanied by the Colonne Orchestra and by her pupils as well, who charmed audiences with their innocence and grace in a group of incidental dances.

Reviewing for *Comoedia Illustré* in February 1909, André Marty described the scene at the Gaîté-Lyrique:

> Let's imagine a stage, completely hung with gray-blue draperies, a carpet of the same color; a soft light facing toward the back of the stage. The curtain parts, and with the first measures of a Gluck air we see emerging from the shadows the strangest, most exquisite of apparitions. Have we

seen her on one of those immortal paintings that adorned Greek vases; does she step live from the land of Tanagra; is she the serene muse on Parnassus out of a Mantegna, the most perfect of Clodion's statuettes? She is none of these, she is all of them; even more, one makes a mistake to compare her with anything else. Her dance is not imitative of other plastic arts, nor an appealing accompaniment for music; it is an art in itself, she attains the beautiful by means all her own.

Marty observed that Isadora, in her expression of feelings and in her representation of human actions, created something simpler and more forceful than reality. He referred to this as a "superior synthesis," a stylization seen in the games she played in the "Aulide" segment—ball and knucklebones. Not literal images, they were devoid of relation to a specific time, place, or period. And when in the "Bacchanale" "she might seem an intoxicated bacchante incited by some god to irrational behavior, we are actually seeing the symbol of divine folly itself."

Pierre Mille started his account of Isadora's concert in the February 1909 issue of *Le Théâtre* by quoting his colleague, Fernand Nozière: "'One wants to get down on the knees and pray, even to cry' . . . It seems insane that a dance, only a dance—two feet, fast or slow, the arms open or folded, and the supple body of a woman could inspire you to pray or cry. Yet this is the truth! Nozière is right. There is a great mystery here." To his own rhetorical questions he provided answers: "What is it that she does, this large woman with long legs, an undulating torso, and muscled like the statues of virgins sculpted by Polycletus?" Whatever it was that she did, Mille was certain of one thing: "She dances and no one has ever danced as she."

To describe her attire, Mille referred to the virgins of the Parthenon frieze, the priestesses in flowing robes standing before the temple of Athena, the winged victory, the seductive folds that cover without concealing, the forms of Botticelli's nymphs. "And then, what is it that she does? Certainly others have danced better, if it were solely a question of . . . beat and step. But what she does is so very open, so very unsophisticated—a simple manner and that is all that is necessary." Utterly convinced that Isadora knew at all times what she wished to achieve, Mille went on to describe the heroine Iphigenia as she played along the shoreline with knucklebones: "They are like flowers in her hands. She tosses them in the air; they fall back downward. She seizes them. So convincing are all her actions that spectators do not question that she truly sees the sea before her and that her eyes are filled with the shape of the waves." With certainty and pride she runs to welcome the victorious Greek fleet, arriving to the reverberations of trumpets, "her bosom heaving, her figure seeming to grow taller."

Still later Isadora returned as a young warrior, dressed in a short red tunic, her arms bare. Then, during the clash of weapons (the "Dance of the Scythians" from *Tauride*), she brought an exaltation to the combat: "How vivid are the simulations of battle, the fist that strikes, the feigned flight, the bold young head warding off the blows, eyes brilliant in valor; and when the final assault fells the foe, her arm is raised in triumph. No longer does she battle, she remains still—a monument to glory."

For the *Finale* Isadora appeared as a bacchante, clumps of ivy and flowers in her hands. "First she tosses the flowers, then brandishes the vines, all the while continuously dancing and ever faster." If the role of the poet and artist was to awaken and to reveal, then "she is indeed artist and poet, this Isadora."

The American dancer and her revolutionary approach to her art created a furor, reported the *New York Times* on May 23, 1909. Her pursuit of acceptance by the French had been a resounding success. "Of all the cities where I have danced, Paris is the one from whom I most wanted admiration. . . ." The extraordinary success of the two Gaîté-Lyrique engagements placed Isadora firmly in the French consciousness. Increasing attention was paid to all aspects of her personal and professional life. Journalists wrote of her individual craft and style, music critics of the aptness of her choice of music, dance experts of balletic tradition vis-à-vis Isadora's more radical concepts. Feature articles spotlighted her choreography, her school of dance, and her young pupils.

One of the few professional women to write on Isadora during this time was Jeanne Gazeau, whose lengthy essay in *Les Entretiens Idéalistes* on December 25, 1909, presented a discriminating and favorable assessment of the philosophical and esthetic underpinnings of the new dance and its theorist. Reacting to the choreographies, Gazeau described moments of wonder and excitement: Isadora's run in the "Scythian Dance" was "steady and fiery as an ephebe"; in the "Bacchanale," "she is possessed"; in her "glide into a Chopin waltz" she effected an easy transformation of mood and form.

Of the Chopin numbers on the dancer's programs, Gazeau considered that Isadora reached the peak of tragic emotion in *The Maiden and Death* to the Mazurka in B minor (opus 33, no. 4). "I know nothing more beautiful than the sudden transformation of this young being dancing with the exuberance of life, who now feels gripped by Death; there is a shudder, then an effort to shake off the icy embrace, finally a desperate stiffening of the entire body, a supreme convulsion, where she seems to raise herself erect like a fragile flower that shoots up from a blow, then falls lifeless. It is the eternal mystery of death in all its simple anguish. . . ."

One of the lengthiest and most detailed examinations of "The Dances of Isadora Duncan" appeared in the March 1910 issue of *Mercure de France*. In analyzing *Iphigénie* the author Ovion was intrigued by its archaeological character and the two distinct classifications of movements at work in this dance: movements of action, descriptive and evocative of the style of Greek art, and gestures expressing human emotion. Ovion did not find these derivative of earlier influences, but personal in nature and decidedly more interesting and original.

The best example of the action motions and the set figurative patterns of Greek origin, were the youthful scenes from *Iphigénie en Aulide:* the Tanagra figurine half-kneeling, counting the score points from the imaginary knucklebones caught on the back of the hand, the recumbent pose in the classic position of the Greeks—underleg bent, upper leg extended—or in the symbolic lamentations of Iphigenia, who, believing Orestes dead, makes her final tribute, articulating maddening grief by simulating the tearing of her hair.

Unmistakably derived from ancient artifacts, Ovion believed, were the physical gestures employed in the warrior's conflict: "One can point out by the hundreds the designs on vases where the poses of Isadora Duncan in this dance . . . can be traced." Ovion drew close parallels between the gestures in this dance, in which Isadora was both the attacker and the attacked, and Plato's description of the Pyrrhic dance in which he had written of those natural bodily modulations employed in battle: ". . . the posture of a man letting fly an arrow or hurling a javelin." Gestures characteristic of the one being attacked were associated with the body's mechanisms for self-defense, "be it flinging oneself to the side, drawing back, leaping, or bending."

But the dances of joy, as in the *air gai,* the delirious climax of the "Bacchanale," even the undulating motions of Isadora's arms in the "Entrance of the Priestesses" in *Tauride,* had the individuality of personal, interpreted gestures. Here one encountered the emotional, expressive movements that Ovion properly credited to Isadora—creative movements of "unusual novelty, a return to symmetrical form, architecture in dance, movements regular and broadly structured, well-proportioned, and evincing a sureness of balance and deliberate control of the emotional dynamics." In the music of Gluck, Isadora seemed to perfect her unusual art, the writer concluded: "She is the remarkable interpreter . . . a gesture from her radiant purity of style remains imprinted on the retina, a joy forever."

French deputy Paul Boncour eulogized "The Art of the Sublime Dancer" in his article for *Le Figaro* on May 22, 1909. When he called for the creation of a society to perpetuate Isadora's work in dance, he caused quite a stir. When his report on the fiscal state of the arts was carried by the newspaper *Excelsior* on November 30, 1910, it raised eyebrows in "parliamentary circles" and upset the "small, charming world of danseuses."

Boncour had provocatively made known his opinion that all ballet had had its day. He cited Isadora as a most important figure among new artists of the dance, sug-

gesting in fact, that her fresh perceptions and innovative ideas had far more contemporary relevance than did ballet and should be considered for a needed renovation of the old system. *Excelsior* also aired the results of a survey it had conducted on the controversial subject: "Tutu vs. Peplum—Will Isadora Duncan Reform Our Corps de Ballet?—Freedom of Art vs. Tradition—What Are the Big Stars Saying?"

The first "big star," Mme. Rosita Mauri, who was then in charge of dance training at the Opéra, spoke well of Isadora, but defended traditionalism. A dancer could no more divorce herself from the established disciplines of the profession than a writer could violate grammatical rules. Opening the doors to innovation, as Boncour suggested, could not work. "Classic dances [ballet] cannot be changed and the tutu remains the only costume appropriate for the dancer." Of course she had seen Isadora and her pupils who were so wonderfully graceful, but never could one of the children accomplish what the children of her own studio did. "Look at her!" She indicated to the *Excelsior* interviewers a thirteen-year-old child in tights and a pink and white tutu, with a strong, supple, arched back, momentarily wobbling to balance herself on left pointe.

The ballet mistress at the Opéra-Comique, Mme. Marquita, was cautious about giving an opinion, not having seen Isadora in concert. "I did not know that she had already become a school."

The reporters next caught up with the famous Mme. Carlotta Zambelli, who was rehearsing on stage at the Opéra. A champion of ballet, she was reluctant to talk, but told them straight away: "What Isadora Duncan does is not very difficult; one has only to move the legs freely. We could perform her work easily, but the reverse is not true." One reporter tenaciously pressed the point further. Isadora Duncan, he advised, had been through a thorough physical training in preparation for her dance and had as strong a technique as she. Zambelli's reply: "You think so? It would show." She terminated the interview with that, and proceeded to transform herself into a Snow Fairy.

"Aflutter, pretty, amiable, and in a feathered hat," Mme. Regina Badet limited her interview to five minutes; she was late for her rehearsal at Gemier's. The subject of Isadora Duncan merited some sympathy from this ballet mistress. Isadora's was an art that offered much of interest, but was unlikely to realize any permanent success because, Mme. Badet explained, "the Opéra is so solidly entrenched an organization that to penetrate it will be most difficult." However, she could recognize the benefits of new ideas on the old traditions. "We are martyrized, you know, in childhood . . . they deform and dislocate us. Very fortunate are Isadora's young girls who are let free to dance and follow their own instincts."

The central figure in the controversy had the final say. Isadora Duncan's studio, where the interview took place, was located in the Hôtel Biron on rue Varennes (the current Rodin Museum). There, she told her visitors, she spent hours daily working on her technique and compositions, "proving well that what she does is not all that easy." (The composition in preparation on that occasion was her new version of *Orphée et Eurydice*.) She professed to not being entirely familiar with Paul Boncour's report on the state of the arts or aware of any investigation into her dance, but, in general, she was of the opinion that most people were mistaken about what she believed.

In the nine years since her arrival in Paris, Isadora claimed to have become much wiser, talking less and doing more. She accepted the fact that her art had no chance of supplanting the classical dance because it was not an art of the theater. Hers was a self-sufficient art expression, and her true ambition was to focus on founding a school of fine arts in a milieu of painters and sculptors, where the plastic arts would become an official study and where she could expound and reveal the principles of her work in dance and train future exponents of her ideas. She expressed distress over "the wretched imitations they do of me," and desired only to be left alone to live quietly, read, and listen to music. "I have nothing more to say now. I have already talked too much."

Isadora's fuller version of Gluck's long-surviving opera, *Orphée et Eurydice* (a short suite of pieces from this opera dated from her early programs, c. 1900), was completed by the close of 1910 and presented at the Châtelet Theater on January 18, 1911, with the participation of singers, a chorus, and the Colonne Orchestra. The *Orphée* was the second Gluck adaptation to reinforce the public's recognition of the dancer as an artist. She was not solely a captivating charmer and invigorating spirit in the music of Strauss, Schubert, Brahms, and Chopin but an earnest interpreter of simple and powerfully beautiful musical scores, capable of integrating great music with human gestures of dramatic truth and eloquence. Whenever it appeared in Paris, Isadora's *Orphée* was announced in the press as a cultural event of commanding magnitude; all were summoned to the theater.

Walter Rummel, Isadora's musical advisor and accompanist, some years later, wrote on the dancer's interpretive approach to Orpheus. Her role was neither representative of the word nor illustrative of the dramatic action. She placed herself within the panorama of the narrative as did the Greek chorus in the performance of ancient tragedies, rendering "the primordial and impersonal emotion that rises from the innermost depths" of the character in the drama. Such emotion, Rummel stressed, could not manifest itself other than through music, and only the dance could make it visible. Thus the chorus (Isadora's role) was not a depiction of the story development; it assumed the silent and concentrated focus of the drama's emotion, "the distillation of its passionate essences."

André Nède's January 18, 1911, article, "Isadora Duncan at the Châtelet," provided a preview of the major scenes of her *Orphée,* a run-through as helpful to his fellow Frenchmen as today's readers:

> The orchestra will play the overture, the curtain will rise, and the chorus will be heard; Orpheus's companions lament the death of Eurydice and Miss Duncan will dance these lamentations. At Eurydice's tomb she becomes Orpheus, who can be recognized by the grief that marks her pantomime. She is alone on stage.

For the performance, there were usually two voices—Orpheus (contralto) and Eurydice (soprano)—and a small chorus, all seated among the orchestra players. On stage, Isadora constituted the entire spectacle.

> The orchestra plays the dance of the lost souls and we are now in Hell. A harp is heard, Orpheus's arrival is announced, and the chorus begins the melody of the lost spirits. Miss Duncan dances the dance of these wretched souls. . . . The following scene transfers to the Elysian Fields, where Miss Duncan, in her dance, reveals the now happy shades leading Orpheus toward Eurydice. . . . The end of the poem is the triumph of love, and Miss Duncan dances the processions, the sacrifices, and the placing of flowers on love's altar.

There was no unanimity among the critics. Paul Souday's response to the Châtelet *Orphée* found Isadora's choice of music faulty. "Even a dancer such as Isadora Duncan cannot alone adequately synthesize a complete lyric drama." He thought her meanings were obscure as she shifted her portrayal from that of Orpheus to that of the Shades who obstruct her entrance into Hades. Strange and disconcerting though, "it was not at all unbecoming or tiresome." As for the rest of Isadora's program, Souday commented that "Miss Duncan merited the most glowing of compliments."

A personal apprehension was disclosed by André Marty in his February 1911 *Comoedia Illustré* article, "Isadora Duncan at the Châtelet." Might she not in her latest undertaking perhaps destroy the sublime memory of her earlier perfection, "treasured in us like a jewel?" His fear that the "new" that might shatter the spell of the "old" dissolved upon seeing "the priestess" once again. Sometimes the same, sometimes different, Isadora was always beautiful to Marty.

Isadora's handling of the beginning of *Orphée*'s second act demonstrated to the reviewer how deep intuition and artistic intelligence could inject art with an exceptional character. While the off-stage voice of the hero was pleading for the return of his Eurydice, the dancer began moving to the haunting theme of the lost souls—she had become one of those pitiful, infernal creatures, wandering along the banks of the Styx. "At no moment in this dance could one say her gestures recreated figures from the Sistine Chapel . . . still, Michaelangelo's name was on everyone's lips. She does not imitate the great creator, but by her energy and superhuman effort she rises to the height of his genius."

Pierre Lalo, the brilliant son of composer Edouard Lalo, was music critic for *Courier Musical, Comoedia,* and *Le Temps.* He was an arch conservative, known for his astuteness and caustic wit. With Isadora he made little progress, despite his undiminished antagonism. His lengthy critique ignored direct reference to the *Orphée* première, tackling instead her ideas and doctrines and their fallacies. Altogether peculiar in view of its past disdain was Paris's unwholesome infatuation with her dances and her bare feet. "There is not in what she does today any less pretension or less mediocrity than at another time." But it was Isadora's remark in *Excelsior,* to the effect that a collection of more or less arbitrary steps does not constitute an art, that incited Lalo to the virulence of his critique.

The classical dance to which the dancer had referred *was* an art, Lalo asserted, because it defined its gestures and attitudes with precision and eliminated "useless, obscure motions." Ballet cultivated, developed, and perfected a style by "logically studied methods based on a body of rules." Citing Gautier and Mallarmé, who were fervent admirers of the ballet, and pointing to Degas, the greatest painter of the day, who esteemed ballet sufficiently to devote a significant portion of his work to studies of it and its practitioners, Lalo challenged Isadora to make such a claim for herself. "Merely fluttering about and trying to express her soul, this presumptuous American, without any understanding of the medium, not even a shadow of technical competence, thinks she is creating a revolution. . . . She seems entirely devoid of a musical sense . . . like one of those Anglo-Saxons of whom Nietzsche said, 'they possess no music in them.'"

Under attack were Isadora's "false simplicity and affected naiveté." Lalo, with his well-known anti-German prejudice, called the children from her school "heavy little girls from beyond the Rhine, whose ankles were as thick as their thighs . . . their naked legs skipping around monotonously while following Miss Duncan in a row." The public, who aided and abetted her successes, were not spared his attack. "They are the dupes of a Parisian pro-Duncan coalition composed of snobs: ringleaders, agitators preying on the bovine throng, who blindly follow the caprices of fashion." He found incomprehensible "their stupid tendency to confuse the amateurish, underdeveloped efforts of the foreigner with those of a genius." Denying any prejudice on his part, he pointed to his acceptance of the foreigner "who is a Wagner, Tolstoi, or an Ibsen—not a Puccini, Caruso, or an Isadora Duncan."

Composer Reynaldo Hahn's music review of an *Orphée* performance given by Isadora in March 1913 at the Trocadéro was critical of her treatment of the Gluck score. "Regretfully, I must confess that this Orpheus is not an example of her notable art I prefer." He faulted her disregard for the composer's tempo markings, the vagueness of her interpretation of Eurydice, of Orpheus, and the Blessed Spirits, which ultimately undermined her artistic intentions. Furthermore, the Gluck music bore characteristics of eighteenth-century operatic style quite incompatible with the dancer's attempt to apply it to movements of the Chorus in Greek tragedy. In Act Three, "The Elysian Fields," mention is made of seven of the pupils led by Isadora, who became the "living realization of all sylvan myths. . . ." The renowned dramatic actor Mounet-Sully recited the prose uniting the narrative extracts, while the distinguished singer Rudolf Plamondon sang the role of Orpheus.

When Hahn turned to the Schubert numbers on the program, his review lightened. There was, in Isadora's ease of rhythms, in her serenity and tranquility of repose, that which excited in the spectator "a penetrating sense of well-being, to be alive and to feel the world so acutely." What irresistible magic in her forms and exhilarations in her vigor, the critic marvelled. He would not find the term "genius" excessive in one who could realize the summit of beauty and emotion attainable by a human being. "In those moments where beauty and emotion fuse and climax, something of the immortal floats about the dancer; she wanders in a divine ray, in a mist where all works of art circle in unison with her . . . As Goethe once said: 'Hold this moment, do not flee, you are so beautiful!'"

One of a favored circle of journalists whose supportive reviews were appreciated by Isadora, Michel Georges-Michel attended her performances in late November 1911 at the Châtelet. In his "Les Ennuis et les Rêves d'Isadora Duncan" ("Isadora Duncan's Anxieties and Dreams") that appeared on December 3 in *Gil Blas,* Georges-Michel made note of the seven young pupils, "the little dancing roses," who entered the stage and stood within the blue shadow of the heavy curtains. At that point Isadora approached the footlights, crossed her arms, and addressed the rather surprised audience: "Look at these children. They are healthy and robust; eyes are clear and no one is tired or weakened. To the contrary, listen as they breathe freely. Do you think it is wrong for them to dance?"

What prompted the brief and unexpected speech became apparent to Georges-Michel when, in her dressing room, Isadora told him: "I am pampering a big dream—my school of dance. I want not 50, not 500, but 5,000 pupils. The dance is play, it is art, health, joy and poetry. I would wish for the whole world to dance with me! And the whole world, even with its idiosyncrasies, delusions, pathos and passions and would come to realize a more pleasurable existence." How should she not be irritated, Georges-Michel wrote, when that very day, she had been informed by a reputable critic that her pupils were to be the subject of an investigation? A prominent society member found objectionable the commercial exploitation in Parisian theaters of young children, parading around in skimpy outfits and baring their naked legs. Moreover, Georges-Michel added, Mme. Duncan was apprised by her informant that all young children dancers in Europe usually wound up as prostitutes—lost by the time they reached the age of fifteen!

There was more to come. Isadora herself was threatened with cancellation of her concerts if she dared to appear in her transparent veils for what was described as her "sensuous" "Bacchanale" from *Tannhäuser*. The daily papers made it known that a police deputy was to be on hand in the theater to enforce the restraining order on her attire (waiting to close the curtain at the first drop of her modesty). The harried dancer tried to put the matter into some rational perspective with a letter to the newspapers. She was hoping to diffuse the situation by clarifying her personal concept of Wagner's score and her choreography. Those familiar with Isadora's interpretation of this music were equally cognizant of her belief that the spirit of the dance must transcend the corporeal, so that in the treatment of the love and carnal themes suggested in the music, only the imagination was titillated, not the flesh. To Georges-Michel she vented her frustrations: "If they annoy me about this, I will dance in a forest naked, naked, naked . . . with the song of birds and elemental noises for an orchestra."

To unruffle feathers, Isadora wore for this performance (according to one source) a double layer of light scarves. Inevitably, with all this commotion, public anticipation was high for the "Bacchanale" and the audience, not disappointed in the overall presentation, had actually awaited a less restrained interpretation. All in all, things proceeded without incident. Isadora was seen leaving the theater wrapped in ermine from head to foot, utterly fatigued and utterly delighted.

The death of Isadora's children in 1913, followed by the four-year war that engulfed first Europe and subsequently the United States, brought years of disruption and turmoil to Isadora's life. She restlessly kept moving with more and more concerts in the United States, as well as South America; in between she returned to France, where she presented in Paris, in April 1916, two benefit performances to aid French war relief and did a short tour of the provinces in recital with a piano accompanist. The French press kept track of it all.

Isadora's first major reappearance in Paris after the war took the form of a year-long Festival of Music and Dance throughout 1920. This year celebrated two decades since the dancer's arrival in Paris in 1900. Art critic Waldemar George, in an article on the new dance, addressed part of his essay on the now familiar and reputable artist and the implications of her dance. A broad and rhetorical question framed the purport of his assessment. Could the dance have the potential for becoming a viable art, one no longer peripheral, but within the scheme of the modern esthetic? He believed it could and found in Isadora the initiator and the

reactivator, evidence of the renewal of this medium and the new spirit infecting the plastic arts. She had, in the twenty years of her opposition to the balletic tradition, brought credibility to a technique at first thought to be based solely on intuition. Surprisingly and more precisely, George viewed this technique as stemming from a perfect knowledge of the rules of rhythmic structure. This is an art, he reasoned, that could be learned and taught with authenticity.

The press had been informed by Isadora that her dance now had a new character. The horrendous events affecting the world had deeply touched her and she desired to express through her dance ideas and emotions more relevant to those experiences shared in common by all people. It was her earnest wish to offer some consolation to the sorrowing and to the afflicted.

Afflicted but not consoled by Isadora's words was Paul Abrams who, in an article in March 1920, vented a wary response. He addressed himself to the men of his generation who were witness, as was he, to two events in the art of choreography—both indelible, "never to be stricken from memory." The first came with the entrance of the Ballets Russes, the decors of Bakst, the performances of Nijinsky, Karsavina, and Rubenstein, and the sumptuousness of the Orient. The second landmark event, less ostentatious but more profound and memorable in its appreciation and alliance with the values of beauty in the classical sense, was the appearance of Isadora Duncan. Then Abrams got to the heart of his displeasure. He and several of his colleagues had received letters from the dancer in which she promised a departure from the earlier character of her dance. He was apprehensive. For Isadora to complicate or even to become pretentious just to produce other effects "which she little needs" worried him. It would be, he commented, "like having grains of pepper thrown into a glass gilden by the Hellenic sun and filled with wine from Samos."

Newspapers carried the announcement of Isadora's concert dates and program schedules with a jubilation befitting the return of Ulysses to Ithaca: "A date in the History of Beauty," "She will reclaim her Apostolic Esthetic." As the momentum gathered, her appearances took on the dimension of immense cultural happenings—masterpieces from the greatest composers and the most acclaimed dancer of her epoch together in the prominent theaters of Paris. Isadora began her concert series at the Trocadéro in March and April, continuing at the Théâtre des Champs-Elysées in May and June, again performing at the Trocadéro in November and December, this time with the Isadorables, finishing at the Champs-Elysées, again with the Isadorables, in January 1921.

Paris resounded with the "big guns" of Isadora's creative achievements, the mainstays of her career and her artistic signature, *Iphigénie* and *Orphée*, the sensitively probed works of her maturity, Tchaikovsky's Symphony

No. 6 in B minor (1916), César Franck's *Redemption* (1916), Liszt's *Les Funérailles* (1918-1919) and his *Bénédiction de Dieu dans la Solitude* (1918-1919), her revised and enlarged excerpts from Wagner's *Parsifal,* and her gestural dramatization of the French anthem *La Marseillaise* (1915-1916). For her numerous "loyalists" Isadora tossed floral bouquets in the form of the beloved Schubert, Brahms, and Chopin waltzes, which rekindled treasured remembrances of the vivacious and nimble Isadora of her younger days.

The cavernous, antiquated, and acoustically faulty Trocadéro did not impede the tumultuous reception accorded Isadora. Across its enormous stage had passed France's great orators, beribboned men of state, and members of L'Académie Française. Isadora now stood there in her light peplum and bare feet, first expressing her gratitude to the full house for so grand a welcome and then announcing her plan to endow Paris with a school of the dance. She called on her faithful followers to aid her in her task. "I have but opened a door. This door must never be allowed to close." On hand and in good number were the members of the press, many familiar figures reconvening for such an auspicious occasion. Seen with some frequency during the gala season were the notables among artists and intellectuals in Paris, several of whom would continue to cast their shadows over cultural events for some time to come: Gabriel Astruc, Henri Bidou, René Blum, Colette, Kees van Dongen, Lanvin, Louis Jouvet, Steinlen, Picasso.

As in the past, eulogistic terms—"Priestess," "Goddess," "Statue"—headlined article after article. Charles Mère described Isadora's effect on the crowds as a "magnetism of intelligence and benevolence." Fontrailles exclaimed: "She's a prodigious thing!" As Isadora danced the *Marche Slav,* Nozière, drama critic for *Gil Blas* and *Au Matin,* was seen standing in his loge, writing and uttering "She is an entire temple, this woman!" The crusty critic of *L'Oeuvre,* known to his colleagues as La Fouchardière, grumbled aloud: "To dance to Wagner with this corpulence . . . this Isadora! I must do an article, but . . . cannot handle it with this woman. She's a national glory!"

Following are some of the collected impressions of the Schubert *Funeral March (Marche Héroïque)* composed by Isadora in 1914 as a memorial to her children.

> The Goddess appears; first, a pale shadow moving against the tall, dark backdrop. . . . The years, heavy with grief and anguishes, have weighed oppressively on the shoulders of the divine Iphigenia who not long ago danced on the shores of Aulis.

> Still and white in long vertical folds and staring with an inexpressible sadness . . . the poses, the walk of the great artist suffice to cause spectators to tremble.

> The sadness and gravity of the Funeral March, a dance? No—it is a mute tragedy.

For Isadora's fans, her return to the Trocadero with her *Orphée* was a time for elation. Her performances of December 11 and 16, 1920, featured singers M. Francell of the Opéra Comique, Rudolphe Plamondon of the Opéra, Mme. Marcelle Doria and an ensemble of Singers from Saint Gervais, and eighty musicians from the Concerts Colonne Orchestra with the much admired conductor Georges Rabani.

Sublime and "hieratic," Isadora took charge, reported critic Guillot de Saix. On this occasion her Orpheus took on a particular dignity. While interpreting the Gluck score, yellow, violet, and red lights created a phantasmagoric atmosphere. Guillot de Saix noted how the composer Gluck had transcended his epoch, but how the dancer in her turn had surpassed the composer. He called attention to how she had rejoined the statuary of antiquity, of how she brought animation to the paintings of da Vinci. She now led her audience as she dreamily wandered from the tomb of Eurydice to the infernal caverns where monsters and furies became tamed by the strumming of Orpheus' divine lyre, and when she guided them into the Elysian Fields studded with flowering narcissus, artists in the hall watched this scene with ecstatic eyes, believing they were seeing live before them, their own dreams.

During Easter week in April 1920, Isadora offered a "Spiritual Concert" that featured the *Childhood of Christ* of Berlioz, the *Redemption* of César Franck, and the *Holy Grail* music from *Parsifal* of Wagner. Leading into his review of the concert, Pierre Scize asked a question: "Who, then, said this woman was a dancer? The most agreeable of mimes, a tragedian, perhaps, a sculptor, as well. A dancer? Truly no!" Appraising Isadora, Scize regarded her as a sculpture of flesh with movements ecstatic and of prayerful supplication; he beheld in her the collision of two worlds—ancient and modern, Dionysus in full sunlight and Jesus in Christian austerity: the reign of humiliation and sacrifice. "And when the splendid statue of flesh finally lies outstretched under its shroud as the bells and fanfares of the Grail ring out a new Assumption, we realize that something august came to pass here—a kind of Mass for paganism crucified. But who, then, who said this woman was a dancer?"

Well regarded and of established reputation within the community of writers was Fernand Nozière, alias Guy Launay. Under either name he was a staunch partisan of Isadora, strongly receptive to her form of dramatic expression and humbled by the physical beauty of her movements. Throughout the year-long extravaganza his reviews recorded some of the details and on-stage actions in the lesser known choreographies. In his sensitivity to his subject, Nozière was able to depict clearly the physical woman as well as her creative spirit, and her intellectual and psychological influence on the spectator.

Observing her during the Easter week concert, Nozière profiled Isadora noting that she had the decorative beauty of the angels imagined by the artists of the Renaissance. Her arms extended were caressing, "heavenly nourishment"; the slope of her neck, the clearness of the gaze, and the smile on her lips were "evocative of those Botticelli compositions . . . of a religious serenity." (César Franck's oratorio in three parts, *Redemption,* was based on a poetic text that set forth and acclaimed the spiritual reformation. Isadora danced only the second part, the "Symphonic Interlude," in which she conveyed the regenerative transformation of mankind's depravity into the age of enlightenment. It was first performed on April 9, 1916, at the Trocadéro for a war charity matinee.) Nozière began by describing Isadora as having risen from the dust. First sitting, then kneeling, she executed a sequence of positions that were forceful and tremendously stirring, "calling to mind Bourdelle's sculptural studies of the torso." With deliberate resolve she steadily pulled herself upward, "as the seed raises itself to the sun. Standing erect, her hand signals the canopy of heaven and the revelation of divinity. It is simple and it is great."

For her picturesque movement images to Berlioz's *L'Enfance du Christ,* Isadora brought a quality of light and the sparkle of joy. Through Nozière's eyes, a woman lingered maternally before the divine child, lovingly regarding his slumber. She smiled to him, rocked him, and suddenly, "accompanied by flutes and harp, she goes off seeking wondrous gifts for him: brilliant, full flowers, fruits of luscious shape and color, rich fragrances." All the while, the critic observed, the dancer scarcely touched the floor, gliding with an ethereal grace that enveloped onlookers, including Nozière, in an atmosphere of awe.

Of Tchaikovsky's Sixth Symphony Nozière reported the following:

> The orchestra plays the Adagio [first movement]. The Scherzo [second movement] inspires Isadora. She is the Isadora Duncan we have known, the one who runs blithely across the green and gathers a flower, who dances in sunlight, and who abandons herself to her youthfulness. It is the Isadora of yesterday—the one numerous ballerinas have imitated; she now appears to be imitating herself. But the Allegro Vivace [third movement] reveals the new Isadora Duncan . . . She has become the very symbol of battle—of its intoxication, its sadness, its glory. With her index finger she seems to have traced on the pediment of the temple a sign of heroic duty. When her forces diminish, when she seems to waver, she returns to this sacred and radiant inscription where she renews her courage and vigor . . . It is no longer a woman who dances—it is a divinity rousing the crowd. Behind her she urges a whole people toward a superhuman task—toward challenges, toward triumph. Alone on stage, nevertheless, a feverish procession follows, walks, and dances with her toward invisible arcs on which are inscribed the superb criteria of heroism, dedication, goodness.

It is the fourth movement, the Adagio Lamentoso, that Nozière gave testimony to Isadora's intense imagination and emotive depths. With forceful symbolism she is earth-mother in a dolorous plaint for the slain in battle. A striking metaphor for maternal grief, she kneels and weeps for the dead children of man, and with an immense, surging movement of torso and arms, she wrests them from the void, pressing them against her body, to shelter within her womb. The critic wrote: "Such feelings demand symphonic scope. Beyond words is the sublimity of these movements; the most moving, most profound and human homage that could have been rendered the dead."

No longer suggestive of Greek sculpture or Botticelli paintings, Isadora's arrangement of the march toward the Holy Grail from Wagner's *Parsifal* transformed her into a Wagnerian hero, "posing the eternal polemic of Dionysus and Christ, earth and heaven, darkness and light, the weight of lust, and liberation through renunciation." There was authority, subtlety, and nobility in her characterization of Kundry: "How she makes us feel the torment of doubt, the invigoration of faith, the hesitancy of anguish, the ascent toward the light." As for her *Death of Isolde* (dramatized on about four square feet of space), Nozière had reached a verbal impasse: "I give up explaining it; I bow before this marvel of intelligence . . . of the sublime artist and the creator [Wagner]."

Neither nymph nor bacchante, Isadora's art had become prouder. She was seen as a powerful sculpture, her gestures more solemn, her stances solid and her expressions intense. Criticized elsewhere for her unsatisfactory conception of the frail Isolde, Nozière questioned whether it was ever Isadora's intention to interpret the legendary princess. "It is not the heroine," Nozière conjectured, "but the very inspiration of the composer that she strives to manifest in the music. There are formidable forces of love and death in evidence here."

Music critic Louis Laloy, however, who justifiably took credit as one of the first critical voices to herald the arrival of Isadora's unusual and earnest talent, now persisted in objecting to her free adaptations from Wagner, whose music was least representational for dance purposes. Meritorious though they may be, her energetic evocations of the *Ride of the Valkyries,* the "Bacchanale" from *Tannhäuser,* or Isolde's *Love-Death,* were not works, Laloy cautioned, to become models for other artists of the dance, or replacements for classical ballets. "Isadora Duncan's dance is not, and cannot be, the whole dance."

Just as Isadora's *Blue Danube* waltz years earlier had brought ecstatic audiences to their feet, her *La Marseillaise,* since its first performance in wartime Paris in 1916 had ignited the public's fervor. Unsurpassed for its sheer theatrical power, this semi-mimed interpretation of man's eternal quest for freedom produced the *tour de force* of her career. It remained a crowd favorite whether performed in Europe, South America or the United States. Audiences wept and went wild.

Allan Ross Macdougall, friend, secretary, and biographer of Isadora, described the emotional outburst that rang through the Trocadéro in 1916 when the dancer, robed in a blood-red tunic and red shawl, mimed with "incredible intensity" the four stanzas of the French anthem: "She stood filled with patriotic fury, her left breast bare as in the Rude statue in the Arc de Triomphe which had been her inspiration . . ."

François Rude's 1836 sculpture relief in stone on the lower right quadrant of the Arc de Triomphe in Paris overwhelms in its personification of Liberty. The central figure of the *Marseillaise* herself "raises high her left arm to rally all the brave to her side. With the other hand she points her sword toward the enemy. Her legs are wide apart. Her mouth of stone shrieks as though to deafen one." An examination of the sculpture and then a closer study of the art and photographic reproductions of Isadora reveal an almost literal transfer from the physical force of the stone's gesture and its embodiment of patriotic ardor to the dancer's bodily stances and expressive demeanor.

For anti-war intellectuals and those on the political left in the United States, the dancer's overpowering effect and success in her *Marseillaise* were a severe disillusionment. Up to now she had been a symbol to them of "life lived frank and free"; they now rebuked their lady of liberty for accelerating American pro-war sentiments.

For quite different reasons, sounds of disapproval came from a small critical enclave in Paris. Isadora's dance translation of the French anthem during her 1920-21 festival once again raised the familiar dichotomous issue: the appropriateness of dancing to certain kinds of music, specifically a literary piece and none other than the supreme pride of France—the national anthem. It was an affront to the public! Tampering with the Rouget de Lisle poem to indulge choreographic whims was an impiety! One did not desecrate a glorious poem by dancing it. "Botch the works of foreign composers," she was told, "but leave their compatriot alone."

Also biased in favor of the French "soul" as alone capable of appreciating and conveying the *Marseillaise,* was Emile Mas. Generally supportive of her other undertakings, he rejected Isadora's dramatization. Her fierce stances, the unattractive facial grimaces, then her unbecomingly lively change were seen as a grievous error. She understood nothing of his anthem! Less mocking than disappointed, he described how at one point in the dance when she had not stirred, one hand was finally raised up and cupped around her ear, leaving the impression that she wanted to telephone. This *Marseillaise* was not theirs!

The excerpt that follows appeared in print after a 1920 performance of the *Marseillaise*. Incomplete, it nevertheless comes closest to being a choreographed text and provides vivid clues to the dancer's movement phrase in correlation with word and music. This choreographic description ends at the point of the galvanizing refrain, "Aux Armes, Citoyens" (To Arms, Citizens), when the entire hall breaks loose into feet stamping, hand clapping, and general commotion climaxing the dance.

LA MARSEILLAISE

ALLONS ENFANTS DE LA PATRIE

The dancer places her right foot in front and raises the right arm. Hand is wide open, fingers separated, palm facing the audience, her fixed glance is in the direction of the first balcony.

LE JOUR DE GLOIRE EST ARRIVÉ

The torso is brought forward, plexus trained on the first balcony, the mouth in the direction of the second balcony and the eyes on the rim of the theater; both arms are flung backwards, lightly raised from the body and forming an angle with it of approximately twenty-two degrees. The right foot rejoins the left foot which has not moved.

CONTRE NOUS DE LA TYRANNIE

Here the dance begins. The dancer steps off with the left foot and executes a half turn of the stage while moving to the right and seeming to hold some invisible cord: it is this "pulling" that designates the "tyranny" of which the poet de Lisle speaks.

L'ÉTENDARD SANGLANT EST LEVÉ

The dancer stops point blank in the rear center stage. She raises both arms high above her head which has been thrown backward. At this moment the spot lights hit her robe with a flaming red color.

ENTENDEZ-VOUS DANS LES CAMPAGNES

The ear is thrust toward the east and the gaze becomes strangely pained; the arm at that side is stretched out to this central point; the foot of that side readies to move.

MUGIR CES FEROCES SOLDATS

The dance begins again here and the dancer does the second half turn on stage while pushing with feet and hands against the on-rushing forces. The forcefulness of the feet is obtained by first causing the thighs, then the calves, to quiver. As for the hands, the powerful vibrations from the upper arm muscles tremble down through the entire arm, through the palms.

ILS VIENNENT JUSQUE DANS NOS BRAS

The dancer has returned to center stage. Starting first with the left arm, she slaps herself across the right arm, then, simultaneously on both arms, each with only four fingers of the opposite hand.

ARRACHER NOS FILS, NOS COMPAGNES

There are gestures of wresting, battle, struggle, resurge, and at the end, despair. The wresting on "arra," the battle on "cher nos," struggle on "fils nos," the resurge on "comp," despair on "gnes." These movements must be synchronized to produce their full effect.

Looming large on the Duncan landscape was Fernand Divoire, editor-in-chief of *L'Intransigeant,* dance critic, and author of works on theater and dance. One of the most consistent and interested of witnesses to the growth of Isadora's influence on twentieth-century theater, Divoire was devoted to "Isadorism." His published writings contain major segments on her dominant choreographies and her individual artistry, on Duncanism as an art ideology, and on the Isadorables as the fruition of an ideal vision. Commenting on Isadora's 1920-1921 Paris appearances, Divoire discerned an ever-evolving artist, surprisingly more supple and diverse, "richer of fine and fluid ease, more replenished. And the curve of her gesture each time seemed larger and bolder." Divoire next saw her in 1923. He sensed, as did others, her bodily fatigue, her spiritual frailty. He made mention of the lost happiness, the many sadnesses, and the greatness: "Have they not withered and wearied her spirit?" Through Divoire's compassionate, humane words could be heard genuine empathy from one long attracted to Isadora as a person and as an artist. The body on stage that had so captivatingly articulated beauty, grace, and strength, now registered the cumulative effect of life's multiple tragedies and thwarted dreams. (Coinciding with Isadora's appearance at the Trocadéro in May 1923 was her realization that her chaotic relationship and marriage to the Russian poet Essenin would have to be dissolved.)

Erudite, aristocratic André Levinson critiqued Isadora's concert of May 27, 1923, explaining first how repugnant it was for him to speak about the physical decay of an artist and the inevitable ravages of time, but then proceeding to do so. From the entire performance a single memory remained with him. "I see again the dancer, arms crossed as on an imaginary crucifix, torso slumped, knees bent, limbs . . . brutally apart. Then the head falls, the torso following it and the short hair brushes the floor. These two positions, while close to the grotesque, attain a painful grandeur." He referred to the Tchaikovsky and Scriabin that Isadora interpreted, as "music of the defeated and frenzied Russians. But it is the music that is necessary for Mme. Duncan; it is the score that provides the emotive shock, the psychological stimulant."

Levinson possessed a refinement and specialized knowledge of the theatrical arts that made his critical essays of the heretic Isadora stand in class by themselves. On record in *Comoedia, Les Nouvelles Littéraires,* and in many published volumes are his contributions distinguished for their precise detailing of Isadora's gesture in its physical character and subtleties of expression, in its mimetic clarity and persuasive manner of projection. But his nineteenth-century elitist sensibility found much to challenge in "the intrinsic value of her reform." He seriously questioned her claim that through the unrestricted movements of the body lay endless paths to one's identity and individuality. With his rational criticism, the sophisticated Levinson intellectualized deeper resentments toward her: her dance vocabulary was too simple, she subjugated the dance to music, she lacked formal elements in her dance, and—the source of blatant irritation to him— she dared to reject the time-honored classic traditions and scorn a distinguished esthetic order, a most venerable discipline. Ultimately, he was certain that Isadora's "negation of all doctrine" would doom her role as evangelist. All the more was his wonderment over the "psychic contagion" by which the barefoot dancer was able to win the "enthusiasm of an immense public."

There was obvious chagrin when Levinson charged Isadora with wrenching theatrical dance out of the gentle and caring hands of the privileged few, democratizing it through her open, revolutionary channels. Her dance, he contended, would release the floodgates of dilettantism and imitation. Levinson could not conceal his private dismay and frustration that the brilliant and royal art of ballet that he loved, his sacred and "golden art," his personal fantasyland, had been invaded, injured, and changed by the woman who, for the integrity of her ideals, "braved all, risked all," and who, "by a miracle of will and faith . . . had imprinted her seal on a whole epoch." How to explain the complacency, the impotence of ballet officialdom in not launching a counteroffensive to Isadora's esthetic onslaught? Almost sheepishly, André Levinson surmised that they, too, had been "captivated by the glowing candor of the intrepid amazon."

Levison did not acknowledge Isadora's dance as a viable art form. His analyses were thoughtful, forthright, penetrating, and beautifully written. In essence, he appreciated her negatively, but for her convictions, her sovereign presence, and her effect on the world's perception of dance, his admiration was boundless.

These men of letters, composers, dramatists, opera and theater critics, poets, and journalists were prominent chroniclers of their time. Out of their own diversities of temperament and esthetic proclivities they presented the many facets of Isadora Duncan, all somehow valid and appropriate for the complex, larger-than-life persona and her individual imprint on a culture in transition. Their words alone, in this instance, have become the conservators of one unique being's creative existence. Collectively, their writings constitute the principal archive of Isadora's twenty-five-year effort to convert the consciousness of the world to the dance as art.

Elizabeth Francis (essay date 1994)

SOURCE: "From Event to Monument: Modernism, Feminism and Isadora Duncan," in *American Studies,* Vol. 35, No. 1, Spring, 1994, pp. 25-45.

[*In the following essay, Francis examines the ways in which Duncan contributed, through her theories about the female body in motion, to women's liberation and the modernist temperament.*]

Many intellectuals and artists who saw Isadora Duncan dance came away believing they had experienced the liberation they longed for in their hopes and dreams for the twentieth century. Duncan returned to the Greek emphasis on balancing ecstasy and harmony and made it "excitingly modern," as one critic put it. Her performances from 1908 and throughout the 1910s excited the imagination of American intellectuals who sought to tear down the barriers of class and sex in order to see their philosophies reflected in a praxis of art and life. Max Eastman, editor of the *Masses,* wrote, "She was an event not only in art, but in the history of life." With their qualities of immediacy and yet recognizable significance, events crystallize moments of consciousness formation—they shock the viewer into a new recognition of identity. Sloughing off the old, embracing the new, Duncan's dances were events through which her viewers recognized themselves as modern. They also were shocking, because Duncan performed the female body differently in a period when the transformation of womanhood was both a source of anxiety and a central element of radical theories of liberation. In this sense, Duncan was an event in the history of women's participation in modernism.

Out of the twentieth century's fragmentation of identity and the division of labor and play into ever smaller pieces, Duncan suggested the possibility of wholeness—the resolution of fundamental dualisms between body and mind, self and world, the individual and social collectivity. She accomplished this resolution through a different signification of the body *as* female. The heavy layers of Victorian clothing were gone. "She ripped off all the corsets and let herself go," as one admirer described the sense of liberation from the prohibition and repression associated with female bodies. Duncan was excitingly modern because she changed woman's place in the artistic process, transforming it from the grounds for representation to an agent *of* representation. In doing so, Duncan set into motion a series of dialectical relations that characterized modernism in the first decades of the century, thereby revealing the gendered dimension of that dialectic. For a variety of reasons, Duncan's career reached an impasse in the twenties. This impasse was emblematic of the pessimism and alienation among intellectuals after World War I. While Duncan established a new relation of women to artistic production by using her body as both the medium and the agent of representation, as Duncan grew older (she died at 50 in 1927), the signs of her body's aging became correspondingly more noticeable signifiers of her decline. Duncan herself used a divisive rhetoric of race and nation to attack the changes in modern culture that increasingly marginalized her. The dialectical interplay of the event of Duncan shifted to a reifying rhetoric that froze Duncan into a monument. By interpreting this shift, we can see the contradictions in the desire for wholeness among cultural radicals after the war and the effects these contradictions had on the perception of Duncan as an artist, a woman and a modernist. Duncan's career thus reveals both the connections and the tensions between feminism and modernism in the early twentieth century.

THE EVENT OF ISADORA DUNCAN

"Everything must be undone," Duncan wrote about 1910, playing on the metaphor of loosening the bonds of clothing to express her critique of dominant aesthetics in dance. Unwrapping the garb of culture from her body, Duncan took off shoes, stockings, and corset, all signifiers of constraints on the female body and its expressive potential. Duncan danced in a sheer, short tunic, secured at the breast and hips, and lined with a leotard. She believed that her tunic, uncorseted form and bare feet replaced constraint with unity and fusion as the basis for beauty. "It has never dawned on me to swathe myself in hampering garments or to bind my limbs and drape my throat, for am I not striving to fuse soul and body in one unified image of beauty?" she asked in the early 1900s. In its signification of transparency, the tunic let the female body be perceived as a unified whole. Her costume also became an emblem of women's emancipation, a radical performance of a woman's body freed from the binding and stifling layers of culture. In contrast to manipulating fashion and appearance to subvert the static perception of gender difference, Duncan sought to reveal an essential body beneath the surface of culture and to mold culture to fit that body. Promoting a universal image of womanhood, Duncan did not use costume as a form of fashion but as a timeless image that placed her outside the particular and various histories of womanhood.

In her appeal to universality and timelessness, however, Duncan sought to blur the static image of womanhood into a dynamic, moving performance. Duncan's "everything" was undone through her transformation of the medium of dance. At a Duncan performance, the stage design was simple—a backdrop of long, blue-gray curtains, a carpet and diffuse lighting. When Duncan appeared unassumingly from the shadowy corners of the stage, audiences saw a form of dancing quite different from the rigid commonplaces of the ballet of the period and the displays of soubrettes at popular revues. Her movements magnified those of everyday life—runs, walks and skips—through which Duncan expressed an unmechanical relation to the world. Duncan also transgressed aesthetic boundaries by performing not to conventional dance music, but to Gluck and Wagner operas, Tchaikovsky and Beethoven symphonies and Chopin concertos. Duncan expressed her dismantling of performance conventions polemically as a rejection of dance altogether. Duncan often and vehemently rejected the cultural connotations of being a dancer, "I hate dancing. I am an expressioniste of beauty. I use my body as my medium, just as the writer uses his words. Do not call me a dancer."

Duncan's transformation of dance was rooted in her struggle to disarm the power of civilization to dominate and control the body. In using her body as a medium, rather than presenting the female body as something to be assimilated and controlled through the vision of others, Duncan placed the body's development at the center of her social critique. Many radical thinkers had argued in the nineteenth century that civilization crippled rather than encouraged individuals to develop, and Duncan extended that argument by claiming that the individual would find in the body the sources of unity and harmony to counteract the negative aspects of civilization. Duncan tells us in her autobiography that early in her career, she stood for hours in front of a mirror and finally discovered the origin of movement within her body, at the solar plexus, rather than from an exterior source. "I was seeking and finally discovered the central spring of all movement, the crater of motor power, the unity from which all diversities of movements are born, the mirror of vision for the creation of the dance." From this central place, movement radiated outward, connecting self and world.

Duncan was an event because her performances suggested—some even said made possible—the experience of coherence and totality. She theorized the coherent self as a way to lighten the pressures of modern life in the first decades of the twentieth century. Coherence meant reuniting the body and the mind, doing away with the split between nature and civilization, and restoring an embodied self lost in the modern world. Duncan also evoked the desire for oneness and wholeness characteristic of appeals to totality. In her 1909 essay, **"Movement is Life,"** Duncan wrote,

> With the first conception of a conscience, man became self-conscious, lost the natural movements of the body; today in the light of intelligence gained through years of civilization, it is essential that he consciously seek what he has unconsciously lost.

Civilization repressed the consciousness of the body, but it was only through civilization—and not an attempt to return to the primitive—that the expressive body could be rediscovered. The individual would rediscover an embodied relation to the world through sense—nerves, muscles and perception—but the senses had to be trained. Duncan theorized that if one was trained to make the most of this encounter with the world, then one also had the means to resist the moral and social prohibitions that dominate the body. In theorizing dance as a way to achieve oneness in a primary and uncorrupted relation to the world, Duncan posed her

interpretation of Greek civilization against the censorship and constraints with which she associated Victorianism. Duncan thus overturned a central tenet of the nineteenth-century world view by arguing that the body must not *be* civilized, but rather that the body *was* the source of civilization. Thus, the body as the medium for self-expression liberated moderns to make and mold civilization, rather than submitting to civilization and its mechanisms of repression.

The shift from repression to self-expression was part of the discourse of personal and social transformation among intellectuals in the early twentieth century. Modernists marked their distance from the Victorian world in their embrace of self-expression. While Duncan appealed to a broad audience at the height of her career in the early 1910s, her performances and her persona had special meaning for cultural radicals in America beyond 1908, because they sought to create a coherent ethos of artistic practice, social relationships and political beliefs. Anxious critics saw fragmentation and disorder in the new portrayals of reality in literature and art but many modernists actually desired wholeness in their insistent demands for cultural transformation. At the core of the modernist appeal to wholeness before the war was a desire for both boundlessness and integration.

Cultural radical Floyd Dell shared these desires for collective and personal transformation, and he understood Duncan's ability to represent this dream through a new aesthetic medium: the body itself. He wrote in 1916,

> A strange and dark century, the nineteenth! . . . When I think that if I had lived and died in the darkness of that century I should never have seen with these eyes the beauty and terror of the human body, I am glad of the daylight of my own time. It is not enough to throw God from his pedestal and dream of superman and the co-operative commonwealth: one must have *seen* Isadora Duncan to die happy.

In Dell's rhetoric of light and vision, Duncan dispelled the "darkness" of the nineteenth century. Yet she is not one of the philosophers of the metaphysical breakdown that shaped modern consciousness; she *embodies* those ideas. Through the shock of "seeing" Duncan's body, Dell recognized himself as modern, albeit with a utopian's sunny view of the twentieth century.

But Duncan's emphasis on liberating the body was shot through with ambivalence about the relationship between modernization and modernity. This ambivalence was shared by many cultural radicals who believed that the development of capitalism had established the preconditions for a classless society and sexual equality, but who found themselves rebelling from the iron cage of modernity, especially from the monotony and dullness of all things bourgeois. Since the late nineteenth century in America, intellectuals had worried over how modernization affected the body and the mind; they sought to loosen the bonds of rationalization and repression and to search for self-fulfillment. Duncan played upon but did not resolve this ambivalence because she believed that the bonds tying the individual to modernity not only could be loosened but that they could be escaped altogether. Her belief in the essential integrity of the body did not acknowledge the body's mediation by the machines of capitalism, either the assembly lines of industry or the telephones, automobiles and cameras of consumer culture.

Instead, Duncan laid claim to the possibility of self-fulfillment and a creative and imaginative space in the machine age by evoking a dialectic between the self and the world. For Duncan, an inner self had to be discovered before the world could be reconstructed. "We do not know how to get down to the depths, to lose ourselves in an inner self, how to develop our visions into the harmonies that attend our dreams. . . . We are always in paroxysms." Those who met Duncan consistently point out that she was calm and self-possessed; she moved with a slow grace, and her voice was melodious and soothing. Duncan's response to modernization was to emphasize depth and harmony to counteract the corrosive effects of an increasingly accelerated and alienated twentieth-century world, what she called "strident, clamorous dissonance." Duncan's aim was to slow things down, to calm the paroxysms of modern life in the first two decades of the twentieth century.

Inner harmony was one way to break free from the constraints of the social world, but it led to a contradictory way of thinking about the interrelations of self and world. Duncan often said her motto was "*sans limites*." The desire to be both unified and without limits—both coherent in self and encompassing the world—was for Duncan the "magnetic center" that redefined her relation to self, world and expression. "Often I thought to myself, what a mistake to call me a dancer—I am the magnetic centre to convey the emotional expression of the Orchestra." The experience Duncan sought to evoke as the center of movement and music was itself contradictory: her body as a medium for expression led away from the centered self. This contradiction also was rooted in a central dilemma among cultural radicals: how to bridge the demand for self-expression within a social movement that included socialism, feminism, and other collective demands for rights.

Duncan appeared to bridge that tension between individualism and collectivity in her performances. She wanted movement to suggest not individual expression but a collective social presence. Duncan's essays claim over and over that she meant to play upon the individual's access to harmony, but also to make the audience aware of itself as a collective presence reflected in the movements on stage, "call and response, bound endlessly in one cadence." Her performances sought to break down the barriers of spectacle and bind the audience and the performer together into a collective event. Like Walt Whitman, whose *Leaves of Grass* she

carried with her everywhere, Duncan wanted her body to "contain multitudes." She expressed collectivity by evoking the impression of a moving chorus rather than the solitary dancer on a spare stage. She claimed, "I have never once danced a solo." Duncan's medium was thus her body, but her theory of expression was not reducible to the body. In suggesting the chorus, she pointed to an arena outside the coherent, solitary self. Her performances also suggested an allegory of revolution, and they could be likened to the dialectical model for socialism and history. Marxist editor Michael Gold wrote in 1929, "She prophesied the future, when in a free society there will be neither money nor classes, and men will seem like gods, when the body and mind will form a radiant unity. Her own mind and body approached that unity."

In evoking collectivity and a socialist body politic, Duncan distanced herself from individual artistic interpretation, equating her own persona with what she believed were universal feelings and drives. Mabel Dodge Luhan, Duncan's friend and backer during her tours in New York, suggested in her memoirs, "[T]his life she let loose up through her body was not good or bad but merely undifferentiated and voluminous." Duncan called this "multiple oneness," and theorized movement as a social force, when she writes:

> In order to realise these dreams, a single gesture of appeal will be able to evoke a thousand extended arms, a single head tossed back will represent a bacchantic tumult. . . . It seems to me that in this music is concentrated the . . . whole cry of desire in the world. . . . I repeat, I do not fulfill it, I only indicate it.

Duncan's career was constructed around fanning the flame of "desire in the world."

Duncan fanned the flame particularly through her challenge to the categories and conventions of gender. She evoked wholeness and unity as a woman at one with her body through dance. She was effective because women had been associated with the splits, fragmentation and divisions of modernity. Duncan's ideas slide back and forth between the universality of woman and her sense of herself as unique, as a woman apart. This slippery relation produced the dialectical relations between self and world, individuality and collectivity, civilization and nature that surface in her theories. Her performances were powerful because the image of woman as emblem for a transformed modern world functioned on both sides of the dualisms. In this, she argued that she acted as a mirror for others: "Nietzsche says, 'Woman is a mirror,' and I have only reflected and reacted to the people and forces that have seized me." But as Duncan also suggests, the process of mirroring was rooted in the belief that she was capable of turning the mirror out upon the audience and projecting an image outside of history by emphasizing her own difference. The ancient Greek motifs in her costume and in her movements signified that outsiderness in their timeless, abstract quality. As Luhan wrote, "She was able to project her vision upon the ether, and others, then, saw as she did." Duncan both sought a unified image of woman, which she saw in the strong stances of the classical statues she imitated, and exposed the extent to which contemporary women had been denied that unity in her critique of marriage and other social institutions. A central aspect of Duncan's ability to fan the flame of desire in the world, then, was to "dance the freedom of woman."

The discourse of women's emancipation thus is central to understanding Duncan's cultural impact. Tied to the body and subjectivity, women's emancipation was the basis for a new civilization, not a civilizing influence. Duncan's was a heroic theory meant to free women from weakness, dependence, and deformity. In Duncan's critique, women had the most to gain from eradicating the prohibitions associated with Victorianism. Her preeminent concern was with women's control over their bodies as the foundation for expression. She thus opposed marriage, encouraged open sexual expression, and believed in free motherhood. Duncan's outspoken critique of marriage and her emancipated lifestyle, however, stood in tension with her view of gender and aesthetics. While she advocated sexual equality and sexual expression in the social realm, Duncan firmly rejected sexuality as a mode of expression in performance, arguing that wholeness and unity could only be experienced when audiences stopped eroticizing the female performer. In representing the female body as a source of wholeness rather than the site of fragmentation, Duncan allied women's emancipation to central ideas of modernism.

Duncan's lecture **"The Dance of the Future,"** which was written in the early 1900s, allows us to look at how Duncan's view of modernity worked with a new definition of womanhood. Duncan composed this essay as a response to critics who attacked the legitimacy of Duncan's redefinition of dance. The rhetoric of the lecture is significant. After moving through two stances that establish the narrator as a figure to be looked at, Duncan reverses that relation, speaking as she herself boldly looks out upon her audience. She ends the speech with a peroration on the ability of woman to dance themselves rather than assigned roles in the trite and eroticized dance repertoire. "She will dance not in the form of nymph, nor fairy, nor coquette, but in the form of woman in her greatest and purest expression."

Duncan separated her own stance as an artist from the sexuality of female performance through the appeal to a seemingly timeless, abstract hellenism. In doing so, she sought to dismantle the twin discourses that structured the perception of women as hopelessly split between body and mind, intelligence and animality. "She will dance the body emerging again from centuries of civilized forgetfulness, emerging not in the nudity of primitive man, but in a new nakedness, no longer at war with spirituality and intelligence, but joining with them in a glorious harmony." For Duncan, the female body did not represent civilization, but *was* its source: "the highest

intelligence in the freest body!" Duncan's superlatives overturned the characterization of women as fundamentally weak and at war with their dual natures. Duncan's fusion of a "new nakedness" from her selective reading of the split between the primitive and the civilized was a central move in the modernist vision of wholeness.

Duncan's emphasis on the wholeness and unity of her body stands in stark contrast to the depiction of nudity at what is usually considered the inception of modernism in the United States, the Armory Show of 1913. Marcel Duchamp's painting, *Nude Descending a Staircase,* which became the unofficial emblem of the show, used the conventions of the nude to demonstrate how fragmentation and multiple points of view actually generated a more complete configuration of reality. In contrast to representations of modern life through fragmented images of the female body, Duncan turned such a schema on its head; she used her body to present an image of the whole. Duncan represents the moment when woman breaks free of her status as the sexual ground for modernist representation.

Significantly, most cultural radicals did not talk about the inspiration that they took away from Duncan's performances in terms of an expressive sexuality—even though liberating sex from the repression associated with Victorianism was a pervasive discourse of the period. Rather, Duncan set into motion another dialectical relation: that of women and the perception of gender difference. In fact, many critics emphasized that Duncan's performances were freed from a relation to sex, a freedom they characterized as androgynous. Carl Van Vechten wrote after seeing her perform in New York, "She called her art the renaissance of the Greek ideal but there was something modern about it, pagan though it might be in quality. Always it was pure and sexless . . . always abstract emotion has guided her interpretations." By evoking ancient statues, Duncan had shifted the emphasis from the female body parts eroticized in her own time to a different image. "Imagine for yourself a woman with a body that suggests the perfection of Greek sculpture, without the slightest resemblance to the modern French figure. . . . Straight, slender as a sapling, robust hips, with legs at once feminine and virile, bust fragile," a French critic wrote. Duncan did not resemble the "modern French figure" because the gaze of the viewer shifted from her bust to her powerful legs. To prove the artistic stature of Duncan's work and to undermine the association of Duncan's performances with her famed lifestyle of "free love," her conductor, Martin Shaw, wrote, "There was no sex appeal in Isadora's dancing."

Duncan's challenge to gender difference, "her sexlessness," opened up more avenues of interpreting the significance of her work, and reviews of her performances are filled with hyperbole and metaphor. Many cultural radicals saw her performances as moving and visual enactments of theories of freedom and revolution. But in doing so, Duncan's body itself became a metaphor. Painter and sketch artist John Sloan was one of many American artists breaking away from the techniques and subjects of academic, genteel art and moving toward representing life as they found it—on the streets and from the rooftops of immigrant neighborhoods—with a style to depict both the beauty in everyday life and the injustice they saw all around them. Duncan was a special subject for Sloan's painting because she helped him to see in aesthetic terms a new iconography of the body different from both mannered portraits of society women and academic conceptions of the nude. Sloan's 1911 painting of Duncan performing on a darkened stage attempted to capture the event of Duncan in paint. Sloan's broad strokes arrest Duncan in a lyrical moment. Her body is figured with head back and arm flung wide with the fluttering tunic draped lightly and transparently over her body. But as he wrote in 1911,

> Isadora as she appears on that big simple stage seems like *all* womanhood—she looms big as the mother of the race. A heavy solid figure, large columnar legs, a solid high belly, breasts not too full and her head seems to be no more important than it should to give the body the chief place.

Sloan used the rhetoric of universality and a eugenic view of civilization to render Duncan back into the ground for a modernist point of view, an object of representation.

Despite Duncan's ability to disrupt the association of eroticism with the female body, the attempts by cultural radicals to make Duncan into a beacon of feminism and emancipation served to disarm the power of Duncan's intervention. Floyd Dell, for example, recognized himself *as* modern in seeing Duncan's dancing body. But when he wrote about Duncan as a feminist, he turned attention away from Duncan's disruption of conventions of representing the body as itself a feminist act. He writes:

> That women should make so much fuss about getting the vote, or that they should so excite themselves over the prospect of working for wages, will appear incomprehensible to many people who have a proper regard for art, for literature, and for the graces of social intercourse.

Duncan, for him, represented the leap from political and social agitation to the realm of "truth" and "beauty." "It is only when the woman's movement is seen broadly . . . that there comes the realization that here is a cause . . . from which sincere lovers of truth and beauty have nothing really to fear." To see the women's movement "broadly" for Dell meant to rewrite its history from its roots in the nineteenth century to the re-orientation of American culture signified by the modern movement in art, literature, and philosophy. In doing so, Dell assimilates feminism into modernism. Dell quotes **"The Dance of the Future,"** to make this point, finally concluding that "In any case, it is to the body that one looks

for the Magna Charta of feminism." Duncan, then, was writing one of the founding texts of feminism with her body; she was a hero, a "world-builder" in her encouragement of women to be that "self-sufficient, broadly imaginative and healthy-minded creature upon whom we have set our masculine desire." While Duncan turned her gaze to the audience and redefined the terms upon which women would inhabit their bodies and thus change the world rhetorically in **"Dance of the Future,"** Dell's appropriation of Duncan's essay reinscribes her performance of womanhood within the terms of masculine desire. In doing so, he re-established her as no threat to those who have a "proper regard for literature and art."

Max Eastman also brought his desire to bear upon his assessment of Duncan. In motion, Duncan was powerful. When she left the stage, however, her stature was literally diminished, he writes:

> She was not of heroic size, as you expected after seeing her on the stage, and her body, though comely in a mellow way, was not excitingly beautiful. She had in supreme degree only the powers of expression and motion. Thus her physical presence in private life did not make up, as an Amazon's should, for a certain overriding force in her—a sort of didactic, almost blue-stocking assertiveness. . . . She was the most advanced outpost of the movement for woman's emancipation. Her position was not too advanced for me—that is not what I am trying to say. But it was an intellectual position; she was invading a field where serious thinking had been done and some was still to do.

Again, Duncan's claim for women's emancipation diverted Eastman's admiration and unleashed a torrent of pejorative labels associated with feminism. Moreover, as soon as Eastman placed Duncan on a frontier of women's emancipation, he reintroduced the split between thinking and the body. Her body was a liberating force, but she could not be taken seriously when she staked out an intellectual position.

Consideration of Duncan thus poses the problem of feminism in relation to the modernist quest for wholeness. Duncan's mode of representing the body appealed to the modernist ideology that sought liberation from social bonds, including those of gender, but modernists were also concerned with the creation of new ideals to counteract the negative aspects of modernity. As in Sloan's painting, the impulse to erase and redraw cultural and aesthetic boundaries met in the moment of watching Duncan perform. The problem that surfaces in the modernist impulse expressed by such cultural radicals as Dell, Eastman, Sloan and others is that Duncan's body was mediated by such conventional metaphors as youth, joy, and beauty and as a feminist she was labeled a bluestocking, Amazon, and intellectual invader in order to assert or diminish her power as a women in modernism.

Duncan acted as a metonymy for utopian aspirations by using her body to depict a whole, unified world, yet she could not sustain this metonymic relation. Duncan began to be recognized not as a dynamic event, but as a monument—an immobile allusion to a lost moment of freedom. Her appeal to totality was divorced from the moment of performance and began to be expressed in a shrill nationalism and attack on popular culture. Just as a monument stands for an abstract thing called the past, the discourse of monumentality separated Duncan from the present moment of transformation.

THE MONUMENT OF ISADORA DUNCAN

The end of Duncan's career in the 1920s, indeed, vividly demonstrates and exposes the contradictions in the modernist quest for wholeness and their view of a unified culture. The visual apprehension of Duncan's performing body as the unity of a new definition of womanhood and utopian aspirations for the twentieth century fragmented as Duncan herself confronted difference and change in modern culture. Duncan saw a widening split between her theory of a whole civilization and elements of popular culture influenced by African-American forms. From the start, Duncan's ideas about civilization had embedded racial theories of evolution that situated the "new" woman in a white, hellenic tradition. She writes in **"The Dance of the Future,"**

> It is not only a question of true art, it is a question of race, of the development of the female sex to beauty and health, of the return to the original strength and to natural movements of woman's body. It is a question of the development of perfect mothers and birth of healthy and beautiful children.

Duncan's eugenic view was at the root of her belief that the emancipated body would allow women to overcome weakness and dependence. Moreover, Duncan's ideas about harmony required that difference dissolve into "multiple oneness."

While Duncan used a rhetoric of universality in her earlier essays, the implications of her division between the "primitive" and the "civilized" became more disturbing and forceful in her manifestos written in the twenties. Her rejection of the conventions of dance took a new polemical turn when she saw how pervasive the culture of popular dances had become in America in the early twenties. She also began to have qualms about her ability to draw an audience when dance crazes were sweeping the country and capturing the imagination of young Americans. Duncan used a divisive racial rhetoric to criticize the "primitivism" of popular dances and music influenced by African-Americans. In attacking popular dances as primitive, not civilized, her rhetoric re-associated dance with race and sexuality. Her later essays also connected her ideas about women to her fear that her conception of dance was being contaminated by popular expression. Her own rhetoric took on a moral, civilizing overtone when she wrote in 1927,

> If, twenty years ago, when I first pleaded with America to adopt my school and my theories of dancing in all the public schools, they had acceded to my request, this deplorable modern dancing, which has its roots in the ceremonies of African primitives, could never have become dominant. It is extraordinary that mothers who would be intensely shocked if their daughters should indulge in a real orgy . . . will look on with smiling complacency at their daughters indulging in licentious contortions upon a dance floor, before their very eyes.

Duncan's protest reasserted the very dualisms she earlier had sought to undo: popular dancing was merely sexual for her. Poet Claude McKay made this clear in describing an argument he had with Duncan in her studio in Nice. "Isadora was . . . severe on Negro dancing and its imitations and derivations. She had no real appreciation of primitive folk dancing, either from an esthetic or an ethnic point of view." Duncan's belief in a utopian philosophy of the integration of art and life was in tension with what she saw as the primitive allure of popular culture.

At the same time, Duncan saw that sexuality, not women's control of their bodies, had become central to the discourse of modern culture in the twenties, but she displaced that distinction onto her rejection of "primitivism." Her emphasis on the licentiousness of popular culture reiterated the division between primitivism and civilization. To convey the perils of an identification between dance and sexuality for young women, she writes:

> A seemingly modest young girl would not think of addressing a young man in lines or spoken phrases which were indecent and yet the same girl will arise and dance these phrases with him in such dances as the Charleston and Black Bottom, while a negro orchestra is playing *Shake that thing!*

Popular culture itself destabilized the essentialized, ideal form Duncan had sought to rejuvenate in her interpretation of the ancient Greeks. The racial signifiers of jazz—the negro orchestra—and popular dances—the Black Bottom—replaced the image of woman as the universal figures in Duncan's rhetoric, but her allusions were highly negative. While her image of the female body freed from its relation to sex and to social constraint had been dynamic and radical, the more this emphasis was displaced in her later rhetoric, the more static her idea of womanhood became.

Further changing her rhetoric of universality, Duncan also began to use nationalism to express her opposition to the direction of youth culture. She wrote in her 1927 autobiography,

> It seems to me monstrous that any one should believe that the Jazz rhythm expresses America. Jazz rhythm expresses the primitive savage. America's music would be something different. . . .

America will be expressed in some Titanic music that will shape its chaos to harmony, and long-legged, shining boys and girls will dance to this music, not the tottering, ape-like convulsions of the Charleston.

Popular dances shook Duncan's philosophy to the core: they challenged Duncan's story of discovering the "motor" of dance in her body at the solar plexus, where the interior center expressed exterior harmony. Instead, popular dances became cultural machines that openly asserted sexuality and accelerated its expression. For all of their loosening of constraint in an expanding consumer culture, they subverted Duncan's emphasis on dance as a productive, generative philosophy of life. For Duncan, popular dances were not universal and had no pretense toward a totality of art and life.

In changing her rhetoric to emphasize her critique of popular culture, Duncan's own self-presentation shifted. The dialectic of subjectivity in **"Dance of the Future"**—the movement from a figure to be looked at to the narrator who looks—hardened into a concrete, stable narrative in such later essays as **"I See America Dancing"** and in *My Life*. Not only did Duncan see herself in a battle with popular culture, she herself was attacked during her performances and in the press for her own mode of displaying the body and her lifestyle on her last tour of the United States in 1922-23. In response, Duncan resorted to a nationalist discourse of identity. She began to tell a story about her own origins as an American often, in essays, speeches and in her autobiography, over and against an oppositional culture. She made herself into a symbol of America but asserted that it was an Anglo-Saxon image, emphatically not "primitive," not African. Duncan began to think of herself as a heroic American at the same time that she felt doomed to exile by its dominant culture, and the story produced a stable identity for Duncan in a sea of cultural contention. Her posture became more and more that of a demagogue, her stance rigid with an ideological notion of America as she denounced materialism and prudery.

Cultural radicals responded in kind: they built rhetorical monuments to Duncan that gestured toward a utopian lost moment but that were not grounded in the conditions of Duncan's career in the changing culture. As if to corroborate Duncan's movement from an abstract collectivity to a rigid Americanism, many writers and artists claimed that Duncan was symbolic of America, and that American ideals would be exhibited by American bodies. Max Eastman wrote, "All the bare-legged girls, and the poised and natural girls with strong muscles, and strong free steps wherever they go—the girls that redeem America and make it worth while to have founded a new world, no matter how badly it was done—they all owe more to Isadora Duncan than to any other person." The shift in rhetoric from the transformative event of Duncan to the monumental Duncan thus is central to the interpretation of Duncan's ideas about the expressive body, her role as an artist and to the historical assessment of gender in modernism.

In this context, the division between being a subject—Duncan's control over the process of being both an artist and a woman—and an object of representation—how others described, photographed, and drew Duncan—asserted itself powerfully in the twenties. This division, however, was channeled metaphorically into the perception that Duncan had aged, a convenient discourse but one that had everything to do with a generation's anxiety over the failure of a cultural idea. As Duncan entered middle age, she no longer signified an artistic, philosophical, cultural unity to others: instead, her body got in the way of the visual apprehension of her ideas. Critic Andre Levinson wrote in 1929,

> The art of Isadora Duncan had aged with her. Those who had not seen her when she was twenty had not seen her. It was at the Trocadero, in May of 1923, that these inexorable ravages were apparent to me for the last time. . . . How I remember from the upright and noble carriage of her small head, to the torso of a robust amazon. . . . Yesterday, tortured, I sought those traits in her heavy face, the nape of her neck, and her massive thighs, revealed by an overly short tunic. . . . The arms, the wrists had lost their suppleness. . . . [A] single memory stays with me. I see the dancer, again with arms crucified as on an imaginary cross, the body weighed down, knees bent, legs broadly, brutally split apart. Then the head rolls back, the chest follows and the short head of hair sweeps the floor.

The stream of metaphors that Duncan's performances had generated in the 1910s stopped abruptly in the 1920s. Her tunic no longer signified transparency and sexlessness, and her body referred to nothing but itself. Rather than as symbolic of abstract concepts such as freedom, unity, nobility, or images drawn from "nature," Duncan was described in terms of her bodily parts: legs, breast and hair. Modernists could not watch her without remembering what they had seen years before in her performances, and they could not brook the comparison. To many, Duncan had become monstrous.

But in their desire to hold onto the possibility of cultural transformation, even though it no longer could be produced through the event of Duncan, her intellectual companions used militaristic as well as utopian imagery in their writing about her. Using his memory of Duncan to explain his own cultural crusade against "puritanism," Eastman cast Duncan in the mold of a militant hero in battle armor, in contrast to the fluidity of the transparent, silky tunics in earlier descriptions. He writes:

> America fighting the battle against Americanism—that was Isadora. From that battle incomparable things are to come—things that will startle and teach the world. And Isadora led the way into the fight all alone, with her naked and strong body and her bold character, beautiful as an Amazon. If America triumphs over itself—over its cheap greed and prudery, its intellectual and moral cowardice, it prurient puerile senility—if America

triumphs over that, Isadora Duncan will be sculptured in bronze at the gate of the Temple of Man in the new day that will dawn.

Even as Eastman built a monument to Duncan's struggle against social constraint, the complexities of her ideas and her performances, not just her polemical posturing, were lost. The image of Duncan as a statue occurred frequently in tributes to her, for example, by a gushing admirer in 1920: "No man who lives is great enough to build a permanent monument to you."

Duncan grew impatient with those who wanted to memorialize her while she was engaged in an ongoing struggle. She said in 1921, "I know you will put up a monument to me fifty years after my death, but what good will that be? I will then be far away from the agony and struggle and unable to give you a great school and a great idea that you cannot understand or appreciate." Making Duncan into a monument was an ideological move that distanced Duncan from an ongoing cultural process and it was a move that was easily codified. Duncan was substituted for that other ideological emblem of freedom, the Statue of Liberty. Victor Seroff, Duncan's companion at the end of her life, claimed, "The time will come when freedom-loving Americans will throw the Statue of Liberty, that symbol of so-called freedom, into the sea, and raise in its place a statue of Isadora Duncan, who was the personification of true freedom and who called for the brotherhood of nations." Eastman makes the association even more boldly: "She looked like a statue of real liberty." The appeal to a national symbol shifted Duncan from an abstract dialectical notion of self to a concrete, stable one as an "American."

This appeal to a national symbol further separated Duncan's project from a younger generation of modernists who found little to value in Duncan's experiment for their own struggles for self-expression. Margaret Anderson, editor of the *Little Review,* castigated Duncan's performance because she saw in it both a frightening nationalism and a sentimental portrayal of the body. Anderson turned her experience of seeing Duncan perform into an opportunity to express how her idea of art differed from Duncan's. She used the metaphor of monument-building to establish her critique of sentimentality: "You must not insist to us that Isadora Duncan is an artist. This generation can't be fed on any such stuff. We are tired of that kind of loose valuation. . . . Isadora Duncan, as you will know after seeing her once, is a . . . monument of undirected adolescent vision, an ingrained sentimentalist."

CONCLUSION: THE SCARF

Others, however, remembered the significance of Duncan's transformation of gender and the conventions of representation, her stance as both an artist and a liberator. For example, Janet Flanner, who wrote cultural criticism for the *New Yorker* and paid particular attention to the participation of women in modernist culture, liked Duncan's performances during her later career. Flanner saw the tension between aging and Duncan's aesthetic project, but believed that modernists such as Levinson saw failure in the midst of their own anxiety over the fate of an artist's career. In Flanner's view, the cultural memory of Duncan neutralized her explosive, uncomfortable presence that had opened a trail for women's artistic expression. "Only Isadora, animator of all these forces, had become obscure. Only she, with her heroic sculptural movements, had dropped by the wayside, where she lay inert like one of those beautiful battered pagan tombs. . . ."

The reification of Duncan from an event significant to the history of women in modernism into a sentimental monument to a lost moment for cultural radicals can be seen clearly in assessments of Duncan's death. In 1942, Eastman wrote about his ambivalence about Duncan as a hero of emancipation. "As an aging woman, she needed a truer and more austere wisdom than she had," he wrote. "She could not live on gestures any longer. . . . If the scarf had really been given life by her dance, it could not have acted more loyally." The scarf that Eastman refers to is the one that broke Duncan's neck when it wrapped around the wheel of a Bugatti sports car in southern France in 1927. While the cruelty of Eastman's statement denied Duncan's humanity and his friendship for her, his statement also referred to Duncan as an image and a character, a symbol of "Isadora Duncan" in a web of ideas about the meaning of cultural intervention in American life in the 1910s and 1920s. The scarf acted loyally to the creation of Duncan into a monument, not to Duncan as an ongoing event. The scarf fluttered gaily in the wind, dropped into the spinning wheel, was pulled tight. Dialectical disorder and fluidity in a moment of abandon was pulled tight into a line of separation in a dualistic framework. For Eastman, then, Duncan was killed by her own contradictions. The ideas that Duncan depicted through her body were worthy of expression for most moderns—oppression and freedom, the desire for oneness—but casting the body into a statue reified her ideas, and has immobilized our perception of Isadora Duncan by making her a legend, outside of history, obscure and inert.

Melissa Ragona (essay date 1994)

SOURCE: "Ecstasy, Primitivism, Modernity: Isadora Duncan and Mary Wigman," in *American Studies,* Vol. 35, No. 1, Spring, 1994, pp. 47-64.

[*In the following essay, Ragona explains Duncan's and Wigman's use of Nietzche's "Dionysian ecstasy" in their dance theories.*]

Ecstatic movement is of a dichotomous nature: it can originate as an inner impulse directed outward, or exist as an outer force directed inward.

It can inspire a seemingly purposeless losing of the self or a surrendering that is determined by a distinct Other. In other words, such movement materializes as self-motivated rhythm or rhythm dependent on a preexisting polarity. In many cases, however, these two forms intersect with one another and appear as one.

Tanzkunst, Fritz Böhme (1926)

Ecstasy: Kandinsky called it "the inner sound"; Kirchner, "an inner vision"; Nolde, "a spiritual state"; and Beckman, "the profound secret." In the early dance theory of Isadora Duncan (1878-1927) and Mary Wigman (1887-1973) the language of ecstasy occupies a central position: it is what allows them to articulate an aesthetic of the body that had both liberating and reactionary repercussions on 20th century formulations of social identity and artistic form in the U.S. and Europe.

For Duncan and Wigman ecstasy connoted a meaning beyond the self. Its intention was not to "express" a subjective state of mind, but rather to communicate the essence, the character, the being of a given phenomenon, an object or a relationship. Duncan and Wigman, in step with the painters Wassily Kandinsky, Ernst-Ludwig Kirchner, Emile Nolde and others associated with an expressionistic movement in art and literature, were informed by a Dionysian ethos made popular by Nietzsche. Both had a vision of dance as a bacchic experience that transgressed traditional western divisions of mind and body, of present and past. Wigman contends: "Dancing is an expression of higher vitality, confession of the present, experience of being, without any intellectual deviations." And, in 1903, Duncan promises: "But the dance of the future will be one whose body and soul have grown so harmoniously together that the natural language of that soul will have become the movement of the body."

Though Duncan was American and Wigman German, they were both reknowned as international pioneers of modern dance. Duncan is often identified as the creator of "free dance," while Wigman is lauded as the initiator of *Ausdruckstanz,* or "expressive dance." Duncan was born nine years before Wigman; her dancing career began more than a decade earlier (Duncan's in the late 1890's, Wigman's in 1914). In 1899 Duncan, discouraged by American audiences apathetic to her new dance forms, left the U.S. for Europe where she accrued international recognition for her performances. She was enthusiastically received by audiences in St. Petersburg, Stockholm, Paris, Budapest, and Berlin. Wigman left her home in Hannover in 1909 to study with the Swiss music and rhythm theoretician Jacques-Dalcroze in Hellerau by Dresden. When the war broke out in 1914, she and her most significant teacher and colleague Rudolf von Laban moved to Zurich where they performed in a program of dramatic masquerades, art "happenings," and dance evenings sponsored by a group of Da Da artists, among them Hugo Ball, at the Cabaret Voltaire. In the 1920s, however, Wigman's professional

centers were Dresden and Berlin. Here, the philosophical origins of her *Ausdruckstanz,* profoundly influenced by the work and theory of German Expressionist artists, first emerged. Duncan founded her first dance school in Berlin in 1905, Wigman in 1920 in Dresden.

Taken together, Duncan and Wigman give us an important cross-cultural, intercontinental vision of an aesthetic theory which strove to transform popular knowledge of the body. In their attempt to theorize a dance form that was not yet accepted into the canon of dance history, Duncan and Wigman reached to the Nietzschean ecstatic as a way of dismantling nineteenth-century precepts of realism, romanticism and subjectivity in art. For both, questioning aesthetic form was a project that examined notions of how social identity was conceived in and defined through a culture of the body. In the early work of Duncan and Wigman the ecstatic is a dynamic that contested the markings of gender and nationality attached to the body. By the end of their careers ecstasy is reduced to myth and esoteric rite, the ecstatic body transposed into an icon of national character, unity and fervor.

NIETZSCHE AND DIONYSIAN MYTH

Wigman and Duncan were not, of course, Nietzsche scholars. Like many of their contemporaries, though, they were taken with Nietzsche. Thus, I don't want to argue that Nietzsche's concept of the Dionysian was extracted, analyzed and subsequently integrated into the choreography and performance of Wigman and Duncan, but instead that popular fragments of Nietzsche's *The Birth of Tragedy* (1872) and *Zarathustra: A Book for Everyone and No-one* (1883) were apparent in their written and performed work. Wigman choreographed Nietzsche's *Zarathustra* as one of her first compositions, while Duncan (apparently after reading Kant's *Critique of Pure Reason,* 1781) had Nietzsche's *Zarathustra* read aloud to her by a German admirer. Moreover, Duncan in *My Life* (1927), referred repeatedly to Nietzsche as one of the most important theoreticians of dance: "I realized that the only dance masters I could have were Jean-Jacques Rousseau ('Emile'), Walt Whitman and Nietzsche," and again: "That was the origin—the root—but afterwards, coming to Europe, I had three great Masters, the three great precursors of the Dance of our century—Beethoven, Nietzsche, and Wagner . . . Nietzsche was the first dancing philosopher."

Duncan and Wigman, as well as many other artists of this period were inspired by Nietzsche's concept of the Dionysian. The artist group "Die Brücke" ("The Bridge"—a group of young German painters who banded together in Dresden in 1905) drew their name from the prologue of Nietzsche's *Zarathustra*:

Man is a rope, tied between beast and Higher Man . . . a rope over an abyss. A dangerous across, a dangerous on-the-way, a dangerous looking back, a dangerous shuddering and stopping. What is great in man is that he is a bridge and not an end: what can be loved in man is that he is an overture and a going under. I love those who do not know how to live, except by going under, for they are those who cross over. I love the great despisers because they are the great reverers, the arrows of longing for the other shore.

Presented here was Nietzche's ecstatic paradigm. The individual or the self, at the center of his paradigm, was presented in a transitional, often precarious state of becoming: "a dangerous on-the-way." The risk of experiencing extremes, one of which is "going under," was in Nietzschean terms, a way of crossing over, of experiencing the new, the "other shore." Nietzsche offered a self that was mobile, amorphous, limitless. The beast and the Higher Man here echoed the Dionysus and Apollo surfacing in Nietzsche's earlier work, *The Birth of Tragedy* (1872) in which Dionysus symbolized a "duality in the emotions," an event where "pain begets joy" and "ecstasy may wring sounds of agony from us."

Apollo and Dionysus were described by Nietzsche as, at once, existing in tremendous opposition to one another and interdependent. In the Greek world, he contends, Apollo represented the art of sculpture, Dionysus, the "nonimagistic," art of music. Their constant antagonism of one another was, Nietzsche argued, what constituted tragedy. Apollo, with his "impulse towards beauty," was continually confronted with the "barbaric" gesturing of Dionysus, that "horrible mixture of sensuality and cruelty," the "most savage (of) natural instincts." But, like the beast and the Higher Man, one could not enter one without finding the other. The Apollonian Greek's consciousness was "like a veil," it concealed the Dionysian world from his vision.

A revival of myth, of the archaic, or a call to reexamine a Dionysian "destruction, change, becoming," was a way of reenvisioning aesthetic consciousness for Nietzsche. His historical thesis about the origin of the Greek tragic chorus in the ancient Greek cult of Dionysus, though it appears to have acquired its critical point for modernity from ideas developed in early Romanticism, does not support a romantic messianism. His Dionysus is not the Christian savior-god. Nietzsche returns to ancient Greece precisely in order to bypass or overwhelm Christian mythology, not to reassert its hegemony. Though his Dionysus is—like the romantic Christian Dionysus, a "god who is coming"—it is a god who is both historical and foreign. This god's absence is not founded upon the guilt of sin, but on the forgetting of an Otherness that has the potential to decenter modern consciousness.

Nietzsche's Dionysian schematic held the contradictions of the modern project that Duncan, Wigman and their contemporaries were striving for early in their careers: the attainment of an aesthetic illusion which would disassemble rational subjectivities that had been defined by a static body. This body, in turn, was inscribed by gender and race. Only in a paradigm of the ecstatic were Duncan and Wigman able to perform a body that not only questioned nineteenth-century notions of female

(non)corporeality, but—in step with Nietzsche—challenged enlightenment rationality. Jürgen Habermas describes Nietzsche's affront to rationalism as an ecstatic moment that questions subjectivity: "the subject loses itself, when it sheers off from pragmatic experience in space and time, when it is stirred by the shock of the sudden, when it considers 'the longing for true presence'" (Octavio Paz). Nietzsche's Dionysus is not only distinguished from all other Greek gods as "the one who is absent, whose return is still to come," but also by his embodiment of the high culture of ancient Greece and the lower impulses of the Primitive. It is precisely this shifting frame of subjective reference and cultural context that moves Duncan and Wigman to incorporate a Dionysian aesthetic into their work which could potentially free the body from a reifying of modern social hierarchies.

GREEK IDEALISM AND THE PRIMITIVE IN DUNCAN AND WIGMAN

Dionysian ecstasy is transformative. It also has the potential to be transgressive. For Duncan and Wigman, ecstasy offered a model through which they could radically critique nineteenth-century precepts of female fashion, movement and desire without sacrificing—*tout court*—the elite status of dance in high culture. In order to displace ballet from its hegemonic position, Duncan and Wigman had to find a way of suggesting that their "new art" possessed both elements from the present and the classical past.

In the texts of Duncan and Wigman, Greek iconography intermingled with the "primitive." Of course, Duncan's evocation of ancient Greece was much more exhaustive than Wigman's: it was the insignia of her popularity as an eccentric. Duncan's donning of sheer Greek tunics, as she describes in *My Life,* even shocked contemporary Greeks when she travelled to Greece in 1903. While Duncan did engage in an extensive study of Greek vases, artifacts, and history, her Greece, in contrast to Wigman's, was a Greece that was more effectively performed than theorized. Wigman, more than ten years after Duncan's pilgrimage to Athens, explored the relationship between Greek myth and dance as a way of abstracting the cultic, of merging it with the Primitive in hopes that it would inform new methods for dance composition.

In spite of their temporal and temperamental differences, Wigman and Duncan's tendency to turn to ancient cultures as a source of rethinking aesthetic assumptions about form and content can be seen as representative of a distinct trend in certain early twentieth-century artistic and intellectual communities, both European and American. Rather than presenting intimate and accurate epistemes of African, Indian, Oceanic, Egyptian, Roman, and Greek cultures, artists in the fine and performing arts created transmutations of social and cultural knowledge. For Duncan and Wigman, as well as their contemporaries, reaching back to the Primitive through the Greek was, perhaps, a way of incorporating the challenges brought on by the entrance of mass culture into a formerly elite discussion of aesthetics.

Here, I will first scrutinize a text from each performer that signals their initial ideas about dance as a traditionally transcendental experience and then turn to examples from their later works that reveal the evolution of these ideas in new historical and career contexts.

ISADORA DUNCAN'S GREECE

"But this is Greece!" I exclaimed.

> But after I examined it more closely I realised that Berlin did not resemble Greece. This was a Nordic impression of Greece. These columns are not the Doric columns which should soar into the skies of Olympian blue. These are the Germanic, pedantic, archaelogical Professors' conception of Greece. And when I saw the Kaiserlich Royal Guard goose-step out of the Doric columns of the Potsdamer Platz, I went home to the Bristol and said, "Geben Sie mir ein Glas Bier. Ich bin müde."

Duncan's texts were maddening, repetitive eulogies to her transmutable self. She was goddess, whore, scholar, angel, pauper, victim, diva. She was "trembling and stammering," she assured her readers, when she delivered her first public lecture which later became her most Dionysian of texts, *The Dance of the Future* (1903). Duncan's use of ancient Greece in this early text was a topos to which she could anchor her arguments against nineteenth-century women's fashion, ideals of beauty, and notions about artistic form. This early essay seesawed between an Apollonian ideal of serene physical perfection (which found its crowning expression in Greek sculpture) and a Dionysian ethos that sacrificed aesthetic harmony for the joy of uninhibited movement and the excitement of the novel.

The category "Natural" was a Duncan trademark. What it accomplished in this text was twofold. First of all, by evoking the "Natural," Duncan was able to use the then popular Darwinism—which pervaded polemics on the left and the right in the U.S. and Europe—in elevating the daily movements of the body to a position of art. "The sole of the foot rests flat on the ground, a position which might be ugly in a more developed person, but is natural in a child trying to keep its balance. One of the legs is half raised: if it were outstretched it would irritate us, because the movement would be unnatural." Like Wigman, she exploited Darwin's "natural" body so that it extended to the movement of women as "natural," she writes: "It is not only a question of true art, it is a question of race, of the development of the female sex to beauty and health, of the return to the original strength and to natural movements of woman's body."

Duncan also drew on Darwin to justify her "return" to Ancient Greece:

> . . . the Greeks were the greatest students of the laws of nature, wherein all is the expression of

unending ever increasing evolution, wherein are no ends and no stops.

The Greek, she argues, was an evolved "Savage":

> So it has been with civilized man. The movements of the Savage, who lived in freedom in constant touch with Nature were unrestricted, natural and beautiful. Only the movements of the naked body can be perfectly natural. Man, arrived at the end of civilization, will have to return to nakedness, not to the unconscious nakedness of the savage, but to the conscious and acknowledged nakedness of the mature Man, whose body will be the harmonious expression of his spiritual being.

One could, of course, read Original Sin into this parable of body consciousness. Here, and, in fact, throughout this early text and in her memoirs, Duncan attempted again and again to make her Dionysian palatable (and acceptable to herself) to an often skeptical late Victorian public.

The effort to exalt the Primitive in aesthetic theory, as a component existing within "civilized man," was a project that had precedent during this period. The Primitivism of the early twentieth century, like the Orientalism of the nineteenth century, included a homogenization of cultural heritages. This was achieved not only through the distancing achieved in their generic naming, but by an ad hoc appropriation of only those aspects of the culture of the Other that seemed to support contemporary Western European social and cultural projects. Examples of this could be seen in expressionist artists' use of "African" and "Asian" masks as a method of decentering the self in painting and sculpture, or the Munich-based artist group Blaue Reiter's fascination with what they saw as a similarity between children's drawings and "Primitive Art." Under the rubric Primitive or Oriental (which will become more apparent in Wigman's use of these ideologies), the Greek was included as a way of "dressing up" the unpresentable Other.

What was "natural" in Duncan's terms, was also "beautiful." The Beautiful was Apollonian: it exhibited "perfect harmony," "form and symmetry," "health," and "strength." It was no surprise that Duncan's reception in Germany was as favorable; in her tribute to the beauty of Greek art, she asked: "Why are its (Ballet's) positions in such a contrast to the beautiful positions of the antique sculptures which we preserve in our museums and which are constantly represented to us as perfect models of ideal beauty?" She was clearly echoing sentiments shared by an influential segment of German intellectual society during the nineteenth and early twentieth centuries who believed that the "good taste which is increasingly spreading through the world was first formed under the Greek skies." Still, while a range of critics—German included—might have accused Duncan of simply mimicking Greek statues, her focus on expressive movement was not in step with one prevailing nineteenth-century German conception of beauty, which stated that it was "opposed to an excess of movement or decorative detail."

Duncan made sweeping, often biologistic statements about movement, such as: the untaught child's "movements are beautiful," "the natural language of that soul will have become the movement of the body;" "the dancer of the future movements will become godlike, mirroring in themselves the waves, the winds, the movements of growing things." However, she included a seemingly harmless anecdote of a Roman girl that radicalized her concepts of both beauty and movement in this piece. Beginning with the notion of the timelessness of movement as it exists in nature ("the movement of waves, of winds, of the earth is ever in the same lasting harmony . . ."), her lecture made it increasingly apparent that her use of an evolutionary argument was, first and foremost, a powerful weapon against the hegemonic, highly formalized, and constricted movement of ballet. Specifically, the word "evolution" gave Duncan the oxymoronic effect for which she was searching. It implied both a stationary and dynamic condition:

> The ideal of beauty of the human body cannot change with fashion but only with evolution. Remember the story of the beautiful sculpture of a Roman girl which was discovered under the reign of pope Innocent VIII and which by its beauty created such a sensation that the men thronged to see it and made pilgrimages to it as to a holy shrine, so that the pope, troubled by the movement which it originated, finally had it buried again.

This, I want to argue, was a very Dionysian moment. This kind of movement had the potential to motivate change, to stir things up. Beauty became transgressive. The statue must be removed and, in a sense, came to represent "the god that is absent."

Duncan's Roman girl digression was a very crucial turning point, a point in the Duncan lecture that also changed the tone of her argument. Duncan attempted to explain that she was not merely mimicking the imagined dances of the old Greeks. Here, she was in accordance with Wigman when she wrote: "We don't have any ritualized cult dances in the same way they existed in antique culture." Nor was Duncan's goal a revival of the dances of "primitive tribes." Still, she set up a linkage that imagined an intimate relationship between civilized high culture and the Primitive. The Greek and the Primitive, however, existed on the same plane and had a valency with which to attack the etiquette of ballet morality. As Habermas argued for Nietzsche, one could also apply to Duncan in her early work: rather than supporting an aesthetic that solely called for a "heightening of the subjective to the point of utter self-oblivion," it attempted to bring the Dionysian of Greek myth into the "experience of contemporary art." In this way, Duncan was able to refigure questions about form that could also challenge conventional categories of so-

cial identity. For instance, commenting on nationality she wrote: "The dancer will not belong to a nation but to all humanity." Or, Duncan envisioned a woman who ventured beyond traditional definitions of femininity when she wrote: "She will dance not in the form of the nymph, nor fairy, nor coquette but in the form of woman in its greatest and purest expression."

MARY WIGMAN'S PRIMITIVE

Wigman's relationship to contemporary art or the historical avant garde in her early theoretical work was much more readily apparent than was Duncan's. This had historical as well as cultural reasons. Duncan was speaking in 1903, before contemporaries were consciously speaking of Cubism, Futurism, Expressionism as "modern" art. Her influences, however, were "towering . . . at the threshold of modernity" and included: Richard Wagner, the Ballet Russe' (with Serge Diaghileff at its fore), Loie Fuller, Auguste Rodin. Wigman made her debut in 1914 with "Hexentanz I", well after Duncan's important 1904 St. Peterburg's performance, Nijinsky's 1912 revolutionary choreography of "Afternoon of a Faun," and the publishing of Kandinsky's Expressionist text, *The Spiritual in Art* (1912). Wigman entered a world already rich with the chaos of redefining of aesthetic categories in and through the culture of the body. Duncan, on the other hand, was present at the start of this aesthetic questioning.

Though Wigman also used Greece as a model for the harmony of body, soul, and intellect—where dance was seen as playing an integrative role—the Dionysian moment of her early work was an eclectic cultural experience. This experience was profoundly influenced by Wigman's proximity to German Expressionism. *Ausdruckstanz*, like Expressionism, emphasized the intrinsic nature of subjectobject relationships. One way of articulating that "inner sound" (Kandinsky's key concept in *The Spiritual in Art*) was to attach it to some kind of ethnic and racial Otherness: the Jewish, the Caribbean, the Peruvian, the Nigerian, the Indian, the Asian. Ethnographic masks, for example, became models of the exotic, and thus, the transcendent for both Nolde and Wigman. Wigman used masks, usually of "oriental" origins, to encourage experimentation with new identities in her choreography.

Like Duncan's Greece, however, the primitive proved problematic in Wigman's work. Wigman functionalized what she considered primitive in order to achieve an ecstatic state that took the subject out of its own cultural context. The body, immersed in the process of becoming the Other, could momentarily transcend itself. And, likewise, the Other was a way of revealing the repressed parts of the self. "The mask he brought me," wrote Wigman in 1926 in *Zerimonielle Gestalt* (Ceremonial Form), "was of a largely demonic character. I loved it at first sight. But as I pulled it over my face an unsettling feeling crept over me. Instead of bringing calm, it elicited uneasiness. The mask emphasized the personal, where it should have estranged." The Orient plays a central role in Wigman's early solo work. For example, "Marche Orientale," (1918-19) and "Vier Tänze nach orientalischen Motiven" (1920) were important in garnering Wigman public recognition and in pushing her to develop a theory of the ecstatic in her writings on dance composition.

In Wigman's first analytical statement, *Komposition* (1925), she conceived the Orient as unchanging and eternal, the silent, knowing Other, and a Primitivism that conjured up a primitive of the wild, the innocent, the impulsive, and the holy. What resulted was a generic "aesthetics of inwardness," which, in turn, informed Wigman's theory of the transcendent in dance. This theory, however, was not only a theory of the Other. It was also an attempt to define dance in terms of language and movement, in terms of its relationship to space and color. Wigman introduced *Komposition* by informing the reader that "there is no technique for producing form." In this piece she attempted to examine how formal structures were created in response to a dancer's *Ausdruckssehnsucht* or desire to express. This desire was located, Wigman argued, in a language inscribed in the moving body: "Dance is language, announcement, language of a body in motion." Dance language was created when one was able to confront modern form with the cult and ritual of the Primitive. Wigman explored this confrontation through the concepts which she termed the "ornamental," the "dynamic," and the "nuanced."

Wigman was much more analytically sophisticated than Duncan. Still, Duncan initiated a discussion of how movement could reevaluate the Beautiful and this, in turn, contributed to a rethinking of form that Wigman could build on. For Wigman, the Beautiful, becomes radically synthetic; she calls it the "ornamental." Wigman questioned what was considered traditionally beautiful. Moreover, she questioned it in a semiotic manner; it became just one more representation of a body which invited a multiplicity of meanings. Wigman defined the ornamental as "illustration, a kind of jewelry, or a changing of dress." Its effect on artistic composition is an "enlargement or enrichment . . . a complicating of the compositional text through playful movement motifs."

The structure of a dance, for Wigman, consisted of a system of "dynamics" and "nuance" resulting from the study of the relationship between motion and the forces affecting motion, between movement and form, between the inner and outer tensions of a composition. Dynamics was "inner breathing," that which made a composition fluid. Nuance was color; it illuminated an especially dynamic *Ausdrucksmoment* (expressive moment).

Wigman, unlike Duncan, did not feel compelled to deliver a diatribe against ballet, though her *Ausdruckstanz* was still considered an affront to ballet by adherents of classical dance even into the 1920s. She did, however, make a qualitative distinction between European social dances of the eighteenth and nineteenth centuries and *Ausdruckstanz*. The "step-dances," as she called the March, the Polonaise, the Gavotte, and the Minuet were "functional dances," formal, traditional structures one could use to increase one's range of opportunities for expression. Likewise, the Mazurka and the Waltz which she called *Springtänze,* dances which utilized a leap, a jump, or a hop also belonged to the category of the functional. They had a "strict rhythmic orientation" and illustrated a "definite theme" that did not vary from a pre-ordained musical structure whose time was ordered and measured.

Wigman clearly saw *Ausdruckstanz*—which she labelled the "emotional dance" and juxtaposed with functional dance—as the more innovative form. It was the text or "song" of the body that could house a variety of forms. This dance-song functioned through a "lyrical content of feeling." In other words, through a particular discursive logic. "There is a main sentence or clause, a middle clause, and a main thesis which is repeated. This is, however, accompanied by a change of the last few movements (or words)." This grammar, however, was always being destroyed, for it was a "free song-form" created anew again and again. It was Wigman's Dionysian, where the "seemingly most varied, most opposing formulations lose definition because of a sudden outbreak of (dance) passion." Differences "flow into one another and work together" and created yet another structural novelty.

Wigman saw the Romance, the Ballad, the Rhapsody, the Cultic, and the Elemental (as in nature-spirit) as the characteristic *Ausdruckstänze*. Wigman intended here, I think, to emphasize the extremes entailed in the ecstatic: *Lust/Leid* (desire/suffering), *Tod/Leben* (death/life) and, thus, its capacity to transcend traditionally polarized sets of meanings. This, however, was an instance where the Dionysian, precisely because of its inherent polymorphism was laid open to a variety of interpretations that could divest it of its transformative qualities. Toward the end of *Komposition,* a kind of gothic romanticism entered Wigman's theoretical inquiry. Wigman isolated the Primitive as cultic so that it was no longer confronted with contemporary form. The Primitive was presented by Wigman as that which "renounces all that is playful," that "concentrates on the big line," that became, at once, "rigid, broad, monumental." Wigman followed this assertion by pointing to a recovering of contemporary experience, "Cultic dances can also be religious forms—religious in the sense that they offer ecstatic-mystical conditions of earlier cultures—but should not be purely formal imitations of this 'previous,' but rather the performance of a real dance experience." That "real dance experience" was composed of particular elements that left the reader hovering on the brink of a gothic romanticism, which, with hindsight, suggests one wellspring for an ideology like *Volk* under National Socialism. How did the notion of

Ausdruck, that push for the expressive in both Duncan and Wigman, lead to an unimaginative and non-regenerative Nationalism?

IS THIS MODERN? A NATIONAL MARKING OF THE DANCE BODY

Despite its radical aesthetic project or ambitions, the early ideology espoused by the creators of modern dance at the beginning of the twentieth century—its conception of the body as an instrument through which one could register the dissonance and unity between movement and space—could appeal to authors of modern nationalistic discourses. Moreover, its evocation of the cult and the festive stirred the imagination of a historical period which contained both a fear of and a fascination of masses coalescing. German fascism, with its emphasis on symbol, myth, festival, found the theories of modern dance useful for its liturgical displays of a national *Volk.*

The intersecting of dance and nationalism in the works of Duncan and Wigman remains complicated. Both performers participated in expanding the ideology of a movement of physical culture that had roots in both the U.S. and Germany at the turn of the century. While it exposed the body as ornamental, gave it a consciousness as a surface upon which gender was displayed and subsequently incorporated, it also reinforced a biological essentialism. It could be easily assimilated as an element of State programs that formulated their nationalism against the Otherness of a body marked by race, gender, and ethnicity.

Wigman, in the adopting of the language of National Socialism in *Deutsche Tanzkunst* (1935), converted her earlier theoretical inquiries into rhetorical caricatures. While her arguments previously toyed with or implied the biologic, they now engaged in a eugenics discourse that sealed emancipatory potential into a national apocalyptic. A static "destiny" replaced Wigman's earlier concepts of "inner urgency" and "expressive desire." The "creative fantasy" of composing was no longer a process, but an essential product of a certain "blood," and the individual "dancer" became the German *Volk.* Group dancing, which had at its center "communal movement and leaping, festive walking, and virile running," became Wigman's primary passion in the later part of her career. Wigman had already theorized about group choreography in *Komposition* in 1925. Her emphasis here, however, was on how group dance "expands the texture and variation" of form. Though she wrote that this leads to "larger compositions," there is no qualitative difference between the group and solo dance. Group dances appealed to Wigman because of the possibility of "multiple authors" for the production of composition ideas. They also interested her because of their "polyphonic possibilities." These "movement temperaments" could also "melt into one another," but here Wigman was not speaking of a preordained unity. Rather her goal was overcoming boundaries, or playing with limits in order to re-imagine artistic form. This

nuance of sophistication was, without question, lost in Wigman's notion of the group in her 1935 *Deutsche Tanzkunst:* "The community presumes leadership. The mass that is self-reflexive never achieves community." For Wigman, the concept "community" acquired a resonance that did not appear in her initial vision of group dances: "What is German? What makes German art, German? . . . The unmistakable features of real German artistic accomplishment are not only present in the materials and themes of art works. They exist much more in the irrational, a place the personal must enter in order to experience something beyond the personal, or real humanity." Wigman's Dionysian became national, propagandistic.

The sentiment that dance should be "choirs of movement," shared by Wigman and Rudolf von Laban in their later work, was realized literally in their choreography of a mass ornament of the German *Volk* for the Olympic Games in 1936 in Berlin:

> It is especially fitting for the times that the cultic ideas of Laban's amateur-dance and movement choirs be momentarily integrated. With his influence a certain amount of frivolous literary convention can be avoided . . . Without his imaginative world, the concept amateur-dancer would not exist. It does not matter if those laymen feel at ease or at one with Laban. He is needed so that the effort for an inaugural cultic festive occasion does not appear to be simply an offering for the needs of the bourgeoisie.

The program was arranged into five parts that extended the above-mentioned effort to appear "close to the people," laymen-like. The first feature presented 2500 "German" girls moving in unison while Gret Palucca (one of the Wigman's most successful students) danced a waltz. Another displayed 500 youth who, with balls and hoops, performed gymnastics. Wigman, accompanied by 80 of her students, appeared as the fourth entry in her "The Lament of Death."

Until 1937 Wigman and Laban, participated in and were accepted as performers and authors of *Volk*-ish work under National Socialism. While it remains unclear exactly why Laban eventually fell out of the good graces of Goebbels and other Nazi-party members, Goebbels has been quoted as punning: "There is only one movement in Germany and that is the National Socialist movement." After 1936, however, the cultural politics of National Socialism measured all artistic expression rigorously against the touchstone *Volk.* Laban was arrested in the summer of 1937 and "allowed" to leave Germany for France. In Paris, he joined the faculty of a dance school belonging to Kurt Joos, a former dance student of Laban's. In 1942 Wigman was forbidden to perform officially in Germany. From this point on, she was considered pro-Jewish, her dances were labelled *entartet* (degenerate), and public funding for her Dresden school was cut off.

Duncan was not confronted with the political choices Wigman faced under National Socialism, nor did she live to react to the Stalin purges of the thirties. But as much as Duncan had rallied in her early writings and performances to free the body from the confinements of nineteenth-century fashion and morality, in her memoirs of 1927 (the year she died), she reverted to a racist, nationalist splitting and hierarchizing of dance into white, classically influenced "modern" dance and black, jazz inspired "nondance":

> It seems to me monstrous that any one should believe that the Jazz rhythm expresses America. Jazz rhythm expresses the primitive savage. America's music would be something different. It has yet to be written. No composer has yet caught this rhythm of America—it is too mighty for the ears of most. But some day it will gush forth from the great stretches of Earth, rain down from the vast sky spaces, and America will be expressed in some Titanic music that will shape its chaos to harmony, and long-legged shining boys and girls will dance to this music, not the tottering, ape-like convulsions of the Charleston, but a striking, tremendous upward movement, mounting high above the Pyramids of Egypt, beyond the Parthenon of Greece, an expression of beauty and strength such as no civilisation has ever known.

I have argued that such a division existed in Duncan's dance philosophy from the onset. It was a duality that—in her early work—she located within herself. The "long-legged shining boys and girls" in this text, however, are presented as radically separate from, and implicitly superior to the "primitive savage." The "unconscious," but "perfectly natural nakedness" of the "savage" is no longer the Dionysian "nakedness" found in the "mature" man or woman of her earlier work. And Duncan's focus is no longer "movement" but rather, a valorizing of the static colossal of monuments: the Pyramids of Egypt, the Parthenon of Greece.

The moment of the sublime that Duncan had located previously in a complex and careful Dionysian—where the concept of beauty was put into question and radicalized becomes an anthem to the national here, as she writes:

> It has often made me smile—but somewhat ironically—when people have called my dancing Greek, for I myself count its origins in the stories which my Irish grandmother often told us of crossing the plains with grandfather in '49 in a covered wagon—she eighteen, he twenty-one, and how her child was born in such a wagon during a famous battle with the Redskins, and how, when the Indians were finally defeated, my grandfather put his head in at the door of the wagon, with a smoking gun still in his hand, to greet his newborn child.

. . . . .

The idea of dance as an ecstatic rite existed in Wigman's and Duncan's arguments from the beginning. It assisted them in recalling the creative Dionysian, in devaluing the traditional (ballet) by exalting the experimental, and in gaining credibility from audiences that had capital and influence by presenting this rite as valuable in its subversion of high art. What, however, began as a critical scrutiny of the subjective and a challenge to high culture reverted to a confirming of the national.

Dionysian ecstasy—popularized through Nietzsche, constituting a model of disruption, change, and expressiveness—was used by Duncan and Wigman to pose questions about content and form, about inner and outer reality, about the plasticity of the body, of language. While the self is left intact by Wigman and Duncan, it became an instrument, at least in their initial pioneering work, through which one could impose a multiplicity of meanings in relation to the biological, the spiritual, the social.

The very precariousness of identity spurred by an awareness of cultural, racial and ethnic difference at the turn of the century, whether it came from the recent experience of colonization or the urbanizing of industrialization, was reflected in Wigman's and Duncan's revising of their earlier subversive Dionysian ecstatic to fit regressive State and National ideologies. Engaging in the aesthetics of ecstasy meant risking the familiar for the unknown. At its most emancipatory, it called for a reexamining of accepted categories of knowing, a moment that Wigman and Duncan were only able to sustain at the very advent of their careers.

FURTHER READING

Biography

Blair, Fredrika. *Isadora: Portrait of the Artist as a Woman.* New York: McGraw-Hill, 1986, 470 p.
> Attempts to place Duncan's life in historical context and present hitherto unavailable information. Blair addresses neither Duncan's relationships with her students nor her years in Russia in much detail, stating that these areas have been covered adequately by others.

Flanner, Janet. "Isadora." *An American in Paris: Profile of an Interlude between Two Wars,* pp. 169-81. Simon and Schuster, 1940.
> Recounts Duncan's last years in Paris.

McVay, Gordon. *Isadora and Esenin.* Ann Arbor, MI: Ardis, 1980, 335 p.
> Examines Duncan's relationship with Russian poet Sergei Esenin and details their lives together both in Russia and abroad.

Schneider, Ilya Ilyich. *Isadora Duncan: The Russian Years.* New York: Harcourt, Brace and World, 1968, 221 p.

Depiction of the time Duncan spent in Russia by an admiring friend and colleague.

Seroff, Victor. *The Real Isadora.* New York: The Dial Press, 1971, 441 p.

Duncan's life as told by a close friend and prolific biographer.

Splatt, Cynthia. *Life Into Art: Isadora Duncan and Her World.* Edited by Dorée Duncan, Carol Pratl, and Cynthia Splatt. New York: W. W. Norton and Company, 1993, 199 p.

Illustrated biography with a foreword by Agnes de Mille.

Terry, Walter. *Isadora Duncan: Her Life, Her Art, Her Legacy.* New York: Dodd, Mead and Company, 1963, 174 p.

Overview of her life with extended comments on her work as a dancer.

Criticism

MacCarthy, Desmond. Review of *My Life,* by Isadora Duncan. *Life and Letters* 1, No. 2 (July 1928): 136-40.

Positive assessment in which he describes *My Life* as "something more" than a biography: "the record of the emotional life of an artist."

Untermeyer, Louis. "Isadora Duncan." *Makers of the Modern World,* pp. 522-32. New York: Simon and Schuster, 1955.

Overview of her life and career and an assessment of her significance as an artist.

Additional coverage of Duncan's life and career is contained in the following sources published by Gale Research: *Contemporary Authors,* Vols. 118, 149.

Joseph Goebbels

1897–1945

Full name, Paul Joseph Goebbels. German politician, propagandist, diarist, editor, novelist, and playwright.

INTRODUCTION

Nazi propaganda minister between the years 1933 and 1945, Goebbels was the only intellectual, next to Adolf Hitler, among the leaders of the German Third Reich. A failed novelist and playwright, Goebbels founded and edited the political newspaper *Der Angriff* in the early years of the Nazi regime. As Hitler's Minister of Propaganda, he headed one of the most pervasive and powerful government-controlled propaganda machines in history. With near total authority over all forms of mass media in Nazi Germany, including newspapers, radio, film, theatre, and book publishing, Goebbels manipulated the opinions of millions of Germans. During World War II he was responsible for maintaining public morale through lies and fabrications, delivered almost daily by print and broadcast media. Intensely anti-Semitic and violently opposed to both the bourgeoisie and Catholic Church, Goebbels organized the infamous *Kristallnacht* pogrom of 1938 and, overall, endeavored to legitimize the slaughter of more than six million Jews between the years 1938-1945 by disseminating the Nazi myth of Aryan racial superiority among the German people. A member of the left-wing of the Nazi Party, he sympathized to a degree with the efforts and methods of Joseph Stalin in the Soviet Union, but was nevertheless fanatically loyal to Hitler and played a key role in promulgating the cult of the *Führer*. His love of Hitler, however, was equally matched by his disdain for most of his fellow Nazi leaders.

Biographical Information

Goebbels was born on October 29, 1897, in Rheydt, Germany, into a working-class, Catholic household. A clubfoot prevented him from joining the army during World War I, so Goebbels instead pursued the study of German literature and philology at the University of Bonn, and later at the University of Heidelberg. He received his doctoral degree from the latter in 1921 and, embittered by his failure to find a publisher for his novel *Michael*, joined the Nazi party. Moving rapidly through the ranks, Goebbels was made *gauleiter* or "district leader" of Berlin in 1927, and founded the Nazi newspaper *Der Angriff* ("The Attack") that same year. He continued to edit the periodical, which was designed to stir popular support for the party, and later acted as Adolf Hitler's campaign manager until 1933, when Hitler was elected Chancellor of Germany and appointed Goebbels as his Minister of Public Enlighten-

ment. The job put Goebbels in control of the mass media, allowing him to launch a sustained campaign of anti-Semitic, anti-Catholic, and anti-bourgeois propaganda. In November, 1938, he orchestrated the *Kristallnacht* pogrom, in which German synagogues were burned, Jewish storefronts destroyed, and thousands of Jews arrested. After the outbreak of war in 1939, Goebbels stepped up his propaganda efforts, providing assurances of a quick German victory; later he attempted to allay fears of defeat by alluding to the existence of powerful super weapons and to the strength of the German people as the modern manifestation of the Aryan or "Master" race. In February of 1943, after the German defeat at Stalingrad, Goebbels—a brilliant speaker, though lacking the extraordinary charisma of Hitler—delivered his "Sports Palace Speech" in which he called for "total war." A little over a year later, as the conflict began to steadily turn against Germany, he was appointed General Commissioner for Total War Measures. He remained by Hitler's side in Berlin as the Soviets began their assault on the German capital in 1945. On May 1, 1945, shortly after Hitler had taken his own life, Goebbels ordered his children poisoned and, along with his wife, committed suicide.

Major Works

The novel *Michael*, adapted from Goebbels's early diaries and reworked after Hitler's rise to power to emphasize Nazi values, has been universally panned by critics as dull and maudlin. The primary source of interest to scholars of Goebbels's works are the numerous volumes of his diary recovered from the ruins of the Reich Chancellery in Berlin after his death. Goebbels had intended to publish his journals after the war, but instead left behind the unrevised and unexpurgated fragments of his daily thought covering much of his adult life. *Vom Kaiserhof zur Reichskanzlei* (*My Part in Germany's Fight*, 1934) details his role in the Nazi ascension to power in Germany, and represents one of the few works Goebbels had the opportunity to edit before publication. Among his diaries now translated into English are entries spanning the war years 1939 to 1945 as well as a collection of fragments from the 1920s, most of which were composed in Goebbels's characteristically overblown style. While the war entries provide summaries of military and political events, critics note that their scholarly value lies in relation to the mass of misleading information that Goebbels and the Ministry of Propaganda presented to the German public during this period. The diaries also reveal Goebbels's self-delusion, his intense feelings of hatred, contempt, and revenge, as well as a his near-fanatical worship of Adolf Hitler alongside emotionally detached observations of the war and the contemporary social and political situation in Germany. The wartime diaries additionally chronicle Goebbels's shifting state of mind as the fighting turned against the Germans, his contempt for his rivals among the Nazi leadership, particularly for the *Luftwaffe* commander Hermann Goering, who he perceived as incompetent, and his deep respect for Stalin's political acumen, if not for his ideological beliefs. Among the most compelling aspects of the diaries, scholars note, are Goebbels's records of his activities as Propaganda Minister—ingenious lies and misrepresentations, subversive attacks against the British, French, Russians, and Americans in print and over the airwaves, hatred campaigns against Jews, and indignant denunciations of those who differed with his opinions. Countless examples of the methods that Goebbels developed to undermine his political and military opponents fill the diaries of a man considered to be among the most gifted and cunning propagandists in history.

PRINCIPAL WORKS

Michael (novel) 1929
Vom Kaiserhof zur Reichskanzlei [*My Part in Germany's Fight*] (diary) 1934

"Sports Palace Speech" (speech) 1943
Goebbels Tagebücher aus den Jahren 1942-43 [*The Goebbels Diaries 1942-43*] (diaries) 1948
Das Tagebuch von Joseph Goebbels 1925-26 (diaries) 1960
The Early Goebbels Diaries (diaries) 1962
Tagebücher 1945. Die letzten Aufzeichnungen [*Final Entries 1945: The Diaries of Joseph Goebbels*] (diaries) 1978
The Goebbels Diaries 1939-41 (diaries) 1982
Die Tagebücher von Joseph Goebbels: Sämtliche Fragmente (diaries) 1987

CRITICISM

William Solzbacher (essay date 1948)

SOURCE: Review of *The Goebbels Diaries: 1942-1943,* in *The Commonweal*, Vol. XLVIII, No. 11, June 25, 1948, pp. 260-62.

[*In the following review, Solzbacher contends that Goebbels's diaries from 1942 and 1943 were designed to further the Nazi cause upon their publication.*]

A comparison of this volume with ***Vom Kaiserhof zur Reichskanzlei,*** the diary which Dr. Joseph Goebbels published in 1934, produces two conclusions: (1) It disperses any doubts regarding the authorship of these diaries; (2) it demonstrates the absurdity of the statement on the publisher's blurb. "As he fabricated his network of lies to the German people and to the world by day, he was telling the truth to his diary by night." There is overwhelming internal evidence that Goebbels is the author of these diaries. Every page shows his style, his way of thinking, his shrewd maneuvering, his art in the distortion of facts. There is not the slightest justification for the assumption that one of the greatest liars in the world's history should have become a fanatical truthseeker in those few minutes every day which he spent on dictating his diary.

The original, several times more voluminous than the more than 500 pages translated by Mr. Lochner, fell into American hands after a junk dealer had carted it away from the courtyard of the Berlin Ministry of Propaganda. The Russians apparently tossed these papers, with many others, out of the window, showing interest only in the filing cabinets which contained them.

Mr. Hugh Gibson, in his "Publisher's Note," mentions evidence showing that Goebbels was in debt to the Nazi Party's Publishing Company (headed by Max Amann, Hitler's drill sergeant in World War I, and owned jointly by Hitler and Amann) to the amount of 226,583.69 marks, which he had drawn as advances against future royalties. Strangely enough, neither Mr.

Gibson nor Mr. Lochner seem to have noticed the obvious relationship between these debts and the *Diaries*. Amann was no philanthropist nor a special friend of Joseph Goebbels, but a hard-headed businessman. As he lent Goebbels money for his life of luxury and his expensive amorous adventures, he could be expected to demand payment in full. Since the *Kaiserhof* Diary had been the most successful of Goebbels's books, from the point of view of sales (this reviewer's copy bears the imprint "261st-280th thousand"), Amann apparently was interested in more books of this type. The writing of his diary was a chore for which Goebbels was being paid by Amann. Mr. Lochner mentions that Goebbels apparently never looked at his diary once it had been typed according to his dictation. This would seem to show that the diary was not meant to be a sentimental, "intimate" and "truthful" record for his own peace of mind, but raw material for books, one out of many tools in his quest for power, money, and fame.

Obviously Goebbels could not have planned to publish his diaries as they were, but was aware of the fact that they would have to be edited in accordance with whatever would be the party line at the time of publication. The *Kaiserhof* Diary, which gave a day-by-day report of events from January 1, 1932, to May 1, 1933, had shown that he was quite good at such a job. The *Kaiserhof* book contained vitriolic attacks against Gregor Strasser, who at the dates under which Goebbels listed his comments was still the Chief Organizer of the Nazi Party, ranking immediately after Hitler. It is quite probable that the "original" diary contained sharp criticism of Goering, Streicher, Rosenberg, Roehm, Feder, etc., as well, but that unfriendly remarks were eliminated because these leaders were riding high in the Nazi hierarchy when Goebbels published his book, while Strasser was helpless; he was assassinated by Hitler's and Goering's thugs a few weeks after the appearance of the book.

It is now known from many sources that during the war Hitler became thoroughly fed up with many of his lieutenants, including Ribbentrop, Ley, Darré, and Rosenberg, and with most of his generals. There would certainly have been a purge in the Nazi Party if Hitler had won the war. In such a case, many of the "deep secrets" in the Goebbels diaries would have been ripe for publication. On the other hand, Goebbels could not know whether Goering, whose power had been declining since 1941, would eventually be "purged" as a "traitor" or reestablished in his role as a national hero. Goebbels was prepared for both possibilities, mingling in his diaries praise and basest flattery with criticism and ridicule. By blue-penciling either the former or the latter, Goebbels could easily adapt the diary to whatever would be required at the time of publication.

The fact that the diaries contain nothing but praise and admiration for Hitler does not necessarily prove anything about the intimate thoughts of the author. It merely shows that Goebbels knew that his fate was inextricably linked with that of the founder of the Nazi movement and that, in the case of Hitler's defeat, his own career would be finished.

The best proof that these diaries are not an "intimate" and "truthful" record of the author's life and innermost thoughts is furnished by the fact that all through these hundreds of pages Goebbels plays the comedy of a faithful husband and father while in fact his love affairs with a number of women, including the film star Lyda Barova, were notorious and he lived mostly separated from his wife. Any mention of Hitler's Eva Braun is also avoided in the diaries.

Many of the "revelations" of these diaries are undoubtedly true. Some Nazi schemes are described with remarkable frankness, e.g. Hitler's plans to annex large parts of France, especially Burgundy, and Goebbels's proposal to annex large parts of Italy, especially Venice. In some matters, Goebbels apparently was more realistic than other Nazis, for instance when he demanded more food and clothing for the slave laborers (to make them cooperative), when he suggested in vain, against Rosenberg's violent opposition, that people in the Nazi-occupied parts of the Soviet Union be offered land and freedom of religion (to win them for the German cause), and when he opposed Hitler's plan to have German troops occupy Vatican City (because of the indignation which this would stir up all over the world).

On the other hand, the diaries contain entries which are obviously false, for instance the one on March 3, 1943: "I learn that the Pope intends to enter upon negotiations with us. He would like to get into contact with us and would even be willing to send incognito to Germany one of the Cardinals with whom he is intimate."

Goebbels boasts in the diaries that he deliberately "planted" items of false information in the German and foreign press. There are indications that he used his diaries for the same purpose. That Mr. Lochner has not remained completely immune against such attempts, may be seen from his comment on p. 252: "The Mr. Cohn here referred to is better known by his pen name of Emil Ludwig." In reality, Mr. Ludwig's father changed his name to Ludwig in 1883, when Emil Ludwig was 2 years old. It has been his legitimate name ever since.

In his Introduction as well, Mr. Lochner appears to have been too much impressed by Goebbels's boastfulness, for instance when he writes: "He spoke night after night, edited his paper, attended to a multitude of details of political organization, and still found time with Gregor Strasser to start the *National-Sozialistische Briefe* (National Socialist Letters)." This is legend, not history. When the semi-monthly *Briefe* was founded (July 1925), Goebbels had no paper to edit and had few speaking engagements; organizational matters were attended to by his boss, Gregor Strasser. Mr. Lochner's reference to a "Goebbels-Strasser duumvirate" is greatly exaggerated. Goebbels was Strasser's employee. Only after his break with Strasser and his entrance into Hitler's service was Goebbels given organizational assignments. One of the reasons for which Hitler sent him to Berlin in November, 1928, was the fact that he knew Gregor and Otto Strasser and could be expected to keep an eye on their activities in Berlin where they were publishing at that time a chain of 7 Nazi weeklies, among them the *Berliner Arbeiterzeituna,* following a "socialist" line.

The Introduction and the notes for this book have obviously been prepared in a hurry. I did not try to count the inaccuracies, but their total is undoubtedly very high. To give just a few examples: It is not correct that the Nazi SD (Security Service) was part of the Gestapo (it was part of the SS storm troops), that ex-Gauleiter Kube was "one of Hitler's earliest disciples" (he fought the Nazis as a member of a rival racist group until he joined them in 1927), that De Valera became Prime Minister of Ireland in 1937 (the correct year is 1932). Walther Rathenau was no *von.* The palace on Peacock Island, where Mr. Lochner attended a Venetian Night organized by Goebbels, cannot possibly have been "erected in 1794 for Frederick William III" (who ascended the throne only 3 years later). It seems very unlikely that Mr. Lochner had the talk with Captain Roehm, which he describes, in 1930, because Roehm spent that entire year in Bolivia, returning to Germany only in January, 1931. Most of these inaccuracies are unimportant in themselves, but their large number impairs the value of the book.

Many of the notes produce confusion rather than clarification. On p. 419, for instance, where Goebbels describes a conversation with Himmler about the conscientious objectors among the International Bible Students, the only comment needed would have been that the sect is now known in its country of origin, America, as Jehovah's Witnesses. Mr. Lochner, however, states: "The International Bible Students were a small sect claiming to be serious searchers into the verities of Holy Script." Has he never heard of Jehovah's Witnesses?

In the Introduction, Mr. Lochner mentions several of Goebbels's books, omitting, however, the most important one, and the only one in diary form, *Vom Kaiserhof zur Reichskanzlei.*

Unquestionably the Goebbels Diaries are of immense interest for students of history. In the perspective of recent events, most of the falsehood which they contain is obvious for everyone. Such is not the case for all of it, however. The critical reader will do well to keep in mind that he is handling poison.

Helmut Heiber (essay date 1962)

SOURCE: "Introduction," *The Early Goebbels Diaries: The Journal of Joseph Goebbels from 1925-1926,* edited by Helmut Heiber, translated by Oliver Watson, Weidenfeld and Nicolson, 1962, pp. 15-26.

[In the following essay, Heiber focuses on Goebbels's diaries for the years 1925 and 1926.]

Throughout his life—it is said, from the time he was twelve—Joseph Goebbels kept a diary. Later, when in power, he probably even kept two diaries—his private notes and also voluminous daily records, dictated to a stenographer and containing descriptions of events and comments; these, for all their candour, were clearly addressed to posterity that would judge his actions. Shortcomings in general and colleagues in particular he criticized acidly; he found little wrong with matters of principle and nothing wrong with Hitler, let alone with himself. These moderate disclosures were intended as raw material for a history of the Third Reich, the writing of which was to give content to Goebbels' years of retirement; when completed the history was to provide financial security for his family.

Probably only very few people, and these are in the East, know what happened to these private and semi-official diaries, for most of what escaped destruction during the fighting in Berlin was presumably captured by the Soviets. Under-Secretary of State Naumann believes that this is certainly true of the microfilms of the semi-official diary, which were made before the collapse, and Hans Fritzsche has testified to having seen in Moscow, at any rate, part of the private notes written in Goebbels' own hand.

Disregarding such inaccessible fragments those portions of the diary are of course known which were published by Goebbels himself under the title *From the Kaiserhof to the Reich Chancellery*. They cover the period from 1st January 1932 to 1st May 1933 and though of course heavily edited they preserve the original diary form. Another portion appears in his *Michael,* a novel written in the form of a diary, in which Goebbels draws on his diary covering the years 1919 and 1920 when he went to the Universities of Freiburg, Munich and Heidelberg. Written in 1921, Goebbels was able to publish this book only in 1929 when Eher, the party publisher, accepted it; it contains his own adventures mixed with those of his friend Richard Flisges. Finally we have a book, *The Struggle for Berlin,* published in 1932, for which the diaries probably provided the source; it begins with 9th November 1926, the day on which the new Gauleiter enters the capital, and describes the first year of his work there.

Far more important than these edited publications are the few available original manuscripts. One of these contains fragments of a typescript taken from dictation and covering the period from 21st January 1942 to 9th November 1943. A heavily cut edition was published by Louis P. Lochner several years ago; it is an important source for the history of that period and for some internal developments in the Third Reich.

But these are meditations of a man written not so much for the sake of recording as for the impression they would make on posterity. Far more important to judge Goebbels, the man, are the 192 diary pages written in his own hand, the only part of the private diaries which fell into western hands after the war. They run from 12th August 1925 to the end of October 1926 without a gap. Apart from the last few pages and a portion in the middle the manuscript is in good condition, although Goebbels' hand makes reading somewhat difficult.

These pages had the same fate as the 1942-43 diary published by Lochner. When the Propaganda Ministry was cleared in 1945 the Russians intended to burn this manuscript, but someone picked it up in the courtyard. It passed through several hands as waste paper until it reached an American well versed in German affairs who, in 1946, passed it on to Herbert Hoover, the former U.S. President. Since then the manuscript has been in the custody of the Hoover Institution on War, Revolution and Peace, Stanford University, California.

These notes have accordingly been known for some time, and they have several times been quoted at length—by Lochner, in his preface, down to the recent Goebbels biography by Manvell and Fraenkel. Transcribing difficulties have probably been responsible for the failure so far to publish these notes which, when seen *in toto,* fully reveal the personality of the author. This book (first published in Germany by the *Institut fuer Zeitgeschichte*) is thus the first full version of the diary.

As we have already mentioned, a small party of the original is in poor condition. Several pages and corners are burnt—particularly entries beginning on 9th September 1926; other pages have been pierced by nails; and a third group—particularly the entries from 12th to 20th July 1926—have been smudged by water. Fire damage has badly affected the part beginning on 16th October 1926, and only tatters remain of the last pages for that month. The transcriber had thus to contend not only with the handwriting, but also with these defects of the material.

The diary has been transcribed from the original word for word; style, spelling and punctuation follow the original. All mistakes due to carelessness have been reproduced to give the flavour of these hastily made notes and to be fair to the author. Doubtful passages have been placed between square brackets, especially names of insignificant persons (many of these were identified by references to reports of meetings in the *Völkischer Beobachter*). Undecipherable passages have been indicated by dots. But to save space the paragraphing in the original has been disregarded, for Goebbels usually started a new paragraph for every or every second sentence or exclamation.

The documents in the Appendix are, with the exception of the letter from Holtz (No 10) and Heinemann's notes (No 11), original typescripts or typed copies. A few typing errors in the documents have been corrected.

Many biographers publishing or using personal diaries have inevitably laid bare events of the diarist's private life which can normally claim exclusion from public discussion. But the case of a man like Joseph Goebbels is different. He belongs to history, and he has influenced and moulded the fate of millions. The personality of such men is a matter of public interest and therefore a proper object of historical research. To answer the question—what manner of man was such a person behind the façade which he erected when in power?—it is exceedingly important to know something about his relations with other people.

What, then, had been the career of that young man at the time when he wrote these pages in his diary, before his twenty years of malignant political power? Biographies make it possible to sketch his life briefly as follows.

Paul Joseph Goebbels was born on 29th October 1897 at Rheydt which, like its twin city of Muenchen-Gladbach (now Moenchen-G.), was dominated by the textile industry. In common with the majority of the population, his parents were Roman Catholics, and not only as a matter of form. It seems difficult to establish the occupation of Friedrich Goebbels, Joseph's father. Older biographies describe him as foreman or charge hand, but according to the most recent biography—which also relies on statements by members of the family—he was an office worker in an incandescent mantle factory, in which he eventually rose to a managerial position. Perhaps all statements are correct, and Goebbels' father started as a manual worker and, by his own efforts, bettered his position. This, at any rate, is how his son once described the situation when he spoke of the sacrifices and stubborn efforts of his parents to help their sons to get on in life and to lift them out of their narrow lower middle-class surroundings into which the parents had emerged from the working class. Not that the Goebbels family can have lived in any luxury—in 1917, when applying for a scholarship, Goebbels said that his father's salary was between 315 and 355 marks. Paul Joseph was one of several children. He had two older brothers, Hans and Konrad, and a sister, Elisabeth, older than himself, but she died in 1915. In later years Goebbels was more attached to his sister Maria, who was twelve years younger, than to his brothers.

Just as the family is uncertain about the occupation of the father, who died in 1929, it is uncertain about the cause of Paul Joseph's club-foot. In this respect, too, the two biographies which are based on detailed interrogation of members of the family differ slightly. According to one version the child, at the age of seven, contracted osteomyelitis and the left thigh had to be operated on; this weakened the left leg and retarded development so that the left leg was in the end three inches shorter than the right one. The second version attributes the affliction expressly to poliomyelitis at the age of four. What both explanations have in common is that they describe the deformity as not congenital, which it was commonly understood to be in the Third Reich.

Whatever the origin of the deformity its effect on the mind of the crippled boy, with his weak and underdeveloped body and huge head, and on his relations with playmates and school-fellows of his own age can be well imagined. No wonder that Joseph Goebbels concentrated all his energy on intellectual work. At play and in physical contacts he was necessarily always beaten, but with his mind he was determined to surpass all others. His good intellectual equipment made success certain. The parents sent Joseph to the grammar school, although this entailed heavy sacrifices; the other children had a secondary school education.

Joseph Goebbels was among the best in his form, although he did not surpass everyone. One of his last reports shows three firsts—in scripture, Latin and German. He was not a popular boy, being considered a careerist and a tell-tale, who wanted to get into the good books of the masters and did not hesitate to inform against the other boys. He was also thought to be arrogant and conceited, but this was no doubt the bastion built by the young weakling, who was always on the defensive.

From his school-leaving examination Goebbels emerged with practically top marks. His German essay was the best and he was allowed to deliver the farewell oration. When it was over the headmaster was said to have clasped his hand, saying: 'Good, Goebbels, very good. Content excellent, but believe me, you will never be a good speaker.'

Not many of those who left school that Easter in 1917 have survived, for many volunteered for military service. Even the cripple presented himself at the recruiting depot—evidence that even then he inclined to the grand and meaningless gesture, or that he deceived himself. The medical officer would hardly look at him: he was quite useless for service at the front, but was accepted for non-combatant duties and served for a while as a clerk. Then the war was over as far as he was concerned.

At Bonn University Goebbels began reading German, history and Latin. His father wanted one of his sons to graduate and Joseph was best qualified to do so. He was given an allowance of fifty marks a month, but even so had to interrupt his very first semester. Later, he supported himself by coaching, and he received a loan from the Roman Catholic Albertus Magnus Society, to which he had applied for help. Not that he received any extravagant funds from that source, barely a thousand marks all told between 1917 and 1920, but the society had to wait ten years for repayment, and recovered the money in 1930 only by taking Goebbels, then the Gauleiter of Berlin, to court.

Despite his financial straits Joseph Goebbels went freely from one university to another. In the summer of 1918 he went from Bonn to Freiburg, where he spent one semester, and he was at Würzburg when Germany collapsed in the winter of that year. He went back to Freiburg for the summer semester of 1919, and on to Munich in the following winter—a long-standing ambition hitherto unattainable because he had been unable to find digs. In 1920 Goebbels settled down in Heidelberg, where, in November 1921, he took the PhD with a thesis, *Wilhelm Schuetz; A Contribution to the History of the Romantic Theatre.*

During those years at the university several events occurred which significantly influenced Goebbels' life. He became estranged from the Church; this developed during his second semester at Freiburg and at Munich, and coincided with the termination of his Albertus Magnus grant. This estrangement led to differences with his devout Catholic parents, especially with his father, who was seriously perturbed and full of reproaches. This cooling of relations between father and son becomes apparent in the diary; the rift had probably not quite closed when the father died.

Simultaneously young Goebbels was acquiring literary ambitions. In a will made at the end of October 1920 he appointed his brother literary executor for his—unpublished—poems and stage-play drafts. Interest in the revolutionary political events seems to have hardly exceeded the degree of patriotism and disappointment felt by most young undergraduates in those years. On the other hand, while in Heidelberg, he probably received a mental wound that was to influence his mind. Vain as he was, and used to leading his fellows in the intellectual field, Goebbels failed to break into the exclusive circle of Friedrich Gundolf, the literary 'Pope' of Heidelberg. This representative of the Stefan George circle was repelled by the bearing of the ambitious young man. And Gundolf—whose original name was Gundelfinger—was a Jew.

Two people who made a deep impression on Goebbels, as can be seen from diary entries several years later, he also met in his student days. It was probably at Freiburg that Goebbels came under the influence of a young man who soon became his friend. Richard Flisges had returned from the war seriously wounded and with high decorations. He wanted to go to the university but failed his entrance examination. This, as he believed, unmerited disqualification, probably made the young man, who may have leaned in the direction before, a rebel against the existing social order—a pacifist, a communist, even a nihilist.

Thus Goebbels, hitherto more or less untroubled by a philosophy of life, was drawn into the whirlpool of opinions passionately expressed and joined together higgledy-piggledy. Flisges introduced Goebbels to the philosophy of Dostoevsky, of Marx and Engels and of Rathenau. The altars built to this dominating friend were probably not destroyed altogether when after a few months Goebbels began to free himself from intellectual shackles; his pride presumably drove him to support an antithesis—nationalism and war. Soon the two young men were completely estranged, but the nimbus of friendship remained, especially when Flisges, who had become a miner, was killed in a mine in Upper Bavaria in July 1923. Goebbels also retained the anti-bourgeois concept of class warfare, latent to the very end though concealed for opportunist reasons. Years later his diary recorded regret at the senseless fight with erring communist class-brothers, and in 1944 and 1945 Goebbels was one of the few National Socialist leaders who dreamed of an 'eastern solution' rather than a 'western solution'.

Finally, there was Anka, Joseph Goebbels' first great love, the first of a long line of women in the life of this man for whom love had become a mania. Goebbels the lover was always active, compensating for his inhibitions by passion. No doubt his physical handicaps contributed to this. In this field at least he wanted to demonstrate his manhood.

Diary entries indicate that Anka came from Itzehoe and later lived in Recklinghausen. Biographers have said nothing about her occupation. In Goebbels' *Michael* she was a student. Her second name has been given as Hellhorn or Stahlhern, but neither tallies with Goebbels' own records. At any rate she was described as beautiful and coming from a good family, and later, during the Third Reich, she was said to have remembered her former lover. The romance, probably begun in Freiburg in the summer of 1918, lasted a fairly long time, until 1922. According to later diary entries, the semester at Würzburg seems to have been closely connected with this girl.

Anka was followed by Else—a 'half-Jew', according to the Nuremberg Laws. The diary that follows prominently records the climax and end of this love affair. Having taken his degree Joseph Goebbels went back to Rheydt. He did not sit for the teaching diploma, for he considered the career of a schoolmaster out of the question, although his subjects would have made this a likely choice. His ambitions were connected with writing, possibly the stage. This was the time when he wrote *Michael,* dedicated to Richard Flisges, on whose life he drew for the 'fateful German character'. The novel's other main character was Anka, portrayed in Hertha Holk, and there was also a Russian, to whom years later Goebbels addressed an open letter on politics. Goebbels offered the novel to Ullstein and Mosse, but these two 'Jewish' publishers returned the manuscript, just as Theodor Wolff, the 'Jewish' editor of *Berliner Tageblatt,* returned a series of articles which Goebbels had written.

The young man lived with his parents. He wrote poems, plays, essays and articles, and earned some money by coaching and book-keeping. Fritz Prang, a friend from his schooldays, had a girl-friend, Alma, who was a teacher; subsequently Goebbels did not hesitate to make advances to her. Alma introduced Goebbels to one of her colleagues, Else, who has already been mentioned. Her home was at Duisburg, but she taught at a school in Rheydt. Goebbels' sister, Maria, went to that school, and so Else came to see the Goebbels family, the two young people fell in love, and the two couples became an inseparable group.

Through Else, Goebbels obtained an appointment with the Cologne branch of the Dresdner Bank, where he worked with distaste for nine months. Then Fritz Prang got him another job, that of price-teller at the Cologne stock exchange. It seems to be well established that Goebbels took no great interest in politics during those years; possibly even the struggle for the Ruhr district and the French occupation affected him little. While Prang joined Hitler's party in 1922, Goebbels, though full of nationalist gestures, would not commit himself. The story that a speech by Hitler in 1922 converted him and that he joined the Munich branch of the party in that year is most probably a later invention of Goebbels himself, like the story that he had written to Hitler while the latter was detained at Landsberg. Goebbels' party membership number, No. 22, was of course subsequently 'acquired'.

In fact, Joseph Goebbels went in for politics as late as 1924. At that time he was going through a period of inner conflict, gaiety and sociable conduct alternating with depression leading to freely advertised suicide threats. The main cause of despair was probably his failure to get on in life, which angered his family. Had they made all those heavy financial sacrifices for a boy who now spent his days doing nothing or, at any rate, doing little more than casual work? Goebbels himself looked at his life in a different way. He considered himself excluded from work to which his ability entitled him, excluded by the Jews who dominated cultural life and would only allow 'their own people' to advance.

In January 1924 Goebbels made a final attempt; he applied for a job on the *Berliner Tageblatt,* but was turned down. He fared similarly with the stage. Meanwhile, Prang had introduced him to nationalist and National Socialist circles, and he had taken part in the discussions at some of their meetings. At last, Franz von Wiegershaus, the Elberfeld nationalist politician and Prussian diet deputy, appointed Goebbels his private secretary at a monthly salary of a hundred marks. His duties included speaking at party meetings and helping with the editing of *Völkische Freiheit,* a small weekly magazine published by von Wiegershaus. At the end of 1924 this work brought him into contact with prominent National Socialists in West Germany.

Early in 1925, when after Hitler's release from Landsberg the NSDAP was re-formed, there was a chance of new work. Goebbels was appointed manager of the Gau Rheinland-Nord, Karl Kaufmann's Gau, with his office at Elberfeld; as such he drew two hundred marks a month. This post was coupled with a kind of secretaryship to Gregor Strasser, the North and West German party leader, who had transferred to Berlin and left his secretary, one Heinrich Himmler, behind in Landshut. Finally, Goebbels was to help with the editing of a magazine which Strasser wanted to bring out and which was intended as the 'intellectual mouthpiece' of the party.

The surviving part of the diary opens at this stage of Goebbels' career; it pictures the events of the following months. What is the broad impression that these pages convey of Goebbels' political conduct and development? First, they show clearly his transition from a mere party member to an unconditional follower of Hitler. Originally Goebbels had had certain fixed political ideas; at any rate, that was what he pretended. Strongly attached to his West German friends, he had even joined the anti-Munich junta and indulged in the most acid criticism of the party leader. Then he suddenly changed course and became an uncritically admiring follower. It is difficult to be sure whether this change of heart was caused by Hitler's magic or by an opportunist assessment of the forces ranged on either side.

Clearly both factors contributed, but it can be assumed that the second factor prevailed. For though easily roused to enthusiasm, Goebbels was essentially a man who, when his personal interests were at stake, kept a cool head. At the same time, it remains doubtful whether at that juncture Goebbels knew that his choice was prompted by a political philosophy which determined his actions to the end. Throughout his life Goebbels was actuated by an anti-capitalist resentment, typical of the *petit bourgeois* intellectual, the intensity of which probably dated from his disappointments as a young writer. It was essentially fortuitous that Goebbels plumped for National Socialism rather than for Marxism or Bolshevism. Moreover, he had no scruples, being quite prepared to turn traitor when it paid. And Hitler paid—that much this shrewd cripple grasped in a flash. This period is covered by the diary which reveals how the mind of Goebbels worked.

The last notes of the diary, written at the end of October 1926, mention the decision just arrived at that Goebbels was to go to Berlin as Gauleiter. Of course, that sounds far grander than it was, for no one could say that the NSDAP was then a particularly imposing force in the city. In his *Struggle for Berlin* Goebbels wrote, not unfairly, that 'what went as the party in Berlin in those days in no way deserved that description. It was a wildly mixed collection of a few hundred people with National Socialist ideas.' Such hostility had developed between the political organization, led by the Strasser brothers, and the SA under Kurt Daluege, later to become chief of police, that their leaders slapped each other's faces at meetings. In this situation Hitler sent Goebbels to Berlin as a kind of umpire. Berlin thus became the scene of a struggle between the Strassers and their erstwhile young

man who suddenly appeared as Hitler's *stadholder* in the centre of 'left-wing deviationists'; earlier there had been a crisis caused by the extreme anti-capitalism, federalism and anti-Munich conduct of the North and West Germans. From this crisis Hitler emerged as victor, and his opponents, gritting their teeth, surrendered unconditionally.

The Berlin Documents Centre papers from the files of the Supreme Party Tribunal . . . and fragments from Goebbels' personal file are good illustrations of the hard but successful struggle of the new Gauleiter. Read in conjunction with the diary for the preceding year they round off the picture of Goebbels' early years in politics and provide a very revealing contribution to the history of the deteriorating relations between Goebbels and the Strasser brothers—a development indicative of the shifting balance of forces in, and the political trend and whole character of, the NSDAP.

Werner J. Dannhauseer (essay date 1963)

SOURCE: "Goebbels's Nature," in *Commentary,* Vol. 34, No. 3, March, 1963, pp. 272-76.

[*In the following review of* The Early Goebbels Diaries, *Dannhauser details Goebbels's shortcomings as a diarist.*]

To readers of history, [**The Early Goebbels Diaries 1925-1926**] will prove disappointing. There is little new historical information to be gained from them, and there are even occasional distortions of the facts we already have. We know, for instance, that during the period spanned by the diary entries—August 24, 1925, to October 30, 1926—the Nazi party was still small and disorganized. But the impression Goebbels gives is the opposite: the entire adult population of Germany seems to be attending the rallies which he describes. Moreover, Goebbels was in no position to impart "inside" information even had he wished to; he was still at this time a long way from becoming "the man next to Hitler." When the book opens, he is a member of the Strasser faction in the Rhineland, "out in the sticks" for the Munich-centered movement; at the time of the final entry fourteen months later, he is about to become *Gauleiter* of a Berlin which is not the stronghold but the Achilles' heel of the movement. It is only from this position that he will begin his rise to prominence. The diaries *do* provide new data on the factionalism within the party—between *national* socialists and national *socialists*—which grew and subsided during this period. But the main outlines of Nazi party affairs in the mid-20's have been known before this, and admirably described by Bullock himself in his book on Hitler. Nevertheless, the book is entirely fascinating.

This is due in large part to the fascination we bring to the figure of Goebbels. I cannot here discuss the meaning and grounds of it, but I know it exists, and especially among Jews. It is compounded by a bizarre nostalgia we have begun to feel even for the *terrible* past. Goebbels was, after all, not a fictional character, but terribly real, and the diaries promise to tell us what this monstrous man "was really like." The reader welcomes the very badness of the book, which proves it to be genuine and not written for publication: nobody could possibly *choose* to appear this way in print.

These journals reveal Goebbels as an abominable diarist. A good diarist is one who makes his journal the battleground of a genuine struggle for self-knowledge, or an austere man who uses the occasion to settle accounts with himself, or a genius for whom a journal is a playground, sometimes the place where he fashions masks. In good diaries, therefore, one expects poignant reflections on the quest for sincerity (which often take the form of reflections on diary-keeping), or the genuine self-reckonings of the ascetic, or the aphorisms and witticisms which are the spontaneous overflow of a great mind. Very few of these things are to be found here. There is no struggle for self-knowledge, but rather the empty praise of struggle (if only because of the title of Hitler's book [*Mein Kampf*]) by a man who thinks he knows what and who he is: tragic figure in a hostile world. There are no austere reckonings, but endless recitals of activities. And his remarks are so far from brilliant that they force one to wonder on what basis so many have agreed that Goebbels, say whatever else you will, was a genius. Is it because we have an Iago complex and assume that evil must always be spectacularly brilliant?

Goebbels was a bad diarist who wanted to be a good one. The result is a parody of a good diary, a diary of adolescent romanticism. All the conventions of the genre are obeyed: The hero is never alone without being lonely and never in company without being alone; he is never tired but always weary to the breaking point. He is not content or gloomy but ecstatic or wretched; he both fears death and yearns for it, and sometimes imagines himself already dead. He addresses his heart and his soul. "Heart, be silent." "Be still, my soul!" Childhood is bliss but not to be recovered; home is bliss, but one can't go home again. On birthdays he reflects on getting old, and on the New Year he Takes Stock. This is Goebbels's entry on January 1, 1926, in its entirety: "I close the old year. It brought me much joy, much consolation, much misery, much despair. Now I am in the midst of everything. And enter the new state with courage! We have progressed! We must progress infinitely further! The struggle continues!" (Almost 70 per cent of the entries end with exclamation points, and almost 90 per cent contain them.)

The days he describes are remarkably alike. There is always too much work, most of it paperwork. With peculiar German thoroughness the Nazis were determined, even by 1925, to be the best-documented political movement of all time. There is usually a speaking engagement. Goebbels's account of it almost never varies. He notes the size and composition of the audience, the length of his speech (totalitarian speakers invariably talk longer than others), and the response to the speech; he *never* mentions what he said. He likes to call himself a preacher. A successful speech "inspires" the audience or makes it shudder.

Within this framework one looks in vain for his inner life. One seeks real passion but finds only artificially stimulated frenzy. The woman of the diaries is Else. When he is not yearning for Else to arrive, he is waiting impatiently for her to leave. When he is pleased by her, he realizes that it is because *she* loves *him,* but this, of course, becomes impossible to bear. He regrets his increasing estrangement from his family, but generally after an experience of failure. What is more surprising is that he does not really hate much either. He can scorn or disdain, and is a master of resentment, but there is no great passion in any of it. Jews, for example, are mentioned in the diary less frequently and much more perfunctorily than one would expect. Instead of passions there are moods ranging from the suicidal to the euphoric. But since they change from day to day, and sometimes between the beginning of an entry and the end, and since they are usually devoid of all discernible consequences, one discounts them. He is capable of certain insights, but never reaches the basic one of seeing himself as actor or poseur. Expecting such a man's emotional life to be demonic, one finds it is only drab.

The landscape of his mind is equally dreary. His view of man is simple: man is an animal, a worm, a beast; man is cowardly and lukewarm; man is evil. To the extent that he is not by nature completely depraved, he has been corrupted and degraded by politics. Significantly, Goebbels does not think of himself as a politician. He shares with other Nazis a contempt for day-to-day politics, a contempt that, in the Right wing of our time, is contained in the distinction between the "great" politics of the future and "petty politics," that is, politics as one really knows it. (The distinction is similar to the one the Left makes between making history and making politics.) His political views, such as they are, circle around the opinion that Russia is fascinating (a view he is soon to surrender without anguish) and that workers are more trustworthy than bosses. He has little interest in the actual politics of the Weimar Republic, except that, characteristically enough, he views Locarno, which marked Germany's re-entry into respectability and the Western community, with scorn. Whatever happens in real politics he must find repulsive, since men are beasts whose beastliness is accentuated by politics. At times he insists on playing the Stock Nazi, a volatile combination of sentimentality and brutality. The reader does not at first realize that the "Benno" Goebbels refers to frequently is the family dog, whom he describes in human terms and prefers to human company. He can enjoy riots in which heads are bashed, he can write of a book, "Cruel and great!" but he is also *shocked* to find prostitution rife on the Hamburg waterfront.

He thinks mechanically, that is, in words. The good words are "fanatic" and "revolutionary." The bad words are "waffler" and "philistine." He discovers that Else, his father, and almost everybody in Berlin and Munich are philistines. He reads a good deal, including novels, glorifications of Germany's past, and crackpot books of the extreme Right (Christ as Aryan, etc.). He likes Schubert and Wagner, does not like Ibsen. He is at least formally educated, and can refer to Thomas Mann, Goethe, Schiller, and Kant. His judgments of people are subject to quick change, and not particularly incisive. Thus he recognizes Feder, an economist of sorts who advocated the abolition of "interest slavery," as a crank, but considers Alfred Rosenberg "brilliant." As for Streicher—for whom the label sex pervert is a kindness—Goebbels knows him to be "a sow," but also calls him courageous and honest.

In rare moments the dreariness and repulsiveness of all this are relieved. In a man like Goebbels all minor vices become endearing because they establish his bonds with humanity: we read almost with pleasure that he worries about excessive smoking, ponders his inability to be true to Else, and is given to sleeping all through Sunday. And rarely, very rarely, he shows the qualities of a poet, as when he writes of the Hamburg harbor, "Out there in fog and smoke lie the ships. There is a feeling of the sea and of America." But even at his most appealing moments he is frightening, for the few remaining vestiges of humanity are clearly withering or being squelched.

Yet one must resist the temptation of picturing Goebbels as the great cynic or even nihilist, for that is to miss the point. It will not do to characterize him as an opportunist who knew he was evil and enjoyed that knowledge, or as a cynical manipulator who deliberately projected a fraudulent image of Hitler and delighted in his own success, or as the cold man who rode to power with Hitler without believing in him. It will not do because, as the diary shows, he was really enchanted by Hitler, turning to him not for ulterior motives but because he had no basis for judging or resisting him.

Strasser, for whom Goebbels worked in 1925, was a competitor for leadership of the party. Hitler opposed the radicalism to which Goebbels was at this time committed. The first mention of Hitler in the diaries (August 21, 1925) shows, however, that Goebbels did not blame Hitler for the opposition. Hitler can be criticized only for excessive kindness in not getting rid of bad advisers. On August 29, Goebbels is reading *Mein Kampf.* He finds it "wonderful."

In October of the same year, the factionalism grows bitter, and Strasser fans the flames. On October 12, Goebbels writes: "Letter from Strasser. Hitler does not trust me. He has abused me. How that hurts." On October 14, he shows that this has *not* lessened his reverence, writing of Hitler: "Who is this man? Half plebeian, half God! Really Christ, or only John?" It is all some misunderstanding that would be solved if only he could break through and "get close to Hitler" (October 19). On November 6, the crisis is over because Hitler was friendly: "Shakes my hand like an old friend. And those big blue eyes, like stars."

Alas, the dispute swells up again. Goebbels is involved in proposing a party program which enrages Hitler. This time Goebbels will fight, even though he now has "a number of new photographs of him [Hitler] on my desk" (February 6, 1926). At a Bamberg rally Hitler comes out against expropriating the property of princes, which Goebbels advocated. A break seems inevitable, *the* crisis is upon him. "I can no longer believe in Hitler absolutely. . . . I have lost my inner support" (February 15).

The crisis begins to wane in less than a month. Goebbels reads a pamphlet by Hitler on the Tyrol question, and many doubts are dispelled. In a month, "Hitler is great . . . I bow to his greatness, his political genius!" (April 13). Six days later Goebbels exorcises his last vestige of independence. Though Hitler "has not yet quite appreciated the Russian problem," what does it matter? For he has "taken me to his heart like no one else . . . Adolf Hitler, I love you, because you are both great and simple. A genius" (April 19). Only in connection with Hitler does Goebbels speak of love, and he does so frequently.

When Goebbels receives the greatest of all possible gifts, a few days with Hitler in the mountains, he is captured forever. He will go to Berlin, because Hitler wants him to go. He does not even resent Strasser's opposition, treating it as understandable envy. On July 24, he records a day spent listening to Hitler: "He is a genius. The natural creative instrument of a fate determined by God. I am deeply moved." At night, Hitler's words sound like prophecy: "Up in the skies a white cloud takes on the shape of the swastika. There is a blinking light that cannot be a star."

That is what Goebbels was "really like." He is neither cynic nor opportunist, for he shows a capacity for selfless devotion that could not possibly be faked. We do not seem to have the proper categories for understanding such a man: to know what he was like is not to understand him. We have only a terrifying clue which the word "selfless" gives us. We work from the surface through a maze of moods and thoughts only to find that the periphery conceals a dead center. In his own words, he has no "inner supports." Goebbels is the man with *nothing* in his soul, and hence there is nothing to understand, except that the man with nothing in his soul is the ideal vessel for that most evil of men, the man with the lie in his soul—Hitler. One can never wrong an empty man enough, but it is an error to attribute to him motives like treachery. We should have known that the celebrated propaganda triumphs of the later years could not have been perpetrated by a cynical man.

Goebbels was fulfilled by Hitler, literally *filled full.* His real intelligence, or cleverness at least, was never directed to seeing Hitler as he was. There was no self to direct it. History bears us out. Though Hitler never completely trusted him, it was Goebbels who proved to be the one trustworthy man in Hitler's inner circle. Only Goebbels chose to remain in the bunker with Hitler, and to imitate Hitler's suicide. It was the most graceful possible act of a type of man who can exhibit grace *only* under pressure. In his death he showed that such a man is capable of only one virtue, the most terribly ambiguous virtue of all: loyalty.

Joachim C. Fest (essay date 1970)

SOURCE: "Joseph Goebbels: Man the Beast," in *The Face of the Third Reich: Portraits of the Nazi Leadership,* translated by Michael Bullock, Pantheon Books, 1970, pp. 93-7.

[*In the following essay, Fest analyzes Goebbels's effectiveness as a propagandist for the Third Reich.*]

Propaganda was the genius of National Socialism. Not only did it owe to propaganda its most important successes; propaganda was also its one and only original contribution to the conditions for its rise and was always more than a mere instrument of power: propaganda was part of its essence. What National Socialism meant is far less easily grasped from the contradictory and nebulous conglomerate of its philosophy than from the nature of its propagandist stage management. Carrying it to an extreme, one might say that National Socialism was propaganda masquerading as ideology, that is to say, a will to power which formed its ideological theorems according to the maximum psychological advantage to be derived at any given moment, and drew its postulates from the moods and impulses of the masses, in the sensing of which it was abnormally gifted. In view of its capacity for mediumistic communication with the 'mind' of the masses, it seemed not to require any real idea, such as had served to gather and hold together every other mass movement in history. Resentments, feelings of protest of the day and the hour, as well as that mechanical attachment which arises from the mere activation of social forces, replaced the integrative effect of an idea, in conjunction with a gift of handling crowds that made use of every technique of psychological manipulation. The majority of the ideological elements absorbed into National Socialism were nothing but material, assessed at varying degrees of effectiveness, for a ceaseless pyrotechnical display of propagandist agitation. Flags, Sieg Heils, fanfares, marching columns, banners and domes of searchlights—the whole arsenal of stimulants, developed with inventive ingenuity, for exciting public ecstasy was ultimately intended to bring about the individual's self-annulment, a permanent state of mindlessness, with the aim of rendering first the party adherents and later a whole nation totally amenable to the leaders' claim to power. The relative status of ideology and propaganda is shown more clearly than anywhere in that phraseology employed by numerous contemporaries that referred to National Socialism as 'experience', a term that tacitly outlawed any cognitive or critical approach. In fact this ideology was literally indisputable and evaded all objective analysis by retreating into the unimpeachable realms of pseudo-religious feelings, where the Führer reigned in solitary metaphysical monumentality. To be sure, this flight into the irrational, into regions where politics became a matter of faith, of *Weltanschauung,* answered a vehement need of the disoriented masses; nevertheless, there was a purposeful Machiavellian guidance behind the direction and forms it took, so that on closer inspection the apparently elemental demand proves to be the planned and repeatedly reawakened irrationalism to which the modern totalitarian social religions owe their support and their existence.

Joseph Goebbels was the brain behind this manipulation of minds, 'the only really interesting man in the Third Reich besides Hitler'. One of the most astonishingly gifted propagandists of modern times, he stood head and shoulders above the bizarre mediocrity of the rest of the regime's top-ranking functionaries. He was one of the few real powers in the movement's leadership, not merely a figurehead drawn into the light of history 'in the wake of the victorious cause'. These two, Hitler and Goebbels, complemented each other in an almost unique manner. For Hitler's sombre, complex-determined visions, his intuitive, ecstatic relationship with the masses, Goebbels found the techniques of persuasion, the rationalisations, the slogans, myths and images. It was from Goebbels that *der Führer,* the term by which Hitler appeared as redeemer, demiurge and blessed saviour, received its visionary content. He astutely turned the initially irresolute Adolf Hitler into *der Führer* and set him on the pillar of religious veneration. With strenuous Byzantinism, consciously mingling the sacred with the profane, he spread around Hitler that messianic aura which so appealed to the emotions of a deeply shaken nation. The cult of the Führer, whose true creator and organiser he was, not only exploited the need for faith and security, as well as the German's latent urge to self-abandonment in the face of a world stripped of its gods, but also gave the rising NSDAP the solid backbone of a hierarchical structure. The evidence of this cult is overwhelming. In *Der Angriff,* the paper he founded as Gauleiter of Berlin, Goebbels wrote, with a significant imitation [in the original] of biblical cadences and alliterations:

> Works of talent are the result of diligence, persistence, and gifts. Genius is self-creative by grace alone. The deepest force of the truly great man is rooted in instinct. Very often he cannot even say why everything is as it is. He contents himself with saying: It is so. And it is so. What diligence and knowledge and school learning cannot solve, God announces through the mouths of those whom he has chosen. Genius in all fields of human endeavour means—to have been called. When Hitler speaks, all resistance breaks down before the magical effect of his words. One can

only be his friend or his enemy. He divides the hot from the cold. But lukewarmness he spits out of his mouth. Many can know, even more can organise, but he alone in all Germany today can construct the political values of the future out of fateful knowledge through the power of the word. Many are called, but few are chosen. We are all unshakably convinced that he is their spokesman and guide. Therefore we believe in him. Over his inspiring human figure we see the grace of destiny at work in this man and cling with all our hopes to his ideal and are thereby bound to that creative force which carries him and all of us forward.

Elsewhere Goebbels described his feelings for the Führer as 'holy and untouchable'. He stated after a speech by Hitler that he had spoken 'profoundly and mystically, almost like a gospel', and affirmed in a protestation of loyalty: 'An hour may come when the mob rages around you and roars, "Crucify him!" Then we shall stand as firm as iron and shout and sing "Hosanna!"' In one of his regular birthday addresses on the eve of April 20, Goebbels declared, 'When the Führer speaks it is like a divine service', while in his early journal, whenever he conjures up the image of Hitler, we find passages in the most unbearably sentimental style, reminiscent of an adolescent's diary:

> We drive to Hitler. He is having his meal. He jumps to his feet, there he is. Shakes my hand. Like an old friend. And those big blue eyes. Like stars. He is glad to see me. I am in heaven. That man has got everything to be a king. A born tribune. The coming dictator.

Or elsewhere:

> Hitler is there. Great joy. He greets me like an old friend. And looks after me. How I love him! What a fellow! Then he speaks. How small I am! He gives me his photograph. With a greeting to the Rhineland. Heil Hitler! I want Hitler to be my friend. His photograph is on my desk.

Hitler's position in the mass party that was being formed was enormously reinforced by and received a positively metaphysical endorsement from such idolatry. The cult developed around his personality destroyed those beginnings of internal democracy which had characterised the party in its old form, and fostered its centralist, authoritarian structure. Hitler now finally became the exclusive central will, 'to whom were directed the party's members' desire for self-surrender, service and subordination, their weariness with responsibility, who alone knew how to pick up this desire and translate it into the redeeming political act'. He rewarded his 'faithful, unshakable shield bearer', as he once called Goebbels, by exceptional advancement at the beginning of his career and by giving him the distinction of being the partner and organiser of his private social life. Later a perceptible reserve entered their relationship. In so far as it was not due to purely tactical

considerations—the wish to undermine the Minister of Propaganda's patently excessive self-confidence by the well-tried method of the cold shoulder—this reserve may have sprung from Hitler's distrust of the practised adroitness with which Goebbels always managed to adapt himself to circumstances.

In fact, these overemotional declarations are by no means to be taken as honest statements of Goebbels' feelings; the exaggeratedly demonstrative accent alone is enough to make them profoundly dubious. All too often Goebbels 'met his Damascus', and his various conversions were never dependent upon an inner voice but upon an opportunist eye for the bigger battalions. 'I am an apostate', he once confessed. It was first and most consistently to himself that he applied that conviction of man's total guidability which later enabled him to organise whatever was asked of him: cheering and riots, pogroms, trust in the Führer, and the will to resist. The only clear brain within the party Old Guard, he was at the same time the least independent, and lacking in any personal core.

> I am only an instrument, / on which the old god Sings his song. / I am only a waiting vessel, Into which Nature pours the new wine / with a smile.

he wrote as a student. Destitute of any inner conviction himself, he merely knew how to place the convictions of others decoratively and effectively on display. He once admiringly confessed that the reason why Hitler was so dangerous was that he believed what he said. He himself, on the other hand, was never in his life able to believe what he said and concealed this shortcoming—which he fully understood to be a weakness—behind a front of cynicism. The soft, sentimental interior side of his nature, which yearned for dull but cosy certainties, was overlaid by a sober scepticism, and nothing that his longing for faith could construct stood up to the probing of his inquisitorial intelligence. The occasional cry of jubilation of the early days, 'I believe again,' or the formula *credo ergo sum* expressed all too clearly the hunger of the rationalist for a share in the heightened emotions and the self-forgetfulness of others, and significantly what the object of his hunger for faith might be was a matter of complete indifference to him. 'What matters is not so much what we believe; only that we believe.'

That the son of a strictly Catholic working-class family from Rheydt in the Rhineland should have found his ostensible certitude of faith, after years of agonising indecision, in the National Socialist movement is a stroke of historical irony. Highly gifted, he was subjected from an early age to a tormenting feeling of physical inadequacy; he had a weak constitution and a crippled foot. When he appeared in Geneva in 1933 as representative of the Reich, a caricature in a Swiss newspaper showed a crippled little man with black hair. Under it was written: 'Who is that?' Oh, that's the representative of the tall, healthy, fair-haired, and blue-eyed Nordic race!' This joke throws light on some of the difficulties Goebbels found himself up against in the midst of the old followers of Hitler, especially the rough SA. As a man with a physical deformity and an intellectual, he was something of a provocation to a party that regarded, not intellectual ability, but muscular strength and racial heritage, fair hair and long legs, as qualifications for genuine membership. The designation 'our little doctor', which quickly established itself, shows the sort of contemptuous esteem in which Goebbels was always held by his well-built, feeble-brained fellow fighters of the early days. In spite of their admiration for his demagogic brilliance, they were always suspicious of him. To their coarse slow-wittedness his rationality, his coldness always appeared strange and even 'un-German', and for a long time he was looked upon as a 'pupil of the Jesuits and a half Frenchman'. It was almost as a challenge to the human type demanded and moulded by the movement when he wrote: 'We are not content with opinions. We seek to confirm and deepen these opinions. We want clarity, clarity. Faith moves mountains, but knowledge alone moves them to the right place. In knowledge we seek clarity and the definition of our feelings.' Sentences such as this mark his intellectual distance from the type of mind predominant in the NSDAP, who, as Goebbels once said, 'has in his heart that which he does not have in his head, and, which is the main thing, has it *in his fists*'.

Undoubtedly Goebbels suffered from not being like everyone else. Above all, at the beginning of his rise to power, as Gauleiter of Berlin—when he depended upon the absolute loyalty of an SA detachment whose criteria of merit were an uncritical activism, an athletic taste for violence and the dullest 'normality'—he found his authority repeatedly subjected to irritating curbs. Like Mirabeau (and equally in vain) he may at times have asked God to bestow upon him that mediocrity from whose simple raptures he felt himself excluded. This was the source of his hatred of the intellect, which was a form of self-hatred, his longing to degrade himself, to submerge himself in the ranks of the masses, which ran curiously parallel with his ambition and his tormenting need to distinguish himself. He was incessantly tortured by the fear of being regarded as a 'bourgeois intellectual' and hence disqualified. His shrill anti-bourgeois complex sprang from this problem, as did his painfully exaggerated attitude of loyalty to the person of Adolf Hitler: it always seemed as though he were offering blind devotion to make up for his lack of all those characteristics of the racial élite which nature had denied him. Because his intellectualism and his physical deformity combined to make him particularly vulnerable among his rivals for power, he developed into an uninhibited opportunist with an exceptional nose for the power relationships in his circle. In the internal conflicts of direction within the party Goebbels, by virtue of his temperament and his intellectual consistency, often found himself on the ideological wing, yet he always managed to switch in good time to the side of the majority.

Tactical moves merely camouflaged the dichotomy, however, and with all his aptitude for self-deception he could not in the long run refrain from calling himself to account, even if more or less involuntarily. 'Everything within me revolts against the intellect,' he wrote early on. And then, betraying the real cause of all his tensions and awkwardness: 'My foot troubles me badly. I am conscious of it all the time, and that spoils my pleasure when I meet people.'

He also tried continually to offset the bitter consciousness of his deformity. His hunger for status and prestige and the strained style of his early literary efforts, based on the language of military commands, bear witness to this. He liked to see himself as hard and manly, but it was the forced hardness of a sensitive young man—who once made a pilgrimage to lay a bunch of wild flowers on the grave of the poet Annette von Droste-Hülshoff. Only in unguarded romantic moods, as for instance in his helplessly sentimental poems, did he allow himself to depart a little from his stern ideals. His whole literary and propaganda output displays three curiously contrasting layers: alongside the stylistic and intellectual succinctness of his day-to-day political contributions is the foolishly strained pose of the fighter and finally the stammering bombast of his private jottings. 'In them dwells a poet and a soldier,' he makes the girl Hertha Holk say in his juvenile work *Michael,* after he himself had been graded 'fit for non-combatant duties only' and had just seen his first literary works fail. The very name of the hero, Michael, to whom he gave many autobiographical features, suggests the way his self-identification was pointing: a figure of light, radiant, tall, unconquerable. He too is the son of a peasant, who strides over 'steaming clods' and feels the blood of his forefathers rising 'slow and healthy' within him. 'I don my helmet, draw my sword and declaim Liliencron. Sometimes I am overcome by a sort of spasm. To be a soldier! To stand sentinel! One ought always to be a soldier,' wrote Michael-Goebbels. The fraudulent claim to having fought at the front which he made in this book, as in his later speeches when he used the phrase 'We who were shot up in the World War,' was intended to suggest that his crippled foot was the result of a war wound. The deception seems to have been successful for an astonishingly long time.

No doubt the same feeling of physical inferiority also provided the essential impulse behind his erotic activity. Both the wide range of his various affairs, as revealed by those parts of his private diary that have been found, and the tone of these confessions very clearly betray the desire to appear 'a hell of a fellow', even if only in his own eyes. 'Alma sends me a postcard from Bad Harzburg,' he notes in his diary. 'The first sign of life since that night. Alma, the teaser and charmer. I quite like this girl. First letter from Else from Switzerland.' (August 14, 1925). 'Little Else, when shall I see you again? Alma, you lithe, lovely flower! Anka, I shall never forget you.' (August 15, 1925). And a little later: 'Yesterday Hagen together with Else. Celebrated my birthday together. She gave me a nice coloured cardigan. A sweet night. She is a good darling. Sometimes I hurt her bitterly. What a budding, bursting night of love. I am loved! Why complain!' (October 28, 1925). But a few days later his mood changes: 'Over me and women there hangs a curse. Woe to those who love you! What an agonising thought. One is ready to despair.' (November 10, 1925). And finally he comes to the conclusion: 'Such is life: many blossoms, many thorns, and—a dark grave.' (July 18, 1926). In any case: 'Marriage would be torment. Eros raises his voice!' (July 29, 1926). Such outpourings by a man who after all was twenty-eight years old contrast with countless affirmations of an excessive self-confidence, which at all times turns abruptly into self-pity or, through a trivial demonisation of his own ego, threatens a plunge into the void. Then he writes, for example:

> I am reading Gmelin's *Temudchin* (the Lord of the Earth). Every woman rouses my blood. I run hither and thither like a hungry wolf. And yet I am shy as a child. Often I can hardly understand myself. I ought to get married and become a philistine! And then hang myself after a week!

The Lord of the Earth, the feelings of a wolf, satiety and a profound insecurity. In so far as it was not sheer necessity, such impulses undoubtedly helped to persuade this academic, whose professional career had so far been a failure, to enter the NSDAP at the end of 1924. To reassure his worried parents he worked for a short time in a bank, after completing his studies, and then took a job as caller on the stock exchange, before finally, as secretary to a nationalist politician, he came into contact with the National Socialists. As a collaborator of Gregor Strasser he belonged first to the social-revolutionary North German wing of the party which, in its 'proletarian' anti-capitalist tendencies, differed markedly from the 'Fascist' South German wing. In Goebbels it found one of its most consistent spokesmen. 'I am the most radical. Of the new type. Man as revolutionary,' he noted, almost ecstatically, in his diary of those years, and in his **'Letters to Contemporaries'** he passionately dissociated himself from the bourgeois half-heartedness of the politicians of the German National People's Party. 'Tools of destruction they will call us,' he wrote in that characteristic tone of self-regarding revolutionary fervour. 'Children of revolt, we call ourselves with a poignant tremor. We have been through revolution, through revolt to the very end. We are out for the radical revaluation of all values'; people would 'take fright at the radicalism of our demands'. Even at that time he announced, 'In the last analysis better go down with Bolshevism than live in eternal capitalist servitude,' and thought it 'horrible that we and the Communists bash in each other's heads'. In an open letter to **'My Friend of the Left'** he listed a whole catalogue of convictions and attitudes in common, among them fundamental agreement on the need for social solutions, common enmity towards the bourgeoisie and the 'lying system', as well as the fight 'for freedom' waged 'honestly and resolutely' by both sides, so that ultimately the only division

remained the tactical question of the most appropriate means. 'You and I,' Goebbels finished his letter, 'we are fighting one another although we are not really enemies. By so doing we are splitting our strength, and we shall never reach our goal. Perhaps the last extremity will bring us together. Perhaps!'

These questions raised by the socialist wing of the movement brought Goebbels into violent conflict, above all, with the so-called 'Munich group', the 'Munich big shots', as he called them. During this controversy, at a party congress in Hanover early in 1926, he made the famous demand 'that the petty bourgeois Adolf Hitler shall be expelled from the National Socialist Party'. But three weeks later, at a meeting called by the 'South Germans' in Bamberg, when he compared the external trappings, the prosperity and the great domestic power around Hitler with the material poverty of the Strasser group, he began for the first time to waver. True, he found Hitler's talk on Bolshevism, foreign policy, redemption of the rights and holdings of the princes and private property 'terrible' and spoke of 'one of the greatest disappointments of my life'; but when Hitler publicly embraced him shortly after a speech, Goebbels called him in gratitude 'a genius' and noted emotionally in his diary: 'Adolf Hitler, I love you'. Six months earlier he had asked himself who this man really was, 'Christ or St John?' Now, notably under the influence of a generous invitation to Munich and Berchtesgaden, his last doubts vanished, while simultaneously his ambition recognised the outlines of the role he might play. If Hitler was really 'Christ', then he wanted to be the one to take the part of the prophet; for 'the greater and more towering I make God, the greater and more towering I am myself'. In this sense it really was apt when he wrote that the days in Munich with Hitler had shown him his 'direction and path': the organiser of the Führer myth had found his mission. During his stay, he wrote in his diary:

> The chief talks about race problems. It is impossible to reproduce what he said. It must be experienced. He is a genius. The natural, creative instrument of a fate determined by God. I am deeply moved. He is like a child: kind, good, merciful. Like a cat: cunning, clever, agile. Like a lion: roaring and gigantic. A fellow, a man. He talks about the state. In the afternoon about winning over the state and the political revolution. It sounds like prophecy. Up in the skies a white cloud takes on the shape of the swastika. There is a blinking light that cannot be a star. A sign of fate?

From this point on he submitted himself, his whole existence, to his attachment to the person of the 'Führer', consciously eliminating all inhibitions springing from intellect, free will and self-respect. Since this submission was an act less of faith than of insight, it stood firm through all vicissitudes to the end. 'He who forsakes the Führer withers away,' he would say. Three months later in the autumn of 1926 Hitler rewarded him for this change of front by making him a Gauleiter 'with special mandatory powers' at the head of the small, conflict-riven party organisation in Berlin. The hectic, noisy atmosphere of the city particularly suited Goebbels' quick, street-urchin nature. Very early on he had realised that 'history is made in the street' that 'the street is the political characteristic of this age'. Now, by following this maxim to the limit, he rose within a few months to be the city's most feared demagogue. First of all, in order to get himself talked about, he and a tough bodyguard organised beer-hall battles, street brawls, and shooting affrays; one chapter in which he described this period carries the title 'Bloody Rise'. Shortly before this he had written: 'Beware, you dogs. When the Devil is loose in me you will not curb him again.' His practice of stirring up fights was the logical application of a new, completely Machiavellian principle of propaganda. The blood which the party's rise cost among its own members was regarded, not as an inevitable sacrifice in the struggle for a political conviction, but as a deliberate means of furthering a political agitation which had recognised that blood always makes the best headlines. As he stated in a speech of this period:

> That propaganda is good which leads to success, and that is bad which fails to achieve the desired result, however intelligent it is, for it is not propaganda's task to be intelligent, its task is to lead to success. Therefore no one can say your propaganda is too rough, too mean; these are not criteria by which it may be characterised. It ought not to be decent, nor ought it to be gentle or soft or humble; it ought to lead to success. If someone says to me, 'Your propaganda is not at a well-bred level,' there is no point in my talking to him at all. Never mind whether propaganda is at a well-bred level; what matters is that it achieves its purpose.

With the aid of these maxims directed exclusively towards success, Goebbels made considerable breaches in the massive front of so-called 'Red Berlin'. In the foreword to a collection of the essays which he had published during this period in his newspaper *Der Angriff,* he speaks with astonishment of the 'incredible freedom' he was allowed by the Republican authorities; and this volume is indeed one of the most damning pieces of evidence of their lack of the will to assert themselves, their infinite helplessness in the face of their sworn enemy. 'Put pressure on your adversary with ice-cold determination,' he says, describing his own demagogic tactics. 'Probe him, search out his weak spot; deliberately and calculatingly sharpen the spear, hurl it with careful aim where the enemy is naked and vulnerable, and then perhaps say with a friendly smile, Sorry, neighbour, but I can't help it! This is the dish of revenge that is enjoyed cold.'

There are countless examples of his method of fighting. For months on end he concentrated his attacks on the Berlin Police President Bernhard Weiss, whom he continually referred to as 'Isodore Weiss'. When the courts forbade him to use this name, he simply attacked the 'Isodore System'. He called Police President Karl Zörgiebel the 'publicity *goy* in the Police Praesidium'; the Reich Chancellor Hermann Müller, who had formerly been in the earthenware industry, a 'traveller in water closets'; Philipp Scheidemann a 'salon simpleton'—all without ever being seriously called to account. When a friend criticised him for his malicious attacks on Bernhard Weiss, who had been a gallant officer and was a man of integrity, he explained cynically that he wasn't in the least interested in Weiss, only in the propaganda effect. 'For our agitation we use whatever is effective.' Through middlemen he circulated scandalous rumours against Carl Severing and was delighted when the democratic press 'fell into the trap'. During the campaign against the Young Reparations plan he openly admitted that he had never read what he was so passionately attacking. 'Propaganda has absolutely nothing to do with truth!' In one article he called the Reichstag a 'stinking dungheap' and blatantly stated that the parliamentary mandate merely served to allow the NSDAP 'to equip itself with democracy's own weapons from the democratic arsenal'. With the same frankness he described the purpose of an election as 'to send a sabotage group into the exalted house', and finally, during the legislative period of 1928, he wrote: 'I am not a member of the Reichstag. I am an IdI. An IdF. An *Inhaber der Immunität* [possessor of immunity], an *Inhaber der Freifahrtkarte* [holder of a free-travel ticket]. What do we care about the Reichstag? We have been elected against the Reichstag, and we shall use our mandate in the spirit of those who gave it to us.' He concluded 'Now you are surprised, eh? But don't think we're already at an end. This is only the overture. You will have a lot more fun with us. Just let the play begin!' A classic example of his mastery of propaganda comes in an article of May 31, 1931, entitled **'The Marshal President'**:

> The presidency of the man to whom we here turn our attention was a deadly tragicomedy; it was based on a fundamental lack of character and an inability, cloaked in a dignified gravity, to see things as they really were. It is indeed painful to have to register the existence of a man merely because he was President of the Republic, a man whose grotesque insignificance raises in us the astonished question: How was it possible for this nincompoop to become Commander of the Imperial Army and President of the Republic?

Only at this point did the article reveal that the man referred to was not, as everyone was bound to think and meant to think, the Reich President von Hindenburg, but the French President MacMahon. When Brüning refused a challenge to a public debate, Goebbels had one of the Chancellor's speeches recorded and refuted it paragraph by paragraph in the Sportpalast, to the accompaniment of yells from his followers. One of his admirers aptly called him the 'Marat of Red Berlin, a nightmare and goblin of history' who wanders 'around the house of this system like a crow around a carcass. A ratcatcher. A conqueror of souls.' With the coming of the world economic crisis the masses flocked to him, and he showed extraordinary skill in mobilising their fears. As early as 1926 he declared in his pamphlet *Die Zweite Revolution* (**The Second Revolution**): 'We shall achieve everything if we set hunger, despair and sacrifice on the march for our goals. It is my will that we light the beacons in our nation till they form a single great fire of Nationalist and Socialist despair.' Now he openly welcomed the collapse, and did all he could to add fuel to the fires of despair. 'To unleash volcanic passions, outbreaks of rage, to set masses of people on the march, to organise hatred and despair with ice-cold calculation': this was how he saw his self-imposed task. And he succeeded. With diabolical flair, continually thinking up new tricks, he drove his listeners into ecstasy, made them stand up, sing songs, raise their arms, repeat oaths—and he did it, not through the passionate inspiration of the moment, but as the result of sober psychological calculation at the desk. Once he had got the reaction he wanted he stood there, small but erect, generally with one hand on his hip, above the tumult, coolly assessing the effect of his stage management. In truth, the 'little Doctor' with the tormenting feeling of physical inadequacy was capable of bending the masses to his will and making them available for any purpose; he could, as he boasted, play upon the national psyche 'as on a piano'. Out of Horst Wessel, the SA leader who was shot by a rival, at least partly for reasons of jealousy, in a fight over a whore, he created the movement's martyr; after a meeting-hall battle in the Pharus rooms in North Berlin he created the heroic type of the 'Unknown SA Man'; with a kind of underworld pride he made the name 'Chief Bandit of Berlin', applied to him by hostile agitators, his honorary title; he invented slogans, hymns and myths, and made capital out of every defeat. Tireless, tenacious, stubborn: propaganda has absolutely nothing to do with truth! Its success rested rather, as he provocatively confessed, on an appeal to the 'most primitive mass instincts'. He played a decisive part in the NSDAP's election successes wrung from the honest routine propaganda of the democratic parties. Immediately after January 30, 1933, he boasted that 'his propaganda had not only operated directly by winning over millions of supporters; equally important was its effect in paralysing opponents. Many had become so tired, so fearful, so inwardly despairing as a result of his onslaughts that in the end they regarded Hitler's chancellorship as fated.' His reward came in the middle of March 1933 when Hitler openly broke the coalition agreement to bestow upon him the long-planned Ministry for National Enlightenment and Propaganda. On taking office Goebbels cheerfully announced that 'the government intends no longer to leave the people to their own devices'. It was the task of the new ministry 'to establish political coordination between people and government'.

Skilfully riding the crest of a wave of consent made up of countless misunderstandings and blindnesses, he achieved this coordination in an amazingly short time and maintained it through all the phases of the regime right up to the end. Certainly the terrorist threat in the background effectively helped, but then the very essence of totalitarian government always lies in the combination of propaganda and terrorism. It is these two together that alone make possible that thoroughgoing psychological and social organisation of man which reduces the scope of individual freedom to the point of immobility. But we must not overestimate the part played by compulsion, and even such a critical observer, not subject to terrorist intimidation, as the American journalist William L. Shirer, has confessed that this propaganda 'made a certain impression on one's mind and often misled it'.

From the way the role of Goebbels in the further history of the Third Reich, after his promising beginning, at first continuously fell in importance and then, towards the end of the war, suddenly and significantly rose again, we can clearly see to what extent he—and with him National Socialism—had made his way to power by mobilising moods of protest and resentment; indeed, it shows the extent to which the totalitarian propagandist needs an enemy. So long as the young minister's energies were absorbed in building a flawless apparatus of propaganda and surveillance and the fight against internal political resistance still furnished the required material for the psychological manipulation of the masses, the problem remained concealed. Then, however, it emerged all the more distinctly, especially as resort to the creation of outside enemies was barred for a long time while the government strove to win recognition for itself.

In consequence Goebbels was pushed into the background, at first almost imperceptibly. His writings at this time also remain curiously dull and empty. He may have realised this, since he did not publish them in a collected edition, as he did his writings during the period of struggle and later during the war years. Explaining his waning influence at that time, he once stated that he often looked back with longing to the years before the seizure of power, when there was something to attack. Only when inner and outer political consolidation had progressed far enough for the control hitherto exercised to be abandoned did Goebbels find in the increasingly unrestrained practice of anti-Semitism by the state new possibilities into which he threw himself with all the zeal of an ambitious man worried by a constant diminution of his power. Thus the man who in earlier years had frequently mocked the primitive anti-Semitism of nationalist politicians now became one of the most relentless Jew-baiters. Unquestionably, personal motives also played a part; possibly his hatred of the Jews was an externalised form of self-hatred. A man who conformed so little to the National Socialist image of the élite and whose fellow pupils are said at one time to have called him 'the Rabbi' may have had his reason, in the struggles for power at Hitler's court, for offering keen anti-Semitism as a counterweight to his failure to conform to a type: ideological rectitude to counterbalance typological deviation. His attitude may also have had something to do with the fact that shortly before the onset of the great wave of anti-Semitism in 1938 he had risked his own prestige and that of the party by a passionate love affair, and was obsessed by the urge to rehabilitate himself. But whatever his real motives, it is fairly certain that Goebbels himself did not take the race theory seriously; one of his colleagues reported that during his twelve-year period in office Goebbels never once 'so much as mentioned it' inside the Ministry. The opportunist and tactical motives behind his anti-Semitism are also evident from the fact that the measures he took to purify German culture of foreign influences were directed predominantly against the representatives of a spirit far nearer his own inclinations than the oppressive National Socialist approach to art, which he himself now propagated. Lastly, everything seems to indicate that in Goebbels' anti-Semitism, over and above individual motives, we must see an example of that dialectic common to all totalitarian propaganda: the need for a barbarically exaggerated image of the opponent. This helps to harness the aggressions within a society while attaching the latent positive energies to emotional idealisations of its own leader figures. Only in this way could propaganda regain that vehemence which had once brought it such success, even if there was always an obvious element of strained artificiality about the demonised figure of the Jew as presented by Goebbels with ever more breathless efforts. All his attempts to paint the universal enemy as a wirepuller at work from Moscow to Wall Street were shattered by the reality of the frightened and harassed human beings wearing the yellow star, who for a time wandered the streets of German cities before suddenly vanishing forever. How much Goebbels' propaganda owed to the friend-enemy stereotype is also shown by a comment of Hitler's, which he proudly noted in his diary in 1943, to the effect that he 'is one of the few who today know how to make something useful out of the war'. The important thing about this first word of praise from Hitler for a long time is that it coincided with the turning-point in the war; for up to that time Goebbels, for all his efforts, had not succeeded in winning back the ground he had lost. Even towards the end of 1939 his rival Rosenberg had noted with satisfaction a statement by Hitler that for the duration of the war the Propaganda Minister must be kept as far as possible in the background. With the first crises and setbacks, on the other hand, when propaganda abandoned the unprofitable tone of confidence in victory in favour of a growing bitterness, and switched from contempt for the enemy to hatred, Goebbels made his long-prepared comeback. He showed once again his old impudent adroitness, his cynical art of sowing confusion, and with an enemy to hate he also regained that great rhetorical fervour which had once won him the reputation of being the party's best speaker, superior even to Hitler.

This was proved not only by his articles in the periodical *Das Reich,* in which he adopted the principle of at least *one* surprising concession to truth each time, but also by the inventiveness with which he wore down the enemy's nerve by broadcasts over the front lines, by mobilising fear of an imaginary fifth column, and other means. He invented new terms, such as 'Coventrisation', and later, according to the state of the war, the formula of the 'advantage of the inner line'. He deftly usurped the enemy's V-sign as a symbol of Germany's own confidence in victory, discouraged undesirable behaviour by the creation of easily understood characters like the 'coal grabber' or that threatening black shadow-man who announced from every wall that the enemy was listening. Finally, faced with the growing hopelessness of the military situation, he invented the 'secret weapon'. The astonishing effect of his ideas once more confirmed Hitler's assertion 'that by the clever and continuous use of propaganda a people can even be made to mistake heaven for hell, and vice versa, the most miserable life for Paradise'. Preoccupied as he was with propaganda, it was, as one of his colleagues confirmed, 'almost a happy day' for him when famous buildings were destroyed in an air raid, because at such times he put into his appeals that ecstatic hatred which aroused the fanaticism of the tiring workers and spurred them to fresh efforts. He strove for hours after the Stalingrad disaster to get Hitler's permission to stage a spectacular requiem, which finally took place in vast and sombre splendour. He achieved one of his greatest triumphs as a speaker when shortly afterwards he put his famous ten 'evocative questions' to an invited audience in the Sportpalast, raising them to a consciousness of being representative of the nation, and 'in a turmoil of wild emotion', as he wrote afterwards, won agreement to total war. Every sentence, every effect, every heightening of the emotional temperature in this speech, down to the electrifying final phrase, 'Now, nation, arise—storm, break loose!' had been carefully calculated days in advance. Even before he set out for this gathering he had confidently predicted: 'Today there will be a demonstration that will make the thirtieth of January rally look like a mothers' meeting.' But he took every care not to allow himself to be carried away, to see to it that he remained the organiser, never the victim, of his own propaganda effects, even if he did not always succeed in this, and occasionally found himself caught in the grip of his own demagogy. When later, faced with the enemy's approaching front, he played on the spectre of the 'Asiatic hordes' with all the means at his disposal, he at the same time called Soviet propaganda 'the best horse in the stable' and toyed with the idea of a separate pact with the East: a Machiavellian through and through, he desired power in exactly the same degree as he despised its objects.

In fact, Goebbels' career can be explained only on the basis of a deeply rooted contempt for humanity. Again and again the revealing expression 'man the beast' (*Canaille Mensch*) occurs in his private jottings, a favourite formula to express his humiliated personality. Opponents, friends, supporters and finally the whole nation never meant more to him than raw material for achieving successful effects and bolstering his self-exaltation and power. The tirades of hate and the festive Sportpalast—they all came from him and in purpose and execution were nothing but cynically admitted gimmicks. He could speak to the hearts of millions although not one word came from his own heart; he manipulated souls and ideas and himself: it was all one. As the coldest and most unscrupulous calculator among the top leadership, he was entirely free from that 'burden of conscience' the removal of which from the whole nation Hitler had announced as his historic mission. What urged him on throughout his life was the hatred felt by the weak, crippled and deformed which found satisfaction only when he could drive 'with ice-cold calculation' the healthy, those who were not crippled, through all the stages of delusion, intoxication and exhaustion. He seemed always anxiously trying to prove to the world that intelligent deformity was superior to dull-witted normality. In a report on a political discussion he noted, 'I dominated'. All his life he sought this consciousness of power. And if his physical weakness was the source of so many sufferings and tensions, it was certainly also one of the essential factors in his rise. He once recalled with amusement the statement of his old form master after his valedictory address that although he was gifted he was not cut out to be an orator, which only proves the point that a shortcoming may be the cause not only of great failure but also of great achievement.

Just as he himself only used other people, so he allowed himself right up to the end to be used without demur, without a thought of revolt. During the last phase of the war, he not only regained and actually heightened his power and prestige but also to a great extent recovered his personal position of trust with Hitler, so that there was no feeling of having been slighted which might have prompted him to follow an independent line. True, he showed a certain tendency to think for himself after realising that Hitler was beginning to lose his earlier intuitive certainty; but the attachment retained its strength, and up to the last he extolled 'the height of good fortune that allowed me to be his contemporary'. Even out of the ruins of the shattered Reich Chancellery he brought up again insanely and against his better knowledge the myth which he had once created that 'together with this man you can conquer the world'. The attempt had failed. But true to his principle that the propagandist must never contradict himself he continued—with Russian tanks already in the suburbs of Berlin—to call Hitler the only man who could point the way to a new and flourishing Europe. If the German people never shouted over Adolf Hitler the dreaded 'Crucify him!' it was largely due to Goebbels. But he himself, when all was manifestly lost, stood among the smoking debris and shouted 'Hosanna!' as he had once predicted, the paradoxical picture of an opportunist who at the last proved to be the most loyal follower. But what looked like loyalty was merely the realisation of his own lack of substance, which all his life, despite all his gifts, forced him into the role of substitute. He liked to hear himself referred to as the movement's Talleyrand, but he was

certainly not that. 'I never pursued a policy of my own,' he repeatedly asserted. Very true!

Unhesitatingly he accepted Hitler's end as his own. Unlike the former comrades in arms who ignominiously fled—Ley, Ribbentrop, Streicher—but also without the naïve self-deception of Göring or Himmler, he had no illusions as to how intensely they had provoked the world. 'As for us,' he wrote in *Das Reich* of November 14, 1943, 'we have burnt our bridges. We cannot go back, but neither do we want to go back. We are forced to extremes and therefore resolved to proceed to extremes.' And later: 'We shall go down in history as the greatest statesmen of all time, or as the greatest criminals.' He was level-headed enough to accept responsibility for the final verdict. For this reason he pressed Hitler, who as always was shrinking from important decisions, to await the end in the Reich Chancellery and add the crowning apotheosis to the artificially constructed myth. His last concern, to which he devoted himself with alert and tenacious resolution, was with a practised hand to make the end itself a spectacle of breathtaking grandeur. His remarks in his farewell conversation with Hans Fritzsche, in which, following Hitler's example, he ascribed the collapse to the failure of the German people, and at the same time the way he strove to intensify the process of destruction, were like a final seal set upon his contempt for humanity. 'When we depart, let the earth tremble!' were the last words with which, on April 21, 1945, he dismissed his associates. What he seemed to fear more than anything else was a death devoid of dramatic effects; to the end, he was what he had always been: the propagandist for himself. Whatever he thought or did was always based solely on this one agonising wish for self-exaltation, and this same object was served by the murder of his children, on the evening of May 1, 1945. They were the last victims of an egomania extending beyond the grave. However, this deed too failed to make him the figure of tragic destiny he had hoped to become; it merely gave his end a touch of repulsive irony. A few hours later he died, together with his wife, in the gardens of the Reich Chancellery.

'The essence of propaganda,' he once remarked, 'consists in winning people over to an idea so sincerely, so vitally, that in the end they succumb to it utterly and can never again escape from it.' By this standard, he undoubtedly failed; for the idea of National Socialism has been forgotten, or is at most only a memory. However, on closer inspection this maxim of propaganda proves to be itself no more than propaganda; in reality, totalitarian propaganda does not count on exercising a permanent influence. It bears witness to its own knowledge of the futility of its efforts in the capricious abruptness with which it alters watchwords and 'granite principles', demands damning judgments or oaths of loyalty, hails the deadly enemy of yesterday as the faithful ally of today, brands the friend a traitor, revokes, annuls, rewrites its history, and obtains from the people protestations of faith in each of its erratic changes of course, wiping out at each switch all previous truths and oaths of loyalty. There can be little doubt that Goebbels was occasionally aware of this, and his early words 'But scratch our names in history, that we shall do,' now sound like an anticipatory reply. Certainly he succeeded in this aim. It was probably a matter of indifference to him whether he figured in history as a criminal or a statesman, but how wretched is his fame compared with what it cost.

Viktor Reimann (essay date 1976)

SOURCE: "From National Bolshevik to Hilterite" and "From Reich Minister to Reich Chancellor," in *Goebbels,* translated by Stephen Wendt, Doubleday & Company, Inc., 1976, pp. 13-66, 210-26.

[*In the following excerpt, Remain examines Goebbels's novel* Michael *and his diaries for the years 1942 and 1943.*]

MICHAEL: A GERMAN FATE

Goebbels' literary output from 1921-24 included several plays, most of them unfinished: one about Christ, *Judas Iscariot;* another, *Heinrich Kämpfert;* and plays called *The Sowing* and **The Wanderer. The Wanderer** was produced on November 6, 1927, by the National Socialist experimental stage company in a matinee performance of a memorial service at the Wallner Theater in Berlin. This play, consisting of a prologue, fourteen scenes, and an epilogue, borrows its form from Dante's *Divine Comedy*. Just as Virgil leads the Italian poet through Inferno, so the wanderer leads the despairing author "over the heights and through the valleys of German history." A repeat performance given five days later was to be the last.

Early in the twenties Goebbels was obsessed by the idea of his literary vocation. In **Michael** he described his powerful creative impulse:

> July 15: I am lying in bed sleepless, wrestling with the powers that press upon me.
>
> There is in me rebellion, indignation, revolution. An idea grows inside me to grandiose proportions. Danse macabre and resurrection.
>
> July 18: I feel as if I no longer belong to this world. I rave in a state of intoxication, in a dream, in anger.
>
> I divine new worlds.
>
> Farawayness grows in me.
>
> Give me the strength, Lord, to say what I suffer.

At first his novel **Michael**—a mere 160 pages—was not published. It was written in the form of a diary and described the spiritual evolution of a young German searching for the meaning of life, for God, for the sense of mankind's true task and calling. Since the German universities with their antiquated system failed to give him an answer, he turns to the common people, becomes a miner, and dies down in the mine, mortally wounded by a falling rock. The story is frequently interrupted by reflections on every kind of topic. These aphorisms are neither particularly original nor well formulated. Most of them are stylistically reminiscent of Nietzsche, though they are sadly lacking in Nietzsche's language and wealth of thought.

There are four main figures in this novel: Michael; Herta Holk, his girl friend; Iwan Wienurowsky, a Russian student; and Michael's school friend, Richard. Michael has much of Goebbels' mental outlook, but Michael's appearance is that of his friend, Richard Flisges, to whom the novel was dedicated. (Flisges had actually died in an accident in a mine in Bavaria in July 1923.)

This composite figure of Goebbels and Flisges is hardly convincing. A Michael who thinks like Goebbels can never be a glorious hero but only pose as such:

> June 20: I put my helmet on, draw my sword and declaim Liliencron.
>
> Sometimes I am overcome by a yearning to be a soldier, to stand guard.
>
> One must be a soldier always.
>
> A soldier serving the revolution of one's people.

On the other hand, a Michael who looks like Flisges cannot think like Goebbels. He will be by nature much more straight, more simple, even if he indulges in his own pessimism, as Flisges used to. Goebbels' failure to present a convincing hero came from his inability to create a living figure rather than a projection of his own wish fulfillment.

While Michael expresses the thoughts of Goebbels, Iwan Wienurowsky presumably represents those of Flisges. But Iwan, too, lacks a clear outline. He remains a cliché—a Russian as Goebbels would imagine him after reading too much Dostoevsky. But compared with Dostoevsky's deep psychological insight and the profound and tortured revelation of his hero's guilt, Goebbels' attempt looks like scraps picked up from the floor of the master's workshop.

Michael liberates himself—as any good German would—from Iwan's influence. And Wienurowsky's last letter to Michael strikes the note of things to come:

> July 8: I wish Russia had created a new world. Rome has come to an end. The new Rome: Russia . . . for me you represent the German youth about to liberate itself, you are strong, but we will be stronger!
>
> Michael: Yes, we will cross swords. The German

and the Russian man. Germans and Slavs!

Michael's school friend, for whom Fritz Prang served as a model, plays only a minor part. He becomes a bourgeois, so Michael loses all interest in him.

> July 2: The political bourgeoisie has no significance and does not wish to have any. All they want is to live, and live in a primitive way. That is why they will perish. I hate the bourgeois because he is a coward and no longer prepared to fight. He is just an animal in a zoo, that is all.

In Michael's view the bourgeoisie should be thrown on the rubbish dump of world history and be replaced by the working class. After his attack on the bourgeoisie, Michael writes:

> July 2: The working class has a mission to fulfill, particularly in Germany. It has to liberate the German people within Germany, as well as in her relationship with the outside world. This is a mission of universal importance. If Germany perishes, then the light of the whole world will go out.
>
> Soldiers, students, and workers will build the new Reich. I was a soldier, I was a student, I want to be a worker. I must pass through all three stages to show the way. . . . The new man will be born in the workshops and not in books.

Alas, Goebbels missed the first and the third stages. He had never been a soldier nor a worker. He was excluded from the former by his physical shortcomings; and as for the latter, it soon would have spoiled his well-groomed hands.

Michael was probably written at the end of 1923 and the beginning of 1924. Its original title was: *Michael Voormann: The Diary of a Man's Fate*. It was published only in 1928, not, as Goebbels had wished, by Ullstein, but by the National Socialist party's official publishers. Both title and content had undergone changes. In the title the name Voormann was dropped and *a Man's Fate* had become *the Fate of a German*. The differences between the original (1923) and the published version (1928) were probably due to the fact that Goebbels had met with Hitler and had meanwhile risen to a high position in the party. The numerous anti-Semitic outbursts in the published version could hardly have been included in the original submitted for publication to the Jewish Ullstein publishing house. In many places one can trace the influence of Hitler's *Mein Kampf*, which was still unpublished when Goebbels wrote the original *Michael*. In the original Goebbels had addressed himself to mankind. In the published version mankind in general was replaced by the Germans in particular. The wings of the idealist have been clipped. Before us stands a meekly conforming member of the party.

Michael is the work of a beginner, with all the corresponding weaknesses. It was Goebbels' first attempt at

creating a hero. But Goebbels absolutely lacked any true feeling for nature and any real curiosity about the intricacies of the human soul. *Michael* is no more than a collection of slogans, not even particularly well presented. But while Goebbels strained to create the book of a true writer, he was neglecting the talent that later made him into the greatest propagandist of all time. Goebbels' new religion was a concoction of Faust, Christ, and Zarathustra. Three books are found in Michael's drawer after his death: Goethe's *Faust,* the Bible, and Nietzsche's *Zarathustra*. The Bible was always an important element in Goebbels' strange *Weltanschauung*. And it is perhaps significant that he left this sentence, "I took with me two books, the Bible and *Faust,*" in the published version. The Bible has first place, and *Zarathustra* isn't even mentioned. It is surprising that no critic has ever remarked on the dominant part the image of Christ plays in Goebbels' *Michael*.

> August 12: . . . in the evening I sit in my room and read the Bible. From afar I can hear the pounding of the sea.
>
> I lie awake for a long time and think of the quiet pale man of Nazareth.

The figure of Christ remained powerfully present in Goebbels' imagination to the very end. Even quite late he was still planning a book about Christ: "I cannot think of a more fascinating personality in history than Christ. . . . I know no more powerful speech than the Sermon on the Mount. Every propagandist ought to study it."

THE WARTIME DIARY

Goebbels' wartime diary of the years 1942-43, like that which he kept in 1925-26, contains observations primarily on contemporary events and personalities; however, the strong personal accent of his earlier diary is absent. In 1942 Goebbels was a mature man. He was no longer beset by griefs of young love, and in any case, times were far too serious for sentimental problems. He was fully preoccupied with the political or military position; everything personal had to take second place.

Historically this diary is interesting, insofar as it differs from that of 1925-26, in that it was written with an eye to posterity. Goebbels might have planned to use it as material for some books he expected to write one day; but as he became increasingly aware of the fact that the war might be lost, the diary more and more assumed the character of a political testament. Perhaps the most striking feature of this wartime diary is the author's complete amoralism. This amoralism had its predecessors in Nietzsche, Machiavelli, and, above all, in Hitler. It appears that Goebbels threw his own moral concepts overboard and adopted Hitler's. Examples are his praise of Heydrich's policy in the protectorate and his open admission that he was more concerned with an ostensible than a real pacification of the subjugated peoples. He did not hesitate to make promises for the future to certain countries, knowing full well they would never be kept. Goebbels' brutal policy of destruction of the Jews, as recorded in his wartime diary, is also new. All this painfully demonstrates his assimilation of Hitler's ideas. In the twenty years that elapsed between the two diaries, Goebbels' thoughts had cleared up considerably, but they had also become far more primitive and brutal. All humanitarian considerations had disappeared.

The wartime diary is also interesting as a critical analysis of that particular period. It covers two years, from January 1942 to December 1943. In these two years the tide turned against Germany. In December 1942 the tragedy of Stalingrad threw its chilling shadow over Germany's fate. In summer 1943 Italy joined the enemy camp. The Anglo-American air forces established their unchallenged superiority and dominated the airspace over the German homeland. One town after another fell in ruins; this, in fact, failed to destroy the morale of the population or diminish production appreciably, but it revealed Germany's impotence. The "Baedeker raids" that obliterated Germany's most beautiful towns and monuments were militarily useless and obviously barbaric, but destroyed much that the Germans were proud of. [The term "Baedeker raids" was used for the first time in connection with Germany's air attacks on English towns of no military importance. They preceded those mentioned here.] On the Eastern front the Soviet advance continued, and Germany's strong ally in the Far East, Japan, had begun its "planned retreat."

Interesting, also, in the diary are Goebbels' judgments of his contemporaries. His views on Churchill and Roosevelt have been mentioned, but they were not the only foreign politicians to get bad marks. Generalissimo Franco is called a "bigoted churchgoer," "an inflated peacock" who permits "Spain to be practically ruled by his wife and his father-confessor." About Quisling, Goebbels says, "I have the impression that Quisling is just Quisling. I cannot feel much sympathy for him."

For Stalin, however, in his diary Goebbels has only admiration. There is a marked divergence between his private entries in his diary and his official pronouncements. He was most impressed with Stalin's brutality. "He got rid of all opposition within the Army and thereby cut out any defeatist tendencies. The introduction of political commissars had a most salutary effect on the fighting capacity of the Red Army."

Goebbels saw other advantages in Bolshevism, such as "the liquidation of all opposition in Russian society." Goebbels also welcomed Stalin's brutal methods used against all opposition within the Church, "which remains a real headache for us."

Goebbels' views on how to deal with France were profoundly deceitful. He had adopted Hitler's line. Reading Goebbels' notes, one never has the feeling that he was seriously concerned with the question of how to build a new Europe, since he proposed to exclude all peoples, including such a highly cultivated nation as the French,

from playing any important role. He drew on Hitler for his moral excuses.

> Whoever possesses Europe will soon lead the world. In this context we cannot even begin to discuss the question of right or wrong. A lost war will put the German people in the wrong; victory will assure us every right. Altogether, only the victor will be in a position to put over to the world the moral justification of this war.

Goebbels accused the Ministry of Foreign Affairs of lacking initiative in its European policy; he published his own statements, promising all European peoples freedom and prosperity after a German victory. At the same time he confided to his diary his views on France, which prove that his promises were brazen lies.

> It would be a mistake to hope for too much from France. The French people are to my mind ill and worm-eaten. They are no longer able to make any significant contribution toward the construction of a new Europe. . . .
>
> The Fuehrer's policy toward France has proved correct in every way. One must put the French on ice. As soon as one flatters them it goes to their heads. The longer one leaves them hanging in the air the readier they will be to submit.

While the Ministry of Foreign Affairs is inclined to support the French demand for a preliminary peace, all the more so since the French government declared its readiness "to actively take part in the war," Goebbels sided with Hitler who, reluctant to play his aces too soon, thought he could do without French armed assistance. He intended to obtain "truly historical results from the war against France."

What are these "historical results"? "Whatever the war may bring, he [Hitler] says France will have to pay dearly; after all, she has caused this war and initiated it. . . . [This statement completely contradicts Goebbels' propaganda line up until the French campaign in May 1940.] France will be reduced to its frontiers of the year 1500 . . . which means that Burgundy will be integrated into the Reich. We will win a territory superior in beauty and riches to almost any other German province."

But woe to any other nation that pursued a similarly egotistical and ruthless policy. This is exemplified by Goebbels' reference to Mussolini's fall. In May 1943 Tunisia had been lost, and on July 10, Anglo-American forces landed in Sicily. This appeared to be the moment for Italy to seek a divorce *à l'Italienne* from her Axis partners. Italy's inner political situation made this relatively easy: The Italians still had a ruling King, not to mention the Pope, in their midst. Mussolini was completely spent after twenty-one years of government. There was precious little left of his animal-of-prey nature, of being "the big wild cat," as Ezra Pound had described him once. Driven by sheer greed, Mussolini had entered the war too hastily. The ignominious defeats the Italian armies sustained in Greece and North Africa only revealed to the world Italy's military and economic weakness. This, in its turn, reduced Mussolini from his position as Hitler's partner to that of Hitler's factotum—if that. And when on July 25, 1943, Mussolini was deposed by the Great Fascist Council and arrested by the King, no one in Italy raised a finger to help Mussolini. Over twenty years of fascism seemed to have been blotted out overnight.

Goebbels had never set great store by Italy or fascism: "The Italians are not only incapable of any valid military effort, but they have also failed to produce anything important in art. One can almost say that fascism had a sterilizing effect on the Italian people. . . ."

But when Goebbels was told of Mussolini's fall, he stared at his press officer "with a mixture of unbelief and horror." Goebbels sat down, incapable of uttering a word, for a quarter hour: "An expression of complete despair appeared on his face, slowly changing into grim bitterness. The first words he then uttered were 'What a shit of a man.' Then he added: 'Fascist Italy was never anything but a blown-up rubber lion. . . . And a clever ventriloquist made him roar, so that some people believed the lion had real teeth and claws. But one little pinprick and—puff—the whole monster collapses.'"

Goebbels immediately left for the Fuehrer's headquarters in Rastenburg. Hitler, too, had been taken by surprise, since the German Diplomatic Service, as well as the Secret Service, had obviously been caught by surprise. As soon as Hitler heard that Marshal Pietro Badoglio had taken over the government, he knew the revolt was directed against Germany. Badoglio's declaration that he would continue the war on the side of the Axis powers could not deceive Hitler.

For once, Hitler managed to keep his composure better than Goebbels who, in his consternation, hardly knew how to break the terrible news to the German people. At first he broadcast that Mussolini had retired "for health reasons." Goebbels refused for three weeks to write an editorial in *Das Reich,* which gave rise to all kinds of rumors.

Events in Italy developed slowly but according to plan. On September 8, an armistice was proclaimed between Italy and the Western powers. Badoglio had already signed the agreement on September 3, when Anglo-American forces landed in southern Italy. Yet on September 8, the Italian marshal told the councilor of the German legation, Rahn, that he had not the slightest intention of quitting the fighting Axis powers. The Germans would see "how an Italian general kept his word."

Goebbels, who before had never missed a chance to employ aristocrats in his entourage, became after the events in Italy a real hater of the aristocracy:

> The conspiracy that was built up against us in Rome consisted of the monarchy, aristocracy, society, high-ranking officers, Freemasons, Jews,

industrialists, and clerics. The Duce fell victim to this conspiracy.

> The Fuehrer is taking all measures to exclude, once and for all, the possibility of anything of this kind happening over here. All German princes are expelled from the German Wehrmacht. I suggested to the Fuehrer that we confiscate without any further delay the great estates belonging to the former ruling families.

Eighteen years earlier, Goebbels and the Strasser group had supported the proposal of the German left parties to dispossess the princes without compensation. At that time Hitler had opposed the Goebbels-Strasser group. Once again, Hitler recoiled from taking this drastic step, while Goebbels more and more reverted to the National Bolshevist ideas of his political beginnings. Goebbels openly leaned toward Stalinist policy, trying to prepare the German people for co-operation with Stalin.

Had Goebbels learned his lesson from the events in Italy? His diary reveals his determination to apply still harsher methods in order to prevent anything similar from happening in Germany. "I will from now on beat up anybody who says anything against the war or against the Fuehrer. Or I will put him before a court, or shut him up in a concentration camp."

Dan Jacobson   (essay date 1978)

SOURCE: "The End of the Road," in *Commentary,* Vol. 66, No. 1, July, 1978, pp. 78-80.

[*In the following review, Jacobson considers the historical value of* Final Entries 1945: The Diaries of Joseph Goebbels.]

Not even the publishers of *Final Entries 1945* claim that the diaries which Joseph Goebbels kept during the last two months of his life, and which have belatedly been made available by the East German government, contain new historical facts of any importance. How could they? By the time these entries begin, the Nazis were in effect defeated; nothing that Adolf Hitler's Minister of Propaganda could say—and little enough that his master could do—would make much difference to what was happening outside the German capital, or even inside it. The Russian and Anglo-American armies would continue to advance; German troops would continue to retreat or to surrender in large numbers; the entire edifice of the Third Reich, and all its systems of command and information, would continue to disintegrate rapidly. The sole interest of the diaries, therefore, lies precisely in their revelation of what a man like Goebbels tells himself at such a time: when he sees slipping away from him, minute by minute, the power which he and his fellow-gangsters had enjoyed almost unchecked for more than a decade.

That the diaries are unspeakably depressing to read goes without saying. Given the nature of the regime Goebbels had both served and helped to inspire, it could not be otherwise. What may come as more of a surprise, however, is their *childishness*. This does not make one feel any better about them. On the contrary.

Consider the situation. The war which had devastated Europe was drawing to its end. Horror upon horror was being uncovered by the Allied armies, as each concentration camp and death factory was overrun. Large parts of Germany itself were in ruins. These were the achievements of the regime of which this man had been the chief agitator and spokesman. Now the hour of—no, not retribution, for no retribution was possible, or even imaginable—but the hour of defeat had arrived. Nevertheless, until about two weeks before his suicide he went on dictating to his secretaries, as he had done for years, a daily record both of the position on the various war fronts, as transmitted to him by the military command, and of his own reactions to these developments, as man, minister, Gauleiter of Berlin, and confidant of the Fuehrer. Of what do these reactions speak? Remorse? None. Self-analysis? None. Political retrospection? None. Impotent rage, irrelevant and inexhaustible blaming of others, fantasies of revenge, expressions of slavish adoration toward the father-figure of his leader, boasts about his own mythical achievements in stemming the crisis, detailed plans for a future which could not under any conceivable circumstances be realized—of these, and of combinations of these, no end.

Let me give some examples. The Allied armies, as I have said, are astride Germany and are advancing steadily, and the Allied air forces have total mastery of the German skies. But—"The workers' strikes now flaring up both in England and the USA, however, are more important." "The situation in the enemy-occupied regions is becoming increasingly menacing. Here is a great opportunity for us." "Our sole great hope at present lies in the U-boat war. Our Western enemies are very worried abut it." "On the enemy side, time presses as never before." "The political crisis in the enemy camp is growing to considerable magnitude." Over and over again, it is true, the writer will admit that none of these factors seems in itself sufficient to change the fundamental drift of events; but one soon realizes that there is something curious about these admissions. They are not made in order genuinely to qualify or to question the assertions they accompany; rather, they are demonstrations by Goebbels to himself that he is in fact being realistic, he is not merely indulging in daydreams. In other words, they are there to reinforce the fantasy, not to destroy it. "I am convinced that this political crisis [among the Allies] could quickly be made to flare up, if it was not continually being pushed into the background by the enemy's military victories."

Who is to blame for these enemy victories? According to the diaries, one man chiefly: Hermann Goering. The general staff are cowards, the mayors and Gauleiters of the devastated German cities are not showing the reso-

lution that could be expected of them, Himmler lacks "the divine spark," there are looters and deserters everywhere. But what has brought these moral failings to the surface is above all else the bombing of the German cities; and for that Goering is responsible. If only he could be shown the door, the position might soon be restored. "Bemedalled idiots and vain perfumed coxcombs have no place in our war leadership." "I rage inwardly when I think that despite all the good reasons and arguments, it is not possible to persuade the Fuehrer to make a change here." "It is simply ridiculous to show any sympathy now for a man who has brought the Reich into such mortal crisis." "All those present at the fire [after an air raid] voiced only scorn and hatred for Goering. . . . I beg the Fuehrer yet again to take action, because things cannot go on like this."

That is as near as he ever comes to criticism of his Fuehrer. For the rest, Hitler's wisdom, strength, and moral and intellectual capacities are beyond all questioning. Full of a habitual, self-vaunting callousness and cruelty though these diaries are, they speak of Hitler in tones of fainting, sentimental veneration. "The Fuehrer gives me a very stalwart impression once more. . . . His steadfastness is admirable. If anyone can master this crisis, he can. Throughout the length and breadth of the land there is no one who can hold a candle to him." But no single quotation or group of quotations can convey the tone of soggy, dog-like worship which informs the pages upon pages of the diary devoted to accounts of his face-to-face meetings with Hitler, or the unction with which he reports Hitler's compliments to him, or the sycophantic glee with which he describes his renewed closeness to Hitler, brought about by the crisis. "The Fuehrer no longer holds back anything from me." "The Fuehrer had high praise for the simplicity and purity of my family life."

In any event, the Fuehrer's praise can always be supplemented by his own praise for himself. "I set out yet again in a calm, totally assured and lofty vein the arguments capable of giving the German people hope of victory." Sometimes he will go even farther, and impute to his audiences, without any supporting evidence, the praise he feels they must be giving to him. The effect of this can be unconsciously comic, on occasion. "The broadcast makes an extraordinarily strong impression, for it radiates a strong fighting spirit." "I give these men [some troops just behind the front-line] watchwords for the present situation, reinforcing them with a series of historical examples which carry much conviction, particularly in this area. One can imagine the effect of such a speech on an assembly such as this."

As for the Jews: "Anyone in a position to do so should kill off these Jews like rats. In Germany, thank God, we have already done a fairly complete job." Other groups, large and small, German and non-German, are unfortunately out of his reach; but he promises himself that their turn will come. Or rather, that his turn will come again. Then they will be made to suffer. In the meantime, he tries to bring that day nearer by magical curses and incantations—some of the kind quoted a few paragraphs above, others more specific in nature. Thus on March 6, 1945 he reports: "There is definite fear of the Rhine [among the Allied commanders]. The British and Americans naturally realize that in the middle of Germany they cannot carry out an amphibious operation like that of last summer. There are far too many obstacles for that." Two days later: "This evening alarming news comes . . . that the Americans have succeeded in forming a small bridgehead on the right-hand bank of the Rhine. I cannot confirm the accuracy of this information, since communications to the west are not working. I regard it as more or less out of the question however." So much for that. "The reports both of Dr. Ley and Speer are extremely alarming. I assume, however, that they are much influenced by what they have seen in the west and cannot look at these matters from the necessary distance. . . . I refuse to be deterred by reports of so-called eye-witnesses." So much for them.

One could go on and on, accumulating such grotesqueries and absurdities. But enough. The psychological processes at work are sufficiently plain and familiar; childish they indeed are. But if that word is to be given the force it should have, there are two important points to be added here. Inevitably both are cheerless. First: among the variety of psychic mechanisms which enabled Goebbels to keep going until the very end, the one which was *not* childish in any way was his impregnable, even crazed, moral self-righteousness. Roosevelt, declares Hitler's propagandist-in-chief, is "megalomaniac" and "reckless"; Churchill "rides roughshod over all criticism"; the allies are full of "victory hysteria" and "victory psychosis," and need (again and again) "to be sobered up"; the foreign workers in Germany "will undoubtedly be our best propagandists after the war"; the behavior of the Allies, who show no respect for Germany's cultural monuments, "literally brings blushes to the cheeks"; the world as a whole is a place "of contradiction, mendacity, and hypocrisy inconceivable in one's wildest dreams." This kind of self-exaltation, this capacity for seeing oneself as the very embodiment of precious moral and cultural values, is quite beyond the reach of any child. For that you need to have had the experience of a protracted literary and religious education, years of embittered failure and struggle, a hate-filled ideology that eventually brings you success, the support of a dictatorial party and state, the hysterical adulation of mass meetings and of hired or terrorized media, the admiration and caresses of kept women, the applause of flunkeys and foreign potentates.

The second point is that to speak of a political leader as "childish" is not in the least to say anything dismissive about him. Far from it. Unimpeded and unashamed access to the crudest emotions and mental processes of early childhood of the kind which Goebbels evidently had, can in fact be a source of immeasurable strength in public life. Hence his power as a propagandist in compelling the world to conform to his own fantasies; hence the tenacity with which he could cling to those fantasies when the world had at last grown recalcitrant. If it be objected that these diaries show him *in extremis,* or virtually so, and that they can therefore offer no guide to his "real" self, I can only reply that they seem to me perfectly continuous with what was revealed in the earlier diaries (1942-43), published about thirty years ago, or the extracts from his execrable, post-adolescent novel, *Michael,* which appear in the biography by Roger Manvell and Heinrich Fraenkel. Of course there are differences too. The circumstances were different. But the man remains the same; so does the deformed, vindictive child within him; and so does the relationship between the two.

It is entirely appropriate that he should have taken his own life, once Hitler was dead. That he should have taken with him his wife and six children is also fitting.

Peter L. Haratonik (essay date 1979)

SOURCE: "Propagandist as Propagandee," in *ETC.: A Review of General Semantics,* Vol. 36, No. 2, Summer, 1979, pp. 204-08.

[*In the following essay, Haratonik considers the extent to which Goebbels himself believed in the principles and ideas that he fostered as propaganda minister for the Third Reich.*]

Diaries are a curious form of literary endeavor. They are simultaneously both a private and public document; private in that the material is quite often initially meant for the use of the author exclusively; public in that, once committed to the page, by that very act, all information is accessible. "Diary"; the very word has always conjured up the image of a small Moroccan leather bound volume, securely sealed with a neat brass hasp, opened with a filagreed key. It seemed the perfect vehicle for Victorian ladies or pubescent girls to document precious moments of social (and sexual) triumph and tragedy. As Oscar Wilde had Gwendolyn tell Cecily in *The Importance of Being Earnest:* "I never travel without my diary. One should always have something sensational to read in the train."

Wilde aside, diaries often hold more significance. They shed light on events which otherwise would not have been documented. Antonio Pigafetta's classic account of Magellan's voice is one historic example. Select diaries such as *Pepys' London* document an entire epoch. Still others transform the medium into a tool for intellectual discourse as do the journals of Thoreau or Emerson. Literary diaries are often viewed as Rosetta stones in terms of deciphering the meaning of a larger body of work. The recent publication of diaries of Virginia Woolf and Edmund Wilson are but two examples. At times, diaries can often overshadow an author's other work, the diaries of Anais Nin being a case in point.

Political and military diaries have traditionally been held to be particularly important in that often such materials are the only sources available which provide an inside view of operations which by their very nature must be clandestine. For a historian a diary can lead to fascinating and intriguing consequences. The recent discovery and subsequent publication of portions of "lost diaries" of Dr. Paul Joseph Goebbels, Reich Minister of Propaganda and Popular Enlightenment, is one such fascinating and intriguing event.

There is an old story that turns out to be both ironic and tragic in relation to these diaries. It tells of the last conversation between Hitler and Goebbels in the Fuehrer's bunker. As Allied bombardment is heard on the outskirts of Berlin and the Nazi command now accepts the inevitable, Dr. Goebbels turns to Hitler and questions, "Mein Fuehrer, if you had to do it all over again, would anything be different?" Hitler pauses and replies, "No Goebbels, not a thing except . . . next time, no more Mr. Nice Guy."

When one completes *The Final Entries* the joke becomes even more ironic and chillingly tragic, for here we are presented, in self-imposed detail, with a portrait of a man consumed by the power of an image he, himself, created.

Professor Hugh Trevor-Roper, editor of the English edition, calls Goebbels "The only interesting man in the Third Reich, other than Hitler." His diary entries certainly support this claim. Goebbels was a compulsive and consistent keeper of these journals, which begin in 1925 and apparently were kept up until three weeks before his death on May 1, 1945. As a student of history, philology, and romantic literature, he had completed his Ph.D. in 1921, an accomplishment which both he and Hitler viewed with a great deal of pride. Goebbels' early diaries reflect youthful social, sexual, and career oriented concerns, but gradually the entries take on more and more of the tenor of Nationalist Socialist propaganda. In many ways, the early diaries become a substitute for more substantive written work, possibly as a result of Goebbels failure as both a novelist and journalist. By the early 1930's he considered the writings to be important enough to include in published texts of Nazi policy and philosophy. All that remains from this period, however, is a single handwritten diary of 1925-26 which was presented to then former president Herbert Hoover during a post World War II visit to Europe. Until the publication of this text, edited down from the first German edition, it was believed that the only other existing material was that of the period of 1942-43, which was translated and edited by journalist Louis Lochner, in 1948. All of the diaries appear to have been in the bunker in 1945, Goebbels having publicly acknowledged that he felt them to be his major contribution to posterity. With the Soviet occupation, most of the documents seem to have been either destroyed or at best transported to the U.S.S.R. and never released. The entries edited by Lochner contained many missing sections and many of the pages had been singed and trampled upon. The recent collection appeared quite unexpectedly, as a result of the fact that all of what the Nazi High Command considered to be valuable was microfilmed during the last months of the war, and a copy later verified by one of Goebbels' stenographers mysteriously found its way to a publisher (leading many to believe that there are indeed other materials in either private or government hands). It should be noted that up until July of 1941 Goebbels wrote all of his own manuscripts by hand. Beginning that month, however, he turned to dictation, given at high speed and typed directly each evening by the stenographer. Often the entries would run as long as eighty pages, with Goebbels practicing a curious approach to diary writing by accounting the previous day's events in the present tense, thus giving him at least a day for reflection and a sense of the future. The entries are consistent, beginning first with an assessment of military situations and then moving on to a broad range of other political and personal concerns.

Every word was taken down verbatim, yet according to both the stenographers he employed, never once did he ask to see any entries again, or to make any corrections. The material was clearly designed for future editing and reference, to be shaped later to create a personalized history of the Reich.

The collection is revealing more for what it confirms than for any new issues it raises. Two major themes remain from the earlier materials. First is Goebbels' unquestioning, unwavering belief in the power and ultimate righteousness of Adolph Hitler, and second is his belief in his personal power as propagandist. On March 7, 1945, less than two months before the final collapse, he wrote that Hitler is "in his best and most resolute form. Though the situation is extraordinarily serious and menacing, he still represents a firm, fixed point round which events revolve. As long as he is at the head of the Reich, we have no need to haul down our flag." In his handling of the last attempts at propaganda, the entries showed Goebbels retreating more and more into the romantic German past. To rally the already depleted sense of German patriotism, he stressed local heroism above anything else and called upon all of the still active elements of the media to devote their columns and airwaves to such historical precedents as the Second Punic War, the inspiration of Frederick the Great, and the military writings of Von Clausewitz.

By April of 1945, Goebbels still clung tenaciously and irrationally to the belief that the Reich would survive. He perpetuated his own mythical creation of the "Werewolf Organization," a supposed resistance front which would continue fighting against any occupation forces. His faith in Hitler likewise never diminished. On April 4, 1945, with the end clearly in sight, he could still write that though he did not know where ultimately the military crisis would lead, he still felt that, "he

[Hitler] will get the better of the situation. He has always known how to await his moment with lofty calm." That moment came less than four weeks later, with Hitler and Goebbels dead and the rest of the Command either having surrendered or in flight. Yet to the end Goebbels expected "ultimate vindication." Three days before his death by suicide, he wrote a letter to his stepson, Harold Quandt. (Goebbels took the lives of his own six children.) In it, he says, "Do not let yourself be disconcerted by the worldwide clamor which will now begin. One day the lies will crumble away of themselves and truth will triumph once more. That will be the moment when we shall tower over all, clean and spotless, as we have striven to be and believe ourselves to be." In the end Goebbels fell victim to his own maniacal approach in rationalizing complex problems, a philosophy he had applied in his earlier efforts. In 1935 he wrote, "By simplifying the thoughts of the masses, and reducing them to primitive patterns, propaganda was able to present the complex process of political and economic life in the simplest terms . . . we have taken matters previously available only to experts and . . . specialists and have carried them into the streets and hammered them into the brain of the little man." The act of simplifying language, in tandem with a total media effort (another principle of Goebbels' propaganda philosophy), can create a semantic environment both devoid of thought and composed of only the most predictable and organized actions. Private opinion becomes totally devalued propaganda. As Jacques Ellul notes, "The more progress we make [in our use of media for purposes of propaganda] the less private opinion can express itself through mass media." Organized media, by their very nature, serve to create organized or public opinion. Ultimately, as in Goebbels' case, even the individual opinion of the mass opinions' creator is subsumed into a generalized response.

One may doubt the sincerity of Goebbels' reflections, noting the ever-present possibility of reprisal for being candid. Such a conclusion fails to recognize the profound influence that the very act of keeping these diaries seems to have had on his self-image and his psychological state. He clearly does not avoid controversy—a point revealed in his criticism of those leaders he believed to be ineffective, such as Goering. Each entry is a curious blending of what E. K. Bransted calls "intense feelings of hatred, revenge, and destruction . . . side-by-side with cool assessments of military, political and social problems."

One problematic aspect of this edition should be noted. Trevor-Roper's introduction to the English edition (playwright Rolf Hochhuth wrote the introduction to the German edition) fails adequately to provide a sense of the complexity of the problem of dealing with this historic period and relies on tracing the roots of Goebbels' fanaticism to his Catholic background and restless radicalism. Goebbels was unsatisfied by the Church, university life, and Socialism; for these reasons, Trevor-Roper

states, he was ripe for Hitler's brand of Fascism. This may be compelling psycho-history but does not in any way adequately confront the ultimate significance of a Goebbels, who Trevor-Roper himself calls, "a man of words, images, gestures," but one who had "no ideas, no beliefs of his own . . . no positive aim . . . even the positive aim of Nazism."

If *The Final Entries* reveal nothing else, they do point out how limited our knowledge is when attempting to explain such a life. They give us a dramatic demonstration of the power of language. George Steiner wrote, "Everything forgets, but not a language." Perhaps closer examination of this text will remind us of the conversation in the bunker, so that we will be prepared for any "next time," nice guys or not.

Dieter Saalmann   (essay date 1986)

SOURCE: "Fascism and Aesthetics: Joseph Goebbel's Novel *Michael*: *A German Fate Through the Pages of a Diary* (1929)," in *Orbis Litterarum,* Vol. 41, No. 3, 1986, pp. 213-28.

[*In the following essay, Saalmann uses Goebbels's novel* Michael *to illustrate parallels between fascist social and political principles and theories of aesthetics.*]

In a recent publication, Adolf Muschg, the Swiss author, literary critic, and *Germanist,* defines fascism as "the aesthetic façade of politics." He further elaborates by ascribing to 'aesthetic' fascism the phenomenon of "holistic phantasies foisted upon society." It is this attempt to artistically shape the masses with the intent of creating a new socio-political entity in terms of a *Gesamtkunstwerk,* or total work of art, that we shall concern ourselves with in this essay. It must be emphasized, however, that the question of fascism and aesthetics should not be construed as constituting an exhaustive analysis of the fascist movement. The artistic perspective is only one aspect of the multi-faceted spectrum of this phenomenon, albeit a highly significant one in that it does address itself to the very substance of the fascist mentality.

The aesthetic inclinations of National Socialism have been noted by a number of critics. Aestheticization, as it applies to the ideology espoused by the Third Reich, ought to be viewed as a "Dekadenzproze," in other words, as a process which involves the corrosion of traditional aesthetic concepts. As thus understood, the effort to analyze this abuse of the conventional aesthetic precepts of bourgeois society must therefore be seen as a contribution to the historico-political debate over German intellectual developments in the twentieth century. Hence, the document analyzed in this essay is substantially more than a piece of *Trivialliteratur.* It is indeed a key to the National Socialist frame of mind and thus a factor in the historical evolution.

Henry Grosshans, in his recent book entitled *Hitler and the Artists,* admonishes the reader that "Hitler as an artist in politics should be taken seriously." This is precisely what our exegesis proposes to accomplish by means of an interpretation of Goebbels' novel *Michael. A German Fate Through the Pages of a Diary* in terms of its anticipatory function as regards the aesthetic attributes of National Socialism. Consequently, *Michael* will reveal itself as something distinctly more portentous than solely a "true literary curiosity." Its principal protagonist will emerge as the embodiment of the nascent "artist in politics" whose most heinous incarnation was to become the scourge of Germany and all of Europe in the years to come. Inasmuch as it has been rumored that Hitler contemplated writing a novel in the 1920's that was to depict the efforts of a man of action to shape and ultimately save his nation, Goebbels' work actually conceived during the National Socialist struggle for supremacy assumes added significance. The published version and the delineation of the main character are clearly modelled on the emergence of Hitler's movement as a force to be reckoned with. As a result, the diary represents, in form of an aesthetic blueprint, what Hitler himself failed to accomplish as a writer but was nevertheless able to realize in the empirical realm. "The attempt to legitimize political rule through aesthetic symbolization," Anson G. Rabinbach states quite unequivocally in this regard, "is perhaps the decisive characteristic distinguishing twentieth century fascist regimes from other forms of authoritarian domination."

As for Goebbels' novel in particular, it was probably written at the end of 1923 and the beginning of 1924. The title chosen at first—*Michael Voormann: The Diary of a Man's Fate*—was later changed to "the fate of a German," that is to say, subsequent to the author's encounter with Hitler. The anti-semitic outbursts were in all likelihood not included in the draft that had been submitted to and rejected by Ullstein and Mosse, two Jewish publishing houses, before being accepted by Eher, the official Nazi publisher. In this context, Ullstein once remarked quite appropriately to Heinrich Fraenkel "that it was a pity that they had never accepted *Michael* and so perhaps diverted Goebbels' energies into literature instead of politics." The influence of *Mein Kampf* can only be traced in the printed version since Hitler's book was still unavailable when Goebbels' novel was being prepared. In the initial phases of the writing process, the narrator in *Michael* addressed himself to mankind in general whereas the book version that appeared in 1929 spoke to the Germans in particular. In view of our conception of fascism in terms of aesthetic attributes it is of especial interest that the author obtained the degree of doctor of philosophy at the University Heidelberg on April 21, 1921 with a dissertation on "Wilhelm Schütz. A Contribution to the History of the Romanticist Drama." He had taken up studies in that city in the fall of 1920 and became acquainted with the works of Friedrich Gundolf on Goethe, George, Caesar, and Shakespeare. All these publications were imbued with the spirit of George, that is to say, with a pronounced reverence for form which had definitely more ominous overtones than being a mere matter of aesthetics.

In the early stages of preparing the manuscript, the author resorted to an almost solemn, if not outright ecclesiastical, style. In the process of revising the preliminary draft the language became remarkably rhythmic, evocative, and exuberant under the obvious influence of Nietzsche. Basically, Michael is a dreamed-up image of Goebbels' life as a myth with the latter in the role of myth-maker: "Vincent van Gogh," one of the diary entries asserts, "is the most modern among moderns. . . . Modernism is a new world feeling. Van Gogh . . . is teacher, preacher, fanatic, prophet, madman. After all, we are all mad when we produce a creative idea."

It behoves us to regard books such as *Michael* not on literary grounds—in this respect the verdict is in—but as a socio-political phenomenon. Thus the protagonist reveals a profound sense of boredom with civilization and an existential malaise in general, a feeling of *ennui* reinforced by the experience of defeat, national humiliation, and frustrated patriotism. A similar sensation of *Weltschmerz* can be found in Wagner, Baudelaire, Carlyle, and other European artists. Basically, *Michael* is a revolt against conventional socialism as well as capitalism. Unlike earlier nationalistic heroes, Michael experiences a deep sense of isolation bordering on autism. Statesmen, according to this credo, are poets and artists *manqués* destined to become the legislators of the world.

By the same token, Hertha Holk, Michael's female pendant who is ultimately sacrificed on the altar of a 'greater' cause, betrays a noteworthy insight into the potentially far-reaching consequences of this explosive concoction of politics and aesthetics: "In politics you think like an artist," she warns, "that is dangerous for your own life and career." It must be noted that these words are put into the mouth of the heroine by the author himself who thus formulates a truth which has haunted him and which has finally been dismissed as irrelevant to the realization of the actual political goal. As if driven by an evil force, Michael succumbs to the lure of his "demon," in others words, to his political 'genius:' "I think and act as I must think and act. That is what everyone does who does not belong to the herd. A demon operates in us who leads us along a preordained path. One can do nothing against this demon." That political ambitions intertwined with the aesthetic inclinations of the idealist are indeed the principal criteria in the protagonist's life, emerges quite unequivocally from a brief exchange between Michael and Hertha: "In you there dwell a poet and a soldier. Are you also a musician?—A bit of each." In the end, he dismisses her as being a "realist" in the pejorative sense of the word to the extent that she fails to experience the sensation of wonderment which, for Michael, is "the origin of all poetry and all philosophy." Such a putatively poetic conception of the world contrasts rather harshly with the *Herrenmenschen* philosophy espoused by the protagonist and his desire, as Michael puts it in a remarkably premonitory fashion, "to reshape the world." In opposition to modern art with its emphasis on the artist's sense of hopeless isolation, Michael styles himself as a crusader for authentically German creative values. Such strictly indigenous criteria impel the artist-turned-politician to restore the nation to its presumed original unity and splendor.

From the point of view of structure, **Michael** is reminiscent of Goethe's *Werther*. Both works express in a first-person narrative very private, intimate confessions in a fragmentary and emotion-laden language. Goebbels' protagonist, a true Faustian nature, also demonstrates the author's turning from Goethe to Nietzsche, from Hertha Holk to Adolf Hitler. Ossian's want of moderation seduces Werther but not his creator. On the other hand, Nietzsche, misunderstood and misconstrued by Michael who relies on fragmentary quotations taken out of context or distorted, intoxicates both Goebbels and his spokesman. As a poet-politician, Michael's principal readings, aside from Goethe's *Faust* and the Bible, consist primarily of Nietzsche's *Zarathustra*. Quite appropriately, it is the following line from this work that concludes Michael's notebook entries: "Many die too late and some too early. Strangely sounds the lesson: die at the right time!"

The diction of Goebbels' **German Diary** is exclamatory, incantatory, and exhortatory. It adjusts itself to the hero's exaltations and depressions. The latter express his "demon" in a pseudo-poetic language which, however, should not simply be dismissed as the product of an inferior talent. It undoubtedly foreshadows the hypnotic power of National Socialist jargon. It is Goebbels the myth-maker extolling the 'blacksmith' of the "new Reich" who propagates the idea of 'forging' a new people and a new nation. This kind of mythical thinking anticipates the later myths surrounding Horst Wessel and Leo Schlageter. In his diary, Goebbels purports to have met Hitler as early as 1922. In reality, however, the two did not become acquainted until 1925. Such a claim is therefore symptomatic of the author's systematic effort to shroud his spiritual awakening to National Socialism with the mysterious veil of a pseudo-mythical past. The attempt to create a new political reality is couched in a mode of thinking and finds its verbalization in a language that are essentially aesthetic in nature: "The true poet," Michael's reasoning goes, "is a kind of amateur photographer of life. For a poem is nothing else but a snapshot taken by the lense of the artistic soul. Art is the expression of feeling. The artist is distinguished from him who is not an artist by the fact that he can express what he feels. . . . The statesman is also an artist. For him the people are that which a stone is for the sculptor. Leader and masses, that is exactly the same problem as painter and color." This creative potential of the prototypical statesman-artist is fundamentally "expressionist" in nature: "Today we are

all expressionists," Michael concludes: "Men who want to make the world outside themselves take the form of their life within themselves. The expressionist builds within himself a new world. His secret and his power are the forces within his own passionate nature. The world of his inner thoughts breaks to pieces on reality. . . . The expressionist world-feeling is explosive. It is an autocratic sensation of its own being." In this manner, Goebbels' novel illustrates the aesthetic connection between Expressionism and National Socialism, a fact which was to become the focal point of the controversy over Expressionism in the exile journal *Das Wort* in 1937-38.

In congruence with such dubious literary precepts, Michael the so-called expressionist-turned-politician engages in the very process that Benjamin has termed the "aestheticization of politics" by transforming "the soul of the expressionist" into the "new macrocosm" of National Socialist ideology. It is indicative of this putatively metaphysical approach to what is fundamentally a political question that the author resorts to a terminology which circumscribes the quintessence of his belief as a sensation of "self-being" that originates in what he calls "a world unto itself." In spite of the claim that the "expressionist feeling is explosive," the inner-directedness of this thinking can therefore not conceal its affinity with salient aspects of a *l'art pour l'art* attitude.

In identifying political activity as "Ausdruckskunst," the author endows the socio-political substance with "historical form," analogous to the activities of poet, painter, and sculptor. Consequently, the "ideological" revolution he propagates continues, according to this way of thinking, the intent of divine genesis in the political sphere as an explicitly "creative act." Its final result is the nation-state as "formgewordenes Volkstum," that is to say, a *Volkstum* forged in accordance with the "Gestaltungswille," or creative will, of the politician-as-artist. It is this congruence of the 'will to power' and the 'will to form,' of the artistic and ideological volition that constitutes the Nietzschean and Schopenhauerian dimension of Goebbels' novel.

The metaphysico-philosophical frame of reference is further reinforced by an open appeal to the Romantic concept of "Unendlichkeit," in other words, the desire to reach the ultimate limits of human endeavor. In this way, political activity and *weltanschaulich* goals are conceptualized in terms of a "Faustian urge." It is this "storm and stress" mentality that the protagonist wishes to emulate, not the mature Goethe but the young disciple of iconoclastic inclinations as the incarnation of Michael's own emotional upheaval along the lines of "turmoil" and "rebellion." In such a vein, the older Goethe is rejected outright—"Not Weimar is our Mecca"—and *Wilhelm Meister* dismissed as being too well-rounded and lacking the rough edges of a truly revolutionary spirit. In contradistinction, the so-called "expressionist," for Michael, is the new macrocosm, not just a faint echo of the larger perspective. Thus Goethe's

"Erlebniswerte," or experiential values, have been replaced by the "Eigenwert," or intrinsic worth, of the new autonomous and "autocratic" personality that strives to re-create the world in its own image.

There can be no doubt that the author of the **German Diary,** at least at the time of the inception of this book, was deeply steeped in Germany's cultural heritage. The following excerpt may serve as proof of our contention that Goebbels, despite the obviously transitional and fermentational nature of these diary entries, was nevertheless unable to resist the lure of an aestheticized view of the contemporary world that was to permeate the further development of National Socialism. A strong undercurrent of profound and genuine empathy for the past can be detected throughout the passage which assumes the character of a rather intimate confession: "In its decline, the gradually collapsing historical class (i.e. the bourgeoisie), for the last time, inspires the finest flowers of its failing creative force. . . . One more time, its exquisiteness and graciousness emanating from nearly exhausted sources of inspiration, manifest themselves in the last examples of a vanishing world. In its final hour, it engenders creations full of delicate beauty and grace." It is true that the author of these words claims to have overcome such allegedly obsolete aesthetic notions. And yet, a close perusal of the entire text leaves no doubt that the cultural legacy extolled in the lines just quoted has left an indelible imprint on this self-proclaimed "revolutionary" as harbinger of the supposedly invincible "strong forces of a new creation."

Michael's perception of the world based on 'beauty' even extends to the realms of production and technology, a characteristic feature of National Socialism. Thus, the protagonist attempts to integrate himself not only politically but also aesthetically into the reality of proletarian life. The 'beauty' of labor—to wit: the Nazi *Amt Schönheit der Arbeit*—therefore assumes symbolic significance. In this sense, then, Michael experiences the facts of existence as they pertain to coal mines and their work force, as a highly stylized and intensely melodramatic scenario. His efforts to bridge the attitudinal gap between his life as a student and his new associates among the miners who initially reject him as a carpetbagger, is an open undertaking to politicize the working class whose alienation inspires in Goebbels a sort of left-wing brand of National Socialism. The politicization of the production process and of the means of production is also depicted as proceeding along aesthetic lines. Consequently, the notion of 'work' is conceived essentially as a formative rather than a merely utilitarian procedure. In this way, the idea of 'beauty of work' as espoused during the Third Reich by the journal bearing the same title receives its initial formulation in Michael's encounter with the working class. The prime function of this concept is one of creating social harmony through the aestheticization of labor relations. The result is an aesthetic illusion underlying concrete social interaction which, in turn, is engendered by political motivation as the principal driving force. The aestheticization of the work environment in **Michael** therefore acts as a potentially calamitous symbol of the aestheticization of politics in general. In this fashion, labor relations evolve into a kind of *l'art pour l'art* endeavor, that is to say, into a social mode for its own sake, "a pure representation of social power." Hence, Michael's encounter with the proletarian milieu falls into the general pattern of experiencing life as a product of the imagination, of viewing the modalities of existence in metaphysical terms, just as the "metaphysical charisma" attributed to Hitler manifested itself in "the omnipresence of his speeches and on the radio . . ."

What emerges from Michael's desire to "forge" the political destiny of the nation—"I want to create . . . bring into being"—is a "Symphonie der Arbeit," a 'symphonic' work wrestled from the shapeless mass that constitutes the people. The ever-expanding and elusive nature of this material must be pressed into a manageable shape until it conforms to the *machtpolitisch* intentions of the creatively inclined statesman. As with the artist proper, the fundamental problem here is one of *Form* versus *Inhalt*. If applied to politics, the dichotomy between form and content can only be overcome through a truly revolutionary spirit that destroys both *Form* and *Inhalt* of the existing order for the sake of realizing the "new . . . German man" as the result of a process of so-called 'organic creation.' Such is the intellectual disposition of the 'idealist' like Michael who, as an 'organic thinker,' endeavors to perceive the "essence behind the appearances" of empirical reality by virtue of his "longing for form, *Gestalt,* and quintessence." What is needed, then, is not "men" but "*a* man," in other words, a *Führer*-like figure who is charged with actualizing Christ's mission of bringing "salvation" to humanity. As Michael defines the proselytizing intent of the 'new gospel:' "My plan: from the individual to the whole, from the realia to the symbol, from brother to *Volk,* and only from *Volk* to the world."

Implicit in these assumptions is the necessity for military action in harmony with Marinetti's praise of war as the perfect incarnation of the ultimate form of human struggle and the nadir of beauty. Military conflict is viewed by Michael as the apotheosis of human existence and justified on account of the cynical premise that nature itself is "undemocratic" and that life as a whole is basically "evil." It is this substratum of militaristic thinking, the conviction that "war is the simplest form of affirming life," which undergirds the protagonist's exhortation of what he calls the necessity of "zum Ausdruck bringen," or giving verbal *Gestalt* to the "artistically tuned soul." From this vantage point, the notion of war embodies a "creative act," the only way, in Michael's thinking, to realize the future German nation as the "grandiose" achievement of a "dance of death." In retrospect, such words sound quite prophetic in view of what transpired in subsequent years which were to echo those premonitory pronouncements uttered by Goebbels' *alter ego:* "The earth shall belong to him who takes it." In this context, Michael's penchant for war and his admiration for Nietzsche go hand in hand in that he vulgarizes the latter's ambivalent disposition of simultaneously criticizing and advocating military action and promoting a social Darwinism of German supremacy based on racial confrontation. The protagonist thus displays the same irrationalism combined with a stress on vitality and a fascination with death that recurs in a much more thoroughly aestheticized version in a number of literary figures. The anti-rational component of Michael's frame of mind is further strengthened by a nature mysticism that borders on the ecstatic. A similarly irrational attitude informs his feeling toward the Soviet Union and the supposed Slavic menace in general. It also fuels his dislike of the bourgeoisie. All these classical *Feindbilder* serve as models of the dreaded threats of societal "corrosion" and "dissolution," that is to say, the disintegration of traditional values because of allegedly un-German influences. "War awakened me from deep slumber. It gave me full consciousness. *Geist* tormented me and drove me into catastrophe: it showed me the depths and the heights of human experience. Work gave me salvation. It made me proud and free. And now I have assumed a new form on the basis of these [criteria]." What distinguishes Michael's intellectual confession is the profoundly artistic nature of the terminology chosen. Using the triad of *Krieg, Geist,* and *Arbeit* and its synthesis as the "new law" and cornerstone of his spiritual evolution, he prophecies Germany's ideological future for which these same premises constitute its very *raison d'être* with their message of "deliverance" through the medium of the 'creator.'

Michael's final words on his death bed after the tragic accident in a coal mine in Southern Bavaria echo such thoughts, with one significant addendum, namely the notion of "opfern," or sacrifice. His life-long struggle with Christianity has now come full circle: his exposure to National Socialism has led him to merge the figure of the anticipated *Führer* with that of the Savior in order to postulate his idea of the most noble form of self-denial, 'für Volk und Vaterland,' to be sure. It thus follows quite logically that he hails the rise of so-called "Christussozialisten" fighting for what could presumably be termed a 'Christussozialismus.' The seminal affinity between Christ, the artist such as Vincent van Gogh, and the statesman is reinforced by the description of Jesus as "Dichter" representing a specific "Zeitgeist," that is to say, the epochal spirit of the creative genius who toils to actualize man's highest ambition: "He who speaks up there places stone upon stone in order to construct the cathedral of the future. What has lived inside me for years is now taking shape and assuming tangible form." It is therefore no accident that the "Mittagsandacht" in *Zarathustra* with its theme of the "Brunnen der Ewigkeit," or fount of eternity, and the concept of a pantheistic sense of perfection, casts its contemplative spell over Michael. This intermingling of notions germane to the Judeo-Christian tradition with secular ideas is the more significant in that investigation into *völkisch* concepts has indisputably demon-strated that it was the pseudo-religious aspirations of National Socialism, its pretense as a *Heilslehre,* or doctrine of salvation, and its insistence on redemption, among other factors, which facilitated acceptance of the 'movement' and its anti-semitic excesses by a large segment of the German population.

"No work of art without creator! No *Volk* without statesman! No world without God!" This dictum synthesizes the *Weltanschauung* that serves as underpinning for Michael's outlook on life. Its essence lies in the total identification of *Schöpfer, Staatsmann,* and *Gott* on the one hand and *Kunstwerk, Volk,* and *Welt* on the other. "The genius," so the argument continues, "is always nothing but the highest expression of the people's will." Being "the very incarnation of creative *Volkstum*" as it were, the genius and his obligation are in perfect congruence with the task that Jesus Christ set himself on earth, at least according to Goebbels' interpretation. In this particular sense, Christianity is viewed as the elitist activity of a select few and the embodiment of an essentially cultural endeavor. It is a fundamentally secularized and aestheticized version of the Christian concept of life as a "Lebensqual," or vale of tears, transformed into a "lebensbildend," or life-giving, factor as it applies to the ideological sphere. In this vein, the exemplary life of Jesus Christ is credited with the ability to arouse the narrator's imaginative propensity as regards the advent of "ein Grösserer." By the same token, the quasi-religious atmosphere that permeates the entire work, conceivably as a compensation for Goebbels' lost Roman Catholicism, is reinforced by the view of Jesus himself as a kind of militant socialist whose spirit might infuse a modern, secular political movement. Such an interpretation of Christianity rests on the assumption that the notion of *Gott,* in the Nietzschen tradition, is ultimately identical with the concept of *Wille.* The latter, in turn, provides the *homo politicus* with the 'divine' prerogative to 'will' the 'form' that the socio-political entity is to take.

In summarizing, then, it can be said that Goebbels' prose reflects the affinities that exist between fascism and the avant-garde. To wit: the irrational tendencies of the *fin-de-siècle*; Nietzsche's plea for *Lebenspathos,* or a vitalistic disposition; moral relativism; the cult of the instinct; an emphasis on action; aristocratic inclinations toward the state as the only purveyor of values; an anti-capitalist mentality nurtured by utopian and romantic notions; an overt racism and virulent anti-semitism; an elitist aestheticism coupled with an occasional extreme form of *Weltfremdheit*; a deep-seated aversion to the parliamentary form of government; a profound anti-modernist conviction exacerbated by capturing, in a very genuine way, a pronounced sense of the loss of national self-esteem and a distinct feeling of distrust vis-à-vis the Western world and the modern age in general; a frame of mind dedicated to the principle of *épater le bourgeois*; an emphasis on the power of the free will reinforced by an anarchist drive to determine the pattern of life as exemplified by Michael's ultimately fateful decision to gain acceptance by the proletariat; a ruthless readiness to cast aside the human element in favor of ideology; a resolute denial of mediocrity and the conforming habits of the herd instinct under the impact of Nietzsche's demand on the individual to conquer himself and to rid himself of his false sense of inferiority; and, finally, the dichotomy between aesthetic and economic considerations, between the spiritual values of the 'new myth' and its plutocratic aspects, a point that figures prominently in Brecht's and Benjamin's discussion of fascist aesthetics.

There can be no denying the fact that artistic considerations were instrumental in shaping fascist ideology. In France, it was Charles Maurras and Thierry Maulnier of the *Action Française* whose interest in aesthetics preceded the genesis of fascism proper. Robert Brasillach, another representative figure of the pan-European specimen of *homo fascista,* regarded Hitler and Mussolini as 'poets' *par excellence* of creative politics whose destiny it was to subdue the masses by virtue of political decisions as poetry and myth made visible. Fascism, to be sure, encompasses a total concept of life. For this reason, man's inner being is likewise subject to the urge of the fascist aesthete to give formal expression to his attitudinal disposition. In this context, Goebbels' verbal visualization of Michael as the prototypical fascist-oriented youth shares the general concern of the European intelligentsia in the early part of the century over the devastating effect of industrial and technological advancement on the artistic sensibilities and the resultant feeling of anomie in the machine age. Like the European adherents of fascism, Michael also identifies his aesthetic leanings with a distinctive sense of combativeness and a predatory tendency. In 1934, Pierre Drieu de la Rochelle, under the immediate impact of a journey across the Rhine, confirms Michael's conviction that Germany is about to embark on a course that will take the country down the path of a thoroughly spiritualized and aestheticized society. To a considerable extent, then, the success of fascism must be attributed to its appeal to man's sensory perception and his longing for creating new forms. In congruence with Brasillach's analysis of fascism, Michael thus sees the 'new order' as a struggle between the senses and metaphysical abstraction.

To be sure, it would be highly inaccurate to limit the attraction of this ideology to its aesthetic perspective, as suggested by Jean Turlais in 1943. Still, the fact of the matter is that Goebbels portrays his protagonist as a man of heroic sensibilities who, in the terminology of Brasillach's characterization of the fascist mind, strives to reconcile the corporeal and the spiritual within himself for the benefit of the 'new faith' he espouses. Notwithstanding the literary mediocrity of the 'German Diary,' its doctrine does indeed reflect what has been called "the poetry of the dictators." By the same token, the analogy between art and politics ought not to be carried to an extreme. Thus, Alfred Fabre-Luce's attempt to present Hitler as a sort of 'presiding artist'

"who betrayed the arts in trying to make them 'useful' and disregarded the laws of his personal art (the political art) which, more than any other, should take into account the resistance of the material employed," unquestioningly exceeds the limits of exegetical sagacity. One therefore wholeheartedly concurs with the caustic assessment that Fabre-Luce's claim "surely is one of the most prudent criticisms of Hitler ever written." Conversely, the significance of the *Führer*'s own statement to the effect that "art and politics belong together as nothing else on earth belongs together" should not be nonchalantly dismissed as the pseudo-intellectual meanderings of a misguided spirit succumbing to the "external trappings of culture."

What Michael indulges in is the kind of "metapolitics" that Peter Viereck defines as an admixture of romanticism, an ill-conceived socialism, racism, and an abiding faith in the concept of *Volk*. Goebbels' book thus portends, in analogy to Nero's desire to turn aesthetic resentment into political animosities and cruelty, the appearance of those "frustrated aesthetes" of the Third Reich who spared no effort to become "aesthetes with brass knuckles." In anticipation of Hitler's confession that "the only things that exist are the works of human genius. This is the explanation of my love of art," Michael introduces the insidious consequences of argumentation by analogy with its inherently vague abstractions and blurring of distinctions. In conformity with H. R. Trevor-Roper's assessment of Hitler's mind—"To him there was no real truth, no objectivity. . . . To him, reality, especially political reality, was not a fact but an artefact; it was made by the human mind, the human will"—the protagonist of the 'German Diary' stresses the point that "what we believe is not as important as the fact that we do believe." To put it differently: 'style' envisaged by Michael as a Synthesis between "precept and expression" is the key term that prefigures later evaluations of Hitler as a "consummate actor, with the actor's and orator's facility for absorbing himself in a role and convincing himself of the truth of what he was saying at the time he said it."

Our critical assessment of fascist ideology as delineated in Goebbels' **Michael** in terms of the endeavor to transpose empirical reality into an artificial construct, to transfigure concrete phenomena into a triumph of the creative but utterly nihilistic will, has demonstrated the *trompe l'oeil* effect of such an effort, that is to say, the mendacious façade of artistic manipulation in the historical realm. The determination of the *homo politicus* to 'act' as a fanatical *homo aestheticus* with presumed prophetic ambitions therefore creates, as Horkheimer and Adorno have recognized, "an ideological curtain" on the political stage "behind which the real evil is concentrated" and perpetrated by what Thomas Mann denounces as the "künstlerischer Bezauberer Europas," in other words, the politician-as-artist turned charlatan and sorcerer who casts his magic spell over his audience. The ultimate aesthetic perversion of the alleged banality of such a self-styled ideologue and bureaucrat with artistic pretensions has recently been expressed by a commentator who characterizes Adolf Eichmann's involvement in racial annihilation as the desire to perform a "creative task." It can thus be observed that the aesthetic component of the politics espoused in Goebbels' novel signals the consummation of the principle of *Fiat ars—pereat mundus* that Benjamin ascribes to fascism.

Tom Clark   (**essay date 1987**)

SOURCE: "The Nazi Wrote a Novel," in *Los Angeles Times Book Review,* October 25, 1987, p. 7.

[*In the following review of* Michael, *Clark discusses Goebbels's novel as a reflection of his Nazi principles and attitudes.*]

Joseph Goebbels wrote [*Michael*] in 1923, at age 26, two years after he'd taken his Ph.D in literature. The book was originally—and rather appropriately, as things turned out—called **Michael: Pages From a German Destiny,** but the subtitle may have caused some queasy moments for the publishers of this first English edition, who have left it off. Variously rejected by German publishers before the author had made a name for himself in politics, it finally came out in Germany in 1929 and by 1945 had gone through 17 printings. Though the author's position as Hitler's propaganda minister certainly didn't hurt his sales figures, he never got around to composing a sequel. That was perhaps his only known act of mercy, considering the literary quality of this early effort—less a novel than a romantic, rhapsodic and rather sophomoric paean to National Socialist revolution.

Goebbels' story seems to be a blend of his own youthful experiences (probably reconstructed from student diaries); those of his close friend Richard Flisges, a veteran of the First World War who'd introduced him to Marx, then died in a mining accident (Goebbels' protagonist suffers a similar fate), and those of Fyodor Dostoevsky, whose louse-under-the-floorboards autobiographical stance in *Notes From the Underground* obviously provided the fledgling novelist with a convenient model.

Michael, this diaristic novel's first-person narrator and hero, returns in 1918 from the Russian front to his university; there he meets an idealistic, blond-haired fraulein named Hertha Holk, with whom he takes rainy strolls through the Black Forest, conducts high-minded discussions about the Fatherland and—in chaste and exalted fashion—falls in love.

Subsequent "action" includes some ranting political arguments with a demonic Russian student-revolutionary (whose Pan-Slavism bumps head-on into Michael's Pan-Germanism), a religious seaside interlude during which Michael writes a verse play about Christ, and a rather anti-climactic tryst between Michael and Hertha Holk in Munich's Latin Quarter, where the hero's *Sturm-und-*

Drang psychic torments and anti-bourgeois fervor drive his middle-class sweetheart away. Alone, he goes off to the mines to pursue his new-found doctrine of redemption through work and self-sacrifice.

All of this is punctuated steadily by Michael's ejaculatory, aphoristic commentary, delivered mostly in one-line paragraphs whose relentless ripple-effects at first hold a certain awful fascination, but soon come to feel like the sledgehammer blows of a baby rattle filled with concrete. And Goebbels' characters never rise above their basic two-dimensionality; they are cardboard cut-outs whose greatest glory is to become sounding boards for the author's lugubrious philosophizing.

Goebbels' literary sources probably included not only Dostoevsky, Nietzsche and Goethe (all revered by Michael) but also such more immediate influences as Knut Hamsun, Ernst Junger and Arnolt Bronnen. But discussing his book in such terms is a little like talking about John Hinckley's diary in relation to the Confessional Tradition, or comparing Howard Hunt's spy novels with Joseph Conrad. In short, his historical role is our only reason for looking into Goebbels' book.

On the face of it, this is not a book about Hitler. Shortly after it was written, in fact, Goebbels, as a National Socialist newspaper editor, demanded the expulsion from the party of "the petty bourgeois Adolf Hitler." A year later, however, the novelist-turned-journalist attended a Hitler speech and immediately abandoned the party's "moderate" wing to follow him; the rest, like they say, is history.

Michael contains a few passages of evangelical, lyric-ecstatic proto-Nazism, hailing an incandescent, unidentified Fuehrer-figure and denouncing Jews, but these passages were likely 11th-hour, brink-of-publication inserts. The novel's testimony about its author's political life is largely a psychological backdrop, a portrait of the Ur-Fascist character achieved quite apart from (and in spite of) Goebbels' confused and self-conscious "revolutionary" intentions.

John Lukacs   (**essay date 1988**)

SOURCE: "In Love with Hitler," in *The New York Review of Books,* Vol. XXXV, No. 12, July 21, 1988, pp. 14-16.

[*In the following essay, Lukacs analyzes Goebbels's characteristics as a man and writer.*]

The diaries of Joseph Goebbels are an extraordinary find, for many reasons, including their size and their history. Goebbels was a truly compulsive writer as well as speaker—an unusual combination. He began to write a regular diary in July 1924 (there are indications of an irregular diary even earlier) at the age of twenty-six. The last entry is probably that of April 9, 1945, three weeks before his suicide along with his wife and children, and the complete collapse of the Third Reich. The total of the retrieved hand- and typewritten material may amount to more than 60,000 pages. When completed, their publication will comprise ten large volumes, of which the first four have now been published by the Institut für Zeigeschichte in cooperation with the West German Federal Archives. These four volumes of Goebbel's diaries from July 1924 to July 1941 are a unit by themselves. Goebbels wrote them by hand, often every day, even when he was at his frenzied work as the minister of propaganda and culture in the Third Reich.

He turned to dictating them to a first-rate stenographer in July 1941. A few months earlier he had the written diaries transported to an underground safe and commissioned the same man to begin transcribing them on a typewriter. Thus there are portions of these diaries of which two or even more transcripts exist. This is one guarantee of their authenticity, about which there should be no question. The extensive introductions of Elke Fröhlich, their compiler and editor, describe the extreme care and precision of their analysis and transcription. (Goebbels's handwriting became increasingly difficult; besides, many of the retrieved pages were damaged by moisture.) In reading these nearly three thousand large printed pages I found only a few, very minor, errors in the annotations.

The story of the recovery and the detection of these manuscripts is long and complicated. Elke Fröhlich has given an account within her 103-page introduction in Vol. 1 (and in an article in the October 1987 number of the *Vierteljahrshefte für Zeitgeschichte*). Some of the material was found by a German woman who had been ordered by the Russians to clean up the *Führerbunker* soon after the fall of Berlin; another portion was found within a mass of paper sold by a junk dealer a year later; much of the material, in large aluminum boxes, was carted away by the Russians; more boxes were found by the East Germans in the late 1960s. The Russians eventually turned over microfilm rolls to the East German authorities, who, after some of the material was leaked to a West German publisher, agreed to their publication. One odd detail is Goebbels's request to a German phototechnician in November 1944 to begin the photographic reduction of these thousands of pages ("I may lose everything, but these personal papers of mine must be preserved for posterity"): the technician was the man who either invented or at least was a pioneer of what much later became known as microfiche to librarians and archivists around the world. By a strange coincidence this man, who is still alive, bears the name of Dr. Joseph Goebel.

What is remarkable, significant, and new in this enormous mass of papers? The answer to the first question is obvious: their bulk. I know of no comparable example of such extensive continuous diaries by any political leader of any country at any time. (There *are* a few important gaps, in 1938 and 1939.) But obviously, too, quantity and quality are different matters. There are not many truly startling revelations in these pages. Most of the interesting revelations involve Goebbels himself. But apart from what these diaries may tell about this frantic and compulsive diarist there are at least two elements—elements, rather than specific individual items—of these diaries that should make historians rethink some matters.

One of these concerns the political history of the German people before, not after, the Depression. The accepted view is that the sudden rise in Nazi votes (the tremendous, ninefold increase in September 1930 from 12 to 108 Nazi seats in the Reichstag) was a result of the economic crisis that befell Germany soon after the New York stock market crash in October 1929. Most historians have attributed most of the Nazi successes to the Depression in Germany. Yet in 1929—which was a prosperous time in the history of the Weimar Republic—the appeal of the Nazis had already begun to grow. In the communal elections of Saxony, Apolda, Coburg, Mecklenburg, and Berlin Nazi votes doubled and trebled. Goebbels of course records these minor (though significant) electoral events. But what is astonishing is the absolute confidence—and, alas, the foresight—that Goebbels and Hitler possessed and that they demonstrated about their prospects, even before the economic and political crisis of the Weimar Republic: that is, before the late summer of 1930, at a time when the Nazi party was only an extremist faction, holding fewer than 3 percent of the seats in the Reichstag. Once the people speak up, we'll be in power—this was Goebbels's conviction as early as 1929.

Later, a year before Hitler's astounding rise to the chancellorship, Goebbels writes (February 4, 1932): "It is wonderful to observe how sure and unhesitating the Führer looks at the coming assumption of power. He does not doubt that for a second, not even in his private thoughts. He speaks and acts and thinks as if we were in power already." He goes on: "Gröner [the anti-Nazi minister of war] must fall. Then Brüning. Then Schleicher"—the exact sequence of what happened. On April 14, 1932, "we are discussing questions of personnel, as if we were already in power." Alas, these were not the daydreams of fanatics. Goebbels and Hitler understood the tides of German popular sentiment. This suggests the need not only to revise (and drastically diminish) the economic interpretation of the crisis of German democracy in the years between 1930 and 1933 but to recognize the political savvy of Hitler and of his cohorts—and also to recognize that National Socialist propaganda, well before 1932 and 1933, had struck deep chords in the consciousness of increasing numbers of Germans, involving sentiments and inclinations that were more powerful and older and deeper than the novel responses to economic need.

Another potential revision suggested by these diaries involves Hitler's relationship to Goebbels. (The converse, that is, Goebbels's relationship to Hitler, is a different matter, to which I shall return.) The accepted opinion is that Goebbels was one of Hitler's closest advisers, and surely his intellectual adviser. But from the evidence of these diaries there can be no question that Goebbels was subordinate to Hitler in every way: not only administratively or psychologically but also intellectually—a condition that Goebbels admits throughout his career, again and again. More important: it appears from the mass of evidence of these diaries that, Hitler's need for Goebbels's propaganda activities notwithstanding, Goebbels's influence on Hitler's decisions—decisions and choices on all level—was minimal.

Perhaps even more important is the evidence accumulated here that confirms something that few people (one exception was General Jodl) remarked: despite his more than occasional volubility, Hitler was a very secretive man. His frequent, and often cunningly planned, monologues and haranguings were not always the result of self-indulgence. He used them to influence, inspire, overwhelm, and, at times, intimidate others. Yet some of his most important political and military decisions he kept entirely to himself. It was Jodl who said in 1946 (and a few fragments of evidence since then support this view) that, contrary to the accepted view, Hitler knew before almost anyone in his circle that he would lose the war: but how could one expect that he would admit this to his staff, let alone to the German people at large? Goebbels's diaries confirm Hitler's secretiveness, well before the war. Yes, he was close to Hitler; but for Hitler to tell him what he, Hitler, was about to do (except for his sometimes dreamy speculations and long-range designs) happened very seldom.

One example is Hitler's decision to attack Russia. Hitler ordered the planning for the invasion to begin nearly eleven months before it took place, and he gave the definite directive for it six months later; but Goebbels was not privy to these plans except shortly before the actual attack. In this respect the meeting of the two men on June 16, 1941, as recorded in these diaries, is significant. It may be the longest of these thousands of diary entries. It contains yet another revelation of Hitler's brutal and amoral convictions of what war was supposed to accomplish ("Right or wrong does not matter. We must conquer [*siegen*]"); but it is another confirmation, too, of the fact that Hitler was less certain about the prospects of a rapid collapse of Russia than were Goebbels and his generals—which may explain why, for once, he was compelled to harangue Goebbels and others about this.

And now: what about Goebbels himself? Again there is reason, supplied by these diaries, to correct the accepted view that this master of propaganda was something of a genius, and "the most interesting of the men around Hitler." This was the view of Alan Bullock, Hitler's first serious biographer, whose views about Hitler have not quite stood the test of time. That this is still the accepted view should appear from the fact that, next to

Hitler, none of the Nazi leaders has been the subject of as many biographies as Goebbels (of these Helmut Heiber's is the best); and during the last forty years at least four portions of Goebbels's diaries—fragmentary, incomplete, and, at least on one occasion, pirated editions—have been published by American and English commercial houses. Was Goebbels really the most interesting man among the Nazis? There was an extraordinary consistency in the vision of this man, the very shape and sound of whose name suggests, like a small rubber ball, the bounce of compressed energy. Yet these diaries show how his mind was more limited in its scope and more shallow than one has been inclined to think.

Goebbels was addicted to the diary form. His two books (the novel *Michael,* written in 1923 and published in 1929, and his account of Hitler's achievement of power, *Vom Kaiserhof zur Reichskanzlei,* published in 1934) were also written in the form of diaries—it is significant how the text of the latter corresponds largely to his diaries of the same period. For many years he scribbled these long diary entries at night, often ending them with sentimental exclamations, and calling his diary "My father confessor!" He appears early as a prototypical example of an unhappy German neo-idealist, a radical revolutionary youth with a Spenglerian cast of mind, an extreme nationalist with sympathies for a nationalist bolshevism. Tearing himself away from his lower-middle-class Catholic family, critical of his father, a factory foreman who rose to be a clerk, filling his mind with a hatred for anything that is middle-class bourgeois, he is extremely moody, too; and his moods, very frequently, involve women.

Large portions of his diaries during the Twenties are devoted to his love affairs. Here, again, a minor revision is in order. Goebbels has had the reputation of an obsessed womanizer, a physically unattractive man who would use his powerful position and prestige to bed women, including young movie actresses. This is not altogether untrue; yet everything indicates that this partially maimed man (it is odd how much Goebbels looked like Joel Grey in *Cabaret:* a swarthy, energetic little man, with a diabolical grin and large, popping eyes) attracted all kinds of women early in life, probably because of his immediately apparent dynamic personality. He needed women (the platitude "women are the motor of life" he repeated often). Yet it was the women who flocked to him, including his future wife, Magda Quandt, the second great love of his life (the first, Anka Stahlherm, kept returning to him after her marriage). Until now it had seemed that the beautiful Frau Quandt, who was something of an upper-middle-class woman, was courted by Goebbels and served as his means of rising in society. It now appears that it was she who seduced Goebbels, not the reverse. (With all of the importance of his erotic drive the only entry in these diaries in which a physical consummation is even suggested occurs when Magda appears at his apartment on the night of February 15, 1931: "And she stays very late.") But—and this is more important—his sexual ambitions were wholly subordinated to his political ones. On June 17, 1931, he wrote: "First comes the Party, then Magda. Love does not restrict me; it drives me on." Around that time he made "a solemn agreement" with Magda that they will not marry "until we have conquered the Reich." (Actually their marriage took place before this.)

But by that time the style and the very purpose of his diary had changed. He wrote less and less about his private life, more and more about his public life. He was much happier than before. Like Hitler, he discovered his talent for public speaking. His references to his speeches are full of self-praise. The fairly vulgar word "*Bombenerfolg*" (whose English translation, "an explosive success," is but a pale version) recurs, over and over again. He now saw himself as the great chronicler of the party; and, after that, of the Third Reich. He said that his diaries will provide his children a substantial inheritance (in 1934 he received a very large advance for their eventual publishing rights); he became more obsessed with his self-appointed task as chronicler of the Reich. The result is a gradual decrease of interesting material. There are two reasons for this. One is his increasing habit of beginning each diary entry with a summary of the military and political events of the previous day. (By this time he was writing his diary every morning, and not at night.) This is especially evident in the later portions, after 1941. Yet these summaries tell us relatively little that is new. The other reason is the already mentioned secretiveness of Hitler.

At this point we must say something about Goebbels's adulation of Hitler. In one of the earliest entries in his diary, on July 4, 1924, Goebbels wrote (it is not certain whether he had met Hitler by that time): "Germany is longing for the One, the Man, as the earth in summer is longing for rain. . . . Could a miracle still save us? Lord, show the German people a miracle! A miracle!! A man!!!" The miracle was coming. It was Hitler. (On July 19: "The people's movement needs an ideal, a great Führer personality. Yes, we are looking for the born Führer.") Then he met Hitler. On October 14, 1925, having finished reading *Mein Kampf*: "Who is this man? Half plebeian, half god! Is he in fact The Christ, or only the John [the Baptist]?"

Yes, there are a few—very few—instances in which the diaries record disappointment with Hitler's tactics. They do not last. From the very beginning Goebbels is wholly under Hitler's sway. The adulatory passages are copious. But they do not only refer to Hitler's ideas. They refer to his private personality. (November 6, 1925: "Hitler now jumps up, he stands before us. He grasps my hand. Like an old friend. And those great, blue eyes. Like stars. He is glad to see me. I am very happy. . . . This man has everything to be a king. The born tribune of a people. The coming dictator." April 13, 1926: "At the end Hitler embraces me. Tears in his eyes. I am so

happy. . . . He is our host. And how great he is in that too!" July 31, 1928: "Hitler is a universal human being. He is a glorious story-teller.") Much later, when Hitler chooses to telephone him on New Year's Eve, Goebbels is in tears. It appears that Hitler knew very well how to deal with him. Goebbels was only eight years younger than Hitler but "he is like my father." (June 22, 1929: "His fatherliness is touching. I love him very much. Of all men I love him most, because he is so good. He has a great heart." Nine years later, August 16, 1938: "The Führer is like a father to me. I am so thankful to him for that.")

Goebbels was not a particularly loyal character, but his loyalty to Hitler remained unbroken until the end. Some time after 1929 his references to Hitler begin to change. He no longer refers to him as "der Chef." Now he writes "der Führer." It was not only National Socialist fanaticism but Goebbels's adulation of Hitler that made him (contrary to Hitler's request that Goebbels abandon the *Führerbunker*) accompany Hitler beyond the end, into death. In their twenty years together there are a few times when Goebbels is disconcerted with Hitler's hesitations. The brutalities of Hitler, his vulgarities, do not trouble Goebbels for a moment. He admires Hitler for them. Hitler is the stronger character and—it is Goebbels who says this—the greater mind.

This tells us something not only about Goebbels's character but about his mind. Was he altogether a good judge of people? It does not seem so. He was very vain. His reactions varied extremely according to how he was seen and treated by others. There was a time when he despised Göring and liked Ribbentrop; later he would reverse himself. His assessments of foreign statesmen were very poor. He knew little of the world beyond Germany. In *Michael* he wrote about the German people: "We are the most intelligent but, alas, also the stupidest nation in the world." If by "intelligent" we mean the original meaning of that word, the ability to read between the lines, then Goebbels does not come out very well. He had a quick mind, and his self-discipline was often amazing. (In 1931 he could write—besides his diary—three hundred typewritten pages in fourteen days.) But his mind was both fanatical and superficial. He wrote his diaries in a feverish haste, with a minimum of contemplation. He had read much in his youth, but after 1929 his main intellectual pleasure and interest were directed to films. (He was an admirer of American movies, especially of *Gone With the Wind*: "a great achievement of the Americans," which he showed several times in his private movie-room, including the agitated night before the invasion of Russia.)

If there was a glimmer of genius in his insights it was in his ideas about propaganda. (February 8, 1932: "The intellectuals think that the more often a theme is repeated the less its effect on the public. This is not true. It depends how one treats that theme. If one has the ability to repeat the same theme over and over again but in different ways, from different sides, with ever increasing drastic arguments, then its [acceptance] by the public will never fade; to the contrary, it will become stronger.")

Goebbels was not a simple person. There were dualities in his character. There was his obsessive erotic drive; yet his relationship to the many women in his life seems fairly normal. He broke away from his Catholic parents early; yet he remained a good son, often to the point of sentimentality. He was a cynic about people (September 25, 1924: "90 percent of people are the gutter, 10 percent halfway decent"); yet his admiration for and faith in German soldiers and workers were excessively strong. Much of the prose of his diaries is sentimental and petty, with many expressions of kitsch; often it seems almost a caricature of German middle-class sentimentalities. Yet the most consistent element in his ideology was his hatred of the sentiments of the bourgeoisie, of the middle-class mentality (which is why both in the beginning and near the end of his public career he favored an alliance with Russia and Communists). Even at the end of the war (which he never opposed, and into which he had thrown himself with enthusiasm), looking at the destruction of German cities, he took some comfort by saying that at least the bourgeois world of Europe had been destroyed forever. He was, fortunately, wrong.

It is a curious coincidence that Goebbels ended his antibourgeois novel ***Michael*** with "that catastrophic day, January 30" when his hero Michael died. Ten years later, in 1933, January 30 was to become the culmination, the greatest triumph, in Goebbels's life, the day Hitler became the chancellor of Germany. From the consequences of that catastrophic thirtieth of January we have not yet recovered—leading as it did to the world war in the shadows of which we still live.

Joseph Goebbels   (excerpt date 1942-43)

SOURCE: *The Goebbels Diaries: 1942-1943*, Fireside Press, edited and translated by Louis P. Lochner, 1948, 566 p.

[*The following excerpts are from diary entries made by Goebbels during the war years of 1942 and 1943.*]

JANUARY 22, 1942

The Japanese Foreign Minister, Togo, delivered an extraordinarily firm, manly, and diplomatically clever speech in Parliament. He rejected the theory of race struggle, stretched out the hand of peace to the South American states, and above all handled the peoples in East Asia, who are oppressed by the English and Americans, with exceptional psychological skill. The Japanese are pursuing a tactical course fraught with extraordinary danger for both England and the United States. It is evident that the Japanese have had considerable political and diplomatic experience. Added to their great military powers this experience is calculated to achieve corresponding successes. . . .

JANUARY 23, 1942

Rommel's boldly conceived attack in North Africa is extremely gratifying. The English are again trying to alibi with weather difficulties. In the course of the day, however, they must nevertheless admit being pushed back quite a distance. Rommel is praised highly by the English press. He is altogether one of our most popular generals. We could well use a few more such big shots. . . .

I am about to release some three hundred officials of my Ministry to the Army and the munitions industry and to replace them by women. That involves some difficulties, but these will be gradually overcome. The Party, especially, will have to help me with this. I should like also to force society ladies and women from our better strata into this work. I therefore had a long discussion about this with Frau von Dirksen [mother of the former German Ambassador to Japan and Great Britain, Herbert von Dirksen, (and) one of the first blue bloods to embrace the Nazi faith] who is very enthusiastic about my plan and who has promised to support me in a big way. . . .

JANUARY 25, 1942

We have issued a special communiqué to the effect that German submarines have succeeded in sinking 125,000 tons of enemy shipping off the American Atlantic coast. That is an exceedingly good piece of news for the German people. It bears testimony to the tremendous activity of our submarines and their widely extended radius of action, as well as to the fact that German heroism conquers even the widest oceans. At last a special bulletin! We certainly needed it, and it acts like rain on parched land. Everybody regards the communiqué as a very effective answer to the warmonger Roosevelt, whom the whole German people curse. Many people are in a quandary as to whether they ought to hate him or Churchill more. . . .

JANUARY 26, 1942

I have received a report from a commanding general at the northern front which is extraordinarily favorable. The general says the Russian forces there are very weak and are being bled white. He believes the Soviet Union will collapse in the spring, provided we are in a position to deliver a few decisive blows. Even though I am not able as yet to share this optimism I nevertheless believe he has something. It may well be that the times through which we now are passing will later be regarded as the most advantageous in the entire history of this war; possibly it is actually true that the Bolsheviks are now using up their last resources and will break down under a severe blow.

But let us not cling too much to such hopes. Our preparations for the coming spring and summer must be made just as though the Bolsheviks still had very great reserves. That will make us immune to surprises and we won't have moral setbacks like those of last summer and autumn. The more difficult we imagine war to be, the easier it will prove in the end. . . .

APRIL 11, 1942

A black day for the enemy side. The Americans must admit they have evacuated Bataan. They now have nothing more to defend in the Philippines except Corregidor. . . .

The whole United States is in a dither. The hero's halo they gave MacArthur is fading. We are naturally going to seize upon this opportunity. This big shot, whom New York only a few days ago still tried to sell as the outstanding genius of the century, will now be unmasked completely by our propaganda.

I have received confidential information to the effect that the Pope has appealed to the Spanish bishops under all circumstances to see to it that Spain stays out of the war. He supports his argument with humanitarian phrases. In reality he thereby gives expression to his enmity for the Axis. It is clear nonsense for a spiritual and ecclesiastical power to meddle so much in political and military questions. After the war we shall have to see to it that as far as our country is concerned at least, such attempts at interference are rendered impossible. . . .

APRIL 20, 1942

All signs indicate that the American public is extremely disappointed at the course of the war thus far. It had expected much more from what Mr. Knox advertised a few months ago as the "beginning of the shooting war." The Americans are therefore bragging about millions of soldiers whom they are training by all rules of the book for every theater of war. It would be better if some tens of thousands of these soldiers were already in the theaters of war where the war is actually being waged, and not on alleged training fields where you merely practice playing at war. . . .

The birthday of the Fuehrer . . . was celebrated in the late afternoon by an impressive demonstration in Berlin Philharmonic Hall. All who have rank or power in the state, the Party, and the Wehrmacht, were assembled there. . . . My speech . . . met with great approval. . . .

APRIL 24, 1942

. . . It is clear that Churchill is once again playing an extraordinarily insolent and impudent game. He can dare play it only with the English population. We would have to beware of doing anything like it to the German people. For instance, if in the autumn of 1940 we had advertised an invasion of the British Isles with so much noise and publicity even though it was not planned and could not be executed, without afterwards starting it, that would have been nothing short of disastrous for our propaganda. The British can do a thing like that. The British people are like children and in addition have the limitless patience of sheep. They stand for having the invasion theme played again and again without compelling Churchill to make good. . . .

APRIL 30, 1942

. . . Roosevelt addressed his people in a fireside chat. He also appealed to the French people. His speech fairly dripped with hypocrisy. That he also turned to the German and Italian people deserves only to be recorded in the margin. He evidently intends to make good what British propaganda has missed and to prove himself a clever pupil of Wilson. . . .

MAY 10, 1942

. . . .News policy is a weapon of war. Its purpose is to wage war and not to give out information. . . .

MAY 13, 1942

The Japanese Foreign Minister, Tojo, delivered a speech in which he came out strongly for the independence of India. The Japanese are showing exceptional wisdom in their approach to the peoples suppressed by the English. We could learn a lot from them; this applies especially to our political leadership in the occupied areas of the East. Unfortunately, Rosenberg has again failed to take this topic up with the Fuehrer. There is nothing left for me to do except to take up this theme the next time I speak with the Fuehrer. . . .

MAY 21, 1942

New Americans have arrived in Ireland. The purpose of this isn't quite clear for the moment. Americans seem determined by demonstrations of this kind to put the English gradually under moral compulsion to create a second front. But the English are merely standing by their guns for the present. They especially lament their heavy shipping losses and believe that in view of the catastrophic tonnage position an invasion of the European continent can scarcely be attempted.

Churchill's conduct of the war is attacked with exceptional vehemence during the debate in the House of Commons. He is standing in the cross fire of criticism by all parties. It is nothing short of a riddle how this man can still be so popular. . . .

MAY 15, 1943

. . . The well-known physics expert, Professor Ramsauer, Director of the Research Institute of the German General Electric Company and chairman of the *Deutsche Physikalische Gesellschaft*, presented me with a report on the status of German and Anglo-Saxon physics. This report is very depressing for us. Anglo-Saxon physical science has completely eclipsed us, especially in research. As a result the Anglo-Saxon powers are very superior to us in the practical application to warfare of the results of research in physics. That is noticeable both in air and submarine warfare. Professor Ramsauer proposed a number of changes which I shall attempt to bring about to the extent of my ability. He, too, believes we can catch up with the Anglo-Saxon physics experts by concentrating our research facilities, by combining the various research institutes which are doing substantial work, by raising the standards of the profession, and by increasing the number of physical scientists, both students and teachers. Of course this will take considerable time. It is better, however, to make a beginning and to count on certain results for the future rather than to let things merely go on as they are now. . . .

MAY 19, 1943

. . . The English and Americans claim they took 109,000 Germans and 63,000 Italians prisoner in Tunisia. It may therefore be presumed that most of our troops there are in captivity. In the last analysis that is a comforting thought. It certainly does not leave so bitter a taste as did the collapse of our defense in Stalingrad.

The psychological pressure which is being brought to bear upon the Italian public at the moment is extremely heavy, and, I suppose, also painful.

A Hollywood movie about the Soviet Union, based on the book, *Mission to Moscow,* by the former American Ambassador in Moscow Davies, has created a great sensation in the United States. It pleads for friendship with the Soviets in such an evil-smelling manner that even the American people are protesting.

The reduction of the meat ration by one hundred grams has, after all, had a very serious psychological effect. Criticism is directed especially at Goering's speech of last autumn in the Sports Palace, in which he claimed that from then on everything would be better. . . .

MAY 27, 1943

Churchill still claims that unconditional surrender is the war aim of the Anglo-Saxon powers. He will have to wait a good long time before he reaches this aim. He praised the superiority of English and especially American production over Axis production, but his estimates are absolutely wrong. We are taking occasion to prove it in our reply to his interview. His language is coarse and cynical as can be. He says he is planning a knockout blow against us. We are planning something quite different for him. Only it is essential that we succeed soon in overcoming England's nervewracking air supremacy. . . .

SEPTEMBER 19, 1943

The Anglo-American press attacked me violently because of my allegedly premature reports of victories. But these didn't come from me; on the contrary, as I have already emphasized, I protested energetically against them. At the Fuehrer's GHQ there were a couple of generals who could not wait. They distributed the skin of the bear before it had been killed and trumpeted to the world a victory that we hadn't achieved. Developments as a matter of fact have been just about the opposite. . . .

I have made it clear both to the responsible men in my Ministry as well as to the Fuehrer's GHQ that I won't stand any longer for such premature and unsubstantiated reports of victories. . . . No military news must hereafter be issued unless it has had my approval. . . .

SEPTEMBER 23, 1943

Shortly after I arrived at GHQ the Fuehrer asked me to accompany him on his morning walk. The Fuehrer seemed to be in exceptionally good health. Apparently he has recuperated well in recent weeks. He told me his morning walks with his dog Blondi did him a lot of good. In contrast to last year he at least gets into the fresh air every morning and every afternoon. That is excellent for his health. His condition gives no hint of the difficult days through which we are now passing; on the contrary, he seems to be in the best of form. That, in my opinion, is the most important thing for our political and military situation. . . .

It is refrshing to note the Fuehrer's optimistic attitude regarding the entire situation at the front. Seldom throughout this whole war have I seen the Fuehrer so tough and aggressive. It proves what I have claimed so often: The more furious the storm, the more determined is the Fuehrer to face it.

The Fuehrer told me in detail about the Duce's visit, which made a deep impression on him. That is, the Duce's personality did not act so strongly on him this time as in their earlier meetings. The main reason may be that the Duce now came to the Fuehrer without any power and that the Fuehrer accordingly looked at him somewhat more critically. The Duce has not drawn the moral conclusions from Italy's catastrophe that the Fuehrer had expected of him. He was naturally overjoyed to see the Fuehrer and to be fully at liberty again. But the Fuehrer expected that the first thing the Duce would do would be to wreak full vengeance on his betrayers. But he gave no such indication, and thereby showed his real limitations. He is not a revolutionary like the Fuehrer or Stalin. He is so bound to his own Italian people that he lacks the broad qualities of a worldwide revolutionary and insurrectionist. . . .

NOVEMBER 10, 1943

The Fuehrer's speech in the Loewenbräu Cellar has simply amazed the enemy. They had expected quite a different song. They thought the Fuehrer was sick, nervous, depressed, and devoid of all confidence in victory. Also, they had already joyfully anticipated that November 9 could be looked on as a day of great triumph for them. Now the English are sitting there like a sorry tanner whose pelts have swum away. Everything they prophesied in their propaganda has failed to happen. . . . Now they suddenly say that the Fuehrer has spoken aggressively and boastfully, that he was a different Hitler from the one known the last few months. . . . Nobody any longer pokes fun at the reprisals threatened by the Fuehrer. On the contrary, the enemy considers this very realistically and without skepticism. . . .

NOVEMBER 27, 1943

Last night it was Frankfurt's turn to suffer fairly heavy attacks. . . . the Goethe House has been hit. One's feelings are already so blunted by air raids that this hardly seems like sacrilege. There's nothing one can do about it anyway! Air raids hang over us like fate. . . .

Michael H. Kater (essay date 1990)

SOURCE: "Inside Nazis: The Goebbels Diaries, 1924-1941," in *Canadian Journal of History,* Vol. XXV, No. 2, August, 1990, pp. 233-43.

[*In the following essay, Kater discusses the public and private aspects of Goebbels's life as reflected in his diaries.*]

Elke Fröhlich of the Munich-based Institut für Zeitgeschichte has done historians of National Socialism and the Third Reich an immense service by transcribing, editing, and publishing all hitherto known fragments of Dr. Paul Joseph Goebbels's surviving diary, which he kept from October 17, 1923, to the spring of 1945. The five volumes, including a register, are marketed by the K. G. Saur publishing company, with offices in Munich, New York, London, and Paris. In this case, Dr. Fröhlich has been able to publish hand-written diaries dating from July 1924 to July 1941. As Fröhlich explains in her introduction, because of the fullness of the events during the war Goebbels decided to dictate his diary after that date, a process that resulted in type-written text for the balance of the dictatorship. Fröhlich's basis for her edition were twenty-two thick binders, constituting anywhere from two-thirds to three quarters of Goebbels's hand-written notes. The rest so far is missing. Parts of the diary from summer 1941 to spring 1945 may also turn out to be absent, depending on the final availability of either originals or copies, but so far Fröhlich is hopeful that she will be able to complete the edition not too long from now, meaning that six more volumes would be added on to the present four (not counting an extant register volume and other registers to follow).

The editor narrates the adventurous fate of the diaries for the benefit of the readers who can consider themselves fortunate to have these sterling transcriptions at their disposal. This story reads like a tall tale, yet undoubtedly is true; it involves Germans, Russians, Swiss, Americans and Britons. After perusing it for the first time shortly after the appearance of the volumes, this reviewer was wondering how the remaining sequels could possibly see print. He was then told that progress had indeed been impeded by the obstinacy of East Germans, who, contrary to prior agreements, were reluctant to send the follow-up material to Munich. The latest in this development is that the current circumstances in

Eastern Europe have led to progress: Fröhlich's subsequent editions should come onto the market shortly.

Elke Fröhlich has spent years deciphering Goebbels's extremely difficult handwritten accounts and gives tantalizing examples of how dozens of expressions in the source could quite easily be mistaken for something radically different. Fröhlich was commissioned to do this work by the Munich Institute, in official conjunction with the Federal Archive of Koblenz. The text was computer-typeset and printed in such a way that a very readable, if not exactly glossy edition resulted. For the benefit of libraries and the researcher, this procedure has kept the price of the five volumes (including the lexical register) down to an affordable minimum.

Fröhlich explains convincingly why Goebbels's text has not been annotated and why only the barest of editing has been done: with the aim of establishing as much authenticity of script as possible. But even this modest-sounding task was hazardous, for apart from the difficulty of Goebbels's capricious hand there often was physical damage to the originals to be overcome, there were non-paginated pieces to be linked, and dates and spellings to be corrected.

The outcome of this labour amounts to a gold mine for the diligent researcher, for this now is by far the most complete personal record we have by any of the major figures of Hitler's movement, and certainly the most voluminous one. The editor is right in pointing out that not even the second largest diary available in print, that of Polish *Generalgouvernement* chief Hans Frank, approximates the Goebbels source in terms of information potential, let alone volume. Other fragmentary diaries exist, such as by Heinrich Himmler (only from his adolescence), Alfred Rosenberg, Hermann Göring, and Franz Halder, but they have been of rather limited service in the past. Commercially the most successful and, with reservations, for the historian the most welcome of the diary and memoir genus has been Albert Speer's venal volume of reflections, *Inside the Third Reich,* which, nonetheless, has blanked out as much as it has revealed about Hitler and his Third Reich.

This definitive edition of one part of the Goebbels diaries makes it mandatory for historians to differentiate carefully between already extant, useful precursors on the one hand, and bogus or redundant versions on the other. It also suggests another close examination of existing Goebbels biographies and related literature. Concerning the first task, one should not lose sight of Helmut Heiber's meritorious 1960 publication of Goebbels's 1925-26 diaries, but nevertheless note that some of his translations or interpretations were faulty. Into the same group of bona fide editions belongs Louis P. Lochner's work of 1948, a German-language Zurich edition as well as a translation into English of diary fragments from January 1942 to December 1943. Apart from the loss of felicity in translation, in principle this book is more reliable than Heiber's because its original

fundament was type-written and hence decipherable. It is also still indispensable because, unlike Heiber's, it has not yet been superseded by Fröhlich's definitive edition. A section of the diaries from early 1945, published not too long ago by a prestigious West German firm, also appears dependable and equally indispensable, until replaced by the forthcoming larger edition. Goebbels's notorious, especially designed version of 1932-33 diaries for official publication is less useful because of its deliberate omissions and distortions, but editor Fröhlich rightly emphasizes what the readers can now see for themselves: that the then *Gauleiter* of Berlin anxiously awaiting Hitler's takeover in the Kaiserhof hotel falsified facts far less than had earlier been thought. The reader can make this judgement because Fröhlich has now published both versions, Goebbels's official and his private one, side by side in volume 2. However, scholars should beware of an English pirate edition of a fragment covering January 1, 1939, to July 8, 1941, brought out by the British Hamish Hamilton and thereafter Penguin companies, and subsequently in the United States by G.P. Putnam's Sons. As Fröhlich explains, the translation and editorial work by Fred Taylor is fraught with errors for reasons of carelessness, lack of German language skills, and the inability to facilitate proper linkages of the original leaves. Thankfully, this misleading volume has now been certified as obsolete.

Regarding biographies, Fröhlich's master edition today is capable of verifying those, at least to a certain degree, even though nothing is bound to change in the presently accepted weighting. Now as before, Helmut Heiber's magisterial Goebbels biography excels, but Fröhlich does shift some of Heiber's hermeneutical accents. Fröhlich dismisses the works of other biographers such as Curt Riess and Manvell and Fraenkel as superficial and sensational, and also makes short shrift of self-serving biographical memoirs penned by former Goebbels aides, notably that of Wilfred von Oven. In this context, it would have been useful had she gauged the memoirs of Goebbels helper Werner Stephan, which this author has had several occasions to rely upon in the past.

The best of these works, in particular Heiber's, are still not expendable, not only for the adduction of other primary and secondary materials, but also for the colour that lies in individual interpretation, and which makes for quite a different quality from the sober authenticity conveyed by Goebbels's own hand. Moreover, historians still need to fill the gap that exists, with few exceptions, for the period from July 1941 to the end of the Third Reich. In addition to reliable secondary sources, there are two primary ones that will help them do that. One consists of Goebbels's regular lead articles in *Das Reich,* the comparatively sophisticated weekly the Reich Propaganda Minister published out of Berlin from the start of the war till April 1, 1945. The other is a two-volume collection of some of Goebbels's more important articles from that paper, as well as other essays and public addresses, for the years 1941 to 1943, both published in 1943 and, unlike *Das Reich,* readily available in libraries. There are, of course, individual locations for Goebbels's publicistic output, such as his article on education and leadership, published as early as 1930, in a Nazi-specific yearbook. Lest we forget, we have recourse to excellent critical treatments of Goebbels's *Kampfzeit* and Third Reich life, for instance the monographs and articles by the American historian Jay W. Baird, but also by others, all of whom have mainly concentrated on the uses of propaganda in a dictatorship.

Goebbels's many pages of memoirs do not throw any new light on the received history of the Nazi movement or the Third Reich, but they deepen our knowledge of certain events, reassign historiographical emphasis, and indeed expose a few hitherto unknown albeit isolated phenomena to scrutiny. As the editor elaborates, there are some irritating lacunae, for example in the case of the Röhm Purge, June-July 1934, about which Goebbels says little more than that he would be on Hitler's side, or on the pre-history of *Reichskristallnacht,* November 1938, which Goebbels leaves shrouded in darkness. The diaries amplify the already rich evidence on two important points of political relevance: first, that the Nazis did *not* abet in the laying of the Reichstag Fire of February 27, 1933, and second, that Hitler was genuinely surprised (and disturbed) by Rudolf Hess's flight to England in April, 1941, and had not, contrary to steadily recurring hearsay, sent his deputy on a secret mission for the sake of a separate peace with London.

Because Goebbels was minister of propaganda and responsible for most of the culture in the Third Reich, the diaries can be best put to use in an evaluation of Nazi public opinion manipulation and cultural administration, especially radio, which he policed very closely, apart from rounding off the personality portrait that we have of the man thus far. On the whole, these intricate notes bear out the long-held contention that this doctor was the preeminent intellectual in Hitler's entourage and, despite his rationality, one of the most fanatical believers in Hitler and his self-proclaimed mission at the same time. This is evident from the very first phase of Goebbels's meetings with Hitler, which was in 1925. The often daily entries also project a romantic Goebbels, in fact a man obsessed with sexuality and the need constantly to prove himself with women. If much has already been written about Goebbels's chronic promiscuity and the impression has been conveyed that he was well-nigh irresistible, the diary reveals the traits of a man not at all certain of his powers of sexual persuasion. A reader looking for saucy details regarding Goebbels's love life will be disappointed, for at the most Joseph was fond of intimating a certain level of success or the lack thereof.

In the pages of the diary, the compulsion about girls and "beautiful women" (a recurring phrase) is on the wane to the extent that ministerial duties keep Goebbels occupied after spring 1933, and even more so after the outbreak of the war in September 1939. About his legend-ary affair with young Czech actress Lyda Baarova from 1936 to 1938 there is little in these pages, but he faithfully records the effect Hitler's man-to-man talk had on him in mid-August of 1938. No question, the negative outcome of this great love almost destroyed the propaganda minister! About Goebbels's various arrangements with film stars and, much more so, starlets, again the volumes are rather silent, but we already know from other sources that he routinely and cynically preyed on women who were dependent on him in the film industry. The Swedish singer Zarah Leander, for instance, has described a would-be seduction in her memoirs, and German film actress Margot Hielscher, in the early 1940s a very young and attractive starlet, has told this author how Goebbels demonstratively once seated her next to him during a private showing of "Gone with the Wind," immediately touching her in the dark, and how the stately Leander, who reportedly could not stand the little doctor, then exchanged seats with Hielscher, in order to rescue her as tactfully as possible. At another time, Goebbels attempted to show young Margot one of his several love nests, but as he proceeded to open the door to the place, the key broke—after having been tampered with by an adjutant with pity to spare for Hielscher. Indeed, as the testimony of a number of self-indulgent actresses validates, Goebbels is supposed to have been no hero in bed, performing the sex act quickly, businesslike and totally normally, thereafter hurrying his paramour to leave.

Goebbels liked personalities from screen and stage, because he identified his own artistic persona with them. This applied to writers and musicians as well. As a writer, despite early setbacks that prevented him from publishing his autobiographical novel **Michael** before 1933, he empathized with current poets and playwrights and took a keen interest in the affairs of the *Reichsschrifttumskammer* (part of his Reich Culture Chamber) led by Hanns Johst. Among all musicians in the Reich, the conductor Wilhelm Furtwängler, long famous before 1933, moved him most. (A good biography of Furtwängler, authored a few years ago by Fred K. Prieberg, which showed the musician as being held at ransom by the Third Reich for the sake of artistic concessions he was constantly seeking, might now be somewhat modified. For in the diaries there is evidence of a larger degree of collaboration on the conductor's part than Prieberg had assumed.) Goebbels was not "remarkably unmusical," as has recently been claimed; on the contrary, he knew the standard fare of the classics well, played the piano passably (often using it strategically in his seduction attempts), and he even injected his own melodic ideas during the composition of a propaganda song by Norbert Schultze, of "Lili Marleen" fame.

It is from the realm of propaganda and culture that entries in the diaries may be used exemplarily to demonstrate how entire sub-themes of Third Reich history can be elucidated. In the first instance, official German attitudes to American phenomena may be probed, and in the second instance, the propaganda ministry's relationship with soldiers fighting at the fronts. In both scenarios, Goebbels's personality is central; this man was truly inside the Nazi body politic.

Contrary to Hans Dieter Schäfer's suggestion some years ago, the Third Reich was not ambivalent toward the United States, possessing a "split consciousness" that allowed all sorts of manifestations of Americanism in Nazi Germany to flourish, for the sake of the social peace. Deep-down the Nazis hated Americans and the modernism they stood for, and they tried to fight symbols of American life-style such as jazz or *Girl-Kultur*. Whenever it seemed that the Nazis embraced something of American origin, they were cynically trying to appropriate or copy it for their own purposes, strictly as a means, never as an end. This signified not ambiguity and confusion, but the realization of necessary compromises. At worst, the Nazis had to acknowledge that even compromises were not possible because they themselves were incapable of maintaining their own position, which, in principle, was always recognized as superior.

Goebbels's diary bears out this situation with graphic clarity. In general, this doctor of philosophy was so contemptuous of American home-bred culture and so convinced of the primacy of German culture that he wanted to use the latter in July of 1935 to attract American sympathies, by staging suitable German events in the United States. About a year later he crassly referred to that country as "this land without culture." Some nine months hence: "The Americans are the most corrupt people on earth." And in February 1938 the minister heartily concurred with Hitler that America was "not really a nation in our sense of the word."

Goebbels denigrated the Americans for their large Negro population and the greater degree of tolerance they exhibited toward racial minorities, in particular Blacks and Jews. When in June 1936 the German boxer idol Max Schmeling defeated Joe Lewis in a dramatic match, Goebbels interpreted the victory of his next-door-neighbour Schmeling as one of the white nordic race over the inferior black race. During the Olympic Games that year in August Goebbels was mortified because in an early round of competitions only one German had won a gold medal, as opposed to three Americans, two of them Blacks.

Juxtaposed to Goebbels's fundamental contempt for America is his apparent admiration of certain of her technical facilities, in constructing machinery, for instance, and especially, in producing films. About American movies, which, according to the diaries, he watched regularly in private showrooms, the chief of all German film companies loved virtually everything, with the sometime important exception of thematic content, characteristically deemed too shallow. Goebbels was intrigued by the American mastery of the camera, by the lavish sets, the cutting and editing in the studios, and, not least, the acting abilities of the stars, wherein he once again admired the physical beauty of such celebri-

ties as Jean Harlow and Eleanor Powell. When colour was introduced in 1937, Goebbels waxed enthusiastic; this, as well as the entire technique of making a successful film, had to be emulated by the Nazis. Significantly, Goebbels viewed the whole phenomenon of American film in the manner of a tough competitor who would one day outdo the originators and beat them at their own game. As far as he was concerned, Germany could not work toward that goal fast enough. And once America was surpassed, she would be humiliated, annihilated. From the vantage point of intense rivalry, then, Goebbels's regard of the United States as champions of film production was closer to hatred than to love; here was a clever foe to be conquered, not unlike the Jews.

Such sentiments are more brashly expressed in the war diaries, which leave us short of America's entry into the conflict by December 1941. This also applies to film, for already in February 1939 Goebbels had decided, after seeing a bad American flick, that "our German films are much better." In 1942 Goebbels had a tap-dance scene cut out of the film "Carnival of Love" because he regarded this as an "Americanism." It is during the war that Goebbels's negative opinion of all things American becomes exalted, as the fragmentary diaries and also the spiteful articles in *Das Reich* illustrate. Today one may be certain that much of that vituperative anti-American propaganda is reflected in Goebbels's personal opinion as dictated to his stenographer from summer 1941, in the yet-to-be published portion of the diaries.

Goebbels admired the Wehrmacht, and in particular its elite formation, the Luftwaffe. The reasons for this are psychological and can in part be gleaned from the pages of his diary. Like Heinrich Himmler, who just missed active duty because of age, Goebbels was a frustrated World War I fighter, in his case one who would not be accepted by the army because of his deformed foot. He therefore fantasized to himself about a possible role as a warrior. His close identification with soldiers as men of bravery, paragons who sprang from the well of Nazi ideology, was the counterpart to Himmler's founding of a private army, the SS; in Freudian terms of reference, Goebbels projected himself into the ranks of the Wehrmacht through what analysts call transference. Later still Goebbels fused an experienced joy of flying, well documented in the diaries, with his adulation of soldiering: air force pilots became role models long before World War II.

For Goebbels the Luftwaffe was, significantly, the "most modern and most revolutionary" of all the Wehrmacht sections. Because to him an air force pilot was the epitome of heroism, Goebbels endowed his persona, totally irrationally, with the highest quality a human being could possess, at least in his own catechism: political astuteness. Thus in September 1940 Goebbels noted that famous war ace Major Mölders based a military judgment "entirely on political sobriety and lack of hallucination [*Phantasielosigkeit*] at the front." In contradistinction and relatively speaking, ordinary army officers were "mere political children"—a phrase used twice by Goebbels in his diaries before summer 1941.

Goebbels ranked the navy just a notch under the air force. He even sent film director Herbert A. Selpin to his doom because he had risked offensive remarks about marine officers who were obstructing his work. Again, a personal preference may have been behind Goebbels's predilection. As the diary explains on numerous occasions, Goebbels preferred holidays at the seaside, he owned villas on the Berlin lakes and enjoyed pleasure boats. Goebbels worshipped marine aces like the 32 year-old Günther Prien, who with his submarine had singlehandedly scuttled the "Royal Oak," a mighty British battle ship, at its home base in Scapa Flow on October 13, 1939, and thereafter thought this "a milestone in my life." The propaganda minister duly cultivated the hero myth of Lieutenant Prien as he had cultivated that of Horst Wessel and Werner Mölders, even after Prien went down somewhere south of Iceland in March of 1941.

Goebbels found such heroes also in the army. Franz Baron von Werra for instance, who in 1941 escaped from a Canadian prisoner-of-war camp via the United States and Mexico and then regaled the minister with tales of his adventures. Goebbels visited the soldiers at the western fronts—only in the safe spots—and was determined, as early as 1940, to heroize "the whole of German soldierdom" in one of his films. (In fact, this would turn into an entire genre of Nazi military films by 1944.) In any case, with a side glance at his model heroes from the Luftwaffe, Goebbels was planning early on in the war "to do something for these boys."

This resolve to accord some sort of special treatment to Wehrmacht staff was motivated, in Goebbels's case, by a mixture of private infatuation with "these boys," and the cool tactician's understanding of the war-psychological value of morale-boosting for the sake of the final victory. Goebbels was in a unique position to act here because of his dual function as minister responsible for propaganda *and* culture: not only did he have the propaganda apparatus in hand, but he also controlled all the facets of culture, high and low, that could be channelled into that machinery.

Hence Goebbels's answer to the needs of the fighting soldier turned out to be *Truppenbetreuung,* a singularly comprehensive program of troop entertainment from the lowest to the highest level of culture and of style. The minister entered into a tacit agreement with Germany's male artists: they would be exempt from active service if they consented to travel to the military bases and outposts, and they would be paid according to their qualifications. Indeed, the missions were risky; artists could come under fire from partisans, and one actor is known to have slipped off a rock on the Mediterranean coast and to have drowned. But if the artists refused to comply or misbehaved, they could be conscripted or worse: this was an additional instrument of Nazi popu-

lation control in time of war. Persuasion and the enticement of wages and camaraderie were used on female artists; many women found those exploits exciting, as did one popular singer who, while performing in occupied Warsaw, was invited by the SS to visit the Jewish ghetto and had a lovely pair of books made there for a farthing. Resourcefully, these programs were linked to select offerings on radio and the installation of exclusive *Soldatensender,* soldiers' stations, at the fronts or in occupied territories, the most famous of which came to be *Soldatensender Belgrad,* as it launched "Lili Marleen" and various broadcasts of officially illicit swing music.

The diaries reveal interesting details about *Truppenbetreuung.* Already in April of 1940 Goebbels was able to register 15,000 individual front shows per month. One of the problems with these was to keep a healthy balance between quantity and quality, in that the spectrum of sophistication among soldiers was so wide as to reflect the factual extremes of formal education within the German populace at large. Typically, the enlisted men longed for cheap, sometimes raunchy diversions, whereas the haughty officers demanded "class." Goebbels was constantly worried about having to sacrifice one of these legitimate desiderates for the benefit of the other, but he clearly repudiated trash among the common soldiers as much as he despised high-brow snobbery in the officer corps.

In the course of the historian's perusal of these matters, particular difficulties surface in the diaries. For example, there were the usual Third Reich competency battles between the propaganda ministry on the one side, and the Wehrmacht staff office (OKW) and Goebbels's partner in the deal, German Labor Front Leader Robert Ley, on the other. As a further example, popular and celebrated artists, buoyed by much success, were becoming overbearing and used to raking in more and more money, so that Goebbels had to decree a fee ceiling. On January 12, 1941, the minister personally received about seventy front artists and sampled some of their expertise; on the whole he was pleased, showing his jovial side, he talked to the men and women and "learned much about their challenges, cares and needs."

How reliable, overall, are the Goebbels diaries as a source of historiography? Did Goebbels not know that they would be used by posterity to judge him and the Third Reich, against the background of aggressive warfare and of Auschwitz? Elke Fröhlich offers a persuasive answer to this most important of all questions. Goebbels started the habit of diary entries when he was an unknown young man, as replacement for church confession he had enjoyed as a pious Catholic child. The confessional character of the document, which insures fidelity, was carried over, though weakened, into the period of the Third Reich, because Joseph became accustomed to treating his diary, perhaps psychotically, in the manner of a personal friend. As his own importance under Hitler grew, he increasingly looked upon himself as a chronicler of the great historic era he thought to be living in, to whom later generations would be grateful for having left a weighty record. Since Goebbels subjectively created this diary with a clear conscience, as an unshaken believer in the idea of National Socialism, he had no reason to pretend or distort anything unduly. And lastly, he wanted his children to believe him. Goebbels, it is obvious from the diary, loved these children as any good father would; that constitutes one of the truly human aspects of the tomes. Whatever one may say about Joseph Goebbels, this father would not ever have been able to bear the thought that he had deceived his children.

Ronald Smelser (essay date 1991)

SOURCE: Review of _Die Tagebücher von Joseph Goebbels: Samtliche Fragmente, Part 1,_ in _The Journal of Modern History,_ Vol. 63, No. 4, December, 1991, pp. 819-21.

[_In the following essay, Smelser examines the scholarly importance of the 1987 German edition of Goebbels's diaries._]

The editor offers us here [in **_Die Tagebücher von Joseph Goebbels: Sämtliche Fragmente,_** Part 1] the definitive edition of Goebbels's diaries—exhaustive, authoritative, well-edited, and user friendly. When the project is completed—six additional volumes are scheduled to complete the wartime period—it will replace all the various previously published fragments, including those edited by Lochner (entries from 1942-43), Heiber (1925-26), Hamilton (1939-41), and Trevor-Roper (1945), all of which contained many incomplete or inaccurate entries.

This first stage of the project, comprising four volumes plus a provisional index with 3,400 names, covers the period from Goebbels's earliest recollections, which he began to put on paper in 1924, to 1941, when, in the midst of the Russian campaign, he went over from handwritten to dictated and transcribed diaries. Although some of the material was lost at the end of the war, these volumes nevertheless represent about two-thirds to three-quarters of the total expanse of the original diaries.

This constitutes an extremely valuable historical document. No other modern political figure—certainly no other prominent Nazi so close to Hitler—produced anything remotely as voluminous as this, even in memoir form. Virtually the entire span of National Socialism, from its earliest days as a struggling, obscure movement to its triumphant seizure of power in 1933 to (when all volumes are complete) its final destruction in 1945 finds expression here.

Froehlich deserves an enormous amount of credit for the painstaking, herculean five-year effort which lies behind this publication. She tracked down every known diary fragment, including that on Russian microfilm, early microfiches, and original handwritten texts; evaluated each source for authenticity; collated the various versions and placed them in chronological order. She also carefully read and transcribed Goebbels's very difficult handwriting, eliminating errors that had been introduced in earlier published versions. Her familiarity with the historical context also enabled her to identify many an obscure figure who appeared in the text.

Having done this, Froehlich then presents the material with only the necessary editorial apparatus (spelling and grammatical errors are indicated as well as missing words and passages) so as not to be an obtrusive presence between the scholar and this primary material. Indeed, in place of extensive editorial comments in the body of the text, she uses a lengthy introduction to put the fragments into the context of earlier published versions; to characterize the content of the diaries and point out gaps; to describe in detail the goals, difficulties, and results of the editorial work; and to give us a brief interpretive sketch of Goebbels and his diaries.

It is unfortunate that missing sections from the diaries leave us in the dark about critical elements both in the history of National Socialism and in Goebbels's own political evolution. Gaps in the earliest segments prevent us from following just how Goebbels became politically active and what initial role Hitler may have had in that process, although the extant entries do give us some indication of the emergence of a "Nazi" mentality. Large gaps from August 1933 to June 1935 allow only an incomplete picture of the consolidation of power as well as the dramatic events surrounding the "Night of the Long Knives" of June 1934. Moreover, significant lacunae in 1938 leave us in the dark with respect to the Austrian _Anschluss,_ to appeasement and, above all, to the critical events leading up to the so-called _Reichskristallnacht_ of November, in which Goebbels's himself played such a critical role. By the same token, large gaps in 1939 conceal Goebbels's reaction to such important foreign policy events as the occupation of Bohemia-Moravia, the Nazi-Soviet pact, and the outbreak of World War II. Once the war broke out, however, a relatively complete section from October 1939 to July 1941 puts Goebbels into the midst of epochal events of which he is clearly aware.

Missing sections notwithstanding, the diaries offer valuable insights into the formative years of National Socialism and the man who would create the Hitler image. The so-called Elberfelder diaries (summer 1925-October 1926) as well as entries from the period of summer 1929 to summer 1933 are particularly useful in this regard, especially since the earlier diaries seem to be more frank and less contrived than later entries. The editor also does a valuable service in juxtaposing the published version of Goebbels's diaries dealing with the period leading up to the _Machtergreifung_ (**_Vom Kaiserhof zur_**

Reichskanzlei) with the originals, so that the reader can immediately follow Goebbels's own editorial process—in itself a revealing exercise.

These volumes are valuable for their completeness, not for any stunning revelations they might offer. What do they reveal about Goebbels? That he was a complex, often contradictory personality—a driven man, deeply insecure, narcissistic, quite impressionable, only superficially reflective, but always anxious to be "somebody." We have had these impressions of Goebbels before; now they are strengthened, particularly in the brief autobiographical notes which precede the diary and in which Goebbels reveals a surprising degree of self-criticism and self-doubt. As the years go by one also perceives an evolution that might sustain a number of interpretations of Goebbels, depending on which years one selects, ranging from the early, as yet unformed and immature man who sees his diary as a "Beichtstuhlersatz" to the more confident propaganda minister, who is, however, more self-conscious in his entries, viewing them as important historical documents to be preserved for posterity. Perhaps most clearly, Goebbels appears nearly throughout as a man who, like several other top Nazis, developed an emotional dependency on Hitler, one so strong that only very rarely does he criticize the man even in this intimate forum. Indeed, he betrays the need for such a dependency even before it develops: "Ich kenne überhaupt noch keinen völkischen Führer. Ich mu bald einen kennen lernen, damit ich mir wieder etwas neuen Mut und neues Selbsvertrauen hole" (June 20, 1924).

Other interesting, if scarcely earthshaking, revelations: that Goebbels's anti-Semitism began quite early ("Und jetzt ist meine Haut doch eine etwas einseitige antisemitische"—July 4, 1924); that the Nazis did not set the Reichstag fire; that Goebbels was a very poor judge of character, particularly concerning his own Nazi contemporaries, about whom his opinion fluctuates wildly from month to month. But his judgments are at least colorful. A sampling: Julius Streicher—"Berserker. Vielleicht etwas pathologisch" (August 19, 1924); Robert Ley—"ein Dummkopf und vielleicht ein Intrigant" (September 30, 1925); Goering—"etwas gedunsen" (June 13, 1928); Alfred Rosenberg—"ein sturer, eigensinniger Dogmatiker" (August 24, 1934); Party treasurer Franz Xaver Schwarz—"abgebauter Beamter, kleiner Idealis-mus, peinlich in Geldsachen, Münchener Schnauze" (April 13, 1926). Then, of course, there was Goebbels's eternal rival, Reich press chief, Otto Dietrich, the "armer Irrer" (December 31, 1935).

One major regret in reading these potentially invaluable entries is that Goebbels chose to write in a telegraphic style and in a common vernacular which often obscures his keen intelligence. One wishes he had written more expository prose; many a thought needs development, many a reference or hint, explanation. But perhaps the man simply lacked the depth.

FURTHER READING

Biography

Manvell, Roger and Heinrich Fraenkel. *Dr. Goebbels: His Life and Death*. New York: Simon and Schuster, 1960, 306 p.
    Details Goebbels's life before and during the Nazi ascendancy in Germany using data from first-hand accounts, letters, and diaries.

Reuth, Ralf Georg. *Goebbels*, translated by Krishna Winston. New York: Harcourt Brace & Company, 1993, 471 p.
    Chronicle of Goebbels's life based upon more recently available primary sources.

Riess, Curt. *Joseph Goebbels*. Garden City, N.Y.: Doubleday & Company, Inc. 1948, 367 p.
    Early biography that recognizes the importance of Goebbels's youth. Riess accepts the thorough evilness of his subject and therefore refuses to make moral considerations on Goebbels's character.

Semmler, Rudolf. *Goebbels—The Man Next to Hitler*, edited by D. McLachlan and G. S. Wagner. London: Westhouse, 1947, 234 p.
    Biography, originally written before the discovery of the Goebbels diaries in the West, based on the journals of Semmler from 31 December 1940 to the end of the Second World War.

Criticism

Bramsted, E. K. "The Propagandist in Private." *Times Literary Supplement*, No. 3970 (May 5, 1978): 506.
    Review of Goebbels's diaries from the period 28 February to 10 April, 1945 occasioned by their translation into English.

Breindel, Eric. Review of *Final Entries 1945: The Diaries of Joseph Goebbels*. *The New Republic* 179, No. 11 (September 9, 1978): 40.
    Review of Goebbels's late diaries notes his admiration for Stalin and "early identification with the more radical 'left-wing' element in the [Nazi] party."

Carsten, F. L. "The Goebbels Diaries." *Historical Journal*, Vol. 32, No. 3, September, 1989: 751-56
    Commentary on Die Tagebücher von Joseph Goebbels, a five-volume edition of Goebbels's diaries published in Germany in 1987.

Crossman, R. H. S. Review of *The Goebbels Diaries*. *The New Statesman and Nation* XXV, No. 891 (April 3, 1948): 277.
    Review of Goebbels's diaries from 1942 to 1943 that highlights the Nazi Propaganda Minister's post-war goals.

Delmer, Sefton. "The Secret Minutes of Dr. Goebbels." *Times Literary Supplement*, No. 3428 (November 9, 1967): 1063-64.
>   Discusses Goebbels's methods of subversion and psychological warfare as revealed in the minutes of his daily meetings with the Nazi propaganda chiefs.

Dulles, Allen W. "A Brilliant, Distorted Mind." *New York Times Book Review* (April 25, 1948): 1, 25.
>   Review of *The Goebbels Diaries 1942-43* that describes the "evil perfection" of his propaganda.

James, Harold. "Minister of Misinformation." *Times Literary Supplement*, No. 4,172 (March 18, 1983): 275.
>   Review of *The Goebbels Diaries 1939-41* that examines evidence about Goebbels's personal life and the propaganda techniques he devised and employed in the early years of World War II.

Lemmons, Russel. *Goebbels and 'Der Angriff.'* Lexington: The University of Kentucky Press, 1994, 172 p.
>   Investigates Nazi propaganda in the years prior to 1933, especially that of Goebbels's Berlin newspaper *Der Angriff.*

Lochner, Louis P. Introduction to *The Goebbels Diaries 1942-43*, pp. 3-30. Garden City, N.Y.: Doubleday & Company, Inc., 1948.
>   Brief summary of Goebbels's rise to power within the Third Reich.

Speier, Hans. Review of *The Goebbels Diaries 1942-43*. *Public Opinion Quarterly* 12, No. 3 (Fall 1948): 500-05.
>   Comments on textual issues, such as authenticity and scholarly value, relating to Louis Lochner's translation of Goebbels's diaries.

Watts, Richard, Jr. "The Evil Men Do." *New Republic* 118, No. 17 (April 26, 1948): 21-3.
>   Review of *The Goebbels Diaries 1942-43* that calls this exploration of "the black and bitter recesses of [Goebbels's] soul" a "repulsive but oddly arresting literary adventure."

Additional coverage of Goebbels's life and career is available in the following sources published by Gale Research: *Contemporary Authors*, Vols. 115, 148.

D. W. Griffith

1875-1948

(Full name David Wark Griffith) American filmmaker.

INTRODUCTION

As the first filmmaker to exploit the potential of film editing to convey the impression of simultaneous action, and for his promotion of a style of acting and innovative uses of the camera that suited the representation of character psychology, Griffith is generally acknowledged by scholars and critics as the most influential figure in film history. Exemplified in his epic silent movies *The Birth of a Nation* (1915) and *Intolerance* (1916), his techniques were copied and refined by the majority of filmmakers in the United States and Europe, and were closely studied by Sergei Eisenstein, Vsevolod Pudovkin, and other directors in pre- and post-revolutionary Russia. Most critics note, however, that as a storyteller Griffith was prone to bombastic thematic pretension, sentimentality, and was capable of only pedestrian insight. Moreover, *The Birth of a Nation,* which is often considered the apotheosis of his technical achievement, can no longer be shown outside of academic settings because it is blatantly racist, depicting blacks as either buffoons or savages and the Ku Klux Klan as heroes. For these reasons, modern critical attention tends to focus on two areas of his career: the early, formative period from 1908 through 1913 when he made over 480 short films for the Biograph Company; and the later phase that included important yet less well-known works such as *Broken Blossoms* (1919), *Way Down East* (1920), and *Isn't Life Wonderful* (1924).

Biographical Information

Griffith was born in Oldham County, Kentucky, to parents whose families had been in the United States since the revolutionary period. His father, Jacob, was a doctor who participated in the California Gold Rush, was a member of the Kentucky legislature, and, prior to the Civil War—in which he served as an officer in the Confederate cavalry—had been a prosperous slave owner with a large plantation. With the family's fortunes greatly diminished after the war, Griffith was born into impoverished circumstances. His father died in 1882 and his mother moved the family to Louisville where she ran a boarding house. Griffith, who never finished high school because of his obligation to help support the family, had decided early in life to be a writer; his temperament and personality, however, led him to pursue the more social and flamboyant art of stage acting. He joined a travelling theatrical company in 1895, and for the following ten years made a meager

living acting and holding odd jobs. In 1906 he married his first wife, the actress Linda Arvidson, who later appeared in many of his films. After the marginal success in Washington, D.C. and Baltimore of a play he wrote called *A Fool and a Girl* (1907), Griffith moved to New York City to resume acting. There he began selling story ideas to various motion picture companies—which at the time were located primarily in that city—and in 1908 he was hired by the Edison Company to act in two films, *Cupid's Pranks* and *Rescued from an Eagle's Nest;* the latter was directed by Edwin S. Porter, director of two much-studied films, *Life of an American Fireman* (1902-1903) and *The Great Train Robbery* (1903). He was then hired by the Biograph Company as a writer and actor. He appeared in at least twenty films before June, 1908, when he was given the opportunity to direct a film, *The Adventures of Dollie*. He became Biograph's principal director, and in the next five years he made over 480 short, very popular films. In this time, because of the success of his work, Griffith gained increasing control over the major aspects of film production at Biograph, from writing, casting, and editing to promotion. In 1913, when the owners of Biograph rejected his demands to make longer, more elaborate, and thus more expensive films, Griffith left the company, taking with him his cameraman, G. W. "Billy" Bitzer, and several of his favorite actors, including Lillian and Dorothy Gish, Robert Harron, and Henry B. Walthall. Relocated in Southern California, Griffith made several films for the Reliance-Majestic company and raised money for *The Birth of a Nation.* This film generated significant controversy upon its release—the protests of a number of black groups and prominent critics impelled Griffith to write a pamphlet, *The Rise and Fall of Free Speech in America* (1915), defending himself and the movie against charges of racism. Nonetheless, *The Birth of a Nation* was widely hailed as "the greatest film ever made." Its success enabled Griffith to make the grandly elaborate *Intolerance,* a two-and-a-half hour film presenting four intertwined historical dramas and employing massive, spectacular sets and hundreds of extras. Although it drew big crowds upon its release and soon after, audiences quickly dwindled as word spread that its four-part structure was confusing. The film was a financial failure and marked the beginning of a gradual decline in Griffith's ability to dictate the terms of his career. In 1919, Griffith, Mary Pickford, Douglas Fairbanks, and Charlie Chaplin formed United Artists, a production company designed to give them the freedom they felt they were losing in the face of the growing, consolidating, and realigning film industry. Griffith's first film released by United Artists was *Broken Blossoms.* Seeking even greater independence, he moved his troupe of actors and technicians out of California to Mamaroneck, New York, where he bought an estate that he turned into a film studio. Facing financial difficulties, Griffith quickly made several lesser films in order to allow the filming of *Way Down East,* which has endured as one of his best works. But continuing and increasing financial problems made it impossible for Griffith to exercise the control over his productions that he once enjoyed. Even with United Artists he was assigned films to make and was overseen by producers wary of his profligate tendencies. After *Isn't Life Wonderful,* Griffith made largely unremarkable films, save for *Abraham Lincoln* (1930), his first film with synchronized sound and featuring Walter Huston in the title role. His last film, *The Struggle* (1931), a melodrama about an alcoholic, impressed neither critics nor audiences. For the next seventeen years, Griffith could not find backers willing to fund his projects; he was offered work and tributes by friends—the director George Cukor unsuccessfully petitioned the owners of Metro-Goldwyn-Mayer to "pension" him for his contributions to the art of film—but Griffith declined what he felt to be charity. He died in Hollywood in 1948.

Major Works

By the standards of its day, Griffith's first film as director, *The Adventures of Dollie,* is typical, well-made, and evidence of the first-time filmmaker's mastery of contemporary film form. In a series of linked vignettes, each consisting of one shot, the film presents the story of a little girl who is kidnapped by an evil gypsy; when the girl's father searches for her at the gypsy camp, she is spirited away in a barrel; the barrel eventually falls into a river and Dollie is carried back to her home. In plot and premise, *The Adventures of Dollie* is typical of many of Griffith's subsequent Biograph films: a tranquil, bourgeois domestic situation is upset; daring measures are undertaken in response; and tranquility is restored. Over the course of his next 480 or so films, Griffith experimented with ways in which to heighten the viewer's identification with the characters' experiences and states of mind. Among the innovations evident in his Biograph films are: 1) the increased and refined use of point-of-view shots, in which the viewer sees what the character sees; an early example of this occurs in Griffith's second film, *The Redman and the Child* (1908), when an Indian witnesses a murder through a telescope; 2) an increasingly restrained and naturalistic style of acting, one that eschewed the broad gestures of the nineteenth-century "histrionic" style; among the many films in which this new style dominates, *The New York Hat* (1912) is often cited because the subtle performances of Mary Pickford and Lionel Barrymore contrast strikingly with the more demonstrative and obviously stylized actions of the rest of the cast; and 3) the use of what has been called "switchback" or "parallel" editing, by means of which two or more events taking place in different locations are presented as occurring simultaneously; Griffith—and most filmmakers after him—used this technique in a variety of ways: from increasing the suspense in a "last minute rescue" sequence, as in *The Lonely Villa* (1909) when a man must race home to prevent criminals from attacking his wife and daughters; to the breaking down of individual scenes into numerous closer and more detailed shots, a technique that creates a "synthetic" space, one that exists as a unified whole only in the viewer's imagination. All of these innovations were adopted by other filmmakers and came to be hallmarks of the Hollywood style. Critics argue, however, that Griffith's own style should not be thought of as synonymous with the "classic realist text" of Hollywood, that his films characteristically employ devices that distance the viewer and prevent the kind of identification and "suspension of disbelief" thought typical of Hollywood. A case in point is *The Birth of a Nation,* the Civil War saga that tells the story of two families—one from the North, one from the South. While the film deploys the realistic techniques mentioned above, and is often described as the culmination of Griffith's experiments in the "narrative integration" of such techniques, the film also explicitly re-creates famous paintings and photographs—for example, those of Abraham Lincoln signing the Emancipation Proclamation—and identifies these re-creations as such on screen. Thus, *The Birth of a Nation* combines two modes of addressing the viewer: one that tries to efface itself through realistic techniques designed to heighten the viewer's identification with the action on screen; and one that calls attention to itself, addressing the viewer directly and reminding him of the unreality of the depicted events. The first mode—which

Griffith did not invent, only refined and exploited on a grand scale—became the dominant one for narrative filmmaking; the second—which was, in fact, the dominant mode of early cinema, before "narrative integration"—influenced Eisenstein and the Soviet filmmakers who were interested in a more didactic approach to film form. This dual approach is also evident in *Intolerance,* an epic film that intertwines four stories: a tale set in the film's present day that depicts what happens when upper-class matrons crusade to "refine" the lower classes; the massacre of the Huguenots; the fall of Babylon; and the life of Jesus. Griffith continuously cuts from one story to another, inviting the viewer to, at once, get caught up in each individual story and set of characters, and to draw thematic, moralistic connections between them. Because of this alternation between identification and intellectual distance, Eisenstein is reported to have been surprised to learn that Griffith was not a communist—so much did this approach mirror and influence his own. Griffith's other major films—including *Hearts of the World* (1918), *Broken Blossoms, True Heart Susie* (1919), and *Way Down East*—emphasize melodrama over didacticism and are romantic, tragic visions of ill-fated love. In criticizing the thematic content of Griffith's films, Eisenstein wrote: "In social attitudes Griffith was always a liberal, never departing far from the slightly sentimental humanism of the good old gentlemen and sweet old ladies of Victorian England, just as Dickens loved to picture them. His tender-hearted film morals go no higher than a level of Christian accusation of human injustice and nowhere in his films is there sounded a protest against social injustice." Finally, Orson Welles once wrote that, toward the end of his life, Griffith "was an exile in his own town, a prophet without honor, a craftsman without tools, an artist without work. No wonder he hated me. I, who knew nothing about films, had just been given the greatest freedom ever written into a Hollywood contract [when he was hired by RKO to make *Citizen Kane* (1941)]. It was the contract he deserved. . . . I never really hated Hollywood except for its treatment of D. W. Griffith. No town, no industry, no profession, no art form owes so much to a single man. Every filmmaker who has followed him has done just that: followed him."

---

*PRINCIPAL WORKS

A Fool and a Girl (drama) 1907
The Adventures of Dolly (film) 1908
After Many Years [adaptor; from the poem "Enoch Arden" (1864) by Alfred Lord Tennyson] (film) 1908
The Fatal Hour (film) 1908
The Greaser's Gauntlet (film) 1908
The Redman and the Child (film) 1908
The Salvation Army Lass (film) 1908
The Song of the Shirt (film) 1908

A Convict's Sacrifice (film) 1909
A Corner in Wheat [adaptor; from the short story "A Deal in Wheat" (1903) by Frank Norris] (film) 1909
The Drive for Life (film) 1909
A Drunkard's Reformation (film) 1909
The Lonely Villa [with Mack Sennett] (film) 1909
The Voice of the Violin (film) 1909
An Arcadian Maid (film) 1910
His Trust (film) 1910
The Newlyweds (film) 1910
Ramona [adaptor; from the novel *Ramona* (1884) by Helen Hunt Jackson] (film) 1910
A Summer Idyll (film) 1910
The Battle (film) 1911
Enoch Arden [adaptor; from the poem "Enoch Arden" (1864) by Alfred Lord Tennyson] (film) 1911
The Last Drop of Water (film) 1911
The Lonedale Operator [with Sennett] (film) 1911
Swords and Hearts (film) 1911
The Girl and Her Trust (film) 1912
His Lesson (film) 1912
The Massacre (film) 1912
The Musketeers of Pig Alley (film) 1912
The New York Hat [with Anita Loos] (film) 1912
The Sands of Dee (film) 1912
The Battle at Elderbush Gulch (film) 1913
†*Judith of Bethulia* (film) 1913
The Mothering Heart (film) 1913
The Reformers, or The Lost Art of Minding One's Business (film) 1913
‡*The Avenging Conscience* [adaptor; from the short story "The Tell-Tale Heart" (1843) and other works by Edgar Allan Poe] (film) 1914
The Battle of the Sexes (film) 1914
The Escape (film) 1914
Home, Sweet Home (film) 1914
The Birth of a Nation [with Frank Woods; based on the novel *The Clansman* (1905) and on its 1906 dramatic adaptation, both by Thomas Dixon] (film) 1915
The Rise and Fall of Free Speech in America (essay) 1915
Intolerance (film) 1916
The Great Love [with Stanner E. V. Taylor] (film) 1918
The Greatest Thing in Life [with Taylor] (film) 1918
Hearts of the World (film) 1918
Broken Blossoms [adaptor; from the short story "The Chink and the Child" by Thomas Burke] (film) 1919
The Girl Who Stayed at Home [with Taylor] (film) 1919
The Greatest Question [with Taylor] (film) 1919
A Romance of Happy Valley (film) 1919
Scarlet Days [with Taylor] (film) 1919
True Heart Susie [with Marion Fremont] (film) 1919
The Idol Dancer [with Taylor] (film) 1920
The Love Flower [adaptor; from the short story "The Black Beach" by Ralph Stock] (film) 1920
Way Down East [with Anthony Paul Kelly; based on the play by Lottie Blair Parker] (film) 1920
Dream Street [adaptor; from the short stories "Gina of the Chinatown" and "The Sign of the Lamp" by Burke] (film) 1921

Orphans of the Storm [adaptor; from the play *The Two Orphans* by Adolphe d'Ennery and Eugene Cormon] (film) 1921

One Exciting Night (film) 1922

The White Rose (film) 1923

America [with Robert W. Chambers; based on Chambers's novel *The Reckoning*] (film) 1924

Isn't Life Wonderful [adaptor; from the short story by Geoffrey Moss] (film) 1924

Sally of the Sawdust [with Forrest Halsey; based on the musical play *Poppy* by Dorothy Donnelly] (film) 1925

That Royle Girl [with Paul Schofield; based on the novel by Edwin Balmer] (film) 1925

The Sorrows of Satan [with Halsey, John Russell, and George Hull; based on the novel *The Sorrows of Satan; or, The Strange Experiences of One Geoffrey Tempest, Millionaire: A Romance* (1895) by Marie Corelli] (film) 1926

The Battle of the Sexes [with Gerrit J. Lloyd; based on the novel *The Single Standard* by Daniel Carson Goodman] (film) 1928

Drums of Love [with Lloyd] (film) 1928

Lady of the Pavements [with Sam Taylor; based on the short story by Karl Volmöller] (film) 1929

Abraham Lincoln [with Lloyd and Stephen Vincent Benét] (film) 1930

The Struggle [with Loos and John Emerson] (film) 1931

§*The Man Who Invented Hollywood: The Autobiography of D. W. Griffith* (autobiography) 1972

*Because Griffith directed over 480 short one- and two-reel films for the Biograph Company between 1908 and 1913, the above list includes only some of the more notable titles from those years. All of the films he made after leaving Biograph are included. Bracketed information following a title refers to screenwriting ("scenario" writing) credit and/or to the literary source of the film.

†This is Griffith's first feature-length film, with a running time of approximately one hour. Released at the beginning of 1914, it was his last film for the Biograph Company.

‡Griffith's films from 1914 and after are all five reels or longer. *The Avenging Conscience* is six reels, or approximately an hour and a half in running time. *Intolerance,* his longest film, is fourteen reels, or nearly three hours long.

§Griffith's autobiography was compiled and edited by James Hart.

CRITICISM

D. W. Griffith (essay date 1924)

SOURCE: "The Movies 100 Years from Now," in *Film Makers on Film Making: Statements on Their Art by*

Thirty Directors, edited by Harry M. Geduld, Indiana University Press, 1967, pp. 49-55.

[*In the following essay, originally published in 1924, Griffith speculates on a number of innovations he believed will occur in filmmaking during the next one hundred years and predicts that movies will become an influential social force.*]

They say I am a realist—a man who functions best when reproducing in the films life as he sees it or knows it. Whereupon the editor promptly assumes that fantasy will be perfectly easy for me, and propounds a question that scarcely can be answered by anything other than a dream. Fortunately, I have my fancies.

"What," asks the editor in substance, "will be the status of the motion pictures one hundred years hence?"

I have wondered that very thing many times myself, and since I am one of those persons who sometimes respond to their own imagery with answers, I can at least give an opinion. I may qualify this by adding that it is the opinion of one who has devoted a large part of his life to the subject.

In the year 2024 the most important single thing which the cinema will have helped in a large way to accomplish will be that of eliminating from the face of the civilized world all armed conflict. Pictures will be the most powerful factor in bringing about this condition. With the use of the universal language of moving pictures the true meaning of the brotherhood of man will have been established throughout the earth. For example, the Englishman will have learned that the soul of the Japanese is, essentially, the same as his own. The Frenchman will realize that the American's ideals are his ideals. All men are created equal.

It is not to be presumed that I believe one hundred years from now the pictures will have had time to educate the masses away from discord and unharmony. What I do mean to say is, by that time war, if there is such a thing, will be waged on a strictly scientific basis, with the element of physical destruction done away with entirely. My theory is that conflict, if and when it arises, will find itself governed by scientific rules and regulations to which both sides of the controversy will subscribe. Armies outfitted with boxing gloves, man to man, may, I think, go into "battle" to determine the victor. I am not smiling with you now. I am quite sincere. It will be a matter of science and fair play to the last letter. I am just as sincere when I predict that after the "battle" the warriors will repair to a prearranged cold-drink canteen and have grape juice. Just as the old English debtors' prison was wiped out by education, so will armed conflict be wiped out by education.

There is little question that a century ahead of us will find a great deal more of the so-called intimate drama presented on the screen, although there will always be a field set apart for the film with a vast background such as *The Birth of a Nation* and *America*.

You will walk into your favorite film theatre and see your actors appearing in twice the size you see them now, because the screens will be twice as large, and the film itself twice as large also. With these enlargements, "close-ups" will be almost eliminated, since it will be relatively easy to picture facial expression along with the full figure of the performer. It will always be necessary to picture the face in pictures. It is the face which reflects the soul of a man.

Our "close-ups," or "inserts," as I call them, are sometimes cumbersome and disconcerting. I invented them, but I have tried not to overuse them, as many have done. It is a mechanical trick, and is of little credit to anyone.

We shall say there are now five elaborate first-run picture theatres on one New York street, Broadway. In 2024 there will be at least forty. Cities of 1,000 will average at least six. Cities of 20,000 and thereabout will have over a hundred. By virtue of its great advantage in scope, the motion picture will be fitted to tell certain stories as no other medium can. But I must add that the glory of the spoken or written word in the intimate and poetic drama can never be excelled by any form of expression.

In the year 2024 our directors of the better order will be men graduated from schools, academies, and colleges carrying in their curriculum courses in motion-picture direction. Our actors and actresses will be artists graduated from schools and colleges either devoted exclusively to the teaching and study of motion-picture acting or carrying highly specialized courses in acting before the camera. This is inevitable.

I am well aware of the fact that the present cumbersome and haphazard method by which screen talent is selected (and by screen talent I mean to say directors, designers, actors, and cameramen) will not endure long. Time will find this matter adjusted upon a basis of merit and equipment.

Probably on an average of a dozen times each week persons ask me if I think color photography in the motion pictures will be perfected and made practical. Most assuredly, I do think so. Certainly all color processes and tint methods at present in use are wrong. They are not arrived at with any degree of inventiveness, and they cannot last. At present the colored pictures we see are made by the use of gelatines on the film or by the use of varicolored lenses which fly before the film. Thus we find a great lack of harmony and accuracy. I am willing to confess that I have tried them. But I should be the last to speak of my color effects seriously. We have been merely exploring and speculating.

Only through one method will color be naturally and properly given to objects and persons in the motion pictures. This is a method which will develop a film so sensitive that it will record the natural tints and colors as the picture is being photographed.

Of course, to the man or woman untrained in these lines, this seems remote and hardly possible. Still, consider the conquering of the air—the discovery of a means whereby the human voice may be projected through air three thousand miles! When we realize what has been done in the wireless it seems utter folly to suppose that color photography—natural, permanent color photography—may not be found for the films. One hundred years from now the color of a woman's eyes and hair, the tint of the sea, the hues of the rainbow itself will be a natural part of every motion-picture play.

On the other hand, I am quite positive that when a century has passed, all thought of our so-called speaking pictures will have been abandoned. It will never be possible to synchronize the voice with the pictures. This is true because the very nature of the films foregoes not only the necessity for but the propriety of the spoken voice. Music—fine music—will always be the voice of the silent drama. One hundred years from now will find the greatest composers of that day devoting their skill and their genius to the creation of motion-picture music.

There will be three principal figures in the production of a picture play—the author first, the director and music composer occupying an identical position in importance.

We do not want now and we never shall want the human voice with our films. Music, as I see it within that hundred years, will be applied to the visualization of the human being's imagination. And, as in your imagination those unseen voices are always perfect and sweet, or else magnificent and thrilling, you will find them registering upon the mind of the picture patron, in terms of lovely music, precisely what the author has intended to be registered there. There is no voice in the world like the voice of music. To me those images on the screen must always be silent. Anything else would work at cross purposes with the real object of this new medium of expression. There will never be speaking pictures. Why should there be when no voice can speak so beautifully as music? There are no dissonant r's and twisted consonants and guttural slurs and nasal twangs in beautiful music. Therefore the average person would much prefer to see his pictures and let the voice which speaks to him be the voice of music—one of the most perfect of all the arts.

I seem a little emphatic on this particular point, and I mean to be.

In the year 2024 we shall have orchestras of many kinds playing for the pictures. Each motion-picture theatre will have several orchestras of diversified character. The big, robust, outdoor pictures will have more than one orchestra in attendance at all times. String quarters will play for the mood of a string quartet; sighing guitars and thumpety banjos will play for their mood in the picture play; symphonic orchestras of greater proportions than we now dream of will be employed for moods to fit the sublime and the grand.

We have scarcely an inkling of what the development of music is going to be in the film play.

It really seems to me a little bit humorous now to realize how narrow a place in our everyday life the film is playing, despite the great rise in attendance in the last few years. One hundred years hence, I believe, the airplane passenger lines will operate motion-picture shows on regular schedule between New York and Chicago and between New York and London. Trains, which will be travelling twice or three times as fast as they do now, will have film theatres on board. Almost every home of good taste will have its private projection room where miniatures, perhaps, of the greater films will be shown to the family, and, of course, families will make their albums in motion pictures instead of in tintypes and "stills." Steamships will boast of first runs, which will be brought to them in mid-ocean by the airplanes, and I may add that almost all subjects in our schools will be taught largely with the use of picture play and the educational animated picture.

By the time these things come to pass, there will be no such thing as a flicker in your film. Your characters and objects in pictures will come upon the screen (which by then may not even be white, and certainly may not be square, or look anything like what it does now), and they will appear to the onlookers precisely as these persons and objects appear in real life. That much-discussed "depth" in pictures, which no one as yet has been able to employ successfully, will long since have been discovered and adopted. The moving canvas will not appear flat, but if a character moves before a fireplace you will recognize the distance as between the character and the fireplace. Likewise, in landscapes, you will feel the proper sense of distance. Your mountain peaks will not appear to rise one on top of the other, but will appear exactly as if you stood and looked at them. Of course these are merely details that will require long and intense study and experiment, but they will come. In other words, from the standpoint of naturalness, motion pictures one hundred years from now will be so nearly like the living person or the existing object pictured that you will be unable, sitting in your orchestra seat, to determine whether they are pictures or the real thing.

By a perfection of the studio lighting system, film will be as smooth before the eye as if it were a stationary lighted picture. By that time the studios will have changed greatly, and instead of actors being forced to work before great blinding lights, which now at times register 117 degrees of heat, we shall have "cold" lights. We are experimenting in these already. Our studios will be great spreading institutions, as large as many of the cities surrounding New York. I think that one hundred years from now there will be no concentrated motion-picture production such as our Hollywood of today. Films will be made in various cities, most of which will be located near to New York.

It nettles me at times when I am asked if I do not think that in time the popularity of the motion pictures will subside. It seems to me ridiculous. As ridiculous as to assume that the popularity of music, or painting, or acting on our spoken stage will go out.

No. I not only do not think the popularity of motion pictures will decrease; I am already on record as predicting that the popularity of pictures will increase and keep on increasing. Consider my own *Birth of a Nation*. It was revived two years ago, after having been off for ten years, and it was as great a success in revival as in the original. The popularity of motion pictures (which are a natural form of dramatic expression) will ride higher and higher as the quality of motion pictures rises higher and higher. One hundred years from today we shall have novelists devoting all their energies toward creating motion-picture originals. By this I mean that the novelists giving their exclusive time to the films will create characters and situations and dramatic plots in terms of pictures. Motion-picture historians will have been developed, and they will be a great help to production. Motion-picture artists of all kinds will have grown up. It will all make for a more natural, dignified, sincere result because we shall have all our different branches devoting their time and efforts toward the completion of a single object—a motion picture.

I have no hesitancy in saying that the radio has claimed its share of amusement audiences. Unquestionably it has kept many persons away from both the films and the spoken stage. It is a great, useful discovery—a glorious medium. One hundred years from now there will be no confusion as between the radio and the motion picture. There cannot possibly be a connection nor a conflict. It is just possible there may be a conflict as between radio and spoken stage, but never between radio and film. Each occupies its own exclusive place in our lives.

Now let us prepare for a small-sized shock. One hundred years from today it will cost perhaps twice as much as it costs today to see the really first-class cinema. It is perfectly proper that it should. Time, effort, energy, and preparation put into pictures at that time will have advanced greatly. I am just honest enough to say that I do not at the moment understand how more time, effort, energy, and preparation could have been put into my own pictures; but, then, for the average large picture play this will hold true. The average supposedly high-class film play in 2024 will be on view at not less than $5 a seat.

In looking into the crystal I have seen many things which I have not touched upon here. Perhaps they would be too tedious to bring out and discuss. But of one thing I may place myself on record plainly and without qualification. The motion picture is a child that has been given life in our generation. As it grows older it will develop marvelously. We poor souls can scarcely visualize or dream of its possibilities. We ought to be kind with it in its youth, so that in its maturity it may look back upon its childhood without regrets.

Peter Noble (essay date 1946)

SOURCE: "A Note on an Idol," in *Sight and Sound,* Vol. 15, No. 59, Autumn, 1946, pp. 81-2.

[*In the following essay, Noble outlines the racist trappings of* The Birth of a Nation.]

Griffith has one of the great poetic minds of the cinema. He ranks with Chaplin, Von Stroheim and René Clair among the immortals of the screen, and it is in no way meant to decry his genius that I draw attention to a facet of his work which has not been fully examined. I refer to his anti-Negro bias, as demonstrated in that otherwise superb film *The Birth of a Nation* and in such of his later films as *One Exciting Night*. He is indeed a pioneer, but a pioneer of prejudice!

The Birth of a Nation is one of the cornerstones of the cinema as we know it now. It is a magnificent and impressive film, containing many lessons applicable to modern film production. Griffith pioneered a number of techniques still used in film-making today, and the immense sweep and power of this epoch-making production (as well as such others as *Intolerance* and *Orphans of the Storm*), will always reserve for him a place among the great ones of the silent screen.

Yet the film has a certain, unsavoury significance which cannot be forgotten when its subject, racial intolerance, is still as urgent today as it was when Griffith directed *The Birth of a Nation*. It was, indeed, the first important movie to devote much of its length to an attack on Negroes, and the monumental achievement of this film was, in the opinion of many critics, marred by its vicious distortion and strongly partisan attitude. Griffith was himself a Southerner, brought up with the conventional Southern States attitude to the coloured man and steeped in an atmosphere of racial hatred. In the majestic sweep of Thomas Dickson's novel *The Clansman* he probably envisaged perfect material for a large-scale epic, and certainly the resultant production was technically and artistically far ahead of any other motion picture of that period. It must be acknowledged that Griffith was a genius, but however great the workmanship, however inspired the direction and however remarkable the acting and production of the film, the fact remains that for sheer vicious distortion *The Birth of a Nation* heads the considerable list of American motion pictures which have consciously maligned the Negro race.

OBSESSIONS

The great theme of *The Clansman* covered the eventful period of the American Civil War, tracing the history of two families, one from the North and another from the South, who are estranged by the struggle. We see the happy home in Piedmont of the Southern Colonel with the inevitable stereotypes, the obsequious black Mammy and the faithful Negro retainer. But after we come to the defeat of the South and the period of Reconstruction Griffith allows his imagination to run riot. The Northern politician, Stoneman, a liberal who is in favour of complete emancipation for the Southern Negroes, is depicted as an egotistic and scheming rascal, while his associate, Silas Lynch the mulatto, is shown in a most unfavourable light. When Stoneman becomes the Lieutenant Governor of Piedmont the Negroes, the former slaves, begin to run riot under the new *regime*; while the Yankee politician, nothing more than a villainous careerist, and the "renegade" Negro leader Lynch plot together to enforce a "black stranglehold" (Griffith's own description) on the defeated South. Also Lynch's lust it seems extends not only to power but to the daughter of Stoneman, and in the final reel the inevitable rape attempt occurs. Villainy and rape—the two main attributes of the coloured man (according to Griffith).

This pathological obsession of some Americans with the Negro rape of white women is remarkable and appears to have occurred with astonishing frequency in American literature of the past hundred years. Griffith's *The Birth of a Nation* made history in that it marked its first appearance on the screen, not once but twice! In addition to Silas Lynch's attempted rape of Elsie Stoneman, there is also the scene where the Negro Gus, a villainous, frothy-mouthed, pop-eyed caricature (played, incidentally, by a white actor in black-face), drives the Little Colonel's sister to her death in an attempt to outrage her.

In all the sequences dealing with the South the coloured people are shown as swaggering black toughs, elbowing white women off the pavements and indulging in all kinds of brutalities to their former white masters. For example, we see the Negro Parliament in session. Here "the new tyrants of the South" (to quote Griffith again), hold sway, lounge back in their chairs, their bare feet up on their desks, a bottle of whisky in one hand and a leg of chicken in the other. These black monsters are not interested in affairs of State; they desire only revenge on the whites, and content themselves with planning retaliation and intimidating white girls with nods, winks and lewd suggestions. This then is the manner in which Griffith handles the first historical attempt by the American Negroes to govern themselves in that tragic post-war period. The monstrous caricatures of coloured politicians, officials, army officers, soldiers and servants in this film rival anything seen on the screen since that time, with the possible exception of *So Red the Rose* and *Gone With the Wind* (both based on novels by Southerners).

The final reel of *The Birth of a Nation* shows that "heroic" organization, the Klu Klux Klan, sweeping the rebellious blacks out of town. A group of coloured soldiers are besieging a hut where the proud and heroic Cameron family is fighting for its very life; as the murdering Negroes, with bulging eyes and fanatical cries, are breaking down the door for the final kill the white-hooded Klu Klux Klan ride to the rescue. To a burst of Wagnerian music the hooded saviours of the South sweep magnificently over the hill, saving the white family from the black terror. Such a distortion has indeed to be seen to be believed, remembering that the Klan invented that fine old Southern custom of lynching! Many younger filmgoers who have been told about **The Birth of a Nation** are by no means aware of its almost unbelievable viciousness.

As Lewis Jacobs writes in *The Rise of the American Film*: "The film was a passionate and persuasive avowal of the inferiority of the Negro. Its viewpoint was narrow and prejudiced. . . . The social implication of this celebrated picture aroused a storm of protest in the North".

Indeed it did; in California the film was banned and it was also refused a licence for exhibition in a dozen other states. Such prominent American leaders as Oswald Garrison Villard, Jane Addams and Charles Elliot spoke bitterly and often against the showing of the film. The Liberal magazine *The Nation* described it as "improper, immoral and injurious, a deliberate attempt to humiliate ten million American citizens and to portray them as nothing but beasts".

Historians were quick to point out the many inaccuracies in the film, and generally the effect of Griffith's film upon intelligent people was that of antagonism and indignation. Griffith himself was greatly incensed by the attack on his beloved film and for many years referred to the public protest as deliberately unfair, even going so far as to write and distribute a pamphlet entitled **"The Rise and Fall of Free Speech in America"**, which included quotations from magazines and newspapers which had endorsed his film and an impassioned defence by the director. Protests apart, however, **The Birth of a Nation** caused a sensation and was successfully shown for the next fifteen years, an admitted landmark in film history. But Griffith, who had poured all his spirit into the film, was greatly influenced by the storm which followed its showing. It is said that he relented somewhat and three years later, in 1918, in **Hearts of the World** he inserted a sequence showing a dying Negro soldier crying for his mother, and a white comrade kissing him as he died. It was a shamelessly sentimental scene, and as Richard Watts, Jr., film critic of *New Theatre*, remarked "It was a pretty shoddy and futile effort to make up for what he had done in **The Birth of a Nation**". In Britain the latter film was received with enthusiasm, but many critics attacked it for its unfair handling of a great theme. Oswald Blakeston remarked in *Close Up*, August 1929: "As a spectacle Griffith's production was awe-inspiring and stupendous; but as a picture of Negro life it was not only false but it has done the Negro irreparable harm. And no wonder since it was

taken from a purile novel, *The Clansman,* a book written to arouse racial hate by appealing to the basest passions of the semi-literate".

THIRTY YEAR CONTROVERSY

The film has caused controversy for thirty years; as late as 1931 it was banned in Philadelphia, after the Mayor had declared it "prejudicial to peace between the black and white races". It is surely ironic that a film which was an enormous financial success and which established Griffith as one of the greatest film directors of all time should have this blot upon its name, and it is indeed a pity that a film which occupies a place of honour among the memorable achievements of the cinema could still bear such responsibility for a great and incalculable harm. Thirty years ago it constituted a direct incitement to race riot, and seeing it today still tends to leave a nasty taste in the mouth.

In 1922 Griffith directed **One Exciting Night,** perhaps the first, certainly the most striking, example of the use of the Negro as the contemptible comic relief. It provides an interesting sidelight on how a director steeped in anti-Negro prejudice can influence his audience. The coloured character in this film, played incidentally by a white actor in black-face—since Griffith apparently would never employ a Negro actor in any role of prominence—commenced the long line of those well-known screen puppets, the cowardly black men whose hair turns white or stands on end when they meet danger in any form. They are afraid of the dark, of thunderstorms, of fire-arms, of animals, of police, and so on. In this film, Griffith showed how to portray the coloured man as a figure of contempt, and for his treatment of the Negro character in **One Exciting Night** he must be accorded the dubious honour of having commenced the long, long trail of celluloid depicting the Negro as a frightened, shivering wretch, lily-livered, weak-kneed, stupid and almost bestial. In **The Birth of a Nation** Griffith portrayed the coloured man with hatred, and nine years later, in **One Exciting Night,** with contempt. He had made some "progress". (And yet he had the presumption to make a film called **Intolerance**!)

At a time when a spate of lynchings in the Southern States and the race-proud and fascist outpourings of such American politicians as the notorious Senator Bilbo it is well to reflect what harm can be wrought by films. It is now a truism to remark, as Thomas Edison once did, "Whoever controls the motion picture industry controls the most powerful medium of influence over the people", for this is well-known and accepted; but it is not perhaps realised to what extent Hollywood has contributed towards the existence of renewed racial prejudice. Today, in these turbulent post-war years, thirteen million Negroes in the United States are waiting anxiously. They want to know whether they are to become full citizens of the U.S.A., or return to those dark days before the war, times of persecution and injustice. And it is as well at this time to take stock of Griffith's contribution to past prejudice. Their artistic merit apart, his two films *The Birth of a Nation* and *One Exciting Night* form the feet of clay of this idol of the cinema, and his shortcomings must never be forgotten whenever his genius is referred to.

Sergei Eisenstein (essay date 1949)

SOURCE: "Dickens, Griffith, and the Film Today," in *Film Form: Essays in Film Theory and The Film Sense,* edited and translated by Jay Leyda, Meridian Books, 1957, pp. 195-255.

[*In the following essay, originally published in 1949, Eisenstein explores Griffith's innovative use of montage as well as film techniques which can be traced in literary form to the works of Charles Dickens.*]

"The kettle began it. . . ."

Thus Dickens opens his *Cricket on the Hearth.*

"The kettle began it. . . ."

What could be further from films! Trains, cowboys, chases . . . And *The Cricket on the Hearth*? "The kettle began it!" But, strange as it may seem, movies also were boiling in that kettle. From here, from Dickens, from the Victorian novel, stem the first shoots of American film esthetic, forever linked with the name of David Wark Griffith.

Although at first glance this may not seem surprising, it does appear incompatible with our traditional concepts of cinematography, in particular with those associated in our minds with the American cinema. Factually, however, this relationship is organic, and the "genetic" line of descent is quite consistent.

Let us first look at that land where, although not perhaps its birthplace, the cinema certainly found the soil in which to grow to unprecedented and unimagined dimensions.

We know from whence the cinema appeared first as a world-wide phenomenon. We know the inseparable link between the cinema and the industrial development of America. We know how production, art and literature reflect the capitalist breadth and construction of the United States of America. And we also know that American capitalism finds its sharpest and most expressive reflection in the American cinema.

But what possible identity is there between this Moloch of modern industry, with its dizzy tempo of cities and subways, its roar of competition, its hurricane of stock market transactions on the one hand, and . . . the peaceful, patriarchal Victorian London of Dickens's novels on the other?

Let's begin with this "dizzy tempo," this "hurricane," and this "roar." These are terms used to describe the United States by persons who know that country solely through books—books limited in quantity, and not too carefully selected.

Visitors to New York City soon recover from their astonishment at this sea of lights (which is actually immense), this maelstrom of the stock market (actually its like is not to be found anywhere), and all this roar (almost enough to deafen one).

As far as the speed of the traffic is concerned, one can't be overwhelmed by this in the streets of the metropolis for the simple reason that speed can't exist there. This puzzling contradiction lies in the fact that the high-powered automobiles are so jammed together that they can't move much faster than snails creeping from block to block, halting at every crossing not only for pedestrian crowds but for the counter-creeping of the cross-traffic.

As you make your merely minute progress amidst a tightly packed glacier of other humans, sitting in similarly high-powered and imperceptibly moving machines, you have plenty of time to ponder the duality behind the dynamic face of America, and the profound interdependence of this duality in everybody and everything American. As your 90-horsepower motor pulls you jerkily from block to block along the steep-cliffed streets, your eyes wander over the smooth surfaces of the skyscrapers. Notions lazily crawl through your brain: "Why don't they seem high?" "Why should they, with all that height, still seem cozy, domestic, small-town?"

You suddenly realize what "trick" the skyscrapers play on you: although they have many floors, each floor is quite low. Immediately the soaring skyscraper appears to be built of a number of small-town buildings, piled on top of each other. One merely needs to go beyond the city-limits or, in a few cities, merely beyond the center of the city, in order to see the same buildings, piled, not by the dozens, and fifties, and hundreds, on top of each other, but laid out in endless rows of one- and two-storied stores and cottages along Main Streets, or along half-rural side-streets.

Here (between the "speed traps") you can fly along as fast as you wish; here the streets are almost empty, traffic is light—the exact opposite of the metropolitan congestion that you just left—no trace of that frantic activity choked in the stone vises of the city.

You often come across regiments of skyscrapers that have moved deep into the countryside, twisting their dense nets of railroads around them; but at the same rate small-town agrarian America appears to have overflowed into all but the very centers of the cities; now and then one turns a skyscraper corner, only to run head on into some home of colonial architecture, apparently whisked from some distant savannah of Louisiana or Alabama to this very heart of the business city.

But there where this provincial wave has swept in more than a cottage here or a church there (gnawing off a corner of that monumental modern Babylon, "Radio City"), or a cemetery, unexpectedly left behind in the very center of the financial district, or the hanging wash of the Italian district, flapping just around the corner, off Wall Street—this good old provincialism has turned inward to apartments, nestling in clusters around fireplaces, furnished with soft grandfather-chairs and the lace doilies that shroud the wonders of modern technique: refrigerators, washing-machines, radios.

And in the editorial columns of popular newspapers, in the aphorisms of broadcast sermon and transcribed advertisement, there is a firmly entrenched attitude that is usually defined as "way down East"—an attitude that may be found beneath many a waistcoat or bowler where one would ordinarily expect to find a heart or a brain. Mostly one is amazed by the abundance of small-town and patriarchal elements in American life and manners, morals and philosophy, the ideological horizon and rules of behavior in the middle strata of American culture.

In order to understand Griffith, one must visualize an America made up of more than visions of speeding automobiles, streamlined trains, racing ticker tape, inexorable conveyor-belts. One is obliged to comprehend this second side of America as well—America, the traditional, the patriarchal, the provincial. And then you will be considerably less astonished by this link between Griffith and Dickens.

The threads of both these Americas are interwoven in the style and personality of Griffith—as in the most fantastic of his own parallel montage sequences.

What is most curious is that Dickens appears to have guided *both* lines of Griffith's style, reflecting both faces of America: Small-Town America, and Super-Dynamic America.

This can be detected at once in the "intimate" Griffith of contemporary or past American life, where Griffith is profound, in those films about which Griffith told me, that "they were made for myself and were invariably rejected by the exhibitors."

But we are a little astonished when we see that the construction of the "official," sumptuous Griffith, the Griffith of tempestuous tempi, of dizzying action, of breathtaking chases—has also been guided by the same Dickens! But we shall see how true this is.

First the "intimate" Griffith, and the "intimate" Dickens.

The kettle began it. . . .

As soon as we recognize this kettle as a typical close-up, we exclaim: "Why didn't we notice it before! Of course this is the purest Griffith. How often we've seen such a close-up at the beginning of an episode, a sequence, or a whole film by him!" (By the way, we shouldn't overlook the fact that one of Griffith's earliest films was based on *The Cricket on the Hearth!*)

Certainly, this kettle is a typical Griffith-esque close-up. A close-up saturated, we now become aware, with typically Dickens-esque "atmosphere," with which Griffith, with equal mastery, can envelop the severe face of life in *Way Down East,* and the icy cold moral face of his characters, who push the guilty Anna (Lillian Gish) onto the shifting surface of a swirling ice-break.

Isn't this the same implacable atmosphere of cold that is given by Dickens, for example, in *Dombey and Son?* The image of Mr. Dombey is revealed through cold and prudery. And the print of cold lies on everyone and everything—everywhere. And "atmosphere"—always and everywhere—is one of the most expressive means of revealing the inner world and ethical countenance of the characters themselves.

We can recognize this particular method of Dickens in Griffith's inimitable bit-characters who seem to have run straight from life onto the screen. I can't recall who speaks with whom in one of the street scenes of the modern story of **Intolerance.** But I shall never forget the mask of the passer-by with nose pointed forward between spectacles and straggly beard, walking with hands behind his back as if he were manacled. As he passes he interrupts the most pathetic moment in the conversation of the suffering boy and girl. I can remember next to nothing of the couple, but this passer-by, who is visible in the shot only for a flashing glimpse, stands alive before me now—and I haven't seen the film for twenty years!

Occasionally these unforgettable figures actually walked into Griffith's films almost directly from the street: a bit-player, developed in Griffith's hands to stardom; the passer-by who may never again have been filmed; and that mathematics teacher who was invited to play a terrifying butcher in *America*—the late Louis Wolheim—who ended the film career thus begun with his incomparable performance as "Kat" in *All Quiet on the Western Front.*

These striking figures of sympathetic old men are also quite in the Dickens tradition; and these noble and slightly one-dimensional figures of sorrow and fragile maidens; and these rural gossips and sundry odd characters. They are especially convincing in Dickens when he uses them briefly, in episodes.

> The only other thing to be noticed about [Pecksniff] is that here, as almost everywhere else in the novels, the best figures are at their best when they have least to do. Dickens's characters

are perfect as long as he can keep them out of his stories. Bumble is divine until a dark and practical secret is entrusted to him. . . . Micawber is noble when he is doing nothing; but he is quite unconvincing when he is spying on Uriah Heep. . . . Similarly, while Pecksniff is the best thing in the story, the story is the worst thing in Pecksniff. . . . [G. K. Chesterton, *Charles Dickens, The Last of the Great Men*]

Free of this limitation, and with the same believability; Griffith's characters grow from episodic figures into those fascinating and finished images of living people, in which his screen is so rich.

Instead of going into detail about this, let us rather return to that more obvious fact—the growth of that second side of Griffith's creative craftsmanship—as a magician of tempo and montage; a side for which it is rather surprising to find the same Victorian source.

When Griffith proposed to his employers the novelty of a parallel "cut-back" for his first version of *Enoch Arden* (*After Many Years*, 1908), this is the discussion that took place, as recorded by Linda Arvidson Griffith in her reminiscences of Biograph days [*When the Movies were Young*]:

> When Mr. Griffith suggested a scene showing Annie Lee waiting for her husband's return to be followed by a scene of Enoch cast away on a desert island, it was altogether too distracting. "How can you tell a story jumping about like that? The people won't know what it's about."
>
> "Well," said Mr. Griffith, "doesn't Dickens write that way?"
>
> "Yes, but that's Dickens; that's novel writing; that's different."
>
> "Oh, not so much, these are picture stories; not so different."

But, to speak quite frankly, all astonishment on this subject and the apparent unexpectedness of such statements can be ascribed only to our—ignorance of Dickens.

All of us read him in childhood, gulped him down greedily, without realizing that much of his irresistibility lay not only in his capture of detail in the childhoods of his heroes, but also in that spontaneous, childlike skill for story-telling, equally typical for Dickens and for the American cinema, which so surely and delicately plays upon the infantile traits in its audience. We were even less concerned with the technique of Dickens's composition: for us this was non-existent—but captivated by the effects of this technique, we feverishly followed his characters from page to page, watching his characters now being rubbed from view at the most critical moment, then seeing them return afresh between the separate links of the parallel secondary plot.

As children, we paid no attention to the mechanics of this. As adults, we rarely re-read his novels. And becoming film-workers, we never found time to glance beneath the covers of these novels in order to figure out what exactly had captivated us in these novels and with what means these incredibly many-paged volumes had chained our attention so irresistibly.

Apparently Griffith was more perceptive . . .

But before disclosing what the steady gaze of the American film-maker may have caught sight of on Dickens's pages, I wish to recall what David Wark Griffith himself represented to us, the young Soviet film-makers of the 'twenties.

To say it simply and without equivocation: a revelation.

Try to remember our early days, in those first years of the October socialist revolution. The fires *At the Hearthsides* of our native film-producers had burnt out, the *Nava's Charms* [*Nava's Charms* (by Sologub) and *At the Hearthside,* two pre-Revolutionary Russian films, as is also *Forget the Hearth*. The names that follow are of the male and female film stars of this period.] of their productions had lost their power over us and, whispering through pale lips, "Forget the hearth," Khudoleyev and Runich, Polonsky and Maximov had departed to oblivion; Vera Kholodnaya to the grave; Mozhukhin and Lisenko to expatriation.

The young Soviet cinema was gathering the experience of revolutionary reality, of first experiments (Vertov), of first systematic ventures (Kuleshov), in preparation for that unprecedented explosion in the second half of the 'twenties, when it was to become an independent, mature, original art, immediately gaining world recognition.

In those early days a tangle of the widest variety of films was projected on our screens. From out of this weird hash of old Russian films and new ones that attempted to maintain "traditions," and new films that could not yet be called Soviet, and foreign films that had been imported promiscuously, or brought down off dusty shelves—two main streams began to emerge.

On the one side there was the cinema of our neighbor, post-war Germany. Mysticism, decadence, dismal fantasy followed in the wake of the unsuccessful revolution of 1923, and the screen was quick to reflect this mood. *Nosferatu the Vampire, The Street,* the mysterious *Warning Shadows,* the mystic criminal *Dr. Mabuse the Gambler,* reaching out towards us from our screens, achieved the limits of horror, showing us a future as an unrelieved night crowded with sinister shadows and crimes. . . .

The chaos of multiple exposures, of over-fluid dissolves, of split screens, was more characteristic of the later 'twenties (as in *Looping the Loop* or *Secrets of a Soul*), but earlier German films contained more than a hint of this tendency. In the over-use of these devices was also reflected the confusion and chaos of post-war Germany.

All these tendencies of mood and method had been foreshadowed in one of the earliest and most famous of these films, *The Cabinet of Dr. Caligari* (1920), this barbaric carnival of the destruction of the healthy human infancy of our art, this common grave for normal cinema origins, this combination of silent hysteria, particolored canvases, daubed flats, painted faces, and the unnatural broken gestures and actions of monstrous chimaeras.

Expressionism left barely a trace on our cinema. This painted, hypnotic "St. Sebastian of Cinema" was too alien to the young, robust spirit and body of the rising class.

It is interesting that during those years inadequacies in the field of film technique played a positive rôle. They helped to restrain from a false step those whose enthusiasm might have pulled them in this dubious direction. Neither the dimensions of our studios, nor our lighting equipment, nor the materials available to us for makeup, costumes, or setting, gave us the possibility to heap onto the screen similar phantasmagoria. But it was chiefly another thing that held us back: our spirit urged us towards life—amidst the people, into the surging actuality of a regenerating country. Expressionism passed into the formative history of our cinema as a powerful factor—of repulsion.

There was the rôle of another film-factor that appeared, dashing along in such films as *The Gray Shadow, The House of Hate, The Mark of Zorro*. There was in these films a world, stirring and incomprehensible, but neither repulsive nor alien. On the contrary—it was captivating and attractive, in its own way engaging the attention of young and future film-makers, exactly as the young and future engineers of the time were attracted by the specimens of engineering techniques unknown to us, sent from that same unknown, distant land across the ocean.

What enthralled us was not only these films, it was also their possibilities. Just as it was the possibilities in a tractor to make collective cultivation of the fields a reality, it was the boundless temperament and tempo of these amazing (and amazingly useless!) works from an unknown country that led us to muse on the possibilities of a profound, intelligent, class-directed use of this wonderful tool.

The most thrilling figure against this background was Griffith, for it was in his works that the cinema made itself felt as more than an entertainment or pastime. The brilliant new methods of the American cinema were united in him with a profound emotion of story, with human acting, with laughter and tears, and all this was done with an astonishing ability to preserve all that gleam of a filmically dynamic holiday, which had been captured in *The Gray Shadow* and *The Mark of Zorro* and *The House of Hate*. That the cinema could be incomparably greater, and that this was to be the basic task of the budding Soviet cinema—these were sketched for us in Griffith's creative work, and found ever new confirmation in his films.

Our heightened curiosity of those years in *construction and method* swiftly discerned wherein lay the most powerful affective factors in this great American's films. This was in a hitherto unfamiliar province, bearing a name that was familiar to us, not in the field of art, but in that of engineering and electrical apparatus, first touching art in its most advanced section—in cinematography. This province, this method, this principle of building and construction was *montage*.

This was the montage whose foundations had been laid by American film-culture, but whose full, completed, conscious use and world recognition was established by our films. Montage, the rise of which will be forever linked with the name of Griffith. Montage, which played a most vital rôle in the creative work of Griffith and brought him his most glorious successes.

Griffith arrived at it through the method of parallel action. And, essentially, it was on this that he came to a standstill. But we mustn't run ahead. Let us examine the question of how montage came to Griffith or—how Griffith came to montage.

Griffith arrived at montage through the method of parallel action, and he was led to the idea of parallel action by—Dickens!

To this fact Griffith himself has testified, according to A. B. Walkley, in *The Times* of London, for April 26, 1922, on the occasion of a visit by the director to London. Writes Mr. Walkley:

> He [Griffith] is a pioneer, by his own admission, rather than an inventor. That is to say, he has opened up new paths in Film Land, under the guidance of ideas supplied to him from outside. His best ideas, it appears, have come to him from Dickens, who has always been his favorite author. . . . Dickens inspired Mr. Griffith with an idea, and his employers (mere "business" men) were horrified at it; but, says Mr. Griffith, "I went home, re-read one of Dickens's novels, and came back next day to tell them they could either make use of my idea or dismiss me."

> Mr. Griffith found the idea to which he clung thus heroically in Dickens. That was as luck would have it, for he might have found the same idea almost anywhere. Newton deduced the law of gravitation from the fall of an apple; but a pear or a plum would have done just as well. The idea is merely that of a "break" in the narrative, a shifting of the story from one group of characters to another group. People who write the long and crowded novels that Dickens did, especially when

they are published in parts, find this practice a convenience. You will meet with it in Thackeray, George Eliot, Trollope, Meredith, Hardy, and, I suppose, every other Victorian novelist. . . . Mr. Griffith might have found the same practice not only in Dumas *père*, who cared precious little about form, but also in great artists like Tolstoy, Turgeniev, and Balzac. But, as a matter of fact, it was not in any of these others, but in Dickens that he found it; and it is significant of the predominant influence of Dickens that he should be quoted as an authority for a device which is really common to fiction at large.

Even a superficial acquaintance with the work of the great English novelist is enough to persuade one that Dickens may have given and did give to cinematography far more guidance than that which led to the montage of parallel action alone.

Dickens's nearness to the characteristics of cinema in method, style, and especially in viewpoint and exposition, is indeed amazing. And it may be that in the nature of exactly these characteristics, in their community both for Dickens and for cinema, there lies a portion of the secret of that mass success which they both, apart from themes and plots, brought and still bring to the particular quality of such exposition and such writing.

What were the novels of Dickens for his contemporaries, for his readers? There is one answer: they bore the same relation to them that the film bears to the same strata in our time. They compelled the reader to live with the same passions. They appealed to the same good and sentimental elements as does the film (at least on the surface); they alike shudder before vice, they alike mill the extraordinary, the unusual, the fantastic, from boring, prosaic and everyday existence. And they clothe this common and prosaic existence in their special vision. [The author adds in a footnote: "as late as April 17, 1944, Griffith still considered this the chief social function of film-making. An interviewer from the Los Angeles *Times* asked him, 'What is a good picture?' Griffith replied, 'One that makes the public forget its troubles. Also, a good picture tends to make folks think a little, without letting them suspect that they are being inspired to think. In one respect, nearly all pictures are good in that they show the triumph of good over evil.' This is what Osbert Sitwell, in reference to Dickens, called the 'Virtue v. Vice Cup-Tie Final.'"]

Illumined by this light, refracted from the land of fiction back to life, this commonness took on a romantic air, and bored people were grateful to the author for giving them the countenances of potentially romantic figures.

This partially accounts for the close attachment to the novels of Dickens and, similarly, to films. It was from this that the universal success of his novels derived. In an essay on Dickens, [in *Three Masters: Balzac, Dickens, Dostoyevsky*] Stefan Zweig opens with this description of his popularity:

The love Dickens's contemporaries lavished upon the creator of Pickwick is not to be assessed by accounts given in books and biographies. Love lives and breathes only in the spoken word. To get an adequate idea of the intensity of this love, one must catch (as I once caught) an Englishman old enough to have youthful memories of the days when Dickens was still alive. Preferably it should be someone who finds it hard even now to speak of him as Charles Dickens, choosing, rather, to use the affectionate nickname of "Boz." The emotion, tinged with melancholy, which these old reminiscences call up, gives us of a younger generation some inkling of the enthusiasm that inspired the hearts of thousands when the monthly instalments in their blue covers (great rarities, now) arrived at English homes. At such times, my old Dickensian told me, people would walk a long way to meet the postman when a fresh number was due, so impatient were they to read what Boz had to tell. . . . How could they be expected to wait patiently until the latter-carrier, lumbering along on an old nag, would arrive with the solution of these burning problems? When the appointed hour came round, old and young would sally forth, walking two miles and more to the post office merely to have the issue sooner. On the way home they would start reading, those who had not the luck of holding the book looking over the shoulder of the more fortunate mortal; others would set about reading aloud as they walked; only persons with a genius for self-sacrifice would defer a purely personal gratification, and would scurry back to share the treasure with wife and child.

In every village, in every town, in the whole of the British Isles, and far beyond, away in the remotest parts of the earth where the English-speaking nations had gone to settle and colonize, Charles Dickens was loved. People loved him from the first moment when (through the medium of print) they made his acquaintance until his dying day. . . .

Dickens's tours as a reader gave final proof of public affection for him, both at home and abroad. By nine o'clock on the morning that tickets for his lecture course were placed on sale in New York, there were two lines of buyers, each more than three-quarters of a mile in length:

The tickets for the course were all sold before noon. Members of families relieved each other in the queues; waiters flew across the streets and squares from the neighboring restaurant, to serve parties who were taking their breakfast in the open December air; while excited men offered five and ten dollars for the mere permission to exchange places with other persons standing nearer the head of the line! [A Philadelphia newspaper, December, 1867]

Isn't this atmosphere similar to that of Chaplin's tour through Europe, or the triumphant visit to Moscow of "Doug" and "Mary," or the excited anticipation around the première of *Grand Hotel* in New York, when an airplane service assisted ticket buyers on the West Coast? The immense popular success of Dickens's novels in his own time can be equaled in extent only by that whirlwind success which is now enjoyed by this or that sensational film success.

Perhaps the secret lies in Dickens's (as well as cinema's) creation of an extraordinary plasticity. The observation in the novels is extraordinary—as is their optical quality. The characters of Dickens are rounded with means as plastic and slightly exaggerated as are the screen heroes of today. The screen's heroes are engraved on the senses of the spectator with clearly visible traits, its villains are remembered by certain facial expressions, and all are saturated in the peculiar, slightly unnatural radiant gleam thrown over them by the screen.

It is absolutely thus that Dickens draws his characters—this is the faultlessly plastically grasped and pitilessly sharply sketched gallery of immortal Pickwicks, Dombeys, Fagins, Tackletons, and others.

Just because it never occurred to his biographers to connect Dickens with the cinema, they provide us with unusually objective evidence, directly linking the importance of Dickens's observation with our medium.

> [John] Forster speaks of Dickens's recollections of his childhood sufferings, and notes, as he could hardly fail to note, Dickens's amazingly detailed memory. He does not note, as he should, how this super-acuteness of physical vision contributed a basic element to Dickens's artistic method. For with that acuteness of physical vision, and that unerring recollection of every detail in the thing seen, went an abnormally complete grasp of the thing in the totality of its natural connections. . . .
>
> And if ever a man had the gift of the eye—and not merely of the eye but of the ear, and of the nose—and the faculty of remembering with microscopic accuracy of detail everything ever seen, or heard, or tasted, smelled, or felt, that man was Charles Dickens. . . . The whole picture arises before us in sight, sound, touch, taste, and pervading odour, just exactly as in real life, and with a vividness that becomes positively uncanny.
>
> To readers less sensitive than Dickens, this very vividness with which he visualizes plain things in plain everyday life appears to be "exaggeration." It is no such thing. The truth is that Dickens always sees instantly, and in every last, least, tiny detail, *all* that there is to be seen; while lesser mortals see only a part, and sometimes a trifling part at that. [T. A. Jackson, *Charles Dickens; The Progress of a Radical*]

Zweig continues the case:

> He cuts through the fog surrounding the years of childhood like a clipper driving through the waves. In *David Copperfield,* that masked autobiography,

we are given reminiscences of a two-year-old child concerning his mother with her pretty hair and youthful shape, and Peggotty with no shape at all; memories which are like silhouettes standing out from the blank of his infancy. There are never any blurred contours where Dickens is concerned; he does not give us hazy visions, but portraits whose every detail is sharply defined. . . . As he himself once said, it is the little things that give meaning to life. He is, therefore, perpetually on the watch for tokens, be they never so slight; a spot of grease on a dress, an awkward gesture caused by shyness, a strand of reddish hair peeping from beneath a wig if its wearer happens to lose his temper. He captures all the nuances of a handshake, knows what the pressure of each finger signifies; detects the shades of meaning in a smile.

Before he took the career of a writer, he was parliamentary reporter for a newspaper. In this capacity he became proficient in the art of summary, in compressing long-winded discussions; as shorthand writer he conveyed a word by a stroke, a whole sentence by a few curves and dashes. So in later days as an author he invented a kind of shorthand to reality, consisting of little signs instead of lengthy descriptions, an essence of observation distilled from the innumerable happenings of life. He has an uncannily sharp eye for the detection of these insignificant externals; he never overlooks anything; his memory and his keenness of perception are like a good camera lens which, in the hundredth part of a second, fixes the least expression, the slightest gesture, and yields a perfectly precise negative. Nothing escapes his notice. In addition, this perspicacious observation is enhanced by a marvellous power of refraction which, instead of presenting an object as merely reflected in its ordinary proportions from the surface of a mirror, gives us an image clothed in an excess of characteristics. For he invariably underlines the personal attributes of his characters. . . .

This extraordinary optical faculty amounted to genius in Dickens. . . . His psychology began with the visible; he gained his insight into character by observation of the exterior—the most delicate and fine minutiae of the outward semblance, it is true, those utmost tenuosities which only the eyes that are rendered acute by a superlative imagination can perceive. Like the English philosophers, he does not begin with assumptions and suppositions, but with characteristics. . . . Through traits, he discloses types: Creakle had no voice, but spoke in a whisper; the exertion cost him, or the consciousness of talking in that feeble way, made his angry face much more angry, and his thick veins much thicker. Even as we read the description, the sense of terror the boys felt at the approach of this fiery blusterer becomes manifest in us as well. Uriah Heep's hands are damp and cold; we experience a loathing for the creature at the very outset, as though we were faced by a snake. Small things? Externals? Yes, but they invariably are such as to recoil upon the soul.

The visual images of Dickens are inseparable from aural images. The English philosopher and critic, George Henry Lewes, though puzzled as to its significance, recorded that "Dickens once declared to me that every word said by his characters was distinctly *heard* by him. . . ."

We can see for ourselves that his descriptions offer not only absolute *accuracy of detail,* but also an absolutely *accurate drawing of the behavior* and actions of his characters. And this is just as true for the most trifling details of behavior—even gesture, as it is for the basic generalized characteristics of the image. Isn't this piece of description of Mr. Dombey's behavior actually an exhaustive regisseur-actor directive?

> He had already laid his hand upon the bell-rope to convey his usual summons to Richards, when his eye fell upon a writing-desk, belonging to his deceased wife, which had been taken, among other things, from a cabinet in her chamber. It was not the first time that his eye had lighted on it. He carried the key in his pocket; and he brought it to his table and opened it now—having previously locked the room door—with a well-accustomed hand. [John Forster, *The Life of Charles Dickens*]

Here the last phrase arrests one's attention: there is a certain awkwardness in its description. However, this "inserted" phrase: *having previously locked the room door,* "fitted in" as if recollected by the author in the middle of a later phrase, instead of being placed where it apparently should have been, in the consecutive order of the description, that is, before the words, *and he brought it to his table,* is found exactly at this spot for quite *un*fortuitous reasons.

In this deliberate "montage" displacement of the time-continuity of the description there is a brilliantly caught rendering of the *transient thievery* of the action, slipped between the preliminary action and the act of reading another's letter, carried out with that absolute "correctness" of gentlemanly dignity which Mr. Dombey knows how to give to any behavior or action of his.

This very (montage) arrangement of the phrasing gives an exact direction to the "performer," so that in defining this decorous and confident opening of the writing-desk, he must "play" the closing and locking of the door with a hint of an entirely different shade of conduct. And it would be this "shading" in which would also be played the unfolding of the letter; but in this part of the "performance" Dickens makes this shading more precise, not only with a significant arrangement of the words, but also with an exact description of characteristics.

> From beneath a heap of torn and cancelled scraps of paper, he took one letter that remained entire. Involuntarily holding his breath as he opened this document, and 'bating in the stealthy action something of his arrogant demeanour, he sat down, resting his head upon one hand, and read it through.

The reading itself is done with a shading of absolutely gentlemanly cold decorum:

> He read it slowly and attentively, and with a nice particularity to every syllable. Otherwise than as his great deliberation seemed unnatural, and perhaps the result of an effort equally great, he allowed no sign of emotion to escape him. When he had read it through, he folded and refolded it slowly several times, and tore it carefully into fragments. Checking his hand in the act of throwing these away, he put them in his pocket, as if unwilling to trust them even to the chances of being reunited and deciphered; and instead of ringing, as usual, for little Paul, he sat solitary all the evening in his cheerless room.

This scene does not appear in the final version of the novel, for with the aim of increasing the tension of the action, Dickens cut out this passage on Forster's advice; in his biography of Dickens Forster preserved this passage to show with what mercilessness Dickens sometimes "cut" writing that had cost him great labor. This mercilessness once more emphasizes that sharp clarity of representation towards which Dickens strove by all means, endeavoring with purely cinematic laconism to say what he considered necessary. (This, by the way, did not in the least prevent his novels from achieving enormous breadth.)

I don't believe I am wrong in lingering on this example, for one need only alter two or three of the character names and change Dickens's name to the name of the hero of my essay, in order to impute literally almost everything told here to the account of Griffith.

From that steely, observing glance, which I remember from my meeting with him, to the capture *en passant* of key details or tokens—indications of character, Griffith has all this in as much a Dickens-esque sharpness and clarity as Dickens, on his part, had cinematic "optical quality," "frame composition," "close-up," and the alteration of emphasis by special lenses.

Analogies and resemblances cannot be pursued too far—they lose conviction and charm. They begin to take on the air of machination or card-tricks. I should be very sorry to lose the conviction of the affinity between Dickens and Griffith, allowing this abundance of common traits to slide into a game of anecdotal semblance of tokens.

All the more that such a gleaning from Dickens goes beyond the limits of interest in Griffith's individual cinematic craftsmanship and widens into a concern with film-craftsmanship in general. This is why I dig more and more deeply into the film-indications of Dickens, revealing them through Griffith—for the use of future film-exponents. So I must be excused, in leafing through Dickens, for having found in him even—a "dissolve." How else could this passage be defined—the opening of the last chapter of *A Tale of Two Cities*:

Along the Paris streets, the death-carts rumble, hollow and harsh. Six tumbrils carry the day's wine to La Guillotine. . . .

Six tumbrils roll along the streets. Change these back again to what they were, thou powerful enchanter, Time, and they shall be seen to be the carriages of absolute monarchs, the equipages of feudal nobles, the toilettes of flaring Jezebels, the churches that are not my Father's house but dens of thieves, the huts of millions of starving peasants!

How many such "cinematic" surprises must be hiding in Dickens's pages!

However, let us turn to the basic montage structure, whose rudiment in Dickens's work was developed into the elements of film composition in Griffith's work. Lifting a corner of the veil over these riches, these hitherto unused experiences, let us look into *Oliver Twist*. Open it at the twenty-first chapter. Let's read its beginning [for demonstration purposes I have broken this beginning of the chapter into smaller pieces than did its author; the numbering is, of course, also mine]:

Chapter XXI

1. It was a cheerless morning when they got into the street; blowing and raining hard; and the clouds looking dull and stormy.
The night had been very wet: for large pools of water had collected in the road: and the kennels were overflowing.
There was a faint glimmering of the coming day in the sky; but it rather aggravated than relieved the gloom of the scene: the sombre light only serving to pale that which the street lamps afforded, without shedding any warmer or brighter tints upon the wet housetops, and dreary streets. There appeared to be nobody stirring in that quarter of the town; for the windows of the houses were all closely shut; and the streets through which they passed, were noiseless and empty.

2. By the time they had turned into the Bethnal Green Road, the day had fairly begun to break. Many of the lamps were already extinguished; a few country waggons were slowly toiling on, towards London; and now and then, a stage-coach, covered with mud, rattled briskly by:
the driver bestowing, as he passed, an admonitory lash upon the heavy waggoner who, by keeping on the wrong side of the road, had endangered his arriving at the office, a quarter of a minute after his time.
The public-houses, with gas-lights burning inside, were already open.
By degrees, other shops began to be unclosed; and a few scattered people were met with.
Then, came straggling groups of labourers going to their work; then, men and women with fish-baskets on their heads: donkey-carts laden with vegetables;
Chaise-carts filled with live-stock or whole carcasses of meat; milk-women with pails;

and an unbroken concourse of people, trudging out with various supplies to the eastern suburbs of the town.

3. As they approached the City, the noise and traffic gradually increased;
and when they threaded the streets between Shoreditch and Smithfield, it had swelled into a roar of sound and bustle.
It was as light as it was likely to be, till night came on again; and the busy morning of half the London population had begun. . . .

4. It was market-morning.
The ground was covered, nearly ankle-deep, with filth and mire; and a thick steam, perpetually rising from the reeking bodies of the cattle, and mingling with the fog,
which seemed to rest upon the chimney-tops, hung heavily above. . . .
Countrymen,
butchers,
drovers,
hawkers,
boys,
thieves,
idlers,
and vagabonds of every low grade,
were mingled together in a dense mass;

5. the whistling of drovers,
the barking of dogs,
the bellowing and plunging of oxen,
the bleating of sheep,
the grunting and squeaking of pigs;
the cries of hawkers,
the shouts, oaths and quarrelling on all sides;
the ringing of bells
and roar of voices, that issued from every public-house;
the crowding, pushing, driving, beating, whooping and yelling;
the hideous and discordant din that resounded from every corner of the market;
and the unwashed, unshaven, squalid, and dirty figures constantly running to and fro, and bursting in and out of the throng; rendered it a stunning and bewildering scene, which quite confounded the senses.

How often have we encountered just such a structure in the work of Griffith? This austere accumulation and quickening tempo, this gradual play of light: from burning street-lamps, to their being extinguished; from night, to dawn; from dawn, to the full radiance of day (*It was as light as it was likely to be, till night came on again*); this calculated transition from purely visual elements to an interweaving of them with aural elements: at first as an indefinite rumble, coming from afar at the second stage of increasing light, so that the rumble may grow into a roar, transferring us to a purely aural structure, now concrete and objective (section 5 of our breakdown); with such scenes, picked up *en passant,* and intercut into the whole—like the driver, hastening towards his office; and, finally, these magnificently typical details, the reeking bodies of the cattle, from which the steam rises and mingles with the over-all cloud of morning fog, or the close-up of the legs in the almost ankle-deep filth and mire, all this gives the fullest cinematic sensation of the panorama of a market.

Surprised by these examples from Dickens, we must not forget one more circumstance, related to the creative work of Dickens in general.

Thinking of this as taking place in "cozy" old England, we are liable to forget that the works of Dickens, considered not only against a background of English literature, but against a background of world literature of that epoch, as well, were produced as the works of a city artist. He was the first to bring factories, machines, and railways into literature.

But indication of this "urbanism" in Dickens may be found not only in his thematic material, but also in that head-spinning tempo of changing impressions with which Dickens sketches the city in the form of a dynamic (montage) picture; and this montage of its rhythms conveys the sensation of the limits of speed at that time (1838), the sensation of a rushing-stage-coach!

> As they dashed by the quickly-changing and ever-varying objects, it was curious to observe in what a strange procession they passed before the eye. Emporiums of splendid dresses, the materials brought from every quarter of the world; tempting stores of everything to stimulate and pamper the sated appetite and give new relish to the oft-repeated feast; vessels of burnished gold and silver, wrought into every exquisite form of vase, and dish, and goblet; guns, swords, pistols, and patent engines of destruction; screws and irons for the crooked, clothes for the newly-born, drugs for the sick, coffins for the dead, church-yards for the buried—all these jumbled each with the other and flocking side by side, seemed to flit by in motley dance. . . . [Dickens, *Nicholas Nickleby*]

Isn't this an anticipation of a "symphony of a big city"?

But here is another, directly opposite aspect of a city, out-distancing Hollywood's picture of the City by eighty years.

> It contained several large streets all very like one another, inhabited by people equally like one another, who all went in and out at the same hours, with the same sound upon the same pavements, to do the same work, and to whom every day was the same as yesterday and tomorrow, and every year the counterpart of the last and the next. [Dickens, *Hard Times*]

Is this Dickens's Coketown of 1853, or King Vidor's *The Crowd* of 1928?

If in the above-cited examples we have encountered prototypes of characteristics for Griffith's *montage exposition,* then it would pay us to read further in *Oliver Twist,* where we can find another montage method typical for Griffith—the method of a *montage progression of parallel scenes, intercut into each other.*

For this let us turn to that group of scenes in which is set forth the familiar episode of how Mr. Brownlow, to show faith in Oliver in spite of his pick-pocket reputation, sends him to return books to the book-seller, and of how Oliver again falls into the clutches of the thief Sikes, his sweetheart Nancy, and old Fagin.

These scenes are unrolled absolutely à la Griffith: both in their inner emotional line, as well as in the unusual sculptural relief and delineation of the characters; in the uncommon full-bloodedness of the dramatic as well as the humorous traits in them; finally, also in the typical Griffith-esque montage of parallel interlocking of all the links of the separate episodes. Let us give particular attention to this last peculiarity, just as unexpected, one would think, in Dickens, as it is characteristic for Griffith!

Chapter XIV

COMPRISING FURTHER PARTICULARS OF OLIVER'S STAY AT MR. BROWNLOW'S, WITH THE REMARKABLE PREDICTION WHICH ONE MR. GRIMWIG UTTERED CONCERNING HIM, WHEN HE WENT OUT ON AN ERRAND.

> . . ."Dear me, I am very sorry for that," exclaimed Mr. Brownlow; "I particularly wished those books to be returned tonight."
>
> "Send Oliver with them," said Mr. Grimwig, with an ironical smile; "he will be sure to deliver them safely, you know."
>
> "Yes; do let me take them, if you please, Sir," said Oliver. "I'll run all the way, Sir."
>
> The old gentleman was just going to say that Oliver should not go out on any account; when a most malicious cough from Mr. Grimwig determined him that he should; and that, by his prompt discharge of the commission, he should prove to him the injustice of his suspicions: on this head at least: at once.
>
> [Oliver is prepared for the errand to the bookstall-keeper.]
>
> "I won't be ten minutes, Sir," replied Oliver, eagerly.
>
> [Mrs. Bedwin, Mr. Brownlow's housekeeper, gives Oliver the directions, and sends him off.]
>
> "Bless his sweet face!" said the old lady, looking after him. "I can't bear, somehow, to let him go out of my sight."
>
> At this moment, Oliver looked gaily round, and nodded before he turned the corner. The old lady smilingly returned his salutation, and, closing the door, went back to her own room.

"Let me see; he'll be back in twenty minutes, at the longest," said Mr. Brownlow, pulling out his watch, and placing it on the table. "It will be dark by that time."

"Oh! you really expect him to come back, do you?" inquired Mr. Grimwig.

"Don't you?" asked Mr. Brownlow, smiling.

The spirit of contradiction was strong in Mr. Grimwig's breast, at the moment; and it was rendered stronger by his friend's confident smile.

"No," he said, smiting the table with his fist, "I do not. The boy has a new suit of clothes on his back; a set of valuable books under his arm; and a five-pound note in his pocket. He'll join his old friends the thieves, and laugh at you. If ever that boy returns to this house, Sir, I'll eat my head."

With these words he drew his chair closer to the table; and there the two friends sat, in silent expectation, with the watch between them.

This is followed by a short "interruption" in the form of a digression:

It is worthy of remark, as illustrating the importance we attach to our own judgments, and the pride with which we put forth our most rash and hasty conclusions, that, although Mr. Grimwig was not by any means a bad-hearted man, and though he would have been unfeignedly sorry to see his respected friend duped and deceived, he really did most earnestly and strongly hope, at that moment, that Oliver Twist might not come back.

And again a return to the two old gentlemen:

It grew so dark, that the figures on the dial-plate were scarcely discernible; but there the two old gentlemen continued to sit, in silence: with the watch between them.

Twilight shows that only a little time has passed, but the *close-up* of the watch, *already twice* shown lying between the old gentlemen, says that a great deal of time has passed already. But just then, as in the game of "will he come? won't he come?", involving not only the two old men, but also the kind-hearted reader, the worst fears and vague forebodings of the old housekeeper are justified by the cut to the new scene—Chapter XV. This begins with a short scene in the public-house, with the bandit Sikes and his dog, old Fagin and Miss Nancy, who has been obliged to discover the whereabouts of Oliver.

"You are on the scent, are you, Nancy?" inquired Sikes, proffering the glass.

"Yes, I am, Bill," replied the young lady, disposing of its contents; "and tired enough of it I am, too. . . ."

Then, one of the best scenes in the whole novel—at least one that since childhood has been perfectly preserved, along with the evil figure of Fagin—the scene in which Oliver, marching along with the books, is suddenly

startled by a young woman screaming out very loud, "Oh, my dear brother!" And he had hardly looked up, to see what the matter was, when he was stopped by having a pair of arms thrown tight round his neck.

With this cunning maneuver Nancy, with the sympathies of the whole street, takes the desperately pulling Oliver, as her "prodigal brother," back into the bosom of Fagin's gang of thieves. This fifteenth chapter closes on the now familiar montage phrase:

The gas-lamps were lighted; Mrs. Bedwin was waiting anxiously at the open door; the servant had run up the street twenty times to see if there were any traces of Oliver; and still the two old gentlemen sat, perseveringly, in the dark parlour: with the watch between them.

In Chapter XVI Oliver, once again in the clutches of the gang, is subjected to mockery. Nancy rescues him from a beating:

"I won't stand by and see it done, Fagin," cried the girl. "You've got the boy, and what more would you have? Let him be—let him be, or I shall put that mark on some of you, that will bring me to the gallows before my time."

By the way, it is characteristic for both Dickens and Griffith to have these sudden flashes of goodness in "morally degraded" characters and, though these sentimental images verge on hokum, they are so faultlessly done that they work on the most skeptical readers and spectators!

At the end of this chapter, Oliver, sick and weary, falls "sound asleep." Here the physical time unity is interrupted—an evening and night, crowded with events; but the montage unity of the episode is not interrupted, tying Oliver to Mr. Brownlow on one side, and to Fagin's gang on the other.

Following, in Chapter XVIII, is the arrival of the parish beadle, Mr. Bumble, in response to an inquiry about the lost boy, and the appearance of Bumble at Mr. Brownlow's, again in Grimwig's company. The content and reason for their conversation is revealed by the very title of the chapter: OLIVER'S DESTINY CONTINUING UNPROPITIOUS, BRINGS A GREAT MAN TO LONDON TO INJURE HIS REPUTATION . . .

"I fear it is all too true," said the old gentleman sorrowfully, after looking over the papers. "This is not much for your intelligence; but I would gladly have given you treble the money, if it had been favourable to the boy."

It is not at all improbable that if Mr. Bumble had been possessed of this information at an earlier period of the interview, he might have imparted a very different coloring to his little history. It was too late to do it now, however; so he shook his head gravely; and, pocketing the five guineas, withdrew. . . .

"Mrs. Bedwin," said Mr. Brownlow, when the housekeeper appeared; "that boy, Oliver, is an impostor."

"It can't be, Sir. It cannot be," said the old lady energetically. . . . "I never will believe it, Sir. . . . Never!"

"You old women never believe anything but quack-doctors, and lying story-books," growled Mr. Grimwig. "I knew it all along. . . ."

"He was a dear, grateful, gentle child, Sir," retorted Mrs. Bedwin, indignantly. "I know what children are, Sir; and have done these forty years; and people who can't say the same, shouldn't say anything about them. That's my opinion!"

This was a hard hit at Mr. Grimwig, who was a bachelor. As it extorted nothing from that gentleman but a smile, the old lady tossed her head, and smoothed down her apron preparatory to another speech, when she was stopped by Mr. Brownlow.

"Silence!" said the old gentleman, feigning an anger he was far from feeling. "Never let me hear the boy's name again. I rang to tell you that. Never. Never, on any pretence, mind! You may leave the room, Mrs. Bedwin. Remember! I am in earnest."

And the entire intricate montage complex of this episode is concluded with the sentence:

There were sad hearts in Mr. Brownlow's that night.

It was not by accident that I have allowed myself such full extracts, in regard not only to the composition of the scenes, but also to the delineation of the characters, for in their very modeling, in their characteristics, in their behavior, there is much typical of Griffith's manner. This equally concerns also his "Dickens-esque" distressed, defenseless creatures (recalling Lillian Gish and Richard Barthelmess in **Broken Blossoms** or the Gish sisters in **Orphans of the Storm**), and is no less typical for his characters like the two old gentlemen and Mrs. Bedwin; and finally, it is entirely characteristic of him to have such figures as are in the gang of "the merry old Jew" Fagin.

In regard to the immediate task of our example of Dickens's montage progression of the story composition, we can present the results of it in the following table:

1. The old gentlemen.

2. Departure of Oliver.
3. *The old gentlemen and the watch. It is still light.*
4. Digression on the character of Mr. Grimwig.
5. *The old gentlemen and the watch. Gathering twilight.*
6. Fagin, Sikes and Nancy in the public-house.
7. Scene on the street.
8. *The old gentlemen and the watch. The gas-lamps have been lit.*
9. Oliver is dragged back to Fagin.
10. Digression at the beginning of Chapter XVII.
11. The journey of Mr. Bumble.
12. *The old gentlemen* and Mr. Brownlow's command to forget Oliver forever.

As we can see, we have before us a typical and, for Griffith, a model of parallel montage of two story lines, where one (the waiting gentlemen) emotionally heightens the tension and drama of the other (the capture of Oliver). It is in "rescuers" rushing along to save the "suffering heroine" that Griffith has, with the aid of parallel montage, earned his most glorious laurels!

Most curious of all is that in the *very center* of our breakdown of the episode, is wedged another "interruption"—a whole digression at the beginning of Chapter XVII, on which we have been purposely silent. What is remarkable about this digression? It is Dickens's own "treatise" on the principles of this montage construction of the story which he carries out so fascinatingly, and which passed into the style of Griffith. Here it is:

It is the custom on the stage, in all good murderous melodramas, to present the tragic and the comic scenes, in as regular alternation, as the layers of red and white in a side of streaky well-cured bacon. The hero sinks upon his straw bed, weighed down by fetters and misfortunes; and, in the next scene, his faithful but unconscious squire regales the audience with a comic song. We behold, with throbbing bosoms, the heroine in the grasp of a proud and ruthless baron: her virtue and her life alike in danger; drawing forth her dagger to preserve the one at the cost of the other; and just as our expectations are wrought up to the highest pitch, a whistle is heard: and we are straightway transported to the great hall of the castle: where a grey-headed seneschal sings a funny chorus with a funnier body of vassals, who are free of all sorts of places from church vaults to palaces, and roam about in company, carolling perpetually.

Such changes appear absurd; but they are not so unnatural as they would seem at first sight. The transitions in real life from well-spread boards to death-beds, and from mourning-weeds to holiday garments, are not a whit less startling; only, there, we are busy actors, instead of passive lookers-on; which makes a vast difference. The actors in the mimic life of the theatre, are blind to violent transitions and abrupt impulses of passion of feeling, which, presented before the eyes of mere spectators, are at once condemned as outrageous and preposterous.

As sudden shiftings of the scene, and rapid changes of time and place, are not only sanctioned in books by long usage, but are by many considered as the great art of authorship: an author's skill in his craft being, by such critics, chiefly estimated with relation to the dilemmas in which he leaves his characters at the end of every chapter: this brief introduction to the present one may perhaps be deemed unnecessary. . . .

There is another interesting thing in this treatise: in his own words, Dickens (a life-long amateur actor) defines his direct relation to the theater melodrama. This is as if Dickens had placed himself in the position of a connecting link between the future, unforeseen art of the cinema, and the not so distant (for Dickens) past—the traditions of "good murderous melodramas."

This "treatise," of course, could not have escaped the eye of the patriarch of the American film, and very often his structure seems to follow the wise advice, handed down to the great film-maker of the twentieth century by the great novelist of the nineteenth. And Griffith, hiding nothing, has more than once acknowledged his debt to Dickens's memory.

We have already seen that the first screen exploitation of such a structure was by Griffith in *After Many Years,* an exploitation for which he held Dickens responsible. This film is further memorable for being the first in which the close-up was *intelligently* used and, chiefly, *utilized.*

Lewis Jacobs has described Griffith's approach to the close-up, three months earlier, in *For Love of Gold,* an adaptation of Jack London's *Just Meat:*

> The climax of the story was the scene in which the two thieves begin to distrust each other. Its effectiveness depended upon the audience's awareness of what was going on in the minds of both thieves. The only known way to indicate a player's thoughts was by double-exposure "dream balloons." This convention had grown out of two misconceptions: first, that the camera must always be fixed at a viewpoint corresponding to that of a spectator in a theatre (the position now known as the long shot); the other, that a scene had to be played in its entirety before another was begun. . . .

> Griffith decided now upon a revolutionary step. He moved the camera closer to the actor, in what is now known as the full shot (a larger view of the actor), so that the audience could observe the actor's pantomime more closely. No one before had thought of changing the position of the camera in the middle of a scene. . . .

> The next logical step was to bring the camera still closer to the actor in what is now called the close-up. . . .

> Not since Porter's *The Great Train Robbery,* some five years before, had a close-up been seen in American films. Used then only as a stunt (the outlaw was shown firing at the audience), the close-up became in *Enoch Arden [After Many Years]* the natural dramatic complement of the long shot and full shot. Going further than he had ventured before, in a scene showing Annie Lee brooding and waiting for her husband's return Griffith daringly used a large close-up of her face.

> Everyone in the Biograph studio was shocked. "Show only the head of a person? What will people say? It's against all rules of movie making!" . . .

> But Griffith had no time for argument. He had another surprise, even more radical, to offer. Immediately following the close-up of Annie, he inserted a picture of the object of her thoughts— her husband, cast away on a desert isle. This cutting from one scene to another, without finishing either, brought a torrent of criticism down upon the experimenter. [Lewis Jacobs, *The Rise of the American film*]

And we have read how Griffith defended his experiment by calling on Dickens as a witness.

If these were only the first intimations of that which was to bring glory to Griffith, we can find a full fruition of his new method in a film made only a year after he began to direct films—*The Lonely Villa.* This is told in Iris Barry's monograph on Griffith:

> By June, 1909, Griffith was already gaining control of his material and moved to further creative activity: he carried Porter's initial method to a new stage of development in *The Lonely Villa,* in which he employed cross-cutting to heighten suspense throughout the parallel scenes where the burglars are breaking in upon the mother and children while the father is rushing home to the rescue. Here he had hit upon a new way of handling a tired device—the last-minute rescue— which was to serve him well for the rest of his career. By March, 1911, Griffith further developed this disjunctive method of narration in *The Lonedale Operator,* which achieves a much greater degree of breathless excitement and suspense in the scenes where the railwayman-hero is racing his train back to the rescue of the heroine attacked by hold-up men in the depot. [Iris Barry, *D.W. Griffith, American Film Master*]

Melodrama, having attained on American soil by the end of the nineteenth century its most complete and exuberant ripeness, at this peak must certainly have had a great influence on Griffith, whose first art was the theater, and its methods must have been stored away in Griffith's reserve fund with no little quantity of wonderful and characteristic features.

What was this period of American melodrama, immediately preceding the appearance of Griffith? Its most interesting aspect is the close scenic entwining of *both* sides that are characteristic for the future creation of

Griffith; of those *two sides,* typical for Dickens's writing and style, about which we spoke at the beginning of this essay.

This may be illustrated by the theatrical history of the original ***Way Down East***. Some of this history has been preserved for us in the reminiscences of William A. Brady. These are particularly interesting as records of the emergence and popularizing of that theatrical genre known as the "homespun" melodrama of locale. Certain features of this tradition have been preserved to our own day. The successes of such keenly modern works as Erskine Caldwell's *Tobacco Road* and John Steinbeck's *The Grapes of Wrath* (in their original and film versions) contain ingredients common to this popular genre. These two works complete a circle of rural poesy, dedicated to the American countryside.

Brady's reminiscences are an interesting record of the scenic embodiment of these melodramas on the stages of that era. For purely as staging, this scenic embodiment in many cases literally anticipates not only the themes, subjects and their interpretations, but even those staging methods and effects, which always seem to us so "purely cinematic," without precedent and . . . begotten by the screen!

> A variety actor named Denman Thompson in the late 'seventies was performing a sketch on the variety circuits called *Joshua Whitcomb*. . . . It happened that James M. Hill, a retail clothier from Chicago, saw *Joshua Whitcomb*, met Thompson, and persuaded him to write a four-act drama around Old Josh. [William A. Brady "Drama in Homespun."]

Out of this idea came the melodrama, *The Old Homestead,* financed by Hill. The new genre caught on slowly, but skillful advertising did its work—recalling sentimental dreams and memories of the good old, and alas! deserted hearth-side; of life in good old rural America, and the piece played for twenty-five years, making a fortune for Mr. Hill.

Another success from the same formula was *The Country Fair* by Neil Burgess:

> He introduced in the play, for the first time on any stage, a horse race on tread-mills. He patented the device and collected royalties the world over when it was used in other productions. *Ben Hur* used it for twenty years. . . . [Brady]

The novelty and attraction of this thematic material cast in scenic devices of this sort quickly made it popular everywhere and "homespun dramas sprung up on every side. . . ."

> Another long-lived earthy melodrama was *In Old Kentucky,* which with its Pickaninny Band made a couple of millions in ten years for its owner, Jacob Litt. . . . Augustus Thomas tried his hand writing a trio of rurals—*Alabama, Arizona,* and *In Missouri.* [Brady]

An energetic all-round entrepreneur like Brady was sure to be drawn towards this new money-making dramatic form:

> All through the 'nineties, I was a very busy person in and around Broadway. I tackled anything in the entertainment line—melodramas on Broadway or the Bowery, prize fights, bicycle races—long or short, six days, twenty-four hours, or sprints—league baseball. . . . Broadsword fights, cakewalks, tugs of war, wrestling matches—on the level and made to order. Masquerade balls for all nations at Madison Square Garden. Matching James J. Corbett against John L. Sullivan and winning the world's heavyweight championship. This put me on the top of the world, and so I had to have a Broadway theatre. [Brady]

Brady leased the Manhattan Theatre with "a young fellow named Florenz Ziegfeld, Jr." and went looking for something to put into it.

> A booking agent of mine named Harry Doel Parker brought me a script called *Annie Laurie* [by his wife, Lottie Blair Parker]. I read it, and saw a chance to build it up into one of those rural things that were cleaning up everywhere. . . . I told him that the play had the makings, and we finally agreed on an outright purchase price of ten thousand dollars, he giving me the right to call in a play doctor. I gave the job to Joseph R. Grismer, who rechristened the play *Way Down East*. . . .
>
> . . . We booked it at our Broadway theater, where it ran seven months, never knowing a profitable week. The critics tore it to pieces. . . . During its Broadway run we used every trick known to the barnstormer to pull them in, but to no avail. . . . We depended on "snow"—sloughing New York and its suburbs with "Pass 2's."
>
> One night a well-known minister dropped in and he wrote us a nice letter of appreciation. That gave us a cue. We sent out ten thousand "minister tickets" and asked them all for tributes and got them. They all said it was a masterpiece—made long speeches from the stage to that effect—and followed it up with sermons from their pulpits. I hired the big electric sign on the triangle building at Broadway and Twenty-third Street (the first big one in New York). It cost us a thousand dollars a month. How it did make the Rialto talk! In one of our weekly press notices, which *The Sun* printed, it stated that *Way Down East* was better than *The Old Homestead*. That gave us a slogan which lasted twenty years. . . . [Brady]

The manager of the Academy of Music, the home of *The Old Homestead,* was asked to put *Way Down East* into his theater.

> He was willing, but insisted that the show and its production was too small for his huge stage. Grismer and I put our heads together and decided on a huge production, introducing horses, cattle, sheep, all varieties of farm conveyances, a monster

sleigh drawn by four horses for a sleigh-ride, an electric snowstorm, a double quartette singing at every opportunity the songs that mother loved—forming, all in all, a veritable farm circus. It went over with a bang, and stayed in New York a full season, showing profits exceeding one hundred thousand dollars. After that, it was easy going. I launched a half-dozen touring companies. They all cleaned up.

The show was a repeater and it took twenty-one years to wear it out. The big cities never seemed to grow tired of it. . . .

The silent movie rights of *Way Down East* were purchased by D. W. Griffith for one hundred and seventy thousand dollars, twenty-five years after its first stage production. [Brady]

In the fall of 1902, exactly a year before the production of *The Great Train Robbery,* a moralistic melodrama entitled *The Ninety and Nine* (the title derives from a familiar hymn by Sankey) opened at the same Academy of Music. Under a striking photo of the climactic scene in the production, *The Theatre Magazine* printed this explanatory caption:

> A hamlet is encircled by a raging prairie fire and three thousand people are threatened. At the station, thirty miles away, scores of excited people wait as the telegraph ticks the story of peril. A special is ready to go to the rescue. The engineer is absent and the craven young millionaire refuses to take the risk to make the dash. The hero springs forward to take his place. Darkness, a moment of suspense, and then the curtain rises again upon an exciting scene. The big stage is literally covered with fire. Flames lick the trunks of the trees. Telegraph poles blaze and the wires snap in the fierce heat. Sharp tongues of fire creep through the grass and sweep on, blazing fiercely. In the midst of it all is the massive locomotive, full sized and such as draw the modern express trains, almost hidden from view in the steam or smoke. Its big drive wheels spin on the track, and it rocks and sways as if driven at topmost speed. In the cab is the engineer, smoke-grimed and scarred, while the fireman dashes pails of water on him to protect him from the flying embers.

Further comment seems superfluous: here too is the tension of parallel action, of the race, the chase—the necessity to get there in time, to break through the flaming barrier; here too is the moral preachment, capable of inflaming a thousand ministers; here too, answering the "modern" interests of the audience, is HOME in all its "exotic fullness"; here too are the irresistible tunes, connected with memories of childhood and "dear old mother." In short, here is laid out the whole arsenal with which Griffith later will conquer, just as irresistibly.

But if you should like to move the discussion from general attitudes of montage over to its more *narrowly specific* features, Griffith might have found still other

"montage ancestors" for himself—and on his own grounds, too.

I must regretfully put aside Walt Whitman's huge montage conception. It must be stated that Griffith did not continue the Whitman *montage tradition* (in spite of the Whitman lines on "out of the cradle endlessly rocking," which served Griffith unsuccessfully as a refrain shot for his **Intolerance**; but of that later).

It is here that I wish, in connection with montage, to refer to one of the gayest and wittiest of Mark Twain's contemporaries—writing under the *nom de plume* of John Phoenix. This example of montage is dated October 1, 1853 (!), and is taken from his parody on a current novelty—illustrated newspapers.

The parody newspaper is entitled "Phoenix's Pictorial and Second Story Front Room Companion," and was first published in the San Diego *Herald*. Among its several items, ingeniously illustrated with the miscellaneous "boiler-plate" found in any small-town newspaper print-shop of the time, there is one item of particular interest for us [a series of pictures with the caption]: "Fearful accident on the Princeton Rail Road! Terrible loss of life!"

"By all the rules of the art" of montage, John Phoenix "conjures up the image." The montage method is obvious: the play of *juxtaposed detail*-shots, which in themselves are immutable and even unrelated, but from which is created the desired *image of the whole*. And particularly fascinating here is the "close-up" of the false teeth, placed next to a "long-shot" of the overturned railway coach, but both given in *equal size,* that is, exactly as if they were being shown on "a full screen"!

Curious also is the figure of the author himself, hiding beneath the pseudonym of Phoenix the honored name of Lieutenant George Horatio Derby, of the United States Army Engineers, wounded at Serro Gordo in 1846, a conscientious surveyor, reporter and engineer till his death in 1861. Such was one of the first American ancestors of the wonder-working method of montage! He was one of the first important American humorists of a new type, who belongs as well to the indubitable forerunners of that "violent" humor, which has achieved its wildest flourish in films, for example, in the work of the Marx Brothers.

I don't know how my readers feel about this, but for me personally it is always pleasing to recognize again and again the fact that our cinema is not altogether without parents and without pedigree, without a past, without the traditions and rich cultural heritage of the past epochs. It is only very thoughtless and presumptuous people who can erect laws and an esthetic for cinema, proceeding from premises of some incredible virgin-birth of this art!

Let Dickens and the whole ancestral array, going back as far as the Greeks and Shakespeare, be superfluous reminders that both Griffith and our cinema prove our origins to be not solely as of Edison and his fellow inventors, but as based on an enormous cultured past; each part of this past in its own moment of world history has moved forward the great art of cinematography. Let this past be a reproach to those thoughtless people who have displayed arrogance in reference to literature, which has contributed so much to this apparently unprecedented art and is, in the first and most important place: the art of viewing—not only the *eye,* but *viewing*—both meanings being embraced in this term.

This esthetic growth from the *cinematographic eye* to the *image of an embodied viewpoint on phenomena* was one of the most serious processes of development of our Soviet cinema in particular; our cinema also played a tremendous rôle in the history of the development of world cinema as a whole, and it was no small rôle that was played by a basic understanding of the principles of film-montage, which became so characteristic for the Soviet school of film-making.

None the less enormous was the rôle of Griffith also in the evolution of the system of Soviet montage: a rôle as enormous as the rôle of Dickens in forming the methods of Griffith. Dickens in this respect played an enormous rôle in heightening the tradition and cultural heritage of preceding epochs; just as on an even higher level we can see the enormous rôle of those social premises, which inevitably in those pivotal moments of history ever anew push elements of the montage method into the center of attention for creative work.

The rôle of Griffith is enormous, but our cinema is neither a poor relative nor an insolvent debtor of his. It was natural that the spirit and content of our country itself, in themes and subjects, would stride far ahead of Griffith's ideals as well as their reflection in artistic images.

In social attitudes Griffith was always a liberal, never departing far from the slightly sentimental humanism of the good old gentlemen and sweet old ladies of Victorian England, just as Dickens loved to picture them. His tender-hearted film morals go no higher than a level of Christian accusation of human injustice and nowhere in his films is there sounded a protest against social injustice.

In his best films he is a preacher of pacifism and compromise with fate (***Isn't Life Wonderful?***) or of love of mankind "in general" (***Broken Blossoms***). Here in his reproaches and condemnations Griffith is sometimes able to ascend to magnificent pathos (in, for example, ***Way Down East***).

In the more thematically dubious of his works—this takes the form of an apology for the Dry Law (in ***The Struggle***) or for the metaphysical philosophy of the eternal origins of Good and Evil (in ***Intolerance***). Metaphysics permeates the film which he based on Marie Corelli's ***Sorrows of Satan***. Finally, among the most repellent elements in his films (and there are such) we see Griffith as an open apologist for racism, erecting a celluloid monument to the Ku Klux Klan, and joining their attack on Negroes in ***The Birth of a Nation***. [In all instances the craftsmanship of Griffith remains almost unaltered in these films, springing as it does from profound sincerity and a full conviction in the rightness of their themes, but before all else I am noting the themes themselves and their ideological aims.]

Nevertheless, nothing can take from Griffith the wreath of one of the genuine masters of the American cinema.

But montage thinking is inseparable from the general content of thinking as a whole. The structure that is reflected in the concept of Griffith montage is the structure of bourgeois society. And he actually resembles Dickens's "side of streaky, well-cured bacon"; in actuality (and this is no joke), he is woven of irreconcilably alternating layers of "white" and "red"—rich and poor. (This is the eternal theme of Dickens's novels, nor does he move beyond these divisions. His mature work, *Little Dorrit,* is so divided into two books: "Poverty" and "Riches.") And this society, perceived *only as a contrast between the haves and the have-nots,* is reflected in the consciousness of Griffith no deeper than the image of an intricate race between two parallel lines.

Griffith primarily is the greatest master of the most graphic form in this field—a master of *parallel montage.* Above all else, Griffith is a great master of montage constructions that have been created in a direct-lined quickening and *increase of tempo* (chiefly in the direction of the higher forms of parallel montage).

The school of Griffith before all else is a school of *tempo,* However, he did not have the strength to compete with the young Soviet school of montage in the field of expression and of relentlessly affective *rhythm,* the task of which goes far beyond the narrow confines of tempo tasks.

It was exactly this feature of *devastating rhythm* as distinguished from effects of *tempo* that was noted at the appearance of our first Soviet films in America. After recognizing the themes and ideas of our works it was this feature of our cinema that the American press of 1926-27 remarked.

But true rhythm presupposes above all organic *unity.*

Neither a successive mechanical alternation of crosscuts, nor an interweaving of antagonistic themes, but above all a unity, which in the play of inner contradictions, through a shift of the play in the direction of tracing its organic pulse—that is what lies at the base of rhythm. This is not an outer unity of story, bringing with it also the classical image of the chase-scene, but that inner unity, which can be realized in montage as an entirely different system of construction, in which so-called parallel montage can figure as one of the highest or particularly personal variants.

And, naturally, the montage concept of Griffith, as a primarily parallel montage, appears to be a copy of his dualistic picture of the world, running in two parallel lines of poor and rich towards some hypothetical "reconcilation" where . . . the parallel lines would cross, that is, in that infinity, just as inaccessible as that "reconciliation."

Thus it was to be expected that our concept of montage had to be born from an entirely different "image" of an understanding of phenomena, which was opened to us by a world-view both monistic and dialectic.

For us the microcosm of montage had to be understood as a unity, which in the inner stress of contradictions is halved, in order to be re-assembled in a new unity on a new plane, qualitatively higher, its imagery newly perceived.

I attempted to give theoretical expression to this *general tendency* of our understanding of montage, and advanced this in 1929, thinking least of all at that time to what degree our method of montage both generically and in principle was in opposition to the montage of Griffith.

This was stated in the form of a definition of the *stages* of relationship between the shot and montage. Of the thematic unity of content in a film, of the "shot," of the "frame," I wrote:

> The shot is by no means an *element* of montage.
>
> The shot is a montage *cell*.
>
> Just as cells in their division form a phenomenon of another order, the organism or embryo, so, on the other side of the dialectical leap from the shot, there is montage.

Montage is the expansion of intra-shot conflict (or, contradiction) at first in the conflict of two shots standing side by side:

> Conflict within the shot is potential montage, in the development of its intensity shattering the quadrilateral cage of the shot and exploding its conflict into montage impulses *between* the montage pieces.

Then—the threading of the conflict through a whole system of planes, by means of which ". . . we newly collect the disintegrated event into one whole, but in *our* aspect. According to the treatment of our relation to the event."

Thus is broken up a *montage unit*—the cage—into a multiple chain, which *is anew gathered into a new*

unity—*in the montage phrase, embodying the concept of an image of the phenomenon.*

It is interesting to watch such a process moving also through the history of language in relation to the word (the "shot") and the sentence (the "montage phrase"), and to see just such a primitive stage of "word-sentences" later "foliating" into the sentence, made up of separately independent words.

V. A. Bogoroditzky writes that ". . . in the very beginning mankind expressed his ideas in single words, which were also primitive forms of the sentence." The question is presented in more detail by Academician Ivan Meshchaninov:

> Word and sentence appear as the product of history and are far from being identified with the whole lengthy epoch of gutturals. They are antedated by an unfoliated state, till this day undetected within the materials of incorporated languages.
>
> Broken up into their component parts, word-sentences show a unity between the original words and their combination into the syntactic complex of the sentence. This gains a diversity of possibilities in expressive word-combinations. . . .
>
> The embryos of syntax, previously laid down, were in a latent form of incorporated word-sentences, then, later during its decomposition, projected outward. The sentence appeared to have been broken down to its chief elements, that is, the sentence is created as such with its laws of syntax. . . . [Ivan I. Meshchaninov, *General Linguistics*]

We have previously stated the particularity of *our* attitude towards montage. However, the distinction between the American and our montage concepts gains maximum sharpness and clarity if we glance at such a difference in principle of the understanding of another innovation, introduced by Griffith into cinematography and, in the same way, receiving at our hands an entirely different understanding.

We refer to the *close-up,* or as we speak of it, the "large scale."

This distinction in principle begins with an essence that exists in the term itself.

We say: an object or face is photographed in "large scale," i.e., *large.*

The American says: *near,* or "close-up." [Griffith himself, in his famous announcement in *The New York Dramatic Mirror* of December 3, 1913, employed both designations: "The large or close-up figures. . . ." But it is characteristic that in habitual American film usage it should be the latter term, "close-up," that has been retained.]

We are speaking of the *qualitative* side of the phenomenon, linked with its meaning (just as we speak of a *large* talent, that is, of one which stands out, by its significance, from the general line, or of *large* print [bold-face] to emphasize that which is particularly essential or significant).

Among Americans the term is attached to *viewpoint.*

Among us—to *the value of what is seen.*

We shall see below what a profound distinction in principle is here, after we have understood the system which, both in method and in application, uses the "large scale" in our cinema in a way distinguished from the use of the "close-up" by the American cinema.

In this comparison immediately the first thing to appear clearly relating to the principal function of the close-up in our cinema is—not only and not so much to *show* or to *present,* as to *signify,* to *give meaning,* to *designate.*

In our own way we very quickly realized the very nature of the "close-up" after this had been hardly noticed in its sole capacity as a means of showing, in American cinema practice.

The first factor that attracted us in the method of the close-up was the discovery of its particularly astonishing feature: to create *a new quality of the whole from a juxtaposition of the separate parts.*

Where the isolated close-up in the tradition of the Dickens kettle was often a determining or "key" detail in the work of Griffith, where the alternation of close-ups of faces was an anticipation of the future synchronized dialogue (it may be apropos here to mention that Griffith, in his sound film, did not freshen a single method then in use)—there we advanced the idea of a *principally new qualitative fusion,* flowing out of the process of *juxtaposition.*

For example, in almost my first spoken and written declarations of the 'twenties, I designated the cinema as above all else an "art of juxtaposition."

If Gilbert Seldes is to be believed, Griffith himself came to the point of seeing "that by dovetailing the ride of the rescuers and the terror of the besieged in a scene, he was multiplying the emotional effect enormously; the whole was infinitely greater than the sum of its parts," but this was also insufficient for us.

For us this *quantitative accumulation* even in such "multiplying" situations was not enough: we sought for and found in juxtapositions more than that—*a qualitative leap.*

The leap proved beyond the *limits of the possibilities* of the stage—a leap beyond the *limits of situation*: a leap into the field of montage *image,* montage *understanding,* montage as a means before all else of revealing the *ideological conception.*

By the way, in another of Seldes's books there appears his lengthy condemnation of the American films of the 'twenties, losing their spontaneity in pretensions towards "artiness" and "theatricality."

It is written in the form of "An Open Letter to the Movie Magnates." It begins with the juicy salutation: "Ignorant and Unhappy People," and contains in its conclusion such remarkable lines as these:

> . . . and then the new film will arrive without your assistance. For when you and your capitalizations and your publicity go down together, the field will be left free for others. . . . Presently it will be within the reach of artists. With players instead of actors and actresses, with fresh ideas (among which the idea of making a lot of money may be absent) these artists will give back to the screen the thing you have debauched—imagination. They will create with the camera, and not record . . . it is possible and desirable to create great epics of American industry and let the machine operate as a character in the play—just as the land of the West itself, as the corn must play its part. The grandiose conceptions of Frank Norris are not beyond the reach of the camera. There are painters willing to work in the medium of the camera and architects and photographers. And novelists, too, I fancy, would find much of interest in the scenario as a new way of expression. There is no end to what we can accomplish.
>
> . . . For the movie is the imagination of mankind in action. . . . [Gilbert Seldes, *The Seven Lively Arts*]

Seldes expected this bright film future to be brought by some unknown persons who were to reduce the cost of films, by some unknown "artists," and by epics, dedicated to American industry or American corn. But his prophetic words justified themselves in an entirely different direction: they proved to be a prediction that in these very years (the book appeared in 1924) on the other side of the globe were being prepared the first Soviet films, which were destined to fulfill all his prophecies.

For only a new social structure, which has forever freed art from narrowly commercial tasks, can give full realization to the dreams of advanced and penetrating Americans!

In technique also, montage took on a completely new meaning at this time

To the parallelism and alternating close-ups of America we offer the contrast of uniting these in fusion; the MONTAGE TROPE.

In the theory of literature a *trope* is defined thus: "a figure of speech which consists in the use of a word or phrase in a sense other than that which is proper to it," for example, a *sharp* wit (normally, a *sharp* sword).

Griffith's cinema does not know this type of montage construction. His close-ups create atmosphere, outline traits of the characters, alternate in dialogues of the leading characters, and close-ups of the chaser and the chased speed up the tempo of the chase. But Griffith at all times remains on a level of *representation and objectivity* and nowhere does he try through the *juxtaposition* of shots to shape *import and image.*

However, within the practice of Griffith there was such an attempt, an attempt of huge dimensions—***Intolerance.***

Terry Ramsaye, a historian of the American film, has definitively called it "a giant metaphor." No less definitively has he called it also "a magnificent failure." For if ***Intolerance***—in its modern story—stands unsurpassed by Griffith himself, a brilliant model of his method of montage, then at the same time, along the line of a desire to get away from the *limits of story* towards *the region of generalization* and metaphorical allegory, the picture is overcome completely by failure. In explaining the failure of ***Intolerance*** Ramsaye claims:

> Allusion, simile and metaphor can succeed in the printed and spoken word as an aid to the dim pictorial quality of the word expression. The motion picture has no use for them because it itself is the event. It is too specific and final to accept such aids. The only place that these verbal devices have on the screen is in support of the sub-title or legends. . . . [Terry Ramsaye, *A Million and One Nights*]

But Terry Ramsaye is not correct in denying to cinematography *all possibility in general of imagistic storytelling,* in not permitting the assimilation of simile and metaphor to move, in its best instances, beyond the text of the sub-titles!

The reason for this failure was of quite another nature; particularly, in Griffith's misunderstanding, that the region of metaphorical and imagist writing appears in the sphere of *montage juxtaposition,* not of *representational montage pieces.*

Out of this came his unsuccessful use of the repeated refrain shot: Lillian Gish rocking a cradle. Griffith had been inspired to translate these lines of Walt Whitman,

> . . . endlessly rocks the cradle, Uniter of Here and Hereafter.

not in the structure, nor in *the harmonic recurrence of montage expressiveness,* but in *an isolated picture,* with the result that the cradle could not possibly be *ab-*stracted into an image of eternally reborn epochs and remained inevitably simply a *life-like cradle,* calling forth derision, surprise or vexation in the spectator.

We know of a nearly analogous blunder in our films, as well: the "naked woman" in Dovzhenko's *Earth.* Here is another example of a lack of awareness that for *imagist* and *extra-life-like* (or *sur*realist) "manipulation" of film-shots there must be *an abstraction of the lifelike representation.*

Such an abstraction of the lifelike may in certain instances be give by the *close-up.*

A healthy, handsome woman's body may, actually, be heightened to *an image of a life-affirming beginning,* which is what Dovzhenko had to have, to clash with his montage of the funeral in *Earth.*

A skillfully leading montage creation with *close-ups,* taken in the "Rubens manner," isolated from naturalism and abstracted in the necessary direction, could well have been lifted to such a "sensually palpable" image.

But the whole structure of *Earth* was doomed to failure, because in place of such montage material the director cut into the funeral *long shots* of the interior of the peasant hut, and the naked woman flinging herself about there. And the spectator could not possibly separate out of this concrete, lifelike woman that generalized sensation of blazing fertility, of sensual life-affirmation, which the director wished to convery of all nature, as a pantheistic contrast to the theme of death and the funeral!

This was prevented by the ovens, pots, towels, benches, tablecloths—all those details of everyday life, from which the woman's body could easily have been freed by *the framing of the shot,*—so that *representational* naturalism would not interfere with the embodiment of the *conveyed metaphorical* task.

But to return to Griffith—

If he made a blunder because of non-montage thinking in the treatment of a recurring "wave of time" through an unconvincing plastic idea of a rocking cradle, then at the opposite pole—in the gathering together of all four motifs of the film along the same principle of his montage, he made another blunder.

This weaving of four epochs was magnificently conceived. Griffith stated:

> . . . the stories will begin like four currents looked at from a hilltop. At first the four currents will flow apart, slowly and quietly. But as they flow, they grow nearer and nearer together, and faster and faster, until in the end, in the last act, they mingle in one mighty river of expressed emotion.

But the effect didn't come off. For again it turned out to be a combination of *four different stories,* rather than *a fusion of four phenomena* in *a single imagist generalization.*

Griffith announced his film as "a drama of comparisons." And that is what **Intolerance** remains—a drama of comparisons, rather than *a unified, powerful, generalized image.*

Here is the same defect again: an inability to abstract a phenomenon, without which it cannot expand beyond the *narrowly representational.* For this reason we could not resolve any "*supra*-representational," "conveying" (metaphorical) tasks.

Only by dividing "hot" from a *thermometer reading* may one speak of "a sense of heat."

Only by abstracting "deep" from *meters and fathoms* may one speak of "a sense of depth."

Only by disengaging "falling" from *the formula of the accelerated speed of a falling body* ($mv^2/2$) may one speak of "a sensation of falling!"

However, the failure of **Intolerance** to achieve a true "mingling" lies also in another circumstance: the four episodes chosen by Griffith are actually un-collatable. The *formal failure* of their mingling in *a single image* of **Intolerance** is only *a reflection of a hematic and ideological error.*

Is it possible that a tiny general feature—a general and superficially metaphysical and vague viewpoint towards **Intolerance** (with a capital *I!*)—can really unite in the spectator's consciousness such obvious historically uncollated phenomena as the religious fanaticism of St. Bartholomew's Eve with labor's struggle in a highly developed capitalist state! And the bloody pages of the struggle for hegemony over Asia with the complicated process of conflict between the colonial Hebrew people and enslaving Mother Rome?

Here we find a key to the reason why the problem of abstraction is not once stumbled upon by Griffith's montage method. The secret of this is not professional-technical, but ideological-intellectual.

It is not that representation cannot be raised with correct presentation and treatment to the structure of metaphor, simile, image. Nor is it that Griffith here altered his method, or his professional craftsmanship. But that he made no attempt at a genuinely thoughtful abstraction of phenomena—at an *extraction of generalized conclusions* on historical phenomena from a wide variety of historical data; that is the core of the fault.

In history and economics it was necessary for the gigantic work of Marx and the continuers of his teaching to aid us in understanding *the laws of the process* that

stand behind miscellaneous *separate data.* Then science could succeed in abstracting *a generalization from the chaos of separate traits* characteristic for the phenomena.

In the practice of American film studios there is a splendid professional term—"limitations." Such a director is "limited" to musical comedies. The "limits" of a certain actress are within fashionable rôles. Beyond these "limitations" (quite sensible in most cases) this or that talent cannot be thrust. Risking departure from these "limitations" sometimes results in unexpected brilliance, but ordinarily, as in commonplace phenomena, this leads to failure.

Using this term, I would say that in the realm of *montage imagery* the American cinema wins no laurels for itself; and it is ideological "limitations" that are responsible for this.

This is not affected by technique, nor by scope, nor by dimensions.

The question of montage imagery is based on a definite structure and system of thinking; it derives and has been derived only through collective consciousness, appearing as a reflection of a new (socialist) stage of human society and as a thinking result of ideal and philosophic education, inseparably connected with the social structure of that society.

We, our epoch—*sharply ideal* and *intellectual*—could not read the content of a shot without, before all else, having read its ideological nature, and therefore find in the *juxtaposition of shots an arrangement of a new qualitative element,* a new *image,* a new *understanding.*

Considering this, we could not help rushing into sharp excesses in this direction.

In *October* we cut shots of harps and balalaikas into a scene of Mensheviks addressing the Second Congress of Soviets. And these harps were shown not as harps, but as an imagist symbol of the mellifluent speech of Menshevik opportunism at the Congress. The balalaikas were not shown as balalaikas, but as an image of the tiresome strumming of these empty speeches in the face of the gathering storm of historical events. And placing side by side the Menshevik and the harp, the Menshevik and the balalaika, we were *extending the frame of parallel montage into a new quality, into a new realm:* from the sphere of *action* into the sphere of *significance.*

The period of such rather naive juxtapositions passed swiftly enough. Similar solutions, slightly "baroque" in form, in many ways attempted (and not always successfully!) with the available palliative means of the silent film to anticipate that which is now done with such case by the music track in the soundfilm! They quickly departed from the screen.

However, the chief thing remained—an understanding of montage as not merely a means of producing effects, but above all as a means of *speaking,* a means of *communicating* ideas, of communicating them by way of a special film language, by way of a special form of film *speech.*

The arrival at an understanding of normal film-speech quite naturally went through this *stage of excess in the realm of the trope and primitive metaphor.* It is interesting that in this direction we were covering methodological ground of great antiquity. Why, for example, the "poetic" image of the centaur is nothing more than a combination of man and horse with the aim of expressing *the image of an idea, directly un-representable by a picture* (but its exact meaning was that people of a certain place were "high speed"—swift in the race).

Thus the very production of simple meanings rises as a process of juxtaposition.

Therefore *the play of juxtaposition* in montage also has such a deep background of influence. On the other hand, it is exactly through elementary *naked juxtaposition* that must be worked out a system of the complicated inner (the outer no longer counts) juxtaposition that exists in each phrase of ordinary normal literate montage speech.

However, this same process is also correct for the production of *any kind of speech* in general, and above all *for that literary speech,* of which we are speaking. It is well known that the metaphor is an abridged simile.

And in connection with this Mauthner has very acutely written about our language:

> Every metaphor is witty. A people's language, as it is spoken today, is the sum total of a million witticisms, is a collection of the points of a million anecdotes whose stories have been lost. In this connection one must visualize the people of the language-creating period as being even wittier than those present-day wags who live by their wits. . . . Wit makes use of distant similes. Close similes were captured immediately into concepts or words. A change in meaning consists in the conquest of these words, in the metaphorical or witty extension of the concept to distant similes. . . . [*Beitrage zu einer kritik der Sprache: Zweiter Band, Zur Sprachwissenschaft*]

And Emerson says of this:

> As the limestone of the continent consists of infinite masses of the shells of animalcules, so language is made up of images, or tropes, which now, in their secondary use, have long ceased to remind us of their poetic origin. ["The Poet"]

At the threshold of the creation of language stands the simile, the trope and the image.

All meanings in language are imagist in origin, and each of these may, in due time, lose its original imagist source. Both these states of words—imagery and non-imagery—are equally natural. If the non-imagery of a word was considered derivative as something elementary (which it is always), that derives from the fact that it is a temporary latency of though (which imagery is its new step), but movement attracts more attention and is more provocative of analysis than is latency.

The calm observer, reviewing a prepared transferred expression of a more complicated poetic creation, may find in his memory a corresponding non-imagist expression, more imagistically corresponding to his (the observer's) mood of thought. If he says that this non-imagery is *communis et primum se offerens ratio* then he attributes his own condition to the creator of imagist expression. This is as if one were to expect that in the midst of a heated battle it is possible thus calmly to deliberate, as at a chess-board, with an absent partner. If one should transfer into the condition of the speaker himself, that would easily reverse the assertion of the cold observer and he would decide that *primum se offerens,* even if not *communis,* is exactly imagist. . . . [A.A. Potebnya, *From Notes on a Theory of Literature*]

In Werner's work on the metaphor he thus places it in the very cradle of language, although for other motives—he links it not with the tendency to *perceive* new regions, familiarizing the unknown through the known, but, on the contrary, with the tendency to *bide,* to substitute, to replace in customary usage that which lies under some oral ban—and is "tabu."

It is interesting that the "fact word" itself is *naturally* a rudiment of the poetic trope:

> Independently from the connection between the primary and derivative words, any word, as an aural indication of meaning, based on the combination of sound and meaning in simultaneity or succession, consequently, is metonymy. [Potebnya]

And he who would take it into his head to be indignant and rebel against this would inevitably fall into the position of the pedant in one of Tieck's stories, who cried out:

> ". . . When a man begins to compare one object with another, he lies directly. 'The dawn strews roses.' Can there be any thing more silly? 'The sun sinks into the sea.' Stuff! . . . 'The morning wakes.' There is no morning, how can it sleep? It is nothing but the hour when the sun rises. Plague! The sun does not rise, that too is nonsense and poetry. Oh! If I had my will with language, and might properly scour and sweep it! O damnation! Sweep! In this lying world, one cannot help talking nonsense!" [Johann Ludwig Tieck, *Die Gemälde*]

The *imagist* transference of thought to simple *representation* is also echoed here. There is in Potebnya a good comment on this:

> *The image is more important than the representation.* There is a tale of a monk who, in order to prevent himself from eating roast suckling during Lent, carried on himself this invocation: "Suckling, transform thyself into a carp!" This tale, stripped of its satirical character, presents us with a universal historical phenomenon of human thought: word and image are the spiritual half of the matter, its essence.

Thus or otherwise the primitive metaphor necessarily stands at the very dawn of language, closely linked with the period of the production of the first transfers, that is, the first words to convey meanings, and not merely *motor* and *objective* understanding, that is, with the period of the birth of the first tools, as the first means of "transferring" the functions of the body and its actions from man himself to the tool in his hands. It is not astonishing, therefore, that the period of the birth of articulate montage speech of the future had also to pass through a sharply metaphorical stage, characterized by an abundance, if not a proper estimation, of "plastic sharpness"!

However, these "sharpnesses" very soon became sensed as excesses and twistings of some sort of a "language." And attention was gradually shifted from curiosity *concerning excesses* towards an interest in *the nature of this language itself.*

Thus the secret of the structure of montage was gradually revealed as a secret of *the structure of emotional speech.* For the very principle of montage, as is the entire individuality of its formation, is the substance of *an exact copy of the language of excited emotional speech.*

It is enough to examine the characteristics of similar speech, in order to be convinced, with no further commentary, that this is so.

Let us open to the appropriate chapter in Vendryes' excellent book, *Language:*

> The main difference between affective and logical language lies in the construction of the sentence. This difference stands out clearly when we compare the written with the spoken tongue. In French the two are so far removed from each other that a Frenchman never speaks as he writes and rarely writes as he speaks. . . .
>
> . . . The elements that the written tongue endeavours to combine into a coherent whole seem to be divided up and disjointed in the spoken tongue: even the order is entirely different. It is no longer the logical order of present-day grammar. It has its logic, but this logic is primarily affective, and the ideas are arranged in accordance

with the subjective importance the speaker gives to them or wishes to suggest to his listener, rather than with the objective rules of an orthodox process of reasoning.

> In the spoken tongue, all idea of meaning in the purely grammatical sense, disappears. If I say, *L'homme que vous voyez la-bas assis sur la greve est celui que j'ai rencontre hier à la gare* (The man that you see sitting down there on the beach is he whom I met yesterday at the station), I am making use of the processes of the written tongue and form but one sentence. But in speaking, I should have said: *Vous voyez bien cet homme—la-bas—il est assis sur la greve—eh bien! je l'ai rencontre hire, il etai à la gare.* (You see that man, down there—he is sitting on the beach—well! I met him yesterday, he was at the station.) How many sentences have we here? It is very difficult to say. Imagine that I pause where the dashes are printed: the words *la-bas* in themselves would form one sentence, exactly as if in answer to a question—"Where is this man?—*Down there.*" And even the sentence *il est assis sur la greve* easily becomes two if I pause between the two component parts: *"il est assis," [il est] "sur la greve"* (or *"[c'est] sur la greve [qu'] il est assis"*). The boundaries of the grammatical sentence are here so elusive that we had better give up all attempts to determine them. In a certain sense, there is but one sentence. The verbal image is one though it follows a kind of kinematical development. But whereas in the written tongue it is presented as a whole, when spoken it is cut up into short sections whose number and intensity correspond to the speaker's impressions, or to the necessity he feels for vividly communicating them to others.

Isn't this an exact copy of what takes place in montage? And doesn't what is said here about "written" language seem a duplication of the clumsy "long shot," which, when it attempts to present something *dramatically,* always hopelessly looks like a florid, awkward phrase, full of the subordinate clauses, participles and adverbs of a "theatrical" *mise-en-scène,* with which it dooms itself?!

However, this by no means implies that it is necessary to chase at any cost after "montage hash." In connection with this one may speak of the *phrase* as the author of "A Discussion of Old and New Style in the Russian Language," the Slavophile Alexander Shishkov wrote of *words:*

> In language both long and short words are necessary; for without short ones language would sound like the long-drawn-out moo of the cow, and without long ones—like the short monotonous chirp of a magpie. [Shishkov, *Collected Works and Translations*]

Concerning "affective logic," about which Vendryes writes and which lies at the base of spoken speech, montage very quickly realized that "affective logic" is the chief thing, but for finding all the fullness of its system and laws, montage had to make further serious creative "cruises" through the "inner monologue" of Joyce, through the "inner monologue" as understood in film, and through the so-called "intellectual cinema," before discovering that a fund of these laws can be found in a third variety of speech—not in *written,* nor in *spoken* speech, but in *inner speech,* where the affective structure functions in an even more full and pure form. But the formation of this *inner speech* is already inalienable from that which is enriched by *sensual thinking.*

Thus we arrived at the primary source of those interior principles, which already govern not only the formation of montage, but the inner formation of all works of art—of those basic *laws of the speech of art in general*—of those general *laws of form,* which lie at the base not only of works of film art, but of all and all kinds of arts in general. But of that—at another time.

Let us return now to that historical stage when montage in our field realized itself as a *montage trope,* and let us follow that path of development which it performed in the field of creating a unity of work, inseparable from that process, in which it became conscious of itself as an independent language.

Thus, in its way, montage became conscious of itself among us with the very first, not imitative, but independent steps of our cinema.

It is interesting that even in the interval between the old cinema and our Soviet cinema, researches were conducted exactly along the line of *juxtaposition.* And it is even more interesting that at this stage they naturally are known as . . . *contrasts.* Therefore on them above all else lies the imprint of *"contemplative dissection"* instead of an *emotional fusion* in some "new quality," as were already characterizing the first researches in the field of the Soviet cinema's own language. Such a speculative play of contrasts fills, for example, the film *Palace and Fortress* as if to carry the principle of contrast from its title into the very style of the work. Here are still constructions of a type of *un-crossed* parallelism: "here and there," "before and now." It is completely in the spirit of the posters of the time, split into two halves, showing on the left, a landlord's house *before* (the master, serfdom, flogging) and on the right—*now* (a school in the same building, a nursery). It is completely such a type of colliding shots that we find in the film: the "points" of a ballerina (the *Palace*) and the shackled legs of Beidemann (the *Fortress*). Similarly speculative in the *order of parallelism* is given also in the combination of shots—Beidemann behind bars and . . . a caged canary in the jailer's room.

In these and other examples there is nowhere any further tendency towards *a union of representations in a generalized image*: they are united neither by a unity of composition nor by the chief element, emotion: they are presented in an even narrative, and not in that degree of emotional excitement when it is only natural for an imagist turn of speech to *arise.*

But pronounced without a corresponding emotional degree, without corresponding emotional preparation, the "image" inevitably sounds absurd. When Hamlet tells Laertes:

> I loved Ophelia; forty thousand brothers
> Could not, with all their quantity of love,
> Make up my sum. . . .

this is very pathetic and arresting; but try taking from this the expression of heightened emotion, transfer it to a setting of ordinary lifelike conversation, that is, consider the immediate objective content of this image, and it will evoke nothing but laughter!

Strike (1924) abounded in "trials" of this new and independent direction. The mass shooting of the demonstrators in the finale, interwoven with bloody scenes at the municipal slaughter-house, merged (for that "childhood" of our cinema this sounded fully convincing and produced a great impression!) in a film-metaphor of "a human slaughter-house," absorbing into itself the memory of bloody repressions on the part of the autocracy. Here already were not the simple "contemplative" *contrasts* of *Palace and Fortress,* but already—though still crude and still "hand-made"—a consistent and conscious attempt at *juxtaposition.*

Juxtaposition, striving to tell about an execution of workers not only in representations, but further also through a generalized "plastic turn of speech," approaching a verbal image of "a bloody slaughter-house."

In *Potemkin* three *separate* close-ups of three different marble lions in different attitudes were merged into *one* roaring lion and, moreover, in another *film-dimension*—an embodiment of a metaphor: *"The very stones roar!"*

Griffith shows us an ice-break rushing along. Somewhere in the center of the splintering ice lies, unconscious, Anna (Lillian Gish). Leaping from ice-cake to ice-cake comes David (Richard Barthelmess) to save her.

But the parallel *race of the ice-break* and of *the human actions* are nowhere brought together by him in a unified image of *"a human flood,"* a mass of people bursting their fetters, a mass of people rushing onward in an all-shattering inundation, as there is, for example, in the finale of *Mother,* by Gorky-Zarkhi-Pudovkin.

Of course, on this path excesses also occur, and also bald failures; of course, in more than a few examples these were good intentions defeated by shortcomings in compositional principles and by insufficient reasons for them in the context: then, in place of a flashing unity of image, a miserable trope is left on the level of an unrealized fusion, on the level of a mechanical pasting together of the type of "Came the rain and two students."

But thus or otherwise the dual *parallel rows* characteristic of Griffith ran in our cinema on the way to realizing themselves in the future *unity of the montage image* at first as a whole series of plays of montage comparisons, montage metaphors, montage puns.

These were more or less stormy floods, all serving to make clearer and clearer the final main task in the montage side of creative work—the creation in it of an inseparable domination of the *image*, of *the unified montage image*, of *the montage-built image, embodying the theme*, as this was achieved in the "Odessa steps" of *Potemkin*, in the "attack of the Kappel Division" of *Chapayev*, in the hurricane of *Storm Over Asia*, in the Dnieper prologue of *Ivan*, more weakly—the landing of *We Are from Kronstadt*, with new strength in "Bozhenko's funeral" in *Shchors*, in Vertov's *Three Songs About Lenin*, in the "attack of the knights" in *Alexander Nevsky. . . .* This is the glorious *independent* path of the Soviet cinema—the path of the creation of the *montage image-episode*, the *montage image-event*, the *montage image-film in its entirety*—of equal rights, of equal influence and equal responsibility in the perfect film—on an equal footing with the *image of the hero*, with the *image of man, and of the people*.

Our conception of montage has far outgrown the classic dualistic montage esthetic of Griffith, symbolized by the two never-convergent parallel racers, interweaving the thematically variegated strips with a view towards the mutual intensification of entertainment, tension and tempi.

For us montage became a means of achieving *a unity of a higher order*—a means *through the montage image of achieving an organic embodiment of a single idea conception, embracing all elements, parts, details of the film-work.*

And thus understood, it seems considerably broader than an understanding of narrowly cinematographic montage; thus understood, it carries much to fertilize and enrich our understanding of art methods in general.

And in conformity with this principle of our montage, *unity and diversity* are both sounded as principles.

Montage removes its last contradictions by abolishing dualist contradictions and mechanical parallelism between the realms of sound and sight in what we understand as audio-visual ("vertical") montage.

It finds its final artistic unity in the resolution of the problems of the unity of audio-visual synthesis—problems that are now being decided by us, problems that are not even on the agenda of American researches.

Stereoscopic and color film are being realized before our eyes.

And the moment is drawing near when, not only through the method of montage, but also through the synthesis of *idea, the drama of acting man, the screen picture, sound, three-dimension and color*, that same great law of *unity and diversity*—lying at the base of our thinking, at the base of our philosophy, and to an equal degree penetrating the montage method from its tiniest link to the fullness of montage imagery in the film as a whole—passes into *a unity of the whole screen image*.

Everett Carter   (essay date 1960)

SOURCE: "Cultural History Written with Lightning: The Significance of *The Birth of a Nation*," *American Quarterly*, Vol. XII, No. 3, Fall, 1960, pp. 347-57.

[*In the following essay, Carter points out thematic flaws in* The Birth of a Nation *which prevent the film from being an artistic success.*]

On February 20, 1915, David Wark Griffith's long film, **The Clansman**, was shown in New York City. One of the spectators was Thomas Dixon, the author of the novel from which it was taken, who was moved by the power of the motion picture to shout to the wildly applauding spectators that its title would have to be changed. To match the picture's greatness, he suggested, its name should be **The Birth of a Nation**. Only by a singular distortion of meaning could the film be interpreted as the story of a country's genesis; the birth it did herald was of an American industry and an American art; any attempt to define the cinema and its impact upon American life must take into account this classic movie. For with the release of **The Birth of a Nation** "significant motion picture history begins" [Seymour Stern, "**The Birth of a Nation** in Retrospect," *International Photographer*]. Its prestige became enormous. It was the first picture to be played at the White House, where Woodrow Wilson was reported to have said: "it is like writing history with lightning." By January 1916 it had given 6,266 performances in the area of greater New York alone. If we conservatively estimate that five hundred patrons saw each performance, we arrive at the astounding total of over three million residents of and visitors to New York who saw the picture, and forever viewed themselves and their country's history through its colorations. And not only does significant motion picture history begin, but most of the problems of the art's place in our culture begin too. The picture projects one of the most persistent cultural illusions; it presents vividly and dramatically the ways in which a whole people have reacted to their history; its techniques in the narrowest sense are the fully realized techniques of the pictorial aspects of the motion picture; in the widest sense, its techniques are a blend of the epical and the symbolically realistic, and each part of this mixture has developed into a significant genre of cinematic art.

Griffith was a Kentuckian, a devout believer in Southern values, and these values, he was certain, were embodied in *The Clansman,* a sentimental novel of the Reconstruction which had appeared in 1905, had been widely read, had been seen in dramatic form throughout the South, and whose author [Thomas Dixon] had dedicated it "To the memory of a Scotch-Irish leader of the South, my Uncle, Colonel Leroy McAfee, Grand Titan of the Invisible Empire Ku Klux Klan." In his introduction, Dixon went on to describe his theme: "How the young South, led by the reincarnated souls of the Clansmen of Old Scotland, went forth under this cover and against overwhelming odds, daring exile, imprisonment, and a felon's death, and saved the life of a people, forms one of the most dramatic chapters in the history of the Aryan race." This strong suggestion that the South's struggle is a racial epic, involving all the people of one blood in their defense against a common ancestral enemy, became, as we shall see, a major influence upon Griffith's conception of his cinematic theme. And, in addition, the novel in so many ways served as what would later be called a "treatment" from which the story would be filmed, that we must examine the book closely before we can understand the significance of the film.

The Clansman told the story of "Thaddeus Stevens' bold attempt to Africanize the ten great states of the American Union . . ." It interpreted the history of the Reconstruction as the great Commoner's vengeance motivated partly by economics: the destruction of his Pennsylvania iron mills by Lee's army; partly by religion: in his parlor there was "a picture of a nun . . . he had always given liberally to an orphanage conducted by a Roman Catholic sisterhood"; but mainly by lust: his housekeeper was "a mulatto, a woman of extraordinary animal beauty . . ." who became, through her power over Austin Stoneman (the fictional name for Stevens) "the presiding genius of National legislation." Stoneman was shown in private conference with Lincoln, whose words in his Charleston debate with Douglas were directly quoted: "I believe there is a physical difference between the white and black races which will forever forbid their living together on terms of political and social equality." Stoneman's instruments in the South were all described as animals, demonstrating that the Civil War was fought to defend civilization against the barbaric and bestial. Silas Lynch, the carpet-bagger, "had evidently inherited the full physical characteristics of the Aryan race, while his dark yellowish eyes beneath his heavy brows glowed with the brightness of the African jungle." The Negro leader, Aleck, had a nose "broad and crushed flat against his face," and jaws "strong and angular, mouth wide, and lips thick, curling back from rows of solid teeth set obliquely . . ." The Cameron family of the Old South were the principal victims; Gus, a renegade Negro, ravished Marion Cameron, the sixteen-year-old ". . . universal favourite . . ." who embodied "the grace, charm, and tender beauty of the Southern girl . . ."; Silas Lynch attempted to violate Elsie Stoneman, the betrothed of Ben Cameron. The actual rape was a climax of a series of figurative violations of

the South by the North, one of which was the entry of Stoneman into the black legislature, carried by two Negroes who made "a curious symbolic frame for the chalk-white passion of the old Commoner's face. No sculptor ever dreamed a more sinister emblem of the corruption of a race of empire-builders than this group. Its black figures, wrapped in the night of four thousand years of barbarism, squatted there the 'equal' of their master, grinning at his forms of Justice, the evolution of forty centuries of Aryan genius." These figurative and literal ravishments provoked the formation of the Ku Klux Klan, whose like ". . . the world had not seen since the Knights of the Middle Ages rode on their Holy Crusades." The Klan saved Elsie, revenged Marion, brought dismay to the Negro, the carpet-bagger and the scallawag and, in the final words of the book, ". . . Civilisation has been saved, and the South redeemed from shame."

The picture followed the book faithfully in plot, character, motivation and theme, and became a visualization of the whole set of irrational cultural assumptions which may be termed the "Plantation Illusion." The Illusion has many elements, but it is based primarily upon a belief in a golden age of the antebellum South, an age in which feudal agrarianism provided the good life for wealthy, leisured, kindly, aristocratic owner and loyal, happy, obedient slave. The enormous disparity between this conception and the reality has been the subject of Gaines's *The Southern Plantation* and Stampp's *The Peculiar Institution.* But our concern is not with the reality but with what people have thought and felt about that reality; this thinking and feeling is the Illusion, and the stuff of the history of sensibility. The Illusion was embodied in Kennedy's *Swallow Barn* (1832), developed through Carruther's *The Cavaliers of Virginia* (1834) and firmly fixed in the national consciousness by Stephen Foster's "Old Folks at Home" (1851), "My Old Kentucky Home" and "Massa's in the Cold, Cold Ground" (1852), and "Old Black Joe," songs which nostalgically describe a "longing for that old plantation . . ." In 1905 Dixon summarized it in the assertion that the South before the Civil War was ruled by an "aristocracy founded on brains, culture, and blood," the "old fashioned dream of the South" which "but for the Black curse . . . could be today the garden of the world."

This was the image realized almost immediately at the beginning of ***The Birth of a Nation.*** A scene of Southern life before the Civil War is preceded by the title: "In the Southland, life runs in a quaintly way that is no more." A primitive cart is shown trundling up a village street, filled with laughing Negroes; there is further merriment as a few children fall from the cart and are pulled up into it; then appears a scene of a young aristocrat helping his sister into a carriage; she is in white crinoline and carries a parasol; the young Southerner helps her gallantly from the carriage, and the title reads: "Margaret Cameron, daughter of the old South, trained in manners of the old school." With the two levels of feudal society established, the scene is then of the porch of the plantation house. Dr. and Mrs. Cameron are rocking; he has a kitten in his arms, and puppies are shown playing at his feet. A pickaninny runs happily in and out among the classic columns while the Camerons look indulgently on; a very fat and very black servant claps her hands with glee.

A corollary of this aspect of the Southern Illusion, one might even say a necessary part of it, is the corresponding vision of the North as the land of coldness, harshness, mechanical inhumanity; expressed most generously, it is the description of the North as "Head" and the South as the warm human "Heart" which was Sidney Lanier's major metaphor in his Reconstruction poems. Although Lanier had called for the reunion of the heart and head, a modern Southerner, John Crowe Ransom, has scolded Lanier for preaching reconciliation when, Ransom said, what should have been preached was the "contumacious resistance" of the warm, agrarian South against the harsh industrialism and rationalism of the North. *The Clansman* had emphasized the contrast between warm South and cold North by rechristening Thaddeus Stevens, "Thaddeus *Stoneman*"—the man of stone; the radical republican who is the obdurate villain of the picture. He has a clubfoot and moves angularly and mechanically; his house, his dress, are gloomy, dark, cold, as opposed to the warmth and lightness of the Southern planation garments and scene. In the novel, Dixon had identified him as the owner of Pennsylvania iron mills, and Griffith took the hint, giving him clothes to wear and expressions to assume which, in their harshness and implacability, suggest the unyielding metal. The sense of commercialism, combined with rigidity and pious hypocrisy is identified with the North, too, by showing the presumed beginnings of slavery in America. We see a Puritan preacher sanctimoniously praying while two of the elect arrange the sale of a cringing slave; the following scene is of Abolitionists demanding the end of slavery; the grouping of the two scenes, the dress and features of the characters in both, make the point strongly that these are the same people; the montage is a dramatization of Ben Cameron's assertion in the novel, that "our slaves were stolen from Africa by Yankee skippers . . . It was not until 1836 that Massachusetts led in Abolition—not until all her own slaves had been sold to us at a profit . . ."

In these opening scenes, too, we have the complete cast of characters of the Plantation Ideal. The Camerons are shown as they go down to the fields to mingle with the happy and trusting slaves. A title tells us that "in the two hour interval for dinner given in their working day from six to six the slaves enjoy themselves"; then appears a view of slaves clapping hands and dancing. Ben Cameron places his hand paternally upon the shoulders of one, and shakes hands with another who bobs in a perfect frenzy of grateful loyalty: in several seconds a wonderful summary of a hundred years of romantic tradition in which "a beautiful felicity of racial contact has been presented, not as occasional but as constant; an imperious kindness on the part of the whites, matched

by obsequious devotion on the part of the blacks" [F. P. Gaines, *The Southern Plantation*].

The Plantation Ideal had to explain the obvious fact that during the war and Reconstruction, many Negroes fought with the Union and greeted Emancipation with joy. The Illusion protected itself by explaining that the true, southern, fullblooded Negro remained loyal throughout and after the war. It expanded the truth of individual instances of this kind into a general rule. In the Civil War sequences of **The Birth of a Nation,** the Camerons' slaves are shown cheering the parade of the Confederate soldiers as they march off to defend them against their freedom. The fat Negro cook and the others of the household staff are described as "The Faithful Souls"; they weep at Southern defeat and Northern triumph; they rescue Dr. Cameron from his arrest by Reconstruction militia.

While the Illusion persistently maintained the loyalty of the true slave, it premised the disaffection of other Negroes upon several causes, all of them explicable within the framework of the Plantation Ideal. The major explanation was the corruption of the Negro by the North. The freed Negro, the Union soldier, is a monster of ingratitude, a renegade from the feudal code, and only evil can be expected of him. The picture shows The Faithful Soul deriding one such abomination; the title reads, "You northern black trash, don't you try any of your airs on me." And a little later, we see her lips saying, and then read on the screen, "Those free niggers from the north sho' am crazy." The second explanation was that the mulatto, the person of mixed blood, was the arch-villain in the tragedy of the South. Stoneman, the radical republican leader, is shown, as he was in the novel, under the spell of his mulatto housekeeper. A scene of Stoneman lasciviously fondling his mistress is preceded by the title: "The great leader's weakness that is to blight a nation." The mistress, in turn, has as a lover another mulatto, Silas Lynch, who is described as the principal agent in Stoneman's plans to "Africanise" the South. This dark part of the Plantation Illusion is further represented in the twin climaxes of the picture, both of which are attempted sexual assaults on blonde white girls, one by a Northern Negro, and the other by the mulatto, Silas Lynch.

The sexual terms into which this picture translated the violation of the Southern Illusion by the North underscores the way in which the film incorporates one of the most vital of the forces underlying the Illusion—the obscure, bewildering complex of sexual guilt and fear which the Ideal never overtly admits, but which are, as Stampp and Cash and Myrdal have pointed out, deeply interwoven into the Southern sensibility. The mulatto, while he occasionally would be the offspring of the lowest class of white woman with Negroes, much more commonly was the result of the debasement of the Negro woman by the white man, and, not infrequently, by the most aristocratic of the characters in the plantation conception. At the very least, then, the deep convictions of the Protestant South about the nature of sin would cause the Southern Illusion to regard a living, visible evidence of a parent's lust as evil in itself, and at the most, and worst, and most debilitating, as a reminder of the burden of guilt the white must bear in the record of sexual aggression against the Negro. *The Birth of a Nation* gives all aspects of these sexual fears and guilts full expression. Typically, the burden of guilt is discharged by making the mulatto the evil force in the picture, evincing both the bestial, animal sensuality of the unrestrained Negro, and the perverted intellectual powers of the white. And the full-blooded, but renegade, black justifies any excess of the Klan, by accomplishing that final most dreaded act of the sexual drama, the violation of the blonde "little sister." The book had made the rape actual: "A single tiger-spring," it narrated, "and the black claws of the beast sank into the soft white throat." The picture shows us the little sister as she jumps off a cliff to escape dishonor; but a scene of Gus, kneeling blackly over the white-clad, broken body, makes the sexual point without the overt act. And this point is further reinforced by a description of Lynch's attempts to possess Elsie Stoneman, by a portrayal of the passage of the first law of the black Reconstruction legislature legalizing miscegenation, and by a scene of Negroes who carry signs reading "Equal rights, equal marriage."

The descriptions of Gus as "tiger-like" and of Stoneman's mistress as a leopard, brings us to the last element of the Plantation Illusion—the defense of the system on the basis of the essential non-humanity of the Negro. The book had been blatant in its statement of this position; the picture projects this attitude by its shots of the eyes of mulatto and Negro displaying animal lust and ferocity, and by its view of Gus as a slinking animal, waiting, crouching, springing.

As the record of a cultural illusion, then, *The Birth of a Nation* is without equal. Furthermore, it is the film to which, as the historian of the art declares, "much of subsequent filmic progress owes its inspiration." In order to understand its significance, one has to remind oneself of the nature of the motion picture art. It is not an art of external events and the people who perform them; it is an art of the camera and the film. Before Griffith, the camera was treated as a fixed position, much like the spectator of the drama. The interpretation was by the actors, by their bodies, by their faces, by physical objects and by the settings before which these performed. Griffith made the ordering and interpretation—the art, in brief—one of the location, the angle, the movement of the camera and of the juxtaposition of the images the camera records by means of cutting and arranging these images to bring out their significance. An example of the first technique—camera position—was the famous scene of Sherman's march to the sea. The camera shows the serpentine line of Union troops in the distance, winding over the landscape. War is distant; it is simply a move of masses over territory; the camera turns slowly until it includes, in the left foreground the figures of a weeping mother and child. Im-

mediately a perspective is achieved; what was remote and inhuman becomes close and humanized; the human implications of such mass movements are illustrated clearly, sharply, poignantly simply by the perspective of the camera.

An example of the second aspect of the purely filmic technique was Griffith's juxtaposition of the two parallel scenes in the introduction to the Plantation Ideal: Negro cart and white carriage. Alone the first shot would be at worst meaningless, at best a bit of atmosphere; the second would serve merely to introduce two characters who might have been presented in an infinite variety of ways. Placed together, both scenes become significant forms because of the two elements they have in common: means of transportation, and the perfect fitness of each group of characters to that means; the juxtaposition thus serves to summarize the feudal theory—the rightness of each part of society in its place.

A second aspect of this editorial technique—the cutting and arranging of images—was also brought to its fullness of possibility in *The Birth of a Nation* after Griffith had experimented with it in earlier films. This was the intercutting of parallel scenes occurring at different locations in space, but at the same location in time, each of which has a bearing upon the other, with the meanings of both carefully interwoven, and with the tensions of either relieved only when the two are finally brought together. The famous example of this, an example which has been followed faithfully from then on, was the intercutting of shots of Lynch's attempted forced marriage to Elsie Stoneman with shots of the gathering of the Klan which will effect her rescue. A series of six shots of Lynch and Elsie is superseded by seven shots of the gathering of the Klan; then two single shots of the Klan and two of the attempted ravishment are quickly alternated; fourteen shots of Lynch and Elsie are followed by one of the Klan; a shot of long duration during which the Elsie-Lynch struggle becomes more intense is then followed by seven shots of the Klan's ride to the rescue; and so it goes until both sequences are joined in space when the Klan finally reaches Elsie. As an early critic described the meaning of this achievement: "Every little series of pictures . . . symbolizes a sentiment, a passion, or an emotion. Each successive series, similar yet different, carries the emotion to the next higher power, till at last, when both of the parallel emotions have attained the nth power, so to speak, they meet in the final swift shock of victory and defeat" [Henry MacMahon, "The Art of the Movies," New York *Times*]. To these epoch-making achievements of camera placement, significant juxtaposition and intercutting, Griffith added the first uses of night photography, of soft-focus photography and moving camera shots, and the possibilities of film art were born.

And with it were born most of the problems of those of us who wish to take the art seriously. For what can we make of so awkward a combination of sentimental content and superb technique? We must admit, first of all, that the effect of the film's detachable content was pernicious. It served the ugliest purposes of pseudo-art—giving people a reflection of their own prejudices, sentimental at best, vicious at worst, and a restatement of their easy explanations of the terrible complexities of their history as Americans. It demonstrated how easily and how successfully the art could pander to the sentimentality of the public, how effectively and profitably it could transfer melodrama from the stage and false values from the novel. The enormous commercial success of the film at a time when men like Louis B. Mayer, later to become the head of the greatest studio, were starting their careers as exhibitors, cannot have but fixed the melodramatic, the cheap and obviously emotional, as the index to the potential economic success of a film.

But it showed, as well, two directions in which the film would move: one is in the direction of the epic, and the other in what may be termed "symbolic realism." Its move in the first direction, of course, was an immense and shocking perversion. Griffith apparently sensed the truth that great epics are involved with the destiny of whole races and nations, and had seized upon Dixon's hint that the South's struggle was part of an "Aryan" saga. The Klan was described in the book, and on the screen, as part of an "Aryan" tradition. The term is used again at a crucial point in the screen narrative, when a mob of Negro soldiers attack the embattled whites. The battle of the Caucasians, the title on the screen tells us, is "in defense of their Aryan birthright." Griffith improved upon Dixon in emphasizing the "epical" quality of the story: before they ride, the Klansmen are shown partaking of a primitive barbaric rite; they dip a flag in the blood of the blonde white virgin before they go out to destroy.

The picture is no epic, but rather an epic *manqué*: partial, fragmentary and therefore necessarily inartistic; in attempting to be the saga of a shattered fragment of a nation, in attempting to erect upon false premises a series of racial responses reputedly instinctive, it was immediately self-defeating. An epic is justified in its radical simplifications, its stereotypes, its primitive terms, by its appeal to a real national unity of belief, and by its power to reinforce that unity. The over-simplifications of *The Birth of a Nation,* however, are not the controlled and ordering images of an art based upon a set of beliefs to which an entire people subscribe, images which emotionally order and control the world of that people's experience; instead it is the projection of images of disorder, an attack upon cultural and moral unity; the images of the film are the debilitating images of a false myth, a pseudo-epic.

The picture did, however, provide another cinematic genre with many of its basic situations. In 1908, with the "Bronco Billie" series, the Western setting had begun to be realized as particularly suitable to the enactment of the drama of simple primitive faiths and national aspirations. After *The Birth of a Nation,* its

images of elemental struggle and black and white moral values, and its techniques for making these exciting and significant, were transferred to the "Western." The epic qualities of *The Birth of a Nation* were false and vicious because they impinge upon contemporary reality, and oversimplify both actual history and contemporary social circumstance; transferred to a realm of pure mythology—the Western scene of Richard Dix, *Stage Coach* and *High Noon,* and to the moral blackness of outlaw and moral whiteness of law, these simplifications, and the techniques for pictorializing them, have given us something much more artistically valid.

But more important, *The Birth of a Nation* pointed in the second, and the major direction of the motion picture art. This direction we can call "symbolic realism"—the apparent imitation of actuality which brings out the symbolic or representational meaning of that apparent reality. This "significant" or "symbolic" realism was demonstrated to be effective in the portrayal of either deep psychological or wide universal meanings. To take a rather titillating example in *The Birth of a Nation* of the first kind of surface realism arranged to illustrate unexpressed psychological truths: Lillian Gish plays an innocent love scene with the hero, returns to her room, and seats herself dreamily on the bed; the bed happens to be a four-poster each of whose posts is almost embarrassingly suggestive of masculinity; she dreamily embraces and caresses the bedpost. Some years later, Greta Garbo, as Queen Christina, after three days in bed with John Gilbert, used the bedpost in similar fashion. More significant, perhaps, is the way in which images were juxtaposed in this pioneering picture so as to bring out the universal significance of the concrete instance. The view of the army winding past the mother and child to symbolize the agony and displacements of war; the cart and the carriage as symbols of feudal levels of society; Stoneman's clubfoot representing the maimed wrathful impotence of the mechanical North; little sister adorning her coarse post-bellum dress with a bit of cotton rescued from the destroyed plantation fields—these were but a few of the large number of symbolic extensions of the surface, and they pointed the way toward the great documentary symbolic realism of Flaherty, and the imaginative symbolic realism of *The Informer, Sous les Toits de Paris, The River* and the whole run of wonderful Italian neo-realistic films: *Open City, Paisan, The Bicycle Thief* and *La Strada.*

A preliminary examination of a significant motion picture, then, has yielded some profit as well as some disappointment. The disappointment is largely in the failure of this pioneering picture to measure up to standards of artistic greatness: its failure to achieve that fusion of content and technique which together make up a great work of art. Its failure is doubly disappointing, because it involves an inversion and debasement of epic powers in which those powers pander to popular taste instead of attempting to reach a whole vision, sinewed with moral responsibility. But in this very failure lies some of its profit for us as students of American civilization; better than any other art work, it summarizes every aspect of the Plantation Illusion which is so vigorous a force in the history of American sensibility; for the student of the art form, it will demonstrate the beginnings of techniques which both rescue *The Birth of a Nation* from ugliness, and which, when used to embody more aesthetically malleable content, give us the possibilities of the art of the movie.

Bosley Crowther (essay date 1967)

SOURCE: "Intolerence: 1916," in *The Great Films: Fifty Golden Years of Motion Pictures,* G. P. Putnam's Sons, 1967, pp. 17-20.

[*In the following review, Crowther praises* Intolerance *for its ambitious scope and complex editing while acknowledging the film's failure to rise above melodrama.*]

Would success spoil D. W. Griffith?

That thought surely never occurred to anyone at the time *The Birth of a Nation* was vaunting the fame of the great director throughout the land. Such a triumph must certainly have seemed evidence of his infallibility. And, of course, people were not then as knowing about the evanescence of screen success as they have since become. But this question has been a speculation of students in later years: Did the great success of *The Birth of a Nation* generate in Griffith such a faith in the responsiveness of the public and in his own capabilities that he was moved to extend his virtuosity in a massive film that strangely proved his undoing?

This may seem a surprising speculation to anyone who has been told only that Griffith was *the* great creative genius of motion pictures in the early days, or to anyone not familiar with his sad decline in a matter of a few years. And it may seem off-key and infelicitous as a prefatory note to this review of what is generally regarded as his greatest (some even call it *the* greatest) of all films.

But felicitous or not, it is a question that inevitably occurs as we come to consider the next project that Griffith undertook. For the evidence is that the assurance *The Birth of a Nation* fired in him, and the parallel indignation caused him by the demonstrations against it in the North, charged him with such a confusion of vanity, vindictiveness and zeal that he was roused to make a film of such proportions that his critics would be overwhelmed. This was his great *Intolerance,* which ironically turned out to be the longtime peak of cinematic creation and the bane of Griffith's career.

Compared to *The Birth of a Nation,* this extraordinarily long and complex film is far and away more ambitious, involved and cinematically mature. Where *The Birth of a Nation* offers a fairly unified story line in which dramatic action is developed within a frame of history and time, *Intolerance* embraces four stories from four different periods of history, each separately evolved and carried forward to a dramatic climax of its own. Yet the unfolding of these four stories is done simultaneously, with cutting from one to another as they go along, so that they all reach their awesome climaxes in one great interweaving of action in the last tempestuous reel. The aim is to show the working of bigotry and injustice throughout time and to make a plea for tolerance, Christian charity and the brotherhood of man.

The construction of this elaborate picture looks comparatively awkward today, raw and elemental in conception and continuity. The stories are crudely motivated, and the development of the characters is weak. The film is mainly melodrama on an involved and spectacular scale. The strength of it lies in the sensations of the occurrence of exciting events and of the viewer's participation in them that Griffith stirs with his command of silent cinema.

Yet so tangled and complicated were the strands of its narrative to audiences uneducated to this kind of cross-cut cinema that it was hard for them to follow its dramatic intricacies for three hours or to grasp the philosophical intentions of Griffith's abstract theme.

As a consequence, though hailed by critics, it failed to be a popular success when it was offered in 1916. It was, in fact, the first big "turkey" that the expanding movie industry turned up. This callous rejection by the public caused Griffith to be even more confused than he was by the criticism that *The Birth of a Nation* drew. He became disillusioned and embittered. He was also financially strained, since he put most of his profits from *The Birth of a Nation* into this mammoth film. It cost more than $2,500,000, a fabulous sum in those days.

The basis of this tremendous project was a modest scenario that Griffith wrote: a drama of social injustice called *The Mother and the Law,* about a working-class mother whose baby was taken from her and her young husband unjustly thrown in jail because of the heartless machinations of certain self-righteous meddlers of the upper class. It was the sort of plaintive story popular in those days, which insinuated social criticism with unblushing sentiment.

Griffith was set to shoot it when the triumph of his Civil War film brought upon him an expanding comprehension of his destiny. He wished now to do something mighty, in keeping with his new-found fame, and to humiliate the detractors who accused him of bigotry. He felt those who criticized his picture and wanted to have it suppressed were the actual bigots, blind and intolerant. In this frame of mind, he got an idea of what to do with *The Mother and the Law.* He would make this fervid story the central strand of a skein of four stories that would be woven together to show how hypocrisy, persecution and religious hatred have always afflicted and tended to destroy civilized men.

To go with this homely exposure of the contemporary oppression of the working class, he decided to have an account of the overthrow of Belshazzar and the destruction of ancient Babylon by the armies of Cyrus of Persia, with Cyrus instigated to this violence by the vindictiveness and treachery of a cabal of Babylonian priests; a drama of the religious persecution of the Huguenots by Catherine de Medici in sixteenth-century France; and, as a line of familiar spiritual reference, a tabloid account of the life of Jesus Christ.

Obviously, something would be needed to provide an introductory thought with which to arrest the audience and serve as a binder and reminder from time to time. For this Griffith hit upon the idea of Eternal Motherhood. Thus, he started his picture with a cameo shot of a mother rocking a cradle, over which is superimposed these lines from Walt Whitman: "Endlessly rocks the cradle, Uniter of Here and Hereafter—Chanter of Sorrows." This simple iconograph serves as a "chapter heading" for the separate dramas and as an occasional transition piece. Lillian Gish plays the Mother.

Today, this device seems stiff and pompous, literary and pretentious in the style of sentimental novels. But that was Griffith's taste. He was mawkish and moralistic, but he also had an exceptionally keen and accurate "camera eye" that accounted for some strikingly natural and trenchant passages.

For instance, he throws us off balance very early in his first episode—the drama of the daughter of a factory worker whose innocent, fun-loving proclivities are wickedly opposed by the blue-nosed sister of the boss of the factory in which her father works—when he breaks away from a romantic and bouncy pictorial style to give a few sharply realistic scenes of a factory strike. This incident is weakly motivated (the workers go on strike because the boss has reduced their wages in order to support his sister's moral crusade), but it has a solid and authentic quality. It could be a recording of the seething labor troubles of the day.

In its substance, the whole romantic drama of the cruelly treated factory girl—the Dear One, as Griffith coyly calls her—is on the preposterous side. It is full of contrivance and coincidence as it recounts how this poor girl loses her father, moves to the nearby city, marries The Boy with whom she was in love back home and has to fend for herself and her baby against vice elements and the relentless do-gooders when her husband is unjustly put in jail.

Likewise, the fustian behavior of and relations among the characters in the Babylonian episode and in the grossly stilted drama of the tyranny of Catherine de Medici must be blinked at—or taken as amusing—in full-value payment for the still-overwhelming explosions of spectacle and action in these episodes.

The Babylonian section is undeniably the most ingenious and impressive in the film. For it, Griffith had constructed a mammoth outdoor set to represent the towers and temples of the city of Babylon. Huge portals adorned with massive sculptures, walls 100 feet high and great vaulted Oriental chambers distinguished this unprecedented facility for spectacle. The conception and dynamism of it were on a scale that was to set the style, and the high mark, for future spectacle films. The elements of personal involvement that Griffith devised for this episode are neither profound nor convincing. It is the clashing, deadly action when the forces of Cyrus assault the walls of the city that is powerful—that and the eye-popping luxury and eroticism displayed at Belshazzar's feast.

Most unsubtle and amusing about the French Huguenot episode is the swaggering arrogance with which a busty Catherine steamrollers a simpering Charles IX into ordering the St. Bartholomew's Day massacre. But once the maneuver is launched and the French soldiers are pouring through the streets, battering down doors and finally nabbing the pretty heroine, the action is fierce and fine.

As for story of Jesus, it is told, or represented, in solemn tableaux that are conventional illustrations of incidents in the last few years of the life of the Messiah.

The ultimate greatness of *Intolerance* is achieved in the momentum with which Griffith builds up the tension and excitement of all the separate dramas at the end—the Mountain Girl racing in her chariot to warn Bel-shazzar that he has been betrayed; the fiancé of the heroine struggling through the crowded Paris streets to try to rescue her before the Huguenot-killers reach her house; Christ groaning toward Calvary; and the Dear One speeding in an automobile to catch a train on which the governor is riding and get a pardon for her husband who is about to be hanged. These actions are flowed together as though they were all parts of one great conglomerate "chase."

It is this aspect of *Intolerance,* this demonstration of how to achieve illusion on several levels that is its genius. At the same time, it must be observed that its clearly conglomerate character is esthetically inharmonious and overwrought. In his great burst of power and ostentation, Griffith tried to do too many things with too little awareness of the necessity of cohesive form and style. He tried to equate a modern social drama and its implications of reality with the romantic and purely escapist exaggerations of pseudo-historical spectacle. He tried, in his surge of ambition, to blend two distinct types of films, apparently without an awareness of how distinctly different they are.

But throughout he is always the master of details that strike the eye and fire the imagination with concentrated emotional pull or shock. Scores of these have the distinction of being models for subsequent clichés—such things as the iron door banging behind The Boy as he is taken into jail and the little window in the door snapping shut with a shuddering finality; or the working of the trapdoor on the gallows being demonstrated by a close-up of the knife being drawn across cords, a simple detail which is repeated to develop great suspense when we are waiting breathlessly for The Boy to be hanged; or the close-up of the hand of the Dear One groping feebly across the floor for a discarded sock of her baby after the child has been taken from her; or the close shot of one of the Persian besiegers having his head completely lopped off by a swinging sword and a bulge of viscera spouting out through his gaping neck!

Inevitably, Griffith's disposition to moralize and preach comes out in an idealistic and grandiloquent epilogue. Having brought his separate illustrations of the evil of intolerance to an end (and having let only one, the modern story, conclude happily for the people involved), he envisions "the day when cannons and prison bars wrought in the fires of intolerance" will no longer prevail and "perfect love shall bring peace forever." A shot of battlefields, a shot of a prison, and then a dissolve to fields of flowers as a superimposed subtitle reads, "Instead of prison walls bloom flowery fields," and we see children playing happily on a grassy slope, clouds drifting serenely in the sky—and, as a final reminder, the mother rocking the cradle endlessly. . . .

Unfortunately for Griffith, unfortunately for the world, this elaborate sentiment for peace was disconcerting to those who saw the film. For even as *Intolerance* was bidding to attract middling audiences, the propaganda drums were beating to pull this country into the First World War. This was but one more reason for the public indifference to the film.

Griffith's disappointment and intransigence, his allegiance to an attitude and style that became "old-fashioned" and unpopular with youthful audiences after the war, arrested his growth beyond this picture. He did make others in which ideas and some scenes reflected his bold imagination and his command of the medium. The rescue of the drowning heroine from an ice-clogged river in *Way Down East* (1920); the stark, poetic beauty in *Broken Blossoms* (1919); the dignity of his last, *The Struggle* (1931), attest to the fact that Griffith was expressive to the end. But he was haunted by the failure of *Intolerance*. It broke his faith and his heart.

George E. Dorris (essay date 1967)

SOURCE: "Griffith in Retrospect," in *Man and Movies,* edited by W. R. Robinson, Louisiana State University Press, 1967, pp. 153-60.

[*In the following essay, Dorris looks back thoughtfully at Griffith's oeuvre.*]

When the Museum of Modern Art announced its D. W. Griffith retrospective in the spring of 1965, I decided to attend the complete series. But I had no real idea of what I was letting myself in for. Like most filmgoers, I knew the legend of the shattered titan, living out the last years of his life as a virtual recluse. I had seen *The Birth of a Nation* and *Intolerance* and been moved by the beauty, the dramatic sweep, and the emotional power of these remarkable films. But of Griffith's other work I knew nothing. I had no prejudice against silent films, having admired many of the classic Russian and German silents as well as a few French and American ones. But, with the exception of the Eisenstein films, I had rarely seen an extensive showing of a single director and never of one who produced mainly silent films. Therefore I was unprepared for what I discovered during those three months when at least twice a week I descended to the small theater in the basement of the museum.

Like any retrospective showing of an important figure, the Griffith cycle tested the art, the artist, and the audience. At times all were found wanting, but it remained a finely conceived tribute to a true artist, although too often it brought out flaws in the audience which were unconnected with the flaws in the artist. From it emerged, finally, an understanding of Griffith's art, still too often misunderstood, and a feeling of pity that such a man could be forced into silence and humiliation by the Hollywood studios and financiers; when he died in 1948, it had been seventeen years since he had completed his last film, *The Struggle,* which revealed his powers virtually unimpaired. What remains is the monument he created, the films themselves, for his greatness is to be found not only in the few famous ones—*The Birth of a Nation, Intolerance, Broken Blossoms, Way Down East, Orphans of the Storm*—but in nearly all he touched.

Griffith remains one of the few masters of the film. From the often primitive one-reelers (technically and artistically primitive), the form he inherited from Edwin S. Porter, he created a style which transcended the anecdotal nature of the twelve-minute film. As he developed actors sensitized to his style, subtleties of detail, of characterization, and of form emerged. Between 1909 and 1913 he built the nucleus of a film repertory company—Blanche Sweet, Mae Marsh, Lillian Gish, Henry Walthall, Robert Harron—performers on whom he could experiment emotionally as his cameraman Billy Bitzer was experimenting technically. At the same time Griffith was also experimenting with cutting, creating the film as an artistic entity. Between *The Lonely Villa, A Corner in Wheat,* and *The Usurer* (1909-10) and *The Lonedale Operator, The Goddess of Sagebrush Gulch,* and *The Musketeers of Pig Alley* (1911-12), as his touch became surer, the films became more complex and emotionally richer. Eventually Griffith overcame most of the problems inherent in the one-reel form, creating suspense, humor, and pathos by his handling of the story and of his developing actors and by his manipulation of the techniques of film.

In these early films many of the traits of the later Griffith can be seen; suspense, humor, and pathos were to remain his stock-intrade. Most of his later films culminate in one version or another of the big chase, however transformed in *Way Down East* or *Isn't Life Wonderful*. Equally typical is a gentle, sometimes pastoral, humor, from the first intellectual's discovery of weapons in *Man's Genesis* (1911) to the warm picture of rural life in *True Heart Susie* (1919). Comedy of the Sennett or Chaplin variety was not Griffith's strength, but his gentler vein could be warm and effective. The pathos speaks for itself, growing from the deep emotionalism of the melodramatic tradition from which Griffith came (he had been both actor and playwright) and which he transformed. Another aspect of this is the idealism which at times leads Griffith to see his characters as Good or Evil, symbolic and often explicitly allegorical. Like the angels who transfigure a battlefield at the end of *The Birth of a Nation* and the pitchfork devil prodding damned souls in *Dream Street* (1921)—a film of Limehouse life in which Good is symbolized by the elder Tyrone Power as an itinerant street preacher and Evil by Morgan Wallace as a masked violinist—his fancy-dress allegories and visionary recreations of Christian symbols are often extremely literal. But they spring directly from his idealism and the deep view of emotion which it reflects and which he hoped to give visual form, moving from a narrative to a moral statement. Conventionality, naïveté, and literalness are the inevitable flaws, early and late, but they are usually suffused with a disarming sincerity.

One other significant aspect of Griffith's thought, seen early in its pristine condition, is a conventional tendency to view social ills as the primary result of individual actions. In *A Corner in Wheat* (1909) the prohibitive price of bread is the direct and sole result of financial manipulation by one greedy man, suitably and symbolically punished by suffocating in a wheat bin; in *The Birth of a Nation* Austin Stoneman's passion for his mulatto mistress leads to the excesses of Reconstruction; the scorned priest of Bel betrays Babylon in *Intolerance*; the British-Indian atrocities during the Revolution are exclusively attributed to the lascivious Walter Butler in *America* (1924); and out of personal pique Robespierre condemns the lovers—and by implication thousands of others—to the guillotine in *Orphans of the Storm*. The lovers' rescue by Danton suggests the other side of this individual view of history and social forces, which is perhaps seen most clearly in the warm treatment of Lincoln both in *The Birth of a Nation* and in the very late *Abraham Lincoln* (1930). Only *Isn't Life Wonderful*, of the social films, is free of this social-biographical simplification: when the starving workers steal the unfortunate lovers' first harvest, they cry, "Yes, beasts we are, beasts they have made us." Here Griffith rises to a maturity of outlook unexpected in his essentially non-intellectual art, suggesting the maturity of the developing artist.

Isn't Life Wonderful (1924), his picture of a family crushed by the inflation in Germany after World War I,

is a late masterpiece, a superb work of social realism, almost documentary in its approach and power. Still it seems untypical of the usually more romantic Griffith. With his tendency to push warmth and emotion toward sentimentality and his often faltering comic interludes—Griffith's greatest faults—goes his distrust of adult physical passion, for which he too often substitutes coyness. But these flaws do not cancel out the emotional power of the great scenes and the exquisite pathos seen especially in the roles designed for Lillian Gish and Mae Marsh, superb actresses who brought out the best in Griffith as he did in them.

In his tendency to emotional excess, as in his equally typical emotional delicacy, his warmth, his ability to create and define character, and his superb feeling for fitting the exact detail and small personal scene into a sweeping action, in both his excess and restraint, virtues and flaws, Griffith is closely comparable to Dickens. Modern audiences seem to fear deep emotion, and anyone who is unwilling to overlook the sentimentality and the comic excesses typical of Dickens and Griffith, in order to find the emotional richness and subtlety beyond, is well advised to avoid both of them. Those who are willing to accept these conventional flaws are abundantly rewarded by the range and power of the world each creates. [This comparison is best explored by Eisenstein in his 1944 essay "Dickens, Griffith, and the Film Today" (reprinted in *Film Form*). His comment on the emotional power of the two masters is especially astute, as when speaking of Nancy in *Oliver Twist:* "By the way, it is characteristic for both Dickens and Griffith to have these sudden flashes of goodness in 'morally degraded' characters and, though these sentimental images verge on hokum, they are so faultlessly done that they work on the most skeptical readers and spectators!" Certainly this is true of Griffith, from the early Biograph films to his powerful last film, *The Struggle* (1931). Perhaps Eisenstein's own silent films are more readily acceptable to present-day audiences because he avoids the "sentimental images" which so often make audiences squeamish, however faultlessly done.]

Not all of Griffith's films are masterpieces. Like Dickens, he produced too much, perhaps too rapidly. But as also is the case with Dickens, from this profusion came some of his best work. In 1919 and 1920, at the peak of his career, he released ten films, from *The Girl Who Stayed at Home,* the last of his war films, to *Way Down East,* a spectacularly successful melodrama. In the first of these he combined two strands of plot, one involving M. France, an unreconstructed Southerner who has lived abroad since the Civil War, a charmingly conceived character who comes to terms with his country through the rescue of his granddaughter and himself by the AEF; the other involves the two sons of a rich American businessman, one son conventionally noble (he rescues and marries M. France's granddaughter), while the other is transformed from "lounge lizard" to war hero and with him transforms the chorus girl he loves. Among the most revealing scenes is one in which the second boy crawls across the battlefield to report the dangerous position of the small party led by his brother; this scene is crosscut with one of his fiancée being tempted by gifts from a former admirer. As she hesitates, the boy crawls. When she overcomes temptation, he reaches safety. This point is never made explicitly, but the emotional effect is the stronger for this restraint. The treatment is typical of the way Griffith transforms a film primarily intended to encourage the war effort (and officially supported by the government) into a work independent of propaganda in its richness, charm, and effectiveness. If less moving than *Hearts of the World* (1918), an earlier film exploring the horrors of war, and less gentle than *True Heart Susie,* which came soon after, *The Girl Who Stayed at Home* stands as a fine example of Griffith's craftsmanship and his ability to work creatively with his actors, especially Robert Harron and Clarine Seymour as the transformed lovers.

Even where the integration of plot fails to come off, the resulting parts can be highly effective. In *The Greatest Question* (1919) the scene in which the beloved son off at sea appears to his mother on the day he dies in action is a profoundly moving one. Such extrasensory experience may be an unfashionable subject now, although it was not following World War I, but I am unable to imagine how that scene could be improved upon or even done any differently without spoiling its simplicity and beauty. Although the Lillian Gish escape plot is largely unconnected with this whole aspect of the film, the effectiveness of each part remains. In later films these double plots are played down, so that, for example, the poor boy-rich girl subplot of *The White Rose* (1923) remains a convention and never interferes with the poor girl and rich, spoiled minister story which forms the main plot of this beautiful and moving relatively late film.

Although now most famous for the epic sweep, the vast panoramas, and the great battle scenes of *The Birth of a Nation, Intolerance,* and *Orphans of the Storm*—and properly famous, it might be added—Griffith's enduring power is also to be found in his individual emotional scenes. The mother's plea to a tired, awkward, gentle Lincoln in *The Birth of a Nation,* Mae Marsh's face as her baby is taken away from her in the modern story in *Intolerance,* and Lillian and Dorothy Gish, the two orphans in *Orphans of the Storm,* fearfully setting out for Paris and the great operation on the blind girl's eyes—these are also moments that remain.

These moments are usually held in a striking visual image, which is another aspect of Griffith's power: his ability to create a visual image which is beautiful in its own right while also embodying dramatic and emotional meaning. Perhaps the most celebrated single image in Griffith's work is the riding of the klan in *The Birth of a Nation,* the long line of white-clad horsemen galloping to the rescue of a small, embattled party. The ambiguities created by the second half of this film in the modern liberal spectator are crystallized in this scene; however much he loathes the klan, he is compelled by the hypnotic effect of suspense building in this rescue sequence to side with these towering figures as they fill the screen. The racial tensions generated by the whole film today are a belated tribute to Griffith's power, but nowhere more so than in this scene, which is so well suited to the silent screen. It is superbly visual and, when properly accompanied by music, all other sound is superfluous. One may regret that Griffith was unable to rise above the prejudices of his Kentucky background and of his age, but even *The Birth of a Nation* is suffused by the warmth and the deep humanity which he showed increasingly in such films as *Broken Blossoms* (with Richard Barthelmess as the gentle Chinese boy) and *Isn't Life Wonderful,* not to speak of *Intolerance*.

Griffith's work consists almost entirely of silent films. The aesthetic of the silent film has often been argued. There was never, of course, a literally "silent" film, supported as it was by its piano or theater orchestra accompaniment, yet the modern filmgoer outside the purlieu of the Museum's invaluable Arthur Kleiner usually sees such films in total silence. Except at the Museum they are usually seen at a slightly faster speed ("sound speed") than was intended, making fast movements jerky. Coupled with the pomposity of some of the "titles"—especially if the subject is unsuited to the silent medium—the effect can be incongruous. For the large audiences at the Museum these incongruities apparently blocked an appreciation of Griffith's richly emotional art; only the two sound films (*Abraham Lincoln* and *The Struggle*) seemed to present no such obstacles. The failure of the audience lay in this breakdown of understanding and sympathy. Unfortunately this reaction is typical of the current approach to silent films.

Of course the failure may lie with those who take Griffith and silent films seriously. But the small group of serious admirers who attended despite the behavior of a vocal part of the audience was too consistently moved and too consistently in agreement to accept such an argument. To watch an artist develop and become aware of his medium was an illumination. To see the camera begin to move, the close-up and the panoramic shots devised and brought together to create a new kind of beauty, was more than a historical thrill. Griffith loved beauty, and his films are full of it, especially when seen on the original tinted stock with its suffused blues, greens, and gold. Even in *Isn't Life Wonderful* one finds a beauty in all its starkness. Part of the pathos of the late films lies in Griffith's attempts to preserve this beauty despite the interference with his films and the inadequacy of the stories forced on him by studios, Griffith in decline takes on a symbolic quality, for much of the pathos of this retrospective view lies in the sense of waste. At the height of his powers this protean artist was trapped by the financial pressures which turned Hollywood into a factory and stifled the few artists who emerged in American films, the von Stroheims and the

Welleses. He tried to come to terms with this, but inevitably he was rejected. There is no indication that the recent Griffith festival was intended as an ironic allegory; Griffith himself probably wouldn't have been amused at that idea either, despite his fondness for allegory. And perhaps the audiences were laughing to keep from crying. One can only hope, finally, that all unawares they caught some of the beauty, the emotional power, and the humanity that made the unique art of D. W. Griffith.

Pauline Kael (essay date 1970)

SOURCE: "A Great Folly, and a Small One," in *Going Steady,* Atlantic-Little, Brown, 1970, pp. 42-8.

[In the following essay, Kael reflects on Griffith's pioneering cinematic accomplishments.]

"She is madonna in an art as wild and young as her sweet eyes," Vachel Lindsay wrote of Mae Marsh, who died on Tuesday of last week. She is the heroine of D. W. Griffith's *Intolerance,* which came out in 1916 and which will soon have its annual showing at the Museum of Modern Art. *Intolerance* is one of the two or three most influential movies ever made, and I think it is also the greatest. Yet many of those who are interested in movies have never seen it. *The Birth of a Nation,* which Griffith brought out in 1915 (with Mae Marsh as the little sister who throws herself off a cliff through "the opal gates of death"), still draws audiences, because of its scandalous success. But those who see it projected at the wrong speed, so that it becomes a "flick," and in mutilated form—cut and in black-and-white or faded color—are not likely to develop enough interest in Griffith's art to go to see his other films. *Intolerance* was a commercial failure in 1916, and it has never had much popular reputation. After the reactions to *The Birth of a Nation,* Griffith was so shocked that people could think he was anti-Negro that he decided to expand some material he had been working on and make it an attack on bigotry throughout the ages. *Intolerance* was intended to be virtuous and uplifting. It turned out to be a great, desperate, innovative, ruinous film—perhaps the classic example of what later came to be known as *cinéma maudit.* Griffith had already, in the over four hundred movies he had made—from the one-reelers on up to *The Birth of a Nation*—founded the art of screen narrative; now he wanted to try something more than simply telling the story of bigotry in historical sequence. He had developed cross-cutting in his earlier films, using discontinuity as Dickens did in his novels. In *Intolerance,* he attempted to tell four stories taking place in different historical periods, crosscutting back and forth to ancient Babylon, sixteenth-century France, the modern American slums, and Calvary. He was living in an era of experiments with time in the other arts, and although he worked in a popular medium, the old dramatic concepts of time and unity seemed too limiting; in his own way he attempted what Pound and Eliot, Proust

and Virginia Woolf and Joyce were also attempting, and what he did in movies may have influenced literary form as much as they did. He certainly influenced them. The events of *Intolerance* were, he said, set forth "as they might flash across a mind seeking to parallel the life of the different ages." It doesn't work. *Intolerance* almost becomes a film symphony, but four stories intercut and rushing toward simultaneous climaxes is, at a basic level, too naïve a conception to be anything more than four melodramas told at once. The titles of *Intolerance* state the theme more than the action shows it, and the four parallel stories were probably just too much and too bewildering for audiences. Also, the idealistic attack on hypocrisy, cruelty, and persecution may have seemed uncomfortably pacifistic in 1916.

No simple framework could contain the richness of what Griffith tried to do in this movie. He tried to force his stories together, and pushed them into ridiculous patterns to illustrate his theme. But his excitement—his madness—binds together what his arbitrarily imposed theme does not. *Intolerance* is like an enormous, extravagantly printed collection of fairy tales. The book is too thick to handle, too richly imaginative to take in, yet a child who loves stories will know that this is the treasure of treasures. The movie is the greatest extravaganza and the greatest folly in movie history, an epic celebration of the potentialities of the new medium—lyrical, passionate, and grandiose. No one will ever again be able to make last-minute rescues so suspenseful, so beautiful, or so absurd. In movies, a masterpiece is of course a folly. *Intolerance* is charged with visionary excitement about the power of movies to combine music, dance, narrative, drama, painting, and photography—to do alone what all the other arts together had done. And to do what they had failed to. Griffith's dream was not only to reach the vast audience but to express it, to make of the young movie art a true democratic art.

Griffith's movies are great not because he developed the whole range of film techniques—the editing, the moving camera, the closeup, the flexible use of the frame so that it becomes a pinpoint of light or a CinemaScope shape at will—but because he invented or pioneered those techniques out of an expressive need for them. When Griffith is at his best, you are hardly aware of how short the shots are, how brilliantly they are edited, how varied the camera angles are. Reaching for color, he not only had the prints of his movies dyed in different hues selected to convey the mood of the sequences but had crews of girls adding extra color by hand, frame by frame. Still dissatisfied, he had the projectionists throw beams of red or blue light to intensify the effects. Reaching for sound, he had scores specially prepared and orchestras playing in the pit. In *Intolerance,*" he overstretched. There is hardly anything that has been attempted in movies since (except for sound effects, of course) that was not tried in *Intolerance. The Birth of a Nation,* the longest American film up to that date, was rehearsed for six weeks, shot in nine weeks, and edited in three months; it cost a hundred thousand dollars—a record-breaking budget in those days. *Intolerance* cost several times as much. The huge statue-cluttered Babylonian set, which is the most famous of all movie sets, is big in the way DeMille's sets were to be big later on—a picture-postcard set—and neither the camera nor any of the players seems to know what to do with it. The steps on this set undoubtedly inspired Eisenstein's Odessa Steps sequence, but the action that Griffith staged on them looks mechanical and confused. The movie had got too big, and even Griffith was crushed by the weight of it. Yet the enormous project released his imagination, and there are incomparable images—for example, the death of the young mountain girl, with the toy chariot drawn by doves at her feet—and miraculously successful sequences: the prison scenes, later imitated in the Warner Brothers social-protest films of the thirties, and almost reproduced in *I Am a Fugitive from a Chain Gang*; the strike scenes, which influenced the Russians; the great night-fighting scenes, originally in red, which are imitated in practically every spectacle.

One can trace almost every major tradition and most of the genres, and even many of the metaphors, in movies to their sources in Griffith. The Ku Klux Klan riders of *The Birth of a Nation* became the knights of Eisenstein's *Alexander Nevsky*; the battle scenes, derived from Mathew Brady, influenced almost all subsequent war films, and especially *Gone with the Wind*. A history of Russian movies could be based on the ice breaking up in Griffith's *Way Down East,* taking that ice through Pudovkin's epic *Mother* up to Chukhrai's *Clear Skies,* where the thaw after Stalin's death is represented literally by the breaking up of ice. One can also trace the acting styles. Mae Marsh returned to us via the young Garbo and other Scandinavian actresses, and Lillian Gish returned to us via Brigitte Helm of *Metropolis,* Dorothea Wieck of *Mädchen in Uniform,* and *most* of the European actresses of the twenties. Griffith's stylized lyric tragedy *Broken Blossoms* (which will also be shown at the Museum of Modern Art), though smaller in scope than *The Birth* or *Intolerance,* is, I think, the third of a trio of great works. It is the source of much of the poignancy of Fellini's *La Strada*. Donald Crisp's brutal prizefighter became Anthony Quinn's Zampano, and Lillian Gish's childish waif must have strongly influenced the conception of Giulietta Masina's role as well as her performance.

Griffith used Lillian Gish and Mae Marsh contrastingly. In his films, Lillian Gish is a frail, floating heroine from romantic novels and poems—a maiden. She is the least coarse of American screen actresses; her grace is pure and fluid and lilylike. She is idealized femininity, and her purity can seem rather neurotic and frightening. Mae Marsh is less ethereal, somehow less actressy, more solid and "normal," and yet, in her own way, as exquisite and intuitive. She is our dream not of heavenly beauty, like Gish, but of earthly beauty, and sunlight makes her youth more entrancing. She looks as if she could be a happy, sensual, ordinary woman. The tragedies that befall her are accidents that could happen to any of us, for she has never wanted more than common pleasures. There is a passage in *Intolerance* in which Mae Marsh, as a young mother who has had her baby taken away from her, grows so distraught that she becomes a voyeur, peeping in at windows to simper and smile at other people's babies. It's horrible to watch, because she has always seemed such a sane sort of girl. When Lillian Gish, trapped in the closet in *Broken Blossoms,* spins around in terror, we feel terror for all helpless, delicate beauty, but when Mae Marsh is buffeted by fate every ordinary person is in danger. Mae Marsh died at seventy-two, but the girl who twists her hands in the courtroom scene of *Intolerance* is the image of youth-in-trouble forever.

It took Griffith years to pay off the disaster of *Intolerance,* and though he later made box-office successes, like *Way Down East,* he wasn't financially strong enough to keep his independence. By 1925, he was forced to go to work for Paramount as a contract director, which meant doing the scripts they handed him, and doing them *their* way. By the thirties, he had sunk even further; he was called in to fix films that other directors had messed up, and he didn't receive screen credits anymore. There was so much emphasis in Hollywood on the newest product that it was feared his name would make people think a picture old-fashioned. Eventually, alcoholic and embittered, he could get no work at all. Until his death, in 1948, Griffith lived in a hotel room in near obscurity in the Hollywood he had created—which was filled with famous directors he had trained and famous stars he had discovered. They could not really help him. Motion pictures had become too big a business for sentiment, or for art.

William Cadbury (essay date 1974)

SOURCE: "Theme, Felt Life, and the Last-Minute Rescue in Griffith After *Intolerance,*" in *Film Quarterly,* Vol. XXVIII, No. 1, Fall, 1974, pp. 39-49.

[In the following essay, Cadbury asserts that a mature artistic vision is present in Griffith's earlier films.]

There have come to be two positions on D. W. Griffith, a modern orthodoxy and a much-needed revisionism. The orthodoxy is a picture of Griffith the great innovator, whose values and intentions however amount only to a style for his times. When those times changed (it happened with startling suddenness, Karl Brown reminisces, between the making and exhibiting of *Intolerance*), Griffith's values and his style fell away from those congenial to his audience. In this view the later films are spasmodic attempts to accommodate the new audience without, however, any aesthetic growth on Griffith's part. Griffith is aesthetically the same throughout his career, and the films only come to look a bit different because they get worse.

The welcome revisionism offered recently by John Dorr challenges both aspects of the orthodoxy. It admits Griffith the early innovator but sees him breaking new aesthetic ground after *Intolerance,* moving to a new style built not on melodramatic action and last-minute rescues but on investigation of spiritual states through close-ups; not on passive victim-heroines but on actively assertive New Women; not on Lillian Gish but on a Carol Dempster quite different from the poor actress of the orthodoxy. In this view, Griffith's real value only emerges after the "great" period is over, and his later films improve in style and content. In effect, Griffith changes and his films get better.

The revisionism is most welcome, as it encourages recognition of the wonderful later films. But I think the earlier films are as wonderful, and render the same rich vision, as the later; and the later ones use just as brilliantly (though often, naturally enough, a little differently) the devices of the early. Dorr misreads key Dempster films to make them seem more different from key Gish films than they are. And he misanalyzes the structural centers of the late films, which simply develop the parallel editing techniques which always were at the heart of Griffith's conception of expressive cinematic form.

Let us first deal with the claim that the late films mark a change in vision. Dorr argues that in *Dream Street* "a decidedly neurotic element enters Griffith's cinema." For instance Billy, the younger brother of Gypsy's (Dempster's) favored Spike, is "pathologically insane." He murders someone, but wins release, to our full approval, by lying about the crime during court-room confession of it. But in fact that is not what Griffith shows us. In the initial presentation of the killing we see Billy first maddened by the demonic violin-player and then in close-up shooting the intruder whom he has found in his room. (The shooting is intercut also with Sam Jones, the incredibly offensively portrayed "black" comic relief, running away from the sound of the shot.) We then see the victim go out of focus and fall, and when we finally return to medium long shot of the room we see that there is a chair overturned on the floor which wasn't there at the start of the sequence, before we went to close-ups and diversions.

Then in the confession Billy tells us remorsefully of the killing, but this time we see the victim in fact hit viciously at Billy with the chair, miss, and come at him again with it; it is only at that point that Billy shoots him. Clearly Billy is not lying; clearly we are seeing what we had not seen before because we cut away from it; clearly the killing was in self-defense. And equally clearly it is appropriate that in Billy's turmoil of mind the fact of the shooting, its quality of matching by its violence the violence of his own motives (half crazy with love for Gypsy, he has just seen her in an impassioned love scene with his brother Spike), would be what we would *rightly* be shown at that point. It is not the fine points of legal culpability which count for Billy

there, but the fact that his assertiveness, always before submerged for his brother's sake, has suddenly gotten out of control and caused him, to his own abject panic, to lash out. But in the clearing of accounts of the confession it is equally appropriate that the extenuating circumstances which actually held might come to Billy's consciousness. There is reconciliation here, not the achievement of a criminal loony's freedom through a false confession.

Similarly, though Dorr says there is doubt about the paternity of Gypsy's baby, Griffith gives us no reason to doubt that the baby is Spike and Gypsy's, and Billy's being included in the domestic scene at the end, when Gypsy and Spike and Billy all watch the baby play, is no "perversion of earlier scenes and situations" but just what you would expect after anguish, repentance, and a last-minute confession which admits and purges moral even as it clears of legal guilt. Likewise, Dorr finds it shocking that Gypsy dances around her father's death-bed; but her action is not some strange rite but because he, knowing himself dying, asks her to dance for him. She does so until she learns that he has died. There is nothing perverse there.

Nor does the dance to quell the panic in the burning theater work as Dorr says. He calls it a "daring and unsettling scene," in which close shots of the rioting audience come to seem "defined and confined" while "Dempster's movement within the larger frame" of the long shots "is anarchy." "Dempster is more out of control than the riot." But what Griffith shows us of the audience is a series of vastly disturbing vignettes of as motley a crew as you could hope to find. They are indeed in close-up, but not thereby confined and defined but rather bursting outwards from a crowded, explosive, painful, ungainly frame. In contrast Gypsy, saying "Sit down, I'm the only fire here!" rushes on to a bare stage and, shot always in clear air with adequate psychological space, does what is far less a dance than a set of acrobatic posturings and steps which all say "Here I am, attend to me and have fun, look, look!" It is ridiculous as a dance, but its effect is immensely charming. The contrast is not between anarchy and control. Rather, Gypsy is personal assertiveness, innocent and gamboling and avowedly sexually appealing, and the riot is inward fantasy, oppressive and oppressed, crushed and crowded and breathless.

In no sense is Gypsy's innocence "tainted and dangerous," as Dorr thinks. Nor is there ambiguity to the themes or the heroine. Spike indeed "demonstrates his love for Gypsy in heavy-handed bullying ways," but this is not because Griffith is rendering a statement about the forms love must sometimes take—how for instance like the violin player it is grotesque under its mask of beauty. Spike must show love in awkward ways, at first, because of the "thoughtlessness of exuberant youth" (this is about the first title defining Spike) and because of the pressures militating against sensitivity in the ghetto. But he learns, he learns—and that he does so is the very theme of the film.

Dorr may say that not "all Griffith films [are] about Lillian Gish and the imminence of rape," but it remains true that in *Dream Street* Spike does try to rape Gypsy, who is saved only by Billy's intervention. "Oh Lord, why won't the men love me right?" asks Gypsy, whose charming desire is frank and open, sexual and innocent. We see her in her street pensive and yearning with a flock of doves, and in her apartment playing with a stuffed rabbit, and it is as natural for her to be shown that way as for Susie of the true heart to be shown with her chickens and cow, or Anna Moore with her pigeons, or Mountain Girl with her goat. There is indeed "animal freedom" in Gypsy's desires, but there is no "moral anarchy"—unless for a woman to be sexually yearning is an anarchic situation. The irony of Gypsy's lot is not that she is "lethal, erotic and demanding," but that men confuse sex with aggression.

Far from *Dream Street* rendering a neurotic perversity, it simply works its way toward a typical Griffith image of the good, a picture of a mutuality only barely achieved against pressures from within and without—tendencies to withdrawal and to insensitivity to others, the tendencies we find in most Griffith films. How is the unprotected person like Gypsy, full of desire for self-expression, to achieve fulfillment when it looks as if the two sorts of character we find in the world are equally powerless to avoid turning monstrous? Spike's jovial, demonstrative assertiveness all too easily becomes brutal because it is unable to accommodate or to respect others. But Billy's responsive reflectiveness, sensitive and concernful, all too easily becomes paranoid because its very valuation of others hinders action.

But it turns out that assertiveness and reflectiveness are not the only character choices. On another level in this world other forces are fighting it out, represented by the violin player in touch with the forces of evil and the preacher in touch with heaven, and themselves supervised by the morning star. What happens is less that Billy loses and Spike wins than that a new organization displaces the hopeless contraries of assertiveness and reflectiveness which had seemed all the world had to offer. There may be selfishness and unselfishness, in free variation with the different character types. Assertiveness may limit itself, and reflectiveness may learn to come forward. Thus Griffith turns what looked like "You can't win either way" into "You can win both ways."

Dream Street's structure works up to rendering the conquering of selfishness first for Spike and then for Billy. We have discussed Billy's climactic confession; the whole first half of the film shows how Spike gets over his problems. When he first courts Gypsy in front of her house, as a "man of action" he bends her wrist back and tries to force a kiss. He even slaps her before she runs into the house to escape and complain to the

Lord about her incompetent suitors. She has been attracted to Spike, leaning toward him as if magnetized when he sings a song for her on the dock, but she claps her head as if to clear it, and one feels that her attraction and his desire will have much trouble coming to terms.

Again on the inner stairs of her house Gypsy is attracted to Spike, only fleeing to her room when he tries to kiss her. Though she tells him not to come into her room he does. She is bothered, but after all she wants to love him; she plays langorously with a piece of string, she claims that his feet don't match (such play amazes Spike, he has no idea how to deal with it), she sits across the room when he pulls up a chair for her, she jumps away from him and does little enticing steps. Griffith makes us understand perfectly the necessary admixtures of aggression in the sexual games, the requirements that integrity be preserved for both people to allow them to let their guards down and let each other in, the tentativeness of it all along with the obvious sexuality of the atmosphere.

But Spike can't sustain it, and he fails her. The violin player sounds for him, and Gypsy's proud testing, by which she will keep her sexual submission from being a defeat, just comes to make Spike mad. The scene of courtship becomes a rape. But though Gypsy is as terrified as later she is of Sway Wan, we have seen enough of Spike to be full of pity for him as well as for Gypsy. He would like to love her right, but knows no other way than force and no other motive than self-gratification. Billy with his roses comes in, and helped by the preacher's voice gets Spike to leave—but Billy is overcome by sentiment, and can merely offer the roses (as earlier he offered a song) and flee. If Spike cannot go towards Gypsy except to force her, Billy cannot go towards her at all but turns everything inside in a very paradigm of self-defeating sentiment.

At home, then, Spike is torn between the voice of the preacher and the violin player, as he visualizes Gypsy terrified as she was when he attacked her and also as she might be, seraphic and lovely. The preacher shows him Gypsy coming to her door and waiting for him outside her house, yearning and ready on the bench in the empty street. Spike goes to her, indicates his rejection of his old ways, and "The first battle won, the pure flame at last," they kiss each other in a holy and sensual ecstacy. No more awkward rough fumbling, but full mutuality—and it is utterly convincing, despite how conventional the description makes it sound, that Gypsy should blush, be embarrassed, hide her head on Spike's chest. The sense of "felt life" is very strong for me in these sequences, as Griffith convinces us of the plausibility of shy retreats from such openness, and of just how hard it is, in unsup-portive surroundings, to get together with others, to get past one's own limiting styles and awkwardnesses.

After following Billy's story for a bit, we return to Gypsy and Spike on their bench. The scene is designed as a contrast to the scene of the near-rape; Gypsy tells Spike not to come in and this time he obeys. She closes the door on him but as he falls on his knees in adoration outside she looks back out. She sees him, laughs as she had laughed before, but goes in again refusing to let him follow: and this time far from being offended Spike is delighted, and struts off down the street comically far more self-satisfied than he could ever have been if his forcefulness had been successful. Above, Gypsy does one of her little dances and sinks in her chair to kiss her stuffed rabbit. As we see Spike walk off happily we realize that though they are separated, though they are withholding, though Gypsy is teasing Spike and he is being teased, both are infinitely satisfied. Griffith here has to prove the case, difficult to make plausible, that there is net gain from abstention. He proves it by embedding the decision to abstain in an emotional context in which not to abstain would have to amount to dominance of the man over the woman and her abject submission to him. Dorr thinks it neuroticism to hold it difficult to "make pure and sweet the dreams" of a "Life [which] is not always what it seems," as the titles have it. But it seems to me that by showing the actual emotional danger of selfishness and the emotional rewards attendant on mutuality, Griffith proves that a forceful but sensitive responsiveness to others can give joys as great as those symbolized by Gypsy's happy little shuffle with her rabbit or Spike's delighted strutting as he leaves Gypsy's door.

But I do not think this proof is higher in quality than those of the best Gish films, nor indeed that it is different in point. Griffith films tend to have the same form, with which they render Griffith's insistent imaginative vision, and the form is supported by the principal actors whoever they are. Characters in Griffith's films are pressed by circumstances into emotional holding actions. From these their natural vitality can only briefly glance out until the issues of accommodation of personal assertiveness and constraining commitment (which each film raises in its own terms) can be brought to resolution. And when they are, the force of the characters' privately held assurance of the good can be implemented and the necessarily hidden power of their buried life can reach the surface of the action.

We knew the force of buried life in **Dream Street** in part through Gypsy's dances, public and private. And Gypsy went out to Spike in quite overt ways. But to think of Gish as "sweet, innocent and cloying," in a way Dempster is not, is simply untrue to Gish's display of inner life bubbling up in a hostile world. **True Heart Susie,** for instance, is as solidly Gishian a film as one could find. And the main sense we have of Susie is of someone who has to suppress her natural spark because of the cloddishness of those around her. Just like Gypsy, Susie isn't loved right, and we keep seeing her worth, like Gypsy's, press against her lover's inadequacy to appreciate it.

Just as Gypsy from the start has a project—to express her sexuality so the men will love her right—so from the start has Susie. "I *must* marry a smart man," she confides to her cow after outspelling William, and sending William to college is her way to make him that man. Susie comes forward sexually to William as much as Gypsy to Spike, though William can no more figure how to love Susie right than Spike can Gypsy. After the spelling bee Susie reaches up to be kissed, but William awkwardly turns aside. When William is going off to college, Susie at her gate tries again for the kiss and William fails her again. After Susie has overheard William's heavy flirtation in her own rose garden with the flapper Bettina (Truffaut recreates Susie's later faint in that garden in *Two English Girls*), she dresses up and "prepares for war," putting on necklace, silk stockings, and cornstarch for make-up. But then she makes "a dangerous move," and goes back to her old clothes and sits on her porch to let William see her as she is and, hopefully, love her right this time. But he misses her quality again and only asks her if she thinks he should marry. She says yes, but he goes away, having Bettina not Susie in mind.

Like Gypsy, Susie offers herself delicately but clearly, and her assertiveness is as plain as her decorum. A girl tries to stop William and flirt with him—Susie plucks insistently at his sleeve until he comes with her. Walking with William, Susie does an amazing little side-kick every three or four steps as she walks. It has no verisimilitude, but it perfectly renders the quality of Susie's inner life, the vitality which pops through the demure surface of her social relations. And that vitality, the sense of Susie with energy to spare, in a context which, like Gypsy's, is not up to appreciating it, charges the film for us.

The assertiveness Susie must suppress is summed up in a climactic scene which is full of felt life. Bettina has sneaked out from William to party with her friends, has lost her key and been caught in a rainstorm coming home (she catches her death, in fact). She comes to Susie, begging to be taken in and to have Susie cover for her. Of all the people in the film, only Bettina has trouble pushing Susie's gate open, and Susie herself is, entirely reasonably, most reluctant to help or to lie for Bettina. But she agrees, and we see the two of them in bed. Susie thinks about it, gets madder and madder, and hauls back to punch Bettina out, with a most disgusted expression.

But we see Bettina in close-up and in troubled sleep, and we see Susie realize her inadequacy and pathos as a person. She shakes her head a little, accepts it all, and cuddles Bettina with open eyes to a fade. And Griffith earns it: the scene is not coy or cloying, since Susie is aware of Bettina's unworthiness of William and that that is just what makes Bettina so annoying and at the same time makes her human appeal so irresistible. Susie's inner life is suppressed here as everywhere not because Griffith intends to praise passivity, but because activity itself, in a world out of tune with one's needs and deserts, must often take this form. In the bind Gypsy is put in by Spike, action becomes yearning and waiting. In the bind Susie is put in by William, it becomes this sort of annoyed amused tolerance.

Of course Griffith renders not just the buried life pushing outwards but also what holds it in. Just as the low point of **Dream Street** is Gypsy finding the very man she longs for turning monstrous before her eyes even as she tries to work out a way to adjust her assertiveness to his, so the low point of **True Heart Susie** is Susie mounting a full-scale effort finally to get William for herself yet finding herself suddenly pressed upon in as nightmarish a way as anything provided by Sway Wan. Susie arrives at a party, all dressed up and ready to charm, only to have to come into a crowded room to congratulate William as he tells her he took her advice to marry and that Bettina has accepted him. Susie must be demure and proper here, and before the scene closes on her surreptitiously wiping her eyes Griffith gives us a virtually Eisensteinian set of close-ups of the people in the room, of Susie's aunt looking disturbed and Bettina's looking triumphantly complacent, of Bettina looking smugly down on William looking fatuous, of various members of the group sitting silently in what amounts, as a series of shots, to a montage tableau. The very treatment renders the complacency, the irrevocable quality, the sense that possibilities have suddenly been exhausted and feeling has been socialized in the worst possible way, which characterize the situation. In its varnished parlor stasis it forms the diametric opposite of the hitch-legged walk down the country path which renders this film's picture of the good. Such kinds of control of feeling through the cinematic surface, and its truth to narrative context, are what make Griffith great.

Both early and late, Griffith invested his films with that felt life which the revisionism of Dorr finds only late, and, both early and late, Griffith structured it by variants of the device of the "last-minute rescue" which the orthodoxy of Casty finds thematically dessicating and which it is the essence of the revisionism to say that Griffith went on beyond. Fundamentally a technique of parallel editing leading to a climax, the rescue is properly neither a category of content nor a mere technique for audience manipulation, but rather a specifically cinematic device for rendering the development of the issues raised by a film in order to give an aspect of their resolution a striking representation whose feeling will match its thematic import.

Thus in **True Heart Susie** the entire sequence leading up to Susie's gesture against and then accepting Bettina is treated in the characteristic rhythms and patterns of the device. We observe Bettina sneak out and enjoy her party, get caught in the storm and come to Susie. But we observe two other locations as well, William agonizing at Bettina's door and Susie caring for her sick aunt. Bettina's charming weakness is played against Susie's charming strength as she sits on the covers to keep her

aunt's restless arm under, and Susie longs for William's house from her own window, toward which William yearns from his. Bettina's dancing and Susie's caring, William's moral unease and the aunt's physical unease, the lost key and the arm out of the covers, all illuminate each other and lead to Susie's sadly going to her bed just while Bettina equally sadly can't find her way to hers. The sense of converging lines and the treatment in mutually revealing shots of decreasing duration are just those of the last-minute rescue, and the climax in Susie's moral triumph of acceptance feels just like the rescue's triumph.

Even in films where action sweeps us up and where there is a literal rescue, the sequence of the last-minute rescue interplays with the issues of the film for enrichment and specification of theme. No one, for instance, would deny that **Way Down East** is overwhelmingly impressive for the rescue from the ice. But the rescue is experienced in the context of the sequences by which Anna Moore has come to be there. Anna's progression from openly sexual delight in Lennox Sanderson, to emotional closedness as she walks toward Bartlett's, her fiercely but restrainedly scornful antagonism to Lennox and her developing feeling for David Bartlett are richly particularized. There is a dogged quality to Anna Moore, more serious because more initially wounded, and more determinedly assertive of her right to happiness, than Susie's youthful quality. It gives consistency and appropriateness to the lovely close-ups of Anna in her party gown and as Elaine of Astolat which would have been impossible for Susie, and gives psychological density to the famous confrontation scene.

It gives also a specific thematic effect to the rescue from the ice. Anna's despair as her possibilities come to nothing, and then her virtually committing suicide on the frozen river, are not mere passivities like those of The Boy being taken to execution in **Intolerance,** but are, like Susie's ironic resignation, the very mode of action of her dogged and serious character in that plight. And David's finally chasing her is an eruption into action of a character whose error (like the errors of all the Billy types) is to turn feeling inward and be ineffectual; but his saving of Anna expresses as it rewards the value of her character as well as of his own.

Like Anna's, Henriette's vitality in **Orphans of the Storm** is squelched between the same alternatives: by Lennox-like aristocrats who press for sensuality during a party, and by rubish revolutionaries who catch Henriette up in a dance of their own but, finding she is not one of themselves, threaten her with their guillotine. (In a doubling, we note that Pierre Frochard and his brother Jacques who threaten Henriette's sister Louise are perfect versions of Billy and Spike.) It might seem, in summary of the action, that Danton's rescue of Henriette from the guillotine is just like David's rescue of Anna from the ice. But it by no means feels that way or renders the same theme; Griffith is not repeating himself even if he is using the same structure. As soon as it happens it is clear to us that David's change of mind, by which he breaks free of his family and cleaves to Anna, represents a counter-assertiveness to the tendencies of his social system to become inflexibly intolerant—and he goes after Anna very much for himself. But Danton's rescue, motivated by his recollection of Henriette's kindness to him and of her lover the Chevalier's having fed the poor, represents rather a selfless submission to the appeal of old values, treasured kindnesses, personal relations. What David does for himself in rejecting his family's stasis, Danton does for others in turning his revolutionary society's chaos in the direction of more humane action. David's action is a personal triumph of assertion of energies, but Danton's is a triumph of the channeling of energies into a broader tolerance.

Even in these avowed spectaculars, the rescues do not replace thought with action, but rather articulate and resolve particularized themes. The Griffith themes, as we have seen, center around issues of social constraint against which, without becoming monstrous, human character must somehow find a way to assert its legitimate demands. Often the solution for the individual is acting morally by refraining from action or by acting counter to his or her own immediate interests. But the force of that moral action impels someone else into activity, for instance a rescue, which will reward it. The last-minute rescues, as well as rewarding the central figure, also thus manifest his or her force, since it is the moral force which made the difference. Thus it is only natural variation that the last-minute rescues may be either by someone else, as in *Orphans of the Storm,* or by the hero or heroine, as in *True Heart Susie*. And as with any device which may be used to render developments of specific issues in terms subtly adjusted to the issues' necessities, the last-minute rescue is capable of other variations as well, to match the particular requirements of specific variants of Griffith's general theme.

In *True Heart Susie* the rescue pattern leads up to Susie's triumph. In *Abraham Lincoln* the rescue pattern is set aside from Lincoln's triumph in order both to manifest it and to keep a clear distinction between its spiritual and social aspects. The film has two strands, one of which is the establishment of Lincoln's value in his sacrifice of himself. As is typical of Griffith's structures, Lincoln's assertiveness is made clear at the start. In John Ford's *Young Mr. Lincoln* Lincoln faces down with stern patriarchal repression a bully who shouts "I'm the buck of this lick," but in Griffith's film it is Lincoln himself who fights a bully and then explodes into shouting the same sentence. But the assertiveness is constrained by the demands of history, and for the bulk of the film Lincoln's inner life can only express itself in acts whose assertiveness is largely to deny assertion. Lincoln pardons a young deserting soldier whose legs ran away with him when he saw his friend's corpse—a reminder of Lincoln's own legs' running away with him when he first tried to marry Mary Todd. The soldier's reluctance is linked, through his dead comrade, to Ann

Rutledge dead, and to the whole weight of Lincoln's personal obligation to a vanished frontier past. It is in this context that Lincoln pardons the South itself, despite the pressures on him not to do so.

But pardonings take their toll. Rather than acting as against a bully, the pardonings are a giving up of what Lincoln might have done as buck of this lick. For all their sense of moral tranquillity they entail also Lincoln giving up a part of himself, becoming less than he was. The assassination is of course the climax of this development towards giving himself up, as it completes the chain by which the heroic and boastful frontier hero becomes an awkward dancer, a president whose legs will not fit under the White House sofas, a rube who cannot be kept in his own shoes. For "The Union, we've saved it at last," Lincoln gives up dignity and life itself; the sacrifice of personal forcefulness for the Union is Lincoln's cost for which we are to be grateful to him.

But Griffith wants Lincoln's movement toward assassination to be seen as an action: it is Lincoln's spirit which leads him inexorably, as the last set of shots makes clear, from log cabin to the Lincoln Memorial. The fact that it is not submissiveness but profound assertiveness which drives that development is shown in another plot strand which presents the feeling appropriate to Lincoln's achievement. In it Lincoln passes on his assertiveness to others like him, whose activity may thus be assigned to him. The war is run at first by a grotesque ineffectual General Scott, a kind of Toby Jug parody of a European general, but Lincoln takes the conduct of the war from him and gives it to Grant—as backwoodsy and disreputable as Lincoln himself. And in turn this assertiveness is passed on to another cut from the same cloth: Sheridan's ride, his turning of the losing army to "rally round the flag, boys, rally once again," is treated in Griffith's best last-minute rescue style, with pounding hooves and all his most stirring techniques of mass action, striking close-ups, and exciting editing. Since these events derive from Lincoln's assigning the war effort to people who are like what he was once himself, it can seem to be Lincoln's best quality (though implemented by others while he sits in the White House in mystic trance) which actually saves the Union through just that forcefulness for which Lincoln earns our gratitude by allowing it to pass out of himself for the general good. He has found the way, as do the heroes of many Griffith films, to socialize assertiveness and to make restraint action.

The case against the last-minute rescue is that it simplifies, so that as a rhetorical pattern obligatorily coming near the ends of films it limits the imagination about what can be in the films which must be ended with it. In the later films especially, says Alan Casty, "even the style seemed to collaborate with the reductive conceptions, restricting the kinds and degrees of felt life that could become the content of the work." But that is simply not true. *Abraham Lincoln* symbolizes a passive-seeming achievement so that its truly active nature will be rendered in the surface of the film; *Isn't Life Wonderful?* goes further and uses the last-minute rescue pattern to raise feelings in us which the whole film will deny. Far from investing all value in the conclusion of the rescue, that film puts into it everything which will turn out to be false. Clearly we must say, faced with cases like these, that Griffith (like any artist) uses the devices he learns to control to make his points; and he employs whatever clever variations on their ordinary use will serve his purpose. That is not being impoverished by one's rhetoric, but enriched.

Inga and Paul in *Isn't Life Wonderful?* have harvested their potatoes, but they are spotted by destitute workers who seek profiteers transporting hoarded food. The chase is treated just like Gus chasing Flora through the woods in *Birth of a Nation*. Paul and Inga are caught and their potatoes are stolen—but it is as clear a moral triumph as Susie accepting Bettina in her bed that Inga creeps up the side of the empty potato wagon, realizes that all is lost, and then decides that life is wonderful after all. The potatoes have been treated as the necessary and sufficient means of Inga's achieving what she wishes most in life, her marriage to Paul. And the marriage will have to be put off because they are stolen. But Griffith does not want just to say that putting off is not renouncing, or that while there is even a life of resignation there is hope. He wants to say that life is wonderful, not just bearable. And for this he sets up a double proof: intensity is what one treasures, moment by moment and success or no; true intensity may entail transformation of its natural drive into a more general understanding than of one's own purposes. The real danger is not of loss, but of truncation. It is a particularly rich version of the general Griffith theme, rendered in a particularly rich treatment of the characteristic Griffith device.

Intensity is provided most obviously in the particularization of experience which has struck so many viewers of this film. Dempster's extraordinary acting, the fully realized personal relations throughout the family, the warm rendition of the festivals of turnips and feasts of liverwurst in gamely struggling lives, and the light-sculptured love scenes between Paul and Inga combine to make us feel the attitude to life which can properly experience such things, and not the goal to which they are directed. As usual in Griffith, the bulk of the film builds up an intensity of felt life to which whatever happens later must be related.

But Griffith means us to see, through his last-minute rescue in which all is gained as all is lost, that this sort of intensity has its psychic hazards, developing attitudes which in their selfishness may be like the monstrous character deformities we have seen in the other films. Throughout the film a disturbing double valuation has been built up toward the pursuing workers. On the one hand, we have a lot more sympathy for them than for most villains. In the very middle of Paul's family's "lucky day" dinner we are shown "the giant" who leads

the chase resolving to spare his wife the suffering of having only rotten meat; that resolution leads to the foray into the woods. Much as we like Paul and Inga, our awareness of the suffering of others makes us aware too that the family's good fortune *is* unusual, and perhaps in a sense unjustified. In the workers we have a brutalism which is simply assertiveness gone too far, and for which, as for Spike's similar case, we feel sympathy.

But on the other hand (and this is characteristic for Griffith), there has been throughout a distinct aura of sexual menace. We were told at the beginning that the giant's righthand man would rob Inga of her greatest earthly possession. A little later, unaware, she is followed home by this man. While she displays lots of leg taking off her stockings in her room the man pauses outside as if entranced—we can see her, and it is distinctly as if he can too. The same man is among the loutish idlers Inga must pass on her way to the meat store, and he is one of those who menace her as she walks her chickens on a leash. The episodes suggest that Inga's most precious possession may be her chastity. So when, with the couple caught, Inga babbles naively to this very man that of course the gang won't hurt a fellow worker like Paul, we fear the worst.

But the giant rejects Paul's union card, and the whole tone changes. The henchman shares in expressing self-loathing and ironic laughter at the justice of their self-description as no longer workers but now made beasts through war and privation. Rape was on no one's mind but ours, and the simple personal threat against Inga dissolves (for her too) into understanding of the straits to which people may be forced by deprivation. It is against that sense of reduction, of the vulnerability of people pressed into turning monstrous, that Griffith sets the assertiveness of Inga's final "Oh, isn't life wonderful?"—since she still has the relation to Paul which matters, and which in this social context is all she may have without selfishness.

Clearly here, as in many other Griffith films, the last-minute rescue has been used to undercut the very expectations of simplification of theme which its use suggests: potatoes are not everything, nor even chastity. Here, as elsewhere, the device supports and renders a striking demonstration of the Griffith theme: that despite pressures towards simplifications of self-gratification or of brutalism, the assertiveness of selfhood can through patience, unselfishness, and love find a way of acting in the world so as to find fulfillment in terms not forced upon it, but its own.

Far from passing beyond the mere melodrama of the last-minute rescue, as Dorr suggests, or from decaying into its mere employment for simplification of response, as Casty argues, Griffith as he develops the technique throughout his career gives the device, as André Bazin said of Hitchcock's development of montage itself, "a relativity and a meaning." And there seems little more we can ask of an expressive device than that it bear exactly what shades of meaning, what relativities to its context in a developing story, its author's subtly developing but stable vision would have it bear.

John Dorr (essay date 1974)

SOURCE: "The Griffith Tradition," in *Film Comment*, Vol. 10, No. 2, March-April, 1974, pp. 48-54.

[*In the following essay, Dorr surveys key movies, by Griffith and other directors, which were inspired by a filmmaking style known as the "Griffith Tradition."*]

The first strain of the American filmmaking tradition grew directly from the all-pervasive influence of the early work of D. W. Griffith. This essentially nationalistic tradition of dramatic narrative was rooted in the simple, direct montage principles that Griffith evolved in his Biograph one- and two-reelers. In 1915, ***The Birth of A Nation*** became the official lexicon of these principles.

The Griffith Tradition was the dominant style of the silent American film and was evolved to a classical perfection by the mid-Twenties. Later, emasculated by the transition to sound, this tradition became a recessive approach to direction best suited for keeping track of uncomplicated narratives over which a performer's personality could easily dominate. It is doubtless because the Griffith Tradition lingered well into the Thirties that the star system came to prevail over the art of the director. When, in the late Thirties, a second approach to filmmaking (the Murnau Tradition) began to unify the potential of the sound medium, the legacy of the Griffith Tradition became the history of the B-picture— until its transfer to television in the Fifties. Even today, when a director wants to analyze simply and quickly the dramatic content of a straightforward narrative, he will fall back upon these principles, now referred to as "television style."

The glory and limitation of the Griffith Tradition, as explained by Griffith himself, was that "Ideas are alright for stage people, but pictures prefer simple straight stories of facts." In the montage tradition, each shot becomes a fact whose meaning is determined by its juxtaposition to another fact. Since the first goal of this tradition was effective storytelling, it was a virtue that each shot retain its singularity of meaning.

The evolution of these montage principles was thus a product of necessity. The camera came to be placed at varying distances from the action for purely utilitarian purposes—namely comprehensible narration. The resulting method of dramatic analysis was an economical, rational, and above all unambiguous response to the challenge of telling a story with a movie camera.

America at this time was not a particularly sophisticated country. Mass communication was limited to the printed word, and storytelling was the folk art most accessible to a nation of immigrants in need of a new heritage on which to rebuild their self-identity. The qualities inherent in the Griffith Tradition embraced such basic American virtues as simplicity, practicality, rationality, straightforwardness, and nonverbalism. The silence of the silent film was not a problem, but a virtue, because it was universally comprehensible.

It was thus that the cinema became the rallying medium of a distinctly American mythological heritage. As an indigenous American folk art, the cinema provided a form and set of conventions perfectly suited to the expression of American themes, folklore, and landscape. Griffith had fused the traditions of American literature to those of American painting. With the addition of parallel-action cutting and the resultant techniques of suspense (added to the basic analytic vocabulary of long shot, medium shot, and close-up), the cinema was fully equipped to evoke the fundamental emotions of the melodramatic and action-adventure genres.

The Griffith Tradition became the medium of the genres—ideal for narratives based on rather strict conventions and animated with mythologies of the American heritage and American dream. These narratives became rituals leading through physical confrontations and complications to the obligatory cathartic endings. The montage tradition was a moralist tradition and the ready instrument of cultural propaganda—in that certain ways of life were portrayed as virtuous, and virtue was invariably rewarded. The action was ritualized, and the characters tended to become types: heroes or villains, virtuous or fallen women. The classical stability of this medium must have been a sustaining influence implying order in the cultural chaos that followed the First World War. For it was the decade of 1918 to 1928 that was the Golden Era of the Griffith Tradition.

In regarding the silent film form as a folk art (as contrasted with personal art), we acknowledge the existence of certain beauties inherent in the medium itself, common to the expressions of all those artists who worked in this medium, and *dominant* over the personal idiosyncrasies of these otherwise diverse artisans. As in the classical period of Greek art, there existed in this classical period of silent filmmaking a formal ideal (a clarity of narrative) toward which all works strove. Also, like classical Greek art, the artisans of the Griffith tradition valued order, balance, graceful proportions, symmetry—ideals of structure and geometry. There were a limited number of elements (types of shots) with which to build a narrative. Thus it was in the graceful ordering of these elements that the skill of a master director was evidenced.

Perhaps because many of the early cameramen had their origins in pictorialist still-photography, a tendency toward pictorialism was added to the rudiments of this montage structure. The High Griffith Tradition movie became a series of largely frontal, largely static, shots, each classically well composed and balanced. The overall movie had a formal grace that distanced the viewer from the characters and the action, mythologizing the narrative. Like the sonnet, the High Griffith Tradition was a rigid form; but it was the form itself that lent beauty and dignity to the work of those who adopted it.

It has been well documented elsewhere that almost all American directors who began their careers previous to 1920 either worked directly under Griffith's personal supervision or openly acknowledged their formal debt to him. Among those who personally apprenticed with Griffith were John Ford, Raoul Walsh, Erich von Stroheim, Allan Dwan, Sidney Franklin, and Donald Crisp, while certainly no less influenced were King Vidor and Cecil B. De Mille. In the early work of these directors can be detected not only the Griffith form, but many of the Griffith mannerisms dutifully copied from the master's example. It was through the work of these (and many, many other) directors, and *not* through Griffith himself, that the Griffith Tradition flourished and evolved into its classical form. It is interesting to note that during their silent careers, Ford and Walsh, in particular, were known more as competent genre directors (i.e., folk artists) than as innovative personal directors. And when Buster Keaton wanted to tie his gags into coherent feature narratives, he would hire a graduate of the Griffith school as co-director to supply this dramatic unity. There was a single, accepted approach to dramatic narrative, and this was the Griffith Tradition.

Because the Griffith Tradition was appropriate to the expression of a vision suited to the needs of a mass American audience (i.e., because these films made reliable money), Hollywood, as the film *industry,* undertook the institutionalization of that tradition. This process of institutionalizing forced the crystallization of the form, at once eliminating error and stifling experimentation. By the mid-Twenties, the only exploratory art of the Griffith Tradition was to be found in the refinement of studio-bound techniques.

In these mid-Twenties, a second strain of the American narrative cinema began to exert its presence. This was the Murnau Tradition, which rallied around the rather advanced expressions of F. W. Murnau's *The Last Laugh* (imported in 1925) and *Sunrise* (1927), it would not be inappropriate to call this strain the Murnau Tradition. This is the tradition ostensibly of the moving camera, but more broadly (as defined by Andrew Sarris) the aesthetic which "implies the continuousness of a visual field outside of the frame of the camera." Whereas the Griffith Tradition *constructs* an emotion, the Murnau Tradition *records* it; and whereas the Griffith analyzes drama, the Murnau synthesizes.

By way of clarification, it should be pointed out that the Griffith Tradition is a specific development of the more general category of the montage aesthetic. For example, Eisenstein's use of montage, while not unrelated, would

not be described as part of the Griffith Tradition, which was specifically a development of the American cinema. On the other hand, in the context of the history of the American cinema, the Griffith Tradition has been roughly synonymous with the montage aesthetic as variously expressed over the years. (See André Bazin's "The Evolution of the Language of Cinema.")

After the Thirties (except in the B-pictures, where the Griffith Tradition remained relatively pure), it becomes increasingly difficult to isolate the montage aesthetic from the moving-camera aesthetic; both coexisted in the collaborative-adaptive tradition that predominated in Hollywood's production from the late Thirties through the Sixties. Also, in defining the Murnau Tradition as representative of the moving-camera aesthetic in the evolution of the American narrative form, we refer more to a point of view (a way of seeing) than to any specific set of directorial techniques. Two directors might make use of the same technique with polar aesthetic implications.

Thus, though we might polarize the two traditions as the battle of the cut versus the shot, we wouldn't attribute absolute meanings to either the cut or the shot. A spiritualist director like Frank Borzage cuts frequently, but so imperceptibly as to imply continuity instead of disjunction. Borzage's cuts within a scene will involve only slight changes of camera angle or distance from subject, such as to avoid those large emotions implied by the usual Griffith Tradition vocabulary of long shot, medium shot, close-up. On the other hand, a formalist like Fritz Lang will make extensive use of the moving camera, yet not lose that sense of an isolating destiny that predominates the montage ethic. Instead of following his characters, Lang's camera pursues them.

Young directors entering the cinema in the mid-Twenties looked to Murnau, and not to Griffith, as the model on whom to build their visual style. For instance, Howard Hawks, in his third film *The Cradle Snatchers* (1926), seems completely oblivious to the Griffith Tradition vocabulary. Hawks is clearly a sound director making a silent film. The titles are not descriptive, but transcripts of dialogue. The pace is fast; but the speed is in the physical action, as recorded in full shots, pans, and dollies, not in the speed of the cutting.

The technological development of synchronized sound fulfilled the Murnau Tradition, but was superfluous to the Griffith Tradition. The ever-multiplying complexity of modern life could be captured (in a poetic sense) with ease through the Murnau Tradition, whereas the frantic pacing of those wonderful special montage sequences of the late Twenties and the Thirties demonstrated the ever-increasing difficulty of dramatic analysis to deal with this complexity. By the late Thirties, screenwriters had learned that a single well-chosen line of dialogue could quickly and less obtrusively express a passage of time than these montages.

The Griffith Tradition was a noble tradition when the dramatic analysis implied order in the universe. The acceleration of montage (Eisenstein notwithstanding) was an ever less satisfying attempt to find a pattern of order in a complexity of events that were evolving faster than man could keep up with. As montage practices broke away from the stability of the Griffith Tradition, the frantic energy of the cutting reflected man's initial inability to cope with the complexities of modern life.

This essentially neurotic use of montage reappeared in the Sixties as an expression of man's violent despair at his inability to construct meaning in his environment. Fragmenting montages isolated diverse elements that refused to unify, refused to offer any hope of order. The rational tools of analysis were not adequate in explaining the phenomena observed. Carried to its logical extreme in such films as Russ Meyer's *Beyond the Valley of the Dolls* and *The Seven Minutes,* the lingering presence of the Griffith Tradition has been viewed as reactionary and simplistic; and yet the lesson of the futility of this extreme analytic violence does aptly and artfully pinpoint the logical crisis of an unbendingly rational approach to modern life.

ALLAN DWAN

Of all the directors of the Griffith Tradition who maintained careers well into the sound period, Allan Dwan was the least affected by the emergence of the Murnau Tradition—perhaps because his theme of temporal resignation was so totally unassailable by either social or cultural evolutions. Dwan's visual style was the purest expression of the Griffith Tradition; and it was certainly the purity of this style (and its thematic implications) that sustained Dwan's creative energy throughout a long B-movie career. In Dwan's later work the mathematical perfection of his visual style best illustrates the primal power inherent in the Griffith Tradition. It is precisely in these films, burdened with the most hopeless scripts and populated by the most crippled performers (projects in which "personal involvement" seemed most out of the question) that Dwan relied most exclusively and abstractly on the beauties of the filmmaking tradition itself, and proved himself the master craftsman of the Griffith Tradition.

Such films as *Belle Le Grand* (1951), *I Dream of Jeanie* (1952), and *Enchanted Island* (1958) become textbook exercises in the American montage tradition. These films are realized with a cinematic precision as intuitively perfect as Eisenstein's montages were calculatedly accurate. Dwan's images are beautiful not so much as formal entities unto themselves, as in their existence as cinematic units. The world captured in the frame is never as important as the relationship of one shot to the next. In ordering these units, Dwan is concerned with those qualities central to the montage tradition rather than that deceptive pictorialist prettification of individual shots that became fashionable in the late silent era. If the craft of directing can be compared to that of writing, then Dwan is the master of cinematic syntax.

Economy, simplicity, and directness characterize the Dwan approach. Each image is selected as a utilitarian response to a narrative challenge. Compared with Dwan's straightforward decisions, the cinema of Howard Hawks looks mannered and expressionistic. Thematically and visually, Dwan is one of the least neurotic of all filmmakers—even in his visualization of such a totally neurotic subject as *Slightly Scarlet* (1956).

To understand the current nostalgic response to Hollywood B-pictures—and to the dubious personalities who acted out the rituals of these films—one must understand those properties of the Griffith Tradition as brought out in the purity of Dwan's use of these practices. The performers in B-pictures were rather unextraordinary people in bigger-than-life roles, unable to summon up emotions as mythic as those suggested by the characters they played. But the conventions of the Griffith Tradition (and the conventional responses evoked by these clichés) were oblivious to the incompetence of these performers. A cut-in to a large close-up, or a cut-back to a long shot, in the primal power of the change in image size alone, suggests a nobility of emotion that is direct and effective. Furthermore, the sympathetic incompetence of the B-performer suggests the essential innocence of the human condition. Vera Ralston's close-ups in *Belle Le Grand* are among the most moving images in the American cinema, and yet simultaneously are a mockery of the traditional process of mimesis we call acting.

The innocence of Allan Dwan's response to such blatant incompetence—his total acceptance of inane situations and performers—transcends our conventional evaluations of theme and character. Dwan's style is characterized by a benign grace that allows his camera to observe and analyze without passing judgment. Because he introduces no element of tension by trying to evoke performances of which his actors are incapable, or to insert deeper meaning into scripts that were not structured to sustain much meaning at all, Dwan avoids the sense of artificiality that can hover over the ambitious aspirations of talented directors contending with incompetent collaborators. As folk art, Dwan's best films are his most dramatically purposeless. They become objects of meditation.

CECIL B. DE MILLE

Surely the best-known practitioner of the Griffith Tradition was Cecil B. De Mille. De Mille was everything that Griffith refused to become; consequently, he enjoyed the successful career that Griffith was denied. De Mille was happy to be a moralist, happy to be a storyteller, happy to parade the spectacle of man's folly, happy to pander emotionalism, happy to give the public everything it thought it wanted. If Dwan fulfilled the Griffith Tradition by seeking its highest implications,

De Mille exploited that tradition by seeking out its logical extremes. While Dwan's films best demonstrate the glories of the Griffith Tradition, De Mille's films best demonstrate its limitations.

De Mille's films are wonderfully satisfying as far as they go, but they lack the transcendence of high art. The earthboundedness of the visual style makes mockeries of the religious themes, but is ideally suited to the detailing of human folly that is so central to most of his work. De Mille reminds us that, when we speak of the Griffith Tradition as folk art, we are looking at the cinema primarily in its function as entertainment. It could be said of De Mille's films that they have no content at all: they are exercises in pure narration. Certainly, De Mille has little involvement in his stories except as a raconteur. Like Otto Preminger, De Mille seeks out large issues and contexts for his narratives and avoids overtly choosing sides in depicting conflicts. But, unlike Preminger, De Mille is not interested in a discussion of the issues. The issues and contexts are merely the canvas on which he illustrates the great American adventure.

De Mille's heyday was the late Twenties and early Thirties, when his outrageous romanticism was synonymous with the folly of the Hollywood ethic. His visual style during this period shows the Griffith Tradition at its most rigid, its most institutionalized, and its most relentlessly formal. De Mille may have been a rather limited craftsman, but he had *total* control over those few elements the Griffith Tradition put at his disposal. His characters have little depth, but they are described with total economy, equipped with only those dimensions of personality that are necessary to the telling of the story. While the tendency of the early sound film was to allow narrative to illustrate characterization, De Mille relentlessly deployed characterization only to illustrate narration.

In De Mille, there is no sense of the profound, no "penetration into the realm of the immaterial." Everything is order. He is the total montage director, with only one associational meaning aligned with each image. In a film like *The Volga Boatman* (1926), he never moves the camera and strenuously avoids depth of focus. Most of his story takes place in medium close-ups with his characters focused in a single plane in the foreground, while the backgrounds function only pictorially. Everything is very flat: long shots have no foregrounds or middle distances, and all objects are focused equidistant from the camera. De Mille has a strong sense of the pictorial. Characters are strictly posed within the frames. Even spectacular long shots have the feeling that every extra has been exactly placed and controlled by the director. Nothing is pictorially or narratively extraneous. The actions are stylized, and the emotions are wildly extreme. The staging is as high style as the plot elements are ridiculous.

Of course, more than any other element, it was De Mille's use of spectacle that sustained his career. Griffith had used spectacle to make concrete the exterior forces over which his characters' love was challenged to triumph. Griffith's spectacle was all the more overwhelming in its relegation to the background of his story. De Mille was interested in spectacle per se. De Mille defines the Griffith Tradition as the exploitation and institutionalization of elements that were at best peripheral to the driving force of Griffith's vision.

D. W. GRIFFITH

After establishing its initial concepts, Griffith himself did not play a major part in the evolution of the Griffith Tradition. After *Intolerance* (1916), his own visual style moved progressively farther away from the elemental montage aesthetic.

Almost all the misunderstanding of Griffith's later work stems from the assumption that Griffith remained a part of this montage tradition. On the contrary, the essential driving force behind much of Griffith's later work was his very conscious desire to find a visual style through which the medium of film would have the potential to become a personal (as opposed to folk) art form, comparable to the other established forms of high art.

By 1928, he was able to look back upon this first narrative solution as a faulty, incomplete medium. He wrote: "So far I believe all our pictures have been written on sand. The medium is perishable. The medium is far from being equal to the medium of words, written or spoken. I welcome talking pictures because it may be through this medium, where we can use words and music, that in the future it may be possible to produce motion pictures which can be classified with great plays, painting, music and the other proper arts. By their faulty medium, the pictures made so far have become obsolete, while the dialogue of Shakespeare is as beautiful and telling as the day it was written."

The commercial failure of *Intolerance* can be seen as the first indication to Griffith that the form he had evolved was insufficient for dealing with the themes he wanted to explore. Griffith wanted to deal with ideas, but he had at his disposal a form suited to deal only with stories. The complexity of the structure of *Intolerance* reinforced the emotions of his narrative, but offered only repetitions and variations, and not the desired deepening, of Griffith's vision. Furthermore, the complexity of *Intolerance* ran contrary to the ideals of simplicity and directness that had so endeared the Griffith Tradition to the American consciousness.

Yet, for Griffith, *Intolerance* was the logical extension of the montage aesthetic. In a formal sense, he had developed a complete medium—and come to a creative dead end. Had Griffith's interests been only in securing a career, he could have rested on his laurels for the rest of the silent period, reworking and refining, with a minimum of creative effort, this narrative solution of dramatic analysis. All other choices involved totally new beginnings. The bulk of Griffith's career in the Twenties can be seen as alternations between new formal explorations and safer refinements of this first narrative solution. The drama of Griffith's evolution as an artist lies in his compulsive search for this new narrative solution.

The crisis that Griffith had to face in finding the montage aesthetic a system inappropriate to the yearnings of his own vision underscores the degree to which the Griffith Tradition was consolidated as a response to a cultural necessity external to Griffith and even antithetical to his vision. Research into the early appearances of the specific elements of this tradition further supports that Griffith did not so much invent these techniques as consolidate them into a workable narrative system. Before he could evolve as an artist along lines dictated by his own interior vision, he had first to secure a medium in which to work. For securing this medium, Griffith has already been appropriately honored.

The point is not to reject the importance of Griffith's editing, but to accept it as a given—the most important given of the silent-film form. But even while Griffith was consolidating the montage principles of the Griffith Tradition, his visual style contained the seeds of a vision that saw beyond the limitations of the montage aesthetic. It is in his unique uses of this montage tradition that we observe a second tendency in Griffith's vision begin to coalesce.

Certainly what distinguished Griffith from the other directors who had adopted the Griffith form, and what made Griffith's work stand apart and above from all his competitors', were those elements of his style which were not integral to the montage tradition and which mere emulation could not duplicate.

Griffith's themes involved subjects which could not easily be captured in simple narratives—thus prompting the poetry of Griffith's title cards. And Griffith's legendary skill in directing actors can be translated, in aesthetic terms, to a preoccupation with the reality of the individual human presence—a concept rather alien to the mythologizing tendencies of the montage tradition. A film like Elmer Clifton's *Down to the Sea in Ships* (1922) might perfectly have imitated Griffith's narrative structure, his spectacle, and even his staging; but the performances are ludicrous, and a high level of ideas is lacking.

From today's perspective, these are the two elements of Griffith's early work—the acting and the titles—that are most difficult to evaluate, alternating as they do between the ridiculous and the sublime. In either regard, it is clear that these two elements were wedded to the montage tradition in a most uneasy relationship in Griffith's work. The broader acting styles and more directly descriptive titles employed by other contemporary directors melded better with the narratives of the montage aesthetic.

Griffith was both a moralist and a spiritualist, and the evolution of his later career can be seen as the battleground between these two tendencies. The vision of Griffith the moralist could be accommodated in the montage system, but the vision of Griffith the spiritualist could not.

As a moralist (like Hitchcock), Griffith's first concern was the effect his film would have upon his audience. The needs of the audience were primary. In the Twenties, the simple, physical reactions created by the suspense of parallel editing gradually became less effective in holding the interests of an ever-more sophisticated audience. Thus, as the needs of his audience changed, so Griffith sought the means of evoking deeper and more subtle emotions. Griffith's vision required a mass audience. If he could not reach the people with his films, there was little reason to make them. The moralist Griffith could hardly indulge in art for art's sake. His cinema eschewed abstraction, humanity being its central preoccupation.

As a spiritualist, Griffith was in no position to make the moral judgments that his montage cinema implied. The spiritualist wanted to record deep emotions, to move the emotions of his audience. For this Griffith, one close-up of Lillian Gish—held while profound emotions subtly animated her body—expressed in a moment all the truths that the moralist Griffith could strive in vain to adequately describe in a lifetime of narratives. The close-up became less a unit of cinematic narration and more the medium of a new intimacy between audience and character that rendered both storytelling and stage-level theatrical observation obsolete.

If the moralist Griffith edited in order to separate the elements of his narrative, the spiritualist Griffith would edit to imply unions between shots and characters otherwise separated by space and time. Griffith would intercut between a man at war and his loved-one at home, not so much to indicate simultaneous actions as to indicate a continuing spiritual bond.

In his later work, Griffith moved his emotional involvement from the cut to the shot itself; and the analysis of individual shots becomes more telling than analysis of the relationships of montage. The technology of the matched cut became less a compulsion than before, and sometimes the actions of shots overlap or are mismatched (perhaps purposefully). Griffith also rejected the classically composed and balanced frames of the pictorialist tradition—a fact that indicates the extent to which he wished to free his characters from the determining forces of a structured frame. Even in the Biograph period, Griffith preferred to let his characters move in depth, emphasizing the three-dimensionality of their space, rather than confining them in single two-dimensioned planes parallel to the camera. When he did stage his action in this frontal plane—as in the dinner scene in *Way Down East,* when Lillian Gish is banished to her fate on the ice floes—the staging itself implies the loss of freedom, and the limiting morality of intolerance.

Well aware of the traditions of the earlier graphic arts, Griffith would reserve the use of classical composition for special moments when a sense of heightened harmony was desired. Often a static camera would hold on a conspicuously unbalanced composition, only to later have a character enter the frame or move within the frame to complete the composition.

While Griffith always tended to employ a static camera, one rarely had the feeling that his actors were confined, for purely formal reasons, to any one spot in front of the camera. The freedom of the actor came first, and it is significant that Griffith would choose to show a character exiting one shot and entering another, rather than employ the simple pan that would be standard today. Some of the most interesting effects, especially in the Biograph films, involve the use of the very edges of the frame. In both cases, the camera is set up not in relation to the characters, but to the environment through which they move. Griffith's most harmonious compositions are his landscapes. His camera discovers the harmonies inherent in man's universe, but sees man himself as undetermined and free to move through that universe without external interference. (Andy Warhol's initial explorations of the static camera in the Sixties are remarkably similar in meaning to those of Griffith in his Biograph period.)

For the moralist Griffith, the disappointing response of his audience to *Intolerance* was an undeniable defeat. *Intolerance*·succeeded as a film of spectacle and as a film of narrative action, but not as a film of ideas. For all the complexity of its form, *Intolerance* had fallen short of the grandeur of its theme. It was the old story of man's greatest monument being ultimately inferior to the profound perfection of a simple flower. This obvious lesson in hubris was not lost on Griffith, who spent the rest of his career pursuing the beauty of the flower.

The second phase of Griffith's career involved a progressive loss of dependency on analytic editing and an increasing dependency on the presence of humanity within the individual shot. For Griffith, it became less and less possible (or necessary) to take the camera off Lillian Gish. The spiritualist studies that which is within, and the illumination of Griffith's later frames comes from within the performers who populate his visions. Griffith chose to forgo the idealizations of pictorialism in order to record the actual vibrations of those objects of nature he found before his camera.

With the evolution of a cinema that would accommodate first of all the presence of his actors, Griffith declared: "The greatest thing in motion pictures is humanity. (Other objects) are beautiful only if we associate them with humanity in a beautiful way. A street might be recalled to us as a beautiful street. If our dreams of the people we met and knew and loved on that street are beautiful, then the street will be beautiful to us. It is the same with everything else. There is nothing in life but humanity."

Just as the early sound directors could not capture the complexity of modern life in montage, so Griffith could not describe the complexities of human emotions, deep to the point of transcendence, with montage. Griffith spent most of his later career trying to push the silent medium beyond its inherent limitations, searching for a freedom that only sound could eventually bring. The Griffith Tradition was capable of mythology, but not psychology; archetypes, but not characterization; pageant, but not intimacy; stability, but not immediacy; abstractions of life, but not that full parallel of life to which Griffith's vision aspired.

The prophets of the cinema—Griffith, Rossellini, Godard, Warhol—have always introduced the techniques to make the cinema more immediate; while the institutionalizing tendencies of the industry have undertaken the formalization of these techniques. The tension between these two tendencies has produced some of the highest glories of the medium. The Griffith Tradition was one of these glories, but the vision of D. W. Griffith himself was in pursuit of higher options.

John B. Kuiper   (essay date 1985)

SOURCE: "The Growth of a Film Director—D. W. Griffith," in *Wonderful Inventions: Motion Pictures, Broadcasting, and Recorded Sound at the Library of Congress,* Library of Congress, 1985, pp. 11-16.

[*In the following essay, Kuiper describes Griffith's early film career at Biograph Studios.*]

During the early part of 1908 an unusual man of thirty-three years began to work at the old Biograph Studios, 11 East 14th Street in New York City. Author, poet, and playwright by predisposition and a reasonably successful actor by practice and experience, David Wark Griffith began his work in the motion-picture medium first by acting in a short picture for the Edison Company and then by offering Biograph scenarios and plots as well as his other Thespian talents.

The activity he must have observed at the 14th Street studio could hardly have inspired serious meditation or even confidence in the expressive capabilities of his newly chosen field. Producing companies then ground out new subjects as quickly as possible, and one day was considered the necessary time to film a "photoplay," as the short, dramatic, seven-to-fifteen-minute films of the day were called.

New York production methods similar to those Griffith must have encountered at Biograph in 1908 were amusingly recorded by William Allen Johnson in the November 13, 1909, issue of *Harper's Weekly*. Johnson reported that out-of-work stage actors congregated in a park at Broadway and 42nd Street where they were told during the morning to report to the studio for shooting at one o'clock in the afternoon. When they arrived, they discovered that they were to work on a set which resembled a wartime naval vessel. First they were outfitted in appropriate clothing; then came the rehearsal as described by Mr. Johnson:

> The regular stage requires many weeks for this sort of production; the moving picture studio takes only as many minutes. The expedition of the thing, the rapid improvisations of the performers, seem very remarkable to a layman . . . The actors ask for explanations, if they require them. Sometimes the stage director changes his plot as he stages it; and, again competition is so keen that each is fearful to make known clearly the title and story for fear it will leak into a competitor's hands before his copyright is obtained. . . . the stage director groups his men about the battleship . . . then he steps back, and folding his arms, regards them thoughtfully.
>
> The first rehearsal takes but two minutes; the second takes less . . . [during the third] the stage director's constant cry is: "Keep moving. Talk, smile, frown, yell—do something—keep awake!" . . .
>
> A hurried test is now made to see if the machine is working properly. . . . Less than fifteen minutes have been consumed and an entire act has been staged and reproduced. Other acts follow in the same quick course of procedure, and before the afternoon sun wanes a complete play has been enacted and transferred to a film one thousand feet in length.

The actors were paid five dollars and dismissed. Within several weeks the photoplay was making the rounds of the theaters. Six months later it was retired or, as one reviewer put it, "stored away until it can be used again as fresh material, after the public has forgotten it."

From the situation just described we get one of our first pictures of an American film director. He had to be a coordinator and a bully. He capitalized on the accidental and incidental to change the plot furnished him by the story writer while always keeping an eye out for camera troubles; he was also expected to trouble-shoot "the machine" if it broke down.

During his tenure at Biograph from June 1908 to October 1913, D. W. Griffith helped bring about substantial changes in the length of time a director could spend on a project and, what is more important, in the sophistication and richness of the end product. It is axiomatic among film historians that Griffith was one of the greatest and most influential of all American motion picture directors. Most of them agree that although his influence was not appreciated until after he left Biograph, his work there was richly productive in terms of the variety of subjects he treated, the story-telling devices he utilized, and the motion picture techniques he spurred

technicians to develop. Griffith developed an extremely effective method of motion picture story-telling, a method that utilized almost every dramatic device he had learned during his apprenticeship as a young actor and playwright on the popular stage of the day. The Biographs he produced served as his notebooks, sketchbooks, and story outlines; a constant source of experimentation in dramatic method which stocked his memory with notes on successes and failures and the methods by which each success was achieved and each failure accounted for.

According to recent estimates, Griffith directed 494 short films and a four-reel feature, *Judith of Bethulia,* while he was at Biograph. The paper positive print collection of the Library of Congress contains 310 of these films, and there are a score of additional Biographs in the Mary Pickford collection. Thus the Library has the largest single group of early Griffith films that has survived the self-destructive tendencies of the celluloid nitrate base upon which all other copies were recorded.

Until the copyright law was amended in 1912 to provide for copyrighting motion pictures, producers obtained protection for their films by depositing a paper print and having it registered as a still photograph. These paper prints, which form the basis of the Library's holdings of early motion pictures, have outlived most of the original cellulose prints. Some original Biograph negatives still survive in other locations, but they are not easily reprinted nor have they been restored consistently or thoroughly. After two decades of planning and work, the Griffith films in the Library's collection, as well as almost three thousand other early titles from 1894 to 1912, have been painstakingly rephotographed, image by image, as a result of a restoration program of the Library and the Academy of Motion Picture Arts and Sciences. Now, too, an index to the entire collection by Kemp R. Niver has been published by the University of California Press. For the first time since they were released nearly sixty years ago, Griffith's legacy has been restored for the new generation of film historians to study, sort, and clarify.

And what is likely to be deduced a decade from now when the bright young film students in colleges and universities have looked, compared, and digested all the early Griffiths available to them today? Although any definite conclusions seem somewhat premature, I believe that certain errors that have been woven into the fabric of the Griffith legend will be promptly eliminated when the films themselves are available. Foremost among these errors are misstatements about Griffith's use of technical devices and his development, seemingly single-handed, of cinematic devices known today as the close-up, long shot, fade-out, and the like. For example, it has often been said that Griffith first used a change of camera setup in the middle of a scene in *For Love of Gold* (1908). A view of the film confirms that no such change takes place.

Students of the motion picture medium will surely note, however, a wonderful development in story-telling power from Griffith's early to his late Biographs. His later films amply demonstrate how he began to break up his scenes into many different shots, often taken from different angles and distances. They will note, for example, that in *The Lesser Evil* (1912) he cut rapidly from one action or set of characters to another and in the process created suspense, contrast, or a startling juxtaposition that efficiently advances the action; and that as early as July 1909, in *The Country Doctor,* he used shots to build atmosphere even though they did not directly advance the story action.

But above all I believe new students of the cinema will notice that what have been called Griffith's "discoveries" deserve mention not because every one of his early films had some of them—many do not—but because Griffith used them in relationship to the response of an audience. Today we may laugh at the obvious mawkishness of the despairing wife in *The Expiation* (1909) or at the oath of the drinking father in *The Drunkard's Reformation* (1909); we may feel embarrassed by the chauvinism of Civil War dramas like *The House with Closed Shutters* (1910); and we may regard *The Two Paths* (1911) as excessively moralistic or *When Kings Were the Law* (1912) and *The Unchanging Sea* (1910) as unduly pretentious and "literary." But it will be a great deal more difficult for the scholars of the coming decade to discount the successful realization of the idealism and high aspirations which went into the making of such films, just as we have already learned not to discount the favorable reception they were accorded when they were originally released. With all his faults and prejudices, Griffith's treatment of humanity is still an affective one.

In my opinion, at least two other qualities of Griffith's work will attract the notice of scholars. The paper print collection contains an unusual number of light-hearted family comedies, most of them directed during the first two years of the Biograph period. Griffith's comedy work, as far as I know, has been completely unsurveyed. Social historians will also be interested in the characterizations and plots of the more "serious" films and the way they seem to describe the social mores and attitudes held in our country during what Walter Lord has called the Good Years, 1900 to 1914.

However, the study of Griffith Biographs by young people whose consuming interest is cinema will reveal that David Wark Griffith's contribution to the motion picture remains solidly in the realm of film direction. When Griffith entered Biograph in 1908, there were only about ten film directors of the coordinator-bully type. But by 1912 there were at least thirty film directors and Epes Winthrop Sargent could write:

> One gratifying change is in the increased number
> of directors in proportion to the number of pictures
> released each week. In some studios a single

director is still required to make one or even two full releases a week, but there is a growing tendency to give a director more time on a subject and this helps the photoplay in that the script may be studied more carefully and the finer points brought out.

There can be little doubt that D. W. Griffith's experimentation and growth at Biograph was one of the central factors behind this change.

Jean E. Tucker (essay date 1985)

SOURCE: "Voices from the Silents," in *Wonderful Inventions: Motion Pictures, Broadcasting, and Recorded Sound at the Library of Congress,* edited by Iris Newsom, Library of Congress, 1985, pp. 31-9.

[*In the following essay, Tucker creates a portrait of Griffith by drawing on memories and reflections from several of his contemporaries.*]

The origins of the motion picture as an art form can be traced to the turn of the century. Since the late 1800s, motion pictures have drawn what they have needed from the other arts—music, literature, and the theater—and have attained an artistic maturity of their own in a relatively short period of time. The artistic attainment has been accompanied by a coincidental evolution of motion picture technology.

The development of a historical record of the motion picture has not kept pace with the advancement of the art and technology, however. Indeed, the history of the motion picture, particularly silent film, was neglected until the mid-1960s and the early 1970s. It is fortunate that film scholars are now beginning to pay attention to the historical development of the art and that more and more people who worked in silent pictures are writing memoirs and consenting to taped interviews, thus sharing their experiences and knowledge. As a consequence, the history of the silent movies is being more fully documented in the voices and words of living persons who were directly involved in devising, developing, and perfecting the acting and production techniques that have become the art of the motion picture.

Oral history especially lends itself to the study of silent film. Taped interviews make it possible to record or reconstruct events which occurred during the silent film era of the motion picture. Interviews enable participants to tell their own particular story and include specific facts about the birth of an industry that might otherwise be lost. They can replace or supplement written documents and clarify differing views of the same event, revealing personality in ways which cannot be represented in written form.

The quality of information revealed in interviews depends upon the analysis made of it. After comparing the information to other interviews and written sources, it can be elaborated, explained, and interpreted, so as to supplement and validate known information and create original documents.

D. W. Griffith's *Intolerance,* a silent film produced in 1916 by the Wark Producing Company, has been particularly neglected by film historians and critics since its release. No definitive work on the film has been published. No one directly involved with the production of the film has written more than a chapter or two about it. And, until the time I began a search for persons associated with the film, no one had recorded a collection of taped conversations with individuals who took part in its production.

The inspiration for this search came from Lillian Gish. I first met and talked briefly with her at the Library of Congress in 1969 at a presentation of her film-lecture *Lillian Gish and the Movies: The Art of Film, 1900-1928.* She made a lasting impression. She seemed so interested and enthusiastic about everyone and everything around her. Her devotion to silent film and D. W. Griffith and her desire to tell his story were clearly genuine.

After a second meeting nearly a year later, I wanted to learn more about the woman who seemed to epitomize the silent screen. I quickly discovered she had been sorely neglected by biographers and other writers. I read all I could find, looked at existing films in the collections of the Library of Congress and the Museum of Modern Art, and eventually interviewed her.

The Recorded Sound Section of the Library of Congress (now part of the Motion Picture, Broadcasting, and Recorded Sound Division) accepted for its collections a copy of the tape of my conversation with her and expressed an interest in the tapes of interviews that I might record with other film personalities.

I discovered there were at least four living persons in addition to Lillian Gish who had been involved directly in the production of D. W. Griffith's film *Intolerance* and that they would be willing to talk with me—not only about the film but about the development of the motion picture, acting and directing techniques, their early careers in silent film, and their relationship with D. W. Griffith. They were Karl Brown, cameraman; Miriam Cooper, actress; Joseph Henabery, actor, researcher, and director; and Anita Loos, who had written titles for the film.

Their stories were told within the framework of their own particular skills, experiences, and contributions. Some bias and differences of opinion were inevitable. The value of the oral history approach was to bring the differing views out in the open where they could be compared. Taken together, the accounts of the experiences of the interviewees present a clearer understanding of why and how the film *Intolerance* was made and assist in interpreting the silent film period.

None of the interviewees knew the full story of the production of *Intolerance* as they evaluated the film from different production aspects and degrees of intimacy with Griffith. If the success or failure of the film is judged on its technical and artistic merits, the interviewees agree it was a success. They also agree that the film would never have popular general audience appeal because it is tediously long. Film historians concur. Only film students flock to see it.

The interviewees express a great depth of feeling toward D. W. Griffith. Their enthusiasm is open and genuine. They share a great sense of pride in their association with him and are all devoted and loyal. They feel close to Griffith even though none of their relationships—with the possible exception of Lillian Gish—were ever on a personal level.

They had courted his pleasure and were deeply appreciative of the smallest of compliments from Griffith. They bore no resentment that he did not credit their work in his films. Griffith treated the women with dignity and courtesy and expected them to be ladies. He encouraged their creativity. In turn, they gave him their undivided loyalty and devotion and worked hard to please him. The men were equally as loyal although somewhat more willing to admit flaws in Griffith.

The intense effect Griffith had on the interviewees is as complex and difficult to explain as the man himself. It can be attributed primarily to the combination of his maturity, father image, personal magnetism, and leadership qualities and his ability to inspire creativity and to generate excitement in the work and the films they produced together.

During the silent film era, the interviewees did not recognize the significant contributions they were making to their craft and the industry. With the passage of time, however, they realized the magnitude of the art they helped create. They were proud of their role and wanted to talk about it. Theirs was a time of great experimentation and development. It is remarkable that except for technical equipment advances and sound, the basic film-making techniques they helped develop stand today.

The interviewees were completely different in temperament and personality, but some common traits—such as pride in self and work, strength of character, tenacity, aggressiveness, desire to achieve, self-confidence, sense of humor, and a respect for one another—come out in the interviews.

All had a natural talent for their work. They succeeded because they seldom considered failure. Lack of formal education did not deter them. They were in movies because they wanted to be. In order to stay there, they had to be the best. They were doing something that very few of their peers were able to do because it was a disgrace in many social circles to work in the movies. But they considered themselves very special people engaged in a very special craft. They all had great confidence in their abilities.

They obviously were not well acquainted with one another when they worked with Griffith but grew to respect and admire one another in old age. They enjoyed being discovered by film historians, students, and others, and liked to share their experiences. They had a sense of history and were eager to get their life stories written or preserved on tape. Miriam Cooper, Joseph Henabery, Lillian Gish, and Anita Loos all arranged for their memorabilia to be deposited either in the Library of Congress or the Museum of Modern Art. Their films have not been as well preserved and many have been lost through deterioration or destruction. Still photographs are the only remaining source of information about many of the films they were involved in producing. The taped words and voices of the interviewees provide the means to experience more closely the period of the silent film.

INTOLERANCE

Intolerance is a long motion picture—on fourteen reels of film, it lasts over two hours. Audiences tend to find it bewildering and exhausting and are confused by the constant intercutting of the four stories representing four different time periods, each with its own set of characters: "The Modern Story" (or *The Mother and the Law*), "The Babylonian Story," "The Medieval French Story (or the St. Bartholomew Massacre)," and "The Judean (or Crucifixion) Story." Intercuts of a woman rocking a cradle are used to tie the stories together.

The film grew out of a five-reel melodrama entitled *The Mother and the Law* that Griffith had almost completed before the release of *The Birth of a Nation*. After the financial success and critical acclaim of *The Birth of a Nation*. Griffith feared that audiences would consider *The Mother and the Law* disappointing. Anxious to live up to his reputation as the greatest genius of the cinema, he took *The Mother and the Law* and intercut it with three other stories to create the epic *Intolerance*.

The Mother and the Law, set in a modern time period, deals mainly with social intolerance, the miscarriage of justice, and class hatred, bleakly revealing the wrongs inflicted by a pious factory owner on his employees and the events that ensue. The Babylonian episode illustrates the intolerance of one people for another and the intolerance of a priest for the beliefs of a different religion. The medieval French story deals with the massacre of French Protestants by Catholics in 1572. The Judean story uses incidents from the life of Christ—Christ and the Pharisees, the marriage of Cana, and the Crucifixion. In each of the stories intolerance is the initial theme but the topic is not expanded or reinforced by the action. As a result, the film turns into a melodrama.

Griffith created the entire film without a written script, despite its length and complexity. It was all in his head. The film took almost two years to make and cost two million dollars to produce. G. W. "Billy" Bitzer, the principal cameraman, was assisted by Karl Brown in shooting the film. Many of the scenes were tinted red, green, blue, and yellow. Unless fading has changed the originals, Griffith used varying intensities and combinations for these tints, which differ on various frames of the film. His use of color was unrealistic and contributes immeasurably to the emotional intensity of the film.

Music for full orchestra accompaniment was arranged by Joseph Carl Breil under Griffith's supervision. The cast included sixty credits and hundreds of uncredited extras. Crowd and battle scenes used thousands of actors and actresses. Some fifteen thousand persons and two hundred and fifty chariots were used for the filming of the "Fall of Babylon" sequence. Griffith drew on the talents of the regular members of the stock company as well as many relative newcomers who went on to become important actors, actresses, and directors.

The giant sets for the film were built without architectural plans on the corner lot of Sunset and Hollywood Boulevards. The structures rose to towering heights, growing from day to day as Griffith had new ideas and told his carpenters what he wanted. They were perhaps the greatest sets ever constructed. Gigantic walls, painted to simulate stone, were built under the supervision of Huck Wortman. The walls rose to a height of one hundred feet and were adorned with reliefs of winged creatures and elephants. Towers reached much higher. The walls were wide and strong enough to hold the weight of racing horses, chariots, and the throngs of soldiers used in battle scenes. Huge heavy gates, built like those of ancient Babylon, were opened by actors portraying slaves pushing big iron wheels on either side of the gates.

Sets were also constructed to resemble ancient Judea and the Paris of Louis IX. Thousands of pieces of furniture, decorative items, swords, guns, and other objects were built or collected. Although the Los Angeles fire department ordered the sets dismantled in 1916, Griffith managed to delay the destruction until 1917. They were so solidly built that parts of them survived on back lots for many years.

Previewed in a theater in Riverside, California, on August 6, 1916, *Intolerance* opened at the Liberty Theatre in New York City on September 4, 1916. As was his custom, Griffith accompanied the film on its first showing in major cities, cutting the prints at the theaters in an effort to improve it. In 1919 he cut into the original negative—somewhere between 13,500 and 13,700 feet in length—without making a duplicate in order to make new films from two of the stories in *Intolerance: The Fall of Babylon* and *The Mother and the Law.* Consequently, it has never been possible to restore the *Intolerance* negative to its original state. The master print in the collections of the Museum of Modern Art is missing two reels and measures only 11,811 feet.

Some critical reviews after the New York opening acclaimed Griffith's genius and declared the film a spectacle. Other reviews were generally favorable to Griffith but expressed some reservations about the film itself, which was a box office failure.

Although attempts have been made from time to time to revive the film, especially in Europe, *Intolerance* has never been a popular success. But the film has had a lasting impact on the art of filmmaking and holds an important place in film history.

THE *INTOLERANCE* THEME

Intolerance cannot be discussed without reference to its predecessor, *The Birth of a Nation,* released the previous year. Some silent film scholars feel *Intolerance* was Griffith's apologia for the racial bigotry portrayed in *The Birth of a Nation* and demonstrated his penitence for the violence the first film engendered wherever it was shown. Others believe that *Intolerance* was strictly a commercial enterprise and in no way reflected any change in Griffith's attitude. Although Lillian Gish, Karl Brown, Miriam Cooper, Joseph Henabery, and Anita Loos all have differing views on Griffith's purpose and accomplishments in both films, they seem to agree that Griffith fought all of his life for the right of freedom of speech and creative expression.

The Birth of a Nation, released in 1915, was a tremendous success for Griffith and established a place for him in film history. The film has been considered by some to be the single most important motion picture ever made. Iris Barry has stated that the picture established the film genre as the "most persuasive of entertainments and compelled the acceptance of the film as art."

First shown as *The Clansman* in Los Angeles on February 8, 1915, and as *The Birth of a Nation* at the Liberty Theatre in New York on March 3, 1915, the film was twelve reels long. It was based on *The Clansman* and *The Leopard's Spots,* both written by the Reverend Thomas Dixon, Jr.

Public response to it was overwhelming, but from the beginning the film was met with extraordinary protests and demands for censorship. Even today it stirs up controversy. Although portions of the film are deemed racist and inflammatory, few have considered Griffith himself as being a racist. Iris Barry states that the film was "a Southerner's honest effort to portray events still very close to the experience of the community in which he grew up." She goes on to say that

> Griffith had the native attitudes of the Southern tradition. At the same time he was a nineteenth-century romantic. But above all he was a dramatist; he was a genius at portraying emotion by means of the language of the screen.

Much of the film's early success can be attributed to the controversy it aroused. Demonstrations and violence flared when the film was shown in Boston, Philadelphia, and other cities across the country. The protests and demands for censure may have angered Griffith, but they also created profits—the more protests, the more publicity, the bigger the crowds, and the larger the take at the box office.

Griffith's public response to the bigotry charges leveled at him was couched in terms of censorship and guaranteed freedoms. The protests and demands to censure *The Birth of a Nation* seemed outrageous to him. He consistently defended the right of the motion picture to share with literature the privilege of free speech. In 1916, he published a pamphlet, *The Rise and Fall of Free Speech in America,* in which he condemned all censorship and defended the extension of the First Amendment to film. The word "intolerance" appears frequently throughout this declaration and lends credence to the notion that the title of Griffith's next film was no coincidence. One paragraph in particular points to a defense of his integrity and challenges his detractors to criticize his second answer to their intolerance—his film *Intolerance*:

> The reason for the slapstick and the worst that is in pictures is censorship. Let those who tell us to uplift our art, invest money in the production of an historic play of the time of Christ. They will find this cannot be staged without incurring the wrath of a certain part of our people. The Massacre of St. Bartholomew, if produced, will tread upon the toes of another part of our people.

Opinions of the interviewees vary as to how they thought public response to *The Birth of a Nation* affected Griffith's decisions on the production of *Intolerance*. Lillian Gish disclaims that *Intolerance* was a response to reactions to *The Birth of a Nation*. Miriam Cooper, on the other hand, claims that it was. Anita Loos states that there was nothing original in intolerance as a theme. Karl Brown and Joseph Henabery both look on the film as a business enterprise and as Griffith's attempt to capitalize on an opportunity.

In her autobiography Lillian Gish tries to dispel the theory that Griffith produced *Intolerance* as an apology for *The Birth of a Nation*. She suggests that Griffith in *The Birth of a Nation* showed on film what he had heard as a boy and believed to be true about the Civil War. Believing that Griffith had no reason to apologize for his film, Gish contends that *Intolerance* "was his way of answering those who, in his view, were the bigots."

Miriam Cooper states that *Intolerance* was a part of Griffith's crusade against intolerance. "He wanted to show intolerance throughout the world through the ages through thousands of years of intolerance." She believes Griffith produced *Intolerance* because of the riots connected with the showing of *The Birth of a Nation* and because "people were so incensed at other people."

In her interview, Anita Loos's reaction to intolerance as a theme for the film is somewhat negative. She does not see anything particularly creative or new about Griffith's idea that intolerance was the cause of everyone's troubles.

Karl Brown agrees with Lillian Gish that Griffith portrayed the Civil War and Reconstruction in *The Birth of a Nation* as he thought the events had taken place. Moreover, he feels that Griffith, a showman and a businessman, produced his pictures to sell. Brown considers the reaction to the film and the riots around the country as "very good business. . . . Every riot meant another million dollars." He says that Griffith gave no indication at the time of filming *Intolerance* that it was in any way a reaction to *The Birth of a Nation*. Rather, Griffith was "just making another film." Although it was a bigger film than Griffith was used to making, Griffith himself, Brown believes, did not have the "faintest conception of what it was going to be like or what the reaction was going to be." Brown further states that Griffith did not care particularly about intolerance as such but had the impression that "everybody else did" and chose the theme because he thought it was popular.

Joseph Henabery states that Griffith created *Intolerance* out of necessity. His impression is that Griffith found himself in an extremely awkward situation after the great popularity of *The Birth of a Nation* because nothing equal to it was ready for release. According to Henabery, Griffith felt the public would expect an even more spectacular film from him. Henabery has difficulty accepting the idea that intolerance is the overall theme of the film. He comments on his feeling in the interview:

> Naturally, people were looking forward to the next work of this great artist who had made *The Birth of a Nation,* What did he have to show? A lousy, old, stinking "quickie." I suppose like most directors he didn't want to show a bum picture. He began to look for ways that he could improve *Intolerance* or *The Mother and the Law,* as it was called. That's where he thought he was being treated unfairly. Intolerably, he said. So he got the idea of making a bigger picture by embellishing it with a few added scenes for the modern period but adding the St. Bartholomew episode, the Crucifixion, and the Babylonian episodes. I would say that first of all the kind of intolerance suffered in *The Mother and the Law* was not religious. But two of the things that he picked were religious intolerance—St. Bartholomew and the Crucifixion. He showed priests who were traitors but the major part of the picture was not devoted to that. Now, what was intolerance? God knows.

One may conclude that after the tremendous reception of *The Birth of a Nation,* Griffith must have had second

thoughts about releasing *The Mother and the Law* and decided to enlarge upon it and to expand the intolerance theme with three additional stories.

THE PRODUCTION OF *INTOLERANCE*

Griffith rarely discussed his scripts, production plans, or financial affairs with anyone except Frank Woods, his business manager. The production plans for *Intolerance* were no exception. They remained one of Griffith's better kept secrets.

Anita Loos calls *Intolerance* the studio mystery. She indicates that no one knew what the film was about except Griffith and Frank Woods. It was a complete mystery to the actors playing in it. The filming went on for month after month, and the constant shifting of sequences from modern to ancient was confusing. The sets became enormous. She says, "We used to say, 'What is D. W. doing?' We never had the nerve to ask him."

When Miriam Cooper was asked if she had any idea while the film was being made what Griffith had in mind, she responded, "He never told us. He never told me anything. [We did] what we were told. He wouldn't describe anything."

Karl Brown concurs:

> No [we didn't know what the film was about], and to compound the felony, we didn't care. That's what he wanted. That's what we gave him. He was happy. So were we. We were all being paid.

Brown recalls that Griffith had no plan or shooting schedule and that Griffith filmed "whatever came next. Whatever was ready next."

> No, there was no straight plan. The only time he was ever stuck with a plan was during the biblical sequences when he had to. He had no choice there. He could put his own interpretation on it, but he had to follow the letter of the Book. That's the one place where he was really tied down.

Lillian Gish believes that even though her role in *Intolerance* took less than an hour to film, she was closer to *Intolerance* than anyone else except Billy Bitzer and Jimmy Smith, the cutter. She feels there was more of her in the picture than any other in which she had ever played. She describes her feelings in her autobiography:

> Perhaps because I wasn't acting a long role, Mr. Griffith took me into his confidence as never before, talking over scenes before he filmed them, having me watch all the rushes, even accepting some of my ideas with the cutting. At night, as I watched the day's rushes, I saw the film take shape and marveled at what Mr. Griffith was creating.

Joseph Henabery describes himself as equally close to Griffith. Besides doing research and assisting in production, he acted in two roles in the film. He says he "very definitely" knew what Griffith had in mind:

> I did ninety-five percent or more of the research work in the picture. I assisted him for over a year. I ran around at his heels or at his side for over a year and I believe I'm safe in saying that nobody is alive today that was as close to him as I was. But there are lots of things that I don't know—that I don't claim to know. I don't know what his business arrangements were or a lot of interesting things. It wasn't part of my job.

Henabery haunted local bookstores and spent hours pouring over materials in researching the film. He particularly liked one bookstore where the owner allowed him to come in on Sunday mornings and "systematically go underneath the counters, pull out . . . and look through everything." He found and purchased many items. For instance, the marriage market scene in *Intolerance* was a replication of a picture he discovered. He found a photograph of a painting which served as a reference source for parts of the Belshazzar episode. He also picked up "bits of fiction about Old Babylon." One he remembered as the *Fall of Ishtar* by a woman author named Porter. Another was called *Semiramas,* he believed. Henabery looked at many Bibles in researching the "Jewish period." He settled on the Tissot Bible as a reference because he believed "Tissot gave the detail of the costumes and the phylactery and all the rituals and all that sort of stuff. Most of the [other] Bibles were illustrated like Dore, which are wonderful drawings, but not authentic."

In his autobiography Brown corroborates Henabery's statement. Henabery, he writes, "became our one-man research department," collecting books, cutting out significant pictures and mounting them in scrapbooks for ready reference. In further support of Henabery, Brown states that Tissot's illustrated Bible was set aside as a standard reference because the illustrations appeared to be more realistic, whereas the Old Masters' paintings presented too many discrepancies to be of much help.

Henabery describes his relationship with Griffith in the day-to-day production of the film:

> I was with him all the time. At the end of the day he would tell me about what he wanted to shoot and I'd get some rough idea of what he wanted. If it was to be a very big day I'd stop my work at noon the preceding day and start in on the logistics. [I would] see that everything that was needed was available. But I had to use my memory more than anything. Nowadays they have production departments where they have it all broken down and everybody takes his whack at it. [The director] knows how many people are needed, what horses are needed, how many chariots are needed, and so on. Well, I didn't, you see.

Lillian Gish, however, presents another story of how research was done for the film in her autobiography, stating that "once again everyone became absorbed in history. . . . Rabbi Meyers helped with the biblical research. Mr. Griffith knew the Bible well but it was his habit to use people as a sounding board. He talked to all of us, and we often came up with sound ideas." She implies that she too had a part in the research when she continues, "research was no chore for me."

Karl Brown's autobiographical account supports Lillian Gish's statement that Rabbi Meyers participated in the research for the biblical wedding scene. He adds that "the equally highly respected Father Dodd, Episcopalian, stood by to make sure no Christian beliefs would be shaken by this purely Jewish ceremony."

Lillian Gish states in an interview with Anthony Slide that Griffith had all of *Intolerance* in his mind. She says that Griffith wrote every bit of it and designed every set and every costume. He did not go on the set not knowing what to do. He did not improvise.

Nevertheless, in the more than one and one-half years that it took to film *Intolerance,* Joseph Henabery says "miles of film" were shot and many episodes were not used. He describes one of the scenes:

> [Griffith] had one episode that wasn't shown about the courts of Hammurabi—the law courts—and he used to laugh himself to death. He had me playing this part and I'd improvise and build it up, you know. I was telling the story. I was a Babylonian soldier. I was walking along and I heard somebody whistle and there was a gal up there. So I went upstairs and I told this. I'm in a law court. I've been arrested. Just a poor dumb fool. I used to tell this story in pantomime and he'd laugh and laugh and laugh. And, I'd say to myself, "Well, what in the world? Why is he so interested in this bit? There's no room for it in the story." Well, that was true of so many things. I don't think many others realized where we were going because they didn't attend all of the rehearsals.

When asked about her involvement in the editing of Griffith's films, particularly **The Birth of a Nation** and **Intolerance,** Lillian Gish replies:

> Oh, I always sat in on all of the pictures because Griffith would make me. He would say, "You go in there and pick your takes, my eyes get tired. Don't discard what you've taken out, but you pick the best ones." So that if I hadn't he would have run the others. No, I helped. I knew cutting.

At the time of the filming of *Intolerance,* Karl Brown had been promoted to second-unit camera. He shot many of the scenes that did not involve principals. He assisted Billy Bitzer on the major scenes. He contends that the big shots—the crowd and battle scenes—were easy to film compared to the close-ups of the Christ character portrayed by Howard Gaye:

The hardest thing were the close-ups of the Christ—to make him to look at all Christian, not like Howard Gaye with a lot of whiskers sticking on his face. The rest of it—those big shots—was easy. There's absolutely no question about that. I shot with fifteen hundred, two thousand people in a good crosslight somewhere. You just set up your scenes. That's all there is to it. There are no reflectors to handle. Nothing. You just take a picture of it. It's the only way you can get into a close-up that big and it calls for some skill.

The Babylonian scene was one of the more extravagant in *Intolerance*. Griffith first tried to film it from a balloon suspended over the action, but the basket rocked too badly. Griffith then constructed a huge dolly with an elevator, which Billy Bitzer describes as being fifteen feet high, about six feet square at the top, and sixty feet wide at the bottom. It was mounted on six sets of four-wheel railroad car trucks and had an elevator in the center. Men pushed the dolly backward and forward on tracks while other workers operated the elevator, which had to descend at a regular rhythm as the railroad car moved. The entire scene was filmed in one continuous shot, in focus at every level, with a single hand-cranked Pathe camera. Bitzer did the tilt and pan cranks while focusing. Karl Brown, seated underneath the camera, did the cranking through a flexible shaft.

Anita Loos was an established writer for Griffith by the time *Intolerance* was released. It was logical that he called on her to assist with its titles. She relates that when *Intolerance* was almost complete Griffith sent for her and asked her to stay late to view a rough cut of the film with him alone in the projection room. She thought the film was "terrible" and that Griffith "had gone out of his mind" with all of "these scrambled sequences."

> And, then, he told me what he wanted to do and I realized that the titles he wanted would more or less pull it together and so I went to work and wrote a full set of titles. He told me where they were needed for time lapses and to connect for bridges between episodes. But he said, "If you see any places where you can put in a laugh, don't hold back."

Griffith himself contributed to the writing of titles, also, and the stylized prose of *Intolerance* titles is typical of his films. The caption "A love blossoms from the prince stricken by her beauty as though struck by white lightning" Loos quickly acknowledges as Griffith's. She says, "That is Griffith. That is D. W. himself. He fancied himself as a poet and his poetry was like his stage writing. It's pretty banal." Another specific title, "The loom of fate weaves death for the young boy's father," she also attributes to Griffith, saying, "Oh, those are pure Griffith."

Loos liked to quote from Voltaire and recalls that her paraphrase of Voltaire, "When women cease to attract men, they often turn to reform as a second choice,"

particularly pleased Griffith. She explains that she did not do research for titles:

> No, I never did any research for anything. I'm deadly against research. I think it bogs you down. I mean if you're a humorist. I don't think you should know the facts too well [because you can't be funny if you do].

Joseph Henabery also contributed to the titles. He relates to Kevin Brownlow that at the preview of *Intolerance* he particularly objected to the titles and told Griffith the next day that the worst feature of the film was that it had so many titles that meant absolutely nothing to the audience. That afternoon Griffith asked Henabery to view the film with him and for about three hours they discussed the titles and reworked a number of them:

> I sat in there for about three hours. I hit the titles I particularly objected to. I made suggestions and they worked my ideas over and revamped the titles. In a way, this was very flattering to me. I'm human and I'm susceptible to flattery.

SUCCESS OR FAILURE?

At the grand openings *Intolerance* was acclaimed by the critics as wonderful, gigantic in spectacle, and novel in presentation. Audiences applauded the brilliant images but found the four concurrent stories confusing and difficult to follow. Theaters were filled for about five months and then attendance fell off to nothing. The film was withdrawn. *Intolerance* was one of the few pictures never to have a second run in neighborhood theaters.

The timing of the film's release was poor. In 1916 the American public was emotionally stirred up for war, but the film was a sermon on peace. As the country became more war conscious the film was censored and barred in many cities. It therefore had little chance for sustained success.

The film had a similar reception in Great Britain. It was enthusiastically received in London by the critics and the public but ran only eight weeks before closing.

During the filming of *Intolerance,* none of the interviewees fully comprehended the total scope of the picture or the full significance of the techniques Griffith employed in the production. All were incredulous at their first viewing, but in later years they realized the magnitude of what they had helped create. They attribute part of the ultimate box office failure to the unfortunate timing of the release of the film when the country was preparing to go to war. They all feel the film was too advanced technically for the average movie-goer to appreciate.

Griffith typically previewed his films at towns in the Los Angeles area. Henabery went with Griffith and several others to the preview of *Intolerance* at Pomona. Henabery was "terribly disappointed—more so than I thought I would be." He thought the picture was "Griffith's biggest flop" and "failed in so many respects." He criticized the film as "too confused for an ordinary audience."

> They didn't know what it was about. They were stunned. They didn't know what to make of these flashes that were that long [indicating a short distance]. They'd just about get their eyes open and [it was] gone.

Henabery also criticizes the idea that the stories in the film run parallel:

> A parallel means that a similar thing happened at these different times. They were not similar things. They were usually quite different things. They talk about the wonderful parallel in the action at the end, but the train ride, the automobile race with the train, and the chariot race in Babylon, and all this. What similarity is there between a run to the rescue and a traitorous opening of the gates to let the invaders in? [And the Crucifixion.] Where is the parallelism? None. To begin with the whole Crucifixion period lacked movement. To me, it was, as I said, his biggest flop.

Brown did not share Henabery's deep disappointment. He describes the reception of the Los Angeles opening as "tremendous because they were looking for something big and they got it." He saw the "picture more than once, mostly to try to find out what all these various critics were talking about." During the shooting of the film he had not been able to make out the stories, "but once assembled and once its theme had been clearly stated in tones of brass from Breil's great orchestra, everything fit together. Griffith had succeeded brilliantly." He disagrees with Henabery's statement that the film does not use parallelism:

> Because [Griffith] had been doing it so long. He had been doing it over and over and over again. In his earlier pictures he'd have three or four stories running parallel or closely related, so finally when he came to this one he decided he'd go all the way—the same story in four different parallels—in four different settings.

Brown believes that *Intolerance* was a big picture in every possible respect. It was designed to be shown as a great theatrical spectacle in full-size theaters at advanced prices. It required a full orchestra of symphonic proportions and a backstage crew of sound effects men to build up the hullabaloo and clamor of battle. But it did not attract the crowds necessary to pay the cost of its screening. Brown admits that the film was a failure at the box office. "It was," he said, "in short, a flop." Griffith had succeeded "with the wrong thing at the wrong time for the world had changed." Griffith could not foresee the war. "I think it was badly timed."

Brown states that a little understood fact about *Intolerance* is that compared to *The Birth of a Nation, Intol-erance* made more money during the first several months after being released. "More people paid more money to go see it." The difference in profit was a direct result of the difference in production cost—seventy-five thousand dollars compared to a million and a half dollars.

Anita Loos rates the success of the film somewhere between Henabery's and Brown's evaluations. She says she had some idea of what the film was about after working on the titles but "was as confused as the audiences were." She believes the film "was a really colossal failure," but that it "was terribly in advance of its time."

> Audiences said what is this thing? You're in a modern courtroom and then you're back in history. It just didn't make any sense. It was long. Up to that time, of course, every story was filmed with a beginning, a middle, and an end. To cut back and forth in time was really so far in advance of anybody.

Loos describes Griffith's theme of intolerance as ordinary, finding nothing new in the idea that "it's intolerance that causes everybody's trouble." She says that while *Intolerance* was being filmed "we all thought it was a big folly and a mistake. We were more than ever convinced after it failed in the theater. But those were pretty gay times when nobody had any cares in the world. So [Griffith] was preaching to a lot of people who weren't listening."

Unlike Henabery, Loos feels that "in later years people have been able to appreciate [*Intolerance*] for what it was."

Miriam Cooper and Lillian Gish strongly support the film and Griffith. Miriam Cooper writes that whatever the film's weaknesses may have been, it still stands as a monument to D. W. Griffith. She attributes the negative reaction to the film to its length, ponderousness, and the timing of its release. It is her feeling that then as today it is difficult for audiences to watch the film because "it was hard to follow four stories at the same time. The extensive cutting jerked the viewer back and forth." She believes there was no response to the film's "strong message against war and for peace," because the national mood of the country supported the war.

Lillian Gish believes that in *Intolerance* Griffith's "genius reached its full expression." Never had his techniques been so fresh and resourceful nor have the dimensions of the film ever been equaled. She told Anthony Slide that she thought it was the greatest film ever made. It is Griffith's monument and the measure of the man himself.

Lillian Gish contends that the film would have been successful had it been shown as Griffith intended. Griffith had planned for the film to be shown in two four-hour screenings, but when exhibitors heard about the film's length, they refused to show it. Griffith therefore cut and edited the film down to two and a half hours. But he should have followed his instincts to defy the exhibitors and presented the film in its entirety, Gish explains. The shortened version was difficult to follow and the climax was particularly bewildering to audiences with the images falling "on them like spent buckshot, without force or direction."

Gish feels there were other reasons for the film's failure. The long months of production and the great financial outlay could have been lessened if Griffith had been willing to turn over more of the planning and directing of other productions to his assistants. The stars should have been given screen credits and the "kind of publicity and exploitation that was by then starting in the industry." Their pulling power might have offset the financial deficit of the film.

How Griffith himself may have felt about the picture while it was under production was revealed in an incident described by Joseph Henabery:

> I used to wait for him at night to come out of the projection room. I was never allowed in there. Nobody was except the editors. One night, probably about 6:30, he came out and he had his big hat pulled down over his face. I knew he felt low. He had to cross a sort of a roadway to come over to where I was up on the stage. I was waiting for orders. He told me, "I wish I had made a Babylonian picture." I didn't know what to say. But, I'm glad he didn't because I never saw a story that was big enough for it. But the next day he'd forgotten all about it. I couldn't understand him in that respect.

In Griffith's conversation and correspondence with Lillian Gish after the box office decline, he referred to *Intolerance* as his "great failure." He confided in her that he may have dreamed too big a dream and stretched his talents too far when he made *Intolerance*. He had tried to influence the entire world with a message of compassion. He thought he should have confined himself to America.

Intolerance was a financial failure but time has vindicated its artistic and technical merit. It has become a film classic. It is shown in classrooms around the world, and filmmakers the world over have adopted and expanded upon its filming techniques. Theodore Huff has called it "the greatest motion picture ever produced. In its original form and properly presented, it is a masterpiece of creative conception and execution."

IMPRESSIONS OF D. W. GRIFFITH

The man who created *Intolerance* was an innovator and genius of the early film industry, yet he died comparatively unknown. He was a complex man. Born and reared in Kentucky, D. W. Griffith valued Southern tradition and courtly manners but occasionally carried these values to the extreme. Aspiring in his youth to be a writer and dramatic actor, he became instead a film director. But he retained the instincts of the writer and actor.

Possibly no one ever knew him intimately. He had business, personal, and family associates, but apparently none became an intimate part of his life, at least not for any length of time. His business associations, except for those with Frank Woods and Billy Bitzer, were not long-standing. He married twice, but both marriages ended in divorce. He loved his family, especially his mother, but his relatives for the most part did not return his love. They showed only a fondness for his money and eagerness to take advantage of his generosity.

Those who worked or associated with Griffith are unable to provide more than a superficial description of the total man but emphasize his personality, voice, and physical characteristics or his creative and technical abilities. They are consistently loyal and respect him as a person and as a creative genius of his time.

Lillian Gish may have known and understood Griffith better than anyone else during his early years of filmmaking. She describes her first impression of him in her book:

> I grope in the files of memory for my first impression of David Wark Griffith. He looked so tall to my young eyes, yet he was two inches under six feet. He was imposing; he held himself like a king. Later I discovered that he could no more slouch than change the color of his blue eyes, which were hooded and deepset. He was vigorous and masculine-looking. Under the wide-brimmed straw hat set on his head with a jaunty curve to the brim, his brown sideburns were rather long. His nose was prominent; his profile seemed to belong on a Roman coin, and he had the heavy lower lip and jaw of the Bourbons. It was an important face.

Just to live in daily contact with Griffith was a notable experience for Anita Loos. She describes him as like an Indian chieftain with a certain dignity and restrained but imposing manner. She thinks there was a certain naivete about him that approached prudery. He was very formal. Nobody was ever called by his or her first name in the studio. "You were always Miss Loos or Mr. Griffith."

Miriam Cooper regards Griffith as a Victorian gentleman. His manner, dress, and the discipline he exercised over the lives of his actresses exemplified to her the Victorian father none of his fatherless actresses had. She recalled that he had a large mouth and a lovely voice.

To many, Griffith's voice was his distinguishing characteristic. Its tones, resonance, and inflections had an almost hypnotic power over an actor's emotions and performance. Brown describes Griffith's voice:

He had a very flexible voice. It varied according to the occasion. He could shout if he had to. He could coax. The one outstanding thing about his voice was his laugh which was almost exactly like that of a jackass. It was a very funny indrawn laugh.

Miriam Cooper describes Griffith as a man of honor and dignity who treated everyone fairly and always kept his word. She liked him and everything about him. "He was one of the most wonderful men I've ever known." "He was just marvelous to all of us." "He had a wonderful disposition. He was very patient and never lost his temper, at least not with me."

A very private man, Griffith seldom discussed anything about his personal life. Miriam Cooper was not aware at the time she was acting under his direction, for instance, that he had been married to Linda Arvidson, one of the Griffith actresses. He seemed to care little for a high style of living or, if he did, he kept it to himself. His activities away from the studio were largely unknown. He seemed to be immune from what Karl Brown called "the rich-man syndrome." Women whom he directed adored him on the set but in his personal relationships with them he seemed inept at times.

Griffith's ability to inspire and mold talent seems to have been unrecognized by himself as well as by others at the time. Anita Loos feels she was much more impressed with Griffith as a man than as an artist but that his enormous imagination had a telling effect in his ability to mold and use "raw human material." She had worked for Griffith for a long time before she had any realization that he was the genius that he was. She did not think he realized himself what he was doing because he always hated the movies and wanted to get away from them. She said he considered himself a playwright, "which he wasn't because the plays of his that exist are just trash. He didn't know his own talent."

Joseph Henabery told Brownlow that Griffith had been an inspiration to him because of Griffith's great appreciation of acting details, not because of his innovations. He believes Griffith was the first director to realize that a good story depends upon characters who are well developed and interesting. He had great insight and a great feeling for contrasts. Griffith worked without any of the aids considered necessary today. He had no art director, no character make-up man, no hairdressers, no special effects department, no scriptwriter—and no script! He was a very appreciative man. Henabery said "he didn't come up and clap you on the back, but something would happen in your favor, and that's how he would show his appreciation."

Griffith had an almost evangelical approach toward film. He spent long hours during the day directing films and equally long hours at night in the cutting room assembling them. He did not take vacations. He told the actors that it was predicted in the Bible that film was the universal language that would make all people

brothers, end wars, and bring about the Millennium. When he overheard an actress make a disparaging remark about working in the flickers he remonstrated that he never wanted to hear that word again in his studio. He told her "what we do here today will be seen tomorrow by people all over America—people all over the world! Just remember that the next time you go before the camera."

Karl Brown characterizes Griffith as a very extraordinary person born in a dark circle with motion pictures as the only slit of light through which he could see. The rest of the world meant nothing to him. But what he could see through that tiny slit nobody else could see and that was his beginning and that was his end.

After *Intolerance* Griffith never again experienced the total freedom to produce and direct as he wanted. He was forced to work for others in order to pay off the huge debts incurred in the production of *Intolerance*. His career declined. He had no purpose in life. Brown conjectures that "Griffith's end began with his loss of freedom. When he lost this freedom, he lost everything. He could not possibly follow anybody else's preconception of what he ought to do with his talent."

Lillian Gish has probably been the most influential person in memorializing D. W. Griffith. She endeavored for years to persuade the U. S. Postal Service to create a commemorative stamp, which was eventually issued in 1975, the centenary of Griffith's birth. She included his name in the title of her autobiography. She helped with the script and contributed the title to *Silver Glory,* a dramatic narrative of Griffith's life with excerpts from his films, produced for television by Fred Coe. She put together and narrated a film, *Lillian Gish and the Movies: The Art of Film, 1900-1928,* in which she paid high tribute to Griffith, and she was instrumental in preserving his papers and films at the Museum of Modern Art.

D. W. Griffith has become important in film history for his technical innovations, but many of his artistic achievements have been overlooked. He strove very hard to perfect the film as a vehicle of ideas. He produced hundreds of films during the years he spent making motion pictures. It is through these films, through the Griffith style, the enthusiasm, the projection of himself into his work, and the tremendous respect of those who worked with him in the early years, that a partial understanding of the complexity and intensity of the man can be realized.

William M. Drew (essay date 1986)

SOURCE: "Artistic Influences," in *D. W. Griffith's* Intolerance: *Its Genesis and Its Vision,* McFarland & Company, Inc., 1986, pp. 63-101.

[*In the following essay, Drew highlights the various artistic influences Griffith drew upon during the making of* Intolerance.]

Utilizing elements from music, painting, theater, poetry and novels, Griffith produced a twentieth-century masterwork, adapting and synthesizing the art forms of the nineteenth century into the new medium of cinema. In addition, he was stimulated by the work of the European filmmakers, absorbing some of their techniques in spectacle and costume productions. As a result, *Intolerance* is a fusion of romanticism and realism. This blending is a distinguishing characteristic of nineteenth-century art, in which intuition, emotion and the exaggeration of incident and action to intensify the theme merges with a commitment to portray life realistically and project believable characters and situations in order to elucidate their social and historical significance.

MUSIC

With Griffith, the use of musical scoring for films attained a new maturity. Deriving from the traditions of the nineteenth-century theater in which music heightened the action and set the mood for popular melodramas and sophisticated stage spectacles such as Sir Henry Irving's productions of Shakespeare, he was meticulous in selecting music to accompany his films. He often worked "for weeks with musicians to find music that would match each character and situation" [Lillian Gish, *The Movies, Mr. Griffith and Me*]. He believed that music was an integral part of cinema presentation:

> Watch a film run in silence and then watch it again with eyes and ears. The music sets the mood for what your eye sees; it guides your emotions; it is the emotional framework for visual pictures. [Gish, *The Movies*]

Convinced that "The only pure art, if pure art exists, is music," he employed live symphony orchestras ranging in size from ninety pieces in the larger theaters to a minimum of twelve instruments in the smaller houses. He was so certain of the importance of the live orchestra in accentuating the effect of the imagery that in the 1940s he observed: "No sound track will reproduce the true melodic interrelation of instruments in an orchestra" [A. R. Fulton, *Motion Pictures: The Development of an Art From Silent Films to the Age of Television*].

The premiere of *Intolerance* at the Liberty Theatre was accompanied by a forty-piece orchestra and a chorus from the Metropolitan Opera House. The use of full-scale symphony orchestras for *The Birth of a Nation* and *Intolerance,* marking the maturation of film scoring, was of enormous assistance in catapulting the cinema from the nickelodeon entertainment of the working classes to an art form capable of attracting the most sophisticated circles.

The score for *Intolerance* included classical themes as well as some popular music. Griffith collaborated with Joseph Carl Breil, a composer and arranger who had worked with him on the score for *The Birth of a Nation*. Film historian A. R. Fulton gives a description of the music used in *Intolerance*:

> The music was varied as well as familiar—Beethoven's *Minuet in G* for the peaceful scene in the Huguenot home before the massacre, Handel's *Largo* for the scene in which Jesus is scorned by the Pharisees, "In the Good Old Summer Time" for a day at Coney Island, etc. The film provides opportunity for considerable use of imitative music, such as bugle calls, bells, and gongs, as well as accompaniment to the various dance scenes. [Fulton, *Motion Pictures*]

Brown remembers that the "Bacchanale" from Saint-Saëns' *Samson and Delilah* was used to accompany scenes of Belshazzar's feast in the Babylonian Story. Newspaper sources of the time record that Griffith and Breil also used excerpts from Wagner and Rimsky-Korsakov and the popular song, "My Wild Irish Rose," which was the theme for the Dear One.

In addition to making use of music as an accompaniment, Griffith was indebted to the heritage of classical music in helping him to evolve cinematic form. While his other film epics are patterned on the symphonic form, *Intolerance* is often called "the only film fugue." Corresponding to the exposition of the fugue, the theme is introduced in the opening sequences of the Modern Story and repeated in succession in the introductory segments of the other three stories. The Modern Story lays out the basic premise, showing the Vestal Virgins of Uplift initiating their plans for a moral reform campaign followed by shots of the workers peacefully pursuing their daily existence. The theme reappears in the succeeding stories with the Pharisees arrogating righteousness as they interrupt the daily tasks of the people in Judea; Catherine de Medici intriguing at court, followed by shots of the wedding procession and the Huguenot couple; and the Mountain Girl playfully spurning the advances of her would-be suitor, the Rhapsode, intercut with the High Priest of Bel angrily looking down from his lofty tower at the ceremonies of Ishtar.

Continuing to pattern the fugue form in which the exposition is succeeded by the discussion or development, Griffith elaborates the theme as the film proceeds. As the intertwined narrative becomes increasingly complex, he counterpoints the theme of intolerance with sub-themes of love, courtship and celebration alternating with violence and loss. Like the windings of the melodic line throughout the fugue, the original theme is always apparent in the various segments of the stories. By the time he reaches the climax of the film, he recapitulates the theme with such rapid intercutting between the stories that, like the stretto of the fugue in which different musical parts overlap, the concluding sequences of each of the stories seem to tumble end over end in a dramatic montage.

PAINTING

First and foremost a visual artist, Griffith adapted the techniques of the painter, transforming the stationary two-dimensional representation "into the twentieth-century world of moving art" [Bernard Honson, "D. W. Griffith: Some Sources"]. His use of composition to draw the spectator's eye to the central subject of the shot and perspective to create the illusion of distance, combined with his skillful manipulation of light and shadow and color tinting to heighten the mood, demonstrates the capacity of the moving picture to rival painting as a visual art. In addition to utilizing specific paintings in the Babylonian Story, his work is reflective in a general sense of the realistic and romantic schools of painting.

No director has taken more pains to use details of composition to rivet the viewer's attention and create a pleasing visual effect. In the long-shot of the court of Charles IX, the eye focuses on the king seated on his throne with Catherine standing to his right at the apex of a triangle formed by a multitude of lords and ladies in the background. The triangular shape is complemented not only by the page boys kneeling on the left in the foreground, but also by the floor design and the fleurs-de-lis beneath the lavish tapestry. Similarly, in a shot of the Babylonian throne room during the Persian conquest, Griffith enhances the dominance of Belshazzar and the Princess Beloved through a series of rectangular units. In the foreground, the rectangles are apparent in the floor tile and in the grouping of the kneeling servants, a pattern which is repeated in the high window in the background and inverted in the throne itself forming a modified rectangle. In a shot of the strike sequence in the Modern Story, the visual composition stresses the guns of the militia by using the parallel lines of the soldiers stretched on the ground to complement their rifles pointed at the strikers.

Throughout his work, Griffith is adept at using space to add depth to the flat, two-dimensional screen. During the siege of Babylon, the setting is given perspective with the high-angled shots of the towers receding into the background of the open sky as the action of the combatants fills the foreground. The eye of the viewer is directed towards the diagonal lines of the towers directly behind the combatants and through the elongated enclosure created by the series of towers. In a long-shot of Cyrus's troops pouring down the road, Griffith deepens the perspective by showing empty space in the foreground, a technique he often employs in his work.

Griffith augments his compositions with lighting effects and color tints to underscore the emotion of the scene. When the Dear One's father dies, their small one-room apartment is "darkly lit with heavy shadows," conveying a sense of grief [Paul O'Dell, *Griffith and the Rise of Hollywood*]. A close shot of the Boy in prison dramatically emphasizes his plight with light playing across his face framed by the bars against the black background of the prison walls. A long-shot of the Massacre of St. Bartholomew's Day is a study in black and white contrasts. The bodies of Huguenots clothed in black and white are strewn across the white cobblestones, reflecting the first rays of the dawn. The armor-clad soldiers on their horses are swathed in the morning light as a white sky can be seen peeking through the dark clouds above the buildings that are framed by houses shrouded in darkness. A. R. Fulton points to another example of black and white contrasts in a scene in the Huguenot home in which the white candles and "the headdresses of the Huguenot women contrast strikingly with the dark background" [Fulton, *Motion Pictures*]. In the original prints, Griffith distinguished the four epochs with specific tints, using amber in the Modern Story, blue in the Judean Story, sepia in the French, and gray-green in the Babylonian. Additionally, moods and atmosphere in each of the four stories were enhanced by the choice of coloring, including flaming red for the shots of conflict in the strike, massacre and war sequences, blue for night scenes and yellow for daylight exteriors.

In a unique adaptation of artistic techniques to the cinema, Griffith employs framing and masking to concentrate on specific details of an image, seldom using "the same shape twice in succession . . . so that the eye of the spectator is kept moving." [Harry M. Gedald, editor, *Focus on D. W. Griffith*] His cameo shots edged in black accentuate the expressions of emotion in his characters such as in the close-up of the delighted Mountain Girl when she meets Belshazzar at the marriage market and the shot of the anguished Dear One at her husband's trial. He uses the vignette, masking the top, bottom, or sides of an image, to add depth and dimension. The long-shot of a train in the Modern Story, masked at the bottom, creates a wide-screen effect comparable to the CinemaScope process introduced in the 1950s. With the iris shot, he duplicates the action of the eye, focusing first on a detail, then gradually enlarging the picture to reveal the full image. For example, he introduces the Babylonian Story with a semi-circular iris shot of a portion of the gate of Imgur-Bel on the lower right of the frame, then opens to encompass the upper left as the full image is disclosed and "the camera retreats through the ages and time rolls backward" [Fulton, *Motion Pictures*].

Although it is difficult to determine the extent to which Griffith was influenced by specific schools of art, his photography in the Modern Story contains striking similarities to contemporaneous American realistic painting. His earlier ***The Musketeers of Pig Alley,*** in the words of Richard J. Meyer, "had the look of the Ashcan School of art," which included the works of painters Robert Henri, George Bellows and John Sloan, who explored the contemporaneous daily life of the city, capturing its essence on canvas. These artists, attracting national attention with their exhibitions in New York in February, 1908 and the Armory Show of 1913, were derisively called the "Ashcan School" of painters by critics who did not appreciate their realistic, unvarnished depictions of the world about them.

In his evocation of the joys and sorrows of lower-class life in the first decades of the twentieth century, Griffith's work parallels John Sloan's, whose paintings and sketches reflect his belief that his mission was to depict the life of his times. Sloan found subject material for his art on the streets of New York. Griffith went to downtown Los Angeles "to search out life at its worst" for scenes in the Modern Story that became, as Brown notes, "one long gray series of pictures in unrelieved monotone." Sloan, who was an art editor and illustrator for the Socialist publication *The Masses* from 1912 to 1916, comments on the same social problems that caught Griffith's attention. In *Before Her Makers and Her Judge,* featured in the August, 1913 issue of *The Masses,* Sloan captures the sternness and hypocrisy of the judge, policeman and onlookers in a sketch of a prostitute in a night-court. "Sloan felt very strongly about the mistreatment" of these women who were regularly entrapped by the police, a procedure condoned by the judicial system [David W. Scott and E. John Bullard, *John Sloan 1871-1951: His Life and Paintings, His Graphics*]. Griffith indicates a similar sentiment in the scene in the Modern Story in which the uplifters and police, after raiding a brothel, herd the prostitutes into a patrol car. *Class War in Colorado,* appearing on the cover of the June, 1914, *Masses,* was Sloan's representation of the infamous Ludlow strike. Depicting a desperate miner firing a revolver as he holds a dead child while a dead woman and her child lie at his feet, it conveys the same powerful emotion as the shot of the Boy in the Modern Story clutching his father who has just been killed by the militia. Reminiscent of Sloan's 1907 *Sixth Avenue and Thirtieth Street,* a painting of New York's Tenderloin District which faithfully records the "drab, shabby, happy, sad and human" surroundings, Griffith's scenes of the mean streets where the Boy first meets the Dear One blends the dreariness and joy of the slums. The simple pleasures of working-class life are subject matter that appeals to both Griffith and Sloan. With a feeling for documentary realism, the painter and director alike are able to catch the exuberant, boisterous atmosphere of the saloons and dance halls where workers found diversion from their monotonous existence.

The love of the sensual and exotic and the taste for violence in the Babylonian Story reflect the romantic school of painting led by Eugène Delacroix, the nineteenth-century master of French romantic art. Delacroix, who inspired many imitators, infused his work with a boldness and intensity of emotionalism that marked a departure from the restraint of the classical tradition. He was intrigued by the Middle East and often chose it as a subject for his art. His paintings *The Massacre at Chios* (1824), showing a Turkish horseman slashing at his helpless victims, and *The Death of Sardanapalus* (1827), with the dying Assyrian king witnessing the suffering of his subjects, are unsparing in their concentration on violence. Similarly, Griffith pictures the carnage in the siege of Babylon with heads being lopped off and fighters impaled. His elaboration of exotic architectural details in the Babylonian settings also bears a resemblance to Delacroix's opulent Moorish interiors and courtyards. Indeed, the French artist's studies of Eastern harem life may have served as a thematic prototype for

Griffith's scenes of temple prostitutes in Ishtar's shrine and the undraped women at Belshazzar's feast.

Besides the overall effect of art traditions on *Intolerance,* Griffith's mise-en-scène encompasses specific paintings. In his detailed study of Griffith's assimilation of artistic sources, Bernard Hanson identifies and describes the director's adaptation of nineteenth-century paintings for the Babylonian Story: *The Fall of Babylon* by Georges Rochegrosse, first exhibited in 1891; *Belshazzar's Feast* by John Martin, initially displayed in 1821; and *The Babylonian Marriage Market* by Edwin Long, exhibited in 1875.

Hanson's research, which appeared in *The Art Bulletin,* shows that Rochegrosse's painting of an orgy on the eve of Babylon's fall received a "mixed review" when it was first exhibited. He contends, however, that looking at one of the reviews provides the clue to its adaptability to the screen. Although he noted that the painting demonstrates a high degree of archaeological knowledge and "ingenuity of reconstruction," the critic cited by Hanson maintained that Rochegrosse's work was so full of details that the central idea was lost, forcing the viewer to scrutinize the "composition piecemeal." When he adapted from the painting, Griffith drew upon its plethoric details, intercutting them between shots of the city being taken by Cyrus's forces and the scenes of the great court of Babylon. While the recreation of "Babylon's last bacchanal" was daring for the time with its scantily clad women, Hanson believes that the filmic adaptation lacks "the grand sweep of the painting . . . so that only the 'piecemeal' details remain and the lush opulence of the late nineteenth-century French vision of decadence is lost" [Hanson, *D. W. Griffith*].

Hailed by David Wilkie, the nineteenth-century critic, for its outstanding treatment of "geometrical properties of space, magnitude and number" and its imaginative reconstruction of architecture, John Martin's *Belshazzar's Feast* provided background particulars for Griffith's spectacular Babylonian set. Thomas Balston, another critic, describes Martin's "multiplication of a few bystanders into an innumerable herd," "the complication of the architecture" and "this wealth of detail and movement." Hanson points out that Wilkie's and Balston's critical evaluations of the painting could also apply to Griffith's Babylon. Griffith, however, was able to free himself from the static confines of Martin's work and, by exploiting movement, give "fuller meaning to the idea behind" the tradition of English historical painting. With the aid of a camera mounted on an elevator, he moves from the vast panorama of the "innumerable herd" of people in the great court of Babylon to close-ups that reveal the characters' emotions.

The influence of Martin's painting can be seen in Griffith's conception of the massive open court of Babylon with its stairways, its columns topped by cornices and its great corbelled arches. Although the painting and the film both create a feeling of "spatial grandeur," the differences between them, according to Hanson, reflect the uniqueness of the respective mediums. The main action in Martin's painting takes place "near the front of the scene and on a terrace reached by a broad flight of stairs above the column-flanked courtyard" while Griffith centers the action "at the top of the stairs and well within the courtyard" in order to utilize the moving camera. His modifications of Martin's design, including the separated cornices and the placement of the stairs between the piers, allow him to make more effective use of space to accommodate camera movement.

With his adaptation of Edwin Long's *The Babylonian Marriage Market,* Griffith, as Hanson states, demonstrates "his genius as an artist who saw in terms of film . . . in the transformation of a static painting into a complex and exciting movie sequence." Hanson notes that Griffith is not only faithful in reproducing the details of the painting, "the slave block, the auctioneer's stance, the metal gate, the gestures, the costumes, and even the expression on the faces of the waiting women," he expands its range of mood by adding a human touch to the scene through the actions of the Mountain Girl on the auction block. Griffith's setting is more crowded than the painting but the director compensates for this, recapturing Long's sweep through skillful use of the moving camera and precise editing. Consisting of sixty shots in all, the sequence is punctuated by three panoramic shots at the beginning, middle and end, evenly spaced between the fifty-seven other shots which are of shorter duration. This rapid cutting enables Griffith to present history "lyrically and humorously transformed, through the looking-glass of nineteenth-century painting, into the reality of the magic world of the movies."

THEATER

Griffith's work reveals his indebtedness to the genres of the nineteenth-century theater, including melodrama, spectacle, dramas of intimate and social realism, and opera. In his book *Stage to Screen,* A. Nicholas Vardac contends that Griffith's cinematic achievements culminated more than a century of experiments in staging which emphasized the pictorial, as opposed to the verbal, aspects of theater. Griffith's work also evolved from a dramaturgy that blended realism and romanticism, combining accurate, lifelike details with action and emotion.

No theatrical genre had more effect on Griffith's techniques than the melodrama, providing an example for his scenes of action including suspense-building situations and last-minute rescues. One of the most popular forms of entertainment in the nineteenth century, the melodrama, with its stereotyped characterizations, thrills and narrow escapes, attracted lower and middle class audiences in both urban and provincial America. It often drew on the novel for plots and devices, and perennial favorites in its repertoire included simplified adaptations of *Uncle Tom's Cabin, The Count of Monte*

Cristo, and the works of Charles Dickens. Vardac maintains that the melodrama anticipated film narrative in its use of "a progression of pictorial episodes defining a single line of action, or . . . crosscutting between two or more parallel lines of action" [Nicholas A. Vardac, *Stage to Screen: Theatrical Method from Garrick to Griffith*].

Although Griffith frequently attributed his development of parallel action to his study of Dickens, his work clearly indicates that the melodrama played a major role in evolving his cinematic skill. Often the melodrama stage was divided into sections to represent simultaneous lines of action, a technique that anticipated Griffith's use of crosscutting in his last-minute rescues. Vardac cites W. J. Thompson's 1883 melodrama, *A Race for Life,* with the action divided between the heroine downstairs, an old woman upstairs, and a menacing villain outside the house. Similarly, in **The Lonely Villa** (1909), one of the first films in which Griffith employed crosscutting, the parallel action alternates between robbers outside a house threatening a family inside while, a few miles away, the father of the family desperately attempts to find a way to rescue them.

Vardac notes that Dion Boucicault's melodrama *Arrah-na-Pogue* (1864) is a salient example of a theatrical method which was "highly suggestive of the camera." He points to "the crosscutting between three simultaneous lines of action" as a precedent for the film language. The lines of action are cut between a Secretary of State's office, the interior of a prison and a mountain setting outside the prison. In the narrative, a secondary character, after receiving a pardon for the hero from the Secretary of State, attempts to reach the prison before the protagonist is executed. The scene switches to the hero's fiancee waiting outside the prison and then to the hero inside his cell preparing to escape. Two last-minute rescues then occur simultaneously, with the hero rushing to save his sweetheart from an attack by the villain while the secondary character arrives at the prison with the pardon in time to prevent the hero's recapture and execution.

Such suspense and last-minute rescues were also a part of Griffith's dramaturgy. A classic melodramatic situation occurs in the Modern Story when the Boy, forcing his way through the door, comes to the rescue of the Dear One, who is being attacked by the Musketeer of the Slums. In the climax of the Modern Story, Griffith employs three parallel lines of action as he switches from the Boy in his prison cell awaiting execution to the train carrying the governor, then to the car conveying the Dear One speeding to the rescue. The lines of action merge as the heroine boards the governor's train, leaving the camera free to focus on the final rescue when the governor and the Dear One arrive at the prison.

While he developed his basic editing structure against the background of the melodrama, Griffith's flair for creating epic films with imposing settings and masses of people grew out of the tradition of the stage spectacle, which flourished in the late nineteenth and early twentieth centuries. Transcending the limitations of conventional methods in staging melodrama, the spectacles were large-scale productions that achieved lavish effects through lighting, the use of crowds, and elaborate sets and costumes. Catering to a more metropolitan audience than the melodramas, their emphasis on realism and accuracy of detail made them perfect vehicles for presenting historical events such as the destruction of Pompeii and the burning of Moscow. Huge painted panoramas fronted by real houses and trees and special lighting effects from fireworks added authenticity to these productions. Producers striving for greater realism developed complex mechanical devices to stage unusual effects. At the turn of the century, dramatizations of *Quo Vadis* and *Ben-Hur* featured rapid scenic changes and chariot races with live horses on treadmills. These spectacular effects whetted the public's appetite for a pictorial theater, setting up a ready market for mammoth film productions.

Griffith, who insisted upon accuracy of details in his historical productions (as he often reminded his audiences in his subtitles and program notes), derived his concern in part from the example of producers of stage spectacles. Outstanding among these producers was Sir Henry Irving, who achieved photographic realism through careful research. Renowned for his Shakespearean productions, Irving included street scenes which were "faithful representations of familiar localities in Venice" in his 1879 presentation of *The Merchant of Venice*. His 1882 production of *Romeo and Juliet* similarly contained "a photographic reproduction of the time, the place, and the very events of the play." Like Griffith's research for the Babylonian Story, Irving's preparation for his 1888 production of *Macbeth* was extensive and encompassed "the British Museum and all known authorities upon archaeology . . . for correct patterns of the costumes, weapons, and furniture of the eleventh century" [Vardac, *Stage to Screen*].

The relationship between the silent cinema and the historical stage spectacle was most clearly defined in the work of the American producer-playwright Steele MacKaye. His experiments in the creation of an epic theater were the most ambitious of any of the theatrical producers, exploiting the potentialities of the stage spectacle to its fullest extent and forming a natural link between the stage and the film.

MacKaye's emphasis on elaborate pictorial art, in the words of a contemporary critic, "spoke to the heart as no words of poet, dramatist or historian could speak," minimizing dialogue in favor of action. Vardac points to MacKaye's 1887 play, *Anarchy: or, Paul Kauver,* set in the French Revolution, as an example of the cinematic qualities of his work. Citing a scene in which the heroine's execution by guillotine is enacted with unsparing realism, the reviewers of the time noted that "the production's most skillful invention is a silent picture."

The play was also distinguished for its crowd scenes, described by Vardac as "a dynamic, personalized mob which, as a unit, became the most significant single dramatis personae." Griffith's skill in creating momentum and adding forcefulness to his work through crowd scenes is characteristics of *Intolerance*. The angry, rebellious strikers in the Modern Story, the jeering onlookers of Christ's Via Crucis in the Judean Story, the cheering celebrants in the French Story, the surging mass of Persian troops attacking the walls of Babylon and the festive multitude celebrating their victory in the great courtyard in the Babylonian Story, all react as a single unit to underscore the drama.

Continuing with his innovations in the early 1890s, MacKaye conceived various devices that correlated his staging methods even more closely with cinematic techniques. These contrivances included huge signs to accompany the action (corresponding to silent film subtitles), an "Illumiscope" and "Colourator" for tinting and lighting effects and telescopic and movable stages for changing from panoramas to closer views and from huge sets to intimate scenes. This form of theater, which he called the Spectatorium, enabled him to "present the facts of history with graphic force." His 1893 production, *The World-Finder,* which utilized all of his devices in developing a cinematic style, was a spectacular recreation of Columbus's voyage to America. Ships carrying fifty-foot masts, actors essentially pantomiming the story accompanied by music and told in titles in "flaming letters . . . a foot long, a sentence at a time" and a curtain of light which produced dissolve effects and hastened changes of scenery, brought the stage spectacle to a height that could be surpassed only by the resources available to filmmakers [Vardac, *Stage to Screen*].

In the 1910s, Griffith, along with the Italian directors, expanded the potentialities of an epic dramatic form envisioned by MacKaye in his Spectatorium but left unfinished by his early death in 1894. Recognizing the relationship between the stage spectacle and the film, Griffith stated that, in comparison to the stage, "the motion picture . . . is boundless in its scope, and endless in its possibilities. The whole world is its stage, and time without end its limitations." He correctly prophesied in 1915 that the cinema was in the process of supplanting the stage as the vehicle for spectacle and the related genre of melodrama:

> The regular theatre . . . will, of course, always exist, but not, I believe, as now. The (moving) pictures will utterly eliminate from the regular theatre all the spectacular features of production. Plays will never again appeal to the public for their scenery, or their numbers of actors and supernumeraries. Pictures have replaced all that.
>
> The only plays that the public will care to see in the regular theatre will be the intimate, quiet plays that can be staged in one or two settings within four walls, and in which the setting is unimportant, while the drama will be largely subjective. Ob-

jective drama, the so-called melodrama, will be entirely absorbed in the pictures . . . [Gedald, *Focus on D. W. Griffith*]

From the genre of intimate domestic drama, Griffith added to his repertoire of cinematic techniques the capacity to evoke from his players a naturalistic, restrained style of acting and attentiveness to careful reproduction of authentic settings. The intimate drama, distinguished for its photographic realism and use of homey details and sentimental themes, enjoyed its greatest success in the late nineteenth and early twentieth centuries with the work of its principal figure, the producer-playwright David Belasco. While Belasco was also noted for his melodramas and spectacles, his most original contributions to the stage came from his quieter productions stressing characterization and realistic representations of daily life. Griffith, who was a great admirer of Belasco, was often called "the David Belasco of the motion pictures" and, like the producer, "could take obscure people and instill confidence into them," according to Griffith's colleague, the director Marshall Neilan. Indeed, Mary Pickford, one of Griffith's most famous actresses, came to him after working under Belasco.

Vardac cites *The Wife* (1887), which Belasco wrote in collaboration with Henry DeMille (the father of Cecil B. DeMille), as an example of the producer's influence on the intimate style adopted by motion pictures. The play was described by a contemporary critic as "the best example of . . . the naturalistic methods of the modern school." Scenes such as the hero courting the heroine as they sat on the bough of an apple tree and, in a room lit only by the fireplace, the wife confessing to her husband she loved another man were so replete with homely details that the play was unique for its uncomplicated but highly personal style.

Griffith adopted this approach throughout his work, delighting in domestic touches to create a sense of intimacy. In the French Story, for example, Griffith presents a picture of domestic tranquility in the Huguenot home in the subtle interaction between Prosper Latour, Brown Eyes, her younger sister and the mother and father: the father reads aloud while the mother rocks a cradle, smiling at her baby; the younger sister munches an apple as Prosper Latour and Brown Eyes exchange tender glances. The silent tête-á-tête of Prosper Latour and Brown Eyes is interrupted when her younger sister throws the core of her apple in their direction. The charming courtship scene in the Modern Story allows the viewer to peer in, as it were, on the romance between the Dear One and the Boy. When the Boy attempts to enter the Dear One's room to say goodnight, she shuts the door in his face, only opening it again to let him kiss her after his promise of marriage.

Zaza, Belasco's 1899 production, demonstrated his ability to give minor characters a life of their own. With his assemblage of sundry characters comprising "a dodder-

ing old rake . . . a boyish loafer . . . a besotted matron . . . [and] a shy young debutante," Belasco made each member of the cast equally important in projecting "an aura of real life" [Vardac]. His expertise in casting was matched by Griffith, who, in the words of Neilan, "could pick types, as Belasco did, with an unerring eye" [Anthony Slide, *The Griffith Actresses*]. Throughout his work, including *Intolerance,* Griffith's minor characters such as the matronly moral reformers, the old men hanging around the bars, or the prisoners on Death Row stand out, like Belasco's, as distinct individuals.

Vardac contends that by exploiting "the intimate and minor details of surface reality," Belasco intensified the effect of his unique, naturalistic style of acting. He notes that David Warfield, who became Belasco's most celebrated actor, "excelled in this itemized pantomime of surface realities." For instance, in *The Auctioneer* (1901), Warfield, surrounded by numerous objects typical of a second-hand store, engaged in lengthy bits of business with these properties, attaining the theatrical effects that Belasco sought.

In both the interior and exterior scenes, Belasco achieved a pictorial reality surpassed only by the film. A reviewer characterized the street scene in *The Auctioneer* as "a simulation of street life as it really exists in busy Gotham" which could be "a motion picture production of the original." *A Grand Army Man,* Belasco's 1907 production, also starring Warfield, was dubbed by a critic "the most realistic play that has been presented in New York City." The "worn benches, bare 'gas fixtures,' strips of dilapidated railing, pulpit-like bench, and a dozen other material details," added to the authenticity of the interior of a rural courthouse [Vardac].

Belasco's precedent inspired Griffith to break with the limitations of the early films. In place of the melodramatic gesticulations of the actors in the first one-reelers, he introduced a restrained style of acting that became the model for subsequent films. Gradually eliminating painted canvas flats for his background settings, he constructed detailed, authentic interiors that included real properties instead of objects painted on a canvas, and filmed exteriors on location. While Griffith absorbed Belasco's art of stagecraft, the camera enabled him to explore the human emotions through the close-up with an intensity denied the theater and made possible the documentation of reality beyond the restrictions of the proscenium arch as he filmed actual streets and natural landscapes.

Vardac sees Griffith's dramaturgy as emanating primarily from the pictorial theater, but Russell Merritt maintains that it also reflects the influence of the more literary social dramas, particularly in choice of subject matter and symbolic use of inanimate objects. The social drama, revolutionizing the stage in the late nineteenth and early twentieth centuries, dealt with a vast range of conflicts and injustices in modern society. Henrik Ibsen, Hermann Sudermann, Gerhardt Hauptmann, Sir Arthur

Wing Pinero, George Bernard Shaw and John Galsworthy were all major social dramatists of the period. As an actor, Griffith had appeared in Ibsen's *Hedda Gabler* and *Rosmersholm* and Sudermann's *Magda* and *The Fires of St. John,* an experience which undoubtedly led to his assimilation of the techniques and thematic dimensions of the social drama.

Galsworthy's plays, *Strife* (1909), depicting a struggle between the forces of capital and labor, and *Justice* (1910), an indictment of the penal system, are built upon themes that parallel the social problems explored by Griffith in the Modern Story. While differing from Griffith in presenting the strike from a neutralist point of view, *Strife,* first produced in the United States in 1910, focuses on the hardships endured by the workers and their families because of the intransigence on both sides of the dispute. Griffith, on the other hand, attributes the misery of the workers solely to the venality of the capitalist. Galsworthy's highly successful *Justice,* staged in the United States in 1916 with John Barrymore in the lead, concerns a young man of good character who, in order to protect the woman he loves, commits his first offense, the relatively minor crime of forgery, and receives unusually harsh treatment from the law. Like Galsworthy, Griffith exposes the inequity built into the penal system, which seems all the more iniquitous when it victimizes an innocent young man.

According to Merritt, Griffith derived from social dramas "a dramaturgy of signs built around costumes, clothes, hand props and decor." Unlike Belasco, the social dramatist frequently employs inanimate objects as symbols to reinforce the thematic implications of the play. Merritt cites the example of the cut wild flowers in *Rosmersholm,* which are symbolically linked to "Rebecca West's schemes to lure Rosmer away from his dead wife." These "evocative trifles," as Merritt terms them, permeate Griffith's work as well, taking on special significance in the context of the film's theme and adding depth to the characterizations. With the inclusion of a scene in which the Dear One examines "the hopeful geranium," the director signifies his belief in the renewal of life: the girl first mourns the nearly-dead plant, then finds hope in a new shoot growing from the old stem. He builds an ironic motif around the handgun the Boy returns to the Musketeer of the Slums when he renounces a life of crime. It is this same gun that the Friendless One uses to kill the Musketeer, an action leading to the conviction and near-execution of the Boy.

While the social drama provided a model for his "iconography of psychological abstractions," grand opera gave Griffith the inspiration to infuse his work with an emotional quality. [Georges Sadaul, *Dictionary of Films*]. The opera's relentless assault on the emotions through the synergetic crescendoing of the music to the unfolding of the plot is analogous to Griffith's heightening of the audience's feelings through rhythmic editing. Whether it is Giacomo Puccini's *La Tosca* with Tosca killing Scarpia to preserve her honor, then jump-ing to her death from a parapet when her lover is shot, Georges Bizet's *Carmen* with the jealous Don José stabbing the faithless Carmen to death, or Giuseppe Verdi's *Il Trovatore* with the Count ordering the execution of a man who is actually his brother, the audience's emotions are raised to the same level of intensity that Griffith evokes with his films. In the trial scene in the Modern Story, he moves the spectator to empathize with the Dear One awaiting the court's decision, cutting from a close-up of her anxious face to a close-up of her hands twisting and turning in the folds of her dress, then continuing the emotional intensity after the verdict, showing her abject despair. The denouement of the Babylonian Story, in which Belshazzar and his consort commit suicide and the Mountain Girl dies amid the debacle of Babylon's conquest, possesses the same kind of crescendo to catastrophe found in many operas, including the destruction of Valhalla in Wagner's *Die Götterdämmerung.*

A devotee of the opera, Griffith chose subject matter for the French and Babylonian Stories suggesting elements of plots from specific operatic works. Giacomo Meyerbeer's spectacular opera, *The Huguenots,* like Griffith's French Story, has fictional lovers who are caught up in the events of 1572. Both narratives conclude with the deaths of the hero and heroine in the massacre of St. Bartholomew's Day. The Babylonian Story is reminiscent of Verdi's early opera, *Nabucco,* which takes place in the Babylon of Nebuchadnezzar and has among its characters an intriguing High Priest of Bel. Verdi's *Aida* also contains similarities to the Babylonian Story. Both are set in ancient Middle Eastern civilizations and have a High Priest as their pivotal villain. In *Aida,* the High Priest of Isis brings about the death of the hero and heroine, while in the Babylonian Story, the High Priest of Bel is responsible for the fall of Babylon. The priests in *Aida* invoke the gods to protect Egypt in its war with the invading Ethiopians just as the priests in Griffith's film beseech Ishtar's aid to defend Babylon from the Persians. In both the opera and the film, the victors celebrate their triumphs with elaborate festivities and gala performances by dancing girls.

For all his stage background, Griffith was no more indebted to the theatre than to any of the other arts. He utilized the rich heritage of the stage, not to imitate it, but to incorporate elements from it to aid him in the creation of a new dramatic-narrative form with its own laws and syntax.

FILMS

Compared to his absorption of elements from the older art forms, Griffith's borrowing from other filmmakers was superficial, primarily limited to such items as costumes and decors. While his basic editing style and approach to historical film evolved independent of foreign influences, Griffith was impressed with the careful staging he saw in the French "Film d'Art" costume dramas and the Italian epic cinema, prompting him to adopt some of their components for his French and Babylonian Stories.

The Film d'Art, developed in France, influenced filmmakers throughout the world in the 1910s. Dealing with literary and historical subjects, the films of this genre were essentially photographed stage plays with little camera ingenuity. The concentration on elaborate settings and costumes along with the histrionics of the stars brought prestige to the cinema in cultured circles. The dominance of the Film d'Art began with the international success of the one-reel film, *The Assassination of the Duc de Guise* (1908) which Griffith later called "my best memory of the cinema" and "a complete revelation." Depicting an incident from the region of Henri III (the prince of the French Story), this film, although theatrical, was distinguished for its fine acting and historically accurate sets. Another celebrated French production in the Film d'Art tradition was the four-reel *Queen Elizabeth* (1912) starring Sarah Bernhardt. The American release of this film simultaneously launched the career of its distributor, Adolph Zukor of Famous Players, and created a market for longer films in the United States. As theatrical as *The Assassination of the Duc de Guise, Queen Elizabeth,* dramatizing the love affair of Elizabeth and Essex, also provided an opportunity for displaying lavish sixteenth-century costumes and sets. Although Griffith's dynamic use of the cinematic language in the French Story went far beyond the stagy techniques of costume productions like *The Assassination of the Duc de Guise* and *Queen Elizabeth,* his choice of a sixteenth-century historical subject with the appropriate costumes and settings owes much to the popularity of the French imports and his own study of them.

Far more cinematic than the Films d'Art were the Italian spectacles which established the genre of the epic film. These epics, surpassing the capabilities of the stage spectacle, recreated historical events including huge battle scenes and natural disasters and featured thousands of extras and monumental ancient architecture. Although *The Fall of Troy* (1910), a two-reeler directed by Giovanni Pastrone and one of the earliest of these films, had attracted American attention as early as 1911, it was not until the 1913 American screenings of the full-length feature *Quo Vadis,* directed by Enrico Guazzoni in 1912, that the public and critics began to recognize the motion picture's capacity to achieve a scale unknown to the theater. Following *Quo Vadis,* other large-scale Italian productions won acclaim from American audiences and critics, including *The Last Days of Pompeii* (1913) directed by Mario Caserini and *Antony and Cleopatra* (1913) and *Julius Caesar* (1914), both directed by Guazzoni. With their awesome reproductions of ancient Rome, these films revealed that the motion picture could bring history to life. They identified the glories of the Roman Empire with the modern renascent nation of Italy, fulfilling a political goal by giving artistic expression to the resurgence of Italian nationalism.

Giovanni Pastrone's *Cabiria* (1914), the masterpiece of the genre, is an epic recreation of the Punic Wars between Rome and Carthage and an ancient analogy to twentieth-century Italian expansion in North Africa. Upon its release in the United States in 1914, *Cabiria* was hailed by reviewers as an outstanding work of art. It was shown in "legitimate" theaters and had a special screening at the White House. Brown recalls that "The reviews of *Cabiria* had such an effect on Griffith that he and key members of his staff took the next train to San Francisco to see it." He incorporated certain elements from *Cabiria,* including soldiers scaling the city walls while defenders hurl missiles at them, and pet leopards adorning the royal court. He also modeled his giant warrior, the Mighty Man of Valor, who is devoted to Belshazzar, after Maciste, the hairy-chested giant who is the Roman hero's friend and protector in *Cabiria.* The two colossal elephant statues flanking the stairway of a palace courtyard in the Italian film inspired the huge elephants on the cornices that dominate the Babylonian set. In addition, Griffith's elaborate experiments with tracking shots in **Intolerance** may have been stimulated by his study of the extensive use of dolly shots in *Cabiria.*

Despite these relatively minor embellishments adapted from foreign filmmakers, Griffith was so far ahead of the Europeans that his overall style was unaffected by the imported productions. Even in *Cabiria,* the most advanced of the early European historical films, "the editing tended merely to link shots which were complete in themselves" [Kevin Brownlow, *The Parade's Gone*]. For all their visual impressiveness, the great Italian epics are primarily generalized visions of patriotism and lack the personal vision of history achieved through dynamic editing so characteristic of Griffith's masterpieces. The most significant effect of the early European films on Griffith was in galvanizing him to compete by producing his own full-length spectacles.

POETRY

Poetry was a major influence on Griffith's artistic development; he drew on the master poets for his themes, his images, his characterizations and even his philosophy. At Biograph, he filmed Robert Browning's "Pippa Passes" in 1909 and "A Blot on the 'Scutcheon" in 1911. He also adapted Alfred, Lord Tennyson's "The Golden Supper" in 1910 and directed two film versions of "Enoch Arden" including **After Many Years** (1908) and the two-reel film of 1911, released under the poem's original title. His fictionalized biography of Edgar Allan Poe, made in 1909, and his full-length feature, **The Avenging Conscience** (1914), based on the works of Poe, reflect his admiration for the American poet. He also demonstrated his love for poetry by frequently quoting verses in his subtitles. For example, in **Intolerance,** a shot of the prisoners in the death-house is accompanied by a quote from Oscar Wilde's *The Ballad of Reading Gaol*: "And wondered if each one of us / Would end the self-same way, / For none can tell to what red Hell / His sightless soul may stray."

The preeminent poetic inspiration for *Intolerance* derived from Alfred, Lord Tennyson and Walt Whitman. While Poe and Browning were suitable sources for the content of earlier Griffith films, their concentration on inner conflicts of man was less relevant to the director's projection of a social-historical vision than Tennyson and Whitman, whose works reflect a visual reality more adaptable to his purposes in *Intolerance.* Representing polar opposites, Tennyson, the great British poet-laureate, and Whitman, the great American poet-rebel, are synthesized in Griffith's aesthetic approach, infusing his work with both Victorianism and sensuality. The Victorian values of chastity and domesticity in Tennyson are tempered by the celebrations of the flesh in Whitman. In both poets, however, Griffith found a common thread of love and idealism that harmonized with his own philosophy.

Familiar with Tennyson from his childhood when his father's "orotund voice poured forth the music of Keats and Tennyson and Shakespeare," Griffith imbues his heroines with a kind of Tennysonian Victorianism. Tennyson's maidens are beautiful, chaste, delicate, incapable of malicious or sinful acts, yet sometimes prone to mischief. The Dear One hopping and skipping about and flirting with the Boy, and the Mountain Girl playfully spurning the Rhapsode's advances and impudently chewing onions to discourage suitors in the marriage market, are reminiscent of Tennyson's verbal portrait of Lilian:

> Airy, fairy Lilian,
> Flitting, fairy Lilian
> When I ask her if she love me,
> Claps her tiny hands above me,
> Laughing all she can;
> She'll not tell me if she love me,
> Cruel little Lilian.
>
> . . . . .
>
> So innocent-arch, so cunning-simple,
> From beneath her gathered wimple
> Glancing with black-beaded eyes,
> Till the lightning laughters dimple
> The baby-roses in her cheeks;
> Then away she flies.

Brown Eyes in the French Story is the quintessential Tennysonian heroine, a frail, angelic creature whose fidelity to her finance causes her to resist the savage lust of the mercenary soldier who is ultimately responsible for her death. Tennyson's description of the perfect wife of "chasten'd purity" in the poem "Isabel" might well apply to the faithful, virtuous Brown Eyes:

> Eyes not down-dropt nor over-bright
>   but fed
> With the clear-pointed flame of chastity,
> Clear, without heat, undying, tended by
>   Pure vestal thoughts in the translucent
>   fane

> Of her still spirit; locks not wide-dispread,
>   Madonna-wise on either side her
>   head;
>   Sweet lips whereon perpetually did
>   reign
> The summer calm of golden charity,
>
>   . . . . .
>
>   Revered Isabel, the crown and head,
> The stately flower of female fortitude . . .

Tennyson's conception of femininity in "Isabel" reflects his belief that woman possesses qualities which extend beyond conformity to a simple moral code. He characterizes Isabel as having "courage," "prudence," "extreme gentleness," and "a bright and thorough-edged intellect" with the intuitive ability "to part error from crime." In Tennyson's view, woman can redeem man through her role as a "maternal wife," capable of giving "subtle-paced counsel in distress" and sustenance with her love. For Griffith, too, the power of woman's love can be redemptive, leading man to a higher level of being. In an illustration of this Tennysonian concept in the Modern Story, the Dear One, entreating the Boy to pray with her for strength, convinces him to renounce his criminal pursuits for an honest and upright life.

Not only does Tennyson's admiration for the virtues of woman in the roles of wife and mother add dimensions to his feminine portraits; his poetry shows a reverence for the family unit as the basis for transmitting the values of Christian piety. Instilled in Griffith's consciousness was a deep, abiding respect for family life, which, like Tennyson's, sprang from his mother's teaching of the Protestant ethic. The serenity in the Huguenot home conveys Griffith's feeling for the stabilizing effect of the family unit amid the encroaching internecine conflict that will soon shatter this peaceful domesticity. In both Tennyson and Griffith, "the delights of familial calm occur against a backdrop of frustration, defeat, and impending death" [Gerhard Joseph, *Tennysonian Love: The Strange Diagonal*].

A poignant illustration of this motif occurs in Tennyson's "Enoch Arden," filmed by Griffith in his own adaptations of the poem, in which the hero, Enoch Arden, returns home from his long sojourn overseas to find his wife remarried. Yearning for the domestic bliss that is no longer his, he peers through the window of the home of his lost love and her new husband, Philip:

> For Philip's dwelling fronted on the
>   street,
>
>   . . . . .
>
> With one small gate that open'd on the
>   waste,
> Flourish'd a little garden square and
>   wall'd:
>
>   . . . . .
>
> And on the right hand of the hearth he
>   saw

Philip, the slighted suitor of old times,
Stout, rosy, with his babe across his
  knees;

. . . . .

And on the left hand of the hearth he
  saw
The mother glancing often toward her
  babe
Hers, yet not his, upon the father's knee,
And all the warmth, the peace, the
  happiness,
And his own children tall and beautiful,
And him, that other, reigning in his place,
Lord of his rights and of his children's
  love . . .

The mother and father surrounded by their children are "exemplars of a harmony that is sanctioned by, and proof of, a benificent God" [Joseph]. Adapting this scene from his own film versions of "Enoch Arden," Griffith shows the Dear One, after her baby has been taken from her, "enjoying the happiness of others" as she gazes longingly through a stranger's window at the tranquil scene of a couple with their child. While undetected by the couple, her smiles and gestures attract the attention of the child who returns her smile. The physical setting of this night scene of a house fronted by a garden so closely replicates Tennyson's description in "Enoch Arden" that Griffith's source for his imagery is unmistakable. In both Tennyson and Griffith, the meanings extend beyond the image to symbolize the melancholy of loss juxtaposed with domestic happiness.

In "Akbar's Dream," one of his last poems, Tennyson manifests a spirit of tolerance that parallels the essence of Griffith's theme in ***Intolerance***. The poem concerns the great Indian Mogul emperor who attempted to bring all religions together in a universal faith. Like Griffith, Tennyson expands his theme of spiritual love to a broader perspective glorifying the virtues of tolerance: "when creed and race / Shall bear false witness, each of each, no more, / But find their limits by that larger light, / And overstep them, moving easily / Thro' afterages in the love of Truth, / The truth of Love." Tennyson's description of Akbar in his notes brings to mind Griffith's religious reformer, Belshazzar:

> His tolerance of religions and his abhorrence of religious persecution put our Tudors to shame. He invented a new eclectic religion by which he hoped to unite all creeds, castes and peoples; and his legislation was remarkable for vigour, justice and humanity.

Besides his theme of spiritualized love, another motif that appears in Tennyson's work is his "passion for the past," which enables him to express the sensuousness he repressed within the context of his own time and culture. His tendency to tinge his presentation of the "far, far away" with an exotic lushness of detail extends not only to his portrayal of the heroines but also to their surroundings. While Griffith felt less restricted by Vic-

torian proprieties than Tennyson, he, too, found that the exoticism of the past offered a freedom to revel in sensuous detail. In the Babylonian Story, he projects a voluptuousness denied him in the more repressive or less resplendent periods of the other stories.

Typical of Tennyson's aesthetic indulgence when he conjures up images of the past is his depiction of the heroine, a Persian girl, in "Recollections of the Arabian Nights": "Serene with argent-lidded eyes / Amorous, and lashes like to rays / Of darkness, and a brow of pearl / Tressed with redolent ebony." Griffith's voluptuous portrait of the Princess Beloved, Belshazzar's favorite, displays the same abandonment from the restraints of Victorianism as Tennyson's Persian girl in Caliph Haroun Alraschid's harem.

Tennyson's loving representation of "A goodly place, a goodly time, / . . . in the golden prime / Of good Haroun Alraschid" compares with Griffith's romantic vision of a lost, glorious civilization. Thus, the pictorial imagery of the mythical Oriental grandeur of Griffith's Babylon is equivalent in its sensual provocativeness to the verbal luxuriousness of the Caliph's palace in Tennyson's poem with its "carven cedarn doors," "spangled floors," "Broad-based flights of marble stairs . . . with golden balustrade," and a room containing "six columns, three on either side, / Pure silver, underpropt a rich throne of the massive ore."

An even more vital influence than Tennyson in molding Griffith's social-historical vision in ***Intolerance*** was Walt Whitman. Exposed to Whitman as an impressionable youth in Louisville, Griffith's assimilation of the radical morality and individualism permeating the work of the poet undoubtedly played a pivotal role in helping him overcome the limitations of his Victorian-Southern background. Griffith, who "could quote pages of his poetry," often declared in later years that "he would rather have written one page of (Whitman's) *Leaves of Grass* than to have made all the movies for which he received world acclaim" [Gish, *The Movies*]. He even attributed his development of tempo and parallel action in his films to his study of Whitman. Although hesitant to openly express his affinity for the work of the robust, sensual poet who had shocked rural America "with his earthy ideas on sex and religion," the director confided to acquaintances that Whitman was even more essential to his evolution as a film artist than Dickens [D. W. Griffith and James Hart, *The Man Who Invented Hollywood*].

A certain coincidental similarity between Griffith the man and Whitman the man may shed light on the director's lifelong fascination with the poet. Raised in the traditions of Jeffersonian and Jacksonian democracy, they both demonstrated an individualistic self-reliance fused with broad social concerns in their personal and political philosophy. With little formal education, both were thrown into the world at an early age, gaining knowledge that would later prove fruitful in their artistic development. Whitman, apprenticing to a printer as a child and later drifting from one editorial position to another, and Griffith, working in a bookstore as a youth and subsequently becoming a traveling actor, exhibited an independence of spirit that typified, not only their lifestyles, but also their conceptions of art. By the time they reached their early thirties, neither had fulfilled his aesthetic aspirations. Not until Whitman, the failed novelist, and Griffith, the failed playwright, abandoned conventional modes of expression to become artistic revolutionaries, did they find their true metier. While their individualism enabled them to expand the horizons of their art forms, their uncompromising adherence to their own inner visions eventually ran counter to the tastes of the mass audience they wished to inspire and led to widely varied critical evaluations.

With their common dedication to the individual, both Whitman and Griffith espoused a form of social democracy that eschewed leftist dogma as well as rightist orthodoxy. Whitman, rejecting the doctrinaire socialism of his day, editorialized in the 1850s that education "is the only true remedy for mobs, emeutes, wild communistic theories, and red-republican ravings" [Gay Wilson Allen, *The Solitary Singer: A Critical Biography of Walt Whitman*]. Griffith, in an introductory subtitle in ***Orphans of the Storm*** (1922), warned the American public to beware of replacing "our democratic government" with "anarchy and Bolshevism." While each was caught up in the great reform movement of his day, each displayed an aversion to what he interpreted as the intellectual tyranny of the left. The intensity with which they opposed the mentality and practices of the traditional oligarchy, however, caused them to fall into a place on the political spectrum that could best be described as "radical social democrats." Paradoxically, their individualistic approach to political philosophy led to greater appreciation for their artistic achievements in the collectivist society of the Soviet Union than in their own country.

Inimical to their sense of social concern and independent spirit were the attempts by government to legislate morality. Griffith's condemnation of those who argue that "we must have laws to make people good" parallels Whitman's attitude towards moral reformers. Denouncing a proposed bill that would punish all practitioners of licentiousness in New York, Whitman stated in an editorial in the 1840s that "You cannot legislate men into morality." This sentiment also appears in his poem "Transpositions," in which he writes that the reformers should "descend from the stands where they are forever bawling" to be replaced by lunatics. He was incensed by another incident in the New York of the 1840s in which fifty prostitutes were arrested and turned again to his editorial pen to protest the "ruffianly, scoundrelly, villainous, outrageous and high handed proceeding, unsanctioned by law, justice, humanity, virtue or religion." His sympathy for prostitutes reappears in his long poem, "Song of Myself" from *Leaves of Grass*:

> The prostitute draggles her shawl, her bonnet
>> bobs on
>> her tipsy and pimpled neck,
> The crowd laugh at her blackguard oaths, the
>> men jeer
>> and wink to each other,
> (Miserable! I do not laugh at your oaths nor jeer
>> you . . .)

Reflecting this same sentiment in the Modern Story, Griffith presents prostitutes as victims of pharasaism, departing from the Tennysonian-Victorian view which draws a sharp distinction between virtuous women and temptresses. Again, in the Babylonian Story, his portrait of temple prostitution seems closer to Whitman's belief in the union of body and soul than to Tennyson's with its inherent dualism. While Griffith is Tennysonian in associating the exotic with the sensual, feeling less constrained in a presentation of a far-away era than in his own time, he goes beyond the mere aesthetic indulgence of an inhibited Victorian, imbuing his scenes of the "Virgins of the Sacred Fire of Life" in the Temple of Ishtar with a Whitmanesque quality that becomes a kind of erotic mysticism uniting the spirit and the flesh.

Whitman's attitude toward the penal system represents another area in which his radical morality coincides with Griffith's views. Joining with death penalty abolitionists in the 1840s, he denounced capital punishment in his editorials. Similarly, Griffith expressed his opposition to the death penalty in statements of the time as well as in his films, including *Intolerance*. In their creative work, both exhibit a great compassion for convicts, whom they view, like prostitutes, as among the oppressed in society. Decrying the plight of prisoners in the following poem, Whitman questions the right of society in light of its own misdeeds to pass judgment on these poor unfortunates:

> You felons on trial in courts,
> You convicts in prison-cells, you sentenced
>> assassins
>> chain'd and handcuff'd with iron,
> Who am I too that I am not on trial or in prison?
> Me ruthless and devilish as any, that my wrists
>> are
>> not chain'd with iron, or my ankles with iron?

Griffith interposes his own commentary on the harshness of the penal system in the prison scenes in the Modern Story and again in the epilogue in which he forecasts a day "when cannon and prison bars wrought in the fire of intolerance" shall be no more. In this sequence, the prison walls disappear, "allowing the prisoners to surge to freedom" where, in the words of the final subtitle, "Instead of prison walls bloom flowery fields" [Paul O'Dell, *Griffith and the Rise of Hollywood*].

Merged with Whitman's radical morality is his belief in religious humanism, a concept that is at the core of Griffith's ***Intolerance***. Whitman, influenced by the teachings of Elias Hicks, the Quaker leader, developed a new religion for himself. Like Griffith, Whitman repudiated original sin and questioned the established church dogmas and official morality as antithetical to the true teachings of Christ. Griffith, however, posits Christ's humanism within the context of a cyclical concept of history, whereas Whitman emphasizes Christ's humanism by freeing him from a historical perspective. The vitality of Griffith's humanism in *Intolerance* emanates from relating Christ's historical experiences and teachings to the present reality. Whitman's contemporary relevance in *Leaves of Grass,* on the other hand, arises from identifying the Christ symbol with himself as the common man who can be his own savior, thereby emancipating Christianity from its Biblical orthodoxy.

The poet's humanism enabled him to embrace all religions, including those regarded as pagan by Christian orthodoxy. He demonstrates his repudiation of traditional Christian claims to exclusive truth in "With Antecedents":

> I respect Assyria, China, Teutonia, and the
>   Hebrews,
> I adopt each theory, myth, god, and demi-god,
> I see that the old accounts, bibles, genealogies,
>   are true, without exception

Again, in "Song of Myself," he pays tribute to all faiths: "My faith is the greatest of faiths and the least of faiths,/ Enclosing worship ancient and modern and all between ancient and modern."

Griffith's assimilation of Whitman's ideas undoubtedly played a role, conscious or unconscious, in liberating him from the confines of the fundamentalist tradition common to the South. In the Babylonian Story, Griffith's depiction of the cult of Ishtar as a religion of love analogous in its essence to Christianity is akin to Whitman's acknowledgment in "With Antecedents" of the verities in all religions, including polytheism. From an orthodox point of view, representing "godless" paganism as possessing spiritual values equivalent to Christianity borders on heresy.

The corollary of this respect for non-Christian religions was the artists' appreciation for ancient civilizations. Just as Griffith found ancient Babylon fascinating, Whitman was captivated by ancient Egypt and included "numerous echoes, allusions and references to Egyptology" in *Leaves of Grass*. His study of the history of the ancient culture at the Egyptian Museum in New York City provided the historic detail appearing in his poetry, and more importantly, gave him "a sense of the continuity of life and human culture," an undercurrent of *Leaves of Grass* [Allen].

A similar feeling for the continuity and unity of human experience through the centuries is basic to the narrative structure of *Intolerance* making Griffith's conception of history more Whitmanesque than Tennysonian. Tennyson views the past as a legendary backdrop for romantic escapism or moralistic allegorizing, while Whitman's invocations of remote civilizations are predicated on the theory that the present is inseparable from the past. Although Griffith is Tennysonian in coloring his depiction of Babylon with exotic detail, his total historical conception remains closer to Whitman.

An integral part of Griffith's historical vision is Whitman's view of "flowing time" which anticipates the director's approach in *Intolerance*. Whitman's conception grew out of his belief in an "eternal present" in which "past and present and future are not disjoined but joined." According to Gay Wilson Allen, Whitman's biographer, the artist is a "time-binder" who transcends the limitations of time and space, preserving the wisdom of the past in order to interpret the present and the future, a technique which is embedded in the narrative and ideological development of *Intolerance*. One of the best examples of Whitman's alternation between the past and the present occurs in "Passage to India." In this poem, his homage to the achievements of the past as preparations for the accomplishments of the present becomes a device for revelation:

> Singing my days,
> Singing the great achievements of the present,
>
>   · · · · ·
>
> Yet first to sound, and ever sound, the cry with
>   thee O soul,
> The Past! the Past! the Past!
>
>   · · · · ·
>
> The past—the infinite greatness of the past!
> For what is the present after all but a growth out
>   of the past?
> (As a projectile form'd, impell'd, passing a
>   certain line,
>   still keeps on,
> So the present, utterly form'd, impell'd by the
>   past.)

Throughout the poem, Whitman conjures up images of Columbus, Vasco da Gama, Alexander the Great and the ancient Orient alongside the great engineering achievements of his own time, the building of the Suez Canal and the transcontinental railroad. Similarly, Griffith frees himself from the boundaries of time and space, shifting from one era to another in *Intolerance* to discover the underlying pattern of human existence that holds the key to truth.

Griffith also resembles the poet in "Passage to India" in his projection of the future. Both the film and the poem conclude with a future millenium of love and brotherhood. While structurally parallel, each beginning in the present, reverting to the past and ending with a vision of the future, they differ in their internal thematic implications. Griffith's underlying and unifying motif is a tension between harmony and disharmony which is resolved by an ultimate return to man's original state of happiness. Whitman, on the other hand, conceives an uninterrupted progression from past to present to future symbolized by modern transportation and communication linking the continents, a metaphor for the love that will eventually bind the human race.

Another characteristic common to the style of the poet and the director is a blending of the lyric with the epic. Throughout *Leaves of Grass,* Whitman evokes images of vast stretches of time and space encompassing innumerable centuries of history and culture and immense distances in the universe interwoven with the homely details of everyday living. Whitman pictures in "Salut au Monde," for example, "a great round wonder rolling through space," its "mountain peaks," its "Libyan, Arabian and Asiatic deserts," its "huge, dreadful Arctic and Antarctic icebergs." But he also sees "flocks of goats feeding," "the fig-tree, tamarind, date," "fields of teff-wheat," "the incomparable rider of horses with his lasso on his arm" and "the seal-seeker in his boat poising his lance."

In a visual language that emulates Whitman's blending of epic and lyric, Griffith likewise alternates between vast panoramas and close-ups of characters or intimate details. In the Babylonian Story, the long-shots of the colossal set are interspersed with lyrical portraits. At the great feast, for instance, the scene in which the Princess Beloved places a white rose in a toy chariot pulled by white doves to send her gift to the prince on the other side of the table is, as Brown notes, "the big moment of this big set with its big everything." Another example of this technique is the simple, homely scene of the Mountain Girl milking a goat intercut with the shots of epic grandeur and the luxury of the Babylonian court. Like Whitman, Griffith, while contemplating the vastness of reality, ponders the significance of the small in the belief that "a leaf of grass is no less than the journey-work of the stars."

From these speculations on the cosmic and the confluence of time, the poet and the director come to understand that the individual is the center of existence, a microcosm of the universe. In *Democratic Vistas,* Whitman asserts that in all things, "sooner or later, we come down to one single, solitary soul" and, reaffirming this idea in "By Blue Ontario's Shore," states: "The whole theory of the universe is directed unerringly to one single individual—namely to You." For Whitman, this realization provides the unity for his lyric epic, *Leaves of Grass.* He, as poet-prophet, becomes a common man whose spirituality issues from his identification with people of other times and other places. It forms the basis for his belief that the fulfillment of democratic ideals will come about only through "a real, vital, spiritual democracy" in which the love of individuals for each other fosters the brotherhood of man [Thomas Edward Crawley, *The Structure of Leaves of Grass*].

Griffith, too, finds the meaning of existence rooted in "the supreme value of the individual" [Seymour Stern, *"The Birth of a Nation"*]. Although *Intolerance* has no

authorial "I" comparable to Whitman's poet-prophet, its truth is revealed in the common experiences of ordinary individuals through the ages. Like Whitman, Griffith believes that the transformation of society occurs through individual acts of kindness that are manifestations of brotherly love.

Whitman's conception of femininity growing out of his belief in individualism may have colored Griffith's portrayal of his heroines. Whitman idealizes the strong, athletic woman who is capable of taking care of herself, a striking contrast to Tennyson's delicate, ethereal women. In "A Woman Waits for Me," Whitman dismisses "impassive women," preferring those who are "warm-blooded and sufficient for me": "They know how to swim, row, ride, wrestle, shoot, run, strike, retreat, advance, resist, defend themselves, / They are ultimate in their own right—they are calm, clear, well-possess'd of themselves."

These Whitmanesque characteristics appear in Griffith's heroines, profoundly modifying a strictly Tennysonian-Victorian attitude towards women. The Mountain Girl is primarily Whitmanesque despite her touches of Tennysonian sprightliness: she fights valiantly against the Persian invaders, deftly using her bow and arrow, and drives a chariot with lightning-like speed to warn Babylon of its impending doom. Although she does not exhibit this same athletic prowess, the Dear One also possesses Whitmanesque qualities that extend the dimensions of her characterization beyond its Tennysonian elements. Undaunted after the death of her father and the imprisonment of her husband, she manages to survive, manifesting the strength and endurance that Whitman so appreciated in women.

The pivotal poem in *Leaves of Grass* is "Out of the Cradle Endlessly Rocking" which, for the first time, sets forth the central themes, representing a transition from materialism and individualism to a spirituality that embraces the totality of existence. In this poem, Whitman uses a mother rocking a cradle as a metaphor for the sea; the sea becomes a symbol for life and death. The persona of the poem is a boy who matures with his understanding of "the absorption of the individual into the soul of nature or the universe" when he observes two nesting mocking-birds on the beach [Allen]. He shares their joy together and their grief when they are forever separated. Contemplating the significance of death as he wanders by the sea, the boy gains insight that enables him to become a poet-prophet.

This poem so profoundly affected Griffith that he adopted its image of a rocking cradle for his own metaphor in *Intolerance*. The image of a young woman rocking a cradle with the indistinguishable three Fates in the background represents the eternal cycle of life and death. Freed from any identification with a specific historical period, this image opens and closes *Intolerance*. Throughout the film, it is used as a transitional device virtually every time Griffith cuts from one era to another, reinforcing the unity of the work. Adapting from Whitman's lines

> Out of the cradle endlessly rocking,
>
> . . . . .
>
> I, chanter of pains and joys, uniter of here and
>   hereafter,
>
> . . . . .
>
> A reminiscence sing.

he either quotes or paraphrases these lines at several points in the film. When the cradle image first appears, it is preceded by the title, "Out of the cradle endlessly rocking" and is followed with the paraphrased title: "Today as yesterday, endlessly rocking, ever bringing the same human passions, the same joys and sorrows." Later in the film, the words "Endlessly rocks the cardle / Uniter of here and hereafter. / Chanter of sorrows and joys" is superimposed over the image. Griffith repeats the lines to underscore the idea of continuity associated with the image. Additionally, the line "Chanter of sorrows and joys" may indicate his wish to enlighten his audience through his authorial presence. Much as Whitman, the poet-prophet, seeks to reveal the truth through his reminiscence of personal experience, Griffith shares with his audience the historical experiences of other human beings.

NOVELS

Griffith's approach to narrative construction, indeed, his overall social and historical vision, owes much to English and American novels of the nineteenth century, particularly the works of Sir Walter Scott, James Fenimore Cooper, Charles Dickens and Frank Norris. As Jack C. Ellis notes in *A History of Film*:

> The fusing of fiction with history . . . was standard with Sir Walter Scott and other historical novelists; Griffith drew more or less consciously on nineteenth-century literary precedents for the shaping of his stories.

Acknowledging his indebtedness to Dickens, Griffith once said he composed novels in pictures. He maintained that "the Motion Picture is a novelizing or storytelling form, not strictly a stage form."

Griffith's assimilation of Scott's methods of depicting historical themes and characters seems to have been largely intuitive, arising from his Southern heritage. The first great novelist of the nineteenth century and the most important since Cervantes, Scott set a literary precedent that radiated across the Western world from America to Russia. In America, he enjoyed particular popularity in the South, where marked similarities to his native Scotland led to identification with the spirit of his work. Compared to the urbanized, industrialized and wealthy northern United States, the South seemed rural, feudalistic, and impoverished, as did Scotland in contrast to the neighboring England. Both had suffered disastrous defeats at the hands of the more advanced adjacent regions. In the South in the aftermath of the Civil War, the vivid narratives of the defeats of heroic Scottish rebellions had a particular appeal to the heart of a Dixie cherishing the memory of a lost cause.

By the time Griffith was growing up in the South, Scott had become central to the literary and cultural heritage of the region. Steeped in Southern traditions, Griffith was introduced to the novelist at an early age when his father read Scott's works aloud to the family. Indeed, the genesis of his treatment of historical narrative can be traced to Scott's example. Like Scott, he intermingles his fictional protagonists with actual historical personages. Also, like Scott, he creates characters representing social forces who articulate his historical perspective of any particular moment in history. David Brown's description of Scott could apply to Griffith as well:

> Scott's great originality . . . lies not only in his intuition that an individual's life is fundamentally affected by the age in which he lives, but also in a complementary intuition that the most significant manifestation of the forces at work in society at any one time will be in the lives of ordinary individuals . . . Scott attempts to illuminate the underlying movements common to society as a whole at the particular moment.

Similarly, Stanley J. Solomon states in *The Classic Cinema* that *Intolerance*, like Griffith's other historical films, concentrates on

> the problems and emotions of ordinary individuals who reflect the values and attitudes of their culture . . . as we watch the Persian assault on the walls of Babylon or the massacre of the innocents on St. Bartholomew's Day, for example, we are always aware of a particular individual's struggle against the dehumanizing forces of his age.

Henry Morton, Scott's hero in *Old Mortality,* exemplifying the forces of Presbyterianism in rebellion against the royalist authority, parallels Griffith's Prosper Latour, who embodies the Huguenots' struggle against the allied forces of church and state. While historical figures like Catherine de Medici in the French Story and Claverhouse in *Old Mortality* symbolize vast forces of repression attempting to thwart and subdue the perceived enemies of the power structure, the narrative emphasis in both Scott and Griffith always returns to the ordinary individuals in their brave struggle against their oppressors. Henry Morton, siding with the Covenanters during their revolt against the crown, twice saves the life of one of his compatriots; Prosper Latour vainly attempts to rescue his sweetheart in the midst of the St. Bartholomew's Day Massacre. The Dear One, manifesting the heroic qualities of the common people as she pleads for her husband's life amid the class conflicts of the Modern Story, recalls Jeannie Deans, the humble peasant girl in Scott's *The Heart of Midlothian* who, caught up in the dissension brought about by the

Porteus riots, endeavors to save her sister, demonstrating "the rich humanity and simple heroism of a really great human being" [A. Norman Jeffares, editor, *Scott's Mind and Art*].

Griffith also seems to have drawn from James Fenimore Cooper, the other great historical novelist of the early nineteenth century. The only direct evidence of Cooper's impact on the director is Griffith's one-reel adaptation of *The Leatherstocking Tales* for Biograph, but, given Cooper's stature as the first great American novelist, it is reasonable to assume that his literary precedent may have been as important as Scott's in shaping Griffith's narrative concepts. In his early films of pioneer and Indian life, his themes and settings suggest he may have used Cooper as a frame of reference. In addition, Cooper's use of action to highlight the recreation of historical events and his tendency to infuse his work with a moral purpose are characteristics that can be found in Griffith's work.

In his stories of frontier life and Indian Wars, Cooper is a master at creating suspense through vivid descriptions of flights, pursuits and rescues to propel the action, providing a prototype adaptable to filmic methods. A typical example of his technique occurs in the climax of *The Last of the Mohicans*. During a wilderness battle in the French and Indian Wars, tension mounts as one dramatic incident follows another. The Indian hero, Uncas, and his friends, Natty Bumppo and a British officer, pursue the villainous Iroquois, Magua, and his fellow tribesman, fleeing through the rugged mountainous terrain with their captive, Cora Munro. Cora, refusing to go farther, is killed by Magua's companion just as Uncas drops from a high ledge to knife Cora's murderer. Magua first stabs Uncas, then attempts to leap to safety only to miss his mark and hang precariously over a precipice. The action concludes with Natty Bumppo shooting the Iroquois, who falls into the abyss below.

In Griffith, too, events coalesce to add momentum and suspense. Griffith's most advanced use of this narrative device, surpassing Cooper in scope, appears in the climax of *Intolerance* when, as Lewis Jacobs observes,

> action follows action . . . as the rhythm sweeps along. Christ is seen toiling up Mount Calvary; the Babylonian Mountain Girl is racing to warn her king of the onrushing enemy; the Huguenot is fighting his way through the streets to rescue his sweetheart from the mercenaries; the wife is speeding in an automobile to the prison with a pardon for her husband who is about to be hung.

Another similarity between Cooper and Griffith is their intense religious moralizing. Although Griffith presents a religious perspective imbued with Whitmanesque humanism that is broader and more eclectic than Cooper's doctrinaire approach, in many of his films he infuses his social and historical view with moral overtones. Iris Barry calls *Intolerance* "an epic sermon" with Griffith citing scriptures to make his point, presenting his moral

conclusions in didactic subtitle, drawing a clear distinction between good and evil in his characters and manifesting his seriousness of purpose in an epilogue prophesying the Millenium. Similarly, Cooper blends breathtaking entertainment and epic historical recreation with his own moral and religious convictions as in the conclusion of *The Deerslayer*:

> We live in a world of transgressions and selfishness, and no pictures that represent us otherwise can be true; though happily for human nature, gleamings of that pure spirit in whose likeness man has been fashioned, are to be seen, relieving its deformities, and mitigating, if not excusing, its crimes.

Cooper, like Griffith, sees the possibility for mankind's redemption amid all its evils. Unlike Griffith, however, Cooper believes that land ownership, the law, the social hierarchy, the traditional high church are sacred and that "the devaluation of the sacred inevitably leads to the degeneration of civilization." Although Cooper's philosophy contrasts with Griffith's prerevolutionary view in *Intolerance,* in which traditional hierarchies pervert or obscure the sacred, moral qualities inherent in the individual; both artists conceived their work and their interpretation of history as a means of reaffirming a moral conception of man originating in the religious experience.

The most singular influence on Griffith among novelists was Charles Dickens. Griffith's favorite novelist, Dickens played an important role not only in the development of his cinematic techniques, but also in shaping his overall social and historical vision. In their use of characterizations, their attitude toward established institutions, their sympathy for the downtrodden in society, their emphasis on pathos to highlight their narratives, and their ability to depict the sweep of historical events through the passion of crowds, Dickens and Griffith show a concern for social justice and a commitment to rectify the wrongs. As Lary May points out, Griffith, like Dickens, sought "to show the way the world ran and inspire the viewer to change it."

Griffith often attributed his development of parallel editing to his study of the great English novelist. While the director's most elemental use of crosscutting in his earliest films may have derived from the melodrama, his more sophisticated narrative construction drew on Dickens's precedent as he stated in 1922:

> It was the reading of his [Dickens's] works that convinced me of the effectiveness of this policy of "switching off." It is to be found throughout his books. He introduces a multitude of characters and incidents, and breaks off abruptly to go from one to another, but at the end he cleverly gathers all the apparently loose-threads together again and rounds off the whole. It occurred to me that the method would be far more suitable to films than the straightforward system borrowed from plays which was then in vogue, and I put it into effect.

An episode in *Oliver Twist* in which Oliver, on an errand for his benefactor, Mr. Brownlow, is recaptured by a gang of thieves illustrates the technique Griffith described. A series of transitions accompanies the action. As the episode begins, Oliver is leaving the Brownlow house where Mr. Brownlow and his friend await the boy's return. The action then cuts to a scene in a tavern disclosing the thieves, Fagin, Bill Sikes and Nancy. After Nancy and Sikes leave, the setting switches to the streets where Oliver is blithely carrying out his mission for Mr. Brownlow when he is suddenly accosted by Nancy and Sikes. A brief cutback to Mr. Brownlow and his friend still waiting for Oliver is followed by the street scene in which the boy is led away by Nancy and Sikes to Fagin's den. Inspired by the Dickensian form, Griffith perfected his method of crosscutting, enabling him to evolve the cinematic editing which became the basis for narrative film.

The link between Dickens and Griffith in delineating characters is analyzed by Sergei M. Eisenstein, the Russian film director, in his famous essay, "Dickens, Griffith and the Film Today." He notes that "striking figures of sympathetic old men, noble figures of sorrow and fragile maidens, rural gossips and sundry odd characters in the Dickens tradition" abound in Griffith's work "and grow from episodic figures into those fascinating and finished images of living people in which his screen is so enriched." Dickens endows even his incidental characters with memorable traits, such as the opinionated old lady in *David Copperfield* who thinks all sailors are nothing but "meanderers" and the disreputable old shopkeeper from the same novel who haggles with David over the price of clothes. These characters, like the myriad others who people the Dickens world, are used by the author for comic relief. Like Dickens, Griffith punctuates his drama with unforgettable incidental characters. In **Intolerance,** the bit-players humanize the theme and make satirical comments on the pretentiousness and hypocrisy around them. For example, in the Judean Story, an old man momentarily stops munching an apple, his face reflecting the absurdity of the situation when the Pharisees demand that all activity cease while they pray in public. Again, in the Modern Story, a grizzled old man's sly wink ridicules the self-righteous Vestal Virgins of Uplift as they lead the police raid on a brothel.

Another similarity in character development between Griffith and Dickens is their preference for youthful protagonists to emphasize the social themes. The innocence of the aspiring young heroes and heroines is accentuated when contrasted with the harshness of their societies. In *Nicholas Nickleby,* Dickens exposes the oppressive nature of provincial schools by juxtaposing the young hero, an assistant teacher, with his overlord, the sadistic schoolmaster, Squeers. Again, in *Bleak House,* Dickens highlights the chicanery of unscrupulous lawyers by showing the downfall of young Richard Carstone, who is destroyed by his entanglement in a lengthy chancery suit. The injustice of debtors' prison is

underscored in *Little Dorrit* as Dickens portrays the heroine growing up in the prison where her father is incarcerated. Griffith likewise strengthens his statement against injustice in the Modern Story by counterpointing the naivete of the Dear One and the Boy reveling in the simple pleasures of life with the self-righteousness of the reformers, the avariciousness of the capitalist, and the impersonal cruelty of the law. The horror of the St. Bartholomew's Day massacre in the French Story is vividly conveyed to the audience through the fate of the young couple who are slaughtered on the eve of their marriage. In the Babylonian Story, the viewer is sensitized to the futility and destructiveness of war through the depiction of the Mountain Girl sacrificing her life in battle for a lost cause.

Both the novelist and the director developed a gallery of villains to project the corrupting and destructive forces in society. Jenkins, his sister and her associates in the Jenkins Foundation display the same kind of pharasaism that Dickens portrays in the arrogant, heartless industrialist, Josiah Bounderby, in *Hard Times,* who loudly proclaims the official morality while boasting that he is a self-made man. Griffith's characterization of the Musketeer of the Slums combines the shrewd, conniving leadership of Fagin, chief of the underworld in *Oliver Twist,* with the menacing appearance and manner of Fagin's chief lieutenant, Bill Sikes. Fagin is able to achieve his ignominious position by recruiting poor boys and girls to carry out his thievery. Like Fagin, the Musketeer of the Slums thrives upon social outcasts to build his empire, enlisting those who have been dispossessed because of the strike. Thus, the criminality of Dickens's and Griffith's underworld figures becomes an indictment of poverty and corruption, the conditions in society which allow the criminals to flourish.

Dickens's and Griffith's inclination to show "morally degraded characters who have sudden flashes of goodness" is apparent in the analogous portraits of Nancy in *Oliver Twist* and the Friendless One in the Modern Story. Both are criminals' mistresses who manifest an inherent goodness enabling them to rise above their sordid milieu. To save Oliver Twist, whom she has befriended, Nancy turns against her gang, an act of self-sacrifice that leads to her death at the hands of Bill Sikes. Her Griffithian counterpart, the Friendless One, redeems herself by saving the innocent Boy from execution on the gallows when her conscience forces her to confess to the murder of her paramour.

Both Dickens and Griffith express an immediate and passionate concern for the social ethos, a motif lacking in Scott's detached historical view and Cooper's religious didacticism. They are able to communicate sympathy for the downtrodden and stimulate outrage at social injustice by creating scenes of pathos to stir the emotions of the audience. Mingling comment on social inequities with a sense of loss is typical of both Dickens and Griffith. In *Great Expectations,* Dickens impresses upon his reader the unnecessary human devastation that results from society extracting its pound of flesh when he creates empathy for Abel Magwitch, an old convict who, after befriending the young hero, Pip, dies a broken man in prison. Dickens poignantly dramatizes the results of society's neglect of the poor in the scene in *Bleak House* in which Jo, the little sweeping-boy, dies from a disease brought on by his life of poverty. Comparable scenes in **Intolerance** arouse the spectator to Griffith's perception of the corrosive effects of poverty: the death of the Dear One's father, reduced to indigence by the suppression of the strike, becomes a strong indictment of the monopolies; the Boy's gravitation to the underworld when he cannot find work after his father's death at the hands of the militia dramatically illustrates Griffith's belief that poverty leads to crime.

An underlying distrust of established institutions is a dominant theme in both Dickens and Griffith. They view the Establishment as a potential instrument for oppression. In his satirical depictions of popular religious and moral movements in *Bleak House* and other novels, in his expose of the alleged "charitable" workhouse system in *Oliver Twist,* in his attack on governmental bureaucracy in *Little Dorrit,* and in his many other indictments of societal injustice and hypocrisy in his works, Dickens established a precedent for the socially conscious artist. Griffith, who had taken up this challenge from his earliest days at Biograph, uses the Modern Story to condemn the motives and practices of capitalist-sponsored charitable foundations, the brutal treatment that labor received at the hands of monopolists, the connection between political corruption and the underworld, and the inequities built into the legal system. He reinforces his expose of twentieth-century abuses through his historical analogies.

Frank Norris, the powerful social novelist who seems to have had the strongest impact on Griffith of any of the turn-of-the-century American writers, augmented the Dickensian legacy. Regarded as a literary revolutionist, Norris was a transitional figure between American Literature of the nineteenth and twentieth centuries, introducing uncompromising realism to portray the life of his time and becoming one of the first voices of Progressivism.

The seeds of the vast organization of the historical and social vision of **Intolerance** can be traced directly to Griffith's 1909 Biograph one-reel film, **A Corner in Wheat,** based on "A Deal in Wheat," a short story by Norris, and several sequences from Norris' great novel *The Octopus,* published in 1901. When he adapted a chapter from *The Octopus* for **A Corner in Wheat,** Griffith greatly advanced film language by using Norris's method of alternating scenes to dramatize an idea. Indeed, before **A Corner in Wheat,** Griffith's experiments in parallel editing or crosscutting had been used primarily for creating suspense and unfolding his narrative.

The Norris model enabled Griffith to express a social vision through parallel editing which went beyond the melodramatic structures of his earlier films. **A Corner in Wheat** manifests "a firm and obvious rhythm . . . based on the ideological content of each shot" [Robert M. Henderson, *D. W. Griffith: The Years at Biograph*]. In *The Octopus,* a novel about the oppression of farmers by the railroad monopoly, Norris repeatedly cuts between feasting at the mansion of a railroad executive and a starving woman and child wandering in the city streets, victims of the railroad's war on the farmers. From this source, Griffith evolved his form of editing to express a philosophical and ideological conception of society in **A Corner in Wheat,** in which he cuts between the banquet of a wealthy wheat capitalist and the breadlines of the poor who suffer from the executive's manipulation of the stock market. In succeeding films, Griffith continued to experiment with this technique. It reached its apogee with his "drama of comparisons" in which he not only cut between the oppressors and the oppressed within the individual stories but used thematic cross-cutting between the four stories to reinforce the unity of his historical vision.

The overwhelming force of industrialism crushing the helpless victims in its path is a dominant theme in both Norris's *The Octopus* and Griffith's Modern Story. Adopting the epic form, Norris presents a struggle between the wheat farmers and the railroad over the land in California's San Joaquin Valley. In the end, the monopoly prevails, leaving the farmers broken men as their ranches are "seized in the tentacles of the octopus." With comparable epic vision, Griffith shows in the Modern Story that the force of capitalism, strewing its course with ruined lives, is able to quell the budding labor movement.

Despite similarities in their perception of social conflict, their basic philosophic values lead them to different conclusions. A sympathetic but detached observer of his time, Norris is an optimistic determinist. He believes that "the individual suffers but the race goes on" as he shows that the wheat harvest is destined to feed thousands of the famished in India. Viewing the railroad as necessary and inexorable to facilitate delivery, Norris concludes that out of evil comes good (the wheat) "untouched, unassailable, undefiled, that mighty worldforce, that nourisher of nations." Griffith, his roots in an agrarian society defeated by industrialism, maintains that the race will survive only through the triumph of the individual. Thus, the optimistic conclusion of **Intolerance** derives, not from any coincidental beneficence of industrialism, but from the survival of the young couple in the Modern Story over the forces of capitalistic oppression. Reflecting the Jeffersonian and Whitmanesque tradition, Griffith believes that the system is good only if it respects the individual.

As artists, Norris and Griffith stand at the conjunction of realism and romanticism. Both combine depictions of the minutiae of daily life and social and historical analysis with action, emotion and intuition. Norris's style, which has been described as "primitivism," stresses "a faith in instinct and emotion" with "action rather than the mind the center of existence." It became "a central force in the modern American novel," and was inherently suited to the visual medium of film. It was through Griffith, intuitively incorporating the more compressed style of the modern novel, that "primitivism" became the characteristic mode of expression in the cinema.

Norris and Griffith held a common belief that, as artists, their mission was to instruct the people in the truth about life as they saw it. Donald Pizer writes that Norris

> believed that the best fiction does not merely describe or amuse. Rather, it serves the practical moral purpose of revealing both the primary truths of human experience and the full extent of human injustice and deprivation, so that man might learn and mend his ways.

In Norris's own words, he saw his role as a novelist as

> one who reaches the greatest audience. Right or wrong the People turn to him the moment he speaks, and what he says they believe . . . The People have a right to the Truth as they have a right to life, liberty and the pursuit of happiness. It is not right that they be exploited and deceived with false views of life . . . (The novelist) has a heavy duty to perform, and tremendous responsibilities to shoulder, and he should address himself to his task, not with the flippancy of the catch-penny juggler at the county fair, but with earnestness, with soberness, with a sense of his limitations, and with all the abiding sincerity that by the favor and mercy of the gods may be his.

Griffith demonstrated a similar earnestness of purpose in commenting on the role of filmmaker in his pamphlet *The Rise and Fall of Free Speech in America,* written as a protest against censorship, which he feared would limit the screen to "slap-stick comedies, the ridiculous, sentimental 'mush' stories, the imitation of the cheap magazines." The director stated:

> The world-wide acceptance of moving pictures means the introduction of the most popular and far-reaching form of education the world has ever known. . . . Censorship demands of the picture makers a sugar-coated and false version of life's truth. . . . We have no wish to offend with indecencies or obscenities, but we do demand, as a right, the liberty to show the dark side of wrong, that we may illuminate the bright side of virtue.

As many commentators have implied, Griffith is a transitional figure, drawing upon nineteenth-century art forms to create a twentieth-century art. His work, then, reflects a continuity with past achievements, yet his choice of artistic models is congruent with his times. In particular, such authors as Dickens and Whitman, with their celebrations of the common man and condemna-tion of injustice, harmonize with the democratic idealism of Jeffersonianism and the spirit of the Progressive Era. Indeed, Griffith's assimilation of nineteenth-century art forms to project a social-historical vision underscores the link between the democratic idealism of the 1800s and the Progressive movement of the early 1900s.

William Rothman   (essay date 1988)

SOURCE: "D. W. Griffith and the Birth of the Movies" and "Judith of Bethulia," in *The "I" of the Camera: Essays in Film Criticism, History, and Aesthetics,* Cambridge University Press, 1988, pp. 11-17, 18-30.

[*In the following essay, Rothman discusses Griffith's early post-Biograph film work, with an emphasis on* Judith of Bethulia.]

Film was not invented to make movies possible. The Lumière brothers' first public screening in 1895 was the culmination of innumerable technical developments that finally allowed films to be made and projected, but the invention of film did not immediately give rise to movies as we know them. Within ten years, film had become a sizeable industry and medium of popular entertainment, but news films, travelogues, films of vaudeville acts, trick films, and gag films were the dominant forms. Even as late as 1907, dramatic narratives constituted only one-sixth of the "product."

The turning point came in 1908. With the sudden growth of nickelodeons, respectable theaters intended primarily for the screening of films, producers turned to such "legitimate" fare as adaptations of novels and stage plays, and the dramatic narrative became the dominant form of film, as it has remained to this day. It was at this critical—and rather mysterious—juncture that the technology of film decisively linked up with the incipient idea of movies. Not entirely coincidentally, it was in 1908 that David Wark Griffith directed his first film.

Griffith was a struggling actor from Kentucky, no longer young, with fading dreams of attaining immortality as a playwright. In desperation, he accepted work with the American Biograph Company as a movie actor. When Biograph needed a new director, he stepped in.

In the next five years, working for Biograph, Griffith directed over five hundred short dramatic films in every imaginable genre—an inexhaustible treasure trove for students of film.

In 1913, Griffith took his next fateful step, breaking with Biograph when the company refused to release his *Judith of Bethulia* as a feature-length film. Striking out on his own, he produced as well as directed a series of extraordinary features culminating in *The Birth of a Nation* (1915), the film that definitively demonstrated to the world how powerful movies could be.

The Birth of a Nation was an astounding commercial success, but controversy surrounded it from the beginning. It was embraced by the resurgent Ku Klux Klan, and the NAACP rallied opposition, attempting to have the film banned. Griffith was shocked at the accusations that his film inflamed racial hatred; by all accounts, that was not his conscious intention. As if in defense against such charges—some would say in atonement—he sank all his profits from *The Birth of a Nation* into *Intolerance,* a colossal, majestic film, but a commercial debacle.

Deeply in debt, Griffith struggled the rest of his life to regain financial independence. In the years after the end of World War I, he made a number of his greatest films, *Broken Blossoms, True Heart Susie* (my personal favorite), *Way Down East,* and *Orphans of the Storm* among them. Yet he never reclaimed his position and power in the film industry.

Movies had become a giant corporate business, centered in Hollywood, with a rationalized system of studio production to which Griffith never fully adjusted. It became increasingly difficult for him to find backing for his projects, and by the last years of his life he was a pathetic figure haunting Hollywood, abandoned by the industry that owed him so much. But this is not the place to dwell on the melancholy denouement of the Griffith story.

Griffith's years at Biograph were like Haydn's years at Esterhazy. Churning out two films a week for over five years provided endless opportunities for experimentation. If an idea didn't work the first time, he tried it again—and again. To study the evolution of Griffith's Biograph films from 1908 to 1913 is to witness movies being born—year by year, month by month, week by week.

Film students once were taught that Griffith singlehandedly invented what is loosely called "the grammar of film"—continuity cutting, close-ups, point-of-view shots, iris shots, expressive lighting, parallel editing, and the other techniques and formal devices that movies have employed for over seventy years. Recent scholarship has made it clear that Griffith did not actually originate any of the inventions that once had been credited to him. Precedents have been found for all his innovations. Although his films were intimately involved in that complex process, Griffith was not the "prime mover" in the development and institution of the set of rules and practices that constitute the grammar of the movies.

Yet the more I ponder film's mysterious history, the deeper my conviction of Griffith's centrality. Without Haydn, the symphony would have developed, but without the examples of Haydn's symphonies and quartets and sonatas, and without the ideas about music manifest in those examples, Beethoven would not have become the Beethoven we know. Without Griffith, movies would have developed their grammar, and Hollywood would have become Hollywood but Chaplin would not have become Chaplin, nor Hitchcock Hitchcock, nor Renoir Renoir. The same can be said for Murnau, Dreyer, von Stroheim, Eisenstein, Ford, or von Sternberg. Griffith's centrality does not reside in a legacy he left to all subsequent movies, but in the inheritance he passed on to the greatest filmmakers of the succeeding generation. To them, Griffith was inescapable. From the period in which movies as we know them were born, it was Griffith's work alone that fully demonstrated the awesome power of the film medium, and it was Griffith's ideas about the conditions of that power that demanded—indeed, still demand—a response.

What movies are and what gives them their power are questions that vexed society at a time when the movies were fighting off their first attacks from would-be censors. Griffith's Biograph films are affirmations of the power of movies—and veiled (sometimes not so veiled) allegories justifying his unleashing of that power.

Consider *A Drunkard's Reformation* (1909), for example, a fascinating early Biograph film. It tells a story about the power of theater, but movies are what Griffith really has in mind. A young girl persuades her alcoholic father, who beats her whenever he is intoxicated, to go with her to a temperance play called *A Drunkard's Reformation*. At the theater, Griffith cuts back and forth between the actors on stage and the father and daughter in the audience. Gradually, the father begins to recognize himself in the drunkard on stage. As the stage father takes a drink and begins to beat his little girl, the father in the audience watches in fascination. His daughter views him warily out of the corner of her eye. Conscious of the play's intoxicating hold over him, she is afraid that theater, like whiskey, will release the monster within him. With the grace of God, this does not happen. Rather, the unfathomable power of theater brings him to his senses and saves his soul.

Griffith's Biograph films declared their innocent intention: to tap the awesome power of film in the hope of saving souls. By the time of *The Birth of a Nation,* however, Griffith's vision had grown darker, as is revealed in the remarkable sequence in which Mae Marsh, ignoring warnings, goes out alone to draw water from the spring. In a natural setting that dwarfs the merely human, Gus, a "renegade Negro," views Mae Marsh as she is absorbed in viewing a squirrel playing in a tree. Griffith cuts from a long shot of the girl to an iris insert of the squirrel. (This is not, strictly speaking, a point-of-view shot, but our view and hers do not essentially differ.)

He cuts back to the delighted and unselfconscious girl, then to a shot, notable for its expressionism, of Gus coming into the foreground to get a better view of something off screen that has struck his attention.

The shot of Mae Marsh that follows is closer than the preceding view of her, registering the menace of Gus's gaze, although, again, this is not literally a shot from his point of view.

Griffith cuts again to the playful squirrel and then back to the girl, delectable and frighteningly vulnerable in her unselfconscious absorption. In this context, the cut to the expressionistically composed tight close-up of Gus is deeply disturbing.

Gus is intoxicated by his views of the innocent girl. The twisted branches turn the frame into an expressive metaphor for the monstrous forces within him that his intoxication threatens to liberate.

In Griffith's dramaturgy, deeply indebted to Victorian melodrama, innocence and monstrousness are eternally at war for possession of the human soul. In the present sequence, Griffith explicitly links the act of viewing to both these opposing forces. But is our viewing, and Griffith's, innocent or monstrous?

The innocent girl is vulnerable to Gus—and vulnerable to the camera. In affirming innocence, the camera violates innocence; this is the most disquieting discovery Griffith passed on to his successors. However innocent their intention, movies emerge out of darkness.

Monstrousness threatens to possess Gus; yet he is not a villain. A dupe of the ambitious mulatto Lynch, himself a victim of Stoneman, the twisted, hypocritical carpetbagger, Gus is a figure of pathos, like the lunatic in *A House of Darkness* (1913).

In this late Biograph film, one of Griffith's most transparent allegories about art's powers of redemption, a lunatic is intoxicated by his views of an innocent woman (Griffith's expressionistic framing of Gus's viewing recalls his framing of the lunatic here).

Wild-eyed, the lunatic advances on the woman. Providentially, at the critical moment, the sound of piano playing drifts in from another room. Music, like theater in *A Drunkard's Reformation,* has the power to save men's souls. The beautiful melody calms the lunatic and saves him—and the woman—from the darkness within. In the world of *The Birth of a Nation,* however, Providence does not intervene to avert the tragedy.

Gus steps forward from his place as a secret viewer and innocently presents himself to Mae Marsh. Heartbreakingly, he declares his love for her and proposes marriage. Reacting in horror, the terrified child flees. Gus runs after her, desperately trying to reassure her that he means no harm. She climbs to the top of a cliff, with the frenzied Gus close behind. When he steps forward again, apparently to stop her from leaping, she jumps to her death.

Moments later, the Little Colonel (Henry Walthall) comes upon his dying sister. Realizing what has hap-

pened, he stares into the camera, his face an expressionless mask.

Walthall, a magnificent actor, plays this as a scene out of Shakespearean tragedy, not melodrama. In his anguish and his despair, he dedicates himself to vengeance; this is what Walthall's acting, under Griffith's direction, expresses. His look to the camera calls upon us to acknowledge his guilt, not his innocence, for he knows in his heart that he has no right to condemn Gus—because he himself at this moment, with the camera as witness, guiltily embraces the dark, monstrous forces within himself.

The last third of *The Birth of a Nation,* with its nightmarish inversion of Griffith's cherished values, follows from this guilty moment. The vengeful Ku Klux Klan, emerging out of darkness, does not and cannot restore the rightful order. All it can do is allow our nation to be born; it cannot save its soul. The burden of *The Birth of a Nation* is that America was born with blood on its hands. Its soul remains to be saved.

Griffith's masterpiece casts movies, as well as America, in shadow. Vanished is his faith that movies will be our salvation. How could they be, when they emerge out of darkness?

Griffith's films after his break with Biograph no longer claim for themselves the power of salvation. Their aspiration is more modest: to help keep alive, during dark times, the distant dream of a world to come in which innocence may be restored to its rightful throne.

. . . . .

Judith of Bethulia (1913) was D. W. Griffith's first feature-length film. Griffith devoted extraordinary energy and attention to its making. Indeed, he broke irrevocably with the Biograph management, for whom he had directed over five hundred short films, by his refusal to shorten it or to release it as two separate two-reelers. The last film of Griffith's long and productive association with Biograph, it remained, in his own estimation, one of his very best films.

Everything points to the conclusion that *Judith of Bethulia* is a key film in Griffith's career. Indeed, it is a film of considerable compositional complexity, thematic directness, and cinematic artistry. In addition, it highlights a fundamental strain in Griffith's filmmaking, perhaps carrying it to the furthest extreme of any of his films. Thus, *Judith of Bethulia* helps provide a perspective on Griffith's work as a whole. Yet the film has received virtually no critical attention.

I shall proceed by first sketching the film's narrative (the division into sections is my own).

I. *Idyllic Prologue:* The film begins with a prologue depicting the life of the peaceful community of Bethulia.

The first shots are of the well outside the city's walls. We see, for example, the innocent flirting of the young lovers, Naomi and Nathan (Mae Marsh and Robert Harron). Then the stout walls of the city are shown, and only then the marketplace within the walls of the city. Judith, the widow of the hero Manasses, is introduced. This prologue ends with a shot of the great "brazen gate" that guards the entrance to the city.

II. *The Assyrian Threat:* The Assyrians, led by Prince Holofernes, capture Bethulia's well. Naomi is among the prisoners taken. The Assyrians attempt to storm the walls, but are repelled. In the Assyrian camp, Holofernes is enraged. He is not placated by the bacchanalian revel staged to please him. There is then a renewed all-out attempt to storm the city's walls and penetrate its gate. A pair of shots (one of the defenders and one of the attackers) is repeated three times, then followed by a shot of Judith watching and then a shot of Holofernes waiting. Then a new pair of shots of defenders and attackers—closer and more dynamic—is intercut with the shot of Judith, now visibly more excited, and the shot of the intent Holofernes. We then get still closer and more violent shots of defenders and attackers, and a wild fusillade of shots encompassing all the setups thus far used in the sequence. Finally the shot of Judith is followed by the image of a giant battering ram brought into place against the gate. Yet the gate holds.

III. *The Siege:* Holofernes takes counsel. The Assyrians lay Bethulia under siege. There are scenes of suffering within Bethulia (for example, doling out water to thirsty Bethulians). The people come to Judith, imploring her to lead them. She is in despair, but then she has a vision of "an act that will ring through the generations." (We are not shown Judith's vision.) She dons sackcloth and ashes and then bedecks herself in her "garments of gladness." At the Assyrian camp, Holofernes takes out his impatience and frustration on his captains. Judith, veiled, leaves for the Assyrian camp to carry out her mysterious plan.

IV. *The Seduction:* Judith enters Holofernes' tent and begins the process of seducing him. Enticingly evading his touch, she finally leaves his tent (". . . his heart ravished with her"). There is prayer in the Bethulian marketplace. Holofernes' eunuch comes to Judith's tent to announce that Holofernes is ready to see her and that she should prepare herself. A title tells us what we can in any case see: Judith is aroused by the prospect of the impending encounter. Shots of Holofernes are intercut with other shots: Judith in excited anticipation; a desperate Pickett's Charge—like attempt by the Bethulians to reach the well, leading to renewed fighting at the walls; the separated Naomi and Nathan. Holofernes dismisses his erotic slave dancers (". . . Famous Fish Dancers from the illustrious Temple of Nin"). Judith, faltering in her resolve, catches sight of her loyal old retainer and prays for strength. The eunuch summons Judith. In Holofernes' tent, Judith seductively entices Holofernes to drink, refilling his chalice until he collapses, dead

drunk. Seeing him helpless, she hesitates, momentarily cradling his head. Then Griffith cuts to images of dead Bethulians, fallen in the attempt to retake the well, and suffering in the marketplace of Bethulia. Griffith cuts back to Judith, who raises Holofernes' sword to strike; then Griffith cuts to the exterior of the tent.

V. *The Bethulians' Triumph:* When the Assyrians discover that their leader has been killed, there is chaos in their ranks. In the market-place of Bethulia, Judith triumphantly unwraps the severed head of Holofernes. The Bethulian soldiers, transformed, pour out of the city's gate, defeat the Assyrians, and raze their camp. Naomi and Nathan are reunited.

VI. *Epilogue:* Judith passes through the marketplace. The Bethulians bow before her. She walks out of the frame.

Any discussion of **Judith of Bethulia** might well begin with a reflection on the character of Judith, in particular, her sexuality. In the context of Griffith's work, Judith's sexuality is noteworthy in two general ways: its "womanliness" and its "manliness." In contrast, for example, to Lillian Gish's "girls," Judith is very much a woman, although Blanche Sweet was only fifteen years old at the time. Judith's womanliness has three aspects.

1. *Judith's womanly beauty.* Griffith presents Judith's womanly beauty directly to the viewer. Griffith gives us images of Judith that are neither his Victorian "Madonna" idealizations nor his patented depictions of "dear" girlish behavior (jumping up and down with enthusiasm, and the like). Nor are they the "familiar" representations so common in Griffith's work (the presentation of Nathan and Naomi is, in this sense, "familiar," with the camera asserting a patriarchal authority over its subjects, exposing their tender cores, treating them as children). In the shots of Judith in sackcloth and ashes, the usual dematerializing effect of Griffith's makeup is eliminated in shots that anticipate Carl Dreyer's *The Passion of Joan of Arc* in their acknowledgment that a woman's face is covered with skin.

Certain shots of Judith preparing to seduce Holofernes, and engaged in that seduction, reflect a frank acknowledgment (again, rare in Griffith's images of women) that a woman has a body made from flesh that includes, say, armpits and breasts.

2. *Judith's knowledge of sexuality.* Complementing Judith's beauty are her knowledge and mastery of every stage of seduction. Her womanly confidence in her own sexuality is manifest in her peacocklike strutting, dressed in her "garments of gladness" in the full ensemble, her beauty enticingly veiled, and in the knowing way she parts her veil. Judith's hands, especially, become instruments of seduction. The focus on hands, effected by the use of the frame line as well as costuming and gesture, is one of the main strategies of the film.

Judith's womanhood is expressed in her hands, and Holofernes' manhood is concentrated in his. For example, when he comes to the entrance of Judith's tent, he enters the frame hands-first.

When Judith enters his tent for the first time, each stage of the seduction is registered in a pose or gesture of their hands. The erotically charged images of Holofernes' hand reaching for Judith's tantalizingly withheld hand are intercut with the Bethulians, begging for water, imploringly holding out their hands.

When Judith kills Holofernes, his death is registered by the cessation of movement of his hands (shades of Hitchcock's *Blackmail*). It is Judith's hands, now transformed, that wield the sword.

3. *Judith's desire.* When the Assyrians make their all-out attempt to penetrate the great brazen gate, the battle is imaged in clearly sexual terms as an attempted rape: Bethulia is, as it were, a woman threatened with violent penetration. The title summing up the sequence makes the underlying parallel all but explicit: "Yet Holofernes could not batten down the brazen gate nor make a single breach." The climax of the sequence is the appearance of the terrible, revelatory image of the giant battering ram.

The shots of fighting, cut in a crescendo of intensity, are intercut with repeated shots of Holofernes waiting in his tent and Judith watching the battle from her window. The shots of Judith and Holofernes are linked in their composition.

Throughout the film, in fact, the left side of the frame tends to be dominated by either Judith's presence or Holofernes' presence, implying the bond between them.

The spectacle, climaxing in the image of the battering ram, fills Judith with ever-increasing excitement. When Judith subsequently places herself in Holofernes' hands, pretending to offer herself, but really meaning to kill him, she finds herself sexually drawn to his majestic, bull-like presence. He has inflamed her passion even before they meet.

Despite Judith's intentions, she is sorely tempted not to kill Holofernes but to make passionate love to him. It is not that, in her intoxication with her enemy, she is motivated by the idea that he is good (as is, for example, the Mountain Girl, infatuated with Belshazzar, in the Babylonian story of *Intolerance*). A title declares ". . . And Holofernes became noble in Judith's eyes," but Griffith is using "noble" in accordance with the pseudobiblical language characteristic of most of the titles in the film ("Nathan could scarce refrain from going to the succor of Naomi" is among the more risible examples) and means nothing more than "splendid." In Holofernes' tempting presence, Judith does not think in moral terms at all, and it is not any idea of marriage or family that inflames her.

That the wiles of the "paint-and-powder brigade" have the power to tempt and/or deceive good men is a basic fact of life in Griffith's narrative universe. It is the strategy of these worldly women to excite eligible men, while at the same time presenting a falsely innocent face to the world. In *True Heart Susie* (1919), William is disillusioned when he learns Bettina's true nature. It is perhaps only in *The White Rose* (1923)—arguably the Griffith film that is most fully worked out thematically—that Griffith presents a good man inflamed by the erotic presence of a woman he knows to be "bad." But the presentation of the good Judith drawn to the splendid yet brutal Holofernes is perhaps unique in all of Griffith's films in its acknowledgment, and acceptance, of the dark side of a woman's sexual desire.

Judith is every inch a woman, yet the second noteworthy aspect of her sexuality is that the people of Bethulia call upon her to act as their leader—that is, as Griffith understands it, to assume a man's role. While Judith watches the spectacle of the battle, she is visibly aroused, as though part of her desires the Assyrians' penetration. But she is also racked with guilt. She wants to answer the Bethulians' call, but she feels powerless to lead them in battle. It is in this state, compounded of arousal and despair, that Judith has her first vision—a vision that, significantly, Griffith withholds from the viewer, although the presentation of holy visions is one of his specialties (as witness, for example, *The Avenging Conscience, Home Sweet Home,* and even *The Birth of a Nation*).

Acting on her vision, Judith puts on her "garments of gladness" and goes to Holofernes as though she were his bride. To complete her envisioned act, she must harden herself, conquering her own desire. Thus, a fateful struggle takes place in Holofernes' tent. How is the outcome of this struggle determined?

Providentially, Judith catches sight of her loyal old retainer. This is nicely presented in a deep-focus shot with Judith in the left foreground, the retainer in the background, and a smoking censer in the right foreground. Visually, the censer is linked with the well outside Bethulia's gate—directly by its shape and inversely by the water/fire opposition that runs through the film.

This shot is intercut with the representation of a simultaneous event: the ambush of a group of brave Bethulians who try to draw water from the captured well. This kind of crosscutting in Griffith's work implies a virtual psychic connection. Although Judith cannot actually see this display of barbarism, the sight of the retainer at this moment is functionally equivalent to such a view, serving to make Judith mindful of her people's suffering. A spasm of disgust passes through Judith—disgust for her own body sinfully drawn to the agency of her people's suffering, I take it. She prays to the Lord for strength.

Judith talks Holofernes into dismissing his eunuch so that she can be his sole "handmaid" for the night. Alone with Holofernes in his tent, she finds herself again in-flamed with desire. Repeatedly, she fills his chalice and goads him into drinking himself into a state of intoxi-cation. For a moment, she cradles his head in her arms, but then a second vision comes to her. The cinematog-rapher Karl Brown describes this moment [in *Adventures with D. W. Griffith*]:

> His highest objective, as nearly as I could grasp it, was to photograph thought. He could do it too. I'd seen it. In *Judith of Bethulia,* there was a scene in which Judith stands over the sleeping figure of Holofernes, sword in hand. She raises the sword, then falters. Pity and mercy have weakened her to a point of helpless irresolution. Her face softens to something that is almost love. Then she thinks, and as she thinks, the screen is filled with the mangled bodies of those, her own people, slain by this same Holofernes. Then her face becomes filled with hate as she summons all her strength to bring that sword whistling down upon the neck of what is no longer a man but a blood-reeking monster.

Actually, what Griffith shows here is not, as it were, natural thought, but a God-given vision. When Judith is transformed by this second vision, the manhood passes out of Holofernes' hands and animates hers.

In Griffith's imagery, the city of Bethulia itself under-goes a parallel sexual metamorphosis. The climactic image of the rout of the Assyrians is a shot of the tri-umphant Bethulians pouring out of the brazen gate. In reversal of the earlier images of Bethulia as a woman, Griffith here images the city as a potent man.

Judith of Bethulia centers on the dramatic struggle within Judith—spiritual, yet imaged in sexual terms and mirrored by the armed struggle between the Bethulians and the Assyrians—to perform an act that appears to deny her womanly nature. How can this struggle, and specifically its triumphant and liberating resolution, be reconciled with the affirmation, fundamental to Griffith's work, of an order in which sexuality can be fulfilled naturally only through love within a marriage?

To begin to answer this question, it is necessary to re-flect on Griffith's understanding of the natural history of a woman. When a woman grows from an infant and baby and becomes a girl, she simultaneously starts to play with dolls and begins to develop (at first unaware) the ability to attract men. When she comes of age and blossoms into a young woman, the change is twofold. Unless tutored in the wily ways of the paint-and-powder brigade (as is, for example, Mae Marsh in *The White Rose*; Lillian Gish, by contrast, is constitutionally un-able to master the simplest wile), she continues to act in public as a girl. But she knows that her girlishness now veils her womanhood, a mystery never to be betrayed.

In defending her "trust"—her virgin womanhood—she is prepared to fight like a man. Only within the privacy

and sanctuary of a marriage may she reveal herself as a woman. Her mystery now revealed, what follows natu-rally is that she becomes transformed into a mother. Her womanhood fulfilled, her trust now passes from her own body to the walls of her home, which enclose and protect her baby, as her womb once did. Evil threatens, no longer rape, but its equivalent, violence to her baby. Now she will fight like a man to protect her home.

The paint-and-powder brigade is made up of women who display their womanhood in public, although what they reveal is not womanhood in all its mystery and beauty but only a monstrous caricature: When a woman betrays her trust, she loses her true beauty. It follows logically that womanliness in Griffith's films—unlike girlishness, manliness, or motherhood—is ordinarily invisible, or at least out of bounds for the camera. How can womanliness be filmed, without violating its sanc-tity? But then what makes Griffith's presentation of Judith possible?

As a childless widow, Judith is no longer a girl, and she is no virgin: She has been initiated into the life of marriage, has revealed her womanhood and given her trust. (If a Griffith virgin were granted Judith's vision, she would not understand it.) Yet she remains childless, denied that natural fulfillment of a woman.

Is Holofernes the man who can fulfill Judith? Griffith takes great pains to present Holofernes as a majestic figure. In general, Griffith's visual treatment of men, the ways in which his camera differentiates among, for example, Henry Walthall, Robert Harron, Richard Barthelmess, Lionel Barrymore, Donald Crisp, Joseph Schildkraut, Ivor Novello, and Walter Huston, is as cru-cial to his filmmaking as his treatment of women. It was no mean feat to transform slight Henry Walthall into such an imposing figure. This is attested to by Karl Brown. At his first meeting with Billy Bitzer, the cin-ematographer of *Judith of Bethulia,* Bitzer at first scoffed when Brown offered himself as an assistant. As Bitzer and Griffith were about to depart, Brown pleaded: "Please, Mr. Bitzer! I know I'm not wanted, but before you go, will you *please* tell me how you managed to make Hank Walthall look so big in *Judith of Bethulia*?' He stopped and stared at me. I continued recklessly. . . . If you'll please tell me, I won't ever bother you any more, honest I won't.' His face softened into kindness. 'Sure, be glad to. But it'll take a little time. Report for work at nine tomorrow and I'll show you what you have to do."

Holofernes' bull-like majesty and the power of his armies—crystallized in the image of the giant battering ram—arouse Judith. If Holofernes is fully a man—one who can take the place of her dead husband—then he can fulfill Judith in the natural way, and she need not carry out her plan. But, of course, Holofernes does not pass this test. If he were fully a man, he would have succeeded in penetrating the gate of Bethulia.

When Judith succeeds in enticing Holofernes to drink himself into a stupor, she knows that he cannot satisfy her. (For Griffith, any man who drinks to intoxication always thereby exposes a weakness of character that is also a sexual weakness.) Her realization of her power over him shatters the illusion of Holofernes' manhood and frees Judith from her temptation.

For a moment, she cradles his sleeping head in her arms, as if her womanly nature tempts her to view him as the child she so passionately desires, or to imagine bearing his child. This temptation cannot be defeated by any display of power over him, but only by another God-given vision: a vision of the death and suffering that Holofernes has wrought on Bethulia.

Once Holofernes' monstrousness is exposed, Judith's womanhood no longer protects him from her. She becomes transformed. Wielding the sword like a man, she slays the monster and cuts off his head, symbolically castrating him. (Like Judith's first vision, this unnatural act is not—cannot be—framed by Griffith's camera.) When she displays the severed head in the marketplace, she acts as Bethulia's triumphant leader, revealing—to her people and to us—that she has assumed her dead husband's place. This revelation is the climax of the film.

By surrendering herself to her visions, Judith assumes a woman's role, as Griffith understands it, in relation to the power that grants her vision. The moment at which she unmasks Holofernes, the moment at which she gives herself completely to this higher power, is the moment of her fulfillment as a woman. Yet, paradoxically, this is also the moment at which she performs a man's act, is transformed into a man. This paradox is fundamental to Griffith's understanding of what it is to be a woman. When her trust is threatened, a true woman reveals that she possesses a man within her.

The man within Judith is Manasses. But although their marriage proves still to be alive, does it remain issueless? Is she left unfulfilled as a woman after all? The film's answer is that Judith's act gives life to the city itself. Judith has become the mother of Bethulia.

Reborn, the city is transformed. Bethulia's soldiers have at last become men: They storm out of the city's gate to rout the disordered Assyrian forces. Naomi and Nathan are reunited, their fruitfulness assured.

This rebirth in turn transforms Judith. Her transformation is reflected in the final shot of the film. In the marketplace, within Bethulia's walls, she passes into, through, and out of the frame. No one looks directly at her. Everyone bows before her. She no longer lives in the city, whose inhabitants are now all as her children. She dwells in a higher realm. She is no longer even the camera's subject.

This final shot invokes the characteristic closing of a Griffith film: a family united within its home—except, of course, that at the end of *Judith of Bethulia* the mother and father are both absent from the frame. This final shot also completes the series of equations between Judith's sexuality and the city of Bethulia. Bethulia is no longer a woman threatened by violation, and no longer a man; it is finally a home (whose walls are the symbolic equivalent of its mother's fulfilled sexuality).

Thus, the film's dramatic struggle is articulated in terms that are, after all, consistent with the laws of Griffith's narrative universe, and the character of Judith can be accounted for in Griffithian terms. Nonetheless, the film's drama, particularly in its resolution, remains extraordinary in Griffith's work. This is reflected in the fact that Judith's act, though inspired by holy visions, is in no sense Christian.

The general point that the film's resolution is not Christian—is, indeed, specifically pre-Christian—is crucial to understanding the place of this film in Griffith's work. *Judith of Bethulia* is Griffith's major Old Testament film.

The grounding of *Judith of Bethulia* in Old Testament tradition and morality is everywhere manifest. The central strategy of identifying a woman's sexuality with a city, for one thing, is familiar from the Old Testament. But also, the outcome of Judith's struggle is not that she softens and forgives Holofernes, redeeming the tyrant through love; her act of retribution for her people's suffering equals Holofernes' acts in its harsh cruelty. The film's eye-for-eye spirit may be seen, at one level, to determine the system of doubling—with symbolic equivalences and reversals—so characteristic of the film. The Assyrians cut off Bethulia from its water supply, and their tents are razed by flames. Holofernes attempts to penetrate Bethulia's gate with his battering ram, and Judith slays him with the sword. Judith's retainer doubles Holofernes' eunuch. And so on. This system of doubling in turn is linked to the doubling of the Judith/Holofernes and the Judith/Manasses pairs, and by the doubling of both by the Naomi/Nathan pair, by the doubling of the city and its captured well, and, most important, by the doubling of Judith and Bethulia.

Judith's consciousness serves as a field of battle for higher forces; up to a point, this reflects the general Griffith dramaturgy, laid out most explicitly in *Dream Street* (1921). Under the all-seeing Morning Star, the symbolic drama of *Dream Street* unfolds, motivated by the figures of the demonic violinist (whose mask of sensual beauty hides a face only an orthodontist could love) and a beatific preacher. The former's mad fiddling has the power to whip mortals into a Dionysian frenzy, whereas the latter's calm voice speaks in Apollonian strains.

The pre-Christian world of *Judith of Bethulia*, however, has no Morning Star to oversee it. This world is ruled by the Hebrew deity, who calls upon Judith to perform an act of violence, not an act of forgiveness; to harden, not soften.

Judith's motherhood is unnatural, for Griffith, in the sense that it is not Christian. It is perhaps only in *Abraham Lincoln* (1930) that Griffith presents a heroic act true to both Old Testament and New Testament morality: The modern-day Abraham gives birth to a nation, not through a liberating, triumphant, but unnatural sexual fulfillment, but through a Christian act of sacrifice.

The presentation of an un-Christian act as heroic is unusual in Griffith's work, but it does not in itself undermine the Christian identity of Griffith's camera. In telling this story of a pre-Christian world, Griffith's camera is freed from certain constraints, because the characters are not Christians, but other constraints remain. Thus, Griffith can film Judith in all her womanliness without betraying his principles, but he cannot show us her vision of the act that will "ring through the generations," or the unnatural act itself.

Of course, by refraining from showing us that vision or that act, Griffith at the same time strongly serves the interests of his narrative, investing the film with a central enigma (What is Judith planning to do?) and suspending its solution (What has Judith done?), intensifying the film's climax.

Thus, although Griffith does not violate his Christian morality in the depiction of Judith's struggle and the resolution of that struggle, that morality does not by itself account for the film, for the nature of Griffith's implication in this pre-Christian world (and the implication of his camera) remains to be determined. But that determination cannot be achieved apart from a critical account of the relationship, in Griffith's work, between his Christian moralizing and his violent eroticism. The latter emerges in a uniquely pure form in *Judith of Bethulia,* in part because it is his major film that asserts no Christian moral. But Griffith could never, in any case, negate his violent eroticism simply by asserting a moral. The tense and complex relationship between these conflicting strains dominates Griffith's work. It manifests itself in various guises: as an opposition between the theatrical and the poetic/transcendental; between the realistic and the dreamlike; between the representation and the symbolization of events; between the extreme linearity of the parallel-edited suspense sequences and a film's organic composition as a whole. It is this tension, above all, that engenders the specific density and texture of Griffith's films and accounts for their form.

Michael Rogin (essay date 1989)

SOURCE: "The Great Mother Domesticated: Sexual Difference and Sexual Indifference in D. W. Griffith's *Intolerance,*" in *Critical Inquiry,* Vol. 15, No. 3, Spring, 1989, pp. 511-54.

[*In the following essay, Rogin analyzes the sexual undercurrents of* Intolerance.]

A giant statue of the mother goddess, Ishtar, presides over *Intolerance* (1916), the movie D. W. Griffith made after his triumph with *The Birth of a Nation* (1915). Ishtar sits above Babylon's royal, interior court, but the court itself is constructed on so gigantic a scale that it diminishes the size of the goddess. Perhaps to establish Ishtar's larger-than-life proportions, Griffith posed himself alongside her in a production still from the movie. The director is the same size as the sculpted grown man who sucks at Ishtar's breast; both males are dwarfed by the goddess' dimensions.

Ishtar connects Griffith to the concern with originary female power current at the turn of the twentieth century. The appearance of the New Woman and the attention to the matriarchal origins of culture were signs of a crisis in patriarchy. But the great mother could support masculine reassertion as well as female power. Ishtar will help us see how.

Ishtar, the naked great mother, displays an unambiguous sexuality. Griffith complicated her sex by posing himself between her legs. Far too small to be the goddess' lover, perhaps he intended to look like her baby—the baby of the mother he'd created. But both Griffith's position in charge of the movie and his position in front of the camera suggest another possibility. Was Griffith supplying the great mother with her missing phallus? Was the director, like Freud at about the same time, linking the absent maternal phallus and the baby?

These questions may seem to have less to do with Griffith than with current critical fashion, and to deflect attention from the director's purposes and from his movie. Griffith, however, had organized his two most important previous films around the real and symbolic male organ. The castration of a black rapist climaxes the original version of *The Birth of a Nation*. And a phallic mother dominates Griffith's first, feature-length movie, *Judith of Bethulia* (1913). The censorship controversy surrounding *Birth,* moreover, the controversy that produced *Intolerance,* posed Griffith (as he saw it) against emasculating female reformers. Attention to Griffith's film history will serve here to introduce *Intolerance* and clarify Ishtar's function in that movie. The subject of the phallic mother in *Intolerance,* far from being foreign to the founder of American film, emerges from Griffith's own preoccupations.

1

Intolerance aside, Griffith made only one feature organized around a dominating female presence. In *Judith of Bethulia* he placed a sword in the widow's hand. The central scene of that movie, organized for a sexual climax between Judith and Holofernes, climaxes when she cuts off his head.

"To decapitate = to castrate," wrote Freud, and *Judith,* I have argued elsewhere, illustrates Freud's links between decapitation, castration, and fetishization. By cutting back and forth between Judith's body parts and the sword in the moments before the beheading, Griffith fetishized Judith's body. He substituted eroticized part-objects for the whole. The fetish, according to Freud, reassured the male viewer that the woman had not lost her penis and that he, therefore, was not in danger of losing his. The fetish was a comforting substitute, wrote Freud, "not . . . for any chance penis, but for a particular quite special penis that had been extremely important in early childhood but was afterwards lost. . . . To put it plainly: the fetish is a substitute for the woman's (mother's) phallus which the little boy once believed in and does not wish to forego—we know why."

The fetish defended against castration anxiety, according to Freud; decapitation evoked it. Freud himself used the Judith story to link decapitation to castration, and Griffith's camera made the same connection. Griffith cut from Judith's raised sword to Holofernes' head bouncing down a step to the king's headless body. The lone limp arm (one arm and not two) suggests at once the single phallic member and its absence. Holofernes is the headless body, Judith the woman with the penis.

Film techniques—close-ups and cross-cutting—are peculiarly suited to display fetishization, since these techniques juxtapose part-objects. Film also depends on another mechanism central to Freud: scopophilia, the pleasure in looking. If fetishization denies sexual difference, however, according to writers in the Freudian tradition, voyeurism establishes it. The male viewer observes what the woman lacks; seeking woman as the bearer of the bleeding wound, his gaze subjugates female desire. Holofernes, watching Judith and the other dancing girls, is the spectator's surrogate inside the film. But Holofernes is disempowered, not empowered, by his male gaze. As *Judith* illustrates the Freudian connections, it fails to reassure the male viewer. Judith relinquishes her sexual desire in order to dismember the man. Whether one sees the movie as denying sexual difference (through the fetish) or establishing it (through the gaze), Judith (contra Freud on the fetish) acquires the phallus from the king.

Judith also subverts Freud's account of female penis envy. The boy fears losing his penis, according to Freud, and the girl wants to acquire one. The boy must give up his mother to keep his penis; the girl must give up her wish for a penis and become a mother. Accepting the "fact" of her castration, the mature woman relinquishes her desire to take the man's penis; she wants it instead to give her a child. "The feminine situation is only established," wrote Freud, "if . . . a baby takes the place of a penis." That female acceptance of sexual difference inscribes heterosexuality and reproduces motherhood.

The exchange of phallus for baby occurs in *Judith,* but it occurs in reverse, accentuating anxiety instead of dis-

pelling it. Lillian Gish plays the domestic mother in *Judith,* as she would in *Intolerance*. Judith admires Gish's baby early in the film. The contrast between the two women points to a future foreclosed for the childless widow, and Judith replaces the baby with the sword. In addition to reversing Freud's normative, developmental direction, this substitution also supplies Judith with a baby of her own. That baby, issued forth from the hole in his torso, is Holofernes' head. A shawl covered Gish's baby so that only its head was visible. Judith wraps Holofernes' head in a shawl, places it in a basket, and carries it away. Like Freud's mature woman, Judith has given up her phallus for a baby. But she has first used Holofernes' sword to turn his phallus into her child.

Links that established sexual difference for Freud are threats to male identity in *Judith*. Why do the founder of psychoanalysis and the founder of film share a symbolism of dismemberment and sexual difference and yet place the opposite valence on it? Why does Griffith ally himself with the black widow? Elsewhere I have located Griffith in the patriarchal crisis of the turn of the twentieth century. Judith, I argued, did not simply confirm male fears about female power; she turned them to rebellious advantage. Creating a modern art form against the conventions of the stage, Griffith made Judith his instrument for parricide. But the alliance of women and youth that was intended to liberate the sons threatened to empower the woman instead.

The New Woman—as figure of power or sexual desire—was taking over Griffith's screen in the films before *Birth*. *The Birth of a Nation,* I have argued, displaced female danger onto black men. The New Woman (from the book on which *Birth* was based and from Griffith's earlier films) is refeminized and made helpless. *Birth* took the sword from Judith and placed it in the hands of the Klan. Judith's sword saved the Jewish nation. The ritualized castration of a black rapist gave birth to America. Judith decapitated a patriarch. *Birth* returned the sword to the father's ghost, the white-sheeted shade who rode with the Klan.

The Birth of a Nation established Griffith, in the words of *Photoplay* magazine, as "the founder of [the] modern motion picture." Amidst anxieties about the power of movies to dissolve ethnic, class, and sexual boundaries, *Birth* created a respectable, mass audience for film. Transcending both the immigrant origins of the early one-reelers and the psychological disintegration threatening Griffith's films, *Birth* brought together in the motion picture palace northerners and southerners, immigrants and natives, cosmopolitans and provincials, workers and bosses, shopgirls, and professional men and leisure-class women in a spectacle of national integration. *The Birth of a Nation,* Griffith claimed—in its unprecedented critical and mass audience appeal, in its unifying social content, and in its cinematic power to stand in for history—gave birth to the modern United States.

But *The Birth of a Nation* also created a split in the forces of reform. Although most cultural guardians endorsed the movie, liberal humanitarians joined the NAACP in a campaign to stop the film from being shown. The conflict over *Birth* was not the only free speech fight being waged in the spring of 1915. "Films and Births and Censorship" ran a headline in the April issue of *Survey* magazine. The same people who believed *Birth* was not "objectionable from the standpoint of public morals'" supported the federal government's ban on Margaret Sanger's paper, *Woman Rebel,* and her indictment for sending obscene matter through the mail. The same vice crusaders who encouraged audiences to see *Birth* jailed Sanger's husband for disseminating information on birth control. *The Birth of a Nation,* concluded the National Board of (Film) Review, was historically accurate and educationally valuable. William Sanger, ruled the judge at his trial, was a "'menace to society.'" As *Birth* swept the country in 1915 and 1916, advocates of birth control went to jail.

Female reformers like Jane Addams who wanted *Birth* banned from the screen opposed censoring birth control information. *Survey* noticed this paradox without resolving it. But beneath the fights over free speech, in which players switched sides, lay a deeper consistency. Although Griffith published a pamphlet, *The Rise and Fall of Free Speech in America,* to attack the censorship of his movie, freedom of speech animated none of the adversaries in the battles over birth control and *Birth*. The two controversies turned, rather, on the control of female sexuality.

Those opposing both birth control and control of *Birth* wanted white men in charge of sex and procreation. *Birth of a Nation* warned against interracial sexuality, the alliance of white women and black men. Birth control, its opponents feared, substituted female pleasure for babies. And those who favored marriage for sexual gratification were compared "'with the Negroes.'" Birth control placed white women in charge of their own sexuality; it stood against the reproductive family and the paternal inheritance.

Birth raised the twin specters of the rapist and the mulatto to warn against interracial mixture. The eroticism generated by birth control, its opponents charged, would produce not mulatto babies but no babies at all. The mulatto and family limitation may thus seem like opposed dangers, the one implying proliferation and the other sterility, but they were united in racialist consciousness by the alleged infertility of the hybrid. They were united in the racial unconscious because both miscegenation and birth control broke the law that tied progeny to the legitimate father. Whether white women produced black children, no children, or children only when they chose, they deprived the white man of his paternity.

Woman, according to Freud, needed to shift her desire from phallus to baby to accept her femininity. The controversies over birth control and *Birth,* by contrast, uncover the father's stake in sexual difference. Both supporters of birth control and critics of *Birth,* in their opponents' view, wanted to sever the connection between the paternal phallus and the baby. *Birth* and birth control, for those supporting the former and opposing the latter, offered alternative forms of castration. *Birth*'s castration restored power to white men. Birth control left the penis intact, but it performed a symbolic castration. Birth control advocates might defend their right to speak, but their speech, it was feared, destroyed the ground of the symbolic order itself in the words, laws, and conventions that sustained the name of the father.

That very alliance of blacks and women imagined by opponents of birth control wanted to suppress *Birth*. In his cartoons for free speech, Griffith depicted the censor and female reformer as allies, who expropriate his control over castration and birth. The censor's scissors cut film in one cartoon and attack a baby in another. Censors (who had already excised *Birth*'s castration scene) threatened to take from the director his power to cut film. The threatened baby stood at once for the movie, *Birth,* for the "infant motion picture industry," and for the nation to which Griffith's movie had given birth.

Opponents of birth control shared Griffith's concern to save babies. They feared birth control would lead to a declining birth rate among Anglo-Saxons and to "race suicide." Germany had won "the warfare of the cradle" in the nineteenth century, complained Theodore Roosevelt; if Anglo-Saxon women did not produce more children, America would be swamped by the proliferating immigrants and blacks. Castration, suggested the uncensored *Birth of a Nation,* was the alternative to race suicide. Whether they used birth control or the scissors of censorship, women must be prevented from either stopping or choosing the male seed. Censorship, like birth control, delivered over to women and blacks the power to make history and make life.

2

The sexual politics of the two birth control controversies produced *Intolerance*. "Intolerance" appeared atop every page of Griffith's pamphlet defending free speech. Griffith was advertising his new film, whose enormous cost and length, and four parallel stories, made it the most grandiose project in the early decades of cinema. The proclaimed subject of *Intolerance* was intolerance in world history, from ancient Babylon through the life of Christ and the Huguenot massacre to the modern metropolis. The actual subject of the movie was female sexuality. The theme of *Intolerance,* like the theme of the film about the Klan, was birth. As opponents of birth control were insisting on the political importance of producing children, Griffith shifted from political regeneration to sexual reproduction. That shift in subject also entailed a shift in point of view, and both emerged from the controversies that generated the new movie. *Birth* wiped out female sexuality; its heroine, Lillian Gish, was an innocent, sexually menaced virgin. *Intolerance* celebrated the goddess of fertility and tied reproduction to heterosexual pleasure.

The Rise and Fall of Free Speech in America, Griffith's anticensorship pamphlet, made blacks into the sources rather than the victims of intolerance. "The malignant pygmy [of intolerance] has matured into a caliban," in Griffith's rhetoric, and behind the mask of virtue in one cartoon lurks the dark shadow of the censor. *Intolerance* in no way retracted the racial politics of *Birth*. In the scenes of universal brotherhood that close both movies, no black faces appear. But *Intolerance* does depart, in a return of the repressed, from *Birth*'s aversion of female sexuality. Prince Belshazzar, an "apostle of tolerance and religious freedom," is introducing goddess worship into Babylon. He worships at "Ishtar's temple of love and laughter." Intolerance is the hatred of heterosexual pleasure. *Intolerance* supports female desire.

In celebrating fertility, *Intolerance* stood with the opponents of birth control. Its sexual displays, however, not only reversed the direction of Griffith's previous movies but antagonized opponents of birth control as well. *Intolerance* undercut the oppositions in the birth control controversies in part, as we will shortly see, because Griffith was responding to the changing relationship of family life to urban public pleasures. He was also responding to the terms of *Birth*'s censorship struggle.

Radical supporters of birth control, like Margaret Sanger and Emma Goldman, placed birth control in the service of free love. No one attacked *Birth of a Nation,* however, by defending interracial sex, for the power of racial sexual taboos made such a position unthinkable. The white women and black men who favored censoring *Birth* did not demand the right to sleep together; they rather opposed those who discredited demands for racial equality by sexualizing them. Sanger led the fight for birth control in 1915, Addams the opposition to *Birth*. But women who opposed sexualizing racial issues were vulnerable to being labelled puritanical. The taboo on interracial sex, which Griffith exploited in *Birth,* now permitted him to depict female reformers as hostile not to racist hysteria but to sexual pleasure. He could present himself as repressing black sexual aggression, not female sexuality. Blacks, the promoters of intolerance in the free speech pamphlet, disappear from *Intolerance,* the movie. Their place is taken by sexually repressive American women, the NAACP's allies in its fight to censor *Birth*.

The Rise and Fall of Free Speech in America depicted censors as witch-burners, the filmmaker as their victim. The persecuted witches in *Intolerance* are women of the street in the modern story and supporters of the goddess cult in the ancient story. Juxtaposed against the female reformer—demanding control over sex in one of the battles behind *Intolerance* and over movies in the other—is the ancient goddess cult of love and fertility. And the effects of that cult subliminally reach into the modern city as well. By making female reformers rather than blacks its target, *Intolerance* opened up a space for urban, public, female-based pleasures. Attacking one negative stereotype of the feminist, the spinster, the movie sympathized with another, the libertine. Female sexual desire normally disturbed Griffith. Yet his deeper fear of female indifference to men, which, as we will see, *Intolerance* locates in lesbian alliances, opened up room for female heterosexuality. Faced with the withdrawal of women's interest in men, Griffith celebrated not simply women who satisfied male desire but women who needed men to satisfy themselves. The campaign against *Birth* had given Griffith back, and for the last time, the sympathy for modern urban women and workers that lay at the basis of his art.

3

Although Ishtar rules Babylon, she appears in only one of the four stories that constitute *Intolerance*. Lillian Gish is supposed to preside over the movie as a whole. Echoing her brief appearance as mother in *Judith,* Gish rocks a cradle in *Intolerance*'s opening scene. "Out of the cradle endlessly rocking" reads the line from Whitman. Repeated to mark transitions between *Intolerance's* four stories, the shot privileges motherhood as the source both of babies and of the movie. But the cradle actually serves to take Gish out of the body of the film. By marginalizing the domestic mother in the name of sanctifying her, Griffith made room for the love goddess and the spinster/lesbian.

These three female archetypes—Demeter, the great mother, Aphrodite, the love goddess, and Artemis, the celibate huntress and killer of men—appear in the concern with originary female power at the turn of the twentieth century. The first two are identified in J. J. Bachofen's *Mother Right*. Bachofen contrasted "the Aphroditean principle of carnal emancipation" to "the chaste, Demetrian character of a life grounded in strict order and morality." Artemis, so D. H. Lawrence believed, signalled the return of the woman under conditions of patriarchal repression. Griffith probably never heard of Bachofen or Lawrence, and *Intolerance*'s world history does not line up in every detail with theirs. But the similarities point to a shared male obsession with the feminine, a fascination that feared and celebrated women and wanted to make their powers available to men. The Aphroditean Ishtar, the Demetrian Gish, and Miss Jenkins the female reformer structure *Intolerance* and embed it in a larger cultural history.

Ishtar is a fertility goddess, and she presides over marriage and reproduction. Love ends in marriage in Griffith's Babylon both in the shots of the marriage market and in the story of Belshazzar's wedding. Ishtar brings forth children, as the opponents of birth control wanted, and she is surely a mother on a pedestal. But

223

she subverts Roosevelt's grounding of motherhood in male respect for "'anything good and helpless.'"

The goddess' size is not disjunctive with other representations of motherhood in turn-of-the-century America. Giant statues of women, most prominently the Statue of Liberty, are a feature of the period. Woman symbolizes the republic in the central building of the 1893 Chicago exposition. She holds aloft an upraised globe surmounted by an eagle and a staff with a liberty cap. Woman blesses the metropolis both in Chicago's White City and in Babylon. A ninety-foot suffragette graced the 1915 San Francisco World's Fair, and women with cornucopias symbolized female nurture throughout the country. Comparable maternal images would soon be produced to support American soldiers in World War I. A magazine advertisement for the Red Cross, for example, pictures a pietà demonstrating concern for suffering soldiers by "The Greatest Mother in the World," and in an advertisement for the Y.M.C.A. the "great . . . mother love" of a *madonna della misericordia* enfolds her fighting sons.

But these Christian icons, like the classical statues, contrast with the oriental Ishtar. Like Gish at the cradle, the classical and Christian representations desexualize motherhood. Ishtar resexualizes it. Ishtar was "'the mother of mankind . . . who awakens passion,'" "'the fruitful goddess of the earth'" and "'the patronness of love'" in the Bachofen-influenced sources on which Griffith drew for his portrait of Babylon. Ishtar blesses marriage, to be sure, whereas Bachofen's Aphrodite presides over a promiscuous sexuality. But bacchanals and the marriage market insist on the sexual origins of motherhood. Ishtar also shatters the opposition between sex and female virginity. "Vestal virgins of love," nearly naked dancing girls, serve the goddess. Each virgin enters the temple of sacred fire (Gish reported in her autobiography) and gives herself to a man who comes to worship there. Griffith shows viewers the sex of his vestal virgins, the source of their future motherhood. He moves his camera up the legs of one seated young woman, for example, to expose the blank, black space between her legs—the space Griffith will himself fill in his production still.

Babylon appeals to the prurient interest. By showing the fall of the city, Griffith may seem to disown responsibility for its revelry. According to that view Griffith, counterposing the destruction of Babylon to the rescue of the endangered modern couple, stands with the family and against the city. The director's other feature-length films would support such an interpretation. But the cultural context for *Intolerance* and the images that dominate the film demand almost exactly the opposite reading.

Urban dangers threatened the family, in the Victorian view, and the home was a refuge from metropolitan life. Urban progressives, by contrast, promoted public activities to transform and strengthen private, conjugal existence. In creating Babylon, Griffith was responding to efforts to break down the opposition between the family and the modern metropolis. He intended a narrative not of binary opposition between the ancient and modern stories, the city and the home, but of incorporation and progress. But Griffith's images undercut the synthesis to which his narrative aspired. Unlike his progressive contemporaries, Griffith could not sublimate the city into the family. The city generated an excess of pleasure, weakening defenses and stimulating repression; pleasure gave way to impersonal, institutional control. Gish stands for the modern family, but Ishtar and the spinster/lesbian take over her movie. Ishtar is the archaic, whole mother. Instead of providing the ground for modern maternity, however, she is simply defeated. Her fall drains woman of heterosexuality and splits her in two. The domestic mother and the reformer supplant Ishtar. Although they battle one another they are also deeply allied, for both signify censorship not simply of male sexuality but of female desire for men as well. The good woman will take over Griffith's cinema in the decade after *Intolerance* and ultimately deprive him of his power to make films. *Intolerance,* Griffith's last stand for the modern metropolis and the New Woman, shows the sources and the limits of his modernism. We turn first to the progressive context for *Intolerance,* then to the interwoven four narratives, and look finally at the images themselves.

4

The modern metropolis and the domestic mother were born together, as opposite sides of the same coin. The confined privacy of the home, in Laura Mulvey's formulation, protected against the chaotic crowd in the street. Severing reproduction from female sexual pleasure, as Thomas Laqueur has shown, Victorians separated biological and cultural maternity within the house from barren sexual excitement outside. But the urban world of entertainment and leisure posed threats to the middle-class family from below and from above. The lower-class city-by-night and the leisure-class, male homosocial tavern both threatened the ties that bound together the middle-class husband and wife.

Popular entertainments such as the pre-Griffith one-reelers, originating on the margins of society, threatened the sanctuary of the home. But domestic melodrama domesticated the city-by-night, first in English theater and then in Griffith's one-reelers, by making the subject of popular entertainment into the danger to the home. Although the metropolis in domestic melodrama justified the family by threatening it, melodrama thereby maintained the family/city opposition. The places of popular, working-class entertainment, moreover, proved dangerously seductive to the middle class. The family triumphed in melodrama, but the city retained its subversive potential.

The middle-class family was under siege from upper-class forms of entertainment as well. Leisure-class culture separated the sexes, leaving women in charge of society and men seeking pleasure outside the home. Respectable men consorted with prostitutes; eating and drinking in taverns, they abandoned their children and wives.

Babylonian prostitution and orgies of food and drink associate the ancient city with modern, leisure-class decadence. *Intolerance*'s modern story, in which the urban underworld threatens the family, had roots in domestic melodrama. But the movie was also part of the post-Victorian effort to bring the family and urban nightlife together. Babylon signified sensual excess and tyranny in the nineteenth-century imagination; it was the city as evil. The 1880s London campaign against child prostitution, for example, labelled the British capital the "modern Babylon." Vice crusaders were invoking "Babylon, the Great, the Mother of Harlots and of the Abominations of the Earth" from the Book of Revelation. The Jews were enslaved in Babylon, but though *Judith of Bethulia* took the side of the Jews against the invading Assyrians, *Intolerance* omits the Babylonian captivity. Griffith's invading Cyrus may "war on vice" like the purity crusaders, but he liberates no Jews, for *Intolerance* stands against the war on vice and with Babylonian pleasure. Griffith presented urban public entertainment not as a threat to conjugal happiness but as an alternative to the restrictive Victorian family.

As progressives saw it, the repressive family generated its opposite, the disruptive city-by-night. Progressives in the new helping professions would mediate between the family and the city. They would organize leisure and drain it of its disruptive potential by sponsoring such institutions as urban parks and planned recreation, the school, the settlement house, the reform state, and the motion picture palace itself. *Intolerance* evoked one of these new institutions in particular: the urban cabaret. Ishtar, the ancient goddess of pleasure, blesses modern cabaret culture.

Cabaret culture strengthened the family by bringing the sexes back together in arenas that offered a good time. The cabaret promised to end the opposition between children and the family on the one hand, and sexual gratification on the other, the opposition enshrined in the birth-control struggle. Lewis Erenberg writes,

> By permitting informal entertainments for respectable women, the cabaret marked a new departure in relations between the sexes and challenged the Victorian confinements that had limited the behavior of both men and women. In an open environment, good women could mix promiscuously with people of unspecified moral character from whom they formerly had been rigidly separated. By opening up an urban, public area, the café opened up respectable culture to a wider, more spontaneous world. [*Steppin Out: New York Nightlife and the Transformation of American Culture*].

The public dance craze of 1915-16, contemporaneous with the filming and release of *Intolerance,* insured the success of the cabaret. Dancing made cabarets profitable, transforming urban nightlife from all-male feats of drinking and eating to heterosexual performance. Public dancing offered a mixture of immediacy and distancing. Audiences observed a show whose dancing stars became celebrities; at the same time, members of the audience also danced, breaking down the audience/performer distinction. A comparable mixture of immediacy and observation characterized the progressive style in journalism, as genteel readers were made to feel present at behind-the-scenes revelations of real life. Movies also drew members of the mass audience into an immediate experience where they participated as observers. With its scenes of dancing and urban entertainment, *Intolerance* mirrored the audience participation in cabarets.

Babylon may have been exotic in progressive America, but new styles of dress brought the foreign into restaurant, cabaret, and boudoir. "Back to Babylon for New Fashions" headlined *Photoplay* in April 1917. "When *Intolerance* brought us Babylonian modes, straightway the designers took notice," announced the magazine. Fashion designers were making "the filmed ladies of Belshazzar's court" into "the real inspiration of the day." *Intolerance* fed a trend that it did not originate. Already in 1914 the New York Follies Marigny had announced an Arabian Night in its series of special balls. "When I turn into Broadway by night and am bathed in its Babylonic radiance," wrote an anonymous contributor to *Atlantic,* "I want to shout with joy, it is so gay and beautiful"

Two displacements made possible this celebration of urban pleasure: the extrusion of class conflict and the excision of the Negro origins of the cabaret. *Intolerance* registers them both, the first by what the screen displays and the second by what it hides. Working-class struggles disrupted urban America at the turn of the twentieth century. The metropolis threatened the middle-class family not only in pleasure-by-night but also in work-by-day. Class conflict at the point of production placed the middle class under siege, threatening the boundaries that insulated the home from the struggle for existence. (The 1894 Pullman strike, for example, kept Jane Addams' ailing sister from being reached by her husband and children before she died.) Like urban nightlife, class conflict corrupted the work ethic and invaded the family.

The cabaret shifted value not only from the restrictive, moralistic family to scenes of public entertainment but also from the conflicted realm of work to what *Billboard* magazine called the leisure-time "eager pursuit of pleasure." *Intolerance* domesticated leisure; and it removed class conflict from the open metropolitan present to the confined rural past.

A strike sets in motion *Intolerance*'s modern story. Although a title places us in a midwestern city, we are shown a pastoral scene. From a traditional perspective it was radical to allow class conflict into the American countryside. Such Griffith one-reelers as *The New York Hat* and *The Painted Lady,* however, had already depicted a repressive, rural familial environment; the city (as in "The Musketeer of the Slums") was a liberating alternative. The strike in *Intolerance* perpetuates that opposition. The patriarchal factory owner, Jenkins, lines up with familial forces of repression. Although "the boy" (Bobby Harron) loses his father in the strike, that tragedy frees him to go to Chicago.

The most important industrial conflicts of the late nineteenth century, the Haymarket riot and the Pullman strike, took place in Chicago. Griffith, however, derived his industrial violence from the Ludlow massacre—the 1915 Colorado mining strike in which company militia killed strikers and their families—and not from an urban labor dispute. John D. Rockefeller, who controlled the Colorado Fuel and Iron Company, was the model for Jenkins. Ludlow was contemporary with *Intolerance*; the struggle and its investigation by the U.S. Commission on Industrial Relations dominated newspaper headlines in the months prior to the first filming of the modern story. But by placing his strike in the rural past (the past symbolically, since the countryside stood for an older America, and the past in the movie's chronology), Griffith freed Chicago to stand for a progressive future.

The war between capital and labor threatened middle-class America. But Griffith's workers are bowed down even before their strike and the director sustained sympathy for the working class by depicting its defeat. He would apply that technique of threat containment, successful at the beginning of the film, to Babylonian sexuality. But Griffith wanted to shift from work to pleasure, to sublimate female sexuality and not simply displace it. As the conjunction of sympathy with defeat slid from working-class victims to the fall of Babylon, it would ultimately undo Griffith's project.

The strike, removed to the countryside, is shown, but the urban blacks who originated cabaret culture entirely disappear from the film. These black entertainers replaced the minstrel show, where whites in blackface had created the first form of American mass culture. The original cabarets retrieved the role of performer from whites playing blacks. Minstrels, moreover, had mocked many targets through the mask that mocked blacks, but even in a comic mode black sexuality was off limits. The urban New Negro in the first cabarets was a sexually explicit entertainer. *Birth of a Nation,* to be sure, had made its whites in blackface libidinal, but only to invent a black sexual menace. *Birth* climaxed and displaced minstrelsy by turning its blackface performers into New Negroes. The movie located the New Negro in the Reconstruction South, where he did not exist, demonized him as a rapist, and punished him. *Intolerance* eliminated New Negroes entirely from the culture they had brought into being.

This excision followed the lead of the cabarets themselves. "Coon songs" featuring sexually active blacks peaked in the 1910s; by 1915 white performers like Sophie Tucker were replacing the blacks who had influenced them. At the same time that whites took over the forms of cabaret entertainment developed by blacks, Griffith eliminated blacks from the modern city. He moved them to his ancient story instead, where "Ethiopians" briefly appear as members of Cyrus' invading army. The blacks play rural primitives, threatening the cosmopolitan culture that was actually being expropriated from them.

Urban nightlife links *Intolerance*'s modern and ancient stories, the two episodes that dominate the film as a whole. Griffith conceived the modern story first and began filming it as a separate movie, "The Mother and the Law." The massive scale and success of *Birth,* however, and the attacks levelled against that film, made "The Mother and the Law" an anticlimax. The director reconceived the modern plot as one of four stories that would cover world history and that his theme and camera technique would unify. The theme of "The Mother and the Law"—the husband faces execution for a crime he did not commit; the wife loses her baby—may seem to have nothing to do with Ishtar. But the metropolis spawns the romance between the young couple, and Ishtar's modern female antagonists generate the family tragedy.

"The dear one" (Mae Marsh) and the boy are both victims of the strike, but they only meet once the workers' defeat drives them into the city. The boy becomes an urban sophisticate under the tutelage of a gangster. The dear one attracts him by imitating the dress and walk of a woman of the streets. From one perspective Jenkins is the bad father, contrasted to the good but helpless fathers in the family. The strike Jenkins provokes kills the boy's father and sends the girl's to die in the city. But the movie also lines up all the fathers on one side of a generational conflict. The fathers stand for restriction, and the new urban family arises from the death of the old.

Prostrated by the first kiss between the boy and the dear one, her father dies soon after. He cannot adjust to the new conditions of urban life, a title announces, but his death offers opportunity as well as danger. The dear one goes out with the boy; when he tries to force his way into her apartment, she bars the door. Her resistance elicits a proposal of marriage, which replaces forced entry with domesticity. The marriage proposal, however, does not eradicate sex. In a shot sequence that deliberately eroticizes the break-in, the dear one opens her door just enough for the boy to place his head in the slit and kiss her.

The dear one and the boy bring street excitement into their room. But their new home will be menaced by the conflict between pleasure-seeking women and the forces of repression, the conflict that dominates both the ancient and modern stories. Griffith juxtaposes Babylon's "vestal virgins of love" to the "vestal virgins of uplift" in modern America. These menacing female reformers, the women who attacked *Birth,* close the public places of pleasure, the saloons and dance halls (and, by implication, the motion picture palace as well). A fine shot of ballroom dancing among the rich, with remarkable depth of field, introduces the modern story. The rich have their pleasures; workers dance in cafes. But working-class pleasure antagonizes the factory owner, Jenkins, and his "unmarried sister." Jenkins is a lonely, dried-up old man; he turns away from the working-class women who flirt with him in the street, retreats behind his desk, and gives his sister the money for reform.

Who are the women who tantalize Jenkins? Single working women in early twentieth-century New York (the city where Griffith made his one-reelers in the years before *Birth* and *Intolerance*) spent their evenings on the streets. They frequented public dance halls and other popular amusements. Seeking adventures with male companions, young women mixed easily with strangers. Their language and behavior broke down the traditional, rural distinction between the loose woman and the good girl. The exchange of sexual favors for gifts, meals, and entertainment was part of this working-class, urban nightlife; but although vice crusaders stigmatized working girls as loose women, and sought to raise the age of sexual consent to control female independence, the women of the streets depicted at the beginning of *Intolerance* are not professional prostitutes.

The law creates prostitutes in *Intolerance* by stamping out public entertainment. The prohibition of public drinking and dancing drives pleasure underground. Instead of going to dances, men pick up prostitutes; instead of frequenting saloons for drinks, each person distills his own. While men look on, women are rounded up and taken off to jail. Prostitution, Griffith's contemporaries believed, originated with the sacred Babylonian fertility rites, and brothels in urban America contributed to the "Modern Babylon." But since Babylonian girls earned their dowries by prostitution, according to Charlotte Perkins Gilman, they were learning to be prostitutes and wives at the same time. Gilman deplored the Babylonian origins of modern marriage; Griffith celebrated it. The vestal virgins of love who display themselves for male pleasure are the ancestors of the modern women of the streets. Griffith in both the ancient and the modern stories places himself on the side of these women. Social purity reformers opposed birth control because, by separating sex from reproduction, it would make all women into prostitutes. *Intolerance,* by contrast, derived the modern family from female sexual availability.

The high priest of Babylon opposes goddess worship. He secretly allies himself with Cyrus and the invading Persians. The bearded Cyrus resembles Holofernes. Like Holofernes and like Jenkins and the Babylonian high priest, Cyrus is a patriarchal villain. Since he is not weakened, as Holofernes is, by sexual ambiguity and desire, he is not in the power of women. And female power is even more menacing than patriarchy. The truly sinister figures in *Intolerance* are Miss Jenkins and her spinster allies. Instead of depicting sympathy for the Ludlow workers by such female reformers as Addams and Florence Harriman, Griffith makes their hard-heartedness cause the strike, as they raise the money to stamp out leisure-time pleasure by convincing Jenkins to cut wages at work.

"When women cease to attract men they often turn to reform," explains a title. The camera contrasts the misshapen "vestal virgins of uplift" to the pleasure-loving women of the streets. The Committee of Seven that orchestrates reform is composed entirely of women. Like the "Female Army" of suffragettes condemned in Walter Heape's *Sex Antagonism* (1913), Griffith's "spinsters" have "usurped" maternal authority. But Griffith opposes his reformers not simply to Victorian mothers but to pleasure-seeking young women as well. He cuts from the virgins of uplift in the modern story to the woman taken in adultery in the movie's third story, the life of Christ. Christ protects the adulteress from those who want to stone her. Cut to the modern prostitutes being taken off to jail. Even in the schematic Christ episode, which contains but five brief scenes, Griffith celebrates domesticity (the marriage at Cana and "suffer the little children") and condemns intolerance of female desire.

Catherine de Medici orchestrates the Huguenot massacre in *Intolerance*'s fourth story, where the theme of religious intolerance also dissolves into sexual discontent. Although the Huguenot massacre supposedly has religious sources, religion is not visible on the screen. Catherine's hostility to romance between Protestant and Catholic derives from sexual perversion, not religious conviction; she opposes not Protestants but heterosexual love. Catherine, a large, mustachioed, masculine woman, is surrounded by effeminate courtiers. She controls "the heir to the throne, the effeminate Monsieur le France." At the massacre's climax Catherine's troops slaughter "bright eyes" and her betrothed.

Sexually punishing women—Catherine de Medici and Miss Jenkins—stand not just against pleasure but against the family as well. Urban nightlife made female sexual pleasure support the family. Catherine and Miss Jenkins, by contrast, embody a female invasiveness freed from masculine control. Female heterosexuality in *Intolerance,* as Bachofen had also argued, binds women to men. In the feminist debate of the early twentieth century, repeated today, over whether free (heterosexual) love liberates or entraps women, Griffith endorses entrapment.

Judith of Bethulia dismembered a king by feigning sexual desire, and flickers of genuine passion for Holofernes threatened her resolve. Ishtar, the mother goddess, blesses heterosexual love. Unlike Judith, moreover, Ishtar is not a human actor but a statue. The actual women with power in *Intolerance,* Catherine de Medici and Miss Jenkins, are demons. Two sympathetic women do take independent initiative in the film. One is the Babylonian mountain girl; the other is "the friendless one," the gangster's girlfriend in the modern story. Both are defeated. The mountain girl's ride to rescue Babylon fails to save the city and the friendless one will be incarcerated for shooting the gangster. Both women are allowed initiative not simply because they fail but also because their desire subordinates them to men. The mountain girl tells the priest's underling to "put away the garments of a female man. I shall love none but a soldier." She acts from her worship of Belshazzar, just as her modern counterpart is in thrall to the gangster. Alone in the city, the friendless one slips from working-class girl into kept woman. She gives herself to "the musketeer of the slums" and remains his sexual slave until she kills him. (A statue of a naked woman grasping a pillar appears on the screen after the friendless one and the gangster become lovers.)

Women without men threaten the family, the family to which the city has given birth. The underworld is part of the city, to be sure, and Griffith twins it with female reformers as opposing threats to the home. The musketeer frames the boy to punish him for leaving the gang, consigning him to the grid of prison and asylum that will also incarcerate his baby. But the threatened family, as we have seen, owes its existence to the underworld. Griffith counterposed the family to the city in his other features, virtue to sexuality. Instead of glorifying the family, however, that contrast made it claustrophobic and fragile. *Intolerance* derived the family from urban, sexual opportunities to give it a stronger foundation.

But Griffith did not believe in the synthesis of family, metropolis, and sexual pleasure to which his movie aspired; he could not imagine a sexually powerful man within the domesticated interior. Domestic melodrama, saving the family at the expense of its erotic urban roots, takes over the form and content of *Intolerance*. For when the boy relinquishes his gun to the musketeer, in order to marry the girl, he surrenders his manly power. Once in the family the boy is innocent victim, not active protagonist. After the gangster assaults the dear one and is shot by the friendless one, police arrest the husband for murder. As he is feminized, the friendless one plays the role of Judith, the female avenger.

Female reformers take the dear one's baby away, and the law condemns the boy to hang. Griffith has retreated to familiar thematic and technical ground. He cuts from preparations for the hanging to the ride of the friendless one to stop it. He intercuts a series of rides to the rescue in the modern story with the ride of the Persians against Babylon and with the mountain girl's ride to warn the city. The Huguenot massacre and the road to Calvary also appear. Babylon is destroyed, the modern family is reunited, and the friendless one faces prison for playing Judith. But *Birth* had already offered, in a more unified

and powerful form, the climax through parallel montage. The four stories add grandiosity rather than cinematic or social complexity.

Melodrama subsumes the world in "an underlying manichaeism," writes Peter Brooks [in *The Melodramatic Imagination: Balzac, Henry James, Melodrama, and the Mode of Excess*], "putting us in touch with the conflict of good and evil played out under the surface of things." Through "heightened dramatic utterance," melodrama supplies "grandiose moral terms" to everyday, domestic life. Since melodrama relies on visual signs and intensified, dreamlike states, it is peculiarly suited to silent film. "The indulgence of strong emotionalism; moral polarization and schematization; extreme states of being, situations, actions; overt villainy, persecution of the good, and final reward of virtue; . . . high emotionalism and stark ethical conflict"—these all characterize *Intolerance* and reach their height in the climax. But since melodrama relies on the "logic of the excluded middle," it can only counterpose opposites and not create something new. As in *Intolerance*'s climax, melodrama offers a return to innocence instead, "the misprision and recognition of virtue." But Griffith's ride to rescue innocence defeats the director's project, for the failure to give birth to new authority leaves behind the splits—between family and city, virtue and pleasure, phallus and female body—that it was the movie's purpose to overcome.

Parallel montage, the juxtaposition of contrasting shots, is the film technique most appropriate to melodrama; Griffith falls back on it to bring his movie to an end. But against the melodrama that drives the narrative forward to its oedipal conclusion in the home stand the female icons Ishtar and Artemis. The two sets of opposed images over which they preside resist reduction to melodrama and give *Intolerance* its moments of power.

One set of images—nightmare distortions, anticipating German expressionist cinema—depicts modern institutional space. The other set—crowd scenes and dynamic montage—anticipate Soviet constructivism. Griffith brings fresh excitement to the populated crowd scenes of strikers, dancers, and revellers. Like the nightmare, institutional visions that are their negative, these scenes embody the movie's originality, for they are where Griffith brings something new into being. But the powerful filmic images undercut the narrative progress that the movie's ideology intends. Griffith wanted to counterpose reform institutions to the family and to sublimate urban public pleasures into domestic happiness. But reform and the family alike survive urban, public defeat. Since the family cannot contain, either thematically or visually, the forces that pull against it, the visual power of *Intolerance* turns Griffith's domestic melodrama upside down.

Postwar German filmmakers borrowed the moving camera from *Intolerance* in the service of visual disorientation. They may have been influenced by the movie's spatial distortions and depersonalized figures as well. *Intolerance*'s expressionist scenes open up into large, empty, misshapen spaces that dwarf the humans within. Like other modern artists, Griffith gives power in these shots not to the figure but to the ground. A long shot shows Jenkins alone behind his desk, a tiny figure stranded, as Robert Sklar puts it, in a sea of floor space. Counterposed to this "positive negative space," in Stephen Kern's term, are crowds of multiplied, uniform figures. A shot of the blank, empty prison exterior when the boy enters jail is followed by the sight of the milling mass of anonymous, replicated prisoners inside. The reproducibility of these figures is meant to condemn impersonal institutions. But the motion picture itself, with its reproducible images, stands implicitly alongside them.

Three vestal virgins of uplift, in the most terrifying expressionist scenes, invade the dear one's room. These women, who dress and move alike, constitute (in Henry Adams' words on the death of his sister) "a vision of pantomime with a mechanical motion." They link the bad mother to the machine. The three women examine the dear one's baby on their first invasion; on their second they knock down the mother, seize the baby, and take it away. (Judith turned Holofernes' head into a baby; the vestal virgins of virtue appropriate the mother's baby for themselves.) Griffith next shows "the Jenkins foundation," a modern, impersonal building. Deep corridors accentuate the large, empty anteroom in the foreground. Tiny, robotlike figures move through the halls. These miniaturized, mechanical women scurrying through empty space accentuate (by contrast) the nurturing function of Ishtar's size. The goddess fills the space left blank by the absent, negative, institutional mother.

The institutional spaces, however, are not completely empty. Barred cribs in which babies lie unattended line the wall of the nursery. Uniformed female attendants ignore the babies to dance with one another while a lone man looks on. The long-angled shot, which shrinks and depersonalizes the figures, accentuates the disturbing effect of women dancing with women. This scene contrasts to the female dancing done with and for men in lively, populated dance halls. Griffith links imprisoning institutional walls to women who neglect babies and men. The walled institutions define the bad mother. Cut from the dancing nurses to the Huguenot massacre, presided over by a gloating Catherine.

Catherine displays masculinity by dominating weak men in Griffith's depiction of degenerate court life. Griffith's court scenes are fantasy, but they accurately indicate that the male nightmare of female erotic bonding post-dates the aristocratic age. Feudal sexual disarray implies male homosexuality. The director's modern lesbians form a community of women. Women also dance with women in Griffith's *True Heart Susie* (1919) to symbolize hostility to the family. But that scene lacks the cinematic and social interest of its counterpart in *Intoler-*

ance. By linking lesbian sexuality to modern institutions, *Intolerance* displays a historically situated male nightmare. Artemis reappears in the modern city as a maiden in uniform.

Just as Griffith's celebration of Ishtar responded to progressive hopes for the family, so his demonization of lesbians made visible contemporary fears. The concept of lesbian identity, Carroll Smith-Rosenberg and Ann Ferguson have argued, emerged in the early twentieth century partly as a response to a new medical discourse of deviance and partly as the self-definition of women in urban subcultures. By weakening the patriarchal power of fathers and husbands, industrial capitalism increased the life chances of women—in wage labor; in urban boarding houses where unmarried women lived without parental supervision; and on the streets and in public places of entertainment. The New Woman in these settings posed the threat not simply of free love and economic autonomy but also of erotic female bonding.

The threat of the New Woman took different forms in progressive America—free, heterosexual or bisexual love in which Aphrodite was faithful to no one man; female independence, where women lived alone or with others of their sex; and self-proclaimed lesbian identity. Griffith was using the mannish lesbian to demonize all female autonomy.

On the one hand Griffith discredited female independence by (homo)sexualizing it. On the other hand, however, the fear of lesbianism expressed anxiety about the sexual turn of women away from men. Late nineteenth-century men had attacked unnatural mothers, who favored birth control and abortion. By the progressive period the New Woman was demonized not just for rejecting motherhood but for rejecting men. Roosevelt had warned against race suicide in 1902 to attack the female college graduates who refused to marry and reproduce. Within a decade such women were labelled lesbians. First-generation New Women like Addams and Gilman had replaced personal with social mothering. The next generation, emerging as Griffith filmed *Intolerance,* made claims for homosexual and not just homosocial satisfaction. Women cross-dressed and danced together in the nineteenth-century homosocial female world before lesbianism was invented. By the progressive period such behavior was pathological from one point of view, a self-proclaimed statement of new sexual identity from another.

The companionate family responded to the threat that women would abandon the home, the threat for which lesbianism stood. By contrast to the Victorian family, the ideology of companionate marriage joined sexuality to domesticity. But by defining the husband as bread-winner and the wife as nurturant and expressive, the companionate family reinscribed gender difference against the lesbian threat. A sexuality tied to fertility would recontain women inside the family.

Intolerance made visible the lesbian threat to the family. Worse yet, it located the danger in the very progressive institutions that were supposed to restore the family. The helping professions—teaching, social work, urban planning—provided careers for progressive women. Reformers saw the public sector and the family in relations of mutual superintendence and support. But the helping professions also provided space for communities of women, working and even (as in Addams' Hull House) living together. Describing such female institutions in turn-of-the-century England, Martha Vicinus writes, "The very idea of an effective women's community was frightening. It implied that women could be self-sufficient and that men were dispensable." Griffith's modern city thus generated two prognoses: heterosexual libido domesticated by public institutions and recontained within the family, or a lesbian alliance of women and the state against the family. Progressive optimists looked forward to the first possibility. They imagined reform women in the helping professions using the state to foster domesticity. *Intolerance* denounced the helping professions for undermining the family; the director wanted to replace female reformers with motion pictures. But in spite of Griffith's wishes, *Intolerance* placed the sexual family not in the American future but in the destroyed, Babylonian past.

Babylon is destroyed, in Griffith's narrative, as domestic melodrama reunites the family against the lesbian menace. The Babylonians celebrate their apparent victory over Cyrus with a bacchanal; it exposes them to Persian invasion. Revellers delay the mountain girl, and her ride to the rescue fails to save the city. The friendless one, by contrast, reaches the governor with her confession before the three hangmen cut the rope that would drop the boy to his death. (Their rehearsal is shown.) Griffith multiplies identical hangmen in his final image of murderous state power. Compare the cutting of the rope in this image with the cutting of film in Griffith's attack on state censorship. The three women barely visible in the background as Gish rocks the cradle move forward to join her in the movie's final shot. The three vestal virgins of uplift who took the dear one's baby away are now domesticated; like Gish, they revolve around the cradle. A priest, helpless to save the boy from the state, was able only to hear his confession. The new institution for the urban masses, the motion picture, replaces the church as the agent of salvation. Film alone can rescue the family from the movies' progressive institutional competitors.

But Griffith's images undercut his domestic restoration. Only the populated, constructivist images have the power to counteract the expressionist ones. This side of *Intolerance*—the active crowds, short shots, and dynamic montage—gave birth to Soviet cinema. Sergey Eisenstein and V. I. Pudovkin were decisively influenced by the film, and the latter abandoned chemistry for moviemaking after he saw it. Lenin himself arranged to have *Intolerance* shown throughout Russia, where it was exhibited for a decade; the movie enjoyed its greatest success in the Soviet Union. But Griffith's revolutionary film technique worked against his narrative intentions. Images that celebrated disorder inverted the cinematic values of *Birth of a Nation*. That reversal might merely have signified a shift in the sources of domesticity between the two movies, from cloistered female victimization to public female pleasure. The populated scenes are tied, however, not to apotheosis but to defeat.

Birth glorified the organized Klan mass and demonized the disorderly Negro mob. *Intolerance* reverses that choice. It first does so in the strike scene early in the film. The mob of strikers resembles *Birth*'s Negroes and the militia lines up like the Klan, but Griffith has switched sides. His camera, instead of celebrating the line of force as in *Birth,* creates a classic example of dynamic montage. Griffith, as Sklar has said, cuts back and forth in shorter and shorter shots from the strikers, to their anxious families, to Jenkins isolated at his desk, to the militia. Jenkins, alone in empty space, gives the order to clear his property. The militia fires on the strikers, in the scene's culmination, and the camera pans over open space as the workers retreat.

The heavily populated spaces in the shots of this scene, like the technique of montage itself, offer more than the eye can see. Griffith displays the industrial conflict in different pieces and from different angles, shattering the illusion of a single, all-encompassing, observer's perspective. Dynamic montage democratizes and pluralizes point of view, decapitating the classic omniscient narrator. At the same time, by throwing images on the screen, dynamic montage puts the director and not the democratic mass in charge. Disorder and multiplicity place the audience in the power of the man behind the camera, for he determines what viewers see. The method of the scene undercuts its message, locating viewers in the relation to the camera that strikers are to the factory owner.

Just as dynamic montage overwhelms the individual viewer, so it does not encourage individual characters to develop and breathe. The technique creates sympathy for people as a mass rather than for individual, working-class lives. Joined with expressionist cinema, therefore, montage techniques place pressure on the traditional, autonomous subject, the individual that progressive reforms hoped to rescue. Expressionist images turn inward, arousing anxiety about a future for man alone; the strike scene celebrates the crowd.

Expressionist cinema dwelt on illness, according to Eisenstein; dynamic montage created something new. Eisenstein aligned the revolutionary film technique with social revolution. Dynamic montage signifies the director's power in *Intolerance,* but it registers the slaughter of the crowd.

Griffith also used dynamic montage to display Babylon's interior court. He celebrated the city by moving his camera freely around it (mounting an elevator on a railroad car to sweep the camera up and over the city walls, the first crane shot in movie history), and by juxtaposing different parts of the urban landscape. *Intolerance* and *Judith,* the two films set in ancient cities and presided over by a woman, are the only two Griffith films to employ dynamic montage. The conjunction of woman and the city in these films freed Griffith from traditional, rural, patriarchal constraints. If the lesbian lies behind Griffith's expressionism, Ishtar presides over his dynamic montage. But the city that lies open before Griffith's camera is equally vulnerable to Cyrus. We see Babylon from the inside only after the illusion of victory has relaxed the city's guard. The opening of the populated bacchanalian spaces foreshadows a city open to invasion.

The Persian/Babylonian battle at the end of the film repeats the strike scene at the beginning. Massed Persians, shown in silhouette and head-on, echo the ride of the Klan. Griffith cuts from the Persians in directed, forceful movement to seminude, exhausted dancing girls. Babylonian revelry has left the city defenseless, but though there are traces of *Birth*'s black mob in the character of the Babylonian crowd, our sympathies now lie with the city. Massed uniformed figures were heroic in *Birth*. Now, as the militia at the beginning of *Intolerance* or the Persians at the end, as the multiplied vestal virgins of uplift or the uniformed prisoners in jail, they are destructive of urban pleasure.

Birth celebrated the sword of castration that reestablished white male power. Cyrus repossesses that sword, "'the most potent weapon forged in the flame of Intolerance.'" "'Seize now the flaming sword,'" Ishtar's priests exhort her, but "'"the warlike Ishtar"'" (in one of Griffith's sources) fails to follow in Judith's footsteps and decapitate the king. The most prominent sword in *Intolerance* is the one the camera dwells on as it runs through the Huguenot ingenue.

The intended moral of *Intolerance* is that Aphrodite the sexual matriarch, threatened by Artemis the cultural superego, must give way to Demeter the domestic mother. Griffith wants to contrast institutional reform to the family, Jenkins alone at his desk to Gish rocking the cradle. But the two shots of single figures behind single pieces of furniture, alone in empty space, echo rather than contradict each other. Both contrast to the populated, teeming, alive urban scenes. The opposition between claustrophobic, vulnerable family interior and empty, impersonal institutional space only emerges once the modern Aphrodite, the modern city, is reformed. After the prostitutes are taken away, Griffith depicts first the dear one threatened in her small room, then the empty institutional space of the orphanage. He cuts to the contrast with Belshazzar's feast, with its eating and sexual display. Other filmmakers would incorporate such scenes into the 1920s celebration of consumption. For Griffith they remained transgressive and forbidden. Cecil B. deMille would make sexualized biblical epics

for family entertainment. Birth control advocates, in a comparable domestication of the subversive, linked contraception to conjugal intimacy, not female sexual freedom. Griffith wanted to bring female sexuality, public pleasure, and the family together, but he could not do so. Griffith bade farewell in *Intolerance* to his embrace of the modern city and his flirtation with female sexuality.

Griffith's failure to move forward into the culture of consumption is more instructive, nonetheless, than the accommodations that succeeded him. The alliance of women and the city retains its subversive potential in *Intolerance,* as the retribution for Belshazzar's feast, the fall of Ishtar, leaves behind only domesticity and the state. That denouement returns us to the production still of Griffith between the great mother's legs, the visual with which this discussion began. What does the narrative of *Intolerance* as undercut by its images say about the fetish, the phallic mother, and Freud's narrative of female sexuality?

5

Ishtar presides over *Intolerance* as the archaic mother attentive to her sons. The modern woman is split between lesbian and domestic; Ishtar is whole. But woman cannot be whole in male fantasy, according to Freud, because she lacks a phallus. In the production still that commented on and completed his movie, Griffith gave her one: himself. Supplying Ishtar with her phallus and baby, Griffith endorsed Freud's equation of the two. But Freud insisted women made that equation; Griffith shows that the need for it is male. By what he shares with Freud, Griffith displaces the doctor from his privileged position as interpreter of sexual fantasies and makes him a patient, too. The production still from *Intolerance,* read as the conclusion of the movie, suggests the place of phallocentrism in establishing sexual difference.

Male gender identity, Nancy Chodorow has argued, is based on difference from the mother. The phallus is the sign of that difference; it signifies the separation of the male child from the original, maternal dual-unity and his entrance into language and culture. That separation, however, is fragile. At the same time that the penis signifies sexual difference and independence from the woman, it invokes the danger of its loss. To imagine a woman with a penis is to restore the originary unity and deny castration fear.

The integrity of the separate male ego, symbolized by possession of a penis, succeeds and defends against an earlier psychic unity, that of the unseparated mother and baby. Freud, however, began not with the mother but with the penis. In analyzing fetishes as substitutes for the penis, he avoided the primary male substitution of a part for the whole, the substitution of the phallus for the union of mother and son. The fetish stands in for the phallus because the phallus is already a fetish.

The original wholeness was the mother/baby symbiosis, the retrospectively imagined all-powerful dual-unity before consciousness of separation. The phallic mother restores that wholeness (Freud, sharing the male wish, had it exactly backwards) by substituting the penis for the baby. The phallus replaces the breast, in Geza Roheim's formulation, as the male identifies his own (fluid-producing) genital with the absent maternal source of pleasure. In posing before the nursing Ishtar, Griffith pointed to the phallic mother's origins in the baby at the breast. By restoring the missing penis to the mother, the son restores her connection to him.

Freud had proposed, like Griffith in *Intolerance,* to free women from sexual inhibition in order to save the conjugal family and to bind women to men. But the doctor lost faith in that enterprise as the early mother forced her way into his work. At that point, instead of analyzing the son's relations to his early mother, Freud turned to the girl's relationship to her missing penis. Insisting on sexual difference, the later Freud celebrated patriarchy. Griffith, unable to restore a credible patriarchy, exposes the mother repressed in Freud's project.

Calling the mother-son bond "altogether the most perfect, the most free from ambivalence of all human relationships" in his writings on female sexuality, and attributing preoedipal conflicts to daughters and not sons, Freud voiced a male wish. Griffith displays the trouble with the early mother against which that wish defends. Freud continued, "A mother can transfer to her son the ambition which she has been obliged to suppress in herself, and she can expect from him the satisfaction of all that has been left over in her of her masculinity complex." Claiming the mother wanted to make the son her extension, Freud voiced the son's wish to complete the mother by becoming her phallus. Griffith, creating *Judith* and posing before Ishtar, represented that desire.

Griffith imagined, with Judith and Ishtar, different versions of the archaic mother. The early mother who is whole by acquiring a sword threatens to turn on the son. Both Freud's and Griffith's Judith placed the phallus/baby equation in the service of female revenge, woman's resistance to sexual difference. Ishtar, the mother goddess, sanctified sexual difference. The phallus turned into baby restores the mother to the son.

On the one hand, then, Ishtar is the great mother who takes care of her creator, her son. But giving Ishtar back a phallus also revealed the failure of *Intolerance* to dissolve the early mother into the companionate family. The phallus stands for the move from identification with to desire for the woman. But in that shift there is a loss. Griffith wanted the family union—father, sexual mother, and baby—to replace the original dual-unity. The progression that began with Judith, the woman with the penis, was to end in the modern home. The failure of the family to include sexuality and empower the father left the early mother as unsublimated excess. Since

the baby could not do all the work of the maternal phallus, Griffith restored that organ to Ishtar.

Women, according to Freud, had to accept the "fact" of their castration. That fact is a male wish to derive female from male development, turn women into lesser men, and make motherhood their fulfillment. Turning women into castrated men, however, destabilizes the sexual difference it is intended to guarantee. The male oscillates between reassurance that woman lacks a phallus and is therefore different and inferior, and the wish that she have a penis so as not to remind him of castration. Phallocentrism, therefore, does not simply establish sexual difference; it enforces sexual hierarchy against the threat of castration, of men becoming women, of the end of the difference between women and men.

Lesbian reformers are the bearers of that threat in *Intolerance*. "What does a woman want?" Freud asked. Ishtar signified what Griffith wanted women to want; the lesbian scenes are the nightmare against which Ishtar as whole mother defends. Lesbian fiction, Sandra Gilbert and Catharine Stimpson have suggested, replaces the binary structure of sexual difference with multiple, fluid relations—like those caricatured in Griffith's communities of mechanical women. Griffith makes those women masculine to claim they want to be men; what he fears (the dancing scene shows) is that they do not want men.

Birth control, its opponents charged, allowed women to behave like men, for it severed sex from reproduction. Lesbianism, a more perfect form of nonreproductive sexuality, allegedly completed the phallicization of women. But the mannish lesbian, as depicted in *Intolerance* and contemporary cultural documents, defended against a still deeper fear that the object of female sexual desire was not the male at all.

In denying female sexuality, the culture that produced Freud and Griffith identified sex with the phallus. When the sexual woman returned, she brought with her in Griffith's production still that same identification. As the woman with the penis/baby, Ishtar insisted on her orientation to men. Disowning the male need for the woman with the penis, *Intolerance* attributed that need to lesbians. But lesbian sexuality, its proponents began to argue in the progressive period, emancipated the woman from desire for the phallus. Lesbianism aimed to establish woman as genuine difference, not as a castrated man who needs penis and baby to complete her. Since the lesbian—she claimed and Griffith feared—required neither the male organ nor his child, she would make the man insignificant. The oedipal mother chooses another man, but the son who has relinquished her can become a father himself. The lesbian lives in a world absolutely closed off to the man. She chooses a love object so different from the son that he cannot replace the object of her desire. The lesbian is the woman fatally and finally lost to the male-child.

"We should be . . . indifferent," says Luce Irigaray, naming Griffith's nightmare. Irigaray gives female indifference the three meanings it has in *Intolerance*: women no longer defined by their difference from men; women indifferent to men, leaving the mirror empty by refusing to reflect them; and women undifferentiated from one another, forming a female community. The distorted, empty spaces in *Intolerance*'s expressionist scenes depict the anxiety of female indifference.

Posing with Ishtar, Griffith filled the empty space between her legs with himself. He filled the empty space in the movie with urban crowds and with the intercutting of dynamic montage. But the family restoration, I have argued, failed to incorporate these alternatives to the bad mother. Griffith's position between Ishtar's legs alludes thematically to Cyrus' invasion and dismemberment of the city, formally to the director's moving camera and dynamic montage. Unable to locate masculine reinsertion within the family, however, Griffith failed to lay the archaic mother to rest. The progressive cultural synthesis between the companionate family, regulatory institutions, and the city-by-night flourished in the urban 1920s. *Intolerance,* conceived as the foundation of that synthesis, could not support it. The movie's disintegration exposes the warring forces—regulatory family and surveillance state, subversive city and independent woman, female sexual self-definition and lesbian identity—that modern American political culture is still trying and failing to contain.

Kenneth S. Lynn (essay date 1990)

SOURCE: "The Torment of D. W. Griffith," in *The American Scholar,* Vol. 59, Spring, 1990, pp. 255-64.

[*In the following essay, Lynn recounts the production history of* Broken Blossoms *and other films, focusing on Griffith's relationship with actor Lillian Gish.*]

The first masterpiece by an American director to emerge from the post-World War I search for a new art of film was D. W. Griffith's *Broken Blossoms,* which had its premiere in New York in May 1919. Filmed in constricted studio settings under artificial lights, rather than in the open expanses of California fields in which Griffith had mounted so many of the scenes in *The Birth of a Nation, Intolerance,* and *Hearts of the World,* the picture was characterized by attention to atmosphere, involuted acting styles, and innovative photography. Yet if *Broken Blossoms* was an exquisite piece of work, it was also excruciating, reaching levels of emotional intensity that were no less frenzied than those which German audiences would begin to encounter eight months later in *The Cabinet of Dr. Caligari* and climaxing in a denouement of uncompromising grimness. Whether *Caligari* was intended to expose fatal tendencies inherent in the German national psyche is a fiercely debated question. The hidden dynamics in *Broken Blossoms,* on the other hand, were indisputably personal. The story of the three principal characters—a Yellow Man, so called, from China, played by Richard Barthelmess; a Limehouse boxer with a cauliflower ear, played by Donald Crisp; and the boxer's fifteen-year-old illegitimate daughter, played by the incomparable Lillian Gish, aged twenty-two—bore a nightmarishly distorted resemblance to a real-life situation involving Gish and Griffith, when the latter at age forty-three was old enough to have been his leading lady's father.

They first met, Gish and Griffith, on a humid summer morning in 1912, when the fifteen-year-old Lillian and her fourteen-year-old sister Dorothy paid a visit to the brownstone mansion on East Fourteenth Street in Manhattan that housed the movie studios of the Biograph Company. They were looking for a childhood friend of theirs named Gladys Smith, whom they had come to know during the period in which all three girls had achieved precocious success on the stage. After years of being out of touch with Gladys, Lillian and Dorothy had recently recognized her in a Biograph one-reeler entitled *Lena and the Geese*.

Their reunion with Mary Pickford—as Gladys Smith now called herself—was warm; but when the director of *Lena and the Geese* came up to be introduced to the pretty visitors, Lillian became very tense. Griffith held himself like a king, she remembered, and his beaknosed profile recalled the images of emperors on Roman coins; underneath his wide-brimmed straw hat, which he wore indoors and out, his hooded, deep-set eyes seemed to be dissecting his new acquaintances. Abruptly, he challenged the Gishes to tell him if they had the talent to act in movies—and then insisted on conducting them to a rehearsal hall to determine the answer for himself. En route, he ordered Mary Pickford to inform Lionel Barrymore, Elmer Booth, and other actors on the Biograph payroll that they must join him in the hall immediately. Once the men had arrived, Griffith gave Lillian a blue bow to wear in her hair and Dorothy a red bow, so that he could refer to them by colors, rather than by their names. Next he announced what he had in mind.

"We will rehearse the story of two girls trapped in an isolated house while thieves are trying to get in and rob the safe. . . . Now, Red, you hear a strange noise. Run to your sister. Blue, you're scared, too. Look toward me, where the camera is. Show your fear. You hear something. What is it? You're two frightened children, trapped in a lonely house by these brutes. They're in the next room." Wheeling around to his group of actors, Griffith pulled the nearest of them into the action. "Elmer, pry open a window. Climb into the house. Kick down the door to the room that holds the safe. You are mean! These girls are hiding thousands of dollars. Think of what *that* will buy! Let your avarice show— Blue, you hear the door breaking. You run in a panic to bolt it—"

"What door?" Lillian cried.

"Right in front of you! I know there's no door, but pretend there is. Run to the telephone. Start to use it. No one answers. You realize the wires have been cut. Tell the camera what you feel. Fear—*more fear!* Look into the lens! Now you see a gun come through the hole as he knocks the stovepipe to the floor. Look scared, I tell you."

According to Lillian's autobiography, she and her sister were already practically paralyzed with fright, so it was not difficult for them to obey Griffith. But still he wasn't satisfied. "No, that's not enough! Girls, hold each other. Cower in the corner." Suddenly the director pulled a real gun from his pocket and began chasing the girls around the room, shooting it off. Neither of the Gishes was aware that the bullets were being aimed at the ceiling. "He's gone mad!" Lillian thought, as she and Dorothy scurried around the room, looking frantically for an exit.

At last, the shooting ceased. Griffith put away his gun. He was smiling. "That will make a wonderful scene," he said. "You have expressive bodies. I can use you. Do you want to work for me? Would you like to make the picture we just rehearsed?" After a brief hesitation, the Gishes accepted the offer, and a few weeks later *An Unseen Enemy,* as the picture was called, went into production.

A vicious man penetrating the confined space in which helpless young women cower in terror: variations on that situation recur with remarkable frequency in Griffith's early movies, and the violence, degradation, and control with which the women are threatened constitute symbolic forms of attempted rape. But fortunately for the maidens, men who love them become conscious of their peril and ride to the rescue in the nick of time. If the menacing villains in these pictures seemed to have come straight out of stage melodrama, it is no wonder, for they were modeled in part on the tramp who figures so importantly either as a sinister or a comic character in the turn-of-the-century plays that Griffith came across in his early career as an actor in touring dramatic companies. The tramp shown in the melodramas was modeled on a contemporary social type, for in the hard period commencing with the panic of 1893, shocking numbers of men had hit the road in the United States, eking out an existence by begging and stealing. Fearsome specimens of these migrant non-workers—and of the non-migrant non-workers succinctly called bums—became personally known to Griffith as a result of his having been forced by dwindling funds to live in malodorous flophouses during an extended stay in New York at the close of the nineties. The villains he conjured up in his Biograph thrillers sprang from his recollection of the thieves he had been frightened of in the flophouses as well as out of his conversance with a memorable character in the melodramatic repertoire.

The dramatic confrontations between villains and virgins that Griffith filmed likewise had a double origin. While such confrontations had long been the stuff of which popular plays were made, his employments of them were energized by his own psychological demons. For the great director was a sexual addict in whom attractive young women aroused violently contradictory impulses. Only by understanding this can we begin to comprehend Griffith's utter fascination with Edgar Allan Poe. In a number of Poe's tales, so the poet Richard Wilbur has observed, a woman's redemptive love or spotless honor is the ground of contention between two men, one of them lofty-minded and the other base or brutish. The observation not only applies to Griffith's movies as well, but to his tormentedly divided personality. When he went after the Gish girls with a live gun blazing, there is good reason to believe, there was something more at work in him than just the desire to administer a screen test.

A link of another sort to Poe is that Griffith's heritage was Southern. His father, Jacob Wark Griffith, popularly known as Thunder Jake, or Roaring Jake, because of the carrying power of his voice, had once owned five slaves and a prosperous farm in Oldham County, Kentucky, and during the Civil War had served with bravery as a Confederate cavalry officer. Upon his return to Kentucky, he bore the scars of at least two wounds, if not the five he boasted of. The years of life that now remained to him were mainly given over to drinking, gambling, and windy reminiscences of war. His son David was born in 1875. Five years later, Thunder Jake died, leaving a wife, seven children—of whom David was the youngest—and many debts.

Young David had adored and idealized his father, yet had never felt able to count on his love. As he confessed in his unfinished autobiography, "I often wondered if [my father] cared anything about me particularly. I am forced to doubt it. As far as I can remember he never seemed to show anybody his feelings toward them." About his mother, Griffith likewise had desolate thoughts: ". . . a silent sort of woman . . . so silent and quiet . . . that I never dreamed she loved me until she was about seventy years old when I discovered that stern, cold, hard exterior covered a tremendous emotional and . . . affectionate nature that was terrible in its intensity." Only from the attentions of his sisters did he receive any sense of female love.

From his excessive shyness as a boy we can judge that he lacked self-esteem, of which an important sign was Griffith's conviction that his big nose made him unattractive to girls. In compensation, he conjured up enormous ambitions; indeed, they were imbued with fantasy. Thus, on the way home from school one day, he experienced a religious vision. As a result of a sleet storm followed by a quick freeze, the branches of the trees were covered with ice. With the morning sun on them, they were radiant with light. In the center of that light, he was sure he saw the face of Christ. Adoringly, he spoke to the Savior. "My name is David, and you know that means dearly beloved. I do hope you may like me a little, that I might even become your dearly beloved, because I love you and always have." That he was marked for a special destiny became the solacing certainty of the youngster's life.

Griffith found his métier as a movie director in 1908. In the course of the next five years, close to 450 films, most of them one-reelers, were improvised by him without shooting scripts, even when his source was a famous poem or piece of fiction. Out of a need for exciting modes of story telling, he also developed an entire grammar of cinematic expression. From the work of other filmmakers, he appropriated and brilliantly refined the close-up shot. Other techniques that are associated with his name, such as the spot-iris opening, the dissolve, and cross-cutting from one scene of action to another, were familiar to him from his days on the stage, for they had been introduced there by theatrical directors who had grown impatient with the lack of plasticity in their medium. Still other techniques, such as backlighting, Griffith worked out himself, with the aid of his gifted cameraman Billy Bitzer. By the time of his departure from Biograph in 1913, his movies had no superiors in technical accomplishment anywhere in the world, and *The Birth of a Nation* in 1915 and *Intolerance* the following year would mark the emergence of the "magician of tempo and montage," as Sergei Eisenstein would later say of him.

But for a man who had once had direct contact with Jesus Christ, technically marvelous story telling was not enough. Some remarks Griffith addressed to Lillian Gish in 1914 disclosed his messianic aspirations. "Do you know," he rhetorically asked her, "that we are playing to the world? What we film tomorrow will strike the hearts of the world. And they will know what we are saying. We've gone beyond Babel, beyond words. We've found a universal language—a power that can make men brothers and end wars forever." On other occasions, he spoke of the movies as operating like "the hand of God" in that they could lift people out of their "commonplace existence" into a realm of "poetic simulations," and he called on his players to think of themselves as vessels containing the same "divine fluid" that had given Napoleon and George Washington the power to transform the world. In accordance with his belief that images of pure beauty could make a movie seem like a message from God Himself, he concluded *The Birth of a Nation* with an image of Jesus. *Intolerance* similarly ends with a vision of perfect love and eternal peace. The newspaper reporter who hailed Griffith as a "prophet" who speaks through "shadow sermons more powerful than the pulpit" was a man after the director's own megalomanic heart.

In the Progressive Era of Theodore Roosevelt and Woodrow Wilson, Griffith also thought of himself as a reformer of manners and morals. Late in life, he would recall that "Reform [in those days] was sweeping the country, newspapers were laying down a barrage against gambling, rum, and light ladies, particularly light ladies . . . so I decided to reform the motion picture industry." To that end, he played the stern Victorian father with his actors and actresses—in his case, I should say the stern Victorian mother—and established strict rules for them, especially for the younger actresses, who were supposed to be chaperoned on the set and were not allowed to receive men in their dressing rooms. Lillian Gish has written that Griffith was also gripped by a virtual "mania for cleanliness." He himself was always impeccably groomed, Gish's account continues, "and he expected the young actresses on the lot to be equally immaculate. A female aspirant would lose out if she weren't scrupulously clean. Once, after an interview with a talented actress whom he had dismissed, he said exasperatedly, 'She just doesn't *look* clean.'" From moral and hygienic lectures to his players, Griffith went on to call for movies that would never "deviate from the Puritan plane," that would always "keep boys and girls along the right lines of conduct." Newspaper talk about youth going away from the old morals was nonsense, in his opinion. "Never since the beginnings of time," he trumpeted, "have there been so many boys and girls who were so clean, so young. . . ."

W. J. Cash observes in his book *The Mind of the South* that, while the "barnyard morality" of male students in Southern colleges and universities following World War I flouted the tradition and forms of Southern Puritanism and the cult of Southern Womanhood, their emancipation was far from complete; and a "subconscious will to escape into being more nearly whole again" filled even the better-known campus seducers with longing for "the old gesturing worship" of feminine virtue and chastity. Griffith, too, was caught between two worlds. Underlying his manic concern with cleanliness lay the haunted knowledge that, by the standards of the moral code he professed, his behavior was filthy.

In 1906, while still trying to make it as an actor in the theater, Griffith had married the actress Linda Arvidson. Five years later, Linda came upon a love letter addressed to her husband, and she sent him an accusatory note about it. In a melancholy reply tinged with self-loathing, Griffith confessed that the author of the love letter was not the first paramour he had ever had, and that "there are sure to be others just as objectionable in every way after her." In conclusion he pleaded, "Let me lead my own life and you yours. . . . I am better off morally, and in all ways, outside of marriage." Just before signing his name, he again emphasized his promiscuity: "Don't think there is some other woman in the case. It is not one, but many." And some of his lovers, he might have added, had he been willing to be fully candid, were nymphets in their early teens. It was a taste that established yet another kinship with Poe, whose tragic life with the fatally consumptive young woman whom he married when she was fourteen and he twenty-seven was sketched by Griffith in a Biograph film entitled *Edgar Allen* [sic] *Poe*. Linda Arvidson, in her wisdom, immediately granted her husband's plea for a separation, but they did not legally terminate their marriage until 1936. Although Griffith remarried at once, this union, too, would end in divorce.

Struggles between his guilt feelings and his resentments of the guilt led Griffith in 1914, shortly after shifting his headquarters to the Reliance-Majestic Studios in Hollywood, to make a four-reel movie called *The Avenging Conscience*. A remarkable attempt at psychological analysis, as Erwin Panofsky has called it, the movie was based on one of Poe's briefest but most memorable stories, "The Tell-Tale Heart," and augmented with references to several of Poe's poems, most notably "Annabel Lee." As of 1914, literary critics in America still thought of "The Tell-Tale Heart" as a tale of insanity, cruelty, self-destructive hysteria, and nothing more. In order, therefore, to highlight its sexual content, which he himself intuitively grasped, he had to alter the plot.

To play the central role, Griffith selected Henry B. Walthall, a physically undersized, heavy-drinking Hollywood actor in his thirties. With his high forehead, pouchy eyes, and curled black locks carelessly combed, Walthall bore a strong resemblance to Poe, as Lillian Gish, among others, has affirmed. In the movie he is a literarily talented fellow who has been raised from infancy by his uncle. The uncle has a useless eye that is covered with a large and ghastly looking black patch, but with his good eye he keeps his nephew under close surveillance. While he does not mind him taking time from his writing to read "The Tell-Tale Heart," his Cyclopean stare communicates stern disapproval of the nephew's attraction to a ripe young woman, played by a full-figured, seventeen-year-old, platinum-blonde actress with the luscious name of Blanche Sweet. The nephew calls the young woman Annabel because he considers her his Annable Lee, an analogy which suggests that, despite her voluptuousness, he likes to think of her as a child. "*I* was a child and *she* was a child / In this kingdom by the sea," Poe wrote, "But we loved with the love that was more than love— / I and my ANNABEL LEE." Why the uncle is upset by his nephew's involvement with this lovely girl is made clear by the disgust he displays at shows of affection by other young couples in the neighborhood. His balefully puritanical attitude is the envy-riddled product of an aging man's loss of sexual potency, the symbol of which is that ghastly eye patch. In a paroxysm of jealousy, he finally denounces Annabel as a loose woman and banishes her from his house.

If Griffith's camera doesn't let us forget either the uncle's eye or his eye patch, its probing of the nephew's moodiness is even more relentless. A fixed stare is the first indication that he is nearing the edge of a nervous breakdown. As he slips into morbidity, Griffith employs eerie combinations of massed shadows and ghostly lights to convey the atmospherics of a tortured inner world. Seized at last by madness, the nephew strangles

his uncle and immures his body in the brick wall of a fireplace, but all too soon the sweetness of revenge is overwhelmed by horrifying visitations, from the uncle's wandering ghost, from a suspicious detective whose tapping foot and tapping pencil have the appalling rhythm of a beating heart, from an apparition of the crucified Christ, and from a blazing tablet of the Law that says, "Thou Shalt Not Kill."

Moments after the nephew's attempt at suicide is thwarted by a posse of armed men who have come to arrest him, we learn that the nightmarish events we have witnessed have merely taken place in his mind, after he dozed off while reading "The Tell-Tale Heart." On awaking, he is greeted effusively by his remorseful uncle, who then makes amends with Annabel as well. The ceaseless war of the superego upon the id, the constant punishment of impulse by conscience, dissolves into a wish-fulfillment vision of harmony.

Ten years after *The Avenging Conscience* was released, Gilbert Seldes, in his survey of American popular culture, *The Seven Lively Arts,* would speak of the film in terms that suggested it was Griffith's greatest work. Although the judgment was extravagant, implicit in it was an important truth: Griffith's genius was better suited to psychological dramas than to such historical epics as *The Birth of a Nation,* to which he turned upon finishing *The Avenging Conscience*.

Ever since its release in 1912, an Italian film company had been raking in heavy profits at foreign box offices with a big-spectacle picture based on Henryk Sienkiewicz's novel *Quo Vadis?*. The twelve reels of *The Birth of a Nation* represented, first of all, an American answer to the Italians; secondly, a celebration of the fiftieth anniversary of the end of the American Civil War; thirdly, the belief of a Kentucky-born director that the United States had not truly become a nation until the overthrow of Reconstruction in the South; and lastly, the dream of a cinematic messiah that by dramatizing the horrors of the battlefield he could inspire a world convulsed by war to lay down its arms.

The movie cost close to $100,000—an unprecedented sum—to produce, and the money bought a lot, including a cast of hundreds of men, women, and children; color tints in an extensive variety of hues that were painstakingly applied to different sections of the filmstrip in order to enhance certain emotional values; and a musical score arranged both for the full orchestras that played in the grander movie houses of the time and for the solitary pianists who worked in most of the rest. This score was made up not only of such American tunes as "Turkey in the Straw" and "Camp-town Races," but of excerpts from Schumann, Wagner, Grieg, and half a dozen other European composers. While the movie's richly disparate materials raised the danger of incoherence, they in fact were wondrously well coordinated by Griffith, even in such complicated scenes as the battle of Petersburg and the burning of Atlanta. He was masterful, too, in establishing narrative connections in the sprawling drama through poignant contrasts, of which the most moving begins with the departure in 1861 of a Confederate cavalry troop (headed by Colonel Ben Cameron) down a village street lined by crowds of white people and slaves laughing and cheering, while the music swells with the strains of "Dixie," and terminates with Cameron's return to the silence of that same street four years later, on foot, alone, and barely recovered from grievous wounds.

The Birth of a Nation is also one of the few dramatic movies ever made that contains scholarly footnotes. The citations on its subtitle cards range from Woodrow Wilson's *History of the American People* to Horace Porter's *Campaigning with Grant* to Civil War and post-Civil War pictorial documents. Nevertheless, as a historical epic the movie is intellectually and artistically inadequate. It does not offer sympathetic insights into the physical and mental suffering of the slaves or their dreams of freedom. In turning Lincoln into a Christ figure, it shuts off the possibility of explaining his part in precipitating and sustaining a bloody conflict. It ascribes the pursuit of legal equality for blacks by Congressman Thaddeus Stevens (thinly disguised as "Master of the Congress" Austin Stoneman) to his vulnerability to the seductive wiles of the sexual tiger cat who is his mulatto housekeeper. And the justly famous ride to the rescue by the hooded horsemen of the Ku Klux Klan—excitingly intercut with scenes of social chaos and personal danger in the Cameron family's hometown of Piedmont, South Carolina—is not shadowed by even the slightest hint of moral ambiguity.

Griffith's shortcomings as a historian, however, were not what made *The Birth of a Nation* the focus of the most furious controversy about a work of the American imagination since the publication of *Uncle Tom's Cabin.* The controversy was a consequence, rather, of Griffith's everlasting need to produce paradigms of his conflicted feelings about women. An abhorrence of miscegenation merely served to intensify a familiar contrast in his work; this time, the opposite of lofty-mindedness would be a subhuman baseness, not far removed from Poe's evocation of the razor-wielding black ourang-outang in "The Murders in the Rue Morgue."

For the heroic role of Colonel Ben Cameron, Griffith chose a most unlikely candidate, Henry Walthall. Although it proved possible to mask the ravages of dissipation in his face with heavy applications of powder, his short stature could not be concealed, so the best of a bad bargain was made by acknowledging it with a nickname, "the little Colonel." But if the choice of Walthall was odd from the point of view of epical plausibility, a Poe look-alike was eminently suited to the phobic episodes of sexual persecution that Griffith had in mind. And another effect of his obsession with sex on his cast selections is that the most vivid performers in a picture filled with masculine derring-do are two young women, Mae Marsh and Lillian Gish.

Eighteen and seventeen years old, respectively, at the time the filming began, Marsh and Gish both were involved with Griffith off the set as well as on. Neither actress offered the pneumatic bliss of Blanche Sweet, but this was to their advantage, for Griffith preferred girl-women with slightly formed figures and an abundance of nervous energy. His ideal of the feminine film star, he told an interviewer for *Photoplay,* had "nothing of the flesh, nothing of the note of sensuousness," and he added that he liked "the nervous type."

Marsh projected a coltish, tomboyish innocence that reminded Griffith of one of the sisters whose collective pampering of him had eased the emotional desolation of his childhood. In *The Birth of a Nation,* the scenario of which was co-authored by Griffith and which departs substantially from the Thomas Dixon novel it is derived from, he assigned Marsh to play a character who does not exist in the novel, Ben Cameron's blonde-haired little sister, Flora. "You remind me so very much of my little sister," he told her. "You are a little sister." In the most arresting of the secondary dramas in the movie, the intimacy between Ben and Flora veers close to the edge of kinkiness. She hugs and nuzzles him and dances about him, her thin legs flashing; after he goes off to war, it is not to his mother or father or other sister that he writes, but to Flora, who dons her last good dress before opening his letter, swings her legs back and forth across her body as she reads it, and then places it in her bosom and pats the place where it is; upon his return home in 1865, Flora alone comes outside to meet him, wearing a dress pathetically adorned with strips of raw cotton, and Ben reaches out his hand and touches the strip on her bosom. By imposing upon Ben and Flora a fond fantasy of his own about brother-sister relations, Griffith set up his audiences for the horror of their final moment together.

In Lillian Gish, a Kentucky Galahad found a spiritual icon come to life, and in picture after picture he paid tribute to the purity of her beauty in ever more prolonged and searching close-ups of her luminous, transparently complexioned face. "I followed [Griffith's] work with intense interest," the great French director Jean Renoir has written. "The marvel of marvels was the close-up. I have never changed my opinion of this. Certain close-ups of Lillian Gish . . . are imprinted on my memory for life."

The silent-film star Colleen Moore has testified that Gish once confided in her that Griffith had asked her to marry him. His love for her, however, never halted his hunt for other women. Underlying the concupiscence of that hunt, moreover, was a fear of his quarries. "He admired and loved women," Lillian Gish has written, "yet he seemed afraid of them. He never saw a girl in his office without a third person present. . . . Hollywood was already filled with ambitious girls who would stop at nothing to get into films. Some unscrupulous young girls, having obtained an interview with a producer, would threaten to remove their clothes and accuse him of rape if he didn't promise them a role in a movie." But while Griffith took steps to avoid being forced to resort to such promises, he had no compunctions about dangling jobs before women in order to assert his control of them. Thus he was wont to humiliate Gish and other actresses who worked for him by creating uncertainties in their minds about whether they would get the parts they coveted. And when such ambitious performers as Mary Pickford announced that they were leaving his employ, he reacted so passively as to suggest that he secretly dreaded being engulfed by their demands on him and was relieved to see them go. The fear that women might victimize him was also kept secret in the movies he made; instead, he portrayed the victimization of women by men, and the terrific power with which he did so reached its peak in his work with Gish, for with her fugitive hands, facial mobility, and agitated body gestures, she could communicate every iota of the vulnerability he was seeking to dramatize.

In *Birth of a Nation,* he placed both Marsh and Gish in situations of sexual terror; indeed, in Marsh's case it involved attempted rape, which he no longer felt constrained to present symbolically. For in 1913, the producer-director George L. Tucker had brought out a picture called *Traffic in Souls,* based on the Rockefeller Commission's findings about white-slave rings in New York City. By this means the theme of sexual violation finally came to the American screen, and the astonishing financial success of *Traffic in Souls* gave Griffith the latitude to deal with it in his own way.

Three characters figure in the rape scene: tomboyish Flora Cameron, her brother Ben, and a low-caste black man named Gus, played in black face by a white actor of no renown, whom Griffith required to walk and run in a crouched-down way that resembled the scuttling of an animal. In a superbly edited sequence of shots, we witness the terrified Flora fleeing through sun-dappled woods from the onrushing Gus, whose foam-specked lips betray his sexual heat. Far in the rear but running hard as well is Ben, his face contorted with concern. He hopes to reach the black man before his sister is harmed, but his hopes are in vain. On the edge of a cliff, Gus closes in on Flora, who leaps to her death just as he is about to touch her. The scene ends at the foot of the cliff with the anguished Ben bent over his little sister's crumpled form.

In Gish's terror scene—which has no counterpart in Dixon's novel—the eye of the camera is mainly fixed on two characters: a young visitor to the South from Pennsylvania, Congressman Stoneman's ethereally ash-blonde daughter, Elsie, played by Gish, and the mulatto lieutenant governor of South Carolina, Silas Lynch, played by a swarthily made-up white actor, George Siegmann, a man of gorilla-like bulk. The town of Piedmont is falling into anarchy under the riotous sway of Negro militia, and in the midst of its breakdown Elsie is cornered by Lynch in a small room. He kisses the hem of her dress and asks her to marry him. Horrified, Elsie

dodges away, her hands fluttering, but Lynch nabs her again. One of his black henchmen enters the room, and Lynch orders him to hurry preparations for a forced marriage. Lynch's lascivious closeness becomes so unbearable to Elsie that she faints. Lynch sweeps her up in his huge arms, gorilla-fashion—so Lillian Gish would later describe the way she was held—and carries her into an inner room; as he does so, her hair becomes unpinned and falls loose. (That particular image of beauty and the beast would return to the screen eighteen years later, in a shot of King Kong and Fay Wray.) After depositing Elsie in a chair, Lynch instructs his orderlies to keep her under guard. The camera cuts to a picture of salvation: units of white-robed Klansmen on horseback, assembling in the countryside for a ride to the rescue of Elsie and other threatened towns-folk. The leader of the ride will be Ben Cameron, who has fallen in love with Elsie.

It was these two scenes that aroused massive rage against the film. The entire Negro population of the United States, cried the urban reformer Frederic C. Howe, has been "degraded" by Griffith's portrayal of Negroes as "lustful" and "depraved"; and the mayor of New York, John Purroy Mitchell, alarmed by mounting social tension in the city, persuaded the manager of the Liberty Theater, where *The Birth of a Nation* was playing, to censor both scenes. In Boston, a group of militant protesters, led by the black newspaper editor William Monroe Trotter, threw stink bombs at the screen during Flora's flight through the woods. At the end of the show, fist fights between whites and blacks broke out in front of the theater and arrests were made. Emerging from the police station after being booked, Trotter told reporters that the movie "will make white women afraid of Negroes and will have white men all stirred up on their account."

The outcry that he was a racist caused Griffith much suffering, Lillian Gish has written. At a public hearing about the movie in Boston, presided over by Mayor James Michael Curley, Griffith offered to give $10,000 to the national president of the NAACP, Moorfield Storey, if he could point to any episode in the picture that was false. But when Storey asked him to name the mulatto lieutenant governor of a Southern state who had tried to force a white woman to marry him, Griffith sat mute. How could he, after all, have explained that *he* was Silas Lynch and the foam-lipped black Gus as well?

The Birth of a Nation, Cecil B. De Mille would remember in 1948, "burst upon the world with atomic force." By the end of 1917, its earnings exceeded sixty million dollars, an all but incredible amount that would have been even higher had not unscrupulous exhibitors such as Louis B. Mayer of Haverhill, Massachusetts, underreported their receipts. Nevertheless, the picture was a tragedy for Griffith, and not merely because accusations of racism would hound him to his grave. It created among movie moguls and moviegoers alike expectations of historical grandeur in his future work, expectations that he, in his megalomania, was all too eager to meet. In the teeth, therefore, of his intellectual naïveté, he went on to make other epics. *Intolerance* appeared in 1916, fourteen reels long and breathtaking in places, but unfortunate in its attempt to encompass the fall of Babylon, episodes in the life of Christ, the St. Bartholomew's Day massacre, and industrial strife in modern America. In 1918, *Hearts of the World* followed, a World War I chronicle partly made in Britain with the cooperation of the British government and nauseatingly propagandistic about the beastly Huns. And in 1922 came the inadvertently self-parodying *Orphans of the Storm,* a laughably inaccurate rendition of the French Revolution made more laughable by an overlay of anti-Bolshevik parable and notable mainly because it marked Lillian Gish's final appearance as an actress for Griffith.

In the final weeks of 1918, Griffith turned away from the seductions of history and in eighteen days and nights of work made *Broken Blossoms,* based in part, but only in part, on Thomas Burke's short story "The Chink and the Child." For all of its lapses into Victorian sentimentality, its low-life tableaux, remarkable transitions of light and shadow and psychopathological outcome gave it the look and feel of some of the greatest pictures of the twenties.

Gish at the time of the filming was still the director's premier actress, but the imminent doom of their association was plain to see in his admiration for the much less talented Carol Dempster—just turned eighteen and his newest mistress. Very soon he would be assigning parts to Dempster that ought by rights to have been Gish's. But although he toyed with the idea, he did not deny Gish the role of the battered fifteen-year-old Lucy in *Broken Blossoms*. Lucy's nightmare relationship with her sadistic father, the boxer known as Battling Burrows, and her dream relationship with a youthfully sensitive Yellow Man contained opportunities for dramatizing how he felt about Gish that were simply too rich for Griffith to pass by, and Gish herself rose to the challenge of the material by giving what she always would regard as her finest performance for him.

As the movie opens, the Yellow Man is preparing to leave China in order to carry Buddha's "glorious message of peace to the barbarian Anglo-Saxons, sons of turmoil and strife." It is an ambition that recalls the idealism of a young man out of Kentucky who believed that he could make the art of the movies serve the cause of universal peace. The sordid realities of life in the Limehouse district of London prove to be impervious, however, to the Yellow Man's plans, and he retreats into opium-intoxicated reveries. In a characteristic pose, he stands outside his small shop, leaning against the wall with his back curved and his arms wrapped around his body in a lonely self-protective embrace. Yet if his gaze often appears to be directed inward, he also is stirred by the sight in his neighborhood of the poignant figure of Lucy Burrows.

Lucy has been raised by Battling Burrows from the time she was a baby, when one of the many women in the boxer's life thrust her into his arms and disappeared. A swaggering bully with a taste for strong drink, Burrows makes Lucy wait on him slavishly, beats her with a whip, and constantly makes threatening gestures in her direction, for her jitteriness acts like a sadomasochistic come-on, inflaming him further. In her moments alone, it becomes clear that she is still a little girl who yearns for her lost mother. Yet she is not dreaming of a traditional woman's role for herself, because a housewife burdened with a large family of children has warned her against such a fate, and even prostitutes have advised her not to follow in their footsteps. Unable to define the liberation she wants, she merely lives from day to day, in the fear that at some point her father's temper will explode cataclysmically—and finally it does.

Faint with pain from a truly ferocious beating, Lucy staggers away and at last collapses in the Yellow Man's shop. He daubs her wounded shoulder with a cloth and impulsively leans forward to kiss her, but withdraws when she offers no sign of consent. Upstairs in an apartment crammed with Oriental bric-a-brac, he wins her wide-eyed gratitude by dressing her in a Chinese robe, giving her a doll to play with, and placing her in his bed. The erotics of voyeurism have taken many notable forms in the movies; this scene is one of them. To begin with, Griffith enlisted the talents of a special-effects cameraman, Hendrik Sartov. Sartov worked with a single-element lens that was full of the aberrations of glasswork. But if stopped down to a certain point, the aberrations not only created a soft focus that eliminated facial wrinkles, but cast an enchanting sparkle on catch lights in the eyes and on the lips. With the camera close in upon her, Lucy's face is a white blossom, irradiated with light. Ravished by her beauty, the Yellow Man leans forward once more to kiss her, only to restrain himself again with an enormous effort. At the same time that *Broken Blossoms* is a plea for international love and understanding, it defines racial difference as a gulf that the Yellow Man cannot bridge.

When informed of Lucy's presence in the Yellow Man's apartment, her father flies into a jealous rage, filling the air with racial epithets. This reaction and those that follow it expose the sexual pathology inherent in his sadism. He goes to the apartment and finds his daughter there alone. The camera shifts back and forth from his glowering face to the terror-stricken Lucy's. He smashes every Oriental object within reach, orders Lucy to put on her old clothes, and force-marches her home. At once he makes clear that he intends to beat her. Lucy runs into a closet and locks the door. The ensuing scene of assault on a young female in an enclosed space looks back to Griffith's suspense thrillers and forward, as Andrew Sarris has observed, to two homages to it from Alfred Hitchcock—Anthony Perkins's murderous strike at Janet Leigh through the translucent shower curtain in *Psycho* and the entrapment of Tippi Hedren in an outdoor phone booth in *The Birds*. As Burrows pounds on the door and shakes the handle, Lucy's agitation becomes almost unbearable to watch. Around and around and around she whirls in a vortex of hysteria, her arms thrashing wildly and her eyes huge. Burrows next attacks the closet with a hatchet. Back inside again, the camera shows us the hatchet blade biting through the wood. At last, Burrows breaks down the door, drags Lucy out, and flings her on a bed. Just for a few seconds, the tempo slows. Quite deliberately, he picks up his whip and oh! so gently taps it several times against her forehead. Then he beats her to death. As the camera cuts away, he is falling upon her, his arm flailing.

His own death, and the Yellow Man's, follow in quick succession. Having discovered the ruination of his shop, the Yellow Man rushes to the boxer's home and finds Lucy's body. Burrows threatens him with his hatchet, but the Yellow Man kills him with a burst of pistol shots. Back in his apartment, the Yellow Man adorns the dead Lucy in a Chinese gown and ceremonially stabs himself to death.

Was such a grim movie doomed to fail with the American public? Griffith was willing to gamble that the audience for movies was now so large that he could profitably pursue a fragment of it. Therefore, he marketed **Broken Blossoms** as an art film that would interest an elite. The New York premiere was staged in a plush legitimate playhouse, the George M. Cohan Theater, and the normal admission price to a first-run movie was tripled. A Russian balalaika orchestra was engaged to play the score of the film, apparently because its instruments made Asiatic sounds. The Cohan Theater was decorated with Chinese ornaments and Chinese costumes were provided to the ushers. Finally, a choreographer was commissioned to create a dance prologue in which a symbolic version of the movie was enacted and Griffith's mistress, Carol Dempster, was cast as the lead dancer. Well-dressed first-nighters packed the playhouse, and the major reviewers loved the movie. "A masterpiece in motion pictures," said the man from the *New York Times,* surpassing "anything hitherto seen on the screen in beauty and dramatic force." In the end, the picture returned $700,000 on an investment of $80,000.

An unusually articulate cameraman, Karl Brown, who worked for Griffith for many years, once said of the characters in **Broken Blossoms** that "they were the creatures of a poetic imagination that had at very long last found its outlet in its own way in its own terms." The result was a haunting fantasy of domination and terror, supplemented by an unforgettable portrait of an alien's emotional repression. That the object of the passions of the two men in the movie is an innocent child of fifteen—the very same age, of course, of Lillian Gish at the time of her first arrival at the Biograph studios—illustrates once again Griffith's dualism about young women. On the one hand, he was obsessed with their sexual allure; on the other hand, he had a Victorian wish to exalt them as morally pure. Directors in the

twenties both at home and abroad—von Stroheim, for instance, and von Sternberg, and G. W. Pabst—would dramatize sexual dynamics in ways that were predicated upon a far more sophisticated understanding of feminine cynicism and indifference than Griffith ever displayed. Nevertheless, D. W. Griffith's vision led to theirs. Lucy's submission to the sick cruelties of a jealous father would flower in time into the pitiless triumphs of Lulu in *Pandora's Box* and of Lola in *The Blue Angel* over older men maddened by desire.

Vance Kepley, Jr. (essay date 1991)

SOURCE: "*Intolerance* and the Soviets: A Historical Investigation," in *Inside the Film Factory: New Approaches to Russian and Soviet Cinema,* edited by Richard Taylor and Ian Christie, Routledge, 1991, pp. 51-9.

[*In the following essay, Kepley evaluates the influence* Intolerance *had on early cinema in the Soviet Union.*]

Tracing lines of influence in film history is one of the most popular endeavours among film scholars; it is also one of the most treacherous. The appearance of similar styles or conventions among different schools of film often invites premature conclusions about direct lines of descent. The historian, therefore, must penetrate below such surface observations to identify the complexities and contradictions of historical continuity if we are truly to understand the links between one cinematic movement and another.

Historians agree that the most influential early filmmaker was D. W. Griffith and that among his most precocious students were the Soviet directors of the 1920s. Furthermore, *Intolerance* is singled out as the most conspicuous link between Griffith and the Soviets, with the explanation that the radical editing style of Griffith's 1916 feature was instrumental in shaping the montage school of film which culminated in the USSR in the middle and late 1920s. *Intolerance* was admired in the Soviet Union. It was reputedly studied in the Moscow Film Institute for the possibilities of montage and 'agitational' cinema [agitfil'm], and leading Soviet directors, including Eisenstein, Pudovkin and Kuleshov, acknowledged a debt to Griffith in their writings.

Such evidence would seem to support the assumption that Griffith and *Intolerance* were of paramount importance to the Soviets. Griffith's most loyal partisans attribute many of the salient characteristics of Soviet cinema to Griffith's legacy. But more balanced studies argue that *Intolerance* was actually one of several sources for the Soviets and that the Soviet montage aesthetic originated in Russian avant-garde art, theatre and literature. An examination of the circumstances and ramifications of the distribution of *Intolerance* in the USSR will considerably qualify our assumptions about Griffith's supposed hold over the Soviets.

I

The Soviet directors of the early post-Revolutionary period were excited primarily by American films. These young artists dismissed the Russian cinema of the tsarist period, with its preponderance of love triangles and uneven literary adaptations, as hopelessly decadent. American adventure and mystery films—to which the Soviets attached the single genre label *detektiv*—captured the fancy of the Soviets. They admired the vitality and frenetic activity of these 'naive' films. Kuleshov noted of the *detektiv* that 'the fundamental element of the plot is an intensity in the development of action, the dynamic of construction'. The Soviets hoped to adapt this energetic style into an aggressive, revolutionary cinema.

The Americans offered no more impressive example of dynamic cinema than *Intolerance,* and various incidents attest to its impact in the USSR; Pudovkin abandoned a scientific career for the cinema after watching the film; *Intolerance* was so popular that in 1921 the Petrograd Cinema Committee organised an extremely successful two-week run of the film to raise funds for victims of the Civil War famine, Soviet representatives reportedly even extended Griffith an invitation to work in the USSR.

Nevertheless, other evidence indicates that we should not overestimate the film's importance—particularly as a stylistic inspiration. It would be incorrect to assume that the idea of film montage for the Soviets originated with *Intolerance*. Rather, it seems that when the film was shown in the Soviet Union in 1919, it merely popularised a style already evolving in the hands of Soviet artists. Kuleshov claims he began to forge his seminal theories well before *Intolerance* appeared in the Soviet Union. His experiments which defined the 'Kuleshov effect' apparently began as early as 1917-18. In March 1918, several months before the Russian première of *Intolerance,* Kuleshov published his theoretical essay 'The Art of Cinema', in which he argued that editing constituted the fundamental feature of film art. Vertov writes that he worked out a rapid montage style in his early film *The Battle of Tsaritsyn* [Boi pod Tsaritsynom, 1919-20]. *Intolerance* played in Russia while he was still at work on the film, and the American picture helped acquaint audiences with the mode he sought to perfect: 'After a short time there came Griffith's film *Intolerance*. After that it was easier to speak.' *Intolerance* may have been less a source than a vindication for these innovators.

Russia's familiarity with Griffith actually predated the Revolution. A number of Griffith's early Biograph shorts circulated in tsarist Russia, and at least one served as the source for a Russian film. Yakov Protazanov used the story of Griffith's *The Lonely Villa* for his *Drama by Telephone* [1914]. Protazanov's tale concerns a young wife who discovers that bandits are trying to break into her home. She immediately telephones her absent husband for help but, as he desper-

ately rushes home, the bandits break in and overpower the wife. Whereas Griffith specialised in the successful rescue, in the Russian version the husband arrives too late and discovers that his wife has been murdered. This is not the only change Protazanov makes. Anyone searching for an early link between Griffith's cross-cutting device and Soviet montage must look elsewhere. Protazanov is not concerned with the rhythm or tension of the attempted rescue, and he does not exploit parallel editing. Rather he examines the psychological states of the characters during the crisis, the terror of the woman and the panic of the husband, and he employs an elaborate split-screen system which permits the audience simultaneously to compare the emotions of the husband, wife and culprits. The Russian artist, in borrowing Griffith's tale, specifically rejects Griffith's most famous stylistic contribution to the genre.

II

The familiar story that *Intolerance* first reached the USSR after it somehow slipped through an anti-Soviet blockade is apocryphal. In fact the film was imported well before the Revolution. When the Italian spectacle *Cabiria* scored a success in Russia in 1915, it was assumed that a potential audience for spectacles existed there, and the Italian Jacques Cibrario, who headed the Transatlantic film distribution firm, brought *Intolerance* into Russia in 1916. But, although *Intolerance* overshadowed *Cabiria* in size and splendour, it was quickly labelled too avant-garde for Russian movie audiences. No Russian exhibitor would agree to handle the film for fear that audiences would be confused by the four-part structure. Consequently, the film gathered dust on a shelf somewhere in Russia until after the Revolution. Not until 1918 did a special government decision clear the way for *Intolerance* to be shown commercially in the RSFSR.

The première of *Intolerance* in Petrograd was a major cinema event for the Soviets. On 17 November 1918 the Petrograd Cinema Committee sponsored a special showing for an audience composed largely of government officials, including the Commissar for Enlightenment, Anatoli Lunacharsky. The 25 May 1919 Moscow première was part of an official celebration. The occasion was the first anniversary of so-called 'Universal Military Training', the government's Civil War programme of training Red Army conscripts. *Intolerance* warranted a special closed showing at the prestigious Moscow movie theatre, the Artistic [Khudozhestvennyi].

The Moscow première inspired an illuminating review in *Izvestiya*. The critic was impressed by the American film's scope and technical virtues, and he noted that it might serve as a model for future Soviet productions. But he dismissed the content as 'bourgeois': the theme of reconciliation and 'notorious tolerance' failed to resolve the issues of class conflict in the modern story. He suggested that *Intolerance* might be reconstructed into a thoroughly 'agitational' film by 'turning scenes around and changing titles'. His remarks identify the ideological reservations that Soviet cinephiles had about the film. The Soviets recognised that *Intolerance* was a humanist, even a somewhat leftist film. But it certainly was not a revolutionary film. For Soviet artists anxious to find a cinematic model which combined the dynamic style of the *detektiv* with the political content of the *agitfil'm*, *Intolerance* was close yet still very far. *Intolerance* had its militant moments—most notably the strike sequence—but its vague sentimental humanism left Griffith's Soviet admirers cold.

The *Izvestiya* critic advocated the re-editing of the film for commercial release to give it a proper slant. It is difficult to determine the extent to which that was done. At least one account indicates that the Christ section was abridged in the public versions of the film. But there is reason to believe that the film was not completely altered by Soviet censors. The Soviet Union was entering the most eclectic years in all Russian intellectual history. Soviet artists were borrowing from numerous cultures and political systems, and as yet there was no Stalin or Zhdanov to enforce rigid conformity.

More important, the Soviets employed a method of dealing with the ideological shortcomings of *Intolerance* that was far more ingenious and exciting than censorship. *Intolerance* was selected for presentation at the Congress of the Comintern in Petrograd in the summer of 1921. The Petrograd Cinema Committee undoubtedly hoped to impress the delegates with the potential of agitational cinema, but they were painfully aware of the film's ideological deficiencies. They decided the occasion required them to 'sharpen the class theme' of the film while at the same time respecting the author's original intentions. Their method was not to censor or cut parts of the film but rather to add to it. Nikolai Glebov-Putilovsky of the Petrograd Cinema Committee prepared a live, dramatised prologue which would 'amplify the anti-exploitation theme of the film'. The practice of adding Soviet propaganda to pre-Revolutionary works of art was common in the young socialist country. Soviet writer Demyan Bedny's satirical poem at the base of a tsarist monument is another example of this method of 'finishing' a work of art. This operation transcends censorship. It respects the integrity of the original work while at the same time allowing the Soviets to make ideological improvements. Indeed, it rather resembles Meyerhold's theatrical practice of staging classic and pre-Revolutionary plays in modern, Constructivist styles which were rich with propaganda.

It speaks well for Griffith that five years after *Intolerance* was made and almost two years after the nationalisation of the Soviet industry, the Soviets singled out this American film of dubious service to the Revolution for presentation at the Comintern Congress. Despite the shortage of celluloid, the Soviets did manage to prepare for the congress a series of documentary films on the work of the socialist government through-

out the Soviet Union. But these apparently were rather pedestrian educational films. For an impressive example of *agitfil'm, Intolerance* may still have seemed the most palatable choice available. Also, the American epic undoubtedly had a more cosmopolitan appeal to the international audience than a strict diet of Soviet films would have had. In any event, the Cinema Committee was willing to sacrifice ideological purity to entertain and edify the socialist audience. The prologue would give the evening the proper dose of revolutionary spirit, and the movie would take care of itself.

The prologue allowed the Soviets to comment on the film and to add their own interpretations to certain scenes. The most glaring problem for the Soviets was the film's insistent theme that history is cyclical. *Intolerance* advances the argument that the same cycles of intolerance and injustice simply recur in different historical dress. Basic impulses and human emotions, the fundamental forces in all human endeavours, are as consistent as the hand that rocks the cradle. Not surprisingly, the same dilemmas appear in epoch after epoch. This is hardly compatible with a Marxist, economic-determinist philosophy which considers history progressive and dialectical.

The prologue goes about uniting Marx and Griffith with considerable finesse. Generally, the prologue seizes on certain vivid images of suffering and injustice in the film and casts these in a Marxist framework. The prologue opens with a call to those assembled:

> Hear ye, hear ye, O people! . . . Hear, ye who have come hither: men and women, young and old—and behold! Beyond your life in the distant depths of history you will see a broad road that the human race has been following for thousands of years.

Already it is clear that the delegates are in for a history class. The prologue emphatically proclaims that the lessons of *Intolerance* are the lessons of the past. The road is the central metaphor of the first half of the prologue, and on it can be seen the bitter teachings of history. A look down the road reveals countless examples of hardship in the lot of the common people. For example, the Girl is 'tossed by the evil hand of life into the mud and dust'.

The road reveals something of a dialectic and a clear class conflict in the constant presence of opposites. The powerful and the weak, the exploiter and the exploited, are always present: 'The ancient patrician and the plebeian, the king and his serf, Babylon and a simple settlement, love and hate, light and darkness'.

The road metaphor disappears in the second half of the prologue and new imagery emerges. Now ancient mountains represent history. Out of these mountains of the past flow four small streams, the four tales of the film. The streams run in separate but parallel paths, suggesting the flux and turmoil of history—a counterpoint to the static, awesome mountains. We again see images of exploitation with the stories of *Intolerance*.

> Millions and billions of riches, created by slave labour and legally accumulated by those who have seized control of the law: the factory owners, the governors, the public prosecutors, the emperors and their fine retinue of concubines and lackeys. . . .
>
> The French Court with its overdressed dolls and a gallows demanding a sacrifice. A smoke-filled episode of religious baseness from the stately priests and St Bartholomew's Eve; a humble carpenter from Galilee; clean-handed Pilate and the wild instincts of the crowd, shouting, 'Crucify Him! Crucify Him!'

The prologue concludes with a promise of ultimate salvation from this history of cruelty. The four currents flow down the mountains unto a gentle plain where they merge into one stream. This is, in a sense, the synthesis, and it leads to the Soviet utopia 'In the beautiful valley of life'. The film shows the ugly lessons of the past, but for the future there is the promise of the Soviet system: from 'the mire and slime and rottenness, from which we emerged with pain and torment towards the radiant Soviets: towards our temples of labour and liberty, through which we shall resurrect everything. The prologue then ends with an affirmation and a rallying cry reminiscent of a varsity cheer:

> The Soviets! The Soviets!—the earth hums.
> The road of the Soviets—the Soviets are our salvation!!!

By insisting that the stories of *Intolerance* represent some dreadful past, the Soviets could fit the film into a Marxist schema which promises a glorious future. The utopian vision in the prologue is no less naive than the film's coda which calls for an era of brotherhood when prison walls will dissolve. Griffith invests his faith in an amorphous notion of brotherly love, and the Soviets celebrate an equally dubious confidence in the ability of socialism to eradicate all strife. The reconciliation between Marx and Griffith proved an ingenious, albeit tenuous one.

The prologue's metaphor of the parallel streams originated in a playbill which accompanied the New York premiére of *Intolerance*:

> Our theme is told in four little stories.
>
> These stories begin like four currents, looked at from a hilltop. As they flow they grow nearer and nearer together, and faster and faster, 'until in the end, in the last act, they mingle in one mighty river of expressed emotion'.
>
> Then you see that, though they seem unlike, through all of them runs one thought, one theme.

The metaphor here is restricted to describing the structure of the film itself. The four stories merge in the last reel of *Intolerance* through cross-cutting to create an emotional climax, 'one mighty river of expressed emotion'. The Soviet prologue expands the metaphor into a historical one. Significantly, Eisenstein's celebrated analysis of *Intolerance* in 'Dickens, Griffith, and the Film Today', specifically cites the American playbill's stream metaphor to analyse Griffith's montage. He argues that Griffith's film, contrary to the claim set out in the playbill, fails to achieve a true synthesis of tales. For him, Griffith's montage is not truly dialectical, and he claims *Intolerance* remains a drama of comparisons—'a combination of *four different stories,* rather than a *fusion of four phenomena* into *a single imagist generalisation*'. The Soviet prologue subtly apologises for the ideological faults of *Intolerance,* and Eisenstein, who borrows the same metaphor from the same source, exposes what he considers the film's formal problems. In honouring Griffith, the Soviets were compelled to criticise him.

This investigation of the early history of *Intolerance* in Russia reveals some of the hazards of too-easy assumptions of historical continuity. The evidence on the Soviet reception of *Intolerance* raises questions about the actual extent of the Soviet debt to Griffith that can only be resolved through meticulous stylistic comparisons of the work of the early Soviets and that of Griffith—not to mention such Griffith contemporaries as Ince, King, Feuillade and Gance. As present it seems clear that for all the attention the Soviets lavished on *Intolerance,* it was as important to them for its flaws as for its virtues.

Scott Simmon (essay date 1992)

SOURCE: "'The Female of the Species': D. W. Griffith, Father of the Woman's Film," in *Film Quarterly,* Vol. XLVI, No. 2, Winter, 1992-93, pp. 8-20.

[*In the following essay, Simmon maintains that Griffith was the progenitor of the "woman's film" and probes the director's use of females in such movies as* A Flash of Light *and* The Painted Lady.]

Traditionally, D. W. Griffith is credited as "father" of a host of cinematic techniques and Hollywood patterns. If he is to be given progenitive tags at all, he deserves a more surprising one as "The Father of the Woman's Film"—and deserves too all the psychosexual conflicts such paternity entails.

"The woman's film" has always been as elusive as its evolving names, from the concise gender/genre affront of "the woman's weepie" to the academically neutered "melodrama." One might suspect that something of the elusiveness arises from its being an oppositional genre, as it were, definable only in opposition to genres tracing the ambitions of male heroes. But such an explanation won't do in Griffith's era: his woman's films reveal mature narrative form *before* the genres centering on goal-driven men. (Earlier Westerns had yet to rely on the lone cowboy hero, significant only gradually after 1909 with the first "Broncho Billy" films.) The unexpected complexity of even the earliest and most cinematically primitive of Griffith's woman's films arises partly from his evident difficulties in wrestling directly with the rapid shifts in family patterns in the opening decade of the twentieth century, shifts he could dramatize more metaphorically elsewhere.

Through close to a hundred one-and two-reelers (the least innocent hundred) of the 450 he made for the Biograph company between 1908 and 1913, Griffith fundamentally outlined the sound-era variations on the woman's film. During its Hollywood heyday in the 1930s and 1940s, the woman's film tended to fall into subgenres loosely defined by whether the woman who suffers within domestic confines was seen as a daughter (e.g., *Now, Voyager, Johnny Belinda*), a wife (*Rebecca, A Letter to Three Wives*), a mother (*Stella Dallas, Imitation of Life*), or a "fallen" woman (*Ladies of Leisure, Back Street*). We can glance here at a few of Griffith's curious opening arguments for the genre through three early one-reelers: *The Fascinating Mrs. Francis* (1909), with its fallen woman; *A Flash of Light* (1910), with its (doubled) wife; and *The Painted Lady* (1912), with its anguished daughter.

There is, it soon becomes clear, an unresolvable conflict at the core of Griffith's project in his woman's films, and we need to acknowledge it if we are to make much sense of our three samples. That conflict might be simply suggested by looking briefly at a one-reel domestic drama of Griffith's from 1909 which is not strictly a woman's film—its main sympathy is with a man's suffering—called *To Save Her Soul*. As it opens, a "little choir singer" (Mary Pickford) seems to have a crush on the minister (Arthur Johnson), although romance is sidetracked when a vaudeville manager, his automobile broken down outside the rural church, hears her voice and offers her a slot at his music hall. After the work of rehearsals, her debut is a triumph, as the increasingly fretful minister discovers through a newspaper review. While visiting the music hall to see her onstage, he overhears a sharply dressed stage-door-Johnny bragging of his after-hours date with the singer. Thus, as a title puts it, the minister "finds her fate is that of the oft told story and resolves to save her." She looks in no particular need of a savior when he bursts into a banquet in honor of her triumph, although he sees her dressed in her stage costume, standing on a chair and drinking champagne in response to a toast. In an anteroom, she shuns his pleas to return to their village, gesturing instead to her body, as if in reference to her new life or achievement. He settles the argument by pulling a gun on her: "Crazed by jealous love, he would kill her that her soul may remain pure." This climax releases, somehow, mutual love. Last seen, the couple is back in the church, hugging while kneeling in prayer.

There are a couple of fairly obvious reasons why this story line might be troubling now, not least of which is the singer's motivation at the climax. The film is also a pretty clear melodramatic parable, reconstituting devout harmony away from threats that arise should women enter into the public space (a worry behind most of Griffith's domestic tales, filmed as the proportion of women in the work force was increasing dramatically). From this angle, *To Save Her Soul* would be at best a retrograde, thoroughly patriarchal, desperately inauthentic little film.

However, the conflict within it runs deeper—deeper even than the familiar complaint that Griffith's story lines are drearily "Victorian" and only redeemed for us by his innovations in cinematic form. Essentially, the conflict within a film such as *To Save Her Soul* is that its morality can't begin to mesh with the whole ontology of the cinema-going apparatus—the situation of spectatorship and film viewing. To put it simply, Griffith is *creating* the very forces that his woman's film story lines most often fight against. *To Save Her Soul,* that is, makes a moralistic argument for traditional, church-centered values and against the dangerous public display and fame of its woman character. However, the film itself gets its genuine verve and wit from the display of Mary Pickford—who indeed is never more freshly seductive than in these Biographs—right from the opening shot, when her character stages a fall off the choir rail, manipulating her way into the minister's not-too-reluctant arms. The conflict in this film and so many like it can be reduced to a content/form split in this sense: the story line takes its stand against what the film-going situation promotes—the public display of women.

To the extent, then, that Griffith's woman's films argue that American society is best served by maintaining women in private, family spaces, those films, almost by the very nature of their being films, are divided against themselves. One would think that it shouldn't be possible to argue for long (in narrative) that a woman had best *not* be displayed and (in form) that she *should* be, without the deepest hypocrisy becoming terribly clear. To put this more positively, however, it is possible that film form *necessarily* subverted Griffith's older moralism, whatever his story lines seemed to argue. He was probably neither so innocent nor so confused about this conflict as I've implied thus far. Even *To Save Her Soul* doesn't treat with anything like a straight face the process through which the minister returns Pickford to her presumably rightful place in the village church. Rather, the film borrows a staple figure from nineteenth-century women-authored, so-called "domestic" fiction—the noble but too intellectual minister who represses his authentic emotions—and, as in many of those novels, converts his male certitude into a source of drama and droll comedy (here represented in his pompously self-dramatizing arm gestures and clenched fists, leading to his eruption with the gun). In domestic novels, the minister was regularly the most sought-after of husbands for his relatively more feminized sensitivity and for the presumption that a minister's wife would share in her husband's work more fully than the wife of a businessman. *To Save Her Soul* doesn't forget this figure of the minister so emotionally repressed that his love can only be explosive (a pattern drawn from popular memory in the ministerial sex scandals of the 1860s and 1870s, notably Henry Ward Beecher's, and remembered in more canonical fiction through *The Scarlet Letter*'s Dimmesdale).

One of the traits that gives the genre of the woman's film such enduring fascination is the way it carries within it certain "resistances" to its overt arguments: the repressive narratives are regularly undercut, partly via mise-en-scène and acting but also by conflicts within the narratives themselves. Such resistances are sometimes presumed to have begun with Douglas Sirk's ironies in his postwar American woman's films, but even the purest examples of the genre, such as King Vidor's 1937 version of *Stella Dallas,* with its story line ending in the social "eradication" of the mother, *also* holds a counter-story of Stella's personal triumph over the patriarchal world around her—or at least of her refusal to submit to it. Part of this resistance to the story line comes via acting—as in Barbara Stanwyck's expression of triumph in the final fade-out—and some of it, as I've suggested, comes from the very ontology of film itself (displaying for us what the world within the film presumes as eradicated). The surprise, in looking back to Griffith, is less that he originates the genre but that he outlines its mature form, with its repressions certainly but with its resistances as well. *To Save Her Soul* reestablishes a patriarchal, indeed phallic, order, but not without mocking the agent who so little understands his motivation for whipping out his gun. Whether Griffith himself knew quite what he was doing must probably remain an open question.

In its eight shots running 417 feet (or about six minutes), *The Fascinating Mrs. Francis* sets forth the essential paradigm of the woman's film. Its primitive style—exclusively proscenium interior shots—only reinforces that this film is present at the creation, a sense deepened by the surrealistically primal emotions arising from various irresistible attractions and fickle changes of heart within unbroken shots. The central figure of the little family drama is the title's "Mrs. Francis," a lovely, dark woman with flowers in her hair, who is surrounded by admiring men in the first shot and left alone and despondent in the final one. As the film opens she is center of attention as a singer in an upper-class private musical evening. Chief among her admirers is the host's tuxedoed son, who is so quickly drawn into obsessive, suicidal desire that (in the film's second shot) Mrs. Francis receives a visit from the wealthy father who pleads with her to, presumably, free his son from her charms. (As with most of Griffith's earliest films, the original intertitles are lost.) Mrs. Francis's room is dominated by a large mirror—the first, unless I'm mistaken, in a Griffith film—evoking, rather uncomplicatedly here, the painterly iconography of vanity and narcissism. After initially resisting the father's

plea, Mrs. Francis puts on a masterful act to make herself less socially attractive by ostentatiously coarsening her habits: drinking liquor out of large mugs (in the company of two of Biograph's broadest buffoons, Mack Sennett and John Cumpson), smoking cigarettes (an act for which, committed in public, she could have been arrested), and generally adopting large, "male" gestures, including wrapping her arm around the son (a gesture he seems to find particularly repugnant). Her masterstroke in repelling the son comes when she instructs another, younger woman in the exact physical tricks necessary to attract him. Thus Mrs. Francis stage-manages the restoration of the family.

In this brief film, Griffith sets up two prototypical images of desire: a complex image of the woman who must finally be avoided and a blander image of the marriageable one. The former is Mrs. Francis (as there is no "Mr. Francis" in evidence, she may be a divorcée), played by the vibrant Marion Leonard, whom Griffith often typecast as the disruptive third side of a love triangle: a "capricious woman" (*The Jilt*), a "discontented" one (*Fools of Fate*), a "cold hearted woman of society" (*Two Memories*) or, worst of all, one in his line of wives who neglect their children for some social frivolity (*Through the Breakers*). Interestingly, Marion Leonard is also "The Gibson Goddess" in his 1909 film of that title (that is, a woman of ideal beauty as arbitrated for his era by the illustrator Charles Dana Gibson), who is pursued at a seaside resort by a pack of harassing men until she has the inspiration to roll cotton into her leggings, leaving the men scurrying away under the discovery of perfection deformed. Gibson's curvaceous image of desire is only evoked by Griffith as a split-reel joke, and his casting of Marion Leonard also hints that Gibson's ideal wasn't his. The Gibson girl may have been on her way out of fashion by 1909 but that's partly Griffith's own doing, to the extent that his films were becoming the most popular mass images of their day, replacing Gibson's sexualized but static images of desire with Griffith's virginal but dynamic charmers.

As stripped down and paradigmatic of the genre as *The Fascinating Mrs. Francis* is, it still has room for "resistances" to its main argument. It is, in particular, keenly aware of its woman's images as artificially created through demeanor and gesture. The wealthy father, after all, first demonstrates to Mrs. Francis exactly how to physically assume the role of loose woman, as in his stumble round her room to teach a mock-drunken gait. Mrs. Francis proves a quick study and extends such manufactured gestures by showing the other woman (Florence Lawrence) exactly how to fake another variety of leg-clutching stumble and thus how to display herself as a weak woman in need of the son's assistance. That second woman is not without her own resourceful touches, adding to her elegant stumble a dropped rose, bait which the son cannot resist.

In the final essential generic moment, all of Mrs. Francis's clever manipulation must, in this domestic context, take its toll. She watches the son walk into the next room arm-in-arm with his newfound ideal, then shakes her head at the dollars offered from his wallet by the father (as unfeeling a man as the genre will regularly feature). Instead, she leans over to pick up and smell the dropped rose, which the new lovers have by now forgotten. As described in the *Biograph Bulletin* (a flyer for theater owners and trade papers), her "act amounts to self-immolation." Mrs. Francis becomes a lonely onlooker of the happiness of others, a happiness made possible by an "act" that extends her image as the "bad woman."

What is so surprising is that even here in 1909, at the origins of the genre, Griffith is producing a woman's film that is both conventional *and* a deconstruction of its images, revealing them as artifices consciously manufactured. In the terms that Mary Ann Doane takes from Luce Irigaray, this 1909 film must be said to contain progressive "double mimesis," enacting cultural notions of femininity in such a way as to "make visible . . . what was supposed to remain invisible." What one has to conclude from finding this reputedly feminist pattern in Griffith's original is that such resistances have *always* been an essential feature of the genre.

With *A Flash of Light* in the following year, 1910, we move into a vastly wilder melodrama—with every emotional and narrative stop pulled—which nevertheless expresses specific social worries about the ideal of "wife" in an era of increasing divorce.

Our attention is initially focused on a young research chemist (Charles West) and his marriage to the younger, more vivacious of two sisters (Vivian Prescott). The older sister (Stephanie Longfellow) is shown crying alone after the wedding, but holds her love a secret as she suffers in silence in the extended household (which includes the chemist's father, his adolescent sister, and servants). Despite efforts by the chemist to interest his wife in his laboratory experiments and the weighty books that go with them, she prefers (an intertitle tells us) "the outside world's glitter" and is off at an elegant party when a chemical explosion leaves her husband blind and deaf, despite the immediate ministrations of her sister. "Annoyed by his helplessness," the wife grabs an opportunity "to shine on the comic opera stage" and, with a new life thus arranged, writes to her husband's father announcing her intention "to get a divorce. Have entered the theatrical profession, where I hope to make a name." She returns home only to toss her wedding ring on a table. In a gesture the film takes as selfless, the good sister slips the wedding ring on her own finger so that the chemist mistakes her for his wife, "to deceive him until his affliction is passed." Some time later, the doctors perform an operation, convinced that they will be able to restore his sight and hearing. With reluctance, the estranged wife agrees to return—and to take back the ring—for the delicate moment when the bandages are to be removed from her husband's eyes. In the superbly melodramatic conclusion, the bandages are

unwound, and the husband is able to see the wife he presumes to have stood by him devotedly, but she, instinctively retreating and stumbling away, knocks down the heavy black curtains, allowing in a flash of sunlight which brings blindness *again,* this time "incurable". But in his instant of sight, the husband has apparently recognized the disdain in his wife and the devotion of the sister. The film ends with the chemist down on his knees, kissing the hem of the long-suffering sister, whose true love is now acknowledged by all. "A strongly dramatic picture, yet not altogether pleasant," in *Moving Picture World*'s understatement (July 30, 1910).

The implications of the astonishing, quite entertainingly played conclusion are worth teasing out. Clearly the wife is no mere bystander to her husband's tragedy but *causes* his blindness, literally so in allowing sunlight to cause the "incurable" condition. And it takes only a small metaphorical leap to assign blame to her for his initial blindness as well, brought by the bright flash of the chemical explosion, which follows hard on her desire to be *seen* outside the home, by her preferring the world's "glitter," by her desire to "shine" on stage. In the visual metaphors of the film, she seeks more light than her husband's eyes can tolerate. That such desire is reprehensible is reinforced by what one might call Griffith's "ethical intercutting" between the wife at her brilliant party and the husband working away in his windowless basement lab. If the ethical contrast looks less stark than in Griffith's more celebrated intercutting between, say, oppressed poor and oppressive stock manipulators in *A Corner in Wheat,* it is nevertheless hardly less difficult to pinpoint the villain of the piece: this would-be independent wife, seeking the light.

The film overtly takes its stand against the tyranny of superficial sight and first appearances by which the vivacious younger sister initially attracts the chemist. The *Biograph Bulletin* for the film glosses it this way: "The sight of a pretty face . . . nearly always intoxicates us to such degree as to make us believe that our impulses are induced by the heart and soul. . . . It is by the sight we are hypnotized." Thus the love of the older sister was ignored by the chemist when he could see. The moral here is familiar enough from a hundred fables. And yet, as a film-maker, Griffith once more runs up against that deep conflict we noted in connection with *To Save Her Soul*: silent film form must again rely on exactly that tyranny of sight against which the conventional morality of the narrative tries to take its stand. "A flash of light" twice blinds the chemist, but the phrase is also definitional of the silent film apparatus, and the wife *will* be seen by us, come what may.

The reverse image of the light-loving wife is the long-suffering sister. Her *worry* about being seen—about what she will have to give up when the husband regains his sight—is signified by her discomfort at the doctor's optimistic prognostications and her stiff-gestured stoicism at the return of the wedding ring before the unbandaging. The long-standing woman's film concern about the *price* of being an object on display—Laura Mulvey's "to-be-looked-at-ness"—is melodramatized in a number of Griffith films, and most profoundly so in the film we will come to next, *The Painted Lady*. Two earlier Griffith woman's films anticipate the good sister's worry about the tyranny of sight in *A Flash of Light: The Way of Man* (1909; whose title refers to a man's repulsion over a tiny scar presumed to disfigure Florence Lawrence's face after a lamp explosion; she nobly fakes her own suicide and runs off to live as a foster mother in an orphan asylum, leaving her man happily wed to her cousin) and *The Light That Came* (1909; in which a woman, despite her anxiety over another facial scar, funds an operation that will restore sight to her blind fiancé).

The nobility in these Griffith heroines comes from not simply a willingness but a *preference* to work unseen, to sacrifice in ways unrecognized. This trait brings Griffith to the venerable dilemma involved in trying to bring such women to the center of heroic narratives *without* violating their defining passivity. *A Flash of Light* resolves the conflict through a device that would have been familiar to readers of the nineteenth-century domestic novel—one that has been labeled "the mutilation of the male"—in which the virtuous woman, who would normally suffer in silence, is paired with a man crippled or otherwise stricken, whose very condition demands from her a more active, nearly equal life. There is a telling gesture at the end of Griffith's *Through Darkened Vales* (1911)—a "male" gesture legitimated, in this one context, for a woman—when Blanche Sweet wraps her arm high over the shoulder of her long-humiliated and now-blind suitor to guide him into her yard. The best-known precursor of the pattern, Rochester's crippling in Charlotte Brontë's *Jane Eyre,* has been taken as a woman's fantasy of revenge through emasculation, but at least in the American tradition, the mutilations also double as social dreams. Helen Papashvily described the pattern in her pioneering and witty study of the domestic novel: "If in some way the power of the male could be diminished or removed, then neither conscience nor society would censure the brave woman forced to act on her own initiative."

Griffith allows the patient sister a triumph on just such terms, justifying through mutilation actions which work out to her own one-sided demand for marriage. (Just what is taking place during the long dark nights between husband and substitute wife is a question this light-obsessed film doesn't go into.) A parallel among the domestic novelists would be Mary Jane Holmes' *Darkness and Daylight* (1864), with its blind young man, who, as Papashvily suggests about Holmes' males generally, is "no longer a protagonist" but "a trophy, a token prize for the victor."

And that is just about how the climax works out in *A Flash of Light,* as interest shifts to the battle between the two sisters and away from a husband who ends the film still maimed (if presumably with *hearing* restored).

Indeed, the two sisters, who double as one woman in the husband's mind, are transformed by melodrama into competing *ideas* about the role of "wife," a split self, as it were. The pattern was vastly popular among domestic novelists, as, famously, with the cold and generous sisters of Mary Jane Holmes' *Tempest and Sunshine* (1854). Those sisters also compete over a young man who (of course) chooses the vivacious, heartless sister ("Tempest") and on his deathbed mistakes the faithful, good sister ("Sunshine") for her. As film, Griffith's *A Flash of Light* is a precursor to a favorite pattern within Hollywood's woman's films: the doppelgänger sisters, one evil, one "normal" (later often played by the same actress), whose opposed personalities and moral positions battle over one very confused man (as with the two Blanche Sweets in *The Secret Sin* [1915] or, in the noir era, the two Bette Davises in *A Stolen Life* and the two Olivia De Havillands in *The Dark Mirror*). In *A Flash of Light,* the "evil twin" is, to simplify her only slightly, the wife whose craze for an independent "name" leads her to the extreme option of divorce, while the "good twin" demonstrates the wifely ideal, even if she must promote marriage on her own initiative from a husband "blind" to her value.

Among the first signs that the restless wife in *A Flash of Light* falls short of the ideal are several shots of her reading or holding a cheap paperbound book. The implication—reinforced by a tradition in painting—is that only an idle woman has leisure unoccupied by procreation or other domestic work. (The moralism is explicit in another Griffith film of 1910, unambiguously titled *A Salutary Lesson,* in which the wife is so "strongly addicted to the reading of cheap novels" that the care of her daughter becomes "odious.") *A Flash of Light* is vague about the length of the marriage before the wife puts down her books to seek her "name" and divorce, but the lack of children may also warn against what Teddy Roosevelt was calling "wilful sterility" or "race suicide" among the upper class. The specific blame assigned to the wife in the film can be found in divorce records of the era, as old complaints over a spouse's indulgence in "night life" were beginning to be voiced not as they had been traditionally by wives, but by husbands (as evening amusements became legitimated for women). The worry that the film takes up is not simply that divorce was rapidly increasing (after remaining almost static through the nineteenth century) but that it was also shifting from a man's to a woman's option.

The contrasting figure of the good wife gets Griffith's most complex portrayal in *The Mothering Heart* (1913). In *A Flash of Light,* she initially hovers at the edge of the frame, with the stoicism of Griffith's women-waiting-at-the-seashore films (*Lines of White on a Sullen Sea* [1909], *The Unchanging Sea* [1910], etc.), until the husband's mutilation provides her with opportunities. Such heroic passivity worked its way to Griffith via nineteenth-century stage melodrama. As the heroine declaims with winning directness in a play by John Howard Payne (whose life is the subject of Griffith's feature *Home, Sweet Home*), "I can only wait patiently for the storm to burst on my head and trust to heaven for deliverance."

The Painted Lady (1912), to my mind one of Griffith's greatest films, is a tragedy of a daughter's attempted rebellion from the family. For a one-reeler it's quite elaborate, and with a camera speed down to approximately 14 frames-per-second it runs, properly projected, to over 18 minutes (in 65 shots, excluding titles).

Even trade journals recognized something rare. "The subtlety of it makes it a very hard picture to comment on; one hesitates as before jumping into a very deep pool," said *Moving Picture World* (November 9, 1912). The focus is on an eldest daughter (Blanche Sweet), favorite of her bearded, black-garbed father. The film opens on the day of a church-supervised "Ice-Cream Festival," a wholesome meeting place for the town's young women and men. The vibrant younger sister (Madge Kirby), primping at home before a mirror, demonstrates face powder and eyebrow plucking for her more primly dressed sister. As if in demonstration of the younger sister's advice that "You must paint and powder to be attractive," the men who crowd around her at the festival pointedly avoid her older sister, who retreats into a secluded bower to weep quietly. She is interrupted by the genial, trusting minister, who introduces her to a handsome "stranger" (Joseph Graybill)—who we have earlier been told is a "plotter." Though her father politely refuses him entry into their home, he soon becomes "her first sweetheart" after she sneaks out the window for clandestine meetings at their bower. Eager for his compliments, especially of her face, she solemnly rubs her cheeks and shakes her head to explain that she uses no makeup. At home, she can now gaze into the mirror with pleasure. Chatting freely at one of their meetings, she apparently reveals the location of her father's strongbox—after which the stranger gives her what seems to be a first kiss. He now has the information he needs to break into the family home, his face hidden by a kerchief. She confronts him at gunpoint and he is killed in their struggle over the gun. At the discovery of his identity, she is "shattered." Weeks go by but she is still sneaking out to reenact imaginary meetings in the bower with her dead lover, obsessively replaying the conversation about her face, unfazed by the mockery of passing children and at one point introducing the invisible figure to an older woman (presumably her nurse, or possibly her mother). Eventually, she is "tempted" by face powder to shade her now even paler face. But following that day's imaginary conversation, she gazes at her powdered face in a small mirror on the base of her purse. Seeing herself proves, somehow, a final, fatal shock. Her father arrives only in time to catch her collapsing body.

It is possible to take this really quite extraordinarily strange film as another in Griffith's cautionary tales: about the conflict between older, authentic, home-centered morality and the threats to it by modern tempta-tions, here represented by cosmetics and all that using them implies in this context about abandoning parental authority for consumer culture. Thus the film would illustrate the sort of puritanical fretting still filling newspaper advice columns well into World War I—as with a concerned young woman writing to the *Jewish Daily Forward* in 1915: "Is it a sin to use face powder? Shouldn't a girl look beautiful? My father does not want me to use face powder. Is it a sin?" From that angle, the film also warns against a growing consumerist faith in "youthful beauty" promoted by the burgeoning cosmetics industry, as sociologists Robert and Helen Lynd found in their study of evolving "Middletown" attitudes between the 1890s and 1920s. One might also see a continuation of Griffith's warnings about the hazards for women of public spaces—even one so apparently innocent as the Ice-Cream Festival—running back to an early Biograph like *The Honor of Thieves* (1909), in which a smooth thief picks up a trusting Jewish girl at a dance hall only in order to rob her pawnbroker father.

If one hesitates to lump *The Painted Lady* among such relatively simple cautionary tales, it's not because Griffith progressed away from them. As late as *The White Rose* (1923), the source of innocent orphan Mae Marsh's sexual tragedy (leading to an illegitimate child) is the moment when she is taught to apply makeup, an ironic reminder of which returns at the wildly melodramatic finale when makeup is applied to cover her pallor at her deathbed marriage. What moves *The Painted Lady* beyond the cautionary tales is partly its complexity in dramatizing the pressures for modern conformity and its way of suggesting, within the claustrophobic bower, the diminishing space for the unmarried woman generally (as the percentage of unmarried women *decreased* in the early years of the century and average marriage age grew younger). Additionally, this mirror-obsessed woman's film takes on complex questions about the price of being gazed upon. As such, it has parallels with sophisticated novels of a few years before, memorably Stephen Crane's *Maggie: A Girl of the Streets* (1893) and Edith Wharton's *The House of Mirth* (1905), which plot ever more confining, ultimately fatal tragedies of women who are "looked" into being, who take their self-definitions from the way they are looked upon by others. Crane's Maggie is deemed a "looker" in the sense that men look her into existence until, abandoned as a little-noticed streetwalker, she loses even her name in the narrative. In *The House of Mirth* (the masterwork among the era's novels about women confined by the gaze), Lily Bart has a beauty that is analyzed or employed as a weapon by everyone, including Lily herself, who begins to be frightened by defects revealed by the mirror, "two little lines near her mouth, faint flaws in the smooth curve of her cheek."

The Painted Lady is structured around five scenes of Blanche Sweet's character gazing at herself in mirrors: with uncertainty after the lessons in makeup from her sister; with satisfaction after the certification of her physical worth by the stranger; and ultimately with horror in her final self-assessment leading to her death. The mirror prop moves beyond the simple symbol of narcissism as in *The Fascinating Mrs. Francis,* and its implications about the woman viewed also move the film beyond those essentially cautionary tales about women who opt for the public space of the musical stage in *To Save Her Soul* and *A Flash of Light*. The mirror scenes in *The Painted Lady* scrutinize women from just the opposite angle, not as public display but rather as secret views of a woman contemplating herself and who presumes herself alone—woman as "surveyor" of her own identity (as John Berger put it in his influential survey of images of woman and mirrors). And the insecurity that keeps Sweet's character returning to the mirror in the first half of the film is not unconnected with her tragedy of obsession in the second half. Griffith here introduces to the movies, via the prop of the mirror, certain psychological interrogations and social inquiries about women's roles which America's best novelists had grappled with not so many years earlier, as in *The House of Mirth*; or Henry James's *The Wings of the Dove* (1902; whose subtly manipulative heroine opens the novel "star[ing] into the tarnished glass too hard indeed to be staring at her beauty alone"); or Theodore Dreiser's *Sister Carrie* (1900; whose heroine practices in the mirror seductive gestures that her man, Drouet, has admired in other women). At its most uncompromising, this novelistic tradition carried its perceptions to a logical end, with heroines who escape visual scrutiny into death, typically suicides by drowning (as with Crane's Maggie and Edna Pontellier of Kate Chopin's *The Awakening*). Griffith tried this narrative, not very convincingly, in *The Sands of Dee* (1912), where the innocent country heroine drowns herself after becoming the subject of a painting by a wandering artist. From this angle, even *Broken Blossoms* (1919) looks like the story of a young woman whose tentative examination of her newly discovered beauty in the Chinese shopkeeper's mirror is a harbinger of her death. In Griffith, as in the artistic tradition from which he draws, mirrors are a dangerous prop less because they signify female narcissism than because they force the heroines to see themselves under the terms of the outside world.

The bizarre conclusion of *The Painted Lady,* where the woman seems to die from the very sight of herself, may only make sense in light of such patterns in the artistic air. Her shock seems to come from seeing herself "painted" with makeup for the first time and thus perhaps succumbing to an image at variance with her obsessive fantasy of a man who would love her for her true face. Such a hope and shock of disillusion is also at the center of Griffith's feature *True Heart Susie* (1919), in which Lillian Gish's title character has a charmingly smug conviction that her rural sweetheart loves her for her open face, free of cosmetics—until he runs off with a "painted" Chicago girl. This prompts pathetic mirror scenes, with Susie caught between her country attempts to match modern ways (with cornstarch as makeup) and

her aunt's moralizing ("Powder! Do you think you can improve on the Lord's work!"). Wherever one places the blame in the ambiguous, last, fatal look into the mirror in *The Painted Lady,* it is a tragedy of being gazed upon.

If Griffith's one-reeler can bear comparisons with sophisticated turn-of-the-century novels, it's in good part because of a complexity in the acting. Blanche Sweet's performance is surely one of the most compelling in the pre-feature era. As she commented nearly 60 years later, she worked within a passive range—"reactions to what life is doing to her"—restrained by the character's repression for the first half of the reel and then by a "shattered" psychopathy for the second half. But dividing these two sides of the film is Sweet's melodramatic tour-de-force at the lover/burglar's death, with her body and facial gestures making for a montage of surprises in an unbroken medium shot. In shock after the shooting, she talks to the clearly unresponsive body, questioning it and explaining; but when her father returns and begins to manhandle the body with something like Old Testament anger, Sweet's character rouses herself with a previously unseen fury, knocking her father's hands aside as she mouths "mine!" in reference to the corpse and caresses her cheeks in a gesture we recognize as her earlier response to her lover's admiration of her face. At this, her grim father rather touchingly shifts his attention from the corpse to wrap his arm around his evidently deranged daughter. Sweet's performance is far beyond realism, communicating by exaggeration and by precise gestural echoes of earlier scenes—as she has said, "We only had a few feet of film to put across an emotion"—but the semaphore style nonetheless infuses an authentic psychology into melodrama.

One doesn't need to make much of a metaphorical leap to read the film as melodramatizing the woman's first experience of sex—an experience portrayed as trauma. The stranger proves himself a rapist, one can say, violating the private space of her home, her trust, and the strongbox; the frenzied struggle over the pistol proves her shattering. It is always difficult to say just how far sexuality enters intentionally into Griffith's work, since the subject is so censored and disguised. But it is probably a mistake to confine even his intentional world to one of Victorian propriety. Undeniably, many of his domestic dramas do take such propriety to extremes that now play only as comic, as with the very early *For a Wife's Honor* (1908), where "a true friend's sacrifice," when caught in the room of another man's wife, is to confess to being a burglar to save her, at least, from taint. Very occasionally, Griffith did allude unmetaphorically to sexual passion, as in *A Victim of Jealousy* (1910), where an unreasonably jealous husband is temporarily subdued by an evening of sex— signified by the wife leaving her girdle on his chair (what the *Biograph Bulletin,* more circumspect than the film, calls "placing within his range delicate reminders of her own gentleness")—after which the film cuts to "The next morning" title card. More explicitness than this one cannot find in Griffith, nor could one expect much more within the era's commercial film-making.

Instead, the sexuality one now sees in his earliest films tends to look like Freudian jokes, so obvious that they can surely only be unconscious (as with the repetition compulsion rape of *The Hindoo Dagger* [1909] or the primal rage of *The Restoration* [1909]). As tempting as it is to read the films this way, it is with a false sense of superiority that one does so, patting their little heads for their naïveté. At least by 1912, the year of *The Painted Lady,* a number of Griffith films do seem to know quite what they're doing as they displace sexuality into narrative, not unlike the transference of dreams. (As subjects for further consideration, one might begin with three one-reelers from 1912: *The Female of the Species,* with its bizarre conflation of archetypes; *The Girl and Her Trust,* with its wild profusion of phallic imagery; and *A Change of Spirit,* with its evocation of sexuality as criminality.)

The pattern of *The Painted Lady* is not so clear, even as sexual parable. On the one hand, as I've suggested, it's Griffith's version of a story variously retold in the era's novelistic cycle about the fatal price paid by the "gazed-upon" woman. But one must also factor in a less progressive reason for the tragedy—because it arises from the point at which the heroine becomes, in a sense, the phallic woman by taking up her father's pistol. This entry into the world of action proves too much for her, and her mental collapse evokes the nineteenth-century presumption of women innately prone to nervous collapse and outright insanity if their delicate mechanisms were strained—especially by an entry into the male world—a hazard to which women were said to be particularly prone during times of sexual change. A basic text here would be Dr. Edward H. Clarke's much reprinted *Sex in Education; or, A Fair Chance for Girls,* full of horrifying case histories of women who allowed the intellectual "college regimen" to get "out of harmony with the rhythmic periodicity of the female organization." Isaac Ray, a prominent pre-Freudian American psychiatrist explained in an article entitled "The Insanity of Women Produced by Desertion or Seduction" that "With women it is but a step from extreme nervous susceptibility to downright hysteria, and from that to overt insanity. In the sexual evolution, in pregnancy, in the parturient period, in lactation, strange thoughts, extraordinary feelings, unreasonable appetites, criminal impulses, may haunt a mind at other times innocent and pure." In this sense, then, our heroine's "sexual evolution" *itself* proves fatal and, in her standing up to the burglar like a phallic man, one would have to place her within another American novelistic tradition of drowned women, via Hawthorne's Zenobia in *The Blithedale Romance,* whose suicide results from attempting to deny her place.

What remains surprising, from Griffith, is that the young woman's acceptance of the ways of her puritani-

cal father is one clear source of the tragedy, not any modern abandon, which is characteristic only of her younger sister, who is both "painted" and thoroughly healthy when we last see her. *The Painted Lady* is not so neat a parable as most of Griffith's woman's films, and therein lies its continuing interest. Like so much of Griffith, it remains caught between two centuries, looking backwards to nineteenth-century medical ideas of women's sexual weaknesses but also ahead to twentieth-century explorations about the price of the gaze.

It is evident from Griffith's woman's films—both from their numbers and their narratives—that women not men were central to his career-long project. This is, of course, not to say he allowed women to claim power, only that their rapidly changing roles were both a worry and a dramatic opportunity. If Griffith borrowed the means of America's nineteenth-century domestic novelists (notably the devout and resourceful, if physically weak, pubescent girl), it was in order to dispute their conclusions. Still, certain points of agreement with those novelists reveal how Griffith is finally a "father" of Hollywood only in certain limited geographic and formalist senses. Prominently absent from his entire body of work is the male success story: the tale of admired willpower and drive which underpins the Hollywood myth in both its positive generic forms (e.g., the Western) and negative (the gangster film). Instead, his films tend most to admire certain passive virtues, of endurance or sacrifice. Where Hollywood came to confine such virtues within the genre of "the woman's film," Griffith had distributed them to heroine and hero alike. It is revealing that when Douglas Fairbanks was signed from Broadway in 1915 and assigned to Griffith's Triangle studio, the director could come up with no significant use for the actor who by the following year would be showing Hollywood its way through his vastly popular tales of energetic striving. With Griffith's active men, we stand ready for the nearly inevitable moment when—as an intertitle from *Brutality* (1912) puts it—"The brutal spirit asserts itself." The phrasing there is precise: not "his" but "the" brutal spirit, a general trait, ever ready, in men, to assert itself. Griffith views male energy, even when it remains this side of rape, from a nearly eighteenth-century aristocratic artistic tradition, where ambition is more liable to be the object of irony than admiration. (Of his many object lessons about male ambition, the most flamboyant is *For His Son* [1912], in which a businessman finds success by adding just a pinch of cocaine to his new soft drink—"for that tired feeling, Dopokoke"—only to have his son fall into fatal addiction.)

In a sense, Griffith's dreams for the woman's film reach a limit in *Intolerance* (1916), whose four eras are linked by the static shots of Lillian Gish as the impassive mother, taking on the full sorrow of history, her cradle endlessly rocking toward some apotheosis of the maternal melodrama. Perhaps surprisingly, in that epic and elsewhere, Griffith tends to rely upon "woman's time" ("cyclical or monumental" patterns of "gestation [and] eternal recurrence," rather than time as "project," in Julia Kristeva's definition) and on the "female plot" (which tends to substitute "an inner drive toward the assertion of selfhood" for male plots of ambition, in Peter Brooks' formulation). Griffith's formative woman's films argue that any expression of female sexuality (as in *The Painted Lady*) or hopes for an independent occupation (as in *A Flash of Light*) can have only tragic consequences. And yet it may be to their credit that while they clung to a pathologically repressive ideal, they somehow couldn't quite ignore the price paid for it.

FURTHER READING

Biography

Brown, Karl. *Adventures with D. W. Griffith*. New York: Farrar, Straus and Giroux, 1973, 252 p.
> Anecdotal reminiscence of working with Griffith. Brown was an assistant cinematographer to G. W. "Billy" Bitzer, Griffith's cinematographer, from 1913 and the making of *The Birth of a Nation* until *Broken Blossoms* and Griffith's return to New York in 1920.

Schickel, Richard. *D. W. Griffith: An American Life*. New York: Simon and Schuster, 1984, 672 p.
> Massive biography that synthesizes the work of many previously published and unpublished accounts and brings new insights to some of Griffith's lesser-known films. Some scholars have noted inaccuracies in Schickel's account of Griffith's career and in his descriptions of the films Griffith made for the Biograph Company.

Criticism

Agee, James. "David Wark Griffith." In his *Agee on Film*, pp. 313-18. New York: McDowell Oblensky, 1958.
> Applauds Griffith's "epic and lyrical" vision as a filmmaker.

Andrew, Dudley. "Broken Blossoms: The Vulnerable Text and the Marketing of Masochism." In his *Film in the Aura of Art*, pp. 16-27. Princeton: Princeton University Press, 1984.
> Considers the artistic merits of *Broken Blossoms*.

Altman, Rick. "Dickens, Griffith, and Film Theory Today." *The South Atlantic Quarterly* 88, No. 2 (Spring 1989): 321-59.
> With frequent references to Griffith's films, discusses various issues in contemporary film theory, particularly those relevant to the notion of "classicism" in the cinema.

Elsaesser, Thomas, and Barker, Adam, eds. *Early Cinema: Space, Frame, Narrative*. London: British Film Institute, 1990, 424 p.
> Collection of essays that addresses a wide range of issues relevant to the earliest period of filmmaking. While there are references to and discussions of his work throughout the book, four essays are devoted specifically to Griffith: Anne Friedberg's "'A Properly Adjusted Window': Vision and Sanity in D. W. Griffith's 1908-1909 Biograph Films"; Tom Gunning's "Weaving a Narrative: Style and Economic Background in Griffith's Biograph Films"; Jacques Aumont's "Griffith—The Frame, the Figure"; and Raymond Bellour's "To Alternate/To Narrate," which analyzes *The Lonedale Operator*.

Friedberg, Anne. "'A Properly Adjusted Window': Vision and Sanity in D. W. Griffith's 1908-1909 Biograph Films." In her *Early Cinema: Space Frame Narrative*, edited by Thomas Elaesser and Adam Barker, pp. 326-35.
> Examines the concept of sanity in relation to Griffith's Biograph films.

Gish, Lillian, and Pinchot, Ann. *The Movies, Mr. Griffith, and Me*. Englewood Cliffs, N.J.: Prentice-Hall, 1969, 388 p.
> Reminiscences throughout to Gish's professional and personal relationship with Griffith. Gish, one of the first "movie stars," appeared in her first film in 1912, Griffith's *An Unseen Enemy*.

Griffith, D. W., and Stern, Seymour. "*The Birth of a Nation*: A Reply to Peter Noble's Article in the Autumn *Sight and Sound*." *Sight and Sound* 16, No. 61 (Spring 1947): 32-5.
> Includes a brief letter to the editor of *Sight and Sound* by Griffith that introduces and endorses Stern's essay, "Griffith Not Anti-Negro," which defends the director and his films against charges of racism. The article that occasioned these replies appeared in the Autumn 1946 issue of *Sight and Sound*. Stern was Griffith's "authorized biographer"; he published several essays on Griffith in the 1950s.

Gunning, Tom. *D. W. Griffith and the Origins of American Narrative Film: The Early Years at Biograph*. Urbana and Chicago: University of Illinois Press, 1991, 316 p.
> Closely examines the development of Griffith's filmmaking from 1908 through 1913, focusing on his increasingly intricate editing schemes, his articulation of both on-screen and off-screen space, and the evolution of what Gunning terms the "narrator system": that is, the coordination of the plastic elements of film—e.g. editing, camera placement and movement, performance style—to convey the impression of the existence of a narrator, or a narrating consciousness responsible for the progression of images. Gunning is a leading authority on Griffith and early cinema.

Henderson, Robert M. *D. W. Griffith: The Years at Biograph.* New York: Farrar, Straus and Giroux, 1970, 250 p.

Chronological account and descriptive analysis of Griffith's work at the Biograph Company from 1908 to 1913. More recent scholarship and historical research have rendered this work somewhat outdated.

Jacobs, Lewis. "The Decline of D. W. Griffith." In his *The Rise of the American Film: A Critical History,* pp. 384-94. New York: Harcourt Brace & Co., 1939.

Attributes Griffith's decline in Hollywood, in part, to the director's inability to change with the times.

Jesionowski, Joyce E. *Thinking in Pictures: Dramatic Structure in D. W. Griffith's Biograph Films,* Berkeley: University of California Press, 1987, 212 p.

Close analysis of Griffith's early films, demonstrating the ways in which he developed his method of cinematic narration.

Johnson, William. "Early Griffith: A Wider View." *Film Quarterly* XXIX, No. 3 (Spring 1976): 2-13.

Reassesses Griffith's importance as a filmmaker based on viewing one hundred of the films he made for the Biograph Company.

Leondopoulos, Jordan. *Still the Moving World: "Intolerance," Modernism and "Heart of Darkness."* New York: Peter Lang, 1991, 208 p.

Against traditional critical opinion, argues that *Intolerance* is a work of "modern" art. Leondopoulos compares the film, the historical circumstances in which it was made, and the artistic development of its creator with those of Joseph Conrad and his novella *Heart of Darkness* (1902), which is generally considered the prototypical modernist narrative.

Merritt, Russell. "Dixon, Griffith, and the Southern Legend: A Cultural Analysis of *The Birth of a Nation.*" *Cinema Journal* 12, No. 1 (Fall 1972).

Examines the literary sources that were the basis for *The Birth of a Nation* and discusses the cultural climate into which the film was received.

Murray, Lawrence L. "History at the Movies during the Sesquicentennial: D. W. Griffith's *America* (1924)." *The Historian* XLI, No. 3 (May 1979): 450-66.

Discusses the production and immediate critical reception of *America.*

Pearson, Roberta E. *Eloquent Gestures: The Transformation of Performance Style in the Griffith Biograph Films,* Berkeley: University of California Press, 1992, 184 p.

Examines the ways in which acting technique changed and was refined over the course Griffith's work at the Biograph Company, complementing and enhancing his refinement of cinematic narrative technique.

Quarterly Review of Film Studies: Special Issue on D. W. *Griffith* 6, No. 1 (Winter 1981): 1-121.

Includes essays by Eileen Bowser, Tom Gunning, Marshall Deutelbaum, Russell Merritt, Nick Browne, Dudley Andrew, James Naremore, Arthur Lennig, and Elaine Mancini.

Silverman, Joan L. "*The Birth of a Nation*: Prohibition Propaganda." *Southern Quarterly* 19, No. 3 (Spring-Summer 1981): 23-30.

Argues that Griffith was an exponent of the temperance movement and that many of his films—particularly *The Birth of a Nation*—can be seen as parables on the evils of drink.

Simmon, Scott. *The Films of D. W. Griffith.* Cambridge: Cambridge University Press, 1993, 179 p.

Presents an overview of Griffith's life and career, with particular emphasis on his work for the Biograph Company between 1908 and 1913. Sim-mon attempts to place Griffith within specific soc-ial and historical contexts, addressing the racism in his films—particularly *The Birth of a Nation*—as well as examining his depictions of city life and women's issues.

Staiger, Janet. "The Birth of a Nation: Reconsidering Its Reception." In her *Interpreting Films: Films: Studies in the Historical Reception of American Cin-ema,* pp. 139-53. Princeton: Princeton University Press, 1992.

Describes the audience reception accorded to *The Birth of a Nation* over the years, beginning with the film's debut in 1915.

Stern, Seymour. "The Cold War Against David Wark Griffith." *Films* VII, No. 2 (February 1956): 49-59.

Attributes the decline in Griffith's reputation and popularity to a worldwide Communist conspiracy.

Wagenknecht, Edward. *The Movies in the Age of Innocence.* Norman, Okla.: University of Oklahoma Press, 1962, 280 p.

Personal survey of American silent film, with a chapter devoted Griffith's career.

——, and Slide, Anthony. *The Films of D. W. Griffith.* New York: Crown Publishers, 1975, 276 p.

Discusses Griffith's major works from *Judith of Bethulia* (1914) to *The Struggle* (1931). Wagen-knecht and Slide devote their first chapter and an appendix to the films Griffith made for the Biograph Company.

Young, Vernon. "Footnote to a Cinematic Primer." In his *On Film: Unpopular Essays on a Popular Art,* pp. 15-21. Chicago: Quadrangle Books, 1972.

Assesses the strengths and weaknesses of *Intolerance.* Young's essay originally appeared in *Southwest Review* in 1954 and is included here with a "Post-script" from 1971.

Additional coverage of Griffith's life and career is contained in the following sources published by Gale Research: *Contemporary Authors*, Vols. 119, 150.

Robert Musil

1880-1942

Full name Robert Edler von Musil; Austrian novelist, novella writer, dramatist, essayist, and poet

INTRODUCTION

Although Musil is little known outside of literary and academic circles, he is considered by many critics to be among the greatest novelists in modern literature, primary because of his voluminous novel *Der Mann ohne Eigenscaften (The Man without Qualities)*. This work occupied him for twenty years but was never completed. The novel's protagonist, Ulrich, has been interpreted as a paradigm of the modern individual and the novel's setting—decadent pre-World War I Austria, with the Austro-Hungarian empire on the brink of collapse—has been seen as symbolic of the whole of twentieth-century existence.

Biographical Information

Musil was born in Klagenfurt, Austria, to an aloof, intellectual father and an emotionally unstable mother. While his father devoted himself to a successful career as a professor of engineering, Musil's mother maintained a forty-year liaison with a teacher who lived with the family. Critic Frederick G. Peters wrote that this strange domestic triangle "had a profoundly adverse effect upon [Musil's] psychological development." Musil was a troubled and withdrawn child who had to be taken out of the third grade for half a year to recover from a nervous breakdown. His father enrolled him in a military academy when he was twelve, and two years later sent him to the senior military academy at Mährisch-Weisskirchen, which Rainer Maria Rilke had attended a few years earlier. Both writers later recounted that they suffered greatly from the rigorous regime of the school and from embarrassment by older students. Rilke claimed that he always meant to write about his ordeal at the school, but was never able to carry out his intention. Musil, however, used his experiences there as the basis for his first novel, *Die Verwirrungen des Zöglings Törless (Young Törless)*. At seventeen, he decided to forgo the military career mapped out for him by his father and began to study engineering, in which he took his degree. Musil later entered the University of Berlin to study philosophy, psychology, and mathematics, and in 1908 submitted his dissertation on the epistemology of the physicist and philosopher Ernst Mach. In 1911 Musil married, and in the same year published his second book, *Vereinigungen (Unions)*, containing the novellas *Die Vollengung der Leibe (The Perfecting of a Love)* and *Die Versuchung der stillen Veronika (The Temptation of Quiet Veronica)*. His father obtained for him a post as librarian at the Technical University of Vienna, which he occupied for two years before moving back to Berlin to become an editor of the periodical *Die neue Rundschau*. During World War I Musil served as an officer, and after the war held various semimilitary positions with the Austrian Foreign Ministry and the War Office. In 1922 he lost his job due to government cutbacks, and afterward lived as a freelance writer, often in extremely impoverished circumstances. Financial pressure, coupled with the tremendous intellectual and emotional stress of composing the massive novel *The Man without Qualities*, led to another nervous breakdown in 1929. Patrons in Berlin and Vienna provided some financial support, and Musil tried repeatedly, but without success, to find a sponsor to aid in his emigration to the United States. In 1938, just before the Nazi invasion of Vienna, Musil and his Jewish wife fled to Switzerland. He died there four years later, embittered by continued poverty and lack of public recognition, his vast final work unfinished.

Major Works

Musil's first novel, *Young Törless*, examines the crises in the life of a schoolboy. Musil critic and biographer Burton Pike has summarized the novel as "an examination of the psychology of an adolescent and, perhaps even more, an examination of the psychology of an adolescent representing a general type of human psychology at a particular stage of development." In *Young Törless* Musil defines an adolescent as someone who has not yet constructed the fiction of character, and Torless has been seen as a precursor of Ulrich in *The Man without Qualities*. Törless is described early in the novel as having no character (or personality or ego, depending upon the translator) of any kind. His part in the sadistic treatment of the hapless, "soft" Basini is often viewed a preparatory stage to Törless's development and to his achievement greater self-knowledge. Because Musil appears to sanction his protagonist's cruelty toward a weaker classmate, the novel has been interpreted in terms of Nietzsche's philosophy of a superior individual who is above conventional morality. Critics also find Freudian themes in *Young Törless*; in fact, Harry Goldgar has said that it may be "the earliest novel of any sort in any language to show specific Freudian influence." However, other critics, notably Frederick G. Peters and Yvonne Isitt, dispute this claim. Peters cites evidence from Musil's diaries and journals that Musil possessed only a minimal grasp of Freudian thought, and that he rejected much of what he did understand. Isitt sates that pertinent Freudian works were not even published at the time of the novel's composition.

Musil produced two volumes of novellas, *Unions* and *Drei Frauen (Three Women)*. In the two novellas that appear In *Unions, The Perfecting of a Love* and *The Temptation of Quiet Veronica*, Musil presented his central characters by describing their successive mental impressions of various situations. Musil's style in writing these two novella's has been likened to impressionism in painting. The closest stylistic comparison in literature is to the stream of consciousness technique as employed by James Joyce and Gertrude Stein. In an attempt to render the feelings of his female characters to his readers, Musil used what has been described as a "stream of emotions" and intended the reader of these novellas to respond to them emotionally, rather than intellectually. Musil told his stories through images and metaphors, omitting the usual fictional elements of plot, physical description, and conventional narrative. Both novellas focus upon the attempts of a central female character to reconcile the varying demands of physical and spiritual love. Claudine, in *The Perfecting of a Love,* reaffirms the bonds of her marriage through a meaningless sexual encounter with an animal-like stranger. Veronica, in the second novella, denies her own sexuality and seeks a purely spiritual union. At one point she believes she has attained this; upon discovering she was mistaken, some critics believe she becomes insane, though Musil's surrealistic narration makes any definitive statement regarding *The Temptation of Quiet Veronica* difficult.

The novellas in Musil's second collection—*Grigia, Tonka,* and *Die Portugiesin (The Lady from Portugal)*—have male protagonists, with the eponymous characters, all women, serving as antagonists. The respective protagonists—an engineer, a scientist, and a soldier—each become involved with an enigmatic woman in a relationship which ultimately demands that the man seek a reconciliation between the rational and the nonrational aspects of life. Only the soldier, through his marriage to the Portuguese lady, achieves a synthesis between the two. The protagonist of *Grigia* cannot strike a balance between the empiricism of his profession and the "andere Zustand"—the mystical state of "other reality"—of the valley where he has gone to work, which is embodied in his peasant mistress. *Grigia* concludes with his death. The protagonist of *Tonka* is a scientist who does not attempt a reconciliation between the rational and nonrational, but chooses scientific reason over mystical faith in his lover, which results in her death. The three male-female relationships explored in the novellas in *Three Women* are often critically interpreted as the antecedents to the union between Ulrich and his sister Agathe in *The Man without Qualities,* a relationship whose success or failure cannot be conclusively judged because of the work's unfinished state.

The Man without Qualities appeared in three volumes over a thirteen-year period, and as it is thought that Musil began the novel in 1922, he devoted about two decades to this unfinished work. As early as 1931 the initial volume of *The Man without Qualities* was described in *The Times Literary Supplement* as the "first part . . . of a monumental work." At the novel's center is the collapse of the Austro-Hungarian empire and its significance as the end of an epoch. However, other elements have been pointed out which are equally important to the structure of the novel. The first of these is the central character, Ulrich, the man without *Eigenschaften*—a difficult term for translators, who have settled upon "qualities"; however, in the same context the word has been alternately translated as "characteristics," "attributes," "properties," and "capacities." Ulrich's age, his background in philosophy, the sciences, and his military experiences are all Musil's own, making the novel autobiographical to some extent. Ulrich, the man of multiple possibilities, has decided to spend a year keeping himself apart while speculating upon which possibility to pursue. His dilemma is seen as representative of the existing social conditions in pre-World War I Europe. Musil depicts a panorama of Austrian, and by extension, European, society in decline. At the same time he shows his quintessential modern European struggling to reconcile the rational with the nonrational aspects of life through his relationship with his sister Agathe. Another important feature of the novel is the presence of the psychotic murderer Moosbrugger, whose upcoming trial is a common topic of conversation. Wilhelm Braun wrote that Moosbrugger is "representative of the mood and the scope of the work" and that he is symbolic of the disintegration of the European people prior to World War I. There is no way of knowing what form the novel would ultimately have taken if Musil could have brought *The Man without Qualities* to a conclusion. In the third volume of the novel, Musil has Ulrich approach a union between "Moglichkeitssinn" and Wirklichkeitssinn" ("possibility" and "reality") in his physical and spiritual union with his sister Agathe.

Critical Reception

As Musil's works become better known through increased critical attention, they are met with an enthusiastic response from critics and readers who find in Musil an author with an idiosyncratic approach to fiction, yet one who addressed his works to basic human problems: whether the morality of a past epoch can be applied to a new age; how the individual is to find an ideal balance between the many alternatives present by life; and how the modern individual is to deal with the potentially limitless possibilities now available. Denis de Rougemont summarized current opinion when he wrote that Musil's work "will continue to rise on the horizon of European literature." Support for this claim is provided by the publication in 1995 of a new English-language translation of *The Man without Qualities* as well as the first translation of *Nachlass zu Lebzeiten (Posthumous Papers of a Living Author)*, a collection of essays and short stories.

PRINCIPAL WORKS

Die Verwirrungen des Zöglings Törless [*Young Törless*]
(novel) 1906
Vereinigungen [*Unions*] (novellas) 1911
Die Schwärmer [first publication] (drama) 1921
Vinzenz und die Freundin bedeutender Männer [first
publication] (drama) 1923
Drei Frauen [*Three Women*] (novellas) 1924
Der Mann ohne Eigenschaften. 3 vols. [*The Man with-
out Qualities*] (novel) 1930-43
Nachlass zu Lebzeiten [*Posthumous Papers of a Living
Author*] (essays) 1936
Tonka, and Other Stories (novellas) 1966
Gesammelte Werke in neun Bänden. 9 vols. (novels,
novellas, essays, journals, dramas, and letters) 1978-81
Selected Writings (fiction and nonfiction) 1986

CRITICISM

D. J. Enright (essay date 1983)

SOURCE: "The Stupendous Cannot Be Easy: On Robert
Musil," in *A Mania for Sentences,* Chatto & Windus,
1983, pp. 23-33.

[*In the following essay, Enright considers Musil's
achievement as both a thinker and a fiction writer.*]

If you were to read **The Man Without Qualities** for the
story, your patience would be much fretted: you would
probably not hang yourself, you would merely want to
hang Robert Musil. The 'story' of the novel ostensibly
concerns the preparations being made in 1913 in the
Austro-Hungarian Empire to celebrate the seventieth
anniversary of the Emperor's accession in December
1918. The preparations are known as the Collateral
Campaign because Germany, that uncomfortable
neighbour, is also planning a celebration: of Kaiser
Wilhelm's jubilee, thirty years on the throne, in July of
the same year. Unfortunately July precedes December,
hence honour requires the Austrians to turn the whole of
the year 1918 into a jubilee. Since, as the author knew
(he began to write the work in the early 1920s and the
first volume was published in 1930), these celebrations
are never going to take place, the story in an obvious
sense bears on a non-event.

The view that the work is a study of decadence, revealing the decay at the heart of the Austrian Empire,
though it endows the project with a respectable-seeming
significance, is a highly doubtful one. It points to what,
though marvellously apt, is the least important element
in the novel: its setting in time and place. By and large
the dramatis personae form an exceptionally bright

set—they could as well win the world as lose their little
piece of it—and the tone of the work is remote from
Orwellian or Brechtian allegory. The inset story of
Moosbrugger the sex-murderer hardly supports the view
either, despite the opening it offers for the question of
whether one is responsible for one's acts, and despite
Ulrich's portentous reflection in one of his grimmer
moments that 'if mankind could dream collectively, it
would dream Moosbrugger'. There being so much civil-
ity in evidence, someone has to stand for violence and
unadorned insanity.

It says something for a country that, although it custom-
arily regards a genius as a lout, a lout is never ('as
sometimes happened elsewhere') regarded as a genius.
No doubt the Empire was ramshackle, tottery and given
to 'muddling through'—the hero Ulrich, we shall see, is
given to thinking through: he however has no other
calls of a pressing nature—but Musil was not interested
in a retrospective analysis of the processes of decline
and downfall. Ulrich even suggests that 'muddling
through' may be Austria's world mission. And in fact,
despite his virtually continuous irony, Musil is careful
to forgo the hindsight wisdom which would have supplied him with irony of the cruder sort in plenty. The
analysis that interests him—obsesses is a better word—
is that of his characters and their situations as individual and yet (on a somewhat elevated plane) representative beings. He is the most relentlessly analytic of
authors, the most sententious (except perhaps for
Wilhelm Meister's), and one of the most intelligent.

He did not finish his 'story' because in one sense, a
minor one, history had already finished it for him, and
in another and major sense it could never end. If his
characters died it would be as if humanity died out.
Death is as immaterial here (but how useful it is to
novelists who have to tell a story and to end it too!) as
in a Freudian casebook. Events too are rather crude
animals, although they do happen, even to representative figures, and might be thought on occasion to be
capable of representativeness themselves. Where events
are concerned Musil can make Proust seem as fast-mov-
ing as James Bond: why, Mme Verdurin gets to be
Princesse de Guermantes and Marcel's grandmother
actually dies . . . Yet, like *A la recherche du temps
perdu,* Musil's novel is a continuous texture, a vast
weave of references back and forth, a seamless expanse
of strands of thought which evince themselves at remote
intervals and yet have been there, imperceptibly growing, all the while. If you skip, and it is very hard never
to do so, you will be made to regret it.

'What this age demonstrates,' the novel tells us, sounding as so often as if it had been written yesterday, in
some intellectually richer yesterday, 'when it talks of
the genius of a race-horse or a tennis-player is probably
less its conception of genius than its mistrust of the
whole higher sphere.' The reader should not let himself
be alarmed by that fearsome expression 'higher sphere',
but merely remind himself that some spheres are higher

than others. What is enjoyable in this novel is, happily, what matters most in it, and not just the sugar round the pill. To that extent the heart of the matter is worn on the sleeve and there is, until we make it, no insuperable problem: the novel is highly entertaining. Or the problem is: how sturdy is our appetite for what we are fairly overtly offered? That is to say, intelligence and insight, an 'unmerciful' shrewdness, outright comedy, wit, an all-embracing but by no means merciless irony—in short, a cast of mind, in motion, that we might think of as world-weary were it not for the sheer energy and gusto it bears and is borne by.

If the first characteristic we note of Musil's style is its leisureliness—Volume I begins with a hefty meteorological paragraph which at last summarizes itself in the words 'In short . . . it was a fine August day in the year 1913'—the second is its succinctness. For speed there is little to beat this sentence: 'Two weeks later Bonadea had already been his mistress for a fortnight.' And in two and a half pages we are given a living portrayal of the reluctant nymphomaniac Bonadea, the stuff of a novel in itself. 'She was capable of uttering the words "the true, the good and the beautiful" as often and as naturally as someone else might say "Thursday".' She has only one fault: 'she was liable to be stimulated to a quite uncommon degree by the mere sight of men'; a good wife and mother, 'she was by no means lustful' but 'sensual in the way that other people have other troubles, such as sweating of the hands or blushing easily'. Comic as the tone of this is, we emerge from the three-page chapter knowing that Bonadea is not merely to be laughed at or despised or condemned. Musil's starting-point, the reminder that Bonadea was a goddess of chastity whose temple suffered a transmogrification into 'a centre of all debaucheries', does not initiate the crushing send-up of a trivial, pretentious light-of-love that we might have expected. Bonadea, when she has no one in her arms, is a 'quiet, majestic woman'. Like the goddess's temple, people too are subject to queer inversions and contradictions, and the only infallible way of preserving an empire, of whatever kind, is by petrifying its inhabitants, reducing them to programmed robots *in perpetuum*. The most perspicacious (and perspicuous) passage in Musil's early novel, **Young Törless,** touches on the boy's experience of 'the failure of language' whereby things, people and processes have been fettered to harmless explanatory words from which they may break loose at any moment.

In Chapter 99 of the Second Book the story is told, in passing, of Ulrich's adoptive Aunt Jane, whose dress resembled a soutane and who smoked cigars and wore a man's wig—not in anticipation of 'the mannish type of woman that was later to come into fashion', but because of her early and passionate admiration for the Abbé Liszt. Aunt Jane's heart was 'womanly' indeed. A music mistress, she had married against her family's wishes an improvident photographer and self-styled 'artist', who at least had a 'superb head' and drank and ran up debts like a genius. To him and then to his illegitimate child

she sacrificed herself utterly. 'She seldom spoke of that past,' the author interposes: 'If life is stupendous one cannot also demand that it should be easy.' This anecdote—it arises out of a family album Ulrich is leafing through and occupies three pages—is a slice of the very body of life: again, the raw material for a substantial novel of its own, one would say, except that Musil is never 'raw'. That he over-cooks is the objection we are more likely to make. In an interesting essay, 'The Ironic Mystic' (*PN Review,* 22) David Heald varies the metaphor: 'His terrier-like habit of chewing every scrap of flesh and sucking the marrow out of every fleeting insight can irritate . . .'

With one sense of the word 'raw' in mind, we are provoked into perceiving before long that, for all the author's well-bred discretion, or because of it, the work carries a powerful sexual charge—in no way defused by the presence of humour, satire and pathos—and especially in the vicinity of his women characters. 'The tender aspects of masculine self-abandonment,' he remarks, 'somewhat resemble the growling of a jaguar over a hunk of meat.' But then, his women are the most original of his creations, and only brute accident, one wants to say, could bring about the downfall of an empire that had such women in it as Agathe, Diotima, Bonadea and Clarisse. It has to be admitted that Musil turns his sardonic gaze even more lovingly on his women than on his men: this detracts from them less than the reader might suppose in his innocence.

Apropos of Diotima, Ulrich animadverts on 'the mind of this woman, who would have been so beautiful without her mind', and it could hardly solace her to hear that Musil is offering her as an exemplary victim of what he calls 'the indescribable wave of skim-romanticism and yearning for God that the machine-age had for a time squirted out as an expression of spiritual and artistic protest against itself.' Diotima is the spiritual and artistic spearhead of the Collateral Campaign—culture, in the circles to which she belongs, being largely left to ladies—and in quest of a Great and Beautiful Idea, something to do with the Ideal and the eternal verities and, if at all possible, involving 'a positively redeeming exaltation of inner life, arising out of the anonymous depths of the nation'. How gratified the Emperor Franz Joseph will be by a whole year of all that! When Ulrich looks at Diotima he sees a fine woman; in his mind's eye, however, she appears in the shape of a 'colossal hen that was about to peck at a little worm, which was his soul'. Musil's women have a peculiarly potent charm, bypassing or overriding one's intellectual judgement of them; their wrong-headedness is richer than male rightmindedness, which by comparison looks cloddish, pompous or ineffectual.

In fact almost all the characters are endowed with a generous share of their creator's acuteness. Even the patently foolish ones, like those of limited brain-power, are allowed such fluent cogitation that they too strike us as preternaturally observant and self-aware. The 'tubby little general' Stumm, fallen under Diotima's sway, goes to the Imperial Library in the hope of locating a 'great redeeming idea' for the Campaign and finds himself faced with three and a half million volumes. 'You may say,' this simple soldier reflects, 'one doesn't really need to read every single book.' But that won't pass muster. 'My retort to that is—in warfare, too, one doesn't need to kill every single soldier, and yet every single one is necessary.' The Prussian industrialist Arnheim is put in his place by the author as a plausible *vulgarisateur* or at best a talented eclectic: none the less he proceeds to put neatly in their place the 'fat species' of solemn idealistic poets who 'puff out great bales of the eternal emotions'.

In conversation, as when Arnheim and Ulrich dispute together, one character's wits strike sparks off another's sagacity and, at times quite unexpectedly, intellectual honours are more or less equal at the end. What respect for—or what rare generosity towards—one's own creations this shows, among them not a single imbecile or swine! The exceptional subtlety thus implied in the differentiation between characters—levels of intelligence, degrees of good intention—doesn't make the reader's task any easier. Whose side is he meant to be on? He will need to be a reader without qualities, apart from those of insatiable curiosity and immense patience. He will need to be nearly as clever as Musil.

'At times he felt just as though he had been born with a gift for which at present there was no function.' The figure of Ulrich is obviously crucial, and also slippery: he is, one supposes, the author, in large measure at any rate, and the reader's zealous though less than wholly accommodating guide. Over this length, he will require to be more than a guide, a stance or a view-point; he will need to be of very considerable appeal, gruesome or charming, in himself. Is he sufficiently so? He describes himself in a typical paradox as 'a man of faith, though one who believed in nothing'. More strongly he asserts (partly, one may suppose, by way of apology to Bonadea, with whom he is breaking off), 'My nature is designed as a machine for the continuous develuation of life!'

Ulrich is or was (like Musil) an engineer and mathematician, earlier a cavalry officer, now taking a year's leave from his life in order to find out what to do with it: a youngish man of promise disillusioned with the promises, a dilettante who loves 'intellectual hardship'. He is a detached observer, a juggler with ideas, an intellectual trouble-maker—as his friends discover—and he can run to tedious sophistry and sterile elaboration— as his readers discover. If he appears sexually cold—he certainly isn't abstinent—this is in part, though only in part, because the author skips over the details (we catch a rare period glimpse of ribbons being untied or tied, hooks being unfastened or fastened) and straight into Ulrich's post-coital musings. Against his coldness we set the quickness of his curiosity, as when he pauses outside a shop window to marvel at 'the countless ver-

sions of nail-scissors' or the processes whereby a goat's skin is transformed into a lady's glove. In the barely definable relationship between him and his sister Agathe which begins to take over Volume III, he reflects, 'there was implicit not more love for each other than distaste for the rest of the world.' Yet when he is out with Agathe, discussing his dislike of the world, and they stroll through a busy market-place, he exclaims: 'Can one help loving the world if one simply sees and smells it?'

Wherever his mind may be, Ulrich has his feet on the ground, and he is less of a pedant, and in truth probably less of a world-disliker, than the windy idealists and Great Lovers whom he mocks. If he is rather too knowing about women, and—even for a personable thirty-two-year-old bachelor—somewhat over-privileged in that sphere, he likes them naturally, with a liking that can only go with a fair amount of respect, and in their company he never declines into baby-talk or sulks or masculine mysteries. He may fall into silence, however. What is exasperating to the reader, as to his female visitors, is his capacity for thinking, at such length and for the greater part so well. This is indeed quite offensive. 'Let's have more conviction!' we protest, when we really mean, 'Less superior intellection if you please!'

The reader's courage may dim a little when, in Volume III, Ulrich is reunited with Agathe ('sister . . . woman . . . stranger . . . friend'), for alas the siblings have long been separated and have so much to talk about. Moreover Agathe is made of sterner stuff—stuff of a less decipherable pattern too—than his other women friends, and she can give as good as she takes. We are told by Musil's expert translators—they deserve the Nobel Prize for Translation—that this is where he originally intended the story to begin, and so the previous thousand pages are only a form of prologue. What is to be narrated now, Musil declares in connection with the siblings and by way of warning to the slow-witted and hence (he assumes) squeamish, is 'a journey to the furthest limits of the possible, skirting the dangers of the impossible and unnatural, even of the repulsive, and perhaps not always quite avoiding them.' This, though one may not be absolutely sure of what it signifies, is possibly a clue to one reason for the novel's unfinishability. The man who is going to travel that far needs to travel light, and as a symbol, no matter what of, no matter how beautifully managed, incest tends towards topheaviness.

However, this volume contains splendid material continuative of the foregoing volumes. On the one hand, such ripe comedy as Bonadea's playing truant from Diotima's high-minded academy of love, where general theory alone is taught, to taste the reality of sex in Ulrich's apartment. On the other, an unforgettably powerful scene in which—at the instigation of Clarisse, a highly-strung 'modern' version of Aunt Jane moved by fiercer artistic aspirations but a lesser lovingness—some of the friends visit the lunatic asylum where Moosbrugger is held. As they progress from ward to ward ('this is idiocy, and that over there is cretinism') General Stumm rambles on about the Collateral Campaign and how the War Ministry finds itself co-operating with both the pacifists and the nationalists, the former keen on universal love and human goodness and the latter on seizing the opportunity to bring the army up to scratch. The General himself is in favour of both parties.

There is no facile suggestion that it is the inmates of the asylum who are 'truly' sane while the outside world is 'truly' insane. Musil compares lunatic asylums, 'the ultimate habitation of the lost', with Hell—which 'is not interesting; it is merely terrible'. Those who have attempted to portray Hell, however imaginative they may be, have never got beyond 'oafish torments and puerile distortions of earthly peculiarities'. And Dante, more discreetly, humanized Hell by populating it 'with men of letters and other public figures, thus distracting attention from the penal technicalities'. Asylums are as uninteresting, as lacking in imagination, as Hell itself, and even Clarisse, fired by self-generated excitement and a head full of Nietzschean ideas ('for her this journey was half philosophy and half adultery'), is left disappointed. On the return journey the General remarks, as he lights up a cigar, that he didn't see a single patient smoking: 'People don't realize how well off they are so long as they're in their right minds.'

The advent of Agathe brings about a new seriousness in Ulrich, or a thinning of the flippancy that has invested his seriousness. For a while we wonder whether he is going to develop qualities. He comments on his own scepticism: 'I don't believe God has been among us yet. I believe He is still to come. But only if we shorten the way for Him': that is, we have to meet God half-way. The comment is indicative of Ulrich's 'mysticism', itself a contributory reason for the novel's length. For that mysticism, in so far as it is describable, is of a scrupulously rational species which allows of no short-cuts by way of 'feeling', no leaps into the unknown, but only of hard and rigorous journeys. There follows a sustained passage of considerable solemnity on the theme of morality, which for Ulrich consists in 'order and integrity of feeling'. 'Morality is imagination' and 'there is nothing arbitrary about the imagination'. Men have introduced a degree of order into the workings of the intellect, which is at least able to weigh theories against facts. Cannot something similar be done for the feelings? For 'we all want to discover what we're alive for . . . it's one of the main sources of all the violence in the world.' When Arnheim interrupts: 'But that would mean an expanding relationship to God!' Ulrich asks mockingly, 'And would that be so very terrible?'

It is tempting at this pointl—but not especially rewarding—to turn back to *Young Törless (Die Verwirrungen des Zöglings Törless,* 1906), a book whose curiously high standing may owe something to the guilty sense that its author wrote another novel, much finer no doubt but very much longer and on the face of it less acces-

sible. For it is hard, I would have thought, to distinguish between the *Verwirrungen,* the confusions, of young Törless and those of the not much older author. The unlikeable youth Beineberg—but who in the novel is likeable?—sounds like a seedy pubescent hanger-on of Diotima and her Great and Beautiful Idea when he talks about the soul and how we should restore our contact with it and make better (in his case, probably worse) use of its powers. But it is the author *in propria persona* who tells us that

> Any great flash of understanding is only half completed in the illumined circle of the conscious mind; the other half takes place in the dark loam of our innermost being. It is primarily a state of soul, and uppermost, as it were, at the extreme tip of it, there the thought is—poised like a flower.

Such Freudian-style talk of light and loam may pass in a boarding school where metaphysics and masochism, soul and sadism, are jumbled up together, but the later Musil is more authentic in his aspiration and more rigorous in his scepticism.

Musil tells us that in his references to the rubble of feelings one age bequeaths to another Ulrich is prophesying the fate of Europe, though without realizing it—'indeed, he was not concerned with real events at all; he was fighting for his own salvation.' The salvation of a representative being is a theme, a concern, which survives 1914-18 and thereafter: the end is not yet nigh, and it is wholly in character that a fourth volume of translation should be in prospect, containing (we are told) the unfinished conclusion of the work and some unfinished chapters.

Musil's mind is a brilliant, speculative and untiring one, but not precisely the mind of a novelist. Yet if such a mind applies itself to a novel—and it is difficult to think what it could apply itself to more profitably—then the result must be, if not a brilliant novel, then still brilliant. In Chapter 112 of the Second Book Arnheim reflects on Ulrich, his Viennese 'counter-influence' in the triangular relationship with Diotima and a man with whom, paradoxically, he is much taken. His diagnosis of what he persuades himself is Ulrich's weakness may stand as a criticism of Musil himself, so long as we keep in mind that it is highly paradoxical to describe as a writer's 'weakness' what is plainly of his essential strength. Ulrich is witty, 'and wit came from witting, knowing, and here was a piece of wisdom on the part of language, for it revealed the intellectual origins of this quality, and how spectral it was, how poor in feeling.' Arnheim continues: 'The witty man is always inclined to live, as it were, by his wits, overriding the ordained frontiers where the man of true feeling calls a halt.'

Yes, we think, more feeling would surely have served to inhibit, to slow down, even to tire out Musil's wits, and thus to call a halt to his novel this side of the ordained frontiers of magnitude and ambition. But therein, as we have seen, lies the burden of Ulrich's—and Musil's—complaint against 'feeling' and its soulful exponents. When they are moved by emotions they think are moving towards truth—and never mind frontiers and halts.

The Man Without Qualities is essentially exploratory and experimental rather than programmatic or predetermined. Yet, as we expect novels to have a conclusion, so we expect thinkers to arrive at conclusions. The truth may well be that Musil couldn't end his novel because he hadn't arrived at his conclusions, he was still inching ruthlessly towards them when he died. If he had arrived—ah, then we should have more than merely a great novel, we should possess the great secret of life.

Anthony Heilbut (essay date 1988)

SOURCE: "The Man with Extraordinary Qualities," in *The New York Times Book Review,* April 10, 1988, pp. 28-9.

[*In the following review, Heilbut outlines Musil's main characteristics as a writer and thinker as evidenced in the essays and fiction collected in* Posthumous Papers of a Living Author.]

Since so little of Robert Musil's work is available in English, this collection's appearance is a major literary event. A congeries of light sketches, composed for Austrian and German newspapers between 1913 and 1929, it was compiled in 1935 when Musil was still living in Austria. But it was first published a year later in Switzerland, the country he fled to in 1938 following the Anschluss. So often ahead of his time, the archivist of social estrangement seems to have anticipated this exile. By 1935 he was both impoverished and horrified by Austrian politics. His audience, never large, had been reduced to a small group, predominantly Jewish and even more endangered than he. Musil's sense that with the destruction of his public he had "outlived himself" underlines the not quite facetious title, *Posthumous Papers of a Living Author.*

Trained as a mathematician, behavioral psychologist and engineer, Musil, who died in 1942, had worked as a journalist, librarian and civil servant before devoting his energies exclusively to literature. With a more academically honed intelligence than any of his peers, he attempted to make of the solitary act of thinking a literary drama. Rather than pursue a Joycean stream of consciousness, he captured the divagation of thought in essays. Indeed, his great novel, *The Man Without Qualities,* is a perfected instance of essayistic fiction. Each qualification of thought is answered by some astonishing image or incident. The transition between dramatic and discursive realms is a seamless one.

The Musilian posture is fraught with contradictions. In the novel, he hails the essay's capacity to regard "a thing from many sides without comprehending it wholly, for a thing wholly comprehended instantly loses its bulk and becomes a concept." For Musil, concepts were dogmatic, totalitarian, destructive of every living pattern. He also found them vulgar and humorless, and thus had no time for the Big Idea men, Freud, Heidegger or Jung. On the other hand, Musil said that the essay's best trait was its reflection of the form "a man's inner life assumes in a decisive thought"—that is, thought that discovers itself in the process of enunciation. But decisiveness is precisely what you don't find in his writing. Ulrich, the hero of *The Man Without Qualities,* possesses so many attributes—professional, national, political, cultural—that they conspire to dissolve him unless he acquires "the passive illusion of spaces unfilled." This capacity for making yourself a receptacle for experience, rather atypical for a male protagonist, allows him to regard his public lives with baffled amusement: grim, moralistic but never entirely serious. The playfulness—and the transcendence—reside in the freedom from concepts.

Musil enjoyed the permutations and combinations produced by the collision of our several roles. But how is "decisive thought" possible amid such chaos? Perhaps not since David Hume has a writer so thoroughly exposed the impossibility of objective thought, and then relied on verbal momentum to steer him out of his cul-de-sac.

Yet a theoretical liability frees the essayist's talent. As he strolls among his several selves, Musil becomes a *flaneur* of thought. He loiters among impressions as much as objects, regarding them with equal amplitude and precision. Having defined our various traits, he has a particular alertness to popular culture, the kitsch and more-than-kitsch that saturate our lives. After years in Berlin and Vienna, he was too shrewd to condemn the masses' entertainment. Though exquisitely refined, he was no cultural elitist. Musil's conceit is that the only alternative to the generalized mess he has revealed is the coherence of his meandering thought. His linguistic facility—the merging of aim, manner and result—is virtuosic. He's such a consummate stylist that after him Kafka may seem immature, Mann chatty, Brecht arch, Rilke precious and Walter Benjamin hermetic.

In these *Posthumous Papers,* Musil's pleasure is to start small. The first essay, **"Flypaper,"** begins with an almost pedantic description of the sticky substance. It proceeds to focus on trapped insects, briefly comparing them to a woman fighting off a strong man's grip, and ends with the image of a fly's moribund twitching, compared to "a minuscule human eye that ceaselessly opens and shuts." This is the patented Musilian cadence. An immensely sensuous and concrete prose carries us from the ordinary to the almost-surreal and near-apocalyptic, a progression that appears logical, if not methodical.

Part wit, part logician, Musil makes us anticipate the invariable rush of qualifications. When he dominates us intellectually, he exhibits a conventionally male sense of authority. But his imagery expresses the "passive sense of unfilled space." A deeply erotic writer, Musil exhibits an astonishing fellow-feeling with women. They are his sisters, literally so in *The Man Without Qualities,* in which Ulrich and his half-sibling Agathe perform a kind of spiritual incest. Musilian eros bypasses consummation. In one sketch, **"Awakening,"** he lies in bed, listening to a woman's footsteps in the streets; never will he share such intimacy with his lover. In **"Clearhearing,"** he becomes so absorbed in the sound of each dropped garment postponing their embrace, that he gives up on "anything imaginable." In another essay, a chambermaid's smile protects her against the "onslaught of desire." At such altitudes of feeling, orgasm would be reductive: Musil told his friend Hans Mayer than Ulrich wouldn't sleep with Agathe because "the characters don't want it."

Musil's social diagnoses are equally surprising. In the novel, Ulrich appears to be the one sane citizen of Kakania, a fictive Austria hectically planning an imperial celebration in 1913. The *Posthumous Papers* indicate that the world war that followed didn't bring people to their senses. If anything, Musil's analyses reveal a deepening confusion of past and present that atomizes our already fractured selves. Industry tampers with both nature and art until one ends up preferring prints to paintings, department stores to Vienna woods. Yet nobody is culpable. Our bad taste is prepackaged for we are generated by language. In **"The Paintspreader,"** words "twist" and shape us, precede our existence and define our responses.

But the words are seldom right. Kitsch "strips language of life" even as it turns sentiments, living feelings, into concepts. How does one escape from this maze, still alert and lucid? Artists could help us but, in truth, they merely swoon to higher orders of kitsch. In **"Surrounded by Poets and Thinkers,"** Musil finds that literary circles thrive all over town, each Vatican with a self-appointed Pope. He prophetically discerns the outcome. Some "genuine paranoiac" will sweep all these amateurs offstage. His will be the latest word, and the last.

Nevertheless, this is no lament for a bygone age; excavations or regrets won't restore these ruins. As for that Viennese specialty, psychoanalysis, Musil considers its sense of emotional history insufficiently inflected, with too many "qualities" missing. He acknowledges Freud's obsession with domesticity, which turned the haven in a heartless world into the arena of a born-again humanism. But the materialist in Musil demolishes Freudian tenets. In **"Threatened Oedipus,"** he traces the famous complex to an 1870's style in skirts. The discarding of folded pleats and their intimation of secret passages, he points out, has simplified the female lap. Today, any lap, even a male one will do, and Orestes nudges Oedipus offstage.

By now, some readers will feel immobilized by irony, and in desperate need of an action that is not so stunningly mental. Anticipating them, Musil ends the collection with a group of stories, though most of them are simply new forms of essay in which a dramatized metaphor artfully replaces the more usual mental loitering. **"A Man Without Character"** provides an entry into the similarly named novel. Its hero is so multifaceted that, when asked to describe his fiancée, he replies, "From the point of view of which character?" He is an athlete gone to seed, although his former, nimble self seems to lurk within the corpulence. In other words, he is Musilian thought rendered visible, his body a palimpsest, character overlaid by the weight of years.

The last story, **"The Blackbird,"** is the book's longest piece. The narrator, Atwo, is a peripatetic fellow; he even spends some years in the Soviet Union where, typically, he likes the system but hates the litany. On three occasions he hears a blackbird: while deciding to leave his wife; while dodging bullets in wartime; and while reading a children's book, after the death of his mother. Demonstrating that sentiment is possible, when no longer kitschified into concepts, Musil ends with an extravagance no professional hack would risk. Believing that his dead mother alone preserved a steady image of him—doubtless a false one, but her error constituted his identity—Atwo determines that she is the blackbird. This conclusion is not entirely satirical. It predicts the impulse that led Musil during a particularly miserable exile to develop a form of "religion without God."

Musil was not the first person exile turned quixotic. Granting that he liked to dart between radical and conservative politics—and recognizing that his Jewish wife and largely Jewish public condemned him in the eyes of the Nazis as a religious fellow-traveler—his political pronouncements can be troubling. He was at times intrigued by fascist forms of social control, equivocal about democracy and convinced that the postwar powers would continue the imperial shenanigans of his native "Kakania" (this was not necessarily an error). Our disappointment with his politics is a perverse tribute; an admirer of Musil may want to follow him everywhere.

Peter Wortsman's translation is splendid, succeeding better than any I've read in capturing this author's unique combination of quizzical authority and austere hedonism. Mr. Wortsman finds colloquial equivalents for Viennese slang and makes available a writer whose accessibility may previously have been in doubt.

John Bayley (essay date 1988)

SOURCE: "Death and the Dichter," in *The New York Review of Books,* Vol. XXXV, No. 14, September 27, 1988, pp. 34-6.

[*In the following review, Bayley discusses two later translations of works by Musil.*]

The German term *Dichter* is not at all readily translatable. It has a wider sense than "poet," and a more transcendental one than "writer." Goethe, the archetypal *Dichter,* created masterpieces in every genre, but was also the model of thinking and being, in the science and ethic of a civilized state. Never much like its English, French, or Russian counterpart, the German novel, coming from the pen of a *Dichter,* has always more resembled an enterprise of the philosophical imagination.

Frank Kermode gave this interpretation of *Dichtung* when he spoke of its "elaborate attempts to use fiction for its true purposes, the discovery and registration of the human world." That might mean much or little. A modest masterpiece, like a novel of Jane Austen's, could be said to achieve such a goal as effectively as a work of vast and deliberate metaphysical scope, if not more so. It's a question for the reader, and for the way his mind works. In the relative world of the novel revelation may come to him from an unexpected quarter. Or the discerning reader may go only for a novelist-*Dichter* with whom revelation is an open promise. Milan Kundera, a lively, but it must be said exceedingly naive, commentator on these matters, assures us that the novelist is an "explorer of existence, . . . man's being, which the novel alone can discover."

In a sense Kundera and Kermode are on sure ground, but there is a snag. By hailing the novelist as a *Dichter* (the word has unfortunate if fortuitous connotations with *Diktat*) they bestow on the novel a conscious and transcendent function, one that goes with the German and Goethean tradition.

A *Dichter* can remain a *Dichter* only by asserting his own absolute preeminence and authority; and, as D.H. Lawrence very sensibly put it, the strength of the novel is that it is "so incapable of the absolute." Nothing is more absolute than an idea, and the naiveté of a lively and creative intellectual like Kundera emerges in his persistent belief that the more striking its ideas, the more effective the novel. All his disclaimers, all his insistence that the novelist is not playing with ideas but exploring human individuality, serve only to emphasize his real allegiance. For him the three great novelists of this century, the ones who really matter, are all men— all, one might say, specifically *masculine*—and all Central Europeans: Broch, Kafka, and Musil. And of these the real intellectual's novelist, the one most committed to ideas, is Musil. He is the apotheosis of the modern *Dichter,* one who has passed beyond life into a world of abstract inquiry about it. In the foreword to his essay collection, **Posthumous Papers of a Living Author,** as in its title, he made a joke of this. "Can a *Dichter* still speak of being alive?"

Well perhaps not. The author of *Axel's Castle* observed that the artist's valet would do his living for him: Musil in the next century allots the same role to thought. He was frank about this. In his diary in 1910 he wrote: "Where I cannot elaborate some special idea, the work immediately becomes too boring for me." In one of the essays and dialogues assembled in his book *The Art of the Novel* Kundera observes that Fielding *tells* a story, Flaubert *describes* a story, and Musil *thinks* a story. The odd and indeed slightly comic paradox in all this is Kundera's insistence, where Musil and the modern novel are concerned, on the Heideggerian existence—*in der Welt sein*—of Musil's apparently "unliving" characters. "Making a character 'alive,'" says Kundera, "means getting to the bottom of his existential problem . . . nothing more."

But people don't walk around with an existential problem. They walk around worrying about a visit to the dentist, buying a pound of sausages, wondering if their husbands are being unfaithful. The novel has always known this and has invented itself accordingly. As Kundera elsewhere implies, and rightly, the novel has always known what the existential thinkers in our time have been preaching as a new gospel: and yet he is himself most impressed and influenced by those novelists who have made the most elaborate attempts to use fiction for the discovery and analysis of "existence." It is a question of which comes first: the novel, or thoughts and ideas about the novel, the metaphysical uses that the form can supply after the event. Walter Benjamin—no mean judge—saw this clearly, and said that Musil was a thinker but not a novelist: a thinker who made use of the novel.

Musil himself might well have agreed. He was not dogmatic on such issues. As *Dichter* he saw himself primarily as an explorer of "the other condition," which is both the goal and the process of thinking about oneself, experiencing oneself. And by experiencing oneself one may reveal one's experience to others. This is the delicate point in our relations with Musil—are we sharing an experience, or being asked to admire a highly complex and specialized one of his own? Is he, like Tolstoy, a solipsist who speaks for us all, or one who is only interested in a unique self?

It is the same kind of contradiction as that between man as an existentialist and as someone who is preoccupied about his pound of sausages; and to do Musil justice he is neither disturbed by it nor even made self-conscious. Of the triad of novelists exalted by Kundera he is closer to Broch than to Kafka, or to other intellectual European novelists like Canetti and Thomas Mann. But he remains very much a writer on his own. It is obvious that when we read Kafka, a very different sort of writer, we are no more meeting fully recognizable individuals than we are in the pages of Musil. Kafka's figures are so compelling because we are at once engrossed in their experience, becoming a beetle with Gregor Samsa in *The Metamorphosis,* or the victim of a mysterious trial with Josef K. What happens to them is so absorbing that we are not interested in what they are like. But with Jane Austen's *Emma,* say, interest is divided between Emma as a personage, presented for our acquaintance and amusement, and Emma as a set of experiences that the author invites us to share. With Musil we have something quite different, none of these more familiar introductions to the world of other people, but simply to the mind of a man who once said that he made fictions because they were the only vehicle for the unphilosophical view that everything in thought and experience can be simultaneously true and false.

Hence the unpositive nature of Musil's world, its lack of "characteristics." Most novels depend on emphasizing, even exaggerating, the characteristics of things and people, so that we soon recognize everything and begin to feel at home in the world the novelist invents for us. Musil's long, unfinished novel, *The Man Without Qualities,* which should really be given in English the clumsier title of "The Man Without Characteristics," pretends to use some of the usual business of the novel. There is the "Collateral Campaign," a society project for rehabilitating the Austrian Empire; there is much satire on bureaucracy; there are investigations of a sex murderer, Moosbrugger, and of the incestuous love between Ulrich, the man without qualities, and his sister Agathe. There is the suggestion of a world on the brink of the disaster of the First World War. There are also portraits *à clef* of powerful women of Musil's acquaintance, such as Lou Andreas-Salomé.

But all this is of little importance beside the play of thought—and it must be said, style—which is the real Musil experience. Musil's triumph ultimately is to do what all other great novelists do: that is to say, compel us to share the authenticity of his world; but it is a world in which fact, event, and consideration are, as it were, ineradicably interchangeable. That is why it would be vulgarly misleading to speak of Musil's world as existing on the brink of the abyss of war and anarchy, because the abyss may cease to exist or turn out to be something quite different. For the same reason the novel could not end, but would merely go on, until its author, impoverished and ill, died in Switzerland in 1942, just after completing a sentence. Like fiction's version of Penelope's web it secretly and mysteriously unraveled itself even while it was being so delicately and carefully woven.

In some metaphysical way that might be considered the highest destiny of the novel form, its ultimate essence; and it is certainly true that highly intelligent people who do not read ordinary novels will read Musil with deep admiration. He is a philosopher's pet, like Wittgenstein, perhaps because philosophers, who try to establish what can be known, are seduced by a world of such palpable intelligence in which knowledge and experience remain absolutely free and uncommitted.

Intelligence, for Musil, is embodied in the erotic, in its sensations and discoveries, and the most graphic passages in all his books deal with sexual musings and intimations as a part of the "other condition," the state that medieval mystics, in whom Musil was much interested, frequently likened to certain kinds of erotic expe-

rience. A tiny essay in *Posthumous Papers* called **"Maidens and Heroes"** muses about the thoughts, or nonthoughts, of servant girls exercising dogs. Is their world one of Zen-like calm, or of "thinking that the movie's about to begin"? Another, in a style even more mesmeric and haunting, describes the narrator going to bed in a hotel room with a slight fever, and listening to the woman with him making her own preparations "in the realm of reality":

> Incomprehensible, all the walking up and down: in this corner of the room, in that. You come over to lay something on your bed; I don't look up but what could it be? In the meantime you open the closet, put something in or take something out; I hear it close again. You lay hard, heavy objects on the table; others on the marble top of the commode. You are forever in motion. Then I recognize the familiar sounds of hair being undone and brushed. Then swirls of water in the sink. Even before that clothes being shed; now again: it's just incomprehensible to me how many clothes you take off. Finally, you've slipped out of your shoes. But now your stockings slide as constantly over the soft carpet as your shoes did before. You pour water into glasses, three or four times without stopping. I can't even guess why. In my imagination I have long since given up anything imaginable, while you evidently keep finding new things to do in the realm of reality. I hear you slip into your nightgown. But you aren't finished yet and won't be for a while. Again there are a hundred little actions. I know that you're rushing for my sake, so all this must be absolutely necessary, part of your most intimate I, and like the mute motions of animals from morning till evening, you reach out with countless gestures, of which you're unaware, into a region where you've never heard my step!

In such explorations of the erotic consciousness, as a form of prolonged meditation, Musil the *Dichter* does indeed seem to forgo the authority of that high poetic intelligence, and take on some of the novel's diffidence, its relative and nonabsolute qualities.

Musil was, like Wordsworth, "a traveller, whose tale is only of myself." And yet like many if not most mystics he was an eminently practical man in daily affairs, by turns a mathematician, engineering student, successful soldier in the first war; and then a prolific reviewer and essayist, and editor of a periodical. He wrote one play that was a failure and another that had a considerable success. It is true that all this brought him little profit. His touchy independence and reluctance to commit himself to offers meant that he and his wife lived on the edge of poverty. Friends even set up a *"Musilgesellschaft,"* into which subscriptions were paid for their support. As *Dichter* on the one hand and day-to-day man of letters on the other he led a double life, one not uncommon in an artistic setting but carried by Musil to extreme lengths. *The Man Without Qualities* was incessantly restarted and revised, and the publisher, Ernst Rowohlt, grew reluctant to pay further advances.

He continued to do so nonetheless, remarking later that though many authors threatened to shoot themselves if support were withdrawn Musil was the only one he thought might really do it.

In all these vicissitudes Musil's wife, Martha Marcovaldi, was both pillar of strength and alter ego. Seven years older than her husband, she had been married twice before, first to a young man who died and then to an Italian merchant by whom she had two children. He made trouble about a divorce, which eventually had to be obtained in Hungary. In all his difficulties Musil came to see her as "another side of himself." He wrote in his diary that she "was someone he had become and who had become him." Fortunately Martha was tough enough to stand up to this most invasive of solipsists. In his helpful study Lowell Bangerter records that Musil's first German biographer, Karl Dinklage, announced in an address that "Martha was for Robert Musil the intellectual, spiritual, physical complement that was necessary for him to become what he is today for us and the world."

In a sense all Musil's fictional situations take for granted such an interchangeability. His characters are all himself, or, as he would probably have put it, he has the power of endowing with himself anyone he creates. The same might, after all, be said of Tolstoy, or any other great novelist. Yet it remains true of Musil in a special sense, the sense in which he can be said to *think* his characters and their "story." His first and most popular novel, *Young Törless,* which came out in 1906, already demonstrates this tendency. Outwardly a more or less conventional *Bildungsroman* concerning the events in a military academy, it represents more convincingly the play of mind in a single person: the brutal cadets Reiting and Beineberg and their victim, the cowardly thief Basini, are acting out the "larval" impulses of young Törless in his search for his true selfhood in the "other condition." But the book owed its success to being received by its readers, in the bourgeois era, as a steamy revelation of what actually went on in such a school.

Musil himself saw the "special idea" of his novel as a kind of microcosm of contemporary society, the idea adumbrated—but also, as was typical with Musil, eluded and contradicted—on a much larger scale in *The Man Without Qualities*. Much later, in a diary entry during the Thirties, he referred to his brutal pair of cadets as "today's dictators *in nucleo,*" but that seems like the hindsight of a writer who was always, and deliberately, pretentious. Musil, as much as Joyce, is an intensely personal and domestic bard, although all great writers can of course be seen, or can see themselves, as prophets of political doom, civilization's collapse. "We cannot halt the deluge," Musil exclaimed in the 1930s. But the way he thinks a story echoes the title he gave his essays: it does not depend on the daily vicissitudes of life and history. The mystically erotic transcends such things, as it transcends conventional sex barriers. Törless's homo-sexual experiences are no more specifically homosexual than the relations of Ulrich and his sister Agathe in *The Man Without Qualities* are specifically incestuous, or Moosbrugger is a real sex murderer.

All these things are in the mind, or, as we should have to say in the case of a cruder writer, in the sexual fantasy. Moosbrugger believes that the world's existence depends on his crimes, an exaggeration of Ulrich's search in incest for his other self, a total relation such as Musil saw in himself and Martha. Musil in fact exemplifies perfectly, on the highest of planes, the way men cannot help imagining women. His female characters, like Joyce's Molly Bloom and Gretta Conroy, are themselves male fantasies. There is a certain irony in the fact that the untrammeled exercise of the intelligence on the novel, by so supreme an intelligence as Musil's, results in a rarefied form of something with which men are all too familiar—dreams of fair women. Shakespeare does not in this sense imagine Lady Macbeth speaking of the tenderness of suckling a child; and Tolstoy does not fantasize about Natasha Rostov's translation from coltish girl into slatternly earth mother. These are matters of universal knowledge and experience, as a down-to-earth genius presents them. But Musil's touchingly and indeed hauntingly objective presentation of Tonka, one of the "Three Women" in a short collection with that title published in 1924, is not quite what it seems.

The real Tonka was a simple workingclass girl called Herma Dietz, with whom Musil lived for a time while working as a young man in technical and scientific institutes. The story explores, thinks as it were, her simplicity; and how it dissolves the distinction between deceit and innocence, so that Tonka can be, in some sense, faithful to the narrator, even when it is obvious that she has made love with another man and contracted VD. The story is not really interested in her as a social being, but in the metaphysical status the narrator confers on her. What fascinates him is that she has no power of speech, and thus embodies something his own intelligence has with infinite subtlety concluded: that an idea or a person—anything in the world—can be simultaneously true and false, existent and nonexistent.

Three Women is now combined in a paperback volume with two earlier *nouvelles,* published in 1911 with the title *Unions*. All are concerned with women of the imagination, Tonka being the most notable, and the most elaborate a meditation entitled **"The Perfecting of a Love."** A woman travels to see her daughter at school, her husband absorbed in his work remaining at home. As in a modern film she encounters the shadowy figure of a man who stands outside her hotel door at night, and with whom she eventually makes love, feeling the moment to be the perfection of her union with her husband, "a state that was like giving herself to everyone and yet belonging only to the one beloved." **"Grigia"** reverses the pattern, a husband parting from his wife to work on a project in the South Tyrol, where he makes love with a peasant woman, whose husband lures them down a mine shaft and blocks the entrance. The girl escapes, but the narrator appears to have been seeking the perfect venue for a mystical *Liebestod* with his own wife, which then takes place, at least in the narrator's and the reader's imagination. Musil certainly puts queer ideas into other people's heads.

Published in Zurich in 1936, the ironically named *Posthumous Papers* contains a number of short sketches and stories written for magazines over the previous years, often terse reminiscences in miniature of the longer *nouvelles*. Some are dry and witty comments in newspaper style. Ably rendered as they are by Peter Wortsman, they cannot convey a great deal, in English, of the elliptical symmetry and richness of Musil's German. As a prose poet he is at his best over short distances, moments of what the critic Frederick Peters, in his study called *Robert Musil: Master of the Hovering Life,* defined as "ultimate narcissism." Nothing of course is "ultimate" in Musil, but "hovering life" conveys very well that flashpoint of the solipsistic and the external worlds which he conveys so marvelously, sometimes in images like that of the gathering of people in *The Man Without Qualities,* who seem to take wing in a myriad mental impressions before alighting "like waders on a sandbank."

An ironic little essay in *Posthumous Papers* called **"Black Magic"** conveys as well as anything in his work its simultaneous feel of density, mathematical logic, and seductive unpredictability. Like Kundera, and indeed like most representatives of the culture in which the expressive word originated, Musil is fascinated by the relation of kitsch to life and to art. Kundera claimed, from extensive experience of the political systems of Eastern Europe, that ideals like "the Brotherhood of Man" were only possible on the basis of kitsch. Musil's more subtle view has the same implication. For him "art is a tool which we employ to peel the kitsch off life." Kitsch may be life's answer to "the horrible gaping contingency of all one does," but art—and especially the art that really explores sex—can do the job much better. Art strips life layer by layer. "That in life which cannot be employed for art's sake is kitsch."

It is the center of Musil's philosophy as *Dichter*. Or is it? Abruptly he switches away into a pattern of serio-comic syllogisms:

> Art peels kitsch off of life.
>
> Kitsch peels life off of language.
>
> And: The more abstract art becomes, the more it becomes art.
>
> Also: The more abstract kitsch becomes, the more it becomes kitsch.
>
> These are two splendid syllogisms. If only we could resolve them!

He proceeds to do so in a few sentences worthy of Alice in Wonderland, or Wittgenstein's *Tractatus* run mad. "Art equals life minus kitsch equals life minus language plus life equals two lives minus language."

Then the essay, one of a collection entitled *"Ill-tempered Observations,"* switches as it concludes into quite another key again:

> A black hussar has it so good. The black hussars swore an oath of victory or death and meanwhile stroll around in this uniform to the delight of all the ladies. That is not art! That's life!

Where do these black hussars come from and what do they mean for Musil? Are they a *Dichter*'s companions, the bodyguard as it were, who protect his genius, or the escort who have him under arrest? The artist swears an oath, but the man who lives continues to stroll around day by day, in his artist's uniform, to the delight of the ladies? Art is like death: it swallows up its devotee, who continues to lead a posthumous life.

Lowell A. Bangerter   (essay date 1988)

SOURCE: "Experimental Utopias: The Man without Qualities," in *Robert Musil,* The Continuum Publishing Company, 1988, pp. 111-30.

[In the following excerpt, Bangerter outlines the principal themes of The Man without Qualities.*]*

All of Musil's other works, including **Young Törless,** the novellas, the plays, and the essays, can be interpreted as preliminary studies to his monumental unfinished novel **The Man without Qualities.** In each creation, the author tested variations of ideas about man's relationship to the world, his self-concept, and the possibilities for realizing greater fulfillment and more perfect humanity within the context of life's experience. The analysis of the human condition, with special reference to the role of the thinking individual in modern technological society, is the common denominator of his literary art and his theoretical writings. **The Man without Qualities** is the grand culminating experiment in his creative-analytic process of exploring the unfixed domain of mortal potentiality.

Musil's masterpiece is not a traditional novel with a clearly defined plot and carefully orchestrated resolution of one or more central problems. It has been variously described as a "compendium of contemporary uncertainty," "a grand satire of the dying Austria," and "the supreme example in Western literature of the novel of ideas." The author himself characterized it as a novel "of a spiritual adventure," and as a "combat document." More than anything else, however, it is his strongest illustration of the creative power of his own sense of possibility.

The uniqueness of **The Man without Qualities** lies in the fact that on one level it is an analysis of historical reality, while on another it is an extremely complex metaphor for something that transcends the limits of specifically defined time and locale.

With reference to the real world, Musil was concerned about the human developments in Austrian society that inevitably led in the direction of World War I. In his notes about the novel's orientation and his approach to the material, he defines its artistic focus by saying that direct portrayal of the period leading up to the war must be the real substance of the narration, the context to which the plot can be tied, and the thought that provides the orientation for everything else.

It is important to understand that what mattered most for Musil were questions of human response to a spiritual atmosphere, and not the details of events. In his interview with Oskar Maurus Fontana in 1926, he disclaimed engagement in the writing of a historical novel, insisting that the actual explanation of concrete events did not interest him. One reason for this posture was that he considered facts to be totally interchangeable. Accordingly, he declared his fascination with what is spiritually typical, "the phantom aspect of the happening." For Musil, that "phantom aspect" is a timeless dimension of human experience. In the impact of events upon the individual, it is the factor that stimulates experimentation with new ideas.

Within the framework of *The Man without Qualities,* Musil treats what he sees as major problems of the immediate prewar years—the search for order and conviction, the role of the "Other Condition" in the life of the individual, the situation of the scientific person—as substance for experiments with ideas about achieving utopian forms of existence. His notes to the novel identify the most important of the projected patterns as three separate utopias. The first of these is the utopia of the given social condition, the second, the utopia of the "Other Condition" as found in love, and the third, a purely refined form of the "Other Condition" with mystical implications. In discussing these possibilities, he suggests that they differ in importance and that they can be reduced to two major utopias, that of real life and that of the "Millennial Kingdom," where the latter is a combination of the respective forms of the "Other Condition" experienced through love and mysticism.

The experiments pertaining to the first alternative receive their greatest emphasis in the early portions of the book. Exploration of the potentialities of the "Other Condition" then follows as the development of ideas for their own sake reaches its strongest intensity. Because Musil believed that attainment of the "Other Condition" could never be permanent in rational mortality, he projected an ending for the novel that would lead the central characters back into reality.

Musil's experiments with the search for utopia take the form of exposing his "guinea pig" to various stimuli and observing the results. The "guinea pig" is Ulrich, a representative specimen of technological man who is characterized by himself and others as a "man without qualities." The stimuli to which he responds include people who stand for different aspects of modern society, social, political, cultural, and intellectual situations that are typical of the times, and ideas that represent possibilities for alternate approaches to life and its questions. In each instance, the object of the experiment is to obtain a solution to a single puzzle. As the novel's male protagonist sums it up for his sister, the problem that troubles him most is concentrated in the question: "How am I to live?"

The outcome of each investigation is at once a function of and a contribution to the view of typical modern scientific man as a "man without qualities." On one level at least, the entire novel revolves around what it means to be such an individual. For Musil, a "man without qualities" is today's manifestation of the man of possibility, unfixed man in all his ambivalence and ambiguity. In defining the title figure as a typical representative of the times, one of his friends describes him as a man who always knows what to do, a man who can look into a woman's eyes, a man who is intelligent and able to use his mental capacities well under all conditions. More striking are the polarities that exist within him. In addition to talents of strength, objectivity, courage, and endurance, he can be either impetuous or cool and cautious. He can laugh when he is angry, reject things that stir his soul, and find good in things that are bad. His relationship to the world is completely unstable, because his surroundings represent infinite changing possibilities.

It is precisely this fluidity of his nature and his lack of a strong sense of reality, however, that make the "man without qualities" the ideal vehicle for Musil's experiments. His sense of possibility is manifested in a conscious utopianism that is a direct product of his intellectual mobility. It permits him to treat life as a laboratory and to contemplate the uniting of opposites to achieve a more fulfilling existence.

Ulrich's attempts to redefine his life are projected against a rich and complex fabric of interpersonal, social, political, and psychological relationships. At the age of thirty-two, he has behind him three unsuccessful endeavors to become a "man of importance," first as an officer, then as an engineer, and finally as a mathematician. These efforts have been in vain because he is more at home in the realm of possibility than in the mundane real world. Accordingly, in response to what he perceives as a lack of order and meaning in his existence as a whole, he decides to take a year's vacation from his normal life. During that period, he hopes to discover the causes of his surrounding reality's progressive collapse and a more suitable direction for his own future. The body of the novel is formed by the composite presentation of what he learns about himself and his environment in the course of this experiment.

To the extent that one can trace even a general story line for the completed portion of the fragment, its substance can be divided into two major sections with numerous subgroupings of connected situations, ideas, events, observations, and characters. The first main portion examines approximately half of the "vacation" year. It is primarily a description of Ulrich's efforts and ultimate failure to find an appropriate niche for himself within the context of Austrian prewar reality.

Diverse aspects of the decaying society are illuminated in a panorama of character types and behavioral patterns, as Musil depicts Ulrich's involvement in an empty political project called "the Collateral Campaign." Ulrich's participation consists primarily of passive observation of and reflection about events and situations. This fact determines the form of the narration. Essayistic integration of ideas, rather than elaboration of action and plot, receives the key emphasis.

In the second half of the narrative, the Collateral Campaign moves into the background as Ulrich abandons his attempt to find the right life for himself within the domain of material reality. His search enters a new phase in the intense exploration of the possibilities for fulfillment offered by the "Other Condition." The problem of finding the proper form of existence becomes that of self-definition as he grapples with the question of his relationship to his sister Agathe.

With this narrowing of focus comes a subtle change in the format of artistic presentation. Ulrich's examinations of a broad spectrum of ideas about love and mysticism are elaborated in long conversations between brother and sister. In the process of these discussions the siblings begin to function as complementary halves of a single spiritual unit.

How the author intended to end the novel is the subject of continuing controversy among Musil scholars. It is clear from unfinished fragments of chapters, notes from different periods of work on the novel, statements in interviews, and comments in letters that he considered many variations and possibilities for concluding his masterpiece. Nevertheless, only two things can be determined with relative certainty: First, Ulrich's experiments with both mysticism and love would fail to yield a final satisfying answer, just as the attempts to adapt to practical reality had done. Second, his "vacation" year would end with the protagonists and their world being swallowed up by the war. In the notes to the novel, where he projects the ultimate collapse of the Agathe-Ulrich relationship, Musil characterizes the combination of Ulrich's decision to participate in the war and the miscarriage of their excursion into the "Other Condition" as the "end of the utopias."

One of the most significant features of *The Man without Qualities* is Musil's general portrayal of prewar Austria as the setting for his "adventure of the spirit."

Kakania, as he calls the dying Austro-hungarian monarchy, is a land for which spiritual inertia is characteristic. In retrospect, he describes the vanished Austria of former years as an unacknowledged model for many things, a place where speed existed, but not very much of it. Despite the genius that it has produced in the past, it has lost its cultural energy: "It was the State that was by now only just, as it were, acquiescing in its own existence." For that reason, it is ripe for some historical event that will bring about radical changes and move things in a new direction.

A major part of Musil's purpose in writing his critical analysis of the times was to demonstrate how such conditions must inevitably lead to the explosive consequences of war. In that respect, the invented characters and situations of the narrative become symbols and metaphors for broad social and political phenomena.

Despite its de-emphasis in the later portions of the novel, the Collateral Campaign provides what Werner Welzig has labeled "the thread of action that holds the work together." On the surface, the project is simply an endeavor to give Austria new visibility in the world, through the creation in 1918 of a yearlong seventieth anniversary celebration of the reign of Emperor Franz Josef. It is conceived as a direct response to the planned Prussian commemoration of Wilhelm II's thirty years on the throne, an event scheduled for the same year. Within the narrative framework, committee meetings and planning sessions, individual responses to the envisioned festivities, and discussions of the action's implications are employed as vehicles for the presentation of a wide variety of representative Austrian social types. The Collateral Campaign thus becomes on a deeper level Musil's focal metaphor for the spirit of the era. That point is hammered home in the author's notes to the final portion of the work, where he says that the Collateral Campaign will lead to the war.

Musil's ironic treatment of the prevailing social, cultural, and political attitudes in prewar Vienna is extremely successful from an artistic point of view. In the diverse reactions to the Collateral Campaign he offers a stark picture of the pathological condition of an Austrian society made up of people great and small, all of whom are concerned only with their own trivial or glorious schemes while the empire staggers on the edge of collapse.

The portrayed perceptions of the grand patriotic endeavor are as disparate as the characters and the parts of the national community that they represent. Count Leinsdorf, for example, views the coming celebration as an opportunity for Austria to reclaim its true essence. Ulrich's friend Clarisse becomes obsessed with the idea of promoting an Austrian Nietzsche Year. Associated with that, she wants to do something for the homicidal maniac Moosbrugger. For still another figure, the appropriate action is the establishment of an Emperor Franz Josef Anniversary Soup Kitchen.

At the same time, broad factions within the society greet the whole idea with skepticism and suspicion. Already-existing tensions are intensified when ethnic minorities come to regard the project as a Pan-Germanic plot, while extremists in the other direction view it as threatening to destroy the German nation both spiritually and intellectually.

Marie-Louise Roth has summarized effectively the function of the proposed patriotic demonstration in exposing the society's mortal weaknesses. She says:

> The Collateral Campaign that was invented by Musil illustrates in its main representatives the false values of an era, the abstract idealism, the confusion of the spirit, the bureaucratism, the phraseology, the impersonalism, the nonsense and the sterility of all endeavors. . . . The leading persons of the Collateral Campaign live and act according to fossilized principles, the unsuitability and falseness of which they feel themselves.

Ulrich's response to the Collateral Campaign is especially important because it illuminates the project as a parody of his own individual quest for life's meaning. As the figures who promote the cause of celebrating the prolonged reign of their "Emperor of Peace" continue to search for a powerful focus for the undertaking, Ulrich makes his own suggestion as to what the movement should accomplish. Speaking to Count Leinsdorf, he proposes that the Collateral Campaign initiate a general spiritual inventory, as though Judgment Day were coming in 1918, signaling the end of the old spiritual era and the dawning of a higher one. He concludes his presentation by stating that until an official institution is created that is responsible for precision and the spirit, other goals remain either unattainable or illusory.

It is significant that nobody takes Ulrich's recommendation seriously, not even Ulrich himself. Just as the very nature of the spirit of the times will not permit a true synthesis of reality and the soul on a national scale, so Ulrich's own goal for himself cannot be realized because his attitude of "active passivism" (Musil's term for passivity masked by meaningless action) prevents a similar synthesis on an individual plane.

There is stark irony in the parallel between the results of Ulrich's "active passivism" approach to his search for the right life and the accomplishments of the Collateral Campaign in its attempt to renew Austria's sense of identity. At one point the protagonist clarifies his stance with respect to external events by comparing it to that of a prisoner who is waiting for the opportunity to escape. While emphasizing the anticipation of action, the image conveys the tension that exists in a situation of static longing for something that never materializes. Pursued to one possible conclusion, it suggests that escape from confinement may occur only as the prisoner experiences his own execution.

Similarly, the progress of the Collateral Campaign is limited to the maintaining of expectation concerning potential future activity. The pattern of "active passivism" is underscored most strongly in what one character calls "the slogan of action." When it becomes apparent that the semiofficial planning committee is accomplishing nothing, Count Leinsdorf utters a hollow watchcry for its continued wheel spinning. He says that something has to be done. Because the Collateral Campaign, like its secretary Ulrich, is representative of the zeitgeist, its response to Leinsdorf's challenge is the same as his. Nothing happens beyond the contemplation of possibilities.

To the extent that the movement's failure to act symbolizes Austria's passivity toward the conditions leading to the war, the outcome is the same as for Ulrich's prisoner. Release from the waiting comes about only through the empire's destruction. As Wilfried Berghahn has pointed out, that fact becomes apparent at the moment when Ulrich first learns of the Collateral Campaign's existence through his father's letter: "For the father's letter, of course, acquires the satirical function that is decisive for the novel only through the dating of the Austrian apotheosis in the death year of the monarchy. With that, the Collateral Campaign is characterized from the first moment on as a burial undertaking. Its protagonists become the masters of ceremonies for a modern *danse macabre*. They just do not know it yet."

The project's function as a metaphor for the disintegration of a stagnant order is further emphasized in the lifelessness of the interpersonal relationships experienced by its actual and wouldbe participants. As Ulrich makes his way back and forth among the "death-dancers," observing and experimenting with them, his encounters reveal both the tenuousness and fragility of existing connections and an increasing inability to establish new, meaningful bonds based on traditional concepts of love and affinity. This accentuation of isolation and alienation is visible not only in the way in which other figures respond to Ulrich, but also in the manner of their interaction among themselves.

A vivid illustration of the Collateral Campaign's lack of power to bring about unifying change is given in the figure of Ulrich's cousin Diotima Tuzzi, whose drawing room is the planning committee's headquarters. In the picture of Viennese society that Musil creates, Diotima is the bourgeois defender of a romantic vision of Austrian culture. She views the Collateral Campaign as a unique opportunity to realize on a practical level the things that are of greatest importance. For her, the paramount goal is the rediscovery of "that 'human unity' in man's life which has been lost because of the advent of modern materialism and scientific reasoning." Yet her inability to achieve anything more than superficial oneness with others is demonstrated clearly in her respective relationships with her husband, Ulrich, and the Prussian Arnheim.

The impractical, idealistic notions that Diotima cultivates in her salon only estrange her from her bureaucrat spouse. Tuzzi, whom Ulrich sees as the embodiment of pure, practical manliness, is totally absorbed in his profession. He feels no kinship at all with those involved in extracurricular intellectual pursuits. Accordingly, in the scenes where he appears, he is an outsider looking in at the peculiar world of Diotima's involvement in the Collateral Campaign.

Diotima is unable to realize any sort of deep personal union with Ulrich for at least two reasons. On a purely matter-of-fact level, the two cousins possess sharply different attitudes and personalities. That is, Ulrich is the embodiment of Musil's idea of healthy, scientific man, while Diotima represents what is unrealistic and decadent in the contemporary world. More important is the fact that for Ulrich, Diotima is simply another subject for detached experimental observation. Ulrich is prepared to enter only an intellectual relationship governed by carefully controlled conditions. He suggests that they try to love each other like fictional characters who meet in a work of literature, leaving out the superficial padding that gives reality a phony appearance of fatness. Because Diotima's spiritual focus is at best counterfeit intellectual, she is incapable of playing the role that Ulrich envisions for her, and the experiment fails before it begins.

In its meaning for the novel as a whole, the most important of Diotima's vain attempts to unite with another individual is her abortive liaison with Arnheim. A Prussian industrialist and writer whom Musil modeled after Walther Rathenau, Arnheim plays the role of Ulrich's spiritual antagonist. His hollow affair with Diotima thus becomes a shadowy parody of the intense Ulrich-Agathe involvement that dominates the second half of *The Man without Qualities*.

During the course of her participation in the Collateral Campaign, Arnheim becomes a peculiar symbol for the irrationality of Diotima's perception of the project. Under the spell of his external facade, she comes to view him as a kindred spirit with whom she can bring to pass the cultural rejuvenation that she sees as the campaign's goal. Her quixotic approach to her self-made task is given its most grotesque manifestation in her grand idea that her Prussian friend must become the spiritual leader of the Collateral Campaign, despite the fact that it competes jealously with a concurrent celebration in Prussia-Germany.

On the surface, Arnheim appears to share Diotima's vision of their common cause, and he does little to discourage her growing attachment to him. As their spiritual relationship grows stronger, the Collateral Campaign becomes for the two of them an island of refuge. It takes on the dimensions of a special destiny that shapes their lives at a critical moment. As they participate in the project, they grow to share the perception that it represents an enormous intellectual opportunity and responsibility. For that reason, Diotima eventually reaches the point where she considers leaving her husband and marrying Arnheim in order to make their apparent spiritual union permanent. That plan collapses under the strain of reality's intrusion into her romantic illusion. The process of events uncovers the fact that Arnheim's real interest in her salon has little or nothing to do with the Collateral Campaign. He has simply exploited the situation to make business contacts. The envisioned union of souls founders on his pragmatism.

In its artistic function as a recurring symbol for Musil's main ideas, the Collateral Campaign spins within the novel a structural thread that binds together key character groups and situations. Parallel to it, although receiving less emphasis, is a second strand of thought that fulfills a similar purpose, reinforcing the author's statements about the prewar Austrian world by illuminating it from an entirely different direction. The resulting contribution to the narrative fabric is one of harsh, chaotic color in sharp contrast to the more subdued, passive hues of the Collateral Campaign's characteristic inaction.

At the center of this more threatening representation of the spirit of the times is a symbol for what one critic has called "the insanity of a world out of control." It takes the form of the homicidal maniac Christian Moosbrugger.

Like the Collateral Campaign, Moosbrugger provides stimuli to which the various figures respond, revealing things about themselves and the society of which they are a part. Through the brutal slaying and mutilation of his prostitute victims, he arouses peculiar feelings within others, feelings that throw into question traditional concepts of social normality. The judicial system's visible inability to ascertain his mental competence and his accountability for his actions becomes a grotesque caricature of what is happening on the other levels of the novel. His apparent rationality in the courtroom parallels the facade of reason that conceals the tragic internal decay of the social order. According to Musil, Moosbrugger reflects the pertinent conditions within the surrounding environment, as if they were seen in a broken mirror.

Ulrich's views concerning him are especially important for the elucidation of Moosbrugger's meaning for the work. For Ulrich, Moosbrugger is the inevitable product of the world's collective irrationality. In one instance, the thought occurs to him that if it were possible for mankind to dream in unison, the resulting vision would be Moosbrugger.

Because the murderer's behavior is not bound by the restrictions of reason, he is able to participate in the life of a realm beyond material reality, where the "goodness" of an action is determined entirely by individual perception. In that respect, he becomes a perverse manifestation of transcendence into the "Other Condition," where the sense of possibility is unfettered by a traditional morality based upon external social standards. As Johannes Loebenstein has observed: "In this murderer . . . Ulrich sees all of humanity's possibilities combined together in a radically paradoxical unity."

Just as Arnheim functions as Ulrich's antagonist in the practical, material world, so Moosbrugger plays the role of his opposite in the domain of the spirit. A significant aspect of Ulrich's search for fulfillment is his attempt to establish his complete identity by finding and uniting with the missing feminine component of his soul. His experiments with a number of different women bring him no closer to that ideal until he finally rediscovers his spiritual "Siamese twin," in his sister Agathe. In the figure of Moosbrugger, on the other hand, the image of a society that rejects and destroys spiritual completeness is given its strongest elaboration. What the murderer achieves in killing his victims is the excision of the unwanted feminine dimension from his own being. That fact is made abundantly clear in the narrator's description of one of the murders.

In the scene in question, Moosbrugger is presented lying rolled up in a ticket booth, with his head in the corner, pretending to be asleep. Next to him lies a prostitute who has attached herself to him during the night. The narrator labels her Moosbrugger's "accursed second self." When the psychopath tries to slip away from her in the dark, she holds him back, wrapping her arms around his neck. His response is to pull out his knife and stab her with it. When she falls with her head inside the booth, he drags her out, stabbing her repeatedly until he is satisfied that he has "cut her completely away from himself."

The behavior of Moosbrugger's victim is especially meaningful for the scene that is presented here. It signals that within the destructively insane world symbolized by the murderer the feminine element seeks undeterably for the union that he rejects. That idea is given even greater emphasis in the descriptions of Ulrich's interactions with Clarisse, Moosbrugger's strongest female spiritual counterpart.

During the course of the novel, Clarisse becomes progressively more obsessed with the idea of a personal mission to transform European society. Within the context of that fixation, she comes to view herself as a "double being." Intrigued by her husband Walter's fear that she is going insane, she associates the awareness of man's inherent doubleness with that insanity, and she concludes that modern "normal" society has lost its knowledge of humanity's true nature. Pointing to what she sees as a precedent in classical antiquity, she talks about representations of Apollo as both man and woman, insisting that human beings, like the Greek gods, are dual in nature. When Walter presses her to define her own duality more specifically, she responds that she is both man and woman. From this time on, she identifies more and more strongly with the concept of the hermaphrodite.

Clarisse's conscious association of insanity with the redemptive power of the dual individual draws her to Moosbrugger. She begins a crusade to set him free. Within her thoughts he becomes a particularly potent example of the double man. Specifically, she views him as the embodiment of her own mission to unite within herself the opposing extremes of the male element, identified in her mind with the figures of Christ and Nietzsche respectively. For that reason, she tries to persuade Ulrich to help her break Moosbrugger out of prison. She believes that if he can be freed, the redemption of the society will be the result.

To a large extent, Clarisse and Moosbrugger are symbols for what Musil saw as the ultimate focal idea of the novel, carried to its pathological extreme. The starkness of their portrayal sets off through contrast a more contemplative, philosophical development of the author's concept of human duality. The latter is presented during the progress of what the narrator describes as "a journey to the furthest limits of the possible, skirting the dangers of the impossible and unnatural, even of the repulsive, and perhaps not always quite avoiding them." This "journey" is Ulrich's final attempt to find the missing portion of his own identity. It takes place as he seeks to enter the "Other Condition" through the increasingly intense relationship with his sister.

In an important passage from his notebook, Musil suggests that the nucleus for *The Man without Qualities* is contained in an early poem that he wrote, entitled "**Isis und Osiris**" (Isis and Osiris). Both for its relevance to the discussion of the Ulrich-Agathe portion of the novel, and as one of few surviving examples of Musil's early awkward experimentation with lyric forms, the poem is presented here in its entirety:

Isis and Osiris

On the leaves of the stars the moon-boy lay
Sleeping silvery dim,
And the sun-wheel on its way
Turned around and gazed at him.
  From the desert came the red wind's wail,
  And along the coast there is no sail.

And his sister softly from the sleeper
Cut his manhood free, did it consume.
And she gave her soft red heart then for it,
Placed it on him in his organ's room.
  And in dream the wound again grew whole.
  And she ate the lovely sex she stole.

Lo, then roared aloud the sunlight,
As the sleeper started from his sleep,
Stars were tossing, just as rowboats
Moored on chains will surge and dart
When the mighty tempests start.

Lo, his brothers, rage asmoulder,
Chased the robber winsome, fair,
And he then his bow did shoulder,
And the blue space broke in there,

Woods collapsed beneath their tread,
And the stars ran with them filled with dread.
  Yet none caught the slim, bird-shouldered
    maiden,
  Not a one, despite how far he ran.

He alone, the young boy whom she called at
    night,
Finds her when the moon and sun are changing,
Of all hundred brothers none but this,
And he eats her heart, and she eats his.

There is a direct textual link between *The Man without Qualities* and the myth presented in the poem. In a conversation with his newly rediscovered sister, Ulrich attempts to describe the startlingly intense attraction that exists between them. In doing so, he refers to a variety of myths, including that of the human being divided into two, Pygmalion. Hermaphroditus, and the legend of Isis and Osiris. He points to these models as examples of a historic human craving for a double of the opposite sex.

The basis for the connection between the poem and the second half of the novel lies in Musil's interest in the Egyptian sun god Osiris and his sister-wife, the moon goddess Isis, as archetypal symbols for the love between brother and sister. The author was fascinated by these particular figures because Isis represents the irrational, metaphysical dimension, while her brother is identified with the opposing material and rational elements. Unification of these separate halves, graphically signified in the poem by the exchange of hearts and in the novel by Agathe's longing to trade bodies with Ulrich, connotes the merging of fundamental antithetical tendencies of mortality through the power of love.

As ultimately developed within the novel, the longing for completion of the self, which is the focus of "**Isis and Osiris**," is Musil's most extreme projection of the sense of possibility. It is the motivation for Ulrich's attempt to join Agathe in the Utopia of the "Other Condition" through actualization of what Marie-Louise Roth has called "the felt inkling of unity between spirit and nature, subject and object, the dream of termination of the duality between 'I' and 'you.'"

Ulrich's first meeting with his sister after their father's death sets the tone for the intimate union that develops between them. The two siblings encounter each other similarly clothed, so that Agathe immediately characterizes them as "twins." As Ulrich forms his initial impression of her, an idea surfaces that is explored in ever-intensifying variation through the remainder of the novel. While considering her attributes, he notes that she is neither patently emancipated nor bohemian, in spite of the peculiar clothing in which she has received him. The more he attempts to penetrate to the essence of her nature, the more he is struck with the idea that there is something hermaphrodite about her.

In the descriptions of subsequent encounters, ever-more emphasis is placed upon the notion that Agathe is Ulrich's female alter ego. One scene presents him as seeing himself approaching in the figure of Agathe as she enters a room. To be sure, this other person is more beautiful than he is, and she has an aura about her that he does not see in himself, but he cannot help but think that she is really himself, repeated and somehow changed. It is this feeling that she embodies the longed for missing aspect of his identity that moves Ulrich to suggest to her the experiment of living together in a new kind of union beyond the restraints of conventional social reality. His vision of their spiritual merging in the ideal realm that he calls "the Millenium, the Kingdom of a Thousand Years" suggests the attainment of fulfillment in absolute interdependence, not only with each other, but also with the world as a whole.

The process of unification is one of withdrawal from the concerns of material reality into a condition of shared contemplation. Together, Ulrich and Agathe explore many ideas about man's physical and spiritual nature, his actual and possible situation in the world, and the means by which the individual may transcend the traditional limits of mortal existence. Dense conversations about love, mysticism, and morality are part of the "search for a state in which the individual is enhanced, in which his ego rises and does not fall."

In the Agathe-Ulrich dialogues Musil presents the elements of his theory of a psychology of feeling, the bases of which are his interpretations of Nietzsche's ideas concerning private and general morality, the era of comparison, the logic of dreams, suffering and compassion, love and justice. In many instances, complete chapters are devoted to essayistic elaboration of theoretical points and abstractions, interrupting the flow of the narrative with material that Musil eventually recognized as being out of place in the novel. Even for the careful reader, these passages form an unnecessary barrier to the clear understanding of the author's artistic objectives.

Through the exchange of ideas, Ulrich and Agathe draw nearer to each other, until they begin to think in concert. As their relationship approaches the peak of its intensity, the narrator describes them as feeling as if they were a single entity, working together in a harmony similar to that of people who play the piano four-handed, or people who read the same material together aloud. On a mystical, dreamlike level, they seem to melt together and become one being, sharing a common personality.

The peculiar ambiguity of their situation at this point is underscored in the designation that they give to themselves: "the unseparated and not united ones." It suggests that their union, despite its spiritual depth, is fragile and unstable. Recognition that the bond between them may collapse causes them first to contemplate suicide, then to continue the experiment to its final extreme. Agathe gives the signal for the beginning of its last stage when she says that they will not kill themselves until they have exhausted every other possibility for resolving their situation.

The climactic event of the novel is a combination of physical and spiritual union, in which incest serves as a catalyst for the final shattering of all boundaries between brother and sister. In one of the novel fragments, Musil describes them as coming together physically like animals seeking warmth. In the process of sexual union, a spiritual merging occurs on another level, and each of them has the feeling of having assimilated the other. Time and space lose their meaning as the lovers transcend all previous experience and enter the absolute realm of the "Other Condition."

Although the protagonists of *The Man without Qualities* do achieve self-completion temporarily, it is clear that Musil did not envision them finding a permanent escape from conventional reality in their mystical utopia. As he expressed it to Oskar Maurus Fontana during their celebrated interview, the attempt to prolong the experience fails because the absolute state cannot be maintained. In that assessment, as in the novel itself, he gave a lasting indictment of a world progressing toward war, in which only a "man without qualities" could survive.

Christian Rogowski (essay date 1994)

SOURCE: "Der Mann ohne Eigenschaften," in *Distinguished Outsider: Robert Musil and His Critics,* Camden House, 1994, pp. 146-75.

[*In the following excerpt, Rogowski surveys the body of critical writings on* The Man without Qualities.]

Scholars of Germanistik seem to like books reputed to be difficult. Musil's *Der Mann ohne Eigenschaften* surely must rank among the books most written about in the field of literature in the German language. Ever since its republication under the editorship of Adolf Frisé in 1952, there has been a steady and incessant stream of articles, essays, and monographs on Musil's unfinished magnum opus from all sorts of different angles and perspectives. Given the sheer volume of criticism—now numbering in the hundreds, if not thousands, of works—it is surprising that there are few close readings of the novel that investigate its form or describe the nature of its language in detailed analysis. On the one hand, this probably has to do with the scope of the novel, which makes comprehensive analysis difficult. On the other hand, it is understandable that most critics seem eager to aim for a kind of master reading of the text rather than attempting to account for specific stylistic or poetic phenomena.

Serious study of Musil's complex and multifaceted work requires a considerable investment of time and intellectual energy on the part of the reader. To many scholars Musil's grand novel appears to present a kind of athletic challenge to display one's intellectual mastery. It is not surprising, then, that the novel is such a popular object for doctoral dissertations, leading to a proliferation of book-length studies that are as well-meaning as they are redundant: a limited number of topics is addressed time and again, with "new" methodologies frequently offering reworkings of familiar points rather than genuine contributions that open new vistas. The pressures of the academic world dictate that minute differences in accentuation be presented as radically new results, encouraging a tendency to subsume the complexity of Musil's text under a general overriding concept.

In the Cold War climate of the 1950s, the tendency of mainstream Germanistik was to downplay the political implications of Musil's art. A particularly telling example is the work of Hermann Pongs. In the second edition of his study on the modern novel (1956), Pongs added a discussion of *Der Mann ohne Eigenschaften* to supplement a work he had undertaken in 1952 in response to what he called "the current existential distress of the Germans" (reprint 1963, 7). Pongs emulates notions derived from Freudian psychoanalysis to describe Musil's protagonist, Ulrich, as a prime representative of the modern existential condition of ambivalence, a neurotic condition that is as acute, if not more so, after the Second World War as it was in Musil's time. While acknowledging Musil's predominantly critical attitude toward the sociohistorical situation depicted in the novel, Pongs renders this attitude essentially apolitical by presenting Musil's work as the diagnosis of a general "disease of the time" (326). In this fashion, he carefully avoids addressing the causal and functional background of the situation. Pongs ascribes to Musil a striving for *Einfalt*—unity and simplicity—that would resolve the polarizations and dichotomies that characterize the predicament of modernity (13). At certain moments in Pongs's writing there emerges a peculiar rhetoric that appears to belie the ostensible concern with existential crisis and mysticism: at one point, for instance, Pongs professes his exasperation with Musil's negative portrayal of the Habsburg military, although, Pongs exclaims, the admirable discipline of the Habsburg army had been the one element that provided cohesion in a society plagued by ethnic tensions, "truly a defective eastern bullwark (*Ostwall*) of Europe" (329). Similarly, Pongs's rhetoric of distrust of "the whole range of the Eastern peoples" ("die ganze Skala der Ostvölker," 329), presumably representing force of destruction and contamination, curiously harks back to those twelve years in the history of the German speaking countries that some representatives of Germanistik were all too eager to forget.

Sometimes the ideological or professional bias of a critic created oddly skewed readings of Musil's novel. Alfred Focke, for instance, writing from his perspective as a Jesuit theologian, eagerly follows ideas proposed by Gerhard Müller in his 1958 Vienna dissertation, hailing Musil's magnum opus as a philosophical and religious myth about the "fundamentally tragic status of human nature as such" (Focke 1957/58, 30). Such lofty ruminations culminate in the thesis that Musil's protagonist Ulrich represents modern man's alienation from God. Ulrich, Focke contends, fails to achieve a metaphysical trust in his maker, remaining unable to take the redeeming "leap into faith" (33). On a more mundane note, Gerhard Irle (1965) places Musil in the context of works by Kafka, William Faulkner, and Virginia Woolf that address the question of sanity in the modern context. Musil's portrayal of individual psychoses in the characters Clarisse and Moosbrugger, Irle proposes, turns the novel into a prime specimen of what Irle defines as a new subgenre, the "psychiatric novel" (148). Such reductive readings are by no means atypical during the 1950s and 1960s, the first two decades of academic Musil criticism.

There were, however, also serious efforts to provide a solid basis for the study of Musil's work. One of the first contributions to a more focused stylistic analysis came from Beda Allemann, whose influential monograph *Irons und Dichtung* (1956) culminates in a lengthy discussion of Musil's use of irony in **Der Mann ohne Eigenschaften**. Allemann attempts to define irony as a selfconscious literary device that all but places literature in a sphere remote from the world of contingencies. His central metaphor is that of a *Spielraum* (4), a realm of poetic activity opened up by the self-canceling effects of ironic configurations. Allemann's notion of irony is indebted to German early Romanticism (particularly as typified by Novalis and Friedrich Schlegel) and is based in large part upon Martin Heidegger's concept of literature as *Dichtung,* a sphere of human activity that transcends everyday concerns. To Allemann, irony is a literary mode that contributes to the erosion of existential certainties by calling into question preestablished thought patterns. The comprehensive loss of certainties is one of the key features of the modern predicament. Musil's grand novel fragment serves Allemann as an ideal illustration of the connection between the experience of modernity thus defined and the essentially ironic nature of modern *Dichtung.* Allemann gives a series of examples from Musil's novel to describe his ironic style as "conciliatory" (173); Musil gently criticizes the world he describes, yet he never establishes a fixed vantage point from which to lay claim to a greater degree of authority. Each issue discussed or character portrayed is conceded a certain validity. Moreover, Musil's use of irony extends to his own poetic endeavor. Allemann argues that the irony in Musil's novel lies not so much in the manner in which particular statements are formulated but in the nature of the overall configurations, such as the relationships between the characters, which establish a network of finely tuned gradations in differences and correspondences.

Both Allemann's approach and his conclusions are highly questionable: he associates irony with the wistful self-awareness of a culture in its late phase, employing notions such as *Spätheit* (lateness) and *Spätzeit* (late phase), inspired by Martin Heidegger. From this

Heideggerian perspective, history—in the sense of concrete material existence as reflected in the novel—evaporates and gives way to lofty notions of the privileged position of Musil as the wise poet-philosopher. Allemann in effect turns Musil into a modern version of the benign sage, very much in the manner of the public image of the late Theodor Fontane prevalent in West Germany in the 1950s. In his pronouncedly apolitical stance, Allemann is representative of a general tendency within Western Germanistik in the Adenauer era. In their insistence on a perspective that supposedly transcended politics (a stance that tended to amount to a general disavowal of the importance of politics altogether), literary critics directly mirrored the overall climate of restoration and conservatism.

Allemann's theses on irony spawned a debate in Musil criticism that in many ways continues to this day. Walter H. Sokel (1960/61) was among the first to respond publicly, noting that Musil's irony is far removed from the kind of all-encompassing conciliatory attitude Allemann ascribes to Musil. Sokel emphasizes Musil's critical attitude toward any kind of rash and superficial attempts at overcoming the existential, cultural, and political crisis depicted in his novel. Musil's irony, Sokel proposes, borders on satire whenever he unmasks and debunks efforts to combat the experience of fragmentation by way of a "feigned totality" (211).

It is easy to see why a younger generation immediately took issue with Allemann in social and political terms. Arntzen's 1956 dissertation on satire in Musil's work, published in book form in 1960, was written very much as a response to Allemann and as a rebuttal. Against Allemann's concept of irony as a literary mode transcending particular epochs and genres, Arntzen offers the concept of satire, stressing the element of hard-edged social criticism in Musil's novel. To Arntzen, Musil's main aim is an analysis of a culture in crisis, an investigation of the numerous factors that led to the collapse of civilization in central Europe. Arntzen is right in stressing that the critical impetus of Musil's project should not be overlooked. Yet his own critical stance, despite its sometimes brilliant rhetoric, lacks political concreteness: the key concept that runs through Arntzen's study is that of Musil's novel as a diagnosis of an unspecified societal *Schizophrenie.* The metaphor, taken from the sphere of psychotherapy, suggests that what Musil describes is a kind of organic illness devoid of concrete historical, political, economic, and ideological causes. Critics have since noted that Allemann's and Arntzen's approaches are not as dissimilar as Arntzen implies, turning much of Arntzen's polemic into a dispute over terminology (Karthaus 1965b, 466; Huber 1982, 99). Still, with his focus on *Gattungsgeschichte* (historical genre studies) and his insistence on what in the widest sense is a political reading of Musil, Arntzen provided useful impulses to Musil scholarship. Alongside a broad discussion of the nature and history of satirical writing, Arntzen presents a wide variety of examples based on close readings of passages from

Musil's book. For this reason alone Arntzen's highly readable book remains one of the most significant contributions to Musil scholarship.

More limited in scope but just as fruitful is Albrecht Schöne's discussion of Musil's use of the subjunctive mood. Originally Schöne's inaugural lecture upon assuming a professorship at the University of Göttingen, it was published as an article in 1961. The essay has since been reprinted several times and ranks as one of the most impressive contributions to a stylistic analysis of Musil's work. In his eloquent and brilliant presentation, Schöne explores the significance of the subjunctive mode in Musil's novel, showing how aspects of grammar and style relate to overriding thematic concerns. He distinguishes the function and significance of the various types of subjunctive (*irrealis, potentialis,* and so on), all of which correspond to particular elements of Musil's overall poetics, such as his interest in experimentation or his focus on a utopian perspective. Such characteristics lead Schöne to place Musil and his work firmly in the tradition of the European Enlightenment. In his drafts and manuscripts, Musil sometimes experimented with putting different sets of characters in the same situation. Such variants, Schöne argues, possess the same degree of validity, since Musil's experimental attitude allows for—in fact, stresses—the coexistence of a variety of possibilities. Schöne does not take sides in the dispute over the continuation of Musil's unfinished novel: in his reading, the fragmentary and open-ended form of the book becomes a corollary of *Experimentier gesinnung,* the experimental attitude of Musil the trained scientist, from which springs the novelist's penchant for the subjunctive mood (reprint 1975, 304). Unfortunately, the scope of Schöne's essay does not allow him to develop his ideas at greater length. Yet the discussion of what superficially may appear to be minor grammatical issues yields a wide range of results of interest not only to the Musil scholar but to anyone concerned with the history of modern German prose.

Werner Hoffmeister's *Studien zur erlebten Rede bei Thomas Mann und Robert Musil* of 1965, based on his 1962 Brown University dissertation, is similar in approach. Like Schöne, Hoffmeister focuses on a particular stylistic phenomenon from which he draws general conclusions about the nature of Musil's art. This method, which Hoffmeister calls "inductive" and "empirical" (8), is enhanced here by an essentially comparative perspective. Musil employs *erlebte Rede,* the narrative technique known in English as free indirect discourse, with particular frequency. Hoffmeister places Musil's use of this stylistic device in the context of an overall tendency in modern literature toward an "interiorization of narration" (160), in which the focus shifts from the depiction of an outside reality to an observation of the operations of individual consciousness. Hoffmeister's book anticipates ideas that were later to be more fully explored in structuralist theories of narrative, such as Dorrit Cohn's *Transparent Minds* (1978), a monograph on modes of representing consciousness in prose fiction, which includes insightful comments on Musil's narrative technique.

Perhaps the most comprehensive thematic interpretation of Musil's novel to emerge from the first phase of Musil criticism is that of Wolfdietrich Rasch (1963). Under eight headings he addresses some of the crucial thematic and formal aspects that continue to occupy Musil scholarship to this day, such as the dissolution of linear narrative, the issue of utopianism, the tension between rationality and mysticism, the question of irony, and the relationship between Ulrich and Agathe. Rasch synthesizes much of the previous scholarship, including Wilfried Berghan's 1956 Bonn dissertation on essayistic narration, and stresses the consistency of Musil's overall design in his discussion of the tricky questions about the envisaged continuation of the unfinished novel. Always mindful of the author's professed intention, Rasch manages to combine an affirmative stance with a perspective critical of the limitations and internal contradictions of Musil's narrative project.

The critical works of Allemann, Arntzen, Schöne, Hoffmeister, and Rasch remain exemplary achievements in Musil studies, regardless of the changes in interests, methods, and theoretical paradigms that Germanistik has undergone in the last thirty-odd years. They stand out in the incipient phase of Musil scholarship, when much energy was absorbed by the notorious dispute over the reliability of Frisé's edition and the need for a "definitive" version of the text, accompanied by innumerable essayistic reflections and appreciations of Musil and his work.

The 1960s brought a gradual reorientation in Musil studies toward *Geistesgeschichte* in the study of ***Der Mann ohne Eigenschaften,*** as scholars began to relate Musil's ideas to larger intellectual traditions or systematically explore Musil's intellectual background. Ulrich Karthaus, in his examination of the connection between the temporal structures of Musil's novel and the *andere Zustand* (1965a), represents the former approach. He employs notions derived from Kant's *Critique of Pure Reason* and Heidegger's *Being and Time* to examine Musil's treatment of time. The first two parts of the novel, he contends, are characterized by a suspension of linear time. Generally, the date and duration of fictional events cannot be easily identified. Instead, time appears as a polydimensional "playing field of poetic time" (156), filtered through the subjective experience of Musil's characters. This process allows a second kind of reality to shine through that eludes rationality. Part three, however, reasserts time as a chronological sequence of occurrences, high-lighting the problem underlying Ulrich and Agathe's quest for the *andere Zustand* and showing their efforts to lend duration to a different mode of experience to be irresolvable. The only way for Ulrich and Agathe to transcend the contingencies of time, Karthaus maintains, would be to take recourse to the faith of an established religious tradition. Without recourse to religious dogma, their experiment is doomed to failure. To Karthaus, it is a sign of Musil's greatness and intellectual integrity that he refused to provide a fictional solution to a conflict that cannot be resolved in material reality. Karthaus thus stands in clear and diametrical opposition to the mystical tendencies of Kaiser and Wilkins (1962), who had claimed that Musil intended a kind of apotheosis of Ulrich and Agathe's spiritual union. At the same time, Karthaus's approach raises methodological problems concerning the applicability of philosophical theorems to an analysis of a literary work. Karthaus does not seem entirely to escape the pressure of systematization, the temptation to fit Musil's novel into a preconceived philosophical model.

Dieter Kühn (1965) is more attentive to the peculiar qualities of Musil's prose in his examination of Musil's characteristic stylistic devices of analogy and variation against the backdrop of some of the traditions that had a formative influence upon his intellectual outlook. To this end, Kühn correlates Musil's characters with the sources of their internal world. With Ulrich, for instance, it is primarily Ernst Mach's empiriocriticism; Nietzsche provides much of the substance that fuels the conflicts between Walter and Clarisse; and the watered down *Lebensphilosophie* of turn-of-the-century Swedish educational reformer Ellen Key is satirized in Diotima. Of particular interest is Kühn's discussion of the affinity between Gottfried von Strassburg and Musil's treatment of the relationship of Ulrich and Agathe, an issue later explored in more depth by Wolfgang Freese (1972). Kühn stresses the connections between Ulrich and the other characters, who all serve as foils of Musil's protagonist. Kühn's book stands out from other dissertations of the period in its focus, conciseness, and overall readability.

The most comprehensive and systematic attempt to place Musil's novel in the context of German intellectual history was undertaken by Renate von Heydebrand in her 1962 Münster dissertation, published in expanded form as a book in 1966. Here von Heydebrand provides a comprehensive overview of the textual sources that make up Ulrich's intellectual world. Though most of the sources and their authors had been known for a while, nobody had previously taken the trouble of actually identifying and analyzing specific references to works and ideas. Combining *Geistesgeschichte* with basic factual research, von Heydebrand assembles an impressive range of references to philosophical and literary works, showing that Musil transformed and assimilated a wide variety of sources. At the basis of Musil's concepts and images stand past thinkers like Nietzsche, Emerson, and Mach alongside divergent contemporary influences such as Gestalt theory, the experimental psychology of Ernst Kretschmer, Lucien Lévy-Bruhl's anthropology, the sociophilosophical theories of Georg Simmel and Max Scheler, and the mystical ideas of such diverse writers as Maurice Maeterlinck, Ludwig Klages, and Martin Buber. With an abundance of material, von Heydebrand convincingly illustrates a tendency in Musil toward what she calls an "escape into quotation" (96): Musil frequently resorts to citing pronouncements from predecessors whenever his own efforts at expressing something and at transcending the limitations of language threaten to fail. Because of this practice, his novel to a large extent amounts to a collage of citations. Unfortunately, von Heydebrand devotes little attention to the manner in which the material is integrated, the concept of intertextuality and a methodology for analyzing it systematically having not yet been developed when she wrote her study. Still, her study is much more than a positivistic exercise in identifying literary and philosophical interconnections. Rather, it places scholarship on the intellectual background of Musil's novel on a firm footing. To this day, von Heydebrand's book remains one of the most important contributions to the study of *Der Mann ohne Eigenschaften*.

During the late 1960s several studies appeared that complement the *geistesgeschichtlich* approach in aiming to explore in greater detail some of the standard poetological issues raised in the preceding one and a half decades. One such analysis is that of Peter Nusser (1967), who attempts to reconstruct Musil's implicit theory of the novel by way of correlating the author's critical utterances from essays, journal entries, and letters with the novel *Der Mann ohne Eigenschaften*. Nusser attempts to describe the formal aspects of the novel, such as the dissolution of linear narrative and the way in which events are not described directly but refracted through a perceiving consciousness. Perhaps not too surprisingly, Nusser's essentially cumulative method yields the expected conclusion—familiar at least since Berghahn's 1956 dissertation—that the essayistic writing style reflects Musil's "possibilitarian attitude" (*Möglichkeitsgesinnung*).

Jörg Kühne's study on Musil's figurative language (1968) is more fruitful. Kühne shows what distinguishes Musil's use of the *Gleichnis*—a stylistic device that encompasses a wide variety of figurative modes of expression such as the simile, the metaphor, or even the extended parable—from that of other authors: a Musilian *Gleichnis* links two distinct notional spheres in a sometimes surprising juxtaposition; yet the analogies suggested do not serve to render the depicted phenomena easier to comprehend by adding plasticity and concreteness. Instead of mainly serving a decorative, illustrative, or explicatory function, Musil's metaphors, as it were, create the fictional reality itself (a view endorsed without significant modification by Gérard Wicht, 1984). On the one hand, linguistic images reflect the subjectivity of the characters. On the other, they make the presence of a narrating consciousness felt. However, this consciousness cannot be associated with a real personage, either within or outside of the fictional world depicted. Alongside theoretical interpolations and reflections, similes and metaphors construct what Kühne, in the tradition of German Idealist philosophy, calls a "transcendental" narrator, a narrating instance in which the distinction between empirical author, fictive narrator, and fictional character becomes blurred. The result is an amalgamation of the three into a narrative trinity that Kühne identifies as the crucial aesthetic basis of Musil's novel (35). This transcendental narrator, Kühne argues, renders impossible interpretations of the novel along the lines of individual psychology. Kühne counters earlier critics such as Michel (1954), who had stressed Musil's essentially ambivalent stance. In Kühne's view, ambivalence is a characteristic not of Musil's style but of the reality his style aims to address (55). Kühne's book is highly technical, but it offers a great deal of insight into the peculiar nature of Musil's style, which he always views as a direct correlate of Musil's philosophical and aesthetic vision.

In her book *Ratio und "Mystik" im Werk Robert Musils* (1968), Elisabeth Albertsen explores one of the novel's central conceptual polarities. Her thematic reading draws on Musil's other works as well as materials from the unpublished *Nachlass* to show how Musil attempts to overcome the binary oppositions he creates. With the exception of Ulrich and Agathe, Albertsen contends, all characters in the novel represent false efforts at a synthesis. Yet even the true or authentic "mystical" experiment of brother and sister eventually leads to failure. Albertsen puts *Mystik* in inverted commas to emphasize the predominantly secular nature of Musil's mysticism, which is expressed not in a longing for unity with a deity but in the "conversational eroticism" (*Gesprächs-Eros*) of Ulrich and Agathe (107). She shows how Musil deferred the inevitable dual catastrophe that looms over the novel—the simultaneous failure of Ulrich and Agathe's spiritual union and the outbreak of the First World War—by expanding a segment of the novel from fifty pages in an early draft to well over a thousand pages. Albertsen stresses the irresolvable unity of Musil's writing and his thinking while denying him the status of a thinker who went beyond the intellectual parameters of his time (15), a notion heavily contested by a generation of scholars that emerged in the ensuing years to claim Musil as a prime spokesman of *Ideologiekritik*. Albertsen's contribution is uneven in quality; the chapter on language, for instance, which she added in the process of revising this Tübingen dissertation into a book, is not well integrated. The author appears to argue from a defensive position, as some of her polemical and combative asides indicate, primarily aimed against the sociopolitical ideas of Frankfurt school *Kritische Theorie* that were making their presence felt in Germanistik at the time.

Perhaps the most outspoken politically charged contribution to Musil studies of the period is the monograph by Klaus Laermann (1970). Laermann radically deviates from the traditionally affirmative approach, which consisted largely of collecting and commenting on a series of pertinent quotations. Instead, he examines Musil's novel from a decidedly neo-Marxist perspective by looking at the sociopolitical implications associated with the Musilian notion of an absence of qualities—*Eigenschaftslosigkeit*. Musil's protagonist Ulrich here emerges as a representative of a segment of the bourgeois intelligentsia at the beginning of the century. Ulrich's detached mode of existence, Laermann finds, is primarily a symptom of the overall alienation of marginalized intellectuals. Up to that point, few critics had so much as even noticed that Ulrich's existence is apparently free of all material concerns. Laermann argues that the fact that Ulrich is able to take one year's *Urlaub vom Leben* (leave from life) clearly indicates that he is economically privileged. That Musil downplayed the economic aspects of the society he portrayed implies to Laermann that the entire literary plan to present a comprehensive analysis of a culture in decline is seriously flawed, since it ignores some of the most important factors. Laermann integrates psychoanalytic concepts into his approach, identifying the predicament of Musil's protagonist with the Freudian notion of narcissism. Ulrich's detachment, which to most critics had thus far signified an enviable stance of openness and freedom from personal and political concerns, in Laermann's reading turns into a socially conditioned psychopathological condition. Laermann is highly critical of what he sees as the subjectivist and aestheticist bias of Musil's novel, implying that Musil did not fully comprehend the factors that determined his own position in the society he confronted. Perhaps the most fruitful discussion to emerge out of Laermann's study is that of Musil's position in the overall context of the various critiques of rationality that emerged in the latter half of the nineteenth century and continued into the twentieth, an issue explored later, with differences in emphasis, by Bernd-Rüdiger Hüppauf (1971), Götz Müller (1972), Hartmut Böhme (1974, 1986), Stephan Howald (1984), and Cornelia Blasberg (1984).

I have already remarked on the conspicuous dearth of contributions to Musil studies based on reader-response criticism. One notable exception is Hans Wolfgang Schaffnit's monograph *Mimesis als Problem* (1971), which views Musil's poetological reflections as an attempt to conceptualize a new kind of reader. Drawing on Roman Ingarden's notion of the essentially interactive process of reading, Schaffnit stresses the role assigned to the reader in the "concretization" of Musil's novel. Yet Schaffnit's discussion, replete with resonances of phenomenological criticism from Emil Staiger and Martin Heidegger, remains on a highly abstract level. Jürgen C. Thöming (1974) is one of the few Musil scholars directly to emulate reader-response criticism, whereas the philosophical component of Schaffnit's phenomenology found its continuation in the work of David Dawlianidse (1978), Dieter Fuder (1979), and Hartmut Cellbrot (1988), among others.

In the vein of *Ideologiekritik,* Götz Müller (1972) bases his analysis of Musil's novel upon Max Horkheimer's definition of ideology as false consciousness. In quoting and parodying pertinent contemporary modes of thought, Musil sets out to critique ideologies as inadequate responses to the social and philosophical problems of the era. To Müller, Musil's montage of heterogeneous linguistic material is "meta-linguistic" in that it reflects on the use of language as purveyor of world views. The dialogues of Arnheim and Diotima, for instance, are composed largely of direct quotations from the works of Walter Rathenau and Maurice Maeterlinck. Musil debunks the false pathos of these writers in placing their lofty ideas into an ironic context. Yet, at the same time, he acknowledges that the pathos of watered down *Lebensphilosophie* is not too far removed from the solutions that he himself is pursuing. Müller argues that this close affinity of ostensibly divergent thought patterns is evidenced, for instance, in the figures of Clarisse, whose madness consists of taking Nietzsche's ideas literally, and Moosbrugger, whose crime represents a thwarted version of the neoromantic quest for some primal unity of experience.

Musil's montage of quotations and allusions, addressed by Müller from a pronouncedly political perspective, is seen by Dietrich Hochstätter (1972) as a decidedly apolitical question of stylistic perspectivism. In retrospect, the central idea that Hochstätter proposes, that of a perspectivism that transcends ideological bias, appears as a correlate, on the level of textual analysis, to the general notion of a methodological pluralism that was advanced at the time by mainstream Germanistik in response to the challenges posed by the politically volatile climate in academia. All the same, Hochstätter develops his stylistic analysis primarily in opposition to traditional Musil criticism: he rejects Arntzen's notion of satire as well as Allemann's concept of constructive irony as too undifferentiated. Musil's method of citing and emulating a multiplicity of linguistic styles, Hochstätter contends, correlates with his multidimensional and "polyvalent" attitudes toward life and toward thinking (7). The examination of stylistic patterns culminates in a description of the "prismatic-essayistic" overall structure of Musil's novel (55). On the thematic level, Hochstätter's enterprise yields results similar to those of Elisabeth Albertsen (1968). Like Albertsen, for instance, Hochstätter stresses the essentially secular nature of Musil's mysticism and utopianism, while at the same time refusing to reflect on any concrete sociopolitical implications of Musil's ideas. In Hochstätter's reading, "interpretive multidimensionality" (147) appears to become a value in itself, posed against critical attempts to appropriate Musil in the interest of any specific ideological agenda.

In a climate characterized by politically charged polemics on the one side and recourse to lofty and supposedly timeless values on the other, Hartmut Böhme's monograph *Anomie und Entfremdung* (1974) marks a clear watershed. Steering clear of both political maneuvering and affirmative paraphrase, Böhme attempts to address the complexity of Musil's work in terms equally sensitive to aesthetic as to nonaesthetic issues. He takes as his starting point Musil's political essays and reads them as responses to the sociopolitical crisis of central Europe during and after the First World War. The project of confronting and analyzing this crisis continued in what was to become ***Der Mann ohne Eigenschaften***.

While Böhme in a way builds here on Marie-Louise Roth's work covering some of the same issues (1972), he develops a highly differentiated methodology. Throughout, he attempts to take into account the sociohistorical context both of his own theoretical position as critic and that of Musil's texts as the subject matter of the investigation.

First and foremost, Böhme takes issue with Laermann's one-sided reading of Musil's works as evidence of narcissistic and escapist tendencies. While Böhme acknowledges that such tendencies certainly are present in Musil, they do not make up the whole picture; in his essays and in the intricate ironic structures of his grand novel, Musil develops a critique of the very social conditions that produce the kinds of psychopathological deformations Laermann had identified. Böhme uses the sociopsychological concept of *anomie* to characterize Musil's analysis of central Europe in the first third of this century; technological developments, ethnic and social tensions, and other factors had eroded the established order and brought about a paradoxical situation in which hectic activity on the part of particular groups was coupled with the stagnation of the social system as a whole. In Böhme's reading, the psychopathology of Musil's characters is motivated by an essentially critical orientation: the extent of their individual alienation (*Entfremdung*) is a symptom of the overall societal *anomie,* the two concepts that make up the title of Böhme's study. Musil, Böhme argues, exposes the ideological causes of the current malaise, with its combination of social inertia and spiritual disintegration, in his portrayal of the array of representatives of the various discourses prevalent in the Habsburg Empire. As far as we know, Musil intended his novel to be divided into four major parts. Böhme identifies the death of Ulrich's father as the axis around which the novel is structured symmetrically. This construct gives the utopian experiments of Ulrich and Agathe the connotation of a rebellion against patriarchy authority on the personal level, corresponding to a rebellion against patriarchy on the general level. To Böhme, Musil is far from advocating escapist withdrawal; rather, he develops critical countermodels in the shape of the various utopian projects envisaged by his protagonists. To do so, however, it is necessary first to probe the full extent of the existential implications of the sociohistorical situation for the individual.

Böhme draws on a multitude of concepts developed in sociology, psychology, and social philosophy. This makes for a multifaceted and highly differentiated discussion that aims to address the issues raised in all their complexity, in many ways already transcending the limitations of the sociopolitical approaches that were being developed at the time. Böhme's writing is dense and not entirely free of certain tendencies to favor jargon over accessibility. All the same, his book is one of the most theoretically sophisticated and fruitful studies of important aspects of Musil's oeuvre. His combination of a multitude of diverse intellectual traditions effectively raised the level of critical discourse on Musil's grand novel, synthesizing Hochstätter's notion of multi-dimensionality with a perspective that places Musil in a larger socio-historical context. Böhme's study represents a welcome change from the excessive adulation of Musil on the part of affirmative Musil criticism and from the potential hostility of neo-Marxist scholars. To be sure, his ideas have not remained uncontradicted: Stephan Howald (1984), for instance, takes issue with what he regards as Böhme's tendency to underestimate Musil's aesthetic achievement. Böhme later augmented his approach in a series of articles that have also had a lasting impact on Musil scholarship. Of particular interest in this context is his seminal essay on methodological issues involved in an analysis of *Der Mann ohne Eigenschaften,* first published in 1976 and reprinted several times in different contexts.

The more traditional method of *Geistesgeschichte* in German studies continued to yield productive results throughout the 1970s. For instance, Dietmar Goltschnigg's *Mystische Tradition im Roman Robert Musils* (1974) presents an extension of part of von Heydebrand's work on the intellectual influences upon Musil's novel. The conversations between Ulrich and Agathe draw heavily on the mystical sources from various centuries collected by Martin Buber in the anthology *Ekstatische Konfessionen* (Ecstatic Confessions) of 1909. Musil, as Marie-Louise Roth (1972) had demonstrated, made elaborate excerpts from a volume by Karl Girgensohn, who had based his reflections on the psychology of religion on material from Buber's anthology. Goltschnigg explores this interconnection in great detail, giving an extensively documented analysis of the manner in which Musil in his turn transformed, modified, and integrated the material into his novel. In this fashion, Goltschnigg provides fascinating insights into Musil's creative process. Goltschnigg is also the author of one of the best short introductions to Musil's novel, a concise essay published in a volume on the twentieth-century German novel edited by Paul Michael Lützeler in 1983.

Equally valuable for an understanding of Musil's novel is Jochen Schmidt's 1975 discussion of the concept of *Eigenschaftslosigkeit,* the "lack" or "absence of qualities" characteristic of modern man. Starting with an analysis of the novella **"Grigia,"** Schmidt delineates the esoteric opposition Musil sets up between the isolated individual and a social reality that is rejected. In this antisocial stance of radical inwardness, Schmidt maintains, Musil's ideas display certain affinities to expressionism on the one hand and the contemporary tendencies of a "conservative revolution" on the other (27). Schmidt then outlines the intellectual sources of Musil's ideas on mysticism. He shows how Musil's reading in the mystic tradition ranged far beyond the Buber anthology singled out by Goltschnigg. For instance, the very concept of *Eigenschaftslosigkeit,* Schmidt proves, derives from the *Deutsche Predigten* (German Sermons) of medieval mystic Meister Eckhart, who rejects the concept of a personal God in favor of a notion of a deity without qualities—"âne eigenschaft" (48). Musil's concept, Schmidt continues, presents a secularized and intellectualized elaboration of Eckhart's idea of a transcendence of personhood in the experience of a *unio mystica.* Schmidt places Musil's interest in the mystical tradition within the context of the contemporary debates about inwardness, deindividuation, and abstraction, an intellectual spectrum ranging from Husserl's phenomenology and Kandinsky's aesthetic theories to the appropriation of mysticism by the protofascist propagator of the notion of a *Rassenseele* (racial soul), Alfred Rosenberg. Schmidt singles out the connection between artistic abstraction and *Eigenschaftslosigkeit,* correlates of Musil's interest in portraying in Ulrich a "prototype of modern man" (78). He also employs Kafka's "Description of a Struggle" as a foil to Musil's project, an alternative response to the challenges presented by modernity. Both authors, Schmidt contends, respond to the dissolution of stable social, spiritual, and psychological orders. In Kafka, the resulting existential uprootedness produces anxiety, whereas Musil views it as potentially liberating. Musil's philosophical leanings, then, give rise to a strange blend of conservative and anarchist tendencies; his excessively theoretical orientation, Schmidt concedes, leads to artistic problems in the integration of reflection into the narrative. Musil, Schmidt writes, seeks to merge abstraction and mysticism: "The theory of radical abstraction is the theory of *Mystik*" (84). Schmidt's study is an important contribution to Musil criticism, although it has to be noted that, while his discussion of the connection between aesthetic concerns and the anthropological question of deindividuation is stimulating, Schmidt has difficulties integrating the elements of irony and satire into his analysis.

In 1975, East German author Rolf Schneider supplemented his edition of *Der Mann ohne Eigenschaften* for the GDR with an accompanying introductory monograph on Musil. Since the 1950s, Schneider had been profoundly influenced by Musil in his own career as a creative writer. His book is thus interesting both as a personal homage to Musil and as a document of the situation of literary criticism in the GDR during the 1970s. Schneider's ideological bias, which was perhaps obligatory, is evident in the manner in which he dismisses the entire tradition of Musil criticism in the West as "bourgeois scholarship" (*bürgerliche Forschung*) supposedly oblivious of the historical and political components of Musil's work, a view that ignores the wide range of aesthetic and ideological positions (including explicitly political readings of Musil) that had already been developed by that time. Despite paying lip service to Georg Lukács's orthodox Marxist position, Schneider is deeply sympathetic to Musil as a writer. In his view, the social and political satire implied in Musil's depiction of the *Parallelaktion* (collateral campaign) makes Musil—alongside Brecht—the most astute critic of the cultural pretensions of bourgeois society. Grouping Musil and Brecht together in this fashion may be surprising, but it does signal an effort to remove the stigma of bourgeois "decadence" from the former. Schneider writes as a fellow author rather than a *Literaturwissenschaftler,* the result being a provocative and immensely readable book full of wit and panache.

Narratorial irony, the overriding concern of Schneider's decidedly unscholarly monograph, became the focus of a study by Alan Holmes (1978). Holmes systematically approaches a problem that long has—or ought to have—vexed critics of Musil's novel, namely the exact nature of the interaction between author, narrator, and protagonist. In his chapters on the genesis and transformation of the concepts of *Möglichkeitssinn* and *Eigenschaftslosigkeit,* Holmes covers much of the same territory as Jochen Schmidt (1975), though from a more pragmatic and text-focused angle. To the naive observer, it would appear that Holmes performs the kind of analysis that would constitute the prime task of Germanistik, an examination of the narrative organizing principles that inform the novel. In their interest in speculation and theorizing, Musil's critics all too often tend to display disdain for the kind of solid and unassuming work of scholars like Holmes. At the same time, it has to be noted that Holmes relies on concepts that had already become outdated by the time of his writing; he does not employ the sophisticated methodologies developed by structuralist and poststructuralist narrative theory, nor does he adequately address the problem of irony. The lack of a differentiated conceptual framework lead Holmes to conclude that protagonist, narrator, and author are essentially identical, a highly problematic assertion (297). The value of Holmes's work is further impaired by the fact that, with the publication of Frisé's new editions of Musil's diaries (1976) and the novel (1978), and especially with that of Musil's entire literary *Nachlass* on CD-ROM (1992), much material has become available that would render desirable a renewed analysis of the narrative technique of Musil's novel along the lines proposed by Holmes and his predecessors such as Wilfried Berghahn (1956) and Peter Nusser (1967). More recently, Peter-André Alt (1985) endeavored to address the problem of narratorial irony in *Der Mann ohne Eigenschaften* through integrating philosophical concepts of irony, once again neglecting the rich narratological research on literary irony. It can only be hoped that Musil scholars will begin to carry out the task outlined by Holmes on a more advanced level, in the light of the new materials and with the help of a more differentiated methodology.

Christiane Zehl-Romero (1978) is among the first critics tentatively to approximate a feminist perspective on Musil's novel. She places the love between Ulrich and his sister Agathe in the context of Romantic and neo-Romantic traditions ascribing to love a redemptory power that would allow the individual to transcend the limits imposed by reality. Musil's novel, Zehl-Romero argues, conducts a critical and comprehensive examination of this cultural construct, which predominates in all of Western civilization and is expressed most promi-

nently in the myth of Tristan and Isolde (see Freese 1969 and 1972). While Ulrich and Agathe's story shares the element of active rebellion against reality, their relationship culminates not in an apotheosis of *amour passion* but in a realization that all human relationships are placed under the constraints of bodily and social existence. To Zehl-Romero, the issue of incest, which hovers over Ulrich and Agathe, is the clearest indication that Musil consciously attempted to avoid embracing a vacuous mysticism of love. Irrespective of whether or not the two consummate their love in a sexual union—as was suggested in the *Reise ins Paradies* (Journey into Paradise) complex from the mid-1920s—Zehl-Romero contends, Musil remains critical of the autistic and narcissistic nature of a relationship that never reaches the quality of a reciprocal encounter with a Thou in Martin Buber's sense. In contradistinction to Kaiser and Wilkins (1962) and Judith Burckhardt (1973), Zehl-Romero emphasizes that Musil dismisses the idea of redemption through love as a solipsistic myth by presenting it as a symptom of, rather than a solution to, the problematic condition of Western civilization.

Dieter Fuder (1979) takes the divergence and multiplicity of opinions on *Der Mann ohne Eigenschaften* as an indication that Musil's novel is designed as an "open" work of art that provokes essentially endless and multifarious processes of reflection. Focusing on the analogy as the basic figure of Musil's writing, Fuder extends the concept of mimesis from the primarily poetological concern it was for Schaffnit (1971) to a comprehensive anthropological principle. According to Fuder, analogical thinking in Musil's work is associated with a new concept of human nature; Musil's use of analogy characterizes a flexible "poetic logic" inherent in human experience that is different from the predominant, discursive logic of rigid binary oppositions (14). Musil's novel, Fuder notes, produces philosophical *Erkenntnis* on three interrelated levels. The openness of Ulrich's mode of thinking corresponds to the structural openness of the novel as a whole, which in turn is reflected in an experience of openness in the process of reading. This openness is the correlate of the force that motivates Musil's literary effort—the representation (mimesis) of human "subjectivity" as such (53). Fuder's study, relying heavily on Kantian philosophy, is perhaps not so much an interpretation of *Der Mann ohne Eigenschaften* as it is a plea for analogical thinking as a viable aesthetic principle that has, in Fuder's opinion, on account of its anthropological universality, claims to general philosophical significance.

In the early 1980s, poststructuralist ideas and methodologies were integrated into Musil studies and brought to bear in examinations of *Der Mann ohne Eigenschaften*. Alongside Peter Henninger's book on *Vereinigungen* (1980), Dieter Heyd's study of the novel (1980) is the boldest foray into speculative interpretation inspired by the psychoanalytic theories of Freud and Lacan. Drawing on Jacques Derrida's notion of *dissémination,* Heyd rejects a method of interpretation whose aim lies in a hermeneutic reconstruction of the author's conscious intention or a text's allegedly objective significance. Instead, he advocates a method of reading that unravels, as it were, the knots in the textures created by Musil's involvement with language. Musil's interest in the pathological, the imaginary, the mystical, and the erotically charged are of particular interest here. Heyd's "psycho-semiological" approach follows the operations of desire hidden in, or repressed by (though present in) Musil's text. On the psychological level, Heyd views recurring motivic patterns, image clusters, and thematic issues as evidence of unconscious forces that motivate Musil's writing. On the aesthetic level, Musil's dissolution of linear narrative techniques, rigid conceptual orders, and traditional ethical values, Heyd maintains, indicates that Musil engages in the *dissémination* of cultural constructs: Musil's work, in its multiperspectivity and its character as fragment, Heyd believes, occupies a crucial position in the critique of what deconstructionist philosophy has labeled "logocentrism," the assumption of the existence of a unified, rationally determinable, and essentially static concept of truth (290).

That poststructuralist theory and traditional academic rigor are not incompatible is shown, for instance, by the work of Walter Moser (1980), who emulates Michel Foucault in his discussion of Musil's novel. The emphasis here is on Foucault's notion of society as a sphere of competing "discourses," codified speech systems that proclaim merely to describe reality but actually create and control social order. Moser's thesis that Musil's novel, by way of essayistic appropriation, undertakes an investigation into the multiplicity of diverse forms of "discourse" in Foucault's sense is highly fruitful. In particular, it serves to place in a different conceptual framework a problem that has plagued Musil criticism from the beginning, that of the distinction between irony and satire and the ensuing terminological entanglements. Musil's novel, in Moser's model, provides a privileged sphere in which discourses from various disciplines (culture, politics, science, philosophy, jurisdiction, psychiatry, and so on) can be brought together and critically examined through various modes of juxtaposition. Moser presents a series of concrete examples to show how Musil's characters are not so much portraits of actual or possible personages, but rather serve as nodes where several types of discourse intersect. Concepts drawn from Foucault, Roland Barthes, and to a lesser extent Mikhail Bakhtin enable Moser to describe the aesthetic dimension of Musil's writing. At the same time, Moser does not fail to point out the limitations of Musil's experimental approach: on the one hand, the metadiscursive investigation into the mechanisms by which discourses circulate in society is in constant danger of turning into a mere pose; on the other hand, the encyclopedic preoccupation of Musil's work takes place in the social vacuum of the unfinished (and unfinishable) essay-novel, which in turn is in danger of becoming an expression of powerlessness vis-à-vis a reality in which discourses have actual practical and empirical effects.

The primarily philosophical and sociological applications of Foucault's discourse analysis in Moser are complemented by a more literary and aesthetic focus in Ulf Eisele. Eisele's contribution was written around the same time as Moser's and published first in Renate von Heydebrand's collections of essays on Musil (1982). Eisele emphasizes the self-referential aspects of the nexus between the writing process and the thematic core of the novel, the quest for meaning in individual existence. Ulrich's well-known ideal of "living the way one reads" (*MoE* 1936) is one of the manifold devices that according to Eisele indicate that the actual topic of Musil's novel is literature itself—its problematic status in society, the modalities of its coming into being, and its philosophical and aesthetic potential. Life and literary discourse, he maintains, are paralleled, and to a certain extent equated, in Musil's novel. In Eisele's reading, the opening chapter, with its extraordinary event (the traffic accident) and the appearance of characters (Diotima and Arnheim, whose presence at the site of the incident, however, is immediately called into question), evokes the impression of a kind of realistic novel that Musil's writing then proceeds to dismantle. The relationship between Ulrich and Agathe indicates a substitution of discourse for action: existence takes place in communicative exchange rather than in a sphere of activity. Ulrich and Agathe's "discourse eroticism" (*Diskurserotik*, 172) represents a sublimation of Oedipal sexuality transferred onto the level of speech. Musil's writing becomes dependent upon the suspension of what his characters experience: the prohibition against incest between Ulrich and Agathe coincides with Ulrich's refusal to become a writer. The nexus of *Inzesttabu* and *Schreibverbot* signals an "interference of the psychical/Oedipal problematic and the specifically literary one" (186). If, for instance, Ulrich himself had begun to write, Musil's novel would have turned into a kind of Bildungsroman, and the experimental nature of Musil's writing would have been destroyed. In highlighting the impasse of story and writing process alike, Eisele contends, Musil shows how a "realistic" novel has become impossible under the given sociohistorical circumstances; in its incompleteness, the novel thus addresses the "impossibility of the poetic" (193). Combining recent poststructuralist discourse theory with German Idealist aesthetics, Eisele's dense and complex essay is one of the most important contributions to a discussion of the relationship between Musil's writing and literary realism.

A monograph by Josef Strutz (1981) adds a welcome note of specificity to the study of the philosophical, aesthetic, and political dimensions of *Der Mann ohne Eigenschaften*. Strutz focuses on an ostensibly minor character, the pacifist poet Feuermaul, who emerges in the second part of Musil's novel as an advocate of lofty notions of human goodness and spiritual renewal. Feuermaul, Strutz demonstrates in a detailed exploration of biographical and intertextual allusions in the novel and in Musil's manuscripts, is an amalgam of expressionist writers like Leonhard Frank, Anton Wildgans, and above all Franz Werfel. In the context of the imminent catastrophe of the First World War and the subsequent collapse of the Habsburg Empire, Musil viewed Werfel's public success as poet and novelist and as pacifist activist as subject to multiple ironies. The significance assigned to the character Feuermaul indicates that despite Musil's preoccupation with the mystical notion of the *other condition,* he never lost interest in concrete historical reality. In fact, Strutz argues, Feuermaul—alongside such characters as the fervent young nationalist Hans Sepp, the mystagogue Meingast, and the racial researcher Bremshuber—becomes one of the indicators that Musil engaged not only in an examination of a past catastrophe but also conceived of his novel as a reflection upon the political realities of the 1930s: the second part of *Der Mann ohne Eigenschaften* in many ways represents a response to the emerging reality of National Socialism, a phenomenon that to a large extent has its historical and ideological roots in the Habsburg monarchy. Musil's observations in his notebooks and journals on Fascism in general and on Adolf Hitler as person and symbol, Strutz argues, provide the foil for the presentation of Feuermaul's empty antirationalist messianic fervor, a general intellectual attitude only too easily co-opted by National Socialism. Strutz has interesting things to say about Musil's assessment of the connection between the economic and ideological aspects of politics. In his focus on the political criticism contained in Musil's novel, he occasionally perhaps displays a tendency toward overstatement—for instance, when he one-sidedly labels Arnheim a money-hungry warmonger (a designation that does not do justice to the complex character of Arnheim nor to its historical model, Walter Rathenau). All the same, Strutz's insistence on Musil's persistent efforts to address concrete historical and political issues in his novel go a long way toward dispelling the myth of Musil as a world-weary mystic.

Like Strutz's study, that of Martin Menges (1982) indicates that, amid all the efforts at post-structuralist innovation, traditionally hermeneutic Germanistik can still produce impressive results. Continuing ideas introduced by Jochen Schmidt (1975), Menges defines the concept of abstraction as the overriding aesthetic and philosophical principle operating in Musil's novel. On three levels—the social, the aesthetic, and the mystical—abstraction indicates both the dissolution of rigid concepts of identity and the possibility of a renewed synthesis. This assessment leads Menges to take issue with Klaus Laermann (1970), who had accused Musil of escapism, and with Hartmut Böhme (1974), who had criticized in Musil a tendency toward viewing historically determined phenomena as ontological givens. Both interpretations, Menges contends, underestimate the critically utopian potential of Musil's aesthetic intentions. Menges proceeds to give the most detailed account of the various utopian models developed in Musil's novel,

stressing that Musil himself reflects upon the failure of the attempt to bestow duration to the *other condition.* Musil, Menges notes, acknowledges that abstract reasoning requires both *Genauigkeit* and *Phantasie,* both an engagement with reality and imaginative reflection, to avoid ethical, intellectual, and spiritual impasse.

Like Menges, Gérard Wicht (1984) singles out one overriding issue as the focus of his analysis. His examination of the *Gleichnis* as the basic unit of Musil's writing to a certain extent complements, with a more philosophical accent, that of Jörg Kühne (1968), who had restricted himself largely to poetological considerations. Wicht evokes the intellectual context of Musil's interest in figurative language, discussing the various theories of the period on the limits and the potential of language. Wicht's broad and necessarily somewhat superficial survey includes the familiar exponents of *Sprachkrise* and *Sprachskepsis* in literature (for example, Hofmannsthal, Rilke, Broch, and Kafka) and philosophy (such as Nietzsche, Mauthner, Landauer, Klages, and Wittgenstein). Musil, Wicht suggests, embraced the figurative potential of the *Gleichnis* as a linguistic device that promises to bridge and at the same time preserve the gap between linguistic expression and intended meaning. In this fashion, a *Gleichnis* fulfills an important epistemological function in that it points to something without subsuming it into a preexisting conceptual system; it creates the described phenomenon and allows it to shine in its uniqueness. The *Gleichnis* thus combines analytic and synthetic or philosophical and poetic capacities, becoming the "purveyor of the highest intellectual density" (111). Wicht defends Musil against charges that the use of figurative language implies a lack of precision and intellectual rigor by stressing that it is "the *object* of the narrative reflection which is polyvalent, not [Musil's] style!" (168, Wicht's emphasis). Wicht traces throughout the novel one particular set of metaphorical constructs, the semantic field centered on the image of the tree. This complex of images, Wicht argues, functions in a manner akin to lyrical poetry, evoking meaning in the interplay of linguistic signs rather than through reference to any extralinguistic belief system. This leads Wicht to the conclusion, among others, that the theological imagery Musil employs in his novel does not indicate that Musil held religious beliefs in the traditional sense (196).

Wicht's study shows that, even in the 1980s, approaches characteristic of mainstream Germanistik, in this case the history of ideas, continue to coexist with the innovative methodologies derived from poststructuralist thinking. The postmodern quasi-anarchistic tendencies latently present in Dieter Heyd (1980) are more pronounced in Lucas Cejpek (1984), who appears to abandon "methodical" literary criticism altogether in favor of a "mad" form of discourse. Taking his cues from the critique of Western rationality by thinkers like Nietzsche and Foucault, Cejpek presents Musil's novel as a reflection of the tension between "reason" and "madness" in European bourgeois civilization. In a collage of motley citations Cejpek freely moves in and out of all kinds of texts from the period in which Musil's novel originated. Cejpek defines this "historical field" of investigation as the "pre-War sphere" (referring to both world wars as one connected event) to distinguish it from his own context, that of a "post-War" perspective. In Cejpek's contention, war is not an unfortunate aberration from the true nature of European rationalistic civilization but a manifestation of it. Moosbrugger, for instance, appears in this light to embody the destructive essence of a male patriarchal system. Similarly, Clarisse illustrates how women internalize the male structures of violence and are driven to self-destruction. Musil, Cejpek suggests, displays in his novel an awareness of the "madness" at the core of Western rationality brought about by the marginalization of what cannot be subsumed under "reason," implying that all utopian models, including those involving the relationship between Ulrich and Agathe, remain confined within the destructive logic of European culture and therefore cannot be viewed as fruitful alternatives. For all his undeniable intelligence and imagination, Cejpek shows little regard for the reader. His book appears to preclude debate, since it does not offer a thesis supported by arguments but rather presents a rhetorical tour de force that the reader can either participate in or reject. Though it is full of fascinating insights and provocative ideas, Cejpek's book, with its pyrotechnic display of metaphors, is perhaps more an exercise in creative speculation than literary criticism.

Hans-Georg Pott (1984) manages to combine scholarly rigor in the traditional sense with an innovative approach that integrates poststructuralist ideas. On one level, he conducts his reading along lines similar to Eisele's, viewing Musil's novel as a laboratory for the examination of "discourses" (ideologies and their manifestations in different speech modes). On another, he focuses on the psychopathology of the characters as examples of failed modes of identity formation that Musil subjects to critical scrutiny. Pott synthesizes discourse analysis and Lacanian psychoanalysis to address the problem of the "ending" of Musil's novel in its aesthetic and psychosexual dimension. In Ulrich's conversations with Agathe, Pott notes, the topic of the exchange becomes secondary; instead, he writes, the endeavor to engage in an endless process of communication and communion through language "functions as the expression of their desire for union and loss of individual boundaries" (122). If the desired *unio mystica* were achieved, however, the conversations would cease, as would the process of exchange—and, ultimately, Musil's book. Pott proposes that a tension underlying Musil's impetus for writing subjects his novel to the paradoxical logic of deferral and postponement. In Musil's subjectivity, Pott suggests, the desire to keep alive is inextricably interwoven with the desire to keep the writing process alive. This constellation brings forth what Pott labels an "endless text," one that undermines the notion of a stable self by refusing closure: "Musil

destroys the narrative model by dismantling the center of its meaning: the ending" (162).

Pott polemically denounces as "ideologues of alienation" (*Entfremdungsideologen,* 161) those critics who insist on the sociopolitical dimension of the aesthetic and psychosexual issues he addresses. However, at least one of the critics he dismisses in this fashion, Hartmut Böhme, has reached conclusions that are quite similar to Pott's, especially with regard to Musil's critique of Western rationality. In an important essay (1986), Böhme emulates recent poststructuralist theories in order to place Musil in the context of current debates on postmodernism. He finds in *Der Mann ohne Eigenschaften* a response to the collapse of European civilization in the First World War. On the aesthetic level, the cataclysm of an entire culture leads Musil to a rejection of realistic mimesis in favor of a semiotic approach: Musil's novel presents a semiotic panopticon in which ideas, ideologies, and values circulate as mere functions of discourse, "quotations" deprived of substance—"simulacrae," in the terminology of Jean Baudrillard. Musil's critique of Western rationality, Böhme contends, bids farewell to the notion that history is characterized by meaningful rational development, anticipating notions about the stasis of postmodern society developed by Michel Foucault and Jean-François Lyotard. In this context, Böhme views Musil's interest in the interconnections between love, mysticism, crime, insanity, and war as an effort to carve out a node of resistance to universal semiotization and commodification: "In a situation of world-wide rationalization Art offers the only space for an exhaustion (*Verausgabung*) and transcendency (*Überschreitung*) of the Ego—closely related to insanity, crime, and excess" (30). Musil's investigation of aspects of culture that resist closure, Böhme argues, places him alongside Georges Bataille among the "intellectual precursors of postmodernism" (25). Böhme's primarily philosophical focus was complemented later by Rolf Günter Renner (1991), for instance, who restricts himself to aesthetic considerations that link Musil's narrative technique with postmodern tendencies. Böhme's dense and stimulating essay goes far beyond the confines of traditional literary criticism in that it links Musil's aesthetic enterprise with a discussion of the situation of our civilization as a whole.

On a more mundane level, there is an abundance of smaller contributions that limit their focus on specific issues concerning Musil's magnum opus. Frequently such contributions have little impact on the discussion of *Der Mann ohne Eigenschaften,* where grand synthesis is usually favored over detailed analysis. A good example is Walter H. Sokel's (1988) essay on the legacy of the eighteenth century in Musil's grand novel. Sokel compares Musil with other important modernist novelists, such as Joyce, Dos Passos, and Döblin, and the manner in which their works represent a break with the realist tradition. According to Sokel, realistic mimesis is characterized by the author's attempt to increase to the fullest the reader's identification with the depicted world by way of eliminating distance and camouflaging the process of narrative mediation. Sokel identifies the origins of this tradition in Lessing's late-Enlightenment poetics of emotional involvement. What distinguishes Musil's critique of realistic mimesis, Sokel suggests, is that his writing in its combination of essayistic philosophical reflection and self-referential, playful irony harks back to the satirical novel of the first half of the eighteenth century by reemphasizing the distance between reader and fictional world.

Musil's novel, Sokel contends, displays affinities with early-Enlightenment authors like Swift, Fielding, Sterne, and Voltaire as well as their common precursor, Cervantes. When Sokel originally gave his paper in 1985, a discussion ensued in which respondents challenged both Sokel's central thesis and its underlying periodization. Yet it seems to me that Sokel's point that many elements of *Der Mann ohne Eigenschaften* can be related to eighteenth-century traditions is well taken (one need only think of the chapter headings, the division into books, the narrator's ironical interventions). Monika Schrader (1975) had anticipated some of Sokel's concerns in her study on Musil's novel within the Bildungsroman tradition. While her study is somewhat marred by an undifferentiated concept of *Bildung* and its historical permutations as reflected in the Bildungsroman genre, her comparison of Musil's work with Wieland's eighteenth-century novel *Agathon* yields a great deal of interesting insights that should be explored further. Perhaps it would be fruitful to place Musil's novel not primarily in the Bildungsroman tradition but, as Sokel suggests, in that of the picaresque novel (particularly with regard to questions of audience address). As far as I can see, however, such interconnections with literary traditions remain largely unexplored in Musil criticism.

In the late 1980s there was a series of attempts to approach Musil's work from a philosophical perspective. Most of these share the thesis that Musil's writing constitutes an intellectual enterprise that can justly be described as philosophical because Musil addresses far-ranging philosophical issues beyond the scope of fiction. Usually, the underlying assumption is that what remains unclear in Musil's thought and his writings can be clarified with the help of a particular philosophical method. Matthias Luserke (1987), for instance, stresses the unity of Musil's work as an "ideographic cosmos" (15) in his analysis of Musil's notion of "possibility" (*Möglichkeit*) with concepts drawn from Kantian modal theory. He proposes that this approach could provide a useful model for the interpretation of literary texts in general. In his enterprise, Luserke dispenses with traditional distinctions such as those between author and narrator and the idea that both narrator and fictional characters function as the sources of utterances in a narrative text. In their place, he distinguishes four abstract modes of representation at work in Musil's *Der Mann ohne Eigenschaften* that correspond to four "types of actual-

ity" (*Tatsächlichkeitstypen,* 69). While Luserke consistently attempts to stress the affinity between these Kantian notions and Musil's intellectual environment (mediated, for instance, via Phenomenology and Gestalt theory), he operates on a level of abstraction that ultimately alienates the reader. Luserke's differentiation between the "really real" versus the "really possible" and the "possibly real" versus the "possibly possible" (74)—later augmented by elaborate charts and formulae—is likely to become a source of consternation even to the staunchest advocate of Musil's philosophical stature. Luserke might better have pursued the more interesting topic of the extent of Musil's indebtedness to Kant, which has—despite the contributions of Ulrich Karthaus (1981a) and Thomas Söder (1988)—thus far not received sufficient attention in Musil scholarship.

In a manner not unlike Luserke's, Ralf Bohn (1988) explores a different philosophical tradition; he seeks to establish parallels between Musil's works and ideas formulated in Romantic philosophy of nature, above all by Friedrich Wilhelm Schelling, that seek to collapse the distinction between philosophy and *Dichtung*. In Bohn's opinion, Musil's *Der Mann ohne Eigenschaften* illustrates, as a *Gleichnis,* the manner in which the philosophical subject constitutes itself as subject in the process of reflection by "inversion"—that is, by tracing its own development back to its origin. This *Ursprung* (73) is both the source and the goal of the intellectual effort. Bohn goes on to relate his notion of inverted conditions to a different idea of inversion, the altered perception of inside and outside relations characteristic of the mystical experience in general and Musil's *anderer Zustand* in particular. His observations may well be accurate, but in his opaque style Bohn tends to postulate rather than explicate such connections. His book is ambitious in scope, yet the lofty philosophical gloss is sometimes marred by slight factual errors—for instance, incorrect datings of some of Musil's diary entries.

Perhaps the most extreme example of a worthwhile topic mired in philosophical opaqueness is Dieter P. Farda's study of phenomenological aspects of Musil's work, originally a dissertation dating from 1982 and published in apparently unrevised form as a book in 1988. In phenomenological terms, the world does not exist as a single, given, "objective" reality. Instead, manifold "worlds" are constructed in a multitude of ways in a constant interaction between sense perceptions and a perceiving consciousness. Musil's notion of *Möglichkeitssinn,* Farda aims to demonstrate, acknowledges and illustrates this philosophical insight into the coexistence of "multiple worlds." The similar notion of "multiple realities" is explored in an interesting and engaging essay by Peter L. Berger (1983) with reference to the phenomenological sociology of Alfred Schütz. In Farda's case, however, an ultracerebral methodology, derived from Heidegger and somewhat presumptuously labeled "transcendental hermeneutics," leads to a convoluted allusive style that shows little regard for the reader.

The aforementioned studies and others, almost invariably doctoral dissertations, raise the question of the envisaged readership. On the one hand, it is unlikely that they will convince the nonliterary reader of Musil's stature as an intellect of significance; on the other, they operate with a specialized and sometimes rather arcane philosophical jargon that is likely to scare off most Musil scholars trained in mainstream Germanistik. The publication pressure on academics notwithstanding, it is a sad phenomenon to be confronted with book-length works that seem to be addressed to nobody in particular and that are destined to do little more than catch dust on library shelves.

One can, of course, write intelligently and intelligibly about Musil from a philosophical perspective. Cases in point are essays relating Musil to Mach (Claudia Monti 1979 and 1981; Manfred Diersch 1990) or to Wittgenstein (Aldo Gargani 1983; Friedrich Wallner 1983; Peter Kampits 1992) as well as some of the various explorations of Musil's indebtedness to Nietzsche (Aldo Venturelli 1980; Roberto Olmi 1981 and 1983; Friedrich Wallner 1984). Most interpretations of **Der Mann ohne Eigenschaften** and Musil's other works touch upon philosophical issues in one way or another, sometimes in highly sophisticated and enlightening manners. Manfred Frank, a student of Hans-Georg Gadamer who gained prominence as a mediator between the German hermeneutic philosophical tradition and the semiotically oriented (primarily French) poststructural approaches, also wrote several lucid essays on the connection between epistemological and mythological concerns in Musil (1981, 1983, 1988). Perhaps it should be no surprise that it is the mature professional philosophers who on the whole display a greater sensitivity to the complexity of Musil's thinking—and a greater regard for the reader—than do young, philosophically trained scholars in their doctoral dissertations.

Harmut Cellbrot's dissertation, published in book form in 1988, likewise proves that theoretical sophistication and readability need not be mutually exclusive. Cellbrot investigates affinities between Musil's work and the phenomenological theories of Edmund Husserl. It is documented that Musil read Husserl, above all the philosopher's *Logische Untersuchungen* (Logical Investigations, 1902), yet Cellbrot refrains from claiming any direct influence or dependence. Instead, he examines Musil's work as an enterprise that on a literary level in many ways parallels Husserl's philosophical ideas. The two thinkers, he points out, share an interest in the nature of cognition and perception; Musil's writing can be viewed as an investigation into the "movement of the processes of consciousness" (42). Musil's attentiveness to the minuscule gradations and shifts in modes of consciousness displays a kind of poetic complement to Husserl's philosophical rigor. Husserl acknowledges that perception and cognition are potentially endless processes, rendering it impossible to arrive at fixed conclusions. Because of its open-endeness, Musil's work, Cellbrot shows, constitutes a poetic analogue to this

mode of thinking that is as legitimate and as fruitful as philosophy proper. Perhaps it is a sign of Cellbrot's sensitivity as a reader that he does not subsume Musil's literary enterprise under a supposedly superior philosophical construction.

The appropriating grip of a given theoretical or philosophical model is the focus of Reinhard Pietsch's deconstructive discussion of Musil's novel (1988). Like Eisele (1982), Pietsch draws on Jacques Derrida's notion of *dissémination* to describe the way in which Musil's text simultaneously invites and calls into question appropriative readings. In its discursive and poetic richness, Musil's novel contains a wealth of details that point in all directions and challenge the reader to integrate them under a unifying conceptual heading; yet at the same time, its character as a fragment renders impossible any attempt to arrive at a unifying interpretation. Pietsch concludes that Musil's text defies hermeneutic approaches that aim to interpret authorial intention or textual meaning; he opts for an approach that focuses instead on the manner in which Musil's text addresses the creation and subversion of meaning in what Pietsch calls "self-implicating structures." He steers clear of the conceptual clichés that have predominated in Musil criticism for decades by developing his own metaphors to describe the peculiar character of Musil's writing, comparing the novel to a Moebius strip and the effect of Musil's prose to interfering "frequencies" (*Eigenfrequenzen*, 3). Pietsch traces the circularity of Musil's process of composition in two detailed analyses of what, because of Musil's untimely death, became the final chapter of Musil's text, "Atemzüge eines Sommertages." The excessive production of figurative language in ceaseless variation and repetition, Pietsch notes, dissolves the narrating instance: it becomes impossible to locate utterances in the text as coming either from the characters or from the narrator. The dissolution of the concept of narrating subject goes hand in hand with a sense of paralysis of the writing process; ending in stasis, Musil's novel seems a fragment bursting at the seams, both infinite and uninterpretable, a self-canceling artifact. While his approach is not free of the kind of totalizing gestures he criticizes in Musil scholarship, Pietsch nevertheless manages to present a refreshing look at Musil's novel. Of particular interest is his observation that the work includes, in addition to its reflections on the nature of the writing process, an extensive examination of the process of reading. Musil's investigation of the nature of reading, here only touched upon, is a topic that would merit closer attention.

The nexus between Musil's interest in mysticism and the processes of writing and reading is explored by Wagner-Egelhaaf, who includes a chapter on **Der Mann ohne Eigenschaften** in her lucid study of the mystical tradition in twentieth-century German prose (1989). In contradistinction to previous scholars, who approached the issue of mysticism mainly from the perspective of a history of ideas by exploring Musil's reception of mystical sources, Wagner-Egelhaaf employs poststructuralist concepts that place mysticism in the overall context of Western culture as a culture based on writing. Medieval mystics, Wagner-Egelhaaf notes, attempt to describe the mystical experience that prompts them to write as a "dictation" from God. This phenomenon leads Wagner-Egelhaaf to suggest that modern mysticism encompasses a specific mode of writing that elicits a particular manner of reading. The relationship between Ulrich and Agathe displays just such a dynamic. Their conversations about the mystical experience circle around their readings in mystical sources; their utterances consist largely of quotations from or intertextual allusions to such sources; Ulrich is induced to write down his reflections in his diary, which Agathe secretly reads. Such aspects of the work, Wagner-Egelhaaf notes, indicate that the mystical communion between Ulrich and Agathe takes place in an interaction of the reading and writing process. God as source and telos of the mystical experience is thus replaced by writing as a medium of communion. Gerd-Theo Tewilt (1990) reaches ostensibly similar conclusions with regard to the *other condition* in ***Der Mann ohne Eigenschaften*** as a phenomenon constituted by and in language. Yet, whereas Tewilt draws on traditional aesthetics and language philosophy, Wagner-Egelhaaf emulates the poststructuralist theories of Jacques Derrida that challenge the primacy of oral language over writing. In their methodological differences, the two studies mark the epistemological divide characteristic of much of Germanistik in the 1980s and 1990s.

The great diversity of approaches derived from poststructuralist theories is indicated in Thomas Pekar's study on the "discourse of love" in Musil (1989), half of which is devoted to an examination of ***Der Mann ohne Eigenschaften***. Pekar notes that in Musil's novel love is subject to division: the love relationships of all the major characters display a split between, on the one hand, the bodily aspects of love as a biologically determined drive and, on the other, its social manifestations, the codifications of desire in socially accepted modes of behavior. Pekar traces Musil's insight into the social organization of amorous emotions to the very beginning of his writing. Even the early "Varieté" sketches from around 1900, show Musil's awareness of what Pekar in contradistinction to *Liebestrieb* (love drive), calls *Liebesbetrieb* (love business). The motif of the *varieté* as a socially sanctioned marginal space where people seek, for a price, gratification of the sexual and scopic urges repressed by bourgeois society at large, survives in Musil's novel in Ulrich's relationship with Leona, the cabaret singer. Leona sells her body but displaces her emotional needs in her eating binges. In Bonadea the split between bodily needs and social dictates is evident in the contradiction between her nymphomania and her lofty ideal of bourgeois respectability. In Diotima, it centers around an idealization of spiritual purity that masks her sexual and spiritual frustration in her marriage to Tuzzi. Arnheim's excessively cerebral nature, Gerda Fischel's hysteria, and Clarisse's manic tendencies are similar indicators of the socially enforced division between body and soul. In part two of the novel,

Pekar argues, the diagnosis of division is replaced by myths of unifying experience, all centering around Ulrich's relationship with Agathe. These take three different forms. The first variant is narcissistic, consisting of an endless process of mutual mirroring through communication; the second is hermaphroditic, encompassing the desire to become one bodily with the beloved in a mystical union; the third is dionysian, aiming toward a dissolution of the self in an intoxicated indulgence of animalistic urges. The three models of unification, Pekar notes, are contradictory and partly mutually exclusive, which may, at least in part, explain the aesthetic and intellectual problems Musil encountered with the continuation, respectively the conclusion of his novel. Pekar's study is richly textured and always attentive to the complexities of the issues involved. It is intellectually stimulating because of its eclectic combination of divergent methodologies and manages to avoid the kind of reductionism found only too often in Musil studies.

Two Swiss dissertations published in 1990 deal with psychological aspects of Musil's novel, to a certain extent reaching conclusions that are diametrically opposed to each other. Ruth Hassler-Rütti (1990) examines the tension between "madness" and "reality" by focusing on three of Musil's main characters: Ulrich, Clarisse, and Moosbrugger. Drawing on various anthropological, sociological, and psychological theories, Hassler-Rütti defines reality as the product of intersubjective communicative interactions in which a clear sense of personal identity, based on an inside-outside dichotomy, is formed. "Madness" in this context refers to a failed or distorted process of identity formation. Besides Agathe, Ulrich is the only character in the novel capable of recognizing that reality is not an external given but a product of the interplay of contingency and constant interpersonal negotiation. This enables him, Hassler-Rütti contends, to escape "madness," which is characterized in part by an effort to impose stasis upon phenomena subject to perpetual fluctuation.

While Hassler-Rütti is sensitive to Musil's text and attentive to detail, her approach skirts some of the more problematic aspects of Musil's novel, such as the connection between individual and collective "madness" (for example, the prospect of war looming over Musil's panorama of "Kakania"). Her largely positive assessment of Ulrich leads her to dismiss, somewhat vehemently, some of the more disturbing complexities of Ulrich's psychosexual disposition, evidenced in his generally destructive relationships with women and in particular in the possibly incestuous component of his relationship with Agathe. Hans-Rudolf Schärer (1990) focuses precisely on such matters and their psychosexual significance in his discussion of Musil's protagonist, employing a range of psychological theories of the self, including those of psychoanalyst Heinz Kohut. Starting with Ulrich's childhood reminiscences, Schärer observes a pattern of socialization that corresponds—almost too neatly—to the development of the narcissistic personality. With Ulrich, the early loss of the mother, in combination with the aloofness of the father, hinders the formation of a stable sense of self. Ulrich's love for Agathe, who as his sister is in a sense both identical to and different from him, thus becomes the emblem of his inability to overcome his narcissistic isolation. From this psychosexual perspective, Schärer views Ulrich's much heralded *Möglichkeitssinn* primarily as the product of the narcissistic phantasm of indeterminacy and omnipotence. Likewise, he all but debunks Ulrich's utopian schemes, traditionally the object of the highest praise in Musil criticism: favoring as they do theoretical speculation over active involvement in concrete, empirical reality, they emerge here as mechanisms that aid the narcissistic personality in maintaining its precarious balance in the face of contingency. Schärer offers a pragmatic elaboration of ideas introduced into Musil criticism by writers such as Klaus Laermann (1970) and outlined in two seminal essays on a more abstract theoretical level by Peter Dettmering (1981) and Hartmut Böhme (1982). Schärer, however, does not address the socio-political aspects of the problem. His objective is not to denounce, as it were, the character, but to offer a reading that puts Musil's protagonist in a critical perspective. He presents Ulrich as a model of modern socialization; the "man without qualities" emerges as the prototypical narcissistically disturbed personality. In his circumspect manner, Schärer manages to avoid a problem that has plagued a great deal of Musil criticism: he does not allow the power of Musil's language to dominate and contaminate his own critical discourse, as many of the affirmative critics do. At the same time, he remains respectful of Musil's artistic achievement.

Such a combination of sensitivity and respect on the one hand and a remarkable degree of freedom from contamination by Musil's language on the other distinguishes Gerhard Meisel's monograph of 1991 as one of the most significant contributions to Musil scholarship in recent years. It is difficult to do justice to Meisel's discussion of *Der Mann ohne Eigenschaften,* which combines a wide range of theoretical impulses in a fascinating exploration of the philosophical, intellectual, and psychosexual dimensions of Musil's novel. Meisel places Musil within the context of the new view of human nature that emerged around the turn of the century, as scientific thinking began to occupy and to absorb spheres of human experience traditionally excluded from the scientific paradigm. Musil's writing, like Freud's psychoanalysis and the emerging discipline of anthropology, constitutes a contribution to a *Wissenschaft vom Menschen,* an exploration of human experience guided by, and established partly in opposition to, natural science. In Meisel's view, Musil is the writer who most radically and consistently responded to the period's "*categorical paradigm shift* of the scientific world view" (217; Meisel's emphasis). Musil most clearly participated in the move away from teleological thinking in terms of linear notions of causality towards complex functional models of thought involving concepts of statistical likelihood and probability.

Meisel traces Musil's awareness of contemporary scientific theories by exploring a multitude of sources, establishing some surprising and insightful connections and parallels. In a brilliant reading of the opening section of Musil's novel, with its combination of meteorological discourse and traditional narrative, Meisel shows how the author draws on a wide range of contemporary scientific ideas. Musil's focus here, Meisel argues, does not lie in a parody of scientific language (as is often assumed); rather, the passage displays the extent to which Musil employs the most advanced epistemological theories of the time, in particular those concerning the nature of systems implied in the laws of thermodynamics. In Meisel's view, the opening of the novel establishes a "systemic equivalence of thermodynamic and narrative 'laboratory conditions'" (258). Scientific motifs reoccur throughout Musil's novel; for instance, combining psychoanalytic and semiotic perspectives, Meisel establishes parallels between the relationship of Ulrich and Agathe and the notion of entropy in modern physics. Both on the individual and on the general level, Musil's experiment ends in entropy: the Ulrich-Agathe relationship is subject to the irresolvable problem of incest; the sociopolitical question concerning the interconnection between *Parallelaktion* and impending war likewise becomes irresolvable. Meisel employs concepts derived from information theory to establish a correlation between the initial impulse of Musil's writing and its ultimate disintegration in a mass of manuscript drafts: in the terms developed by information theory, an ideal order—which Musil appears to be striving for—is identical with a maximum of disturbance (292). Viewed from this perspective, Meisel suggests, Musil's enterprise of collecting and analyzing a potentially infinite number of pieces of contingent minutiae in his analysis of the historical predicament of his era turned into an unwinnable race against time.

Over the decades, Musil criticism has shown signs of petrification and fatigue. It appears as though the ever-same issues and questions are repeatedly recycled in modified form. Yet works such as Meisel's revive the hope that it will become possible to address Musil's oeuvre in all its complexity, its grandeur, and its limitations without falling prey to the allure of the writer's extraordinarily powerful metaphorical language. In recent years, studies by younger Musil scholars have offered fresh perspectives and signs of intellectual independence from the pull exerted by Musil's conceptual apparatus. Good examples are a monograph by Gabriele Dreis (1992) on the impact of Jean-Jacques Rousseau's pedagogical ideas on Musil and a book by Frank Maier-Solgk (1992) on *Der Mann ohne Eigenschaften* as Musil's investigation into the nature and philosophy of history. Other recent contributions that provide innovative impulses to an elucidation of Musil's novel include an essay by Alexander Honold (1993) on the notion of leisure time and an analysis of the work in terms of chaos theory by Axel Krommer and Albert Kümmel (1993).

Musil's lifework, enthusiastically hailed by Claudio Magris as "the greatest book of our time" (1983, 60), is incomplete. Most interpretations of *Der Mann ohne Eigenschaften* explicitly or implicitly seek to address its significance and stature as a novel fragment. In one way or another, each critic quite literally constructs his or her own object of investigation, rewriting and "finishing" the book that Musil left uncompleted. The ceaseless efforts of the scholarly community to wrestle with the issues raised by Musil's monumental work may be an indication that perhaps the most food for thought is offered precisely by books that, like *Der Mann ohne Eigenschaften,* may have a beginning but no ending.

George Steiner   (essay date 1995)

SOURCE: "The Unfinished," in *The New Yorker,* Vol. LXXI, No. 8, April 17, 1995, pp. 101-06.

[*In the following essay, Steiner discusses* The Man without Qualities *in the context of modern world literature and provides a close examination of the new Wilkins-Pike translation of this work.*]

The Anglo-Saxon temperament has a weakness for innocence, even a touch of grossness, in its novelists. It bridles at intellectuality, at the application to fiction of systematic philosophy. The teller of tales—of sophisticated, psychologically refined tales—is one thing. The logician, the metaphysician, the mind trained in philosophy or science, quite another. The term "thinker," crucial to European and Russian culture, rings awkwardly in Anglo-American. It savors of cold coffee cups in what was Central Europe or of Gauloises on the Left Bank. This is particularly so when the term is attached to a novelist. And there *is* more than a grain of perception in this prejudice. The intelligence in great art and literature is something of a mystery. Such intelligence is obviously formidable in its capacity to organize, to edge out of common focus, to recreate our reading of the world. But the preëminent feat in fiction—the presentation of rounded, autonomous characters, of situations both specific and suddenly universal—can occur in works neither formally cultured nor cerebrally intelligent. Indeed, an enigma of naïveté, even of physical immediacy, often generates literary or visual invention: do not listen to a great sculptor or painter on politics or aesthetics; watch his or her hands. The wisdom of numerous classic novelists is of a peculiarly visceral, instinctive order. Their work is shaped at depths below conscious articulation, let alone reflection—depths that are inaccessible to the rest of us. All this makes more fascinating the exceptions: the writers of fiction who are also major, systematic intellects.

There have been two in the twentieth century: Marcel Proust and Robert Musil. There are, of course, other writers who present themselves as candidates. Elias Canetti, a fervent admirer of Musil, is a special case inasmuch as he produced only one novel, and at an early

age. Thomas Mann carried within himself a fair portion of Western culture, and his narrative genius was manifest. But there is in that towering mastery a perennial conservatism; what he had was an expository brilliance in the adaptation of already available philosophies, such as those of Schopenhauer, Nietzsche, and Freud. Henry James's critique of society and his anatomy of human relations are of the finest. But they are those of a master impressionist, and he more or less uneasily left philosophical argument to his brother. The political instincts and the feel for the turbulence of history in an André Malraux, a Graham Greene, and a Saul Bellow are acute. Yet we would not look to these witnesses for any original contribution to philosophy, to the development of logic or epistemology in any ordered—let alone systematized—way. Joyce mimes ideas, parodies them, dramatizes them, sets them to incomparable verbal music; he does not have them. By contrast, if the notion of literature should itself disappear, Proust's place in intellectual life would remain eminent. He is, after Aristotle and Kant, one of the seminal thinkers on aesthetics, on the theoretical and pragmatic relations between form and meaning. His analyses of the psychosomatic texture of human emotions, of the phenomenology of experience, are of compelling philosophical interest. Even in his lifetime, it became a cliché to set "Proust on time" beside Einstein and the new physics. *À la Recherche du Temps Perdu* is interwoven with motifs of epistemology, philosophy of art (including music), and ethical debate which nevertheless have their own independent status. Only Musil provides a counterpart.

This is, at an obvious level, a matter of biography. Musil was a highly trained and qualified mechanical engineer with a keen grasp of mathematics and mathematical logic. His thesis bore on the technical aspects of Ernst Mach's philosophy of physics. (Einstein shared with him an engagement with Mach.) From 1903 to 1908, Musil was also occupied with the study of experimental clinical psychology and of theories of behavior. There is hardly a page in his immense oeuvre—so much of it as yet unpublished in English—that does not argue, by precept and example, for the radical unison of the philosophical and the poetic. (The German *Dichtung* makes this symbiosis easier to express.) For Musil, thought—be it mathematical, analytic, discursive, or aesthetic—is form. To think rigorously is to shape rigorously: the concordance between genre and content should be as logical and as inevitable in a novella or a play as it is in the blueprint of a machine tool or in an algebraic proof. There is nothing cold or mandarin about this heroic conviction. It gives to Musil's stories and to *The Man Without Qualities,* which has been newly translated by Sophie Wilkins and Burton Pike, a subtle lustre, a summons to adult response, an imaginative authority of the rarest force. Musil honors his readers by the demands he makes of them.

For an American public in the nineteen-nineties, they may prove onerous. Musil grounds the world of his analytic imaginings wholly in that of *Kakanien,* the lavatory term he invented to designate the Austro-Hungarian dual monarchy. His texts swarm with allusions, sometimes covert and sometimes oblique, to Austrian politics and society, to the philosophical-sociological debates in Vienna before the First World War, to incidents of criminality or fashion in the city of Mahler and Freud, and to the diverse styles of rhetoric and jargon in fin-de-siècle Vienna-Budapest-Prague. No less than Joyce, Musil constructs the fabric of his vast design around minutiae of exact local reference. But his motive is not Joyce's. The pressure of abstraction on Musil was such—the temptation of the philosophical essay or epistemological investigation was so constant—that he strove to give to his fiction the concreteness of locality. It is the unresolved tension between the alternatives of the systematic and the poetic, the scientific and the literary—or, rather, a staunch refusal to acknowledge that they *are* divergent alternatives—that confers on his writings their unsettling power.

Both the power and the disturbance emanate from his early masterpiece, **Young Törless,** published in 1906. The German title tells of *Verwirrungen*—of the maddening disorders, confusions, vertigos—that afflict the adolescent hero in the erotic-sadistic atmosphere of the military academy. Musil himself was familiar with this scene. His portrait of the artist as a young cadet belongs to a widespread genre—one that extends from *Tom Brown's School Days* all the way to *The Catcher in the Rye.* But Musil's portrait has a much higher purpose. Consciously or not, Musil has already sensed his archtheme: that of psychological, sexual, and social disorder in the doomed culture of Central Europe. Already, the clairvoyant in him is unmistakable: the episodes of ritual humiliation—of sadomasochistic practices in this tight-buttoned hell, of choosing a scapegoat with "alien" traits—anticipate, almost unbearably, events to come. **"Die Versuchung der Stillen Veronika"**—where *Versuchung,* "temptation," evokes *Versuch,* a "trial," or "attempt"—was completed in 1911. It may well be the single greatest short story in German. (There is more than one element of inspired kitsch in Mann's *Death in Venice.*) Behind this uncannily charged miniature lies the less concentrated canvas of Goethe's *Elective Affinities.* Musil's tale and Goethe's novel depict a shift toward reflexes within us which we register in even the most direct of erotic encounters. The title of the short book in which Musil's story is included, **Vereinigungen**—meaning "unions," or "concordances"—is bitterly ironic: there are none to be found. It is in sexual encounters that solitude is sharpest, that the imagined wealth of remembered, alternative, or illusory possibilities devastates the pretended truth of the moment. Men and women sleep not with each other but with the memories, the regrets, the hopes of unions yet to come. Our adulteries are internal; they deepen our aloneness.

Even beyond Proust's, Robert Musil's sensibility was hermaphroditic. He could focus on the unspoken or subliminal current of feminine consciousness, on women's speech to themselves, with an exactitude, a caring precision, that no other modern writer has quite matched. **"The Temptation of Quiet Veronica"** and its companion piece **"The Perfecting of Love,"** concise as they are, required years of strained labor. They demonstrate, as do the novellas gathered in **Three Women** (1924), that it is possible for an exceptional intellect and imagination to pass through the Freudian tunnel and emerge into a light altogether more scrupulous in its reading of human enclosedness. Had we only these shorter fictions, the occasional lectures (such as the one on stupidity, delivered in the teeth of Nazi Vienna), and the voluminous notebooks, diaries, shards of literary-social criticism and satire, Musil's place in literary history would be considerable. As it is, these *opera minora* seem to stand in the bright shade of the colossus: **Der Mann ohne Eigenschaften**. Translated into English, "Eigenschaften" has, unavoidably, been rendered as "qualities." It is a rendering that omits crucial connotations of selfness, of singular appropriation to oneself, almost of "self-possession," with all its philosophical-moral-economic attributes. "Qualities" lets drop the decisive analogies with the ontological-psychological investigations into the ego not only in Freud but in Husserl and Heidegger. "The Man Whose 'I' Is in Search of His 'Me'" would be an absurdly awkward paraphrase, but it might be more exact.

When Robert Musil died suddenly in Geneva, on April 15, 1942, he was in exile (his wife was Jewish) and was virtually destitute. His publications were, in the main, pulped or out of print, and many of his papers, left behind in Vienna, were destroyed in the war. His magnum opus, on which he was working only moments prior to his death, lay hopelessly unfinished. Musil's very name seemed to ring a bell—and then a muted one—only with a few eminent contemporaries, such as Mann and Broch; with a handful of fellow-refugees; and with the bureaucrats in various relief organizations, who had become increasingly weary of his desolate applications for help. Today, however, there is an academic-critical Musil industry. A series of monographs devoted to his work has now passed twenty volumes. Already, the bibliography of scholarly commentary is vast, and theses are cascading. The claim that **The Man Without Qualities,** even as we have it, towers over modern fiction in the German language is near to being a banality.

Yet there is a good deal that remains confused. The first volume of the novel, comprising a hundred and twenty-three chapters, appeared in 1930. Sales were hardly massive, but critical attention was immediate and almost entirely positive. Critical consensus held it to be the book after *Ulysses.* In 1933, however, when the thirty-eight chapters that make up the second tome were published, few reviewers took note. This lack of attention was due only in part to Hitler's assumption of power in Germany and to prompt Nazi denunciations of Musil as an obscurantist, decadent pessimist, useless to readers in the new dawn. Even sympathetic critics were baffled by the second volume's myriad complexity of narrative strands, by the palpable indecisions of structure and tone. What followed were twenty chapters, which Musil revised in galleys between 1937 and 1938 but then withdrew from his publisher, and the enormous *Nachlass*—the posthumous material, comprising, in different Musil archives, some twenty thousand pages. The Knopf claim, emblazoned on the dust jacket of the new edition, that this translation is "the first in English to provide a *complete* text" is simply not true. There can be no "complete" text of a work that remains drastically incomplete; quite different editorial arrangements are and will continue to be possible. What we have here is a translation, by Sophie Wilkins, breaking off with Chapter 38 of Part 3, followed by some six hundred further pages from the *Nachlass,* dating from 1920 to 1942, and selected and translated by Burton Pike. Particularly with regard to the first two panels of the triptych, this enterprise is essentially based on the German edition issued by Rowohlt in 1978. Though the Rowohlt Musil supersedes previous attempts, it is itself necessarily incomplete and selective as to posthumous matter. Unsurprisingly, it has provoked scholarly-critical doubts. Despite thirty-four megabytes of data on CD-ROM, which appeared in 1992, there can be no definitive **The Man Without Qualities**.

As is well known, Musil sets out to chronicle, to elucidate critically, the death of Europe and its culture. (Spengler was a significant influence.) The philosophical epic begins in August, 1913, exactly a year before the catastrophe. If there is a structural keel, it is Musil's acidly ironic invention—though an invention based on fact—of the "Parallel Campaign." The reign of Emperor William II of Germany would reach its thirtieth glorious year in 1918. Preparations for this august event were actually under way in Berlin. How, then, could Austria do less than celebrate, also in 1918, the seventieth anniversary of Emperor Franz Joseph's accession to the throne—surely a nobler and more blessed' event? The committee that was assembled to study and develop this inspired proposal functions as the pivot of the novel, bringing many of its main characters into ideological, social, political, and sexual interaction. The ultimate fatuousness of the project, given the as yet unknown realities of 1918, and the deep-lying hypocrisies and illusions that it exposes serve Musil as a touchstone for his encompassing thesis of spiritual decay.

This thesis is argued further in a number of ancillary plots, each prodigal enough to form a novel in its own right. Moosbrugger, the sadistic sex murderer, fascinates the elegant, emancipated circles of mundane Vienna. His crimes are, in one sense, enactments of the fantasies of the disturbed, Nietzschean Clarisse (whose androgynous impulses mirror something central in Musil). Dr. Paul Arnheim—based, in part, on the German-Jewish statesman and thinker Walther Rathenau—exhibits those gifts for detachment and for ironic vision which were at once the glory of the Central European life of the mind and a symptom of its incapacity for direct political action in the face of the inhuman. As in

Balzac or Proust, the cast in Musil is large. It spans every social condition, from slums to *palais,* from bohemia to military eminence. Musil's combinatorial techniques, especially in Volume I, are awesome.

When Agathe—the sister of "the man without qualities," Ulrich—enters the novel, what was previously a kaleidoscope narrows to a laser. The siblings have scarcely seen each other since childhood. Agathe is drifting away from a second marriage. Ulrich's sexual affairs have, like Musil's, been numerous and instructive, but they have left him disposable and at the surface of himself. Agathe is a vibrant sleepwalker, who takes care not to exceed the sheltering distances that separate her from awakening. The philosophical armature of her somnambular élan is set out by the novelist. It is that of the cult of authentic life, of finally declared feeling, at whatever private or social risk; it relates Nietzsche to Bergson, and is dramatized in writers as otherwise diverse as Henry James (witness the hymn to "only living" in *The Ambassadors*) and D. H. Lawrence. The secret of recovered life lies, in part, in a knowing retrieval of childhood. Proust is the supreme strategist of this spiralling return. Ulrich and Agathe find themselves journeying homeward, to the "unsealing of a crypt" that is also a cradle or a box of magical toys, masks, mementos. The other motion of recovery, of authentication in the face of the constraints of the social-normative order, is that of the quantum leap. "Leap" is the wrong word, in that the forward thrust can be one of almost impalpable nuance and gradations. But there is a *salto mortale* nevertheless—a step into the void.

The Man Without Qualities is the narrative-psychological apex of an aesthetic of brother-sister relations—an aesthetic that takes its modern guise in Byron, in Shelley, in Baudelaire's incantation to *mon enfant, ma sœur.* Specifically, Musil follows on the mythology and, one can almost say, the politics of love between brother and sister set out in Wagner's "Ring." Musil presses toward a new intensity of metaphysical and ethical valuation the ancient intuition that a brother's passion for his sister, a sister's for her brother, can alone satisfy the ache of eros for total oneness. Love between organic strangers, however vehement, cannot abolish the paradox of solitude, of the unbridgeable. Love between those whom blood and inheritance conjoin fuses the needs of narcissism (self-love) with those of total intimacy with another. "Now I know what you are: you are my self-love!" And this very insight, being communicable, defies aloneness.

In retrospect, the entirety of Musil's genius—the rigor of psychological notation, the eerie depths of the novellas, the ability to make intimate detail representative of philosophical argument and social crisis—can be seen as a prelude to the Ulrich-Agathe chapters. Nothing in modern literature, except the saga of the Narrator and Albertine in Proust, comes close. Step by step, Musil unfolds the hesitant ecstasy of soul and spirit which inspires the Siamese twins as they probe the complex wonder of mutual rediscovery. They proclaim an elective affinity so unguarded as to make of them twins of different gender and age, but twins nonetheless. Gender, moreover, flickers uncertainly. There is something radically boyish in Agathe's lithe charm, in her smiling cynicism, whereas what Ulrich feels crowding upon him is not only his sister's femininity but his own, now liberated from conventional restraints. Within a shared idiom, simultaneously impressionistic, encoded, and strangely resonant with the metaphysical discourse on eros as we know it from Plato or from Nietzsche, "dream" and charged immediacy alternate. Is theirs a joint self-delusion, an infinitely gentle folie à deux? Agathe says, "But it does happen in one's sleep! There you do sometimes see yourself transformed into something else. Or meet yourself as a man. And then you're much kinder to him than you are to yourself. You'll probably say that these are sexual dreams, but I think they are much older."

Agathe's intimation of a primal archetype is given shape, famously, in the "garden episodes" from the chapters withdrawn by Musil in 1938 and still unpublished at his death. Their setting is deliberately Edenic. Theological fantasies play in Ulrich's mind even as the air is toying with Agathe's hair—with her "blond head like light on light against the sky." What if God Himself would devalue the world if He were to come closer to it by even the tiniest step? This esoteric notion is a figuration of Ulrich's unease about the finality of his love for Agathe. "A deep moat from some other world seemed to enclose them both in a nowhere world of their own." But, precisely because "it is imagination" (one of Musil's key doctrines), morality continues to exercise its questioning role. The closer the twins are to each other, the more demanding the conditions of possibility. An unexamined love is not worth living. "Moonbeams by Sunlight," the title of Chapter 46, aims at suggesting something of the countercurrents, the "reflections," in both the optical and the psychological vein, that attach to this pas de deux. (The hint of choreography, of an intricate but also self-ironizing pavane, is compelling.)

These chapters are the cruellest of tests for any translator. The closest analogy in English might be the sections miming Eden in Henry James's *The Golden Bowl*. But with a constant difference: in Musil the analytic-philosophical lineaments are persistently vital. Perhaps one should think of Santayana's fiction, but at a much higher pitch of authority. It would be otiose to anatomize this or that passage of the Pike rendering in the word-for-word light of the German original. A translation of this scope needs to be lived with. What we are given here manifestly supersedes previous attempts. It may well turn out to be the best Musil available to an English-language readership. The comic strands, notably in a personage such as Tuzzi or Diotima, are strikingly recaptured. Passing vignettes show Wilkins' virtuosity: "Then it occurred to him that one could just as well say that a woolen blanket resembled a night in October. He felt a gentle uncertainty on his skin and

drew Bonadea closer." Or the delicious sketch of Diotima reading, brushing back her sumptuous black hair from her forehead, "which gave her a logical air." Grasp the full connotations of the apposition of these two words, and you will be at the heart of Musil.

Why the incompletion? This, of course, is the "Musil question." Why the incapacity or unwillingness to choose between alternative endings when these are more or less fully set out in the vastness of the posthumous papers? Material circumstances mattered, undoubtedly. Musil's *misère*, his pariahdom, the disappearance of his name and works from a Europe whose collapse into barbarism he had so acutely foreseen made him feel that the formal completion of his labors, let alone their publication in any conventionally accomplished form, was a wholly unrealistic prospect. Moreover, what meaning would his own reduced existence have if **The Man Without Qualities** were out of his hands? (The parallels with Proust are evident.) But it can also be argued that incompletion is of the essence, that it was latent in the celebrated initial sentence about the barometric pressure hanging low over the Atlantic and moving inexorably eastward. Time has no stop; nor does human history, even where it is apocalyptic. There are no last judgments—only attempts, as in differential calculus, to get nearer to the truth, to the finally incommensurable. Musil explored and pondered a finale of incest for Ulrich and Agathe. Rightly, he balked at the simplemindedness, at the novelettish flavor, of any such solution. Already, they cohabit far beyond the flesh. Musil was familiar with *The Magic Mountain,* and was himself an excombatant who was ascetically at home in uniform; and so he could easily have closed on a scene of world war. But one senses that Mann's precedent did not convince him. Even the horrors of 1914–18 had proved to be only an unfinished chapter of Europe's tragedy. Thus there is something strangely right about the "interminability" of **The Man Without Qualities** and the aleatory challenge posed by the archive, containing, as it does, pages of the highest interest and the highest art. Completion might have diminished the unbounded life of the torso.

FURTHER READING

Criticism

Bernstein, Michael André. "Precision and Soul." In *The New Republic* 212, No. 22 (29 May 1995): 27-36.
  Provides an overview of Musil's life and career, analysis of *The Man without Qualities,* and an evaluation of the strengths and shortcomings of the new Sophie Wilkins-Burton Pike translation of Musil's unfinished novel.

Drabble, Dennis. "In the Twilight of the Empire." In *Washington Post Book World* (16 April 1995): 1, 10.

Reviews the Wilkins-Pike translation of *The Man without Qualities* and examines the biographical and historical background to Musil's masterwork.

Hoffmann, Michael. "A Never-Ending Story." In *The New York Times Book Review* (14 May 1995): 1, 27.
Praises the Sophie Wilkins-Burton Pike translation of *The Man without Qualities*.

Luft, David S. *Robert Musil and the Crisis of European Culture: 1880-1942*. Berkeley: University of California Press, 1980, 323 p.
Discusses Musil in relation to his historical and cultural milieu.

Peters, Frederick G. *Robert Musil: Master of the Hovering Life: A Study of the Major Fiction*. New York: Columbia University Press, 1978, 286 p.
Lengthy study of Musil's major fictional works.

Pike, Burton. *Robert Musil: An Introduction to His Work*. Ithaca: Cornell University Press, 1961, 214 p.
Critical survey focusing on Musil's major fiction.

Additional coverage of Musil's life and career is contained in the following sources published by Gale Research: *Contemporary Authors,* Vol. 109; *Contemporary Authors New Revisions*, Vol. 55; *Dictionary of Literary Biography*, Vols. 81, 124; *Short Story Criticism*, Vol. 18; and *Twentieth-Century Literary Criticism*, Vol. 12.

Elizabeth Madox Roberts

1881-1941

American novelist, poet, and short story writer.

INTRODUCTION

A prominent figure in American literature of the South, Roberts is best known for her novel *The Time of Man* (1926), which Ford Madox Ford described as "the most beautiful individual piece of writing that has yet come out of America." While various contemporary critics rank Roberts along with such prominent southern writers as William Faulkner, Robert Penn Warren, and Eudora Welty, she never attained either the critical or popular recognition of her peers.

Biographical Information

Roberts was born in Perryville, Kentucky, and raised in Springfield. Her father held a variety of semi-skilled jobs and, like Roberts's grandmother, was an avid storyteller. A sensitive and physically frail child, Roberts was keenly interested in literature from an early age. After graduating from high school, she briefly attended the State College of Kentucky; Roberts withdrew because of ill-health and lack of money. In the succeeding decade she earned a living as a school teacher. In 1917, following time spent in Colorado and California, during which she recovered from a case of tuberculosis, Roberts entered the University of Chicago on a scholarship. She established herself as a central figure in the Poetry Club, started lifelong friendships with Glenway Westcott and Yvor Winters, and graduated with honors in 1921. Roberts spent the rest of her life in Springfield, writing full-time until her death from Hodgkin's disease in 1941.

Major Works

Roberts's first published work, *In the Great Steep's Garden* (1915), is a collection of seven poems. Written while she was in Colorado, the poems were inspired by the flowers of the Rocky Mountains. While at the University of Chicago, she wrote the poems collected in *Under the Tree* (1922). Roberts called these "child poems" because they represent her adult attempt to imagine, or remember, what the experience of childhood was like. Most critics consider *The Time of Man* Roberts's masterpiece. The novel is a kind of *bildungsroman* which tells the story of Ellen Chesser, a young woman from a poor family whose forebears were Kentucky pioneers. The narrative recounts the harsh and difficult circumstances of her life, detailing her withdrawal from the world around her and her subsequent spiritual renewal as she learns acceptance and love. *The Time of Man* has been praised for its skillful and poignant evocation of Ellen's consciousness and for the poetry of its prose style. Somewhat similar to this work is *My Heart and My Flesh* (1927). This novel documents the fortunes of Theodosia Bell, a southern woman who loses her wealth and social standing, attempts suicide, and ultimately experiences a reaffirmation of life. Written while these two novels were still unfinished, *Jingling in the Wind* (1928) is an allegorical satire on the state of the modern world and the inadequacy of Christianity to deal with commercialism, decadence, and the corruption of the human spirit. Set during the revolutionary period in Virginia and Kentucky, *The Great Meadow* (1930) concerns the choice of Diony Hall to leave the comfort and stability of her family's farm for a life in the wilderness. The novel's main theme involves the wresting of order from a chaotic world. *A Buried Treasure* (1931) is about Andy and Philly Blair and the impact exerted on their lives by a found cache of gold coins. Thematically the novel examines the emergence of Andy and Philly's own self knowledge and their understanding of the depth of their love. *The Haunted Mirror* (1932) and *Not by Strange Gods* (1941) are both collections of short stories that critics regard as artistically less successful than her novels. *He Sent Forth a Raven* (1935) is set during World War I and concerns the personal and philosophical conflicts that arise between the people in the small town of Wolflick, Kentucky. The chaos represented by the war sets the beliefs and moral codes of the main characters in stark relief. *Black Is My Truelove's Hair* (1938) is a somewhat allegorical novel about a woman's redemption. With main characters who, on one level, stand for the figures in the story of Genesis, the novel describes the rise and fall and return to grace of the protagonist, Dena, who is an everyman figure. *Song in the Meadow* (1940), a poetry collection, was the last work published during Roberts's lifetime. Some of the works collected here are "child poems" similar to the ones in *Under the Tree*; others are love lyrics, narratives about folk heroes, and poems expounding philosophical positions, particularly those concerned with self-discovery and the idealism of Bishop Berkeley.

PRINCIPAL WORKS

In the Great Steep's Garden (poetry) 1915
Under the Tree (poetry) 1922; revised edition published in 1930
The Time of Man (novel) 1926

My Heart and My Flesh (novel) 1927
Jingling in the Wind (novel) 1928
The Great Meadow (novel) 1930
A Buried Treasure (novel) 1931
The Haunted Mirror (short stories) 1932
He Sent Forth a Raven (novel) 1935
Black Is My Truelove's Hair (novel) 1938
Song in the Meadow (poetry) 1940
Not by Strange Gods (short stories) 1941
I Touched White Clover (poetry) 1981

CRITICISM

Robert Morss Lovett (review date 1926)

SOURCE: Review of *The Time of Man,* in *The New Republic,* Vol. XLVIII, No. 614, September 8, 1926, pp. 74-5.

[*In the following review, Lovett describes* The Time of Man *as "an almost perfect blending of idea and substance, of soul and body."*]

A recent school of criticism has made much of the fact that American literature has so rarely sprung directly from the American soil, has contained so meagrely the elements of folk culture: love of the land that sweetens the labor upon it; love of the life it brings forth, plant and animal; love of tools and material things fashioned by the hand of man for his work upon the earth; instinctive affection for fellow-men who born of the same mother, share the same inheritance. Pioneering has played a great part in American fiction, but the theme of the pioneer has been the conquest, not the growth of the soil. It has been our boast that we have never had a peasantry—social change and promotion have been too rapid to permit human life to sink its roots deeply into the earth. American treatment of the land has tended toward exploitation, not cultivation; and it is exploitation which is recorded in our literature. A sense of this poverty in the native sources of culture has shown itself in an attempt to claim for ourselves the civilization of the Indians of the Southwest and find in it the basis of a truly American art. Again, the racial inheritance of foreign peasant stocks has been laid under contribution, notably in Miss Cather's fine novel *My Antonia.* The recognition of the richness of Negro life in the primary sources of art is a sign of the same awakening. It is Miss Roberts's distinction that in her first novel she has followed a strain of American life which contains the elements in which American fiction has been so often lacking, seen them with the eyes of a poet, and entered into them with an instinctive knowledge and feeling which are the gifts of a true imagination.

The Time of Man is the story of Ellen Chesser, daughter of Henry and Nellie Chesser, poor whites, wanderers upon the Kentucky roads, sojourners here and there by chance on the land by which and for which they live. An instinct for permanence leads them in each new tarrying place to make a home of the two-roomed cabin which is allotted to them, to gather tools and utensils and household gear, a little stock—a cow, a few hens—to plant flowers. Then the sense of failure in permanent adjustment, the lack of ownership of the soil which they till, vaguely working, drives them forth. This is the pathos of their poor lives—the instinct for home constantly defeated yet constantly renewed.

Ellen at ten is a social being. When the wagon breaks down and the family is thrown on the land of Hep Bodine her first thought is to rehearse her story to tell to a woman, another wagon dweller, whom she has met on the road and lost again. For a long time she has no companions but the turkeys she tends and the heifer which she saved at birth. She cries out against her loneliness.

> All at once she lifted her body and flung up her head to the great sky that reached over the hills and shouted:
>
> "Here I am!"
>
> She waited, listening:
>
> "I'm Ellen Chesser! I'm here!"
>
> Her voice went up in the wind out of the plowed land. For a moment she searched the air with her senses and then she turned back to the stones again.
>
> "You didn't hear e'er a thing," she said under breath. "Did you think you heard something a-callen?"

Gradually at each settlement she makes friends, first the boys and girls of neighboring farms, then the men and women whose labor and sorrow she shares. Love comes to her, and desertion, and again love and children and betrayal and new hope. But always there is the call of the land. Ellen and the man she has taken are talking in the sweet, rhythmical speech of the country that falls on the ear like verse.

> "By spring," says Jasper Kent, "I aim to find some fields worth a man's strength. I'm plumb tired trafficken about good land and bad as it comes. I aim to go a long piece from here."
>
> "Once when I was a youngone Pappy went to Tennessee and I saw cotton in bloom. We saw cotton grow."
>
> "I'm plumb tired trafficken about."
>
> "Saw cotton a-growen. The people gathered it after a while in big baskets, piled up white."
>
> "We'll go to some pretty country where the fields lay out fair and smooth. A little clump of woodland. Just enough to shade the cows at noon."

"Smooth pasture is a pretty sight in a country, rollen up and cows dotted here and yon over it, red shorthorns and white and dun."

"And you won't say 'I know a prettier country in Adair or in Shelby or Tennessee.' Mountains or not."

"Smooth pastures, we'll have."

"Whatever I can do to pleasure you, Ellie. The house like the way you want."

"And the house fixed up, the shutters mended and the porch don't leak. To sit on a Saturday when the work is done. A vine up over the chimney. Once I saw a far piece from here . . ."

And always there is the answer of the road, beckoning away from the land which they do not own, inviting them with new promise, forbidding them to stay. Ellen's deepest, unconscious memories are bound up with it.

Going about the rough barnlot of the farm above Rock Creek, calling in the hens, breaking them corn, Ellen would merge with Nellie in the long memory she had of her from the time when she had called from the fence with so much prettiness, through the numberless places she had lived or stayed and the pain she had known, until her mother's life merged into her own and she could scarcely divide the one from the other, both flowing continuously and mounting. . . . It had seemed forever that she had traveled up and down roads, having no claim upon the fields but that which was snatched as she passed. Back of that somewhere in a dim, darkened dream like a prenatal vision, she saw a house under some nut trees, a place where she lived, but as clearly seen as this she could see her brother Davie and the others, the more shadowy forms of the older children, although all of them were dead before she was born. So that this house with the odor about it of nut shells was all imbedded now in the one dream that extended bedimmed into some region where it merged with Nellie's memories. Life began somewhere on the roads, traveling after the wagons where she had claim upon all the land and no claim, all at once, and where what she knew of the world and what she wanted of it sparkled and glittered and ran forward quickly as if it would always find something better.

At the end of her story as at the beginning she is in flight, her goods piled about her on the wagon, her children beside her, seeking the new fair land which is the goal of her pilgrimage.

It is needless to mark further the fine literary quality of Miss Roberts's novel. It will be said, indeed, that the book is written to theme, the great pervading theme of man's seeking; but so abundant and so real is the material in which the experience is rendered, so homely and intimate the background, so vivid the picturing of nature through its succession of seasons, so deep the sense of humanity in the characters, especially in the epic figure of Ellen, above all so perfect is the unity of tone, marred by no note of falseness or exaggeration that one feels in this book an almost perfect blending of idea and substance, of soul and body. It is life, not fiction, or rather it is the higher fiction which is the meaning of life.

Glenway Wescott (review date 1927)

SOURCE: "Miss Roberts' First Novel," in *The Dial,* Chicago, Vol. 83, July, 1927, pp. 73-5.

[*In the following review, Wescott praises Roberts for the "artfulness" of* The Time of Man.]

In the beginning Miss Roberts was a poet, and a number of years ago Mr Huebsch published for her an admirable book of rhymed verses called *Under the Tree.* It is not merely a collection but a slight cycle exquisitely arranged—one little girl speaking in the first person from beginning to end. One might almost think it primarily intended for children; in any case, it is more like a lyric *Alice in Wonderland* than like *A Child's Garden of Verses,* containing neither any sentiments of a grown person wistfully regretting his childhood nor any morally uplifting couplets. The versification, founded throughout upon the cadences of a child's voice "speaking a piece," is graceful though monotonous. Every line has its delightful rhetorical trick; every stanza has been composed with a poet's thoroughness, even in affectation. But Miss Roberts' purpose seems to have been less to put the reader under a spell or a series of spells—the poet's purpose—than to inform him about matters too spiritual to be dealt with in plainer phrases. Conceits about nature and what are called "pathetic fallacies" serve to make clear, in miniature, mystical ideas. The delicately comical people about whom the little girl protagonist in pigtails talks to us do indeed suggest, now a sabbath of a child's witches, now a ring of rural angels; but they touch our emotions only as comical people. Roughly speaking, philosophy and character are the subjects of fiction; and in *Under the Tree* the powerful novelist which Miss Roberts has now shown herself to be was scarcely concealed by the accomplished poet she was then.

The Time of Man is the biography of a woman from childhood until her children begin to repeat her story. Ellen Chesser is the daughter and finally the mother of one of those families in Kentucky bred for centuries for bad luck, wandering poor-whites as unpleasantly impressive as the Wandering Jew. Through the eyes of the strange girl one sees the least leaf and mist and sparkle of a countryside which is crowded with the strangest men, women, and children, and birds and animals:

"That's Judge Gowan," she whispered. "And when he died there was marchen and white plumes on hats. . . . And when he was a-liven he used to ride up to town in a high buggy with a big shiny horse, a-steppen up the road and him a-sitten big, and always had a plenty to eat and a suit of clothes to wear and a nigger to shine his shoes for him of a weekday even. . . . He's Judge Gowan in court, a-sitten big, but I'm better'n he is. I'm a-liven and he's dead. I'm better. And bells a-ringen and banners go by and people with things in pokes to sell and apples a-rollen out on the ground and butter in buckets and lard to sell and pumpkins in a wagon, and sheep a-cryen and the calves a-cryen for their mammies and little mules a-cryen for their mammies, and a big man comes to the courthouse door and sings out the loudest of all: O yes! O yes! The honorable judge James Bartholomew Gowan (It must 'a been) is now asitten. . . ."

Ellen Chesser leads a life of imaginary dignity, with the heartbreaking credo of all men and women who die a little every day until the day of their death: "I'm lovely now. It's unknowen how lovely I am. I saw some mountains standen up in a dream, a dream that went down Tennessee." A life of filth: "A quick memory of Screw, of the time he caught her behind a wagon and hugged her close. . . . Whiskey smells came out of him, and man smells, sweat and dirt, different from woman dirt." A life of exquisite craving: "In their kiss the froth of the high tide of summer arose and frayed. It was as if they sang a comehither-come-hither to all the summer and all the countryside." There is a suicide by hanging; there is a witch; there is a lynching with whips, when Ellen stands in her night-gown in the mud and curses the men who are lashing her husband, her husband adulterous at last. A life of hard labour and fecundity. . . .

So far as I can remember, no book written in English since the war gives rise to so troubling a sense of reality, miserable and adorable reality—which is hideous without being ugly, like a fine animal that has just killed someone and will do it again, which is elegant in its unhurried moderation, which is profoundly instructive but not to be theorized about, which is adorable only because it is always victorious. It makes me think of those "triumphs" of the Caesars—not their successful battles, but the processions when they got back to Rome, in which the rulers, the resources, the customs, the fruits, and the animals of a vanquished kingdom were displayed or represented in simulacrum. In it, reality is Caesar. Therefore, of course, it is a tragic work.

Many modern realists whimper, though their readers must have suffered as well as they, or demand justice, though there is, on earth at least, no judge. Miss Roberts reminds us that even the author who seems to undertake nothing but a report of experiences not his own should be asked to bring to his task a certain personal nobility. For all her lovely or painful material would have been spoiled by the least pusillanimity, and the least vulgarity of over-emphasis would have made a gross and nightmarish book. So much for character; the rest is art—artfulness, artistry, artifice.

By some mysterious transposition or distillation of poor-white speech, Miss Roberts has created one of the most remarkable dialects in literature—as remarkable as Synge's and as appropriate to the slowly flowing chronicle-novel as his was to the rowdy theatre—which gives a fantastic veracity to the conversations and, penetrating the body of the text, colours or perfumes or accompanies with monotonous and peculiar folk-music, the entire story. This prose is suave and supple even when very violent things are taking place. One is drawn on from page to page less by the anxiety of suspense or by variety of interest than by enchantment, by sheer sober pleasure—as if it were an idyll. Daphnis and Chloe in Kentucky, and in distress. . . . Only when one lifts one's eyes from the Kentucky of the book to the actual world full of the same pain, does one realize that there has been printed on every page a most desperate and unforgiving cry.

Donald Davidson (review date 1930)

SOURCE: "Elizabeth Madox Roberts," in *The Spyglass: Views and Reviews, 1924-1930,* edited by John Tyree Fain, Vanderbilt University Press, 1963, pp. 44-8.

[*In the following review of* The Great Meadow, *originally published on March 16, 1930, Davidson determines that Roberts "does show the excellences and advantages of provincial art at its best."*]

Elizabeth Madox Roberts's fourth novel, ***The Great Meadow,*** shows all her fine qualities at their best. . . . What is the subject matter? In general, this time it is the westward push of the pioneers from Virginia across the mountains that brought the Watauga and Cumberland settlements into Tennessee, and Boone's Fort and Harrod's Fort into Kentucky. Of course Miss Roberts is writing specifically about Kentucky, which is her own state, and about people that are her own people in a real ancestral sense. ***The Great Meadow*** is thus as historical a novel as I ever read before. What made the Albemarle people want to go into Kentucky; how did they feel about going; what did they think and feel about their journeying and arriving and settling down; how did they behave in all the dangerous shifts of wilderness life?— these, I take it, constitute the matter that Miss Roberts is interested in giving. All the time, it is evident, she wants to be inside the minds of the Kentucky pioneers, and is not much concerned about telling a brisk story, with the wilderness a stage—which is what James Fenimore Cooper or Winston Churchill would have done.

What happens, then, in the novel, for something must happen in any novel? A great deal, when one comes to think about it. Diony Hall, a girl of an Albemarle family who has "the marryen mouth," marries bold Berk Jarvis and sets forth with him on the very day of her wedding, to follow Dan'l Boone's Trace into the Promised Land of Kentucky. When the long journey is over, they settle at Harrod's Fort, and experience all the hardships of pioneer life. Diony is saved from prowling Indians by the sacrificial devotion of Elvira Jarvis, Berk's mother, who is slain and scalped. Berk goes against the Indians to avenge his mother's death and does not return for a long period. And in the meanwhile Diony, thinking him dead, marries Evan Muir, who is devoted to her in her loneliness. But finally Berk does return, worn and spent with captivity among Ojibways, and the rough pioneer code decrees that Diony must choose between her two husbands. It is a wilderness version of the old Enoch Arden story, boldly and beautifully handled, with the American Revolution but a rumor of wars in the far-off background and the privations of Indian warfare and settlement building furnishing the main episodes.

Yet there are really no episodes. *The Great Meadow* is no tale of action. All this passes as in a glamorous dream where all things pass with the slow, equal intensity of thought. The narrative is like the bright steady flow of a river which does not change even while it changes. All is in the mind of Diony. And this leads to the next question:

What is the manner of the telling? It is the same as in *The Time of Man,* but more carefully shaped and confined to a unity, less straggling, and therefore less tedious. Seek for words to describe the effect, and you will have to say somewhat about reveries, or trance, or even hypnosis. Perhaps the second word is best. In this style, people, things, events are fixed as in the soft glow of a trance. It is as if these figures of wilderness people struggling and loving in the magic land of "Kaintuck" never had more than the muted reality of a dream spun in the thought of Diony Hall, like bright or dark threads on a smoothly humming wheel whose sound is a simple melody yet is rich with overtones.

The overtones, which are not to be separated from the melody, are to be found in the language and in the sharpness and particularity of the physical detail. What Elizabeth Roberts does is to make archaisms of speech, which appear quite forthrightly in the dialogue, the basis of an entire prose style which is not in itself archaic. The archaisms somehow strike a pitch for the sweet monotone of the prose; lying beneath it, they still invade and color it. And into this monotone are worked the thousands of little ways of life, as a painter would work in bits of color to make a harmonious composition—the manner of dress, the talk of distant happenings, the look of forests, the sounds of human and animal life, the strands of social behavior. It is all so skillfully done that I am quite at a loss how to describe it.

Then how does one estimate the performance in general? Certainly it is far above even the average good performance in contemporary English and American fiction of today. Miss Robert's writing has an excellence all its own. There is nobody to compare her with, unless it would be Virginia Woolf, with whom, in method at least, she has some slight kinship. Whether or not she is founding a literary tradition that may be used by others is another question.

How she differs from her contemporaries is an easier question to answer. First of all, she has no special prejudice, so far as we can tell, for which she is making her novel a vehicle, and she is not writing about country people or pioneer people because it happens to be the fashion to write about them. Somehow one feels that in writing as she does she is doing the perfectly natural and inevitable thing, which has come spontaneously out of herself as a natural-born Kentucky person.

This, I suppose, is what one calls literary sincerity. No doubt it is what Glenway Wescott is driving at when he writes of Elizabeth Madox Roberts at the University of Chicago:

> There was the young Southern woman, alone, absolutely original, unimpressed by the setting of evils and plagiaries, meek and insinuatingly affirmative, untouched by but kindly toward all our half-grown basenesses. [Or again] Wherever she was, it (Kentucky) evidently underlay the outbranching experience, folded shadowily into the typical scenes of an author's life—an immense territorial ghost.

(One must somewhat cruelly observe that Mr. Wescott, the author of *Goodbye, Wisconsin,* does not have a similar feeling for his own state, which, instead, he patronizes.)

And being, so far as we can tell, without social programs and preconceptions, Elizabeth Madox Roberts does show the excellences and advantages of provincial art at its best. Happily, she has never learned to abhor nature and simple things; they are not for her something to reform or to condescend to, nor have they for her the false romantic attraction of offering a convenient literary attitude. What they are, she is. Her subjects, her vocabulary, her style, her thought, and herself must surely be all in harmony. Out of this harmony come her scrupulous and beautiful books and her sureness of purpose, which contrast so remarkably with the works of our numerous muscle-bound and befuddled literary athletes.

Is the critique all praise, then? This question might be side-stepped by saying that her work has definite limits. Certain things it does well; it cannot do everything. Perhaps at times it is dangerously near to fastidiousness and affectation. It is of course absurd that a young pioneer woman could be metaphysical, as Diony seems to be. Hardly does it seem possible that the pioneers thought so intensely, and Bishop Berkeley's theories of mind and matter, which provide one of the minor motifs of this curious novel, could hardly have been in the conscious purpose of the Long Knives who won Kaintuck. There is a mystical strain in Miss Roberts that is a little confusing and strange. One fears that the poetic richness it provides carries with it a risk of downright queerness. But Miss Roberts will probably slide safely between Scylla and Charybdis by virtue of a quiet sense of humor.

Sara Teasdale (review date 1931)

SOURCE: "A Child Sings," in *Poetry,* Vol. XXXVIII, No. 4, July, 1931, pp. 227-29.

[*In the following review, Teasdale enthusiastically assesses of the verse in* Under the Tree.]

[*Under the Tree*] is as fresh and full of music as an April morning. A child is overheard singing, and we listen, afraid that the song will end. The little girl, perhaps five or six years old, is as much in love with life as the heroines of Miss Roberts' novels are, and as sensitive as they are to the moods of the earth and to the other creatures living on its surface. She seems to herself and to us an inevitable part of the rich life of the farms and the woods.

The magic of this book lies in its lovely freedom from self-consciousness. It is the heart of a child who knows life at its clearest and happiest. Verses about childhood are frequently sicklied o'er with pathos, or they are encumbered with nurses, governesses, Board Walks and a gaiety that is conscious of its immaculate pinafore. But here one escapes into the broad American countryside, into the life of a child to whom everything that she sees and hears becomes part of a delicious adventure all the keener for being savored chiefly alone.

These poems are as neatly spun as a cobweb and delicately jewelled as a web weighed down with rain-drops. They flash now with an exact observation, now with humor, but they are never consciously naive. Their music has variety, sure little tunes simply modulated as in **"The Branch"** or this evanescent song, **"The Star"**:

> O little one away so far,
> You cannot hear me when I sing.
>
> You cannot tell me what you are,
> I cannot tell you anything.

And here are the last lines from **"The Hens"**:

> I stopped inside, waiting and staying,
> To try to hear what the hens were saying.
>
> They were asking something, that was plain,
> Asking it over and over again.
>
> One of them moved and turned around,
> Her feathers made a ruffled sound,
>
> A ruffled sound, like a bushful of birds,
> And she said her little asking words.
>
> She pushed her head close into her wing,
> But nothing answered anything.

The present edition is bound in bright printed cloth and quaintly illustrated by F. D. Bedford. It is larger by half a dozen poems than the original edition published in 1922, which was admirably reviewed by Yvor Winters in *Poetry* for April, 1923.

Under the Tree has more than its intrinsic interest. It is the early work of a great artist. The best of Miss Roberts' novels, *My Heart and My Flesh,* is a supremely fine full-length portrait of a woman, the finest that I am aware of since that of Milly Theale in Henry James' *The Wings of the Dove.* Nothing could be farther from the impassioned intricacy of *My Heart and My Flesh* than the cool melodies of *Under the Tree,* yet they are both destined for the long journey toward immortality.

Mark Van Doren (essay date 1932)

SOURCE: "Elizabeth Madox Roberts: Her Mind and Style," in *The Private Reader: Selected Articles & Reviews,* Henry Holt and Company, 1942, pp. 97-109.

[*In the following essay, originally published in 1932, Van Doren comments on how Roberts's writing style adds another dimension to her novels.*]

A reader of any novel by Elizabeth Madox Roberts is certain sooner or later to remark the presence of a style. Her style, say those who do not like it, is more than present; it is obtrusive. But even those who like it very much have it uppermost in their minds as they proceed, and when they have finished it is the language, or the way of writing, which they are most likely to mention in favor of the artist they have discovered. *The Time of Man* struck attention largely because of the novelty of its accent. It had other qualities, of course, since it is impossible for a piece of fiction to go far without substance of some sort. But it had an individual voice; and it is this voice which is the most interesting thing about Miss Roberts.

It is truly interesting, indeed, only because it expresses a character in the speaker. There is probably no such thing as a voice which is "beautiful" in itself; our perception of its beauty is a perception of something human behind it. So with styles, which are merely tiresome when they do not reveal a mental or moral character of greater or less distinction. The style of Miss Roberts is worth discussing because it in itself is a sort of substance. It is more than a way of saying things; it is something said, something which would not otherwise have been said at all, something, we suspect, which could not be said unless it were said in this way. So an interesting person is a person who not merely does things interestingly; his doing them is almost the most interesting thing about him.

The clearest feature of Miss Roberts's style is, strangely enough, its monotony. Her books murmur. And there are those who do not like this. They say she puts them to sleep, that she sends out a cloud through which they walk with groping difficulty, that they find themselves reading on, page after page, with very little notion of what is happening or being said. They complain of a lack of emphasis, a failure ever to be quite sharp or plain enough. They admit that it is all very skillful and nice; but they deny that it gets them anywhere, and they assert that after the book is closed they remember only that it was well written: not what the story was, or what the persons were named, or what they did. To show what they mean they might open *The Time of Man* at almost any page and read:

> When he was gone she went into the house, moving dreamily through the moonlit rooms. To marry and go away, the idea came into her mind slowly, spreading unevenly through her sense of the half-lit kitchen and her own room which was bright with a square of white light on the floor. She fell asleep with no formed wish in her mind and no decision, but when Nellie called her out of sleep soon after dawn, while she dressed quickly in the faded blue garment, she heard a catbird singing clear fine phrases on a post near her window, clear phrases that were high and thin, decisive and final, and she knew at the instant that she would marry Jasper and go with him wherever he went, and her happiness made a mist that floated about her body as she carried the feedings to the hogs and opened the chicken boxes.

The lack of emphasis, of course, is deliberate. Not only do these sentences flow into one another with a studied sweetness; they make an endeavor at the same time to conceal the importance of the things they are saying. Imbedded in the third sentence, for instance, is the crucial clause of the entire novel: the clause conveying the information that Ellen, the heroine, has decided to marry Jasper, the hero. But it hides there, it almost defies the reader to note its significance. And a reader whose attention has been lulled by the pages that have gone before is indeed very likely to miss this significance. He is likely to say to himself: This is a paragraph which the author for some reason or other has seen fit to fill with pleasant little details; I shall skim through it and get the general impression she wants me to have. The decision to marry Jasper seems to the outer ear no more important than the color of Ellen's dress, or the patch of white light on the floor, or the necessity of going out to feed the hogs. And over all runs the ripple of a style which has not modified its pace in more than two hundred pages.

A reading of the second novel, however, *My Heart and My Flesh,* will accustom one to this quality; and a reading of *Jingling in the Wind, The Great Meadow,* and *A Buried Treasure* will bring one to the realization that it is a necessary quality in anything Miss Roberts would write. Or at any rate to the realization that it is involuntarily achieved. For Miss Roberts's work is very much of a piece. Every page of it has been strained through the same mind. And her mind is her character.

She has been called philosophical, even metaphysical. And there is no question that she is somehow disposed in the direction of philosophy. But "metaphysical" is hardly the word. I should call her an epistemologist, because there is no other word which will precisely describe the habits of her mind or fully account for her style. An epistemologist is less interested in what we know than in how we know it, if we do. The "if" is usually a big word with him. The epistemologist is likely to be a skeptic also. Not that he doubts the truth of this or that; he simply doubts its knowability. In his most familiar form he is one who challenges us to prove that the mind within the body has any satisfactory way of being certain that anything besides itself exists. Objects are phantoms; truths are impressions; and the perceiving brain may be only a machine that plays with itself, pretending that it perceives.

My conception of Miss Roberts—not necessarily of the woman herself, but of the novelist within her—is that she finds very fascinating the game of observing, comparing, criticizing, measuring, explaining, and doubting her impressions of the external world. The world for her is not the simple thing, with hard outlines and knowable surfaces, which it is for the average person, the average reader. It exists somehow at a series of removes from her, so that she must make an effort to reach it and see or feel it. She has that most curious equipment for a novelist, a doubt that the world exists. Or if she does not really doubt this, she finds the world composed on a fluid principle, so that objects melt and flow into each other even while they are being experienced. Every thing, every person, is perceived and understood with difficulty, as through a veil. And this veil, furthermore, is of such a weave that it has the special property of rendering the sounds and sights which come through it strangely uniform in pitch and vividness. No sound is louder than any other; no outline is clearer than its neighbor. It is a beautiful world behind that screen, since it is a world imagined in the mind; but it is relatively dim.

This might easily account for the monotony in Miss Roberts's pages. They murmur in the same way that the world they deal with does, and they pass in the same way a procession of ghostly images. Not that the writing itself, if examined word by word, is anything but precise. But the impression of the whole is not precise. Who is more eager to be definite than the groper after something which he fears is not there? And who is less able to be vivid than he who never can be quite convinced?

Miss Roberts cannot be really interested in a character who is unlike herself. So we find her heroes and heroines epistemologists too. They are deeply involved in the problem of knowledge, inveterately concerned with their personal mental processes. It is not without significance, surely, that the heroine of *The Great Meadow,* Diony Hall, grows up in the shadow of a father who reads aloud to her from Bishop Berkeley.

Some truths there are so near and obvious to the mind that man need only open his eyes to see them. Such I take this important one to be, namely, that all the choir of heaven and furniture of the earth, in a word, all those bodies that compose the mighty frame of the world, have not any substance without a mind, that their being is to be perceived or known . . . , that, consequently, as long as they are not actually perceived by me, or do not exist in my mind, or that of any other created spirit, they must either have no existence at all, or else subsist in the mind of some Eternal Spirit.

This is Diony's Bible; these are the words which control her every movement throughout the book, and for the simple reason that they fit her. She has always been concerned with the problem of her own identity. The novel begins:

1774, and Diony, in the spring, hearing Sam, her brother, scratching at a tune on the fiddle, hearing him break a song over the taut wires and fling out with his voice to supply all that the tune lacked, placed herself momentarily in life, calling mentally her name, Diony Hall. "I, Diony Hall," her thought said, gathering herself close, subtracting herself from the diffused life of the house that closed about her.

"Her thought said." A characteristic phrase, not only for Diony Hall but for her creator, who has made her so perfectly in her own image. *The Great Meadow* is only superficially about the settlement of Kentucky and the marriage of Diony to Berk, and later on the necessity Diony is under of choosing between the two husbands she finds she has: Muir and the Berk who has returned from Indian captivity. It is really about the thoughts which Diony has. Her decisions are intellectual. The dark and bloody ground into which she goes with Berk is dramatic ground for her because her entry into it is an entry into a world which hitherto has not existed for her because she has not been able to perceive it. Away from it she has not been able to experience it because it has not been part of herself. Yet there is the desire to experience it. "Her whole body swayed toward the wilderness, toward some further part of the world which was not yet known or sensed in any human mind, swayed outward toward whatever was kept apart in some eternal repository, so that she leaped within to meet this force halfway and share with it entirely." When she arrives there and begins her life of hardship she is not like the other women of the settlement. She is introspective; she is always learning the new world; she is forever thinking about it and watching the way it comes into her mind. Her reason for admiring Daniel Boone is a reason which no other woman could have understood: no woman, shall we say, except Miss Roberts. The simple fact about Boone was that he was never lost. No part of this world was strange to him; anything seen became at once, and without any effort, a part of himself; or if it did not he was not worried. "It's curious," she said to herself. "I'm not the Boone kind. I never was. . . . I'd be more at home somewheres else. . . . I don't know where. . . ."

Of course such a person is never at home anywhere. If effort is necessary before this consummation can be reached, then it can never be reached at all. Much thinking and feeling may enrich the person within; they will never, however, bring the outside world any closer—rather, perhaps, they will thicken the wall between. Miss Roberts's best people are on the other side of a thick wall which shuts them away from the things most people see satisfactorily and simply. Her heroines, for instance, lack that directness of attack which makes for success in encounters with men. Ellen in *The Time of Man,* Theodosia Bell in *My Heart and My Flesh,* and even the simple-minded Philly of *A Buried Treasure* can do nothing save stand back and watch certain women of the world throw nets around their husbands and lovers. They themselves have not the art, for they have not that knowledge of the world which would tell them that there is no such art. Speaking to themselves while the conquest goes on, they say strained, melodramatic things about their successful rivals—flatter them by attributing powers to them which perhaps no person ever had. As for themselves, they can only wait and hope that their men will return to them. Hoping may bring them and it may not; sometimes, as a matter of fact, it does. But this is only one of those accidents of life which are intended not to be understood. It has nothing to do with the laws of the mind.

Diony and Ellen have this characteristic in common, namely, that they require a great deal of time to absorb and so after their fashion understand the universe about them. This is why the novels in which they appear move slowly, as if through a viscous atmosphere, a resisting current of life. This universe of course does not exist for them until they see it. But even then it comes only gradually into being, like mist taking shape. Meanwhile they feel the face of life as a blind person feels surfaces which he wants not only to identify but to penetrate and remember; feeling this face monotonously, stroking it over and over with a fine, silent solemnity, and, although coming upon many things there, coming never with sudden discovery upon the One Thing, whatever it is. Ellen has met a strange woman on the road several times, and has talked with her. But she does not know her yet. "The woman had been seen now a half-dozen times and had become a mass of characteristic motions and friendly staring eyes. Ellen longed to fix her into a thought, to know what she would say now that she knew how she would look saying it." Such a mind does not make swift headway in the world. Yet it is capable of intense experiences, once it can experience anything at all; and so the second half of *The Time of Man* is powerfully charged with emotion—though the reader and Miss Roberts are the only ones who are conscious of the fact. To her husband and children and to all her neighbors Ellen remains to the end an incommunicable mystery.

Philly, feeling with her fingers in *A Buried Treasure* for the little sack of pearls which Andy has secreted under his clothing, might be taken as a symbol of all the searching which goes on in Miss Roberts's books.

> In the night Philly fingered again for the sack of pearls, wanting comfort. Her hand went lightly to Andy's side and moved up and down over his hip to find the little tape that would lead to the small treasure. She thought that she must have fallen asleep in the search, for her hand had found nothing. Then she stirred lightly to assure herself that she was awake, and she set upon the task more carefully. . . . . When she was still and light again she went swiftly over the whole of Andy's middle, over his trunk and legs, but there was no tape and no little sack of pearls. She felt then at his neck and his breast, his arms and his ankles, but there was nothing.

Even in other respects Andy has his mysteries for Philly. There could scarcely be a simpler man in all fiction, yet his wife finds herself admitting that "when he said nothing there was a curious thing, as if it would be a mystery about him or near him." She might have remembered a neighbor woman saying earlier in the book:

> Sometimes you hardly seem acquainted with the man you're married to twenty years, and all the time you know every thought inside his head and every act his body can do or is likely ever to do. And there he is, strange. So strange you wonder sometimes if it's a man or a horse or a hay-baler or what kind anyway you're wedded with all your life.

The humor in that last sentence is a reminder of qualities which Miss Roberts richly has in addition to the one quality which has so far been spoken of. Her language, it should be said at once, is in itself a thing of perpetual delight, tart with wit as well as languorous with longing for certitude. It is the mixture of these elements in it that accounts for its pre-eminence over the language of other southern novelists today who try perhaps to do the same thing Miss Roberts is doing. They fail because they lack her complexity of mind—which, after everything else is said, is the thing we come back to when we are explaining the excellence of a novelist or artist of any kind. Her language is the language of her own mind; and so is everything in her novels typical of her own character.

Jingling in the Wind will be puzzling, for instance, to one who expects it to be a satire on contemporary civilization such as anyone else would write. It is the satire that Miss Roberts alone would write: fantastic yet shrewd, fragile yet funny, stylized yet recognizable. And even its hero, by the way, is in the habit of watching his mind. "As he sang," we hear of Jeremy the rain-maker, "he ruminated. It was often his custom and his very great pleasure to arrange his thoughts, or some of them, in decent and orderly periods." So *My Heart and My Flesh* can be contrasted with any of those novels in which another southerner, William Faulkner, has dealt with the decay of his section. The difference between Mr. Faulkner as a Mississippian and Miss Roberts as a Kentuckian is not the chief difference between them; there is the larger difference which results in the fact that the horrors of *My Heart and My Flesh* take their due place, and only their due place, in the procession of Theodosia Bell's thoughts. They are not painful because they are shrouded in intellect; they arrive through layer upon layer of impression.

It is of course not surprising that the chief personage in *He Sent Forth a Raven* should be represented as confined to his house and condemned to know the rest of life by hearsay. Stoner Drake, vowing at his wife's death never to set foot on the green earth again, keeps his vow; and keeps it under the handicaps which Miss Roberts would of course set up. For the women, Martha and Jocelle, through whom Drake sees and hears the world are anything but a transparent medium. When Jocelle was a little girl "a faint haze of things known and unknown spread around her. Those things which she could never bring together into a pattern of thought were left unrelated, floating in a fog." Well, Miss Roberts brings her up that way, too; and so all goes on as it should go on, through mists and veils.

Yet here an attempt is made to record the large, the indubitably solid world. This time it is the world of the great war, and it comes to the fine ears of Miss Roberts's people with such a ruthless crash of sound that the recording instrument can scarcely endure the strain. It is as if lightning had struck some child's receiving set. Miss Roberts's only resort, in the absence of any ability to indicate the sheer volume of this catastrophe, is to set her people talking wildly; not loudly, but wildly. A mad chorus of three men—Drake himself, the carpenter Dickon, and the preacher Briggs—philosophizes and mythologizes in broken sentences of weird power while Martha plays Cassandra in an upstairs chamber. The novel all but goes to pieces in the eloquence of these men, as it had gone to pieces, incidentally, for Martha in her prime; when the hearing of too much from Stoner Drake had rendered her deaf. It seems a question, therefore, whether Miss Roberts should attempt such subjects as world wars, since they obviously are too much for her. Yet the answer is not easy. Perhaps she should. For in making the attempt, and failing, she reminds us of her own best work and of how well it is done; and she does after all say something about the world we live in, if it is only that the truth concerning it cannot possibly be spoken.

Harry Modean Campbell and Ruel E. Foster (essay date 1956)

SOURCE: "Elizabeth Madox Roberts as Poet," in *Elizabeth Madox Roberts: American Novelist,* University of Oklahoma Press, 1956, pp. 251-72.

[In the following essay, Campbell and Foster survey Roberts's poetry.]

As a child of eight, Miss Roberts saw a picture of Elizabeth Barrett Browning under which was printed the single word, "Poet." She was so impressed by this that she pointed to the word and said, "That's what I want to be, a poet." And that she became. The very essence of her art is her poetry. The real key to the subtle appeal of her novels is poetry. [We will discuss] her two published volumes of poetry—*Under the Tree* and *Song in the Meadow*—and attempt to describe here the nature and value of these volumes.

We need to discuss briefly Miss Roberts' beliefs about the nature of poetry. . . .

Since Miss Roberts made an explicit statement about her poetic theory, we will quote from it at some length as an introduction to our discussion of her poetry:

> I find that I have tried for a poignant speech, as direct as cause and effect is direct. . . .
>
> Poetry must appeal to the emotions each time it appears, with the freshness and vigor and the charm of a clear first impression. It flashes into media where the intellect goes crawling and groping. . . .
>
> . . . Poetry is forever trying to make clear obscure relations in the worlds and systems of things and ideas. . . .
>
> . . . I believe that it is the high function of poetry to search into the relation between mind and matter, into the oneness of flesh and thin air . . . spirit.
>
> . . . I have discarded all poetic fancies and pathetic fallacies and have kept close to my own experience and the truth of American life as we live it here in Kentucky. . . .
>
> I have avoided all literary words and all literary phrases.
>
> I have worked for a poignant statement. . . .
>
> I have tried for organic rhythms. . . . I have used contemporary speech and contemporary thought.
>
> I have used child speech and child psychology for my images. . . .
>
> If I can, in art, bring the physical world before the mind with a greater closeness, richer immediacy than before, so that mind rushes out to the very edges of sense—then mind turns about and sees itself mirrored within itself.

The preceding statement is an excellent analysis of exactly what Miss Roberts achieved in her best poetry. Perhaps the chief distinction of her poetry lies in its double impact. It is at one and the same time children's verse of the highest quality and adult poetry with a distinctly metaphysical character and appeal. That these two qualities coexist in a true imaginative unity in her best verse is an achievement of no mean consequence. True, in her later poetry, there is a break down in some of the poems where social propaganda is implied without a true integration of image and concept. A look at her two volumes of poetry will, we believe, show the justness of her self-analysis.

The first volume, *Under the Tree,* is very likely the better of the two. Done mostly in her Chicago period, it presents with great clarity her "remembrance of things past." Here, however, the things are not really past; they are present, eternally present, in the first clarity of a small child's world. The point of view throughout is that of a small child, say five to eight years old. Most of the poems are in the present tense, a few are in the simple past.

If we ask what the specific subject matter of this child's world is, we find it to be first the physical objects she discovers in her home and in the small Kentucky town at the turn of the century. She sees the cornfield, the cow at milking time, the red-hooded woodpecker, the crescent moon, a child asleep, and an August night. She has a vivid imagination, so she composes fantasies about the "little people" who live in the pulpit at church, about a night fear in the form of a panther who crawls under her bed at sleep time, and about a strange tree that looks at her as she walks by it. She has a grandmother who tells her fascinating stories of how it was in the old days, of her ancestors who lived in Maryland and came through the "Gap" long ago into Kentucky. All these strands are worked into the rich cloth of the child's world.

This world is a pristine world, a clear, transparent world where the viewing senses are washed clean of all impurities. It is T. S. Eliot's first world, "Through the first gate, into our first world, shall we follow the deception of the thrush," and it has some of the white innocence of Blake's world. It is even analogous to that blessed state of childhood frequently referred to in the New Testament in such passages as, "Suffer the little children to come unto me for of such is the kingdom of Heaven." This primal childhood innocence appears with effortless sincerity in such a poem as **"Christmas Morning,"** particularly in the last three stanzas quoted below:

> I'd watch his breath go in and out.
> His little clothes would all be white.
> I'd slip my finger in his hand
> To feel how he could hold it tight.
>
> And she would smile and say, "Take care,"
> The mother, Mary, would, "Take care";
> And I would kiss his little hand
> And touch his hair.
>
> While Mary put the blankets back

The gentle talk would soon begin.
And when I'd tiptoe softly out
I'd meet the wise men going in.

There is yet another dimension to this child's world, which, in a sense, is man's world too, since man is but a child in the vast scope of the universe. Thus, as the little girl probes aspects of her village world, she is man probing the pitiless universe. We see this dual import in **"August Night."**

August Night

We had to wait for the heat to pass,
And I was lying on the grass,

While Mother sat outside the door,
And I saw how many stars there were.

Beyond the tree, beyond the air,
And more and more were always there.

So many that I think they must
Be sprinkled on the sky like dust.

A dust is coming through the sky!
And I felt myself begin to cry.

So many of them and so small,
Suppose I cannot know them all.

Here the child becoming poignantly aware of one of the grand mysteries of the universe is recapitulating an archetypal racial experience; thus, she is man, suddenly and frighteningly aware that the fixity of the world crumbles, that mind as a knowing instrument is inadequate and recoils appalled before the horrors of what we know as space.

This dual appeal in a single poem, appealing truly and directly to the child mind and by overtones to the adult mind, must be assessed as one of her fine accomplishments in poetry. Anyone who has attempted poetry knows the almost insuperable difficulty of such double allegiance. Surely Miss Roberts displays in **Under the Tree** clear evidence that she possessed a unique poetic knowledge of the subject matter discussed above. Jacques Maritain, in *Creative Intuition in Art and Poetry,* says that poetic knowledge is a particular kind of knowledge through inclination or connaturality (connaturality, i.e., you know a virtue, fortitude, because you possess and practice that virtue and *are* that virtue yourself). Thus Miss Roberts knew this unique mind expressed in **Under the Tree** through connaturality; the book is, in effect, an anatomy of her own mind. Such poetic knowledge can be fully expressed only in the work. **Under the Tree** expresses a dual subject matter, reflecting the dual character of her mind.

Of equal interest with her subject matter is the form she employs to express that subject matter. First, there is the strong physical element of her poetry. Some of her po-

etry is purely a poetry of things. She employs great skill to give the exact look and "feel" of the object or scene. It is her desire to present the physical world with absolute immediacy, to see small things clearly, exactly. She would have mind rush out to the very edge of sense. To this end, she employs a terse, monosyllabic, Anglo-Saxon diction, pared to the quick. The physical effect is extreme and immediate, as in **"Little Rain."**

Little Rain

When I was making myself a game
Up in the garden, a little rain came.

It fell down quick in a sort of rush,
And I crawled back under the snowball bush.

I could hear the big drops hit the ground
And see little puddles of dust fly round.

A chicken came till the rain was gone;
He had just a very few feathers on.

He shivered a little under his skin,
And then he shut his eyeballs in.

Even after the rain had begun to hush
It kept on raining up in the bush.

One big flat drop came sliding down,
And a ladybug that was red and brown

Was up on a little stem waiting there,
And I got some rain in my hair.

This physical exactness is one of the major factors in guarding these poems from the sentimentality, coyness, and posturing which so frequently mar children's verse. Certainly Miss Roberts has succeeded in avoiding this pitfall. There are other reasons for her success besides the physicality of the poetry. One is the unaltered use of the child's point of view. She establishes it at the beginning and never allows adult condescension suddenly to appear within the poem. Another factor is what we might call "control." The sense of "control" is very fine and exact in **"Little Rain."** Her usual technique is (1) to describe at the beginning of the poem a physical object or scene, then (2) place herself in the poem in a particular relationship to that object or scene, and then (3) conclude the poem by a meditation which suddenly lifts the poem to the level of a haunting emotionalism (frequently close to mysticism) which implies far more than it says on the surface. This conclusion adds great power to the poem, having the effect of music which goes on in the imagination long after it ceases to sound to the physical ear—"*Heard melodies are sweet but those unheard are sweeter.*" Her sense of control and proportion in unifying these three elements of the poem and preventing any one from being exaggerated at the expense of the others definitely contributes to the "guarding" effect of her form. Her short poem, **"The Pilaster,"** is a fair enough example of this controlled style and the techniques of controlling it.

The Pilaster

The church has pieces jutting out
Where corners of the walls begin.
I have one for my little house,
And I can feel myself go in.

I feel myself go in the bricks,
And I can see myself in there.
I'm always waiting all alone,
I'm sitting on a little chair.

And I am sitting very still,
And I am waiting on and on
For something that is never there,
For something that is gone.

In terms of rhyme and meter, Miss Roberts has been content to remain within conventional forms—this in spite of the fact that literary Chicago led the revolt against poetic conventions during her stay there. *Under the Tree* stays well within the bounds of traditional English poetry: the most frequent stanzaic form is a quatrain rhyming either *a b a b* or *a b c b,* and the prevailing meter is iambic tetrameter, employing frequent substitutions. Next to the quatrain in frequency come rhyming couplets, varying from a four- to seven-beat meter. A few iambic tetrameter triplet stanzas appear, but these are exceptional. There is no use of free verse. Rhymes are usually perfect rhymes. Miss Roberts has realized that conventions need not be dead weight, but that, properly used, they are a means of gaining new strength and freedom. These traditional forms blend well with the strong song element of the poems. Probably their strongly incantative character is their outstanding formal mark. Song lay at the very base of Miss Roberts' imagination. Poetry, in the broad sense of imaginative literature in general, may be thought of as moving in the three fields of song, novel, and drama. Miss Roberts' forte was poetry as song, and *Under the Tree* is a prime exhibit of this fact. A great many of these poems have been set to music and sung successfully. There is a strong sound element in the majority of these poems, but it is not used to override and obliterate the meaning and sense of the poems. The sound and the sense reinforce each other, and we savor them together. Both are simple and straightforward on the surface. Almost all the poems in *Under the Tree* seem to be on the verge of song. The sense of musical form, so strong in all of Miss Roberts' imaginative experience, is especially apparent in these poems. We cite the poem **"On the Hill,"** emblematic of the mind trying to see itself in relation to physical objects, as an example of this blend of song and meaning.

On the Hill

Mother said that we could go
Upon the hill where the strawberries grow.

And while I was there I looked all down,
Over the trees and over the town.

I saw the field where the big boys play,

And the roads that come from every way,

The courthouse place where the wagons stop,
And the bridge and the scales and the blacksmith
  shop.

The church steeple looked very tall and thin,
And I found the house that we live in.

I saw it under the poplar tree,
And I bent my head and tried to see

Our house when the rain is over it,
And how it looks when the lamps are lit.

I saw the swing from upon the hill,
The ropes were hanging very still.

And over and over I tried to see
Some of us walking under the tree,

And the children playing everywhere,
And how it looks when I am there.

But Dickie said, "Come on, let's race";
And Will had found the strawberry place.

To sum up our observations, we can say that *Under the Tree* is a book of strong, simple poems appealing to both children and adults. Its delicate psychological probings and metaphysical overtones suggest very closely the quality of the inner reverie and pure sensory imagery of the inner world of Ellen Chesser in *The Time of Man*. The poems usually proceed in a simple, straightforward diction with a strong lilting quality. The object or scene is stated and then begins to glow (her magic is in making it glow). This incandescence is an attribute of the entire poem; it grows from the total effect. The poems are little flames which flare up in our imagination and then glow for a long time in our memories. We will not soon forget them.

In 1940, eighteen years after the publication of *Under the Tree,* Miss Roberts brought out *Song in the Meadow,* her second and last volume of poems. As we would expect, it bears definite similarities to *Under the Tree,* but shows new and different influences at work. It is more experimental than *Under the Tree;* there is a wider range of ideas and verse forms, and a new note of social propaganda appears. More is attempted here than in the earlier volume; yet there are occasional failures, which is certainly not true of *Under the Tree*. Her technical experimentation seems motivated primarily by Gerard Manley Hopkins, whom she discovered in the 1930's. Obvious also is the influence of Whitman and, to some extent, Carl Sandburg; this latter influence is less fortunate. The folk song continued to interest and influence her, as is evident in the latter part of this volume.

Much that we have said about the formal characteristics of her earlier poems would apply equally well to these later ones. To avoid repetition we will touch primarily on some of the new influences which appear here. For example, the dedicatory poem is a sonnet, **"Sonnet of Jack,"** and it is particularly reminiscent of Hopkins. It is Petrarchan in its octave and sestet and in its rhyme scheme—as were most of Hopkins' sonnets. The meter is like Hopkins' "sprung rhythm," having usually five or six beats to the line and an irregular number of unaccented syllables (running up to eleven for one line). Her great use of alliteration, consonance, and assonance, her coinage of compound words and extreme use of Saxon diction, along with familiar Hopkins figures of speech (e.g., "bony house")—all these display the influence of the British poet. Her very title, **"Sonnet of Jack,"** suggests an affinity with Hopkins' poems of the common man, "Tom's Garland" and "Harry Ploughman"—particularly with the conclusion to his "That Nature is a Heraclitean Fire and of the Comfort of the Resurrection," which reads:

> In a flash, at a trumpet crash,
> I am all at once what Christ is, since he was
>   what
>   I am, and
> This Jack, joke, poor potsherd, patch,
>   matchwood, immortal diamond,
> Is immortal diamond.

If we compare the above conclusion with the final couplet of **"Sonnet of Jack,"** . . . see the probable source of Miss Roberts' title in "This Jack," and a further analogy in the startling peripeteia which closes both poems:

> Spread free of the bony house toward
>   heaven, their joy, his or theirs, say
> What you will,—dead Friday and
>   born again already on Thursday.

The poem **"Summer Is Ended"** is another excellent example of the Hopkins influence on Miss Roberts, as the first stanza quoted below will indicate.

Summer Is Ended

> Summer is ended.
> Leaves a-tatter and stippled with rust,
> Great leaves and little, brown brittle
>   and green,
> Red, yellow and bitten, frost-eaten,
> Summered and weathered, full-seasoned,
>   clattered and cluttered,
> A dust in the winds, sweet mass,
>   Leafmas.

Somewhat noticeable, though quite secondary to that of Hopkins, is the influence of Whitman. It is most easily seen in her **"Conversations beside a Stream."** The form of the poem is reminiscent of Whitman's "Song of Myself," employing a loose, free-verse line, frequent catalogings, Indian names for their romantic effect, and some rather vague generalizing about "the people." The same poem echoes portions of Carl Sandburg and Vachel Lindsay and seems less like her best vein and certainly is not among her best poems.

Her interest in the tradition of folk song shows itself in a number of the poems in this volume. She frequently employs the ballad stanza, ballad techniques, and diction reminiscent of the Middle English lyric. **"The Fox Hunt"** uses the question and answer monologue of the folk song with fine effect, while in **"Tapestry Weaving, A Ballad Song of Mary,"** the diction and phrasing are strongly Saxon with an admixture of archaic words like "sweven" and "stear." Both these poems are good. In general, the folk song influence has been more fruitful for her poetry than has the influence of the moderns.

The experimentalism of *Song in the Meadow* displays itself primarily in the use of slant rhymes, long poetic lines, free verse, sprung rhythm, mixtures of different stanzaic forms in the same poem, and a diction which is frequently more stylized and abstract than that of *Under the Tree*. Also, there is a tendency to write on broad social or political questions, to engage in a type of poetry which is overtly a propaganda poetry. Examples of this would be such poems as **"Corbin the Cobbler,"** **"Man Intolerant,"** and **"Conversations beside a Stream."** These are not among her most successful poems. Her best poetry in this volume is an extension of the mode she inaugurated in *Under the Tree*. This observation is supported by a look at the three categories into which she divided this volume.

The categories indicate their content by their titles. The first category, "Maidens and Loves," is the largest of the three, and its tone is nearest to that of *Under the Tree*. The early poems in this section represent the little girl of *Under the Tree* grown slightly older and indulging further her idealistic probing of the universe in such poems as **"Self-Haunted Girl"** and **"The Fox-Hunt."** Then comes the idyllic poem of harvest time, **"Love in the Harvest,"** marked by its exuberant love of life and its strong singing quality.

Love in the Harvest

> Harvest now, and all are in the hay.
> All the men at work now and all
>   the teams a-jingle.
> The cutting knives are quick and the
>   bright traces dangle
> And tinkle with the swingle-tree, to
>   put the grass away.
>
> Windrows now, and the heat is from
>   the South.
> All the boys are gay now and sing
>   along the raking.
> They shout it from the bottom
>   land and make a play of stacking.
> A song in the meadow and a song
>   in the mouth.

The poems of love—a clear, simple, untroubled love—come now with many echoes of the refrains and singing syllables of Middle English and Elizabethan song. Then the more somber note of **"The Lovers"** appears, in which the speaker thinks of slipping into the ease of death to escape the pain of life, but is saved by her instinctive vitality:

> But I loved life
> And life loved me.

Then back to a praise of the sweet mass of the summer for which we "Praise Now the Lord!" in the poem **"Summer is Ended."** The "Maidens and Loves" section concludes with a series of five, softly lilting cradle songs, including the very beautiful **"Blessed Spirit, Guard"** with its fine last stanza—

> At thy cradle side adoring,
> Life renewed and here restoring
> Blessed spirit guard thy sleeping.

Altogether, this first section, "Maidens and Loves," creates a tone of positive love, a tone of the joy of life, and at the same time a feeling of the perpetual mystery of life which is present in all our knowledge. The scene is pastoral—always and deeply so. The love is love of man and love of life; it is a happy love, and from this clear mood arise the **"Song in the Meadow"** and the **"Song in the Mouth."** Although the poems do vary in aesthetic importance, many being relatively minor, they all are completely realized; that is, they accomplish what the poet set out to do.

The second category of poems, "The World and the Earth," is more disturbing artistically than the first—disturbing for the note of social protest. We, of course, do not object to social protest in poetry; we object here because the poetry seems forced and strained. It lacks the air of complete inevitability, of total integration, achieved in her successful poetry. This sense of incompleteness appears in such poems as **"Corbin the Cobbler," "Man Intolerant," "A Man,"** and **"Conversations beside a Stream."** In reading these, we have the uneasy feeling that Miss Roberts is writing not what she really intends, but what she thinks she should intend under these circumstances.

Yet another note intrudes here—darker emotionally but finer poetically. This note is that of an old time, a time running back to a prehistoric past, long before the human race had appeared. This note expresses itself in images of the ancient sea and rock, of cold and nonhuman seasons, of fossil shells bearing witness to an ancient and lost flow of life—a note that lies below the floor of preracial memory but never breaks through. Sad and resigned but not bitter, it is what man thinks of after the glad exuberance of the **"Song in the Meadow"** passes into the mood of reflection and meditation. This vein is well exemplified in such a poem as **"The Ancient Gulf."**

The Ancient Gulf

The shells are packed into the rock
Life has eaten into the stone, edged
Its way through the hard lime,

Seen now where the fields are ledged.

A lean time under the grass.
A cold season for the rock.
A perilous wait in the still cliff
Where the hard beams of stone lock

To hold the leavings of some leaping tide,
The wash of gulf fog, and the swift
Tang of salt spume on a shore,
Now sealed in fossil and drift.

This emotion leads naturally to the pantheistic mysticism of **"Child in the Universe,"** where the speaker feels herself to be merging with the physical universe. It passes on to the organistic idea of the universe expressed in **"A Man."** The theory here, in brief, is that everything is implicit in anything, so it doesn't matter where you start because you will always be led inevitably to the answer. This idea was attractive to Miss Roberts as an artistic theory as well as a way of life. Its general import is expressed in the first stanza of **"A Man."**

A Man

Start anywhere.
Build on the eyes or the feet or the hair,
Build on the want of a pen or a ring.
His name, Ben, Bob, Jack, or Jim.
Start with the gallows beam . . .
Start anywhere.
Start with his hat.
Start with his face.
This way or that.
Start any place.
Start with his end or his plan.
Start anyplace to construct a man.

This poem leads naturally to the extended effort of **"Conversations beside a Stream,"** in which two voices speaking antiphonally attempt to sum up America in an impressionistic mélange of bits of folk song, historical allusions, and democratic mottos. The poem, while it has fine phrases, suffers from too many passages like this:

Of George Washington and his Gentlemen.
The signers who wrote their names, large
and small, to the mighty document of
Jefferson's brain. George Washington
and his ragged regimentals, they of the
bare feet and blood-stained tracks on the
frozen ground.

Or, like this:

Start with democracy
In county, in township, in hundred,
    and shire.
His first aspire.
He, strong speaking and singing
    his will.

Fortunately, this section closes with an excellent poem, a little prayer, **"Evening Hymn,"** which is complete and satisfying.

Evening Hymn

The day is done;
The lamps are lit;
Woods-ward the birds are flown.
Shadows draw close—
Peace be unto this house.

The cloth is fair;
The food is set.
God's night draw near.
Quiet and love and peace
Be to this, our rest, our place.

Part three of *Song in the Meadow* is a brief section bearing the title, "Legends"; it is the slightest of the three sections both in length and aesthetically. The first poem, **"The Meeting,"** presents a situation familiar to those who read Miss Roberts closely. The poem is a brief dramatic lyric describing a meeting between the speaker and an unnamed entity within the house. The poem is plainly symbolic, and Miss Roberts herself suggests that it represents the consciousness meeting the soul. It is a twinning of the ego, a dramatizing of the two personalities within each of us. It is suggestive of the scene at the climax of her short story, **"The Haunted Palace,"** when, Jess, in attacking her own image in the glass, is attacking the brute fear that lurks in her own mind. The poem builds up through six stanzas to a symbolic meeting which comes thus in the last two stanzas:

My hand goes up
To reach for the latch,
And a hand inside
With identical touch.

Blue eyes look in
At the cloudy glass;
Blue eyes inside
Look out of the house.

After this dramatic psychology, the poems turn to racial legends such as Cinderella and Adam and then to the family legend dealing with Miss Roberts' great-grandfather seven generations removed. The story of this ancestor's stowaway voyage to America is told impressionistically in **"Sailing to America."** The Orpheus legend is domesticated in Kentucky in a series of three poems, followed by three others on Daniel Boone. The Boone poems are simple, lilting poems dealing with Boone as a woodsman; they have no suggestion of Boone as the symbolic omnicompetent figure to lead us from the chaos of modern thought—the theme which her notes indicate she hoped to develop in an epic composition on Boone.

The last poem in this section and in the book is **"Jack the Giant Killer,"** a ten-page poem and a fairly long one for Miss Roberts. It tells a folk-idiom version of the story, with symbolic overtones, suggesting that Jack, in a certain sense, is Everyman; and the Giant is the great forces of nature which are subjugated by Jack Everyman in the nature-myth ending of the last two stanzas.

The earth made a cave of the giant's mouth,
And a mountain out of his stomach.
His legs became two mountain chains,
And his head became a hummock.

Then Jack brought up his trusty plow
And he plowed himself a field.
He grew his corn on the giant's breast,
And he reaped a mighty good yield.

It is on these two volumes, then, that her reputation as a poet must rest at present. There are other poems, as yet unpublished, which are not represented in this discussion. Those unpublished poems in the Roberts Papers would in no way alter the judgments made [here]. There are yet other poems which are in the possession of the family and remain an unknown quantity. Presumably, they will one day be published, and they may enhance even further their author's name as poet.

The first volume seems the better, all in all. It is a clear, direct poetry, less troubled by the overt intellectualizing that sometimes obtrudes into *Song in the Meadow*. The experimentalism of the second volume is interesting and frequently effective (as in the organic rhythms of **"The Meeting"** and **"Jack the Giant Killer,"** where the beat and rhyme clearly suggest the appropriate physical movement of the poem's story) though occasionally forced. Both volumes, however, have the magic feel and incandescence of good poetry, and they are pre-eminently a singing poetry. And as we listen to the unique cadence of this poetry, our hearts lift up, and we too sing, "A Song in the Meadow and a Song in the Mouth."

Earl H. Rovit (essay date 1960)

SOURCE: "A Few Hard, Tender Sayings," in *Herald to Chaos: The Novels of Elizabeth Madox Roberts,* University of Kentucky Press, 1960, pp. 129-48.

[*In the following essay, Rovit concludes that Roberts's intricate style serves an important purpose in her prose, allowing the reader to identify more closely with the consciousness of her characters.*]

Almost without exception, every literary review or critical analysis of Miss Roberts' work makes mention of her prose style, the inference being that somehow or other, her "style" is an element in her writing which thrusts itself obtrusively on the reader. Even those critics who make more than a superficial attempt to analyze the stylistic devices which Miss Roberts employs fail to integrate their analysis with the functional intention of this style. They forget that "style" is not an isolated segment of a piece of writing, but that it pervades the entire shape of the writing, integral to that shape at all points. This is true, I suppose, for all writing, but additionally significant for an author who is so persistent in her avowal of aesthetic organicism. Thus, a critical comment that "Miss Roberts is fond of Fra Angelico, and her style often mingles the Italian's blues and golds" [Grant C. Knight, *American Literature and Culture*] is of some biographical interest, but hardly helpful in evaluating the quality of her work. To try to go beyond this kind of impressionistic critical reverie which implies that "style" is something like the frosting on a cake, we may begin with Mark Van Doren's astute perception: "her style being most clearly the expression of a mind which is interesting in its own right. Her style is worth discussing because it in itself is a sort of substance. It is more than a way of saying things; it is something said, something which would not otherwise have been said at all, something, we suspect, which could not be said unless it were said in this way." ["Elizabeth Madox Roberts: Her Mind and Style," *The Private Reader: Selected Articles and Reviews,* 1942]

With this attitude toward "style," let us review for a moment the kind of stylistic problem with which Miss Roberts was faced. We have seen that for Miss Roberts the interest in life is not focused on the external world of things, but on the inner world of sensations becoming ideas. The balance which she tried to attain between poetry and realism requires the literary existence of an active, perceiving, remembering, willing, imagining mind expressing its ideations through sensuous symbols and images. And the "style" which is reflective of such a mind will tend more to the characteristics of lyric poetry than to what is generally regarded as novelistic prose. To take an extreme antithetical example, the modern "hard-boiled" realists, who take their accents and rhythms from Hemingway, have a very different stylistic problem. Since their accent is on the physical causation of sensation, they tend to minimize the creative potential of the mind; the world of things is presented as fixed and absolute, and the human condition is, in varying degrees, determined and doomed. The style which results from this kind of philosophic perspective calls for clipped, staccato sentences, unadorned by qualifying gradations. Flesh is soft and the things of the world are hard, and so action and violent collision become the polarity of the style. Active verbs, interjections, and "tough" vocabulary are the excitement-making ingredients of the prose, and highly dramatic dialog becomes a premium as a technique of setting the human figures apart from the impersonal forces which move them, much as the traditional disciplines of the theater have differentiated between dramatic physical action and the fixed enveloping stage. It is probably with this kind of novel in mind that Alexander Buchan writes: "One concedes Miss Roberts the title of novelist because the title is ample enough, these days, to include almost anything written about incident. In every one of her tendencies of style, however, she does not write novels, but narrative poems." ["Elizabeth Madox Roberts"]

Conceivably she might have employed the stream-of-consciousness method to give free play to her belief in the image-creating mind, but she found this method unconvincing: "The exact content or condition of the mind could not, he supposed, be reproduced by speech either written or spoken, however broken the jargon or immediate the rendering" [*Jingling in the Wind*]. The Jamesian novel, on the other hand, which invites the reader to participate in a strenuous exercise of what we may call "the moral imagination," she valued: "Henry James seems to induce many high opinions and varying degrees of inspiration. He is excellent material as offering points of departure for those delvings into meanings and half meanings which we like to make in an effort to enlarge the capacity for experience and to revalue the human race." But it should be obvious that the Jamesian setting and atmosphere would be incompatible with her interests. So committed to realism was she that she rated Dostoevsky's *The Brothers Karamazov* a failure; in her journal she noted that she admired its psychological penetration, but felt that its characters and interplay of action were too unrealistic to capture the reader. Her creation of a successful style, then, may be the pivotal point on which the evaluation of her novels will rest. And her present inferior reputation may be, as Buchan suggests, a result of inadequate critical response to her style: "In the criticisms . . . , much of the failure to understand the books came from a completely vague appreciation of 'poetic style,' and of the skill with which words—the words of narrative and of soliloquy—were combined to create the effect intended."

Miss Roberts' personal solution to the problem of combining realism and poetry in a narrative form is found in her characteristic combination of the traditional third-person impersonal narrator with the autobiographical point of view. To illustrate this, let us examine the opening paragraph of *The Great Meadow*:

> 1774, and Diony, in the spring, hearing Sam, her brother, scratching at a tune on the fiddle, hearing him break a song over the taut wires and fling out with his voice to supply all that the tune lacked, placed herself momentarily in life, calling mentally her name, Diony Hall. "I, Diony Hall," her thought said, gathering herself close, subtracting herself from the diffused life of the house that closed about her. Sam was singing, flinging the song free of the worried strings, making a very good tune of it.

The first sentence places Diony Hall in a space-time situation, in the act of perceiving and asserting her identity. Thus far, there is no special innovation in narrative technique; the omniscient narrator has merely established his right to go inside the mind of one of his characters and objectively record her mood. The second sentence poses a problem as it moves the focus closer to Diony Hall, transcribes her thought within impersonal quotation marks, and then adds two participial phrases. If the participles are used to modify the subject "thought," the use of the reflexive pronoun "herself" is unnecessarily ungrammatical; and further, the impersonal narrator has surrendered his "objectivity." Continuing with the third sentence, the problem which germinated in sentence two becomes full-blown. Whose perception is it that Sam, while singing, "was flinging the song free of the worried strings"? It cannot be Sam's, because we have had no preparation that would justify thrusting his sensibilities abruptly into the scene; if it is the narrator's, then the narrator must be a character involved in the action to some degree who acts as a sympathetic storyteller and has a very subjective angle of vision. If it is neither Sam nor the omniscient third person, it must be Diony, but there is no connective link between Diony and the descriptive phrase. As we read the passage over, and especially as we continue reading, we discover that the perception was Diony's, although it has been appropriated by the narrator. Miss Roberts' impersonal narrative voice and her heroine Diony have identical attitudes of perception, imagination, and sensitivity.

In order to perceive this more clearly, let us examine several sentences at the beginning of Chapter III. Berk Jarvis has asked for permission to marry Diony and carry her with him into the wilderness of Kentucky. Thomas Hall, Diony's father, has violently refused to let her go, and has gone to the smithy to take out his anger on the blacksmith's anvil.

> The blows on the anvil had become little and thin, put there by a careful hand, and between each stroke there was a long pause while the hand waited on the reflective part of a man. Noon had passed and the odor of cooking foods floated through the room, the dinner being prepared in the kitchen. The day outside was warm in the sun, but within the coolness of the morning still lingered and the dull embers gave out a subdued warmth. Diony scarcely lifted her gaze above the globular billows her skirts made. . . . The anvil had left off its outcry altogether, and presently her father's broken step came on the stones behind the house and he was heard asking for her at the kitchen door.

At first glance the above passage seems traditionally realistic and objective in its presentation. Three sensations—sound, odor, and thermal touch—are recorded, and then the main character is visualized. But if one reads the above passage substituting the pronoun "I" for Diony, and making the appropriate changes in the personal pronouns, the identification of attitudes between Diony and the narrator becomes quite apparent. Nothing is perceived that is beyond Diony's field of perception; all the metaphorical content ("the blows . . . little and thin," "anvil's outcry," "father's broken step") is such that Diony alone could have thought of these things in this way. The verb forms in this passage are also characteristic: "had become," "had passed," "being prepared," "still lingered," "scarcely gazed," "had left off," "was heard." The imperfect tenses and the adverbially qualified past tenses place the action in a limbo of time between present and past; it is action just being completed. The effect is one of immediacy, but an immediacy slowed down to a point where we do not actually hear the blows on the anvil, but we do hear the echoes. The verb forms also create through their accumulation a

sense of anticipation, muted, it is true, by the rhythmic fall of the cadences. This anticipation directs itself toward the main figure, Diony, as though the verb forms were animated sensations and were marching toward the human character to be perceived.

The function of this narrative technique is to enable Miss Roberts to tell her story in a loosely realistic frame, while giving her ample latitude, at the same time, to let the mind of her main character order the details of the action. There is literally nothing, no detail, in *The Great Meadow,* which is not under the direct perception of Diony Hall, and yet the novel has been acclaimed as our finest historical novel. When this technique is working well, it is a perfect instrument for attaining "precision in rendering sensuous contacts"; when it is working not so well, it can be a source of confusion and, sometimes, even preciosity. Its limitations are rather rigid; only one character can be fully visualized at one time; if more than one is to be fully developed, some such device as the alternating chapters in *A Buried Treasure* must be used. The subordinate characters take on life only when they become absorbed into the main character's field of perception. But that main character can be artistically realized with a fullness unequaled in the more objective techniques of narration. Thus Miss Roberts' comment on Ellen Chesser is one that many readers can share:

> Writing *The Time of Man* I saw Ellen functioning in many situations which I did not use in making the design. She was to me always an organic whole, and I should have known how she looked at all periods of her life and how she would react to any being or event, what she would have said in speaking and what she would have felt in mind or senses.

And since . . . . Miss Roberts' philosophic perspective is based on the mind of an individual human being— "The most continually present integer"—we must admit that no other technique of narration could have been as suitable for her purposes.

However, it should also be pointed out that Miss Roberts' style does more than merely direct the reader's attention to the main character; it is also carefully graded to differentiate that character and delineate character change. In reference to Chapter I in *The Time of Man,* the placing of Ellen Chesser into the medium of the novel, Miss Roberts writes: "The sentences are short, the movement staccato, and beauty and ugliness are sharply opposed, set continually in swift contrast, as is the way in the life of a child." A random paragraph from Chapter I will substantiate this analysis:

> Ellen went further up the creek, jumping from white stone to white stone, feeling safe in the narrow ravine hidden among the willow bushes. She heard quails calling over in the fields, and farm sounds came into the hollow, a calf or a mule crying out. After a little she knew that the

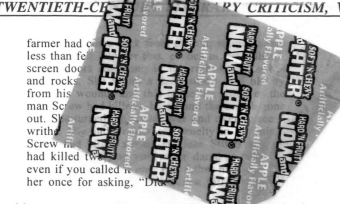

farmer had c[...]
less than fe[...]
screen doo[...]
and rocks[...]
from his wou[...]
man Sc[...]
out. S[...]
writhe[...]
Screw [...]
had killed tw[...]
even if you called [...]
her once for asking, "D[...]

In this passage the cadences are short and clipped, giving a sense of the immediate rush of impressions that would ostensibly occur in a child's mind. The sensations themselves are sharp and strident, allowing little room for gradation and qualification: the slamming of screen doors, the finality of the bloody snake. The sudden juxtaposition of the serenity of the ravine, the brook, and the gentle sounds of quail with the violence of the Screw memory is satisfying motivated by the transition through the finding of the snake, an episode logically connected with the pastoral beginning and the brutal memory which ends the passage. We also notice the limitations of Ellen's capacity for amalgamating her sensations into herself; they come and just as swiftly they are gone.

Notice the difference in style in the following passage, as Ellen rides with Jasper to their new married home the day after the wedding:

> Some little pointed birds in a flock twitted from branch to branch in the sun, and the road went up a hilltop and lay along a ridge where a woman standing by a great gate stopped to watch them pass, her hand stayed on the latch pin. A woman sat before the door of her house among withering hollyhock stems where the road fell gently down to the valley again, and beside the bridge a kingfisher flew from a limb and darted behind the white of a plane tree, the departure of the bird standing out upon the air as something never seen before by man. Ellen looked at her hands as they lay before the folds of her cloak, her hands acutely recognized and the cloak, hardly her own, folded strangely about her, her body stilled and muffled under the strangeness of the old cloak and the kindness of Jasper whose hand touched her sleeve. The day lay outstretched laterally, no marks upon it, and she greeted herself intently.

This is a very different prose and a very different Ellen Chesser, although the narrative point of view and the basic alertness of mind are the same. The cadences are longer and more gentle in their blending one into the other. The sensations perceived are much more subtly colored with gradations of significance. And, most important, the sensations are selected in terms of significant reference to Ellen Chesser; they are not, as in the former passage, the indiscriminate rush of whatever is in her field of perception. Her combination feeling of beauty and strangeness as a brand new bride is deli-

cately implied by her attitude toward the cloak and her awed wonder at the beauty of the bird's flight. The two women she sees at their house gates are perceived under the aspirations of her own dream of a secure domestic hearth. And the last sentence, her realization of herself at the dawn of a new life, ties all her other perceptions into a whole. Commenting on *The Time of Man,* Miss Roberts writes: "The drama of the first part is the drama of the immediacy of the mind, the swift flow of impression. This element being used less as the work moves forward, drama is then projected by the use of dramatic dialogue." The stylistic devices of *The Time of Man* can thus be seen as very conscious attempts on the part of the author to make her prose functionally implement the development of her character, while moving the action of the novel forward as well.

Like her narrative technique, Miss Roberts' sentence structure is organically related to her philosophic and aesthetic perspectives. In what is easily the best critical analysis of her style, Alexander Buchan points out: "Her favorite sentence is simple, a plain subject-predicate assertion followed by a participial construction. . . . When the participle is used not only as a connective, but as a substantive . . . the style appears to move across a regular succession of *-ings*." In the opening lines from *The Great Meadow* quoted above, there are, counting the rhyming words, fourteen *-ing* sounds. These, of course, are unusually frequent in this selection, but it is true that the characteristic sound of her prose is a muted roll, giving an effect of what both Buchan and Van Doren have called "an agreeable monotony." For example, let us look at the following passage from *My Heart and My Flesh,* which describes Theodosia playing the violin:

> Striving to divide her being, to set bounds upon parts, she would turn a half-whimsical gaze inward as she strove to achieve the singing tone and to bow the indefinite legato. "Does the music come out of me really, out of some inner unit, myself, all mine?" she would question, "or do I simply imitate, skillfully or not, what the teacher does?" She wanted to lay her finger on this integer and say, "This is mine." She wanted to go past the bounding of blood in arteries and the throb of her pride in her grandfather's witnessing of her advancing skill. The tone sang more true and she took a great impatient joy in it, searching, as she was, more deeply for the answer to the riddle. Or, in the coming of Albert into her senses, her questioning thought would swim in a pool of inattention and semi-consciousness.

The participial clauses and the repetitive constructions create a liquid rush of sound, subtly cadenced, beginning *in medias res,* tonally, and drifting off at the end with a kind of sibilant indefiniteness. But although the total effect is one of monotony, there are several crisp phrases imbedded in the passage, which seem to be carefully set off and emphasized by their contrast. To illustrate this, I shall take the liberty of attempting to transcribe this prose into cadenced verse, along the lines of Whitman's *Leaves of Grass*. The result is something like this:

> Striving to divide her being, to set bounds upon parts,
> She would turn a half-whimsical gaze inward as she strove to
>   achieve the singing tone and to bow the indefinite legato.
> Does the music come out of me really, out of some inner unit,
> *Myself, all mine?*
> Or do I simply imitate, skillfully or not, what the teacher does?
> She wanted to lay her finger on this integer and say,
> *This is mine.*
> She wanted to go past the bounding of blood in arteries
> And the throb of her pride in her grandfather's witnessing of her advancing skill.
> The tone sang more true and she took a great impatient joy in it,
> *Searching*, as she was, *more deeply* for the answer to the riddle.
> *Or, in the coming of Albert into her senses,*
> Her questioning thought would swim in a pool of inattention and semi-consciousness.

It is quite possible that others would transcribe this passage differently, but I think it is clear that the prose is subject to transcription on the basis of repetition and cadenced sound units. Secondly, it is clear that this combination of sound units has a musically monotonous flow, rising and falling in succession, but never falling to a complete finality, or rising to an abruptly high pitch. And thirdly, I think any transcription would have to recognize the emphatic relation of the sound units I have italicized to the less emphatic sounds which surround them. The unit, "This is mine," is quite clearly the most important in the passage, marking a climax in the tonal pattern. The other italicized phrases are of slightly less importance, echoing in a minor key, as it were, the triumphal major chord of the "This is mine."

The musical patterning of these sentences is clearly designed to evoke emotional responses which will deepen the reader's sense of the meaning. Dorothea Brande points toward this in her comment: "This prose is a kind of incantation; the meaning does not reach the reader through his intellect alone. Mind and emotion are equally engaged" ["Four Novels"]. And, like individual barbs aimed to pierce the reading mind, the significant items, or "the few hard, tender sayings," in this passage closely related to Theodosia Bell's attempts toward self-realization, are isolated from the musical monotony of the background. The prose style is thus thoroughly functional in its attempt to parallel the actual process of a mind perceiving sensation, and gradually transforming it into realized experience. And further, through the incantation effect of the prose, the reader himself is drawn into the process, participating in the immediate experience, and emerging, ideally,

with a truly enlarged vision and a heightened sense of life.

In her diction also Miss Roberts is consistent to the pattern of thought we have described. She is deeply aware of language as the cumulative achievement of countless generations of experiencing human beings. She was fluent in French, had studied a little German, and was an amateur scholar in Middle English. But her view of words was that of the poet, not the linguist. She writes:

> I like to think of the origin of the word, "the world"—*wer,* the root meaning man and *eld* giving old or age—the long life of man on the earth, the were-eld then. . . . Words are poor dumb things when it is the whole yearning of a race, a kind, that tries to speak, but poor as they are they are our most pleasant toy, our most ready delight.

She can be seen playing with words in the delightful passage in which Jeremy reflects on the insistent love letters he has been receiving from the Dark Lady:

> ". . . I cannot understand the nature of this torture into which she drives me with her scented sinister invitations and offers of sympathy. Whether her skin is swart or her hair raven, whatever is the power of her darkness, whether it lies in her eyes or her soul or her breath, she is despised for a corybantic quean, a toad-in-a-hole, a spayed orgiastic whop, a strumpet-widgeon. A chuff-cat trull, a cootish doltish drab from a trugginghouse. A lustic lymphy gluttish homager, a slipshod thousandleg, an earthen galleyworm. . . ." [*Jingling in the Wind*]

She was drawn to the rural speech of her countryside and the dialect which she so beautifully transformed, not because this speech was quaint, but because it was musical; it was more lineally related to the powerful speech of Chaucerian and Shakespearean England than was her nonrural contemporary American language; and it had the marks of earth experience on it. In the following journal note, remembering a group of composition papers which she once had to correct, she comments:

> The papers, in a mass . . . I felt to indicate the soil. These young were lumps of clay become animated. They had the marks of the soil upon them, marks of generations of soil, of closeness to the ground, of the struggle with clods and hard earth. . . . Out of the rocky, strong parts of the country came hard, crude, twisted bitten speech. The richer lands yielded in general the standardized speech of schools and teachers.

However, although her strong preference was for the Anglo-Saxon derivations, she was too much the artist to neglect the advantages of contrast. A reexamination of the passage from *My Heart and My Flesh* which was quoted above will show that the significant phrases are Anglo-Saxon in derivation: "Myself, all mine," "This is mine," "Searching more deeply." There is a fairly large preponderance of Latinate words in the rest of the passage, although not as many as might be expected. Still, the less gnarled words, like "divide," "indefinite," "imitate," "integer," "arteries," "inattention," and "semiconsciousness," offer a polysyllabic liquid vagueness, which points up the spondaic definiteness of the "realization" words. And this, of course, is a functional technique of making diction work in an organic cooperation with the other stylistic devices already discussed.

Miss Roberts' particular preference among the parts of speech is for nouns. Indeed, it is not unusual for her to dispense with verbs altogether, transforming a verb form into a participle as in the sentence: "A woman walking a narrow roadway in the hour of dawn." This habit of Miss Roberts' may be related to the primitive attitude which invests a name with an almost sacred significance, faint traces of which can be seen in the names of some of her characters—Diony Hall, Theodosia Bell, Berk Jarvis, and Luce Jarvis. However, this preference can be more directly related to the importance which Miss Roberts gives to the perceiving mind. Sensations are not significant until they have been realized or re-created, or, to put it another way, the life outside is absorbed within only when it is named. Going one step further, Miss Roberts will combine two nouns, locking them together with a hyphen in order to create a composite noun, without losing the strength of either unit in a prepositional possessive or adjective: "man-pleasure," "Memory-realization," "word-touch." This habit is proportionally more frequent in her poetry, and it may be the result of the influence of Anglo-Saxon "kennings," or the byproduct of her absorbed delight in the poems of Gerard Manley Hopkins.

The effects of her handling of dialog should also be mentioned briefly. Because of her subjective narrative technique, she characteristically employs two different renderings of dialog. When her main character is in a situation of relative stasis, the dialog is conventionally handled, often with brilliance. Thus the scene in which Henry Chesser recounts the story of his life to Ellen and Jonas Prather, or the exchange of lovers' vows between Ellen and Jasper, exhibits a dramatic dialog perfectly compatible with the ordinary third-person narrative point of view. However, when her principal character is apart from the dialog, either because of inner dissociation or incapacity to understand—as in so much of the dramatic dialog of *He Sent Forth a Raven*—the effects brilliantly synchronize with the immediate presentation of a character in the jagged process of developing.

It may be instructive here to analyze a fairly representative specimen of Miss Roberts' dialog to observe more closely the kinds of effects she manipulates. The following is a love scene between Ellen and Jasper in the early stages of their relationship:

> "Hear the dogs howl," she said, "off toward Stigall's it is. It's a lonesome sound, like the end of the world. Are you afeared of the end of the world?"

"I feel like I could pick up a hill or I could break open a mountain with my fist, and what call have I got to be afeared of a lonesome sound tonight? But it's a lonesome one."

"Lonesome like doves a-callen in trees to each other. Did you ever in your time hear a dove call and then another one answers?"

"I could pick up a hill with my strength."

"One asks the question, the doves, and then the other comes right along with the next call."

"I could pick up a hill or I could break open a rock with my fist."

"It's the sorrowfulest sound there is, as if it knowed what would come. Fair and sorrowful all together. It calls to mind good times that are lost and bad sorrowful ones, both gone together somehow."

"I take notice of doves a heap in spring. A dove call denotes spring is come for sure, and it's safe then to plant corn."

"And a dove has got one drop of human blood in its body somewheres, they say."

"By spring I aim to find some fields worth a man's strength. I'm plumb tired trafficken about, good land and bad as it comes. I aim to go a long piece from here."

"Once when I was a youngone Pappy went to Tennessee and I saw cotton in bloom. We saw cotton grow."

"I'm plumb tired a-trafficken about."

"Saw cotton a-growen. The people gathered it after a while in big baskets, piled up white."

"We'll go to some pretty country where the fields lay out fair and smooth. A little clump of woodland. Just enough to shade the cows at noon."

"Smooth pasture is a pretty sight in a country, rolling up and cows dotted here and yon over it, red shorthorns and white and dun."

"And you won't say 'I know a prettier country in Adair or in Shelby or Tennessee.' Mountains or not."

"Smooth pastures we'll have."

"Whatever I can do to pleasure you, Ellie. The house like the way you want."

"And the house fixed up, the shutters mended and the porch don't leak. To sit on a Saturday when the work is done. A vine up over the chimney. Once I saw a far piece from here . . ."

The dialog continues, but to no conclusions beyond what is already reached. The most obvious characteristic of the preceding is its powerful musical quality, the repetition of words and phrases which interweave between the two speakers as in an operatic duet, leaving them apart even as it knits them together. Both Ellen and Jasper reveal and maintain their own personalities in their speeches: his, masculine and practical, hers, feminine and imaginative. And yet the dialog which seems to be carried out at cross-purposes succeeds in manifesting not only a tonal, but an emotional harmony between the two. Like the doves to which Ellen refers, one calls and the other answers, and although the questions and responses fail to follow one another in logical sequence, there is a dialectic of communion established between them. And this kind of dialog is admirably suited to Miss Roberts' novelistic needs where physical action is always subordinate to the inner drama of self-realization.

Her use of metaphor is the element of her style most difficult to isolate because it is so pervasive. Since the novels are all narrated through an active, imagining consciousness, expository passages devoid of metaphor are almost impossible to find. Indeed, it would probably be fair to suggest that each novel with the exception of *A Buried Treasure* is a very elaborate single metaphor of the experience of its heroine. The mind perceives by combining its new perception with an older remembered perception, and thus, sound is given shape and color, or shape is rendered in terms of nonphysical description. The chaos of sensation in Miss Roberts' novels is continually being yoked into order by the imaginative capacities of her protagonists, and the rhetorical device which expresses the order is the metaphor. Let us examine a sample prose passage from *The Great Meadow:*

> When she awoke the moon had set and the dawn was beginning to light the sky. A planet, performing like a small moon, made a crescent in the east. The birds began to arouse, and the cruel, restless dawn began in the trees, the long slow dawn when the birds were insatiable in their pronouncements. The birds arose above the life of the herbs and declared themselves superior, but their declarations needed to be continual. Diony lay in the soft decaying log and heard the clamor among the birds, feeling the vegetable life awake with the sun, each kind standing still in some lewd demand of the light. She came cautiously out of the log and looked about to discover what way she had come there.

The first thing we notice is that the metaphorical content of the passage is related completely to Diony. The coming of the dawn is described, not in order to describe a dawn, but to expose Diony's feelings as she experiences this particular dawn. Factually we know only that the sun is coming up, the birds are singing, and Diony awakes from her night in the woods. More importantly, we know that Diony feels isolated from this activity of nature. The planet, "performing like a small moon," insinuates the idea of spectacle and spectator,

with Diony, the insignificant spectator, lost in the vast amphitheater of nature. The "cruel, restless . . . long, slow dawn" chanted in by the "insatiable" birds dispels the concealing blanket of night which had allowed Diony to curl up within herself and fill her whole world with herself—something knowable and controllable. The dawn is "cruel" because it extends the planes of the world, showing Diony to herself as just another speck in the vast forest. The birds make "pronouncements" and "declarations." They blatantly assert their belongingness to the whole scene with irritating little cries of braggadocio. Even the vegetable life makes "lewd demands" of the sun; it too belongs and is part of the order. Diony is apart from the whole, and this the reader knows only from the metaphorical texture of the passage. This kind of metaphorical writing is, as I said, constant throughout all Miss Roberts' prose, unostentatious, but insistently buzzing at the fringe areas of the reader's consciousness. Indeed, her entire stylistic technique is founded on this indirect metaphorical method of exposition.

Miss Roberts will also, from time to time, employ the more conventional kind of metaphor to emphasize a point, or to shock a reader into awareness, or to vary the pace of her narration. For example, in *A Buried Treasure,* Philly Blair catches her hen sucking on the insides of one of its new-laid eggs: "The day seemed unjointed and delayed. The old pullet had eaten a hole into the morning; she had bitten with her hard bill a flaw into the steady world that lay outside. . . . She had made a crack in time itself and in the illusions people hold together." The same devices are at work as in the preceding quoted passage, but the fused images are more incongruous and direct. Or, in the following description of Dickon the carpenter from *He Sent Forth a Raven,* where Miss Roberts somewhat playfully caricatures the character by expanding the metaphor from a simple descriptive statement to a ludicrously cosmic significance: "There were oaths in his speech. His words seemed to burst from his roughly-shaven face and his stiff throat as if they were pinned together with threats that would crack the day into splinters and rip apart the earth itself."

The test of a novelist's style is ultimately the individual reader's, and the writer who chooses to create a distinctive style will inevitably run the danger of alienating some readers who will prejudge uniqueness as affectation. The effects of style are cumulative; the rhythms of a prose work must sustain a prolonged pattern at the fringes of the reader's consciousness before they can begin to function as an integral element of the total work. Stylistic analysis can only point a direction; it can neither "prove" authoritatively, nor make discoveries. But from this discussion I think we can conclude that the extraordinary degree of functional consistency which Miss Roberts' style possesses serves her aesthetic aim by luring her reader into a participative position, where the reading experience may bring a true enlargement of perspective and a heightened sense of reality.

Frederick P. W. McDowell (essay date 1963)

SOURCE: "The New Beginning," in *Elizabeth Madox Roberts,* Twayne Publishers, Inc., 1963, pp. 85-106.

[*In the following essay, McDowell examines the characters, structure, and symbolism of* The Great Meadow.]

I "A HALF-MYTHICAL LAND"

The spectacle of the pioneer surge westward had long played about the edges of Miss Roberts' mind; she once wrote that this subject had in fact fascinated her "almost . . . since first I began to think at all." In notes to the article written for the Literary Guild in 1930 when *The Great Meadow* was a selection, she told of the spell which the exploits of the Kentucky pioneers had cast over her imagination:

> In 1921, in the spring, walking back across the Midway, behind me the square gray towers of Harper Memorial Library and before me the brave new wind that swept up from the south, that swayed the dainty elms and bent the vivid grass, my mind filled with the patterns of Giovanni Beeline who lived forever in Venice, who was learning fresh ways to paint and fresh ways to see the world, even after he was seventy—and I said, speaking inwardly, "Will it be done with ballad? . . . Or will it be some other kind which I cannot now think?"

> Or farther back, in 1919, perched in my little birdcage of a room high above Fifty-Eighth Street, in an old stone ruin where there was a grand opera stairway which induced song whenever it was mounted, seeing over the trees and towers of the campus, far down in the east, seeing the dome of the old Field Museum, a wreck and a relic of the Columbian Exposition, where it floated as a bubble against the blue mist over the lake—and I said, speaking within, "Will it be narrative poetry, or ballad that will fuse the old matter I have in mind into tangible form?"

> Or back, going farther again, in Colorado, walking over strange mountain sand, coming home from a lonely summit where I had climbed all afternoon among alien stones that had become some near part of myself through much familiarity, and the tohee cried out lovely repetitious song among the scrub oaks. I set my feet down among sand lilies and larkspur and mountain lupin, I brushed cactus thorns and soap-weed on the sunny slopes, and I said, not needing then to speak in inner whispers, shouting aloud to the dear familiar peaks and the fraternal mesas. "But that other country is mine . . . we came there . . . thus . . . and will I ever be able to say, to tell, to state, our coming with some sufficient words . . . what words? . . . how can it be done?"

Since the westward movement of her ancestors seemed to be for her a saga, it was inevitable, once she had written successful fiction, that she should amplify this subject in a novel which she once described as "the most simple, direct, elementary, national, and local of all my books." Figures like Daniel Boone, Simon Kenton, Benjamin Logan, and James Harrod, with their strength and their gentleness, she said, "entice the mind to make heroic patterns." Or as one of the nameless pioneers declares in the novel, "In each fort [Boonesborough, Fort Logan, and Harrods Fort], all three, is a man you could take for a pattern to make men by." Immersing her mind in these materials, a "heroic" pattern emerged in the completed organism of *The Great Meadow:* "the design mounted and swayed, flowed and receded to its own consummation." The design for *The Great Meadow,* in accordance with the large contours of its subject, was to unfold slowly; the book, as originally conceived, was to serve between *My Heart and My Flesh* and *He Sent Forth a Raven* as an "adagio" or slow movement in the Luce cycle.

The spaciousness of sparsely settled eighteenth-century America is reflected not only in the descriptions of the wilderness, as others report it and as Diony Jarvis (Miss Roberts' protagonist) at last sees it, but in the delineation of the chief characters. Even Diony's parents, ending their tranquil days on Five Oaks plantation at Albemarle, Virginia, have large outlines, which suggest the heroic. The Halls are fit descendants of heroic progenitors and are not far removed, in temper and moral strength, from the settlers of the wilderness which continually encroaches upon the plantation.

To Diony the farm is at the parting of the ways, on the divide between Tidewater amenities and frontier rawness, where "the tilled land and the unbroken forests touched their parts" about her. Thus Diony—even before the stranger startles her imagination by painting the land beyond the mountains—not only projects herself backward into the gracious routines of her Tidewater relatives but outward into the expeditions of her brothers as they hunt in the wild Blue Ledge region in the western distance. Her ancestry reflects a divided heritage which sometimes frustrates her but which gives her in the end increased power over herself and her surroundings and increased knowledge of reality. Her mother's people are Methodist mountain folk, having come to the Virginia frontier from Pennsylvania. From her mother, Polly Hall, Diony derives her vigor of constitution and a complete knowledge of domestic life and crafts. On the other hand, her father's people go back many generations in the Tidewater. From Thomas Hall, Diony acquires her respect for knowledge and mental culture and her speculative turn of mind.

Diony is a representative and symbolic figure, since she embodies these contrasting strains, and since she takes this heritage with her into a new country and allows it to govern her actions there. In her article for the Literary Guild Miss Roberts accordingly dwelt upon Diony's rich endowment:

> The elements back of this Diony were carefully chosen. Tidewater gentry, scholarship, pagan lore,

English communicants and Catholics, wealth and ease, family pride, these are met by sturdy races of tradesmen and farmers, Methodists—most despised sect of the century—Puritanic, Quaker, provident, holy and aggressive, of great bodily vigor and a sturdy beauty. They were on fire with their own flame. These elements gathered into the parents of this woman Diony.

Polly Hall, Diony's mother, is of imposing presence and regal beauty; her faith is vibrant and her orthodox ideas are expressed with vigor and determination. Her objection on moral grounds to the white man's pre-empting Kentucky from the heathen Indians disturbs the company, and even Thomas Hall's rationalization that the new land should be reserved for the most enterprising race fails to dispel completely the doubts which she has implanted. She is an embodiment of piety mixed with common sense and creative domesticity. Under her direction is woven the intricate footmantle which protects Diony in the wilderness; and Diony has from her the gourd seeds which flourish and grow into a fine crop in Kentucky. Polly, coming from "a strong race of women," acknowledges Diony as her fit successor; she perceives her other daughter Betty to be small and fragile. The implication is that Betty would be destroyed by the dangers and challenges which Diony eagerly confronts:

> . . . Betty was somehow fashioned for great love and . . . there was nothing at hand which was sufficient to share her need. On the instant the air seemed split apart and the day severed, the sunshine slashed open, she and Betty standing apart in the rent, alike but hostile, and she saw that she herself was fashioned likewise in some curious way, and that there was nothing between the hills of Albemarle which was enough to use all her strength, until it seemed that the whole of the wilderness beyond the mountains, the whole of Kentucky, would not appease her, that she would love it all and still have love to spare.

Betsy Dodd, whose frail and charming femininity at Harrods Fort recalls Betty to Diony's mind, is killed in an Indian raid; her force, like Betty's, would have been unequal in any event to the demands of the frontier.

About Diony's father gather overtones not only of the heroic but of the mythic. His limp and his activity about the forge, most intense while he protests Diony's emigration to Kentucky with her lover Berk Jarvis, recall Vulcan or Hephaestos, the old god of fire and of the arts deriving from the smithy's craft. As a tender of the fire, he is also a Promethean figure; thus Thomas Hall respects the uses of civilization and is their proponent, and he is the source of intellectual light in the novel, with his fervent idealism and advocacy of Berkeley. He is both submerged in the life of the plantation and withdrawn, by his lameness, from it; he is vitally identified with the members of his family and also removed from them, as he raises his hand to comment aloud upon Berkeley's "The Principles of Human Knowledge," for

example, and then thinks better of it. He is an oracle, much of whose wisdom is self-contained except when he can talk to his temperamental equals like Diony. When he finally gives his consent to her going west, he talks of Rhea (who is sometimes to be identified with the earth or Gaea) as an aboriginal deity who signifies "succession" and who is apparently synonymous with the Divine Mind or "the great Mover and Author of Nature" of Berkeley. He also implies that Rhea's children—Jupiter, Vesta, Neptune, Ceres, Juno, and Pluto, and by extension all creatures—reveal in their several ways the traits of the goddess Earth, their mother. As a Vulcan figure, Thomas Hall takes a place among this divine company.

So does his daughter whose name derives from that of a Titan, Dione. Dione was coexistent in time with Rhea; she was the mother by Jupiter of Venus, who of course embodies the elemental force of sex and love which Diony also exemplifies in a new country. As a dynamic feminine presence Diony ministers to the sick during the hard winter of 1778; her own children arouse strong protectiveness in her; and in a moment of deep revelation she feels herself to be the "common mother" rather than the enemy of all the people in the Ojibway Indian lodge with whom her husband Berk dwelt in the North. As a Titan, she regards herself as a descendant of Uranus and Terra, of Heaven and Earth and, like them, as a supplanter of Chaos.

In Kentucky, as if illustrating this mythic ancestry, Diony feels herself to be "the beginning before the beginning," the well-spring of all future developments in the land. She holds in "a chaotic sense of grandeur" these truths concerning her putative descent from the old gods and is "grateful for a name of such dignity" as Dione. As a symbolic source of later abundance and harmony, she has, before Berk's departure from Harrods Fort on his mission of vengeance, an apocalyptic vision in which all promises that had led the settlers westward are fulfilled. This vision is epical, for it represents the common aspirations of a whole people as they begin their civil activities in the wilderness. Diony's vision of the future, in fact, has something of the scope of the archangel Michael's in *Paradise Lost* when he foretells the future of the human race or of Anchises' in the Sixth Book of the *Aeneid* when he prophesies to Aeneas the glories of the Roman state.

If the other characters are not explicitly identified with actual gods, they are imposing—"half-mythical heroes walking the earth as gods walk." Their deeds soon became legendary and the foundation for an indigenous mythology. Boone, the most electrifying of these figures, is a kind of benevolent God walking among men and a power behind the scenes as he goes through the wilderness, alone and powerful, self-sufficient and large-minded. Accordingly, he became for Miss Roberts "a symbol of man leaping apart from men, thrusting forward to a lonely and hazardous freedom among the natural and chaotic things of the unmapped earth."

Truly "a wonder among men," he commands his environment by rising superior to it, towering "without hate above the beasts and above savage men" In his freedom from rancor he is superior to Berk Jarvis who for a time loses himself in his hate. Boone's commanding presence seems to Diony the essence of this land; and she feels, as he talks casually to her, "the breadth of the outreaching land as she had had report of it from one and another, as if it had been there beside her at the gate, as if it had come in the flesh to breathe and smile, to speak to her". He does miraculous feats; for example, he escapes from the Shawnees, when all had thought him lost, in time to help his people at Boonesborough during the Indian and British siege of 1778.

"There were giants in the earth in those days," or so it seems, with Harrod "a big man that never tires, and a heart in him like pure gold" and with Logan "his body made big to hold his big heart". If these men are humble, they are capable of heroic deeds as Logan was when he traveled for a week through the wilderness to secure ammunition for his beleagured fort: "a great man, a giant, a hero, walked out of a half-mythical land, striding down through an unbroken way to get ammunition for his people". Early in the novel the listeners at Five Oaks to Nathan Jones's report of a surveyor's description of Kentucky express as a conjecture what was in fact to happen: "Such a country would breed up a race of heroes, men built and knitted together to endure . . . a new race for the earth".

Since the purpose of these pioneers was as selfless as it was absorbing, their virtues suggest the transcendent: "their fineness was superior to time and their departure a sure token that they had been but caught in it in ephemeral bondage. . . ." "The people had not the faith in commerce now prevailing. . . . They were fundamental, moving among the fundamentals. The substitute is heroic solitude, trees, faith."

Berk and his mother Elvira partake of this heroic mold. Both are large-framed, and both have quiet confidence. The glancing smile which crosses the lips of both mother and son is emblematic of power held in reserve and of a tacitly acknowledged competence. The first time Diony sees Elvira she is impressed by her height, her dignity, and the large "planes" in her face. The two women meet when the Halls play host to a Methodist revival meeting and Elvira comes to help Polly. Symbolically, Diony goes back and forth between her mother and her future mother-in-law, the two women who mean most in her life. At present, she fetches for both of them, but she will later go from her mother and cleave to Elvira. Elvira's moral qualities are exceptional: she takes her place immediately with "the strong women of the fort," and her "superhuman goodness"—in sacrificing herself that she may rescue her pregnant daughter-in-law from the Indian marauders—ends by oppressing Diony. Elvira in her death becomes a legend with the Indians as the "fighting squaw" with strength enough to kill a buffalo.

In his repeated farewells to Diony, Thomas Hall often quotes from the opening lines of the *Aeneid,* discoursing "of arms and the man," as if to identify Berk Jarvis with the Aeneas who in ancient times, according to legend, founded the new nation of Italy. Thomas Hall thus recognizes that the wilderness will be the scene of feats performed by epic heroes—a land which will see, as he had previously declared, "brave men, a brave race." Before Berk takes Diony to the wilderness, he had done great deeds in fighting the British and the Indians at the Watauga forts on the Holston River. His military exploits have been scarifying rather than exhilarating. Diony feels more keenly identified with Berk and his dangers than does her father who is too willing, she thinks, to philosophize about war and to disregard its cruelties. Berk's ventures give him a remote, abstracted gaze; it is as if the reality he had been through makes all other experience pallid; and he attains, perhaps without realizing it, some of his mother's remoteness from the ordinary.

Just as Desdemona fell in love with Othello, so Diony does with Berk: "she would love him with a rush of passion that almost stilled her heart in its beat, would love him for the dangers he had passed and the cruel images that were pictured on his mind . . ." Their understanding is perfected on an autumn morning at Albemarle when, under the early sun, frost and mist become a golden cloud to include the lovers and when Berk appears to Diony, as Jupiter did to Danae, in a shower of golden light and falling golden leaves.

On the journey to Kentucky Berk is the epitome of a masculine strength so fundamental as only to be described in sexual terms, "in the thrust, the drive, in action"; and old Bethel, at the frontier clearing, fashions for him a powder horn, which seems to be in part a phallic emblem, an image of his virility. Berk is always the head of the party, strong-limbed, never showing fatigue, his slow elusive smile "outrunning fatigue and despair." In the forward position, pushing always further into the wilderness, he is thus elemental as well as civilized man. In her subordinate place, Diony is elemental as well as civilized woman; her strength is the woman's in a sexual embrace, "lateral, in the plane, enduring, inactive but constant". Utilizing the contrasting strengths of the sexes, Berk and Diony are typical of those who find themselves masters of a new world, "possessing themselves of it by the power of their courage, their order, and their endurance".

They regard the Kentucky frontier as a land of marvels, an earthly paradise, and are fascinated by the prospect of "the great wash of grass and life over the rolling plains, mountains, and valleys of the vast meadow." The stranger whom Berk brings with him to Five Oaks discusses the wonders he has known and fires the imaginations of those who hear him. He is a figure of mystery himself, an aloof and dignified man, but one compelled, like the Ancient Mariner, to repeat to those who will listen the great things he has known. He seems overawed by the strangeness of his experience, he conducts himself with tranquil dignity, and he is so conversant with the elemental realities of nature that civilized ways sit upon him awkwardly: "He weighed each speech with care, making each phrase with pains, as is the way with men who have lived alone and have made decisions without the use of words or speeches". He describes, for example, the bones of mammoths and vast caves, the ghosts of the Alleghwi which frighten the red men away from the region, the fabulous richness of the cane-lands, and the primeval beauty of the woodlands in the region.

Stirred by these reports and by the legend of an ivory-billed woodcock to be found in Kentucky, Berk and Diony exchange looks which mean that they want to go to this land of beauty, "to paradise, so beautiful and good, attaining something beyond themselves." The actuality does not disappoint, although as Miss Roberts said in her journal, it was less a fruition for the pioneers than "the new beginning." The land is rich, animal life is abundant, the woodlands are imposing, the beauty of the land is enthralling, so that Diony is "shaken with delight and wonder," at "the delirium of a fine land, level expanses delicately tilted to fine curves, here and there cane patches of rich fat growth, here and there noble trees". This is truly God's original Eden, or the land of Canaan lying on the other side of the wilderness. That sinful man corrupts a veritable Eden is, however, the all too disquieting truth. White men have debased the Indians, as Diony learns when Blackfox and his companion push at the door of the cabin to get at her and Elvira and utter the vile oaths they have been taught.

II "OVER THE TRACE": STRUCTURE OF THE GREAT MEADOW

The Great Meadow is organized by chronology and spans the years 1774 to 1781, roughly the era of the Revolutionary War which hovers in the background always as a sinister accompaniment to the central drama of reclaiming the wilderness. The war reaches west to the new region and is more savage there since the British arm and lead the Indians, often reluctant to fight, in campaigns against the settlers. The progression of this novel is forward since the actual moment is all-important in the pioneer struggle for survival. There are few flashbacks, for a rigorous life in the present dims even the memory of the past.

The structure of **The Great Meadow** is firmly balanced among three main masses of material, each comprising three chapters of the novel. The first group of three chapters, covering the years 1774-77, presents Diony's life at Albemarle, her qualities of character, and the personalities of those to whom she reacts and adjusts. Except for Berk's absence at the Watauga forts and his return, there is little direct action. Three years pass, but little transpires that involves Diony's direct participation until she must choose between Berk's pioneer daring and her sister Betty's civilized amenity.

The next three chapters cover the years 1777-78 and describe Diony's journey over the Trace to the Kentucky wilderness and her life at Harrods Fort. This middle section has two centers of interest: the daily lives and adjustments of the pioneers to a primitive existence, and the scalping of Elvira by two predatory Indians. Chapter VI records the struggle between Diony and Berk over his mission of vengeance against the Indians and his abandonment of Diony.

The concluding three chapters treat Diony's life in Kentucky during the years 1778-81, when she is placed on her own after Berk leaves. In Chapter VII (1778-79) Diony concludes that Berk must be dead, for if he were alive his indomitable spirit would not let him stay away from her. With some reluctance but with increasing tenderness she attends to Evan Muir, Berk's friend, and marries him. Her own need for male protection in a wild land and Evan's steadiness and "life-furthering goodness" are, in the end, stronger than her faith in Berk's superhuman powers. Perhaps also that "apathy which comes when the emotions or possibilities of emotion are exhausted" overpowers Diony at this point—apathy which, as Miss Roberts writes in her journal, "surpasses our powers to endure." Chapter VIII (1779-81) is somewhat huddled; it covers in short compass two years of Diony's life with Evan Muir in the house which Berk had built for her.

Because Diony's relations with Evan are not fully developed, the scene in Chapter IX when the rival husbands confront each other lacks complete urgency, relevance, and force. Chapter IX begins with Diony's sense of material well-being with Evan; Berk disrupts this harmony by his return after a three-year span of captivity among the Shawnees. Diony's neighbors, the Harmons, suggest the only possible course of action in a new land: the woman will choose the man she will live with. Though this scene has been much admired by Miss Roberts' critics, I agree with Rovit that it is much less effective than other parts of the book. He alleges that the differences between the men are not so clearly drawn in the novel as Miss Roberts had summed them up in her notes: Berk "the forward darting, hazardous spirit"; Muir "domestic, quiet, easily predicted."

But I feel this scene lacks impact for still another reason. Miss Roberts had so well realized Diony's sense of isolation and frustration at Berk's departure, had so consummately analyzed Diony's despair during the night she spends in the hostile forest, and had so completely conveyed the truth that those like Berk who take up the sword in vengeance perish by it, that his reappearance is, to say the least, anticlimactic. There is also something specious in his accounts of his hardships and travels. He has, of course, some of Diony's own sense of the spirit's sanctity when he discloses that the Indians could not have benefited by his "thinking part" if they had killed and eaten him. On his return, however, he is uncomprehending and unremorseful as to the consequences of his desertion of Diony for what was, after all, a fool's errand. If Berk possesses force, he still lacks, after his travels and sufferings, judgment and insight; and there is much to be said for Muir's industry and dependability. The image of Berk is not completely blurred, but his heroism is much less imposing at the end of the novel than it had been on the outward move into the wilderness and in the building of his spacious house. The image of Muir, moreover, is never quite in focus; as a main character he does not become a force until Chapter VII, and his individualizing qualities are not sharply defined even then. The worth of the book depends upon Diony's consistent psychology, a sustained seriousness until this last chapter, and a combination of the clear realism and the stirring poetry that had also been remarkable in *The Time of Man*.

The chronological method is straightforward rather than devious and indirect; and it records, besides Diony's pilgrimage to the wilderness, the journey of a whole people. Thomas Hall had consented to Diony's going with Berk mainly because the Divine plan, as he perceives it, dictates that "historic man" must give men who have no history the benefits and order of those who do: "Civilized Man is forever spreading more widely over the earth, historic Man bringing such men as have no history to humble themselves and learn their lesson". In such a light, Berk and Diony are archetypal pioneers and explorers. In Miss Roberts' design Diony especially sums up in her personal life the larger experience of the race:

> I saw these people coming over the Trace, some of them coming early when there were hundreds of miles of scarcely broken forests to be passed. The drama was brief, but it was full and picturesque. I thought it would be an excellent labor if one might gather all these threads, these elements, into one strand, if one might draw these strains into one person and bring this person over the Trace and through the Gateway in one symbolic journey.

Diony's complex origin in different cultural strands increases her awareness of her unique destiny. She perceives that these inherited tendencies dictate her passion for Berk, causing her to regard him as the person who will help her "move all the past outward now" into the wilderness. It was Miss Roberts' intent, according to her journal, to have Diony perceive the related truth that her own character, woven from different strands, would provide her with her sole resource in a new land. Her parents "found forms into which they fitted themselves—courts, trials, wills, worship, property, family, amenities. But in the wilderness I found nothing of this but what I brought. I found, but look what I found. Simple and elemental life, sensation, danger."

Though Diony lacks the main strength of Berk and Boone, she has a more sophisticated sense of her historic role than they do. Although these men of action set up the framework for civil order, they prize, for the most part, an institutional law, important enough in its place, but less significant than the intuitive harmony men may achieve with one another. Legal justice is a necessity, but more urgent still is the modulation of institutions by the spirit within, with the aim of securing a more flexible, altruistic, ideal kind of polity. One time, making soap in Berk's absence, Diony thinks of justice and pursues the inquiry, ever more deeply, to some diminishing point of knowledge. Before she abandons this inward search, however, she catches sight of "a little harmony which men are able to make with one another or with a few kinds".

This is the ultimate civilizing influence, represented by Diony more than by Berk, by Thomas Hall more than by Boone. Father and daughter espouse an ineffable law that is superior to but comprehends the written law by which the majority of men—including even Berk and Boone, pioneers in the world's work—are governed: "Diony represents ordered life and the processes of the mind, the mind life. She is not of the Boone kind. She feels lost in an indefinite universe. She wants ordered ways. She wants beauty and dignity and ceremony and the reasons of all things." Symbolically both Berk and Diony are needed to conquer a wilderness; Berk's strength in the long run would count for little were it not to be supplemented by Diony's insight and influence, of the "tame" rather than the "wild" sort.

III *DIONY'S SYMBOLIC JOURNEY, "MOVING ALWAYS MORE INWARDLY"*

Externally, *The Great Meadow* records events in their actual sequence. In actuality, as we saw in discussing the first three chapters, structure is a matter principally of Diony's consciousness. Or put another way, the true measure for time is internal. For the sensitive individual the great moment is the only significant one, and the psychological impression made by an event is the only lasting one. Because in Chapter IX Diony is so much affected by what happens after Berk's return, it seems that many years, instead of one evening, have passed since she lit the candles before his arrival. If the outer organization of *The Great Meadow* features the geographical journey of the pioneers in which Diony takes part, the more subtle organization of the novel records Diony's spiritual journey. The inner "line" of the novel is psychological; it is also ethical and philosophical. As in Miss Roberts' other novels, the psychological aspect of *The Great Meadow* is basic to its rhythm and also provides the groundwork for the development of Diony's moral and speculative ideas.

In a phrase about a minor character—a hunter James Ray, who bravely goes through the Indian lines to get game—Miss Roberts revealed her primary bias in this novel, as in her others. Ray's physique is lank and light, his bones "gracefully notched and fitted together," and at the service of his mind, "the sovereign part of any man". For Diony also the mind is "sovereign" and the mental assimilation of a fact all-important. The "garment of sense" is the outward integument of reality; to get to its core, one must go "within again and yet again, a hushed voice farther within saying some mute word as 'come,' or 'here you will find me.'" So Diony's journey westward becomes an ever more intense realization of the self, a broadening of spiritual perspectives, a deepening of the inner consciousness, a struggle "to isolate the conscious part." For Miss Roberts "Diony is a creature of the mind, moving always more inwardly."

On the journey westward, Diony feels herself restored each morning after the hardships of the day before—"renewed life welling up in her vital part". After the tragedy in which Elvira is killed and Diony is severely wounded, Diony's spirit once again lifts up in affirmation the following spring—at that time the spring winds are "bathing all her flesh with a quick desire for more life and a delight in all that she had". From one point of view, Diony sees the individual as finite, almost insignificant in the cosmic scheme of things: "Men seemed of little account, measured by the breath of a throat which was lightly taken and lightly quenched. Light breath huddled within the stockade, desiring life, but when some sudden crack-of-doom snuffed light out it went without protest". Contrary to this is Diony's more characteristic sense of herself as "eternal, as if all that she did now were of a kind older than kings, older than beliefs and governments". Although nature sometimes seems the only great reality, at other times it is a changeful and fluctuating force; and then the human gives the only fixed principle. In any event the human consciousness interprets and illuminates experience.

Like Miss Roberts' other heroines, Diony has a sensibility so acute as to approach at times the neurasthenic. So intense are her reactions to the world that she seems always at the point of exhaustion, except that her inner resources are endless. Even before she knows that she will go to Kentucky, "her whole body swayed toward the wilderness" in answer to the deepest aspirations of her being. On the actual trip much strain accompanies new vistas as they appear to her and as she projects herself forward into each perspective with a nervous, eager spirit: "She entered each view, thrust forward from within, as if the mind of the Spirit beyond herself were unfolding itself to her continually, as if she went forward eagerly to meet each disclosure".

Her imagination is excessively active when she strains to reach the truth; as a result, one element of her experience, regarded obsessively, frequently distorts her total vision, though new discriminations may thereby result. When Berk comes home from the Watauga forts and describes the brutal realities of war, Diony is disturbed almost to the point of hysteria by the fascination of his audience with his tale—an interest that ignores, she senses, some of the grosser aspects of battle:

> Thomas was talking now and Diony glanced from mouth to mouth and saw these instruments distorted, mouths become some strange flutes or horns, shaped cunningly to play out war, to cry out battles. Thomas Hall's mouth bent and twisted now as a clattering bugle blowing the science of war, making philosophy out of stories of death.
>
> Mouths were hungry instruments that bent about reports of killed men.

Diony's mind broods, even to morbid excess. When she is convinced of Berk's death, she is unable to accept this knowledge until it has entered deep into her psyche, "her inner part feeding forever on what it lacked".

For Diony, as for the other Roberts' heroines, a charged significance also invests the perceptions of the senses, the ultimate source of our inner knowledge. In Kentucky Diony knows her tools by the kinesthetic impress they have made upon her nerves, "each one intimately sensed at the ends of her fingers and in the lifting parts of her arms and shoulders". Similarly, she feels that, in order to understand another's soul, one must work inward from the individual's outward aspect. Thus Diony feels that, in order to know Berk's spirit, she must know more of him as a person: "A deep wish arose within her on the instant, a wish to know more of the structure of his being, to know all that he remembered and all that he saw as he looked outward, and to touch all with her own knowledge, and to know what it would be to him to go".

In an opposite sense, one's life in the imagination can only be discerned exactly when it is translated into the impression of sense. When Diony at the beginning of the novel thinks of herself as living in cultured ease in the Tidewater, she realizes the experience only after she imagines herself at the spinet as "the tunes tingled in her arms and in her shoulders, wanting an outlet by way of her hands . . ." The re-creation of emotional experience is also incisive. When Berk is fitting a new handle to his knife and fashioning his axe for the journey of revenge, Diony gives in to fear, to helplessness, and to a sense of the irrationality of what is taking place; she feels with startling effect "a sudden chill spread through her to stiffen her bones and put minute bristling fine hairs of pain over her skin".

Diony's mind tends to express emotional and intellectual experience in terms of sense impressions. The Roberts heroines are all of them, in essence, poets. The image, as in poetry, often exerts a spell in Miss Roberts' books that the abstract idea or the naked emotion would lack. Accordingly, the Revolutionary War becomes a reality to Diony only when she pictures it as a great bird overspreading the land, with one wing representing the eastern battlefields and the other the frontier skirmishes. This same image of a gigantic fowl with outstretched wings sums up for Diony the opposition expressed at Five Oaks to her going with Berk after Thomas Hall gives his consent: one wing represents the silent Sallie Tolliver, whose frontier life has been traumatic; the other, Betty, who rejects the wilderness as something too stark for her comprehension.

Diony's pilgrimage to the West results not only in her psychological enlargement but in her moral development. The journey to the wilderness tests her spirit, and she is adequate to most crises though she often feels unequal to some of the other women. She is not one of those who hang back, however, from going past the Wall to the wilderness road beyond. Through Elvira's death Diony grows to her greatest stature; the dying woman, as it were, transferred her own great strength to her.

The difficulties the individual encounters in attaining command over nature and the self are all the more terrifying for being subjectively felt. The struggle for survival is acute. To the terror and loneliness and weariness of the long passage other hardships succeed which further test the strength of the pioneers. Children cry for milk in the winter of 1777-78, when little food of any kind exists; in the second year clothing becomes rags, and nothing is available to weave new cloth from. Even animal skins for moccasins are lacking so that Diony's feet are continually bare. Certain external aspects of "the promise land" reflect the hard struggles of human beings to survive. When Berk describes the Lick where the rock has been worn thin by the tongues of animals through centuries and where the bones of the slain animals lie strewn about, Diony immediately envisions herself crushing the innumerable skulls underfoot as she walks there. The skulls are not only a sign of nature's profuseness but of the failure of innumerable animals to survive in a cruel struggle for existence. Diony's scattering the remains with her feet is, in essence, as casual as nature's attitude toward the fate of her creatures.

Not only beasts but men must struggle for survival as hostile forces continually close in upon the stockade from without. The Indians commanded by British officers besiege all the forts except Harrods, skirmishes with the Indians are routine, the much-prized cane becomes a place of ambush for the red men, and even a man of peace like Muir cries out in his sleep when the memories of war leap up from deep within. The menace to security is greatest during the fall season when life in the wilderness is outwardly the most peaceful and beautiful. The autumn of 1778 had been, however, a time of drought; and a smokelike haze had hung over the wilderness as if "the known world" were smoldering away, to be followed by a new mode of life, suitable for only the hardiest of the settlers: "A new way of being was required to meet the burnt-out lifeless hills".

Miss Roberts uses the vivid image, often at widely separated points in the novel, to express the harshness of frontier existence. The references to wolves sum up the savagery the pioneers must withstand and conquer. Hearing them the first night of her marriage, Diony knows her way would be "toward the way of the wolves"; and she only feels secure from the "danger and blood-hunger and hate" which they signify when she nestles close to Berk. Berk, to qualify as leader, must have animal shrewdness and cunning; sometimes he

actually seems vulpine in aspect: "lean as the wolf—man assuming the wolf to overcome the wolf". Wolves cry in the distance by Elvira's grave when Diony has her vision of a civilized future for Kentucky, and their cries add to her terror the night she is locked out from the fort and spends the time in the forest.

Similarly, the supposed owl cries (in reality, two Indians signalling one another) reveal all that is sinister, ominous, and mysterious about the wilderness. They awaken Diony at the pass before the Great Wall; and she hears them again when she is locked out of the fort. The Tory Tree with the three swaying bodies which Muir had seen in the spring of 1777, the scalps triumphantly hanging over the Watauga forts as mementos of the bloody fights of the year before, Elvira's scalp with its one silver lock which becomes Blackfox's prize, the three scalps which Berk sends home to Diony and which she hangs over the fire-board, and the burning of these scalps as a sign of the uselessness of Berk's errand when Diony accounts him lost—all keep before us the nearness of death in the everyday life of these people. Over the forest, when Berk's absence is prolonged, there is for Diony no star of hope, but "a great star . . . , a bright token of loneliness and cold and danger" to convey the actualities of pioneer life.

The wall image is used at many points in the novel to indicate the great obstacles which the pioneers must surmount in their journey westward and as a sign of these obstacles overcome by their courage, resourcefulness, and strength. The great cliff Wall to the West, barring the entrance to Kentucky, is present early in the novel when the stranger mentions it. As Diony and the pioneers go forward, the Wall stands up in front of them, "a wonder to dread"; it makes "the heart leap and lie down still in the breast", inspiring awe and dread at the same time. The cliffs become an overhanging presence, causing night to come quickly and bringing out the travelers' latent fears and insecurity: "Hardness settled over the camp, hate and despair and fright".

Whereas the rock wall signifies that the wilderness keeps people at a distance, other types of wall keep the encroaching forest out of settled areas. The high stockade walls provide a barricade against the wilderness, and viewed from outside, they seem "unyielding and secure." Powerful as they are, their strength is of little moment compared to the power of what lies outside. This Diony realizes on the night she spends in the forest thinking of Berk's undoubted death: "The stockade stood, straight and stark, as of little account in the night, but shut within itself, involuted to secure its way of being from what lay outside". After her marriage to Evan, Diony is glad to be living in the house which Berk built with its high protective walls, and she is relieved to be free from the boundaries of the stockade. The sides of the house are equal to the pressures placed upon them by the wall of trees behind, the vanguard of the wilderness which stretches beyond the cleared farm.

The most significant sign of Diony's increased maturity in Kentucky, as she analyzes her own mind, is a greater understanding of her father's thought. So the inner journey in the novel is not only psychological and moral but philosophical and spiritual as well; it is a journey toward the realization of "grand thoughts . . . from some power beyond the world". Without the enlargement of her perspectives which then takes place, she would not have been able to bring her experiences into relation with what she gleaned from her father's books. She had learned that, until they are perceived by the mind, objects do not properly exist: "For as to what is said of the absolute existence of unthinking things without any relation to their being perceived, that seems perfectly unintelligible. Their *esse* is *percipi,* nor is it possible they should have any existence, out of the minds or thinking things which perceive them." Mind, at both the human and divine levels, is creative. We as human beings create by actually perceiving and thinking.

Thus as new scenes unroll to Diony's view on the way westward, she in essence creates that toward which she rides; a new world comes into existence for her gradually, "like mist taking shape." The eternal spirit, "the great Mover and Author of Nature," creates also by an active process, by bringing to actuality what has been latent within its vast body, where "all unimagined and unwilled and unremembered acts" or objects reside until someone calls them into being. The wilderness is a kind of vast repository of unknown experience—unknown because it has not been experienced by the receptive and sensitive mind; known only as yet to "the Great Author of Nature." By going to the wilderness one may come at some aspects of the Divine Mind he could not find elsewhere. Partly, this is why Diony is fascinated with the West and why Thomas lets her go with Berk.

Diony's metaphysical desire to make a world out of chaos also finds actual expression in her westward journey. In Thomas Hall's philosophy the tendency of Creation is toward order, "the eternal aptitude of matter [revealing] the wholesomeness of the necessities inherent in things". Like the Great Author of Nature, Diony would also evolve pattern from disorder; she learns from her father that "the kept law" is greater than "the deflected law"; she sees in Berk and Boone—and herself— "the power of reason over the wild life of the earth" and she feels that with war's end, discord has lessened and that a new, more disciplined age is about to come into being.

Diony finds the irresistible connection between the outer and inner worlds by subjecting the most imposing outer reality—nature—to the workings of her mind. She had, in fact, learned from her father that the Author of Nature both speaks through men and reveals himself to them in their perceptions of the universe: "Men . . . were the mouths of the earth, and through them the earth spoke in general; but a man, in the particular instance, might understand and interpret and might see the signs put forth by the Author and Designer to reveal what lay under the outer show of properties and kinds". Diony, as one such sensitive individual, is in deep accord with the wonders she finds in the new world; an example is her vibrant reaction to the beauty of spring in the wilderness, when Berk comes back from salt-making to find his newborn son.

Nature is almost lavish in her bounty to the pioneers, flaunting for them the resources of a rich land. Diony is impressed by the bounty of nature and by the possibilities of the future here; the land seems fair to her as she contemplates it from the stockade walls. The men are making homes and security is coming to the wilderness; so Diony's vision of farms with stone walls and rail fences and lush crops is partly realized by the end of the novel. The flourishing corn, described in sexual terms, symbolically defines the great fertility of the land. The identification of the settlers with the growing plants as representing their own flesh "held in abeyance" is a notable example of Miss Roberts' habitual uniting in her fiction of the psychological with the concrete:

> There were delicate shoots at the side of the stalk growing out of the sappy stem, the female element having come now, taking form on the surface of the everlasting mother, the corn itself. Within the sheath were the delicate beginnings of husks, as yet pale and green and tender, scarcely unlike the buds prepared to hold the pollen above on the top of the strand. Within the pale, tender, female husks would flow the fine white milk of the corn which would congeal to be their food.

There is division from, as well as identity with, the land. When Diony is convinced that Berk is dead, she has her dark night of the soul at a time when "the new life in the earth leaped and quivered with the throbbing leaves and the swaying herbs". This is also a season of death as of promise: "The night was full of spring and death, birth coming forth by compulsion to meet death on the way". Ordinarily receptive to nature's beauty and bounty, Diony is oppressed now by a sense of the impersonal, incessant energies in nature, which operate according to law but to a law rigorous and often inexplicable. She does not reject her Berkeleyan idealism, but she has doubts as to the beneficence of Nature's great Author. For a time, she loses her accustomed sense of rapport with the power behind nature and feels herself alone in the world, as she is now physically alone in the wilderness with her boy Tom:

> She continually remembered on her side that the whole mighty frame of the world had no being without a mind to know it, but over this lay another way of knowing, and she saw clearly how little she could comprehend of those powers on the other side, beyond the growth of the herbs and the trees, and to sense the hostility of the forest life to her life, and to feel herself as a minute point, conscious, in a world that derived its being from some other sort. The indefiniteness of the outside earth, beyond herself, became a terror.

Her abstract fears are given concrete form in the sequence which follows when she awakes in terror and senses the promiscuous life surrounding her in the forest. Diony's sense of pattern and order return when she hurries back to the fort, but she knows, more certainly than before, that chaos lies at the outer fringes of civilization to undermine it upon slight provocation.

Nature is not the only means through which Miss Roberts bridges the inner and outer worlds. She also makes use of a cluster of images based upon weaving and spinning. Throughout the novel, clothmaking is symbolic of the civilized crafts through which the pioneers make an ordered life in the wilderness. The degree to which, on the outside, the land is mastered is to be measured by the progress of clothmaking within the home. The footmantle, woven at Albemarle by Polly and Diony Hall, stands for the arts of civilization; and it survives hard usages which take the lives of some settlers. Order finally comes to Harrods Fort when, after abortive attempts at clothmaking through the use of buffalo wool and of fibers from nettles, flax is cultivated, Elvira's wheel is put to use, and sheep become a part of the pioneer farm.

The weaving of cloth not only measures the visible progress of civilization; the process is also used metaphorically to describe Diony's efforts to reach spiritual reality. As Rovit says, weaving in Miss Roberts' work connotes the expansive aspects of the experiential process itself. The intricate manipulating of the threads and the emergence of a design represent for Diony her incremental endeavors to possess a continually elusive truth. In fact, her mental responses to external stimuli parallel the process of the textile craft: her thought rides on the currents set in motion by the rhythms of weaving, and the news that Berk will some day go to Kentucky (she is spinning while his brother Jack delivers a message from him) "spread outward through the threads of her nerves to the last fine web of sense".

Characteristically while she works, words like "I Diony," where-by she affirms the reality of her being, are interwoven into the threads as she forms her web, and the finished web becomes part of an attained inner harmony. The recurrent rhythms when she is spinning wool cause her also to think of her father's volumes of Berkeley and their meaningful phrases. The words and the wool are merged to form a composite fabric in her mind. All this is prelude to a still more arresting revelation. Spinning flax in Betty's company, Diony has a profound sense of spiritual illumination when, after thinking of her father's books, she holds with firmness for a moment "the inner thought, the inmost realization" and then falls into a dreaming trance, "her senses a web of unknowing fibers that reached into and among the fibers of flax".

Considering, then, the extent to which Miss Roberts brings in the psychological and the metaphysical, we might be justified in viewing *The Great Meadow* as only incidentally an historical novel. That history serves mainly as setting for the drama of the inner life Miss Roberts herself acknowledged. While she respected factual accuracy, she also intended to use "as little history as I required to make my motive run. But I have been obliged to keep much in mind to fit these fictitious happenings between authentic reports in a life-like way."

Louis Auchincloss (essay date 1965)

SOURCE: "Elizabeth Madox Roberts," in *Pioneers & Caretakers: A Study of 9 American Women Novelists,* University of Minnesota Press, 1965, pp. 123-35.

[*In the following essay, Auchincloss remarks on key novels and short stories by Roberts.*]

If Emily Brontë had survived the publication of *Wuthering Heights* to write a series of obscure and ponderous allegorical novels, would her reputation be as splendid as it is today? One may doubt it. There is something about the image of a life seemingly offered up on the altar of literature as the price of one perfect book that becomes part of the atmosphere in which the book is read. If Elizabeth Madox Roberts had disappeared from the literary scene after the publication of her first novel, *The Time of Man,* in 1926, she might stand today in the company of Willa Cather and Ellen Glasgow. For as a lyrical evocation of the farmer's relation to the soil it is quite the equal of *My Ántonia* and *Barren Ground.*

Her life was dogged by poverty and ill health, and she was born amid bitter memories. Her father, Simpson Roberts, at fourteen saw his own father shot in cold blood for refusing to join the National Guard and at sixteen joined the Confederate Army. He and his wife, both of pioneer stock, struggled through a Kentucky reconstruction and survived with a small grocery on the first floor of their house in Springfield and with Mr. Roberts' ultimate appointment as engineer and surveyor of the county. The county was in the fertile and hilly farm region that his daughter was to describe so vividly.

She was born in 1881, the first of eight children, and had to start early to help with the household work. She did well at school and yearned to go to college; she did enroll at the State College of Kentucky but her uncertain health and the family's lack of means kept her from completing the course. A shy, frail, introverted, rather lovely girl, she lived with her family and opened a small private school for children at a tuition of three dollars per month. She taught from a rocking chair and sometimes fainted in the classroom. Later, when her health improved, she taught in the public schools and published some poetry. In 1917, when she was thirty-six, there was at last enough money to enable her to realize her dream and enroll as a freshman in the University of Chicago. Harry M. Campbell and Ruel E. Foster, authors of the deeply perceptive if perhaps overlaudatory *Elizabeth Madox Roberts, American Novelist,* describe her at this period: "She had an original, quiet intelligence with an inward poetic cast. Her sensibility was a complex one. There was in the world of her mind a long wind blowing out of the past, out of Virginia and Maryland and Harrodsburg, Kentucky, from the days of Daniel Boone and James Harrod: a wind bringing old phrases, old talk, and the personalities of long-dead ancestry to life."

She made many good friends, despite her age difference, in what turned out to be an exceedingly talented class; she specialized in English literature and the philosophic idealism of Bishop Berkeley, and she was elected to Phi Beta Kappa. Her classmate Glenway Wescott recalls her as "the young southern woman, alone absolutely original, unimpressed by the setting of evils and plagiaries, meek and insinuatingly affirmative, untouched by but kindly toward all our half-grown baseness." She was drawn to Catholicism, an attraction that was to endure for life, but she never became a convert.

After college Miss Roberts returned to her family in Springfield. At the age of forty-one, in the fall of 1922, her education was at last completed, and she devoted her mornings to the composition of *The Time of Man.* Three years later, with considerable interludes for writing poetry, it was completed, accepted by the Viking Press, and chosen by the Book-of-the-Month Club. It had an immediate critical and popular success, and Miss Roberts found herself at once relieved of obscurity and financial need. She could never induce her parents to abandon their old home, so she added a large brick wing containing a study and library. There, amid high shelves of books, she was to spend the bulk of her days, although in the later years her health drove her to Florida in the winter.

Miss Roberts' notes for *The Time of Man* show that she conceived it as an Odyssey, with her heroine as the eternal wanderer. The six parts into which she divided the book do not correspond to any chapter division in the text, but rather to the symphonic movements of her idea of the story:

> I. A Genesis. She comes into the land. But the land rejects her. She remembers Eden (Tessie).
>
> II. She grows into the land, takes soil or root. Life tries her, lapses into lovelessness . . .
>
> III. Expands with all the land.
>
> IV. The first blooming.
>
> V. Withdrawal—and sinking back into the earth.
>
> VI. Flowering out of stone.

Ellen Chesser, the sole surviving child of itinerant farmers, Henry and Nellie, is constantly on the move with her parents through the rural areas of Kentucky. She yearns for permanent things, for houses that are more than shacks, with drawers to put things in, and friends who are more than passing acquaintances. This yearning centers in Tessie, a loquacious semi-gypsy given to flights of imagination, from whom Ellen is separated and whom she vainly seeks, running away from the farm on which her father settles for a time. After this single rebellion, her one practical attempt to recapture Eden, she settles down, "growing into the land," and Jonas Prather seems to offer marriage and "blooming." But after he has confided in her the secret of his affair with a prostitute and of the child that he believes to be his own, he identifies her with the guilt of which he has made her the repository and deserts her for another. Ellen rejects the temptation of suicide, the example of which is offered by Mrs. MacMurtrie, of the local gentry, who hangs herself when her husband goes off with her cousin, and finds the blooming that Jonas Prather had seemed to offer with Jasper Kent, a strong, violent man and an itinerant farmer like her father.

She and Jasper have several children, and she seems at last in tune with the natural things that surround her. But the withdrawal, the "sinking back into earth," occurs suddenly and horribly when Jasper, an adulterer himself, wildly and irrationally accuses her of infidelity and repudiates the child she is carrying. Only when the child is born, a shrunken, sickly bit of a thing, does he repent, but it is too late. The child, suffering from its mother's shock, lives three miserable years and dies. And then Jasper is beaten up by night riders who mistakenly believe him to be a barn burner, and he insists on packing up and moving on. The "flowering out of stone" occurs when Ellen, realizing that her destiny is irretrievably linked with his, refuses to be left behind, and the Kents move away together in their old wagon with all their few poor goods, asking no directions on the road, taking their own turnings.

To tell this story Miss Roberts limits her points of view to Ellen Chesser's and her own, but she does not pretend to limit herself to Ellen Chesser's simple vocabulary. Ellen, after all, is uneducated. Miss Roberts uses her lyrical prose to convey to the reader the state of being Ellen, which is a far more complicated thing than Ellen could possibly articulate. Ellen loves the countryside and all its creatures, even the pigs that must be slaughtered; she is vitally aware of sound and color, of sun and seasons, of affection and distrust. Her extreme sensitivity is conveyed in a prose-poetry that is at times full of sharp, precise imagery and at times dreamlike in its flowing smoothness.

Ellen Glasgow doubted that rural people talked like the characters in *The Time of Man.* Perhaps they do not. Miss Roberts was searching in her dialogue for a rhythm that would convey the inner as well as the outer man and that would give a sense of the people as a unit and a fraction of the geography. It was part of what she called the "poetic realism" that she tried to achieve in all her prose. "Somewhere there is a connection between the world of the mind and the outer order. It is the secret of the contact that we are after, the point, the moment of the union. We faintly sense the one and we know as faintly the other, but there is a point at which they come together and we can never know the whole of reality until we know these two completely."

Ellen Chesser has such an experience when she sees the mountains of the new region to which her family are moving. It is a complex experience, and she could not possibly have described it to another person. Yet its happening depends not on intellect but on awareness, not on knowledge but on sensitivity. Here is how Miss Roberts describes it: "The mountains grew more definite as she looked back to them, their shapes coming upon her mind as shapes dimly remembered and recognized, as contours burnt forever or carved forever into memory, into all memory. With the first recognition of their fixity came a faint recognition of those structures which seemed everlasting and undiminished within herself, recurring memories, feelings, responses, wonder, worship, all gathered into one final inner motion which might have been called spirit; this gathered with another, an acquired structure, fashioned out of her experience of the past years, out of her passions and the marks put upon her by the passions of others, this structure built up now to its high maturity."

What makes *The Time of Man* a great novel is the extraordinary sense conveyed of Ellen as an almost unseparated part of the tissue of living things, with horses, cows and pigs, and people, beneficent people and hateful people, as if the whole landscape, stretching to the mountains and made up of organisms growing or dying, of corn and grass and animals and humanity and even rocks ("Rocks grow," Ellen's father tells her), were part of a single carpet on the earth. Ultimately this continuity is sensed in time as well as material. Jasper Kent seems to move into Ellen's life just where Jonas Prather has left off, so that both men, without in the least losing their individuality, seem at times simply to express the male aspect of nature. Similarly Ellen, in the end, feels that her life is so innately an extension of her mother's that she can share her mother's memories: "Going about the rough barnlot of the farm above Rock Creek, calling in the hens, breaking them corn, Ellen would merge with Nellie in the long memory she had of her from the time when she had called from the fence with so much prettiness, through the numberless places she had lived or stayed and the pain she had known, until her mother's life merged into her own and she could scarcely divide the one from the other, both flowing continuously and mounting."

There is none of the solemn hymning to the land in *The Time of Man* that we find in Ellen Glasgow and Willa Cather. That was to appear in her fiction soon enough, but in the beginning she was free of it. Campbell and Foster point out the interesting twist that Miss Roberts

gave to the philosophy of Bishop Berkeley which she had adopted for her own: "For Miss Roberts indeed there is no contrast between knowledge of the earthy and that of the spiritual; epistemologically, the two were the same for her, as they were for Berkeley, but the emphasis of the artist and her philosophical master, as might be expected, is different: whereas Berkeley as a philosopher is engaged in transforming what is called the physical into that on which it is dependent for its existence, the spiritual, Miss Roberts as an artist seems at one level to be transforming the spiritual into the physical, the sensuous."

But the sensuous has far greater significance in her work than it does in that of an ordinary realist. As Miss Roberts put it herself: "We go into the unseen by way of the visible, into the unknown by way of the known, into nous by way of the flesh and the dust."

The first symptoms of the attenuation of power which Emily Brontë escaped are observable in her very next book, *My Heart and My Flesh* (1927), which introduced the theme that she was to work over and over in the next years: the baffled, humiliated, at times actually violated heroine, after a volume of sleepwalking and groping, punctuated with nightmares, finds a spiritual rebirth in the arms of a strong man who has remained close enough to the soil to be uncorrupted. It is the ancient legend of death, burial, and rebirth, but that is no excuse for solemnity that is always verging on the tedious. Theodosia Bell, the heroine of *My Heart and My Flesh,* suffers two shocks amounting to traumatic experiences: she is brutally deserted by her lover who, overnight, and without even a decent shadow of subterfuge, turns his ardor to another girl, and she discovers that her dissolute father is also the parent of three Negroes, two girls by one woman and a half-witted boy by a second. In an effort to discover her own identity, which has become confused in her mind as a result of these new relationships, she befriends the Negro girls. When the older one murders her lover and the younger sleeps with the idiot brother, Theodosia becomes unbalanced and goes off to live in the country with a crazy aunt who half-starves her. Rescued by the local doctor, she recovers and regains her mental and physical health in a simple rustic atmosphere and with the admiration of a fundamental man. In Caleb Burns, the farmer, "there was a sense of the whole country, of the rolling farms as owned up and down the watercourses and farther, including the town, Anneville and beyond, other towns, Lester, Quincy, all the reach of the entire region."

Miss Roberts' solution of a reconciliation with natural things is expressed in the final paragraph, where Caleb wanders about the farm at night: "The leaves of the poplar tree lifted and turned, swayed outward and all quivered together, holding the night coolness. The steps returned to the pasture, going unevenly and stopping, going again, restless. They went across the hollow place and came back again toward the rise where the cows lay.

They walked among the sleeping cows, but these did not stir for it was a tread they knew."

Glenway Wescott wrote a description of Miss Roberts at this period (1927-28) which may give a clue to what was happening to her writing. She had a patrician aloofness, "something blue-blooded, almost Russian, in her bearing," like one of "antique gentry brought low." "I saw her . . . down one of those wild New York streets scarcely occidental in mood, where the workers go half-naked and negro boys throw balls . . . in a darkened, hot but never warming room, seated with her yellow-crowned head bowed almost between her knees as are figures in certain Blake drawings; now signalling from the window with a towel when she had need of human attendance, now like royalty in a convent drawing apart in an arrogant and pious self-communion; abstractions forming out of the tedium, the shadows of past persons becoming the flesh of future characters—thinking, thinking, remembering, biding her time, uttering extensive, dreamy theories and troubling witticisms, with an occasional incorrectness of folk-songs in her speech."

She laughed so hard in reading the manuscript of *Jingling in the Wind* aloud to a friend that she had to stop reading. Such remoteness from others and enchantment with self can have disastrous results on art that must, in the last analysis, be communicated. At the same time Miss Roberts was becoming the most extreme of valetudinarians. She went in now for every kind of fad, believing that the sun was a cure-all, carrying her own drinking water, checking on the temperature of her dentist's office before she would make an appointment. A neurotic can perfectly well be a literary genius, but his greatest danger is always that he will not recognize when he is dull.

Jingling in the Wind (1928) is one of the dullest novels ever written by a first-rank American novelist. Its allegorical character may remove the need for flesh and blood in its people, but allegories should be very sharp and very funny, and it is neither. Jeremy and Tulip, as rainmakers, represent the synthetic, half-baked modern world that cannot wait for the clouds to supply water but must set up machinery to precipitate the precipitations. The novel is shrill and silly, like the later fiction of Edith Wharton, in its denunciation of the cheapness of contemporary American life. The only way that Miss Roberts could demonstrate what America had lost was to show, not what America was, but what America had been, and this, with much happier results, she accomplished in *The Great Meadow* (1930).

After *The Time of Man,* it is the best of her novels. It is inferior only in that it shows the hymnal quality of which *The Time of Man* is so happily free. Miss Roberts makes it only too clear that she is celebrating the courage and the endurance of the first settlers of Kentucky; Daniel Boone himself is one of the characters. Diony Hall and Berk Jarvis, with their silent understanding and deep love of each other, with their un-

flinching heroism and dedication to the development of a new land, might be figures in a mural of pioneers in a post office. But having said this, let one try to rob the statement of some of its denigration by insisting that it is a *good* mural. The pace of the story is slow until Diony and Berk arrive at Fort Harrod, but thereafter it is tensely exciting. The murder of Berk's mother by Indians, his leaving his wife and child in a dogged, solitary pursuit of revenge, his long absence and ultimate return, a sullen, possessive Enoch Arden, to take back his wife from another, is as gripping a tale as exists in the fiction of the American frontier.

As in *The Time of Man* the characters are a part of the land which they love and for which they have abandoned the relative ease of Virginia. Diony is a magnificent study of a frontier woman. She loves Berk passionately and tries to persuade herself that he is living long after the rest of the stockade community take for granted that he is dead, but there is no place in that primitive world for a young woman without a man, and her economic need for a second husband is soon enough followed by the pricking of her physical desire for one. Such infidelity would be scarcely imaginable among the embittered heroines of Ellen Glasgow. Diony's abandonment of her interim husband to return to Berk when he reappears at Fort Harrod makes a remarkably effective ending. Few indeed are the writers who could carry it off without impairing the epic quality of the saga. But Miss Roberts, it should be emphasized, was a good poet as well as a good novelist. . . .

"*The Time of Man* was my *Hamlet,*" Miss Roberts wrote; "*Jingling in the Wind* was my *Midsummer-Night's Dream* and *The Great Meadow* was my *Romeo and Juliet.*" But *A Buried Treasure* (1931) seems to belong more to the dramaturgy of our own time. It is a dreary little tale, once more allegorical, full of fantastic characters who foreshadow the world of Tennessee Williams and Carson McCullers. Andy and Philly Blair, the old couple who dig up a pail of gold coins and bury it again in fear of robbers, Ben Shepherd who comes to town to transcribe the dates of his ancestors from the tombs in the cemetery and finds a bone of one which he carries about in his pocket, a hen that eats her own eggs, a father who claims that his daughter is illegally married in order to get her home to be his cook—we begin to recognize the whimsical southern cast that has fascinated later audiences. But they fail to come alive.

The Haunted Mirror (1932) is a collection of short stories, one of which, "**The Sacrifice of the Maidens,**" about a young boy watching the ceremony in which his sister becomes a nun, plays up a fascinating conflict of pagan and Christian values, but it was written before *The Time of Man. He Sent Forth a Raven* (1935), written in this later period, is another allegorical novel, this time a dark one, with a World War I setting. Stoner Drake vows that he will never set foot on the soil if his second wife dies, and she does, and he executes his oath by staying indoors for the rest of his days. He gathers about him a group of loquacious characters who represent the folly of a mechanical world at war, who have lost their connections with simplicity, with nature, with God. The plot seems to offer diversions and possibilities: the crazy old Lear whose granddaughter, Jocelle, brutally raped by a cousin, at last finds peace and hope in marriage to the good, simple man who takes over the operation of Lear's farm; but it is very tediously worked out.

In the three years preceding publication of *He Sent Forth a Raven* Miss Roberts' health had been deteriorating, and in 1936 a specialist finally diagnosed her ailment as Hodgkin's disease. The remaining five years of her life were spent in a struggle with an enemy that she knew must win. It was in this shadow that she wrote *Black Is My Truelove's Hair* (1938), and her genius, no longer distracted by the irritants of modern society, went back again to work for her almost as effectively as in the beginning. Her last novel is a rich, ordered, beautiful symphonic piece of writing which gives a fine satisfaction to the careful reader, though at moments some of the vividness of the characterizations may seem sacrificed to the symbolism.

Dena Janes, before the novel opens, has run off from her native village, Henrytown, with a truck driver, Langtry, a dark, dangerous, tattooed man who symbolizes the empty world of nervous motion that exists beyond the rural areas. As soon as she has discovered what a terrible man her seducer is, she has told him that she will return home, but he has warned her that if he ever hears of her going with another man he will hunt her down and shoot her. In the first chapter we see Dena, distraught with terror at the threat, hurrying back to Henrytown where she is only too grateful to be put up by her sister Fronia, older, twice-widowed, domineering, and to do the chores. The local girls are friendly, even chatty, but it is entirely understood that she is disgraced and "different," and the men either avoid her altogether or ogle and leer at her as a loose woman. Dena, however, does not mind this; there may even be safety in her semi-ostracism. She does her work and diverts herself by taking long sunbaths, naked, behind the house. It is a passive half-life with a certain sluggish peace, better, at any rate, than the hell that Langtry offered.

Life, however, will not allow Dena to escape. Fronia loses a gold thimble given her by a former lover, an obvious sex symbol, and frantically hunts it high and low, even threatening to kill her favorite goose and search for the lost object in its gizzard. Dena, younger and sexually ready, finds the thimble, but before she can give it to Fronia it is stolen by a little boy who sells it to Cam Elliot, the beautiful but shy farm lad, the perfect mate. It is the instrument of fate that draws them together, and Dena and Cam become engaged, but when the banns are published Langtry returns. Dena has now acquired courage and confidence; after a first brief panic, when she tries to hide from him, and he shoots at her and misses, she confronts her former lover boldly

and challenges him to do what he must. He repents, and a brave future is left for Dena and Cam. As one can see from this outline, despite the subtlety of the novel's symbolism—its squawking geese, its haunting night cries, its old horses and its new cars—it veers close in the end to the hammy. Yet it never quite reaches that point; that is precisely its artistry. It leaves one with a sense of unity and concord, of nature disturbed and put in order again.

The reviewers felt that *Black Is My Truelove's Hair* was good, but not as good as *The Time of Man*. Poor Miss Roberts learned what so many authors have learned: that a masterpiece is not always a friend. "Would I want to write *The Time of Man* over and over, or even once again?" she protested. But her energy was now running out. The planned epic play for stage and radio on Daniel Boone had to be abandoned. She died in Florida early in 1941.

In the last year of her life she put together the little volume of short stories, *Not by Strange Gods,* that appeared almost simultaneously with her death. Two of these shine with all of her early brilliance.

"The Haunted Palace" is an eerie sketch of poor farmers who move their sheep into the great rooms of a deserted mansion. The wife routs what she believes to be the ghost of the old aristocrat, "the creature or the thing," moving among the sheep with a club and a light, by striking at it, and so shatters the great mirror. It is, of course, her own reflection that she has seen, but she does not know this and is now at ease, and she and her husband count the new lambs born that night and are "pleased with the number they had counted."

"The Betrothed" is a wonderful psychological study, seen from inside the mind of Rhody, of her doubts and panics at the prospect of impending marriage to the man she loves. Her old grandmother gives her a desperate shock by reading her fortune in the entrails of a hog:

> "She prodded into the wet and bloody mass, muttering. It would be thus and thus, she said. The beast, turned wrong side out, danced still his life dance, blood having run into pans on the ground. Life sat, as a dismembered bird, in the vat of the entrails, still throbbing within itself. You are thus and thus, the grandmother said. . . . She would begin a story of mortality, of bloody bearings, the origin of life acting thus alone in a tub of entrails. She leaned over the mass muttering, the mole on her chin beating lightly with the working of her mouth, it uttering jaunty prophecies of blood. For a moment Rhody wanted to push the old one into the tub of quivering intestines, to thrust her forward and downward into the medium of blood and fat."

Overcome with revulsion, Rhody leaves home to visit her married sister, determined to break off the match. She finds herself an upsetting element in an already tense marriage. Joe, her brother-in-law, is attracted to her, and there are ugly scenes. Rhody flees home and discovers at last that she truly loves her betrothed, Kirk Brown, when her younger sisters burn a letter from him which she has not opened. "'Me and you, Rhody,' that's what it says in the letter," they jeer. And then everything is all right again. "Life seemed very simple to her when Kirk was near, as if only those things of which he took account had reason or being. Now value was thus focused at the point where his hand closed upon her own, and as he walked he looked at her continually."

Nature can be a nightmare, as when an old witch of a woman grubs in a pig's entrails, or a sister sleeps with her idiot half-brother, or a man commits rape, but peace can follow nightmare if a proper adjustment is made between man and his natural physical environment. What is hard to understand is why the form of the short story did not strike Miss Roberts as a better tool for her purpose than the allegorical novel. **"The Betrothed"** expresses all that *My Heart and My Flesh* attempts to say.

Still, Elizabeth Madox Roberts accomplished in the best of her fiction, long and short, the object that she set for herself, which should keep her name permanently in the front rank of American novelists: "If I can, in art, bring the physical world before the mind with a greater closeness, richer immediacy than before, so that mind rushes out to the very edge of sense—then mind turns about and sees itself mirrored within itself."

Herman E. Spivey (essay date 1965)

SOURCE: "The Mind & Creative Habits of Elizabeth Madox Roberts," in . . . *All These to Teach: Essays in Honor of C. A. Robertson,* edited by Robert A. Bryan and others, University of Florida Press, 1965, pp. 237-48.

[*In the following essay, Spivey points out the strengths and weaknesses in Roberts's prose.*]

Elizabeth Madox Roberts (1881-1941) deserved and deserves more readers than she had or has for her twelve books: seven novels, two volumes of short stories, and three volumes of poetry. [*In the Great Steep's Garden* (poems, 1913), *Under the Tree* (poems, 1922), *The Time of Man* (a novel, 1925), *My Heart and My Flesh* (a novel, 1927), *Jingling in the Wind* (a satirical fantasy, 1928), *The Great Meadow* (a historical novel, 1930), *A Buried Treasure* (a novel, 1931), *The Haunted Mirror* (stories, 1931), *He Sent Forth a Raven* (a novel, 1935), *Black Is My True Love's Hair* (a novel, 1938), *Song in the Meadow* (poems, 1940), and *Not by Strange Gods* (stories, 1941).] Only two of these twelve were well received, and a third fairly well: *The Time of Man, The Great Meadow,* and *Under the Tree.* Readers now are better able to understand and appreciate her nine volumes of fiction, not only because

of the illuminating books of Campbell and Foster, Rovit, and McDowell [Harry M. Campbell and Ruel E. Foster, *Elizabeth Madox Roberts, American Novelist* (1956), Earl H. Rovit, *Herald to Chaos: The Novels of Elizabeth Madox Roberts* (1960), and Frederick P. W. McDowell, *Elizabeth Madox Roberts* (1963).], but also because the vogue of the novel of violence and of the staccato style, so noticeable in the 1920's through the 1950's, is passing. Although her achievements were greater than was realized by her contemporary readers, her handicaps as literary artist were probably greater than she understood or was able to overcome.

It is the purpose of this essay to suggest a few of the strengths and weaknesses which justify this judgment. The briefest way to do this, perhaps, is to take a close look at her second novel, *My Heart and My Flesh* ["crieth out for the living God," Psalms lxxxiv:2], on which Miss Roberts worked for sixteen months and about which she wrote her publisher (Viking) thirty-seven letters, only a few of which have been published. For the most part, the novel was composed on two water fronts: three-fourths of it by the Pacific in Santa Monica in the winter of 1926-1927 and the rest in Chicago in the spring and early summer of 1927. The last major parts to be rewritten before sending the manuscript away were the long symbolic prologue (which, to the uninitiated reader, is an unfortunately bewildering and mysterious introduction to the novel) and the passages dealing with music, one of the major motifs of the novel.

Although *My Heart and My Flesh* is not extraordinarily subtle, to the first readers the profoundly significant theme and philosophic implications were not fully clear or impressive. One reason is the vagueness of the long symbolic prologue, better omitted or read last even by the later reader; and another reason is the relatively small amount of external conflict and action in the narrative. Yet the close reader of 1927, particularly if he remembered *The Time of Man,* perceived that this second novel continued the theme of spiritual death and rebirth, but with the material circumstances of the leading character and the sequence of happenings reversed. In this respect *My Heart and My Flesh* is complementary to *The Time of Man,* with contrasting social class, tempo, and direction of movements, as Miss Roberts points out in a note left among her manuscripts.

The Time of Man is organized around the age-old journey motif, or, more noticeably, employs the American motif of extreme mobility, especially the Southern rural tradition of the wandering individual with a hungry heart, "down one road and up another and down again," "aways a-looken at everything in the world and expecting to see something more," "on and on, without end, going, day and night and day and rain and windy weather, and sun and then rain again, wanting things and then having things and then wanting," the eye never satisfied with seeing nor the ear filled with hearing. This first novel, featuring the peasant class, but only as poetic symbol, is a story of irregular additions,

Ellen Chesser beginning with scarcely anything more than the breath of life and slowly adding, to quote a manuscript note of the author, "minute particle by minute particle . . . sounds, sights, friends, lovers, material possessions, memories, intuitions, defeat followed by renewal."

In contrast, her second novel, *My Heart and My Flesh,* though set in the same rural area, was designed as an experiment in reverse. It is as if she were now writing a novel, not about poor whites but about the patrician landowners mentioned in the first novel, the Wakefields and the MacMurtries, as she notes in a fragmentary letter written while she was just getting under way with the novel. But these landowners are now conceived of as in gentle decay, again symbolic of a great Southern social change of the nineteenth century. The accent is not on social change, however, but on individual character as affected by the way she reacts to drastic reverses. *My Heart and My Flesh* is a story of *subtraction,* the central character (Theodosia Bell) beginning with family prestige and property but already headed toward relentless loss until she is left with scarcely more than the breath of life, and she tries to destroy even that before she is resurrected. Among her notes Miss Roberts left an undated, revealing comment to herself about her method and intent in this second novel:

> The method here was a steady taking away until there was nothing left but the bare breath of the throat and the simplified spirit. The work begins with a being who has been reared in plenty and security. She has the pride of family, of wealth (as such goes in the South of our country), a pride in being the honored and petted child of parents, a pride in personal charm and in popularity with friends and associates, and finally a pride in musical skill and in a boundless ambition to play the fiddle well. All these gentle conceits are gathered into the person of Theodosia.

> One by one these things are taken from her to the upbuilding of her understanding and the growth of tolerance and wisdom through suffering. Each of these is lost and more. Lover, pride in ambition and the fiddle hand, pride in family, and at length the house in which her family had dwelt—all of these go from her. Friends are lost. Stability is lost and she gives herself in loveless passion. Food is taken from her and health goes. Finally half crazed or more by her condition she lives a brief hell of confusion and despair, warmed and fed by only the stupid lover and his passions. Sunk to the degradation of the nether hell, she lived thus for a winter.

> It is the story of a woman who went to hell and returned to walk among you.

> Out of the icy waters of the frozen pond where she had gone in spirit and determination, being ready to make the last dash from the door that would sweep her into the water to drown, she experienced a resurrection. Spirit asserted itself

over the necessities of death. She prepared an orderly departure from her hell, informed by judgment or the knowing and thinking, the associative entity of her being. She went from the aunt's farm and let chance find a way for her again among living men. In the end is the rare lover, the maker of fine cows, the adoring voice among the distant barns singing, or the hand that led her about over the pasture to show her the cattle and the mind to offer her companionship and a shared living among these excellent things.

These contrasting terms, "addition" as applied to *The Time of Man* and "subtraction" as applied to *My Heart and My Flesh,* like all opposites, are relative and reciprocal terms. Neither one has meaning except as it is related to the other. Both Ellen in the first novel and Theodosia in the second lost; both gained. Both reacted to their experiences in such a manner as to gain strength and wisdom. This is the main point the novelist keeps making: the significance is not the precise thing which happened to the characters but how they reacted to what happened to them. Throughout her writing career Miss Roberts kept suggesting the polarities of experience (as did one of her favorite writers, Jules Laforgue), the cooperation of opposites, life's contradictions, the dualism between election and damnation which is a part of the American Puritan tradition.

My Heart and My Flesh introduces several related themes. It may be considered a study in the decay of gentility, the fall of the House of Bell, miscegenation and incest, the transformation of adolescence into maturity, the mysteriousness of memories, the presentness of the past, the capacity to prevail through endurance as if man's first duty were to live, the effects upon character of various reactions to suffering where there is not the will to suffer (as there is in some Hemingway novels), or catharsis achieved through suffering when aided by sensitivity to phenomenal nature and responsiveness to simple human affection—all themes which were to recur often in her eight remaining books. Two other parallel themes, however, seem nearer the central intent of the author. One is a longing for the identification of spirit, or a yearning to discover a reality beyond fact (what life essentially is, so elusive, so bewildering), an intense search for the permanent underlying so much change. Like Ellen in her first novel, Theodosia is "aways a-looken at everything in the world and expecting to see something more." Theodosia was always "looking more deeply within, parting thought and thought, parting the semi-dark which lies between," to use the author's words. The title of the novel features this search: "My heart and my flesh crieth out for the living God." This is the theme stressed in the first half of the book, and it is made appealing by the haunting pathos of Theodosia's absolute aloneness, her mother dead, her father a lecherous and conscienceless reprobate, her grandfather impoverished and defeated by the decay of the world he loved, one lover jilting her and another burned up accidentally. This near-desperate search for the meaning of life is dramatized for the reader about a third of the way through the novel by an image of lonely Theodosia before a waning fire in the bedroom of her dying grandfather: "When all the subtractions were made, the naked man was left. . . . There should be a soul there somewhere, she thought, and she searched into the withered leavings of crippled body and quavering voice. When she had found this entity in her grandfather she would, she thought, be able to identify it within herself." This haunting search is intensified by Theodosia's primary mode of self-expression (the violin) and also by the associative imagery of the highly symbolic prologue, about which more will be said shortly. Theodosia is in somewhat the same mood as Pascal was three hundred years before: "When I consider the brief span of my life, swallowed up in the eternity before and behind it, the small space that I fill, or even see, engulfed in the infinite immensity of spaces which I know not, and which know not me, I am afraid, and wonder to see myself here rather than there, for there is no reason why I should be here rather than there, now rather than then" [*Pensées*]. The more clearly central theme, however, as has been mentioned, is the age-old one of withdrawal and return, or death and rebirth, which was to be a recurring theme in her later writing and the central one in her seventh novel, ***Black Is My True Love's Hair***. Professors Campbell and Foster comment on the frequent recurrence of this theme in Miss Roberts' books and also its prominence in the Old Testament, one of the strong influences on Miss Roberts: in the stories of Noah, for instance, Jonah, Joseph, and especially Job. Theodosia dies and is recreated. She answered affirmatively Job's echoing question: "If a man die, shall he live again?" None of the American naturalists (Crane, Norris, or Dreiser) would have depicted this new birth, even if they could understand it, because they did not believe in being born again. Theodosia survives, not because of her physical fitness or accident or luck, but because of her moral progress in working toward the will to live as a dignified and divine human being. The two simple but great influences in effecting this therapy, in bringing about this resurrection, are sensitivity to rural nature and responsiveness to unsophisticated true love, the ego having established a working relationship with the non-ego. From a letter which Miss Roberts wrote to Louise McElroy in Springfield, Kentucky, when she was just getting a good start on this novel, we know that these two themes (search for a reality beyond fact, and death and rebirth) were at the heart of her intention: "I have tried to develop some essence," she wrote her friend, "such as we may call 'the human spirit.' . . . It is a story of a woman . . . who went to hell and came back, who was impaled on the very topmost and last and most excruciating pinprick of suffering and privation. By moving all accessories I hope to make live a spirit, a most inner essence, a will-to-live. It is a large problem, a difficult undertaking perhaps, but necessary."

Miss Roberts mistakenly thought she could help communicate this double theme by experimenting with an ambitious narrative technique in the prologue, beyond her full mastery, but interesting; and now with the benefit of her notes clear enough. This thirty-three-page, over-subtle prologue is a fantasy employing associative imagery, and the cosmic consciousness of Luce (symbolically "light"), ranging over time past, time present, and hinting at time to come. This long stream-of-consciousness introduction is supposed to represent timelessness and omniscience, as the main part of the novel, coming to us through Theodosia, represents transiency. As she wrote to Harriet Monroe, she intended this symbolic prologue to serve as the introduction to a whole cycle of novels she had already in mind, and indeed her fourth novel, ***The Great Meadow***, does serve as an introduction to the House of Bell, here in her second novel falling. Luce lives in Mome (which represents Covington, Kentucky, where Miss Roberts went to high school), whereas the world of Theodosia is probably in Washington County, Kentucky. Among the Library of Congress papers is a long manuscript called "The Book of Luce," showing Miss Roberts' lifelong fascination with this method of treating symbolically whole cycles of time. Professors Campbell and Foster aptly compare this intriguing prologue in her second novel to the prelude of a symphony. By the time the reader gets to the end of the prologue he has left the infinite consciousness of Luce and is supposed to be entering the finite, sensitive consciousness of Theodosia. In a note, Miss Roberts says of her technique: "The mind here to be entered is the mind of the woman, Theodosia. The process begins with a Knower, an Observer, Luce, a sensitive onlooker. The narrative moves slowly into Theodosia's mind, beginning in the mind of Luce, seeing Theodosia first from the outside, moving more closely and intently into her experience until it becomes identical with her consciousness."

Other interesting characteristics of Miss Roberts' style here and elsewhere are her abundant use of symbolism, her use of music as a major motif, her strange attraction to dreams as a means of deepening meaning (not immediately clear to the hasty reader of ***My Heart and My Flesh***), surrealistic dialogue, her large use of appropriate folklore, and her lyric prose. Her use of symbols throughout her writing, influenced by her liking for Laforgue, Corbière, and Virginia Woolf, is too pervasive for treatment here. Three years before her first novel she had written a note of advice to herself which might be taken as the aptest possible motto for all her work: Cultivate, she says, "the way of symbolism working through poetic realism."

The symbolic use of dreams is illustrated vividly in this novel by Theodosia's four blurred and prescient dreams on the night her lover burned up, and more suggestively by the dream . . . [Roberts's] publisher objected to and got her to modify a little: one she has in a moment of nodding as she is becoming nauseated at her repulsive father's recollections of lechery; she saw a parade of vague haggard women in the midst of whom her naked father appeared, blown up into a gigantic symbol of excessive sexual vitality.

As with her symbolism, Miss Roberts' large use of appropriate folklore can only be suggested here. It pervades all her books and provides the title of her most elusive book, ***Black Is My True Love's Hair***. In the novel we are discussing she uses folk speech, Negro work songs, proverbial sayings ("See them-there hens out eaten grass in the rain? When you see hens out in the morning eaten grass in the rain, that's a sure sign hit'll rain all day"), folk health practices (like drinking hog's blood), and folk songs.

Characteristically, Miss Roberts couldn't find a title conveying precisely the right thematic implication. Some of the titles she considered before settling on ***My Heart and My Flesh*** are: "L'Abondante," "The Abundant Woman," "Plenitude," "Behind Green Pastures," "Field Lovers," "Proud Fields," "Without a Name," "The Glittering Sword" (from Job), "The Sparks Fly Upward" ("Man is born unto trouble as the sparks fly upward," Job), "The Chronicle," "The Season's Return," and "Full Circle." No subject occurs so often in her thirty-seven letters to her publishers about this novel. These are fascinating letters because they tell so much about her intent as literary artist. There is room here for only a third of one of these letters, addressed to Mr. Huebsch of Viking and now in the publisher's files:

August 7, 1927

Dear Mr. Huebsch:

I have worked on titles all week and have written three full pages of them only to scratch most of them out after a little. The difficulty is this. A title throws an emphasis somewhere and this book is already complete in itself. I see it lie out before me continually as a complete design. There are only a few ideas that I seem willing to stress. One is the person, the woman involved. Another is the land.

Many thanks for the suggestion, "As the Sparks Fly Up-ward." It is indeed all the things you say of it. It throws an emphasis on the idea of trouble, however, and seems to me to throw the design out of plumb a little. It is good, though, and I lean toward it. My ideal title would center to the woman and her abundance as a sensitive body and mind. It would be such a word as the French adjective *abondante* used as a noun *L'abondante,* and I have cast about to try to find an English equivalent, but there is not any. "The Abundant Woman" and all such are rejected. "The Time of Man" gets in the way of any title with "woman" in it. Such an idea as this word would convey is exactly what I want. It would cover the abundance of the woman's trouble or sorrow and her discipline. It would include her as a lover and a living spirit. It is a great title and I wish the book might go into French so that it might be used. . . .

I wish I had the musician's privilege of merely numbering my work. A title is an impertinence. . . .

Though not popular, ***My Heart and My Flesh*** is a significant novel, as is most of Miss Roberts' fiction. Why, then, was it (is it) not more popular? Here are half a dozen suggested reasons.

1. Miss Roberts was too much concerned with man in general and too little with individual man. After her first novel, she let a veil come between herself and the coarse-grained world. Because of her unmarried, somewhat shy, and solitary nature, she lived and wrote as one removed from life in action. Like one of her favorite writers, Virginia Woolf, she lived in an ambiance of ideality, to borrow a phrase coined by Elizabeth Bowen. Rovit considers her second novel more like a case history than the presentation of a struggling individual.

2. In most of her fiction there is too little external action and possibly too little internal tension, especially physical tension. The internal action is probably intense, but more like a severe and unremitting headache and heartache than a shock, and readers in her day wanted to be shocked. Theodosia, for instance, suffers acutely, but she is an enduring sufferer rather than a defiant one; until the end, she *undergoes* rather than acts. The reader misses the appeal of overt, urgent struggle.

3. Like most of her other fiction, ***My Heart and My Flesh*** is a novel of erosion and rebuilding in an age when we were experiencing an epidemic of violence, whether in international war, labor disputes, or gangsterdom, and when the novel of violence was understandably in vogue. ***My Heart and My Flesh*** is devoid of overt violence. In fact, there is in it too much humble acceptance and too little rebellion, ranting, and disillusionment for the American public of the 1920's. As in the novel of violence, Miss Roberts reveals our animality, but unlike most specialists in this genre she also reveals the human capacity for self-sacrifice and love. A novel like ***My Heart and My Flesh*** takes time to show the process of the *development* of character, whereas the novels we preferred when Miss Roberts was writing are those beginning near the climax (like a short story or drama) and featuring strenuous and dangerous action, not growth. As Professor Frohock points out, the plot of the novel of violence is like that of a drama more than the conventional novel: it is concerned with mounting tension, climax, and then resolution of tension.

4. McDowell thinks the chief weakness of her second novel is the lack of forceful "subsidiary characters and setting" to reinforce the theme.

5. The carefully modulated sentences, her poetic diction and imagery, and her successful attempt at symbolism through poetic realism were out of harmony with the staccato style of the Hemingway school and also the rhetorical exuberance and vehemence of Faulkner. This, let us hope, will come to be to her honor and glory. ***My Heart and My Flesh*** is poetic in a period when the

content and the mood of the strenuous novels we bought were not suited to poetry.

6. Miss Roberts' unmastered technical experiments (especially in this her second novel, in the fantasy *Jingling in the Wind*, and in *Black Is My True Love's Hair*) hindered public understanding. Without a little help, the average reader does not fully comprehend her aims in most of her novels, except *The Time of Man* and *The Great Meadow*. With only a small amount of help, however, provided by recent studies, her rich experimentation can be understood and appreciated.

One could mention half a dozen commendable features equally compelling. Miss Roberts deserves, and probably will come to receive, more favorable attention than she experienced when living. She is better than our literary historians have discovered yet.

John J. Murphy (essay date 1966)

SOURCE: "Elizabeth Madox Roberts and the Civilizing Consciousness," in *The Register of the Kentucky Historical Society,* Vol. 64, No. 2, April, 1966, pp. 110-20.

[*In the following essay, Murphy discusses Roberts's blending of historical fact with fiction in* The Great Meadow, *and her use of stream of consciousness in* The Time of Man.]

In writing *The Great Meadow,* first published in 1930, Miss Roberts faced the common problem of the historical novelist, that of integrating fiction and historical fact. The excellence of this work, written in the tradition of Cooper's *The Spy* and countless novels dealing with the American Revolution and Civil War, resides in the novelist's unique method of fusing the two unmatched halves of the historical novel through the search for identity and conscious patterning of experiences of Diony Hall Jarvis, her heroine.

The plot of *The Great Meadow* possesses the simplicity of a chronicle. It was derived from material Miss Roberts spent some time gathering through travel in her native Kentucky, in the archives of the Filson Club of Louisville, and by study of John Filson's *The Discovery, Settlement and Present State of Kentucke,* 1784, which contains "The Adventures of Colonel Daniel Boon" and a narrative of the wars of Kentucky. It records the end of Diony Hall's adolescence in Albemarle County, Virginia, on the upper waters of the James; her marriage to Berk Jarvis; their journey along the Wilderness Road in 1777 through Cumberland Gap to Kentucky; the trials and tribulations at Fort Harrod; the scalping of Berk's mother, Elvira, by the Shawnees; Berk's capture by the same tribe; his travels among the Ojibways (this account reminiscent of Boone's memoir); his adoption by the Shawnees and his eventual escape; Diony's marriage to Evan Muir; Berk's return; Diony's choice between her two husbands, and the coming of peace to the frontier

land. These events are either immediate to the novel or narrated to Diony; as such they are confined to Diony's experiences, and she endeavors to discover herself by evaluating them according to the "Great Design of an Eternal Spirit," which is detected in manifestations of Nature and events in the history of man.

The key to Miss Roberts' successful integration of fact and fiction lies in Thomas Hall's readings and lectures to his daughter on Berkeley's idealism. Diony is frequently obsessed with her father's beliefs: "Stepping back and forth in the dance of spinning, she would recall words from her father's books, from one book [*The Principles of Human Knowledge*]: 'It is evident to anyone who takes a survey of the objects of human knowledge, that they are either ideas actually imprinted on the senses or else such as are perceived by attending to the passions and operations of the mind. . . .'" Diony begins to actualize, create or order her experiences from chaos by searching for their reality deeply within herself.

Because the possibilities of human creation are infinite, Miss Roberts suggests a double infinity, the infinity outside the self leading to the infinity within. (Diony, knitting wool in the house at the plantation "Five Oaks," is "aware of infinity outward going and never returning.") The self becomes as precious as it is powerful as the fountainhead of reality: ". . . [A]s long as they ['all the choir of heaven and furniture of the earth, in a word, all those bodies that compose the mighty frame of the world'] are not actually perceived by me, or do not exist in my mind, or that of any other created spirit, they must either have no existence at all, or else subsist in the mind of some Eternal Spirit." Creative inspiration accompanies Diony's personal responsibility to actualize the vast contents of this eternal mentality: "Her thought leaped then beyond articulation and settled to a vast passion of mental desire. Oh, to create rivers by knowing rivers, to move outward through the extended infinite plane until it assumed roundness. Oh, to make a world out of chaos." Within this philosophical context, the characters and events of *The Great Meadow,* whether fictional or factual, must be re-created by Diony, in whose search for identity they become united.

As Diony matures, her role as integrator of the novel's material is realized. Her role is developed in four stages: Discovery of Self, Extension of Self, Awareness of the Great Design, Interpretation of the Great Design.

In the first stage, Diony becomes aware of the separateness of her identity. While taking a bath "she saw the whole of herself at one time, a revelation." From a hilltop she strains to detect the pattern of "Five Oaks," and in her mind she travels to the main house of the plantation and to her sleeping place in it, that physical spot closest to self: "There, surrounded, she passed more inwardly, wrapped in the warm throb of her blood, her brown hair drawn over her face. Shut securely within, wrapped in a garment of sense, she went within again and yet again, a hushed voice farther within saying some mute words, as 'come,' or 'here you will find me.'" In this early stage of self-awareness, Diony remains powerless to include within it that which is not intrinsically personal.

Because the vista of Diony's personal experience is severely limited, she must extend it by increasing her awareness of other people and by personalizing experiences outside but parallel to her own. The girl's inability in initial attempts at extension is obvious in the first half of the novel, even when Miss Roberts so orders the material that the relationship between personal experiences and those not intrinsically so is implicit in the text. Donning her mother's full dress, comparing it to the childhood frock of her sister and recognizing the fact of her own adolescence, Diony fails to relate her situation to that of the American colonies, even though she is very aware of current events: "Diony felt the year go past and once, for a moment, she heard the great ticking. There was war in Boston, the colony fighting the King's men. Some said that all the colonies would snatch themselves free."

Miss Roberts depicts in her heroine the individual's struggle to extend the search within by including contemporary men and events in awareness of self. The girl's compulsion to create or recreate others becomes obvious with Berk Jarvis: "A deep wish arose within her on the instant, a wish to know more of the structure of his being, to know all that he remembered and all that he saw as he looked outward, and to touch all with her own knowledge, and to know what it would be to him to go." When Berk returns to Virginia from Kentucky before his marriage to Diony, she attempts to personalize the frontier savagery of his tale by blending it with her own response and the physical reactions of his audience: "Thomas was talking now and Diony glanced from mouth to mouth and saw these instruments distorted, mouths become some strange flutes or horns, shaped cunningly to play out war, to cry out battles. Thomas Hall's mouth bent and twisted now as a clattering bugle blowing the science of war, making philosophy out of stories of death."

The growth of Diony's powers of extension prepares her for marriage to Berk, enables her to detect in Nature what corresponds to her new experiences, and to discover a universal pattern residing in an eternal mentality. The girl's growth is evident when Thomas Hall refuses to allow her to travel with Berk into the wilderness of Kentucky and begins his "great musical protest" on the anvil. Despite this protest, Diony is able to see in the dispersion of the morning mist that she would finally go with Berk. The sunlight corresponds to the knowledge that she would go, the mist to the doubt and anxiety caused by her father's opposition: "The sunlight fell broadly, widely dispersed after the brilliant mystery of the early morning, and Diony knew that she would finally go with Berk wherever he desired, the clear fine light of the morning being spread over the whole ground

with equality and evenness." Thomas Hall's protest is the inability of age to cope with progress and in Nature is paralleled by the falling leaves: "The morning had cleared and the bright mist was gone, and the last of the leaves were falling."

It is old Thomas Hall, however, who communicates to Diony the responsibility of individuals to seek a pattern in their individual lives harmonious with the "Great Design of an Eternal Spirit." He maintains that it is the duty of each man to try to understand and interpret the events of history and the laws of Nature to discover among them his place is the universal plan.

> Men, he said, were the mouths of the earth, and through them the earth spoke in the general; but a man, in the particular instance might understand and interpret and might see the signs put forth by the Author and Designer to reveal what lay under the outer show of properties and kinds. He told of one wonder after another, of deviations from the natural law, but he told again of how the kept law is a greater marvel than the deflected law, and how it, by its sufferance of the other, continually reveals a purpose beyond the knowledge of men. He would not stand in Diony's way, he said, smiling, although she had planned to take a long step and to go a long journey.

Diony's attempts to pattern the events of her life depict the individual's struggle to satisfy the demands of reason. She is aware of a lapse in understanding when order is not to be found in her activities. During her journey over the Wilderness Road, the havoc of her surroundings troubles her deeply within until she can replace it with order: "But presently the evenness of their going, Berk to the fore, Muir, herself, and Jack, moving in the design already known to her by the way of the plodding horses, restored a design of evenness and order to her mind, and their going became of the order of law, as if they carried the pattern of law in their passage."

As Diony develops in creative power, minor compromises to her reasoning part become unnecessary. Such development is evident before her departure from Albemarle County, when Thomas Hall gives her his mother's pin, one with a delicate tracery of leaves and stems and "made in someplace beyond the sea." Diony is able to evaluate the heirloom, that it is a link, like herself, between the past and the future, a symbol of the inevitability of the journey she has undertaken. "She accepted the pin at last without regret, taking it to herself completely because she was going far away from any report of her grandmother Luce and would henceforth have of her only what she then had in her being." A bit later, as she rides away from "Five Oaks," she celebrates, to the tinkling of the pack horse bells, the full meaning of her journey to Kentucky:

> Suddenly, in the tinkling of the bells, she knew herself as the daughter of many, going back through

> Polly Brook through the Shenandoah Valley and the Pennsylvania clearings and roadways to England, Methodists and Quakers, small farmers and weavers, going back through Thomas Hall to tidewater farmers and owners of land. In herself then an infinity of hopes welled up, vague desires and holy passions for some better place, infinite regrets and rending farewells mingled and lost in the inner tinkle and clatter. These remembrances were put into her own flesh as a passion, as if she remembered all her origins, and remembered every sensation her forebears had known, and in the front of all this mass arose her present need for Berk and her wish to move all the past outward now in conjunction with him. They went quickly along the road, the seven pack horses making a seven-keyed music that played about her choice and wrapped it in a fine pride. The air was pleasant, the hills vividly seen, the water in the creek being bright over the brown of the stones.

As Diony gains facility in evaluating the significance of her experiences and in patterning them with what she has included within herself of the universal plan, she moves toward the fulness of her maturity and begins to realize her place among the strong women of the frontier. This is dramatized when she meets Daniel Boone. He tells Diony that he has never been lost in the wilderness: "'I was bewildered right bad once for as much as a week, but not lost. I never felt lost the whole enduren time.'" Diony applies his words to his place in the Great Design. "'You always felt at home in the world. . . . You felt at home with what way the sun rises and how it stands overhead at noon, at home with the ways rivers run and the ways hills are. It's a gift you have, to be natured that way.'" At this encounter, Diony herself has not been blessed with Boone's illumination, is not able to detect the inevitable pattern of her life. "'I'm not the Boone kind. . . . I never was. . . . I'd be more at home somewheres else . . . I don't know where. . . .'"

Diony's discovery of her place in the universal plan, her becoming Boone's kind, results in the limitation of her freedom of will and marks the final stage in her development. Her acceptance of Berk's death and decision to marry Muir dramatize her attempt to be guided by what she interprets as signs of the universal will. Frantically searching for a pattern to guide her in the above decision, she leaves her spinning to contemplate the moon. The text reads: "The night was full of spring and death, birth coming forth by compulsion to meet death on the way." The death mentioned suggests Berk's, Diony's sense of loss, her widowhood, while the spring death confronts is that of Diony and of Kentucky. Straying outside the gate of Harrod's fort, Diony recalls her conversation with Boone: "'Boone said he was never lost in a wild country, not in his whole enduren life,' she cried, walking aimlessly. 'I'm a strong woman, but I'm not of the Boone kind. I'm of the other sort.' She cried and wept, shuddering without tears."

When Diony attempts to return to the fortification, she finds the gate locked for the night; thus Diony, due to her widowhood, is symbolically shut out from participation in life. Her disharmony with the joyful expectancy of the people of the new nation and with the renewal of Nature becomes obvious: "Dead sticks and old leaves broke under her tread but the undetermined life that blew about in the spring air was nowhere broken." She realizes, as she sits on a log and listens to the owls crying around her, the significance of being a discordant note in the universal harmony. Basing her decision upon what she can sense and understand, she relegates Berk to the past and accepts the proposal of Muir. "The cry of the owl was known to her as something true or false, and she loaned her ear to it acutely to try to discover if this were the true sort or the other kind." Diony's choice manifests the extension of her creation of self. To discover her inevitable role, she must grope toward forces outside herself:

> She continually remembered on her side that the whole mighty frame of the world had no being without a mind to know it, but over this lay another way of knowing, and she saw clearly how little she could comprehend of those powers on the other side, beyond the growth of the herbs and the trees, and to sense the hostility of the forest life to her life, and to feel herself as a minute point, conscious, in a world that derived its being from some other sort. The indefiniteness of the outside earth, beyond herself, became a terror.

Berk's return does not indicate Diony's complete failure to read the signs of destiny and make the right decision regarding her marriage to Muir. Her second marriage and the birth of Muir's son, Michael, had successfully tapped the resources of her womanhood, resources precious to frontier life, which would have been wasted during the years of Berk's absence. Diony recognizes, however, the inevitability of her final choice of Berk over Muir, for it is the reasonable choice, his having had first claim to her. After Berk relates to his wife the story of his escape from the Shawnee cannibals and how he convinced them of the indestructibility of his reasoning part, she recognizes that, as in her decision to marry Muir, reason must guide her. Having at last found her way and become one of Daniel Boone's kind, she celebrates the dawn of reason upon her own life and the coming of civilization to the frontier: ". . . [S]he felt that the end of an age had come to the world, a new order dawning out of the chaos that beat through the house during the early part of the night. Her thought strove to put all in order before she lay down to sleep. She felt the power of reason over the wild life of the earth."

The last pages of *The Great Meadow* are reminiscent of the conclusion of Boone's memoir in the Filson history. The great pioneer also celebrates the extension of civilization:

> Many dark and sleepless nights have I been a companion for owls, separated from the chearful society of men, scorched by the Summer's sun,

and pinched by the Winter's cold, an instrument ordained to settle the wilderness. But now the scene is changed: Peace crowns the sylvan shade.

What thanks, what ardent and ceaseless thanks are due to that all-superintending Providence which has turned a cruel war into peace, brought order out of confusion, made the fierce savages placid, and turned away their hostile weapons from our country.

REASON AND CONSCIOUSNESS IN *THE TIME OF MAN*

Elizabeth Madox Roberts' *The Time of Man,* first published in 1926, includes three connected stages of human development, from the discovery of identity to the awareness that the discovered self forms a link in the unbroken chain of human history. These three stages include: the discovery of identity through the rational ordering of rudimentary consciousness; the blending of identity with another in love; the blending of identity, through the procreation of children, with human history. My treatment of this novel will concern three levels of the first stage: the ordering of conscious states through rhythms and patterns; the attempt to grasp such states by contrast with opposite states; the attempt to grasp such states through analogies and symbols.

Although consciousness indicates the entire area of mental attention, what has come to be called stream of consciousness fiction is chiefly concerned with rudimentary rather than highly rational states of consciousness. Stream of consciousness fiction is concerned, therefore, with what is termed the pre-speech level of consciousness, that level engaging the least amount of reason, not ordered enough by reason, in other words, to be communicable in the spoken word. The first stage in *The Time of Man* concerns Ellen Chesser's attempts to bring reason to her pre-speech consciousness, to order that level of consciousness toward awareness of her own identity. Ellen's attempt toward self-definition from the pre-speech level is demonstrated during a dough-mixing scene when, wasted by domestic hardship, she strives to recover the sense of self:

Circles flowing outward through thick oily dough, flowing outward through heavy pliant matter, rising and falling, nearer and farther, renewed and sinking back and renewed, over and over, in a perpetual orbit. She watched the flow as she stirred and stirred, looking at the motions and leaning a little nearer. Suddenly a soft whisper came to her lips as she looked, as she penetrated the moving mass, a whisper scarcely breathed and scarcely articulated, as would say, "Here . . . I am . . . Ellen . . . I'm here."

The movement from the pre-speech to a higher level of consciousness is not necessarily to the speech level. (This is particularly true in Ellen's case, for, being the daughter of a migrant tenant farmer, she is not articulate. For example, she is completely incapable of ex-

pressing her feelings in a letter to her fiance: "In the end she wrote that when he came she would have much to tell, trusting that she would then find a way." The advance of reason can be evidenced by the discovery of rhythms or patterns in rudimentary consciousness. Ellen's ability to associate musical rhythms with her vague sense of physical development occurs when, during the planting season at Wakefield's farm, she takes the throbbing sound of a guitar into the pulse of her own awakening body: "Strong rhythms came beating in the rich harmonies, coming out of the pasture that all day had been sopping mud—tonk tonk a-tonk tonk; quick notes danced under the firm beat of the chords and other quick notes ran lightly down while the mellow chord waited. The tones came very beautifully over her waking body, but they were scarcely recognized until they began to recede into the night, growing less vividly present as consciousness came."

Ellen's attempt to control the apparent chaos of experience is dramatized when she tries to understand the feelings of her future husband, Jasper Kent, when he is falsely accused by an enemy of intentional barn burning: "She tried to assume his chaos of anger and his confusion and to bring her more ordered knowing to it." Because such rescuing from chaos implies the personalizing of experience, rational control becomes equated with the discovery and extension of identity. Ellen's ability to organize mentally what she cannot fully grasp is evident in situations like the one in which the conversation of older women on marriage takes on the pattern of an operatic trio, quartet or quintet. When she hears this conversation at a dance, she desires marriage, and the pessimistic voices take the form of a disillusionment which drums into an order in her consciousness:

"If the girls only knowed what they wanted they'd take the fellow that could make, that had property."

Another voice, high pitched: "And easy-goen, not stingy."

"When I was a gal they was six horses tied to Pappy's fence of a Sunday. But I set my head on Joe and looked like I never see any the rest."

"If gals only knowed one is as good as another, but you couldn't tell a gal e'er a word."

"A good provider is what you want."

"When I was a gal they was six horses tied to Pappy's fence and one of them was Sol Beemen's. He lives over in Nelson now and look, he owns a fine farm. His wife gets ten dozen eggs a day, they say. Sol Beemen."

"Over and above that, one man is as good as another, and all about alike if gals only knowed."

"But lands sake! I must have Joe. I never see Sol When Joe is by."

"I ain't never been sorry I took Dan, though. I never see the day I'd take anybody else."

"Hear Lute O'Shay talk!"

"When they say, 'Come see the bride,' I always say, 'I'd rather see her in ten year. I'll wait my time,' I say."

"Yes, teeth all gone. Back crooked."

"I say I'd rather see her in ten year from now."

It is in the fugal patterning of various strains of consciousness, rather than in this direct ordering of dialogue as it penetrates the ear, that Elizabeth Madox Roberts demonstrates most sophistication as a stream of consciousness writer. Her achievement in such patterning is obvious when Ellen weaves the delight she takes in the new wedding hat of her friend Rosie O'Shay with talk over the closing of a road by Scott MacMurtrie, an important land-owner. These two strains of thought resemble the voices in a contrapuntal musical composition. The development of the first voice occurs when Ellen's delight in the wedding hat is coupled with her feelings for Jonas Prather, who is present at the time. The second voice provides a counter melody and a counter development when the mutterings of the men over Scott MacMurtrie's closing of the road develop into plans for an appeal to Scott's wife, Cassie Beal MacMurtrie, who is unknowingly being betrayed by her husband and sister, Amanda Cain. As the men talk of Cassie, Ellen becomes conscious of the despair of that woman's love. This awareness of despair provides a contrast to the hopeful love for Jonas, which is simultaneously entertained by Ellen: "Jonas smiled across at her in the way of the summer that was past and her need for him grew with the deep glow of the flower and with the soft rich mesh of the velvet petals. 'Let Cassie MacMurtrie do hit,' a voice was muttering. 'Let Cassie.' It came to her then, looking into the heart of the blossom as she held the hat in her hand, that it could only be a short while now until Miss Cassie would know the thing she herself knew, for everybody now seemed to know of Scott and Amanda Cain. 'Let Cassie.' They had only to wait, a voice said. 'Bide your time and don't say e'er a word more about that-there road. I give Scott a week now and that's all.' Another voice, high-pitched and angered, foretelling, 'I know Cassie Beal. I went to school along with her down on the creek.' . . . 'Let Cassie MacMurtrie do hit for us. I know Cassie Beal. She's made outen fire and hell. Bide your time.'"

The movement toward rational control becomes evident in Ellen's ability to contrast one strain of consciousness with its opposite. This ability is obvious in the above passage at the point where she becomes aware of the despair of Cassie's marriage, as she [Ellen] is conscious of it, against the hope of her own love for Jonas. In the following passage Miss Roberts isolates the contrast suggested in the previous one. While she explains the state of Ellen's consciousness in rational terms, this

state, as it deepens, falls below one of communicable awareness. As Ellen reviews the MacMurtrie situation and begins to be vaguely aware of Miss Cassie's feelings, her reason becomes incapable of embracing them and jumps to her own opposite feelings. The hope that Ellen cherishes for Jonas' return and her marriage to him, the nucleus of her feelings, closes about her consciousness and squeezes out the hazy notions she entertains about Miss Cassie. Ellen then begins to attach herself to items of objective reality in harmony with her hope. She associates the return of Jonas with a spring thaw:

> Miss Cassie would know soon and when she knew there would be a different feel in the air and another way of thinking. . . . Her own reverie closed about her and she left Miss Cassie out, centering about her ribbon and her bit of lace, her hems and buttons made neat, and, as her reverie grew and became real, the air grew mild and the hold of the frost, at first loosened, became lax and then fell away. The ice would rot away altogether and the earth become pliable, and her reverie grew intense, remembering each moment of the night when Jonas had stayed long with her, distilling each moment of its sweeter fruit.

Ellen's ability to control various states of consciousness by making analogies between them and external objects or situations introduces the final section in her progression from the pre-speech to a higher rational level of consciousness. This ability is apparent in its simplest form when she parallels her own mental states with times of the day and year: for example, Jonas' departure to seek another job becomes associated with night; the alienation caused by Jonas' guilt for siring another woman's child becomes associated with winter, and Jonas' failure to write or return becomes associated with the grass growing tall at MacMurtrie's farm after the cheated Cassie hanged herself.

The handling of Miss Cassie's suicide is significant because it enhances the development of Ellen's consciousness rather than furthers the plot of the novel. Although Ellen had been one of those who rushed to MacMurtrie's farm when the old Negress servant rang the bell for help, Miss Roberts withholds the details of the suicide for forty pages, until the time Ellen discovers that Jonas has married another woman, Sallie Lou Seay. In her attempt to rationalize the painful effects of being the victim of Jonas' unfaithfulness, Ellen identifies with the dead Cassie, and the details of the hanging are revealed as they drum through her consciousness. The dead face evolves into a symbol of Ellen's grief:

> She saw even more vividly the face on the floor, two men leaning over it, one preparing it for life and the other for death; and then the coroner, "Yes, she tied the rope herself, that's plain," and to herself, sworn to speak the truth, "Do you know any reason why Cassie MacMurtrie would hang herself?" Every human relation faded out and every physical tie. Up was no more than down

and out undistinguished from in. Friends and possessions and relatives were gone, and hunger and need. She was leaning over Miss Cassie as she lay on the floor—Ellen and Miss Cassie and no other. She leaned over the dead face until she was merged with its likeness, looking into the bulging eyes, the blackened mouth, and the fallen jaw.

Immediately preceding the passage quoted above, there is another which connects Miss Roberts' concern with stream of consciousness to the general meaning of *The Time of Man:* "She could never be the same, could never go back. What had some withered, ancient past, tenderly remembered but dry, flat, apart, to do with this life she had now? Let it get out. Let it go. She could never be the same as before. Jonas had been in her thought too long so that her very breath had grown up around him." The fact that Ellen will never be the same after her experience with Jonas implies at once the discovery and development of her identity, the basic theme of this novel. The logical conclusion of discovery of self is the discovery of the necessity to include within one's identity the identity of another. Thus Ellen feels a compulsion to love, and when she loves she feels the identity of her lover pervading her identity. This marriage of identities and the experience of parenthood which results from it are accompanied by the awareness of a more universal identity shared by one's children and, in turn, with one's parents. Ellen Chesser eventually identifies herself, therefore, as part of an unending chain of humanity, as an instant in the time of man.

Mary Niles   (essay date 1969)

SOURCE: "Social Development in the Poetry of Elizabeth Madox Roberts," in *The Markham Review,* Vol. 2, No. 1, September, 1969, pp. 16-20.

[*In the following essay, Niles addresses the theme of social awareness in Roberts's poetry.*]

An examination of the poetry of Elizabeth Madox Roberts makes evident that she attempted to develop in this genre many of the same thematic concerns which she forcefully presented in her novels. Therefore, if one is to study thematic variations and development in these poems, wherein thematic ideas of the novel are somewhat fore-shadowed, it is helpful to have studied at least Roberts' four major prose works—*The Time of Man, The Great Meadow, My Heart and My Flesh,* and *He Sent Forth a Raven*. (For a discussion of which of Roberts' novels are her best, see Campbell and Foster's *Elizabeth Madox Roberts: American Novelist,* Earl Rovit's *Elizabeth Madox Roberts,* and Wagenknecht's *Cavalcade of the American Novel.*) It is also expedient to be acquainted with her Journal, in which the poet sets down information helpful in explicating her themes.

However, even without knowledge of Miss Roberts' other writings, it is still possible to see that in her po-

etry this woman most essentially is again attempting to develop what may loosely be termed her social theme. Other thematic concerns are of course present in her poetry. But it is this idea of man's need to grow more socially aware, an idea that is first generally suggested in *Under The Tree* and then slowly expanded in *Song in the Meadow,* that forms the thematic backbone of the Kentuckian's poetry volumes.

To understand this social development it is valuable to glance briefly at the social thematic concerns that Miss Roberts develops in the four novels. Here, the author moves from *The Time of Man,* an introspective novel which is almost a-social, through *The Great Meadow,* a book that introduces readers to geographic and historical and social insights beyond an internal consciousness. This social theme becomes even more prominent in *My Heart and My Flesh,* a novel that begins to probe sociological matters such as the racial problem and society's response to it. And, this thematic concern finally blossoms forth in *He Sent Forth a Raven,* a book filled with questions of war, the future of man in a war-filled world, and the effect which this disturbance has on individual lives.

For various stylistic and thematic reasons, ones which could be explored at another time, the poet does not as clearly present her social theme in the poems as she does in her novels. However, her attempt to make a social statement in poetry is still vigorous and successful enough so that these poems may be studied in terms of her attempt at a "social evolution." Therefore, it will be the purpose of this paper to generally suggest how this evolution is structured, to indicate a few of the poems which mark its stepwise development, as well as to mention several related themes concerning the beauties of the physical world, and the need to introspect, to wonder, about it and its people.

In the strictest sense of the word, *Under The Tree* is not a collection of "social" poems. However, in its emphasis on observation and introspection, this collection remotely prepares the reader for the more obvious social themes of the 1940 collection, and for being able to make some sort of response to them. Many of these 1922 poems are ones which can most easily be appreciated and explained as simple children's lyrics. The majority are carefully constructed short works which admit the reader into a world of childhood innocence and pristine beauty. These lyrics, as Campbell and Foster indicate (*Elizabeth Madox Roberts*), are ones which capture the freshness and vigor and charm of clear first impressions, whether these be visual, auditory, tactile or gustatory.

Roberts' clear impressions of various colorful sights are exemplified in her depiction of various natural objects. In **"Horse"** one notes the long brown nose of a horse that stands beneath a little shade tree, his mane splashed with the patches of sunlight that have filtered through the leaves. In **"The Worm,"** a worm whose skin is "soft and wet" puckers himself into "a little wad," soon to go "back home inside the clod." A panther whose "streaks are moving on his back" is seen in **"In the Night."** **"The Branch"** depicts little black spiders that walk on the top of the water, "keen-eyed, hard and stiff and cool", while the poet's eye catches on a "moth wing that was dry / and thin . . . hung against a burr" in **"Cold Fear."**

In her description of people, Miss Roberts' vision is also keen. **"A Beautiful Lady"** presents a lady wearing little pointed shoes, her best hat one "silvered on the crown." **"Miss Kate-Marie"** also mentions a lady whose dress is "very soft and thin," and adds that "when she talked her little tongue / Was always wriggling out and in." Also, in **"Autumn Fields"** the old man has "stick tights on his clothes / and little dusts of seeds and stems."

The sort of physical awareness which the poet wants her readers to develop—especially if they are to grow socially sensitive—is embodied in the more complex feelings of the child in **"My Heart."** In lines which involve both the auditory and tactile sense, the poem presents the child as thinking,

> My heart is beating up and down,
> Is walking like some heavy feet
> My heart is going every day.
> And I can hear it jump and beat.
> At night before I go to sleep,
> I feel it beating in my head;
> I hear it jumping in my neck
> And in the pillowcase on my bed.

Another manifestation of sound appears as the hens rub their feathers in **"The Hens"** and as the brook in **"Water Noises"** gurgles on its way. The tactile sense is again invoked in **"The Dark."** Here, Roberts writes, "a night fly comes with powdery wings / That beat on my face—it's a moth that brings a feel of dust . . ."

Smell comes alive in **"Autumn Field"** as the little girl "can smell the shocks and clods / and the land where the old man had been." **"At the Water"** offers "five little smells and one big smell . . . One was the water, a little cold smell." Finally, a poem which contains a number of these sensual images is **"Christmas Morning,"** a work often anthologized in children's magazines and readers. Its final four stanzas well indicate the aura of child-like innocence which these early poems are capable of evoking. Another poem interesting, direct and immediate in its effect on the reader is **"Little Rain."** Not only rich in succinct detail and verisimilitude, but also somewhat comic are the lines "A chicken came till the rain was gone; / He had just a few feathers on. / He shivered a little under his skin, / And then shut his eyeballs in."

However, as Campbell and Foster point out, *Under the Tree* is not merely a group of simple children's lyrics. It does contain poems which have distinct adult appeal. In the words of these two critics, this collection is "both children's verse of the highest quality and adult poetry

with a distinctly metaphysical character and appeal." Admittedly, these poems with a deeper character are few, but this select number of them is vitally important for several reasons. First, it is these poems which serve as vehicles for Roberts' poetic statements about man's ability to introspect, to wonder about his physical world. It is in these poems too, that the child who before only just saw, or felt, or heard, is now beginning to question the limits of this sensual knowledge, and to question whether there be any person with whom one can fully communicate, or fully understand. Also, it is with these few poems that some sort of thematic bridge between the merely sensory poetry of the first part of this collection, and the poems of the 1940 volume may be erected.

The sense of wonder which Roberts considered essential if any child or adult were to develop as a sentient, alive, and vibrant human being, one socially aware of other men, is depicted most noticeably in **"Mr. Pennybaker at Church"** and **"Shell in Rock."** In the former the little child studies Mr. Pennybaker as he sings out of key and rhythm, and wonders if "he knows it all / About Leviticus and Shem / And Deuteronomy and Saul." In the latter, the majesty of the powerful, swirling sea is pondered. **"The Pulpit"** again mentions wonder in a church setting, and **"A Child Asleep"** presents a child looking at, and then wondering about a playmate who is sleeping. **"In the Night"** recalls the fear and terror experienced by a little child whose imagination has created a vicious panther out of a clothes-laden chair. In a similar vein, **"Strange Tree"** recreates the terror felt by a vividly imaginative child on his way alone through a dark deserted wood. Finally, on a more metaphysical level, **"The Star"** simply states a truth that is often sensed by children and adults who realize that they and their world are only very small ingredients in a vast universe. "Oh little one away so far / You cannot tell me what you are, / I cannot tell you anything," says the lone helpless child who gazes heavenward. **"August Night"** also mentions the wonder and fear felt by someone contemplating the unknown reaches of space.

In summary, then, the majority of the poems in *Under the Tree* are interesting only because they are rich in the keen sensual images of the land and people that Roberts knew and loved. A few verses of the collection, however, are important because they operate on both the physical-descriptive and the psychological or metaphysical levels. These few are introspective poems rich in inner reverie, but ones still quite a-social in the strictest sense of the word. However, it is "metaphysical" poems like these that Miss Roberts develops for the 1940 collection, into ones even more introspective and more strictly social in theme.

Song in the Meadow, as Campbell and Foster suggest, can be divided into three sections. The first is a grouping of love lyrics, ones which are again introspective and filled with the joy and mysterious wonder of love. The second is the section which finally brings the reader to Miss Roberts' poems of social protest. Part three, called "Legends," contains only a few poems, many of which are experimentally symbolic. For purposes of this discussion, the poems of this final short section need not be considered.

The awareness of the physical world which marked *Under the Tree* is also evident in this second volume. However, in this 1940 collection, the poet does not nearly so often devote a poem solely to depiction of a lovely vista, the smell of a field, or the laugh of frolicking children. Here, along with the sharp physical images the poet so deftly creates, there often appears mention of unsettled emotions and various social problems. In other words, whereas *Under the Tree* with its lovely images and child's point of view could be considered a children's book, this second volume, with its serious, often pessimistic thematic statements, is more adult reading.

In Part I of *Song in the Meadow* poems like **"The Song of the Dove," "Summer is Ended,"** and **"A Girl at Twilight"** are again most "purely" descriptive. **"A Girl at Twilight"** offers some strikingly beautiful thought-provoking images of dusk falling over the Kentucky farmland. And **"Summer is Ended,"** along with the two cradle songs **"Sleep, My Pretty, My Dear"** and **"Blessed Spirit, Guard,"** exemplify the rich fullness of love, the joy to be derived from being alive to one's environment, and the mystery which surrounds life and love. **"Love in Harvest,"** which again contains the spirit of innocence that characterized the pristine world of *Under the Tree,* is also ultimately concerned with the joy derived from the good harvest and the good rural life. This rich, joyful world is set forth, too, in **"Love Newborn"** and **"Ellen Chesser's Dream of Italy."**

However, with **"The Lovers,"** this mood of happy innocence is lost. In this poem, constant thoughts of slipping "down deep / to the cold river bed / Where pulse is still / And breath is shed" keep haunting the "I" of the poem. It is only a final surge of love of life—an exuberant burst like that in **"Love in Harvest"**—that prevents a suicide from occurring. As the last optimistic lines say, "But life held me close/ In a firm embrace, / Life cradled my feet / and kissed my face."

It is with **"And What, Dear Heart"** that an even more outspoken transition is made from poems concerned mainly with love and delight to the more socially thematic Section II of *Song in the Meadow.* In this two-part poem, "And What, dear heart, will we see / As we take the road to the town" is the refrain spoken by one lover to another as they walk through the countryside. In answer to this query the first three stanzas of the poem depict some delightful rural sights that will be seen, heard, or smelled by the pair. "Men will be sowing and planting and taking / The cattle to graze, or the clover be stacking, / And off in the barn be mending and grinding, and down in the wheat will the reapers be binding." Also, hounds and cattle will be calling, birds will be mating, men will be telling of their joys, and

happily singing about their loves. However, the last twelve lines of the poem present a change in tone and mood. It is revealed here that in addition to these simple joys, the lovers also hear and see men speak of problems of a bleaker, more pessimistic nature. Roberts writes,

> Men will be speaking together to tell of the wars,
>   and be asking, and leaving
> Their labors to hear.
> And the hearing be grieving.
> The voice of the air loud speaking and making
> Of hunger and death, and our brothers be dying,
> And over the earth will the war witch be flying
> With pestilence . . . wrath,
> With famine and pillage and death

It is mention of these problems of war, hunger, and death and the grim reality that men, our brothers, are dying, that characterizes most of Section II.

It must be emphasized here that for Miss Roberts, the appreciation of the various sights and sounds of one's world, though vitally important to an individual's becoming more deeply alive, was not sufficient by itself. As she often indicated in her novels, in addition to perceiving the variety and flux of one's world, man could best attain fuller human stature by attempting to somehow order some of the disharmonies in his milieu. Though this attempt would possibly involve some suffering, it was this try at eradicating disorder, at being concerned for others, that was the key to man's maturation as a human. Developing this concern—actually a process of learning to love others—was absolutely necessary in a world that so often had forgotten how to understand and love, a world, which as a consequence of this lack, was now struggling with the burdens of wars, famine and other forms of human injustices.

It is essentially this message about the necessity that man love man—a message clearly set forth in *He Sent Forth a Raven*—that the poet here attempts to give us, in "The World and the Earth," the second section of *Song in the Meadow.* To clearly depict the plight of many contemporary men—men essentially all equal, who should be treated as equals (**"A Man"**)—Roberts fills these poems with images of cold, various sorts of deformation, and death. In **"Disconsolate Morning"** the setting is "the sparse season, the lean time before the cold spring." Here, the "cold birds," the "silver-black" water in the mill, "gaunt foxes," "gaunt hounds" and "spent boughs" are part of the "lean day," a day in which "the wood-path leads nowhere." **"The Ancient Gulf"** also speaks of "a lean time under the grass / A cold season for the rock." In **"Night and Storm,"** the wind howls, "the stricken bell . . . shrieks along the storm," while "the turning sky is black."

Against this symbolic landscape, Miss Roberts points up the injustice involved in men receiving insufficient and unfair wages, in their resulting poverty, and hunger, and also notes the horrors of the awful situation of war. Although in **"Man of the Earth"** a "little beggar woman," a "one-legged clown," and the "poorhouse yard" are strikingly juxtaposed, it is in **"The Lean Year"** that the harsh realities of poor wages and poverty are most succinctly set forth. Here the farmers with "knotty hands and sinewy limb" stand in tatters and wonder "Why" or "What for." Line twelve, "Who pinched and squeezed and drained them thin?" powerfully summarizes the mood, tone, and thesis of this poem. **"Man Intolerant"** discusses another form of injustice. Here, "brothers in flesh" are slaughtering each other in the "act of hatred and intoleration." Here, Miss Roberts states that each man is responsible "before the nations" for the edicts and practices "being bartered." She further reminds the reader that although man's spirit has waned in modern times, and his "poor small hold on God's favor is loosed," he still must see that he is adrift on some course that he must try to chart to the best of his ability. For man not to care where he himself or his fellowman may wander is to hurl the human race "toward the last holocaust, the infinite merciless first-last unknowing abyss."

Finally, the horrible nature of war is revealed in **"The Battle of Perryville,"** and **"Corbin the Cobbler."** In the former, a man reminisces about a long ago battle until "his face is bent and turns to tears." In the latter a bitter cobbler remembers the gas of the Argonne forest and says that today "a man couldn't trust they'd keep the war down." In lines heavy with understatement and irony this artisan, who has "left his important intentions / Along with his leg in the far side of the water," continues to state his feeling that "there'd always be war to take the boys," "there'd still be a new way to line up the nations."

For Miss Roberts, the only hope for such a pessimistic, problematic world seems to be man himself, and his awakening to man. In **"Conversations Beside a Stream"** she offers her reminder that in life—that "multiple flow of human onward-going being" from which no one escapes—"the dread-sick world is not all." For the poet, there is more to life than dissatisfaction and failure. There is also hope. But if one is to hope and realize any tangible rewards from hoping, it must be remembered that "one man himself alone / Cannot make a song." Man needs man, and must come to realize this truth if the race is to survive. In the last poem of this section Miss Roberts tries to show clearly to others what she herself so clearly sees about man and this hope for him. She writes, "We are sitting beside the stream, beside the River of Man's flowing / life, his time, his way on the earth." For her, the hour is late, so man must immediately begin to build a new world, one wherein man will not be burdened with the woes we now suffer. To create this place one can "start anywhere! . . . start with man's liberty . . . his democracy or . . . warm love." What could become a reality, the Kentuckian believes, is that the peace and love described in **"Evening Hymn,"** the last poem of this section, could extend to all men. It is the poet's great hope that all men could grant to each other the wish "Quiet and love

and peace / Be to this, our rest, our place," when "the day is done; / the lamps are lit."

This, then, is but a cursory look at Miss Roberts' attempt to develop a social message through two volumes of her poetry. The scope of this survey has been quite broad; therefore, it is hoped that some idea of the general thematic direction in which the poet tried to move has been established—without losing sight of the social thematic value and lyric beauty of specific lines. Of course, to best understand this social trend, one must read and analyze as much poetry as is available, as well as several of her novels. Hopefully, as more of Roberts' poems are located and published, it will become possible to further substantiate and clarify the social thesis of this paper.

Wade Tyree (essay date 1977)

SOURCE: "Time's Own River: The Three Major Novels of Elizabeth Madox Roberts," in *Michigan Quarterly Review,* Vol. XVI, No. 1, Winter, 1977, pp. 33-46.

[*In the following essay, Tyree assesses the strengths and weaknesses of* The Time of Man, The Great Meadow, *and* My Heart and My Flesh.]

In 1926, at the age of 45, Elizabeth Madox Roberts published her first novel, *The Time of Man*. It was immediately not only a popular success but a critical one, widely reviewed and praised. Sherwood Anderson said of it, "A wonderful performance. I am humble before it" [cited in Harry Modeen Campbell and Ruel E. Foster's *Elizabeth Madox Roberts: American Novelist,* 1956]. Two years later, Ford Madox Ford wrote in *The Bookman* that it was "the most beautiful individual piece of writing that has yet come out of America." By 1938, Miss Roberts had to her credit six more novels as well as volumes of poetry and short stories. One of the novels, *The Great Meadow,* is still considered among the best American historical novels ever written. Since her death in 1941, however, she has received little attention. In part, this can be traced to the reception given her 1935 novel, *He Sent Forth A Raven*. While this book probed more deeply into contemporary problems than her other works, its complexity and symbolic density presented formidable difficulties for her readers. Critic and general reader alike pronounced the book confusing and incoherent, a failure both philosophically and artistically. Her reputation continued to decline until today, 35 years later, she is in such obscurity that few recognize her name. Yet she has a style which is extraordinarily lyrical, precise, and intense, and an insight both profound and moving. She mastered the novel of sensibility and achieved her desire to combine realism and poetry—to get down on paper the inner consciousness of her heroines. She is a fine, interesting novelist who deserves reappraisal by present-day critics, particularly for the three novels considered here. I think it probable that with such attention she will eventually be judged as in the first rank of twentieth-century American novelists.

Elizabeth Madox Roberts was born on October 30, 1881, in Perryville, Kentucky. She was a descendent of Anglo-Saxon pioneers who had settled in Virginia during the eighteenth century, then migrated over the Wilderness Road into Kentucky soon after Daniel Boone blazed the trail into that virgin country. Reared in genteel poverty, a situation not uncommon in the post-Civil War South, she was interested in writing from early childhood. Though an excellent student, lack of funds along with a delicate constitution and frequent ill health prevented her from continuing her formal education beyond an abortive first year at what later became the University of Kentucky. She turned to school teaching and from 1900 to 1910 taught in remote country schools around Springfield, Kentucky. She continued to write poetry privately and never gave up hope of going to college. Finally, 18 years after her first attempt, she was able to make a second, successful, try for college. She matriculated at the University of Chicago in 1917 and graduated four years later with a Bachelor of Philosophy with honors, as a member of Phi Beta Kappa, and as the recipient of the Fiske Poetry Prize. She was 40 years old. The rest of her life, which was to be less than 20 years, she spent writing novels, poetry, and short stories. Unfortunately it was also spent battling constant illness and the malady, Hodgkin's disease, which eventually killed her in March, 1941.

Three underlying themes form the basis of all Roberts' works. First, her heroines are always engaged in a search for self, and their success in life depends upon their success in self-identification. A second theme is that the land is the wellspring of man's life. Only by maintaining a closeness to the soil can life be either productive or satisfying. Her heroines cannot sustain their balance nor can they embrace others in love unless they are a part of the dynamic powers of nature; if they lose this rapport they become disoriented, ill, and finally unable to function. The third major theme is that man's life on earth is but part of a cycle and has a meaning far beyond itself. As Roberts wrote in her journal notes, "The life design is one of birth, rise, decline, rise, decline . . . with the rise and fall again through the growth of these new beings spreading outward like Time's own river." The two novels generally agreed upon as Roberts' outstanding works, *The Time of Man* (1926) and *The Great Meadow* (1930), explicate these themes fully and with authority. However, there is a third novel, less well-known and not so well-received, which deserves equal attention—*My Heart and My Flesh* (1927). While the usual Roberts' themes are not as perfectly developed here as in her most famous works, the powerful treatment of the evils of miscegenation make this an important book in American literature and a fascinating link between Twain's *Pudd'nhead Wilson* and Faulkner's "The Bear."

The first of Roberts' books, *The Time of Man*, is stylistically and thematically the most perfect of her works. This is the story of Ellen Chesser, daughter and wife of wandering Kentucky tenant farmers. The story line is simple; it is in the method of presentation that the uniqueness of the book lies. While there is an external chronological narrative, the book is really the story of Ellen Chesser's soul, of the expanding of her sensibility and her consciousness—the story of the development of a woman seen from the point of view of her inner self. Nothing is real until it is realized in the mind of the heroine, and the book follows her outward journey by charting her inward one. Ellen herself is a representative of wandering man in a life cycle that is never ending. Roberts knew the tenant farmers from first-hand knowledge; she had lived among them and taught their children. But she felt the presentation of her material could not be effectively handled in a straightforward manner if the theme were to be of universal implication. "Admonitions for a plan—it is not to be autobiography. It must be higher art than that. Myself against the chaos of the world. Art before chaos." One way Roberts conveys Ellen's inner state is to put the girl's mental life in physical terms. Ellen's abstract thoughts and her emotions are made concrete, are articulated as physical images and actions. The opening sentence of the book, "Ellen wrote her name in the air with her fingers, Ellen Chesser . . . ," is a picture of a child physically articulating an unspoken inner thought—that she is a separate, identifiable being. Had Roberts simply said, "When Ellen Chesser was fourteen, she realized that she was a separate person," it would not have given a picture of Ellen actually perceiving the thought. Roberts' technique is much more dramatic, and therefore more effective.

The most graphic illustration of Ellen's mental life reflected in physical aspects occurs when her husband carries on an adulterous affair with a neighbor woman. He coincidentally impregnates Ellen, and in order to assuage his own guilt falsely accuses her of adultery. Ellen suffers a difficult and uncomfortable pregnancy as a result of her knowledge of his infidelity. The strife and discord of the family during this time are outward manifestations of Jasper's sin. Concomitantly, Ellen's suppressed violence poisons the helpless body within her own. Her inability to either control or ignore her husband's actions shatters her inner life as well. When she thinks of Jasper lying with Hester Shuck

> in the crab thicket she wanted to go there and take her by the throat and choke the life back into her body until it hardened for death at last. At night, lying alone in her bed, she would want to go to the thicket with a knife in her hand, and her mind would keep remembering the knife in the kitchen beside the cups on the shelf. . . . Then she would . . . know that she would never so fall from her pride as to quarrel with Hester Shuck or to spy on the thicket or the river.

Ellen's hate and her pride combine to enthrall her in a destructive, frustrated state which destroys the health of the body within her body. She is unable to eat or to work or to sustain her family's physical needs until she can free herself from her emotional dependance upon Jasper. When the baby is born sickly and doomed to die, it is apparent that the child has been blighted by the ugliness of Jasper's conduct and Ellen's bitter acceptance of this. The baby's first cry, "a strange wail, the thin cry of the new-born, seemed to be coming from Jasper as an old withered man, and Ellen covered the child with her arms and hid it in her bosom." These two physical acts, the stoical suffering alone and the acceptance of the wretched result of hate, make clear Ellen's inner consciousness of what is happening in her life. There is for her a fusion of experience and action that is more "real" than any fact of knowing, for it is the essence of knowledge.

Ellen's life is one of extreme poverty and enduring struggle; she never owns a home, not even temporarily. But though her life is one of wandering and of unceasing toil, it is not a tragedy but rather, a triumph over mundane reality. At the end of the book, Ellen thinks of life and muses,

> Life and herself, one, comprehensible and entire, without flaw, with beginning and end, and on the instant she herself was imaged in the lucid thought. A sense of happiness surged over her and engulfed her thinking until she floated in a tide of sense and could not divide herself from the flood and could not now restore the memory of the clear fine image, gone in its own accompanying joy.

Man's life on earth is important because he can create his own kind and pass on life itself. Ellen does emerge triumphant, for though she has but meager material possessions, she has independence, love, and the ability to create intact and strengthened by her own experiences. The stark simplicity emphasizes the cyclical nature of Ellen's life, and the universality of her concerns gives the story its epic sweep and focuses the reader's awareness of Ellen as not just a simple folk figure, but the symbol of mankind and his wandering over the earth. The intense subjectiveness of the narrative sustains Ellen in the reader's consciousness while the style, unaffected and limpid, adds to the verisimilitude of an inarticulate though sensitive country girl.

The Great Meadow is the story of the early pioneers who followed Daniel Boone over the Trace into Kentucky and fashioned life out of the wilderness. But the book is more than an historical novel: it is an epic story of the eternal pioneers who are always going forward to create new worlds out of raw nature, of the Adam and Eve put down into a garden of Eden to make out of the fusion of themselves a civilization. The book also shows the typical Roberts heroine on a journey of inward discovery, and again the narrative structure is simple and direct. The time span is from 1774-1781, the period of

the Revolutionary War, and there is a tripartite structural balance of Diony as a girl in settled Virginia, as a bride travelling to the wilderness and making a life there for her new family, and finally as a widow confronted with the necessities of increased self-reliance and the ultimate choice of her own destiny.

Roberts' theme in *The Great Meadow* was "to make a world out of chaos," and Berk and Diony were to typify the male and the female elements that were necessary to coalesce in order to produce this world. In her own words, "Berk . . . the type . . . who would drive Diony beyond herself, driving man forward, thrusting outward and forward through the trees and the stones. Attaining something beyond themselves. But when they arrive there it becomes the new beginning. The cycle of man on earth." This is the same theme as in *The Time of Man*—the endless, perfect cycle of perpetual labor to fashion life from experience and to always start anew—but this time it is to be shown as a dual effort of man and woman together. Furthermore, there is added significance here in the goal itself. It is not just the new and better place to live that Ellen Chesser was reaching for; it is Kentucky, the garden of Eden, the promised land. As such, it is a symbol of the goal of all American pioneers who pushed westward and settled the country. The Great Meadow is Kentucky, but it is also Ohio or Oregon or anywhere that people went to build a good and fruitful life for themselves and their children.

Roberts' secondary theme in this book, the necessity of the interaction of the male and the female, adds to the richness of both plot and characterization. The wilderness cannot be tamed, a new world cannot be made, unless Diony and Berk go forward together. Only by a spiritual combining of the sexes is civilization born, just as the physical combining produces a child. Diony, the essential woman, would be content to realize new worlds within herself, but her inner needs compel her to go beyond safe contemplation into dangerous action because she has a greater need—to find her being in the man she loves. And Berk is the essential man, the one who in spite of a need and a tenderness for woman would leave her behind because of his overwhelming drive to assert his physicalness upon the outside world. Roberts develops this theme by portraying Berk as the activist on an unending quest and Diony as the tender of the hearth, the one who faithfully waits behind.

As with Ellen Chesser, the development of Diony is shown internally. In this book, there is a specific mention of Bishop George Berkeley and of his book, *The Principles of Human Knowledge*. Berkeley was one of the major philosophical influences on Roberts, and Diony illustrates graphically this tenet that matter is of no importance until it is perceived by the senses. Nothing has any real existence outside the mind for Diony, and this is how she views all her experiences. Only as she perceives the wilderness internally does it become real to her. Concomitantly, she visualizes what will be made of the wilderness because of Berk and her and people like them. When she sets out on her bridal journey over the Trace, she understands in a blinding flash of insight that she is "the daughter of many" and the symbol of those who carry life forward to new lands. When they surmount the great wall of stone that is the last obstacle to the promised land, Diony is so overwhelmed with the experience that the physical hardships of the journey are forgotten and she feels only "a freshness as if the world were new-born."

Another significant aspect of the novel is the rooting of Diony and Berk and of all nature in sexual terms. The book does more than just portray Diony and Berk as Man and Woman; the relationship is explicitly physical and sexual. A basic metaphor throughout the book, this treatment of sex as an elemental life force is beautifully and powerfully handled. In passages reminiscent of D. H. Lawrence, Roberts concretizes the emotional abstraction of sex and at the same time poeticizes its physical element. When Diony looks at Berk her emotional response to him wells up in a physical reaction that makes her body, quite literally, feel her love. "Then her eyes would search his averted face and his drooping eyes, his unguarded mouth, and she would love him with a rush of passion that almost stilled her heart in its beat . . ." When her father refuses his consent to let Diony go with Berk, he denies Diony the right of her love as well. She feels this stifling of her passion as a physical thing and his words cause her to be "sickened by them until her breath was slow in her throat and her head bowed." Just before Diony and Berk's child is born, Berk must go farther into the wilderness to make salt and find game, and they know that Diony will probably bear the child before he returns.

> "You're a strong man, Berk Jarvis," she said. "But one strength you have not got." She stood, large and full, beside the door.
>
> "A woman's work is woman's work," he said. He smiled then, and of the beauty of his delayed smile went swiftly to some hidden part of her and made life beat more swiftly there.

Roberts clearly intends Berk, the male, to be characterized as a person of action and not words. Berk was "a quiet man" and part of his contrast to Diony lies in his very inarticulateness, emphasizing therefore his physical prowess. Unfortunately, this characterization is shattered at the supposed climax of the novel. Berk's mother has been killed in one of the numerous Indian raids. Determined to secure revenge, he goes off in search of the war party and is captured. After he has been gone for three years, Diony is persuaded he is dead and remarries. A year later, he suddenly reappears; just as suddenly Roberts gives him the tongue of a backwoods Homer. His eloquent rendering of his odyssey in the far country and struggles to return wins Diony back. But the reader balks. That the silent Berk would emerge from years of privation and grim survival on an animal level suddenly gifted with a golden tongue is beyond the credibility of the most willing imagination.

In spite of the failure of the novel to end with a glorious climax that would have given it the epic sweep Roberts intended, *The Great Meadow* is still an impelling book. It convincingly depicts an incident of American history as a chapter in the story of man's civilization of the world, and it does this solely through the slowly expanding consciousness of the heroine. The novel thus is metaphysical as well as historical.

My Heart and My Flesh is a psychological and tortured Faulknerian work with a shocking subject delineated in gothic horror. Theodosia Bell, a pampered and neurotic young woman of superior birth, is forced by the profligacy of her family to lose her mind and nearly her life. "It is the story of a woman who went to hell and returned to walk among you." In spite of obvious differences, there is a great similarity between this novel and *The Time of Man*. The basic theme is much the same: man's time on earth is one of continual wandering and searching in the face of adversity for a better life. The ultimate goal is the discovery of the supremacy of the inner self and one's ability to express love which can happen only by remaining close to nature. But there is in this second novel an emphasis on a theme not found in *The Time of Man*. It is the danger of overweening pride, the fatal *hubris* of Greek tragedy. There is a knowledge of the self as evil and of the nature of evilness. Theodosia is just the opposite of gentle, humble Ellen Chesser who never expected to achieve more than the most modest position in life. When she does realize the power of her own affirmative nature, Ellen is really changed only in the sense of discovering something which she had possessed from the beginning. Conversely, Theodosia Bell has been born in an advantaged situation and she takes great pride in her family, personal charm, security, talent, and ambition. She is, like Ellen, extraordinarily sensitive, but her sensitivity serves as a selfish attribute, for she views others in the context of her ambitions. So, unlike Ellen, Theodosia must undergo a profound change; she must lose everything of which she is most proud, especially her high opinion of herself. She must learn that only her own spirit affirmatively rooted in love can overcome death. Until she is forced by the inexorable diminishing of her life to accept this bitter lesson, she is doomed to a process of degradation that carries her to the far side of hell. Roberts described Ellen Chesser's journey in search of her soul as one of "accretion" while she described Theodosia's as one of depletion:

> The method here was a steady taking away until there was nothing left but the bare breath of the throat and the simplified spirit. The work begins with a being who has been reared in plenty and security . . . Family . . . Wealth . . . charm . . . popularity . . . musical skill and . . . a boundless ambition. All these gentle conceits are gathered into the person of Theodosia.
>
> One by one these things are taken from her to the upbuilding of her understanding and the growth

of tolerance and wisdom through suffering. Each of these is lost and more.

The tone of *My Heart and My Flesh* is, until the last chapter, one of extreme tension. Theodosia's search into the meaning of life is violent, anguished, and ruthless. At the nadir of her despair she cries out, "Oh God, I believe and there's nothing to believe." The horror of Theodosia's life is depicted by the horrible things that happen to her: one lover is burned to death, another callously and openly jilts her, a third seduces her when she is too weak to resist him. Her friends desert her and her family dies or disappears. Her father attempts to seduce her repeatedly, with the monstrous climax coming the moment after her grandfather (*his* father) dies and father and daughter are standing at the deathbed. The most staggering blow comes when she discovers she has three black, illegitimate siblings, for in the South of her day this was a shame not to be acknowledged. Still more terrible, the black brethren were the result of a liaison without any human tenderness or even fleeting concern; rather, they had been spawned in a moment of ruttish and casual carnality, her father having simply relieved himself into the female body most available when his lust pulled him into bestiality. One of those animal couplings was with a half-wit who lived in the alley behind the jail and it produced an animal of its own—the idiot stable boy, Stiggens. The horror is compounded for Theodosia when she finds she is not only heir to the results of her father's evil, she is heir to his propagation of evil. This is illustrated in a frantic and terrible scene where she incites one black half-sister to murder while bringing together the other with their black half-brother, Stiggins, in drunken incest. She is responsible for carrying to an awful conclusion the evil that her father begat.

This theme of miscegenation is the primary interest of the book today. It appears in no other Roberts' work and, in fact, her treatment of what was to become one of the dominant themes of Southern fiction is one of the first and most powerful of any artist. Except for Mark Twain's *Pudd'nhead Wilson* (1894), no book by a major writer discussing miscegenation openly had yet appeared. Because Roberts' treatment is so much more ruthless and direct than Twain's, the impact has a searing intensity that shows more clearly what a tragedy this was for the South. The writer who most immediately comes to mind as comparable in this regard is Faulkner, and the interesting thing here is to realize that this novel was published (1927) long before anything which Faulkner wrote on the subject appeared. Though Roberts' handling of this theme is not entirely successful since she does not pursue the evil to its ultimate end as does Faulkner, its inclusion makes this novel a major work.

Structurally, however, the book is flawed. The tone of her novel is uneven, ranging from a *Wuthering Heights* intensity to the calmness of a pastoral idyll. The moment of Theodosia's salvation is an unconvincing climax because at this point Roberts turns aside from her clear perception that miscegenation inevitably begats evil and violence and that the sins of the fathers can never be fully atoned for but must be passed on to each new generation. However, in spite of its flaws, *My Heart and My Flesh* is of great importance, both historically and intrinsically.

All three of these novels are fine enough to be compared favorably with the best of American fiction. At the same time, they illustrate Roberts' main problem as an artist. While she is able to portray her female characters sharply, deeply, and totally convincingly, her male figures never seem quite real. Her most memorable male is Stiggins, the half-witted Negro stable boy in *My Heart and My Flesh;* but, though powerfully drawn, he is hardly a man as much as he is an animal. Jasper and Jonas, the two men most central to Ellen Chesser's life in *The Time of Man,* are depicted with such vagueness that it is as though they are the same man wearing different masks, or perhaps different men wearing the same mask. In *The Great Meadow,* Diony is fully developed at the expense of Berk. Since he is never seen as an entity or a force apart from her, the lopsided portrayal of the characters weakens an intended theme of the novel: that male and female need to equally interact to successfully wrest life from the earth. Roberts' women are more than real; they are reality—the perfect unity whose very existence is self-expression. They swallow up the actuality of others by the beingness of themselves. In this light, it is fascinating to read the following note Roberts wrote to herself:

> There is so much more to a woman than there is to a man. More complication. A woman is more closely identified with the earth, more real because deeper gifted with pain, danger, and a briefer life. More intense, richer in memory and feeling.
>
> A man's machinery is all outside himself. A woman's deeply and dangerously inside. Amen.

It is interesting that she felt this way. It is also interesting to realize that all Roberts heroines are either raped or seduced or deserted by the men they love. One is arrested at the power and anger of the scenes of defloweration. It is in these scenes that Roberts reaches her strongest and most vivid effects. I am not suggesting that she had a psychological bias against men; she was not a feminist like Ellen Glasgow, and many of her male characters are warm and good. Journeyman, in the novel, *Black Is My Truelove's Hair,* is one of her most appealing characters. What I am suggesting is that Roberts' ability to turn inward and see life in the Berklerian sense is not only her greatest strength but her greatest weakness, for she could see only what was inside herself. When she depicts men as vulgar and brutal, it is a reflection of what she specifically knew about them—that their "machinery" (interesting word) was "outside."

Nevertheless, this flaw is not a fatal one, for there is much to appreciate in Roberts' best work. Nothing has been said here of her stylistic perfection and she could justly be praised for that alone. Haunting phrases and richly evocative descriptions can be found on any page of her books. Furthermore, the content of her work is of first importance. The problems with which she concerned herself are basic to humanity and she probes deeply into the meaning of life. Elizabeth Madox Roberts was a serious artist who felt keenly the responsibility of "art to enlarge one's experience, to add to man more tolerance, more forgiveness, to increase one's hold on all the out-lying spaces which are little realized in the come and go of every day." She was dedicated in her desire to expand the ability of the novel to add to man's understanding. While she is certainly a Southern writer, she is no more "regional" than is Twain or Frost. Indeed, she is more than merely an American writer, for her depictions of wandering man and the eternal quest for the meaning of life are both universal and timeless.

Anne K. McBride (essay date 1985)

SOURCE: "The Poetry of Space in Elizabeth Madox Roberts' *The Time of Man*," in *The Southern Literary Journal*, Vol. XVIII, No. 1, Fall, 1985, pp. 61-72.

[*In the following essay, McBride demonstrates the symbolism between the various homes of Ellen Chesser in* The Time of Man *and the character's stages of maturity.*]

As Elizabeth Madox Roberts' novel, ***The Time of Man***, nears its conclusion, the outer appearance of the heroine, Ellen Chesser Kent, reflects her inner wholeness. Indeed, the jubilant words of young Luke Wimble capture the aura of her full self-awareness when he exclaims, "You're a bright shiny woman, Ellen Kent . . . You got the very honey of life in your heart." Despite the fact that Ellen, her husband Jasper, and their five children are again journeying into the unknown, her spiritual pilgrimage flows securely toward completion.

The common areas of space and the "o'nary" objects of home—as Ellen would describe them in her backcountry way—have nourished this inner growth. Ellen's steady movement toward spiritual unity rests on her total willingness to allow her psyche to encounter and absorb whatever lies closest at hand; she is always open to a direct experience of things in themselves. By imagining actual events and places in the life of a struggling Kentucky tenant farmer, Miss Roberts is able to depict a psychological drama unfolding under the humblest of circumstances. Thus, Ellen Chesser lives with her parents Henry and Nellie in three homes before her marriage to Jasper Kent, and these simple homes, particularly her own bedroom in each house, firmly establish the wholesome pattern of Ellen's interior development. As protective spaces, these houses also have corresponding implications for the creative activity of the artist.

The works of French phenomenologist Gaston Bachelard express most effectively the importance of such an openness to the ordinary elements of life. A pioneer in the field of phenomenological studies, Bachelard regards the immediate receptivity to images as the key both to the nurturing of the creative imagination and to the understanding of how the imagination produces poetic works. In particular, his observations in *The Poetics of Space* can suggest to us how Ellen's innate ability to respond to the spaces and objects in her life has guided her way and enlivened her imagination. At the same time, they can aid in discovering the poetry with which Miss Roberts narrates Ellen's experiences as a young girl in a one-room house or a bedroom in the loft or beside the kitchen. Illustrating his remarks with examples from such poets as Rainer Maria Rilke, Arthur Rimbaud, and Charles Baudelaire, Bachelard conveys forcefully the significance of that interaction between the sensitive mind and the common areas of space it encounters: "Space that has been seized upon by the imagination cannot remain indifferent space . . . It has been lived in . . . with all the particularity of the imagination." His comments and poetic samples also enable us to see how Miss Roberts' novel demonstrates a keen perception of the workings of the human mind. The author, as well as the heroine of ***The Time of Man***, displays a rich imagination through her receptivity to the nuances of space.

As an artist, Miss Roberts' foremost concern in all her fiction is the dramatic portrayal of the inner psychic journey. For her, ultimate reality exists in the realm of the spirit; the outer physical world reflects and symbolizes the real absolutes, which originate in the human mind. The landscape of the soul is then made concrete by events and things that confront the mind in the world. She phrases her philosophical convictions this way:

> Somewhere there is a connection between the world of the mind and the outer order. It is the secret of the contract that we are after, the point, the moment of union. We faintly sense the one and we know as faintly the other, but there is a point at which they come together and we can never know the whole of reality until we know these two completely [quoted in Harry Modean Campbell and Ruel E. Foster, *Elizabeth Madox Roberts: American Novelist*, 1956].

Although all human beings attempt to make these connections, the writer is compelled to fashion the process into literary form. In ***The Time of Man***, Ellen's acute consciousness of the variety of spaces in her homes—their inner rooms, corners, stairways, and even their outer appearances—become, for her, moments of union between the two orders, and because as an artist Miss Roberts perceives the secret of these contacts, she is able to shape them into poetic form. She presents the unfolding of Ellen's separate self with all the emotional intensity and structural perfection that accompany great musical compositions. Symbol and image, prose and plot, combine to produce an experience akin to the full orchestration of a work by Beethoven or Mozart, two composers she often listened to while she was writing. As her biographers, Harry Campbell and Ruel Foster, describe it, her artistry "transforms what is called spiritual into the physical, the physicalizing which we have called the artistic word made flesh."

The Chesser family's tenant homes—small, poorly-equipped cabins on the farms of the Bodines, the Wakefields, and the Orkeys, respectively—reflect and nurture young Ellen's spirit. Although more or less formally unknown to her, she comes to intuitive understandings through her contact with them. For example, when by the light of the moon, she observes the glittering frost on her bedroom window, the image somehow symbolizes her own inherent awareness of the frigid barrier that arises between individuals, no matter how close they may appear to be. Despite the intimacy that has evolved between Ellen and Jonas Prather, and despite the spirit of friendship that has developed among the members of their youthful group, she instinctively apprehends the permanent and impenetrable separation dividing one human being from another. As in her mind that winter "the distances in the little room were magnified by the crystal of the cold," so also did the wall between people seem to be enlarged when she viewed the frost. While Ellen slept during the extreme cold of December, this "frost stood between herself and Jonas, . . . and between herself and Dorine was the frost and ice." In this way, spiritual realities that she gradually and often painfully learns to accept are made physical. Through the narrator of another novel, *Jingling in the Wind,* Miss Roberts insists that "life is from within, and thus the noise outside is a wind blowing in a mirror." Guided by this philosophy, she also makes full use of the changing of the seasons, the tilling of the soil, and the fixity of the mountains in order to embody particular truths that exist in Ellen's mind. But the emergence of these absolutes, the beginning of the psychic journey, occurs for Ellen, as it does for all of us, in the house.

The house, as a primary image in human life, represents a guardian of mental as well as material needs. The house provides the spirit with a haven for solitude and dreaming just as it offers the body protection from nature's extremes of hot and cold, rain and drought. Bachelard reminds us that the house, like "all great, simple images," reveals "a psychic state"; the house "bespeaks intimacy" because it connotes shelter and safe-keeping. The very essence of the house, Bachelard states, is "protected intimacy" because it shields the fragile emerging self. Also, the straight lines and right angles of even the humblest home somehow fulfill our need for "discipline and balance"; "our consciousness," says Bachelard, "is drawn toward verticality." This comforting structure, then, is an especially important place as well as an essential image for the beginning of an individual's physical and spiritual journey through life, an insight that distinguishes Miss Roberts as an artist who foreshadowed in 1926 the principle ideas set forth

by Bachelard in 1958. She understood the prime importance of the house for early spiritual nourishment. When her heroine, fourteen-year-old Ellen, looks at Hep Bodine's farm house, the young girl intuitively reacts to the sight in this deeply human way:

> In her mind the house touched something she almost knew . . . something settled and comforting in her mind, something like a drink of water after an hour of thirst, like a little bridge over a stream that ran out of a thicket, like cool steps going up into a shaded doorway.

A natural contemplative like the writer who created her, Ellen responds instinctively to the world about her, recognizing in the house a sanctuary for both the outer and the inner life.

The importance of the house in the human psyche begins with its confirmation of an individual's basic notion of being. We are born with the capacity to comprehend our own existence, and, as our first cradle, the house activates this inherent concept. However primitive, the house then helps to further the distinction between the I and the Not-I. No longer trailing clouds of glory, the developing child comes to recognize her own existence as a separate entity that is distinct from all other objects in the world. As a very young child, Ellen had recognized her separateness from the other articles and creatures in her first home: the brick floor, the boiling teakettle, the "tall white cat." This fundamental awareness of individual being enables her to proclaim triumphantly throughout the novel that she is "a-liven!" Alone in her room in the house on the Wakefield farm, for instance, she can avow that despite her painful rejection by a lover she is "still herself." "I'm Ellen Chesser," she says, "and I'm here, in myself." In the face of the many assaults against her sensitive nature, she is consistently able to affirm her own existence as meaningful because it has been nurtured within the protective walls of a simple structure.

Ellen's receptiveness to the sight of nooks and corners continues to protect her awareness of existence. Of this instinctive need for privacy, Bachelard observes that "one can undoubtedly become more aware of existence by escaping from space"; the walls of a corner, for instance, form a "chamber of being." He offers one of Rainer Maria Rilke's poems ["Mein Leben ohne mich"—"My Life Without Me"] as an illustration of the role of the corner in strengthening the concept of selfhood:

> Suddenly, a room with its lamp appeared to me, was almost palpable in me. I was already a corner in it, but the shutters sensed me and closed.

Ellen is immediately attracted to such a cozy place during the family's first night in the one-room house on Bodine's land. She imagines herself describing the experience to Tessie, her friend-from-the-road, and so, as Ellen and her parents prepare to sleep on the floor, she mentally relates to Tessie that "before night I saw a cubby hole against the chimney and a cubby hole is good to put away in." Without attempting to rationalize her reaction, she somehow comprehends that the warm arms of the corner will satisfy her need for solitude, which in turn, as Bachelard asserts, will nourish and individualize her imagination.

In times of personal crisis, our being is again confirmed as the memories of our own childhood resurface in our minds. When we experience this remembrance of houses past, Bachelard explains, we again "participate in this original warmth." Ellen comforts herself this way on two occasions. Frightened by strange happenings in each instance, she unwittingly seeks reassurance by recalling the comfort and security of her earliest protective space. First, when she moves on to the Wakefield's property, her family's unfamiliar tenant house provokes a recollection of her childhood home. As she moves about in this new home, she suddenly remembers events and objects from the long-forgotten one:

> She had been six years old then and she had lived in a house under some nut trees. . . . She could remember the strange smell that hung about the nut trees.

Later, Ellen again participates in this same type of warmth during the depths of her despair after Jonas Prather forsakes her to marry Sally Lou Brown. Intuitively, the rejected young woman explores her memories more deeply this time because she has a greater need for them:

> She had turned her mind upon some happenings of her infancy. She had lived in a house under a nut tree. The rinds of the nuts broke off in beautiful smooth segments and inside was the pale yellow hickory nut to be laid away to dry for the winter.

The memories of the invisible embrace of her first house and the roundness of the hickory nut (an example of the circularity which Bachelard describes as also confirming our being) help Ellen to recover from the psychic wound she has received.

This primary image, an ordinary house, however, not only confirms and protects a sense of being; it also nurtures and enriches the imagination, mostly through the seemingly non-productive activity of daydreaming. And in spite of—or perhaps because of—her meager surroundings, Ellen Chesser displays a rich, creative imagination, which Miss Roberts illustrates in dramatic ways. The roof that leaks in the cabin at the Wakefield farm allows the water to run down the walls of Ellen's bedroom. The resulting brown stains on the walls change with each rainfall, assuming various shapes, such as "monsters," and "demons impaled on trees" or a "woman in a long shawl . . . walking through the crosses. . . ." Each new precipitation brings fresh material with which her imagination can experiment. The

stairs in this two-story house also provide ample opportunity for Ellen to rehearse graceful movements as she imagines herself "to be stepping down hard white stairs, walking on wide stairs, a low wind fluttering her sleeve." When she actually mounts these stairs, she yields to her "sense of pageantry" as she attempts "different methods of descent, walking demurely, gliding down stiffly, or tripping down with dancing steps." The knobs, latches, and closets in this house also provide her with opportunities for investigations and discoveries. Her day-dreams, which feast upon all the objects about her, nourish her self-individualization, a necessary element for her spiritual development. With her portrayal of Ellen's imaginative mind, Miss Roberts reminds us of the essential qualities of the house so that we may not forget that even the plainest of homes can provide these basic opportunities.

Ellen's imagination, as it develops from girlhood to young womanhood, is frequently engaged in fantasizing about ideal houses, an activity which in itself signals her approaching maturity. To convey this inner growth, Miss Roberts presents a vivid stream of ever-changing images: Fifteen-year-old Ellen would dwell in a brown house with large stairs, a tower, and a "fountain a-drippin out in front"; her own room in the small cabin would be "pink and blue," and she would have "things to put in drawers and drawers to put things in. . . ." This is the romantic house of the teenager; the house of the young woman who is making plans for marriage takes on a more practical appearance. As she sits with Jasper Kent, the bride-to-be envisions a structure with mended shutters and a porch that does not leak, a fine parlor for sitting in and a full view of hills, some of them rolling "and some plowed." Thus, although her ideals become more realistic, she does not lose her capacity for creative imagination.

An important element of Ellen's imaginative faculty is her appreciation of form, which is evident from the beginning of the novel. She is attracted to the Bodine house, especially to the relationship of the house to the trees that appear at first to be part of the structure itself. She wonders if the farmer realizes "how the yellow gables came out of the tree boughs, all set and still, fixed behind boughs, gables fitting into each other, snug and firm." When Ellen moves closer, however, she realizes that her perception of these relationships is inaccurate; she sees that "the trees that had belonged to the gables when she had seen the house from the field now stood off along a fence to the rear." These trees were not really attached to the house itself, and this new arrangement somehow violates her sense of form, her notion of how the lines of a fine house ought to be configured. To show her displeasure she sticks out her tongue and then labels the house "a poor trash sort of house." In the next cabin, at Wakefield's farm, Ellen places a glass jar containing a branch of thorn blossom on a shelf above the fireplace. Like the speaker of Wallace Stevens' poem, "Anecdote of the Jar," she proposes to tame the wilderness by satisfying her own sense of form and proportion.

The persona of the poem speaks metaphorically of placing a jar on a hill in the wilderness of Tennessee so that this artistic object takes "dominion everywhere" [Wallace Stevens, *The Palm at the End of the Mind*], whereas Ellen graces the living room of a tenant home with the beauty of a growing plant. Both arrangers, however, are concerned with the aesthetics of relationships. Ellen's intuitive attempt to bring order and design to the chaos of the harsh physical planes is analogous to her instinctive struggle to wrest an orderly pattern from the emotional events of her life.

As an artist, Elizabeth Madox Roberts shares with her heroine this appreciation of form, this desire to bring order and design to chaos both visually and mentally. Her papers at the Library of Congress reveal just how compelling this idea was to her; she describes it as "one evidence of an unseen power at work" and as

> the apprehension of form by the mind, the comprehension of pure form, the mind demanding that things, lines, masses of matter be placed in certain relations to give satisfaction or pleasure . . .

She further states that she believes "that the great value of sacred writing is . . . in their [sic] aesthetic and comforting design, their approach to pure form." Again, in reference to her own preference for line and design over color, Miss Roberts writes elsewhere that ". . . if I were an artist, I should like to be a fine draftsman rather than a painter . . . in the line I see the absolute, the making of design" [cited in Frederick P.W. McDowell, *Elizabeth Madox Roberts,* 1963]. And finally, of her own literary attempts, she observes,

> The difficulty is to choose material from the chaos about me and the apparent chaos that is myself . . . if I cannot trust the fibers of my being to make the pattern, to write in its delicate traceries, there *will be no pattern*. [cited in Campbell and Foster]

As Ellen's perceiving mind attempts to force her sense impressions into meaningful patterns, so also did her creator struggle to select and place certain images and events in a pleasing artistic arrangement that would convey her sense of the importance of any individual's development through an imaginative ordering of his or her surroundings.

This preoccupation with masses of matter, things, and lines in pleasing relationships is the real problem for artists, states Susanne Langer [in *Philosophy in a New Key,* 1942]; their ultimate quest is "the *perfection of form.*" A study of Roberts' seven novels, according to Isabel Hawley, reveals that "the concern for the imposition of 'aesthetically satisfying' form is one of the most prominent and characteristic aspects of Elizabeth Madox Roberts' thinking," though in Hawley's opinion, this tendency exerted a "negative" influence on her later works. In *The Time of Man,* however, Miss Roberts is in total control of this concern. "Structurally," claims

Earl Rovit [in *Herald to Chaos: The Novels of Elizabeth Madox Roberts,* 1963], "it is an almost perfect book. . . ." The desire for perfection of form is perhaps what most attracted Miss Roberts to the works of Beethoven and Mozart; their masterpieces represent a balance between the rational and the irrational, the classical and the romantic, which the human mind constantly craves. In Ellen's story, the artist's search for significant form results in a successful balancing of two elements—form and content—in order to convey the unfolding of her heroine's realizations.

To dramatize the wholesome evolution of Ellen's inner life more fully and to depict the restorative powers of ordinary places more authentically, Miss Roberts draws from the insights that depth psychologists confirm. By her judicious use of dream imagery, she is able to portray what C.G. Jung terms the compensatory nature of dreams. Jung stipulates [in *Man and His Symbols*], that the "general function of dreams is to try to restore our psychological balance by producing dream material that re-establishes, in a subtle way, the total psychic equilibrium." Thus, when deeply hurt by the superior attitude and deliberate snubbing of Joe Trent, fifteen-year-old Ellen climbs up to her small room in the loft of the cabin at Bodine's farm, and eventually, the "well-being of sleep" comforts her body. This same "well-being" speaks to her, reminding her of her beauty and repeating to her, "it's unknowen how lovely I am." The rippling anapestic rhythm of the words themselves reinforce the harmonious flow of a mind that welcomes the information offered to it by the unconscious—an example of how Miss Roberts' poetic prose contributes to the meaning.

In the Chesser's second cabin, on the Wakefield farm, Ellen's dreams continue to restore her psychic balance. Heavy with the gloom of adolescent despondency over the meaning of existence and weary from the physical demands of farm work, she sobs over the threatening images of a futile old age. But, during her sleep, the "comforter" returns to remind her of her loveliness, and she is again able to rejoice because she is "a-liven." Three years later, the voice again reminds a dejected and listless Ellen that despite her rejection by Jonas, she is still worthy and beautiful. In her dreams, "a deep sense of eternal and changeless well-being suffused the dark, a great quiet structure reported of itself. . . ." In this dream, the voice alone is sufficiently strong and deep, requiring no image at all to convey its metaphysical truth.

Ellen's bedroom in the third house, on the Orkey property, is the epitome of a room that can function as a space for healing her psyche and, at the same time, act as a symbol of the whole process. Withdrawn into herself because of Jonas's desertion, she finds her small room snug and dry while she awaits the wet relief that will come later with her own tears. In this haven, Ellen feels the womb-like protection of "the enclosing walls," while, at the same time, the room and its contents represent her state of mind. Here Miss Roberts captures that distinctive atmosphere we often give to a place when we are experiencing a strong emotion. Our own sorrow may fill a room as it enshrouds every object and invades every space. The white-wash on the walls reflects both Ellen's attempted obliteration of the memory of Jonas and her sterility of mind, and the chest standing alongside of the wall opposite her bed becomes a casket in which she buries her love for Jonas. For her, "it was a pleasure to lock the chest and slip the key onto the high shelf where it lay out of sight." Bechelard again articulates for us the significance of such use of the space within a chest:

> Every important recollection . . . is set in its own casket . . . The pure recollection, the image that belongs to us alone, we do not *want* to communicate . . . [e]very secret has its own little casket.

This observation also points out just how conscious Miss Roberts was of the poetry that inhabits ordinary areas of space. Now, because Ellen is open to the sight of places and objects that can contribute to her own healing, she is able to survive what to other young women in her society might be the onset of an embittered life. She has allowed the poetry of space to minister to her spirit.

Gradually, therefore, Ellen begins to open the chest more frequently to put in the money that Jasper Kent entrusts to her. And when her father's accident and Jasper's subsequent help with the farmwork promote the gradual process of healing, the trunk begins to lose its hold on her mind. For, as Bachelard further remarks, "chests . . . are objects *that may be opened* . . . from the moment the casket is opened . . . a new dimension—the dimension of intimacy has just opened up." Her spirit thus restored, Ellen hurls Jasper's name "at the stiff white walls" one night, and later in the season in her moonlit room, she realizes that she will marry Jasper and go with him wherever he chooses. She understands that she must return to life, that she must begin the journey again. Her restored unity is suggested by the "square of white light on the floor," for as Jung tells us, "quadrangular forms symbolize conscious realization of inner wholeness." When Jasper is forced to flee the area, Ellen returns the money he had given to her, and does so, finally, because she was rid of the memory of Jonas:

> The chest was no longer locked for it was empty of any treasure. Its key lay on the floor and its lid stood open . . .

Confident that Jasper will return for her in secret, Ellen is ready to begin life anew, having been strengthened in a room that is also emblematic of her renewal.

The design of the novel then presents Ellen, assisted by the basic qualities of her three homes, developing into a wholly integrated, mature human being, a bright and shining woman. She does not have to cling desperately to any single moment or idea and demand that it remain in a petrified state, because she is aware that other moments and ideas of equal or greater significance will follow. To a certain degree, she no longer needs a permanent house for psychic shelter since she has somehow become her own house—a separate, independent, and sound structure. Ellen can now withstand impermanency and travail because she has learned to depend on her own inner resources. When we remember "'houses' and 'rooms,'" Bachelard points out, "we learn to 'abide' within ourselves."

Although the last section of *The Time of Man* is more compressed than the earlier parts and includes many serious family problems, the conclusion does not appear abrupt or somber. Ellen and Jasper Kent, with their growing children and few possessions, load a wagon in the darkness to begin anew in another place. But the final sentence—"They asked no questions of the way but took their own turnings"—conveys a sense of their appreciation of the present moment and their confidence in a future place. The wandering tenant farmers gradually grow dimmer in our minds as the characters in a film would slowly disappear from our sight, leaving only the impact of their unending odyssey. Their constant journeying is the final image as it emphasizes that the movement of life must always be forward. The Kent family, as well as we the readers, are forever pilgrims, and all our sojourns are more enriching when we become aware of the poetic power that exists in "o'nary" places.

Wade Hall (essay date 1986)

SOURCE: "Place in the Short Fiction of Elizabeth Madox Roberts," in *The Kentucky Review,* Vol. VI, No. 3, Fall, 1986, pp. 3-16.

[*In the following essay, Hall discusses the importance of place in short stories by Roberts.*]

Picture this:

> Joan went down the path to the henyard, her mother's voice still telling her to feed the brooding hen. Away from the voices of the house she entered into the mid-morning quiet of the farm. She stopped at the hen's nest and she ran her hand among the soft feathers of the brooding mother, her sense of the place spiced with the odors of sweet lime and the odors of feathers that lay decaying in the dry dust under foot.

Or this:

> The path wound as feet had made it, swerving to the right or to the left. Infinities of rises, hillocks, low difficulties which the feet met, all feet, daily, and she was at the back door under the arbor where the old grapevines twined stiffly, her ear ready for the cry of the door when it should come at the end of the beating of her footsteps. She

touched all these things without care, happy among them, feeling them with the senses and with memory.

These passages are from the opening of **"The Scarecrow,"** one of the seven stories in Elizabeth Madox Roberts's first collection of short fiction, *The Haunted Mirror,* published in 1932. They demonstrate Roberts's sure talent for establishing quickly a sense of place in her stories. It is a talent she exhibited in all her fiction—long and short—as well as in her poetry. It is a talent she shares with other writers, of course, particularly those from her native South.

Place is where things happen. In fiction it is not especially significant in itself. But when it informs, shapes, and reinforces what people do, then it becomes critically important. This is the kind of importance that place had to Roberts and to her work. Her stories—what happens and to whom—are shaped by place, just as she was shaped by the circumstances of her birth in Perryville and her growing up in Springfield and Washington County, Kentucky. Her world is as ordinary and as extraordinary, as predictable and as unpredictable, as good and as evil, as the people and the land she well knew.

Roberts was so skilled in creating credible places that we believe her—at least we suspend our disbelief—when she introduces us to people and plots that may be beyond our usual experience. We will accept fantastic incidents, incredible characters, poetic folk speech. We even believe such a story as **"Children of the Earth,"** her Kentucky version of the medieval *Second Shepherd's Play.* The world of that story is one where the attempt to pass off a bleating sheep as a crying child could happen. And in **"Love by the Highway"** she creates another world in which it is reasonable to expect people to talk like the lyrics of a folk song. Here a young wife works by the side of the road in a potato patch. As she waits for her elderly husband to die, she sings a ballad about a lover "who will come from the highway." Indeed, he does. And when she asks who he is, he answers: "Sing a song of one in want of a lover and I came, is who I am." He continues to speak in lines of ballad poetry, and we continue to read because in the world of this story, it could happen.

In Roberts's short fiction, place can determine many things, and it can mean many things. It can determine and demonstrate tone, speech, folkways, history, psychological maturation. It can even lead to a mystical identification with the total universe.

Roberts published only a handful of stories, thirteen in all, in two collections. There are seven stories in *The Haunted Mirror,* published in 1932: **"On the Mountainside," "Sacrifice of the Maidens," "Record at Oak Hill," "The Scarecrow," "Children of the Earth," "Death at Bearwallow,"** and **"The Shepherd's Interval."** Overall, this collection appears the stronger of the two. The second was published in March

1941, the month of her death in Orlando, Florida. It is entitled *Not by Strange Gods* and contains **"The Haunted Palace," "I Love My Bonny Bride," "Swing Low, Sweet Chariot," "Holy Morning," "The Betrothed,"** and **"Love by the Highway."**

Does Roberts merit serious study as a writer of short fiction? Frederick McDowell judges that "Miss Roberts was . . . an accomplished but not an outstanding writer of short stories" [*Elizabeth Madox Roberts*]. He even quotes Roberts, who wrote, in an undated letter to Marshall A. Best in the early 1930's, "I do not think that the 'short story' is a satisfactory form or that anything very good can be done with it."

Harry M. Campbell and Ruel Foster disagree. And so do I. They conclude that "Eleven of the thirteen stories in these two volumes are excellent, and even the two relative failures—'Record at Oak Hill' and 'Love by the Highway'—reveal careful craftsmanship marred by effects that seem, in spite of their simplicity—too much contrived" [*Elizabeth Madox Roberts: American Novelist*]. While a major reputation in short fiction cannot be based on thirteen stories, these thirteen can at least hold respectable standing in the company of the best stories written in the twentieth century. Many of them are long stories, even approaching the length of novellas. They are long enough, certainly, for Roberts to create large worlds and people who do significant things. There is also considerable range in the stories, in character types, subjects, tone, time, and despite the fact that most of them are set in her Pigeon River country—even in setting.

Much of the excellence of her stories, however, can be attributed to their sense of place, a concern that derives from Roberts's life in Springfield, Covington, and rural Kentucky; her sensitivity to it; her close observation of it; and her desire to interpret and record it. As Annie Steger Harrison points out in her M.A. thesis at Vanderbilt, Roberts's country is a three or four county section of central Kentucky, centered in Washington County. It is a section called Pigeon River, the older name for Salt River. In his dissertation at the University of Kentucky, Woodridge Spears is even more specific about her use of Washington County locales, particularly in her novel *The Time of Man:*

> The land about Springfield, Valley Hill, Cartwright Creek, and the Maud-Mooresville-Litsey neighborhood provided a convenient map for the artist describing the Chessers on their journey. James Still has recalled that when he rode with Miss Roberts near Springfield, several years after the publication of *The Time of Man,* she would point out along the way the places she had associated with—details of physical scenery—carried over to the use in some cases of the actual names, Cornishville, for example.

Her use of this region in the short stories, as well as of actual Kentucky place names, is just as obvious. In fact, in **"Death at Bearwallow,"** she uses the real name of St. Rose. A man is plowing in the fields. "The bell ringing at St. Rose came faintly across many hills and was dispersed among the stony rises and bushy hollows, shallow and thin. Hearing the bell he remembered the mission that would begin at St. Rose in two weeks, and a vague excitement surged in his breast and in his throat, for the mission would be someplace to go every night."

This story—as well as several others—is a reminder of the Catholic presence in this part of Kentucky, a state that is otherwise predominantly Protestant, especially in the rural areas. Names like Dominic and Piety are common in her stories. In **"Death at Bearwallow"** the Catholic presence is seen in the candles burning around the body of a dead girl, the crucifix on the mantel of the room, the prayers read for the repose of the dead, and the prayers prayed from the circle of the rosary. **"Sacrifice of the Maidens"** is the story in which a young girl takes her first vows as a Dominican nun. It is set in the old chapel at St. Catharine College, near Springfield.

An interesting vantage point from which to view her primary country is provided by her only story set in the Kentucky mountains, **"On the Mountainside."** These lines describe the home country of Lester Hunter, a teacher who has come to the mountains, and they show the way a mountain boy envisions the lower country:

> Lester had come from one of the low counties of the rolling plain where the curving creeks of the Pigeon River spread slowly, winding broadly to gather up many little rills. Newt had learned somewhere, in his own blood, to hate the lower country for its pleasantness. There the fields rolled out smoothly and the soil was deep. The grass of any roadside was bluegrass mingled, perhaps, with rich weeds. Fat cattle, fine beasts, ate in the mythical pastures. Smooth roads ran between the farms.

The mountain youth's vision suggests an orderly world beyond the mountains, and indeed it is—at least it is in Roberts's fiction, where roads lead somewhere, fields are carefully marked off, and boundary lines are clear.

Annie Steger Harrison includes in her thesis a letter from Celina M. Bosley, a pianist and music teacher who lived next door to the Roberts home in Springfield in 1910. Mrs. Bosley reports that she encouraged Elizabeth Roberts to go to college at the University of Chicago. As the letter continues, Mrs. Bosley relates that upon learning Elizabeth Madox Roberts was writing a novel, she in jest told the author to be sure to include her neighbor. After the Springfield keyboard teacher had read *The Time of Man,* Roberts asked her if she had recognized herself. Indeed, her home, the one behind the elms, where Ellen had heard a piano and rung the bell, was her own. The description of the street, records Mrs. Bosley, was a very accurate one. Harrison's perceptive

thesis focuses on the novels, but her conclusions regarding their record as social history are equally valid for the short fiction.

One of the most apparent ways in which place affects Roberts's short fiction is the speech of her characters. Her people are good talkers, even the semi-literate ones. In **"Children of the Earth"** Dovie Green berates her "cockroach" husband, as she calls him, for being a sorry provider. And he responds, mostly in Anglo-Saxon monosyllables, reminding her that he has covered up her stealing before:

> I have already lied enough for you, Dovie Green, to go to perdition three times over. I even lied in court the day Jake McNab lost the gilt, swore in the magistrate's house with my hand in the air, 'S'elp me God' we never seen a sign of hit, and hit salted down in our cellar hole under the house then, and your insides full of tripe and hog-heart hash that very minute. If the court had 'a' given you a vomit right then, it would 'a' seen a sight, would 'a' seen Jake McNab's hogmeat run outen your mouth.

A slightly vulgar episode also occurs in **"Death at Bearwallow"** when a man accuses another of slobbering in the water bucket. He says: "You threw back your slobbers inside the water bucket You can just go to the spring and get more water now." And the other says: "I'll not do it. I never threw back my slobbers. I didn't have no slobbers left. I drank it up to the bottom of the dipper." Harrison, incidentally, quotes from Woodridge Spears's dissertation a letter Roberts wrote to Harriet Monroe, in which she said: "My people here are close to the soil and their talk is talk out of the clods." In addition, Campbell and Foster report that Roberts collected archaic expressions while she was teaching in Washington County rural schools.

Indeed, the speech of her characters is sprinkled with such archaic words as *lief.* In **"The Scarecrow"** a man says, "Which buzzards do you like best?" The answer is: "As lief one kind as the other." A man jailed in **"The Shepherd's Interval"** uses the word *ruction* when he speaks of a man who "got killed in a ruction with his uncle over whether a man can have double pneumonia twice." **"On the Mountainside"** is filled with unusual words like *bodacious* and *swivet* and *broguen.* A mother says of the imminent departure of the schoolteacher: "My little tad, the least one, Becky, is plumb bereft over 'im." Others ask the teacher: "Did you come up the gorge to borrow fire you're in such a swivet to get on?" Another says: "There's a big meeten over to Kitty's branch next light moon. Why don't you stay? No harm in you to be broguen about a small spell."

At other times her characters speak a ceremonial folk speech, a country speech in high gear that, as already noted, is sometimes akin to the wording and rhythms of folk music. In **"On the Mountainside"** a boy approaches a strange cabin chanting these words as if they were a charm to bring good luck and welcome from an unfamiliar place:

> Right hands across and howdy-do,
> Left and back and how are you.
>
> Oh, call up yo' dog, oh, call up yo' dog,
> Ring twang a-whoddle lanky day.

And in **"The Scarecrow"** a father keeps calling his daughter in words that begin to sound like the refrain of a folk song: "Joan, Joan, where's Joan? Come, come! The crows are in the new corn!" In many instances place dictates the wording and rhythm of the narrative language. Here are two examples from **"On the Mountainside"**: "While he [Newt Reddix] listened, the knowledge that Lester Hunter [the schoolteacher] would soon go out of the country . . . brought a loneliness to his thought." And later in the story: "The schoolteacher was stepping about in the dance . . . and the fiddle was scraping the top of a tune."

Another feature of placeness in Roberts's work has to do with the creative relationship between character and place. There is frequently the sense that her characters create places as they pass through space; that is, their perception of place gives it quickened reality. **"Swing Low, Sweet Chariot,"** for instance, opens with these lines: "A young woman driving a roan nag hitched to a shining new phaeton came swiftly down the street. . . . With the coming of this belle the afternoon life of the town began to stir." Shortly we discover, however, that it is "merely Kitty Jones showing off her new buggy." The sense that a landscape is real only if it is filtered through the consciousness of a character is seen also in the opening of **"Children of the Earth."** Here the good-for-nothing farmer Eli Green has been to town to beg and is returning home: "He passed farm after farm, each one owned: Bancroft, Blackburn, McNab, his mind being aware of each change of ownership as he passed from one to the next."

But sometimes a person loses hold on a landscape, even one that is familiar. In **"Death at Bearwallow"** a young boy goes to see his grandmother in the country. He starts home as the sun is going down and the darkness remakes familiar places into places of terror: "The thorn bushes at the roadside were familiar, known in all their contours and sensed in all their power, known too well. The hills beyond the running line of the fence and the field sank into the dark of the sky, cool and even, a terror, going to the night too easily, joining the dark."

In **"The Shepherd's Interval,"** it seems as if creation were following in the footsteps of Flynn Thompson, as he walks home to his farm from a four-month jail sentence for making and selling moonshine. As he walks joyously through the countryside, it becomes real. He passes through a hamlet, with five or six scattered houses, and by a blacksmith's shop. Finally, he sees his own place: "The red and gold spread halfway across the

heavens by the time the remembered hills and knolls of his own ridge came to him where familiar trees stood above familiar patches of briars and stiff cliffs of dark stone. In the hollows were running streams." As he comes "in sight of his own land," he sees "his own pasture, dotted with scrubby trees, rolling unevenly backward toward a bluff and tilting evenly forward with the running of the road." Then he sees his sheds and shelters, a white barn to the right, his cattle and the swine at the trough. Soon he is on the flagstones that lead straight to the door of his house. And he is at home, in time for the shearing of his sheep and the wedding of his daughter.

But place is more than physical. In **"I Love My Bonny Bride,"** it becomes psychological. It is a child, Lena, who reaches out to know the world, its possible places and experiences, including a place called Covington, where she is to go to see her aunt married. As she waits for her aunt Patty to arrive for a visit, she thinks the place she came from into existence: "Lena sat here to wait for the stage, and she thought across the miles to the other house, where Patty lived. The other house became very vivid on an instant because Patty had come out of it that morning." Throughout the story Lena makes places out of space, creating people, things, rooms, houses from her memory and imagination.

In Roberts's short fiction time is also place. The setting for **"Record at Oak Hill"** is an antebellum mansion house, and behind it is the log cabin in which the present owner's ancestors had first lived. For a while it was used as a kitchen and workroom, then for storage only. The owner is Morna Trigg, who rents the land to her great-nephew Richard Dorsey. One day at dinner, as he listens to his elderly relative talk, "Richard's thought leaped about among many objects, trailing among such old things that had never been concealed, that had merely been dropped away into forgotten corners and out-of-the-way places, to be found a long while afterward." One day Richard is feeding the hounds in the log cabin, and, as he takes his coat from a peg beside the fireplace, he pricks his fingers on something sticking through the plaster chinked between the logs. Later, Morna tells of her father, Richard's great-grandfather, who came home from service in the Confederate army with twenty men remaining of the more than fifty who had left in his company. They wanted peace, the old woman says, but times were hard, especially for men who had worn the gray, and "some were mad with victory and anger." One man who cruelly exploited the times was named Buchman, her father's enemy. Then Buchman was found dead in his own garden.

Following the threshing of the grain, Richard returns to the cabin, and pries what turns out to be a twelve-inch, three-sided dagger from the plaster—a dagger with his great-grandfather's name on it, the dagger which killed the man named Buchman. The year is 1932, and times are bad again. Will Neal, Richard's brother-in-law who has lost his farm, remarks sarcastically that at least in those days there was "something firm to stick a sword into . . . something to kill." Now, he laments, there is only "high-priced machinery" and "low-priced wheat and tobacco" and no visible enemy to kill to right the balance.

Another aspect of place in Roberts's fiction is that place tends to be that part of the world that you know, possess, control, and truly live in. It is the true landscape of one's life, as **"The Haunted Palace"** illustrates. In this story a poor farmer's family moves into a wing of the old Wickley place, Wickwood, once a grand and prosperous plantation now in partial ruins. "What manner of place is this?" asks the young wife Jess. "She had no names for all the buildings that lay about her. She was frightened of the things for which she had no use. . . ." She wants to destroy them. Then, after a lambing session in the vast unoccupied central section of the mansion, and after Jess has attacked an apparition coming at her through a larger mirror, the place is hers. "It was near midnight. Jess felt accustomed to the place now and more at ease there, she and Hubert being in possession of it." They have carved out now their own place within what *was* an alien world.

In all of Roberts's stories there is the sense of definite, immediate places—places close-by and up-close. There is also a tendency in these stories for places to open up and out into a grander landscape. There is the feeling that the world beyond the immediate setting is full and complete. There is the sense that the world continues even beyond the borders of the story. This continuity is seen everywhere in her short fiction. From **"Death at Bearwallow,"** for example, there is this casual line: "The beasts dragged at the heavy plow over the hill's rim, and the earth lay away, hill following hill, each interlocking with another." **"The Haunted Palace"** opens with this sentence: "The house stood at the head of a valley where the hollow melted away into the rolling uplands." Indeed, many of her stories open with vista-like descriptions. **"I Love My Bonny Bride"** begins this way: "Four children were at a window looking out upon a village street." And this is the way **"Love by the Highway"** starts: "A young woman, Perry Lancer, was digging potatoes in a small field in a mid-morning. Beside the field a highway lifted gently and rounded for the beginning of a slight curve that took it toward the left and out of view."

In one of Roberts's best stories, **"Sacrifice of the Maidens,"** Felix Barbour sits in a convent chapel awaiting the ceremony that will make his sister a Dominican nun. The setting is the old chapel at St. Catharine, a very definite place, "the organ in the loft at the rear of the chapel," the postulants dressed as brides, the priest at the altar "rapidly intoning: Hail Mary, full of grace . . . ," the congregation responding "in a rushing chant," and finally the sister who was Anne Barbour is now Sister Magdalen. And yet inside the chapel, inside this timeless, placeless place that could as easily be a village in France or Germany, the places outside intrude upon the consciousness of Felix Barbour. As most critics have pointed out, the story's tension is between the Christian demands of the spirit and the pagan demands of the flesh. As his sister renounces the world of flesh, the brother remembers: "Summer and winter and Anne, they were running down the channel of the year. The year spread widely then, as if it flowed abroad to fill a wide field with corn. There was sweetness in the high blades of the corn and abundance in the full shucks as he tore each ear from the ripe stem." And he sees Anne "playing with the dog in the yard, saw her running after a chicken to drive it into a coop, saw her making herself a dress to wear to the convent school." Further: "He heard Anne running down the yard at their farm to drive a hen away from the little turkeys while they had their food under the lilac bush, and he heard her shout in the wind and heard her laugh when the old hen flew wildly over a fence to escape her clamor." Time and places outside intrude even here.

As improbable as it may seem, Roberts's most direct and eloquent tribute to place is perhaps her one story set in the Kentucky mountains, **"On the Mountainside."** It is the story of a young mountain boy, Newt Reddix, who has received a taste of education and wants more. He decides to leave his home in the mountains and go to the "settlements." After two weeks of walking towards the lowlands, he stops at a cabin to spend the night. There he meets an old man who is finally going home to the mountains after a lifetime spent in the alien settlements of the low country. Like some Old Testament prophet he warns the boy against leaving. These are his words, his sermon:

> I was a plumb traitor to my God when I left the mountains and come to the settlements. Many is the day I'd study about that-there and many is the night I lay awake to study about the way back over Coster Ridge, on past Bear Mountain, past Hog Run, past Little Pine Tree, up and on past Louse Run, up, then on over Long Ridge and up into Laurel, into Grady Creek and on up the branch, past the Flat Rock, past the sawmill, past the grove of he-balsams, and then the smoke a-comen outen the chimney and the door open and old Nomie's pup a-comen down the road to meet me . . . then I'd come to myself and there I'd be, a month's travel from as much as a sight of the Flat Rock, and I'd groan and shake and turn over again. I was a trailor to my God.

When the boy tells the old man that he drank from a familiar spring a few days before, the man is overjoyed:

To think you been there! You are a-setten right now in hearen of my voice and yet a Tuesday 'twas a week ago you was in the spot I call home . . . and to think you tasted them waters Tuesday 'twas a week ago!

The old man is about to go to sleep before the fire, but suddenly he alerts himself and says, "with kindling eyes, his hand uplifted":

You come . . . from the place I hope to see if God Almighty sees fitten to bless me afore I lay me down and die. You walked, I reckon, right over the spot I pined to see a many is the year, God knows, and it was nothing to you.

Indeed, home is the ultimate good place for Roberts's characters. And she describes kitchens, dining rooms, halls with attention and love. Even outbuildings are consecrated. In **"Holy Morning"** the good place is a barn, where on Christmas Eve an injured ewe gives birth to a lamb. Before that event, however, with its symbolic implications, a girl goes out to the barn to check on the animals:

> She looked to the safety of their two ewes and the old ram, and she found them huddled together near the inner wall that divided the cow's shed from the place where the wagon was kept. When the cow had eaten the last of her hay she went slowly to the place where the sheep were and stood against the inner wall as if she found warmth for herself in the brown boards.

She sees the hens, the cock, the horse, and, overhead, pigeons. "All together," she writes; "the beasts made a gentle warmth . . . of their bodies." It is just such a scene that will make you believe the legend that the girls have been discussing—that on Christmas Eve the animals will kneels in obeisance to the Christchild.

In **"The Betrothed"** a young couple anticipate making a place of their own, setting off their place from the world. The young man promises his intended:

> I'm a-goen to rent a piece of the Cooksey land next year . . . Rhody, you and me, we'll live in the little red house on the branch. We'll have a whole mess of chickens and a pa'sel of hogs and cows. And I'll raise corn and 'backer till I fair split my sides. I'll do hit. And next year or year after I'll fair buy a piece of land, and you and me, we'll be fixed for life.

In such a passage, place is the essence of human realization.

Finally, in at least one story, home has eschatological dimensions. At the end of **"Children of the Earth,"** when the stolen lamb has been freed and the surprise party is over at Eli Green's cabin, the people all go outside and look up at the clear sky.

> The stars were a myriad of small sparks over the great roof of the sky, receding and multiplying if the eye tried to fathom or count the number. The fields on every side were lost in blackness.

The people look up at the sky and begin to talk of the stars, about stars falling, and where they go, and whether people live up there.

> Eli looked upward with the guests, standing in the middle of the throng. Some of the points of

light were so bright that they seemed vocal, as if they were speaking or singing together. The sounds of the speaking people were blended with his sight of the stars so that he could scarcely tell whether the star or the person had spoken.

Then someone plunks the fiddle, and the people begin to sing, mostly hymns which they all know: "Shall We Gather at the River," "When the Roll Is Called Up Yonder," and especially "Beulah Land": "Oh, Beulah Land, sweet Beulah land, / As on a higher mount I stand, / I look away across the sea / Where mansions are prepared for me. . . ." And they sing a new song the fiddler half makes up about "the faraway home of the soul." The rescued lamb is lying "down in the cool grass at the roadside" and the people sing of "eternity and jasper walls," the people "looking from one to another with pleasure, assuming his talent to themselves, and they sang standing near together, filled with wonder and delight, feeling themselves to be a part of the great body of the stars and the world without end." And they sing at the story's conclusion, their songs adding sounds to the music of the spheres.

And so place is a vital element in the short fiction of Elizabeth Madox Roberts. It has a bearing on who her characters are, how they talk and behave, what happens in the stories—even how the stories are structured and written. The literal places of her stories are as familiar as a field of Kentucky tobacco, as concrete as the old chapel still standing on the campus of St. Catharine College, as historical as a pioneer cabin, as ordinary as a shed where a setting hen broods, and as grand as the Milky Way on a clear night in Washington County.

Linda Tate (essay date 1987)

SOURCE: "Against the Chaos of the World: Language and Consciousness in Elizabeth Madox Roberts's *The Time of Man*," in *The Mississippi Quarterly*, Vol. XL, No. 2, Spring, 1987, pp. 95-111.

[*In the following essay, Tate investigates the integration of style and theme in* The Time of Man.]

In a letter to Harriet Monroe, Elizabeth Madox Roberts wrote that she had "poured into [*The Time of Man*] the notes which might otherwise have gone into the making of many bits of verse." For her, the novel was the result of her theory of "poetic realism," as she sought to find points of union between the spiritual and the physical, the inner world and the outer. Roberts defined her theory of "poetic realism" thus:

> Somewhere there is a connection between the world of the mind and the outer order—it is the secret of the contact that we are after, the point, the moment of union. We faintly sense the one and we know as faintly the other, but there is a point where they come together, and we can never know the whole of reality until we have these

two completely. [Quoted in Robert Penn Warren, "Elizabeth Madox Roberts: Life Is from Within," *Saturday Review,* March, 1963]

For Roberts, language was one of these "moments of union."

Given the incredible power language has to synthesize the inner and the outer, it follows that language would be an important element in one's psychological development. Hence, the novel's protagonist, Ellen Chesser, grows psychologically through linguistic experiences which give her an increasing sense of being a distinct and separate individual. That this is of utmost importance to Roberts is indicated by the opening of the novel in one of the most striking unions of the inner and the outer, the psychological and the physical: "Ellen wrote her name in the air with her finger, *Ellen Chesser,* leaning forward and writing on the horizontal plane." Later, we see Ellen, like the narrator in Charlotte Perkins Gilman's short story, trying to impose a pattern on her room's yellow wallpaper [see Gilman's "Yellow Wallpaper," in *The Charlotte Perkins Gilman Reader,* edited by Ann J. Lane, 1980]. The paper takes on many shapes, among them "trees, women, letters, women, crosses, unfeathered birds, swords, demons." It does not seem coincidental that "letters" is bordered on either side by the only pattern repeated: "women." That women—in this case, Ellen—use letters and, in a larger sense, language to impose patterns on their world is at the heart of Roberts's message. *The Time of Man,* then, takes as one of its large concerns the operation of language—the tool which we use to achieve a union between the psychological and the physical—as a means of ordering a chaotic world. *The Time of Man* is, as Roberts called it, a "drama of the immediacy of the mind."

But, even if language has the ability to provide a point of union between the psychological and the physical, the difficulty still remains for Roberts and her characters: how to choose, as Roberts put it, "from the chaos about me and the apparent chaos that is myself." Indeed, in describing her plan for *The Time of Man,* she said, the novel must be "[m]yself against the chaos of the world." Many critics, in writing about Roberts's style and Ellen's development of the self, have reached only a partial sense of the fusion between style and theme. William H. Slavick points out [in "Ellen Chesser: A Journey of the Mind," his introduction to the 1926 edition of the novel] that Ellen's psychological development is a result of the assimilation of her inner voices into a whole, while Kenneth Burke says that Ellen's "monologues . . . seem to be a personal discovery of the author" ["A Decade of American Fiction," *Bookman,* 69, 1929]. Earl H. Rovit, likewise, notes [in *Herald to Chaos: The Novels of Elizabeth Madox Roberts,* 1960] that Roberts's style is more than just "frosting on a cake"; it is crucial to her theme of "the inner world of sensations becoming ideas." He writes, "The balance which she tried to attain between poetry and realism requires the literary existence of an active, perceiving,

remembering, willing, imagining mind expressing its ideations through sensuous symbols and images." And, as Frederick P. W. McDowell puts it, [in *Elizabeth Madox Roberts,* 1963] Ellen has "sensitivity, inner strength, and a restless mind which works from confusion to clarity." While all of these critics have seen either Roberts's preoccupation with words or Ellen's developing self, only Victor A. Kramer has noted, to any extent, that Ellen's use of language is essential to her creation of self; his analysis, however, focuses primarily on the life rhythms language produces. What Roberts's novel demands is a close and detailed reading which uncovers Ellen's working through linguistic stimuli to a point of seeing herself as a separate and unique identity. Through such an analysis, we can see more clearly how Ellen works from "confusion to clarity" and how she uses language to order her world.

Ellen's first act of the novel is, as we have seen, a foremost example of the fusion of the inner and the outer, as is her first truly assertive act in the book. Throughout the first chapter, Ellen has repeatedly wished to communicate with her older friend and linguistic role model, Tessie, but her parents' decision to settle down renders Ellen's desires hopeless. Finally, she takes decisive action by walking to town the night before court day, and the climax of the scene and the moment of Ellen's small, but definite, triumph is her sending of a message to Tessie. Her inner desire to "tell" Tessie becomes tangible reality when she makes the desire physical:

> The paper was in the pocket of the waist; Ellen had seen fingers push it in beside a little dull pocketbook and a piece of orange peel and a bit of a bright rag. . . . One sob shook her throat and then peace came after the hours of strain. She had sent a message to Tessie. She had sent word.

The odds that Ellen's message will ever reach Tessie are marginal at best, and this scene foreshadows another important moment of an attempt at written communication—her correspondence with Jonas.

While the sending of the message to Tessie can be seen as a triumphant act of self-assertion, if a failed one of communication, Ellen's exchange of letters with Jonas bears little success and is one of the most devastating incidents in the novel since verbal communication proves inadequate. When Jonas leaves Ellen, he senses a need to affirm his love for her, but his oaths seem but pathetic attempts at putting into words what has been heretofore largely nonverbal. Likewise, their attempts at letter-writing are doomed to failure. Ellen reads Jonas's letter over and over, "following each phrase to its last degree of meaning and searching out each connoted thought." Her reply is even more of a failure, as she unsuccessfully tries to come up with the words which would express her emotion: "On the paper the words seemed hard and dumb, or given freedom they were sugared and easy and light." For Ellen, Jonas's letter is partially successful, since its existence can represent in a small way his existence (hence, she keeps his letter pinned next to her body just as he kisses the letters of her name), but her own attempt to find a meaningful expression of her inner thoughts fails.

Other written forms of language are more effective. For Ellen as a child and, later, for her children, books represent a means to wonder. As a young girl, she often recalls things she has read in books, particularly those which focus on other people and places. She prides herself on her knowledge, saying, "'I know a right smart of pieces now, for a fact'"; and, when imagining how her life will change when she becomes a woman, she visualizes not only a house but also "herself reading a book by the window." Womanhood, however, brings not more time for books but even less; yet her son Dick carries on her love for books, frequently proclaiming, "'I aim to read a heap of books. It's in books is found the wisdom of the world, they say.'" At first this desire in Dick "bewilder[s]" and "sadden[s]" Ellen, but soon it "pass[es] into . . . rapture," "for she felt her own being, in Dick, pushed outward against the great over-lying barrier, the enveloping dark." Books, then, become a tangible and physical manifestation of the possibilities for other worlds and provide a means of groping with larger, innately felt existential questions.

Finally, highly stylized—or ceremonial—language also has quite a powerful impact on Ellen and the people around her as it juxtaposes their weaknesses and mortality against larger forces. On court day, Ellen is very much aware of the words the town crier is shouting— "Act fitted into act and turned upon a word. . . ."— reinforcing her growing sense of social distinctions. When telling what she knows of Cassie's death, she is required to take an oath and trembles "before the solemn". . . . Jasper's summons to court is even more powerful, as it fuses this higher level of language with written language. The impact upon Jasper and Ellen clearly reflects the power of official written language— the imposing of order upon them by a higher force: ". . . a letter came to their letterbox that cut into the inner fiber of Ellen's new life and made it more intense with purpose. She carried the letter across the field to Jasper where he worked at the fences and they read it together in the crisp cold."

Even their marriage—hinted at in Ellen's dream the night of the heavily veiled consummation of their relationship—is touched by ceremonial words, words which are necessary as a means of making legitimate the emotional and sexual union Jasper and Ellen have experienced. Again, the impact of the words and their power to create structure is not lost upon the two:

> . . . the man faced them, and joining their hands, said ceremonial words. . . . Fixed forever, pronounced, finished, said and unrevoked, his words flowed through the great hardness of his voice, a ground-work on which to lean, a foundation beneath a foundation. . . .

The fact that Jasper and Ellen's names are written on a piece of paper—again, as if to lend legitimacy to the union by making its physical existence tangible—underlines the importance of names in the novel. Since they represent the most pointed union of the inner and the outer, names are a means of assigning identity to outside stimuli, particularly other people, and to oneself. Noting that Roberts prefers using noun phrases even if she has to transform an active verb into a participle to do so, Rovit writes, "Sensations are not significant until they have been realized or re-created, or, to put it another way, the life outside is absorbed only when it is named." Naming—or, more accurately, learning the names of—other people helps Ellen to perceive their existence more readily. The potentiality of people she might know is emphasized by listing their names. For example, when Ellen moves to Wakefield's, Roberts writes, "She might get to know Ben the Negro, and John Bradshaw the hand who looked after the mules and horses; she might get to know Josie the yellow girl, even Mr. Al Wakefield, or even Miss Tod, his wife." While one might argue that such a passage is merely an authorial device to introduce a new cast of characters, at other times Roberts notes the same phenomenon while not specifically noting names. For example, Effie Turpin's friendship is of particular value to Ellen, because Effie tells "the names of all the people who lived up and down the roads and who owned land and who rented." A page later we see Ellen's ever-growing knowledge of the people around her merging with her closeness to the land: ". . . Ellen . . . [kept] a rich sense of the land, all the land about, as filled with an ever-increasing people, gathering into her knowledge incessantly. . . . [H]er knowledge . . . spread even farther and caught at the farms in the glen where names and faces were now known a little." At Dorine's party, she is introduced to a large set of her peers, and the need to assign identities is even stronger. Later, she recalls that it was Jonas who had told her the names of the people at the party, and her growing comfort with the group comes partially from connecting names to "figures and faces." Later, we see the importance of names again as Ellen and Jasper carefully choose the names of each of their children in an effort to honor those they love and respect. The sickly infant, conceived during a time when its parents' very marriage is in question and whose birth represents one of the most chilling scenes in the novel, proves to be an exception. In the most vivid example of the link between one's name and one's identity, this child transcends traditional nomenclature: "The infant was soon very much endeared to the other children, who began to call him Chick as they played about him, and after a little that name was established and the child seemed much too precious to be encumbered with any name less light."

While names and the identities they represent are crucial, so are other verbal valuations. Early in the novel, Ellen learns that you are what people say you are. As the driver tells passersby that his passengers are "The new tenants for Wakefield's," Ellen feels "herself and all of them become what they were said to be . . ." Later, she tries to visualize how the MacMurtries view her by imagining phrases that they would attribute to her: "She would be 'that girl that works on Wakefield's place,' and 'that white girl over at Wakefield's.'" Later, Jasper becomes "'the man who burned down Wingate's barn,'" and even his children make value judgements about him based on statements others have made. And, as if to punish Jasper's mistress, Ellen's "throat ache[s] with the words that would label Hester Shuck as a foul and bestial creature."

Given the importance of names, then, it is not surprising to see Ellen moving through certain stages of development in her preoccupation with them. As a young girl, the names of her dead siblings seem to make them more real to her, and the repetition of Jock's and Tessie's names, along with her statement "Tessie is my folks," affirms her emotional and formative ties to her friend. A bit later, Dorine's name comes to have special significance for Ellen, coming "often to her mind as holding much generous grace and much music." In fact, her own identity in the group is solidified as her name is transformed into Elleen, so that she and the name take on aspects of Dorine. When she moves to Wingate and acquires the trunk, her ability to store away secret things and, symbolically, to have private thoughts is linked to her knowledge of a new group of people and their names. Again, this represents another stage in her development as a separate identity:

> The key of the trunk lay on the shelf before the clock print. Names would play in her mind as she moved about in the tight little room in the midst of a stone-tight land surrounded by steep hills, the people speaking but little and that little in a close hard speech. . . . The names, Regina Donahue, Pius Donahue, Pius, Pius, Regina, Old Mrs. Wingate, Leo Shuck, Mag Mudd, Kate Bannan, she would say them in mind, thinking nothing.

Her mental play with the names and the image of the trunk call up the memory of a childhood friend, Fanny B., whose lack of a full name makes her less an individual and more an abstract idea. Ellen's memory of Fanny B.'s interest in words also calls to mind "all the secret things and the half-known put snugly away in the forgetting parts of the mind . . ." As a young girl, Ellen was not only conscious of names but also, like Fanny B., acutely aware of language, particularly of the sounds and rhythms language produces. What she remembers about Fanny B. is her fondness for words, and the description of her friend could also describe Ellen's own childhood activities: ". . . one could, being young, sing out words one minute and forget all about them the next . . ." At this stage, language is purely sound whose meaning need not be retained. Early in the novel, we see Ellen

> singing a jargon of many phrases that were remembered for the pictures they preserved or the tones they carried.

> *Hounds on my track,*
> *Chicken on my back,*
> *Oh, Brother Andrew have you got a G fiddle string?*
> *Oh, Brother Andrew, have you got a G string?*

As the first chapter progresses, we continue to see Ellen toying with words; this is an especially useful tool on journeys, as phrases like "Not once but ten times" and words such as "sycamores" help her to set a rhythm for walking. At this point in her life, these transformations of words into sounds are harmless, doing nothing more than exercising her innate sense of rhythm.

As she grows older, the sounds take on more meaning, but her inexperience with the ramifications of remembered phrases leaves her incapable of recognizing those most worthwhile: "Her mind gave equal and diffused values to the voices within and without." Since she has not yet fully developed a sense of her own identity or established clear boundaries between herself and the world, hostile encounters with other people have the potential to be quite damaging to her self-esteem. When she has the confrontation with Mrs. Bodine, she is not able to respond adequately in a way that will affirm her own personhood. Instead, she reverts to her stock of phrases as a kind of mental defense: "A nausea spread up from the pit of her stomach and died in her mouth, diffused. 'And you'll live a long and happy life. Only ten cents more, one dime. A long life, a happy life, a long life. Happy happy long long. Long and happy life.'"

A few pages later her inner struggle over the concept of sexuality is marked by remembered, and repulsive, phrases. Haldeen Stikes's lewd words recur in Ellen's mind, tainting her perspective on sex. Then, in her first romantic encounter (with Joe Trent), remembered phrases determine Ellen's responses. Here, positive phrases ("He might be somebody I'd know all my whole enduren life," "Any day you say," "There's no knowen how lovely I am," and "Take a walk") are juxtaposed indiscriminately against negative ones ("What I want with you, Louse Patch?," "Lousy rags," and "I'd be afraid to touch"). Again, Ellen's inability to make sense out of the phrases or to categorize them makes it difficult for her to conceive her own identity. At best, these phrases take her out of her tense existence and set her mind on another plane: "The trees spread upward. . . . She would have something pink to wear . . ."

Words which cause Ellen pain continue to underline her doubts about her sexuality and about her romantic relationships. Her mother's question, "'Where's the fellows that ought to be acomen?,'" becomes a taunt in Ellen's mind instead of a fair question. This phrase represents something which Ellen has difficulty facing: "It was expected of her, something undefined and expected, she would think, abashed, something stated boldly through the words of a hard voice." Later, when trying to work through her quite complicated memories of Jonas's leaving and Cassie's suicide, simultaneous incidents each symbolizing Ellen's sexual doubts, the words of both occasions play upon her mind repeatedly. The memory of Jonas's words—"'Me and you, Elleen. Before summer, Elleen'"—create a desire to murder Jonas, yet also bring back with full force the memory of that night:

> Then words that were printed into her memory long ago began to run forward, and this hour lost its identity before the force of another, long past, until she swam back into the past as if she were an apparition, without presence of its own. The voices spoke aloud, voices of men, filling the room with their terror, speaking sharply, speaking with authority or fright.

Throughout the lengthy scene, Ellen's past and present intersect. In a manner which recalls Proust and anticipates Faulkner, Roberts allows the past to come alive in Ellen's mind. All dialogues collapse into one, and Ellen becomes a part of all of them in the present.

But spoken language and verbal interactions—aside from these few intense scenes—provide another means for Ellen to define her identity and her place in the group. As a young girl, she waits for farmers at new locations to speak to her with "upward-bending words"; "strange voices outside" can make "her breath [leap] with joy"; and voices grown familiar can make her adjustment to a new situation come more easily. At Dorine's party, she wishes "that she could say something pleasing and quick and that one or two would look at her and know what she meant," and it is her singing of a ballad which gains her respect and a place in the group. As she walks home from the party, the voices of the others envelop her until she feels herself become a sixth identity in the group.

Conversation with other women can also, if infrequently, provide a means of psychological identification. Ellen's need to "tell" Tessie the events of her life is indicative of this aspect of female/female communication, as is her friendship with Effie Turpin, when she tries to become Effie and to see through her eyes: "Ellen tore off the leaves carefully and laid them in their piles, a joy in her being because someone had come, another, almost herself but separate in body, a girl her own age. Wanting the girl to stay, she asked her a question now and then to keep her." However, such interaction as a positive step towards self-identification seems part of female/female exchanges only at a young and formative age. As the girls move into womanhood, their dialogues begin to reflect an implicit competition. Put more colloquially, their conversations take on a "catty" aspect. Gossip, harsh evaluations of women not present, and unsolicited advice are the staples of women's dialogues at church, at social occasions such as the fish fry, and at home, as when Nellie and Dorine's whispered comments are used to exclude Ellen.

Since Roberts's main concern is with the female's developing sense of language and communication and since we see the action of the novel through Ellen's

eyes, male/male dialogues are not included very frequently. What few glimpses we do have of communication between males, however, show us that the men are primarily concerned with politics, farming, and other economic concerns. The juxtaposition of the male sense of the practical and the female sense of the beautiful can be uncomfortable, as we see in the scene where Ellen tries on Rosie O'Shay's new hat:

> The men about the fire talked with low muttering, complaining at the closing of the road. The hat was fresh and fragrant, a promise of Rosie's wedding, but the low muttering of the men came into her pleasure in the hat, a faint menace that lay under the air, so that her joy in the hat was magnified as it stood out brightly before their threatenings.

While communication between any two individuals is difficult, communication between males and females proves to be the most complex. As a young girl, Ellen, remembering verbal attention paid her, can respond happily: "She often felt the smile come to her mouth, always when she remembered any of his phrases" and remembering the "tones of a [boy's] voice she had heard many days back" can, as before, cause her to smile. As her unions with men become more substantial, non-verbal communication begins to take on increasing importance. This becomes a key part of her relationship with Jonas: ". . . his free hand reach[ed] for her hand and she, consenting, walked beside him but neither spoke on the way." More often, however, when Ellen and her lovers engage in verbal exchanges, the real communication is happening nonverbally. Jonas, for example, tells her news of other farms, but it is the quality of his voice—"his slow, half-dreaming speech," "the droning of his voice," "the quiet of his careless words"—which Ellen notices. The same form of communication continues in her relationship with Jasper, but we increasingly see her attempts to "merge with his sorrows and his pleasures," "to push her knowing through his knowing to try to see as he had seen," and her ability to calm Jasper with her talk.

Perhaps the most striking example of verbal miscommunication merged with non-verbal communication is the many two edged dialogues which fill the book. These conversations, which almost always occur between Ellen and her lovers, pit the male's perception (strength, seduction, admiration of Ellen's beauty) against Ellen's (wonder, awe, aesthetic appreciation of the actual world and potential worlds). Rovit points to these exchanges, noting that they establish "a dialectic of communion" between the lovers and that they allow Roberts to show once again that "physical action is always subordinate to the inner drama of self-realization."

Given all these stimuli from the outer world—new people to whom she must connect names and make judgments about, remembered phrases which linger in her mind, and complicated modes of conversation between herself, other women, and men—it is not surprising that Ellen has difficulty formulating and articulating her desires. In the first chapter, we see her first encounter with this phenomenon:

> Her own want was undefined, lying out among the dark trees and their dark images, and she reached for it with a great wish that shook her small body. After a while she whispered a little, brokenly, almost without breath, but the words were Tessie's words, borrowed now because her own words were stricken.

This pattern of imposing words supplied by others upon her own articulated desires continues throughout the novel, but, from here on, she will order these desires by attributing them to a man's name. We see this first in her relationship with Joe Trent:

> The name, Joe Trent, went out of her being slowly. For weeks the mention of it brought a first flush of warmth to her mind and a gentle flow of momentary joy to all her members. "Friend" lay in thought with the word, "Somebody I might know all my life. A body to tell things to." But finally the chord was cut. By the time the tobacco was ripe the name no longer caught at her nerves when Artie Pinkston called it in her gossip.

When the relationship with Jonas does not work out, a similar phenomenon occurs. Trying to name a "faint recognition" of internal structures, she cannot, "for the word Jonas had been denied her. . . ." Later, she tests herself and the extent to which her wounds are healed by repeating Jonas's name over and over. Although at first it seems to be "nothing but a word, gone out of her body, as gone as last year's breath," she concentrates on the exercise a bit too long, and the name proves to have the continuing power to call up old memories and tears.

Finally, she finds a name which becomes a permanent articulation of her desire: Jasper. Again, as before, we see her working through her unnamed desire to a realization of this individual's significant importance to her:

> She sat on the side of her cot, her mind pursuing some word that was unnamed and could not gather itself into form, the hands of her mind reaching and straining to shape the nebula. . . . Then a cry came from her lips and she was suddenly awake in the moonlight of the whitewashed room, raised to her elbow, hearing the word ring through the walls. . . . The word of her outcry receded from her, going in waves of remembered sound, throbbing on her ears as she searched from wall to wall to find some real and present token of it. The word, "Jasper," still throbbed in her own voice, still fitted itself into her throat, and beat at the stiff white walls.

After she decides to marry Jasper, "his name [comes] often to her throat and linger[s] there, on the verge of utterance, the word her mind had been seeking, now grown fixed and eternal."

Although the inability to articulate her inner needs causes problems for Ellen and on several important occasions leads her to conclude that her strength or destiny lies in the existence of someone else, her most powerful moments in the novel are all her own. Frequently, they are sparked by her mantra-like repetition of the saying "the time of man" and are almost always punctuated by her avowal of her own name. The first realization of herself as a separate and mortal entity occurs in the first chapter:

> Then out of nothing she came into a quick and complete knowledge of the end. You breathe and breathe, on and on, and then you do not breathe any more. For you forever. Forever. It goes out, everything goes, and you are nothing. The world is all there, on and on, but you are not there, you, Ellen. The world goes on, goes on without you. Ellen Chesser. Ellen.

This sudden awareness of her mortality is punctuated by the repetition of her name as is her first major moment of affirmation, when she realizes by looking at Judge Gowan's tombstone that, while she may be mortal, she is alive in the here and now. While she is at first awed by the pomposity of the judge's name versus the plainness of her own and the class distinction which this difference represents, she soon realizes that there exists an even more important difference between them: "'He's Judge Gowan in court, a-sitten big, but I'm better'n he is. I'm a-liven and he's dead. I'm better. I'm Ellen Chesser and I'm a-liven and you're Judge James Bartholomew Gowan, but all the same I'm better. I'm a-liven.'" Almost all of Ellen's reaffirmations of her belief in life, or "a-liven," are accentuated by her emphatic statement, "I'm Ellen Chesser," a signal that the name represents both her existence and the unique identity she is.

Another stage in her development is also marked earlier in the novel, when her first perception of her self as beautiful and worthwhile is again connected to the repetition of her name. Difficult to articulate and fused almost indistinguishably with the "spreading . . . sweetness" of the white clover around her, the emotion nevertheless makes it onto the page: "Feeling could not take words, so melted in and merged it was with the flowers of the grass, but if words could have become grass in Ellen's hand: 'It's pretty stuff, clover a-growen. And in myself I know I'm lovely. It's unknowen how beautiful I am. I'm Ellen Chesser and I'm lovely.'" A short time later, Roberts writes of another of Ellen's communions with nature: "'The time of man,' as a saying, fell over and over in Ellen's mind," and, a bit later, "the afternoon seemed very still back of the dove calls and the cries of the plovers, back of a faint dying phrase, 'in the time of man.'" This immediately leads into another sudden, yet sweeping, awareness of her existence:

> All at once she lifted her body and flung up her head to the great sky that reached over the hills and shouted:

"Here I am!"

She waited listening.

"I'm Ellen Chesser! I'm here!"

Much later in the novel, after speaking with the charm woman and learning of Jonas's marriage to Sallie Lou, Ellen has a similar experience. When she returns home, she sits "among dry leaves . . . , a faint dying wind seem[ing] to blow over her and a faint phrase blow with it, dimly sensed with the fanning of the wind, 'In the time of man, in the time of man.'" As the wind blows the phrase over her, she is lulled to sleep, and she lapses into a dream in which her spirit seems to have separated itself from her body. Such a removal allows her to gain a new perspective on her life and on "the time of man," and, as she awakens from the dream, she wants to stab Jonas to death. Her whole being becomes filled with anger and an idea that, like it or not, Jonas has permanently affected her: "She could not be the same, could never go back and be the same she had been before Jonas." Finally, however, in the climax and resolution of the scene she comes to feel that her essential and integral identity will remain and that she does have the ability to return to her former self: "She would make her breath come quietly in and out, for she was still herself, Ellen Chesser." This new sense of her self continues, as we see a few pages later: ". . . a deep sense of eternal and changeless well-being suffused the dark, a great quiet structure reported of itself, and sometimes out of this wide edifice . . . a sweet quiet voice would arise . . . , saying with all finality, 'Here I am.'" The chapter ends with Ellen's recognition of the internal structures she has created despite her failed relationship with Jonas. Two kinds of structures—those which are "everlasting and undiminished within herself" and those which are "fashioned out of her experience"—combine to give her a sense of having meaningfully ordered her world, of having reached a "high maturity."

Finally, we are not to see these moments of discovery and affirmation as belonging solely to her developmental years. While the earlier parts of the novel do seem fuller in terms of psychological development (and this only makes sense as it is the early and formative years during which the forging of one's identity takes place), a few powerful moments of reaffirmation do occur in her adult life. While she has usually resorted to the use of a man's name to articulate her desires, her relationship with Jasper changes the pattern just a bit. The one word entirely her own—"no"—comes to her in her one true moment of utter strength, in which she uses her mental and emotional power, "her inner 'no,'" to bring Jasper back. Despite this emphatic assertion of "no," Ellen later reaches a place of positive affirmation. Near the end of the novel, as she is performing household duties, we see again this inner drive to insist on both her existence in the living present and her own and unique identity. Roberts writes: "Suddenly a soft whisper came to her lips as she looked [at the batter], as she pen-

etrated the moving mass, a whisper scarcely breathed and scarcely articulated, as would say, 'Here . . . I am . . . Ellen . . . I'm here.'"

While Ellen as a heroine does not provide Roberts with a consciousness that articulates itself very frequently, she does provide the author with a mind that articulates occasionally and, on those occasions, powerfully. As we have seen, Ellen's innate ear for sounds and rhythms, her receptivity to the power of remembered phrases, and her sensitivity to the voices of those around her show us that, while she is not very literate, she is using language to achieve a sense of herself as a growing and separate identity unique from all others. We see her at the end of the novel, working the farm, yet still trying to articulate "a lasting question that gathered around some unspoken word such as 'why' or 'how.' . . . [H]er lasting inquiry, her questioning anguish, would gather about this remote image, this phrase, and ask it, and beg it for redress, for remission, for pity." Her "more ordered knowing" has helped Jasper work through "his chaos of anger and his confusion" and has had much to do with the marriage's survival. Her children, the people who have come out of her "forever," have been linked in her mind to Luke Wimble's words, and, so, while she may not have given life to a structured unit of words, she has become a worthy creator in her own right. Their lives, their jokes, their laughter, their wonder—all of these have come from her and through her. Lest we forget, though, her powerful capacity to see herself in psychological terms, Roberts reminds us one more time:

> As she sewed at some garment, rocking softly to and fro with the sway of her needle, she stopped, the seam stayed and the thread taut in her hand, stopped and remembered life. Life and herself, one, comprehensible and entire, without flaw, with beginning and end, and on the instant she herself was imaged in the lucid thought.

Lewis P. Simpson (essay date 1994)

SOURCE: "History and the Will of the Artist: Elizabeth Madox Roberts," in *The Fable of the Southern Writer,* Louisiana State University Press, 1994, pp. 54-72.

[*In the following essay, Simpson traces the development of Roberts's female protagonists as artists and as representations of artistic consciousness.*]

"I feel myself to be a Kentuckian," Elizabeth Madox Roberts said, "and all my work . . . centers around Kentucky objects." Just as her younger contemporary William Faulkner took as his subject the history of the Deep South state of Mississippi, Roberts took as her subject the history of the border state of Kentucky. As with Faulkner, this choice was dictated by the discovery that her imaginative reaction to life in her native state defined the encompassing experience of the modern literary artist: the experience of a constant tension between the self and history.

Roberts' historical sensibility was formed by a singular circumstance of her education: her early acquaintance with an eighteenth-century philosophical treatise, Bishop Berkeley's *The Principles of Human Knowledge.* She was introduced to this book by her father, Simpson Roberts, a Confederate veteran who had a penchant for philosophical speculation. Having early in his education developed an obsessive devotion to Berkeley, he made a strong effort to mold his sensitive, precocious daughter in the image of his discipleship. How seriously the child took her father is indicated by the way her entire career as a novelist suggests a struggle to repudiate Berkeley and, one supposes, not less her father. The major motive of Elizabeth Madox Roberts' fiction, to be sure, may be taken as her sense, seldom overt but constantly implied, of the pathos of the effort to transcend the constraint the modern subjectivity of history imposes on the imagination of the literary artist.

I do not mean to imply that as she developed the matter of Kentucky the novelist Elizabeth Madox Roberts came to question a formal commitment to Berkeleian idealism. Her struggle against Berkeley arose from her realization of what the Berkeleian idealism her father had attempted to indoctrinate her with fundamentally represents: the registration—more directly so in Berkeley than in any other post-Baconian philosopher—of a profound internalization of being. Bacon, advising that nature be referred to mind, said mind must put nature on the torture rack and extract all her secrets. Locke, referring mind to mind, said mind must look "into mind and see how it works." Berkeley said mind must "consult" itself; then, conceiving a stronger imperative than either Bacon or Locke, added that mind must "ransack" itself. It is interesting that Berkeley tried his hand at poetry only once, when—under pressure of the strongest desire that ever gripped him, to establish a university in the New World—he set down his vision in the famous poem "On the Prospect of Planting Arts and Learning in America." Originally called "America, or the Muse's Refuge: A Prophecy," Berkeley's poem is conventional in its treatment of the paired themes of the transfer of empire and the transfer of letters and learning from East to West.

> There shall be sung another Golden Age,
> The rise of Empire and of Arts,
> The good and great inspiring epic rage,
> The wisest heads and noblest hearts.
> Not such as Europe breeds in her decay;
> Such as she bred when fresh and young,
> When heavenly flames did animate her clay,
> By future poets shall be sung.
> Westward the course of empire takes its way;
> The four first acts already past,
> A fifth shall close the drama with the day;
> Time's noblest offspring is the last.

> [*Works of George Berkeley,* edited by
> Alexander Campbell Fraser, 1901]

What moves Berkeley's poem is not its treatment of an ancient commonplace, as compelling as this may be.

The force of Berkeley's idea derives from the vision Bacon had a century earlier of the direct equation in the new age between knowledge and power. When he said knowledge is power, Bacon implicitly recognized that the old notion of a transfer of arts and learning from East to West had been replaced by the concept of a momentous, progressive transference of God, man, nature, and mind itself into mind; that, in short, mind had become the key to history, the source and model of historical order. In Berkeley's vision of the Baconian implication, the progress of letters, learning, and the various arts, or the succession of knowledge, will no longer be conceived to be an aspect of the succession of empire. Empire, mind, power, and history will be indivisibly related. The succession of knowledge *is* the succession of empire. Symbolized by Berkeley's dream of founding a university in the New World, the American destiny will be the fulfillment of the last act in the drama of history: the succession of knowledge to America and the subsequent American incarnation of the imperial power of mind.

The awareness of mind as the creating source and model of American history has been inescapably the major aspect of the literary imagination in America from the age of the American Enlightenment to the present. The evolvement of the literary imagination in America has been altogether a part of the movement of all things into mind. I am thinking at this point not simply of the literary perception of the rational mind as the model of our history but also about the unhappy imposition mind makes on the individual imagination and on the self of the writer when, as Berkeley suggested, it follows its imperative to ransack itself. Probably implying more than he intended to about the character of mind, Berkeley suggested what was later to become clear: in its seemingly infinite manifestations of itself, both conscious and unconscious, mind had begun by the seventeenth century, as is evident in Marlowe and Shakespeare, to experience the uncertainty of its own motives, to become burdensome to itself. The uncertainty was especially vexing and distressing to the poetic and artistic faculties of mind, which had always located mind's creative sources in transcendent, supermental, suprahistorical models of order. Through their embodiment in the particular poets and artists of a particular time and place, the transcendent, universal models of order controlled the visible society. The ancient and medieval bards, together with the sculptors, architects, and painters, all these inspired by the muses, had each served as portrayers and interpreters of transcendent formulations of order; in no sense had they served as originators of models, and surely in no sense as models themselves. Now the arts and especially literature had become chief agencies for the act of transforming existence into mind, and not simply the elucidators of the drama of self and history but intimate participants in it. The redoubtable Elizabethan Captain John Smith speaks in his *Generall Historie of Virginia* about the actor who becomes the relator. Even a bluff adventurer like Smith sensed, with Shakespeare and Donne, what Berkeley intimates so clearly in *The Practice of Human Knowledge:* history has become an act of thought. Acting and relating—the actor and the relator, the hero and the storyteller—have become one in the historical act. Smith might almost be said to have intuited that the colony of Virginia would directly produce the actions of thought that resulted in the American Revolution, the new republic, and the creation of the first trans-Allegheny state of the United States, Kentucky.

It was as an eminently self-conscious participant in the act of thought that was, and is, Kentucky that Elizabeth Madox Roberts achieved her extraordinary novels. Envisioning Kentucky as the result of the modern mind's transference of a wilderness into itself, she envisioned her own part in this act; of her own part—to apply to her case the language of Robert Penn Warren—in living and making "the big myth of history." Let us turn to some analysis of Roberts' vision in its leading manifestation, its embodiment in her heroines.

Four of these are figures of the artist and, to an appreciable degree, I believe, surrogates of the author. In each instance the heroine represents the mind—the consciousness—of the artist figure as the crux of the relation between self and history; each artist figure, moreover, represents the model of history in the consciousness of the feminine artist. The heroines I am referring to are Ellen Chesser in *The Time of Man* (1926), Theodosia Bell in *My Heart and My Flesh* (1927), Diony Hall Jarvis in *The Great Meadow* (1930), and Jocelle Drake in *He Sent Forth a Raven* (1935). A shadowy presence among these figures, it must be added, is a woman whose first name is Luce. The novelist had large intentions for Luce, evidently planning to make her the center of a Kentucky saga and call the whole "The Book (or Books) of Luce." But save for the prologue to *My Heart and My Flesh,* in which Luce is called Luce Jarvis, this idea remained unfulfilled.

I shall return to Luce. I shall also comment in a moment on one heroine who is outside the Kentucky books, the female spider who spins her web in the blackthorn bush in *Jingling in the Wind* (1928). But first let us consider Ellen Chesser and Theodosia Bell. In 1923, three years before *The Time of Man* was published, Elizabeth Madox Roberts set down a curious reflection on the "argument" (her term) she wanted to work out in the novel.

> It could never be an analysis of society or of a societal stratum because it keeps starkly within one consciousness, and that one being not an analytical nature of a "conscious" consciousness. There is a tryst here, a bargain between two, and two only, and these are Ellen and Life, and then there is Life. Life uses her. What is this unit, this not-life substance which Life uses and breaks to its end?
>
> Life runs in form, design, alike for all instances. Ellen is the variant, the ego, the wonder, the asking unit.

Asserting a difference between the naturalistic life force and a transcending "not-life substance" that is yet "used" by life (symbolized by Ellen), the novelist seems to posit a spiritual power that, to use the Heideggerian term, is "radically immanent" in life. Although it is doubtful that she was directly acquainted with Heidegger's longing for transcendence within immanence, Roberts shows an affinity with the philosopher who in *Being and Time* distills the pervasive dilemma of a culture moving toward a final collapse of transcendence into immanence—toward the conviction that not only the earth and its inhabitants but the idea of God and the realm of the supratemporal is subject to historical analysis. *The Time of Man* turns on the tension present in the "unconscious conscious" attributed to Ellen by the author in her notes. She is a contrary presence in her world. She is incapable of analytical consciousness, yet her mind consciously registers the places and people that mark her encounter with life. The drama of Ellen's awareness of life, in other words, presents a symbolic situation far beyond her intellectual comprehension but germane to her creator's way of thinking and feeling: the problematic assumption that life transcends history comes up against the evidence that the tenant sharecroppers of the Kentucky tobacco country are immutably creatures of history. Neither peasants (self-supporting land laborers and cultivators living in small village communities) nor, in the European sense, a "folk" (a people who live in a traditionalist culture rooted in Christianity yet are more fundamentally rooted in the timeless thought patterns of a pre-Christian culture), the Kentucky croppers are the descendants of those who only a few generations back had emigrated from an older New World to a newer one to participate in the Jeffersonian dream of dividing a wilderness into self-subsistent freeholds, each freehold being in the Jeffersonian view a symbol of the free mind. But even in its representation in Jefferson, the mind that served as the model of the Republic was divided against itself. On the one hand it associated its freedom with the right to use slaves (or, later, sharecroppers) to work the land, and on the other it identified its freedom with the independence of the freeholder. The eventual result was a conflict of unprecedented ferocity. Permanently displaced by the political and economic circumstances of the American Civil War, the great-great-grandchildren of the original actors in the Jeffersonian dream appear in *The Time of Man* as uneducated tenant farmers. Wandering from farm to farm and landlord to landlord, they are unaware that the identity with the land known to their forebears has been lost. Actors in a dream turned nightmare, they do not know it. Connected to the land solely through the cash nexus, they have neither a sacramental nor an intellectual obligation to it.

But Ellen Chesser—called in the author's notes "the ego, the wonder, the asking unit"—has epiphanic moments of self-identity. Helping her father clear land for a field on a "virgin hill," she hears him remark, "No plow ever cut this here hill afore, not in the whole time of man." Later her father goes to get seeds to plant, and she is alone.

> She piled stones from the plowed soil and piled them in her neat mound, and the wind continued to blow off the hilltop. . . . To the northeast the hills rolled away so far that the sight gave out, and still they went, fading into blue hazes and myths of faint trees; delicate trees stood finer than hair lines on a far mythical hill. The rocks fell where she laid them with a faint flat sound, and the afternoon seemed very still back of the dove calls and the cries of the plovers, back of a faint dying phrase, "in the time of man." The wind lapped through the sky, swirling lightly now, and again dashing straight down from the sun. She was leaning over the clods to gather a stone, her shadow making an arched shadow on the ground. All at once she lifted her body and flung up her head to the great sky that reached over the hills and shouted:
>
> "Here I am!"
>
> She waited listening.
>
> "I'm Ellen Chesser! I'm here!"

Completely attached to the society in which she lives, Ellen, who, as she must, becomes the wife of a tenant farmer, is yet strangely detached. At times, her beauty moving among the men and the animals, she resembles Eula Varner in Faulkner's *The Hamlet.* But unlike Faulkner in the case of Eula, Elizabeth Madox Roberts—although she suggests a certain ambiguity about whether Ellen is innocent of history or simply ignorant of it—does not quite allow the ambivalent suggestion that she is an earth goddess displaced in history. Ellen's innocence, or ignorance, of history simply confirms her immanence in history, her innocence or ignorance being only the reverse of the conscious awareness of history. Thus Ellen figures in *The Time of Man* not, as some of her interpreters would have it, as a symbolic representation of the restoration of the sense of wonder and mythic consciousness, but as a symbol of the isolation of the poetic self in history which occurred once the irreversible transfer of being and existence into mind and history began.

Underlying Ellen's presence in *The Time of Man* is the recognition of the pathos of any effort to restore the prehistorical consciousness. The time of man is the time of history. At the end of the novel, Elizabeth Madox Roberts obliquely but surely confirms her realization of this truth. Ellen and her sharecropper husband Jasper and their brood are on the road at night, once again on the way, to a "somewheres" that will, they hope, be better for them. The children are watching the stars as the wagon moves along. One of the boys, Dick, observes to his brother Hen that you could learn the names of the stars if you had a book. Scientific knowledge, little Dick recognizes, is the power unto life. Longing for knowledge, which in all likelihood is in his case unattainable,

Ellen's child ironically implies the pathos of a kind of ultimate isolation of the human spirit. Aspiring to be a self, the human spirit existing in the world of the sharecroppers—which is, after all, a part of the historical world created by the Baconian imperative—lacking both the power of mythic consciousness and the power of rational knowledge, cannot participate in the world of which it is a part.

While *The Time of Man* may be taken as a discovery of the defeat by history of instinctive wonder and delight, *My Heart and My Flesh* may be read as the discovery of a situation more profound and more distressing. "My protagonist here," Roberts comments in her notes, "is a more self-conscious person than my Ellen was, and thus the book moves in a more inward way." An important but subordinate theme in *The Time of Man,* sexuality, is the dominant motive in *My Heart and My Flesh,* reminding us that Elizabeth Madox Roberts, like Joyce, Lawrence, and Faulkner, belonged to the age of Freud. Understanding what we may take to be Freud's central insight—namely, that the transference of being into mind has meant the transference of sexuality into history—Roberts grasped the possibility that the self-conscious, rational recognition of the implication of sexuality in history may be the leading aspect of modern historiography. Whereas sexual behavior—controlled by an elaborate, transcendent symbolism derived from an amalgam of classical and Hebraic-Christian myths—had been external to self-consciousness, in Freud it becomes integral to self-consciousness. Identifying self with the imperatives of sexuality, mind's search for the meaning of sexual behavior encloses the self in history with finality.

Among American novelists the struggle against the demythologizing of sex is written largest in Faulkner, being the core of his first great work, *The Sound and the Fury.* This novel was published in 1929, but the first truly compelling depiction of the struggle against the demythologizing of sex by an American writer had appeared two years before *The Sound and the Fury* in *My Heart and My Flesh.* Possessing the refined self-consciousness of an educated and passionate artist, the heroine of this story is frustrated in her career as a violinist by a simple genetic impairment: her hands, it turns out, are not adequately structured for the instrument she plays. But the physical impediment to Theodosia Bell's career is no more than a symbol of a more absolute constraint: the deformation of her consciousness by the cruel sexuality of the demythicized historical society in which she strives for her identity as an artist. Sexual disasters multiply in Theodosia's life. Her true lover dies in a fire (and then is falsely accused of having fathered a bastard by one of the girls in the community); she learns that she has two half sisters and a half brother who are mulattoes (and at one point finds her half brother in bed with one of his sisters); her grandfather, with whom she has her sole secure relationship, dies; and as he is dying, she becomes aware that her own father has an incestuous desire for her.

Emotionally shattered, Theodosia is on the edge of suicide. But she is saved—redeemed, so to speak, from the sexuality of history—by a moment of spiritual ecstasy. The "sudden spasm of movement" that would have taken her through the door to plunge into the dark waters of the pond is suddenly, miraculously transformed into an orgasmic entrance into a new life: "At once a vivid appearance entered her mind, so brilliant and powerful that her consciousness was abashed. Larger than the world, more spacious than the universe, the new apparition spread through her members and tightened her hands so that they knotted suddenly together. . . . Her body spread widely and expanded . . . and the earth came back, herself acutely aware of it."

Ellen Chesser experiences the infinite as "a sweet quiet voice" that, "harmonious and many-winged" and "released from all need or obligation," says, "Here I am." One might say that Theodosia's experience sexualizes Berkeleian metaphysics. Furthermore, it subtly asserts a reversal of the masculine and feminine power in the act of creativity. In her epiphanic moment, she not only experiences an orgasmic awakening to a new life but acquires a phalliclike power to penetrate the womb of the universe: "She had shifted her gaze so that she looked now into the fire. She sat leaned forward, tense with new life, with the new world, and she penetrated the embers with her gaze and saw into the universe of the fire, the firmament of dimly glowing heat that receded, world on worlds, back into infinities, atoms, powers, all replete with their own abundance."

After her resurrection Theodosia assumes the qualities of a fertility goddess. The birds on the farm where she is living sing "as if it were to celebrate the coming of Aphrodite among the herds, to announce the beginnings of fine desires and the passing of Aphrodite among the pastures." Her life merges with that of the cows— Queen, Mollie, Betty, Hawthorne, and Princess—creatures described in sensuous images that suggest that they, and Theodosia, bear a relation to the ancient mythology of the powerful, often aggressive, and terrifying cow goddesses like Io, Europa, and Pasiphae. How much more Roberts was up to in *My Heart and My Flesh* than a comforting pastoral resolution of Theodosia's sufferings is intimated in a note in her papers on the significance of Horace Bell, Theodosia's father: "Horace Bell is not an accurate [*i.e.,* actual?] portrait, but I have known men as brutal. During the process of writing I have always a great deal of machinery off stage which makes the performance move. Writing of him, then, I thought of him as a great Jovian thunderer lacking Jove's benignant paternality. He is the Don Juan ideal of freedom carried to the end of its logic. Beyond him lies the spider that is eaten by his female, and a new world."

Engaged in writing the satirical fantasy *Jingling in the Wind* at the same time she was working on *My Heart and My Flesh,* Roberts must have had in mind the scene in *Jingling in the Wind* when Jeremy the rainmaker discovers an exquisite, enigmatic spider in a blackthorn bush by a pool and learns from her that she is spinning the whole design of life out of herself. Hurt because his beloved Tulip McAfee has derisively called him a "Rain-bat," Jeremy decides the masculine sex has been too submissive and that he will institute a "Masculine Renaissance." The spider says to go ahead, that this event, like all things, is woven into the web; but then she quietly announces that she will not be weaving tomorrow.

"Tomorrow I expect to eat my husband."

"Where is your husband?" Jeremy asked.

"I have not seen him yet," said the spider, "but he will turn up tomorrow. I will eat him down to the last mouthful. Then I will begin a new race of spiders, each one as complex as myself. It is all very intricate."

What is actually woven into the web, it would seem, is the intricate and unceasing aggression of the female against the masculine will. Thus the overall design of existence makes Jeremy's idea of a masculine renaissance absured. Although the spider deprecates Jeremy's commonplace moralism that "history teaches," she herself and her web constitute the emblem of an equation between the "life design" and history. Determined by the life design, history moves ruthlessly toward its fulfillment in the self-will of the feminine artist.

The closure of history in the life design spun out of the belly of the spider—the Supreme Author and Designer, the Ultimate Cause—is perfected at the end of *Jingling in the Wind*. Jeremy's delusion that he has restored chivalry and masculine domination and has returned woman to her proper and subordinate role (though he had yielded utterly to Tulip) is celebrated by the singing of old love ballads. The singing ended, "that most exquisite spider that crouched at the hub of the web that is the mind stirred, feeling a tremor pass over the web as if some coil were shaken by a visitation from without. Life is from within, and thus the noise outside is a wind blowing in a mirror. But love is a royal visitor which that proud ghost, the human spirit, settles in elegant chambers and serves with the best." Although the human spirit with its capacity for love can still be visited by love, *Jingling in the Wind* implies, it is a ghost in the house of mind (or the house of history, or the house of the life design). The noise love makes in the house is as silent as the wind blowing in a mirror. The spider's web is finally a symbol of the separation of mind from spirit. It may be taken—I suppose more ominously—as a symbol of the isolation and death of love in the will to make the feminine the fulfillment of history.

In *Jingling in the Wind,* Elizabeth Madox Roberts reached a potential crisis in the relationship between making the little myth of poetry and living the big myth of history. Abstracting the drama of self and history in fantasy and allegory was a way of exploring the historical and philosophical implications of the stories of Ellen

Chesser and Theodosia Bell, but it threatened to dissociate the author from her primary material, the matter of Kentucky. In *The Great Meadow* she turned toward providing a rationale for the stories of Ellen and Theodosia in the historical origin of their world, the settlement of Kentucky during the age of the American Revolution. The result was a historical fantasy, in which, far more than in *My Heart and My Flesh,* an ancient goddess is associated with the mind's interiorization of the historical will to power. I am speaking of Diony Hall Jarvis' reincarnation of Dione—"a great goddess . . . the mother of Venus by Jupiter, in the lore of Homer, an older report than that of the legendary birth through the foam of the sea . . . one of the Titan sisters, the Titans being earth-men, children of Uranus and Terra." Diony's father, the blacksmith-scholar Thomas Hall, obviously an oblique personification of Roberts' own father, associates his daughter with Rhea, mother of gods, who signifies "succession." A disciple of Berkeley, Hall takes *The Principles of Human Knowledge* as his Bible and inculcates the philosopher's teachings in his daughter. He conceives that when Diony leaves her home in Virginia for Kentucky, the newest New World, with her new husband, Berk Jarvis, she is an instrument of the succession of history. A powerful goddess and a disciple of Berkeley, Diony is fulfilling the mission of "historic Man" to bring "such men as have no history to humble themselves and learn their lesson." Although neither Hall nor his daughter mentions Berkeley's "On the Prospect of Planting Arts and Learning in America," they are embodiments of Berkeley's dream of America.

Diony's representation of Berkeley—and of mind in the New World—is symbolized in her work at the loom, an act invested with an aura of sexuality.

> Her eyes followed the flaxen web which was a yellowish gray like some woman's hair, and as such it clung to her thought and twined gray spirals about any words her throat contrived but left unsaid. Her mind slipped to her father's books and tried to bring this idolatrous devotion into relation with what she had read [in Berkeley], and she divided the several processes of willing, imagining, and remembering, and placed the supreme act in one governing Spirit where all unimagined and unwilled and unremembered acts are kept before they are called into being. Having come to the inmost thought, the inmost realization, she held it one instant before it slipped swiftly beyond her most penetrating reaching.

But in her art as a weaver Diony has penetrated the "governing Spirit." Judging from the resourcefulness with which she meets the supreme crisis of the story, she is even in a sense the custodian of acts not yet called into being. The resolution of the crisis is already within the fabric. When Berk returns to the frontier community, long after being given up for dead, to find Diony remarried, it is not the two men who, by fist or knife, decide whose wife she is. By the law of the wilderness—

by the law of a new world—it is Diony who chooses between the two, both worthy fathers of her children. Although Berk left a squaw and Indian children behind when he escaped from captivity, Diony regards this as having been a physical necessity and admits it as no impediment to her decision. When she acknowledges Berk as her husband, she chooses squarely on the basis of his greater psychic strength, responding to her sense of a will that is mated to her own. And yet in the very act of choosing she asserts the dominance of her will—a will that is sanctioned by the law of the wilderness, by the basic nature of things. Figuratively speaking, she eats her mates. As the narrative consciousness of *The Great Meadow*—the interpreter of the motives and meaning not only of her husbands but of the leading figure in the legend of Kentucky, Daniel Boone, the prototype of the prime American hero Leatherstocking—she conceives her idea of the world and wills the idea into being. Choosing between Berk and Muir, she defies history as a naturalistic life design. Diony does not simply live the myth of history, she makes the myth she lives.

At this juncture in her career—having in *The Great Meadow* correlated civilization and the inward movement of history, having portrayed the heroic differentiation of history from chaos through the power of the feminine mind, having made a feminine literary imagination formed in Kentucky and the American South the model of American history—Roberts might well have turned toward assimilating her vision of history in the will, imagination, and remembrance of her dream character, the woman called Luce. According to indications in her papers, she had this in view at the beginning of her work as a novelist; for she had intended to introduce into *The Time of Man* two or three digressive episodes. In these passages Luce, I judge, would have appeared in the role Diony occupies in *The Great Meadow*. Relator of and actor in the heroic age of Kentucky, Luce would have served as a counterpoint to Ellen, their stories suggesting dramatic comparisons and contrasts, continuities and discontinuities between the heroic age and a time a century and a half later.

Having dropped Luce from the scheme of *The Time of Man,* Roberts brought her into the prologue of *My Heart and My Flesh*. Here she appears as a young girl named Luce Jarvis. But she is not the Luce of the pioneer period; she is one of Theodosia's childhood companions. Nobody seems to know quite what to make of this introductory portion of *My Heart and My Flesh*. Perhaps it conveys the notion that Theodosia is an aspect of Luce, just as Luce in the abandoned sections of *The Time of Man* may have served to suggest that the Luce of Kentucky's heroic era is an aspect of Ellen. But Diony is not an aspect of Luce. She is herself. Having in *The Great Meadow* created a strong character to replace the Luce of the early time, the novelist, one would think, would have been ready to develop an account of the generations between Diony Hall Jarvis and the Luce Jarvis of the twentieth century. If Roberts had stayed within Diony's imagination of history, she could have plunged ahead with an epic version of Diony's later life, and the years of the children and grandchildren; bringing in the coming of the Civil War, the war epoch, and the bitter aftermath, she could have given the epic story coherence and force by relating it to the original vision of a strong feminine actor and relator and its fulfillment in her successors. But as far as I can tell this was never a possibility. The Luce sketched in the notebooks had a firm hold on the imagination of her creator.

In Roberts' first conception of Diony, her story was to have been told as part of a larger reconstruction of the Kentucky past by the twentieth-century Luce Jarvis. One note in the Roberts Papers reads: "Luce Jarvis. Has in her possession or in their possession, one pewter spoon marked with a rude free hand, Diony, and a few leaves of a journal. Out of this Luce reconstructs the past. The ink faded into the brown of the paper which is burnt by air and light and time to be a frail dry chip. A strong fine hand is written. An Eighteenth Century hand writing an Eighteenth Century way of thought, setting it beside an Eighteenth Century anxiety." Elsewhere among the notes we find a more specific description of the spoon Luce will use as one way of reconstructing the past: "A spoon shaped to fit into a mouth. It has the hollow of a hungry tongue. It is fitted and cupped to meet the hunger of lips." (In its first form the last sentence read "fitted and cupped to meet the hunger of tongues," but *tongues* is scratched out and the less suggestive *lips* substituted.) One has the impression that the novelist was contemplating a novel of more complicated dimensions than *The Great Meadow*. It would have been something like a Proustian quest for the past in the present and the present in the past, more specifically perhaps a Proustian effort to define the sexuality of modern history.

Among other jottings concerning Luce are two that invite juxtaposing. One is a declaration by Luce: "I will be something of my own right, of myself, I Luce Jarvis." The other is a conjuration of Luce by the author: "I look in the glass and I see a form having a clearly defined color against the dark of the watery air that hangs about me. I see Luce Jarvis myself." The *myself* can be taken merely as intensive, yet it has reflexive force. In the observations on Luce in the Roberts notes, we also come across a couple of attempts to estimate her personal qualities. One stresses Luce's "clarity" and "frankness," calls her "simple and honest" and "straightforward." But a longer entry suggests a much more complex Luce.

> She could find within herself little to identify with what she read of experience in love or family experience, little to coincide with the fixed emotions and patterns of the old stories. She thought she must herself be wrong and her way of life out of all relation to the truth as she read it. She could not find her way. This and that was continually true in her own flesh. She could not find the fixed pattern. She thought her life must not be real and herself wrong, her love wrong.

Some of the notes I have been drawing on may have been made as early as 1927. The novel that ultimately came out of them in 1935, *He Sent Forth a Raven,* is a story centering in Jocelle Drake and her father, Stoner Drake, a man who has taken a vow never to set his foot on the earth again. The chief characters were first conceived as Luce Jarvis and her father, Stone Jarvis. The conception of the father remained the same after he became Stoner Drake; but the conception of the daughter was altered considerably when Luce became Jocelle. Apparently the Luce Jarvis-Stone Jarvis novel would have responded to the elaborate concern for the past that the author demonstrated by her devotion to the genealogies of her fictitious Kentuckians. It would have responded to her vision of a saga based on the progression of a family out of the Old World into Virginia, then in a later generation across the dangerous Trace into Kentucky; then in still later generations the fate of the family as Kentucky entered into the history of the continental nation. Among the succession of family members would be William Jarvis, born in 1865. As one device in the story, Luce would have an old-fashioned loom. While her father stomped about overhead, blowing his horn and commanding his farm hands, she was to weave a tapestry symbolizing the heroic period of the Jarvises. Depicting a blockhouse within a stockade and Indians and their artifacts, the tapestry was to be a work of great care and devotion. Its woven-in title—replete with a large measure of irony between pastoral ideal and historical actuality—would be "The Great Meadow, 1774." But this concept of presenting the story of the settlement of Kentucky was drastically altered. The device of the tapestry was abandoned. The story of the settlement was assigned to the consciousness of Diony Jarvis. When she took this step, the author of the projected Book of Luce effectively abandoned both the book and its heroine. Her reason for rejecting Luce for Diony, I surmise, is basically that Luce was too close to the doubt and anxiety that haunted her creator's inmost consciousness. The heroic element in Luce was insufficient; she lacked the power to overcome the terror of modern existence. There is a stark gloss in Roberts' hand on one of the several genealogical charts in her papers: "Appalled at Life." Like Faulkner, Elizabeth Madox Roberts was nearly overwhelmed by the disorder of history. Seeking a redemption from it, she sought a character who had what she thought she herself did not sufficiently have—an executive will, or, as one might say, an executive sexuality.

Roberts did not entirely relinquish Luce. She comes back as an aspect of Jocelle Drake. I think it is not farfetched to believe that the intention was through Jocelle to invest Luce with a commanding will. As in *My Heart and My Flesh,* the heroine of *He Sent Forth a Raven* is almost overpowered by the masculinity of her society, becoming at last the victim of rape committed by a cousin on his way to the war. Her redemption from this traumatic incident involves her becoming an embodiment, not of Dione, but, like Theodosia, of Aphrodite, a daughter of the primal goddess. Only this time the emblems of the heroine's state of renewal are not cows, nor even the doves usually associated with Aphrodite, but creatures without mythic status, white Plymouth Rock chickens. The pastoral realism contributes rather than detracts from the believability of Jocelle's discovery, in the epiphanic moment in *He Sent Forth a Raven,* that she is not isolated from being but shares what all human beings share: a "common mental pattern where individual traits merge," a community of the human spirit. Yet this comforting revelation is not so significant in the redemption of Jocelle as a force more fundamental than her attraction to "communal devotions and emotions": "the lonely will, the wish, the desire [for] . . . the underlying complexity reducible within itself and of itself to the one simple determinate, lonely among its fellows, aloof, arising now to a super-life, the will to believe, to live, to hate evil, to gather power out of emotion, to divide hate from love where the two are interlocked in one emotion, the will to love God the creator."

Now anyone who is sensitive to the elementary themes of Christian theology will sense in Jocelle's vision of the will to the "super-life" the gravest heresy. In affirming the efficacy of the autonomous will in her redemption, Jocelle denies the efficacy of God's grace. One cannot deliberately will to love God without identifying the human will and God's will. Since Jocelle is not an artist, and may be taken as a rather ordinary Kentucky girl of her time, we may not readily relate her to the complicated quest for transcendence by the artist Elizabeth Madox Roberts. But let us set Jocelle's moment of illumination beside a kind of epiphanic moment that came to the writer herself. I refer again to a note in her papers.

> There is finally and at first, last and first, the aesthetic requirement, the desire to be completed. Beyond theses and plot, beyond history and the daily real, is a thematic design—this final satisfaction to be met. The mind requires fulfillment. One cannot avoid the demand. Some ultimate and fit design beyond all the uses of the mind, some necessity inherent in human works, calls for the consummation. Shall we say the "categorical aesthetic." It is the message from beyond life. The hand of God writing on the walls of the cosmos.

To declare a design beyond history—beyond the human mind—by drawing an analogy between the modern aesthetic imperative and the Kantian moral imperative is to appeal to Kant's mediation between the external and the internal, the objective and the subjective. But in the transference of existence into itself and of itself into itself, mind, as Roberts knew, had rejected Kant. In an account of her vision of art as the act of God, she had written: "The mind requires fulfillment. The tragedy must follow if it is begun. One cannot avoid the de-

mand." No doubt aware that with this declaration she had established a highly ironic, a tragic, tension between the will of the artist to creative action and the action of God, the only creator, Roberts drew a line through "The tragedy must follow as it is begun." But she could not blot the implication. Present everywhere in her work, it is summed up in Theodosia Bell's cry of desperation: "O, God, I believe, and there's nothing to believe." This desperate plea occurs in a portrait of an artist who, whether she is called Luce or Theodosia, is also to be called Elizabeth.

Pursuing the manifestations of the artistic will in Elizabeth Madox Roberts, I find myself wondering if I am guilty of unduly denigrating the spirit of hope that, at least in the days in which she was still read, many found in her stories. I have intended, however, to pay tribute to an artist who, more or less misread in her own day, presents the possibility of being read correctly in our day, when we discover her sense of history. Doing so we discover the significance of a series of novels in which in her struggle with history the author is the peer of William Faulkner, Allen Tate, and Robert Penn Warren. Of course she wrote stories other than the ones I have touched on. Some of these show a relaxation of the concern with the artistic will and the historical imperative. *A Buried Treasure* ends with an almost medieval delight in the garden of the world. The more complex *Black Is My True Love's Hair* poses the nostalgic possibility of recovering the balladic world. But even these novels turn on the sense of what intervenes between the self of the modern artist and a sacramental connection with "the simple and uncomplicated earth": to wit, a terrible intimacy with history that has dissolved both metaphysical and physical reality into illusions generated by the self-consciousness that is history and the history that is self-consciousness. Having modeled order on the society of science and history—on mind—Elizabeth Madox Roberts discovered what we are like: we believe in the idea but not in the fact: in the idea of the heart but not in the heart; in the idea of the flesh but not in the flesh; in the idea of the community but not in community; in the idea of responsibility for one another but not in the responsive, and thus responsible, act of sympathy; in the idea of love but not in the act of love.

FURTHER READING

Bibliography

Tate, Linda. "Elizabeth Madox Roberts: A Bibliographical Essay." *Resources for American Literary Study* 18, No. 1 (1992): 22-43.
> Detailed discussion of Roberts's publishing history that includes an extended survey of critical reactions to her work.

Criticism

Adams, J. Donald. "Elizabeth Madox Roberts." *Virginia Quarterly Review* 12, No. 1 (January 1936): 80-90.
  Generally favorable assessment of Roberts's novels and an extended examination of her place in contemporary world literature at the time.

Bernstein, Stephen. "Comprehension, Composition, and Closure in Elizabeth Madox Roberts's *The Time of Man.*" *The Kentucky Review* X, No. 1 (Spring 1990): 21-37.
  Argues that the structure of Roberts's novel mirrors its themes and that earlier criticism of her work failed to recognize its formal dimension.

Bishop, John Peale. "Spirit and Sense." *The Collected Essays of John Peale Bishop,* pp. 313-16, edited by Edmund Wilson. New York: Charles Scribner's Sons, 1948.
  Brief, generally favorable assessment of *Song in the Meadow.*

Buchan, Alexander M. "Elizabeth Madox Roberts." *Southwest Review* XXV, No. 4 (July 1940): 463-81.
  Examines Roberts's use of language in attempt to account for various critical misunderstandings about her work.

Davidson, Donald. "Elizabeth Madox Roberts." *The Spyglass: Views and Reviews, 1924-1930,* pp. 16-20, edited by John Tyree Fain. Nashville: Vanderbilt University Press, 1963.
  Positive review of *The Time of Man* in which Davidson compares Roberts to Glenway Westcott, asserting that she writes beautifully about "country people." The review was originally published in the Nashville *Tennessean* on 5 September 1926.

Gray, Richard. "The Good Farmer: Some Variations on a Historical Theme." *The Literature of Memory: Modern Writers of the American South,* pp. 106-49. Baltimore: The Johns Hopkins University Press, 1977.
  Chapter section headed "Womanchild in a Promised Land: Elizabeth Madox Roberts" deals with the ways in which Roberts attempted to reconcile a mythological and a reportorial approach to fiction writing.

Hardwick, Elizabeth. Introduction to *Black Is My True-love's Hair.* New York: Arno Press, 1977
  Brief overview of the novel and of Roberts's career.

McIlwaine, Shields. "Sensibility and Realism: Edith S. Kelley, Elizabeth Madox Roberts, and Paul Green." *The Southern Poor-White: From Lubberland to Tobacco Road,* pp. 199-217. Norman, OK: University of Oklahoma Press, 1939.
  Discusses the different kinds of realism employed by the three authors in their depictions of certain Southern character types.

Smith, William Jay. "A Tent of Green (Elizabeth Madox Roberts)." *The Streaks of the Tulip: Selected Criticism,* pp. 113-18. Delacorte Press, 1972.
  Highly favorable review of *Under the Tree.*

Smith, Jo Reinhard. "New Troy in the Bluegrass: Vergilian Metaphor and *The Great Meadow. The Mississippi Quarterly* XXII, No. 2 (Spring 1969): 39-46.
  Discusses the ways in which an understanding of Virgil's *Aeneis* (first century BC; *The Aeneid*) is essential to reading *The Great Meadow.*

"Elizabeth Madox Roberts." *Southern Review* 20, No. 4 (October 1984): 749-835.
  Nine essays devoted to various aspects of Roberts's life and works.

Wagenknecht, Edward. "The Inner Vision: Elizabeth Madox Roberts." *Cavalcade of the American Novel: From the Birth of the Nation to the Middle of the Twentieth Century,* pp. 389-96. New York: Henry Holt, 1952.
  Overview of Roberts's fiction.

Winters, Yvor. "*Under the Tree.*" *Yvor Winters: Uncollected Essays and Reviews,* pp. 16-18, edited by Francis Murphy. Chicago: The Swallow Press, 1973.
  Positive review of *Under the Tree.* The review was originally published in *Poetry,* Vol. XXII, No. 1, 1923.

Twentieth-Century
Literary Criticism

Cumulative Indexes
Volumes 1-68

How to Use This Index

The main references

Calvino, Italo
1923-1985.....CLC 5, 8, 11, 22, 33, 39,
73; SSC 3

list all author entries in the following Gale Literary Criticism series:

BLC = *Black Literature Criticism*
CLC = *Contemporary Literary Criticism*
CLR = *Children's Literature Review*
CMLC = *Classical and Medieval Literature Criticism*
DA = *DISCovering Authors*
DC = *Drama Criticism*
HLC = *Hispanic Literature Criticism*
LC = *Literature Criticism from 1400 to 1800*
NCLC = *Nineteenth-Century Literature Criticism*
PC = *Poetry Criticism*
SSC = *Short Story Criticism*
TCLC = *Twentieth-Century Literary Criticism*
WLC = *World Literature Criticism, 1500 to the Present*

The cross-references

See also CANR 23; CA 85-88;
obituary CA 116

list all author entries in the following Gale biographical and literary sources:

AAYA = *Authors & Artists for Young Adults*
AITN = *Authors in the News*
BEST = *Bestsellers*
BW = *Black Writers*
CA = *Contemporary Authors*
CAAS = *Contemporary Authors Autobiography Series*
CABS = *Contemporary Authors Bibliographical Series*
CANR = *Contemporary Authors New Revision Series*
CAP = *Contemporary Authors Permanent Series*
CDALB = *Concise Dictionary of American Literary Biography*
CDBLB = *Concise Dictionary of British Literary Biography*
DLB = *Dictionary of Literary Biography*
DLBD = *Dictionary of Literary Biography Documentary Series*
DLBY = *Dictionary of Literary Biography Yearbook*
HW = *Hispanic Writers*
JRDA = *Junior DISCovering Authors*
MAICYA = *Major Authors and Illustrators for Children and Young Adults*
MTCW = *Major 20th-Century Writers*
NNAL = *Native North American Literature*
SAAS = *Something about the Author Autobiography Series*
SATA = *Something about the Author*
YABC = *Yesterday's Authors of Books for Children*

Literary Criticism Series
Cumulative Author Index

Abasiyanik, Sait Faik   1906-1954
See Sait Faik
See also CA 123

Abbey, Edward   1927-1989 . . . . . . CLC 36, 59
See also CA 45-48; 128; CANR 2, 41

Abbott, Lee K(ittredge)   1947- . . . . . . CLC 48
See also CA 124; CANR 51; DLB 130

Abe, Kobo
1924-1993 . . . . CLC 8, 22, 53, 81;
DAM NOV
See also CA 65-68; 140; CANR 24; MTCW

Abelard, Peter   c. 1079-c. 1142 . . . CMLC 11
See also DLB 115

Abell, Kjeld   1901-1961 . . . . CLC 15
See also CA 111

Abish, Walter   1931- . . . . CLC 22
See also CA 101; CANR 37; DLB 130

Abrahams, Peter (Henry)   1919- . . . . . CLC 4
See also BW 1; CA 57-60; CANR 26;
DLB 117; MTCW

Abrams, M(eyer) H(oward)   1912- . . . CLC 24
See also CA 57-60; CANR 13, 33; DLB 67

Abse, Dannie
1923- . . . CLC 7, 29; DAB; DAM POET
See also CA 53-56; CAAS 1; CANR 4, 46;
DLB 27

Achebe, (Albert) Chinua(lumogu)
1930- . . . . . CLC 1, 3, 5, 7, 11, 26, 51, 75;
BLC; DA; DAB; DAC; DAM MST,
MULT, NOV; WLC
See also AAYA 15; BW 2; CA 1-4R;
CANR 6, 26, 47; CLR 20; DLB 117;
MAICYA; MTCW; SATA 40;
SATA-Brief 38

Acker, Kathy   1948- . . . . CLC 45
See also CA 117; 122; CANR 55

Ackroyd, Peter   1949- . . . . CLC 34, 52
See also CA 123; 127; CANR 51; DLB 155;
INT 127

Acorn, Milton   1923- . . . . CLC 15; DAC
See also CA 103; DLB 53; INT 103

Adamov, Arthur
1908-1970 . . . . CLC 4, 25; DAM DRAM
See also CA 17-18; 25-28R; CAP 2; MTCW

Adams, Alice (Boyd)
1926- . . . . CLC 6, 13, 46; SSC 24
See also CA 81-84; CANR 26, 53;
DLBY 86; INT CANR-26; MTCW

Adams, Andy   1859-1935 . . . . TCLC 56
See also YABC 1

Adams, Douglas (Noel)
1952- . . . . CLC 27, 60; DAM POP
See also AAYA 4; BEST 89:3; CA 106;
CANR 34; DLBY 83; JRDA

Adams, Francis   1862-1893 . . . . NCLC 33

Adams, Henry (Brooks)
1838-1918 . . . . . . TCLC 4, 52; DA; DAB;
DAC; DAM MST
See also CA 104; 133; DLB 12, 47

Adams, Richard (George)
1920- . . . . CLC 4, 5, 18; DAM NOV
See also AAYA 16; AITN 1, 2; CA 49-52;
CANR 3, 35; CLR 20; JRDA; MAICYA;
MTCW; SATA 7, 69

Adamson, Joy(-Friederike Victoria)
1910-1980 . . . . CLC 17
See also CA 69-72; 93-96; CANR 22;
MTCW; SATA 11; SATA-Obit 22

Adcock, Fleur   1934- . . . . CLC 41
See also CA 25-28R; CAAS 23; CANR 11,
34; DLB 40

Addams, Charles (Samuel)
1912-1988 . . . . CLC 30
See also CA 61-64; 126; CANR 12

Addison, Joseph   1672-1719 . . . . LC 18
See also CDBLB 1660-1789; DLB 101

Adler, Alfred (F.)   1870-1937 . . . . . . TCLC 61
See also CA 119

Adler, C(arole) S(chwerdtfeger)
1932- . . . . CLC 35
See also AAYA 4; CA 89-92; CANR 19,
40; JRDA; MAICYA; SAAS 15;
SATA 26, 63

Adler, Renata   1938- . . . . CLC 8, 31
See also CA 49-52; CANR 5, 22, 52;
MTCW

Ady, Endre   1877-1919 . . . . TCLC 11
See also CA 107

Aeschylus
525B.C.-456B.C. . . . . CMLC 11; DA;
DAB; DAC; DAM DRAM, MST

Afton, Effie
See Harper, Frances Ellen Watkins

Agapida, Fray Antonio
See Irving, Washington

Agee, James (Rufus)
1909-1955 . . . . TCLC 1, 19; DAM NOV
See also AITN 1; CA 108; 148;
CDALB 1941-1968; DLB 2, 26, 152

Aghill, Gordon
See Silverberg, Robert

Agnon, S(hmuel) Y(osef Halevi)
1888-1970 . . . . CLC 4, 8, 14
See also CA 17-18; 25-28R; CAP 2; MTCW

Agrippa von Nettesheim, Henry Cornelius
1486-1535 . . . . LC 27

Aherne, Owen
See Cassill, R(onald) V(erlin)

Ai   1947- . . . . CLC 4, 14, 69
See also CA 85-88; CAAS 13; DLB 120

Aickman, Robert (Fordyce)
1914-1981 . . . . CLC 57
See also CA 5-8R; CANR 3

Aiken, Conrad (Potter)
1889-1973 . . . . CLC 1, 3, 5, 10, 52;
DAM NOV, POET; SSC 9
See also CA 5-8R; 45-48; CANR 4;
CDALB 1929-1941; DLB 9, 45, 102;
MTCW; SATA 3, 30

Aiken, Joan (Delano)   1924- . . . . CLC 35
See also AAYA 1; CA 9-12R; CANR 4, 23,
34; CLR 1, 19; DLB 161; JRDA;
MAICYA; MTCW; SAAS 1; SATA 2,
30, 73

Ainsworth, William Harrison
1805-1882 . . . . NCLC 13
See also DLB 21; SATA 24

Aitmatov, Chingiz (Torekulovich)
1928- . . . . CLC 71
See also CA 103; CANR 38; MTCW;
SATA 56

Akers, Floyd
See Baum, L(yman) Frank

Akhmadulina, Bella Akhatovna
1937- . . . . CLC 53; DAM POET
See also CA 65-68

Akhmatova, Anna
1888-1966 . . . . CLC 11, 25, 64;
DAM POET; PC 2
See also CA 19-20; 25-28R; CANR 35;
CAP 1; MTCW

Aksakov, Sergei Timofeyvich
1791-1859 . . . . NCLC 2

Aksenov, Vassily
See Aksyonov, Vassily (Pavlovich)

Aksyonov, Vassily (Pavlovich)
1932- . . . . CLC 22, 37
See also CA 53-56; CANR 12, 48

Akutagawa, Ryunosuke
1892-1927 . . . . TCLC 16
See also CA 117; 154

Alain   1868-1951 . . . . TCLC 41

Alain-Fournier . . . . TCLC 6
See also Fournier, Henri Alban
See also DLB 65

Alarcon, Pedro Antonio de
1833-1891 . . . . NCLC 1

Alas (y Urena), Leopoldo (Enrique Garcia)
1852-1901 . . . . TCLC 29
See also CA 113; 131; HW

Albee, Edward (Franklin III)
1928- . . . . . . CLC 1, 2, 3, 5, 9, 11, 13, 25,
53, 86; DA; DAB; DAC; DAM DRAM,
MST; WLC
See also AITN 1; CA 5-8R; CABS 3;
CANR 8, 54; CDALB 1941-1968; DLB 7;
INT CANR-8; MTCW

Alberti, Rafael   1902- . . . . CLC 7
See also CA 85-88; DLB 108

Albert the Great   1200(?)-1280 . . . . CMLC 16
See also DLB 115

Alcala-Galiano, Juan Valera y
See Valera y Alcala-Galiano, Juan

Alcott, Amos Bronson 1799-1888 .. **NCLC 1**
See also DLB 1

Alcott, Louisa May
1832-1888 ..... **NCLC 6, 58; DA; DAB;
DAC; DAM MST, NOV; WLC**
See also CDALB 1865-1917; CLR 1, 38;
DLB 1, 42, 79; DLBD 14; JRDA;
MAICYA; YABC 1

Aldanov, M. A.
See Aldanov, Mark (Alexandrovich)

Aldanov, Mark (Alexandrovich)
1886(?)-1957 .... **TCLC 23**
See also CA 118

Aldington, Richard 1892-1962...... **CLC 49**
See also CA 85-88; CANR 45; DLB 20, 36,
100, 149

Aldiss, Brian W(ilson)
1925- ...... **CLC 5, 14, 40; DAM NOV**
See also CA 5-8R; CAAS 2; CANR 5, 28;
DLB 14; MTCW; SATA 34

Alegria, Claribel
1924- .... **CLC 75; DAM MULT**
See also CA 131; CAAS 15; DLB 145; HW

Alegria, Fernando 1918-......... **CLC 57**
See also CA 9-12R; CANR 5, 32; HW

Aleichem, Sholom .... **TCLC 1, 35**
See also Rabinovitch, Sholem

Aleixandre, Vicente
1898-1984 .... **CLC 9, 36; DAM POET;
PC 15**
See also CA 85-88; 114; CANR 26;
DLB 108; HW; MTCW

Alepoudelis, Odysseus
See Elytis, Odysseus

Aleshkovsky, Joseph 1929-
See Aleshkovsky, Yuz
See also CA 121; 128

Aleshkovsky, Yuz .... **CLC 44**
See also Aleshkovsky, Joseph

Alexander, Lloyd (Chudley) 1924- .. **CLC 35**
See also AAYA 1; CA 1-4R; CANR 1, 24,
38, 55; CLR 1, 5; DLB 52; JRDA;
MAICYA; MTCW; SAAS 19; SATA 3,
49, 81

Alexie, Sherman (Joseph, Jr.)
1966- .... **CLC 96; DAM MULT**
See also CA 138; NNAL

Alfau, Felipe 1902-............... **CLC 66**
See also CA 137

Alger, Horatio, Jr. 1832-1899..... **NCLC 8**
See also DLB 42; SATA 16

Algren, Nelson 1909-1981 .... **CLC 4, 10, 33**
See also CA 13-16R; 103; CANR 20;
CDALB 1941-1968; DLB 9; DLBY 81,
82; MTCW

Ali, Ahmed 1910- .... **CLC 69**
See also CA 25-28R; CANR 15, 34

Alighieri, Dante 1265-1321 .... **CMLC 3, 18**

Allan, John B.
See Westlake, Donald E(dwin)

Allen, Edward 1948-.............. **CLC 59**

Allen, Paula Gunn
1939- .... **CLC 84; DAM MULT**
See also CA 112; 143; NNAL

Allen, Roland
See Ayckbourn, Alan

Allen, Sarah A.
See Hopkins, Pauline Elizabeth

Allen, Woody
1935- .... **CLC 16, 52; DAM POP**
See also AAYA 10; CA 33-36R; CANR 27,
38; DLB 44; MTCW

Allende, Isabel
1942- .... **CLC 39, 57, 97; DAM MULT,
NOV; HLC**
See also AAYA 18; CA 125; 130;
CANR 51; DLB 145; HW; INT 130;
MTCW

Alleyn, Ellen
See Rossetti, Christina (Georgina)

Allingham, Margery (Louise)
1904-1966 .... **CLC 19**
See also CA 5-8R; 25-28R; CANR 4;
DLB 77; MTCW

Allingham, William 1824-1889 ... **NCLC 25**
See also DLB 35

Allison, Dorothy E. 1949- .... **CLC 78**
See also CA 140

Allston, Washington 1779-1843.... **NCLC 2**
See also DLB 1

Almedingen, E. M. .... **CLC 12**
See also Almedingen, Martha Edith von
See also SATA 3

Almedingen, Martha Edith von 1898-1971
See Almedingen, E. M.
See also CA 1-4R; CANR 1

Almqvist, Carl Jonas Love
1793-1866 .... **NCLC 42**

Alonso, Damaso 1898-1990 .... **CLC 14**
See also CA 110; 131; 130; DLB 108; HW

Alov
See Gogol, Nikolai (Vasilyevich)

Alta 1942-...................... **CLC 19**
See also CA 57-60

Alter, Robert B(ernard) 1935-...... **CLC 34**
See also CA 49-52; CANR 1, 47

Alther, Lisa 1944-.............. **CLC 7, 41**
See also CA 65-68; CANR 12, 30, 51;
MTCW

Altman, Robert 1925-............. **CLC 16**
See also CA 73-76; CANR 43

Alvarez, A(lfred) 1929-.......... **CLC 5, 13**
See also CA 1-4R; CANR 3, 33; DLB 14,
40

Alvarez, Alejandro Rodriguez 1903-1965
See Casona, Alejandro
See also CA 131; 93-96; HW

Alvarez, Julia 1950-.............. **CLC 93**
See also CA 147

Alvaro, Corrado 1896-1956 .... **TCLC 60**

Amado, Jorge
1912- .... **CLC 13, 40; DAM MULT,
NOV; HLC**
See also CA 77-80; CANR 35; DLB 113;
MTCW

Ambler, Eric 1909-............ **CLC 4, 6, 9**
See also CA 9-12R; CANR 7, 38; DLB 77;
MTCW

Amichai, Yehuda 1924- ...... **CLC 9, 22, 57**
See also CA 85-88; CANR 46; MTCW

Amiel, Henri Frederic 1821-1881 .. **NCLC 4**

Amis, Kingsley (William)
1922-1995 ..... **CLC 1, 2, 3, 5, 8, 13, 40,
44; DA; DAB; DAC; DAM MST, NOV**
See also AITN 2; CA 9-12R; 150; CANR 8,
28, 54; CDBLB 1945-1960; DLB 15, 27,
100, 139; INT CANR-8; MTCW

Amis, Martin (Louis)
1949- .... **CLC 4, 9, 38, 62**
See also BEST 90:3; CA 65-68; CANR 8,
27, 54; DLB 14; INT CANR-27

Ammons, A(rchie) R(andolph)
1926- .... **CLC 2, 3, 5, 8, 9, 25, 57;
DAM POET; PC 16**
See also AITN 1; CA 9-12R; CANR 6, 36,
51; DLB 5, 165; MTCW

Amo, Tauraatua i
See Adams, Henry (Brooks)

Anand, Mulk Raj
1905- .... **CLC 23, 93; DAM NOV**
See also CA 65-68; CANR 32; MTCW

Anatol
See Schnitzler, Arthur

Anaya, Rudolfo A(lfonso)
1937- .... **CLC 23; DAM MULT, NOV;
HLC**
See also CA 45-48; CAAS 4; CANR 1, 32,
51; DLB 82; HW 1; MTCW

Andersen, Hans Christian
1805-1875 .... **NCLC 7; DA; DAB;
DAC; DAM MST, POP; SSC 6; WLC**
See also CLR 6; MAICYA; YABC 1

Anderson, C. Farley
See Mencken, H(enry) L(ouis); Nathan,
George Jean

Anderson, Jessica (Margaret) Queale
.... **CLC 37**
See also CA 9-12R; CANR 4

Anderson, Jon (Victor)
1940- .... **CLC 9; DAM POET**
See also CA 25-28R; CANR 20

Anderson, Lindsay (Gordon)
1923-1994 .... **CLC 20**
See also CA 125; 128; 146

Anderson, Maxwell
1888-1959 ...... **TCLC 2; DAM DRAM**
See also CA 105; 152; DLB 7

Anderson, Poul (William) 1926- .... **CLC 15**
See also AAYA 5; CA 1-4R; CAAS 2;
CANR 2, 15, 34; DLB 8; INT CANR-15;
MTCW; SATA 90; SATA-Brief 39

Anderson, Robert (Woodruff)
1917- .... **CLC 23; DAM DRAM**
See also AITN 1; CA 21-24R; CANR 32;
DLB 7

Anderson, Sherwood
1876-1941 .... **TCLC 1, 10, 24; DA;
DAB; DAC; DAM MST, NOV; SSC 1;
WLC**
See also CA 104; 121; CDALB 1917-1929;
DLB 4, 9, 86; DLBD 1; MTCW

Andier, Pierre
   See Desnos, Robert

Andouard
   See Giraudoux, (Hippolyte) Jean

Andrade, Carlos Drummond de . . . . . . **CLC 18**
   See also Drummond de Andrade, Carlos

Andrade, Mario de 1893-1945 . . . . . **TCLC 43**

Andreae, Johann V(alentin)
      1586-1654 . . . . **LC 32**
   See also DLB 164

Andreas-Salome, Lou 1861-1937 . . . **TCLC 56**
   See also DLB 66

Andrewes, Lancelot 1555-1626 . . . . **LC 5**
   See also DLB 151, 172

Andrews, Cicily Fairfield
   See West, Rebecca

Andrews, Elton V.
   See Pohl, Frederik

Andreyev, Leonid (Nikolaevich)
      1871-1919 . . . . **TCLC 3**
   See also CA 104

Andric, Ivo 1892-1975 . . . . **CLC 8**
   See also CA 81-84; 57-60; CANR 43;
      DLB 147; MTCW

Angelique, Pierre
   See Bataille, Georges

Angell, Roger 1920- . . . . **CLC 26**
   See also CA 57-60; CANR 13, 44; DLB 171

Angelou, Maya
      1928- . . . . **CLC 12, 35, 64, 77; BLC; DA;**
      DAB; DAC; DAM MST, MULT, POET,
                                             POP
   See also AAYA 7; BW 2; CA 65-68;
      CANR 19, 42; DLB 38; MTCW;
      SATA 49

Annensky, Innokenty Fyodorovich
      1856-1909 . . . . **TCLC 14**
   See also CA 110

Anon, Charles Robert
   See Pessoa, Fernando (Antonio Nogueira)

Anouilh, Jean (Marie Lucien Pierre)
      1910-1987 . . . . . . **CLC 1, 3, 8, 13, 40, 50;**
                                             DAM DRAM
   See also CA 17-20R; 123; CANR 32;
      MTCW

Anthony, Florence
   See Ai

Anthony, John
   See Ciardi, John (Anthony)

Anthony, Peter
   See Shaffer, Anthony (Joshua); Shaffer,
      Peter (Levin)

Anthony, Piers 1934- . . **CLC 35; DAM POP**
   See also AAYA 11; CA 21-24R; CANR 28;
      DLB 8; MTCW; SAAS 22; SATA 84

Antoine, Marc
   See Proust, (Valentin-Louis-George-Eugene-)
      Marcel

Antoninus, Brother
   See Everson, William (Oliver)

Antonioni, Michelangelo 1912- . . . . . **CLC 20**
   See also CA 73-76; CANR 45

Antschel, Paul 1920-1970
   See Celan, Paul
   See also CA 85-88; CANR 33; MTCW

Anwar, Chairil 1922-1949 . . . . **TCLC 22**
   See also CA 121

Apollinaire, Guillaume
      1880-1918 . . . . **TCLC 3, 8, 51;**
                                       DAM POET; PC 7
   See also Kostrowitzki, Wilhelm Apollinaris
      de
   See also CA 152

Appelfeld, Aharon 1932- . . . . . . **CLC 23, 47**
   See also CA 112; 133

Apple, Max (Isaac) 1941- . . . . **CLC 9, 33**
   See also CA 81-84; CANR 19, 54; DLB 130

Appleman, Philip (Dean) 1926- . . . . . **CLC 51**
   See also CA 13-16R; CAAS 18; CANR 6,
      29

Appleton, Lawrence
   See Lovecraft, H(oward) P(hillips)

Apteryx
   See Eliot, T(homas) S(tearns)

Apuleius, (Lucius Madaurensis)
      125(?)-175(?) . . . . **CMLC 1**

Aquin, Hubert 1929-1977 . . . . **CLC 15**
   See also CA 105; DLB 53

Aragon, Louis
      1897-1982 . . . . . **CLC 3, 22; DAM NOV,**
                                             POET
   See also CA 69-72; 108; CANR 28;
      DLB 72; MTCW

Arany, Janos 1817-1882 . . . . **NCLC 34**

Arbuthnot, John 1667-1735 . . . . **LC 1**
   See also DLB 101

Archer, Herbert Winslow
   See Mencken, H(enry) L(ouis)

Archer, Jeffrey (Howard)
      1940- . . . . **CLC 28; DAM POP**
   See also AAYA 16; BEST 89:3; CA 77-80;
      CANR 22, 52; INT CANR-22

Archer, Jules 1915- . . . . **CLC 12**
   See also CA 9-12R; CANR 6; SAAS 5;
      SATA 4, 85

Archer, Lee
   See Ellison, Harlan (Jay)

Arden, John
      1930- . . . . . **CLC 6, 13, 15; DAM DRAM**
   See also CA 13-16R; CAAS 4; CANR 31;
      DLB 13; MTCW

Arenas, Reinaldo
      1943-1990 . . . . . . **CLC 41; DAM MULT;**
                                             HLC
   See also CA 124; 128; 133; DLB 145; HW

Arendt, Hannah 1906-1975 . . . . . **CLC 66, 98**
   See also CA 17-20R; 61-64; CANR 26;
      MTCW

Aretino, Pietro 1492-1556 . . . . **LC 12**

Arghezi, Tudor . . . . **CLC 80**
   See also Theodorescu, Ion N.

Arguedas, Jose Maria
      1911-1969 . . . . **CLC 10, 18**
   See also CA 89-92; DLB 113; HW

Argueta, Manlio 1936- . . . . **CLC 31**
   See also CA 131; DLB 145; HW

Ariosto, Ludovico 1474-1533 . . . . **LC 6**

Aristides
   See Epstein, Joseph

Aristophanes
      450B.C.-385B.C. . . . . **CMLC 4; DA;**
      DAB; DAC; DAM DRAM, MST; DC 2

Arlt, Roberto (Godofredo Christophersen)
      1900-1942 . . . . . **TCLC 29; DAM MULT;**
                                             HLC
   See also CA 123; 131; HW

Armah, Ayi Kwei
      1939- . . . . **CLC 5, 33; BLC;**
                                       DAM MULT, POET
   See also BW 1; CA 61-64; CANR 21;
      DLB 117; MTCW

Armatrading, Joan 1950- . . . . **CLC 17**
   See also CA 114

Arnette, Robert
   See Silverberg, Robert

Arnim, Achim von (Ludwig Joachim von
      Arnim) 1781-1831 . . . . **NCLC 5**
   See also DLB 90

Arnim, Bettina von 1785-1859 . . . . **NCLC 38**
   See also DLB 90

Arnold, Matthew
      1822-1888 . . . . . **NCLC 6, 29; DA; DAB;**
      DAC; DAM MST, POET; PC 5; WLC
   See also CDBLB 1832-1890; DLB 32, 57

Arnold, Thomas 1795-1842 . . . . . . **NCLC 18**
   See also DLB 55

Arnow, Harriette (Louisa) Simpson
      1908-1986 . . . . **CLC 2, 7, 18**
   See also CA 9-12R; 118; CANR 14; DLB 6;
      MTCW; SATA 42; SATA-Obit 47

Arp, Hans
   See Arp, Jean

Arp, Jean 1887-1966 . . . . **CLC 5**
   See also CA 81-84; 25-28R; CANR 42

Arrabal
   See Arrabal, Fernando

Arrabal, Fernando 1932- . . . **CLC 2, 9, 18, 58**
   See also CA 9-12R; CANR 15

Arrick, Fran . . . . **CLC 30**
   See also Gaberman, Judie Angell

Artaud, Antonin (Marie Joseph)
      1896-1948 . . . **TCLC 3, 36; DAM DRAM**
   See also CA 104; 149

Arthur, Ruth M(abel) 1905-1979 . . . . **CLC 12**
   See also CA 9-12R; 85-88; CANR 4;
      SATA 7, 26

Artsybashev, Mikhail (Petrovich)
      1878-1927 . . . . **TCLC 31**

Arundel, Honor (Morfydd)
      1919-1973 . . . . **CLC 17**
   See also CA 21-22; 41-44R; CAP 2;
      CLR 35; SATA 4; SATA-Obit 24

Arzner, Dorothy 1897-1979 . . . . **CLC 98**

Asch, Sholem 1880-1957 . . . . **TCLC 3**
   See also CA 105

Ash, Shalom
   See Asch, Sholem

Baker, Russell (Wayne) 1925-...... **CLC 31**
See also BEST 89:4; CA 57-60; CANR 11,
41; MTCW

Bakhtin, M.
See Bakhtin, Mikhail Mikhailovich

Bakhtin, M. M.
See Bakhtin, Mikhail Mikhailovich

Bakhtin, Mikhail
See Bakhtin, Mikhail Mikhailovich

Bakhtin, Mikhail Mikhailovich
1895-1975 .... **CLC 83**
See also CA 128; 113

Bakshi, Ralph 1938(?)-........... **CLC 26**
See also CA 112; 138

Bakunin, Mikhail (Alexandrovich)
1814-1876 .... **NCLC 25, 58**

Baldwin, James (Arthur)
1924-1987 ...... **CLC 1, 2, 3, 4, 5, 8, 13,
15, 17, 42, 50, 67, 90; BLC; DA; DAB;
DAC; DAM MST, MULT, NOV, POP;
DC 1; SSC 10; WLC**
See also AAYA 4; BW 1; CA 1-4R; 124;
CABS 1; CANR 3, 24;
CDALB 1941-1968; DLB 2, 7, 33;
DLBY 87; MTCW; SATA 9;
SATA-Obit 54

Ballard, J(ames) G(raham)
1930- .... **CLC 3, 6, 14, 36; DAM NOV,
POP; SSC 1**
See also AAYA 3; CA 5-8R; CANR 15, 39;
DLB 14; MTCW

Balmont, Konstantin (Dmitriyevich)
1867-1943 .... **TCLC 11**
See also CA 109

Balzac, Honore de
1799-1850 .... **NCLC 5, 35, 53; DA;
DAB; DAC; DAM MST, NOV; SSC 5;
WLC**
See also DLB 119

Bambara, Toni Cade
1939-1995 ...... **CLC 19, 88; BLC; DA;
DAC; DAM MST, MULT**
See also AAYA 5; BW 2; CA 29-32R; 150;
CANR 24, 49; DLB 38; MTCW

Bamdad, A.
See Shamlu, Ahmad

Banat, D. R.
See Bradbury, Ray (Douglas)

Bancroft, Laura
See Baum, L(yman) Frank

Banim, John 1798-1842 .... **NCLC 13**
See also DLB 116, 158, 159

Banim, Michael 1796-1874 ...... **NCLC 13**
See also DLB 158, 159

Banks, Iain
See Banks, Iain M(enzies)

Banks, Iain M(enzies) 1954-....... **CLC 34**
See also CA 123; 128; INT 128

Banks, Lynne Reid .... **CLC 23**
See also Reid Banks, Lynne
See also AAYA 6

Banks, Russell 1940- .... **CLC 37, 72**
See also CA 65-68; CAAS 15; CANR 19,
52; DLB 130

Banville, John 1945-.............. **CLC 46**
See also CA 117; 128; DLB 14; INT 128

Banville, Theodore (Faullain) de
1832-1891 .... **NCLC 9**

Baraka, Amiri
1934- .... **CLC 1, 2, 3, 5, 10, 14, 33;
BLC; DA; DAC; DAM MST, MULT,
POET, POP; DC 6; PC 4**
See also Jones, LeRoi
See also BW 2; CA 21-24R; CABS 3;
CANR 27, 38; CDALB 1941-1968;
DLB 5, 7, 16, 38; DLBD 8; MTCW

Barbauld, Anna Laetitia
1743-1825 .... **NCLC 50**
See also DLB 107, 109, 142, 158

Barbellion, W. N. P.............. **TCLC 24**
See also Cummings, Bruce F(rederick)

Barbera, Jack (Vincent) 1945-...... **CLC 44**
See also CA 110; CANR 45

Barbey d'Aurevilly, Jules Amedee
1808-1889 .... **NCLC 1; SSC 17**
See also DLB 119

Barbusse, Henri 1873-1935 .... **TCLC 5**
See also CA 105; 154; DLB 65

Barclay, Bill
See Moorcock, Michael (John)

Barclay, William Ewert
See Moorcock, Michael (John)

Barea, Arturo 1897-1957 .... **TCLC 14**
See also CA 111

Barfoot, Joan 1946-.............. **CLC 18**
See also CA 105

Baring, Maurice 1874-1945 .... **TCLC 8**
See also CA 105; DLB 34

Barker, Clive 1952- ... **CLC 52; DAM POP**
See also AAYA 10; BEST 90:3; CA 121;
129; INT 129; MTCW

Barker, George Granville
1913-1991 ..... **CLC 8, 48; DAM POET**
See also CA 9-12R; 135; CANR 7, 38;
DLB 20; MTCW

Barker, Harley Granville
See Granville-Barker, Harley
See also DLB 10

Barker, Howard 1946-............ **CLC 37**
See also CA 102; DLB 13

Barker, Pat(ricia) 1943-......... **CLC 32, 94**
See also CA 117; 122; CANR 50; INT 122

Barlow, Joel 1754-1812 .... **NCLC 23**
See also DLB 37

Barnard, Mary (Ethel) 1909-....... **CLC 48**
See also CA 21-22; CAP 2

Barnes, Djuna
1892-1982 ... **CLC 3, 4, 8, 11, 29; SSC 3**
See also CA 9-12R; 107; CANR 16, 55;
DLB 4, 9, 45; MTCW

Barnes, Julian (Patrick)
1946- .... **CLC 42; DAB**
See also CA 102; CANR 19, 54; DLBY 93

Barnes, Peter 1931- .... **CLC 5, 56**
See also CA 65-68; CAAS 12; CANR 33,
34; DLB 13; MTCW

Baroja (y Nessi), Pio
1872-1956 .... **TCLC 8; HLC**
See also CA 104

Baron, David
See Pinter, Harold

Baron Corvo
See Rolfe, Frederick (William Serafino
Austin Lewis Mary)

Barondess, Sue K(aufman)
1926-1977 .... **CLC 8**
See also Kaufman, Sue
See also CA 1-4R; 69-72; CANR 1

Baron de Teive
See Pessoa, Fernando (Antonio Nogueira)

Barres, Maurice 1862-1923 .... **TCLC 47**
See also DLB 123

Barreto, Afonso Henrique de Lima
See Lima Barreto, Afonso Henrique de

Barrett, (Roger) Syd 1946- .... **CLC 35**

Barrett, William (Christopher)
1913-1992 .... **CLC 27**
See also CA 13-16R; 139; CANR 11;
INT CANR-11

Barrie, J(ames) M(atthew)
1860-1937 .... **TCLC 2; DAB;
DAM DRAM**
See also CA 104; 136; CDBLB 1890-1914;
CLR 16; DLB 10, 141, 156; MAICYA;
YABC 1

Barrington, Michael
See Moorcock, Michael (John)

Barrol, Grady
See Bograd, Larry

Barry, Mike
See Malzberg, Barry N(athaniel)

Barry, Philip 1896-1949.......... **TCLC 11**
See also CA 109; DLB 7

Bart, Andre Schwarz
See Schwarz-Bart, Andre

Barth, John (Simmons)
1930- ...... **CLC 1, 2, 3, 5, 7, 9, 10, 14,
27, 51, 89; DAM NOV; SSC 10**
See also AITN 1, 2; CA 1-4R; CABS 1;
CANR 5, 23, 49; DLB 2; MTCW

Barthelme, Donald
1931-1989 ...... **CLC 1, 2, 3, 5, 6, 8, 13,
23, 46, 59; DAM NOV; SSC 2**
See also CA 21-24R; 129; CANR 20;
DLB 2; DLBY 80, 89; MTCW; SATA 7;
SATA-Obit 62

Barthelme, Frederick 1943-........ **CLC 36**
See also CA 114; 122; DLBY 85; INT 122

Barthes, Roland (Gerard)
1915-1980 .... **CLC 24, 83**
See also CA 130; 97-100; MTCW

Barzun, Jacques (Martin) 1907- .... **CLC 51**
See also CA 61-64; CANR 22

Bashevis, Isaac
See Singer, Isaac Bashevis

Bashkirtseff, Marie 1859-1884 ... **NCLC 27**

Basho
See Matsuo Basho

Bass, Kingsley B., Jr.
See Bullins, Ed

Bass, Rick 1958-................. **CLC 79**
See also CA 126; CANR 53

Bassani, Giorgio 1916-............. **CLC 9**
See also CA 65-68; CANR 33; DLB 128;
MTCW

Bastos, Augusto (Antonio) Roa
See Roa Bastos, Augusto (Antonio)

Bataille, Georges 1897-1962 .... **CLC 29**
See also CA 101; 89-92

Bates, H(erbert) E(rnest)
1905-1974 .... **CLC 46; DAB;**
DAM POP; SSC 10
See also CA 93-96; 45-48; CANR 34;
DLB 162; MTCW

Bauchart
See Camus, Albert

Baudelaire, Charles
1821-1867 .... **NCLC 6, 29, 55; DA;**
DAB; DAC; DAM MST, POET; PC 1;
SSC 18; WLC

Baudrillard, Jean 1929-........... **CLC 60**

Baum, L(yman) Frank 1856-1919 ... **TCLC 7**
See also CA 108; 133; CLR 15; DLB 22;
JRDA; MAICYA; MTCW; SATA 18

Baum, Louis F.
See Baum, L(yman) Frank

Baumbach, Jonathan 1933-...... **CLC 6, 23**
See also CA 13-16R; CAAS 5; CANR 12;
DLBY 80; INT CANR-12; MTCW

Bausch, Richard (Carl) 1945-...... **CLC 51**
See also CA 101; CAAS 14; CANR 43;
DLB 130

Baxter, Charles
1947-........ **CLC 45, 78; DAM POP**
See also CA 57-60; CANR 40; DLB 130

Baxter, George Owen
See Faust, Frederick (Schiller)

Baxter, James K(eir) 1926-1972 .... **CLC 14**
See also CA 77-80

Baxter, John
See Hunt, E(verette) Howard, (Jr.)

Bayer, Sylvia
See Glassco, John

Baynton, Barbara 1857-1929...... **TCLC 57**

Beagle, Peter S(oyer) 1939-........ **CLC 7**
See also CA 9-12R; CANR 4, 51;
DLBY 80; INT CANR-4; SATA 60

Bean, Normal
See Burroughs, Edgar Rice

Beard, Charles A(ustin)
1874-1948 .... **TCLC 15**
See also CA 115; DLB 17; SATA 18

Beardsley, Aubrey 1872-1898 ..... **NCLC 6**

Beattie, Ann
1947-........... **CLC 8, 13, 18, 40, 63;**
DAM NOV, POP; SSC 11
See also BEST 90:2; CA 81-84; CANR 53;
DLBY 82; MTCW

Beattie, James 1735-1803 .... **NCLC 25**
See also DLB 109

Beauchamp, Kathleen Mansfield 1888-1923
See Mansfield, Katherine
See also CA 104; 134; DA; DAC;
DAM MST

Beaumarchais, Pierre-Augustin Caron de
1732-1799 .... **DC 4**
See also DAM DRAM

Beaumont, Francis
1584(?)-1616 .... **LC 33; DC 6**
See also CDBLB Before 1660; DLB 58, 121

Beauvoir, Simone (Lucie Ernestine Marie
Bertrand) de
1908-1986 .... **CLC 1, 2, 4, 8, 14, 31, 44,**
50, 71; DA; DAB; DAC; DAM MST,
NOV; WLC
See also CA 9-12R; 118; CANR 28;
DLB 72; DLBY 86; MTCW

Becker, Carl 1873-1945 .... **TCLC 63:**
See also DLB 17

Becker, Jurek 1937-............ **CLC 7, 19**
See also CA 85-88; DLB 75

Becker, Walter 1950-............. **CLC 26**

Beckett, Samuel (Barclay)
1906-1989 ...... **CLC 1, 2, 3, 4, 6, 9, 10,**
11, 14, 18, 29, 57, 59, 83; DA; DAB;
DAC; DAM DRAM, MST, NOV;
SSC 16; WLC
See also CA 5-8R; 130; CANR 33;
CDBLB 1945-1960; DLB 13, 15;
DLBY 90; MTCW

Beckford, William 1760-1844 .... **NCLC 16**
See also DLB 39

Beckman, Gunnel 1910-.......... **CLC 26**
See also CA 33-36R; CANR 15; CLR 25;
MAICYA; SAAS 9; SATA 6

Becque, Henri 1837-1899......... **NCLC 3**

Beddoes, Thomas Lovell
1803-1849 .... **NCLC 3**
See also DLB 96

Bede c. 673-735................ **CMLC 20**
See also DLB 146

Bedford, Donald F.
See Fearing, Kenneth (Flexner)

Beecher, Catharine Esther
1800-1878 .... **NCLC 30**
See also DLB 1

Beecher, John 1904-1980........... **CLC 6**
See also AITN 1; CA 5-8R; 105; CANR 8

Beer, Johann 1655-1700............. **LC 5**
See also DLB 168

Beer, Patricia 1924-.............. **CLC 58**
See also CA 61-64; CANR 13, 46; DLB 40

Beerbohm, Max
See Beerbohm, (Henry) Max(imilian)

Beerbohm, (Henry) Max(imilian)
1872-1956 .... **TCLC 1, 24**
See also CA 104; 154; DLB 34, 100

Beer-Hofmann, Richard
1866-1945 .... **TCLC 60**
See also DLB 81

Begiebing, Robert J(ohn) 1946-..... **CLC 70**
See also CA 122; CANR 40

Behan, Brendan
1923-1964 .... **CLC 1, 8, 11, 15, 79;**
DAM DRAM
See also CA 73-76; CANR 33;
CDBLB 1945-1960; DLB 13; MTCW

Behn, Aphra
1640(?)-1689 ...... **LC 1, 30; DA; DAB;**
DAC; DAM DRAM, MST, NOV,
POET; DC 4; PC 13; WLC
See also DLB 39, 80, 131

Behrman, S(amuel) N(athaniel)
1893-1973 .... **CLC 40**
See also CA 13-16; 45-48; CAP 1; DLB 7,
44

Belasco, David 1853-1931 .... **TCLC 3**
See also CA 104; DLB 7

Belcheva, Elisaveta 1893-......... **CLC 10**
See also Bagryana, Elisaveta

Beldone, Phil "Cheech"
See Ellison, Harlan (Jay)

Beleno
See Azuela, Mariano

Belinski, Vissarion Grigoryevich
1811-1848 .... **NCLC 5**

Belitt, Ben 1911-................. **CLC 22**
See also CA 13-16R; CAAS 4; CANR 7;
DLB 5

Bell, Gertrude 1868-1926........ **TCLC 67**
See also DLB 174

Bell, James Madison
1826-1902 .... **TCLC 43; BLC;**
DAM MULT
See also BW 1; CA 122; 124; DLB 50

Bell, Madison Smartt 1957-........ **CLC 41**
See also CA 111; CANR 28, 54

Bell, Marvin (Hartley)
1937-......... **CLC 8, 31; DAM POET**
See also CA 21-24R; CAAS 14; DLB 5;
MTCW

Bell, W. L. D.
See Mencken, H(enry) L(ouis)

Bellamy, Atwood C.
See Mencken, H(enry) L(ouis)

Bellamy, Edward 1850-1898 ...... **NCLC 4**
See also DLB 12

Bellin, Edward J.
See Kuttner, Henry

Belloc, (Joseph) Hilaire (Pierre Sebastien
Rene Swanton)
1870-1953 ... **TCLC 7, 18; DAM POET**
See also CA 106; 152; DLB 19, 100, 141,
174; YABC 1

Belloc, Joseph Peter Rene Hilaire
See Belloc, (Joseph) Hilaire (Pierre Sebastien
Rene Swanton)

Belloc, Joseph Pierre Hilaire
See Belloc, (Joseph) Hilaire (Pierre Sebastien
Rene Swanton)

Belloc, M. A.
See Lowndes, Marie Adelaide (Belloc)

Bellow, Saul
1915-......**CLC 1, 2, 3, 6, 8, 10, 13, 15,**
25, 33, 34, 63, 79; DA; DAB; DAC;
DAM MST, NOV, POP; SSC 14; WLC
See also AITN 2; BEST 89:3; CA 5-8R;
CABS 1; CANR 29, 53;
CDALB 1941-1968; DLB 2, 28; DLBD 3;
DLBY 82; MTCW

Belser, Reimond Karel Maria de   1929-
   See Ruyslinck, Ward
   See also CA 152

Bely, Andrey . . . . TCLC 7; PC 11
   See also Bugayev, Boris Nikolayevich

Benary, Margot
   See Benary-Isbert, Margot

Benary-Isbert, Margot   1889-1979 . . . CLC 12
   See also CA 5-8R; 89-92; CANR 4;
   CLR 12; MAICYA; SATA 2;
   SATA-Obit 21

Benavente (y Martinez), Jacinto
   1866-1954 . . . . . TCLC 3; DAM DRAM,
                                              MULT
   See also CA 106; 131; HW; MTCW

Benchley, Peter (Bradford)
   1940- . . . . . CLC 4, 8; DAM NOV, POP
   See also AAYA 14; AITN 2; CA 17-20R;
   CANR 12, 35; MTCW; SATA 3, 89

Benchley, Robert (Charles)
   1889-1945 . . . . TCLC 1, 55
   See also CA 105; 153; DLB 11

Benda, Julien   1867-1956 . . . . TCLC 60
   See also CA 120; 154

Benedict, Ruth   1887-1948 . . . . TCLC 60

Benedikt, Michael   1935- . . . . CLC 4, 14
   See also CA 13-16R; CANR 7; DLB 5

Benet, Juan   1927- . . . . CLC 28
   See also CA 143

Benet, Stephen Vincent
   1898-1943 . . . . . . TCLC 7; DAM POET;
                                              SSC 10
   See also CA 104; 152; DLB 4, 48, 102;
   YABC 1

Benet, William Rose
   1886-1950 . . . . . . TCLC 28; DAM POET
   See also CA 118; 152; DLB 45

Benford, Gregory (Albert)   1941- . . . . CLC 52
   See also CA 69-72; CANR 12, 24, 49;
   DLBY 82

Bengtsson, Frans (Gunnar)
   1894-1954 . . . . TCLC 48

Benjamin, David
   See Slavitt, David R(ytman)

Benjamin, Lois
   See Gould, Lois

Benjamin, Walter   1892-1940 . . . . . . TCLC 39

Benn, Gottfried   1886-1956 . . . . TCLC 3
   See also CA 106; 153; DLB 56

Bennett, Alan
   1934- . . . CLC 45, 77; DAB; DAM MST
   See also CA 103; CANR 35, 55; MTCW

Bennett, (Enoch) Arnold
   1867-1931 . . . . TCLC 5, 20
   See also CA 106; CDBLB 1890-1914;
   DLB 10, 34, 98, 135

Bennett, Elizabeth
   See Mitchell, Margaret (Munnerlyn)

Bennett, George Harold   1930-
   See Bennett, Hal
   See also BW 1; CA 97-100

Bennett, Hal . . . . CLC 5
   See also Bennett, George Harold
   See also DLB 33

Bennett, Jay   1912- . . . . CLC 35
   See also AAYA 10; CA 69-72; CANR 11,
   42; JRDA; SAAS 4; SATA 41, 87;
   SATA-Brief 27

Bennett, Louise (Simone)
   1919- . . . . . CLC 28; BLC; DAM MULT
   See also BW 2; CA 151; DLB 117

Benson, E(dward) F(rederic)
   1867-1940 . . . . TCLC 27
   See also CA 114; DLB 135, 153

Benson, Jackson J.   1930- . . . . CLC 34
   See also CA 25-28R; DLB 111

Benson, Sally   1900-1972 . . . . CLC 17
   See also CA 19-20; 37-40R; CAP 1;
   SATA 1, 35; SATA-Obit 27

Benson, Stella   1892-1933 . . . . TCLC 17
   See also CA 117; 154; DLB 36, 162

Bentham, Jeremy   1748-1832 . . . . . NCLC 38
   See also DLB 107, 158

Bentley, E(dmund) C(lerihew)
   1875-1956 . . . . TCLC 12
   See also CA 108; DLB 70

Bentley, Eric (Russell)   1916- . . . . . . CLC 24
   See also CA 5-8R; CANR 6; INT CANR-6

Beranger, Pierre Jean de
   1780-1857 . . . . NCLC 34

Berdyaev, Nicolas
   See Berdyaev, Nikolai (Aleksandrovich)

Berdyaev, Nikolai (Aleksandrovich)
   1874-1948 . . . . TCLC 67
   See also CA 120

Berendt, John (Lawrence)   1939- . . . . CLC 86
   See also CA 146

Berger, Colonel
   See Malraux, (Georges-)Andre

Berger, John (Peter)   1926- . . . . . . CLC 2, 19
   See also CA 81-84; CANR 51; DLB 14

Berger, Melvin H.   1927- . . . . CLC 12
   See also CA 5-8R; CANR 4; CLR 32;
   SAAS 2; SATA 5, 88

Berger, Thomas (Louis)
   1924- . . . . CLC 3, 5, 8, 11, 18, 38;
                                              DAM NOV
   See also CA 1-4R; CANR 5, 28, 51; DLB 2;
   DLBY 80; INT CANR-28; MTCW

Bergman, (Ernst) Ingmar
   1918- . . . . CLC 16, 72
   See also CA 81-84; CANR 33

Bergson, Henri   1859-1941 . . . . TCLC 32

Bergstein, Eleanor   1938- . . . . CLC 4
   See also CA 53-56; CANR 5

Berkoff, Steven   1937- . . . . CLC 56
   See also CA 104

Bermant, Chaim (Icyk)   1929- . . . . . . CLC 40
   See also CA 57-60; CANR 6, 31

Bern, Victoria
   See Fisher, M(ary) F(rances) K(ennedy)

Bernanos, (Paul Louis) Georges
   1888-1948 . . . . TCLC 3
   See also CA 104; 130; DLB 72

Bernard, April   1956- . . . . CLC 59
   See also CA 131

Berne, Victoria
   See Fisher, M(ary) F(rances) K(ennedy)

Bernhard, Thomas
   1931-1989 . . . . CLC 3, 32, 61
   See also CA 85-88; 127; CANR 32;
   DLB 85, 124; MTCW

Berriault, Gina   1926- . . . . CLC 54
   See also CA 116; 129; DLB 130

Berrigan, Daniel   1921- . . . . CLC 4
   See also CA 33-36R; CAAS 1; CANR 11,
   43; DLB 5

Berrigan, Edmund Joseph Michael, Jr.
   1934-1983
   See Berrigan, Ted
   See also CA 61-64; 110; CANR 14

Berrigan, Ted . . . . CLC 37
   See also Berrigan, Edmund Joseph Michael,
   Jr.
   See also DLB 5, 169

Berry, Charles Edward Anderson   1931-
   See Berry, Chuck
   See also CA 115

Berry, Chuck . . . . CLC 17
   See also Berry, Charles Edward Anderson

Berry, Jonas
   See Ashbery, John (Lawrence)

Berry, Wendell (Erdman)
   1934- . . . . CLC 4, 6, 8, 27, 46;
                                              DAM POET
   See also AITN 1; CA 73-76; CANR 50;
   DLB 5, 6

Berryman, John
   1914-1972 . . . . . . CLC 1, 2, 3, 4, 6, 8, 10,
                                 13, 25, 62; DAM POET
   See also CA 13-16; 33-36R; CABS 2;
   CANR 35; CAP 1; CDALB 1941-1968;
   DLB 48; MTCW

Bertolucci, Bernardo   1940- . . . . CLC 16
   See also CA 106

Bertrand, Aloysius   1807-1841 . . . . NCLC 31

Bertran de Born   c. 1140-1215 . . . . . CMLC 5

Besant, Annie (Wood)   1847-1933 . . . TCLC 9
   See also CA 105

Bessie, Alvah   1904-1985 . . . . CLC 23
   See also CA 5-8R; 116; CANR 2; DLB 26

Bethlen, T. D.
   See Silverberg, Robert

Beti, Mongo . . . . CLC 27; BLC; DAM MULT
   See also Biyidi, Alexandre

Betjeman, John
   1906-1984 . . . . CLC 2, 6, 10, 34, 43;
                                 DAB; DAM MST, POET
   See also CA 9-12R; 112; CANR 33;
   CDBLB 1945-1960; DLB 20; DLBY 84;
   MTCW

Bettelheim, Bruno   1903-1990 . . . . . . CLC 79
   See also CA 81-84; 131; CANR 23; MTCW

Betti, Ugo   1892-1953 . . . . TCLC 5
   See also CA 104

Betts, Doris (Waugh)   1932- . . . . CLC 3, 6, 28
   See also CA 13-16R; CANR 9; DLBY 82;
   INT CANR-9

Bevan, Alistair
   See Roberts, Keith (John Kingston)

Bialik, Chaim Nachman
   1873-1934 . . . . TCLC 25

Bickerstaff, Isaac
See Swift, Jonathan

Bidart, Frank 1939- .... CLC 33
See also CA 140

Bienek, Horst 1930- .... CLC 7, 11
See also CA 73-76; DLB 75

Bierce, Ambrose (Gwinett)
1842-1914(?) ...... TCLC 1, 7, 44; DA;
DAC; DAM MST; SSC 9; WLC
See also CA 104; 139; CDALB 1865-1917;
DLB 11, 12, 23, 71, 74

Biggers, Earl Derr 1884-1933 ..... TCLC 65
See also CA 108; 153

Billings, Josh
See Shaw, Henry Wheeler

Billington, (Lady) Rachel (Mary)
1942- .... CLC 43
See also AITN 2; CA 33-36R; CANR 44

Binyon, T(imothy) J(ohn) 1936- .... CLC 34
See also CA 111; CANR 28

Bioy Casares, Adolfo
1914- .... CLC 4, 8, 13, 88;
DAM MULT; HLC; SSC 17
See also CA 29-32R; CANR 19, 43;
DLB 113; HW; MTCW

Bird, Cordwainer
See Ellison, Harlan (Jay)

Bird, Robert Montgomery
1806-1854 .... NCLC 1

Birney, (Alfred) Earle
1904- .... CLC 1, 4, 6, 11; DAC;
DAM MST, POET
See also CA 1-4R; CANR 5, 20; DLB 88;
MTCW

Bishop, Elizabeth
1911-1979 ...... CLC 1, 4, 9, 13, 15, 32;
DA; DAC; DAM MST, POET; PC 3
See also CA 5-8R; 89-92; CABS 2;
CANR 26; CDALB 1968-1988; DLB 5,
169; MTCW; SATA-Obit 24

Bishop, John 1935- .... CLC 10
See also CA 105

Bissett, Bill 1939- .... CLC 18; PC 14
See also CA 69-72; CAAS 19; CANR 15;
DLB 53; MTCW

Bitov, Andrei (Georgievich) 1937-... CLC 57
See also CA 142

Biyidi, Alexandre 1932-
See Beti, Mongo
See also BW 1; CA 114; 124; MTCW

Bjarme, Brynjolf
See Ibsen, Henrik (Johan)

Bjornson, Bjornstjerne (Martinius)
1832-1910 .... TCLC 7, 37
See also CA 104

Black, Robert
See Holdstock, Robert P.

Blackburn, Paul 1926-1971 ..... CLC 9, 43
See also CA 81-84; 33-36R; CANR 34;
DLB 16; DLBY 81

Black Elk
1863-1950 ..... TCLC 33; DAM MULT
See also CA 144; NNAL

Black Hobart
See Sanders, (James) Ed(ward)

Blacklin, Malcolm
See Chambers, Aidan

Blackmore, R(ichard) D(oddridge)
1825-1900 .... TCLC 27
See also CA 120; DLB 18

Blackmur, R(ichard) P(almer)
1904-1965 .... CLC 2, 24
See also CA 11-12; 25-28R; CAP 1; DLB 63

Black Tarantula
See Acker, Kathy

Blackwood, Algernon (Henry)
1869-1951 .... TCLC 5
See also CA 105; 150; DLB 153, 156

Blackwood, Caroline 1931-1996 ... CLC 6, 9
See also CA 85-88; 151; CANR 32;
DLB 14; MTCW

Blade, Alexander
See Hamilton, Edmond; Silverberg, Robert

Blaga, Lucian 1895-1961 .... CLC 75

Blair, Eric (Arthur) 1903-1950
See Orwell, George
See also CA 104; 132; DA; DAB; DAC;
DAM MST, NOV; MTCW; SATA 29

Blais, Marie-Claire
1939- .... CLC 2, 4, 6, 13, 22; DAC;
DAM MST
See also CA 21-24R; CAAS 4; CANR 38;
DLB 53; MTCW

Blaise, Clark 1940- .... CLC 29
See also AITN 2; CA 53-56; CAAS 3;
CANR 5; DLB 53

Blake, Nicholas
See Day Lewis, C(ecil)
See also DLB 77

Blake, William
1757-1827 .... NCLC 13, 37, 57; DA;
DAB; DAC; DAM MST, POET; PC 12;
WLC
See also CDBLB 1789-1832; DLB 93, 163;
MAICYA; SATA 30

Blake, William J(ames) 1894-1969 ... PC 12
See also CA 5-8R; 25-28R

Blasco Ibanez, Vicente
1867-1928 .... TCLC 12; DAM NOV
See also CA 110; 131; HW; MTCW

Blatty, William Peter
1928- .... CLC 2; DAM POP
See also CA 5-8R; CANR 9

Bleeck, Oliver
See Thomas, Ross (Elmore)

Blessing, Lee 1949- .... CLC 54

Blish, James (Benjamin)
1921-1975 .... CLC 14
See also CA 1-4R; 57-60; CANR 3; DLB 8;
MTCW; SATA 66

Bliss, Reginald
See Wells, H(erbert) G(eorge)

Blixen, Karen (Christentze Dinesen)
1885-1962
See Dinesen, Isak
See also CA 25-28; CANR 22, 50; CAP 2;
MTCW; SATA 44

Bloch, Robert (Albert) 1917-1994 ... CLC 33
See also CA 5-8R; 146; CAAS 20; CANR 5;
DLB 44; INT CANR-5; SATA 12;
SATA-Obit 82

Blok, Alexander (Alexandrovich)
1880-1921 .... TCLC 5
See also CA 104

Blom, Jan
See Breytenbach, Breyten

Bloom, Harold 1930- .... CLC 24
See also CA 13-16R; CANR 39; DLB 67

Bloomfield, Aurelius
See Bourne, Randolph S(illiman)

Blount, Roy (Alton), Jr. 1941- ..... CLC 38
See also CA 53-56; CANR 10, 28;
INT CANR-28; MTCW

Bloy, Leon 1846-1917........... TCLC 22
See also CA 121; DLB 123

Blume, Judy (Sussman)
1938- ... CLC 12, 30; DAM NOV, POP
See also AAYA 3; CA 29-32R; CANR 13,
37; CLR 2, 15; DLB 52; JRDA;
MAICYA; MTCW; SATA 2, 31, 79

Blunden, Edmund (Charles)
1896-1974 .... CLC 2, 56
See also CA 17-18; 45-48; CANR 54;
CAP 2; DLB 20, 100, 155; MTCW

Bly, Robert (Elwood)
1926- .... CLC 1, 2, 5, 10, 15, 38;
DAM POET
See also CA 5-8R; CANR 41; DLB 5;
MTCW

Boas, Franz 1858-1942........... TCLC 56
See also CA 115

Bobette
See Simenon, Georges (Jacques Christian)

Boccaccio, Giovanni
1313-1375 .... CMLC 13; SSC 10

Bochco, Steven 1943- .... CLC 35
See also AAYA 11; CA 124; 138

Bodenheim, Maxwell 1892-1954 ... TCLC 44
See also CA 110; DLB 9, 45

Bodker, Cecil 1927- .... CLC 21
See also CA 73-76; CANR 13, 44; CLR 23;
MAICYA; SATA 14

Boell, Heinrich (Theodor)
1917-1985 .... CLC 2, 3, 6, 9, 11, 15, 27,
32, 72; DA; DAB; DAC; DAM MST,
NOV; SSC 23; WLC
See also CA 21-24R; 116; CANR 24;
DLB 69; DLBY 85; MTCW

Boerne, Alfred
See Doeblin, Alfred

Boethius 480(?)-524(?) .... CMLC 15
See also DLB 115

Bogan, Louise
1897-1970 .... CLC 4, 39, 46, 93;
DAM POET; PC 12
See also CA 73-76; 25-28R; CANR 33;
DLB 45, 169; MTCW

Bogarde, Dirk .... CLC 19
See also Van Den Bogarde, Derek Jules
Gaspard Ulric Niven
See also DLB 14

Brandes, Georg (Morris Cohen)
1842-1927 .... TCLC 10
See also CA 105

Brandys, Kazimierz 1916- .... CLC 62

Branley, Franklyn M(ansfield)
1915- .... CLC 21
See also CA 33-36R; CANR 14, 39;
CLR 13; MAICYA; SAAS 16; SATA 4,
68

Brathwaite, Edward Kamau
1930- .... CLC 11; DAM POET
See also BW 2; CA 25-28R; CANR 11, 26,
47; DLB 125

Brautigan, Richard (Gary)
1935-1984 .... CLC 1, 3, 5, 9, 12, 34, 42;
DAM NOV
See also CA 53-56; 113; CANR 34; DLB 2,
5; DLBY 80, 84; MTCW; SATA 56

Brave Bird, Mary 1953-
See Crow Dog, Mary (Ellen)
See also NNAL

Braverman, Kate 1950- .... CLC 67
See also CA 89-92

Brecht, Bertolt
1898-1956 ...... TCLC 1, 6, 13, 35; DA;
DAB; DAC; DAM DRAM, MST; DC 3;
WLC
See also CA 104; 133; DLB 56, 124; MTCW

Brecht, Eugen Berthold Friedrich
See Brecht, Bertolt

Bremer, Fredrika 1801-1865 ..... NCLC 11

Brennan, Christopher John
1870-1932 .... TCLC 17
See also CA 117

Brennan, Maeve 1917- .... CLC 5
See also CA 81-84

Brentano, Clemens (Maria)
1778-1842 .... NCLC 1
See also DLB 90

Brent of Bin Bin
See Franklin, (Stella Maraia Sarah) Miles

Brenton, Howard 1942- .... CLC 31
See also CA 69-72; CANR 33; DLB 13;
MTCW

Breslin, James 1930-
See Breslin, Jimmy
See also CA 73-76; CANR 31; DAM NOV;
MTCW

Breslin, Jimmy .... CLC 4, 43
See also Breslin, James
See also AITN 1

Bresson, Robert 1901- .... CLC 16
See also CA 110; CANR 49

Breton, Andre
1896-1966 ..... CLC 2, 9, 15, 54; PC 15
See also CA 19-20; 25-28R; CANR 40;
CAP 2; DLB 65; MTCW

Breytenbach, Breyten
1939(?)- ...... CLC 23, 37; DAM POET
See also CA 113; 129

Bridgers, Sue Ellen 1942- .... CLC 26
See also AAYA 8; CA 65-68; CANR 11,
36; CLR 18; DLB 52; JRDA; MAICYA;
SAAS 1; SATA 22, 90

Bridges, Robert (Seymour)
1844-1930 ...... TCLC 1; DAM POET
See also CA 104; 152; CDBLB 1890-1914;
DLB 19, 98

Bridie, James .... TCLC 3
See also Mavor, Osborne Henry
See also DLB 10

Brin, David 1950- .... CLC 34
See also CA 102; CANR 24;
INT CANR-24; SATA 65

Brink, Andre (Philippus)
1935- .... CLC 18, 36
See also CA 104; CANR 39; INT 103;
MTCW

Brinsmead, H(esba) F(ay) 1922- .... CLC 21
See also CA 21-24R; CANR 10; MAICYA;
SAAS 5; SATA 18, 78

Brittain, Vera (Mary)
1893(?)-1970 .... CLC 23
See also CA 13-16; 25-28R; CAP 1; MTCW

Broch, Hermann 1886-1951 .... TCLC 20
See also CA 117; DLB 85, 124

Brock, Rose
See Hansen, Joseph

Brodkey, Harold (Roy) 1930-1996 .. CLC 56
See also CA 111; 151; DLB 130

Brodsky, Iosif Alexandrovich 1940-1996
See Brodsky, Joseph
See also AITN 1; CA 41-44R; 151;
CANR 37; DAM POET; MTCW

Brodsky, Joseph .. CLC 4, 6, 13, 36, 50; PC 9
See also Brodsky, Iosif Alexandrovich

Brodsky, Michael Mark 1948- ..... CLC 19
See also CA 102; CANR 18, 41

Bromell, Henry 1947- .... CLC 5
See also CA 53-56; CANR 9

Bromfield, Louis (Brucker)
1896-1956 .... TCLC 11
See also CA 107; DLB 4, 9, 86

Broner, E(sther) M(asserman)
1930- .... CLC 19
See also CA 17-20R; CANR 8, 25; DLB 28

Bronk, William 1918- .... CLC 10
See also CA 89-92; CANR 23; DLB 165

Bronstein, Lev Davidovich
See Trotsky, Leon

Bronte, Anne 1820-1849 .... NCLC 4
See also DLB 21

Bronte, Charlotte
1816-1855 ..... NCLC 3, 8, 33, 58; DA;
DAB; DAC; DAM MST, NOV; WLC
See also AAYA 17; CDBLB 1832-1890;
DLB 21, 159

Bronte, Emily (Jane)
1818-1848 .... NCLC 16, 35; DA; DAB;
DAC; DAM MST, NOV, POET; PC 8;
WLC
See also AAYA 17; CDBLB 1832-1890;
DLB 21, 32

Brooke, Frances 1724-1789 .... LC 6
See also DLB 39, 99

Brooke, Henry 1703(?)-1783 .... LC 1
See also DLB 39

Brooke, Rupert (Chawner)
1887-1915 .... TCLC 2, 7; DA; DAB;
DAC; DAM MST, POET; WLC
See also CA 104; 132; CDBLB 1914-1945;
DLB 19; MTCW

Brooke-Haven, P.
See Wodehouse, P(elham) G(renville)

Brooke-Rose, Christine 1926- ...... CLC 40
See also CA 13-16R; DLB 14

Brookner, Anita
1928- .... CLC 32, 34, 51; DAB;
DAM POP
See also CA 114; 120; CANR 37; DLBY 87;
MTCW

Brooks, Cleanth 1906-1994 ..... CLC 24, 86
See also CA 17-20R; 145; CANR 33, 35;
DLB 63; DLBY 94; INT CANR-35;
MTCW

Brooks, George
See Baum, L(yman) Frank

Brooks, Gwendolyn
1917- ...... CLC 1, 2, 4, 5, 15, 49; BLC;
DA; DAC; DAM MST, MULT, POET;
PC 7; WLC
See also AITN 1; BW 2; CA 1-4R;
CANR 1, 27, 52; CDALB 1941-1968;
CLR 27; DLB 5, 76, 165; MTCW;
SATA 6

Brooks, Mel .... CLC 12
See also Kaminsky, Melvin
See also AAYA 13; DLB 26

Brooks, Peter 1938- .... CLC 34
See also CA 45-48; CANR 1

Brooks, Van Wyck 1886-1963...... CLC 29
See also CA 1-4R; CANR 6; DLB 45, 63,
103

Brophy, Brigid (Antonia)
1929-1995 .... CLC 6, 11, 29
See also CA 5-8R; 149; CAAS 4; CANR 25,
53; DLB 14; MTCW

Brosman, Catharine Savage 1934-.... CLC 9
See also CA 61-64; CANR 21, 46

Brother Antoninus
See Everson, William (Oliver)

Broughton, T(homas) Alan 1936- ... CLC 19
See also CA 45-48; CANR 2, 23, 48

Broumas, Olga 1949- .... CLC 10, 73
See also CA 85-88; CANR 20

Brown, Charles Brockden
1771-1810 .... NCLC 22
See also CDALB 1640-1865; DLB 37, 59,
73

Brown, Christy 1932-1981........ CLC 63
See also CA 105; 104; DLB 14

Brown, Claude
1937- ..... CLC 30; BLC; DAM MULT
See also AAYA 7; BW 1; CA 73-76

Brown, Dee (Alexander)
1908- .... CLC 18, 47; DAM POP
See also CA 13-16R; CAAS 6; CANR 11,
45; DLBY 80; MTCW; SATA 5

Brown, George
See Wertmueller, Lina

Brown, George Douglas
1869-1902 .... TCLC 28

Brown, George Mackay
    1921-1996 .... **CLC 5, 48**
    See also CA 21-24R; 151; CAAS 6;
    CANR 12, 37; DLB 14, 27, 139; MTCW;
    SATA 35

Brown, (William) Larry 1951- ...... **CLC 73**
    See also CA 130; 134; INT 133

Brown, Moses
    See Barrett, William (Christopher)

Brown, Rita Mae
    1944- ..... **CLC 18, 43, 79; DAM NOV,**
                                                    POP
    See also CA 45-48; CANR 2, 11, 35;
    INT CANR-11; MTCW

Brown, Roderick (Langmere) Haig-
    See Haig-Brown, Roderick (Langmere)

Brown, Rosellen 1939- .... **CLC 32**
    See also CA 77-80; CAAS 10; CANR 14, 44

Brown, Sterling Allen
    1901-1989 .... **CLC 1, 23, 59; BLC;**
                                        DAM MULT, POET
    See also BW 1; CA 85-88; 127; CANR 26;
    DLB 48, 51, 63; MTCW

Brown, Will
    See Ainsworth, William Harrison

Brown, William Wells
    1813-1884 .... **NCLC 2; BLC;**
                                                DAM MULT; DC 1
    See also DLB 3, 50

Browne, (Clyde) Jackson 1948(?)- ... **CLC 21**
    See also CA 120

Browning, Elizabeth Barrett
    1806-1861 ..... **NCLC 1, 16; DA; DAB;**
        DAC; DAM MST, POET; PC 6; WLC
    See also CDBLB 1832-1890; DLB 32

Browning, Robert
    1812-1889 .... **NCLC 19; DA; DAB;**
                            DAC; DAM MST, POET; PC 2
    See also CDBLB 1832-1890; DLB 32, 163;
    YABC 1

Browning, Tod 1882-1962 .... **CLC 16**
    See also CA 141; 117

Brownson, Orestes (Augustus)
    1803-1876 .... **NCLC 50**

Bruccoli, Matthew J(oseph) 1931- .. **CLC 34**
    See also CA 9-12R; CANR 7; DLB 103

Bruce, Lenny .... **CLC 21**
    See also Schneider, Leonard Alfred

Bruin, John
    See Brutus, Dennis

Brulard, Henri
    See Stendhal

Brulls, Christian
    See Simenon, Georges (Jacques Christian)

Brunner, John (Kilian Houston)
    1934-1995 ...... **CLC 8, 10; DAM POP**
    See also CA 1-4R; 149; CAAS 8; CANR 2,
    37; MTCW

Bruno, Giordano 1548-1600 .... **LC 27**

Brutus, Dennis
    1924- ..... **CLC 43; BLC; DAM MULT,**
                                                    POET
    See also BW 2; CA 49-52; CAAS 14;
    CANR 2, 27, 42; DLB 117

Bryan, C(ourtlandt) D(ixon) B(arnes)
    1936- .... **CLC 29**
    See also CA 73-76; CANR 13;
    INT CANR-13

Bryan, Michael
    See Moore, Brian

Bryant, William Cullen
    1794-1878 ..... **NCLC 6, 46; DA; DAB;**
                                DAC; DAM MST, POET
    See also CDALB 1640-1865; DLB 3, 43, 59

Bryusov, Valery Yakovlevich
    1873-1924 .... **TCLC 10**
    See also CA 107

Buchan, John
    1875-1940 .... **TCLC 41; DAB;**
                                                DAM POP
    See also CA 108; 145; DLB 34, 70, 156;
    YABC 2

Buchanan, George 1506-1582 .... **LC 4**

Buchheim, Lothar-Guenther 1918- ... **CLC 6**
    See also CA 85-88

Buchner, (Karl) Georg
    1813-1837 .... **NCLC 26**

Buchwald, Art(hur) 1925- .... **CLC 33**
    See also AITN 1; CA 5-8R; CANR 21;
    MTCW; SATA 10

Buck, Pearl S(ydenstricker)
    1892-1973 .... **CLC 7, 11, 18; DA; DAB;**
                                DAC; DAM MST, NOV
    See also AITN 1; CA 1-4R; 41-44R;
    CANR 1, 34; DLB 9, 102; MTCW;
    SATA 1, 25

Buckler, Ernest
    1908-1984 .. **CLC 13; DAC; DAM MST**
    See also CA 11-12; 114; CAP 1; DLB 68;
    SATA 47

Buckley, Vincent (Thomas)
    1925-1988 .... **CLC 57**
    See also CA 101

Buckley, William F(rank), Jr.
    1925- .... **CLC 7, 18, 37; DAM POP**
    See also AITN 1; CA 1-4R; CANR 1, 24,
    53; DLB 137; DLBY 80; INT CANR-24;
    MTCW

Buechner, (Carl) Frederick
    1926- ...... **CLC 2, 4, 6, 9; DAM NOV**
    See also CA 13-16R; CANR 11, 39;
    DLBY 80; INT CANR-11; MTCW

Buell, John (Edward) 1927- .... **CLC 10**
    See also CA 1-4R; DLB 53

Buero Vallejo, Antonio 1916- ... **CLC 15, 46**
    See also CA 106; CANR 24, 49; HW;
    MTCW

Bufalino, Gesualdo 1920(?)- .... **CLC 74**

Bugayev, Boris Nikolayevich 1880-1934
    See Bely, Andrey
    See also CA 104

Bukowski, Charles
    1920-1994 .... **CLC 2, 5, 9, 41, 82;**
                                            DAM NOV, POET
    See also CA 17-20R; 144; CANR 40;
    DLB 5, 130, 169; MTCW

Bulgakov, Mikhail (Afanas'evich)
    1891-1940 .... **TCLC 2, 16;**
                            DAM DRAM, NOV; SSC 18
    See also CA 105; 152

Bulgya, Alexander Alexandrovich
    1901-1956 .... **TCLC 53**
    See also Fadeyev, Alexander
    See also CA 117

Bullins, Ed
    1935- .... **CLC 1, 5, 7; BLC;**
                                DAM DRAM, MULT; DC 6
    See also BW 2; CA 49-52; CAAS 16;
    CANR 24, 46; DLB 7, 38; MTCW

Bulwer-Lytton, Edward (George Earle Lytton)
    1803-1873 .... **NCLC 1, 45**
    See also DLB 21

Bunin, Ivan Alexeyevich
    1870-1953 .... **TCLC 6; SSC 5**
    See also CA 104

Bunting, Basil
    1900-1985 .... **CLC 10, 39, 47;**
                                                DAM POET
    See also CA 53-56; 115; CANR 7; DLB 20

Bunuel, Luis
    1900-1983 .... **CLC 16, 80;**
                                        DAM MULT; HLC
    See also CA 101; 110; CANR 32; HW

Bunyan, John
    1628-1688 ...... **LC 4; DA; DAB; DAC;**
                                DAM MST; WLC
    See also CDBLB 1660-1789; DLB 39

Burckhardt, Jacob (Christoph)
    1818-1897 .... **NCLC 49**

Burford, Eleanor
    See Hibbert, Eleanor Alice Burford

Burgess, Anthony
    . **CLC 1, 2, 4, 5, 8, 10, 13, 15, 22, 40, 62,**
                                            81, 94; DAB
    See also Wilson, John (Anthony) Burgess
    See also AITN 1; CDBLB 1960 to Present;
    DLB 14

Burke, Edmund
    1729(?)-1797 ...... **LC 7, 36; DA; DAB;**
                                DAC; DAM MST; WLC
    See also DLB 104

Burke, Kenneth (Duva)
    1897-1993 .... **CLC 2, 24**
    See also CA 5-8R; 143; CANR 39; DLB 45,
    63; MTCW

Burke, Leda
    See Garnett, David

Burke, Ralph
    See Silverberg, Robert

Burke, Thomas 1886-1945 .... **TCLC 63**
    See also CA 113

Burney, Fanny 1752-1840 .... **NCLC 12, 54**
    See also DLB 39

Burns, Robert 1759-1796 .... **PC 6**
    See also CDBLB 1789-1832; DA; DAB;
    DAC; DAM MST, POET; DLB 109;
    WLC

Burns, Tex
    See L'Amour, Louis (Dearborn)

Burnshaw, Stanley 1906- ..... **CLC 3, 13, 44**
    See also CA 9-12R; DLB 48

Burr, Anne 1937- .... **CLC 6**
    See also CA 25-28R

Burroughs, Edgar Rice
1875-1950 .... **TCLC 2, 32; DAM NOV**
See also AAYA 11; CA 104; 132; DLB 8;
MTCW; SATA 41

Burroughs, William S(eward)
1914- .... **CLC 1, 2, 5, 15, 22, 42, 75;**
DA; DAB; DAC; DAM MST, NOV,
POP; WLC
See also AITN 2; CA 9-12R; CANR 20, 52;
DLB 2, 8, 16, 152; DLBY 81; MTCW

Burton, Richard F. 1821-1890.... **NCLC 42**
See also DLB 55

Busch, Frederick 1941- ... **CLC 7, 10, 18, 47**
See also CA 33-36R; CAAS 1; CANR 45;
DLB 6

Bush, Ronald 1946- .... **CLC 34**
See also CA 136

Bustos, F(rancisco)
See Borges, Jorge Luis

Bustos Domecq, H(onorio)
See Bioy Casares, Adolfo; Borges, Jorge
Luis

Butler, Octavia E(stelle)
1947- ..... **CLC 38; DAM MULT, POP**
See also AAYA 18; BW 2; CA 73-76;
CANR 12, 24, 38; DLB 33; MTCW;
SATA 84

Butler, Robert Olen (Jr.)
1945- .... **CLC 81; DAM POP**
See also CA 112; DLB 173; INT 112

Butler, Samuel 1612-1680 .... **LC 16**
See also DLB 101, 126

Butler, Samuel
1835-1902 ...... **TCLC 1, 33; DA; DAB;**
DAC; DAM MST, NOV; WLC
See also CA 143; CDBLB 1890-1914;
DLB 18, 57, 174

Butler, Walter C.
See Faust, Frederick (Schiller)

Butor, Michel (Marie Francois)
1926- .... **CLC 1, 3, 8, 11, 15**
See also CA 9-12R; CANR 33; DLB 83;
MTCW

Buzo, Alexander (John) 1944- ...... **CLC 61**
See also CA 97-100; CANR 17, 39

Buzzati, Dino 1906-1972 .... **CLC 36**
See also CA 33-36R

Byars, Betsy (Cromer) 1928- .... **CLC 35**
See also AAYA 19; CA 33-36R; CANR 18,
36; CLR 1, 16; DLB 52; INT CANR-18;
JRDA; MAICYA; MTCW; SAAS 1;
SATA 4, 46, 80

Byatt, A(ntonia) S(usan Drabble)
1936- ... **CLC 19, 65; DAM NOV, POP**
See also CA 13-16R; CANR 13, 33, 50;
DLB 14; MTCW

Byrne, David 1952- .... **CLC 26**
See also CA 127

Byrne, John Keyes 1926-
See Leonard, Hugh
See also CA 102; INT 102

Byron, George Gordon (Noel)
1788-1824 ..... **NCLC 2, 12; DA; DAB;**
DAC; DAM MST, POET; PC 16; WLC
See also CDBLB 1789-1832; DLB 96, 110

Byron, Robert 1905-1941 .... **TCLC 67**

C. 3. 3.
See Wilde, Oscar (Fingal O'Flahertie Wills)

Caballero, Fernan 1796-1877 ..... **NCLC 10**

Cabell, Branch
See Cabell, James Branch

Cabell, James Branch 1879-1958 ... **TCLC 6**
See also CA 105; 152; DLB 9, 78

Cable, George Washington
1844-1925 .... **TCLC 4; SSC 4**
See also CA 104; DLB 12, 74; DLBD 13

Cabral de Melo Neto, Joao
1920- .... **CLC 76; DAM MULT**
See also CA 151

Cabrera Infante, G(uillermo)
1929- ..... **CLC 5, 25, 45; DAM MULT;**
HLC
See also CA 85-88; CANR 29; DLB 113;
HW; MTCW

Cade, Toni
See Bambara, Toni Cade

Cadmus and Harmonia
See Buchan, John

Caedmon fl. 658-680 .... **CMLC 7**
See also DLB 146

Caeiro, Alberto
See Pessoa, Fernando (Antonio Nogueira)

Cage, John (Milton, Jr.) 1912- ..... **CLC 41**
See also CA 13-16R; CANR 9;
INT CANR-9

Cain, G.
See Cabrera Infante, G(uillermo)

Cain, Guillermo
See Cabrera Infante, G(uillermo)

Cain, James M(allahan)
1892-1977 .... **CLC 3, 11, 28**
See also AITN 1; CA 17-20R; 73-76;
CANR 8, 34; MTCW

Caine, Mark
See Raphael, Frederic (Michael)

Calasso, Roberto 1941- .... **CLC 81**
See also CA 143

Calderon de la Barca, Pedro
1600-1681 .... **LC 23; DC 3**

Caldwell, Erskine (Preston)
1903-1987 .... **CLC 1, 8, 14, 50, 60;**
DAM NOV; SSC 19
See also AITN 1; CA 1-4R; 121; CAAS 1;
CANR 2, 33; DLB 9, 86; MTCW

Caldwell, (Janet Miriam) Taylor (Holland)
1900-1985 .... **CLC 2, 28, 39;**
DAM NOV, POP
See also CA 5-8R; 116; CANR 5

Calhoun, John Caldwell
1782-1850 .... **NCLC 15**
See also DLB 3

Calisher, Hortense
1911- ..... **CLC 2, 4, 8, 38; DAM NOV;**
SSC 15
See also CA 1-4R; CANR 1, 22; DLB 2;
INT CANR-22; MTCW

Callaghan, Morley Edward
1903-1990 ..... **CLC 3, 14, 41, 65; DAC;**
DAM MST
See also CA 9-12R; 132; CANR 33;
DLB 68; MTCW

Callimachus
c. 305B.C.-c. 240B.C........ **CMLC 18**

Calvino, Italo
1923-1985 ..... **CLC 5, 8, 11, 22, 33, 39,**
73; DAM NOV; SSC 3
See also CA 85-88; 116; CANR 23; MTCW

Cameron, Carey 1952- .... **CLC 59**
See also CA 135

Cameron, Peter 1959-............. **CLC 44**
See also CA 125; CANR 50

Campana, Dino 1885-1932....... **TCLC 20**
See also CA 117; DLB 114

Campanella, Tommaso 1568-1639 .... **LC 32**

Campbell, John W(ood, Jr.)
1910-1971 .... **CLC 32**
See also CA 21-22; 29-32R; CANR 34;
CAP 2; DLB 8; MTCW

Campbell, Joseph 1904-1987 .... **CLC 69**
See also AAYA 3; BEST 89:2; CA 1-4R;
124; CANR 3, 28; MTCW

Campbell, Maria 1940-...... **CLC 85; DAC**
See also CA 102; CANR 54; NNAL

Campbell, (John) Ramsey
1946- .... **CLC 42; SSC 19**
See also CA 57-60; CANR 7; INT CANR-7

Campbell, (Ignatius) Roy (Dunnachie)
1901-1957 .... **TCLC 5**
See also CA 104; DLB 20

Campbell, Thomas 1777-1844 .... **NCLC 19**
See also DLB 93; 144

Campbell, Wilfred................. TCLC 9
See also Campbell, William

Campbell, William 1858(?)-1918
See Campbell, Wilfred
See also CA 106; DLB 92

Campion, Jane................... CLC 95
See also CA 138

Campos, Alvaro de
See Pessoa, Fernando (Antonio Nogueira)

Camus, Albert
1913-1960 .... **CLC 1, 2, 4, 9, 11, 14, 32,**
63, 69; DA; DAB; DAC; DAM DRAM,
MST, NOV; DC 2; SSC 9; WLC
See also CA 89-92; DLB 72; MTCW

Canby, Vincent 1924-............. **CLC 13**
See also CA 81-84

Cancale
See Desnos, Robert

Canetti, Elias
1905-1994 .... **CLC 3, 14, 25, 75, 86**
See also CA 21-24R; 146; CANR 23;
DLB 85, 124; MTCW

Canin, Ethan 1960-................ **CLC 55**
See also CA 131; 135

Cannon, Curt
See Hunter, Evan

Cape, Judith
See Page, P(atricia) K(athleen)

Capek, Karel
1890-1938 ...... **TCLC 6, 37; DA; DAB;**
DAC; DAM DRAM, MST, NOV; DC 1;
WLC
See also CA 104; 140

Capote, Truman
1924-1984 ...... **CLC 1, 3, 8, 13, 19, 34,**
38, 58; DA; DAB; DAC; DAM MST,
NOV, POP; SSC 2; WLC
See also CA 5-8R; 113; CANR 18;
CDALB 1941-1968; DLB 2; DLBY 80,
84; MTCW; SATA 91

Capra, Frank 1897-1991.......... **CLC 16**
See also CA 61-64; 135

Caputo, Philip 1941-............. **CLC 32**
See also CA 73-76; CANR 40

Card, Orson Scott
1951- ...... **CLC 44, 47, 50; DAM POP**
See also AAYA 11; CA 102; CANR 27, 47;
INT CANR-27; MTCW; SATA 83

Cardenal, Ernesto
1925- .... **CLC 31; DAM MULT,**
POET; HLC
See also CA 49-52; CANR 2, 32; HW;
MTCW

Cardozo, Benjamin N(athan)
1870-1938 .... **TCLC 65**
See also CA 117

Carducci, Giosue 1835-1907...... **TCLC 32**

Carew, Thomas 1595(?)-1640....... **LC 13**
See also DLB 126

Carey, Ernestine Gilbreth 1908-.... **CLC 17**
See also CA 5-8R; SATA 2

Carey, Peter 1943-......... **CLC 40, 55, 96**
See also CA 123; 127; CANR 53; INT 127;
MTCW

Carleton, William 1794-1869...... **NCLC 3**
See also DLB 159

Carlisle, Henry (Coffin) 1926-...... **CLC 33**
See also CA 13-16R; CANR 15

Carlsen, Chris
See Holdstock, Robert P.

Carlson, Ron(ald F.) 1947-......... **CLC 54**
See also CA 105; CANR 27

Carlyle, Thomas
1795-1881 .... **NCLC 22; DA; DAB;**
DAC; DAM MST
See also CDBLB 1789-1832; DLB 55; 144

Carman, (William) Bliss
1861-1929 .... **TCLC 7; DAC**
See also CA 104; 152; DLB 92

Carnegie, Dale 1888-1955 .... **TCLC 53**

Carossa, Hans 1878-1956......... **TCLC 48**
See also DLB 66

Carpenter, Don(ald Richard)
1931-1995 .... **CLC 41**
See also CA 45-48; 149; CANR 1

Carpentier (y Valmont), Alejo
1904-1980 .... **CLC 8, 11, 38;**
DAM MULT; HLC
See also CA 65-68; 97-100; CANR 11;
DLB 113; HW

Carr, Caleb 1955(?)-.............. **CLC 86**
See also CA 147

Carr, Emily 1871-1945........... **TCLC 32**
See also DLB 68

Carr, John Dickson 1906-1977 ...... **CLC 3**
See also CA 49-52; 69-72; CANR 3, 33;
MTCW

Carr, Philippa
See Hibbert, Eleanor Alice Burford

Carr, Virginia Spencer 1929-....... **CLC 34**
See also CA 61-64; DLB 111

Carrere, Emmanuel 1957- .... **CLC 89**

Carrier, Roch
1937- ... **CLC 13, 78; DAC; DAM MST**
See also CA 130; DLB 53

Carroll, James P. 1943(?)-......... **CLC 38**
See also CA 81-84

Carroll, Jim 1951- .... **CLC 35**
See also AAYA 17; CA 45-48; CANR 42

Carroll, Lewis .... **NCLC 2, 53; WLC**
See also Dodgson, Charles Lutwidge
See also CDBLB 1832-1890; CLR 2, 18;
DLB 18, 163; JRDA

Carroll, Paul Vincent 1900-1968.... **CLC 10**
See also CA 9-12R; 25-28R; DLB 10

Carruth, Hayden
1921- ...... **CLC 4, 7, 10, 18, 84; PC 10**
See also CA 9-12R; CANR 4, 38; DLB 5,
165; INT CANR-4; MTCW; SATA 47

Carson, Rachel Louise
1907-1964 .... **CLC 71; DAM POP**
See also CA 77-80; CANR 35; MTCW;
SATA 23

Carter, Angela (Olive)
1940-1992 ...... **CLC 5, 41, 76; SSC 13**
See also CA 53-56; 136; CANR 12, 36;
DLB 14; MTCW; SATA 66;
SATA-Obit 70

Carter, Nick
See Smith, Martin Cruz

Carver, Raymond
1938-1988 .... **CLC 22, 36, 53, 55;**
DAM NOV; SSC 8
See also CA 33-36R; 126; CANR 17, 34;
DLB 130; DLBY 84, 88; MTCW

Cary, Elizabeth, Lady Falkland
1585-1639 .... **LC 30**

Cary, (Arthur) Joyce (Lunel)
1888-1957 .... **TCLC 1, 29**
See also CA 104; CDBLB 1914-1945;
DLB 15, 100

Casanova de Seingalt, Giovanni Jacopo
1725-1798 .... **LC 13**

Casares, Adolfo Bioy
See Bioy Casares, Adolfo

Casely-Hayford, J(oseph) E(phraim)
1866-1930 .... **TCLC 24; BLC;**
DAM MULT
See also BW 2; CA 123; 152

Casey, John (Dudley) 1939-........ **CLC 59**
See also BEST 90:2; CA 69-72; CANR 23

Casey, Michael 1947-.............. **CLC 2**
See also CA 65-68; DLB 5

Casey, Patrick
See Thurman, Wallace (Henry)

Casey, Warren (Peter) 1935-1988 ... **CLC 12**
See also CA 101; 127; INT 101

Casona, Alejandro................. **CLC 49**
See also Alvarez, Alejandro Rodriguez

Cassavetes, John 1929-1989........ **CLC 20**
See also CA 85-88; 127

Cassill, R(onald) V(erlin) 1919-... **CLC 4, 23**
See also CA 9-12R; CAAS 1; CANR 7, 45;
DLB 6

Cassirer, Ernst 1874-1945 .... **TCLC 61**

Cassity, (Allen) Turner 1929- .... **CLC 6, 42**
See also CA 17-20R; CAAS 8; CANR 11;
DLB 105

Castaneda, Carlos 1931(?)-......... **CLC 12**
See also CA 25-28R; CANR 32; HW;
MTCW

Castedo, Elena 1937- .... **CLC 65**
See also CA 132

Castedo-Ellerman, Elena
See Castedo, Elena

Castellanos, Rosario
1925-1974 ...... **CLC 66; DAM MULT;**
HLC
See also CA 131; 53-56; DLB 113; HW

Castelvetro, Lodovico 1505-1571..... **LC 12**

Castiglione, Baldassare 1478-1529 ... **LC 12**

Castle, Robert
See Hamilton, Edmond

Castro, Guillen de 1569-1631........ **LC 19**

Castro, Rosalia de
1837-1885 ...... **NCLC 3; DAM MULT**

Cather, Willa
See Cather, Willa Sibert

Cather, Willa Sibert
1873-1947 .... **TCLC 1, 11, 31; DA;**
DAB; DAC; DAM MST, NOV; SSC 2;
WLC
See also CA 104; 128; CDALB 1865-1917;
DLB 9, 54, 78; DLBD 1; MTCW;
SATA 30

Catton, (Charles) Bruce
1899-1978 .... **CLC 35**
See also AITN 1; CA 5-8R; 81-84;
CANR 7; DLB 17; SATA 2;
SATA-Obit 24

Catullus c. 84B.C.-c. 54B.C. ..... **CMLC 18**

Cauldwell, Frank
See King, Francis (Henry)

Caunitz, William J. 1933-1996 ..... **CLC 34**
See also BEST 89:3; CA 125; 130; 152;
INT 130

Causley, Charles (Stanley) 1917-..... **CLC 7**
See also CA 9-12R; CANR 5, 35; CLR 30;
DLB 27; MTCW; SATA 3, 66

Caute, David 1936-.... **CLC 29; DAM NOV**
See also CA 1-4R; CAAS 4; CANR 1, 33;
DLB 14

Cavafy, C(onstantine) P(eter)
1863-1933 .... **TCLC 2, 7; DAM POET**
See also Kavafis, Konstantinos Petrou
See also CA 148

Cavallo, Evelyn
See Spark, Muriel (Sarah)

Cavanna, Betty .... **CLC 12**
See also Harrison, Elizabeth Cavanna
See also JRDA; MAICYA; SAAS 4;
SATA 1, 30

Cavendish, Margaret Lucas
1623-1673 .... **LC 30**
See also DLB 131

Caxton, William 1421(?)-1491(?) . . . . . **LC 17**
See also DLB 170

Cayrol, Jean 1911- . . . . **CLC 11**
See also CA 89-92; DLB 83

Cela, Camilo Jose
1916- . . . . . **CLC 4, 13, 59; DAM MULT;**
HLC
See also BEST 90:2; CA 21-24R; CAAS 10;
CANR 21, 32, DLDY 09, IIW, MTCW

Celan, Paul . . . . . . **CLC 10, 19, 53, 82; PC 10**
See also Antschel, Paul
See also DLB 69

Celine, Louis-Ferdinand
. . . . **CLC 1, 3, 4, 7, 9, 15, 47**
See also Destouches, Louis-Ferdinand
See also DLB 72

Cellini, Benvenuto 1500-1571 . . . . **LC 7**

Cendrars, Blaise . . . . **CLC 18**
See also Sauser-Hall, Frederic

Cernuda (y Bidon), Luis
1902-1963 . . . . **CLC 54; DAM POET**
See also CA 131; 89-92; DLB 134; HW

Cervantes (Saavedra), Miguel de
1547-1616 . . . . **LC 6, 23; DA; DAB;**
DAC; DAM MST, NOV; SSC 12; WLC

Cesaire, Aime (Fernand)
1913- . . . . **CLC 19, 32; BLC;**
DAM MULT, POET
See also BW 2; CA 65-68; CANR 24, 43;
MTCW

Chabon, Michael 1963- . . . . **CLC 55**
See also CA 139

Chabrol, Claude 1930- . . . . **CLC 16**
See also CA 110

Challans, Mary 1905-1983
See Renault, Mary
See also CA 81-84; 111; SATA 23;
SATA-Obit 36

Challis, George
See Faust, Frederick (Schiller)

Chambers, Aidan 1934- . . . . **CLC 35**
See also CA 25-28R; CANR 12, 31; JRDA;
MAICYA; SAAS 12; SATA 1, 69

Chambers, James 1948-
See Cliff, Jimmy
See also CA 124

Chambers, Jessie
See Lawrence, D(avid) H(erbert Richards)

Chambers, Robert W. 1865-1933. . . **TCLC 41**

Chandler, Raymond (Thornton)
1888-1959 . . . . **TCLC 1, 7; SSC 23**
See also CA 104; 129; CDALB 1929-1941;
DLBD 6; MTCW

Chang, Jung 1952- . . . . **CLC 71**
See also CA 142

Channing, William Ellery
1780-1842 . . . . **NCLC 17**
See also DLB 1, 59

Chaplin, Charles Spencer
1889-1977 . . . . **CLC 16**
See also Chaplin, Charlie
See also CA 81-84; 73-76

Chaplin, Charlie
See Chaplin, Charles Spencer
See also DLB 44

Chapman, George
1559(?)-1634 . . . . . **LC 22; DAM DRAM**
See also DLB 62, 121

Chapman, Graham 1941-1989 . . . . . . **CLC 21**
See also Monty Python
See also CA 116; 129; CANR 35

Chapman, John Jay 1862-1933 . . . . . **TCLC 7**
See also CA 104

Chapman, Lee
See Bradley, Marion Zimmer

Chapman, Walker
See Silverberg, Robert

Chappell, Fred (Davis) 1936- . . . . **CLC 40, 78**
See also CA 5-8R; CAAS 4; CANR 8, 33;
DLB 6, 105

Char, Rene(-Emile)
1907-1988 . . . . **CLC 9, 11, 14, 55;**
DAM POET
See also CA 13-16R; 124; CANR 32;
MTCW

Charby, Jay
See Ellison, Harlan (Jay)

Chardin, Pierre Teilhard de
See Teilhard de Chardin, (Marie Joseph)
Pierre

Charles I 1600-1649 . . . . **LC 13**

Charyn, Jerome 1937- . . . . **CLC 5, 8, 18**
See also CA 5-8R; CAAS 1; CANR 7;
DLBY 83; MTCW

Chase, Mary (Coyle) 1907-1981 . . . . . . **DC 1**
See also CA 77-80; 105; SATA 17;
SATA-Obit 29

Chase, Mary Ellen 1887-1973 . . . . **CLC 2**
See also CA 13-16; 41-44R; CAP 1;
SATA 10

Chase, Nicholas
See Hyde, Anthony

Chateaubriand, Francois Rene de
1768-1848 . . . . **NCLC 3**
See also DLB 119

Chatterje, Sarat Chandra 1876-1936(?)
See Chatterji, Saratchandra
See also CA 109

Chatterji, Bankim Chandra
1838-1894 . . . . **NCLC 19**

Chatterji, Saratchandra . . . . **TCLC 13**
See also Chatterje, Sarat Chandra

Chatterton, Thomas
1752-1770 . . . . **LC 3; DAM POET**
See also DLB 109

Chatwin, (Charles) Bruce
1940-1989 . . **CLC 28, 57, 59; DAM POP**
See also AAYA 4; BEST 90:1; CA 85-88;
127

Chaucer, Daniel
See Ford, Ford Madox

Chaucer, Geoffrey
1340(?)-1400 . . . . **LC 17; DA; DAB;**
DAC; DAM MST, POET
See also CDBLB Before 1660; DLB 146

Chaviaras, Strates 1935-
See Haviaras, Stratis
See also CA 105

Chayefsky, Paddy . . . . **CLC 23**
See also Chayefsky, Sidney
See also DLB 7, 44; DLBY 81

Chayefsky, Sidney 1923-1981
See Chayefsky, Paddy
See also CA 9-12R; 104; CANR 18;
DAM DRAM

Chedid, Andree 1920- . . . . **CLC 47**
See also CA 145

Cheever, John
1912-1982 . . . . . . **CLC 3, 7, 8, 11, 15, 25,**
64; DA; DAB; DAC; DAM MST, NOV,
POP; SSC 1; WLC
See also CA 5-8R; 106; CABS 1; CANR 5,
27; CDALB 1941-1968; DLB 2, 102;
DLBY 80, 82; INT CANR-5; MTCW

Cheever, Susan 1943- . . . . **CLC 18, 48**
See also CA 103; CANR 27, 51; DLBY 82;
INT CANR-27

Chekhonte, Antosha
See Chekhov, Anton (Pavlovich)

Chekhov, Anton (Pavlovich)
1860-1904 . . . . . **TCLC 3, 10, 31, 55; DA;**
DAB; DAC; DAM DRAM, MST; SSC 2;
WLC
See also CA 104; 124; SATA 90

Chernyshevsky, Nikolay Gavrilovich
1828-1889 . . . . **NCLC 1**

Cherry, Carolyn Janice 1942-
See Cherryh, C. J.
See also CA 65-68; CANR 10

Cherryh, C. J. . . . . **CLC 35**
See also Cherry, Carolyn Janice
See also DLBY 80

Chesnutt, Charles W(addell)
1858-1932 . . . . **TCLC 5, 39; BLC;**
DAM MULT; SSC 7
See also BW 1; CA 106; 125; DLB 12, 50,
78; MTCW

Chester, Alfred 1929(?)-1971 . . . . **CLC 49**
See also CA 33-36R; DLB 130

Chesterton, G(ilbert) K(eith)
1874-1936 . . . . **TCLC 1, 6, 64;**
DAM NOV, POET; SSC 1
See also CA 104; 132; CDBLB 1914-1945;
DLB 10, 19, 34, 70, 98, 149; MTCW;
SATA 27

Chiang Pin-chin 1904-1986
See Ding Ling
See also CA 118

Ch'ien Chung-shu 1910- . . . . **CLC 22**
See also CA 130; MTCW

Child, L. Maria
See Child, Lydia Maria

Child, Lydia Maria 1802-1880 . . . . **NCLC 6**
See also DLB 1, 74; SATA 67

Child, Mrs.
See Child, Lydia Maria

Child, Philip 1898-1978 . . . . **CLC 19, 68**
See also CA 13-14; CAP 1; SATA 47

Childers, (Robert) Erskine
1870-1922 . . . . **TCLC 65**
See also CA 113; 153; DLB 70

Childress, Alice
    1920-1994 .... **CLC 12, 15, 86, 96; BLC;**
    DAM DRAM, MULT, NOV; DC 4
    See also AAYA 8; BW 2; CA 45-48; 146;
    CANR 3, 27, 50; CLR 14; DLB 7, 38;
    JRDA; MAICYA; MTCW; SATA 7, 48,
    81

Chislett, (Margaret) Anne 1943- .... **CLC 34**
    See also CA 151

Chitty, Thomas Willes 1926-....... **CLC 11**
    See also Hinde, Thomas
    See also CA 5-8R

Chivers, Thomas Holley
    1809-1858 .... **NCLC 49**
    See also DLB 3

Chomette, Rene Lucien 1898-1981
    See Clair, Rene
    See also CA 103

Chopin, Kate
    .... **TCLC 5, 14; DA; DAB; SSC 8**
    See also Chopin, Katherine
    See also CDALB 1865-1917; DLB 12, 78

Chopin, Katherine 1851-1904
    See Chopin, Kate
    See also CA 104; 122; DAC; DAM MST,
    NOV

Chretien de Troyes
    c. 12th cent. - .... **CMLC 10**

Christie
    See Ichikawa, Kon

Christie, Agatha (Mary Clarissa)
    1890-1976 ...... **CLC 1, 6, 8, 12, 39, 48;**
    DAB; DAC; DAM NOV
    See also AAYA 9; AITN 1, 2; CA 17-20R;
    61-64; CANR 10, 37; CDBLB 1914-1945;
    DLB 13, 77; MTCW; SATA 36

Christie, (Ann) Philippa
    See Pearce, Philippa
    See also CA 5-8R; CANR 4

Christine de Pizan 1365(?)-1431(?) .... **LC 9**

Chubb, Elmer
    See Masters, Edgar Lee

Chulkov, Mikhail Dmitrievich
    1743-1792 .... **LC 2**
    See also DLB 150

Churchill, Caryl 1938-... **CLC 31, 55; DC 5**
    See also CA 102; CANR 22, 46; DLB 13;
    MTCW

Churchill, Charles 1731-1764........ **LC 3**
    See also DLB 109

Chute, Carolyn 1947-.............. **CLC 39**
    See also CA 123

Ciardi, John (Anthony)
    1916-1986 .... **CLC 10, 40, 44;**
    DAM POET
    See also CA 5-8R; 118; CAAS 2; CANR 5,
    33; CLR 19; DLB 5; DLBY 86;
    INT CANR-5; MAICYA; MTCW;
    SATA 1, 65; SATA-Obit 46

Cicero, Marcus Tullius
    106B.C.-43B.C................ **CMLC 3**

Cimino, Michael 1943-............. **CLC 16**
    See also CA 105

Cioran, E(mil) M. 1911-1995....... **CLC 64**
    See also CA 25-28R; 149

Cisneros, Sandra
    1954- ..... **CLC 69; DAM MULT; HLC**
    See also AAYA 9; CA 131; DLB 122, 152;
    HW

Cixous, Helene 1937-............. **CLC 92**
    See also CA 126; CANR 55; DLB 83;
    MTCW

Clair, Rene...................... **CLC 20**
    See also Chomette, Rene Lucien

Clampitt, Amy 1920-1994 .... **CLC 32**
    See also CA 110; 146; CANR 29; DLB 105

Clancy, Thomas L., Jr. 1947-
    See Clancy, Tom
    See also CA 125; 131; INT 131; MTCW

Clancy, Tom..... **CLC 45; DAM NOV, POP**
    See also Clancy, Thomas L., Jr.
    See also AAYA 9; BEST 89:1, 90:1

Clare, John
    1793-1864 .... **NCLC 9; DAB;**
    DAM POET
    See also DLB 55, 96

Clarin
    See Alas (y Urena), Leopoldo (Enrique
    Garcia)

Clark, Al C.
    See Goines, Donald

Clark, (Robert) Brian 1932-........ **CLC 29**
    See also CA 41-44R

Clark, Curt
    See Westlake, Donald E(dwin)

Clark, Eleanor 1913-1996 .... **CLC 5, 19**
    See also CA 9-12R; 151; CANR 41; DLB 6

Clark, J. P.
    See Clark, John Pepper
    See also DLB 117

Clark, John Pepper
    1935- .... **CLC 38; BLC; DAM DRAM,**
    MULT; DC 5
    See also Clark, J. P.
    See also BW 1; CA 65-68; CANR 16

Clark, M. R.
    See Clark, Mavis Thorpe

Clark, Mavis Thorpe 1909-........ **CLC 12**
    See also CA 57-60; CANR 8, 37; CLR 30;
    MAICYA; SAAS 5; SATA 8, 74

Clark, Walter Van Tilburg
    1909-1971 .... **CLC 28**
    See also CA 9-12R; 33-36R; DLB 9;
    SATA 8

Clarke, Arthur C(harles)
    1917- .... **CLC 1, 4, 13, 18, 35;**
    DAM POP; SSC 3
    See also AAYA 4; CA 1-4R; CANR 2, 28,
    55; JRDA; MAICYA; MTCW; SATA 13,
    70

Clarke, Austin
    1896-1974 ...... **CLC 6, 9; DAM POET**
    See also CA 29-32; 49-52; CAP 2; DLB 10,
    20

Clarke, Austin C(hesterfield)
    1934- .... **CLC 8, 53; BLC; DAC;**
    DAM MULT
    See also BW 1; CA 25-28R; CAAS 16;
    CANR 14, 32; DLB 53, 125

Clarke, Gillian 1937- .... **CLC 61**
    See also CA 106; DLB 40

Clarke, Marcus (Andrew Hislop)
    1846-1881 .... **NCLC 19**

Clarke, Shirley 1925-............. **CLC 16**

Clash, The
    See Headon, (Nicky) Topper; Jones, Mick;
    Simonon, Paul; Strummer, Joe

Claudel, Paul (Louis Charles Marie)
    1868-1955 .... **TCLC 2, 10**
    See also CA 104

Clavell, James (duMaresq)
    1925-1994 .... **CLC 6, 25, 87;**
    DAM NOV, POP
    See also CA 25-28R; 146; CANR 26, 48;
    MTCW

Cleaver, (Leroy) Eldridge
    1935- ..... **CLC 30; BLC; DAM MULT**
    See also BW 1; CA 21-24R; CANR 16

Cleese, John (Marwood) 1939- ..... **CLC 21**
    See also Monty Python
    See also CA 112; 116; CANR 35; MTCW

Cleishbotham, Jebediah
    See Scott, Walter

Cleland, John 1710-1789 .... **LC 2**
    See also DLB 39

Clemens, Samuel Langhorne 1835-1910
    See Twain, Mark
    See also CA 104; 135; CDALB 1865-1917;
    DA; DAB; DAC; DAM MST, NOV;
    DLB 11, 12, 23, 64, 74; JRDA;
    MAICYA; YABC 2

Cleophil
    See Congreve, William

Clerihew, E.
    See Bentley, E(dmund) C(lerihew)

Clerk, N. W.
    See Lewis, C(live) S(taples)

Cliff, Jimmy..................... **CLC 21**
    See also Chambers, James

Clifton, (Thelma) Lucille
    1936- .... **CLC 19, 66; BLC;**
    DAM MULT, POET
    See also BW 2; CA 49-52; CANR 2, 24, 42;
    CLR 5; DLB 5, 41; MAICYA; MTCW;
    SATA 20, 69

Clinton, Dirk
    See Silverberg, Robert

Clough, Arthur Hugh 1819-1861.. **NCLC 27**
    See also DLB 32

Clutha, Janet Paterson Frame 1924-
    See Frame, Janet
    See also CA 1-4R; CANR 2, 36; MTCW

Clyne, Terence
    See Blatty, William Peter

Cobalt, Martin
    See Mayne, William (James Carter)

Cobbett, William 1763-1835 ..... **NCLC 49**
    See also DLB 43, 107, 158

Coburn, D(onald) L(ee) 1938-...... **CLC 10**
    See also CA 89-92

Cocteau, Jean (Maurice Eugene Clement)
    1889-1963 .... **CLC 1, 8, 15, 16, 43; DA;**
    DAB; DAC; DAM DRAM, MST, NOV;
    WLC
    See also CA 25-28; CANR 40; CAP 2;
    DLB 65; MTCW

Copeland, Stewart (Armstrong)
    1952- .... CLC 26

Coppard, A(lfred) E(dgar)
    1878-1957 .... TCLC 5; SSC 21
    See also CA 114; DLB 162; YABC 1

Coppee, Francois 1842-1908 ...... TCLC 25

Coppola, Francis Ford 1939-........ CLC 16
    See also CA 77-80; CANR 40; DLB 44

Corbiere, Tristan 1845-1875 ..... NCLC 43

Corcoran, Barbara 1911-........... CLC 17
    See also AAYA 14; CA 21-24R; CAAS 2;
    CANR 11, 28, 48; DLB 52; JRDA;
    SAAS 20; SATA 3, 77

Cordelier, Maurice
    See Giraudoux, (Hippolyte) Jean

Corelli, Marie 1855-1924........ TCLC 51
    See also Mackay, Mary
    See also DLB 34, 156

Corman, Cid........................ CLC 9
    See also Corman, Sidney
    See also CAAS 2; DLB 5

Corman, Sidney 1924-
    See Corman, Cid
    See also CA 85-88; CANR 44; DAM POET

Cormier, Robert (Edmund)
    1925- .... CLC 12, 30; DA; DAB; DAC;
                      DAM MST, NOV
    See also AAYA 3, 19; CA 1-4R; CANR 5,
    23; CDALB 1968-1988; CLR 12; DLB 52;
    INT CANR-23; JRDA; MAICYA;
    MTCW; SATA 10, 45, 83

Corn, Alfred (DeWitt III) 1943-.... CLC 33
    See also CA 104; CAAS 25; CANR 44;
    DLB 120; DLBY 80

Corneille, Pierre
    1606-1684 .... LC 28; DAB; DAM MST

Cornwell, David (John Moore)
    1931- .... CLC 9, 15; DAM POP
    See also le Carre, John
    See also CA 5-8R; CANR 13, 33; MTCW

Corso, (Nunzio) Gregory 1930-... CLC 1, 11
    See also CA 5-8R; CANR 41; DLB 5, 16;
    MTCW

Cortazar, Julio
    1914-1984 ...... CLC 2, 3, 5, 10, 13, 15,
        33, 34, 92; DAM MULT, NOV; HLC;
                                    SSC 7
    See also CA 21-24R; CANR 12, 32;
    DLB 113; HW; MTCW

CORTES, HERNAN 1484-1547..... LC 31

Corwin, Cecil
    See Kornbluth, C(yril) M.

Cosic, Dobrica 1921- .... CLC 14
    See also CA 122; 138

Costain, Thomas B(ertram)
    1885-1965 .... CLC 30
    See also CA 5-8R; 25-28R; DLB 9

Costantini, Humberto
    1924(?)-1987 .... CLC 49
    See also CA 131; 122; HW

Costello, Elvis 1955-.............. CLC 21

Cotter, Joseph Seamon Sr.
    1861-1949 .... TCLC 28; BLC;
                                DAM MULT
    See also BW 1; CA 124; DLB 50

Couch, Arthur Thomas Quiller
    See Quiller-Couch, Arthur Thomas

Coulton, James
    See Hansen, Joseph

Couperus, Louis (Marie Anne)
    1863-1923 .... TCLC 15
    See also CA 115

Coupland, Douglas
    1961- .... CLC 85; DAC; DAM POP
    See also CA 142

Court, Wesli
    See Turco, Lewis (Putnam)

Courtenay, Bryce 1933-........... CLC 59
    See also CA 138

Courtney, Robert
    See Ellison, Harlan (Jay)

Cousteau, Jacques-Yves 1910-...... CLC 30
    See also CA 65-68; CANR 15; MTCW;
    SATA 38

Coward, Noel (Peirce)
    1899-1973 .... CLC 1, 9, 29, 51;
                                DAM DRAM
    See also AITN 1; CA 17-18; 41-44R;
    CANR 35; CAP 2; CDBLB 1914-1945;
    DLB 10; MTCW

Cowley, Malcolm 1898-1989 .... CLC 39
    See also CA 5-8R; 128; CANR 3, 55;
    DLB 4, 48; DLBY 81, 89; MTCW

Cowper, William
    1731-1800 ...... NCLC 8; DAM POET
    See also DLB 104, 109

Cox, William Trevor
    1928- .... CLC 9, 14, 71; DAM NOV
    See also Trevor, William
    See also CA 9-12R; CANR 4, 37, 55;
    DLB 14; INT CANR-37; MTCW

Coyne, P. J.
    See Masters, Hilary

Cozzens, James Gould
    1903-1978 .... CLC 1, 4, 11, 92
    See also CA 9-12R; 81-84; CANR 19;
    CDALB 1941-1968; DLB 9; DLBD 2;
    DLBY 84; MTCW

Crabbe, George 1754-1832....... NCLC 26
    See also DLB 93

Craddock, Charles Egbert
    See Murfree, Mary Noailles

Craig, A. A.
    See Anderson, Poul (William)

Craik, Dinah Maria (Mulock)
    1826-1887 .... NCLC 38
    See also DLB 35, 163; MAICYA; SATA 34

Cram, Ralph Adams 1863-1942.... TCLC 45

Crane, (Harold) Hart
    1899-1932 .... TCLC 2, 5; DA; DAB;
        DAC; DAM MST, POET; PC 3; WLC
    See also CA 104; 127; CDALB 1917-1929;
    DLB 4, 48; MTCW

Crane, R(onald) S(almon)
    1886-1967 .... CLC 27
    See also CA 85-88; DLB 63

Crane, Stephen (Townley)
    1871-1900 ...... TCLC 11, 17, 32; DA;
        DAB; DAC; DAM MST, NOV, POET;
                                SSC 7; WLC
    See also CA 109; 140; CDALB 1865-1917;
    DLB 12, 54, 78; YABC 2

Crase, Douglas 1944-............. CLC 58
    See also CA 106

Crashaw, Richard 1612(?)-1649...... LC 24
    See also DLB 126

Craven, Margaret
    1901-1980 .... CLC 17; DAC
    See also CA 103

Crawford, F(rancis) Marion
    1854-1909 .... TCLC 10
    See also CA 107; DLB 71

Crawford, Isabella Valancy
    1850-1887 .... NCLC 12
    See also DLB 92

Crayon, Geoffrey
    See Irving, Washington

Creasey, John 1908-1973.......... CLC 11
    See also CA 5-8R; 41-44R; CANR 8;
    DLB 77; MTCW

Crebillon, Claude Prosper Jolyot de (fils)
    1707-1777 .... LC 28

Credo
    See Creasey, John

Creeley, Robert (White)
    1926- ..... CLC 1, 2, 4, 8, 11, 15, 36, 78;
                                DAM POET
    See also CA 1-4R; CAAS 10; CANR 23, 43;
    DLB 5, 16, 169; MTCW

Crews, Harry (Eugene)
    1935-.................... CLC 6, 23, 49
    See also AITN 1; CA 25-28R; CANR 20;
    DLB 6, 143; MTCW

Crichton, (John) Michael
    1942- .... CLC 2, 6, 54, 90; DAM NOV,
                                        POP
    See also AAYA 10; AITN 2; CA 25-28R;
    CANR 13, 40, 54; DLBY 81;
    INT CANR-13; JRDA; MTCW; SATA 9,
    88

Crispin, Edmund .... CLC 22
    See also Montgomery, (Robert) Bruce
    See also DLB 87

Cristofer, Michael
    1945(?)-......... CLC 28; DAM DRAM
    See also CA 110; 152; DLB 7

Croce, Benedetto 1866-1952 ...... TCLC 37
    See also CA 120

Crockett, David 1786-1836 .... NCLC 8
    See also DLB 3, 11

Crockett, Davy
    See Crockett, David

Crofts, Freeman Wills
    1879-1957 .... TCLC 55
    See also CA 115; DLB 77

Croker, John Wilson 1780-1857 .. NCLC 10
    See also DLB 110

Crommelynck, Fernand 1885-1970 .. CLC 75
    See also CA 89-92

Davies, (William) Robertson
1913-1995 ..... **CLC 2, 7, 13, 25, 42, 75, 91; DA; DAB; DAC; DAM MST, NOV, POP; WLC**
See also BEST 89:2; CA 33-36R; 150; CANR 17, 42; DLB 68; INT CANR-17; MTCW

Davies, W(illiam) H(enry)
1871-1940 .... **TCLC 5**
See also CA 104; DLB 19, 174

Davies, Walter C.
See Kornbluth, C(yril) M.

Davis, Angela (Yvonne)
1944- .... **CLC 77; DAM MULT**
See also BW 2; CA 57-60; CANR 10

Davis, B. Lynch
See Bioy Casares, Adolfo; Borges, Jorge Luis

Davis, Gordon
See Hunt, E(verette) Howard, (Jr.)

Davis, Harold Lenoir 1896-1960.... **CLC 49**
See also CA 89-92; DLB 9

Davis, Rebecca (Blaine) Harding
1831-1910 .... **TCLC 6**
See also CA 104; DLB 74

Davis, Richard Harding
1864-1916 .... **TCLC 24**
See also CA 114; DLB 12, 23, 78, 79; DLBD 13

Davison, Frank Dalby 1893-1970 ... **CLC 15**
See also CA 116

Davison, Lawrence H.
See Lawrence, D(avid) H(erbert Richards)

Davison, Peter (Hubert) 1928- ..... **CLC 28**
See also CA 9-12R; CAAS 4; CANR 3, 43; DLB 5

Davys, Mary 1674-1732............. **LC 1**
See also DLB 39

Dawson, Fielding 1930- .... **CLC 6**
See also CA 85-88; DLB 130

Dawson, Peter
See Faust, Frederick (Schiller)

Day, Clarence (Shepard, Jr.)
1874-1935 .... **TCLC 25**
See also CA 108; DLB 11

Day, Thomas 1748-1789............. **LC 1**
See also DLB 39; YABC 1

Day Lewis, C(ecil)
1904-1972 .... **CLC 1, 6, 10; DAM POET; PC 11**
See also Blake, Nicholas
See also CA 13-16; 33-36R; CANR 34; CAP 1; DLB 15, 20; MTCW

Dazai, Osamu .... **TCLC 11**
See also Tsushima, Shuji

de Andrade, Carlos Drummond
See Drummond de Andrade, Carlos

Deane, Norman
See Creasey, John

de Beauvoir, Simone (Lucie Ernestine Marie Bertrand)
See Beauvoir, Simone (Lucie Ernestine Marie Bertrand) de

de Brissac, Malcolm
See Dickinson, Peter (Malcolm)

de Chardin, Pierre Teilhard
See Teilhard de Chardin, (Marie Joseph) Pierre

Dee, John 1527-1608 .... **LC 20**

Deer, Sandra 1940-................ **CLC 45**

De Ferrari, Gabriella 1941-........ **CLC 65**
See also CA 146

Defoe, Daniel
1660(?)-1731 .... **LC 1; DA; DAB; DAC; DAM MST, NOV; WLC**
See also CDBLB 1660-1789; DLB 39, 95, 101; JRDA; MAICYA; SATA 22

de Gourmont, Remy(-Marie-Charles)
See Gourmont, Remy (-Marie-Charles) de

de Hartog, Jan 1914-............. **CLC 19**
See also CA 1-4R; CANR 1

de Hostos, E. M.
See Hostos (y Bonilla), Eugenio Maria de

de Hostos, Eugenio M.
See Hostos (y Bonilla), Eugenio Maria de

Deighton, Len .... **CLC 4, 7, 22, 46**
See also Deighton, Leonard Cyril
See also AAYA 6; BEST 89:2; CDBLB 1960 to Present; DLB 87

Deighton, Leonard Cyril 1929-
See Deighton, Len
See also CA 9-12R; CANR 19, 33; DAM NOV, POP; MTCW

Dekker, Thomas
1572(?)-1632 ..... **LC 22; DAM DRAM**
See also CDBLB Before 1660; DLB 62, 172

Delafield, E. M. 1890-1943 ...... **TCLC 61**
See also Dashwood, Edmee Elizabeth Monica de la Pasture
See also DLB 34

de la Mare, Walter (John)
1873-1956 .... **TCLC 4, 53; DAB; DAC; DAM MST, POET; SSC 14; WLC**
See also CDBLB 1914-1945; CLR 23; DLB 162; SATA 16

Delaney, Franey
See O'Hara, John (Henry)

Delaney, Shelagh
1939- .... **CLC 29; DAM DRAM**
See also CA 17-20R; CANR 30; CDBLB 1960 to Present; DLB 13; MTCW

Delany, Mary (Granville Pendarves)
1700-1788 .... **LC 12**

Delany, Samuel R(ay, Jr.)
1942- .... **CLC 8, 14, 38; BLC; DAM MULT**
See also BW 2; CA 81-84; CANR 27, 43; DLB 8, 33; MTCW

De La Ramee, (Marie) Louise 1839-1908
See Ouida
See also SATA 20

de la Roche, Mazo 1879-1961 ...... **CLC 14**
See also CA 85-88; CANR 30; DLB 68; SATA 64

Delbanco, Nicholas (Franklin)
1942- .... **CLC 6, 13**
See also CA 17-20R; CAAS 2; CANR 29, 55; DLB 6

del Castillo, Michel 1933-......... **CLC 38**
See also CA 109

Deledda, Grazia (Cosima)
1875(?)-1936 .... **TCLC 23**
See also CA 123

Delibes, Miguel .... **CLC 8, 18**
See also Delibes Setien, Miguel

Delibes Setien, Miguel 1920-
See Delibes, Miguel
See also CA 45-48; CANR 1, 32; HW; MTCW

DeLillo, Don
1936- ..... **CLC 8, 10, 13, 27, 39, 54, 76; DAM NOV, POP**
See also BEST 89:1; CA 81-84; CANR 21; DLB 6, 173; MTCW

de Lisser, H. G.
See De Lisser, H(erbert) G(eorge)
See also DLB 117

De Lisser, H(erbert) G(eorge)
1878-1944 .... **TCLC 12**
See also de Lisser, H. G.
See also BW 2; CA 109; 152

Deloria, Vine (Victor), Jr.
1933- .... **CLC 21; DAM MULT**
See also CA 53-56; CANR 5, 20, 48; MTCW; NNAL; SATA 21

Del Vecchio, John M(ichael)
1947- .... **CLC 29**
See also CA 110; DLBD 9

de Man, Paul (Adolph Michel)
1919-1983 .... **CLC 55**
See also CA 128; 111; DLB 67; MTCW

De Marinis, Rick 1934-........... **CLC 54**
See also CA 57-60; CAAS 24; CANR 9, 25, 50

Dembry, R. Emmet
See Murfree, Mary Noailles

Demby, William
1922- ..... **CLC 53; BLC; DAM MULT**
See also BW 1; CA 81-84; DLB 33

Demijohn, Thom
See Disch, Thomas M(ichael)

de Montherlant, Henry (Milon)
See Montherlant, Henry (Milon) de

Demosthenes 384B.C.-322B.C. .... **CMLC 13**

de Natale, Francine
See Malzberg, Barry N(athaniel)

Denby, Edwin (Orr) 1903-1983 ..... **CLC 48**
See also CA 138; 110

Denis, Julio
See Cortazar, Julio

Denmark, Harrison
See Zelazny, Roger (Joseph)

Dennis, John 1658-1734............ **LC 11**
See also DLB 101

Dennis, Nigel (Forbes) 1912-1989.... **CLC 8**
See also CA 25-28R; 129; DLB 13, 15; MTCW

De Palma, Brian (Russell) 1940-.... **CLC 20**
See also CA 109

De Quincey, Thomas 1785-1859 ... **NCLC 4**
See also CDBLB 1789-1832; DLB 110; 144

du Gard, Roger Martin
See Martin du Gard, Roger

Duhamel, Georges 1884-1966 . . . . . . **CLC 8**
See also CA 81-84; 25-28R; CANR 35;
DLB 65; MTCW

Dujardin, Edouard (Emile Louis)
1861-1949 . . . . **TCLC 13**
See also CA 109; DLB 123

Dumas, Alexandre (Davy de la Pailleterie)
1802-1870 . . . . **NCLC 11; DA; DAB;**
DAC; DAM MST, NOV; WLC
See also DLB 119; SATA 18

Dumas, Alexandre
1824-1895 . . . . **NCLC 9; DC 1**

Dumas, Claudine
See Malzberg, Barry N(athaniel)

Dumas, Henry L. 1934-1968 . . . . . **CLC 6, 62**
See also BW 1; CA 85-88; DLB 41

du Maurier, Daphne
1907-1989 . . . . **CLC 6, 11, 59; DAB;**
DAC; DAM MST, POP; SSC 18
See also CA 5-8R; 128; CANR 6, 55;
MTCW; SATA 27; SATA-Obit 60

Dunbar, Paul Laurence
1872-1906 . . . . . **TCLC 2, 12; BLC; DA;**
DAC; DAM MST, MULT, POET; PC 5;
SSC 8; WLC
See also BW 1; CA 104; 124;
CDALB 1865-1917; DLB 50, 54, 78;
SATA 34

Dunbar, William 1460(?)-1530(?) . . . . **LC 20**
See also DLB 132, 146

Duncan, Dora Angela
See Duncan, Isadora

Duncan, Isadora 1877(?)-1927 . . . . . **TCLC 68**
See also CA 118; 149

Duncan, Lois 1934- . . . . **CLC 26**
See also AAYA 4; CA 1-4R; CANR 2, 23,
36; CLR 29; JRDA; MAICYA; SAAS 2;
SATA 1, 36, 75

Duncan, Robert (Edward)
1919-1988 . . . . **CLC 1, 2, 4, 7, 15, 41, 55;**
DAM POET; PC 2
See also CA 9-12R; 124; CANR 28; DLB 5,
16; MTCW

Duncan, Sara Jeannette
1861-1922 . . . . **TCLC 60**
See also DLB 92

Dunlap, William 1766-1839 . . . . **NCLC 2**
See also DLB 30, 37, 59

Dunn, Douglas (Eaglesham)
1942- . . . . **CLC 6, 40**
See also CA 45-48; CANR 2, 33; DLB 40;
MTCW

Dunn, Katherine (Karen) 1945- . . . . . **CLC 71**
See also CA 33-36R

Dunn, Stephen 1939- . . . . **CLC 36**
See also CA 33-36R; CANR 12, 48, 53;
DLB 105

Dunne, Finley Peter 1867-1936 . . . . **TCLC 28**
See also CA 108; DLB 11, 23

Dunne, John Gregory 1932- . . . . **CLC 28**
See also CA 25-28R; CANR 14, 50;
DLBY 80

Dunsany, Edward John Moreton Drax
Plunkett 1878-1957
See Dunsany, Lord
See also CA 104; 148; DLB 10

Dunsany, Lord . . . . **TCLC 2, 59**
See also Dunsany, Edward John Moreton
Drax Plunkett
See also DLB 77, 153, 156

du Perry, Jean
See Simenon, Georges (Jacques Christian)

Durang, Christopher (Ferdinand)
1949- . . . . **CLC 27, 38**
See also CA 105; CANR 50

Duras, Marguerite
1914-1996 . . **CLC 3, 6, 11, 20, 34, 40, 68**
See also CA 25-28R; 151; CANR 50;
DLB 83; MTCW

Durban, (Rosa) Pam 1947- . . . . **CLC 39**
See also CA 123

Durcan, Paul
1944- . . . . **CLC 43, 70; DAM POET**
See also CA 134

Durkheim, Emile 1858-1917 . . . . . . **TCLC 55**

Durrell, Lawrence (George)
1912-1990 . . . . **CLC 1, 4, 6, 8, 13, 27, 41;**
DAM NOV
See also CA 9-12R; 132; CANR 40;
CDBLB 1945-1960; DLB 15, 27;
DLBY 90; MTCW

Durrenmatt, Friedrich
See Duerrenmatt, Friedrich

Dutt, Toru 1856-1877 . . . . **NCLC 29**

Dwight, Timothy 1752-1817 . . . . . . **NCLC 13**
See also DLB 37

Dworkin, Andrea 1946- . . . . **CLC 43**
See also CA 77-80; CAAS 21; CANR 16,
39; INT CANR-16; MTCW

Dwyer, Deanna
See Koontz, Dean R(ay)

Dwyer, K. R.
See Koontz, Dean R(ay)

Dylan, Bob 1941- . . . . . . **CLC 3, 4, 6, 12, 77**
See also CA 41-44R; DLB 16

Eagleton, Terence (Francis) 1943-
See Eagleton, Terry
See also CA 57-60; CANR 7, 23; MTCW

Eagleton, Terry . . . . **CLC 63**
See also Eagleton, Terence (Francis)

Early, Jack
See Scoppettone, Sandra

East, Michael
See West, Morris L(anglo)

Eastaway, Edward
See Thomas, (Philip) Edward

Eastlake, William (Derry) 1917- . . . . . **CLC 8**
See also CA 5-8R; CAAS 1; CANR 5;
DLB 6; INT CANR-5

Eastman, Charles A(lexander)
1858-1939 . . . . . **TCLC 55; DAM MULT**
See also NNAL; YABC 1

Eberhart, Richard (Ghormley)
1904- . . **CLC 3, 11, 19, 56; DAM POET**
See also CA 1-4R; CANR 2;
CDALB 1941-1968; DLB 48; MTCW

Eberstadt, Fernanda 1960- . . . . **CLC 39**
See also CA 136

Echegaray (y Eizaguirre), Jose (Maria Waldo)
1832-1916 . . . . **TCLC 4**
See also CA 104; CANR 32; HW; MTCW

Echeverria, (Jose) Esteban (Antonino)
1805-1851 . . . . **NCLC 18**

Echo
See Proust, (Valentin-Louis-George-Eugene-)
Marcel

Eckert, Allan W. 1931- . . . . **CLC 17**
See also AAYA 18; CA 13-16R; CANR 14,
45; INT CANR-14; SAAS 21; SATA 29,
91; SATA-Brief 27

Eckhart, Meister 1260(?)-1328(?) . . **CMLC 9**
See also DLB 115

Eckmar, F. R.
See de Hartog, Jan

Eco, Umberto
1932- . . . **CLC 28, 60; DAM NOV, POP**
See also BEST 90:1; CA 77-80; CANR 12,
33, 55; MTCW

Eddison, E(ric) R(ucker)
1882-1945 . . . . **TCLC 15**
See also CA 109; 154

Edel, (Joseph) Leon 1907- . . . . . . **CLC 29, 34**
See also CA 1-4R; CANR 1, 22; DLB 103;
INT CANR-22

Eden, Emily 1797-1869 . . . . **NCLC 10**

Edgar, David
1948- . . . . **CLC 42; DAM DRAM**
See also CA 57-60; CANR 12; DLB 13;
MTCW

Edgerton, Clyde (Carlyle) 1944- . . . . **CLC 39**
See also AAYA 17; CA 118; 134; INT 134

Edgeworth, Maria 1768-1849 . . . **NCLC 1, 51**
See also DLB 116, 159, 163; SATA 21

Edmonds, Paul
See Kuttner, Henry

Edmonds, Walter D(umaux) 1903- . . **CLC 35**
See also CA 5-8R; CANR 2; DLB 9;
MAICYA; SAAS 4; SATA 1, 27

Edmondson, Wallace
See Ellison, Harlan (Jay)

Edson, Russell . . . . **CLC 13**
See also CA 33-36R

Edwards, Bronwen Elizabeth
See Rose, Wendy

Edwards, G(erald) B(asil)
1899-1976 . . . . **CLC 25**
See also CA 110

Edwards, Gus 1939- . . . . **CLC 43**
See also CA 108; INT 108

Edwards, Jonathan
1703-1758 . . . . **LC 7; DA; DAC;**
DAM MST
See also DLB 24

Efron, Marina Ivanovna Tsvetaeva
See Tsvetaeva (Efron), Marina (Ivanovna)

Ehle, John (Marsden, Jr.) 1925- . . . . **CLC 27**
See also CA 9-12R

Ehrenbourg, Ilya (Grigoryevich)
See Ehrenburg, Ilya (Grigoryevich)

Ehrenburg, Ilya (Grigoryevich)
1891-1967 . . . . **CLC 18, 34, 62**
See also CA 102; 25-28R

Ehrenburg, Ilyo (Grigoryevich)
See Ehrenburg, Ilya (Grigoryevich)

Eich, Guenter 1907-1972 . . . . **CLC 15**
See also CA 111; 93-96; DLB 69, 124

Eichendorff, Joseph Freiherr von
1788-1857 . . . . **NCLC 8**
See also DLB 90

Eigner, Larry . . . . **CLC 9**
See also Eigner, Laurence (Joel)
See also CAAS 23; DLB 5

Eigner, Laurence (Joel) 1927-1996
See Eigner, Larry
See also CA 9-12R; 151; CANR 6

Einstein, Albert 1879-1955 . . . . **TCLC 65**
See also CA 121; 133; MTCW

Eiseley, Loren Corey 1907-1977 . . . . . **CLC 7**
See also AAYA 5; CA 1-4R; 73-76;
CANR 6

Eisenstadt, Jill 1963- . . . . **CLC 50**
See also CA 140

Eisenstein, Sergei (Mikhailovich)
1898-1948 . . . . **TCLC 57**
See also CA 114; 149

Eisner, Simon
See Kornbluth, C(yril) M.

Ekeloef, (Bengt) Gunnar
1907-1968 . . . . **CLC 27; DAM POET**
See also CA 123; 25-28R

Ekelof, (Bengt) Gunnar
See Ekeloef, (Bengt) Gunnar

Ekwensi, C. O. D.
See Ekwensi, Cyprian (Odiatu Duaka)

Ekwensi, Cyprian (Odiatu Duaka)
1921- . . . . . . **CLC 4; BLC; DAM MULT**
See also BW 2; CA 29-32R; CANR 18, 42;
DLB 117; MTCW; SATA 66

Elaine . . . . **TCLC 18**
See also Leverson, Ada

El Crummo
See Crumb, R(obert)

Elia
See Lamb, Charles

Eliade, Mircea 1907-1986 . . . . **CLC 19**
See also CA 65-68; 119; CANR 30; MTCW

Eliot, A. D.
See Jewett, (Theodora) Sarah Orne

Eliot, Alice
See Jewett, (Theodora) Sarah Orne

Eliot, Dan
See Silverberg, Robert

Eliot, George
1819-1880 . . . . . **NCLC 4, 13, 23, 41, 49;
DA; DAB; DAC; DAM MST, NOV;
WLC**
See also CDBLB 1832-1890; DLB 21, 35, 55

Eliot, John 1604-1690 . . . . **LC 5**
See also DLB 24

Eliot, T(homas) S(tearns)
1888-1965 . . . . . **CLC 1, 2, 3, 6, 9, 10, 13,
15, 24, 34, 41, 55, 57; DA; DAB; DAC;
DAM DRAM, MST, POET; PC 5;
WLC 2**
See also CA 5-8R; 25-28R; CANR 41;
CDALB 1929-1941; DLB 7, 10, 45, 63;
DLBY 88; MTCW

Elizabeth 1866-1941 . . . . **TCLC 41**

Elkin, Stanley L(awrence)
1930-1995 . . . . . . **CLC 4, 6, 9, 14, 27, 51,
91; DAM NOV, POP; SSC 12**
See also CA 9-12R; 148; CANR 8, 46;
DLB 2, 28; DLBY 80; INT CANR-8;
MTCW

Elledge, Scott . . . . **CLC 34**

Elliot, Don
See Silverberg, Robert

Elliott, Don
See Silverberg, Robert

Elliott, George P(aul) 1918-1980 . . . . . **CLC 2**
See also CA 1-4R; 97-100; CANR 2

Elliott, Janice 1931- . . . . **CLC 47**
See also CA 13-16R; CANR 8, 29; DLB 14

Elliott, Sumner Locke 1917-1991 . . . **CLC 38**
See also CA 5-8R; 134; CANR 2, 21

Elliott, William
See Bradbury, Ray (Douglas)

Ellis, A. E. . . . . **CLC 7**

Ellis, Alice Thomas . . . . **CLC 40**
See also Haycraft, Anna

Ellis, Bret Easton
1964- . . . . **CLC 39, 71; DAM POP**
See also AAYA 2; CA 118; 123; CANR 51;
INT 123

Ellis, (Henry) Havelock
1859-1939 . . . . **TCLC 14**
See also CA 109

Ellis, Landon
See Ellison, Harlan (Jay)

Ellis, Trey 1962- . . . . **CLC 55**
See also CA 146

Ellison, Harlan (Jay)
1934- . . . . . . **CLC 1, 13, 42; DAM POP;
SSC 14**
See also CA 5-8R; CANR 5, 46; DLB 8;
INT CANR-5; MTCW

Ellison, Ralph (Waldo)
1914-1994 . . . . **CLC 1, 3, 11, 54, 86;
BLC; DA; DAB; DAC; DAM MST,
MULT, NOV; WLC**
See also AAYA 19; BW 1; CA 9-12R; 145;
CANR 24, 53; CDALB 1941-1968;
DLB 2, 76; DLBY 94; MTCW

Ellmann, Lucy (Elizabeth) 1956- . . . . **CLC 61**
See also CA 128

Ellmann, Richard (David)
1918-1987 . . . . **CLC 50**
See also BEST 89:2; CA 1-4R; 122;
CANR 2, 28; DLB 103; DLBY 87;
MTCW

Elman, Richard 1934- . . . . **CLC 19**
See also CA 17-20R; CAAS 3; CANR 47

Elron
See Hubbard, L(afayette) Ron(ald)

Eluard, Paul . . . . **TCLC 7, 41**
See also Grindel, Eugene

Elyot, Sir Thomas 1490(?)-1546 . . . . . **LC 11**

Elytis, Odysseus
1911-1996 . . . . **CLC 15, 49; DAM POET**
See also CA 102; 151; MTCW

Emecheta, (Florence Onye) Buchi
1944- . . **CLC 14, 48; BLC; DAM MULT**
See also BW 2; CA 81-84; CANR 27;
DLB 117; MTCW; SATA 66

Emerson, Ralph Waldo
1803-1882 . . . . . **NCLC 1, 38; DA; DAB;
DAC; DAM MST, POET; WLC**
See also CDALB 1640-1865; DLB 1, 59, 73

Eminescu, Mihail 1850-1889 . . . . . **NCLC 33**

Empson, William
1906-1984 . . . . **CLC 3, 8, 19, 33, 34**
See also CA 17-20R; 112; CANR 31;
DLB 20; MTCW

Enchi Fumiko (Ueda) 1905-1986 . . . . **CLC 31**
See also CA 129; 121

Ende, Michael (Andreas Helmuth)
1929-1995 . . . . **CLC 31**
See also CA 118; 124; 149; CANR 36;
CLR 14; DLB 75; MAICYA; SATA 61;
SATA-Brief 42; SATA-Obit 86

Endo, Shusaku
1923-1996 . . . . **CLC 7, 14, 19, 54;
DAM NOV**
See also CA 29-32R; 153; CANR 21, 54;
MTCW

Engel, Marian 1933-1985 . . . . **CLC 36**
See also CA 25-28R; CANR 12; DLB 53;
INT CANR-12

Engelhardt, Frederick
See Hubbard, L(afayette) Ron(ald)

Enright, D(ennis) J(oseph)
1920- . . . . **CLC 4, 8, 31**
See also CA 1-4R; CANR 1, 42; DLB 27;
SATA 25

Enzensberger, Hans Magnus
1929- . . . . **CLC 43**
See also CA 116; 119

Ephron, Nora 1941- . . . . **CLC 17, 31**
See also AITN 2; CA 65-68; CANR 12, 39

Epsilon
See Betjeman, John

Epstein, Daniel Mark 1948- . . . . **CLC 7**
See also CA 49-52; CANR 2, 53

Epstein, Jacob 1956- . . . . **CLC 19**
See also CA 114

Epstein, Joseph 1937- . . . . **CLC 39**
See also CA 112; 119; CANR 50

Epstein, Leslie 1938- . . . . **CLC 27**
See also CA 73-76; CAAS 12; CANR 23

Equiano, Olaudah
1745(?)-1797 . . . . **LC 16; BLC;
DAM MULT**
See also DLB 37, 50

Erasmus, Desiderius 1469(?)-1536 . . . . **LC 16**

Erdman, Paul E(mil) 1932- . . . . **CLC 25**
See also AITN 1; CA 61-64; CANR 13, 43

Feiffer, Jules (Ralph)
1929-...... **CLC 2, 8, 64; DAM DRAM**
See also AAYA 3; CA 17-20R; CANR 30;
DLB 7, 44; INT CANR-30; MTCW;
SATA 8, 61

Feige, Hermann Albert Otto Maximilian
See Traven, B.

Feinberg, David B. 1956-1994...... **CLC 59**
See also CA 135; 147

Feinstein, Elaine 1930-............. **CLC 36**
See also CA 69-72; CAAS 1; CANR 31;
DLB 14, 40; MTCW

Feldman, Irving (Mordecai) 1928-.... **CLC 7**
See also CA 1-4R; CANR 1; DLB 169

Fellini, Federico 1920-1993..... **CLC 16, 85**
See also CA 65-68; 143; CANR 33

Felsen, Henry Gregor 1916-....... **CLC 17**
See also CA 1-4R; CANR 1; SAAS 2;
SATA 1

Fenton, James Martin 1949-....... **CLC 32**
See also CA 102; DLB 40

Ferber, Edna 1887-1968........ **CLC 18, 93**
See also AITN 1; CA 5-8R; 25-28R; DLB 9,
28, 86; MTCW; SATA 7

Ferguson, Helen
See Kavan, Anna

Ferguson, Samuel 1810-1886..... **NCLC 33**
See also DLB 32

Fergusson, Robert 1750-1774 .... **LC 29**
See also DLB 109

Ferling, Lawrence
See Ferlinghetti, Lawrence (Monsanto)

Ferlinghetti, Lawrence (Monsanto)
1919(?)-............. **CLC 2, 6, 10, 27;**
DAM POET; PC 1
See also CA 5-8R; CANR 3, 41;
CDALB 1941-1968; DLB 5, 16; MTCW

Fernandez, Vicente Garcia Huidobro
See Huidobro Fernandez, Vicente Garcia

Ferrer, Gabriel (Francisco Victor) Miro
See Miro (Ferrer), Gabriel (Francisco
Victor)

Ferrier, Susan (Edmonstone)
1782-1854 .... **NCLC 8**
See also DLB 116

Ferrigno, Robert 1948(?)-.......... **CLC 65**
See also CA 140

Ferron, Jacques 1921-1985 ... **CLC 94; DAC**
See also CA 117; 129; DLB 60

Feuchtwanger, Lion 1884-1958 ..... **TCLC 3**
See also CA 104; DLB 66

Feuillet, Octave 1821-1890 ...... **NCLC 45**

Feydeau, Georges (Leon Jules Marie)
1862-1921 ..... **TCLC 22; DAM DRAM**
See also CA 113; 152

Ficino, Marsilio 1433-1499 .... **LC 12**

Fiedeler, Hans
See Doeblin, Alfred

Fiedler, Leslie A(aron)
1917-.................. **CLC 4, 13, 24**
See also CA 9-12R; CANR 7; DLB 28, 67;
MTCW

Field, Andrew 1938-.............. **CLC 44**
See also CA 97-100; CANR 25

Field, Eugene 1850-1895 .... **NCLC 3**
See also DLB 23, 42, 140; DLBD 13;
MAICYA; SATA 16

Field, Gans T.
See Wellman, Manly Wade

Field, Michael .... **TCLC 43**

Field, Peter
See Hobson, Laura Z(ametkin)

Fielding, Henry
1707-1754 ...... **LC 1; DA; DAB; DAC;**
DAM DRAM, MST, NOV; WLC
See also CDBLB 1660-1789; DLB 39, 84,
101

Fielding, Sarah 1710-1768 .... **LC 1**
See also DLB 39

Fierstein, Harvey (Forbes)
1954- ..... **CLC 33; DAM DRAM, POP**
See also CA 123; 129

Figes, Eva 1932-.................. **CLC 31**
See also CA 53-56; CANR 4, 44; DLB 14

Finch, Robert (Duer Claydon)
1900-.......................... **CLC 18**
See also CA 57-60; CANR 9, 24, 49;
DLB 88

Findley, Timothy
1930- ...... **CLC 27; DAC; DAM MST**
See also CA 25-28R; CANR 12, 42;
DLB 53

Fink, William
See Mencken, H(enry) L(ouis)

Firbank, Louis 1942-
See Reed, Lou
See also CA 117

Firbank, (Arthur Annesley) Ronald
1886-1926 .... **TCLC 1**
See also CA 104; DLB 36

Fisher, M(ary) F(rances) K(ennedy)
1908-1992 .... **CLC 76, 87**
See also CA 77-80; 138; CANR 44

Fisher, Roy 1930-................. **CLC 25**
See also CA 81-84; CAAS 10; CANR 16;
DLB 40

Fisher, Rudolph
1897-1934 .... **TCLC 11; BLC;**
DAM MULT
See also BW 1; CA 107; 124; DLB 51, 102

Fisher, Vardis (Alvero) 1895-1968.... **CLC 7**
See also CA 5-8R; 25-28R; DLB 9

Fiske, Tarleton
See Bloch, Robert (Albert)

Fitch, Clarke
See Sinclair, Upton (Beall)

Fitch, John IV
See Cormier, Robert (Edmund)

Fitzgerald, Captain Hugh
See Baum, L(yman) Frank

FitzGerald, Edward 1809-1883 .... **NCLC 9**
See also DLB 32

Fitzgerald, F(rancis) Scott (Key)
1896-1940 .... **TCLC 1, 6, 14, 28, 55;**
DA; DAB; DAC; DAM MST, NOV;
SSC 6; WLC
See also AITN 1; CA 110; 123;
CDALB 1917-1929; DLB 4, 9, 86;
DLBD 1; DLBY 81; MTCW

Fitzgerald, Penelope 1916-... **CLC 19, 51, 61**
See also CA 85-88; CAAS 10; DLB 14

Fitzgerald, Robert (Stuart)
1910-1985 .... **CLC 39**
See also CA 1-4R; 114; CANR 1; DLBY 80

FitzGerald, Robert D(avid)
1902-1987 .... **CLC 19**
See also CA 17-20R

Fitzgerald, Zelda (Sayre)
1900-1948 .... **TCLC 52**
See also CA 117; 126; DLBY 84

Flanagan, Thomas (James Bonner)
1923- .... **CLC 25, 52**
See also CA 108; CANR 55; DLBY 80;
INT 108; MTCW

Flaubert, Gustave
1821-1880 .... **NCLC 2, 10, 19; DA;**
DAB; DAC; DAM MST, NOV; SSC 11;
WLC
See also DLB 119

Flecker, Herman Elroy
See Flecker, (Herman) James Elroy

Flecker, (Herman) James Elroy
1884-1915 .... **TCLC 43**
See also CA 109; 150; DLB 10, 19

Fleming, Ian (Lancaster)
1908-1964 ...... **CLC 3, 30; DAM POP**
See also CA 5-8R; CDBLB 1945-1960;
DLB 87; MTCW; SATA 9

Fleming, Thomas (James) 1927- .... **CLC 37**
See also CA 5-8R; CANR 10;
INT CANR-10; SATA 8

Fletcher, John 1579-1625...... **LC 33; DC 6**
See also CDBLB Before 1660; DLB 58

Fletcher, John Gould 1886-1950 ... **TCLC 35**
See also CA 107; DLB 4, 45

Fleur, Paul
See Pohl, Frederik

Flooglebuckle, Al
See Spiegelman, Art

Flying Officer X
See Bates, H(erbert) E(rnest)

Fo, Dario 1926-..... **CLC 32; DAM DRAM**
See also CA 116; 128; MTCW

Fogarty, Jonathan Titulescu Esq.
See Farrell, James T(homas)

Folke, Will
See Bloch, Robert (Albert)

Follett, Ken(neth Martin)
1949- ...... **CLC 18; DAM NOV, POP**
See also AAYA 6; BEST 89:4; CA 81-84;
CANR 13, 33, 54; DLB 87; DLBY 81;
INT CANR-33; MTCW

Fontane, Theodor 1819-1898..... **NCLC 26**
See also DLB 129

Foote, Horton
1916- .... **CLC 51, 91; DAM DRAM**
See also CA 73-76; CANR 34, 51; DLB 26;
INT CANR-34

Foote, Shelby
1916- ...... **CLC 75; DAM NOV, POP**
See also CA 5-8R; CANR 3, 45; DLB 2, 17

Forbes, Esther 1891-1967 .... **CLC 12**
See also AAYA 17; CA 13-14; 25-28R;
CAP 1; CLR 27; DLB 22; JRDA;
MAICYA; SATA 2

Forche, Carolyn (Louise)
1950- .... **CLC 25, 83, 86; DAM POET;**
PC 10
See also CA 109; 117; CANR 50; DLB 5;
INT 117

Ford, Elbur
See Hibbert, Eleanor Alice Burford

Ford, Ford Madox
1873-1939 .... **TCLC 1, 15, 39, 57;**
DAM NOV
See also CA 104; 132; CDBLB 1914-1945;
DLB 162; MTCW

Ford, John 1895-1973 .... **CLC 16**
See also CA 45-48

Ford, Richard 1944- .... **CLC 46**
See also CA 69-72; CANR 11, 47

Ford, Webster
See Masters, Edgar Lee

Foreman, Richard 1937- .... **CLC 50**
See also CA 65-68; CANR 32

Forester, C(ecil) S(cott)
1899-1966 .... **CLC 35**
See also CA 73-76; 25-28R; SATA 13

Forez
See Mauriac, Francois (Charles)

Forman, James Douglas 1932- ...... **CLC 21**
See also AAYA 17; CA 9-12R; CANR 4,
19, 42; JRDA; MAICYA; SATA 8, 70

Fornes, Maria Irene 1930- ...... **CLC 39, 61**
See also CA 25-28R; CANR 28; DLB 7;
HW; INT CANR-28; MTCW

Forrest, Leon 1937- .... **CLC 4**
See also BW 2; CA 89-92; CAAS 7;
CANR 25, 52; DLB 33

Forster, E(dward) M(organ)
1879-1970 ..... **CLC 1, 2, 3, 4, 9, 10, 13,**
15, 22, 45, 77; DA; DAB; DAC;
DAM MST, NOV; WLC
See also AAYA 2; CA 13-14; 25-28R;
CANR 45; CAP 1; CDBLB 1914-1945;
DLB 34, 98, 162; DLBD 10; MTCW;
SATA 57

Forster, John 1812-1876 .... **NCLC 11**
See also DLB 144

Forsyth, Frederick
1938- .. **CLC 2, 5, 36; DAM NOV, POP**
See also BEST 89:4; CA 85-88; CANR 38;
DLB 87; MTCW

Forten, Charlotte L. .... **TCLC 16; BLC**
See also Grimke, Charlotte L(ottie) Forten
See also DLB 50

Foscolo, Ugo 1778-1827 .... **NCLC 8**

Fosse, Bob .... **CLC 20**
See also Fosse, Robert Louis

Fosse, Robert Louis 1927-1987
See Fosse, Bob
See also CA 110; 123

Foster, Stephen Collins
1826-1864 .... **NCLC 26**

Foucault, Michel
1926-1984 .... **CLC 31, 34, 69**
See also CA 105; 113; CANR 34; MTCW

Fouque, Friedrich (Heinrich Karl) de la Motte
1777-1843 .... **NCLC 2**
See also DLB 90

Fourier, Charles 1772-1837 ...... **NCLC 51**

Fournier, Henri Alban 1886-1914
See Alain-Fournier
See also CA 104

Fournier, Pierre 1916- .... **CLC 11**
See also Gascar, Pierre
See also CA 89-92; CANR 16, 40

Fowles, John
1926- ...... **CLC 1, 2, 3, 4, 6, 9, 10, 15,**
33, 87; DAB; DAC; DAM MST
See also CA 5-8R; CANR 25; CDBLB 1960
to Present; DLB 14, 139; MTCW;
SATA 22

Fox, Paula 1923- .... **CLC 2, 8**
See also AAYA 3; CA 73-76; CANR 20,
36; CLR 1; DLB 52; JRDA; MAICYA;
MTCW; SATA 17, 60

Fox, William Price (Jr.) 1926- ..... **CLC 22**
See also CA 17-20R; CAAS 19; CANR 11;
DLB 2; DLBY 81

Foxe, John 1516(?)-1587 .... **LC 14**

Frame, Janet
1924- .... **CLC 2, 3, 6, 22, 66, 96**
See also Clutha, Janet Paterson Frame

France, Anatole .... **TCLC 9**
See also Thibault, Jacques Anatole Francois
See also DLB 123

Francis, Claude 19(?)- .... **CLC 50**

Francis, Dick
1920- .... **CLC 2, 22, 42; DAM POP**
See also AAYA 5; BEST 89:3; CA 5-8R;
CANR 9, 42; CDBLB 1960 to Present;
DLB 87; INT CANR-9; MTCW

Francis, Robert (Churchill)
1901-1987 .... **CLC 15**
See also CA 1-4R; 123; CANR 1

Frank, Anne(lies Marie)
1929-1945 .... **TCLC 17; DA; DAB;**
DAC; DAM MST; WLC
See also AAYA 12; CA 113; 133; MTCW;
SATA 87; SATA-Brief 42

Frank, Elizabeth 1945- .... **CLC 39**
See also CA 121; 126; INT 126

Frankl, Viktor E(mil) 1905- .... **CLC 93**
See also CA 65-68

Franklin, Benjamin
See Hasek, Jaroslav (Matej Frantisek)

Franklin, Benjamin
1706-1790 ..... **LC 25; DA; DAB; DAC;**
DAM MST
See also CDALB 1640-1865; DLB 24, 43,
73

Franklin, (Stella Maraia Sarah) Miles
1879-1954 .... **TCLC 7**
See also CA 104

Fraser, (Lady) Antonia (Pakenham)
1932- .... **CLC 32**
See also CA 85-88; CANR 44; MTCW;
SATA-Brief 32

Fraser, George MacDonald 1925- .... **CLC 7**
See also CA 45-48; CANR 2, 48

Fraser, Sylvia 1935- .... **CLC 64**
See also CA 45-48; CANR 1, 16

Frayn, Michael
1933- .... **CLC 3, 7, 31, 47;**
DAM DRAM, NOV
See also CA 5-8R; CANR 30; DLB 13, 14;
MTCW

Fraze, Candida (Merrill) 1945- ..... **CLC 50**
See also CA 126

Frazer, J(ames) G(eorge)
1854-1941 .... **TCLC 32**
See also CA 118

Frazer, Robert Caine
See Creasey, John

Frazer, Sir James George
See Frazer, J(ames) G(eorge)

Frazier, Ian 1951- .... **CLC 46**
See also CA 130; CANR 54

Frederic, Harold 1856-1898 ...... **NCLC 10**
See also DLB 12, 23; DLBD 13

Frederick, John
See Faust, Frederick (Schiller)

Frederick the Great 1712-1786 ...... **LC 14**

Fredro, Aleksander 1793-1876 ..... **NCLC 8**

Freeling, Nicolas 1927- .... **CLC 38**
See also CA 49-52; CAAS 12; CANR 1, 17,
50; DLB 87

Freeman, Douglas Southall
1886-1953 .... **TCLC 11**
See also CA 109; DLB 17

Freeman, Judith 1946- .... **CLC 55**
See also CA 148

Freeman, Mary Eleanor Wilkins
1852-1930 .... **TCLC 9; SSC 1**
See also CA 106; DLB 12, 78

Freeman, R(ichard) Austin
1862-1943 .... **TCLC 21**
See also CA 113; DLB 70

French, Albert 1943- .... **CLC 86**

French, Marilyn
1929- .... **CLC 10, 18, 60;**
DAM DRAM, NOV, POP
See also CA 69-72; CANR 3, 31;
INT CANR-31; MTCW

French, Paul
See Asimov, Isaac

Freneau, Philip Morin 1752-1832 .. **NCLC 1**
See also DLB 37, 43

Freud, Sigmund 1856-1939 .... **TCLC 52**
See also CA 115; 133; MTCW

Friedan, Betty (Naomi) 1921- ...... **CLC 74**
See also CA 65-68; CANR 18, 45; MTCW

Friedlander, Saul 1932- .... **CLC 90**
See also CA 117; 130

Friedman, B(ernard) H(arper)
1926- .... **CLC 7**
See also CA 1-4R; CANR 3, 48

Friedman, Bruce Jay 1930- .... **CLC 3, 5, 56**
See also CA 9-12R; CANR 25, 52; DLB 2,
28; INT CANR-25

Friel, Brian 1929-.......... **CLC 5, 42, 59**
See also CA 21-24R; CANR 33; DLB 13;
MTCW

Friis-Baastad, Babbis Ellinor
1921-1970 .... **CLC 12**
See also CA 17-20R; 134; SATA 7

Frisch, Max (Rudolf)
1911-1991 ..... **CLC 3, 9, 14, 18, 32, 44;**
DAM DRAM, NOV
See also CA 85-88; 134; CANR 32;
DLB 69, 124; MTCW

Fromentin, Eugene (Samuel Auguste)
1820-1876 .... **NCLC 10**
See also DLB 123

Frost, Frederick
See Faust, Frederick (Schiller)

Frost, Robert (Lee)
1874-1963 .... **CLC 1, 3, 4, 9, 10, 13, 15,**
26, 34, 44; DA; DAB; DAC; DAM MST,
POET; PC 1; WLC
See also CA 89-92; CANR 33;
CDALB 1917-1929; DLB 54; DLBD 7;
MTCW; SATA 14

Froude, James Anthony
1818-1894 .... **NCLC 43**
See also DLB 18, 57, 144

Froy, Herald
See Waterhouse, Keith (Spencer)

Fry, Christopher
1907- ..... **CLC 2, 10, 14; DAM DRAM**
See also CA 17-20R; CAAS 23; CANR 9,
30; DLB 13; MTCW; SATA 66

Frye, (Herman) Northrop
1912-1991 .... **CLC 24, 70**
See also CA 5-8R; 133; CANR 8, 37;
DLB 67, 68; MTCW

Fuchs, Daniel 1909-1993 .... **CLC 8, 22**
See also CA 81-84; 142; CAAS 5;
CANR 40; DLB 9, 26, 28; DLBY 93

Fuchs, Daniel 1934-.............. **CLC 34**
See also CA 37-40R; CANR 14, 48

Fuentes, Carlos
1928- ...... **CLC 3, 8, 10, 13, 22, 41, 60;**
DA; DAB; DAC; DAM MST, MULT,
NOV; HLC; SSC 24; WLC
See also AAYA 4; AITN 2; CA 69-72;
CANR 10, 32; DLB 113; HW; MTCW

Fuentes, Gregorio Lopez y
See Lopez y Fuentes, Gregorio

Fugard, (Harold) Athol
1932- .... **CLC 5, 9, 14, 25, 40, 80;**
DAM DRAM; DC 3
See also AAYA 17; CA 85-88; CANR 32,
54; MTCW

Fugard, Sheila 1932- .... **CLC 48**
See also CA 125

Fuller, Charles (H., Jr.)
1939- .... **CLC 25; BLC; DAM DRAM,**
MULT; DC 1
See also BW 2; CA 108; 112; DLB 38;
INT 112; MTCW

Fuller, John (Leopold) 1937-....... **CLC 62**
See also CA 21-24R; CANR 9, 44; DLB 40

Fuller, Margaret .... **NCLC 5, 50**
See also Ossoli, Sarah Margaret (Fuller
marchesa d')

Fuller, Roy (Broadbent)
1912-1991 .... **CLC 4, 28**
See also CA 5-8R; 135; CAAS 10;
CANR 53; DLB 15, 20; SATA 87

Fulton, Alice 1952-.............. **CLC 52**
See also CA 116

Furphy, Joseph 1843-1912....... **TCLC 25**

Fussell, Paul 1924-.............. **CLC 74**
See also BEST 90:1; CA 17-20R; CANR 8,
21, 35; INT CANR-21; MTCW

Futabatei, Shimei 1864-1909..... **TCLC 44**

Futrelle, Jacques 1875-1912 ...... **TCLC 19**
See also CA 113

Gaboriau, Emile 1835-1873...... **NCLC 14**

Gadda, Carlo Emilio 1893-1973 .... **CLC 11**
See also CA 89-92

Gaddis, William
1922- ..... **CLC 1, 3, 6, 8, 10, 19, 43, 86**
See also CA 17-20R; CANR 21, 48; DLB 2;
MTCW

Gage, Walter
See Inge, William (Motter)

Gaines, Ernest J(ames)
1933- .... **CLC 3, 11, 18, 86; BLC;**
DAM MULT
See also AAYA 18; AITN 1; BW 2;
CA 9-12R; CANR 6, 24, 42;
CDALB 1968-1988; DLB 2, 33, 152;
DLBY 80; MTCW; SATA 86

Gaitskill, Mary 1954-............. **CLC 69**
See also CA 128

Galdos, Benito Perez
See Perez Galdos, Benito

Gale, Zona
1874-1938 ...... **TCLC 7; DAM DRAM**
See also CA 105; 153; DLB 9, 78

Galeano, Eduardo (Hughes) 1940-... **CLC 72**
See also CA 29-32R; CANR 13, 32; HW

Galiano, Juan Valera y Alcala
See Valera y Alcala-Galiano, Juan

Gallagher, Tess
1943- .. **CLC 18, 63; DAM POET; PC 9**
See also CA 106; DLB 120

Gallant, Mavis
1922- .... **CLC 7, 18, 38; DAC;**
DAM MST; SSC 5
See also CA 69-72; CANR 29; DLB 53;
MTCW

Gallant, Roy A(rthur) 1924- .... **CLC 17**
See also CA 5-8R; CANR 4, 29, 54;
CLR 30; MAICYA; SATA 4, 68

Gallico, Paul (William) 1897-1976 ... **CLC 2**
See also AITN 1; CA 5-8R; 69-72;
CANR 23; DLB 9, 171; MAICYA;
SATA 13

Gallo, Max Louis 1932-........... **CLC 95**
See also CA 85-88

Gallois, Lucien
See Desnos, Robert

Gallup, Ralph
See Whitemore, Hugh (John)

Galsworthy, John
1867-1933 ...... **TCLC 1, 45; DA; DAB;**
DAC; DAM DRAM, MST, NOV;
SSC 22; WLC 2
See also CA 104; 141; CDBLB 1890-1914;
DLB 10, 34, 98, 162

Galt, John 1779-1839........... **NCLC 1**
See also DLB 99, 116, 159

Galvin, James 1951-.............. **CLC 38**
See also CA 108; CANR 26

Gamboa, Federico 1864-1939...... **TCLC 36**

Gandhi, M. K.
See Gandhi, Mohandas Karamchand

Gandhi, Mahatma
See Gandhi, Mohandas Karamchand

Gandhi, Mohandas Karamchand
1869-1948 ..... **TCLC 59; DAM MULT**
See also CA 121; 132; MTCW

Gann, Ernest Kellogg 1910-1991.... **CLC 23**
See also AITN 1; CA 1-4R; 136; CANR 1

Garcia, Cristina 1958- .... **CLC 76**
See also CA 141

Garcia Lorca, Federico
1898-1936 ... **TCLC 1, 7, 49; DA; DAB;**
DAC; DAM DRAM, MST, MULT,
POET; DC 2; HLC; PC 3; WLC
See also CA 104; 131; DLB 108; HW;
MTCW

Garcia Marquez, Gabriel (Jose)
1928- .... **CLC 2, 3, 8, 10, 15, 27, 47, 55,**
68; DA; DAB; DAC; DAM MST,
MULT, NOV, POP; HLC; SSC 8; WLC
See also AAYA 3; BEST 89:1, 90:4;
CA 33-36R; CANR 10, 28, 50; DLB 113;
HW; MTCW

Gard, Janice
See Latham, Jean Lee

Gard, Roger Martin du
See Martin du Gard, Roger

Gardam, Jane 1928-.............. **CLC 43**
See also CA 49-52; CANR 2, 18, 33, 54;
CLR 12; DLB 14, 161; MAICYA;
MTCW; SAAS 9; SATA 39, 76;
SATA-Brief 28

Gardner, Herb(ert) 1934-.......... **CLC 44**
See also CA 149

Gardner, John (Champlin), Jr.
1933-1982 ..... **CLC 2, 3, 5, 7, 8, 10, 18,**
28, 34; DAM NOV, POP; SSC 7
See also AITN 1; CA 65-68; 107;
CANR 33; DLB 2; DLBY 82; MTCW;
SATA 40; SATA-Obit 31

Gardner, John (Edmund)
1926- .... **CLC 30; DAM POP**
See also CA 103; CANR 15; MTCW

Gardner, Miriam
See Bradley, Marion Zimmer

Gardner, Noel
See Kuttner, Henry

Gardons, S. S.
See Snodgrass, W(illiam) D(e Witt)

Garfield, Leon 1921-1996.......... **CLC 12**
See also AAYA 8; CA 17-20R; 152;
CANR 38, 41; CLR 21; DLB 161; JRDA;
MAICYA; SATA 1, 32, 76;
SATA-Obit 90

Garland, (Hannibal) Hamlin
1860-1940 . . . . **TCLC 3; SSC 18**
See also CA 104; DLB 12, 71, 78

Garneau, (Hector de) Saint-Denys
1912-1943 . . . . **TCLC 13**
See also CA 111; DLB 88

Garner, Alan
1934- . . . . . . **CLC 17; DAB; DAM POP**
See also AAYA 18; CA 73-76; CANR 15;
CLR 20; DLB 161; MAICYA; MTCW;
SATA 18, 69

Garner, Hugh 1913-1979 . . . . **CLC 13**
See also CA 69-72; CANR 31; DLB 68

Garnett, David 1892-1981 . . . . **CLC 3**
See also CA 5-8R; 103; CANR 17; DLB 34

Garos, Stephanie
See Katz, Steve

Garrett, George (Palmer)
1929- . . . . **CLC 3, 11, 51**
See also CA 1-4R; CAAS 5; CANR 1, 42;
DLB 2, 5, 130, 152; DLBY 83

Garrick, David
1717-1779 . . . . **LC 15; DAM DRAM**
See also DLB 84

Garrigue, Jean 1914-1972 . . . . **CLC 2, 8**
See also CA 5-8R; 37-40R; CANR 20

Garrison, Frederick
See Sinclair, Upton (Beall)

Garth, Will
See Hamilton, Edmond; Kuttner, Henry

Garvey, Marcus (Moziah, Jr.)
1887-1940 . . . . **TCLC 41; BLC;**
DAM MULT
See also BW 1; CA 120; 124

Gary, Romain . . . . **CLC 25**
See also Kacew, Romain
See also DLB 83

Gascar, Pierre . . . . **CLC 11**
See also Fournier, Pierre

Gascoyne, David (Emery) 1916- . . . . **CLC 45**
See also CA 65-68; CANR 10, 28, 54;
DLB 20; MTCW

Gaskell, Elizabeth Cleghorn
1810-1865 . . **NCLC 5; DAB; DAM MST**
See also CDBLB 1832-1890; DLB 21, 144,
159

Gass, William H(oward)
1924- . . . **CLC 1, 2, 8, 11, 15, 39; SSC 12**
See also CA 17-20R; CANR 30; DLB 2;
MTCW

Gasset, Jose Ortega y
See Ortega y Gasset, Jose

Gates, Henry Louis, Jr.
1950- . . . . **CLC 65; DAM MULT**
See also BW 2; CA 109; CANR 25, 53;
DLB 67

Gautier, Theophile
1811-1872 . . . . **NCLC 1, 59;**
DAM POET; SSC 20
See also DLB 119

Gawsworth, John
See Bates, H(erbert) E(rnest)

Gay, Oliver
See Gogarty, Oliver St. John

Gaye, Marvin (Penze) 1939-1984 . . . **CLC 26**
See also CA 112

Gebler, Carlo (Ernest) 1954- . . . . **CLC 39**
See also CA 119; 133

Gee, Maggie (Mary) 1948- . . . . **CLC 57**
See also CA 130

Gee, Maurice (Gough) 1931- . . . . **CLC 29**
See also CA 97-100; SATA 46

Gelbart, Larry (Simon) 1923- . . . **CLC 21, 61**
See also CA 73-76; CANR 45

Gelber, Jack 1932- . . . . **CLC 1, 6, 14, 79**
See also CA 1-4R; CANR 2; DLB 7

Gellhorn, Martha (Ellis) 1908- . . **CLC 14, 60**
See also CA 77-80; CANR 44; DLBY 82

Genet, Jean
1910-1986 . . . . . . **CLC 1, 2, 5, 10, 14, 44,**
46; DAM DRAM
See also CA 13-16R; CANR 18; DLB 72;
DLBY 86; MTCW

Gent, Peter 1942- . . . . **CLC 29**
See also AITN 1; CA 89-92; DLBY 82

Gentlewoman in New England, A
See Bradstreet, Anne

Gentlewoman in Those Parts, A
See Bradstreet, Anne

George, Jean Craighead 1919- . . . . . . **CLC 35**
See also AAYA 8; CA 5-8R; CANR 25;
CLR 1; DLB 52; JRDA; MAICYA;
SATA 2, 68

George, Stefan (Anton)
1868-1933 . . . . **TCLC 2, 14**
See also CA 104

Georges, Georges Martin
See Simenon, Georges (Jacques Christian)

Gerhardi, William Alexander
See Gerhardie, William Alexander

Gerhardie, William Alexander
1895-1977 . . . . **CLC 5**
See also CA 25-28R; 73-76; CANR 18;
DLB 36

Gerstler, Amy 1956- . . . . **CLC 70**
See also CA 146

Gertler, T. . . . . **CLC 34**
See also CA 116; 121; INT 121

gfgg . . . . **CLC XvXzc**

Ghalib . . . . **NCLC 39**
See also Ghalib, Hsadullah Khan

Ghalib, Hsadullah Khan 1797-1869
See Ghalib
See also DAM POET

Ghelderode, Michel de
1898-1962 . . . . **CLC 6, 11; DAM DRAM**
See also CA 85-88; CANR 40

Ghiselin, Brewster 1903- . . . . **CLC 23**
See also CA 13-16R; CAAS 10; CANR 13

Ghose, Zulfikar 1935- . . . . **CLC 42**
See also CA 65-68

Ghosh, Amitav 1956- . . . . **CLC 44**
See also CA 147

Giacosa, Giuseppe 1847-1906 . . . . . . **TCLC 7**
See also CA 104

Gibb, Lee
See Waterhouse, Keith (Spencer)

Gibbon, Lewis Grassic . . . . **TCLC 4**
See also Mitchell, James Leslie

Gibbons, Kaye
1960- . . . . **CLC 50, 88; DAM POP**
See also CA 151

Gibran, Kahlil
1883-1931 . . . . **TCLC 1, 9; DAM POET,**
POP; PC 9
See also CA 104; 150

Gibran, Khalil
See Gibran, Kahlil

Gibson, William
1914- . . . . **CLC 23; DA; DAB; DAC;**
DAM DRAM, MST
See also CA 9-12R; CANR 9, 42; DLB 7;
SATA 66

Gibson, William (Ford)
1948- . . . . **CLC 39, 63; DAM POP**
See also AAYA 12; CA 126; 133; CANR 52

Gide, Andre (Paul Guillaume)
1869-1951 . . . . **TCLC 5, 12, 36; DA;**
DAB; DAC; DAM MST, NOV; SSC 13;
WLC
See also CA 104; 124; DLB 65; MTCW

Gifford, Barry (Colby) 1946- . . . . **CLC 34**
See also CA 65-68; CANR 9, 30, 40

Gilbert, W(illiam) S(chwenck)
1836-1911 . . . . . **TCLC 3; DAM DRAM,**
POET
See also CA 104; SATA 36

Gilbreth, Frank B., Jr. 1911- . . . . **CLC 17**
See also CA 9-12R; SATA 2

Gilchrist, Ellen
1935- . . . . **CLC 34, 48; DAM POP;**
SSC 14
See also CA 113; 116; CANR 41; DLB 130;
MTCW

Giles, Molly 1942- . . . . **CLC 39**
See also CA 126

Gill, Patrick
See Creasey, John

Gilliam, Terry (Vance) 1940- . . . . **CLC 21**
See also Monty Python
See also AAYA 19; CA 108; 113;
CANR 35; INT 113

Gillian, Jerry
See Gilliam, Terry (Vance)

Gilliatt, Penelope (Ann Douglass)
1932-1993 . . . . **CLC 2, 10, 13, 53**
See also AITN 2; CA 13-16R; 141;
CANR 49; DLB 14

Gilman, Charlotte (Anna) Perkins (Stetson)
1860-1935 . . . . **TCLC 9, 37; SSC 13**
See also CA 106; 150

Gilmour, David 1949- . . . . **CLC 35**
See also CA 138, 147

Gilpin, William 1724-1804 . . . . **NCLC 30**

Gilray, J. D.
See Mencken, H(enry) L(ouis)

Gilroy, Frank D(aniel) 1925- . . . . **CLC 2**
See also CA 81-84; CANR 32; DLB 7

Grenville, Pelham
    See Wodehouse, P(elham) G(renville)

Greve, Felix Paul (Berthold Friedrich)
    1879-1948
    See Grove, Frederick Philip
    See also CA 104; 141; DAC; DAM MST

Grey, Zane
    1872-1939 .... **TCLC 6; DAM POP**
    See also CA 104; 132; DLB 9; MTCW

Grieg, (Johan) Nordahl (Brun)
    1902-1943 .... **TCLC 10**
    See also CA 107

Grieve, C(hristopher) M(urray)
    1892-1978 .... **CLC 11, 19; DAM POET**
    See also MacDiarmid, Hugh; Pteleon
    See also CA 5-8R; 85-88; CANR 33;
    MTCW

Griffin, Gerald 1803-1840 .... **NCLC 7**
    See also DLB 159

Griffin, John Howard 1920-1980.... **CLC 68**
    See also AITN 1; CA 1-4R; 101; CANR 2

Griffin, Peter 1942- .... **CLC 39**
    See also CA 136

Griffith, D(avid Lewelyn) W(ark)
    1875(?)-1948 .... **TCLC 68**
    See also CA 119; 150

Griffith, Lawrence
    See Griffith, D(avid Lewelyn) W(ark)

Griffiths, Trevor 1935-........ **CLC 13, 52**
    See also CA 97-100; CANR 45; DLB 13

Grigson, Geoffrey (Edward Harvey)
    1905-1985 .... **CLC 7, 39**
    See also CA 25-28R; 118; CANR 20, 33;
    DLB 27; MTCW

Grillparzer, Franz 1791-1872...... **NCLC 1**
    See also DLB 133

Grimble, Reverend Charles James
    See Eliot, T(homas) S(tearns)

Grimke, Charlotte L(ottie) Forten
    1837(?)-1914
    See Forten, Charlotte L.
    See also BW 1; CA 117; 124; DAM MULT,
    POET

Grimm, Jacob Ludwig Karl
    1785-1863 .... **NCLC 3**
    See also DLB 90; MAICYA; SATA 22

Grimm, Wilhelm Karl 1786-1859 .. **NCLC 3**
    See also DLB 90; MAICYA; SATA 22

Grimmelshausen, Johann Jakob Christoffel
    von 1621-1676 .... **LC 6**
    See also DLB 168

Grindel, Eugene 1895-1952
    See Eluard, Paul
    See also CA 104

Grisham, John 1955- .. **CLC 84; DAM POP**
    See also AAYA 14; CA 138; CANR 47

Grossman, David 1954- .... **CLC 67**
    See also CA 138

Grossman, Vasily (Semenovich)
    1905-1964 .... **CLC 41**
    See also CA 124; 130; MTCW

Grove, Frederick Philip .... **TCLC 4**
    See also Greve, Felix Paul (Berthold
    Friedrich)
    See also DLB 92

Grubb
    See Crumb, R(obert)

Grumbach, Doris (Isaac)
    1918- .... **CLC 13, 22, 64**
    See also CA 5-8R; CAAS 2; CANR 9, 42;
    INT CANR-9

Grundtvig, Nicolai Frederik Severin
    1783-1872 .... **NCLC 1**

Grunge
    See Crumb, R(obert)

Grunwald, Lisa 1959-............. **CLC 44**
    See also CA 120

Guare, John
    1938- .... **CLC 8, 14, 29, 67;**
    DAM DRAM
    See also CA 73-76; CANR 21; DLB 7;
    MTCW

Gudjonsson, Halldor Kiljan 1902-
    See Laxness, Halldor
    See also CA 103

Guenter, Erich
    See Eich, Guenter

Guest, Barbara 1920-............. **CLC 34**
    See also CA 25-28R; CANR 11, 44; DLB 5

Guest, Judith (Ann)
    1936- .... **CLC 8, 30; DAM NOV, POP**
    See also AAYA 7; CA 77-80; CANR 15;
    INT CANR-15; MTCW

Guevara, Che .... **CLC 87; HLC**
    See also Guevara (Serna), Ernesto

Guevara (Serna), Ernesto 1928-1967
    See Guevara, Che
    See also CA 127; 111; DAM MULT; HW

Guild, Nicholas M. 1944-.......... **CLC 33**
    See also CA 93-96

Guillemin, Jacques
    See Sartre, Jean-Paul

Guillen, Jorge
    1893-1984 ...... **CLC 11; DAM MULT,**
    POET
    See also CA 89-92; 112; DLB 108; HW

Guillen, Nicolas (Cristobal)
    1902-1989 .... **CLC 48, 79; BLC;**
    DAM MST, MULT, POET; HLC
    See also BW 2; CA 116; 125; 129; HW

Guillevic, (Eugene) 1907-.......... **CLC 33**
    See also CA 93-96

Guillois
    See Desnos, Robert

Guillois, Valentin
    See Desnos, Robert

Guiney, Louise Imogen
    1861-1920 .... **TCLC 41**
    See also DLB 54

Guiraldes, Ricardo (Guillermo)
    1886-1927 .... **TCLC 39**
    See also CA 131; HW; MTCW

Gumilev, Nikolai Stephanovich
    1886-1921 .... **TCLC 60**

Gunesekera, Romesh............... **CLC 91**

Gunn, Bill .... **CLC 5**
    See also Gunn, William Harrison
    See also DLB 38

Gunn, Thom(son William)
    1929- .... **CLC 3, 6, 18, 32, 81;**
    DAM POET
    See also CA 17-20R; CANR 9, 33;
    CDBLB 1960 to Present; DLB 27;
    INT CANR-33; MTCW

Gunn, William Harrison 1934(?)-1989
    See Gunn, Bill
    See also AITN 1; BW 1; CA 13-16R; 128;
    CANR 12, 25

Gunnars, Kristjana 1948-.......... **CLC 69**
    See also CA 113; DLB 60

Gurganus, Allan
    1947- .... **CLC 70; DAM POP**
    See also BEST 90:1; CA 135

Gurney, A(lbert) R(amsdell), Jr.
    1930- .... **CLC 32, 50, 54; DAM DRAM**
    See also CA 77-80; CANR 32

Gurney, Ivor (Bertie) 1890-1937... **TCLC 33**

Gurney, Peter
    See Gurney, A(lbert) R(amsdell), Jr.

Guro, Elena 1877-1913.......... **TCLC 56**

Gustafson, Ralph (Barker) 1909-.... **CLC 36**
    See also CA 21-24R; CANR 8, 45; DLB 88

Gut, Gom
    See Simenon, Georges (Jacques Christian)

Guterson, David 1956-............. **CLC 91**
    See also CA 132

Guthrie, A(lfred) B(ertram), Jr.
    1901-1991 .... **CLC 23**
    See also CA 57-60; 134; CANR 24; DLB 6;
    SATA 62; SATA-Obit 67

Guthrie, Isobel
    See Grieve, C(hristopher) M(urray)

Guthrie, Woodrow Wilson 1912-1967
    See Guthrie, Woody
    See also CA 113; 93-96

Guthrie, Woody................... **CLC 35**
    See also Guthrie, Woodrow Wilson

Guy, Rosa (Cuthbert) 1928-........ **CLC 26**
    See also AAYA 4; BW 2; CA 17-20R;
    CANR 14, 34; CLR 13; DLB 33; JRDA;
    MAICYA; SATA 14, 62

Gwendolyn
    See Bennett, (Enoch) Arnold

H. D. .... **CLC 3, 8, 14, 31, 34, 73; PC 5**
    See also Doolittle, Hilda

H. de V.
    See Buchan, John

Haavikko, Paavo Juhani
    1931- .... **CLC 18, 34**
    See also CA 106

Habbema, Koos
    See Heijermans, Herman

Hacker, Marilyn
    1942- .... **CLC 5, 9, 23, 72, 91;**
    DAM POET
    See also CA 77-80; DLB 120

Haggard, H(enry) Rider
    1856-1925 .... **TCLC 11**
    See also CA 108; 148; DLB 70, 156, 174;
    SATA 16

Hagiosy, L.
    See Larbaud, Valery (Nicolas)

Hagiwara Sakutaro 1886-1942 . . . . TCLC 60

Haig, Fenil
See Ford, Ford Madox

Haig-Brown, Roderick (Langmere)
1908-1976 . . . . CLC 21
See also CA 5-8R; 69-72; CANR 4, 38;
CLR 31; DLB 88; MAICYA; SATA 12

Hailey, Arthur
1920- . . . . CLC 5; DAM NOV, POP
See also AITN 2; BEST 90:3; CA 1-4R;
CANR 2, 36; DLB 88; DLBY 82; MTCW

Hailey, Elizabeth Forsythe 1938- . . . CLC 40
See also CA 93-96; CAAS 1; CANR 15, 48;
INT CANR-15

Haines, John (Meade) 1924- . . . . CLC 58
See also CA 17-20R; CANR 13, 34; DLB 5

Hakluyt, Richard 1552-1616 . . . . LC 31

Haldeman, Joe (William) 1943- . . . . . CLC 61
See also CA 53-56; CAAS 25; CANR 6;
DLB 8; INT CANR-6

Haley, Alex(ander Murray Palmer)
1921-1992 . . . . CLC 8, 12, 76; BLC; DA;
DAB; DAC; DAM MST, MULT, POP
See also BW 2; CA 77-80; 136; DLB 38;
MTCW

Haliburton, Thomas Chandler
1796-1865 . . . . NCLC 15
See also DLB 11, 99

Hall, Donald (Andrew, Jr.)
1928- . . CLC 1, 13, 37, 59; DAM POET
See also CA 5-8R; CAAS 7; CANR 2, 44;
DLB 5; SATA 23

Hall, Frederic Sauser
See Sauser-Hall, Frederic

Hall, James
See Kuttner, Henry

Hall, James Norman 1887-1951 . . . TCLC 23
See also CA 123; SATA 21

Hall, (Marguerite) Radclyffe
1886-1943 . . . . TCLC 12
See also CA 110; 150

Hall, Rodney 1935- . . . . CLC 51
See also CA 109

Halleck, Fitz-Greene 1790-1867 . . NCLC 47
See also DLB 3

Halliday, Michael
See Creasey, John

Halpern, Daniel 1945- . . . . CLC 14
See also CA 33-36R

Hamburger, Michael (Peter Leopold)
1924- . . . . CLC 5, 14
See also CA 5-8R; CAAS 4; CANR 2, 47;
DLB 27

Hamill, Pete 1935- . . . . CLC 10
See also CA 25-28R; CANR 18

Hamilton, Alexander
1755(?)-1804 . . . . NCLC 49
See also DLB 37

Hamilton, Clive
See Lewis, C(live) S(taples)

Hamilton, Edmond 1904-1977 . . . . CLC 1
See also CA 1-4R; CANR 3; DLB 8

Hamilton, Eugene (Jacob) Lee
See Lee-Hamilton, Eugene (Jacob)

Hamilton, Franklin
See Silverberg, Robert

Hamilton, Gail
See Corcoran, Barbara

Hamilton, Mollie
See Kaye, M(ary) M(argaret)

Hamilton, (Anthony Walter) Patrick
1904-1962 . . . . CLC 51
See also CA 113; DLB 10

Hamilton, Virginia
1936- . . . . CLC 26; DAM MULT
See also AAYA 2; BW 2; CA 25-28R;
CANR 20, 37; CLR 1, 11, 40; DLB 33,
52; INT CANR-20; JRDA; MAICYA;
MTCW; SATA 4, 56, 79

Hammett, (Samuel) Dashiell
1894-1961 . . . . CLC 3, 5, 10, 19, 47;
SSC 17
See also AITN 1; CA 81-84; CANR 42;
CDALB 1929-1941; DLBD 6; MTCW

Hammon, Jupiter
1711(?)-1800(?) . . . . NCLC 5; BLC;
DAM MULT, POET; PC 16
See also DLB 31, 50

Hammond, Keith
See Kuttner, Henry

Hamner, Earl (Henry), Jr. 1923- . . . CLC 12
See also AITN 2; CA 73-76; DLB 6

Hampton, Christopher (James)
1946- . . . . CLC 4
See also CA 25-28R; DLB 13; MTCW

Hamsun, Knut . . . . TCLC 2, 14, 49
See also Pedersen, Knut

Handke, Peter
1942- . . . . CLC 5, 8, 10, 15, 38;
DAM DRAM, NOV
See also CA 77-80; CANR 33; DLB 85,
124; MTCW

Hanley, James 1901-1985 . . . CLC 3, 5, 8, 13
See also CA 73-76; 117; CANR 36; MTCW

Hannah, Barry 1942- . . . . CLC 23, 38, 90
See also CA 108; 110; CANR 43; DLB 6;
INT 110; MTCW

Hannon, Ezra
See Hunter, Evan

Hansberry, Lorraine (Vivian)
1930-1965 . . . . . . CLC 17, 62; BLC; DA;
DAB; DAC; DAM DRAM, MST,
MULT; DC 2
See also BW 1; CA 109; 25-28R; CABS 3;
CDALB 1941-1968; DLB 7, 38; MTCW

Hansen, Joseph 1923- . . . . CLC 38
See also CA 29-32R; CAAS 17; CANR 16,
44; INT CANR-16

Hansen, Martin A. 1909-1955 . . . . . TCLC 32

Hanson, Kenneth O(stlin) 1922- . . . . CLC 13
See also CA 53-56; CANR 7

Hardwick, Elizabeth
1916- . . . . CLC 13; DAM NOV
See also CA 5-8R; CANR 3, 32; DLB 6;
MTCW

Hardy, Thomas
1840-1928 . . . . . . TCLC 4, 10, 18, 32, 48,
53; DA; DAB; DAC; DAM MST, NOV,
POET; PC 8; SSC 2; WLC
See also CA 104; 123; CDBLB 1890-1914;
DLB 18, 19, 135; MTCW

Hare, David 1947- . . . . CLC 29, 58
See also CA 97-100; CANR 39; DLB 13;
MTCW

Harford, Henry
See Hudson, W(illiam) H(enry)

Hargrave, Leonie
See Disch, Thomas M(ichael)

Harjo, Joy 1951- . . . CLC 83; DAM MULT
See also CA 114; CANR 35; DLB 120;
NNAL

Harlan, Louis R(udolph) 1922- . . . . . CLC 34
See also CA 21-24R; CANR 25, 55

Harling, Robert 1951(?)- . . . . CLC 53
See also CA 147

Harmon, William (Ruth) 1938- . . . . . CLC 38
See also CA 33-36R; CANR 14, 32, 35;
SATA 65

Harper, F. E. W.
See Harper, Frances Ellen Watkins

Harper, Frances E. W.
See Harper, Frances Ellen Watkins

Harper, Frances E. Watkins
See Harper, Frances Ellen Watkins

Harper, Frances Ellen
See Harper, Frances Ellen Watkins

Harper, Frances Ellen Watkins
1825-1911 . . . . TCLC 14; BLC;
DAM MULT, POET
See also BW 1; CA 111; 125; DLB 50

Harper, Michael S(teven) 1938- . . CLC 7, 22
See also BW 1; CA 33-36R; CANR 24;
DLB 41

Harper, Mrs. F. E. W.
See Harper, Frances Ellen Watkins

Harris, Christie (Lucy) Irwin
1907- . . . . CLC 12
See also CA 5-8R; CANR 6; DLB 88;
JRDA; MAICYA; SAAS 10; SATA 6, 74

Harris, Frank 1856-1931 . . . . TCLC 24
See also CA 109; 150; DLB 156

Harris, George Washington
1814-1869 . . . . NCLC 23
See also DLB 3, 11

Harris, Joel Chandler
1848-1908 . . . . TCLC 2; SSC 19
See also CA 104; 137; DLB 11, 23, 42, 78,
91; MAICYA; YABC 1

Harris, John (Wyndham Parkes Lucas)
Beynon 1903-1969
See Wyndham, John
See also CA 102; 89-92

Harris, MacDonald . . . . CLC 9
See also Heiney, Donald (William)

Harris, Mark 1922- . . . . CLC 19
See also CA 5-8R; CAAS 3; CANR 2, 55;
DLB 2; DLBY 80

Harris, (Theodore) Wilson 1921- . . . . CLC 25
See also BW 2; CA 65-68; CAAS 16;
CANR 11, 27; DLB 117; MTCW

Harrison, Elizabeth Cavanna 1909-
See Cavanna, Betty
See also CA 9-12R; CANR 6, 27

Harrison, Harry (Max) 1925- ...... **CLC 42**
See also CA 1-4R; CANR 5, 21; DLB 8;
SATA 4

Harrison, James (Thomas)
1937- .... **CLC 6, 14, 33, 66; SSC 19**
See also CA 13-16R; CANR 8, 51;
DLBY 82; INT CANR-8

Harrison, Jim
See Harrison, James (Thomas)

Harrison, Kathryn 1961- .... **CLC 70**
See also CA 144

Harrison, Tony 1937- .... **CLC 43**
See also CA 65-68; CANR 44; DLB 40;
MTCW

Harriss, Will(ard Irvin) 1922- ...... **CLC 34**
See also CA 111

Harson, Sley
See Ellison, Harlan (Jay)

Hart, Ellis
See Ellison, Harlan (Jay)

Hart, Josephine
1942(?)- .... **CLC 70; DAM POP**
See also CA 138

Hart, Moss
1904-1961 ...... **CLC 66; DAM DRAM**
See also CA 109; 89-92; DLB 7

Harte, (Francis) Bret(t)
1836(?)-1902 .... **TCLC 1, 25; DA; DAC;
DAM MST; SSC 8; WLC**
See also CA 104; 140; CDALB 1865-1917;
DLB 12, 64, 74, 79; SATA 26

Hartley, L(eslie) P(oles)
1895-1972 .... **CLC 2, 22**
See also CA 45-48; 37-40R; CANR 33;
DLB 15, 139; MTCW

Hartman, Geoffrey H. 1929- .... **CLC 27**
See also CA 117; 125; DLB 67

Hartmann von Aue
c. 1160-c. 1205 .... **CMLC 15**
See also DLB 138

Hartmann von Aue 1170-1210.... **CMLC 15**

Haruf, Kent 1943- .... **CLC 34**
See also CA 149

Harwood, Ronald
1934- .... **CLC 32; DAM DRAM, MST**
See also CA 1-4R; CANR 4, 55; DLB 13

Hasek, Jaroslav (Matej Frantisek)
1883-1923 .... **TCLC 4**
See also CA 104; 129; MTCW

Hass, Robert 1941- ..... **CLC 18, 39; PC 16**
See also CA 111; CANR 30, 50; DLB 105

Hastings, Hudson
See Kuttner, Henry

Hastings, Selina .... **CLC 44**

Hatteras, Amelia
See Mencken, H(enry) L(ouis)

Hatteras, Owen .... **TCLC 18**
See also Mencken, H(enry) L(ouis); Nathan,
George Jean

Hauptmann, Gerhart (Johann Robert)
1862-1946 ...... **TCLC 4; DAM DRAM**
See also CA 104; 153; DLB 66, 118

Havel, Vaclav
1936- .... **CLC 25, 58, 65;
DAM DRAM; DC 6**
See also CA 104; CANR 36; MTCW

Haviaras, Stratis .... **CLC 33**
See also Chaviaras, Strates

Hawes, Stephen 1475(?)-1523(?) ..... **LC 17**

Hawkes, John (Clendennin Burne, Jr.)
1925- ...... **CLC 1, 2, 3, 4, 7, 9, 14, 15,
27, 49**
See also CA 1-4R; CANR 2, 47; DLB 2, 7;
DLBY 80; MTCW

Hawking, S. W.
See Hawking, Stephen W(illiam)

Hawking, Stephen W(illiam)
1942- .... **CLC 63**
See also AAYA 13; BEST 89:1; CA 126;
129; CANR 48

Hawthorne, Julian 1846-1934 ..... **TCLC 25**

Hawthorne, Nathaniel
1804-1864 ...... **NCLC 39; DA; DAB;
DAC; DAM MST, NOV; SSC 3; WLC**
See also AAYA 18; CDALB 1640-1865;
DLB 1, 74; YABC 2

Haxton, Josephine Ayres 1921-
See Douglas, Ellen
See also CA 115; CANR 41

Hayaseca y Eizaguirre, Jorge
See Echegaray (y Eizaguirre), Jose (Maria
Waldo)

Hayashi Fumiko 1904-1951 ...... **TCLC 27**

Haycraft, Anna
See Ellis, Alice Thomas
See also CA 122

Hayden, Robert E(arl)
1913-1980 ...... **CLC 5, 9, 14, 37; BLC;
DA; DAC; DAM MST, MULT, POET;
PC 6**
See also BW 1; CA 69-72; 97-100; CABS 2;
CANR 24; CDALB 1941-1968; DLB 5,
76; MTCW; SATA 19; SATA-Obit 26

Hayford, J(oseph) E(phraim) Casely
See Casely-Hayford, J(oseph) E(phraim)

Hayman, Ronald 1932- .... **CLC 44**
See also CA 25-28R; CANR 18, 50;
DLB 155

Haywood, Eliza (Fowler)
1693(?)-1756 .... **LC 1**

Hazlitt, William 1778-1830 ...... **NCLC 29**
See also DLB 110, 158

Hazzard, Shirley 1931- .... **CLC 18**
See also CA 9-12R; CANR 4; DLBY 82;
MTCW

Head, Bessie
1937-1986 .... **CLC 25, 67; BLC;
DAM MULT**
See also BW 2; CA 29-32R; 119; CANR 25;
DLB 117; MTCW

Headon, (Nicky) Topper 1956(?)- ... **CLC 30**

Heaney, Seamus (Justin)
1939- ...... **CLC 5, 7, 14, 25, 37, 74, 91;
DAB; DAM POET**
See also CA 85-88; CANR 25, 48;
CDBLB 1960 to Present; DLB 40;
DLBY 95; MTCW

Hearn, (Patricio) Lafcadio (Tessima Carlos)
1850-1904 .... **TCLC 9**
See also CA 105; DLB 12, 78

Hearne, Vicki 1946- .... **CLC 56**
See also CA 139

Hearon, Shelby 1931- .... **CLC 63**
See also AITN 2; CA 25-28R; CANR 18,
48

Heat-Moon, William Least .... **CLC 29**
See also Trogdon, William (Lewis)
See also AAYA 9

Hebbel, Friedrich
1813-1863 .... **NCLC 43; DAM DRAM**
See also DLB 129

Hebert, Anne
1916- .... **CLC 4, 13, 29; DAC;
DAM MST, POET**
See also CA 85-88; DLB 68; MTCW

Hecht, Anthony (Evan)
1923- ...... **CLC 8, 13, 19; DAM POET**
See also CA 9-12R; CANR 6; DLB 5, 169

Hecht, Ben 1894-1964 .... **CLC 8**
See also CA 85-88; DLB 7, 9, 25, 26, 28, 86

Hedayat, Sadeq 1903-1951 .... **TCLC 21**
See also CA 120

Hegel, Georg Wilhelm Friedrich
1770-1831 .... **NCLC 46**
See also DLB 90

Heidegger, Martin 1889-1976 ...... **CLC 24**
See also CA 81-84; 65-68; CANR 34;
MTCW

Heidenstam, (Carl Gustaf) Verner von
1859-1940 .... **TCLC 5**
See also CA 104

Heifner, Jack 1946- .... **CLC 11**
See also CA 105; CANR 47

Heijermans, Herman 1864-1924 ... **TCLC 24**
See also CA 123

Heilbrun, Carolyn G(old) 1926- ..... **CLC 25**
See also CA 45-48; CANR 1, 28

Heine, Heinrich 1797-1856 .... **NCLC 4, 54**
See also DLB 90

Heinemann, Larry (Curtiss) 1944- .. **CLC 50**
See also CA 110; CAAS 21; CANR 31;
DLBD 9; INT CANR-31

Heiney, Donald (William) 1921-1993
See Harris, MacDonald
See also CA 1-4R; 142; CANR 3

Heinlein, Robert A(nson)
1907-1988 ...... **CLC 1, 3, 8, 14, 26, 55;
DAM POP**
See also AAYA 17; CA 1-4R; 125;
CANR 1, 20, 53; DLB 8; JRDA;
MAICYA; MTCW; SATA 9, 69;
SATA-Obit 56

Helforth, John
See Doolittle, Hilda

Hellenhofferu, Vojtech Kapristian z
See Hasek, Jaroslav (Matej Frantisek)

Heller, Joseph
1923- .... **CLC 1, 3, 5, 8, 11, 36, 63; DA;
DAB; DAC; DAM MST, NOV, POP;
WLC**
See also AITN 1; CA 5-8R; CABS 1;
CANR 8, 42; DLB 2, 28; DLBY 80;
INT CANR-8; MTCW

Hellman, Lillian (Florence)
1906-1984 ...... **CLC 2, 4, 8, 14, 18, 34,
44, 52; DAM DRAM; DC 1**
See also AITN 1, 2; CA 13-16R; 112;
CANR 33; DLB 7; DLBY 84; MTCW

Helprin, Mark
1947- .... **CLC 7, 10, 22, 32;
DAM NOV, POP**
See also CA 81-84; CANR 47; DLBY 85;
MTCW

Helvetius, Claude-Adrien
1715-1771 .... **LC 26**

Helyar, Jane Penelope Josephine 1933-
See Poole, Josephine
See also CA 21-24R; CANR 10, 26;
SATA 82

Hemans, Felicia 1793-1835 ...... **NCLC 29**
See also DLB 96

Hemingway, Ernest (Miller)
1899-1961 .... **CLC 1, 3, 6, 8, 10, 13, 19,
30, 34, 39, 41, 44, 50, 61, 80; DA; DAB;
DAC; DAM MST, NOV; SSC 1; WLC**
See also AAYA 19; CA 77-80; CANR 34;
CDALB 1917-1929; DLB 4, 9, 102;
DLBD 1; DLBY 81, 87; MTCW

Hempel, Amy 1951- .... **CLC 39**
See also CA 118; 137

Henderson, F. C.
See Mencken, H(enry) L(ouis)

Henderson, Sylvia
See Ashton-Warner, Sylvia (Constance)

Henley, Beth .... **CLC 23; DC 6**
See also Henley, Elizabeth Becker
See also CABS 3; DLBY 86

Henley, Elizabeth Becker 1952-
See Henley, Beth
See also CA 107; CANR 32; DAM DRAM,
MST; MTCW

Henley, William Ernest
1849-1903 .... **TCLC 8**
See also CA 105; DLB 19

Hennissart, Martha
See Lathen, Emma
See also CA 85-88

Henry, O. .... **TCLC 1, 19; SSC 5; WLC**
See also Porter, William Sydney

Henry, Patrick 1736-1799 .... **LC 25**

Henryson, Robert 1430(?)-1506(?). ... **LC 20**
See also DLB 146

Henry VIII 1491-1547 .... **LC 10**

Henschke, Alfred
See Klabund

Hentoff, Nat(han Irving) 1925- ..... **CLC 26**
See also AAYA 4; CA 1-4R; CAAS 6;
CANR 5, 25; CLR 1; INT CANR-25;
JRDA; MAICYA; SATA 42, 69;
SATA-Brief 27

Heppenstall, (John) Rayner
1911-1981 .... **CLC 10**
See also CA 1-4R; 103; CANR 29

Herbert, Frank (Patrick)
1920-1986 ...... **CLC 12, 23, 35, 44, 85;
DAM POP**
See also CA 53-56; 118; CANR 5, 43;
DLB 8; INT CANR-5; MTCW; SATA 9,
37; SATA-Obit 47

Herbert, George
1593-1633 .... **LC 24; DAB;
DAM POET; PC 4**
See also CDBLB Before 1660; DLB 126

Herbert, Zbigniew
1924- .... **CLC 9, 43; DAM POET**
See also CA 89-92; CANR 36; MTCW

Herbst, Josephine (Frey)
1897-1969 .... **CLC 34**
See also CA 5-8R; 25-28R; DLB 9

Hergesheimer, Joseph
1880-1954 .... **TCLC 11**
See also CA 109; DLB 102, 9

Herlihy, James Leo 1927-1993 ...... **CLC 6**
See also CA 1-4R; 143; CANR 2

Hermogenes fl. c. 175- .... **CMLC 6**

Hernandez, Jose 1834-1886 ...... **NCLC 17**

Herodotus c. 484B.C.-429B.C..... **CMLC 17**

Herrick, Robert
1591-1674 ..... **LC 13; DA; DAB; DAC;
DAM MST, POP; PC 9**
See also DLB 126

Herring, Guilles
See Somerville, Edith

Herriot, James
1916-1995 .... **CLC 12; DAM POP**
See also Wight, James Alfred
See also AAYA 1; CA 148; CANR 40;
SATA 86

Herrmann, Dorothy 1941- .... **CLC 44**
See also CA 107

Herrmann, Taffy
See Herrmann, Dorothy

Hersey, John (Richard)
1914-1993 .... **CLC 1, 2, 7, 9, 40, 81, 97;
DAM POP**
See also CA 17-20R; 140; CANR 33;
DLB 6; MTCW; SATA 25;
SATA-Obit 76

Herzen, Aleksandr Ivanovich
1812-1870 .... **NCLC 10**

Herzl, Theodor 1860-1904........ **TCLC 36**

Herzog, Werner 1942- .... **CLC 16**
See also CA 89-92

Hesiod c. 8th cent. B.C.- .... **CMLC 5**

Hesse, Hermann
1877-1962 .... **CLC 1, 2, 3, 6, 11, 17, 25,
69; DA; DAB; DAC; DAM MST, NOV;
SSC 9; WLC**
See also CA 17-18; CAP 2; DLB 66;
MTCW; SATA 50

Hewes, Cady
See De Voto, Bernard (Augustine)

Heyen, William 1940- .... **CLC 13, 18**
See also CA 33-36R; CAAS 9; DLB 5

Heyerdahl, Thor 1914-............ **CLC 26**
See also CA 5-8R; CANR 5, 22; MTCW;
SATA 2, 52

Heym, Georg (Theodor Franz Arthur)
1887-1912 .... **TCLC 9**
See also CA 106

Heym, Stefan 1913-.............. **CLC 41**
See also CA 9-12R; CANR 4; DLB 69

Heyse, Paul (Johann Ludwig von)
1830-1914 .... **TCLC 8**
See also CA 104; DLB 129

Heyward, (Edwin) DuBose
1885-1940 .... **TCLC 59**
See also CA 108; DLB 7, 9, 45; SATA 21

Hibbert, Eleanor Alice Burford
1906-1993 .... **CLC 7; DAM POP**
See also BEST 90:4; CA 17-20R; 140;
CANR 9, 28; SATA 2; SATA-Obit 74

Hichens, Robert S. 1864-1950..... **TCLC 64**
See also DLB 153

Higgins, George V(incent)
1939- .... **CLC 4, 7, 10, 18**
See also CA 77-80; CAAS 5; CANR 17, 51;
DLB 2; DLBY 81; INT CANR-17;
MTCW

Higginson, Thomas Wentworth
1823-1911 .... **TCLC 36**
See also DLB 1, 64

Highet, Helen
See MacInnes, Helen (Clark)

Highsmith, (Mary) Patricia
1921-1995 .... **CLC 2, 4, 14, 42;
DAM NOV, POP**
See also CA 1-4R; 147; CANR 1, 20, 48;
MTCW

Highwater, Jamake (Mamake)
1942(?)- .... **CLC 12**
See also AAYA 7; CA 65-68; CAAS 7;
CANR 10, 34; CLR 17; DLB 52;
DLBY 85; JRDA; MAICYA; SATA 32,
69; SATA-Brief 30

Highway, Tomson
1951- ..... **CLC 92; DAC; DAM MULT**
See also CA 151; NNAL

Higuchi, Ichiyo 1872-1896....... **NCLC 49**

Hijuelos, Oscar
1951- .... **CLC 65; DAM MULT, POP;
HLC**
See also BEST 90:1; CA 123; CANR 50;
DLB 145; HW

Hikmet, Nazim 1902(?)-1963....... **CLC 40**
See also CA 141; 93-96

Hildegard von Bingen
1098-1179 .... **CMLC 20**
See also DLB 148

Hildesheimer, Wolfgang
1916-1991 .... **CLC 49**
See also CA 101; 135; DLB 69, 124

Hill, Geoffrey (William)
1932- ... **CLC 5, 8, 18, 45; DAM POET**
See also CA 81-84; CANR 21;
CDBLB 1960 to Present; DLB 40;
MTCW

Hill, George Roy 1921-.......... **CLC 26**
See also CA 110; 122

Hill, John
See Koontz, Dean R(ay)

Hill, Susan (Elizabeth)
1942- .. CLC 4; DAB; DAM MST, NOV
See also CA 33-36R; CANR 29; DLB 14,
139; MTCW

Hillerman, Tony
1925- .... CLC 62; DAM POP
See also AAYA 6; BEST 89:1; CA 29-32R;
CANR 21, 42; SATA 6

Hillesum, Etty 1914-1943 .... TCLC 49
See also CA 137

Hilliard, Noel (Harvey) 1929-...... CLC 15
See also CA 9-12R; CANR 7

Hillis, Rick 1956-................. CLC 66
See also CA 134

Hilton, James 1900-1954........ TCLC 21
See also CA 108; DLB 34, 77; SATA 34

Himes, Chester (Bomar)
1909-1984 .... CLC 2, 4, 7, 18, 58; BLC;
DAM MULT
See also BW 2; CA 25-28R; 114; CANR 22;
DLB 2, 76, 143; MTCW

Hinde, Thomas .... CLC 6, 11
See also Chitty, Thomas Willes

Hindin, Nathan
See Bloch, Robert (Albert)

Hine, (William) Daryl 1936- .... CLC 15
See also CA 1-4R; CAAS 15; CANR 1, 20;
DLB 60

Hinkson, Katharine Tynan
See Tynan, Katharine

Hinton, S(usan) E(loise)
1950- .... CLC 30; DA; DAB; DAC;
DAM MST, NOV
See also AAYA 2; CA 81-84; CANR 32;
CLR 3, 23; JRDA; MAICYA; MTCW;
SATA 19, 58

Hippius, Zinaida .... TCLC 9
See also Gippius, Zinaida (Nikolayevna)

Hiraoka, Kimitake 1925-1970
See Mishima, Yukio
See also CA 97-100; 29-32R; DAM DRAM;
MTCW

Hirsch, E(ric) D(onald), Jr. 1928-... CLC 79
See also CA 25-28R; CANR 27, 51;
DLB 67; INT CANR-27; MTCW

Hirsch, Edward 1950- .... CLC 31, 50
See also CA 104; CANR 20, 42; DLB 120

Hitchcock, Alfred (Joseph)
1899-1980 .... CLC 16
See also CA 97-100; SATA 27;
SATA-Obit 24

Hitler, Adolf 1889-1945.......... TCLC 53
See also CA 117; 147

Hoagland, Edward 1932-.......... CLC 28
See also CA 1-4R; CANR 2, 31; DLB 6;
SATA 51

Hoban, Russell (Conwell)
1925- .... CLC 7, 25; DAM NOV
See also CA 5-8R; CANR 23, 37; CLR 3;
DLB 52; MAICYA; MTCW; SATA 1,
40, 78

Hobbes, Thomas 1588-1679........ LC 36
See also DLB 151

Hobbs, Perry
See Blackmur, R(ichard) P(almer)

Hobson, Laura Z(ametkin)
1900-1986 .... CLC 7, 25
See also CA 17-20R; 118; CANR 55;
DLB 28; SATA 52

Hochhuth, Rolf
1931- ..... CLC 4, 11, 18; DAM DRAM
See also CA 5-8R; CANR 33; DLB 124;
MTCW

Hochman, Sandra 1936-........... CLC 3, 8
See also CA 5-8R; DLB 5

Hochwaelder, Fritz
1911-1986 ...... CLC 36; DAM DRAM
See also CA 29-32R; 120; CANR 42;
MTCW

Hochwalder, Fritz
See Hochwaelder, Fritz

Hocking, Mary (Eunice) 1921-..... CLC 13
See also CA 101; CANR 18, 40

Hodgins, Jack 1938-............. CLC 23
See also CA 93-96; DLB 60

Hodgson, William Hope
1877(?)-1918 .... TCLC 13
See also CA 111; DLB 70, 153, 156

Hoeg, Peter 1957-................ CLC 95
See also CA 151

Hoffman, Alice
1952- .... CLC 51; DAM NOV
See also CA 77-80; CANR 34; MTCW

Hoffman, Daniel (Gerard)
1923- .... CLC 6, 13, 23
See also CA 1-4R; CANR 4; DLB 5

Hoffman, Stanley 1944-............ CLC 5
See also CA 77-80

Hoffman, William M(oses) 1939- ... CLC 40
See also CA 57-60; CANR 11

Hoffmann, E(rnst) T(heodor) A(madeus)
1776-1822 .... NCLC 2; SSC 13
See also DLB 90; SATA 27

Hofmann, Gert 1931-............. CLC 54
See also CA 128

Hofmannsthal, Hugo von
1874-1929 .... TCLC 11; DAM DRAM;
DC 4
See also CA 106; 153; DLB 81, 118

Hogan, Linda
1947- .... CLC 73; DAM MULT
See also CA 120; CANR 45; NNAL

Hogarth, Charles
See Creasey, John

Hogarth, Emmett
See Polonsky, Abraham (Lincoln)

Hogg, James 1770-1835.......... NCLC 4
See also DLB 93, 116, 159

Holbach, Paul Henri Thiry Baron
1723-1789 .... LC 14

Holberg, Ludvig 1684-1754 .... LC 6

Holden, Ursula 1921-............. CLC 18
See also CA 101; CAAS 8; CANR 22

Holderlin, (Johann Christian) Friedrich
1770-1843 .... NCLC 16; PC 4

Holdstock, Robert
See Holdstock, Robert P.

Holdstock, Robert P. 1948-........ CLC 39
See also CA 131

Holland, Isabelle 1920- .... CLC 21
See also AAYA 11; CA 21-24R; CANR 10,
25, 47; JRDA; MAICYA; SATA 8, 70

Holland, Marcus
See Caldwell, (Janet Miriam) Taylor
(Holland)

Hollander, John 1929-...... CLC 2, 5, 8, 14
See also CA 1-4R; CANR 1, 52; DLB 5;
SATA 13

Hollander, Paul
See Silverberg, Robert

Holleran, Andrew 1943(?)-......... CLC 38
See also CA 144

Hollinghurst, Alan 1954-....... CLC 55, 91
See also CA 114

Hollis, Jim
See Summers, Hollis (Spurgeon, Jr.)

Holly, Buddy 1936-1959 .... TCLC 65

Holmes, John
See Souster, (Holmes) Raymond

Holmes, John Clellon 1926-1988.... CLC 56
See also CA 9-12R; 125; CANR 4; DLB 16

Holmes, Oliver Wendell
1809-1894 .... NCLC 14
See also CDALB 1640-1865; DLB 1;
SATA 34

Holmes, Raymond
See Souster, (Holmes) Raymond

Holt, Victoria
See Hibbert, Eleanor Alice Burford

Holub, Miroslav 1923-............. CLC 4
See also CA 21-24R; CANR 10

Homer
c. 8th cent. B.C.-..... CMLC 1, 16; DA;
DAB; DAC; DAM MST, POET

Honig, Edwin 1919-.............. CLC 33
See also CA 5-8R; CAAS 8; CANR 4, 45;
DLB 5

Hood, Hugh (John Blagdon)
1928-..................... CLC 15, 28
See also CA 49-52; CAAS 17; CANR 1, 33;
DLB 53

Hood, Thomas 1799-1845........ NCLC 16
See also DLB 96

Hooker, (Peter) Jeremy 1941-...... CLC 43
See also CA 77-80; CANR 22; DLB 40

hooks, bell .... CLC 94
See also Watkins, Gloria

Hope, A(lec) D(erwent) 1907-.... CLC 3, 51
See also CA 21-24R; CANR 33; MTCW

Hope, Brian
See Creasey, John

Hope, Christopher (David Tully)
1944-...................... CLC 52
See also CA 106; CANR 47; SATA 62

Hopkins, Gerard Manley
1844-1889 .... NCLC 17; DA; DAB;
DAC; DAM MST, POET; PC 15; WLC
See also CDBLB 1890-1914; DLB 35, 57

Hopkins, John (Richard) 1931-...... CLC 4
See also CA 85-88

Hunter, Evan
1926- .... CLC 11, 31; DAM POP
See also CA 5-8R; CANR 5, 38; DLBY 82;
INT CANR-5; MTCW; SATA 25

Hunter, Kristin (Eggleston) 1931-... CLC 35
See also AITN 1; BW 1; CA 13-16R;
CANR 13; CLR 3; DLB 33;
INT CANR-13; MAICYA; SAAS 10;
SATA 12

Hunter, Mollie 1922- .... CLC 21
See also McIlwraith, Maureen Mollie
Hunter
See also AAYA 13; CANR 37; CLR 25;
DLB 161; JRDA; MAICYA; SAAS 7;
SATA 54

Hunter, Robert (?)-1734............. LC 7

Hurston, Zora Neale
1903-1960 .... CLC 7, 30, 61; BLC; DA;
DAC; DAM MST, MULT, NOV; SSC 4
See also AAYA 15; BW 1; CA 85-88;
DLB 51, 86; MTCW

Huston, John (Marcellus)
1906-1987 .... CLC 20
See also CA 73-76; 123; CANR 34; DLB 26

Hustvedt, Siri 1955- .... CLC 76
See also CA 137

Hutten, Ulrich von 1488-1523....... LC 16

Huxley, Aldous (Leonard)
1894-1963 ..... CLC 1, 3, 4, 5, 8, 11, 18,
35, 79; DA; DAB; DAC; DAM MST,
NOV; WLC
See also AAYA 11; CA 85-88; CANR 44;
CDBLB 1914-1945; DLB 36, 100, 162;
MTCW; SATA 63

Huysmans, Charles Marie Georges
1848-1907
See Huysmans, Joris-Karl
See also CA 104

Huysmans, Joris-Karl.............. TCLC 7
See also Huysmans, Charles Marie Georges
See also DLB 123

Hwang, David Henry
1957- .... CLC 55; DAM DRAM; DC 4
See also CA 127; 132; INT 132

Hyde, Anthony 1946-............. CLC 42
See also CA 136

Hyde, Margaret O(ldroyd) 1917-... CLC 21
See also CA 1-4R; CANR 1, 36; CLR 23;
JRDA; MAICYA; SAAS 8; SATA 1, 42,
76

Hynes, James 1956(?)-............ CLC 65

Ian, Janis 1951- .... CLC 21
See also CA 105

Ibanez, Vicente Blasco
See Blasco Ibanez, Vicente

Ibarguengoitia, Jorge 1928-1983.... CLC 37
See also CA 124; 113; HW

Ibsen, Henrik (Johan)
1828-1906 .... TCLC 2, 8, 16, 37, 52;
DA; DAB; DAC; DAM DRAM, MST;
DC 2; WLC
See also CA 104; 141

Ibuse Masuji 1898-1993........... CLC 22
See also CA 127; 141

Ichikawa, Kon 1915-.............. CLC 20
See also CA 121

Idle, Eric 1943-.................. CLC 21
See also Monty Python
See also CA 116; CANR 35

Ignatow, David 1914-...... CLC 4, 7, 14, 40
See also CA 9-12R; CAAS 3; CANR 31;
DLB 5

Ihimaera, Witi 1944- .... CLC 46
See also CA 77-80

Ilf, Ilya........................ TCLC 21
See also Fainzilberg, Ilya Arnoldovich

Illyes, Gyula 1902-1983............ PC 16
See also CA 114; 109

Immermann, Karl (Lebrecht)
1796-1840 .... NCLC 4, 49
See also DLB 133

Inclan, Ramon (Maria) del Valle
See Valle-Inclan, Ramon (Maria) del

Infante, G(uillermo) Cabrera
See Cabrera Infante, G(uillermo)

Ingalls, Rachel (Holmes) 1940-..... CLC 42
See also CA 123; 127

Ingamells, Rex 1913-1955 .... TCLC 35

Inge, William (Motter)
1913-1973 .. CLC 1, 8, 19; DAM DRAM
See also CA 9-12R; CDALB 1941-1968;
DLB 7; MTCW

Ingelow, Jean 1820-1897 .... NCLC 39
See also DLB 35, 163; SATA 33

Ingram, Willis J.
See Harris, Mark

Innaurato, Albert (F.) 1948(?)- .. CLC 21, 60
See also CA 115; 122; INT 122

Innes, Michael
See Stewart, J(ohn) I(nnes) M(ackintosh)

Ionesco, Eugene
1909-1994 .... CLC 1, 4, 6, 9, 11, 15, 41,
86; DA; DAB; DAC; DAM DRAM,
MST; WLC
See also CA 9-12R; 144; CANR 55;
MTCW; SATA 7; SATA-Obit 79

Iqbal, Muhammad 1873-1938 ..... TCLC 28

Ireland, Patrick
See O'Doherty, Brian

Iron, Ralph
See Schreiner, Olive (Emilie Albertina)

Irving, John (Winslow)
1942- ..... CLC 13, 23, 38; DAM NOV,
POP
See also AAYA 8; BEST 89:3; CA 25-28R;
CANR 28; DLB 6; DLBY 82; MTCW

Irving, Washington
1783-1859 ..... NCLC 2, 19; DA; DAB;
DAM MST; SSC 2; WLC
See also CDALB 1640-1865; DLB 3, 11, 30,
59, 73, 74; YABC 2

Irwin, P. K.
See Page, P(atricia) K(athleen)

Isaacs, Susan 1943- ... CLC 32; DAM POP
See also BEST 89:1; CA 89-92; CANR 20,
41; INT CANR-20; MTCW

Isherwood, Christopher (William Bradshaw)
1904-1986 .... CLC 1, 9, 11, 14, 44;
DAM DRAM, NOV
See also CA 13-16R; 117; CANR 35;
DLB 15; DLBY 86; MTCW

Ishiguro, Kazuo
1954- ...... CLC 27, 56, 59; DAM NOV
See also BEST 90:2; CA 120; CANR 49;
MTCW

Ishikawa, Hakuhin
See Ishikawa, Takuboku

Ishikawa, Takuboku
1886(?)-1912 .... TCLC 15;
DAM POET; PC 10
See also CA 113; 153

Iskander, Fazil 1929-............. CLC 47
See also CA 102

Isler, Alan .... CLC 91

Ivan IV 1530-1584 .... LC 17

Ivanov, Vyacheslav Ivanovich
1866-1949 .... TCLC 33
See also CA 122

Ivask, Ivar Vidrik 1927-1992....... CLC 14
See also CA 37-40R; 139; CANR 24

Ives, Morgan
See Bradley, Marion Zimmer

J. R. S.
See Gogarty, Oliver St. John

Jabran, Kahlil
See Gibran, Kahlil

Jabran, Khalil
See Gibran, Kahlil

Jackson, Daniel
See Wingrove, David (John)

Jackson, Jesse 1908-1983 .... CLC 12
See also BW 1; CA 25-28R; 109; CANR 27;
CLR 28; MAICYA; SATA 2, 29;
SATA-Obit 48

Jackson, Laura (Riding) 1901-1991
See Riding, Laura
See also CA 65-68; 135; CANR 28; DLB 48

Jackson, Sam
See Trumbo, Dalton

Jackson, Sara
See Wingrove, David (John)

Jackson, Shirley
1919-1965 .... CLC 11, 60, 87; DA;
DAC; DAM MST; SSC 9; WLC
See also AAYA 9; CA 1-4R; 25-28R;
CANR 4, 52; CDALB 1941-1968; DLB 6;
SATA 2

Jacob, (Cyprien-)Max 1876-1944 ... TCLC 6
See also CA 104

Jacobs, Jim 1942-................. CLC 12
See also CA 97-100; INT 97-100

Jacobs, W(illiam) W(ymark)
1863-1943 .... TCLC 22
See also CA 121; DLB 135

Jacobsen, Jens Peter 1847-1885 .. NCLC 34

Jacobsen, Josephine 1908-......... CLC 48
See also CA 33-36R; CAAS 18; CANR 23,
48

Jacobson, Dan 1929- .... CLC 4, 14
See also CA 1-4R; CANR 2, 25; DLB 14;
MTCW

Jacqueline
See Carpentier (y Valmont), Alejo

Jagger, Mick 1944-.............. CLC 17

Jakes, John (William)
1932- ...... **CLC 29; DAM NOV, POP**
See also BEST 89:4; CA 57-60; CANR 10,
43; DLBY 83; INT CANR-10; MTCW;
SATA 62

James, Andrew
See Kirkup, James

James, C(yril) L(ionel) R(obert)
1901-1989 .... **CLC 33**
See also BW 2; CA 117; 125; 128; DLB 125;
MTCW

James, Daniel (Lewis) 1911-1988
See Santiago, Danny
See also CA 125

James, Dynely
See Mayne, William (James Carter)

James, Henry Sr. 1811-1882 ..... **NCLC 53**

James, Henry
1843-1916 ...... **TCLC 2, 11, 24, 40, 47,**
64; DA; DAB; DAC; DAM MST, NOV;
SSC 8; WLC
See also CA 104; 132; CDALB 1865-1917;
DLB 12, 71, 74; DLBD 13; MTCW

James, M. R.
See James, Montague (Rhodes)
See also DLB 156

James, Montague (Rhodes)
1862-1936 .... **TCLC 6; SSC 16**
See also CA 104

James, P. D. .... **CLC 18, 46**
See also White, Phyllis Dorothy James
See also BEST 90:2; CDBLB 1960 to
Present; DLB 87

James, Philip
See Moorcock, Michael (John)

James, William 1842-1910 ..... **TCLC 15, 32**
See also CA 109

James I 1394-1437 .... **LC 20**

Jameson, Anna 1794-1860 .... **NCLC 43**
See also DLB 99, 166

Jami, Nur al-Din 'Abd al-Rahman
1414-1492 .... **LC 9**

Jandl, Ernst 1925- .... **CLC 34**

Janowitz, Tama
1957- .... **CLC 43; DAM POP**
See also CA 106; CANR 52

Japrisot, Sebastien 1931- .... **CLC 90**

Jarrell, Randall
1914-1965 .... **CLC 1, 2, 6, 9, 13, 49;**
DAM POET
See also CA 5-8R; 25-28R; CABS 2;
CANR 6, 34; CDALB 1941-1968; CLR 6;
DLB 48, 52; MAICYA; MTCW; SATA 7

Jarry, Alfred
1873-1907 .... **TCLC 2, 14;**
DAM DRAM; SSC 20
See also CA 104; 153

Jarvis, E. K.
See Bloch, Robert (Albert); Ellison, Harlan
(Jay); Silverberg, Robert

Jeake, Samuel, Jr.
See Aiken, Conrad (Potter)

Jean Paul 1763-1825 .... **NCLC 7**

Jefferies, (John) Richard
1848-1887 .... **NCLC 47**
See also DLB 98, 141; SATA 16

Jeffers, (John) Robinson
1887-1962 .... **CLC 2, 3, 11, 15, 54; DA;**
DAC; DAM MST, POET; WLC
See also CA 85-88; CANR 35;
CDALB 1917-1929; DLB 45; MTCW

Jefferson, Janet
See Mencken, H(enry) L(ouis)

Jefferson, Thomas 1743-1826 .... **NCLC 11**
See also CDALB 1640-1865; DLB 31

Jeffrey, Francis 1773-1850 .... **NCLC 33**
See also DLB 107

Jelakowitch, Ivan
See Heijermans, Herman

Jellicoe, (Patricia) Ann 1927- ...... **CLC 27**
See also CA 85-88; DLB 13

Jen, Gish .... **CLC 70**
See also Jen, Lillian

Jen, Lillian 1956(?)-
See Jen, Gish
See also CA 135

Jenkins, (John) Robin 1912- .... **CLC 52**
See also CA 1-4R; CANR 1; DLB 14

Jennings, Elizabeth (Joan)
1926- .... **CLC 5, 14**
See also CA 61-64; CAAS 5; CANR 8, 39;
DLB 27; MTCW; SATA 66

Jennings, Waylon 1937- .... **CLC 21**

Jensen, Johannes V. 1873-1950 .... **TCLC 41**

Jensen, Laura (Linnea) 1948- ...... **CLC 37**
See also CA 103

Jerome, Jerome K(lapka)
1859-1927 .... **TCLC 23**
See also CA 119; DLB 10, 34, 135

Jerrold, Douglas William
1803-1857 .... **NCLC 2**
See also DLB 158, 159

Jewett, (Theodora) Sarah Orne
1849-1909 .... **TCLC 1, 22; SSC 6**
See also CA 108; 127; DLB 12, 74;
SATA 15

Jewsbury, Geraldine (Endsor)
1812-1880 .... **NCLC 22**
See also DLB 21

Jhabvala, Ruth Prawer
1927- .... **CLC 4, 8, 29, 94; DAB;**
DAM NOV
See also CA 1-4R; CANR 2, 29, 51;
DLB 139; INT CANR-29; MTCW

Jibran, Kahlil
See Gibran, Kahlil

Jibran, Khalil
See Gibran, Kahlil

Jiles, Paulette 1943- .... **CLC 13, 58**
See also CA 101

Jimenez (Mantecon), Juan Ramon
1881-1958 ..... **TCLC 4; DAM MULT,**
POET; HLC; PC 7
See also CA 104; 131; DLB 134; HW;
MTCW

Jimenez, Ramon
See Jimenez (Mantecon), Juan Ramon

Jimenez Mantecon, Juan
See Jimenez (Mantecon), Juan Ramon

Joel, Billy .... **CLC 26**
See also Joel, William Martin

Joel, William Martin 1949-
See Joel, Billy
See also CA 108

John of the Cross, St. 1542-1591 .... **LC 18**

Johnson, B(ryan) S(tanley William)
1933-1973 .... **CLC 6, 9**
See also CA 9-12R; 53-56; CANR 9;
DLB 14, 40

Johnson, Benj. F. of Boo
See Riley, James Whitcomb

Johnson, Benjamin F. of Boo
See Riley, James Whitcomb

Johnson, Charles (Richard)
1948- .... **CLC 7, 51, 65; BLC;**
DAM MULT
See also BW 2; CA 116; CAAS 18;
CANR 42; DLB 33

Johnson, Denis 1949- .... **CLC 52**
See also CA 117; 121; DLB 120

Johnson, Diane 1934- .... **CLC 5, 13, 48**
See also CA 41-44R; CANR 17, 40;
DLBY 80; INT CANR-17; MTCW

Johnson, Eyvind (Olof Verner)
1900-1976 .... **CLC 14**
See also CA 73-76; 69-72; CANR 34

Johnson, J. R.
See James, C(yril) L(ionel) R(obert)

Johnson, James Weldon
1871-1938 .... **TCLC 3, 19; BLC;**
DAM MULT, POET
See also BW 1; CA 104; 125;
CDALB 1917-1929; CLR 32; DLB 51;
MTCW; SATA 31

Johnson, Joyce 1935- .... **CLC 58**
See also CA 125; 129

Johnson, Lionel (Pigot)
1867-1902 .... **TCLC 19**
See also CA 117; DLB 19

Johnson, Mel
See Malzberg, Barry N(athaniel)

Johnson, Pamela Hansford
1912-1981 .... **CLC 1, 7, 27**
See also CA 1-4R; 104; CANR 2, 28;
DLB 15; MTCW

Johnson, Samuel
1709-1784 ..... **LC 15; DA; DAB; DAC;**
DAM MST; WLC
See also CDBLB 1660-1789; DLB 39, 95,
104, 142

Johnson, Uwe
1934-1984 .... **CLC 5, 10, 15, 40**
See also CA 1-4R; 112; CANR 1, 39;
DLB 75; MTCW

Johnston, George (Benson) 1913- ... **CLC 51**
See also CA 1-4R; CANR 5, 20; DLB 88

Johnston, Jennifer 1930- .... **CLC 7**
See also CA 85-88; DLB 14

Jolley, (Monica) Elizabeth
1923- .... **CLC 46; SSC 19**
See also CA 127; CAAS 13

Jones, Arthur Llewellyn   1863-1947
    See Machen, Arthur
    See also CA 104

Jones, D(ouglas) G(ordon)   1929-....   **CLC 10**
    See also CA 29-32R; CANR 13; DLB 53

Jones, David (Michael)
    1895-1974 ....   **CLC 2, 4, 7, 13, 42**
    See also CA 9-12R; 53-56; CANR 28;
    CDBLB 1945-1960; DLB 20, 100; MTCW

Jones, David Robert   1947-
    See Bowie, David
    See also CA 103

Jones, Diana Wynne   1934- ....   **CLC 26**
    See also AAYA 12; CA 49-52; CANR 4,
    26; CLR 23; DLB 161; JRDA; MAICYA;
    SAAS 7; SATA 9, 70

Jones, Edward P.   1950-...........   **CLC 76**
    See also BW 2; CA 142

Jones, Gayl
    1949-....   **CLC 6, 9; BLC; DAM MULT**
    See also BW 2; CA 77-80; CANR 27;
    DLB 33; MTCW

Jones, James   1921-1977....   **CLC 1, 3, 10, 39**
    See also AITN 1, 2; CA 1-4R; 69-72;
    CANR 6; DLB 2, 143; MTCW

Jones, John J.
    See Lovecraft, H(oward) P(hillips)

Jones, LeRoi ....   **CLC 1, 2, 3, 5, 10, 14**
    See also Baraka, Amiri

Jones, Louis B. ....   **CLC 65**
    See also CA 141

Jones, Madison (Percy, Jr.)   1925- ...   **CLC 4**
    See also CA 13-16R; CAAS 11; CANR 7,
    54; DLB 152

Jones, Mervyn   1922- ....   **CLC 10, 52**
    See also CA 45-48; CAAS 5; CANR 1;
    MTCW

Jones, Mick   1956(?)- ....   **CLC 30**

Jones, Nettie (Pearl)   1941- ....   **CLC 34**
    See also BW 2; CA 137; CAAS 20

Jones, Preston   1936-1979 ....   **CLC 10**
    See also CA 73-76; 89-92; DLB 7

Jones, Robert F(rancis)   1934-.......   **CLC 7**
    See also CA 49-52; CANR 2

Jones, Rod   1953- ....   **CLC 50**
    See also CA 128

Jones, Terence Graham Parry
    1942- ....   **CLC 21**
    See also Jones, Terry; Monty Python
    See also CA 112; 116; CANR 35; INT 116

Jones, Terry
    See Jones, Terence Graham Parry
    See also SATA 67; SATA-Brief 51

Jones, Thom   1945(?)-.............   **CLC 81**

Jong, Erica
    1942- ....   **CLC 4, 6, 8, 18, 83;**
                                    DAM NOV, POP
    See also AITN 1; BEST 90:2; CA 73-76;
    CANR 26, 52; DLB 2, 5, 28, 152;
    INT CANR-26; MTCW

Jonson, Ben(jamin)
    1572(?)-1637 ......   **LC 6, 33; DA; DAB;**
        DAC; DAM DRAM, MST, POET;
                                         DC 4; WLC
    See also CDBLB Before 1660; DLB 62, 121

Jordan, June
    1936- .....   **CLC 5, 11, 23; DAM MULT,**
                                              POET
    See also AAYA 2; BW 2; CA 33-36R;
    CANR 25; CLR 10; DLB 38; MAICYA;
    MTCW; SATA 4

Jordan, Pat(rick M.)   1941- ....   **CLC 37**
    See also CA 33-36R

Jorgensen, Ivar
    See Ellison, Harlan (Jay)

Jorgenson, Ivar
    See Silverberg, Robert

Josephus, Flavius   c. 37-100 ......   **CMLC 13**

Josipovici, Gabriel   1940-........   **CLC 6, 43**
    See also CA 37-40R; CAAS 8; CANR 47;
    DLB 14

Joubert, Joseph   1754-1824 ....   **NCLC 9**

Jouve, Pierre Jean   1887-1976......   **CLC 47**
    See also CA 65-68

Joyce, James (Augustine Aloysius)
    1882-1941 ....   **TCLC 3, 8, 16, 35, 52;**
        DA; DAB; DAC; DAM MST, NOV,
                               POET; SSC 3; WLC
    See also CA 104; 126; CDBLB 1914-1945;
    DLB 10, 19, 36, 162; MTCW

Jozsef, Attila   1905-1937.........   **TCLC 22**
    See also CA 116

Juana Ines de la Cruz   1651(?)-1695 ...   **LC 5**

Judd, Cyril
    See Kornbluth, C(yril) M.; Pohl, Frederik

Julian of Norwich   1342(?)-1416(?) ....   **LC 6**
    See also DLB 146

Juniper, Alex
    See Hospital, Janette Turner

Junius
    See Luxemburg, Rosa

Just, Ward (Swift)   1935- ....   **CLC 4, 27**
    See also CA 25-28R; CANR 32;
    INT CANR-32

Justice, Donald (Rodney)
    1925- ....   **CLC 6, 19; DAM POET**
    See also CA 5-8R; CANR 26, 54;
    DLBY 83; INT CANR-26

Juvenal   c. 55-c. 127 ....   **CMLC 8**

Juvenis
    See Bourne, Randolph S(illiman)

Kacew, Romain   1914-1980
    See Gary, Romain
    See also CA 108; 102

Kadare, Ismail   1936- ....   **CLC 52**

Kadohata, Cynthia.................   **CLC 59**
    See also CA 140

Kafka, Franz
    1883-1924 ....   **TCLC 2, 6, 13, 29, 47, 53;**
        DA; DAB; DAC; DAM MST, NOV;
                                       SSC 5; WLC
    See also CA 105; 126; DLB 81; MTCW

Kahanovitsch, Pinkhes
    See Der Nister

Kahn, Roger   1927-...............   **CLC 30**
    See also CA 25-28R; CANR 44; DLB 171;
    SATA 37

Kain, Saul
    See Sassoon, Siegfried (Lorraine)

Kaiser, Georg   1878-1945 ....   **TCLC 9**
    See also CA 106; DLB 124

Kaletski, Alexander   1946-.........   **CLC 39**
    See also CA 118; 143

Kalidasa   fl. c. 400- ....   **CMLC 9**

Kallman, Chester (Simon)
    1921-1975 ....   **CLC 2**
    See also CA 45-48; 53-56; CANR 3

Kaminsky, Melvin   1926-
    See Brooks, Mel
    See also CA 65-68; CANR 16

Kaminsky, Stuart M(elvin)   1934- ...   **CLC 59**
    See also CA 73-76; CANR 29, 53

Kane, Francis
    See Robbins, Harold

Kane, Paul
    See Simon, Paul (Frederick)

Kane, Wilson
    See Bloch, Robert (Albert)

Kanin, Garson   1912-..............   **CLC 22**
    See also AITN 1; CA 5-8R; CANR 7;
    DLB 7

Kaniuk, Yoram   1930-.............   **CLC 19**
    See also CA 134

Kant, Immanuel   1724-1804 ......   **NCLC 27**
    See also DLB 94

Kantor, MacKinlay   1904-1977 ......   **CLC 7**
    See also CA 61-64; 73-76; DLB 9, 102

Kaplan, David Michael   1946- ......   **CLC 50**

Kaplan, James   1951- ....   **CLC 59**
    See also CA 135

Karageorge, Michael
    See Anderson, Poul (William)

Karamzin, Nikolai Mikhailovich
    1766-1826 ....   **NCLC 3**
    See also DLB 150

Karapanou, Margarita   1946-.......   **CLC 13**
    See also CA 101

Karinthy, Frigyes   1887-1938......   **TCLC 47**

Karl, Frederick R(obert)   1927-.....   **CLC 34**
    See also CA 5-8R; CANR 3, 44

Kastel, Warren
    See Silverberg, Robert

Kataev, Evgeny Petrovich   1903-1942
    See Petrov, Evgeny
    See also CA 120

Kataphusin
    See Ruskin, John

Katz, Steve   1935-................   **CLC 47**
    See also CA 25-28R; CAAS 14; CANR 12;
    DLBY 83

Kauffman, Janet   1945-............   **CLC 42**
    See also CA 117; CANR 43; DLBY 86

Kaufman, Bob (Garnell)
    1925-1986 ....   **CLC 49**
    See also BW 1; CA 41-44R; 118; CANR 22;
    DLB 16, 41

Kaufman, George S.
    1889-1961 ......   **CLC 38; DAM DRAM**
    See also CA 108; 93-96; DLB 7; INT 108

Kaufman, Sue ....   **CLC 3, 8**
    See also Barondess, Sue K(aufman)

Killens, John Oliver 1916-1987..... **CLC 10**
See also BW 2; CA 77-80; 123; CAAS 2;
CANR 26; DLB 33

Killigrew, Anne 1660-1685.......... **LC 4**
See also DLB 131

Kim
See Simenon, Georges (Jacques Christian)

Kincaid, Jamaica
1949-.............. **CLC 43, 68; BLC;**
DAM MULT, NOV
See also AAYA 13; BW 2; CA 125;
CANR 47; DLB 157

King, Francis (Henry)
1923-.......... **CLC 8, 53; DAM NOV**
See also CA 1-4R; CANR 1, 33; DLB 15,
139; MTCW

King, Martin Luther, Jr.
1929-1968 .... **CLC 83; BLC; DA; DAB;**
DAC; DAM MST, MULT
See also BW 2; CA 25-28; CANR 27, 44;
CAP 2; MTCW; SATA 14

King, Stephen (Edwin)
1947-............. **CLC 12, 26, 37, 61;**
DAM NOV, POP; SSC 17
See also AAYA 1, 17; BEST 90:1;
CA 61-64; CANR 1, 30, 52; DLB 143;
DLBY 80; JRDA; MTCW; SATA 9, 55

King, Steve
See King, Stephen (Edwin)

King, Thomas
1943-..... **CLC 89; DAC; DAM MULT**
See also CA 144; NNAL

Kingman, Lee..................... **CLC 17**
See also Natti, (Mary) Lee
See also SAAS 3; SATA 1, 67

Kingsley, Charles 1819-1875..... **NCLC 35**
See also DLB 21, 32, 163; YABC 2

Kingsley, Sidney 1906-1995....... **CLC 44**
See also CA 85-88; 147; DLB 7

Kingsolver, Barbara
1955-......... **CLC 55, 81; DAM POP**
See also AAYA 15; CA 129; 134; INT 134

Kingston, Maxine (Ting Ting) Hong
1940- .... **CLC 12, 19, 58; DAM MULT,**
NOV
See also AAYA 8; CA 69-72; CANR 13,
38; DLB 173; DLBY 80; INT CANR-13;
MTCW; SATA 53

Kinnell, Galway
1927-........... **CLC 1, 2, 3, 5, 13, 29**
See also CA 9-12R; CANR 10, 34; DLB 5;
DLBY 87; INT CANR-34; MTCW

Kinsella, Thomas 1928-......... **CLC 4, 19**
See also CA 17-20R; CANR 15; DLB 27;
MTCW

Kinsella, W(illiam) P(atrick)
1935-.............. **CLC 27, 43; DAC;**
DAM NOV, POP
See also AAYA 7; CA 97-100; CAAS 7;
CANR 21, 35; INT CANR-21; MTCW

Kipling, (Joseph) Rudyard
1865-1936 ...... **TCLC 8, 17; DA; DAB;**
DAC; DAM MST, POET; PC 3; SSC 5;
WLC
See also CA 105; 120; CANR 33;
CDBLB 1890-1914; CLR 39; DLB 19, 34,
141, 156; MAICYA; MTCW; YABC 2

Kirkup, James 1918- .... **CLC 1**
See also CA 1-4R; CAAS 4; CANR 2;
DLB 27; SATA 12

Kirkwood, James 1930(?)-1989 ...... **CLC 9**
See also AITN 2; CA 1-4R; 128; CANR 6,
40

Kirshner, Sidney
See Kingsley, Sidney

Kis, Danilo 1935-1989 .... **CLC 57**
See also CA 109; 118; 129; MTCW

Kivi, Aleksis 1834-1872......... **NCLC 30**

Kizer, Carolyn (Ashley)
1925-..... **CLC 15, 39, 80; DAM POET**
See also CA 65-68; CAAS 5; CANR 24;
DLB 5, 169

Klabund 1890-1928.............. **TCLC 44**
See also DLB 66

Klappert, Peter 1942-............. **CLC 57**
See also CA 33-36R; DLB 5

Klein, A(braham) M(oses)
1909-1972 .... **CLC 19; DAB; DAC;**
DAM MST
See also CA 101; 37-40R; DLB 68

Klein, Norma 1938-1989 .... **CLC 30**
See also AAYA 2; CA 41-44R; 128;
CANR 15, 37; CLR 2, 19;
INT CANR-15; JRDA; MAICYA;
SAAS 1; SATA 7, 57

Klein, T(heodore) E(ibon) D(onald)
1947-............................ **CLC 34**
See also CA 119; CANR 44

Kleist, Heinrich von
1777-1811 .... **NCLC 2, 37;**
DAM DRAM; SSC 22
See also DLB 90

Klima, Ivan 1931-..... **CLC 56; DAM NOV**
See also CA 25-28R; CANR 17, 50

Klimentov, Andrei Platonovich 1899-1951
See Platonov, Andrei
See also CA 108

Klinger, Friedrich Maximilian von
1752-1831 .... **NCLC 1**
See also DLB 94

Klopstock, Friedrich Gottlieb
1724-1803 .... **NCLC 11**
See also DLB 97

Knebel, Fletcher 1911-1993........ **CLC 14**
See also AITN 1; CA 1-4R; 140; CAAS 3;
CANR 1, 36; SATA 36; SATA-Obit 75

Knickerbocker, Diedrich
See Irving, Washington

Knight, Etheridge
1931-1991 .... **CLC 40; BLC;**
DAM POET; PC 14
See also BW 1; CA 21-24R; 133; CANR 23;
DLB 41

Knight, Sarah Kemble 1666-1727 ..... **LC 7**
See also DLB 24

Knister, Raymond 1899-1932...... **TCLC 56**
See also DLB 68

Knowles, John
1926-...... **CLC 1, 4, 10, 26; DA; DAC;**
DAM MST, NOV
See also AAYA 10; CA 17-20R; CANR 40;
CDALB 1968-1988; DLB 6; MTCW;
SATA 8, 89

Knox, Calvin M.
See Silverberg, Robert

Knye, Cassandra
See Disch, Thomas M(ichael)

Koch, C(hristopher) J(ohn) 1932- ... **CLC 42**
See also CA 127

Koch, Christopher
See Koch, C(hristopher) J(ohn)

Koch, Kenneth
1925-....... **CLC 5, 8, 44; DAM POET**
See also CA 1-4R; CANR 6, 36; DLB 5;
INT CANR-36; SATA 65

Kochanowski, Jan 1530-1584........ **LC 10**

Kock, Charles Paul de
1794-1871 .... **NCLC 16**

Koda Shigeyuki 1867-1947
See Rohan, Koda
See also CA 121

Koestler, Arthur
1905-1983 .... **CLC 1, 3, 6, 8, 15, 33**
See also CA 1-4R; 109; CANR 1, 33;
CDBLB 1945-1960; DLBY 83; MTCW

Kogawa, Joy Nozomi
1935- ...... **CLC 78; DAC; DAM MST,**
MULT
See also CA 101; CANR 19

Kohout, Pavel 1928-.............. **CLC 13**
See also CA 45-48; CANR 3

Koizumi, Yakumo
See Hearn, (Patricio) Lafcadio (Tessima
Carlos)

Kolmar, Gertrud 1894-1943....... **TCLC 40**

Komunyakaa, Yusef 1947-...... **CLC 86, 94**
See also CA 147; DLB 120

Konrad, George
See Konrad, Gyoergy

Konrad, Gyoergy 1933- ...... **CLC 4, 10, 73**
See also CA 85-88

Konwicki, Tadeusz 1926-..... **CLC 8, 28, 54**
See also CA 101; CAAS 9; CANR 39;
MTCW

Koontz, Dean R(ay)
1945- ...... **CLC 78; DAM NOV, POP**
See also AAYA 9; BEST 89:3, 90:2;
CA 108; CANR 19, 36, 52; MTCW

Kopit, Arthur (Lee)
1937- ...... **CLC 1, 18, 33; DAM DRAM**
See also AITN 1; CA 81-84; CABS 3;
DLB 7; MTCW

Kops, Bernard 1926-.............. **CLC 4**
See also CA 5-8R; DLB 13

Kornbluth, C(yril) M. 1923-1958.... **TCLC 8**
See also CA 105; DLB 8

Korolenko, V. G.
See Korolenko, Vladimir Galaktionovich

Korolenko, Vladimir
See Korolenko, Vladimir Galaktionovich

L'Amour, Louis (Dearborn)
1908-1988 .... **CLC 25, 55; DAM NOV,**
POP
See also AAYA 16; AITN 2; BEST 89:2;
CA 1-4R; 125; CANR 3, 25, 40;
DLBY 80; MTCW

Lampedusa, Giuseppe (Tomasi) di ... **TCLC 13**
See also Tomasi di Lampedusa, Giuseppe

Lampman, Archibald 1861-1899 .. **NCLC 25**
See also DLB 92

Lancaster, Bruce 1896-1963........ **CLC 36**
See also CA 9-10; CAP 1; SATA 9

Landau, Mark Alexandrovich
See Aldanov, Mark (Alexandrovich)

Landau-Aldanov, Mark Alexandrovich
See Aldanov, Mark (Alexandrovich)

Landis, Jerry
See Simon, Paul (Frederick)

Landis, John 1950-............... **CLC 26**
See also CA 112; 122

Landolfi, Tommaso 1908-1979... **CLC 11, 49**
See also CA 127; 117

Landon, Letitia Elizabeth
1802-1838 .... **NCLC 15**
See also DLB 96

Landor, Walter Savage
1775-1864 .... **NCLC 14**
See also DLB 93, 107

Landwirth, Heinz 1927-
See Lind, Jakov
See also CA 9-12R; CANR 7

Lane, Patrick
1939- .... **CLC 25; DAM POET**
See also CA 97-100; CANR 54; DLB 53;
INT 97-100

Lang, Andrew 1844-1912........ **TCLC 16**
See also CA 114; 137; DLB 98, 141;
MAICYA; SATA 16

Lang, Fritz 1890-1976 .... **CLC 20**
See also CA 77-80; 69-72; CANR 30

Lange, John
See Crichton, (John) Michael

Langer, Elinor 1939- .... **CLC 34**
See also CA 121

Langland, William
1330(?)-1400(?) ...... **LC 19; DA; DAB;**
DAC; DAM MST, POET
See also DLB 146

Langstaff, Launcelot
See Irving, Washington

Lanier, Sidney
1842-1881 ...... **NCLC 6; DAM POET**
See also DLB 64; DLBD 13; MAICYA;
SATA 18

Lanyer, Aemilia 1569-1645 ..... **LC 10, 30**
See also DLB 121

Lao Tzu .... **CMLC 7**

Lapine, James (Elliot) 1949-....... **CLC 39**
See also CA 123; 130; CANR 54; INT 130

Larbaud, Valery (Nicolas)
1881-1957 .... **TCLC 9**
See also CA 106; 152

Lardner, Ring
See Lardner, Ring(gold) W(ilmer)

Lardner, Ring W., Jr.
See Lardner, Ring(gold) W(ilmer)

Lardner, Ring(gold) W(ilmer)
1885-1933 .... **TCLC 2, 14**
See also CA 104; 131; CDALB 1917-1929;
DLB 11, 25, 86; MTCW

Laredo, Betty
See Codrescu, Andrei

Larkin, Maia
See Wojciechowska, Maia (Teresa)

Larkin, Philip (Arthur)
1922-1985 .... **CLC 3, 5, 8, 9, 13, 18, 33,**
39, 64; DAB; DAM MST, POET
See also CA 5-8R; 117; CANR 24;
CDBLB 1960 to Present; DLB 27;
MTCW

Larra (y Sanchez de Castro), Mariano Jose de
1809-1837 .... **NCLC 17**

Larsen, Eric 1941- .... **CLC 55**
See also CA 132

Larsen, Nella
1891-1964 .... **CLC 37; BLC;**
DAM MULT
See also BW 1; CA 125; DLB 51

Larson, Charles R(aymond) 1938-... **CLC 31**
See also CA 53-56; CANR 4

Las Casas, Bartolome de 1474-1566.. **LC 31**

Lasker-Schueler, Else 1869-1945 .. **TCLC 57**
See also DLB 66, 124

Latham, Jean Lee 1902-........... **CLC 12**
See also AITN 1; CA 5-8R; CANR 7;
MAICYA; SATA 2, 68

Latham, Mavis
See Clark, Mavis Thorpe

Lathen, Emma................... **CLC 2**
See also Hennissart, Martha; Latsis, Mary
J(ane)

Lathrop, Francis
See Leiber, Fritz (Reuter, Jr.)

Latsis, Mary J(ane)
See Lathen, Emma
See also CA 85-88

Lattimore, Richmond (Alexander)
1906-1984 .... **CLC 3**
See also CA 1-4R; 112; CANR 1

Laughlin, James 1914-............ **CLC 49**
See also CA 21-24R; CAAS 22; CANR 9,
47; DLB 48

Laurence, (Jean) Margaret (Wemyss)
1926-1987 .... **CLC 3, 6, 13, 50, 62;**
DAC; DAM MST; SSC 7
See also CA 5-8R; 121; CANR 33; DLB 53;
MTCW; SATA-Obit 50

Laurent, Antoine 1952- .... **CLC 50**

Lauscher, Hermann
See Hesse, Hermann

Lautreamont, Comte de
1846-1870 .... **NCLC 12; SSC 14**

Laverty, Donald
See Blish, James (Benjamin)

Lavin, Mary 1912-1996 .. **CLC 4, 18; SSC 4**
See also CA 9-12R; 151; CANR 33;
DLB 15; MTCW

Lavond, Paul Dennis
See Kornbluth, C(yril) M.; Pohl, Frederik

Lawler, Raymond Evenor 1922- .... **CLC 58**
See also CA 103

Lawrence, D(avid) H(erbert Richards)
1885-1930 .... **TCLC 2, 9, 16, 33, 48, 61;**
DA; DAB; DAC; DAM MST, NOV,
POET; SSC 4, 19; WLC
See also CA 104; 121; CDBLB 1914-1945;
DLB 10, 19, 36, 98, 162; MTCW

Lawrence, T(homas) E(dward)
1888-1935 .... **TCLC 18**
See also Dale, Colin
See also CA 115

Lawrence of Arabia
See Lawrence, T(homas) E(dward)

Lawson, Henry (Archibald Hertzberg)
1867-1922 .... **TCLC 27; SSC 18**
See also CA 120

Lawton, Dennis
See Faust, Frederick (Schiller)

Laxness, Halldor................... **CLC 25**
See also Gudjonsson, Halldor Kiljan

Layamon fl. c. 1200-............ **CMLC 10**
See also DLB 146

Laye, Camara
1928-1980 .... **CLC 4, 38; BLC;**
DAM MULT
See also BW 1; CA 85-88; 97-100;
CANR 25; MTCW

Layton, Irving (Peter)
1912- .... **CLC 2, 15; DAC; DAM MST,**
POET
See also CA 1-4R; CANR 2, 33, 43;
DLB 88; MTCW

Lazarus, Emma 1849-1887........ **NCLC 8**

Lazarus, Felix
See Cable, George Washington

Lazarus, Henry
See Slavitt, David R(ytman)

Lea, Joan
See Neufeld, John (Arthur)

Leacock, Stephen (Butler)
1869-1944 .. **TCLC 2; DAC; DAM MST**
See also CA 104; 141; DLB 92

Lear, Edward 1812-1888 .... **NCLC 3**
See also CLR 1; DLB 32, 163, 166;
MAICYA; SATA 18

Lear, Norman (Milton) 1922- ...... **CLC 12**
See also CA 73-76

Leavis, F(rank) R(aymond)
1895-1978 .... **CLC 24**
See also CA 21-24R; 77-80; CANR 44;
MTCW

Leavitt, David 1961-... **CLC 34; DAM POP**
See also CA 116; 122; CANR 50; DLB 130;
INT 122

Leblanc, Maurice (Marie Emile)
1864-1941 .... **TCLC 49**
See also CA 110

Lebowitz, Fran(ces Ann)
1951(?)-................. **CLC 11, 36**
See also CA 81-84; CANR 14;
INT CANR-14; MTCW

Leverson, Ada   1865(?)-1936(?) .... **TCLC 18**
See also Elaine
See also CA 117; DLB 153

Levertov, Denise
  1923- ...... **CLC 1, 2, 3, 5, 8, 15, 28, 66;**
                DAM POET; PC 11
See also CA 1-4R; CAAS 19; CANR 3, 29,
50; DLB 5, 165; INT CANR-29; MTCW

Levi, Jonathan.................. **CLC 76**

Levi, Peter (Chad Tigar)   1931- ..... **CLC 41**
See also CA 5-8R; CANR 34; DLB 40

Levi, Primo
  1919-1987 .... **CLC 37, 50; SSC 12**
See also CA 13-16R; 122; CANR 12, 33;
MTCW

Levin, Ira   1929- ..... **CLC 3, 6; DAM POP**
See also CA 21-24R; CANR 17, 44;
MTCW; SATA 66

Levin, Meyer
  1905-1981 .... **CLC 7; DAM POP**
See also AITN 1; CA 9-12R; 104;
CANR 15; DLB 9, 28; DLBY 81;
SATA 21; SATA-Obit 27

Levine, Norman   1924- .... **CLC 54**
See also CA 73-76; CAAS 23; CANR 14;
DLB 88

Levine, Philip
  1928- .... **CLC 2, 4, 5, 9, 14, 33;**
                 DAM POET
See also CA 9-12R; CANR 9, 37, 52;
DLB 5

Levinson, Deirdre   1931-........... **CLC 49**
See also CA 73-76

Levi-Strauss, Claude   1908- .... **CLC 38**
See also CA 1-4R; CANR 6, 32; MTCW

Levitin, Sonia (Wolff)   1934- .... **CLC 17**
See also AAYA 13; CA 29-32R; CANR 14,
32; JRDA; MAICYA; SAAS 2; SATA 4,
68

Levon, O. U.
See Kesey, Ken (Elton)

Levy, Amy   1861-1889........... **NCLC 59**
See also DLB 156

Lewes, George Henry
  1817-1878 .... **NCLC 25**
See also DLB 55, 144

Lewis, Alun   1915-1944........... **TCLC 3**
See also CA 104; DLB 20, 162

Lewis, C. Day
See Day Lewis, C(ecil)

Lewis, C(live) S(taples)
  1898-1963 ..... **CLC 1, 3, 6, 14, 27; DA;**
            DAB; DAC; DAM MST, NOV, POP;
                                   WLC
See also AAYA 3; CA 81-84; CANR 33;
CDBLB 1945-1960; CLR 3, 27; DLB 15,
100, 160; JRDA; MAICYA; MTCW;
SATA 13

Lewis, Janet   1899-............... **CLC 41**
See also Winters, Janet Lewis
See also CA 9-12R; CANR 29; CAP 1;
DLBY 87

Lewis, Matthew Gregory
  1775-1818 .... **NCLC 11**
See also DLB 39, 158

Lewis, (Harry) Sinclair
  1885-1951 ..... **TCLC 4, 13, 23, 39; DA;**
          DAB; DAC; DAM MST, NOV; WLC
See also CA 104; 133; CDALB 1917-1929;
DLB 9, 102; DLBD 1; MTCW

Lewis, (Percy) Wyndham
  1884(?)-1957 .... **TCLC 2, 9**
See also CA 104; DLB 15

Lewisohn, Ludwig   1883-1955...... **TCLC 19**
See also CA 107; DLB 4, 9, 28, 102

Leyner, Mark   1956-.............. **CLC 92**
See also CA 110; CANR 28, 53

Lezama Lima, Jose
  1910-1976 .... **CLC 4, 10; DAM MULT**
See also CA 77-80; DLB 113; HW

L'Heureux, John (Clarke)   1934-.... **CLC 52**
See also CA 13-16R; CANR 23, 45

Liddell, C. H.
See Kuttner, Henry

Lie, Jonas (Lauritz Idemil)
  1833-1908(?) .... **TCLC 5**
See also CA 115

Lieber, Joel   1937-1971............ **CLC 6**
See also CA 73-76; 29-32R

Lieber, Stanley Martin
See Lee, Stan

Lieberman, Laurence (James)
  1935-..................... **CLC 4, 36**
See also CA 17-20R; CANR 8, 36

Lieksman, Anders
See Haavikko, Paavo Juhani

Li Fei-kan   1904-
See Pa Chin
See also CA 105

Lifton, Robert Jay   1926-.......... **CLC 67**
See also CA 17-20R; CANR 27;
INT CANR-27; SATA 66

Lightfoot, Gordon   1938-.......... **CLC 26**
See also CA 109

Lightman, Alan P.   1948- .... **CLC 81**
See also CA 141

Ligotti, Thomas (Robert)
  1953- .... **CLC 44; SSC 16**
See also CA 123; CANR 49

Li Ho   791-817.................... **PC 13**

Liliencron, (Friedrich Adolf Axel) Detlev von
  1844-1909 .... **TCLC 18**
See also CA 117

Lilly, William   1602-1681.......... **LC 27**

Lima, Jose Lezama
See Lezama Lima, Jose

Lima Barreto, Afonso Henrique de
  1881-1922 .... **TCLC 23**
See also CA 117

Limonov, Edward   1944-.......... **CLC 67**
See also CA 137

Lin, Frank
See Atherton, Gertrude (Franklin Horn)

Lincoln, Abraham   1809-1865..... **NCLC 18**

Lind, Jakov .... **CLC 1, 2, 4, 27, 82**
See also Landwirth, Heinz
See also CAAS 4

Lindbergh, Anne (Spencer) Morrow
  1906- .... **CLC 82; DAM NOV**
See also CA 17-20R; CANR 16; MTCW;
SATA 33

Lindsay, David   1878-1945 .... **TCLC 15**
See also CA 113

Lindsay, (Nicholas) Vachel
  1879-1931 .... **TCLC 17; DA; DAC;**
                DAM MST, POET; WLC
See also CA 114; 135; CDALB 1865-1917;
DLB 54; SATA 40

Linke-Poot
See Doeblin, Alfred

Linney, Romulus   1930- .... **CLC 51**
See also CA 1-4R; CANR 40, 44

Linton, Eliza Lynn   1822-1898.... **NCLC 41**
See also DLB 18

Li Po   701-763................. **CMLC 2**

Lipsius, Justus   1547-1606 .... **LC 16**

Lipsyte, Robert (Michael)
  1938-............. **CLC 21; DA; DAC;**
                     DAM MST, NOV
See also AAYA 7; CA 17-20R; CANR 8;
CLR 23; JRDA; MAICYA; SATA 5, 68

Lish, Gordon (Jay)   1934-.. **CLC 45; SSC 18**
See also CA 113; 117; DLB 130; INT 117

Lispector, Clarice   1925-1977....... **CLC 43**
See also CA 139; 116; DLB 113

Littell, Robert   1935(?)- .... **CLC 42**
See also CA 109; 112

Little, Malcolm   1925-1965
See Malcolm X
See also BW 1; CA 125; 111; DA; DAB;
DAC; DAM MST, MULT; MTCW

Littlewit, Humphrey Gent.
See Lovecraft, H(oward) P(hillips)

Litwos
See Sienkiewicz, Henryk (Adam Alexander
Pius)

Liu E   1857-1909................ **TCLC 15**
See also CA 115

Lively, Penelope (Margaret)
  1933- .... **CLC 32, 50; DAM NOV**
See also CA 41-44R; CANR 29; CLR 7;
DLB 14, 161; JRDA; MAICYA; MTCW;
SATA 7, 60

Livesay, Dorothy (Kathleen)
  1909- .... **CLC 4, 15, 79; DAC;**
                DAM MST, POET
See also AITN 2; CA 25-28R; CAAS 8;
CANR 36; DLB 68; MTCW

Livy   c. 59B.C.-c. 17 .... **CMLC 11**

Lizardi, Jose Joaquin Fernandez de
  1776-1827 .... **NCLC 30**

Llewellyn, Richard
See Llewellyn Lloyd, Richard Dafydd
Vivian
See also DLB 15

Llewellyn Lloyd, Richard Dafydd Vivian
  1906-1983 .... **CLC 7, 80**
See also Llewellyn, Richard
See also CA 53-56; 111; CANR 7;
SATA 11; SATA-Obit 37

Llosa, (Jorge) Mario (Pedro) Vargas
See Vargas Llosa, (Jorge) Mario (Pedro)

Lloyd Webber, Andrew 1948-
See Webber, Andrew Lloyd
See also AAYA 1; CA 116; 149;
DAM DRAM; SATA 56

Llull, Ramon c. 1235-c. 1316 . . . . . **CMLC 12**

Locke, Alain (Le Roy)
1886-1954 . . . . **TCLC 43**
See also BW 1; CA 106; 124; DLB 51

Locke, John 1632-1704 . . . . **LC 7, 35**
See also DLB 101

Locke-Elliott, Sumner
See Elliott, Sumner Locke

Lockhart, John Gibson
1794-1854 . . . . **NCLC 6**
See also DLB 110, 116, 144

Lodge, David (John)
1935- . . . . **CLC 36; DAM POP**
See also BEST 90:1; CA 17-20R; CANR 19,
53; DLB 14; INT CANR-19; MTCW

Loennbohm, Armas Eino Leopold 1878-1926
See Leino, Eino
See also CA 123

Loewinsohn, Ron(ald William)
1937- . . . . **CLC 52**
See also CA 25-28R

Logan, Jake
See Smith, Martin Cruz

Logan, John (Burton) 1923-1987 . . . . . **CLC 5**
See also CA 77-80; 124; CANR 45; DLB 5

Lo Kuan-chung 1330(?)-1400(?) . . . . . . **LC 12**

Lombard, Nap
See Johnson, Pamela Hansford

London, Jack . . **TCLC 9, 15, 39; SSC 4; WLC**
See also London, John Griffith
See also AAYA 13; AITN 2;
CDALB 1865-1917; DLB 8, 12, 78;
SATA 18

London, John Griffith 1876-1916
See London, Jack
See also CA 110; 119; DA; DAB; DAC;
DAM MST, NOV; JRDA; MAICYA;
MTCW

Long, Emmett
See Leonard, Elmore (John, Jr.)

Longbaugh, Harry
See Goldman, William (W.)

Longfellow, Henry Wadsworth
1807-1882 . . . . . **NCLC 2, 45; DA; DAB;
DAC; DAM MST, POET**
See also CDALB 1640-1865; DLB 1, 59;
SATA 19

Longley, Michael 1939- . . . . **CLC 29**
See also CA 102; DLB 40

Longus fl. c. 2nd cent. - . . . . **CMLC 7**

Longway, A. Hugh
See Lang, Andrew

Lonnrot, Elias 1802-1884 . . . . **NCLC 53**

Lopate, Phillip 1943- . . . . **CLC 29**
See also CA 97-100; DLBY 80; INT 97-100

Lopez Portillo (y Pacheco), Jose
1920- . . . . **CLC 46**
See also CA 129; HW

Lopez y Fuentes, Gregorio
1897(?)-1966 . . . . **CLC 32**
See also CA 131; HW

Lorca, Federico Garcia
See Garcia Lorca, Federico

Lord, Bette Bao 1938- . . . . **CLC 23**
See also BEST 90:3; CA 107; CANR 41;
INT 107; SATA 58

Lord Auch
See Bataille, Georges

Lord Byron
See Byron, George Gordon (Noel)

Lorde, Audre (Geraldine)
1934-1992 . . . . **CLC 18, 71; BLC;
DAM MULT, POET; PC 12**
See also BW 1; CA 25-28R; 142; CANR 16,
26, 46; DLB 41; MTCW

Lord Jeffrey
See Jeffrey, Francis

Lorenzini, Carlo 1826-1890
See Collodi, Carlo
See also MAICYA; SATA 29

Lorenzo, Heberto Padilla
See Padilla (Lorenzo), Heberto

Loris
See Hofmannsthal, Hugo von

Loti, Pierre . . . . **TCLC 11**
See also Viaud, (Louis Marie) Julien
See also DLB 123

Louie, David Wong 1954- . . . . **CLC 70**
See also CA 139

Louis, Father M.
See Merton, Thomas

Lovecraft, H(oward) P(hillips)
1890-1937 . . . . **TCLC 4, 22; DAM POP;
SSC 3**
See also AAYA 14; CA 104; 133; MTCW

Lovelace, Earl 1935- . . . . **CLC 51**
See also BW 2; CA 77-80; CANR 41;
DLB 125; MTCW

Lovelace, Richard 1618-1657 . . . . **LC 24**
See also DLB 131

Lowell, Amy
1874-1925 . . . . **TCLC 1, 8; DAM POET;
PC 13**
See also CA 104; 151; DLB 54, 140

Lowell, James Russell 1819-1891 . . **NCLC 2**
See also CDALB 1640-1865; DLB 1, 11, 64,
79

Lowell, Robert (Traill Spence, Jr.)
1917-1977 . . . **CLC 1, 2, 3, 4, 5, 8, 9, 11,
15, 37; DA; DAB; DAC; DAM MST,
NOV; PC 3; WLC**
See also CA 9-12R; 73-76; CABS 2;
CANR 26; DLB 5, 169; MTCW

Lowndes, Marie Adelaide (Belloc)
1868-1947 . . . . **TCLC 12**
See also CA 107; DLB 70

Lowry, (Clarence) Malcolm
1909-1957 . . . . **TCLC 6, 40**
See also CA 105; 131; CDBLB 1945-1960;
DLB 15; MTCW

Lowry, Mina Gertrude 1882-1966
See Loy, Mina
See also CA 113

Loxsmith, John
See Brunner, John (Kilian Houston)

Loy, Mina . . . . **CLC 28; DAM POET; PC 16**
See also Lowry, Mina Gertrude
See also DLB 4, 54

Loyson-Bridet
See Schwob, (Mayer Andre) Marcel

Lucas, Craig 1951 . . . . **CLC 64**
See also CA 137

Lucas, George 1944- . . . . **CLC 16**
See also AAYA 1; CA 77-80; CANR 30;
SATA 56

Lucas, Hans
See Godard, Jean-Luc

Lucas, Victoria
See Plath, Sylvia

Ludlam, Charles 1943-1987 . . . . . **CLC 46, 50**
See also CA 85-88; 122

Ludlum, Robert
1927- . . . **CLC 22, 43; DAM NOV, POP**
See also AAYA 10; BEST 89:1, 90:3;
CA 33-36R; CANR 25, 41; DLBY 82;
MTCW

Ludwig, Ken . . . . **CLC 60**

Ludwig, Otto 1813-1865 . . . . **NCLC 4**
See also DLB 129

Lugones, Leopoldo 1874-1938 . . . . . **TCLC 15**
See also CA 116; 131; HW

Lu Hsun 1881-1936 . . . . . . **TCLC 3; SSC 20**
See also Shu-Jen, Chou

Lukacs, George . . . . **CLC 24**
See also Lukacs, Gyorgy (Szegeny von)

Lukacs, Gyorgy (Szegeny von) 1885-1971
See Lukacs, George
See also CA 101; 29-32R

Luke, Peter (Ambrose Cyprian)
1919-1995 . . . . **CLC 38**
See also CA 81-84; 147; DLB 13

Lunar, Dennis
See Mungo, Raymond

Lurie, Alison 1926- . . . . **CLC 4, 5, 18, 39**
See also CA 1-4R; CANR 2, 17, 50; DLB 2;
MTCW; SATA 46

Lustig, Arnost 1926- . . . . **CLC 56**
See also AAYA 3; CA 69-72; CANR 47;
SATA 56

Luther, Martin 1483-1546 . . . . **LC 9**

Luxemburg, Rosa 1870(?)-1919 . . . . **TCLC 63**
See also CA 118

Luzi, Mario 1914- . . . . **CLC 13**
See also CA 61-64; CANR 9; DLB 128

L'Ymagier
See Gourmont, Remy (-Marie-Charles) de

Lynch, B. Suarez
See Bioy Casares, Adolfo; Borges, Jorge
Luis

Lynch, David (K.) 1946- . . . . **CLC 66**
See also CA 124; 129

Lynch, James
See Andreyev, Leonid (Nikolaevich)

Lynch Davis, B.
See Bioy Casares, Adolfo; Borges, Jorge
Luis

Lyndsay, Sir David   1490-1555 ..... LC 20

Lynn, Kenneth S(chuyler)   1923- .... CLC 50
    See also CA 1-4R; CANR 3, 27

Lynx
    See West, Rebecca

Lyons, Marcus
    See Blish, James (Benjamin)

Lyre, Pinchbeck
    See Sassoon, Siegfried (Lorraine)

Lytle, Andrew (Nelson)   1902-1995 .. CLC 22
    See also CA 9-12R; 150; DLB 6; DLBY 95

Lyttelton, George   1709-1773 .... LC 10

Maas, Peter   1929- .... CLC 29
    See also CA 93-96; INT 93-96

Macaulay, Rose   1881-1958 ..... TCLC 7, 44
    See also CA 104; DLB 36

Macaulay, Thomas Babington
    1800-1859 .... NCLC 42
    See also CDBLB 1832-1890; DLB 32, 55

MacBeth, George (Mann)
    1932-1992 .... CLC 2, 5, 9
    See also CA 25-28R; 136; DLB 40; MTCW;
    SATA 4; SATA-Obit 70

MacCaig, Norman (Alexander)
    1910- ..... CLC 36; DAB; DAM POET
    See also CA 9-12R; CANR 3, 34; DLB 27

MacCarthy, (Sir Charles Otto) Desmond
    1877-1952 .... TCLC 36

MacDiarmid, Hugh
    .... CLC 2, 4, 11, 19, 63; PC 9
    See also Grieve, C(hristopher) M(urray)
    See also CDBLB 1945-1960; DLB 20

MacDonald, Anson
    See Heinlein, Robert A(nson)

Macdonald, Cynthia   1928- ...... CLC 13, 19
    See also CA 49-52; CANR 4, 44; DLB 105

MacDonald, George   1824-1905 ..... TCLC 9
    See also CA 106; 137; DLB 18, 163;
    MAICYA; SATA 33

Macdonald, John
    See Millar, Kenneth

MacDonald, John D(ann)
    1916-1986 .... CLC 3, 27, 44;
                        DAM NOV, POP
    See also CA 1-4R; 121; CANR 1, 19;
    DLB 8; DLBY 86; MTCW

Macdonald, John Ross
    See Millar, Kenneth

Macdonald, Ross ..... CLC 1, 2, 3, 14, 34, 41
    See also Millar, Kenneth
    See also DLBD 6

MacDougal, John
    See Blish, James (Benjamin)

MacEwen, Gwendolyn (Margaret)
    1941-1987 .... CLC 13, 55
    See also CA 9-12R; 124; CANR 7, 22;
    DLB 53; SATA 50; SATA-Obit 55

Macha, Karel Hynek   1810-1846 .. NCLC 46

Machado (y Ruiz), Antonio
    1875-1939 .... TCLC 3
    See also CA 104; DLB 108

Machado de Assis, Joaquim Maria
    1839-1908 ..... TCLC 10; BLC; SSC 24
    See also CA 107; 153

Machen, Arthur .... TCLC 4; SSC 20
    See also Jones, Arthur Llewellyn
    See also DLB 36, 156

Machiavelli, Niccolo
    1469-1527 .... LC 8, 36; DA; DAB;
                        DAC; DAM MST

MacInnes, Colin   1914-1976 ...... CLC 4, 23
    See also CA 69-72; 65-68; CANR 21;
    DLB 14; MTCW

MacInnes, Helen (Clark)
    1907-1985 ..... CLC 27, 39; DAM POP
    See also CA 1-4R; 117; CANR 1, 28;
    DLB 87; MTCW; SATA 22;
    SATA-Obit 44

Mackay, Mary   1855-1924
    See Corelli, Marie
    See also CA 118

Mackenzie, Compton (Edward Montague)
    1883-1972 .... CLC 18
    See also CA 21-22; 37-40R; CAP 2;
    DLB 34, 100

Mackenzie, Henry   1745-1831 .... NCLC 41
    See also DLB 39

Mackintosh, Elizabeth   1896(?)-1952
    See Tey, Josephine
    See also CA 110

MacLaren, James
    See Grieve, C(hristopher) M(urray)

Mac Laverty, Bernard   1942- .... CLC 31
    See also CA 116; 118; CANR 43; INT 118

MacLean, Alistair (Stuart)
    1922-1987 .... CLC 3, 13, 50, 63;
                        DAM POP
    See also CA 57-60; 121; CANR 28; MTCW;
    SATA 23; SATA-Obit 50

Maclean, Norman (Fitzroy)
    1902-1990 .... CLC 78; DAM POP;
                        SSC 13
    See also CA 102; 132; CANR 49

MacLeish, Archibald
    1892-1982 .... CLC 3, 8, 14, 68;
                        DAM POET
    See also CA 9-12R; 106; CANR 33; DLB 4,
    7, 45; DLBY 82; MTCW

MacLennan, (John) Hugh
    1907-1990 .... CLC 2, 14, 92; DAC;
                        DAM MST
    See also CA 5-8R; 142; CANR 33; DLB 68;
    MTCW

MacLeod, Alistair
    1936- ...... CLC 56; DAC; DAM MST
    See also CA 123; DLB 60

MacNeice, (Frederick) Louis
    1907-1963 ...... CLC 1, 4, 10, 53; DAB;
                        DAM POET
    See also CA 85-88; DLB 10, 20; MTCW

MacNeill, Dand
    See Fraser, George MacDonald

Macpherson, James   1736-1796 ...... LC 29
    See also DLB 109

Macpherson, (Jean) Jay   1931- ...... CLC 14
    See also CA 5-8R; DLB 53

MacShane, Frank   1927- .... CLC 39
    See also CA 9-12R; CANR 3, 33; DLB 111

Macumber, Mari
    See Sandoz, Mari(e Susette)

Madach, Imre   1823-1864 .... NCLC 19

Madden, (Jerry) David   1933- .... CLC 5, 15
    See also CA 1-4R; CAAS 3; CANR 4, 45;
    DLB 6; MTCW

Maddern, Al(an)
    See Ellison, Harlan (Jay)

Madhubuti, Haki R.
    1942- .... CLC 6, 73; BLC;
                        DAM MULT, POET; PC 5
    See also Lee, Don L.
    See also BW 2; CA 73-76; CANR 24, 51;
    DLB 5, 41; DLBD 8

Maepenn, Hugh
    See Kuttner, Henry

Maepenn, K. H.
    See Kuttner, Henry

Maeterlinck, Maurice
    1862-1949 ...... TCLC 3; DAM DRAM
    See also CA 104; 136; SATA 66

Maginn, William   1794-1842 .... NCLC 8
    See also DLB 110, 159

Mahapatra, Jayanta
    1928- .... CLC 33; DAM MULT
    See also CA 73-76; CAAS 9; CANR 15, 33

Mahfouz, Naguib (Abdel Aziz Al-Sabilgi)
    1911(?)-
    See Mahfuz, Najib
    See also BEST 89:2; CA 128; CANR 55;
    DAM NOV; MTCW

Mahfuz, Najib .... CLC 52, 55
    See also Mahfouz, Naguib (Abdel Aziz
    Al-Sabilgi)
    See also DLBY 88

Mahon, Derek   1941- .... CLC 27
    See also CA 113; 128; DLB 40

Mailer, Norman
    1923- ...... CLC 1, 2, 3, 4, 5, 8, 11, 14,
    28, 39, 74; DA; DAB; DAC; DAM MST,
                        NOV, POP
    See also AITN 2; CA 9-12R; CABS 1;
    CANR 28; CDALB 1968-1988; DLB 2,
    16, 28; DLBD 3; DLBY 80, 83; MTCW

Maillet, Antonine   1929- ...... CLC 54; DAC
    See also CA 115; 120; CANR 46; DLB 60;
    INT 120

Mais, Roger   1905-1955 .... TCLC 8
    See also BW 1; CA 105; 124; DLB 125;
    MTCW

Maistre, Joseph de   1753-1821 .... NCLC 37

Maitland, Frederic   1850-1906 ..... TCLC 65

Maitland, Sara (Louise)   1950- ...... CLC 49
    See also CA 69-72; CANR 13

Major, Clarence
    1936- .... CLC 3, 19, 48; BLC;
                        DAM MULT
    See also BW 2; CA 21-24R; CAAS 6;
    CANR 13, 25, 53; DLB 33

Major, Kevin (Gerald)
    1949- .... CLC 26; DAC
    See also AAYA 16; CA 97-100; CANR 21,
    38; CLR 11; DLB 60; INT CANR-21;
    JRDA; MAICYA; SATA 32, 82

Maki, James
    See Ozu, Yasujiro

Meltzer, Milton 1915- . . . . **CLC 26**
See also AAYA 8; CA 13-16R; CANR 38;
CLR 13; DLB 61; JRDA; MAICYA;
SAAS 1; SATA 1, 50, 80

Melville, Herman
1819-1891 . . . . . NCLC 3, 12, 29, 45, 49;
DA; DAB; DAC; DAM MST, NOV;
SSC 1, 17; WLC
See also CDALB 1640-1865; DLB 3, 74;
SATA 59

Menander
c. 342B.C.-c. 292B.C. . . . . CMLC 9;
DAM DRAM; DC 3

Mencken, H(enry) L(ouis)
1880-1956 . . . . TCLC 13
See also CA 105; 125; CDALB 1917-1929;
DLB 11, 29, 63, 137; MTCW

Mercer, David
1928-1980 . . . . CLC 5; DAM DRAM
See also CA 9-12R; 102; CANR 23;
DLB 13; MTCW

Merchant, Paul
See Ellison, Harlan (Jay)

Meredith, George
1828-1909 . . TCLC 17, 43; DAM POET
See also CA 117; 153; CDBLB 1832-1890;
DLB 18, 35, 57, 159

Meredith, William (Morris)
1919- . . CLC 4, 13, 22, 55; DAM POET
See also CA 9-12R; CAAS 14; CANR 6, 40;
DLB 5

Merezhkovsky, Dmitry Sergeyevich
1865-1941 . . . . TCLC 29

Merimee, Prosper
1803-1870 . . . . NCLC 6; SSC 7
See also DLB 119

Merkin, Daphne 1954- . . . . **CLC 44**
See also CA 123

Merlin, Arthur
See Blish, James (Benjamin)

Merrill, James (Ingram)
1926-1995 . . . . CLC 2, 3, 6, 8, 13, 18, 34,
91; DAM POET
See also CA 13-16R; 147; CANR 10, 49;
DLB 5, 165; DLBY 85; INT CANR-10;
MTCW

Merriman, Alex
See Silverberg, Robert

Merritt, E. B.
See Waddington, Miriam

Merton, Thomas
1915-1968 . . CLC 1, 3, 11, 34, 83; PC 10
See also CA 5-8R; 25-28R; CANR 22, 53;
DLB 48; DLBY 81; MTCW

Merwin, W(illiam) S(tanley)
1927- . . . . . . CLC 1, 2, 3, 5, 8, 13, 18, 45,
88; DAM POET
See also CA 13-16R; CANR 15, 51; DLB 5,
169; INT CANR-15; MTCW

Metcalf, John 1938- . . . . **CLC 37**
See also CA 113; DLB 60

Metcalf, Suzanne
See Baum, L(yman) Frank

Mew, Charlotte (Mary)
1870-1928 . . . . TCLC 8
See also CA 105; DLB 19, 135

Mewshaw, Michael 1943- . . . . **CLC 9**
See also CA 53-56; CANR 7, 47; DLBY 80

Meyer, June
See Jordan, June

Meyer, Lynn
See Slavitt, David R(ytman)

Meyer-Meyrink, Gustav 1868-1932
See Meyrink, Gustav
See also CA 117

Meyers, Jeffrey 1939- . . . . **CLC 39**
See also CA 73-76; CANR 54; DLB 111

Meynell, Alice (Christina Gertrude Thompson)
1847-1922 . . . . TCLC 6
See also CA 104; DLB 19, 98

Meyrink, Gustav . . . . TCLC 21
See also Meyer-Meyrink, Gustav
See also DLB 81

Michaels, Leonard
1933- . . . . CLC 6, 25; SSC 16
See also CA 61-64; CANR 21; DLB 130;
MTCW

Michaux, Henri 1899-1984 . . . . . . CLC 8, 19
See also CA 85-88; 114

Michelangelo 1475-1564 . . . . **LC 12**

Michelet, Jules 1798-1874 . . . . . . **NCLC 31**

Michener, James A(lbert)
1907(?)- . . . . CLC 1, 5, 11, 29, 60;
DAM NOV, POP
See also AITN 1; BEST 90:1; CA 5-8R;
CANR 21, 45; DLB 6; MTCW

Mickiewicz, Adam 1798-1855 . . . . . **NCLC 3**

Middleton, Christopher 1926- . . . . . . **CLC 13**
See also CA 13-16R; CANR 29, 54;
DLB 40

Middleton, Richard (Barham)
1882-1911 . . . . TCLC 56
See also DLB 156

Middleton, Stanley 1919- . . . . CLC 7, 38
See also CA 25-28R; CAAS 23; CANR 21,
46; DLB 14

Middleton, Thomas
1580-1627 . . . . . . LC 33; DAM DRAM,
MST; DC 5
See also DLB 58

Migueis, Jose Rodrigues 1901- . . . . . **CLC 10**

Mikszath, Kalman 1847-1910 . . . . . **TCLC 31**

Miles, Josephine (Louise)
1911-1985 . . . . CLC 1, 2, 14, 34, 39;
DAM POET
See also CA 1-4R; 116; CANR 2, 55;
DLB 48

Militant
See Sandburg, Carl (August)

Mill, John Stuart 1806-1873 . . NCLC 11, 58
See also CDBLB 1832-1890; DLB 55

Millar, Kenneth
1915-1983 . . . . CLC 14; DAM POP
See also Macdonald, Ross
See also CA 9-12R; 110; CANR 16; DLB 2;
DLBD 6; DLBY 83; MTCW

Millay, E. Vincent
See Millay, Edna St. Vincent

Millay, Edna St. Vincent
1892-1950 . . . . . . TCLC 4, 49; DA; DAB;
DAC; DAM MST, POET; PC 6
See also CA 104; 130; CDALB 1917-1929;
DLB 45; MTCW

Miller, Arthur
1915- . . . . CLC 1, 2, 6, 10, 15, 26, 47, 78;
DA; DAB; DAC; DAM DRAM, MST;
DC 1; WLC
See also AAYA 15; AITN 1; CA 1-4R;
CABS 3; CANR 2, 30, 54;
CDALB 1941-1968; DLB 7; MTCW

Miller, Henry (Valentine)
1891-1980 . . . . CLC 1, 2, 4, 9, 14, 43, 84;
DA; DAB; DAC; DAM MST, NOV;
WLC
See also CA 9-12R; 97-100; CANR 33;
CDALB 1929-1941; DLB 4, 9; DLBY 80;
MTCW

Miller, Jason 1939(?)- . . . . **CLC 2**
See also AITN 1; CA 73-76; DLB 7

Miller, Sue 1943- . . . . . CLC 44; DAM POP
See also BEST 90:3; CA 139; DLB 143

Miller, Walter M(ichael, Jr.)
1923- . . . . CLC 4, 30
See also CA 85-88; DLB 8

Millett, Kate 1934- . . . . **CLC 67**
See also AITN 1; CA 73-76; CANR 32, 53;
MTCW

Millhauser, Steven 1943- . . . . CLC 21, 54
See also CA 110; 111; DLB 2; INT 111

Millin, Sarah Gertrude 1889-1968 . . **CLC 49**
See also CA 102; 93-96

Milne, A(lan) A(lexander)
1882-1956 . . . . TCLC 6; DAB; DAC;
DAM MST
See also CA 104; 133; CLR 1, 26; DLB 10,
77, 100, 160; MAICYA; MTCW;
YABC 1

Milner, Ron(ald)
1938- . . . . . CLC 56; BLC; DAM MULT
See also AITN 1; BW 1; CA 73-76;
CANR 24; DLB 38; MTCW

Milosz, Czeslaw
1911- . . . . CLC 5, 11, 22, 31, 56, 82;
DAM MST, POET; PC 8
See also CA 81-84; CANR 23, 51; MTCW

Milton, John
1608-1674 . . . . . . LC 9; DA; DAB; DAC;
DAM MST, POET; WLC
See also CDBLB 1660-1789; DLB 131, 151

Min, Anchee 1957- . . . . **CLC 86**
See also CA 146

Minehaha, Cornelius
See Wedekind, (Benjamin) Frank(lin)

Miner, Valerie 1947- . . . . **CLC 40**
See also CA 97-100

Minimo, Duca
See D'Annunzio, Gabriele

Minot, Susan 1956- . . . . **CLC 44**
See also CA 134

Minus, Ed 1938- . . . . **CLC 39**

Miranda, Javier
See Bioy Casares, Adolfo

Mirbeau, Octave 1848-1917 . . . . . . **TCLC 55**
See also DLB 123

Morgan, Seth   1949(?)-1990 . . . . **CLC 65**
See also CA 132

Morgenstern, Christian
1871-1914 . . . . **TCLC 8**
See also CA 105

Morgenstern, S.
See Goldman, William (W.)

Moricz, Zsigmond   1879-1942 . . . . . **TCLC 33**

Morike, Eduard (Friedrich)
1804-1875 . . . . **NCLC 10**
See also DLB 133

Mori Ogai . . . . **TCLC 14**
See also Mori Rintaro

Mori Rintaro   1862-1922
See Mori Ogai
See also CA 110

Moritz, Karl Philipp   1756-1793 . . . . . . **LC 2**
See also DLB 94

Morland, Peter Henry
See Faust, Frederick (Schiller)

Morren, Theophil
See Hofmannsthal, Hugo von

Morris, Bill   1952-. . . . . **CLC 76**

Morris, Julian
See West, Morris L(anglo)

Morris, Steveland Judkins   1950(?)-
See Wonder, Stevie
See also CA 111

Morris, William   1834-1896 . . . . **NCLC 4**
See also CDBLB 1832-1890; DLB 18, 35,
57, 156

Morris, Wright   1910-. . . **CLC 1, 3, 7, 18, 37**
See also CA 9-12R; CANR 21; DLB 2;
DLBY 81; MTCW

Morrison, Chloe Anthony Wofford
See Morrison, Toni

Morrison, James Douglas   1943-1971
See Morrison, Jim
See also CA 73-76; CANR 40

Morrison, Jim . . . . **CLC 17**
See also Morrison, James Douglas

Morrison, Toni
1931- . . . . . **CLC 4, 10, 22, 55, 81, 87;**
BLC; DA; DAB; DAC; DAM MST,
MULT, NOV, POP
See also AAYA 1; BW 2; CA 29-32R;
CANR 27, 42; CDALB 1968-1988;
DLB 6, 33, 143; DLBY 81; MTCW;
SATA 57

Morrison, Van   1945- . . . . **CLC 21**
See also CA 116

Mortimer, John (Clifford)
1923- . . . . . . **CLC 28, 43; DAM DRAM,**
POP
See also CA 13-16R; CANR 21;
CDBLB 1960 to Present; DLB 13;
INT CANR-21; MTCW

Mortimer, Penelope (Ruth)   1918-. . . . **CLC 5**
See also CA 57-60; CANR 45

Morton, Anthony
See Creasey, John

Mosher, Howard Frank   1943-. . . . . . **CLC 62**
See also CA 139

Mosley, Nicholas   1923-. . . . . **CLC 43, 70**
See also CA 69-72; CANR 41; DLB 14

Mosley, Walter
1952- . . . . . **CLC 97; DAM MULT, POP**
See also AAYA 17; BW 2; CA 142

Moss, Howard
1922-1987 . . . . **CLC 7, 14, 45, 50;**
DAM POET
See also CA 1-4R; 123; CANR 1, 44;
DLB 5

Mossgiel, Rab
See Burns, Robert

Motion, Andrew (Peter)   1952-. . . . . . **CLC 47**
See also CA 146; DLB 40

Motley, Willard (Francis)
1909-1965 . . . . **CLC 18**
See also BW 1; CA 117; 106; DLB 76, 143

Motoori, Norinaga   1730-1801 . . . . **NCLC 45**

Mott, Michael (Charles Alston)
1930- . . . . **CLC 15, 34**
See also CA 5-8R; CAAS 7; CANR 7, 29

Mountain Wolf Woman
1884-1960 . . . . **CLC 92**
See also CA 144; NNAL

Moure, Erin   1955- . . . . **CLC 88**
See also CA 113; DLB 60

Mowat, Farley (McGill)
1921- . . . . . . **CLC 26; DAC; DAM MST**
See also AAYA 1; CA 1-4R; CANR 4, 24,
42; CLR 20; DLB 68; INT CANR-24;
JRDA; MAICYA; MTCW; SATA 3, 55

Moyers, Bill   1934- . . . . **CLC 74**
See also AITN 2; CA 61-64; CANR 31, 52

Mphahlele, Es'kia
See Mphahlele, Ezekiel
See also DLB 125

Mphahlele, Ezekiel
1919- . . . . . **CLC 25; BLC; DAM MULT**
See also Mphahlele, Es'kia
See also BW 2; CA 81-84; CANR 26

Mqhayi, S(amuel) E(dward) K(rune Loliwe)
1875-1945 . . . . **TCLC 25; BLC;**
DAM MULT
See also CA 153

Mrozek, Slawomir   1930-. . . . . **CLC 3, 13**
See also CA 13-16R; CAAS 10; CANR 29;
MTCW

Mrs. Belloc-Lowndes
See Lowndes, Marie Adelaide (Belloc)

Mtwa, Percy   (?)-. . . . . **CLC 47**

Mueller, Lisel   1924-. . . . . **CLC 13, 51**
See also CA 93-96; DLB 105

Muir, Edwin   1887-1959 . . . . **TCLC 2**
See also CA 104; DLB 20, 100

Muir, John   1838-1914 . . . . **TCLC 28**

Mujica Lainez, Manuel
1910-1984 . . . . **CLC 31**
See also Lainez, Manuel Mujica
See also CA 81-84; 112; CANR 32; HW

Mukherjee, Bharati
1940- . . . . **CLC 53; DAM NOV**
See also BEST 89:2; CA 107; CANR 45;
DLB 60; MTCW

Muldoon, Paul
1951- . . . . **CLC 32, 72; DAM POET**
See also CA 113; 129; CANR 52; DLB 40;
INT 129

Mulisch, Harry   1927-. . . . . **CLC 42**
See also CA 9-12R; CANR 6, 26

Mull, Martin   1943-. . . . . **CLC 17**
See also CA 105

Mulock, Dinah Maria
See Craik, Dinah Maria (Mulock)

Munford, Robert   1737(?)-1783 . . . . **LC 5**
See also DLB 31

Mungo, Raymond   1946-. . . . . **CLC 72**
See also CA 49-52; CANR 2

Munro, Alice
1931- . . . . . . **CLC 6, 10, 19, 50, 95; DAC;**
DAM MST, NOV; SSC 3
See also AITN 2; CA 33-36R; CANR 33,
53; DLB 53; MTCW; SATA 29

Munro, H(ector) H(ugh)   1870-1916
See Saki
See also CA 104; 130; CDBLB 1890-1914;
DA; DAB; DAC; DAM MST, NOV;
DLB 34, 162; MTCW; WLC

Murasaki, Lady. . . . . **CMLC 1**

Murdoch, (Jean) Iris
1919- . . . . . . **CLC 1, 2, 3, 4, 6, 8, 11, 15,**
22, 31, 51; DAB; DAC; DAM MST,
NOV
See also CA 13-16R; CANR 8, 43;
CDBLB 1960 to Present; DLB 14;
INT CANR-8; MTCW

Murfree, Mary Noailles
1850-1922 . . . . **SSC 22**
See also CA 122; DLB 12, 74

Murnau, Friedrich Wilhelm
See Plumpe, Friedrich Wilhelm

Murphy, Richard   1927- . . . . **CLC 41**
See also CA 29-32R; DLB 40

Murphy, Sylvia   1937-. . . . . **CLC 34**
See also CA 121

Murphy, Thomas (Bernard)   1935-. . . **CLC 51**
See also CA 101

Murray, Albert L.   1916- . . . . **CLC 73**
See also BW 2; CA 49-52; CANR 26, 52;
DLB 38

Murray, Les(lie) A(llan)
1938- . . . . **CLC 40; DAM POET**
See also CA 21-24R; CANR 11, 27

Murry, J. Middleton
See Murry, John Middleton

Murry, John Middleton
1889-1957 . . . . **TCLC 16**
See also CA 118; DLB 149

Musgrave, Susan   1951- . . . . **CLC 13, 54**
See also CA 69-72; CANR 45

Musil, Robert (Edler von)
1880-1942 . . . . **TCLC 12, 68; SSC 18**
See also CA 109; CANR 55; DLB 81, 124

Muske, Carol   1945- . . . . **CLC 90**
See also Muske-Dukes, Carol (Anne)

Muske-Dukes, Carol (Anne)   1945-
See Muske, Carol
See also CA 65-68; CANR 32

Pereda y Porrua, Jose Maria de
See Pereda (y Sanchez de Porrua), Jose
Maria de

Peregoy, George Weems
See Mencken, H(enry) L(ouis)

Perelman, S(idney) J(oseph)
1904-1979 ..... CLC 3, 5, 9, 15, 23, 44,
49; DAM DRAM
See also AITN 1, 2; CA 73-76; 89-92;
CANR 18; DLB 11, 44; MTCW

Peret, Benjamin 1899-1959 ...... TCLC 20
See also CA 117

Peretz, Isaac Loeb 1851(?)-1915 ... TCLC 16
See also CA 109

Peretz, Yitzkhok Leibush
See Peretz, Isaac Loeb

Perez Galdos, Benito 1843-1920 ... TCLC 27
See also CA 125; 153; HW

Perrault, Charles 1628-1703 .... LC 2
See also MAICYA; SATA 25

Perry, Brighton
See Sherwood, Robert E(mmet)

Perse, St.-John .... CLC 4, 11, 46
See also Leger, (Marie-Rene Auguste) Alexis
Saint-Leger

Perutz, Leo 1882-1957 .... TCLC 60
See also DLB 81

Peseenz, Tulio F.
See Lopez y Fuentes, Gregorio

Pesetsky, Bette 1932- .... CLC 28
See also CA 133; DLB 130

Peshkov, Alexei Maximovich 1868-1936
See Gorky, Maxim
See also CA 105; 141; DA; DAC;
DAM DRAM, MST, NOV

Pessoa, Fernando (Antonio Nogueira)
1888-1935 .... TCLC 27; HLC
See also CA 125

Peterkin, Julia Mood 1880-1961 .... CLC 31
See also CA 102; DLB 9

Peters, Joan K. 1945- .... CLC 39

Peters, Robert L(ouis) 1924- .... CLC 7
See also CA 13-16R; CAAS 8; DLB 105

Petofi, Sandor 1823-1849 .... NCLC 21

Petrakis, Harry Mark 1923- .... CLC 3
See also CA 9-12R; CANR 4, 30

Petrarch
1304-1374 .... CMLC 20; DAM POET;
PC 8

Petrov, Evgeny .... TCLC 21
See also Kataev, Evgeny Petrovich

Petry, Ann (Lane) 1908- ...... CLC 1, 7, 18
See also BW 1; CA 5-8R; CAAS 6;
CANR 4, 46; CLR 12; DLB 76; JRDA;
MAICYA; MTCW; SATA 5

Petursson, Halligrimur 1614-1674 .... LC 8

Philips, Katherine 1632-1664 .... LC 30
See also DLB 131

Philipson, Morris H. 1926- .... CLC 53
See also CA 1-4R; CANR 4

Phillips, Caryl
1958- .... CLC 96; DAM MULT
See also BW 2; CA 141; DLB 157

Phillips, David Graham
1867-1911 .... TCLC 44
See also CA 108; DLB 9, 12

Phillips, Jack
See Sandburg, Carl (August)

Phillips, Jayne Anne
1952- .... CLC 15, 33; SSC 16
See also CA 101; CANR 24, 50; DLBY 80;
INT CANR-24; MTCW

Phillips, Richard
See Dick, Philip K(indred)

Phillips, Robert (Schaeffer) 1938-... CLC 28
See also CA 17-20R; CAAS 13; CANR 8;
DLB 105

Phillips, Ward
See Lovecraft, H(oward) P(hillips)

Piccolo, Lucio 1901-1969 .... CLC 13
See also CA 97-100; DLB 114

Pickthall, Marjorie L(owry) C(hristie)
1883-1922 .... TCLC 21
See also CA 107; DLB 92

Pico della Mirandola, Giovanni
1463-1494 .... LC 15

Piercy, Marge
1936- .... CLC 3, 6, 14, 18, 27, 62
See also CA 21-24R; CAAS 1; CANR 13,
43; DLB 120; MTCW

Piers, Robert
See Anthony, Piers

Pieyre de Mandiargues, Andre 1909-1991
See Mandiargues, Andre Pieyre de
See also CA 103; 136; CANR 22

Pilnyak, Boris .... TCLC 23
See also Vogau, Boris Andreyevich

Pincherle, Alberto
1907-1990 ..... CLC 11, 18; DAM NOV
See also Moravia, Alberto
See also CA 25-28R; 132; CANR 33;
MTCW

Pinckney, Darryl 1953- .... CLC 76
See also BW 2; CA 143

Pindar 518B.C.-446B.C. .... CMLC 12

Pineda, Cecile 1942- .... CLC 39
See also CA 118

Pinero, Arthur Wing
1855-1934 ..... TCLC 32; DAM DRAM
See also CA 110; 153; DLB 10

Pinero, Miguel (Antonio Gomez)
1946-1988 .... CLC 4, 55
See also CA 61-64; 125; CANR 29; HW

Pinget, Robert 1919- .... CLC 7, 13, 37
See also CA 85-88; DLB 83

Pink Floyd
See Barrett, (Roger) Syd; Gilmour, David;
Mason, Nick; Waters, Roger; Wright,
Rick

Pinkney, Edward 1802-1828 ..... NCLC 31

Pinkwater, Daniel Manus 1941- .... CLC 35
See also Pinkwater, Manus
See also AAYA 1; CA 29-32R; CANR 12,
38; CLR 4; JRDA; MAICYA; SAAS 3;
SATA 46, 76

Pinkwater, Manus
See Pinkwater, Daniel Manus
See also SATA 8

Pinsky, Robert
1940- .. CLC 9, 19, 38, 94; DAM POET
See also CA 29-32R; CAAS 4; DLBY 82

Pinta, Harold
See Pinter, Harold

Pinter, Harold
1930 ..... CLC 1, 3, 6, 9, 11, 15, 27, 58,
73; DA; DAB; DAC; DAM DRAM,
MST; WLC
See also CA 5-8R; CANR 33; CDBLB 1960
to Present; DLB 13; MTCW

Piozzi, Hester Lynch (Thrale)
1741-1821 .... NCLC 57
See also DLB 104, 142

Pirandello, Luigi
1867-1936 ...... TCLC 4, 29; DA; DAB;
DAC; DAM DRAM, MST; DC 5;
SSC 22; WLC
See also CA 104; 153

Pirsig, Robert M(aynard)
1928- .... CLC 4, 6, 73; DAM POP
See also CA 53-56; CANR 42; MTCW;
SATA 39

Pisarev, Dmitry Ivanovich
1840-1868 .... NCLC 25

Pix, Mary (Griffith) 1666-1709 ...... LC 8
See also DLB 80

Pixerecourt, Guilbert de
1773-1844 .... NCLC 39

Plaidy, Jean
See Hibbert, Eleanor Alice Burford

Planche, James Robinson
1796-1880 .... NCLC 42

Plant, Robert 1948- .... CLC 12

Plante, David (Robert)
1940- .... CLC 7, 23, 38; DAM NOV
See also CA 37-40R; CANR 12, 36;
DLBY 83; INT CANR-12; MTCW

Plath, Sylvia
1932-1963 ..... CLC 1, 2, 3, 5, 9, 11, 14,
17, 50, 51, 62; DA; DAB; DAC;
DAM MST, POET; PC 1; WLC
See also AAYA 13; CA 19-20; CANR 34;
CAP 2; CDALB 1941-1968; DLB 5, 6,
152; MTCW

Plato
428(?)B.C.-348(?)B.C..... CMLC 8; DA;
DAB; DAC; DAM MST

Platonov, Andrei .... TCLC 14
See also Klimentov, Andrei Platonovich

Platt, Kin 1911- .... CLC 26
See also AAYA 11; CA 17-20R; CANR 11;
JRDA; SAAS 17; SATA 21, 86

Plautus c. 251B.C.-184B.C. .... DC 6

Plick et Plock
See Simenon, Georges (Jacques Christian)

Plimpton, George (Ames) 1927-..... CLC 36
See also AITN 1; CA 21-24R; CANR 32;
MTCW; SATA 10

Plomer, William Charles Franklin
1903-1973 .... CLC 4, 8
See also CA 21-22; CANR 34; CAP 2;
DLB 20, 162; MTCW; SATA 24

Plowman, Piers
See Kavanagh, Patrick (Joseph)

Plum, J.
See Wodehouse, P(elham) G(renville)

Plumly, Stanley (Ross) 1939- ...... CLC 33
See also CA 108; 110; DLB 5; INT 110

Plumpe, Friedrich Wilhelm
1888-1931 .... TCLC 53
See also CA 112

Poe, Edgar Allan
1809-1849 .... NCLC 1, 16, 55; DA;
DAB; DAC; DAM MST, POET; PC 1;
SSC 1, 22; WLC
See also AAYA 14; CDALB 1640-1865;
DLB 3, 59, 73, 74; SATA 23

Poet of Titchfield Street, The
See Pound, Ezra (Weston Loomis)

Pohl, Frederik 1919- .... CLC 18
See also CA 61-64; CAAS 1; CANR 11, 37;
DLB 8; INT CANR-11; MTCW;
SATA 24

Poirier, Louis 1910-
See Gracq, Julien
See also CA 122; 126

Poitier, Sidney 1927-............. CLC 26
See also BW 1; CA 117

Polanski, Roman 1933- .... CLC 16
See also CA 77-80

Poliakoff, Stephen 1952- .... CLC 38
See also CA 106; DLB 13

Police, The
See Copeland, Stewart (Armstrong);
Summers, Andrew James; Sumner,
Gordon Matthew

Polidori, John William
1795-1821 .... NCLC 51
See also DLB 116

Pollitt, Katha 1949- .... CLC 28
See also CA 120; 122; MTCW

Pollock, (Mary) Sharon
1936- .... CLC 50; DAC; DAM DRAM,
MST
See also CA 141; DLB 60

Polo, Marco 1254-1324 .... CMLC 15

Polonsky, Abraham (Lincoln)
1910- .... CLC 92
See also CA 104; DLB 26; INT 104

Polybius c. 200B.C.-c. 118B.C. .... CMLC 17

Pomerance, Bernard
1940- .... CLC 13; DAM DRAM
See also CA 101; CANR 49

Ponge, Francis (Jean Gaston Alfred)
1899-1988 ..... CLC 6, 18; DAM POET
See also CA 85-88; 126; CANR 40

Pontoppidan, Henrik 1857-1943 ... TCLC 29

Poole, Josephine .... CLC 17
See also Helyar, Jane Penelope Josephine
See also SAAS 2; SATA 5

Popa, Vasko 1922-1991 .... CLC 19
See also CA 112; 148

Pope, Alexander
1688-1744 ...... LC 3; DA; DAB; DAC;
DAM MST, POET; WLC
See also CDBLB 1660-1789; DLB 95, 101

Porter, Connie (Rose) 1959(?)- ..... CLC 70
See also BW 2; CA 142; SATA 81

Porter, Gene(va Grace) Stratton
1863(?)-1924 .... TCLC 21
See also CA 112

Porter, Katherine Anne
1890-1980 ...... CLC 1, 3, 7, 10, 13, 15,
27; DA; DAB; DAC; DAM MST, NOV;
SSC 4
See also AITN 2; CA 1-4R; 101; CANR 1;
DLB 4, 9, 102; DLBD 12; DLBY 80;
MTCW; SATA 39; SATA-Obit 23

Porter, Peter (Neville Frederick)
1929- .... CLC 5, 13, 33
See also CA 85-88; DLB 40

Porter, William Sydney 1862-1910
See Henry, O.
See also CA 104; 131; CDALB 1865-1917;
DA; DAB; DAC; DAM MST; DLB 12,
78, 79; MTCW; YABC 2

Portillo (y Pacheco), Jose Lopez
See Lopez Portillo (y Pacheco), Jose

Post, Melville Davisson
1869-1930 .... TCLC 39
See also CA 110

Potok, Chaim
1929- .... CLC 2, 7, 14, 26; DAM NOV
See also AAYA 15; AITN 1, 2; CA 17-20R;
CANR 19, 35; DLB 28, 152;
INT CANR-19; MTCW; SATA 33

Potter, Beatrice
See Webb, (Martha) Beatrice (Potter)
See also MAICYA

Potter, Dennis (Christopher George)
1935-1994 .... CLC 58, 86
See also CA 107; 145; CANR 33; MTCW

Pound, Ezra (Weston Loomis)
1885-1972 ...... CLC 1, 2, 3, 4, 5, 7, 10,
13, 18, 34, 48, 50; DA; DAB; DAC;
DAM MST, POET; PC 4; WLC
See also CA 5-8R; 37-40R; CANR 40;
CDALB 1917-1929; DLB 4, 45, 63;
MTCW

Povod, Reinaldo 1959-1994 .... CLC 44
See also CA 136; 146

Powell, Adam Clayton, Jr.
1908-1972 .... CLC 89; BLC;
DAM MULT
See also BW 1; CA 102; 33-36R

Powell, Anthony (Dymoke)
1905- .... CLC 1, 3, 7, 9, 10, 31
See also CA 1-4R; CANR 1, 32;
CDBLB 1945-1960; DLB 15; MTCW

Powell, Dawn 1897-1965 .... CLC 66
See also CA 5-8R

Powell, Padgett 1952-............. CLC 34
See also CA 126

Power, Susan..................... CLC 91

Powers, J(ames) F(arl)
1917- .... CLC 1, 4, 8, 57; SSC 4
See also CA 1-4R; CANR 2; DLB 130;
MTCW

Powers, John J(ames) 1945-
See Powers, John R.
See also CA 69-72

Powers, John R. .... CLC 66
See also Powers, John J(ames)

Powers, Richard (S.) 1957- .... CLC 93
See also CA 148

Pownall, David 1938-............. CLC 10
See also CA 89-92; CAAS 18; CANR 49;
DLB 14

Powys, John Cowper
1872-1963 .... CLC 7, 9, 15, 46
See also CA 85-88; DLB 15; MTCW

Powys, T(heodore) F(rancis)
1875-1953 .... TCLC 9
See also CA 106; DLB 36, 162

Prager, Emily 1952-.............. CLC 56

Pratt, E(dwin) J(ohn)
1883(?)-1964 .... CLC 19; DAC;
DAM POET
See also CA 141; 93-96; DLB 92

Premchand...................... TCLC 21
See also Srivastava, Dhanpat Rai

Preussler, Otfried 1923-.......... CLC 17
See also CA 77-80; SATA 24

Prevert, Jacques (Henri Marie)
1900-1977 .... CLC 15
See also CA 77-80; 69-72; CANR 29;
MTCW; SATA-Obit 30

Prevost, Abbe (Antoine Francois)
1697-1763 .... LC 1

Price, (Edward) Reynolds
1933- .... CLC 3, 6, 13, 43, 50, 63;
DAM NOV; SSC 22
See also CA 1-4R; CANR 1, 37; DLB 2;
INT CANR-37

Price, Richard 1949- .... CLC 6, 12
See also CA 49-52; CANR 3; DLBY 81

Prichard, Katharine Susannah
1883-1969 .... CLC 46
See also CA 11-12; CANR 33; CAP 1;
MTCW; SATA 66

Priestley, J(ohn) B(oynton)
1894-1984 .... CLC 2, 5, 9, 34;
DAM DRAM, NOV
See also CA 9-12R; 113; CANR 33;
CDBLB 1914-1945; DLB 10, 34, 77, 100,
139; DLBY 84; MTCW

Prince 1958(?)-.................. CLC 35

Prince, F(rank) T(empleton) 1912- .. CLC 22
See also CA 101; CANR 43; DLB 20

Prince Kropotkin
See Kropotkin, Peter (Aleksieevich)

Prior, Matthew 1664-1721........... LC 4
See also DLB 95

Pritchard, William H(arrison)
1932- .... CLC 34
See also CA 65-68; CANR 23; DLB 111

Pritchett, V(ictor) S(awdon)
1900- .... CLC 5, 13, 15, 41;
DAM NOV; SSC 14
See also CA 61-64; CANR 31; DLB 15,
139; MTCW

Private 19022
See Manning, Frederic

Probst, Mark 1925- .... CLC 59
See also CA 130

Prokosch, Frederic 1908-1989 .... CLC 4, 48
See also CA 73-76; 128; DLB 48

Ransom, John Crowe
1888-1974 . . . . **CLC 2, 4, 5, 11, 24;**
DAM POET
See also CA 5-8R; 49-52; CANR 6, 34;
DLB 45, 63; MTCW

Rao, Raja 1909- . . . **CLC 25, 56; DAM NOV**
See also CA 73-76; CANR 51; MTCW

Raphael, Frederic (Michael)
1931- . . . . **CLC 2, 14**
See also CA 1-4R; CANR 1; DLB 14

Ratcliffe, James P.
See Mencken, H(enry) L(ouis)

Rathbone, Julian 1935- . . . . **CLC 41**
See also CA 101; CANR 34

Rattigan, Terence (Mervyn)
1911-1977 . . . . **CLC 7; DAM DRAM**
See also CA 85-88; 73-76;
CDBLB 1945-1960; DLB 13; MTCW

Ratushinskaya, Irina 1954- . . . . **CLC 54**
See also CA 129

Raven, Simon (Arthur Noel)
1927- . . . . **CLC 14**
See also CA 81-84

Rawley, Callman 1903-
See Rakosi, Carl
See also CA 21-24R; CANR 12, 32

Rawlings, Marjorie Kinnan
1896-1953 . . . . **TCLC 4**
See also CA 104; 137; DLB 9, 22, 102;
JRDA; MAICYA; YABC 1

Ray, Satyajit
1921-1992 . . . **CLC 16, 76; DAM MULT**
See also CA 114; 137

Read, Herbert Edward 1893-1968 . . . . **CLC 4**
See also CA 85-88; 25-28R; DLB 20, 149

Read, Piers Paul 1941- . . . . . . **CLC 4, 10, 25**
See also CA 21-24R; CANR 38; DLB 14;
SATA 21

Reade, Charles 1814-1884 . . . . **NCLC 2**
See also DLB 21

Reade, Hamish
See Gray, Simon (James Holliday)

Reading, Peter 1946- . . . . **CLC 47**
See also CA 103; CANR 46; DLB 40

Reaney, James
1926- . . . . . . **CLC 13; DAC; DAM MST**
See also CA 41-44R; CAAS 15; CANR 42;
DLB 68; SATA 43

Rebreanu, Liviu 1885-1944 . . . . . . **TCLC 28**

Rechy, John (Francisco)
1934- . . . . **CLC 1, 7, 14, 18;**
DAM MULT; HLC
See also CA 5-8R; CAAS 4; CANR 6, 32;
DLB 122; DLBY 82; HW; INT CANR-6

Redcam, Tom 1870-1933 . . . . **TCLC 25**

Reddin, Keith . . . . **CLC 67**

Redgrove, Peter (William)
1932- . . . . **CLC 6, 41**
See also CA 1-4R; CANR 3, 39; DLB 40

Redmon, Anne . . . . **CLC 22**
See also Nightingale, Anne Redmon
See also DLBY 86

Reed, Eliot
See Ambler, Eric

Reed, Ishmael
1938- . . . . **CLC 2, 3, 5, 6, 13, 32, 60;**
BLC; DAM MULT
See also BW 2; CA 21-24R; CANR 25, 48;
DLB 2, 5, 33, 169; DLBD 8; MTCW

Reed, John (Silas) 1887-1920 . . . . . . **TCLC 9**
See also CA 106

Reed, Lou . . . . **CLC 21**
See also Firbank, Louis

Reeve, Clara 1729-1807 . . . . **NCLC 19**
See also DLB 39

Reich, Wilhelm 1897-1957 . . . . **TCLC 57**

Reid, Christopher (John) 1949- . . . . . **CLC 33**
See also CA 140; DLB 40

Reid, Desmond
See Moorcock, Michael (John)

Reid Banks, Lynne 1929-
See Banks, Lynne Reid
See also CA 1-4R; CANR 6, 22, 38;
CLR 24; JRDA; MAICYA; SATA 22, 75

Reilly, William K.
See Creasey, John

Reiner, Max
See Caldwell, (Janet Miriam) Taylor
(Holland)

Reis, Ricardo
See Pessoa, Fernando (Antonio Nogueira)

Remarque, Erich Maria
1898-1970 . . . . **CLC 21; DA; DAB; DAC;**
DAM MST, NOV
See also CA 77-80; 29-32R; DLB 56;
MTCW

Remizov, A.
See Remizov, Aleksei (Mikhailovich)

Remizov, A. M.
See Remizov, Aleksei (Mikhailovich)

Remizov, Aleksei (Mikhailovich)
1877-1957 . . . . **TCLC 27**
See also CA 125; 133

Renan, Joseph Ernest
1823-1892 . . . . **NCLC 26**

Renard, Jules 1864-1910 . . . . **TCLC 17**
See also CA 117

Renault, Mary . . . . **CLC 3, 11, 17**
See also Challans, Mary
See also DLBY 83

Rendell, Ruth (Barbara)
1930- . . . . **CLC 28, 48; DAM POP**
See also Vine, Barbara
See also CA 109; CANR 32, 52; DLB 87;
INT CANR-32; MTCW

Renoir, Jean 1894-1979 . . . . **CLC 20**
See also CA 129; 85-88

Resnais, Alain 1922- . . . . **CLC 16**

Reverdy, Pierre 1889-1960 . . . . **CLC 53**
See also CA 97-100; 89-92

Rexroth, Kenneth
1905-1982 . . . . . . **CLC 1, 2, 6, 11, 22, 49;**
DAM POET
See also CA 5-8R; 107; CANR 14, 34;
CDALB 1941-1968; DLB 16, 48, 165;
DLBY 82; INT CANR-14; MTCW

Reyes, Alfonso 1889-1959 . . . . **TCLC 33**
See also CA 131; HW

Reyes y Basoalto, Ricardo Eliecer Neftali
See Neruda, Pablo

Reymont, Wladyslaw (Stanislaw)
1868(?)-1925 . . . . **TCLC 5**
See also CA 104

Reynolds, Jonathan 1942- . . . . **CLC 6, 38**
See also CA 65-68; CANR 28

Reynolds, Joshua 1723-1792 . . . . **LC 15**
See also DLB 104

Reynolds, Michael Shane 1937- . . . . **CLC 44**
See also CA 65-68; CANR 9

Reznikoff, Charles 1894-1976 . . . . **CLC 9**
See also CA 33-36; 61-64; CAP 2; DLB 28,
45

Rezzori (d'Arezzo), Gregor von
1914- . . . . **CLC 25**
See also CA 122; 136

Rhine, Richard
See Silverstein, Alvin

Rhodes, Eugene Manlove
1869-1934 . . . . **TCLC 53**

R'hoone
See Balzac, Honore de

Rhys, Jean
1890(?)-1979 . . . . **CLC 2, 4, 6, 14, 19, 51;**
DAM NOV; SSC 21
See also CA 25-28R; 85-88; CANR 35;
CDBLB 1945-1960; DLB 36, 117, 162;
MTCW

Ribeiro, Darcy 1922- . . . . **CLC 34**
See also CA 33-36R

Ribeiro, Joao Ubaldo (Osorio Pimentel)
1941- . . . . **CLC 10, 67**
See also CA 81-84

Ribman, Ronald (Burt) 1932- . . . . **CLC 7**
See also CA 21-24R; CANR 46

Ricci, Nino 1959- . . . . **CLC 70**
See also CA 137

Rice, Anne 1941- . . . . . **CLC 41; DAM POP**
See also AAYA 9; BEST 89:2; CA 65-68;
CANR 12, 36, 53

Rice, Elmer (Leopold)
1892-1967 . . . . **CLC 7, 49; DAM DRAM**
See also CA 21-22; 25-28R; CAP 2; DLB 4,
7; MTCW

Rice, Tim(othy Miles Bindon)
1944- . . . . **CLC 21**
See also CA 103; CANR 46

Rich, Adrienne (Cecile)
1929- . . . . **CLC 3, 6, 7, 11, 18, 36, 73, 76;**
DAM POET; PC 5
See also CA 9-12R; CANR 20, 53; DLB 5,
67; MTCW

Rich, Barbara
See Graves, Robert (von Ranke)

Rich, Robert
See Trumbo, Dalton

Richard, Keith . . . . **CLC 17**
See also Richards, Keith

Richards, David Adams
1950- . . . . **CLC 59; DAC**
See also CA 93-96; DLB 53

Rohmer, Eric . . . . CLC 16
    See also Scherer, Jean-Marie Maurice

Rohmer, Sax . . . . TCLC 28
    See also Ward, Arthur Henry Sarsfield
    See also DLB 70

Roiphe, Anne (Richardson)
    1935- . . . . CLC 3, 9
    See also CA 89-92; CANR 45; DLBY 80;
    INT 89-92

Rojas, Fernando de 1465-1541 . . . . . . LC 23

Rolfe, Frederick (William Serafino Austin
    Lewis Mary) 1860-1913. . . . . . TCLC 12
    See also CA 107; DLB 34, 156

Rolland, Romain 1866-1944. . . . . . . TCLC 23
    See also CA 118; DLB 65

Rolvaag, O(le) E(dvart)
    See Roelvaag, O(le) E(dvart)

Romain Arnaud, Saint
    See Aragon, Louis

Romains, Jules 1885-1972 . . . . CLC 7
    See also CA 85-88; CANR 34; DLB 65;
    MTCW

Romero, Jose Ruben 1890-1952 . . . TCLC 14
    See also CA 114; 131; HW

Ronsard, Pierre de
    1524-1585 . . . . LC 6; PC 11

Rooke, Leon
    1934- . . . . CLC 25, 34; DAM POP
    See also CA 25-28R; CANR 23, 53

Roper, William 1498-1578. . . . . LC 10

Roquelaure, A. N.
    See Rice, Anne

Rosa, Joao Guimaraes 1908-1967 . . . CLC 23
    See also CA 89-92; DLB 113

Rose, Wendy
    1948- . . . . CLC 85; DAM MULT; PC 13
    See also CA 53-56; CANR 5, 51; NNAL;
    SATA 12

Rosen, Richard (Dean) 1949- . . . . CLC 39
    See also CA 77-80; INT CANR-30

Rosenberg, Isaac 1890-1918. . . . . . . TCLC 12
    See also CA 107; DLB 20

Rosenblatt, Joe . . . . CLC 15
    See also Rosenblatt, Joseph

Rosenblatt, Joseph 1933-
    See Rosenblatt, Joe
    See also CA 89-92; INT 89-92

Rosenfeld, Samuel 1896-1963
    See Tzara, Tristan
    See also CA 89-92

Rosenstock, Sami
    See Tzara, Tristan

Rosenstock, Samuel
    See Tzara, Tristan

Rosenthal, M(acha) L(ouis)
    1917-1996 . . . . CLC 28
    See also CA 1-4R; 152; CAAS 6; CANR 4,
    51; DLB 5; SATA 59

Ross, Barnaby
    See Dannay, Frederic

Ross, Bernard L.
    See Follett, Ken(neth Martin)

Ross, J. H.
    See Lawrence, T(homas) E(dward)

Ross, Martin
    See Martin, Violet Florence
    See also DLB 135

Ross, (James) Sinclair
    1908- . . . . . . CLC 13; DAC; DAM MST;
                                             SSC 24
    See also CA 73-76; DLB 88

Rossetti, Christina (Georgina)
    1830-1894 . . . . . NCLC 2, 50; DA; DAB;
            DAC; DAM MST, POET; PC 7; WLC
    See also DLB 35, 163; MAICYA; SATA 20

Rossetti, Dante Gabriel
    1828-1882 . . . . NCLC 4; DA; DAB;
                DAC; DAM MST, POET; WLC
    See also CDBLB 1832-1890; DLB 35

Rossner, Judith (Perelman)
    1935- . . . . CLC 6, 9, 29
    See also AITN 2; BEST 90:3; CA 17-20R;
    CANR 18, 51; DLB 6; INT CANR-18;
    MTCW

Rostand, Edmond (Eugene Alexis)
    1868-1918 . . . . . . TCLC 6, 37; DA; DAB;
                DAC; DAM DRAM, MST
    See also CA 104; 126; MTCW

Roth, Henry 1906-1995 . . . . . . CLC 2, 6, 11
    See also CA 11-12; 149; CANR 38; CAP 1;
    DLB 28; MTCW

Roth, Joseph 1894-1939. . . . . TCLC 33
    See also DLB 85

Roth, Philip (Milton)
    1933- . . . . . . CLC 1, 2, 3, 4, 6, 9, 15, 22,
            31, 47, 66, 86; DA; DAB; DAC;
            DAM MST, NOV, POP; WLC
    See also BEST 90:3; CA 1-4R; CANR 1, 22,
    36, 55; CDALB 1968-1988; DLB 2, 28,
    173; DLBY 82; MTCW

Rothenberg, Jerome 1931- . . . . CLC 6, 57
    See also CA 45-48; CANR 1; DLB 5

Roumain, Jacques (Jean Baptiste)
    1907-1944 . . . . TCLC 19; BLC;
                                             DAM MULT
    See also BW 1; CA 117; 125

Rourke, Constance (Mayfield)
    1885-1941 . . . . TCLC 12
    See also CA 107; YABC 1

Rousseau, Jean-Baptiste 1671-1741 . . . LC 9

Rousseau, Jean-Jacques
    1712-1778 . . . . LC 14, 36; DA; DAB;
                DAC; DAM MST; WLC

Roussel, Raymond 1877-1933 . . . . . TCLC 20
    See also CA 117

Rovit, Earl (Herbert) 1927- . . . . CLC 7
    See also CA 5-8R; CANR 12

Rowe, Nicholas 1674-1718. . . . . LC 8
    See also DLB 84

Rowley, Ames Dorrance
    See Lovecraft, H(oward) P(hillips)

Rowson, Susanna Haswell
    1762(?)-1824 . . . . NCLC 5
    See also DLB 37

Roy, Gabrielle
    1909-1983 . . . . CLC 10, 14; DAB; DAC;
                                             DAM MST
    See also CA 53-56; 110; CANR 5; DLB 68;
    MTCW

Rozewicz, Tadeusz
    1921- . . . . CLC 9, 23; DAM POET
    See also CA 108; CANR 36; MTCW

Ruark, Gibbons 1941- . . . . CLC 3
    See also CA 33-36R; CAAS 23; CANR 14,
    31; DLB 120

Rubens, Bernice (Ruth) 1923- . . . CLC 19, 31
    See also CA 25-28R; CANR 33; DLB 14;
    MTCW

Rubin, Harold
    See Robbins, Harold

Rudkin, (James) David 1936- . . . . . . CLC 14
    See also CA 89-92; DLB 13

Rudnik, Raphael 1933-. . . . . CLC 7
    See also CA 29-32R

Ruffian, M.
    See Hasek, Jaroslav (Matej Frantisek)

Ruiz, Jose Martinez . . . . CLC 11
    See also Martinez Ruiz, Jose

Rukeyser, Muriel
    1913-1980 . . . . CLC 6, 10, 15, 27;
                                             DAM POET; PC 12
    See also CA 5-8R; 93-96; CANR 26;
    DLB 48; MTCW; SATA-Obit 22

Rule, Jane (Vance) 1931-. . . . . CLC 27
    See also CA 25-28R; CAAS 18; CANR 12;
    DLB 60

Rulfo, Juan
    1918-1986 . . . . CLC 8, 80; DAM MULT;
                                             HLC
    See also CA 85-88; 118; CANR 26;
    DLB 113; HW; MTCW

Rumi, Jalal al-Din 1297-1373 . . . . CMLC 20

Runeberg, Johan 1804-1877. . . . . . . NCLC 41

Runyon, (Alfred) Damon
    1884(?)-1946 . . . . TCLC 10
    See also CA 107; DLB 11, 86, 171

Rush, Norman 1933-. . . . . CLC 44
    See also CA 121; 126; INT 126

Rushdie, (Ahmed) Salman
    1947- . . . . . CLC 23, 31, 55; DAB; DAC;
                DAM MST, NOV, POP
    See also BEST 89:3; CA 108; 111;
    CANR 33; INT 111; MTCW

Rushforth, Peter (Scott) 1945- . . . . . CLC 19
    See also CA 101

Ruskin, John 1819-1900. . . . . TCLC 63
    See also CA 114; 129; CDBLB 1832-1890;
    DLB 55, 163; SATA 24

Russ, Joanna 1937-. . . . . CLC 15
    See also CA 25-28R; CANR 11, 31; DLB 8;
    MTCW

Russell, George William 1867-1935
    See Baker, Jean H.
    See also CA 104; 153; CDBLB 1890-1914;
    DAM POET

Russell, (Henry) Ken(neth Alfred)
    1927- . . . . CLC 16
    See also CA 105

Russell, Willy 1947-. . . . . CLC 60

Rutherford, Mark . . . . TCLC 25
    See also White, William Hale
    See also DLB 18

Ruyslinck, Ward 1929-. . . . . CLC 14
    See also Belser, Reimond Karel Maria de

Ryan, Cornelius (John) 1920-1974 ... CLC 7
See also CA 69-72; 53-56; CANR 38

Ryan, Michael 1946- .... CLC 65
See also CA 49-52; DLBY 82

Rybakov, Anatoli (Naumovich)
1911-..................... CLC 23, 53
See also CA 126; 135; SATA 79

Ryder, Jonathan
See Ludlum, Robert

Ryga, George
1932-1987 .. CLC 14; DAC; DAM MST
See also CA 101; 124; CANR 43; DLB 60

S. S.
See Sassoon, Siegfried (Lorraine)

Saba, Umberto 1883-1957 .... TCLC 33
See also CA 144; DLB 114

Sabatini, Rafael 1875-1950 .... TCLC 47

Sabato, Ernesto (R.)
1911- .... CLC 10, 23; DAM MULT;
HLC
See also CA 97-100; CANR 32; DLB 145;
HW; MTCW

Sacastru, Martin
See Bioy Casares, Adolfo

Sacher-Masoch, Leopold von
1836(?)-1895 .... NCLC 31

Sachs, Marilyn (Stickle) 1927- ..... CLC 35
See also AAYA 2; CA 17-20R; CANR 13,
47; CLR 2; JRDA; MAICYA; SAAS 2;
SATA 3, 68

Sachs, Nelly 1891-1970 .... CLC 14, 98
See also CA 17-18; 25-28R; CAP 2

Sackler, Howard (Oliver)
1929-1982 .... CLC 14
See also CA 61-64; 108; CANR 30; DLB 7

Sacks, Oliver (Wolf) 1933- .... CLC 67
See also CA 53-56; CANR 28, 50;
INT CANR-28; MTCW

Sade, Donatien Alphonse Francois Comte
1740-1814 .... NCLC 47

Sadoff, Ira 1945-................. CLC 9
See also CA 53-56; CANR 5, 21; DLB 120

Saetone
See Camus, Albert

Safire, William 1929-............ CLC 10
See also CA 17-20R; CANR 31, 54

Sagan, Carl (Edward) 1934-........ CLC 30
See also AAYA 2; CA 25-28R; CANR 11,
36; MTCW; SATA 58

Sagan, Francoise .... CLC 3, 6, 9, 17, 36
See also Quoirez, Francoise
See also DLB 83

Sahgal, Nayantara (Pandit) 1927-... CLC 41
See also CA 9-12R; CANR 11

Saint, H(arry) F. 1941- .... CLC 50
See also CA 127

St. Aubin de Teran, Lisa 1953-
See Teran, Lisa St. Aubin de
See also CA 118; 126; INT 126

Sainte-Beuve, Charles Augustin
1804-1869 .... NCLC 5

Saint-Exupery, Antoine (Jean Baptiste Marie
Roger) de
1900-1944 .... TCLC 2, 56; DAM NOV;
WLC
See also CA 108; 132; CLR 10; DLB 72;
MAICYA; MTCW; SATA 20

St. John, David
See Hunt, E(verette) Howard, (Jr.)

Saint-John Perse
See Leger, (Marie-Rene Auguste) Alexis
Saint-Leger

Saintsbury, George (Edward Bateman)
1845-1933 .... TCLC 31
See also DLB 57, 149

Sait Faik .... TCLC 23
See also Abasiyanik, Sait Faik

Saki .... TCLC 3; SSC 12
See also Munro, H(ector) H(ugh)

Sala, George Augustus .... NCLC 46

Salama, Hannu 1936-............ CLC 18

Salamanca, J(ack) R(ichard)
1922-................... CLC 4, 15
See also CA 25-28R

Sale, J. Kirkpatrick
See Sale, Kirkpatrick

Sale, Kirkpatrick 1937-........... CLC 68
See also CA 13-16R; CANR 10

Salinas, Luis Omar
1937- ..... CLC 90; DAM MULT; HLC
See also CA 131; DLB 82; HW

Salinas (y Serrano), Pedro
1891(?)-1951 .... TCLC 17
See also CA 117; DLB 134

Salinger, J(erome) D(avid)
1919- ...... CLC 1, 3, 8, 12, 55, 56; DA;
DAB; DAC; DAM MST, NOV, POP;
SSC 2; WLC
See also AAYA 2; CA 5-8R; CANR 39;
CDALB 1941-1968; CLR 18; DLB 2, 102,
173; MAICYA; MTCW; SATA 67

Salisbury, John
See Caute, David

Salter, James 1925- .... CLC 7, 52, 59
See also CA 73-76; DLB 130

Saltus, Edgar (Everton)
1855-1921 .... TCLC 8
See also CA 105

Saltykov, Mikhail Evgrafovich
1826-1889 .... NCLC 16

Samarakis, Antonis 1919- .... CLC 5
See also CA 25-28R; CAAS 16; CANR 36

Sanchez, Florencio 1875-1910 ..... TCLC 37
See also CA 153; HW

Sanchez, Luis Rafael 1936-........ CLC 23
See also CA 128; DLB 145; HW

Sanchez, Sonia
1934- ...... CLC 5; BLC; DAM MULT;
PC 9
See also BW 2; CA 33-36R; CANR 24, 49;
CLR 18; DLB 41; DLBD 8; MAICYA;
MTCW; SATA 22

Sand, George
1804-1876 .... NCLC 2, 42, 57; DA;
DAB; DAC; DAM MST, NOV; WLC
See also DLB 119

Sandburg, Carl (August)
1878-1967 .... CLC 1, 4, 10, 15, 35; DA;
DAB; DAC; DAM MST, POET; PC 2;
WLC
See also CA 5-8R; 25-28R; CANR 35;
CDALB 1865-1917; DLB 17, 54;
MAICYA; MTCW; SATA 8

Sandburg, Charles
See Sandburg, Carl (August)

Sandburg, Charles A.
See Sandburg, Carl (August)

Sanders, (James) Ed(ward) 1939- ... CLC 53
See also CA 13-16R; CAAS 21; CANR 13,
44; DLB 16

Sanders, Lawrence
1920- .... CLC 41; DAM POP
See also BEST 89:4; CA 81-84; CANR 33;
MTCW

Sanders, Noah
See Blount, Roy (Alton), Jr.

Sanders, Winston P.
See Anderson, Poul (William)

Sandoz, Mari(e Susette)
1896-1966 .... CLC 28
See also CA 1-4R; 25-28R; CANR 17;
DLB 9; MTCW; SATA 5

Saner, Reg(inald Anthony) 1931- .... CLC 9
See also CA 65-68

Sannazaro, Jacopo 1456(?)-1530...... LC 8

Sansom, William
1912-1976 ...... CLC 2, 6; DAM NOV;
SSC 21
See also CA 5-8R; 65-68; CANR 42;
DLB 139; MTCW

Santayana, George 1863-1952 ..... TCLC 40
See also CA 115; DLB 54, 71; DLBD 13

Santiago, Danny .... CLC 33
See also James, Daniel (Lewis)
See also DLB 122

Santmyer, Helen Hoover
1895-1986 .... CLC 33
See also CA 1-4R; 118; CANR 15, 33;
DLBY 84; MTCW

Santos, Bienvenido N(uqui)
1911-1996 ...... CLC 22; DAM MULT
See also CA 101; 151; CANR 19, 46

Sapper .... TCLC 44
See also McNeile, Herman Cyril

Sappho
fl. 6th cent. B.C.- .... CMLC 3;
DAM POET; PC 5

Sarduy, Severo 1937-1993 .... CLC 6, 97
See also CA 89-92; 142; DLB 113; HW

Sargeson, Frank 1903-1982 .... CLC 31
See also CA 25-28R; 106; CANR 38

Sarmiento, Felix Ruben Garcia
See Dario, Ruben

Saroyan, William
1908-1981 ..... CLC 1, 8, 10, 29, 34, 56;
DA; DAB; DAC; DAM DRAM, MST,
NOV; SSC 21; WLC
See also CA 5-8R; 103; CANR 30; DLB 7,
9, 86; DLBY 81; MTCW; SATA 23;
SATA-Obit 24

Scumbag, Little Bobby
See Crumb, R(obert)

Seabrook, John
See Hubbard, L(afayette) Ron(ald)

Sealy, I. Allan 1951- . . . . **CLC 55**

Search, Alexander
See Pessoa, Fernando (Antonio Nogueira)

Sebastian, Lee
See Silverberg, Robert

Sebastian Owl
See Thompson, Hunter S(tockton)

Sebestyen, Ouida 1924- . . . . **CLC 30**
See also AAYA 8; CA 107; CANR 40;
CLR 17; JRDA; MAICYA; SAAS 10;
SATA 39

Secundus, H. Scriblerus
See Fielding, Henry

Sedges, John
See Buck, Pearl S(ydenstricker)

Sedgwick, Catharine Maria
1789-1867 . . . . **NCLC 19**
See also DLB 1, 74

Seelye, John 1931- . . . . **CLC 7**

Seferiades, Giorgos Stylianou 1900-1971
See Seferis, George
See also CA 5-8R; 33-36R; CANR 5, 36;
MTCW

Seferis, George . . . . **CLC 5, 11**
See also Seferiades, Giorgos Stylianou

Segal, Erich (Wolf)
1937- . . . . **CLC 3, 10; DAM POP**
See also BEST 89:1; CA 25-28R; CANR 20,
36; DLBY 86; INT CANR-20; MTCW

Seger, Bob 1945- . . . . **CLC 35**

Seghers, Anna . . . . **CLC 7**
See also Radvanyi, Netty
See also DLB 69

Seidel, Frederick (Lewis) 1936- . . . . . **CLC 18**
See also CA 13-16R; CANR 8; DLBY 84

Seifert, Jaroslav
1901-1986 . . . . **CLC 34, 44, 93**
See also CA 127; MTCW

Sei Shonagon c. 966-1017(?) . . . . . . **CMLC 6**

Selby, Hubert, Jr.
1928- . . . . **CLC 1, 2, 4, 8; SSC 20**
See also CA 13-16R; CANR 33; DLB 2

Selzer, Richard 1928- . . . . **CLC 74**
See also CA 65-68; CANR 14

Sembene, Ousmane
See Ousmane, Sembene

Senancour, Etienne Pivert de
1770-1846 . . . . **NCLC 16**
See also DLB 119

Sender, Ramon (Jose)
1902-1982 . . **CLC 8; DAM MULT; HLC**
See also CA 5-8R; 105; CANR 8; HW;
MTCW

Seneca, Lucius Annaeus
4B.C.-65 . . . . . . **CMLC 6; DAM DRAM;
DC 5**

Senghor, Leopold Sedar
1906- . . . . . **CLC 54; BLC; DAM MULT,
POET**
See also BW 2; CA 116; 125; CANR 47;
MTCW

Serling, (Edward) Rod(man)
1924-1975 . . . . **CLC 30**
See also AAYA 14; AITN 1; CA 65-68;
57-60; DLB 26

Serna, Ramon Gomez de la
See Gomez de la Serna, Ramon

Serpieres
See Guillevic, (Eugene)

Service, Robert
See Service, Robert W(illiam)
See also DAB; DLB 92

Service, Robert W(illiam)
1874(?)-1958 . . . . . . **TCLC 15; DA; DAC;
DAM MST, POET; WLC**
See also Service, Robert
See also CA 115; 140; SATA 20

Seth, Vikram
1952- . . . . **CLC 43, 90; DAM MULT**
See also CA 121; 127; CANR 50; DLB 120;
INT 127

Seton, Cynthia Propper
1926-1982 . . . . **CLC 27**
See also CA 5-8R; 108; CANR 7

Seton, Ernest (Evan) Thompson
1860-1946 . . . . **TCLC 31**
See also CA 109; DLB 92; DLBD 13;
JRDA; SATA 18

Seton-Thompson, Ernest
See Seton, Ernest (Evan) Thompson

Settle, Mary Lee 1918- . . . . **CLC 19, 61**
See also CA 89-92; CAAS 1; CANR 44;
DLB 6; INT 89-92

Seuphor, Michel
See Arp, Jean

**Sevigne, Marie (de Rabutin-Chantal) Marquise
de** 1626-1696 . . . . **LC 11**

Sexton, Anne (Harvey)
1928-1974 . . . . **CLC 2, 4, 6, 8, 10, 15, 53;
DA; DAB; DAC; DAM MST, POET;
PC 2; WLC**
See also CA 1-4R; 53-56; CABS 2;
CANR 3, 36; CDALB 1941-1968; DLB 5,
169; MTCW; SATA 10

Shaara, Michael (Joseph, Jr.)
1929-1988 . . . . **CLC 15; DAM POP**
See also AITN 1; CA 102; 125; CANR 52;
DLBY 83

Shackleton, C. C.
See Aldiss, Brian W(ilson)

Shacochis, Bob . . . . **CLC 39**
See also Shacochis, Robert G.

Shacochis, Robert G. 1951-
See Shacochis, Bob
See also CA 119; 124; INT 124

Shaffer, Anthony (Joshua)
1926- . . . . **CLC 19; DAM DRAM**
See also CA 110; 116; DLB 13

Shaffer, Peter (Levin)
1926- . . . . . . **CLC 5, 14, 18, 37, 60; DAB;
DAM DRAM, MST**
See also CA 25-28R; CANR 25, 47;
CDBLB 1960 to Present; DLB 13;
MTCW

Shakey, Bernard
See Young, Neil

Shalamov, Varlam (Tikhonovich)
1907(?)-1982 . . . . **CLC 18**
See also CA 129; 105

Shamlu, Ahmad 1925- . . . . **CLC 10**

Shammas, Anton 1951- . . . . **CLC 55**

Shange, Ntozake
1948- . . . . **CLC 8, 25, 38, 74; BLC;
DAM DRAM, MULT; DC 3**
See also AAYA 9; BW 2; CA 85-88;
CABS 3; CANR 27, 48; DLB 38; MTCW

Shanley, John Patrick 1950- . . . . **CLC 75**
See also CA 128; 133

Shapcott, Thomas W(illiam) 1935- . . **CLC 38**
See also CA 69-72; CANR 49

Shapiro, Jane . . . . **CLC 76**

Shapiro, Karl (Jay) 1913- . . **CLC 4, 8, 15, 53**
See also CA 1-4R; CAAS 6; CANR 1, 36;
DLB 48; MTCW

Sharp, William 1855-1905 . . . . **TCLC 39**
See also DLB 156

Sharpe, Thomas Ridley 1928-
See Sharpe, Tom
See also CA 114; 122; INT 122

Sharpe, Tom . . . . **CLC 36**
See also Sharpe, Thomas Ridley
See also DLB 14

Shaw, Bernard . . . . **TCLC 45**
See also Shaw, George Bernard
See also BW 1

Shaw, G. Bernard
See Shaw, George Bernard

Shaw, George Bernard
1856-1950 . . . **TCLC 3, 9, 21; DA; DAB;
DAC; DAM DRAM, MST; WLC**
See also Shaw, Bernard
See also CA 104; 128; CDBLB 1914-1945;
DLB 10, 57; MTCW

Shaw, Henry Wheeler
1818-1885 . . . . **NCLC 15**
See also DLB 11

Shaw, Irwin
1913-1984 . . . . **CLC 7, 23, 34;
DAM DRAM, POP**
See also AITN 1; CA 13-16R; 112;
CANR 21; CDALB 1941-1968; DLB 6,
102; DLBY 84; MTCW

Shaw, Robert 1927-1978 . . . . **CLC 5**
See also AITN 1; CA 1-4R; 81-84;
CANR 4; DLB 13, 14

Shaw, T. E.
See Lawrence, T(homas) E(dward)

Shawn, Wallace 1943- . . . . **CLC 41**
See also CA 112

Shea, Lisa 1953- . . . . **CLC 86**
See also CA 147

Snyder, Zilpha Keatley 1927- ...... **CLC 17**
See also AAYA 15; CA 9-12R; CANR 38;
CLR 31; JRDA; MAICYA; SAAS 2;
SATA 1, 28, 75

Soares, Bernardo
See Pessoa, Fernando (Antonio Nogueira)

Sobh, A.
See Shamlu, Ahmad

Sobol, Joshua................... **CLC 60**

Soderberg, Hjalmar 1869-1941 .... **TCLC 39**

Sodergran, Edith (Irene)
See Soedergran, Edith (Irene)

Soedergran, Edith (Irene)
1892-1923 .... **TCLC 31**

Softly, Edgar
See Lovecraft, H(oward) P(hillips)

Softly, Edward
See Lovecraft, H(oward) P(hillips)

Sokolov, Raymond 1941- .... **CLC 7**
See also CA 85-88

Solo, Jay
See Ellison, Harlan (Jay)

Sologub, Fyodor .... **TCLC 9**
See also Teternikov, Fyodor Kuzmich

Solomons, Ikey Esquir
See Thackeray, William Makepeace

Solomos, Dionysios 1798-1857 ... **NCLC 15**

Solwoska, Mara
See French, Marilyn

Solzhenitsyn, Aleksandr I(sayevich)
1918- ...... **CLC 1, 2, 4, 7, 9, 10, 18, 26,**
34, 78; DA; DAB; DAC; DAM MST,
NOV; WLC
See also AITN 1; CA 69-72; CANR 40;
MTCW

Somers, Jane
See Lessing, Doris (May)

Somerville, Edith 1858-1949 ...... **TCLC 51**
See also DLB 135

Somerville & Ross
See Martin, Violet Florence; Somerville,
Edith

Sommer, Scott 1951- .... **CLC 25**
See also CA 106

Sondheim, Stephen (Joshua)
1930- .... **CLC 30, 39; DAM DRAM**
See also AAYA 11; CA 103; CANR 47

Sontag, Susan
1933- .... **CLC 1, 2, 10, 13, 31;**
DAM POP
See also CA 17-20R; CANR 25, 51; DLB 2,
67; MTCW

Sophocles
496(?)B.C.-406(?)B.C..... **CMLC 2; DA;**
DAB; DAC; DAM DRAM, MST; DC 1

Sordello 1189-1269............ **CMLC 15**

Sorel, Julia
See Drexler, Rosalyn

Sorrentino, Gilbert
1929- .... **CLC 3, 7, 14, 22, 40**
See also CA 77-80; CANR 14, 33; DLB 5,
173; DLBY 80; INT CANR-14

Soto, Gary
1952- .... **CLC 32, 80; DAM MULT;**
HLC
See also AAYA 10; CA 119; 125;
CANR 50; CLR 38; DLB 82; HW;
INT 125; JRDA; SATA 80

Soupault, Philippe 1897-1990 ...... **CLC 68**
See also CA 116; 147; 131

Souster, (Holmes) Raymond
1921- ... **CLC 5, 14; DAC; DAM POET**
See also CA 13-16R; CAAS 14; CANR 13,
29, 53; DLB 88; SATA 63

Southern, Terry 1924(?)-1995 .... **CLC 7**
See also CA 1-4R; 150; CANR 1, 55;
DLB 2

Southey, Robert 1774-1843 .... **NCLC 8**
See also DLB 93, 107, 142; SATA 54

Southworth, Emma Dorothy Eliza Nevitte
1819-1899 .... **NCLC 26**

Souza, Ernest
See Scott, Evelyn

Soyinka, Wole
1934- .... **CLC 3, 5, 14, 36, 44; BLC;**
DA; DAB; DAC; DAM DRAM, MST,
MULT; DC 2; WLC
See also BW 2; CA 13-16R; CANR 27, 39;
DLB 125; MTCW

Spackman, W(illiam) M(ode)
1905-1990 .... **CLC 46**
See also CA 81-84; 132

Spacks, Barry (Bernard) 1931- ..... **CLC 14**
See also CA 154; CANR 33; DLB 105

Spanidou, Irini 1946- .... **CLC 44**

Spark, Muriel (Sarah)
1918- ..... **CLC 2, 3, 5, 8, 13, 18, 40, 94;**
DAB; DAC; DAM MST, NOV; SSC 10
See also CA 5-8R; CANR 12, 36;
CDBLB 1945-1960; DLB 15, 139;
INT CANR-12; MTCW

Spaulding, Douglas
See Bradbury, Ray (Douglas)

Spaulding, Leonard
See Bradbury, Ray (Douglas)

Spence, J. A. D.
See Eliot, T(homas) S(tearns)

Spencer, Elizabeth 1921- .... **CLC 22**
See also CA 13-16R; CANR 32; DLB 6;
MTCW; SATA 14

Spencer, Leonard G.
See Silverberg, Robert

Spencer, Scott 1945- .... **CLC 30**
See also CA 113; CANR 51; DLBY 86

Spender, Stephen (Harold)
1909-1995 ...... **CLC 1, 2, 5, 10, 41, 91;**
DAM POET
See also CA 9-12R; 149; CANR 31, 54;
CDBLB 1945-1960; DLB 20; MTCW

Spengler, Oswald (Arnold Gottfried)
1880-1936 .... **TCLC 25**
See also CA 118

Spenser, Edmund
1552(?)-1599 .... **LC 5; DA; DAB; DAC;**
DAM MST, POET; PC 8; WLC
See also CDBLB Before 1660; DLB 167

Spicer, Jack
1925-1965 .... **CLC 8, 18, 72;**
DAM POET
See also CA 85-88; DLB 5, 16

Spiegelman, Art 1948- .... **CLC 76**
See also AAYA 10; CA 125; CANR 41, 55

Spielberg, Peter 1929- .... **CLC 6**
See also CA 5-8R; CANR 4, 48; DLBY 81

Spielberg, Steven 1947- .... **CLC 20**
See also AAYA 8; CA 77-80; CANR 32;
SATA 32

Spillane, Frank Morrison 1918-
See Spillane, Mickey
See also CA 25-28R; CANR 28; MTCW;
SATA 66

Spillane, Mickey .... **CLC 3, 13**
See also Spillane, Frank Morrison

Spinoza, Benedictus de 1632-1677 .... **LC 9**

Spinrad, Norman (Richard) 1940-... **CLC 46**
See also CA 37-40R; CAAS 19; CANR 20;
DLB 8; INT CANR-20

Spitteler, Carl (Friedrich Georg)
1845-1924 .... **TCLC 12**
See also CA 109; DLB 129

Spivack, Kathleen (Romola Drucker)
1938- .... **CLC 6**
See also CA 49-52

Spoto, Donald 1941- .... **CLC 39**
See also CA 65-68; CANR 11

Springsteen, Bruce (F.) 1949- ...... **CLC 17**
See also CA 111

Spurling, Hilary 1940- .... **CLC 34**
See also CA 104; CANR 25, 52

Spyker, John Howland
See Elman, Richard

Squires, (James) Radcliffe
1917-1993 .... **CLC 51**
See also CA 1-4R; 140; CANR 6, 21

Srivastava, Dhanpat Rai 1880(?)-1936
See Premchand
See also CA 118

Stacy, Donald
See Pohl, Frederik

Stael, Germaine de
See Stael-Holstein, Anne Louise Germaine
Necker Baronn
See also DLB 119

Stael-Holstein, Anne Louise Germaine Necker
Baronn 1766-1817 .... **NCLC 3**
See also Stael, Germaine de

Stafford, Jean 1915-1979 ... **CLC 4, 7, 19, 68**
See also CA 1-4R; 85-88; CANR 3; DLB 2,
173; MTCW; SATA-Obit 22

Stafford, William (Edgar)
1914-1993 ... **CLC 4, 7, 29; DAM POET**
See also CA 5-8R; 142; CAAS 3; CANR 5,
22; DLB 5; INT CANR-22

Staines, Trevor
See Brunner, John (Kilian Houston)

Stairs, Gordon
See Austin, Mary (Hunter)

Stannard, Martin 1947- .... **CLC 44**
See also CA 142; DLB 155

Stanton, Maura   1946- . . . . CLC 9
See also CA 89-92; CANR 15; DLB 120

Stanton, Schuyler
See Baum, L(yman) Frank

Stapledon, (William) Olaf
1886-1950 . . . . TCLC 22
See also CA 111; DLB 15

Starbuck, George (Edwin)
1931-1996 . . . . CLC 53; DAM POET
See also CA 21-24R; 153; CANR 23

Stark, Richard
See Westlake, Donald E(dwin)

Staunton, Schuyler
See Baum, L(yman) Frank

Stead, Christina (Ellen)
1902-1983 . . . . CLC 2, 5, 8, 32, 80
See also CA 13-16R; 109; CANR 33, 40;
MTCW

Stead, William Thomas
1849-1912 . . . . TCLC 48

Steele, Richard   1672-1729 . . . . LC 18
See also CDBLB 1660-1789; DLB 84, 101

Steele, Timothy (Reid)   1948- . . . . CLC 45
See also CA 93-96; CANR 16, 50; DLB 120

Steffens, (Joseph) Lincoln
1866-1936 . . . . TCLC 20
See also CA 117

Stegner, Wallace (Earle)
1909-1993 . . . CLC 9, 49, 81; DAM NOV
See also AITN 1; BEST 90:3; CA 1-4R;
141; CAAS 9; CANR 1, 21, 46; DLB 9;
DLBY 93; MTCW

Stein, Gertrude
1874-1946 . . . . . . TCLC 1, 6, 28, 48; DA;
DAB; DAC; DAM MST, NOV, POET;
WLC
See also CA 104; 132; CDALB 1917-1929;
DLB 4, 54, 86; MTCW

Steinbeck, John (Ernst)
1902-1968 . . . . . . CLC 1, 5, 9, 13, 21, 34,
45, 75; DA; DAB; DAC; DAM DRAM,
MST, NOV; SSC 11; WLC
See also AAYA 12; CA 1-4R; 25-28R;
CANR 1, 35; CDALB 1929-1941; DLB 7,
9; DLBD 2; MTCW; SATA 9

Steinem, Gloria   1934- . . . . CLC 63
See also CA 53-56; CANR 28, 51; MTCW

Steiner, George
1929- . . . . CLC 24; DAM NOV
See also CA 73-76; CANR 31; DLB 67;
MTCW; SATA 62

Steiner, K. Leslie
See Delany, Samuel R(ay, Jr.)

Steiner, Rudolf   1861-1925 . . . . TCLC 13
See also CA 107

Stendhal
1783-1842 . . . . NCLC 23, 46; DA; DAB;
DAC; DAM MST, NOV; WLC
See also DLB 119

Stephen, Leslie   1832-1904 . . . . TCLC 23
See also CA 123; DLB 57, 144

Stephen, Sir Leslie
See Stephen, Leslie

Stephen, Virginia
See Woolf, (Adeline) Virginia

Stephens, James   1882(?)-1950 . . . . . . TCLC 4
See also CA 104; DLB 19, 153, 162

Stephens, Reed
See Donaldson, Stephen R.

Steptoe, Lydia
See Barnes, Djuna

Sterchi, Beat   1949- . . . . CLC 65

Sterling, Brett
See Bradbury, Ray (Douglas); Hamilton,
Edmond

Sterling, Bruce   1954- . . . . CLC 72
See also CA 119; CANR 44

Sterling, George   1869-1926 . . . . TCLC 20
See also CA 117; DLB 54

Stern, Gerald   1925- . . . . CLC 40
See also CA 81-84; CANR 28; DLB 105

Stern, Richard (Gustave)   1928- . . . CLC 4, 39
See also CA 1-4R; CANR 1, 25, 52;
DLBY 87; INT CANR-25

Sternberg, Josef von   1894-1969 . . . . . CLC 20
See also CA 81-84

Sterne, Laurence
1713-1768 . . . . . . LC 2; DA; DAB; DAC;
DAM MST, NOV; WLC
See also CDBLB 1660-1789; DLB 39

Sternheim, (William Adolf) Carl
1878-1942 . . . . TCLC 8
See also CA 105; DLB 56, 118

Stevens, Mark   1951- . . . . CLC 34
See also CA 122

Stevens, Wallace
1879-1955 . . . . TCLC 3, 12, 45; DA;
DAB; DAC; DAM MST, POET; PC 6;
WLC
See also CA 104; 124; CDALB 1929-1941;
DLB 54; MTCW

Stevenson, Anne (Katharine)
1933- . . . . CLC 7, 33
See also CA 17-20R; CAAS 9; CANR 9, 33;
DLB 40; MTCW

Stevenson, Robert Louis (Balfour)
1850-1894 . . . . . NCLC 5, 14; DA; DAB;
DAC; DAM MST, NOV; SSC 11; WLC
See also CDBLB 1890-1914; CLR 10, 11;
DLB 18, 57, 141, 156, 174; DLBD 13;
JRDA; MAICYA; YABC 2

Stewart, J(ohn) I(nnes) M(ackintosh)
1906-1994 . . . . CLC 7, 14, 32
See also CA 85-88; 147; CAAS 3;
CANR 47; MTCW

Stewart, Mary (Florence Elinor)
1916- . . . . CLC 7, 35; DAB
See also CA 1-4R; CANR 1; SATA 12

Stewart, Mary Rainbow
See Stewart, Mary (Florence Elinor)

Stifle, June
See Campbell, Maria

Stifter, Adalbert   1805-1868 . . . . . . NCLC 41
See also DLB 133

Still, James   1906- . . . . CLC 49
See also CA 65-68; CAAS 17; CANR 10,
26; DLB 9; SATA 29

Sting
See Sumner, Gordon Matthew

Stirling, Arthur
See Sinclair, Upton (Beall)

Stitt, Milan   1941- . . . . CLC 29
See also CA 69-72

Stockton, Francis Richard   1834-1902
See Stockton, Frank R.
See also CA 108; 137; MAICYA; SATA 44

Stockton, Frank R. . . . . TCLC 47
See also Stockton, Francis Richard
See also DLB 42, 74; DLBD 13;
SATA-Brief 32

Stoddard, Charles
See Kuttner, Henry

Stoker, Abraham   1847-1912
See Stoker, Bram
See also CA 105; DA; DAC; DAM MST,
NOV; SATA 29

Stoker, Bram
1847-1912 . . . . TCLC 8; DAB; WLC
See also Stoker, Abraham
See also CA 150; CDBLB 1890-1914;
DLB 36, 70

Stolz, Mary (Slattery)   1920- . . . . CLC 12
See also AAYA 8; AITN 1; CA 5-8R;
CANR 13, 41; JRDA; MAICYA;
SAAS 3; SATA 10, 71

Stone, Irving
1903-1989 . . . . CLC 7; DAM POP
See also AITN 1; CA 1-4R; 129; CAAS 3;
CANR 1, 23; INT CANR-23; MTCW;
SATA 3; SATA-Obit 64

Stone, Oliver (William)   1946- . . . . . . CLC 73
See also AAYA 15; CA 110; CANR 55

Stone, Robert (Anthony)
1937- . . . . CLC 5, 23, 42
See also CA 85-88; CANR 23; DLB 152;
INT CANR-23; MTCW

Stone, Zachary
See Follett, Ken(neth Martin)

Stoppard, Tom
1937- . . . . . . CLC 1, 3, 4, 5, 8, 15, 29, 34,
63, 91; DA; DAB; DAC; DAM DRAM,
MST; DC 6; WLC
See also CA 81-84; CANR 39;
CDBLB 1960 to Present; DLB 13;
DLBY 85; MTCW

Storey, David (Malcolm)
1933- . . . . . CLC 2, 4, 5, 8; DAM DRAM
See also CA 81-84; CANR 36; DLB 13, 14;
MTCW

Storm, Hyemeyohsts
1935- . . . . CLC 3; DAM MULT
See also CA 81-84; CANR 45; NNAL

Storm, (Hans) Theodor (Woldsen)
1817-1888 . . . . NCLC 1

Storni, Alfonsina
1892-1938 . . . . . TCLC 5; DAM MULT;
HLC
See also CA 104; 131; HW

Stout, Rex (Todhunter)   1886-1975 . . . CLC 3
See also AITN 2; CA 61-64

Stow, (Julian) Randolph   1935- . . CLC 23, 48
See also CA 13-16R; CANR 33; MTCW

Stowe, Harriet (Elizabeth) Beecher
    1811-1896 ..... **NCLC 3, 50; DA; DAB;**
    DAC; DAM MST, NOV; WLC
    See also CDALB 1865-1917; DLB 1, 12, 42,
    74; JRDA; MAICYA; YABC 1

Strachey, (Giles) Lytton
    1880-1932 .... **TCLC 12**
    See also CA 110; DLB 149; DLBD 10

Strand, Mark
    1934- .. **CLC 6, 18, 41, 71; DAM POET**
    See also CA 21-24R; CANR 40; DLB 5;
    SATA 41

Straub, Peter (Francis)
    1943- .... **CLC 28; DAM POP**
    See also BEST 89:1; CA 85-88; CANR 28;
    DLBY 84; MTCW

Strauss, Botho 1944- .... **CLC 22**
    See also DLB 124

Streatfeild, (Mary) Noel
    1895(?)-1986 .... **CLC 21**
    See also CA 81-84; 120; CANR 31;
    CLR 17; DLB 160; MAICYA; SATA 20;
    SATA-Obit 48

Stribling, T(homas) S(igismund)
    1881-1965 .... **CLC 23**
    See also CA 107; DLB 9

Strindberg, (Johan) August
    1849-1912 ...... **TCLC 1, 8, 21, 47; DA;**
    DAB; DAC; DAM DRAM, MST; WLC
    See also CA 104; 135

Stringer, Arthur 1874-1950 .... **TCLC 37**
    See also DLB 92

Stringer, David
    See Roberts, Keith (John Kingston)

Strugatskii, Arkadii (Natanovich)
    1925-1991 .... **CLC 27**
    See also CA 106; 135

Strugatskii, Boris (Natanovich)
    1933- .... **CLC 27**
    See also CA 106

Strummer, Joe 1953(?)- .... **CLC 30**

Stuart, Don A.
    See Campbell, John W(ood, Jr.)

Stuart, Ian
    See MacLean, Alistair (Stuart)

Stuart, Jesse (Hilton)
    1906-1984 .... **CLC 1, 8, 11, 14, 34**
    See also CA 5-8R; 112; CANR 31; DLB 9,
    48, 102; DLBY 84; SATA 2;
    SATA-Obit 36

Sturgeon, Theodore (Hamilton)
    1918-1985 .... **CLC 22, 39**
    See also Queen, Ellery
    See also CA 81-84; 116; CANR 32; DLB 8;
    DLBY 85; MTCW

Sturges, Preston 1898-1959 .... **TCLC 48**
    See also CA 114; 149; DLB 26

Styron, William
    1925- .... **CLC 1, 3, 5, 11, 15, 60;**
    DAM NOV, POP
    See also BEST 90:4; CA 5-8R; CANR 6, 33;
    CDALB 1968-1988; DLB 2, 143;
    DLBY 80; INT CANR-6; MTCW

Suarez Lynch, B.
    See Bioy Casares, Adolfo; Borges, Jorge
    Luis

Su Chien 1884-1918
    See Su Man-shu
    See also CA 123

Suckow, Ruth 1892-1960 .... **SSC 18**
    See also CA 113; DLB 9, 102

Sudermann, Hermann 1857-1928 .. **TCLC 15**
    See also CA 107; DLB 118

Sue, Eugene 1804-1857 .... **NCLC 1**
    See also DLB 119

Sueskind, Patrick 1949- .... **CLC 44**
    See also Suskind, Patrick

Sukenick, Ronald 1932- ..... **CLC 3, 4, 6, 48**
    See also CA 25-28R; CAAS 8; CANR 32;
    DLB 173; DLBY 81

Suknaski, Andrew 1942- .... **CLC 19**
    See also CA 101; DLB 53

Sullivan, Vernon
    See Vian, Boris

Sully Prudhomme 1839-1907 ...... **TCLC 31**

Su Man-shu .... **TCLC 24**
    See also Su Chien

Summerforest, Ivy B.
    See Kirkup, James

Summers, Andrew James 1942- ..... **CLC 26**

Summers, Andy
    See Summers, Andrew James

Summers, Hollis (Spurgeon, Jr.)
    1916- .... **CLC 10**
    See also CA 5-8R; CANR 3; DLB 6

Summers, (Alphonsus Joseph-Mary Augustus)
    Montague 1880-1948 .... **TCLC 16**
    See also CA 118

Sumner, Gordon Matthew 1951- .... **CLC 26**

Surtees, Robert Smith
    1803-1864 .... **NCLC 14**
    See also DLB 21

Susann, Jacqueline 1921-1974 .... **CLC 3**
    See also AITN 1; CA 65-68; 53-56; MTCW

Su Shih 1036-1101 .... **CMLC 15**

Suskind, Patrick
    See Sueskind, Patrick
    See also CA 145

Sutcliff, Rosemary
    1920-1992 .... **CLC 26; DAB; DAC;**
    DAM MST, POP
    See also AAYA 10; CA 5-8R; 139;
    CANR 37; CLR 1, 37; JRDA; MAICYA;
    SATA 6, 44, 78; SATA-Obit 73

Sutro, Alfred 1863-1933 .... **TCLC 6**
    See also CA 105; DLB 10

Sutton, Henry
    See Slavitt, David R(ytman)

Svevo, Italo .... **TCLC 2, 35**
    See also Schmitz, Aron Hector

Swados, Elizabeth (A.) 1951- .... **CLC 12**
    See also CA 97-100; CANR 49; INT 97-100

Swados, Harvey 1920-1972 .... **CLC 5**
    See also CA 5-8R; 37-40R; CANR 6;
    DLB 2

Swan, Gladys 1934- .... **CLC 69**
    See also CA 101; CANR 17, 39

Swarthout, Glendon (Fred)
    1918-1992 .... **CLC 35**
    See also CA 1-4R; 139; CANR 1, 47;
    SATA 26

Sweet, Sarah C.
    See Jewett, (Theodora) Sarah Orne

Swenson, May
    1919-1989 .... **CLC 4, 14, 61; DA; DAB;**
    DAC; DAM MST, POET; PC 14
    See also CA 5-8R; 130; CANR 36; DLB 5;
    MTCW; SATA 15

Swift, Augustus
    See Lovecraft, H(oward) P(hillips)

Swift, Graham (Colin) 1949- .... **CLC 41, 88**
    See also CA 117; 122; CANR 46

Swift, Jonathan
    1667-1745 ...... **LC 1; DA; DAB; DAC;**
    DAM MST, NOV, POET; PC 9; WLC
    See also CDBLB 1660-1789; DLB 39, 95,
    101; SATA 19

Swinburne, Algernon Charles
    1837-1909 ...... **TCLC 8, 36; DA; DAB;**
    DAC; DAM MST, POET; WLC
    See also CA 105; 140; CDBLB 1832-1890;
    DLB 35, 57

Swinfen, Ann .... **CLC 34**

Swinnerton, Frank Arthur
    1884-1982 .... **CLC 31**
    See also CA 108; DLB 34

Swithen, John
    See King, Stephen (Edwin)

Sylvia
    See Ashton-Warner, Sylvia (Constance)

Symmes, Robert Edward
    See Duncan, Robert (Edward)

Symonds, John Addington
    1840-1893 .... **NCLC 34**
    See also DLB 57, 144

Symons, Arthur 1865-1945 .... **TCLC 11**
    See also CA 107; DLB 19, 57, 149

Symons, Julian (Gustave)
    1912-1994 .... **CLC 2, 14, 32**
    See also CA 49-52; 147; CAAS 3; CANR 3,
    33; DLB 87, 155; DLBY 92; MTCW

Synge, (Edmund) J(ohn) M(illington)
    1871-1909 .... **TCLC 6, 37;**
    DAM DRAM; DC 2
    See also CA 104; 141; CDBLB 1890-1914;
    DLB 10, 19

Syruc, J.
    See Milosz, Czeslaw

Szirtes, George 1948- .... **CLC 46**
    See also CA 109; CANR 27

Tabori, George 1914- .... **CLC 19**
    See also CA 49-52; CANR 4

Tagore, Rabindranath
    1861-1941 .... **TCLC 3, 53;**
    DAM DRAM, POET; PC 8
    See also CA 104; 120; MTCW

Taine, Hippolyte Adolphe
    1828-1893 .... **NCLC 15**

Talese, Gay 1932- .... **CLC 37**
    See also AITN 1; CA 1-4R; CANR 9;
    INT CANR-9; MTCW

Thomas, Piri 1928-. . . . . **CLC 17**
See also CA 73-76; HW

Thomas, R(onald) S(tuart)
1913- . . . . **CLC 6, 13, 48; DAB;**
DAM POET
See also CA 89-92; CAAS 4; CANR 30;
CDBLB 1960 to Present; DLB 27;
MTCW

Thomas, Ross (Elmore) 1926-1995 . . **CLC 39**
See also CA 33-36R; 150; CANR 22

Thompson, Francis Clegg
See Mencken, H(enry) L(ouis)

Thompson, Francis Joseph
1859-1907 . . . . **TCLC 4**
See also CA 104; CDBLB 1890-1914;
DLB 19

Thompson, Hunter S(tockton)
1939- . . . . **CLC 9, 17, 40; DAM POP**
See also BEST 89:1; CA 17-20R; CANR 23,
46; MTCW

Thompson, James Myers
See Thompson, Jim (Myers)

Thompson, Jim (Myers)
1906-1977(?) . . . . **CLC 69**
See also CA 140

Thompson, Judith . . . . **CLC 39**

Thomson, James
1700-1748 . . . . . **LC 16, 29; DAM POET**
See also DLB 95

Thomson, James
1834-1882 . . . . . **NCLC 18; DAM POET**
See also DLB 35

Thoreau, Henry David
1817-1862 . . . . . **NCLC 7, 21; DA; DAB;**
DAC; DAM MST; WLC
See also CDALB 1640-1865; DLB 1

Thornton, Hall
See Silverberg, Robert

Thucydides c. 455B.C.-399B.C. . . . . **CMLC 17**

Thurber, James (Grover)
1894-1961 . . . . **CLC 5, 11, 25; DA; DAB;**
DAC; DAM DRAM, MST, NOV; SSC 1
See also CA 73-76; CANR 17, 39;
CDALB 1929-1941; DLB 4, 11, 22, 102;
MAICYA; MTCW; SATA 13

Thurman, Wallace (Henry)
1902-1934 . . . . **TCLC 6; BLC;**
DAM MULT
See also BW 1; CA 104; 124; DLB 51

Ticheburn, Cheviot
See Ainsworth, William Harrison

Tieck, (Johann) Ludwig
1773-1853 . . . . **NCLC 5, 46**
See also DLB 90

Tiger, Derry
See Ellison, Harlan (Jay)

Tilghman, Christopher 1948(?)- . . . . . **CLC 65**

Tillinghast, Richard (Williford)
1940- . . . . **CLC 29**
See also CA 29-32R; CAAS 23; CANR 26,
51

Timrod, Henry 1828-1867 . . . . **NCLC 25**
See also DLB 3

Tindall, Gillian 1938- . . . . **CLC 7**
See also CA 21-24R; CANR 11

Tiptree, James, Jr. . . . . **CLC 48, 50**
See also Sheldon, Alice Hastings Bradley
See also DLB 8

Titmarsh, Michael Angelo
See Thackeray, William Makepeace

Tocqueville, Alexis (Charles Henri Maurice
Clerel Comte) 1805-1859 . . . . . **NCLC 7**

Tolkien, J(ohn) R(onald) R(euel)
1892-1973 . . . . **CLC 1, 2, 3, 8, 12, 38;**
DA; DAB; DAC; DAM MST, NOV,
POP; WLC
See also AAYA 10; AITN 1; CA 17-18;
45-48; CANR 36; CAP 2;
CDBLB 1914-1945; DLB 15, 160; JRDA;
MAICYA; MTCW; SATA 2, 32;
SATA-Obit 24

Toller, Ernst 1893-1939 . . . . **TCLC 10**
See also CA 107; DLB 124

Tolson, M. B.
See Tolson, Melvin B(eaunorus)

Tolson, Melvin B(eaunorus)
1898(?)-1966 . . . . **CLC 36; BLC;**
DAM MULT, POET
See also BW 1; CA 124; 89-92; DLB 48, 76

Tolstoi, Aleksei Nikolaevich
See Tolstoy, Alexey Nikolaevich

Tolstoy, Alexey Nikolaevich
1882-1945 . . . . **TCLC 18**
See also CA 107

Tolstoy, Count Leo
See Tolstoy, Leo (Nikolaevich)

Tolstoy, Leo (Nikolaevich)
1828-1910 . . . . . . **TCLC 4, 11, 17, 28, 44;**
DA; DAB; DAC; DAM MST, NOV;
SSC 9; WLC
See also CA 104; 123; SATA 26

Tomasi di Lampedusa, Giuseppe 1896-1957
See Lampedusa, Giuseppe (Tomasi) di
See also CA 111

Tomlin, Lily . . . . **CLC 17**
See also Tomlin, Mary Jean

Tomlin, Mary Jean 1939(?)-
See Tomlin, Lily
See also CA 117

Tomlinson, (Alfred) Charles
1927- . . . . **CLC 2, 4, 6, 13, 45;**
DAM POET
See also CA 5-8R; CANR 33; DLB 40

Tonson, Jacob
See Bennett, (Enoch) Arnold

Toole, John Kennedy
1937-1969 . . . . **CLC 19, 64**
See also CA 104; DLBY 81

Toomer, Jean
1894-1967 . . . . . . **CLC 1, 4, 13, 22; BLC;**
DAM MULT; PC 7; SSC 1
See also BW 1; CA 85-88;
CDALB 1917-1929; DLB 45, 51; MTCW

Torley, Luke
See Blish, James (Benjamin)

Tornimparte, Alessandra
See Ginzburg, Natalia

Torre, Raoul della
See Mencken, H(enry) L(ouis)

Torrey, E(dwin) Fuller 1937- . . . . **CLC 34**
See also CA 119

Torsvan, Ben Traven
See Traven, B.

Torsvan, Benno Traven
See Traven, B.

Torsvan, Berick Traven
See Traven, B.

Torsvan, Berwick Traven
See Traven, B.

Torsvan, Bruno Traven
See Traven, B.

Torsvan, Traven
See Traven, B.

Tournier, Michel (Edouard)
1924- . . . . **CLC 6, 23, 36, 95**
See also CA 49-52; CANR 3, 36; DLB 83;
MTCW; SATA 23

Tournimparte, Alessandra
See Ginzburg, Natalia

Towers, Ivar
See Kornbluth, C(yril) M.

Towne, Robert (Burton) 1936(?)- . . . . **CLC 87**
See also CA 108; DLB 44

Townsend, Sue 1946- . . **CLC 61; DAB; DAC**
See also CA 119; 127; INT 127; MTCW;
SATA 55; SATA-Brief 48

Townshend, Peter (Dennis Blandford)
1945- . . . . **CLC 17, 42**
See also CA 107

Tozzi, Federigo 1883-1920 . . . . **TCLC 31**

Traill, Catharine Parr
1802-1899 . . . . **NCLC 31**
See also DLB 99

Trakl, Georg 1887-1914 . . . . **TCLC 5**
See also CA 104

Transtroemer, Tomas (Goesta)
1931- . . . . **CLC 52, 65; DAM POET**
See also CA 117; 129; CAAS 17

Transtromer, Tomas Gosta
See Transtroemer, Tomas (Goesta)

Traven, B. (?)-1969 . . . . **CLC 8, 11**
See also CA 19-20; 25-28R; CAP 2; DLB 9,
56; MTCW

Treitel, Jonathan 1959- . . . . **CLC 70**

Tremain, Rose 1943- . . . . **CLC 42**
See also CA 97-100; CANR 44; DLB 14

Tremblay, Michel
1942- . . . . . . **CLC 29; DAC; DAM MST**
See also CA 116; 128; DLB 60; MTCW

Trevanian . . . . **CLC 29**
See also Whitaker, Rod(ney)

Trevor, Glen
See Hilton, James

Trevor, William
1928- . . . . . **CLC 7, 9, 14, 25, 71; SSC 21**
See also Cox, William Trevor
See also DLB 14, 139

Trifonov, Yuri (Valentinovich)
1925-1981 . . . . **CLC 45**
See also CA 126; 103; MTCW

Trilling, Lionel 1905-1975 . . . . **CLC 9, 11, 24**
See also CA 9-12R; 61-64; CANR 10;
DLB 28, 63; INT CANR-10; MTCW

Trimball, W. H.
See Mencken, H(enry) L(ouis)

Tristan
See Gomez de la Serna, Ramon

Tristram
See Housman, A(lfred) E(dward)

Trogdon, William (Lewis) 1939-
See Heat-Moon, William Least
See also CA 115; 119; CANR 47; INT 119

Trollope, Anthony
1815-1882 ..... NCLC 6, 33; DA; DAB;
DAC; DAM MST, NOV; WLC
See also CDBLB 1832-1890; DLB 21, 57,
159; SATA 22

Trollope, Frances 1779-1863 ..... NCLC 30
See also DLB 21, 166

Trotsky, Leon 1879-1940 .... TCLC 22
See also CA 118

Trotter (Cockburn), Catharine
1679-1749 .... LC 8
See also DLB 84

Trout, Kilgore
See Farmer, Philip Jose

Trow, George W. S. 1943- .... CLC 52
See also CA 126

Troyat, Henri 1911- .... CLC 23
See also CA 45-48; CANR 2, 33; MTCW

Trudeau, G(arretson) B(eekman) 1948-
See Trudeau, Garry B.
See also CA 81-84; CANR 31; SATA 35

Trudeau, Garry B. .... CLC 12
See also Trudeau, G(arretson) B(eekman)
See also AAYA 10; AITN 2

Truffaut, Francois 1932-1984 .... CLC 20
See also CA 81-84; 113; CANR 34

Trumbo, Dalton 1905-1976 .... CLC 19
See also CA 21-24R; 69-72; CANR 10;
DLB 26

Trumbull, John 1750-1831 .... NCLC 30
See also DLB 31

Trundlett, Helen B.
See Eliot, T(homas) S(tearns)

Tryon, Thomas
1926-1991 ...... CLC 3, 11; DAM POP
See also AITN 1; CA 29-32R; 135;
CANR 32; MTCW

Tryon, Tom
See Tryon, Thomas

Ts'ao Hsueh-ch'in 1715(?)-1763 ...... LC 1

Tsushima, Shuji 1909-1948
See Dazai, Osamu
See also CA 107

Tsvetaeva (Efron), Marina (Ivanovna)
1892-1941 .... TCLC 7, 35; PC 14
See also CA 104; 128; MTCW

Tuck, Lily 1938- .... CLC 70
See also CA 139

Tu Fu 712-770 .... PC 9
See also DAM MULT

Tunis, John R(oberts) 1889-1975 ... CLC 12
See also CA 61-64; DLB 22, 171; JRDA;
MAICYA; SATA 37; SATA-Brief 30

Tuohy, Frank .... CLC 37
See also Tuohy, John Francis
See also DLB 14, 139

Tuohy, John Francis 1925-
See Tuohy, Frank
See also CA 5-8R; CANR 3, 47

Turco, Lewis (Putnam) 1934- ... CLC 11, 63
See also CA 13-16R; CAAS 22, CANR 24,
51; DLBY 84

Turgenev, Ivan
1818-1883 .... NCLC 21; DA; DAB;
DAC; DAM MST, NOV; SSC 7; WLC

Turgot, Anne-Robert-Jacques
1727-1781 .... LC 26

Turner, Frederick 1943- .... CLC 48
See also CA 73-76; CAAS 10; CANR 12,
30; DLB 40

Tutu, Desmond M(pilo)
1931- ..... CLC 80; BLC; DAM MULT
See also BW 1; CA 125

Tutuola, Amos
1920- .... CLC 5, 14, 29; BLC;
DAM MULT
See also BW 2; CA 9-12R; CANR 27;
DLB 125; MTCW

Twain, Mark
..... TCLC 6, 12, 19, 36, 48, 59; SSC 6;
WLC
See also Clemens, Samuel Langhorne
See also DLB 11, 12, 23, 64, 74

Tyler, Anne
1941- .... CLC 7, 11, 18, 28, 44, 59;
DAM NOV, POP
See also AAYA 18; BEST 89:1; CA 9-12R;
CANR 11, 33, 53; DLB 6, 143; DLBY 82;
MTCW; SATA 7, 90

Tyler, Royall 1757-1826 .... NCLC 3
See also DLB 37

Tynan, Katharine 1861-1931 ...... TCLC 3
See also CA 104; DLB 153

Tyutchev, Fyodor 1803-1873 ..... NCLC 34

Tzara, Tristan
1896-1963 .... CLC 47; DAM POET
See also Rosenfeld, Samuel; Rosenstock,
Sami; Rosenstock, Samuel
See also CA 153

Uhry, Alfred
1936- ..... CLC 55; DAM DRAM, POP
See also CA 127; 133; INT 133

Ulf, Haerved
See Strindberg, (Johan) August

Ulf, Harved
See Strindberg, (Johan) August

Ulibarri, Sabine R(eyes)
1919- .... CLC 83; DAM MULT
See also CA 131; DLB 82; HW

Unamuno (y Jugo), Miguel de
1864-1936 ... TCLC 2, 9; DAM MULT,
NOV; HLC; SSC 11
See also CA 104; 131; DLB 108; HW;
MTCW

Undercliffe, Errol
See Campbell, (John) Ramsey

Underwood, Miles
See Glassco, John

Undset, Sigrid
1882-1949 .... TCLC 3; DA; DAB;
DAC; DAM MST, NOV; WLC
See also CA 104; 129; MTCW

Ungaretti, Giuseppe
1888-1970 .... CLC 7, 11, 15
See also CA 19-20; 25-28R; CAP 2;
DLB 114

Unger, Douglas 1952- .... CLC 34
See also CA 130

Unsworth, Barry (Forster) 1930- .... CLC 76
See also CA 25-28R; CANR 30, 54

Updike, John (Hoyer)
1932- ...... CLC 1, 2, 3, 5, 7, 9, 13, 15,
23, 34, 43, 70; DA; DAB; DAC;
DAM MST, NOV, POET, POP;
SSC 13; WLC
See also CA 1-4R; CABS 1; CANR 4, 33,
51; CDALB 1968-1988; DLB 2, 5, 143;
DLBD 3; DLBY 80, 82; MTCW

Upshaw, Margaret Mitchell
See Mitchell, Margaret (Munnerlyn)

Upton, Mark
See Sanders, Lawrence

Urdang, Constance (Henriette)
1922- .... CLC 47
See also CA 21-24R; CANR 9, 24

Uriel, Henry
See Faust, Frederick (Schiller)

Uris, Leon (Marcus)
1924- .... CLC 7, 32; DAM NOV, POP
See also AITN 1, 2; BEST 89:2; CA 1-4R;
CANR 1, 40; MTCW; SATA 49

Urmuz
See Codrescu, Andrei

Urquhart, Jane 1949- .... CLC 90; DAC
See also CA 113; CANR 32

Ustinov, Peter (Alexander) 1921- .... CLC 1
See also AITN 1; CA 13-16R; CANR 25,
51; DLB 13

Vaculik, Ludvik 1926- .... CLC 7
See also CA 53-56

Valdez, Luis (Miguel)
1940- ..... CLC 84; DAM MULT; HLC
See also CA 101; CANR 32; DLB 122; HW

Valenzuela, Luisa
1938- ... CLC 31; DAM MULT; SSC 14
See also CA 101; CANR 32; DLB 113; HW

Valera y Alcala-Galiano, Juan
1824-1905 .... TCLC 10
See also CA 106

Valery, (Ambroise) Paul (Toussaint Jules)
1871-1945 .... TCLC 4, 15;
DAM POET; PC 9
See also CA 104; 122; MTCW

Valle-Inclan, Ramon (Maria) del
1866-1936 ..... TCLC 5; DAM MULT;
HLC
See also CA 106; 153; DLB 134

Vallejo, Antonio Buero
See Buero Vallejo, Antonio

Vallejo, Cesar (Abraham)
1892-1938 .... TCLC 3, 56;
DAM MULT; HLC
See also CA 105; 153; HW

Vallette, Marguerite Eymery
See Rachilde

Valle Y Pena, Ramon del
See Valle-Inclan, Ramon (Maria) del

Van Ash, Cay 1918- .... CLC 34

Vanbrugh, Sir John
1664-1726 ...... LC 21; DAM DRAM
See also DLB 80

Van Campen, Karl
See Campbell, John W(ood, Jr.)

Vance, Gerald
See Silverberg, Robert

Vance, Jack .... CLC 35
See also Vance, John Holbrook
See also DLB 8

Vance, John Holbrook 1916-
See Queen, Ellery; Vance, Jack
See also CA 29-32R; CANR 17; MTCW

Van Den Bogarde, Derek Jules Gaspard Ulric
Niven 1921-
See Bogarde, Dirk
See also CA 77-80

Vandenburgh, Jane .... CLC 59

Vanderhaeghe, Guy 1951- .... CLC 41
See also CA 113

van der Post, Laurens (Jan) 1906- ... CLC 5
See also CA 5-8R; CANR 35

van de Wetering, Janwillem 1931- .. CLC 47
See also CA 49-52; CANR 4

Van Dine, S. S. .... TCLC 23
See also Wright, Willard Huntington

Van Doren, Carl (Clinton)
1885-1950 .... TCLC 18
See also CA 111

Van Doren, Mark 1894-1972..... CLC 6, 10
See also CA 1-4R; 37-40R; CANR 3;
DLB 45; MTCW

Van Druten, John (William)
1901-1957 .... TCLC 2
See also CA 104; DLB 10

Van Duyn, Mona (Jane)
1921- .... CLC 3, 7, 63; DAM POET
See also CA 9-12R; CANR 7, 38; DLB 5

Van Dyne, Edith
See Baum, L(yman) Frank

van Itallie, Jean-Claude 1936-....... CLC 3
See also CA 45-48; CAAS 2; CANR 1, 48;
DLB 7

van Ostaijen, Paul 1896-1928 ..... TCLC 33

Van Peebles, Melvin
1932- .... CLC 2, 20; DAM MULT
See also BW 2; CA 85-88; CANR 27

Vansittart, Peter 1920-............ CLC 42
See also CA 1-4R; CANR 3, 49

Van Vechten, Carl 1880-1964 ...... CLC 33
See also CA 89-92; DLB 4, 9, 51

Van Vogt, A(lfred) E(lton) 1912-..... CLC 1
See also CA 21-24R; CANR 28; DLB 8;
SATA 14

Varda, Agnes 1928- .... CLC 16
See also CA 116; 122

Vargas Llosa, (Jorge) Mario (Pedro)
1936- .... CLC 3, 6, 9, 10, 15, 31, 42, 85;
DA; DAB; DAC; DAM MST, MULT,
NOV; HLC
See also CA 73-76; CANR 18, 32, 42;
DLB 145; HW; MTCW

Vasiliu, Gheorghe 1881-1957
See Bacovia, George
See also CA 123

Vassa, Gustavus
See Equiano, Olaudah

Vassilikos, Vassilis 1933-......... CLC 4, 8
See also CA 81-84

Vaughan, Henry 1621-1695........ LC 27
See also DLB 131

Vaughn, Stephanie................. CLC 62

Vazov, Ivan (Minchov)
1850-1921 .... TCLC 25
See also CA 121; DLB 147

Veblen, Thorstein (Bunde)
1857-1929 .... TCLC 31
See also CA 115

Vega, Lope de 1562-1635........... LC 23

Venison, Alfred
See Pound, Ezra (Weston Loomis)

Verdi, Marie de
See Mencken, H(enry) L(ouis)

Verdu, Matilde
See Cela, Camilo Jose

Verga, Giovanni (Carmelo)
1840-1922 .... TCLC 3; SSC 21
See also CA 104; 123

Vergil
70B.C.-19B.C...... CMLC 9; DA; DAB;
DAC; DAM MST, POET; PC 12

Verhaeren, Emile (Adolphe Gustave)
1855-1916 .... TCLC 12
See also CA 109

Verlaine, Paul (Marie)
1844-1896 .... NCLC 2, 51;
DAM POET; PC 2

Verne, Jules (Gabriel)
1828-1905 .... TCLC 6, 52
See also AAYA 16; CA 110; 131; DLB 123;
JRDA; MAICYA; SATA 21

Very, Jones 1813-1880........... NCLC 9
See also DLB 1

Vesaas, Tarjei 1897-1970.......... CLC 48
See also CA 29-32R

Vialis, Gaston
See Simenon, Georges (Jacques Christian)

Vian, Boris 1920-1959 .... TCLC 9
See also CA 106; DLB 72

Viaud, (Louis Marie) Julien 1850-1923
See Loti, Pierre
See also CA 107

Vicar, Henry
See Felsen, Henry Gregor

Vicker, Angus
See Felsen, Henry Gregor

Vidal, Gore
1925- ..... CLC 2, 4, 6, 8, 10, 22, 33, 72;
DAM NOV, POP
See also AITN 1; BEST 90:2; CA 5-8R;
CANR 13, 45; DLB 6, 152;
INT CANR-13; MTCW

Viereck, Peter (Robert Edwin)
1916-....................... CLC 4
See also CA 1-4R; CANR 1, 47; DLB 5

Vigny, Alfred (Victor) de
1797-1863 ...... NCLC 7; DAM POET
See also DLB 119

Vilakazi, Benedict Wallet
1906-1947 .... TCLC 37

Villiers de l'Isle Adam, Jean Marie Mathias
Philippe Auguste Comte
1838-1889 .... NCLC 3; SSC 14
See also DLB 123

Villon, Francois 1431-1463(?) .... PC 13

Vinci, Leonardo da 1452-1519...... LC 12

Vine, Barbara .... CLC 50
See also Rendell, Ruth (Barbara)
See also BEST 90:4

Vinge, Joan D(ennison)
1948- .... CLC 30; SSC 24
See also CA 93-96; SATA 36

Violis, G.
See Simenon, Georges (Jacques Christian)

Visconti, Luchino 1906-1976....... CLC 16
See also CA 81-84; 65-68; CANR 39

Vittorini, Elio 1908-1966...... CLC 6, 9, 14
See also CA 133; 25-28R

Vizinczey, Stephen 1933-.......... CLC 40
See also CA 128; INT 128

Vliet, R(ussell) G(ordon)
1929-1984 .... CLC 22
See also CA 37-40R; 112; CANR 18

Vogau, Boris Andreyevich 1894-1937(?)
See Pilnyak, Boris
See also CA 123

Vogel, Paula A(nne) 1951-......... CLC 76
See also CA 108

Voight, Ellen Bryant 1943- .... CLC 54
See also CA 69-72; CANR 11, 29, 55;
DLB 120

Voigt, Cynthia 1942- .... CLC 30
See also AAYA 3; CA 106; CANR 18, 37,
40; CLR 13; INT CANR-18; JRDA;
MAICYA; SATA 48, 79; SATA-Brief 33

Voinovich, Vladimir (Nikolaevich)
1932-.................... CLC 10, 49
See also CA 81-84; CAAS 12; CANR 33;
MTCW

Vollmann, William T.
1959- ...... CLC 89; DAM NOV, POP
See also CA 134

Voloshinov, V. N.
See Bakhtin, Mikhail Mikhailovich

Voltaire
1694-1778 ..... LC 14; DA; DAB; DAC;
DAM DRAM, MST; SSC 12; WLC

von Bingen, Hildegard
1098(?)-1179 .... CMLC 20

Warren, Robert Penn
1905-1989 .... **CLC 1, 4, 6, 8, 10, 13, 18, 39, 53, 59; DA; DAB; DAC; DAM MST, NOV, POET; SSC 4; WLC**
See also AITN 1; CA 13-16R; 129; CANR 10, 47; CDALB 1968-1988; DLB 2, 48, 152; DLBY 80, 89; INT CANR-10; MTCW; SATA 46; SATA-Obit 63

Warshofsky, Isaac
See Singer, Isaac Bashevis

Warton, Thomas
1728-1790 .... **LC 15; DAM POET**
See also DLB 104, 109

Waruk, Kona
See Harris, (Theodore) Wilson

Warung, Price 1855-1911........ **TCLC 45**

Warwick, Jarvis
See Garner, Hugh

Washington, Alex
See Harris, Mark

Washington, Booker T(aliaferro)
1856-1915 .... **TCLC 10; BLC; DAM MULT**
See also BW 1; CA 114; 125; SATA 28

Washington, George 1732-1799...... **LC 25**
See also DLB 31

Wassermann, (Karl) Jakob
1873-1934 .... **TCLC 6**
See also CA 104; DLB 66

Wasserstein, Wendy
1950- .... **CLC 32, 59, 90; DAM DRAM; DC 4**
See also CA 121; 129; CABS 3; CANR 53; INT 129

Waterhouse, Keith (Spencer)
1929- .... **CLC 47**
See also CA 5-8R; CANR 38; DLB 13, 15; MTCW

Waters, Frank (Joseph)
1902-1995 .... **CLC 88**
See also CA 5-8R; 149; CAAS 13; CANR 3, 18; DLBY 86

Waters, Roger 1944-.............. **CLC 35**

Watkins, Frances Ellen
See Harper, Frances Ellen Watkins

Watkins, Gerrold
See Malzberg, Barry N(athaniel)

Watkins, Gloria 1955(?)-
See hooks, bell
See also BW 2; CA 143

Watkins, Paul 1964-.............. **CLC 55**
See also CA 132

Watkins, Vernon Phillips
1906-1967 .... **CLC 43**
See also CA 9-10; 25-28R; CAP 1; DLB 20

Watson, Irving S.
See Mencken, H(enry) L(ouis)

Watson, John H.
See Farmer, Philip Jose

Watson, Richard F.
See Silverberg, Robert

Waugh, Auberon (Alexander) 1939- .. **CLC 7**
See also CA 45-48; CANR 6, 22; DLB 14

Waugh, Evelyn (Arthur St. John)
1903-1966 ...... **CLC 1, 3, 8, 13, 19, 27, 44; DA; DAB; DAC; DAM MST, NOV, POP; WLC**
See also CA 85-88; 25-28R; CANR 22; CDBLB 1914-1945; DLB 15, 162; MTCW

Waugh, Harriet 1944- .... **CLC 6**
See also CA 85-88; CANR 22

Ways, C. R.
See Blount, Roy (Alton), Jr.

Waystaff, Simon
See Swift, Jonathan

Webb, (Martha) Beatrice (Potter)
1858-1943 .... **TCLC 22**
See also Potter, Beatrice
See also CA 117

Webb, Charles (Richard) 1939-...... **CLC 7**
See also CA 25-28R

Webb, James H(enry), Jr. 1946-.... **CLC 22**
See also CA 81-84

Webb, Mary (Gladys Meredith)
1881-1927 .... **TCLC 24**
See also CA 123; DLB 34

Webb, Mrs. Sidney
See Webb, (Martha) Beatrice (Potter)

Webb, Phyllis 1927-................ **CLC 18**
See also CA 104; CANR 23; DLB 53

Webb, Sidney (James)
1859-1947 .... **TCLC 22**
See also CA 117

Webber, Andrew Lloyd.............. CLC 21
See also Lloyd Webber, Andrew

Weber, Lenora Mattingly
1895-1971 .... **CLC 12**
See also CA 19-20; 29-32R; CAP 1; SATA 2; SATA-Obit 26

Webster, John
1579(?)-1634(?) ...... **LC 33; DA; DAB; DAC; DAM DRAM, MST; DC 2; WLC**
See also CDBLB Before 1660; DLB 58

Webster, Noah 1758-1843 .... **NCLC 30**

Wedekind, (Benjamin) Frank(lin)
1864-1918 ...... **TCLC 7; DAM DRAM**
See also CA 104; 153; DLB 118

Weidman, Jerome 1913-............ **CLC 7**
See also AITN 2; CA 1-4R; CANR 1; DLB 28

Weil, Simone (Adolphine)
1909-1943 .... **TCLC 23**
See also CA 117

Weinstein, Nathan
See West, Nathanael

Weinstein, Nathan von Wallenstein
See West, Nathanael

Weir, Peter (Lindsay) 1944- .... **CLC 20**
See also CA 113; 123

Weiss, Peter (Ulrich)
1916-1982 .... **CLC 3, 15, 51; DAM DRAM**
See also CA 45-48; 106; CANR 3; DLB 69, 124

Weiss, Theodore (Russell)
1916- .... **CLC 3, 8, 14**
See also CA 9-12R; CAAS 2; CANR 46; DLB 5

Welch, (Maurice) Denton
1915-1948 .... **TCLC 22**
See also CA 121; 148

Welch, James
1940- ..... **CLC 6, 14, 52; DAM MULT, POP**
See also CA 85-88; CANR 42; NNAL

Weldon, Fay
1933- .... **CLC 6, 9, 11, 19, 36, 59; DAM POP**
See also CA 21-24R; CANR 16, 46; CDBLB 1960 to Present; DLB 14; INT CANR-16; MTCW

Wellek, Rene 1903-1995.......... **CLC 28**
See also CA 5-8R; 150; CAAS 7; CANR 8; DLB 63; INT CANR-8

Weller, Michael 1942-.......... **CLC 10, 53**
See also CA 85-88

Weller, Paul 1958-.............. **CLC 26**

Wellershoff, Dieter 1925-.......... **CLC 46**
See also CA 89-92; CANR 16, 37

Welles, (George) Orson
1915-1985 .... **CLC 20, 80**
See also CA 93-96; 117

Wellman, Mac 1945- .... **CLC 65**

Wellman, Manly Wade 1903-1986 .. **CLC 49**
See also CA 1-4R; 118; CANR 6, 16, 44; SATA 6; SATA-Obit 47

Wells, Carolyn 1869(?)-1942 ...... **TCLC 35**
See also CA 113; DLB 11

Wells, H(erbert) G(eorge)
1866-1946 .... **TCLC 6, 12, 19; DA; DAB; DAC; DAM MST, NOV; SSC 6; WLC**
See also AAYA 18; CA 110; 121; CDBLB 1914-1945; DLB 34, 70, 156; MTCW; SATA 20

Wells, Rosemary 1943-............ **CLC 12**
See also AAYA 13; CA 85-88; CANR 48; CLR 16; MAICYA; SAAS 1; SATA 18, 69

Welty, Eudora
1909- ...... **CLC 1, 2, 5, 14, 22, 33; DA; DAB; DAC; DAM MST, NOV; SSC 1; WLC**
See also CA 9-12R; CABS 1; CANR 32; CDALB 1941-1968; DLB 2, 102, 143; DLBD 12; DLBY 87; MTCW

Wen I-to 1899-1946 .... **TCLC 28**

Wentworth, Robert
See Hamilton, Edmond

Werfel, Franz (V.) 1890-1945 ...... **TCLC 8**
See also CA 104; DLB 81, 124

Wergeland, Henrik Arnold
1808-1845 .... **NCLC 5**

Wersba, Barbara 1932-............ **CLC 30**
See also AAYA 2; CA 29-32R; CANR 16, 38; CLR 3; DLB 52; JRDA; MAICYA; SAAS 2; SATA 1, 58

Wertmueller, Lina 1928- .... **CLC 16**
See also CA 97-100; CANR 39

Wescott, Glenway 1901-1987....... **CLC 13**
See also CA 13-16R; 121; CANR 23; DLB 4, 9, 102

Wilhelm, Kate .... **CLC 7**
See also Wilhelm, Katie Gertrude
See also CAAS 5; DLB 8; INT CANR-17

Wilhelm, Katie Gertrude 1928-
See Wilhelm, Kate
See also CA 37-40R; CANR 17, 36; MTCW

Wilkins, Mary
See Freeman, Mary Eleanor Wilkins

Willard, Nancy 1936- .... **CLC 7, 37**
See also CA 89-92; CANR 10, 39; CLR 5;
DLB 5, 52; MAICYA; MTCW;
SATA 37, 71; SATA-Brief 30

Williams, C(harles) K(enneth)
1936- .... **CLC 33, 56; DAM POET**
See also CA 37-40R; DLB 5

Williams, Charles
See Collier, James L(incoln)

Williams, Charles (Walter Stansby)
1886-1945 .... **TCLC 1, 11**
See also CA 104; DLB 100, 153

Williams, (George) Emlyn
1905-1987 ...... **CLC 15; DAM DRAM**
See also CA 104; 123; CANR 36; DLB 10,
77; MTCW

Williams, Hugo 1942- .... **CLC 42**
See also CA 17-20R; CANR 45; DLB 40

Williams, J. Walker
See Wodehouse, P(elham) G(renville)

Williams, John A(lfred)
1925- ... **CLC 5, 13; BLC; DAM MULT**
See also BW 2; CA 53-56; CAAS 3;
CANR 6, 26, 51; DLB 2, 33;
INT CANR-6

Williams, Jonathan (Chamberlain)
1929- .... **CLC 13**
See also CA 9-12R; CAAS 12; CANR 8;
DLB 5

Williams, Joy 1944- .... **CLC 31**
See also CA 41-44R; CANR 22, 48

Williams, Norman 1952- .... **CLC 39**
See also CA 118

Williams, Sherley Anne
1944- ..... **CLC 89; BLC; DAM MULT,
POET**
See also BW 2; CA 73-76; CANR 25;
DLB 41; INT CANR-25; SATA 78

Williams, Shirley
See Williams, Sherley Anne

Williams, Tennessee
1911-1983 ..... **CLC 1, 2, 5, 7, 8, 11, 15,
19, 30, 39, 45, 71; DA; DAB; DAC;
DAM DRAM, MST; DC 4; WLC**
See also AITN 1, 2; CA 5-8R; 108;
CABS 3; CANR 31; CDALB 1941-1968;
DLB 7; DLBD 4; DLBY 83; MTCW

Williams, Thomas (Alonzo)
1926-1990 .... **CLC 14**
See also CA 1-4R; 132; CANR 2

Williams, William C.
See Williams, William Carlos

Williams, William Carlos
1883-1963 .... **CLC 1, 2, 5, 9, 13, 22, 42,
67; DA; DAB; DAC; DAM MST, POET;
PC 7**
See also CA 89-92; CANR 34;
CDALB 1917-1929; DLB 4, 16, 54, 86;
MTCW

Williamson, David (Keith) 1942- .... **CLC 56**
See also CA 103; CANR 41

Williamson, Ellen Douglas 1905-1984
See Douglas, Ellen
See also CA 17-20R; 114; CANR 39

Williamson, Jack .... **CLC 29**
See also Williamson, John Stewart
See also CAAS 8; DLB 8

Williamson, John Stewart 1908-
See Williamson, Jack
See also CA 17-20R; CANR 23

Willie, Frederick
See Lovecraft, H(oward) P(hillips)

Willingham, Calder (Baynard, Jr.)
1922-1995 .... **CLC 5, 51**
See also CA 5-8R; 147; CANR 3; DLB 2,
44; MTCW

Willis, Charles
See Clarke, Arthur C(harles)

Willy
See Colette, (Sidonie-Gabrielle)

Willy, Colette
See Colette, (Sidonie-Gabrielle)

Wilson, A(ndrew) N(orman) 1950- .. **CLC 33**
See also CA 112; 122; DLB 14, 155

Wilson, Angus (Frank Johnstone)
1913-1991 .. **CLC 2, 3, 5, 25, 34; SSC 21**
See also CA 5-8R; 134; CANR 21; DLB 15,
139, 155; MTCW

Wilson, August
1945- .... **CLC 39, 50, 63; BLC; DA;
DAB; DAC; DAM DRAM, MST,
MULT; DC 2**
See also AAYA 16; BW 2; CA 115; 122;
CANR 42, 54; MTCW

Wilson, Brian 1942- .... **CLC 12**

Wilson, Colin 1931- .... **CLC 3, 14**
See also CA 1-4R; CAAS 5; CANR 1, 22,
33; DLB 14; MTCW

Wilson, Dirk
See Pohl, Frederik

Wilson, Edmund
1895-1972 .... **CLC 1, 2, 3, 8, 24**
See also CA 1-4R; 37-40R; CANR 1, 46;
DLB 63; MTCW

Wilson, Ethel Davis (Bryant)
1888(?)-1980 .... **CLC 13; DAC;
DAM POET**
See also CA 102; DLB 68; MTCW

Wilson, John 1785-1854 .... **NCLC 5**

Wilson, John (Anthony) Burgess 1917-1993
See Burgess, Anthony
See also CA 1-4R; 143; CANR 2, 46; DAC;
DAM NOV; MTCW

Wilson, Lanford
1937- ..... **CLC 7, 14, 36; DAM DRAM**
See also CA 17-20R; CABS 3; CANR 45;
DLB 7

Wilson, Robert M. 1944- .... **CLC 7, 9**
See also CA 49-52; CANR 2, 41; MTCW

Wilson, Robert McLiam 1964- ..... **CLC 59**
See also CA 132

Wilson, Sloan 1920- .... **CLC 32**
See also CA 1-4R; CANR 1, 44

Wilson, Snoo 1948- .... **CLC 33**
See also CA 69-72

Wilson, William S(mith) 1932- ..... **CLC 49**
See also CA 81-84

Winchilsea, Anne (Kingsmill) Finch Counte
1661-1720 .... **LC 3**

Windham, Basil
See Wodehouse, P(elham) G(renville)

Wingrove, David (John) 1954- ...... **CLC 68**
See also CA 133

Winters, Janet Lewis .... **CLC 41**
See also Lewis, Janet
See also DLBY 87

Winters, (Arthur) Yvor
1900-1968 .... **CLC 4, 8, 32**
See also CA 11-12; 25-28R; CAP 1;
DLB 48; MTCW

Winterson, Jeanette
1959- .... **CLC 64; DAM POP**
See also CA 136

Winthrop, John 1588-1649 .... **LC 31**
See also DLB 24, 30

Wiseman, Frederick 1930- .... **CLC 20**

Wister, Owen 1860-1938 .... **TCLC 21**
See also CA 108; DLB 9, 78; SATA 62

Witkacy
See Witkiewicz, Stanislaw Ignacy

Witkiewicz, Stanislaw Ignacy
1885-1939 .... **TCLC 8**
See also CA 105

Wittgenstein, Ludwig (Josef Johann)
1889-1951 .... **TCLC 59**
See also CA 113

Wittig, Monique 1935(?)- .... **CLC 22**
See also CA 116; 135; DLB 83

Wittlin, Jozef 1896-1976 .... **CLC 25**
See also CA 49-52; 65-68; CANR 3

Wodehouse, P(elham) G(renville)
1881-1975 ... **CLC 1, 2, 5, 10, 22; DAB;
DAC; DAM NOV; SSC 2**
See also AITN 2; CA 45-48; 57-60;
CANR 3, 33; CDBLB 1914-1945;
DLB 34, 162; MTCW; SATA 22

Woiwode, L.
See Woiwode, Larry (Alfred)

Woiwode, Larry (Alfred) 1941- ... **CLC 6, 10**
See also CA 73-76; CANR 16; DLB 6;
INT CANR-16

Wojciechowska, Maia (Teresa)
1927- .... **CLC 26**
See also AAYA 8; CA 9-12R; CANR 4, 41;
CLR 1; JRDA; MAICYA; SAAS 1;
SATA 1, 28, 83

Wolf, Christa 1929- .... **CLC 14, 29, 58**
See also CA 85-88; CANR 45; DLB 75;
MTCW

Author Index

Literary Criticism Series
Cumulative Topic Index

This index lists all topic entries in Gale's *Classical and Medieval Literature Criticism, Contemporary Literary Criticism, Literature Criticism from 1400 to 1800, Nineteenth-Century Literature Criticism,* and *Twentieth-Century Literary Criticism.*

Topic Index

Cumulative Nationality Index

Nationality Index

TCLC 68 Title Index